THE
EDINBURGH
HISTORY
of the SCOTS
LANGUAGE

the
EDINBURGH
HISTORY
of the SCOTS
Language

EDITED BY CHARLES JONES

Edinburgh University Press

For Isla

© The contributors, 1997

Transferred to digital print 2012

Edinburgh University Press
22 George Square, Edinburgh

Typeset in 10 on 12pt Ehrhardt
by Hewer Text Composition Services, Edinburgh, and
Printed and bound by CPI Group (UK) Ltd, Croydon, CR0 4YY

A CIP record for this book is available from the British Library

ISBN 0 7486 0754 4

Contents

Editor's Preface

The historical evolution of the English language has held and continues to hold a central position in modern linguistic research. The shelves of university libraries groan under the weight of general English histories dating from the nineteenth to the late twentieth century. In recent years in particular, the interest in the shape and form of English outside its USA and Great Britain heartlands has provided further insights into the developmental pathways of change and innovation at all levels of the language's grammar. Indeed, for better or worse, the bulk of our ever-increasing knowledge of the causes for and processes of general linguistic mutation through time are provided by and large from English-based materials in the widest sense.

Yet there has always existed the anomaly that a major branch of the English language – Scots – has been denied its own specific History. The reasons for this are complex and not always transparent. A contributing factor might be the perceived closeness of the language spoken by the vast majority of the inhabitants of Scotland to the general English of the British Isles, to the extent that its historical development warrants mere footnote status in the record. Scots is seen as divergent only in a few limited and easily-defined areas, and there is still a widely-held view that Scots is merely 'English with a Scottish accent'. Again, the supposed lack (especially for the early period) of extensive and coherent historical data has also led to the perception that there is not enough Scots to survive to merit any full-scale, dedicated survey of its historical development. The contents of this volume should go a long way to dispel such facile and misleading notions.

Whatever the underlying reasons, the fact remains that this volume represents the first full-scale, detailed and comprehensive attempt to provide a history of the Scots language from the time of its earliest records to the modern period. There was never any intention on my part that this history should present a homogeneous theoretical approach to the linguistic data that it encompasses. The scholarly backgrounds of the contributors are too diverse for that, even were such a thing desirable. This volume sets out to be a collection of the most recent research by some of the foremost contemporary exponents of historical Scots language and literary studies. Each chapter is intended to be read as a self-contained unit, although there are nevertheless certain areas – notably in the treatment of regional variation and syntax/morphology – where generalisations across the entire temporal span can be made. While we have to await an exhaustive, theoretically consistent history of the Scots language from the hand of a single author, there is a real sense in which the diversity of approach taken in this volume can be said to offer advantages in the ways in which it highlights problems of data interpretation which may well be missed or disguised in a single-model approach.

The volume is (somewhat arbitrarily) divided into three parts: the first two treat respectively of the language from its earliest beginnings to 1700 and its development from that time to the present day. Where possible, there are parallel chapters dealing with the main elements of the grammar in these periods: phonology, syntax, morphology and lexis, while in the post-1700 period in particular, sociolinguistic criteria underlying linguistic innovation and its transmission are prominent. I also felt it important to include an essay on the special characteristics of the language in the early Scots literary materials.

The third part of the volume encompasses the historical interrelationship between the Scots and Gaelic languages as well as the 'overseas' manifestations of Scots in a historical context. No history of Scots would be complete without reference to the language's relationship with Ulster Scots and the particular ways in which that form of the language has developed over time. At the same time, the important part played by Scottish settlers in the colonisation of Australia is highlighted in a chapter dedicated to the history of the development and influence of the Scots language in that continent.

My main purpose in taking on what has proved to be a daunting project (for all concerned) is to encourage further study of the history of the Scots language. Every area of the language discussed in this volume contains suggestions for further research and study in Scots historical linguistics, and if even a fraction of these is taken up, then the production of this volume will be justified. As in all undertakings of this type, the simplicity of the original concept was quickly belied by the complexity of its implementation. I have shamelessly pursued contributors, even when I knew that they had other, more pressing responsibilities and commitments. That they are still on speaking terms with me is a tribute to their patience and forbearance and no reflection upon my own tolerance.

I have had direct and indirect assistance from a number of sources and individuals in the production of this volume. My especial thanks must go to the University of Edinburgh's Faculty of Arts Computing Service and to Edmund Rooney, who so speedily and effectively rendered the plethora of different formats of word-processed documents which I received from the contributors into a form readable by my own machines. Without that kind of help, this book would have taken much longer to produce. I am also grateful to the Lorimer Trust for the provision of substantial financial assistance towards the production costs of this volume, and to that great Scotophile, Murray Forbes of Boston, whose Navigator Foundation supplied timely resources to enable additional typing work to be done.

Edinburgh University Press must be heartily thanked for undertaking the production of a major work of this kind. Its involvement on this occasion is yet another instance of its invaluable commitment to the publication of work dealing with Scottish materials. Thanks are due especially to Jonathan Price for setting the whole project in motion, and to Jackie Jones for unstinting encouragement at every stage. At the same time, Ivor Normand's detailed and constructive copy-editing and Nicola Pike's assiduous proof-reading helped enormously in the production of the final version of the manuscript.

While every effort has been made to ensure that the volume is as free as possible from errors, any which remain must be laid at the door of the editor.

Charles Jones
Edinburgh, March 1997

Notes on Contributors

Dr Joan Beal is a lecturer in English Language in the School of English at the University of Newcastle upon Tyne. Her previous publications include a chapter on 'The grammar of Tyneside and Northumbrian English' in *Real English*, ed. J. and L. Milroy (1993) and 'The Jocks and the Geordies: modified standards in eighteenth-century pronouncing dictionaries' in *English Historical Linguistics 1994*, ed. D. Britton (1996).

Robert J. Gregg is Professor Emeritus of Linguistics at the University of British Columbia, Vancouver, and is one of the foremost experts on Ulster Scots. His 1961 Edinburgh doctoral dissertation *The Distribution and Boundaries of the Scots Language in the Province of Ulster* was published in 1985 by the Canadian Federation for the Humanities. He has written many papers on the Scots language in Ulster and is a major contributor to the *Concise Ulster Dictionary*, ed. C. I. Macafee (1996). He is Honorary President of the Ulster Scots Language Society.

Ronald D. S. Jack is Professor of Scottish and Medieval Literature at the University of Edinburgh and has published widely in both of these areas. He is editor of the first volume (*Origins to 1660*) of the four-volume *History of Scottish Literature* (1988) and senior editor of the forthcoming *Mercat Anthology of Early Scottish Literature: 1370–1707*.

Paul Johnston is Associate Professor of English at Western Michigan University. He received his Ph.D. from Edinburgh in 1989. While there, he completed full-scale sociolinguistic studies on Border Area and Edinburgh dialects, which spawned several articles and are now being updated and prepared for book publication. He has also written extensively on the history of Germanic (including Scots) vowel shifts, to be published shortly as a book.

Charles Jones is Forbes Professor of English Language at the University of Edinburgh. He is the author of several books on the history of English, notably *A History of English Phonology* (1989), *Grammatical Gender in English 950 to 1250* (1988) and *A Language Suppressed: The Pronunciation of the Scots Language in the Eighteenth Century* (1996), and is the editor of *A Treatise on the Provincial Dialect of Scotland, by Sylvester Douglas* (1991).

Dr Anne King lectures in Scots language in the Department of English Language at the University of Edinburgh. She has written papers on English historical linguistics (particularly Old English) and Scots.

Dr Veronika Kniezsa is Reader in Historical Linguistics in the School of English and American Studies, Department of English Language and Literature at the Eötvös Loránd University, Budapest. She has published widely on Scots orthographic systems, and her scholarly interests include national varieties of English, historical dialectology and sociolinguistics as well as medieval English literature.

Dr C. I. Macafee is Director of the North-East Language Project in the University of Aberdeen. She is the author of *Traditional Dialect in the Modern World: A Glasgow Case Study* (1994), editor of the *Concise Ulster Dictionary* (1996) and one of the editors of *The Scots Thesaurus* (1990), and author of many papers on the Scots language.

Dr Anneli Meurman-Solin is a member of the Department of English, University of Helsinki. She has published widely in the fields of sociohistorical linguistics, historical stylistics and corpus linguistics. She has compiled the *Helsinki Corpus of Older Scots, 1450–1700*. An outline of diachronic developments in fifteen different genres included in the corpus is given in her monograph *Variation and Change in Early Scottish Prose* (1993).

Lilo Moessner is Professor of Historical English Linguistics and Medieval Studies at the Institut für Anglistik, University of Aachen. Her main fields of research are in English syntax, Medieval and Early Modern English, and varieties of English and Scots. Her previous publications on Scots include: 'Is the subject–verb concord in Scots a number concord?'; 'A critical assessment of Tom Scott's poem *The Seavaiger* as an exercise in translation'; ' "Besyde Latyn our langage is imperfite": the contribution of Gavin Douglas to the development of the Scots lexicon'.

Michael B. Montgomery is Professor of English and Linguistics at the University of South Carolina. He has written extensively and edited seven books on varieties of English in the American South. Since 1987 he has sought to reconstruct the language patterns brought by Scottish and Irish emigrants to North America and to establish their influence on American English. A major part of this has involved archival work to document earlier stages of Scots and English in Ulster. At present he is finishing a dictionary of the English spoken in the southern Appalachian mountains in the USA.

Colm Ó Baoill is Professor of Celtic in the Department of Celtic, University of Aberdeen. He is joint author of volume 4 (1969) of Heinrich Wagner's *Linguistic Atlas and Survey of Irish Dialects*, and his book on linguistic relationships between Ulster Irish and Scottish Gaelic appeared in 1978.

Dr Graham Tulloch is Reader in English in the School of English and Drama, Flinders University of South Australia, Adelaide. His major publications dealing with Scots are *The Language of Walter Scott: A Study of his Scottish and Period Language* (1980) and *A History of the Scots Bible with Selected Texts* (1989). He has also written a number of articles on the literary use of Scots and has edited several Scottish and Australian texts.

Part 1

The Beginnings to 1700

1

Differentiation and Standardisation in Early Scots

Anneli Meurman-Solin

1.1 LANGUAGE DIFFERENTIATION AND LANGUAGE STANDARDISATION

In this chapter, the concepts 'differentiation' and 'standardisation' are used as hypernyms or umbrella terms which refer to complex processes of selection between sets of linguistic variants (Milroy 1994). On the level of individual texts, these processes are reflected in varying degrees of divergence and convergence from a norm which is itself a variable. Scots is traditionally mirrored against the Southern English Standard. The concepts 'anglicisa-tion' and 'de-anglicisation' can therefore be used to specify the direction of diachronic developments in the history of Scots; the latter term refers to the divergence of Scots from the Northern English dialect starting from the fifteenth century, the former to its convergence reflected in the preference of English variants in certain contexts and situations later in its history.

The criteria for defining a standard, that a standard is imposed from above, involves legislation and contains an ideology of standardisation (Milroy 1994: 4), are not directly applicable to Older Scots, as the Scottish 'regional norm standard' did not result from any articulate prescriptivist regulation. Therefore, when we look at the direction of change from the traditional perspective of what became Standard English, both the diverging and the converging trends in Scots illustrate features characteristic of the first phase of standardi-sation, where functional reasons, rather than ideological or attitudinal matters, play an important role (Milroy 1994: 25–6; Stein and Tieken-Boon van Ostade 1994: 8; Klein 1994). The intensification of developments towards divergence in the fifteenth century is linked with the increase of Scotland's political and sociocultural independence. This process seems to have created a climate of consensus among those with access to wielders of political and economic power; such a climate supported the rise of a multi-purpose regional norm standard.

In the case of Older Scots, prestige is not a central motivating factor in differentiation and standardisation processes (Aitken 1979: 93–5; Devitt 1989: 13–14). As has been shown in earlier studies (Murison 1979b: 9; Aitken 1979: 91–3; Meurman-Solin 1993a: 49, 140, 214–15), pragmatic concerns related to social and political changes are more important. For example, conservative or uniformitarian pressures can be found in closed communities

where there are strong ties between a restricted number of literate people who represent a
thin top layer in the social hierarchy. In contrast, innovative language use is motivated by
the interest in appealing to wider audiences outside one's own community; later this is often
supported by the awareness that the adoption of a particular norm creates new opportunities
to climb up the social ladder and allows the enjoyment of privileges related to social
acceptability. Also factors such as directly or indirectly prescriptive conventions of genres
can be significant, since they often strengthen either the conservative or the innovative
tendencies in language use.

If 'prestige' is referred to, it is noteworthy that the concept can be simultaneously
applicable to various norms. In the case of Scots, the norm considered prestigious may
consist of practices followed by the local administration (in the royal burghs of Scotland) or
those adopted by the regional central administration (in Edinburgh); later, the norm could
also be set by the national central administration (in London) (Milroy and Milroy 1985;
Devitt 1989: 49). Thus the label 'prestige' is not necessarily attached only to what becomes
the majority variety; complex processes of language change cannot be interpreted in terms
of the dichotomy, 'low prestige' as against 'high prestige'. The history of Scots, not only in
the periods discussed in this chapter but also in the eighteenth and nineteenth centuries,
sheds light on the coexistence of a number of prestige varieties or subvarieties. Ideally, as a
result of a detailed internal reconstruction of Older Scots, each variety can be shown to have
been a preferred variety in a closely definable context in a particular communicative
situation. In the choice of the preferred norm in written language, established features of
genres, particularly those related to style, register and degree of interactiveness are believed
to have a major regulating effect (Meurman-Solin 1994b).

Older Scots is not an internally uniform variety of English (Aitken 1971a; Murison 1977;
McIntosh 1978 [1989]; Macafee 1989). In my terminology, 'regional' refers to language use
in the whole area of English-speaking Scotland, as opposed to England, and, for purely
practical reasons, the words Scottish and English are used here as cover terms to refer to
these internally heterogeneous varieties in the two geographical areas. Within the regional
norm, standard 'localised' norms can be identified throughout the history of Scots
(McIntosh 1978 [1989]; Meurman-Solin 1993a: 136–7; see section 1.2.2 below).

On the basis of the preceding arguments, I define developments towards a differentiated
regional standard as a case of standardisation. The assumption is that this divergence took
place both in written and in spoken language. In contrast, the later anglicisation process was
chiefly realised in written Scots and can be viewed as change on a more conscious level of
language use. Motivated by a political and socioeconomic unification process, an important
number of features in a majority variety, namely Southern English, were substituted for
those in a minority variety, namely Scots, at least in certain linguistic and/or extralinguistic
environments. However, the pattern of change remains multidirectional (Milroy 1992;
Romaine 1984b: 250–1), but the description of the various developments will inevitably
remain somewhat flawed due to scarcity of material, problems in its availability and absence
of evidence as regards spoken language.

Anglicising trends in Scots are assumed to manifest themselves in written language
before expanding to other linguistic contexts, and there is some evidence, provided by a
number of linguistic features, that this claim may also apply to processes of divergence in
the fifteenth and early sixteenth centuries (for speech-based texts, see section 1.2.4).
Written language is also believed to have had a central role in strengthening and intensifying
standardisation and anglicisation processes: see pp. 14 and 15–16. However, straightforward

generalisations about a higher level of formality leading towards the rejection of local and regional features have been shown to be unjustified, as we shall see when we discuss the findings relating to administrative texts in Table 1.1 (p. 11; see also Devitt 1989: 67–8). The social and communicative function of a text or a genre in a given time and situation, and features related to the tenor, mode and field of discourse (Halliday 1985), are also relevant in categorising written texts in a way that serves to explain differences in diachronic developments (Meurman-Solin 1993d, 1994b, 1995a and forthcoming c).

1.1.1 Text Corpora and the Study of Variation and Change

A description of a non-standard variety of English traditionally contains a random set of findings illustrating how that variety differs from the Standard variety. In this chapter, an attempt is made to give a somewhat more systematic account of some diachronic developments in fifteenth-, sixteenth- and seventeenth-century Scots; but a detailed reconstruction of Early and Middle Scots, 'an up-to-date large-scale grammar' (McIntosh 1978: 85), which is free from any preselection of data, will have to await discussion elsewhere.

A variationist approach to sociohistorically-conditioned language use in the history of Scots has been made possible by the compilation of computer-readable corpora which embody a wide range of genres and text categories, and which also provide information relating to extralinguistic variables such as the author's rank, age and sex, the potential audience of a text, whether it was printed or remained in manuscript, whether it is speech-based (trials) or a script (sermons), and whether, in letters, the participant relationship is intimate (for example, between members of the family) or distant (for example, between a citizen and a government official). For a further discussion, see Meurman-Solin 1993a: 180–3.

The tools of corpus linguistics were introduced into the field of Scottish studies by A. J. Aitken.[1] More recently, two important corpus projects, one in Edinburgh, another in Helsinki, have begun a new era in the study of the history of Scots. The Institute for Historical Dialectology in Edinburgh is continuing the work represented by the *Linguistic Atlas of Late Medieval English* (LALME) and aims at a detailed linguistic analysis of Middle English and Older Scots texts. Laing (1994: 121, 127) points out that 'both linguistic entities share the characteristic that in their surviving written manifestations there is a considerable variation in form' as regards not only spelling variation but also variation in lexis and morphology, and she stresses that the use of computer-based tools allows the analysis of '*all* the linguistic data' instead of 'a pre-selected set of dialectal discriminants'. The decision to base the texts on manuscripts and to tag them to produce text and item profiles providing information for dialectal mapping serves to illustrate the ambitiousness of the project (Laing 1994: 127–40).

At present, only the computer-readable but untagged version of the *Helsinki Corpus of Older Scots* (HCOS) is available for the analysis of variation and change in late medieval and Renaissance Scottish prose in a way which allows the presentation of statistically significant findings.[2] The HCOS differs from the Edinburgh corpus by using only edited texts or early prints, by covering a wider selection of genres, by extending the time-span up to 1700 and by coding a system of extralinguistic variables into the corpus.[3] The earliest texts in the HCOS are official letters dating from 1400 and 1405. There are a few early eighteenth-century letters, but the majority of the texts date from the years 1450–1700. This time-span is divided into the following subperiods: 1450–1500, 1500–70, 1570–1640 and 1640–1700.[4]

The internationally-distributed version, which appeared in 1995, contains approximately 850,000 words of running text, including seventy-four prose texts, representing fifteen primarily non-literary genres: law (Acts of Parliament), local records, trial proceedings, sermons, pamphlets, handbooks, scientific treatises, educational treatises, histories, travelogues, biographies, diaries, the Bible, private letters and official letters. These are further grouped into five different text categories: statutory, religious instruction, secular instruction, expository and argumentative.[5] Private letters in the corpus are represented by twenty-five writers and official letters by forty-four writers.

Prose texts are particularly appropriate for the study of language change in Scots, since prose has been claimed to retain vernacular Scottish features longer than verse (Aitken 1971a: 181; Templeton 1973: 8; Romaine 1982a: 24). Priority was given to non-literary prose texts in the corpus, as they have more varied social functions in the sphere of 'private' versus 'public' (Meurman-Solin 1993a: 63, 71–2). Earlier claims concerning the interchangeability of variant forms and about a generally high degree of tolerance as regards variation in fifteenth- and sixteenth-century Scots have been based on a limited set of data (Aitken 1971: 190). However, the availability of quantitatively and qualitatively more representative data has revealed systematically-ordered distributions of variants (Chambers 1995: 1–33), and has also served to position idiolectal practices in a wider context both synchronically and diachronically. In recent studies, based on corpora of different sizes (Devitt 1989; Meurman-Solin 1993a, forthcoming c), patterns of variation and change have emerged; these reflect varying degrees of inner homogeneity in the choice of linguistic features in a particular idiolect or quillect, in a text or a group of texts. Ideally, these patterns have then been shown to be conditioned by identifiable socio-historical factors and/or features reflecting textual histories and various stages in the evolution of genres.

The general hypothesis in this computer-based approach is that the diffusion of particular sets of features – whether markedly Scottish or markedly English – can be described as a specialisation of distributions which positions idiolects, texts and genres close to 'common core' or not far from it, or in a more or less remote periphery (Meurman-Solin forthcoming a) with the drawing of multidimensional maps to display diatopic patterning (Laing 1994: 121). With localisable texts such as burgh records, the position of a text on a map of this kind may reflect its geographical position and ultimately the political and socioeconomic role of a particular locality in the centre or in the periphery (see section 1.2.2). On the level of language variety, processes of redistribution and specialisation in texts can be seen to lead to a new patterning of variants rather than to an absolute decrease of variation. Consequently, the rise of a standard, or a replacement of one standard by another, at least in a number of genres and settings, are mainly visible in written texts close to 'common core', whereas the complete account of a variety will inevitably give evidence of continued variation.

In summary, the findings in a number of preliminary studies based on all the available data suggest that what have been traditionally viewed as unidirectional differentiation or standardisation processes, leading to a minimum degree of variation, are in reality complex patterns of variation and change which reflect redistributions of variants. These become identifiable only when a sufficiently wide range of data are looked at. Synchronically, each of the resulting new patterns of variation will be shown to be both systematic and orderly. Despite the apparent systematicity and/or a high degree of uniformity in the frequencies and distributions of features in a number of texts, differences between certain idiolects or genres can remain conspicuous.

1.2 DIACHRONIC DEVELOPMENTS IN SCOTS

1.2.1 Patterns of Change

The linguistic history of Scots usually begins with a description of those features which reflect uniformity and dependence in the Early Scots period when the language resembled the Northern English dialect; there then follows a process of tracing differentiation and the achievement of relative independence; later, after the rise of what can be called the regional Scottish English Standard, anglicising tendencies are highlighted (for the political and sociocultural factors conditioning such processes, see Meurman-Solin 1993a: 41–8).

To place the various types of change into a framework of general trends in the history of Scots, individual texts can be positioned chronologically on a scale indicating to what extent they demonstrate a preference for a Scottish variant rather than an English equivalent. Ideally, evidence of this kind should be based on text profiles (Meurman-Solin forthcoming a). As the HCOS is not yet tagged, the reconstruction of the general trends depicted in Figure 1.1 is based on a set of preselected data. In addition to ⟨i⟩ digraphs, ⟨oi⟩ for ⟨-e⟩ (*adoire/ adore*), ⟨ei⟩ for ⟨e-e⟩ (*eis/ese*; later *ease*), ⟨ai⟩ for ⟨a-e⟩ (*cais/case*) and ⟨ui⟩ for ⟨u-e⟩ (*buik/buke, boke*; later *book, refuis(e)/refuse*), the following pairs of features were included in the analysis: ⟨-it, yt⟩ for ⟨-ed⟩, ⟨quh-⟩ for ⟨wh-⟩, *tha(i)* for *they*, ⟨aw/ow⟩ (*knaw/know*), /a:/ /o:/ (*sa/so*), ⟨ch/gh⟩ representing the sound /x/ (*richt/right*), ⟨sch/sh⟩ (*sche/she*) and the variant with or without *l* or *n mouillé* (*spoilze/spoil*; *distrenze/distrain*). The first variant in each pair is considered diagnostic of divergence from the Northern English dialect, whereas the second variant either is shared by this dialect and Early Scots or, in later texts, heralds the increase of Southern English influence. Thus, for example, the variant *gude* is considered non-differentiated, *guid* a markedly Scottish variant and *good* a Southern English variant.[6]

On the basis of this set of data, individual texts, each represented by a dot in Figure 1.1, can be shown to be highly deviant with respect to the chronology of change[7]. After the prominent divergence from Northern English reflected in mid-fifteenth-century texts as compared with the two early texts, a significant degree of variation over a manifestly long period of time can be attested. At the same time, despite the low number of features included in the analysis, the general trend to prefer English variants in the latter half of the seventeenth century is shown to be counterbalanced by a significant number of texts which reflect tolerance towards 'mixed speech' – the co-occurrence of English and distinctively Scottish variants.

In order to relate these findings to extralinguistic factors, the following tentative explanations can be given. A time-lag is recorded in the process towards divergence in the lower percentages of Scottish features in Aberdeen records (54 per cent), representing the periphery, as compared with the contemporary Parliamentary Acts (71 per cent) (cf. section 1.2.2). Peebles records (78 per cent) is the most differentiated pre-1500 text. Variants in the highly derivative *Porteous of Noblenes* (60 per cent), which is a translation from French, are differentiated to a lesser extent than in Ireland's *Meroure of Wyssdome* (72 per cent). There seems to be a systematic difference between religious and secular instruction, so that the four texts representing the former category contain somewhat higher percentages of Scottish variants than those that belong to the latter. Nisbet's

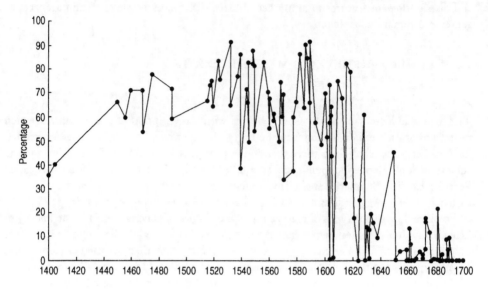

Figure 1.1 Percentages of distinctively Scottish variants in the individual texts in the Helsinki Corpus of Older Scots.

scotticisation of Purvey's *New Testament* (65 per cent) is less Scottish than Gau's *Richt Vay to the Kingdom of Heuine* (92 per cent).

The texts representing the peaks in Figure 1.1, those where the percentage of Scottish variants is at least 80 per cent, are the following: in the subperiod 1500–70, Stirling records, *Acts of Parliament*, Gau, *The Complaynt of Scotland*, Lamb's *Resonyng* and three male writers and the women writers in *The Correspondence of Mary of Lorraine*; in the subperiod 1570–1640, *Criminal Trials of Scotland*, trials from the proceedings of St Andrews Kirk Sessions, letters and a journal by Sir Patrick Waus, Melville of Kilrenny's diary and letters by Alexander Gordon in *The Sutherland Book*. In contrast, low percentages of Scottish variants have been attested in Sir Patrick Waus' letters from school to his parents (39 per cent), John Lesley's diary (34 per cent) and Bruce's sermon (41 per cent).

That the shape of the curve reflects an approximate chronology of change in Older Scots is borne out by findings which can be explained by a number of language-external factors (for information on the influence of printing and author- and audience-related variables, see also sections 1.2.4 and 1.2.5). For example, passages known to have been extracted from English sources in Lindsay of Pitscottie's history reflect a lower degree of Scottishness (38 per cent) than those which are from his own pen (61 per cent). Stirling records (1519–29; 84 per cent), produced in a burgh which is a site of a royal castle and located close to Edinburgh, resemble Parliamentary Acts (1525–55; 87 per cent), in contrast with Peebles records (1555–73; 59 per cent), a contrast which may also be due to the time difference between the first two texts and the third. There is a dramatic decrease of Scottish variants in the *Acts of Parliament* after the Union of the Crowns, whereas texts dealing with regional topics such as John Spalding's history (c. 1650) remain conservative in contrast with those written for a wider audience, such as stories about witches in *Satan's Invisible World Discovered* (1685) by George Sinclair, or texts discussing a topic of general interest among professional people such as his *Natural Philosophy* (1672/1683).

The shape of the curve changes when the linguistic features are looked at separately. Figure 1.2 illustrates the distributions of *quh*-variants (for example *quha/quho*, *quhilk*, *quhile* and *quhite*) as against *wh*-variants (*who*, *which*, *while* and *white*) in the HCOS. This figure shows that there is almost no variation in the pre-1600 texts of the corpus (for differences between pronouns, see Devitt 1989: 18–21). While a number of texts may use the English variant sporadically, only Patrick Bothwell in *The Correspondence of Mary of Lorraine*, John Lesley in his diary, and Bruce in his sermon choose it in more than 5 per cent of the possible contexts. The pattern of 'mixed speech' (see p. 8), which is evident in Figure 1.2 particularly in the sixteenth century, changes into a categorical preference for either of the two sets of variants. In fact, the presentation of the findings for each individual text is necessary in order to stress, on the one hand, the uniformity of practice in the majority of idiolects, and on the other, the conspicuous differences between them. Charts illustrating s-curves (Devitt 1989) fail to demonstrate heterogeneity of this kind. However, in addition to the highly conservative history by John Spalding, the co-occurrence of both variants can be attested to a prominent degree in Melville of Halhill's *Memoirs of his Own Life* (1610) and in a number of private and official letters as late as 1670.[8]

A somewhat similarly shaped curve results from an analysis of the distributions of the Scottish variants *tha, thai* and *thay* for *they*: see Figure 1.3. A tendency to anglicise the third person plural subject pronoun is earlier than the introduction of *wh*-variants. A pattern of complementary distribution in the second half of the seventeenth century is heralded by a longer period of a high degree of variation, as compared with the distributions of variant forms in Figure 1.2.

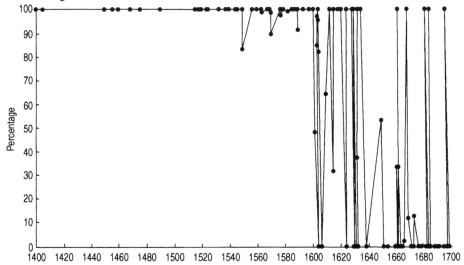

Figure 1.2 Percentages of *quh*-variants, instead of *wh*-variants, in the individual texts in the Helsinki Corpus of Older Scots.

The use of the variant *thir*, 'these', reflects a similar rhythm of change: it is the dominant variant up to the mid-seventeenth century, except in texts which reflect early wholesale anglicisation: James VI's *Counterblaste to Tobacco* (1604), William Birnie's *Blame of Kirk-buriall* (1606), Alexander Huntar's *Weights and Measures* (1624) and William Lithgow's travelogue (1632). On the other hand, a number of histories and diaries

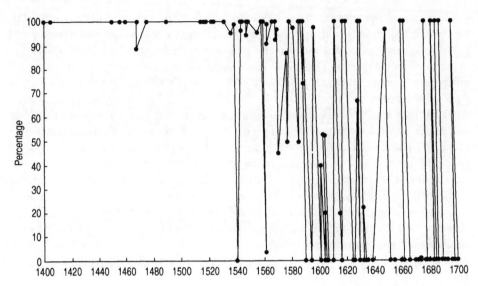

Figure 1.3 Percentages of the variants *tha*, *thai* and *thay*, instead of *they*, in the individual texts in the Helsinki Corpus of Older Scots.

(Melville, Lesley and Moysie) and some official letters illustrate 'mixed speech'. It is noteworthy that *thir* has been attested in a total of nine texts in the subperiod 1640–1700; in addition to the North-Eastern texts, it occurs in legal documents and in Sir John Lauder's *Journals* (1665–76), *The Tryal of Philip Standsfield* (1688), James Brodie's diary (1680–5) and Somerville's memoirs (1679).

However, as we can see in Figure 1.4, a significantly more varied pattern of preferences emerges in the choice of the past tense or past participle morpheme, *-it/ -yt* or *-ed*. The

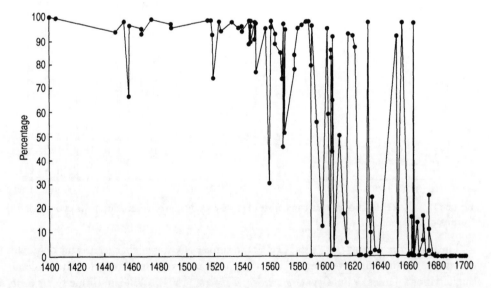

Figure 1.4 Percentages of the variant *-it/-yt*, instead of *-ed*, in the past tense and past participle forms of verbs in the individual texts in the Helsinki Corpus of Older Scots.

phenomenon of 'mixed speech' is manifested as early as the 1520s, and, after 150 years of a high degree of variation, a wholesale adoption of the English variant seems to have occurred. Yet the Aberdeen records dating from 1660–85 are an important exception, with 75 per cent of the variants remaining distinctively Scottish (see Table 1.1).[9]

1.2.2 Dialectal Variation within Scots

The majority of the texts in the HCOS originate from the Central Scots area (East-Mid Scots in Murison 1977), but there are a few texts which represent a North-East Scots regional variety. There is a considerable time-lag in the actualisation of both diverging and converging trends, in the texts extracted from the *Council Register of the Burgh of Aberdeen* (1450–89, 1519–56, 1590–1620 and 1660–85) as well as in the other North-Eastern texts in the HCOS, such as *Porteous of Noblenes* (1490), Gilbert Skeyne's *Descriptioun of the Pest* (1568) and *Descriptioun of the Well* (1580) and John Spalding's history (c. 1650) (Meurman-Solin 1993a: 91–2; 136–7). Table 1.1 illustrates the chronology of change and degree of variation in Parliamentary Acts and local records as assessed by the percentages of the markedly Scottish variants analysed in Figures 1.1–1.4. The *Acts of Parliament* are here viewed as documents produced by the central government; records of Stirling represent the dialect area of Central Scots and Aberdeen records that of North-East Scots, a politically peripheral area. As there are no samples from fifteenth-century Stirling records, Peebles records here represent Central Scots in the subperiod 1450–1500.

Table 1.1 shows how the differentiation process began later in the Aberdeen records than in the texts representing the Central Scots area, whereas local records in general, and

Table 1.1 Percentages of distinctively Scottish variants in the *Acts of Parliament* and Peebles, Stirling and Aberdeen records in the Helsinki Corpus of Older Scots.

	-it -yt	quh-	tha(i) thay	others
1450–1500				
Parliament	96	100	100	71
Peebles	100	100	100	78
Aberdeen	94	100	89	54
1500–1570				
Parliament	98	100	99	87
Stirling	99	100	100	84
Aberdeen	97	100	95	77
1570–1640				
Parliament	88	85	53	74
Stirling	84	97	20	58
Aberdeen	94	100	52	61
1640–1700				
Parliament	2	0	0	5
Stirling	11	13	0	18
Aberdeen	26	0	1	17

Aberdeen records in particular, retain vernacular Scottish features longer than Parliamentary Acts. That divergence has only just started in the Aberdeen records can be illustrated by distributions of variants shared with the Northern English dialect such as *gret*, *gud*, *buk* and *mene*; variants with an ⟨i⟩ digraph (*greit*, *guid* and so on) are in the minority. The spelling ⟨ai⟩ for /a:/ is clearly the earliest ⟨i⟩ digraph adopted in Aberdeen records, with twenty-seven instances against two of ⟨ui⟩ and five of ⟨ei⟩. *Porteous of Noblenes*, translated by Andrew Cadiou from Aberdeen, is in its adoption of markedly Scottish variants later than the contemporary *Meroure of Wyssdome* by Ireland, representing Central Scots. The different pace of change in the north is also evidenced by the high percentages of these variants in Spalding at a time when the majority of Central Scots texts reflect a significantly lower frequency of vernacular features. These results stress the necessity of distinguishing between documents originating from different areas of Scotland. At the same time, the internal heterogeneity of Scots highlights the importance of producing a linguistic atlas of Older Scots on principles of the kind that the Edinburgh project has decided to pursue.

1.2.3   Process of Differentiation

In general terms, divergence from the Northern English dialect towards the rise of a Scottish regional norm can be dated from the fifteenth century and the first half of the sixteenth century. The Edinburgh computerised atlas of Older Scots, with its coverage of Early Scots, will lend itself admirably to the study of pre-1450 differentiation processes, while the Helsinki Scots Corpus offers a relatively modest number of texts in the subperiod 1450–1500 (Meurman-Solin 1995a). However, considering that the earliest vernacular prose texts are extant from as late as the 1370s, the eleven pre-1500 texts in the Helsinki material are perhaps sufficiently representative, since nine of them illustrate language use in two central genres in fifteenth-century prose: legal documents and – either secular or religious – instructive texts. In addition, there are two important letters by George, Earl of March, and James Douglas, Warden of the Marches, addressed to Henry IV and dating from 1400 and 1405 respectively.

As shown in Figure 1.1, the direction of change is well documented in the HCOS. Trends towards divergence are reflected quite systematically, especially in the frequencies and distributions of ⟨i⟩ digraphs, for example in their total absence in the early fifteenth-century official letters and their infrequency as late as the first decades of the sixteenth century. Gavin Douglas (1515–18) uses no ⟨ai⟩ or ⟨oi⟩ variants, whereas in *The Correspondence of Mary of Lorraine* (1542–60), variants with an ⟨i⟩ digraph are the preferred choice in 83–100 per cent of the potential variant pairs.[10] The conditioning factor of date is as important as that of dialect area (see section 1.2.2).

The same trend can be illustrated through a comparison of pre-1500 instructive texts, notably of John Ireland's *Meroure of Wyssdome* (1490) and John Gau's *Richt Vay to the Kingdom of Heuine* (1533). The former clearly shows a preference for an ⟨ai⟩ spelling for /a:/, while ⟨ei⟩ is chosen instead of ⟨e–e⟩ in only 20 per cent of the cases; no instances have been attested of ⟨oi⟩ or ⟨ui⟩. In contrast, Gau consistently prefers spelling variants with ⟨ai⟩ and ⟨oi⟩; he uses ⟨ei⟩ in two-thirds of the possible contexts and ⟨ui⟩ in thirty-six out of forty-three instances (84 per cent). Extracts from Gilbert Hay's *Buke of Knychthede* and *Buke of the Governaunce of Princis*, which date from 1456, also show that variants with ⟨ai⟩ (90 per cent) occur much earlier than the other ⟨i⟩ digraphs (there are no instances of the latter in Hay). When the later developments are analysed in the texts of the first version of the corpus (Meurman-Solin 1993a: 127–9, 199–210), the following results appear. In the subperiod 1500–70, in seventeen out of nineteen texts an ⟨i⟩ digraph was chosen in more than 50 per cent of the possible contexts; in fact, in fifteen texts out of nineteen it is at least 80 per cent.

The dominant variants in the sixteenth century, *quh-* for *wh-*, *tha*, *thai* and *thay* for *they*, and *-it/-yt* for *-ed*, are also almost exclusively used in all pre-1500 texts. In fact, on the basis of the limited evidence available, it seems that only ⟨i⟩ digraphs and, to a lesser extent, *l* and *n mouillé* are still in the process of diffusion in the first subperiod, whereas the other features listed above (pp. 7–8) are already well established in the variety.

It is particularly noteworthy that processes of continuing divergence, or de-anglicisation, and of convergence, or anglicisation, can be found overlapping in the second half of the sixteenth century. The further developments in the use of ⟨i⟩ digraphs confirm this pattern of change, with a number of texts reflecting an increase of Scottish variants at the same time as others give evidence of their rapid decrease. In 1570–1640, the impetus for favouring variants prevalent in the Southern English Standard is reflected in the number of texts (seven) with no ⟨i⟩ digraphs. However, twenty-two out of thirty-eight texts still choose an ⟨i⟩ digraph in more than 50 per cent of the possible contexts; the number of texts with a lower percentage has increased. In the last subperiod, thirty-three texts out of a total of fifty-one use no ⟨i⟩ digraphs at all.[11]

The following examples give further evidence of the continuously varying shape of the curve which depicts processes of change in Older Scots. The diffusion of the ⟨i⟩ digraph *thaim(e)/thaym(e)*, 'them', does not follow the pattern described above. Five pre-1500 texts, the early official letters, *Craft of Deying*, *Vertewis of the Mess* and Aberdeen records, use only the variant *thaim*, while *Dicta Salomonis* clearly prefers it. Hay and Ireland use mostly or exclusively the Northern English variant *thame*; *tham* is used in the majority of instances in Peebles records and in *Porteous of Noblenes*. On the other hand, *Acts of Parliament* reflect a high degree of variation in 1455–83 (*þam* 4 per cent, *thame/þame* 67 per cent, *thai* 1 per cent and *them* 28 per cent). *Thame* remains the most frequent variant in the sixteenth century as well: in the period 1500–70, it is chosen in 55 per cent of the total as against *thaim* (23 per cent), *tham* (10 per cent) and *them* (12 per cent). However, the dominance of the ⟨i⟩ digraph is conspicuous in Gau (more than 99 per cent) and, to a lesser extent, in *Basilicon Doron* (59 per cent). Only *them* occurs in *The Complaynt of Scotland*. In fact, *thame* remains the typically Scottish form, so that this spelling is the preferred shape in 68 per cent of the total of instances in Spalding as late as 1650.

A very homogeneous practice emerges when the Scottish subject–verb constraint is analysed.[12] The rule is applied almost categorically in all pre-1570 texts. Suffixed and suffixless verbs may co-occur in later texts; the total number of suffixless forms increases after 1640 (Meurman-Solin 1992 and 1993a: 203–8, 246–58). The Southern ending *-(e)th* in the third person singular is absent in pre-1500 texts, and there are only three instances in the subperiod 1500–70, whereas 227 instances have been attested in the following subperiod (Meurman-Solin 1992: 250–1).

1.2.4 Degree of Uniformity in the Regional Standard

What degree of uniformity results from the trends towards divergence described in the preceding section? Is it possible to identify statistically significant quantities of distinctive features to enable us to consider the differentiation sufficiently advanced and to describe the outcome as a regional norm standard? To what extent are the uniform practices within the norm conditioned by specific extralinguistic factors? Can they be shown to be established features in a wide range of texts?

In the discussion which follows, special attention will be paid to whether linguistic differences between texts can be meaningfully related to extralinguistic variables. In this chapter, the following extralinguistic parameters seem particularly relevant: dialect, printed versus manuscript, sex of author, audience description, participant relationship, genre and text category (for a complete list of parameters, see Meurman-Solin 1993a: 62–3). The hypothesis is that, if these variables succeed in explaining the position of each text in the general framework of continued linguistic variation, the Scottish variety has reached the status of a regional norm despite the apparent lack of uniformity reflected, for example, in Figures 1.1–1.4. Unless stated otherwise, evidence in this section is based on information illustrated in Figure 1.1; in Figures 1.2–1.4, the degree of variation is very low in pre-1600 texts.

In the sixteenth-century texts of the HCOS, the percentages of Scottish variants vary from John Lesley's diary (1571; 34 per cent) to Gau and St Andrews Kirk Sessions dating from 1589–92 (92 per cent). It is quite evident that date alone cannot explain such a high degree of variation, and further study will be necessary to describe the patterns of variation in more detail and to identify any extralinguistic variables that may account for them. At this stage, it is possible to suggest that genre may condition some of the positions of texts on the scale of variation. Earlier proposals along such lines (Devitt 1989: 68, Meurman-Solin 1993a: 131) can be given further support by the more extensive selection of legal documents in the expanded and revised HCOS. With the exception of early sixteenth-century *Criminal Trials* and contemporary Peebles records, all pre-1600 legal documents, including texts extracted from trial proceedings, contain at least 70 per cent of Scottish variants. Moreover, there is a conspicuous increase in the degree of Scottishness in the late sixteenth-century trials. This is perhaps related to the assumption that the development of the regional standard norm in Scotland first manifested itself chiefly in the well-established genres in written language. Recordings of trial proceedings are labelled 'speech-based' (Kytö 1993; Meurman-Solin 1993a: 79) in the HCOS, and the time-lag in the increase of markedly Scottish features in them (in recordings from St Andrews Kirk Sessions from 71 to 92 per cent, in *Criminal Trials* from 62 to 87 per cent) may be due to this relationship to spoken language.

Subject matter may also explain differences within idiolects: Skeyne's *Descriptioun of the Pest* (50 per cent) reflects a lower degree of Scottishness than his somewhat later tract *Descriptioun of the Well* (67 per cent). The former is written in a learned fashion and in a more Latinate style than the latter, which discusses the beneficial effects of the water of a well near Aberdeen (Meurman-Solin 1993a: 91–2). A similar difference between Quintin Kennedy's *Litil Breif Tracteit* (56 per cent) and his *Compendious Ressonyng* (68 per cent) may be due to the latter being written in dialogue form. The conservative influence of genre conventions may have a more important role in the *Litil Breif Tracteit*, whereas the *Compendious Ressonyng* may be claimed to belong to a less established subgenre. John Lesley's diary is much less Scottish (34 per cent) than his contemporary history (61 per cent). More texts need to be examined to appraise idiolectal variation of this kind, and, in the case of Lesley, both editions need to be checked against manuscripts, to exclude the possibility that different scribes or, for that matter, different editorial principles explain the lack of uniformity in this particular idiolect.

Of the total of seventy-four texts in the Helsinki Scots Corpus, only seventeen are based on first or contemporary prints. On the basis of frequencies and distributions of diagnostic variants, the first half of the seventeenth century seems to be a period of relatively rapid change. Is this because more texts were printed? Table 1.2 gives data relating to differences between unprinted and printed texts (for a more detailed analysis of findings, see Meurman-Solin 1993a: 137–48). In the light of these findings, printing seems to have had an important function in establishing the regional norm: Scottish variants prevail in the sixteenth-century printed texts, sometimes even more regularly than in the unprinted ones (compare, on the one hand, Lesley's and Moysie's histories, and on the other Skeyne's tracts and Fowler's *Answer to Hamiltoun*). However, the role of printing as a means of reaching a wider audience becomes evident in texts of the seventeenth century. There is a clear difference between the language of seventeenth-century private records (see Melville's and Birrel's diaries), which remained in manuscript, and the language in the four printed texts dating from 1600–40.

In the same way, the Scottish subject–verb constraint reflects a tendency to adopt English practices more readily in printed texts than in manuscripts, so that the mean of suffixed forms occurring with other than adjacent pronoun subjects is 4 in manuscripts and

Table 1.2 Percentages of distinctively Scottish variants in a selection of unprinted and printed texts in the HCOS. The texts are in chronological order.

	-it/-yt	quh-, tha(i), thay	others
Unprinted texts			
1570–1600			
Buchanan	99	100	70
Criminal Trials	96	98	87
Pitscottie	85	75	58
Lesley	47	98	53
St Andrews K. Sess.	98	100	94
Moysie	58	66	58
Basilicon Doron	14	99	48
1600–1640			
Stirling records	85	69	61
Melville	42	58	62
Roy trial	98	93	72
Birrel	66	69	28
Printed texts			
1570–1600			
Skeyne	89	100	81
Fergusson	98	96	75
Fowler	82	93	63
1600–1640			
Birnie	1	0	1
Huntar	0	0	0
Lithgow	2	0	0
Row	2	0	10

0.4 in printed texts. Yet this tendency becomes prevalent as late as the seventeenth century, when printing has become a vehicle for anglicisation. Printing is assumed to correlate significantly with other language-external parameters such as genre and audience. Therefore, when Devitt (1989: 63) points out that 'all printed texts were found to be significantly more highly anglicised than all texts in manuscript', her finding cannot be considered conclusive, as all of the printed texts in her material are sermons or religious treatises.

It is no coincidence that the early printed texts represented genres such as handbooks, scientific treatises, pamphlets, travelogues and sermons, as these genres appealed to a more general readership. In contrast, as a result of absence of addressee-orientation (Meurman-Solin 1994b and forthcoming b), genres such as the documentary public records (burgh records), regional histories and introvert private records (diaries and autobiographies) seem to remain linguistically conservative.

The evidence is too limited to consider the explanatory force of some of the extra-linguistic variables. That Sir Patrick Waus' early letters are less Scottish than his letters more than forty years later may be a case of differentiation; that he uses a more Scottish repertoire of spellings than his wife Katherine Kennedy, Lady Barnbarroch, cannot be due to the nature of the participant relationship, labelled 'intimate down' in the HCOS (Meurman-Solin 1993a: 180–3), as a similar set of spellings is also found in his journal. As we shall see, there is some evidence that women may have been linguistically more conservative than men. In the subperiod 1570–1640 (see Table 1.3), some women seem to apply a non-differentiated system of spellings in their private letters, as opposed to a differentiated one in earlier official letters (included in *The Correspondence of Mary of Lorraine*). Perhaps this finding only suggests that the majority of these official letters were written by men (Meurman-Solin forthcoming c).[13]

Table 1.3 Percentages of distinctively Scottish variants in a selection of private letters in the HCOS in the period 1540–1640.

Writer	Date	-it/-yt	quh-, thai(i), thay	Others	i-digraphs only
Patrick Waus	1540	96	80	60	84
William Scott	1569	100	100	75	50
Katherine Kennedy	1586–7	100	95	65	35
Patrick Waus	1587–90	100	100	80	89
Juliana Ker	1613–29	89	100	32	93
John Sutherland	1615	4	28	35	50
Alexander Gordon	1616	95	69	84	85
Jane Sutherland	1616–23	97	100	90	95
Thomas Haddington	1625	0	89	30	25
Lilias Grant	1630	100	100	14	0
John Grant	1631–5	33	20	18	17

1.2.5 Processes towards Convergence with the Southern Standard

The present study confirms that the diffusion of Southern variants through a wider range of Scottish prose texts took place after the first two decades of the seventeenth century. However, the shape of the curve depicting these processes of change in Scots varies to a considerable extent depending on what linguistic features are included in the analysis and what language-external factors condition linguistic choices in individual texts. This has also been made evident by earlier studies: for example, diachronic developments in the subject–verb constraint (Montgomery 1994a; Meurman-Solin 1993a: 203–8, 246–58), the *do*-periphrasis (Meurman-Solin 1993a: 208–11, 259–75), the distribution of variants of the preterite and past-participle morpheme (Devitt 1989) and those of <i> digraphs (Meurman-Solin 1993a: 199–200) all reflect significant differences in the pace and pattern of change, as well as anglicisation processes in the seventeenth century. As stated earlier, linguistic developments in Scots in the sixteenth century are characterised by overlapping processes of de-anglicisation and anglicisation. According to the HCOS, numerous post-1640 texts also use markedly Scottish variants, so that no wholesale adoption of English variants can be claimed to have taken place in all written texts; nor is it possible to say that anglicisation was virtually completed by 1700.

Our findings stress the independence of diachronic developments in Scots, as they are shown to follow a pace and direction of change which are different from developments in contemporary Standard English. The introduction of periphrastic *do* seems to be of Southern influence in Scots (Meurman-Solin 1993d), but there is a significant time-lag in its diffusion. The first occurrences of periphrastic *do* in Scottish prose are as late as the 1550s, that is to say at a time when the device was at its most frequent in Southern English (Rissanen 1991, on the basis of evidence in the early Modern English part of the *Helsinki Corpus of English Texts*). The first occurrences in Scots have been recorded from argumentative texts, labelled 'pamphlets' in the HCOS (for example, *Swa ʒe do transforme ʒour estait ryale als oft as Protheus did change formis* in William Lamb's *Ane Resonyng of ane Scottis and Inglis Merchand*).[14] Its use continued to increase in Scots when a decline could be recorded in English. This increase is particularly conspicuous in trials, educational treatises, diaries and private letters. It appears likely that the construction showed no signs of becoming functionally or stylistically redundant towards the end of the seventeenth century, as high frequencies have been attested in texts dating from the last decade of the century (Meurman-Solin 1993a: 263). In fact, these initial findings for legal documents in 1640–1700 will have to be adjusted, as, according to the expanded HCOS, periphrastic *do* frequently occurs in the *Acts of Parliament* and in Aberdeen records in this subperiod.[15]

Variation in the choice of the indefinite article illustrates yet another pattern of change where Scottish practices are often retained. Devitt (1989: 23–6) shows how the complementary distribution of the variant *a* before consonant and *an* or *ane* before vowel or *h* gains ground rather gradually and less regularly than the shift from *-it* to *-ed* or from *quh-* to *wh-*. It is also less complete by 1659, with the variant *a* having risen to only 74 per cent by that time. In the subperiod 1640–1700 in the HCOS, Stirling records retain *ane* before consonant in 44 per cent of the total, while the percentage is as high as 75 per cent in contemporary Aberdeen records. The lateness of change in the north is also highlighted by the finding in Spalding, where *ane* before consonants represents 60 per cent of the total. That the *Acts of Parliament* dating from 1661–86 are not completely anglicised can be illustrated, for example, by the occurrence of *ane* before consonants in 9 per cent of the total, and there is also variation between *an* (2 per cent) and *ane* (14 per cent) before vowels. In addition, in late seventeenth-century private records such as Andrew Hay's (1659–60) and William Cunningham's diary (1673–80) and Somerville's memoirs, *ane* before consonants is retained in 3 per cent of the instances; Hay and Somerville also prefer this variant, rather than *an*, before vowels.

The co-occurrence of Scottish and English variants in late seventeenth-century letters illustrates the important differences as regards when and how anglicisation can affect different idiolects. In Thomas Stewart's letters to his son (1668–70), *ane* is used before consonants in 50 per cent of the total of indefinite articles; his letters may contain a higher degree of vernacular features because of the intimate relationship between the author and the addressee (on participant relationship, see pp. 5–6; for other features in Thomas Stewart's language, see Meurman-Solin 1993a: 180–3). Uses of *ane* before a consonant and before a vowel are recorded more often in seventeenth-century women's letters than in men's, with the exception of late seventeenth-century official letters by William Glencarne, Donald M'Donald and particularly by John Fletcher, in which the choice of variants resembles that of contemporary women's private correspondence.

Two text types, private and official letters, are a useful source for tracing change over periods of time shorter than the subperiods of the corpus and especially in periods of rapid change. Table 1.3 shows that the percentage of English spelling variants increases in 1615–25, male writers being more eager to adopt the English *-ed, wh-* and *they* than women (compare, for example, Jane and John Sutherland, or Lilias and John Grant). Evidently, both sex and date correlate with the degree of anglicisation.[16] In Table 1.3, this is illustrated by the prevalence of vernacular features in all sixteenth-century letters and in early seventeenth-century letters by female writers. In post-1640 private letters (see Meurman-Solin 1993a: 154–5), eight writers use only English variants; the rest (seven writers) use Scottish variants more or less sporadically. What is interesting is that Scottish features occur only in women's letters or in letters written by men to their social inferiors. The latter are letters in which the writer–addressee relationship is labelled 'intimate down', a parameter value used for letters written by parent to child or by husband to spouse (Meurman-Solin 1993a: 180–3). The relevance of the variable 'participant relationship' is stressed by a clear difference in the degree of Scottishness between letters labelled 'intimate down' and those labelled 'intimate up'. As regards differences between private and official letters, markedly Scottish features are absent in Thomas Haddington's official letters (compare his private letters in Table 1.3). The advanced degree of anglicisation in his official letters may be explained by his social status and his contacts; as a high government official, he served on many Parliamentary commissions and was appointed as a negotiator for the Union of the Crowns.

Women seem to be more conservative in their spelling practices during the period of intense anglicisation in the Scots language, namely in the subperiod 1570–1640, particularly as regards the choice of inflectional endings and pronoun forms, and low standard deviation figures reflect remarkable homogeneity of usage among women compared with male writers (Meurman-Solin 1993a: 160–4). However, a more detailed study (Meurman-Solin forthcoming c), which is based on all data in a selection of sixteenth- and early seventeenth-century letters, has shown that a number of phonetic spellings in women's letters position at least some women among the forerunners in phonological change. The data also highlight the fact that Scottish features occur in both types of letters by women at the very end of the seventeenth century. The analysis of a wider selection of eighteenth-century letters might provide more interesting evidence of the occurrence of Scotticisms in written language later than has usually been assumed; it would also be highly desirable to include more information on the writers' social status, social mobility and social networks.

Meurman-Solin (1993a) introduces the problem of characterising the readership of the texts. The variable 'description of audience' was given the parameter values 'administration' (legal documents), 'official' (letters addressed to officials), 'professional' (most scientific treatises), 'general public' (secular and religious instruction) and 'family' (family memoirs). In addition, information is given about specific addressees (for example, in James VI's *Basilicon Doron* written in the advice-to-princes tradition).[17] Yet variables like 'audience description', 'text category', 'genre' and 'printed' versus 'manuscript' are interrelated in various ways. While within the scope of this chapter it is not possible to examine this topic in detail, the general trend seems to be that unprinted documentary texts (text category 'statutory' with the audience description 'administration') tend to be linguistically conservative, whereas interactive texts (in most texts the audience description is 'general public'), both narrative and argumentative, have been found to be more innovative. The more frequent choice of standard English variants in seventeenth-century texts that aim at appealing to a wider audience would seem to reflect changes in the social functions of texts. Non-interactive statutory texts, which have a purely documentary function, are more conservative, as they fulfil their social function despite their linguistic conservatism. Perhaps we could say that they retain their Scottishness just because their function is restricted to the Scottish context.

As regards periphrastic *do*, its use seems to correlate with addressee-orientation. The group of texts addressed to the general public contains argumentative pamphlets which have been shown to be characterised by a high degree of involvement based on a high frequency of linguistic features in the semantic role of evidentiality; possibility modals and adverbials commenting on truth value are particularly frequent in these texts (Meurman-Solin 1993a: 208–11, 259–75, 292–3, 308–10). The high frequency of periphrastic *do*, for example, in administrative texts from 1640–1700, may be due to the change in the way in which legal proceedings were recorded. Trials, some of which contain judicial depositions partly in direct, partly in indirect speech, range from legal documents, written to be used as precedents in later legal proceedings, to detailed narratives which were printed to receive a wider circulation. The earlier trials in the HCOS represent the former type. Their function seems, however, to have become more diversified towards the end of the seventeenth century. *The Tryal of Philip Standsfield* (1688) was reprinted several times in the seventeenth and eighteenth centuries; this may be the result of the popular appeal enjoyed by trial cases. It is perhaps no coincidence that George Sinclair's contemporary accounts of witches (1685) were also published with a wider readership in mind.

1.3 DIFFUSION OF MARKEDLY SCOTTISH LEXICAL ITEMS

To apply the principle of random sampling, the assumed decrease of markedly Scottish lexical items in the seventeenth-century texts of the corpus was traced by creating a file of words and word-forms which, according to the *Dictionary of the Older Scottish Tongue*, are only or chiefly Scottish. For the purposes of this chapter, the material was restricted to all words and word-forms with an initial ⟨k-⟩, ⟨n-⟩ or ⟨o-⟩. In this analysis of lexis, the findings generally confirm the pattern of distributions of distinctively Scottish features, so that texts reflecting a preference of Scottish variant spellings and morphosyntactic variants also contain a higher frequency (both type- and tokenwise) of primarily or exclusively Scottish words and word-forms. Sporadic uses of Scottish lexical items have, however, been attested in texts which are otherwise highly anglicised.

The material contained only eighteen distinctively Scottish words; the majority of features labelled as only or chiefly Scottish were variant word-forms. Nevertheless, the distributions of the former show that highly anglicised printed texts such as Robert Bruce's sermon *Vpon the Sacrament of the Lord's Supper* (1590) and William Birnie's *Blame of Kirk-buriall* (1606) contain exclusively Scottish lexical items (*out-gaite/outgait* in the former, *kempes*, 'champions' in the latter). The vernacular features of James VI's language are highlighted by his use of *kythe* (one's *clemencie, loue, hatred, contempt, zeale and affectioun*) both in *Basilicon Doron* (pp. 63, 111, 112, 113) and in his letters (*Memorials of the Family of Wemyss of Wemyss*, p. 30). Among the seventeenth-century materials, Aberdeen records (1660–85) and John Spalding's history (c. 1650), two texts, both representing North-East Scots, stand out; but, despite his anglicised spellings and most of his morphosyntactic features, Skene of Hallyard also uses words established in the local community (such as *outfeild/outfield*) in his *Of Husbandrie* (*ante* 1669).

The findings relating to variant word-forms are statistically more significant. The general trend is reflected in the decrease of types from 1.6–1.7 per 1,000 words of running text in pre-1570 texts to 1.1 in 1570–1640, and finally to 0.3 in 1640–1700. As regards tokens, a similar development has been attested (5, 5.5, 3.3 and 0.8). While the number of types and tokens remains the same, for example, in the late fifteenth-century and early sixteenth-century *Acts of Parliament* (one type and five tokens per 1,000 words), the number of types is halved by the period 1587–1621, to fall as low as 0.1, with one token per 1,000 words, in the samples from 1661–86.

However, the frequency of Scottish word-forms varies quite considerably in the individual texts, which partly explains the low mean frequencies above. The differences are particularly significant in texts dating from 1500–1640. Both type- and tokenwise the *Carnwarth Barony Court Book* and Patrick Waus' letters from school stand out, but the number of tokens is twice as high as the mean in four other pre-1570 texts as well – Peebles and Aberdeen records, the Mar Lodge translation of Hector Boece's history and John Gau's *Richt Vay to the Kingdom of Heuine*. Throughout the corpus, the number of types remains high in letters; a case in point is Sir Patrick Waus, in whose letters dating from 1587–90, addressed to his wife, the Scottish variant word-forms represent the same type/token ratio as that attested in his letters addressed to his parents forty years earlier. Scottish and English variant forms co-occur in compilations of texts such as *Criminal Trials* (1561–7) – where, in 52 per cent of the instances, an English variant form is preferred – and in the 'mixed speech' of a number of writers (William Lamb, Quintin Kennedy, Archibald Johnston). Nevertheless, among the total of seventy-two pre-1640 texts in which only or chiefly Scottish variant word-forms have been attested, forty use no corresponding English variants, and in a further nineteen the proportion of English variants is less than 10 per cent.

The claim that lexis would suggest a higher degree of regional features than, for example, spelling variation is supported by our findings; in the set of diagnostic features applied in this chapter, only lexical items serve to reveal the presence of vernacular features in texts such as Skene's *Of Husbandrie* and in a number of letters. Sporadic use of distinctively Scottish features in late seventeenth-century texts can be illustrated by *(malt) kill* (for *kiln*) in John Lamont's diary, *noo(c)k*, eModE *nuk(e)*, in Sir John Lauder's *Journals*, *oulk*, for *week*, in Skene, *obleis*, for *oble(d)ge*, in William Cunningham's diary and expenditure book, and *outrin, outrun* in the anonymous travelogue *Prince of Tartaria* (1661). The otherwise highly anglicised *Acts of Parliament* in the subperiod 1640–1700 contain variant forms such as *nixt* for *next* and *nichbour* for *neighbour*, but the Scottish variants *anly* for *only, necessar* and *ordinar* for *necessary* and *ordinary* are receding features; the English variants by far outnumber the Scottish.

A study of word-forms confirms a pattern of complementary distribution in the use of Scottish or English variants. For example, only very rarely do variants such as the Scottish *awe, aucht, awand, ald, ait, aittis, ath(e)/aith/aicht* and *outhir* co-occur with the English *owe, ought, owing, old, oat, oates, oath* and *either* in the same text (for variant spellings, see DOST). Likewise, the variant *ald* only very sporadically co-occurs with *old* (in five texts, for example two instances out of twenty-five in Quintin Kennedy, two out of thirty-six in *Acts of Parliament* (1587–1621)); in contrast, the Scottish variant seems to have completely disappeared from post-1640 texts. The word *church* for *kirk* appears in Scottish diaries and letters starting from 1571. The latter variant is quite resistant; it has been attested in twelve post-1640 texts. The same is true as regards the use of Scottish *bairn* for *child* (as late as the period 1640–1700 in *Acts of Parliament*, Aberdeen records, *The Tryal of Philip Standsfield* and private letters). *Bide* for *remain* occurs in Alexander Brodie's diary from 1652–80. An investigation of a wider selection of entries labelled as only or chiefly Scottish in DOST would undoubtedly identify further significant distinctions between texts as regards retention of vernacular features.

1.4   CONCLUDING REMARKS

This chapter is based on a corpus of prose genres, *The Helsinki Corpus of Older Scots*, and samples from the *Dictionary of the Older Scottish Tongue* (DOST). Despite its limitations, the HCOS provides a wider range of texts than has previously been available for the study of the history of Scots. On the basis of this evidence, the following observations can be made.

Continued variation characterises the history of Scots. The degree of uniformity which can be recorded when statistical data are presented by grouping the texts in various ways is often considerably lower or absent when texts are looked at individually. Differences between texts can be at least partly explained with reference to extralinguistic factors which relate to textual history, the author, audience, subject matter or the social and communicative function of a text. As numerous fifteenth-, sixteenth- and seventeenth-century texts reflect a high degree of derivativeness, and as even more numerous texts are characterised by contextual styles which add to their inner heterogeneity, an attempt to classify them tends to be misleading in one way or another. The important role of text traditions, stylistic conventions in certain genres, and the intensity of innovative pressures in others, all result in multidirectional developments over time.

In the majority of diagnostic features, differentiation from the Northern English dialect manifests itself in the latter half of the fifteenth century. In this process, there is however a considerable time-lag in texts representing the geographical and/or political periphery as compared with those produced in the vicinity of the centres of national government in Scotland. The pace and pattern of change differ depending on which linguistic feature is analysed: for example, some pronoun variants dominate from the earliest texts dating from the beginning of the fifteenth century up to the end of the sixteenth century, whereas each of the ⟨i⟩ digraphs seems to have a chronology of its own.

A high degree of variation has been recorded in the sixteenth century, as tendencies towards divergence coincide with those leading towards convergence with the Southern English Standard. The first signs of intensified variation can be identified in a number of texts in the second half of the sixteenth century, but the internal heterogeneity of Scots is most prominent during the first decades of the seventeenth century. Addressee-oriented text types reflect a more intense need to appeal to a wider audience and therefore avoid possibly stigmatised linguistic features, preferring the shared or prestigious features of the majority variety. In other words, it is in the more interactive and the more involved texts that the different communicative functions of genres and the social factors related to writers and addressees play an important role. In contrast, in administrative texts which have a purely documentary function, the language may remain conservative as a result of the neutralisation of the roles of both author and addressee. Textual roles of authors and addressees may be conventionalised, so that they have become established generic characteristics. In instances of this kind, the roles may decelerate change. On the other hand, textual roles may reflect actual social roles and give an impulse to the choice of prestige variants or variants which are most appropriate from a pragmatic point of view.

Variation is manifested also in the subperiod 1640–1700, so that those texts which especially show primarily local or regional relevance or those letters written by and addressed to members of closed speech communities with strong ties tend to contain more vernacular features than texts appealing to wider audiences.

It is to be hoped that further diachronic studies will be based on grammatically tagged computer-readable texts which allow the production of a detailed linguistic atlas of Scots.

NOTES

1. As editor of the *Dictionary of the Older Scottish Tongue*, A. J. Aitken launched *The Older Scots Text Archive*, now available through the Oxford Text Archive. In his study on variation and variety in Middle Scots (Aitken 1971a), he advocated the need for quantitatively more representative evidence to support his findings, which in his opinion remained impressionistic.
2. Findings in Meurman-Solin (1992–4) are based upon the first version of the HCOS; for the statistics in this chapter, the expanded and revised version of the Corpus (Meurman-Solin 1995a) has been used.
3. The quality of the editions varies and, when regarding a reading as doubtful, the user of the HCOS should check the manuscript(s). No information is included in the Corpus concerning the editorial principles or the textual history given in the editions. Unfortunately, in a number of texts no detailed introduction is provided by the editor.
4. The periodisation is due to decisions made in the Early Modern English part of the *Helsinki Corpus of English Texts* (Nevalainen and Raumolin-Brunberg 1989).
5. The parameter value is left unspecified in a number of texts (Meurman-Solin 1993a: 148–51; Kytö 1993; Meurman-Solin 1995a).
6. These diagnostic features reflect a time-conditioned pattern of change which allows the conflation of items shared by English and Scots before the rise of the Scottish regional norm and the later English variants reflecting anglicisation. In further studies based on all the data, shared features and those diagnostic of anglicisation should preferably be kept separate.
7. Detailed bibliographical information on the source texts is given in the WordCruncher version of the HCOS. A booklet listing this information has also been made available. Please contact the Oxford Text Archive (archive@vax.oxford.ac.uk) or the Norwegian Computing Center for the Humanities (icame@hd.uib.no).
8. English and distinctively Scottish variants co-occur, with no clear preference given to either of the two, in private letters by John Sutherland (1615) and Thomas Stewart (1668–70), and in official letters by James VI (1587–1618), Alexander Leslie (1631–2) and William Glencarne (1660–2).
9. The early text containing only 67 per cent of Scottish variants in Figure 1.4 is *The Vertewis of the Mess* (1460). For further details on findings for individual texts, see Table IV in Meurman-Solin 1993a.

10. As regards *The Correspondence of Mary of Lorraine*, the Helsinki Scots Corpus contains letters by Patrick Bothwell, George Douglas, Alexander Gordon, Robert Maxwell, Henry Methven and Adam Otterburn, and seventeen letters by eleven female writers.

11. For the diffusion of the variant spelling <ea> (as in *great*, instead of *gret(e)*, *greit*), see Table XXXVII in Meurman-Solin 1993a: 201–2.

12. According to the subject–verb-constraint rule, in the third person plural, adjacent pronoun subjects are followed by suffixless verbs, whereas adjacent noun subjects, all non-adjacent subjects, and relative pronoun subjects with plural antecedents are followed by suffixed verbs (for example, *To this comand pertenis al thingis quhilk ar contenit in the halie writ* (Gau, p. 23); *it behouis zow to tak thame as thay ar, with all thingis that of necessitie belangis vnto thame, or lawfully dependis on thame* (Fergusson, p. 71).

13. Letters by four women in *The Correspondence of Mary of Lorraine* are known to be autographs.

14. Periphrastic *do*, in affirmative statements, and auxiliary *do*, in negative statements and questions, were introduced simultaneously into Scots (Meurman-Solin 1993a: 208–11).

15. In Aberdeen records, periphrastic *do* often occurs in stereotypical expressions, such as *the present Commissioners . . . did ordaine, and heirby ordaines that . . .* (1660 Aberdeen B. Rec., p. 194), an example which also illustrates the Scottish subject–verb constraint with a suffixed verb occurring after a non-adjacent plural noun.

16. The interesting findings regarding gender-based differences in language use (see Meurman-Solin 1993a: 160–3) suggest that the coverage of women's language should be extended to the eighteenth century. A supplementary part to the core corpus is being planned, and the selections made for its first draft stress the importance of private letters, diaries and autobiographies as evidence of women's language.

17. Instead of being based on subclasses, extralinguistic variables such as 'description of audience' could consist of a network of bipolar dimensions where different degrees would reflect various realisations of abstract concepts, such as life-mode characterised by close contacts with speakers of other varieties or other languages versus life-mode characterised by strong ties only with representatives of the writer's own speech community. The role of audience as a sociohistorical phenomenon will be studied further.

2

The Origins of Scots Orthography

Veronika Kniezsa

2.1 BACKGROUND

It is not an easy task to write about the history of Scots orthography, because there is hardly any material to draw from. The history of orthography of the English language seems to be one of the most neglected areas of its historical analyses. To this day there have been only two attempts at the history of English spelling, neither of them even trying to be comprehensive. There are descriptions of some of the Middle English notational innovations in German doctoral theses, but they have attracted little scholarly attention. It is difficult to reconstruct scribal traditions; and, though there are usually orthographic remarks in text editions or papers dealing with the grammar of individual texts, these tend to treat spelling mainly in connection with phonology and thus are scanty and not too reliable. It is a great shortcoming of historical studies of the English language that their main interest lies in the description of the standard, be it in the Old English or the Modern period, to the neglect of the language and writing of areas which at the time were not considered to represent the mainstream of a given period. Thus the Northumbrian dialect of the Old English period has been completely neglected, and very few and sometimes quite misleading statements have been written about its continuation and about the developments of the northern dialects to which, through its origins, Scots also belongs.

No scholar has ever been interested either in giving a complete inventory of the graphemes or in establishing the chronology of their appearance or their regional distribution (Scragg 1974 and Bourcier 1978 are too general in their treatment). Since 1986, with the publication of the *Linguistic Atlas of Late Medieval English* (LALME), we have had much help in placing Scots orthographic features into reliable patterns, and we are now able to see which of them are unique or which are shared with adjacent areas. Unfortunately, however, some features, which are central to any debate about the history of Scots spelling, namely the ⟨i⟩ digraphs and vowel-length marking in general, are not among the 248 features which LALME takes into consideration.

While there are some useful sources to rely on when trying to draw up the development of the Scots orthographic system, there are however some important limitations, which may have something to do with a concern for the Standard. For instance, even when they speak about Older Scots, these sources deal with the Middle Scots period, and nobody seems to be interested in the earliest sixty-odd years of Scots literacy. It is not that there are no documents: this is the period which can provide us with the most reliable type of data taken from original non-literary writings, all dated and marked for their location. These are usually the most prized kind of medieval writings, in contrast to the much-copied and therefore much-altered literary pieces; however, these documents have not raised linguistic interest. The Middle Scots period has been more helpfully treated. James Murray (1873) himself wrote much about this period; there is also a short summary on Middle Scots spelling and phonology in G. G. Smith's (1902) anthology, and another more comprehensive one in the introduction to Kuipers (1964). Alexander Craigie's (1935) article collected important data on non-systemic differences between Scots and Standard (London) English spelling. In 1971, A. J. Aitken wrote an important article in which he criticised earlier writings on the subject and listed a vast number of points to investigate and numerous roads to be taken by future researchers of the subject. *The Dictionary of the Older Scottish Tongue* is useful because it lists the usual spelling variants in the case of each word, so that tendencies can be observed; but it offers no information upon the relationship between these variants, whether they were written, or which were written in the same text and what the difference was in frequency among them. Statistical analysis seems to be a very satisfactory method in dealing with spelling variants, because in this way tendencies can be observed. Meurman-Solin has used such a method in her analysis of the material of the *Helsinki Corpus of Older Scots*, but again she focused on Middle Scots, and thus we cannot gain insight into how the well-known and well-described Middle Scots orthographic system had developed.

Scots can be treated as an independent form of the English language and its features described on their own, without reference to other varieties, for example to London English. If we choose this process, we will have to be satisfied with a synchronic description of the spelling habits of the various periods of the development of Scots, without trying to relate changes in phonology to changes in the representations of forms. One of the difficulties lies in the fact that ever since the time of Henry Sweet, historians of the English language seem to have been mainly interested in describing the developments towards a standard language, which in the Old English period was considered to be the West Saxon dialect and in the Middle English period the language of London. Other dialects, however literary they were, were completely neglected: thus the Northumbrian dialect of Old English has not yet been described, neither is anyone especially interested in the Middle English developments of the northern area, even though York was an important cultural centre all through the Middle Ages, while at the end of the Middle English period, as LALME can bear witness, there were three important scribal traditions available: southern English (London), northern English – York, but also Durham: see Vikar (1922) – and Scots. As Murray (1873) has pointed out, Scots developed out of the Northumbrian dialect of Old English, and one should presume that it inherited the written traditions of the north as well, language developments and writing traditions which have never been seriously studied. Thus Murray's generalisations could never have been satisfactorily put right and the true nature of Northern English and Early Scots satisfactorily described. It is only recently that a useful schema for the presentation of the taxonomy of Scots orthography has been drawn up (Agutter 1987).

2.2 THE BEGINNINGS

For Europeans, the beginning of writing is usually connected with conversion to Christianity; and, depending on whether they accepted its form as taught in Byzantium or Rome, they adopted either the Greek alphabet (or its developments: the Cyrillic script, Gothic script and so on) or the Latin alphabet. After conversion, writing started in Latin, and later there were attempts to use the Latin alphabet to represent words in the vernacular. These notations were modelled on Latin, the native sounds marked by the symbols used for the Latin equivalents or, as in most of the cases, the nearest equivalents; and, when already whole texts were being written in the vernacular, special notations were devised for such phonemes as were unknown in Latin and which thus had no special symbols available for them.

In the establishment of the various vernacular orthographies, external influences also played an important role, since in medieval Europe Latin pronunciation was not uniform, and speakers of every language slightly modified it according to their own phonetic rules. Thus it is not enough to know what was the general pronunciation of Latin at the time of the first attempts to use the alphabet when writing in a vernacular: it is also necessary to know what native language the missionaries spoke who converted the people and transmitted Latin to them. For example, in Old English, the marking of fricatives was by graphs representing voiced stops (⟨b⟩ = /f/, as taught by the Irish scribes), and the use of ⟨y⟩ = /ü/ was due to the influence of the Greek members of the Canterbury mission sent from Rome). And while the Latin alphabet (a modification of the Greek one, which in its turn is an adaptation of a Semitic writing system traditionally referred to as Phoenician) satisfied the notational requirements of the Latin language, it was not without ambiguities, as there were redundant graphs marking the same sound (for example, /k/ = ⟨c⟩, ⟨k⟩, ⟨q⟩ and so on), while on the other hand important contrasts were not differentiated in writing (for example, short and long vowels were marked by the same graph).

When the Latin alphabet was used for writing in another language, the number of symbols often proved to be insufficient, as there were more distinctive phonemes than letters in the alphabet. The usual process was to use the same letter for several phonemes which shared certain phonetic features (for example ⟨s⟩ for /s/, /ʃ/, /ʒ/, /z/ in Hungarian). It seems that medieval scribes, even if they were not trained phoneticians, were not the poor scholars that Jespersen believed them to be: they seemed to have a fairly good ear for analysing speech sounds. Later, in most orthographies there was an attempt to realise the principle of one phoneme – one symbol. This could be carried out by:

1. a combination of letters, which again was based on phonetic analysis: for example /θ/ = ⟨th⟩, with ⟨t⟩ characterising the voiceless dental sound and ⟨h⟩ marking the fricative character of the phoneme;
2. the use of diacritics, most frequently accents (acute, grave and circumflex), or the modified form of Latin ⟨ð⟩ in Old English to mark the interdental fricative;
3. introducing characters not belonging to the Latin alphabet: for example, ⟨þ⟩ 'thorn' = /θ/, ⟨ƿ⟩ 'wynn' = /w/ from the old Germanic runic script.

Writing was thus based on pronunciation, but due to its function of preserving messages and thoughts it is conservative in its appearance. Speech, on the other hand, undergoes slow but constant changes. In most languages, these changes of pronunciation surface sooner or later in writing in the form of changes of spelling; usually a time-lag of fifty to 100 years is assumed for spelling to reflect such changes in speech. Sometimes it is difficult to decide how to value orthographic changes, because not only are the ever-present internal language developments reflected in them but external forces are also at play: historical, social and cultural events and influences may supply explanations for some spelling modifications. An example is the attempt to distinguish long from short vowels in languages where quantitative oppositions were linguistic realities of their sound systems; it was, for instance, a defect of the Latin alphabet that this feature was not expressed in its early orthography. The function of writing will be defined differently from nation to nation. Consequently, speakers of various languages will have contrasting ideas about the relationship of script and speech depending on their national practices, and if they discuss orthography on a theoretical level they will judge its phenomena in other languages very much according to the characteristics of their native traditions.

Continental practice frequently tended to regularise spelling according to pronunciation, with learned societies taking as their remit continuous 'maintenance' of orthography, suggesting minor modifications if these were deemed to serve the purposes of a changed attitude towards earlier practices (such as in Hungarian, and to some extent in German orthography). In English, on the other hand, writing seems to have a different status, and the attitude towards spelling shows a markedly different pattern throughout the history of the language. The Anglo-Saxons started to write in the vernacular at a very early period of their history, in the seventh century, preserving types of literature (for example, *Beowulf*, charms, riddles and so on) which were considered unsuitable for preservation in most parts of the continent; at the same time, they began the custom of writing official documents in English (laws, chronicles, grammars and so on) which, for considerably later periods elsewhere in Europe, were to be written in Latin. The West Saxon cultural boom in the ninth century developed a written tradition which is usually described as a literary standard, with marked West Saxon orthographic conventions among other standardised features; it was a written norm which remained more conservative during the Old English period than probably the spoken language could have been. A written standard would entail that the conventions once developed – be they in spelling, morphology or syntax – would remain little altered throughout the period and also the region, having been accepted and applied also in those areas where the spoken dialect differed from West Saxon.

If this description of the standard character of written West Saxon is correct, it would mean that by the end of the ninth century – more probably at the beginning of the tenth, but in any case at an unusually early time – writing had already developed into an independent system of the West Saxon dialect, so that when we make declarations and analyses of it, we do so without a proper knowledge of the spoken medium, and without the knowledge of the relationship between the two forms. The standardised nature of literary West Saxon is all the more clear when it is viewed against the systems found in early Middle English texts, and by the sudden changes in the notational conventions which they display.

It seems that, after the Norman Conquest, the West Saxon written tradition was replaced by the practice of Norman scribes, which was an amalgamation of elements of continental Latin, Central French and specially devised Norman French spelling conventions in which some features of West Saxon spelling were mixed (although there is evidence to suggest that Old English was preserved in its more classical form up to the first half of the twelfth century). Under continental influence, Middle English orthography involved notations which more closely reflected pronunciation: even the morphological changes which had appeared in the spoken language – but which had remained hidden as a result of the adherence to a standardised West Saxon orthographic convention – came to the surface, as did regional variants. The general tendency throughout the Middle English period was twofold: on the one hand there was the ever-growing standardising influence of royal chancery practice through the emission of official writs, and on the other there was the development of local orthographic forms and systems in the various scriptoria all over the country. By the end of the period, these regional orthographies were so systematic that an analysis of them *qua* orthographic systems (without any reference to the phonetics which they represent) can offer a fairly firm basis for localisation of manuscripts (McIntosh 1966; Jones 1972: 193–216). It was also during the Middle English period that attempts to mark vowel length began. Again the various possibilities were used in the different parts of the country in different ways and to differing extents, but again the appearance of these new forms (for example, doubling of graphs: *good*; digraphs: *boat, friend*; the use of 'mute -e' or 'discontinued grapheme': *here*; and so on) became regionally characteristic (for example, the ⟨i⟩ digraphs: *laird, Leith, muir* in the northern manuscripts and Scotland; see section 2.3 below).

The Germanic-speaking peoples departed from the European norm by developing their own writing system, one which involved runic characters. The twenty-four-symbol runic alphabet is one where each symbol represents a speech sound, with some symbols also representing individual lexical items: thus ⟨ᛗ⟩ = *man* and /m/. When employed for writing texts, most frequently memorial inscriptions, the symbols were used as a phonemic alphabet. In the Old English period, an increase in the use of runic characters seems to reflect phonological innovations in Old English, the additional runes often representing newly-developed sounds corresponding to the spelling forms used in texts written with the Latin alphabet, since the two types of writing were used in parallel. A similar tendency can be observed in the Scandinavian languages, where the usual development was to reduce the number of the runes to sixteen, thus giving up the marking of voiced/voiceless oppositions of the consonants and boiling down the marking of the vowel sounds to the oppositions low/ non-low and rounded/unrounded. When the Latin alphabet started being used, the number of runic symbols was increased and arranged following the order of the Latin alphabet. The origin of the runic characters themselves has not yet been satisfactorily explained. It is noteworthy, however, that diphthongs are represented by digraphs and that vowel length was not marked in any way, although there is one instance of doubling on the Ruthwell Cross, namely *riice*. However, it is believed that this had an aesthetic rationale – to fill in the space available – rather than reflecting any orthographic or phonological significance (King 1986).

2.3   OLD AND MIDDLE ENGLISH SPELLING CONVENTIONS

Texts written in the vernacular appear from the seventh century onwards. It is of interest that the earliest extant texts are written in the Northumbrian dialect of Old English, which shows certain differences from the later West Saxon scribal practice. Most of the Old English speech sounds (phonemes and also allophones) could be written with the graphemes offered by the Latin alphabet; or, as in the case of the diphthongs, the old custom of using digraphs based on sound analysis was employed. Two phonemes, /θ/ and /w/, which were specifically Germanic and thus had no graphemes ready, were represented by their runic symbols, thorn and wynn respectively; there was also an allograph for Old English /θ/ which was a diacritical form of Latin d: ⟨ð⟩. Old English scribes retained the Latin custom of not differentiating between short and long vowels in writing, thus *god* (noun, with a short vowel) and *god* (adjective, with a long one) appear as homographs all through the period. In general, according to the conservative character of West Saxon writing, sound changes very reluctantly appear as changes in spelling, and regional speech variation was rarely accounted for. The graphemes used in Old English manuscripts are as follows: for vowels, single graph: ⟨a⟩, ⟨æ⟩, ⟨e⟩, ⟨i⟩, ⟨o⟩, ⟨y⟩; digraphs: ⟨io⟩, ⟨eo⟩, ⟨ea⟩, ⟨ie⟩. For consonantal sounds, we find: ⟨b⟩, ⟨c⟩, ⟨d⟩, ⟨f⟩, ⟨ʒ⟩, ⟨h⟩, (⟨k⟩), ⟨l⟩, ⟨m⟩, ⟨n⟩, ⟨p⟩, (⟨q⟩), ⟨r⟩, ⟨s⟩, ⟨t⟩, (⟨z⟩), ⟨þ⟩ thorn, ⟨ƿ⟩ wynn, with the forms in parentheses being rare.

Even after the West Saxon scribal tradition had been discontinued, the Old English orthographic system was preserved for at least a time. The early graphemes kept their original value, and it was only later that new graphemes were adopted to mark phonological innovations or to suit new ideas about the ways in which speech sounds had to be represented. That is, not all spelling changes were the result of changes in pronunciation. In the Middle English period, phonemic writing came into the foreground again, not only representing the changes occurring during the life of the language but also allowing regional variation to appear. Middle English vowel graphs include (Fisiak 1968: 14) ⟨a⟩, (⟨æ⟩), ⟨e⟩, ⟨i⟩, ⟨o⟩, ⟨u⟩, ⟨y⟩; digraphs: ⟨ai⟩, ⟨ay⟩, ⟨ea⟩, ⟨ee⟩, ⟨ei⟩, ⟨ey⟩, ⟨ie⟩, ⟨oi⟩, ⟨oy⟩, ⟨oo⟩, ⟨ou⟩, ⟨ow⟩. Consonantal graphs include ⟨b⟩, ⟨c⟩, ⟨d⟩, ⟨f⟩, ⟨ʒ⟩, ⟨g⟩, ⟨h⟩, ⟨j⟩, ⟨k⟩, ⟨l⟩, ⟨m⟩, ⟨n⟩, ⟨q⟩, ⟨p⟩, ⟨r⟩, ⟨s⟩, ⟨t⟩, ⟨v⟩, ⟨w⟩, ⟨z⟩; digraphs: ⟨ch⟩, ⟨dg⟩, ⟨gh⟩, ⟨qu⟩, ⟨sh⟩, ⟨th⟩, ⟨wh⟩.

2.3.1   The Genesis of Early Scots Orthography: Early Northern English Spelling

In this and the following sections, the aim will be to provide an account of how the Scots orthographic system developed, and the choice of notational elements which it made. The analysis of the development of spellings which can be treated as the forerunners of Scots spelling will be carried out on the principle that writing is a second language, an independent system: that is, no phonetic or phonological description will be deemed necessary for drawing up the use of the various notational forms. As we have no overview of the history of English spelling in the northern areas, our description must needs be sketchy. Still, it can offer some chronology of the graphemes in the periods prior to the appearance of texts written in the English language (Scots) in Scotland.

2.3.2   The Old English Period

The earliest texts written in the Anglo–Saxon language are written in the Northumbrian dialect. We have information about a close cultural relationship between the monasteries of Northumbria and those of northern Ireland, thus we can explain the earliest spelling forms as having developed under the influence of Irish spelling conventions. The most important features were the use of ⟨th⟩ and ⟨u⟩, where later West Saxon scribes used the symbols adopted from the old Germanic runic alphabet – ⟨þ⟩ thorn and ⟨ƿ⟩ wynn – or the diacritical Latin ⟨d⟩, ⟨ð⟩: examples are *tha, aeththa, uundrum, gihues* from the eighth- and ninth-century texts of *Cædmon's Hymn* and from *Bede's Death-Song*, where their West Saxon variants have *þa, wundrum, gehwæs* and so on (Sweet 1966: 148–9). On the evidence of later Northumbrian texts, of which the best-known are the interlinear glosses of the *Lindisfarne Gospels* from the late tenth century, we learn that even the northern scribes changed over to the use of the runic graphemes. To mark Old English ⟨w⟩, the *Lindisfarne* glossators preserved the old ⟨u⟩ spellings as well as the more general Old English notation ⟨ƿ⟩, and both graphemes were used in both vowel and semivowel marking, that is for Old

English ⟨u⟩ and ⟨w⟩. There are several examples of ⟨uu⟩, ⟨wu⟩ for Old English ⟨u⟩: *gwurnun, wuðuotto* (Füchsel 1901: 45); if regarded separately, ⟨uu⟩ can be explained as vowel-length marking by doubling the vowel grapheme (which is quite frequent in the glosses) but ⟨wu⟩ is quite different. On the other hand, Old English ⟨w⟩, which is usually marked with wynn, appears quite frequently written with ⟨u⟩ in all positions – initially, medially or word-finally – but also appears as ⟨wu⟩ and ⟨uu⟩: *wureðia, wuræcce, ge-wurito, fulwuiht* (Lea 1894: 115). This means that there are three identical allographs ⟨u⟩, ⟨uu⟩, ⟨wu⟩ to represent both the vowel and the semivowel. In the glosses, diacritical ⟨ð⟩ appears as the regular grapheme instead of ⟨þ⟩. The use of ⟨þ⟩ seems to have been restricted to abbreviations of *þte = þætte* and otherwise in grammatical words: *þat, þone* and so on. The digraph ⟨th⟩, however, is written only in foreign words – *bethania, martha, bethsaiða, nazareth* – and only sporadically in native words: *throuung* (Lea 1894: 126; Füchsel 1901: 52). New notational forms also appear, some of which will be quite regular in later texts and which will become the usual spelling form in the Middle English period. Old English ⟨ht⟩ and ⟨h⟩ sporadically appear as ⟨ch⟩: *lecht, inlichtet, ðæch*; but also the first examples for ⟨gh⟩ come also from these glosses: *mæghte, ænight, aghðanam, gesægh* (Lea 1894: 130; Füchsel 1901: 56). Palatal /k/ is sometimes written already as ⟨ch⟩: *mech, michil, michelo, carchern, iuch* (Lea 1894: 128; Füchsel 1901: 54). Another feature where the glosses differ considerably from other Old English texts is their frequent attempts at the marking of vowel length, either by the use of diacritics, a kind of acute ⟨ ´ ⟩ or circumflex ⟨ ˆ ⟩, or by doubling the vowel graph: *ân, huér, slaa* (Lea 1894: 88).

2.3.3   The Middle English Period

From the mid–eleventh to the mid-twelfth century, new scribal traditions were introduced in the English-speaking areas of the British Isles. The sound representations used by scribes with Norman French training appear in English texts written in the period. These features soon spread all over the speech area and became generally accepted features characteristic of the Middle English period without carrying the usual regional stamps, for which the texts written in the period are especially noted. The digraph ⟨ei⟩ representing the diphthong arising from the vocalisation of the earlier vowel + voiced fricative [ej] – graphically ⟨eg⟩ – starts to appear in the late eleventh century: *weg/wei*; ⟨ai⟩ in the twelfth: *dæg/dai, lai, mai*; ⟨ei⟩: *Teine, Yeines, Bolenei, hei*; and also ⟨oi⟩ in *ætbroiȝden* (Schlemilch 1914: 41ff.). Of the new consonant graphemes, ⟨ch⟩ appears for earlier ⟨c⟩: *cild → child, chyrchen, sechan, bitechan, echere, ich, ilch*; the use of ⟨th⟩, which in the earlier texts was mainly found in foreign words, appears in native words, and starts spreading at the expense of ⟨þ⟩ and ⟨ð⟩: *doth, ahthe, ȝestathelien, feath* (Schlemilch 1914: 49, 56). The grapheme ⟨qu⟩ was very rare in Old English texts, again used mainly in Latin words (such as *reliquia*), but it began slowly creeping into native words too (for example, *quartern*), though there are authors who treat this word also as a Latin borrowing (Plummer 1892: 157, 264). Old ⟨-h(t)⟩ became more and more frequently represented by ⟨ch(t)⟩. Another innovation, also ascribed to Anglo-Norman scribal practice, is the increasingly frequent use of ⟨u⟩ for earlier intervocalic ⟨f⟩: *næure, ræuede, lauerd, yuel* (Clark 1970).

    The *Domesday Book*, a late eleventh-century Anglo-Norman document, is also worthy of investigation, since it throws light on the provenance of some of the digraph graphemes described as special Scottish inventions by Murray (1873). It has been noticed that Old English names with earlier ⟨ea⟩ and ⟨eo⟩ frequently appear written with ⟨ei⟩: *Eideta*

< *Eadgyð, Eidieua* < *Eadgifu, Leiuegar* < *Leofgar, Leimar* < *Leodmær, Walteif* < *Wælþeof.*
Anglo-Norman ⟨ie⟩ is written in *Lieuegar* < *Leofgar, Lieueric* < *Leofric* (Feilitzen 1937: 60,
64). Other manuscripts of the transition period also have examples with ⟨ie⟩ for earlier ⟨e⟩
(Schlemilch 1914: 22). Both graphemes ⟨ei⟩ and ⟨ie⟩ are explained as part of Anglo-
Norman scribal convention, and their sound representation is connected to certain changes
which happened in the Norman French dialect.

It is especially important to have a close look at the spelling forms of words with Old
English [a:], which appear written as both ⟨a⟩ and ⟨ai⟩, in the *Domesday Book* data. Such
spellings appear to represent native English (with ⟨a⟩) and Scandinavian (with ⟨ai⟩)
cognates: *stan – stain*. After the middle of the twelfth century, however, ⟨ai⟩ spellings
appear instead of earlier ⟨a⟩ quite regularly in words where an Old English (and
Scandinavian) [a:] can be reconstructed: *rai* < Old Scandinavian *vrá* and so on. There
are also some Old English personal names with ⟨ai⟩, though these are somewhat uncertain:
Ail- elements which appear frequently are identified with earlier *Æþel-*, and *Aisil* <
Æþelsige, Aildeig, Ailid and so on (Feilitzen 1937: 141–2). Thus the digraph which
originally represented the Scandinavian pronunciation of certain words had become in a
later period, when Scandinavian had already ceased to be a spoken language, a general
northern vowel-length marker, fairly regularly used in texts written in the northern part of
England, especially Yorkshire and Durham (Kniezsa 1989).

Especially relevant evidence for northern orthographic developments comes from the end
of the twelfth century, from the *Ormulum*, one of the few autograph manuscripts from the
Middle English period. It is customary to refer to Orm's peculiar orthography in connection
with alleged vowel-length marking, and less notice is paid to the way in which he used
graphemes for the notation of consonants. *Ormulum* is the first text we know which uses the
grapheme ⟨sh⟩ for earlier ⟨sc⟩: *flessh, englissh, shollde* and so on. Orm also uses quite
regularly the new grapheme ⟨ch⟩: *child*. His system makes a tripartite distinction between
/j/ (represented by ⟨ʒ⟩, an Insular grapheme used in Old English), /g/ written with the
Carolingian grapheme, and intervocalic ⟨-g-⟩ with ⟨ʒh⟩. He seems to be the first to make a
set of consonant digraphs with ⟨h⟩ as their second element: ⟨ch⟩, ⟨sh⟩, ⟨ʒh⟩ (though he
still keeps ⟨þ⟩ and ⟨ht⟩ throughout), and he was the first to add older ⟨hw⟩ to this list by
writing ⟨wh⟩.

After the excellent autographical evidence of the *Ormulum*, there is a lacuna of almost a
century, where we lack original texts. It has become customary therefore to resort to official
non-literary documents, which contain reliable regional spelling forms. Thus the *Subsidy
Rolls* of the six northern counties: Northumbria, Cumberland, Westmorland, Lancashire,
Yorkshire (North, West and East Riding) and Durham – with Lincolnshire as an addition –
provide important information on spelling practice in the early Middle English period
(1290–1350), before the appearance of dated and located regional documents (Kristensson
1967). The Anglo-French spelling innovations became general: ⟨ch⟩: *child*, ⟨th⟩: *Thatford*.
The grapheme ⟨-h(t)⟩ appears usually as ⟨gh⟩, with the important exception of Northumbria, Durham and the East Riding, where the representation is ⟨ch⟩: *Haluchton*. The
usual spelling of Old English ⟨hw⟩ is ⟨wh⟩, but in Northumberland, Cumberland,
Durham, Lancashire, Westmorland and North Riding ⟨qu, qw, qwh⟩ also appear from
the end of the thirteenth century onwards: *Qualton, Qwhom, Qwithill*. It seems noteworthy
that words with original Old English ⟨cw⟩ also appear written with ⟨wh⟩ in these areas,
thus ⟨qu⟩ and ⟨wh⟩ serve as allographs for both Old English /hw/ and /kw/. Old English
⟨sc⟩ appears regularly either as ⟨sh⟩ or ⟨sch⟩, and in an unstressed syllable in word-final

position it also appears as ⟨s⟩, ⟨ss⟩: *Schipwas* (*sheepwash*). For initial /f/, ⟨ff⟩ is frequent, sometimes alternating with upper-case ⟨F⟩. Old English intervocalic /f/, which is regularly represented by ⟨u⟩ in Middle English, is sporadically written ⟨f⟩, ⟨ff⟩: *Syffewryth*. Initial ⟨w⟩ sometimes has ⟨v⟩ as its allograph: *Valter*, *Votton*; ⟨u⟩ is regular before and after consonants: *Eluardeby*. Middle English /v/ is frequently written with ⟨w⟩: *Lewediman*, *Prowost*. Thus ⟨w⟩–⟨v⟩–⟨u⟩ may form a threesome of allographs to represent the vowel /u/, the semivowel /w/ and the fricative /v/. Middle English /j/ is usually written ⟨y⟩, but ⟨yh⟩ also appears (*yhung*), although ⟨j⟩, which counts as an Anglo-Norman grapheme, can also be found: *Jong*.

Vowel-length marking is achieved by the doubling of graphemes, especially in mono-syllables in open syllables: *Graa*. We also find ⟨ai⟩ spellings especially in words where there is the English monophthong/Old Scandinavian diphthong difference (*Haytefeld*); most such examples occur in West and East Riding documents.

2.3.4   The Late Middle English Period

The most recent source for Middle English orthography is the *Linguistic Atlas of Late Medieval English* (LALME). With its diagnostic features, it provides the largest sample of orthographic features with which to plot regional spelling variants, establishing the distribution of the various forms and at the same time the influences of medieval scriptoria. One of the most important conclusions which we can draw from the maps of the second volume is that the whole English-speaking area from the English Channel to the Firth of Forth (the northernmost area as represented in LALME, but we could easily expand it to the northernmost point of Scotland) belongs to one orthographic continuum. Studying the maps, we also realise that features which so far have been counted as Scotticisms, such as the use of the trigraph ⟨sch⟩, were by no means restricted to Scotland, nor even to the northern area in general, but were far more frequent in the whole of the island than was earlier thought; ⟨sh⟩, for instance, appears as the characteristic spelling form of a restricted south-eastern region. The question of the contrast of ⟨wh⟩ versus ⟨quh⟩ is also more intricate than the usual Scottish descriptions: according to LALME, the ⟨qu(h)⟩, ⟨qw(h)⟩ spellings are regular northern features, although the City of York usually shows ⟨wh⟩. However, if we look at the data of the linguistic profiles in the third volume, we see that the City of York ⟨wh⟩ represents a transition between north and south, because the ⟨wh⟩, by which it is connected to the south, is used in conjunction with other consonant and vowel spellings characteristic of the north:

North/Scots	York	South/London
quhilk	*whilk*	*which*
qhua(i)	*wha*	*who*

So far, no mention has been made of the spelling of grammatical markers, although these too are part of the diagnostic features of regional spellings (Meurman-Solin 1993a: 125). Here, LALME shows the Yorkshire area to be the domain of the southern (*-es*, *-ed*, *-en*)/Scots *-is*, *-it*, *-in* isogloss. We find the interchange of *es/en* with *is/in* forms, with the past-tense marker developing a true intermediate form consisting of the southern consonant and the northern vowel marking: *-id*.

When analyzing a spelling system isolated as a special form of second, independent

THE ORIGINS OF SCOTS ORTHOGRAPHY

language, that is, separated from the underlying or coexisting spoken system, we can carry out the investigation in two ways. One is to focus only on the system in question, treating it as a system on its own, unrelated to any other. If we choose this process, we realise that we have to refrain from some – important – statements, mainly concerning the probable origin of the individual graphemes. What we can establish with any certainty is the date when certain graphemes started being used in the system and also their frequency, and which of the variants became a major spelling feature of the system or were only marginal. In the case of such an approach, it is dangerous to attempt to associate sound changes with the appearance of a new grapheme, because there is no information as to whether and when and in what context the same grapheme started being used in related systems.

Again, if we consider Scots in isolation, we shall never be able to explain why particular spelling variants became so productive and frequent in Scots writing. If we do not wish to go further than describing Scots orthography, we have to remain content with stating the dates of appearance of the various graphemes and allographs, establishing their frequency and eventually their span of life as represented in the writings. However, it is also essential to have a look round and make a similar analysis not only of the neighbouring dialects, in our case northern English, but of all languages whose speakers played an important historical-cultural role in the life of Scotland: French, Dutch/Flemish and so on. This is because writing can be influenced externally, and the adoption of a certain spelling habit does not necessarily mean the adoption of the underlying pronunciation, let alone a parallel process in sound changes. The analysis in section 2.3 above has made it evident that all the spelling features which count as diagnostic in Scottish orthography were already found in Northern English texts, and earlier than the examples written in Scotland. Murray's claim that the origin of Scots has to be looked for in Northern English is therefore correct, but his idea that the written form developed independently in Scotland appears to be mistaken: the Scottish scribes learned their writing tradition from the north, and it forms a spelling continuum in the first appearance of texts written in the vernacular. Since no reliable analysis was available in his time about early Middle English in the northern area, Murray believed that whatever difference there is between southern (London) orthography and Scottish writing must necessarily be the result of special Scottish sound developments: hence his influential opinion on the origin of the ⟨i⟩ digraphs. A comprehensive discussion of English spelling which considered the earliest departures from the West Saxon tradition, as well as those found in the northern part of the speech area in the early Middle English period, would have given a clearer picture of the origin and development of several orthographic systems for the English language as a whole – not just for those of London and Scotland. It was pointed out soon after Murray's work became well known that various versions of ⟨i⟩ digraphs appeared at different times in Scottish texts, and the lack of early reversed spellings among them, such as ⟨a⟩ for original /ai/, casts doubt upon a theory of monophthongisation as their origin. A scrutiny of contemporary York and Durham texts also provides many examples of ⟨i⟩ digraphs, some of them earlier than the Scots types (Vikar 1922), while a study of the place-names of the northern area can provide the necessary phonemic background for the changes (Kniezsa 1989).

2.4 THE DEVELOPMENT OF SCOTS ORTHOGRAPHY

2.4.1 The Beginnings: Early Scots (1350–1440)

The first writing in Scotland, as in England, was in Latin. As usual, English words at first appeared in somewhat latinised forms embedded into the Latin of the texts, and these were mostly personal and geographical names or titles. The earliest examples can be dated to about the end of the Old English and the beginning of the Middle English period (Sharp 1927). Thus those orthographic features can be expected which developed during that period in the northern part of the island (see section 2.3 above). The *Scone Lease* of 1350 is generally looked upon as the first document which contains a considerable number of Scots words. It is a document in Latin, and the names of the relevant landmarks are written in Scots above the Latin words between the lines of the text. From that time on, however, there is a continuous and increasing flow of Scots texts of a non-literary type, original documents of deeds, letters and wills, and so on, all clearly dated and located, thus offering a sure basis to describe the beginnings of Scots orthography.

Basing our analysis on the material collected and edited by Jane Slater (1952), we can divide the graphemes used into four layers. The first concerns elements belonging to an 'old-fashioned' notational tradition, such as spelling forms still preserved from Old English (⟨sc⟩ instead of Middle English ⟨sch⟩): there are forty-four examples of *scyr*, representing about one third of all the examples for *shire* and 12 per cent of all initial Old English ⟨sc⟩; and there are eight examples of ⟨ht⟩ written instead of ⟨cht⟩: *wiht, moht, noht* (representing 2.5 per cent of all the examples). The Old English initial sequence ⟨wer + C⟩ appears as ⟨wor⟩ in Middle English. However, in the early documents we can still find the older form: it is regularly written as *werc, werld* and so on. A more general early Middle English feature is the use of the single grapheme to mark both the short and long vowels, exemplified by the Old English examples ⟨god⟩, noun *god*; ⟨god⟩, adjective *good*; or ⟨for⟩, preposition; ⟨for⟩, past singular of the verb *faran*, and so on. This kind of marking still represents more than half of the spellings of long Middle English vowels: ⟨bath⟩ *both*; ⟨blak⟩; ⟨lat⟩; ⟨cler⟩ *clear*; ⟨son⟩ *soon*; ⟨tok⟩; ⟨befor⟩; ⟨dwt⟩ *doubt* and so on. Some of these spellings do not yet show ⟨ou/ow⟩, the general English representation of Middle English /u:/: ⟨dwt⟩ (see section 2.4.3 below).

The second layer of graphemes contains a number of general Middle English notational features shared by all Middle English writings across the speech area, graphemes which had been introduced by scribes with a Norman French training, and which represent features characteristic of eleventh- and twelfth-century Norman French and Central (Parisian) French scribal traditions (see section 2.4.4 below). The third set of graphemes appears in the first thirty years of Scottish writing representing special northern notational forms, some of which Scots shared with most of the Northern English orthographic traditions, such as the so-called ⟨i⟩ digraphs (see section 2.4.3 below). Other graphemes were shared with a more restricted geographic area, notably the region from northern Lancashire to Northumbria, such as the grapheme(s) with ⟨q⟩ instead of more southern ⟨wh⟩ for Old English ⟨hw⟩. Finally, there are graphemes which are either special Scots inventions or represent earlier more general northern spellings which had disappeared from the orthographic systems of the neighbouring northern English areas. There are, too, examples of non-Scots spelling forms in some documents. Of these, Slater remarks that it is known that there were scribes of English origin employed in Scotland in the late fourteenth and early fifteenth centuries. The graphemes which they used were those general in the northern English area, especially Yorkshire. These features will be discussed in sections 2.4.3 and 2.4.4 below.

It seems that Scots chose spelling forms which developed in the direct geographical vicinity and in some cases retained graphemes long lost in other systems (such as ⟨ch⟩ for earlier ⟨h⟩ (+t), thus rendering the digraph ambiguous). The uniqueness of the orthography therefore lies not so much in the invention of entirely new notational forms, but in being a special system which Scots scribes developed from shared features and the later developments of major variants out of earlier marginal ones. Early Scots non-literary documents (Slater 1952) already show the orthographic system in its completion. Indeed, if we consider Agutter's four groups of spelling types, both Type I Basic type and Type II Additional Spellings are already there, together with the English graphemes, with the possible exception of ⟨oa⟩ which is a late development in southern English and did not appear in Scots earlier than the sixteenth century (Müller 1908).

2.4.2 The System of the Middle Scots Period (1440–1700)

By the second half of the fifteenth century, the Scots orthographic system had developed all its characteristic features. The following is an inventory of vowel and consonantal graphemes culled from poetic and prose texts.

```
a  a–e  ai  ay  au  aw
e  e–e  ei  ey  eu  ew  (ea, ee)
i  y  i–e  ie  ye
o  o–e  oi  oy  ou  ow
u  (v  w)  u–e  v–e  w–e  ui  uy  wi  wy  vi  vy

w  (u  v)
ʒ  ʒh  (i)  ih  y  yh
b  d  m  p  pp  r
c  ch  k  qu  quh  h  kk  x  g
f  ff  (u  v  w)
l  ll  lʒ
n  ne  nʒ
s  ss
t  th  (tht)
```

2.4.3 The Vowels

Middle Scots short vowels are marked in the traditional way, using the grapheme correspondences inherited together with the Latin script: /a/ = ⟨a⟩, /e/ = ⟨e⟩, /o/ = ⟨o⟩: *ask, best, dog*. The grapheme representing short /i/ has the allographs ⟨i⟩ and ⟨y⟩: *boundis, likand, bryng, confermys, contrary, bodyly*. Though there is no definitive rule, ⟨y⟩ appears more frequently at word-final position or in the neighbourhood of 'minims'; that is, ⟨y⟩ has the function of lending easier legibility to the manuscript. Similarly, /u/ is also written in several ways: ⟨u⟩, ⟨v⟩ and ⟨w⟩. It is usual to use ⟨v⟩ especially in word-initial position to mark /u/ (a custom general up to the eighteenth century): *vre, vsis, vngodlie*. The appearance of ⟨w⟩ in a similar function is described as especially Scottish: *ws, wnder*. The appearance of

⟨u⟩ in initial position is exceptional: *unitie, unto, use, utterlie*. In word-medial position, ⟨u⟩ is general: *sturdy*, but also ⟨w⟩: *cwmyn, fwrth*, and ⟨v⟩ appears: *cvmpany, cvrage*. It is only frequency which makes a difference between the variants.

These three graphemes have consonant representations as well: word-initially in French words: ⟨v⟩: *voce, vanite*, ⟨w⟩: *werray*; in medial position both in words of French origin: *resauit, resavit, remowe, reprevis* and as an alternation to earlier intervocalic Old English ⟨f⟩: *gave, gevin, have*. Old English ⟨w⟩ is also rendered with an alternation of ⟨u⟩/⟨v⟩/⟨w⟩, with ⟨u⟩: *uerse, uarres, urittin*; ⟨v⟩: *vantoness, vapynis, vastit*; ⟨w⟩: *wand, welcum, wryte*. In medial contexts, we find ⟨u⟩: *alsua, ansuer, betuix, tuenty*, but also ⟨w⟩: *answer, betwix, twa*. From the earliest periods of Middle English, there was an alternation between ⟨u⟩ and ⟨w⟩ (⟨v⟩ is merely a graphic variant of ⟨u⟩, which is why it appears as a place-conditioned allograph), and the Old and early Middle English developments in the northern areas mentioned in section 2.0 above were generalised and preserved in Scots.

A general Middle English feature is the digraphic representation of the new Middle English diphthongs. There are two sets depending on the second element of the digraph. The first is with ⟨i/y⟩: /ai/ in English and Scandinavian words: *away, rayse*, and in French borrowings: *maister, playnt*; and mostly French /oi/: *poyntis*. The second is with ⟨u⟩: ⟨au/w⟩: *awne, draw, kawin*; ⟨eu/w⟩: *new, trew*; ⟨ou⟩: *follow, how*. There is also the variation ⟨i⟩/⟨y⟩ and ⟨u⟩/⟨v⟩/⟨w⟩ in the marking of the glide. However, there appears to be a tendency observable whereby the more marked forms ⟨y⟩ and ⟨w⟩ are preferred in morpheme-final position: *slay, slayis; row, rowyng*, the ⟨i⟩ and ⟨u⟩ variants occurring mainly in closed syllables: *curtais, commoun, four* and so on.

It is interesting to analyse those notational forms which count as Middle English innovations in orthography, which offer the greatest variation and are the more regionally specific, namely the spelling forms of Middle English long vowels. Long vowels are not especially marked in the early centuries of English literacy, and the simple vowel grapheme was used to represent the long vowel as well. It was an innovation of the later Middle English period that various modes of indicating vowel length were introduced by the scribes, who usually chose from three options: graph-doubling, for example ⟨ee⟩ 'meet', ⟨oo⟩ 'door'; digraphs with the second element: ⟨a⟩: ⟨ea⟩, ⟨oa⟩: 'meat', 'boat'; ⟨ie⟩ 'field'; ⟨i,y⟩ ⟨ai⟩, ⟨ei⟩, ⟨oi⟩, ⟨ui⟩ and so on; ⟨ou, ow⟩: 'house', 'town'; or finally ⟨-e⟩, 'discontinued graph' or 'mute ⟨e⟩'. The general marking form of long vowels is that which goes back to the original Old English tradition, that is, where there is no special indication concerning the length of the vowel, and the simple graphs ⟨a⟩, ⟨e⟩, ⟨i⟩, ⟨o⟩ are written, in early texts both in closed syllables *rad, ner, rid, mot* and in word-final position in monosyllabic words: *na, he, my, do*. In monosyllabic words with an open syllable, the old Germanic rule of vowel lengthening remained in operation, thus these words have preserved their simple grapheme spellings in every English orthographic system: *be, me, my, do, to*, most of which have been preserved up to the present day. Other words with long vowel segments still spelled with the simple graph in the early documents are: ⟨sa⟩ *so*; ⟨de⟩ *die*; ⟨fre⟩ *free*; ⟨ga⟩ *go*; ⟨fe⟩ *fee*. In some instances, digraphs were introduced to avoid homographs: ⟨do⟩ (verb) versus ⟨doe⟩ (noun). The French digraph ⟨ou⟩ (ow) for Old English [uu] seems to be one of the first instances of a digraph spelling to indicate vowel length. In Middle English too, it was the general representation of [uu], appearing as ⟨ou⟩ and ⟨ow⟩. Similar to the ⟨y/w⟩ distribution in the glides of diphthongs, ⟨ou⟩ is found generally in medial position in a closed syllable, while ⟨ow⟩ is more frequently written at the ends of morphemes: *ȝour, ȝow; court, boundys, mounday, Dowglas*. The so-called 'discontinued grapheme' or 'mute ⟨e⟩' also starts appearing with the function of indicating vowel length in words which in the Old English period were not disyllabic with two short open syllables, the classical condition for the phenomenon referred to as '*Middle English Open Syllable Lengthening*' (MEOSL), for example, *name, write, mete*. There are examples too where the ⟨-e⟩ is used as a vowel-length marker in words which originally had a long vowel: *ʒere, before, bene, bathe*. This grapheme gained in frequency during the various periods of the language, and special forms developed over the centuries: *fut/fute* words with digraph spelling were also written with ⟨-e⟩: *houise, maire*.

In Scots texts, ⟨u⟩ is the usual grapheme for the northern development of Middle English /o:/: *fut, buk, furth*, and also Old French /ü/: *duk*. The grapheme in its early form is ambiguous, written both for Middle English /u/ and northern Middle English /o:/, which is probably why in later texts the spelling is extended with ⟨-e⟩: *fute*, and why it is also written with the digraph ⟨ui⟩, ⟨uy⟩ or even ⟨ui⟩⟨-e⟩: *buike*. Though the ⟨i⟩ digraph is considered to be more Scottish than ⟨u⟩ or ⟨u-e⟩, ⟨ui⟩ is the last to appear of the list of ⟨i⟩ digraphs (see below). There are no examples of it in the early documents, where indeed ⟨o⟩ as in *fot* is still alternating with ⟨u⟩: *forth – fwrth, god – gud*. In the fifteenth century, the alternation appears as ⟨u⟩ and ⟨u-e⟩: for example, *gud – gude* in the texts of Hay. It is only at the end of the century that ⟨ui⟩ and its possible allographs (u, v, w + i, y) start to appear. In the sixteenth century, the alternation is between ⟨u-e⟩ and ⟨ui⟩. It must be noted that while ⟨ai⟩, ⟨ei⟩, ⟨oi⟩ are frequent, ⟨ui⟩ may be missing from texts: for example, in two poems (*Howlat, Sagis*) in the Asloan manuscript from the early sixteenth century, there are no examples of the digraph.

The general spelling of Old English [ii] is the discontinued grapheme: *wife, mine*. By the sixteenth century, there are examples for analogical digraphs: ⟨yi⟩, and also ⟨ie⟩. While the former is usually written in closed syllables, ⟨ie, ye⟩ became the digraph used at the ends of words in open syllables: *accustomablie, appeirandlie, Dvndie, helplie*. In its use of ⟨ie⟩, Scots differs from southern English practice, where the grapheme is an allograph of ⟨ee⟩.

Anglian Old English /a + ld/ appears as *ald* in the early texts, and later ⟨a⟩ and ⟨au⟩ spellings alternate, to give way to the digraph spelling *auld, bauld, tauld* by the sixteenth century. A similar alternation ⟨a⟩/⟨au⟩ can be observed in French words, where Old French /a + l + C/ varies between ⟨al⟩ and ⟨au, aw⟩: ⟨realte/reawte⟩, ⟨awter⟩ 'altar', ⟨defawtyt⟩, ⟨hawtane⟩. There are further variant spellings in the French formative elements, as ⟨ou⟩ alternates with ⟨o⟩ in '-oun': *abandonyt – abandownyt, enchesoun – encheson, fellone – felloun*, while in '-ous' ⟨ou⟩ alternates with ⟨u⟩: *dispitous – dispitusly; campanus, chevalrusly, wigorusly*. In the fifteenth century, earlier Middle English ⟨ai⟩ starts being written as ⟨a⟩, in both native and French words. It appears especially before ⟨n⟩: *agane, certane*, but also before an original French ⟨ll⟩ it becomes frequent: earlier *bataljе, bataille* becomes *batall, assalle*. Another context for earlier ⟨ai⟩ being written as ⟨a⟩ is in word-final position: ⟨va⟩ 'way'. French ⟨oi⟩ is also sometimes written with a simple ⟨o⟩: *voce*. Ackerman (1898) found examples of early loss of ⟨i/y⟩ in the word ⟨forsade⟩ 'foresaid', but since the spelling appears only in two documents and only once in each, it cannot be considered to be a real argument for an early development of ⟨ai⟩ → ⟨a⟩.

2.4.4 The Consonants

There are some consonants which are used in the traditional way without any apparent variation: ⟨b⟩, ⟨d⟩, ⟨g⟩, ⟨m⟩, ⟨n⟩, ⟨r⟩, ⟨t⟩. Some are doubled in well-defined conditions: ⟨p⟩ if another morpheme is added: *ship – shippes*; ⟨l⟩ in word-final position in di- or polysyllabic words: *litill, fabill*; both ⟨s⟩ and ⟨f⟩ in word-final position. In the case of ⟨s⟩, it is doubled mostly when a voiceless fricative is meant either in grammatical markers, for example *storiss, androwss*, or in monosyllabic words: *Bruss, causs, horss*; in the case of French words, it may be an alternative to French ⟨-ce⟩: *Bruce, aboundance, awncetry, certane*. The case for doubled ⟨ff⟩ is more complicated. It appears in ⟨giff⟩ *give*, that is, usually at the ends of morphemes: *haff, haffis, giffis, giffyn*, where it alternates with single ⟨f⟩: *hafis, gifyn*. This latter spelling is the continuation of the Old English one. In words where Old English ⟨f⟩ was in an intervocalic position, ⟨ff⟩ alternates with the new ⟨u⟩ notation (with all its Scots allographs) introduced by Anglo-Norman scribal tradition: *haue, have, hawe*. In the Slater material, where ⟨ff⟩ is fairly frequent, apart from the above two verbs, ⟨ff⟩ is written in *schyreff, Fiffe, lyffe, Affiril, resaffit, wochesaff, wyffis, Mureff*. In ⟨ft⟩ clusters too, Old English ⟨f⟩ usually appears reduplicated, as in *affter, offt*.

The Old English sequence ⟨hw⟩ was written with di- or trigraphs with ⟨q⟩ as their first element. As has been explained in section 2.3.3 above, this is a special extreme northern development. The embarrassing variety of allographs for whatever is represented by this spelling indicates that the notation took a long time to settle down to any one grapheme, showing that the system was still in the making. In the earliest times in Scots, for example in the Slater material, there were four different spelling forms with further allographs: ⟨qu/w⟩, ⟨qu/wh⟩, ⟨qh⟩, ⟨qhu/w⟩, all of which were also used in the neighbouring areas (LALME vol. 3): *quilk, qwilk, quhilk, qvhilk, qwhilk, qhilk, qhuilk, qhwilk*. Of the variants, ⟨qh⟩ and ⟨qhu⟩ are fairly rare, the two main spelling forms being ⟨qwh⟩ (200 examples, 41 per cent) and ⟨qw⟩ (135 examples, 28 per cent). (It should be recalled that ⟨qu/w⟩ created ambiguity, being the same spelling as ⟨qu/w⟩ for Old English ⟨cw⟩.) All through the period in question, there is a struggle between ⟨quh⟩ and ⟨qhu⟩. The Latin digraph ⟨qu⟩ was very sporadically used in English writings (for example, *reliquia*), replacing earlier Old English ⟨cw⟩ and becoming regular in native words too: *quen*, and in borrowings: *quietly, question*.

Old English ⟨ð⟩ and ⟨þ⟩ are replaced by the grapheme ⟨th⟩, introduced under French influence in the whole speech area (though, for its history in the north of England, see section 2.3.3 above). It appears in all positions in words: *thaim, thingis, thousand, tothir, rather, with, worth*, and in foreign names: *Thomas*. All through the period, however, ⟨þ⟩ was preserved in a slightly modified form (usually represented by ⟨y⟩ in modern editions). Sometimes this form cannot be told apart from ⟨y⟩, thus rendering this grapheme ambiguous due to the similar context in which some words may appear: for example ⟨ye⟩ can represent either the definite article *the* or the subjective form of the second personal pronoun *thee*. This defectively formed ⟨þ⟩ is written mainly in grammatical words well into the fifteenth century: ⟨yat⟩ *that*, ⟨oyir⟩ *other*, as well as frequently in abbreviated forms: ⟨y^t⟩ *that*.

Old English ⟨c⟩ has several representations. One is ⟨c⟩: *callit, comfort, couth*; the other ⟨k⟩, an allograph in marginal use in the Old English period but more frequent in Middle English: *knokyt*. While ⟨k⟩ is unambiguous in its sound value, ⟨c⟩ marks also the voiceless fricative [s] in French words: *certane, Bruce*. Old English ⟨c⟩ followed by a palatal element is written by the grapheme ⟨ch⟩ in Middle English, which became general both in native words: *chese, chosin*, as well as in French loanwords: *change, chartir, chaunceler*. Word-initial Old English ⟨h⟩ remained an unambiguous marking all through Middle English: *he, hawe*. On the other hand, ⟨ht⟩ and word-final ⟨h⟩ were regularly represented by ⟨ch⟩: *betaucht*, *licht, nicht.* This spelling sometimes rendered word-final ⟨ch⟩ ambiguous, the same grapheme representing two different speech sounds: *bowrch* (= /x/) – *branch* (= /t/); *drewch* (= /x/) – *fech* (= /t/). Old English ⟨sc⟩ is written ⟨sch⟩ in the northern regions: *schip.* In words in syntactically unstressed positions it appears as ⟨s⟩: initially *sall, suld*; in word-final position *Inglis, Scottis.* The last two instances count as diagnostic variants for Scots but also represent, as we shall see, an important northern dialectal isogloss.

In Old English orthography, ⟨ȝ⟩ represented Germanic [g] and its Old English developments [g] and [j]. In Middle English, the two phonemes had been separated in spelling, ⟨g⟩ the grapheme marking the voiced stop [g], in native words *gate*, as well as in loanwords: *grace.* Old English ⟨cg⟩ is also written ⟨g⟩ in Scottish writings: *brig.* In medial position, the grapheme marked the palatalised consonant [dʒ]/[ʒ] in French words: *heritage.* In word-initial position, [dʒ] occurs in French words, although these have usually kept their original spelling in ⟨i⟩: *iugis*, with the allograph ⟨j⟩: *James, Jon*; there were digraph modifications too: ⟨ih⟩: *Ihon*, ⟨jh⟩: *Jhames, Jhon.* Both Germanic [j] and the palatalised Old English fricative retained ⟨ȝ⟩, the original Old English grapheme, or its allograph ⟨ȝh⟩: *ȝeid, ȝheid, ȝe, ȝhistirday, ȝoung*, although in the fifteenth century ⟨y⟩, yh⟩ were also introduced: *ye, yhe.*

There is much written about the representation of the French *mouillé* consonants /l'/ and /n'/. Since the two consonants are the result of several Old French developments, from the outset there was a profusion of spelling variants. These alternatives were adopted by scribes writing in English: that is, the French words were adopted together with their written form. It has been suggested that, in Scotland, certain variants were preferred to others. Even if this is the case, it is difficult to find one single preferred spelling form. At the end of the fifteenth century, French /l'/ is represented by ⟨l, ll, ile, ill, ilȝe, ilȝhe, lȝ⟩; however, the frequencies are very varied: ⟨ill⟩ *assaill* 51.8 per cent; ⟨ilȝe⟩ *assailȝe* 25.9 per cent are the most frequent forms, the others representing minor variants. In some words, the original palatal /l'/ is not marked, for example *battle* is regularly written ⟨batal(l)⟩ replacing earlier ⟨bataill⟩. French /n'/ is also represented by a variety of forms: ⟨ne, nyhe, nȝe, ngȝe, nȝȝe, nȝhe, ⟨ngne⟩. The frequencies again are uneven: ⟨ngȝe⟩: *mengȝe* and ⟨nȝe⟩: *menȝe* are the two most frequent forms, with an equal percentage of tokens, while the other five again are only marginal. Of the above allographs, ⟨lȝ⟩, ⟨nȝ⟩ are considered to be the typically Scottish ones. This is, however, not a clear-cut case, because ⟨lȝ⟩ and ⟨nȝ⟩ represent only a small percentage of the spellings among an embarrassing variety of forms. It is true that when ⟨lȝ⟩, ⟨nȝ⟩ are used they appear only in Scots texts; however, their application is not general, and there are texts which otherwise show several Scots diagnostic features, but which nevertheless prefer one or rather a number of other graphemes to mark /l'/ and /n'/. We cannot say that all Scottish texts have ⟨lȝ⟩, ⟨nȝ⟩ for French /l'/ and /n'/, only that if these graphemes appear, they signal a text written in Scotland.

2.5 DIAGNOSTIC VARIANTS

Of the graphemes listed above in section 2.4.2, there is a selection of spelling variants which together form the characteristic Scots orthographic system. These features, contrasted with the ones typical of London writings, can be used either to point out the Scottishness of a text or to explain the extent of the influence of the southern variant. The features employed

in this chapter are taken from an article by Alexander Craigie (1935) and from the list
compiled by Meurman-Solin (1993a: 126). The two lists correspond in their main
characters and usefully complement each other, and were checked against the data in
LALME. In Table 2.1, the graphemic differences are listed, with an extra column for such
spellings shared by both variants. The two systems differ in the notation of both vowels and
consonants:

Table 2.1 Diagnostic orthographic variants in Older Scots.

	Scots	*Scots/English*	*English*
OE a + ld	au, o	a	o
OE [a:]	a, a–e, ai, ay		o, o–e, oa
OE [e:]	ei, ey	e, e–e	ee, ie, ea
OE [i:]	yi, ie, ye	y, i–e	
OE [o:]	oi, oy, u, u–e, ui, uy	o, o–e	oo
OE #u	w	u, v	
OE w	u, v	w	
OE h#	ch		gh
OE ht	ch		gh
OE hw	quh, qwh		wh
ME v	f, ff, w	u, v	
OE g + pal.	ʒ, ʒh, yh	y	
OE cg	g		dg
OF #dʒ	ih, jh	i, j	
OE s#	ss	s	
OE sc	sch		sh
Unstressed # [ʃ]	s		sh
[ʃ] #	s, ss		sh
[θ] #	th, t	th	
w + u, w + o	wa		wou, wo

2.5.1 The Vowels

Since the 'Scottishness' of a text is established according to the presence of the above
diagnostic variants, namely the appearance of ⟨i⟩ digraphs as contrasted with the other
types of digraphs as well as the forms shared by both varieties (single graph and
discontinued grapheme), it is worthwhile analysing the history of these special graphemes
in Scottish writing. As we have already noted, all the above graphemes were in use from the
earliest texts written in English and the difference in time can be expressed only as a change
in the proportion of the allographs. Table 2.2 shows the development of such proportions.
The first item shows the general proportion of the characteristically Scottish ⟨i⟩ digraphs;
the single graph and ⟨-e⟩ are considered to be features shared by the Scottish and London
systems, and 'other' means all the spelling forms characteristic of the south. The texts
chosen in Table 2.2 are considered to be especially Scottish in their orthography. As a
contrast, there are the examples from the writings of John Knox, who was regarded as one
of the most anglicised authors in the sixteenth century.

Table 2.2 The relative distribution of Scots and English orthographic features in some Older Scots texts (percentages).

	i	*single*	*-e*	*other*
Slater	8	59	18	15
Bruce MS E	12	73	12	2
Millar 1508	43	30	20	7
Asloan MS a	30	44	12	14
Asloan MS b	20	61	14	5
Lepreuik	49	37	12	2
Knox	26	12	19	43

There is direct evidence that Scottish writers were quite aware of the differences between Scots and southern English, and also of the fact that, after all, both were varieties of the same language. Bald quotes Napier of Merchiston, who wrote in 1593: 'I presse not to follow the particular ornate tearmes of neither Scottes nor Englishmen; but rather contrarily, for both their instructions, I vse so much as I can these wordes and tearmes, that be more common and sensible to them both, then proper or ornate to any one of them' (Bald 1928: 166). What was true for the 'tearmes' was also true for the spelling: from Tables 2.1 and 2.2, it is evident that most of the orthographic systems consisted of elements characteristic of English orthography in general. However, if we consider Table 2.2, we notice that no matter whether it was the development of writing in the Scottish style, or the use of anglicised spellings by individual authors, it was the regionally more marked forms which gained ground at the expense of the more neutral, shared allographs. It is noteworthy that the proportion of the discontinued grapheme remained more or less stable throughout the period, and it was the single-graph spelling which became less and less used. In the writings of another greatly anglicised author, Alexander Hume (1617), not only was the number of specially Scots forms reduced (where he avoided the ⟨i⟩ digraphs completely and wrote, for example, ⟨ae⟩ instead), but he hardly used any single-graph or discontinued grapheme at all, replacing them with southern digraphs such as ⟨oe⟩. As we have already suggested, all the possible allographs were used for /l'/ and /n'/, therefore it would be difficult to claim any of the variants as a specially English grapheme, and the contrast lies rather in whether the ones with ⟨ʒ⟩ are employed or not.

In addition to the graphemes representing speech sounds, the marking of certain grammatical endings and formative elements can show regional differences, as in Table 2.3. Only the *-s* form of the present indicative third person singular offers itself for comparison, since the regular southern marker *-(e)th* represents a difference in morphology; similarly, the northern form of the present indicative *-is*, *-ys* has also been omitted, because it again belongs to the area of morphology. The Scots form contrasts with the following English forms: *-en* (hence *-0*) in the Midlands and *-eth* in the south. Of the endings with a difference in Scots and southern English, there are the *-ar* forms of *nomen agentis*: *millar*, and the comparative of the adjectives: *lattar*. These features are shared with the other northern English regions. It would be more appropriate to speak about the difference between Scots *-ill* and English *-le* forms, without restriction to the French formative element *-able*, since the contrast appears in native words too: *litill* – *little*.

Table 2.3 Grammatical endings and formative elements showing regional differences.

Past, past participle	–it, –yt	–ed
Present 3rd person singular	–is,–ys	–(e)s
Past participle	–in, –yn	–en
Genitive plural	–is, –ys	–(e)s, –'s
Nomen Agentis	–ar	–er
OFr ⟨a(b)l⟩	–(a)bill	–(a)ble

In addition to the above two sets of differences, Craigie gives a long list of individual lexical items, the spellings of which differ in the two regions. In most of the cases, the variants are not due to any underlying systemic differences. As a diagnostic feature, only a few have been selected, words which do not belong to any specialised vocabulary and thus can be expected to appear more frequently in any type of text:

bot	but
amang	among
ony/mony	any/many
Ing(land)	Eng(land)
ane	an
sic, mekil	such, much
cum	come

Although, as has been stated, most of the above pairs of words do not represent a special system in the differences between Scots and English, it is evident that some of them have more general underlying characteristics of pronunciation which apply to more than the one word mentioned in the above list: for example, *amang – among* does not simply represent an individual case but a type, of which other members exist: Scots *lang, strang* as opposed to southern *long, strong* and so on. Since monosyllabic words such as *man, can* also regularly feature ⟨a⟩, the rule may be written as: on the morpheme boundary /a/ + N#, or when followed by a consonant /a/ + NC, ⟨a⟩ was preserved: *man, lang*. This rule can be complemented: if followed by a vowel /a/ + nasal + V, ⟨a⟩ became ⟨o⟩: *ony, mony* appearing regularly, for example in the fifteenth century. In the same way, the opposition of Scots *sic, mikil* to English *such, much* is again a case where the spelling difference is not restricted to one single word but forms a whole set of examples: *kirk* and so on. This notation indicates an increase in the frequency and difference in the distribution of the grapheme ⟨c⟩/⟨k⟩ in Scots.

2.5.2 Minor Developments

The Middle Scots period begins in 1440, and from the point of view of orthography the fully developed Scots system can be found in the second half of the fifteenth century. Apart from the graphemes which appear regularly in every type of writing in every period of Scots, there are spelling variants which are less common. One of the frequently-quoted variants is ⟨tht⟩ as an allograph of ⟨th⟩ in word-final position. Though it is fairly conspicuous when one meets it in a text, one could easily class it as a feature of minor importance. One of the reasons is that there are comparatively few words in which it can appear. Meurman-Solin (1993a: 240) writes that there were no ⟨tht⟩ spellings in the *Helsinki Corpus of Older Scots* before 1500, and after 1570 it practically went into disuse. Unfortunately, Meurman-Solin fails to give an account of the text types in which the grapheme occurs, or of the region of origin, and nor do we learn anything of the frequency or the proportion of ⟨tht⟩ and ⟨th⟩ in the appropriate graphemic context. Contrary to Meurman-Solin's opinion, ⟨tht⟩ was already used in the Early Scots period: in the Slater material, there are twenty examples in nine documents. The most frequent word is *witht* (eleven examples), and we also find *assitht* (two), *monetht* (two), *moutht, atht, Rossitht, Pertht, Mentetht* (one each). Ackerman adds *batht, hundretht* (eight examples altogether) to the list from the period 1410–40 (Ackerman 1898: 57); Glawe (1908: 80) also found ⟨tht⟩ spellings in MS Adv. Libr. 25.4.16 (c. 1455): *atht, batht, clatht, witht* (twelve examples). It would appear that the grapheme counted as a most marginal allograph in the copies of documents in the Slater material, the first copy has some ⟨tht⟩, the other copy none (Slater 1952: 10, 11, 12, 14, 22, 85, 126, 128, 172, 175, 180, 207).

The grapheme ⟨cht⟩ for word-final ⟨ch⟩ provides a parallel to the above problem, and both could be combined under the heading 'intrusive ⟨t⟩'. Ackerman quotes *broucht, laucht, nychtbouris* and others from between 1387 and 1440. According to Meurman-Solin (1993a: 240), ⟨cht⟩ and ⟨tht⟩ were written in the same texts and went out of use about the same time, while Murray (1873: 128) believes that the intrusive ⟨t⟩ can be connected to the disappearance of postconsonantal /t/ in the pronunciation expressed by such forms as ⟨t⟩-less *perfec*. There are other instances of the loss of consonants, and of intruding consonants. All through the fifteenth century and in the writings of non-anglicised authors, ⟨g⟩ is regularly omitted from the cluster ⟨ngth⟩: *strenth, lenth*. There is also to be found an ⟨al⟩/⟨au⟩ alternation in French words which becomes frequent in native words, resulting in the appearance of intrusive ⟨l⟩ (Agutter 1987). However, it has to be stated that this does not seem to represent a general tendency in the texts analysed, perhaps depending on time, region or text type.

There is a mysterious grapheme which surfaces in the sixteenth century – at least, mention is made of it in connection with texts written in this period. It is the digraph ⟨ae⟩, an allograph of Scots ⟨a⟩–⟨a–e⟩–⟨ai/y⟩: *maer, sae* and so on. Though DOST always gives ⟨ae⟩ as a possible allograph for various lexical items, in most of the cases there are no quotations given with this spelling. In the few instances where there are quotations, these are usually from the sixteenth century. Müller (1908) has some examples of the form in his sixteenth-century Aberdeen records: *waegeris, paement, thaeme, faer, aeir, eschaeting* (from documents dated 1532–84), with the remark that it occurs only sporadically. He explains the origin of the grapheme as an analogical construction, 'the carrying of final *-e* in medial position', that is like ⟨oe⟩ in *doe*, ⟨ie⟩ in *onlie* and so on. Although ⟨ae⟩ may have been in general a grapheme of marginal frequency, ample use of it is made by Alexander Hume, one of the most anglicised writers at the very beginning of the seventeenth century. The Slater documents already have some examples, such as *frae*, suggesting that the grapheme either was invented at an early period of Scots and went out of use for a while, or has been completely neglected by the scholarly descriptions. The relevance of a better knowledge of its use is shown by the fact that from the eighteenth century it gained ground and became an important part of the non-anglicised Scots orthography. From the sixteenth century onwards small variations occur to an increasing extent. A. J. Aitken claims that certain spelling variants represent dialectal differences in underlying pronunciation (Aitken 1971a), while Meurman-Solin's analysis reveals the relationship between the appearance of variants and text types.

2.6 ANGLICISATION: THE SIXTEENTH AND SEVENTEENTH CENTURIES

The history of the relationship between Scotland and England is one of constant political, linguistic and cultural influence of the south upon its northern neighbour. From the sixteenth century onwards, there were some developments in Scottish writing which led away from a distinctive Scottish orthography towards a more general, all-English one by the end of the seventeenth century. In the 1920s, Marjorie Bald produced a series of articles in which she analysed the history of the anglicisation of Scottish writing (Bald 1926, 1927, 1928). She claimed that the process was connected to the introduction of printing in Scotland in the early sixteenth century. The spread and also the printing of English texts in Scotland was due to the accession of Mary Tudor and her persecution of Protestants. Protestant printers and authors fled to Scotland, with the result that English became the accepted medium of religious and other types of academic prose writing. Bald describes how printers changed the Scots language of the manuscripts to English not only with respect to spelling but also grammatically and to a small extent also in points of usage. She remarks that, as a rule, poetry had been left untouched by printers, a practice differing considerably from that of manuscript copyists, who generally 'translated' texts into their own variety of language. Bald gives interesting statistics of the ratio of Scots to English texts printed in Scotland between 1508 (when Chapman and Millar first set up their printing press in Edinburgh) to 1625, where she ended her investigation: over these 117 years, the proportion of anglicised texts grew from all-Scots texts of the first decades to a 3:1 quota of anglicised ones in the last years of the period investigated (Bald 1927). Two questions arise: to what extent do orthographic forms used in printed texts influence the practice of their readers, and how far do printed texts and manuscripts agree in using or omitting Scots spelling forms?

It would appear that, in general, Bald means London English as the influencing force of what she calls the process of 'anglicisation': the early printing presses were set up in London, with William Caxton using London English as the medium to 'standardise' the language of his publications. In some of her remarks, however, it is not clear what variety is meant when the term 'anglicisation' is used, whether it is specifically London English, or any variety of English south of the Scottish border. In connection with the first thirty years of Scottish writing, Jane Slater observed that there were scribes of English origin or at least scribal training among Scottish-based scribes. Indeed, there are spelling forms which do not count as Scots in her material. Judging from the spelling forms, we can conclude that these scribes came from or were trained in the northern area, because the spelling forms which they used are common in the City of York papers. The problem of anglicisation arises particularly in the evaluation of the application of certain consonant graphemes. Bald claimed that the appearance of any ⟨gh⟩ and ⟨wh⟩ in Scots texts was the result of southern influence. The representations of Old English ⟨hw⟩ usually described as Scots show ⟨q(u)h⟩ in contrast to southern ⟨wh⟩ types: *quhat – what, quhy – why*; however, as we have already seen, in LALME ⟨wh⟩ was also extensively used in north-eastern English areas, ⟨q(u)h⟩ being a feature of the north-western areas and Scotland (LALME, vol. 2, p. 177).

In the evaluation of such spelling forms in Scots texts, it is difficult to decide whether they represent northern English forms or southern English proper. In the case of the ⟨wh⟩ forms, however, there are some indicative factors: in the northern texts, ⟨wh⟩ writings are paired off with vowel notations characteristic to northern spelling: ⟨whai, whais, whair⟩, or with the palatal stop: ⟨whilk⟩, as contrasted to London English ⟨who, whose, where⟩ and

⟨which⟩. In the writings of anglicised authors, the marking of Old English ⟨hw⟩ shows mixed forms: southern spellings with ⟨wh⟩: ⟨who⟩, ⟨whom⟩, ⟨whose⟩, ⟨where⟩, ⟨which⟩ are mixed with pure Scots ⟨quh⟩ spellings: ⟨quha, quhaim, quhais, quhair, quhilk⟩, although these words can occur mixed with the southern vowel: ⟨quhom⟩, ⟨quhois⟩, ⟨quher⟩, or consonant: ⟨quhich⟩. At the same time, we find incidental northern forms intermixed: ⟨wha, whais, whaim⟩, ⟨whair⟩, ⟨whilk⟩ and so on. While the case for the southern and the mixed spellings seems to be unambiguous, with the former representing a fully anglicised spelling and the latter a partial one, the incidental northern forms present the problem that these forms may be existing regional varieties, not simply a confused mixture of two different traditions. In addition, there are other hybrid forms used by anglicised authors: Scots suffixes added to stems with an English spelling, or the other way round, for example *amanges* (*amang* = Scots, *-es* = English), *amongis* (*among* = English, *-is* = Scots); or an English sound with a Scots spelling: *moist* (Scots *maist*). In general, it seems that the Scots morphological markers are mixed and are the earliest to be lost, with southern English *-(e)s*, *-(e)d*, *-er* replacing Scottish *-is*, *-id*, *-ar*. The application of southern forms did not necessarily happen systematically: there are authors who used Scots ⟨-is⟩ almost throughout, both as a verbal and as a noun marker, but preferring ⟨-ed⟩ for the past-tense marker of verbs, while others show the opposite pattern. It is interesting that, though ⟨id/yd⟩ spellings are frequent (a form also used in northern England), ⟨*-et⟩ forms are nowhere in evidence; that is, only existing spellings are used and not individual hybrids. The mixing of the two types of spelling of the grammatical markers and formative elements also appears frequently in those texts which otherwise use the traditional Scots notation, and thus represent the most frequent form of anglicisation.

Considered one of the major proofs of southern influence is the replacement of the Scots notation of Old English /a:/: ⟨a, ai, ay⟩ by ⟨o, o–e, oa⟩, especially salient since it does not represent a mere orthographic difference but also involves phonological difference. It is interesting therefore to note that, from the very beginning of Scottish writing, that is, ever since the 1370s, ⟨o⟩ spellings for Old English /a:/ occur. In most of the cases, it represents words like ⟨so⟩ instead of *swa*, *sa*, or ⟨no⟩ for *na*, and so on, but it is noteworthy that the word *lord* is constantly written in its southern form, *lord*, and that the native *lard*, *laird* hardly appear even in the most traditional Scottish texts. Müller found some Scots *la(i)rd* spellings in his sixteenth-century Aberdeen documents, but where the ⟨o⟩ and ⟨a(i)⟩ spellings represented semantic differences (Slater 1952; LALME, vol. 3, pp. 681–90; Müller 1908). Other vowel-length markings, again representing the southern tradition, which appear from the earliest period are ⟨ea⟩ and ⟨ee⟩. Once more, it has to be noted that in early texts such spellings are restricted to certain lexical items: ⟨ea⟩ in *realm*, *seal*, ⟨ee⟩ in *fee*; in general, it seems that the vocabulary of law was adopted together with its spelling, so that such shapes do not necessarily represent orthographic influence. In later texts, the digraph ⟨ee⟩ is used only in French words to mark the word-final long vowel: *citee* and so on; and it is only in the writings of the most anglicised later seventeenth-century texts that ⟨ea⟩ and ⟨ee⟩ replace ⟨ei, ey⟩. In the late sixteenth and early seventeenth centuries, even those authors who are counted as considerably anglicised restrict the use of southern spellings to individual lexical items rather than mix the two systems: for example, Alexander Hume (1617?) writes ⟨oa⟩: *boar, boat, coat, loadstar, moat, oares, roar*, and *broake, noat, spoaken*; but also appearing in his work are Scots forms with old-fashioned ⟨a⟩: *spak, dar*; ⟨a-e⟩: *hame, nane*; ⟨au/w⟩: *awn, knau*; and quite frequently the otherwise fairly rare ⟨ae⟩: *maed, maest, quhae, baeth, sae*. Variants such as ⟨more⟩ and ⟨maer⟩, ⟨so⟩ and ⟨sae⟩ count as exceptions in his text. The abandonment of special Scots orthographic features other than the above can also be taken as a sign of anglicisation. Thus certain consonant doublings and trigraphs ⟨tht⟩#, ⟨ss⟩ or ⟨β⟩# show a rapid decline in use from the late sixteenth century, with ⟨tht⟩# going entirely out of use after 1570 (Meurman-Solin 1993a: 240).

Stylistically speaking, the appearance of anglicised spelling depends on the typology of writing; it is generally stated that the most anglicised texts were the religious treatises, while the most conservatively Scottish were official papers, such as those of the Privy Council, local authorities and so on. The spelling in private papers seems to depend on the personal history of the authors, and whether and for how long they lived in England (for example, John Knox and Alexander Hume), and even there their early training wins considerable ground against later English influence. Later authors, such as Bailly, seem to have been trained in southern writing traditions, and their texts cannot be differentiated from those written by contemporary Londoners. Meurman-Solin also repeats the frequent claim that poetry, both in manuscripts and in print, had a stronger tendency to be anglicised than some types of prose. However, when one analyses the spelling system of some well-known poems, they tend to show basically Scottish characteristics, although we might exclude such texts as *Lancelot of the Laik* which is neither Scottish nor English, but a curious mixture of the two. Even the Cambridge manuscript of Barbour's *The Bruce*, which is accepted as an anglicised text, shows only some extra examples for southern ⟨o⟩ instead of northern ⟨a⟩: *more*, *one*; and a few ⟨ea⟩, ⟨ee⟩ spellings; but no ⟨gh⟩ or ⟨wh⟩ forms surface at all.

2.7 CONCLUSIONS

The above discussion attempts to cover the mainstream developments in early Scots orthography. Following in the footsteps of earlier discussions of the topic, it seemed more fruitful to try to describe here the path towards a standard Scots spelling system than to attempt a discussion of varied and manifold subsystems resulting from regional and stylistical variation. Original Scots orthography, as it appeared in its most pristine forms in the manuscripts written at the end of the fifteenth century, was a blending of common Middle English spelling, special northern English scribal traditions and, in some cases, native innovations or graphemes not evidenced elsewhere. From the earliest texts onwards, that is, ever since the 1370s, notational forms, believed to be characteristic of the southern region of the speech area, began to crop up in smaller or greater numbers. In the early period, the influence can be described within the same framework as dialect differences appearing in other Middle English texts, and can probably be ascribed to the individual scholarly history of the scribe himself. After the introduction of the printing press in England in 1476, a more direct influence of London orthography can be expected, and the importance of London English increased in Scotland through the attempt at anglicisation of books printed there. The results of text analyses corroborate Bald's (1927) conclusions that anglicisation increases in the sixteenth century so that, by the end of the seventeenth century, Scots seems to have fallen practically into disuse in all official writing.

3

Older Scots Phonology and its Regional Variation

Paul Johnston

3.1 INTRODUCTION

3.1.1 Doing Medieval Dialectology

The length of Chapter 11, on Modern Scots dialectology, and the number of works to which it alludes, bear witness that there is certainly no shortage of material with which to chart out the dialects of modern Scots varieties. Full-scale linguistic surveys such as the *Linguistic Survey of Scotland* publications (Mather and Speitel 1975, 1977, 1986; Wright 1905; Ellis 1889), sociolinguistic works done in Scotland and Northern Ireland (Macafee 1983, 1988, 1994c; Melchers 1985, 1986; Pollner 1985a–c; Johnston 1980, 1983a, 1983b, 1985a, 1985b; Hettinga 1981; Romaine 1978; Reid 1978; Douglas-Cowie 1978; Macaulay and Trevelyan 1977; Macaulay 1991, traditional dialect monographs (Zai 1942; Wettstein 1942; Dieth 1932; Wilson 1915, 1923; Mutschmann 1908; Murray 1873) and dialect glossaries and dictionaries (Graham and Murison 1979; Robinson 1985; Grant 1931–76; G. Watson 1923) give more than enough information to identify which forms are characteristic of certain areas, and to place the dialect into some kind of sociolinguistic context which would identify the users of Scots, their attitudes towards their localised form of language, and how Scots and Standard Scottish English coexist for these users. One can also provide apparent-time and, if the area has been covered more than once before, real-time comparisons between studies dealing with a single, specific area, to identify recent changes implemented within the last century or so. This record is not gap-free or error-free: not every Scots-speaking town, or even dialect region, has been covered as much as others, and focus and methodology vary considerably from study to study, as does the quality of data collection. However, it can be said that researchers of Scots have, wherever possible, incorporated advances in approach, interview technique and questionnaire design to try to obtain accurate data on dialect forms (Petyt 1980; Aitken 1981b), and that such forms were therefore, for the most part, authentically given by flesh-and-blood speakers who used Scots as a part of their repertoire in daily life, and recorded on tapes and in notebooks. Should there be any questions as to the authenticity of a given form in, say, North Angus, we should be able to return to the locality in which that form was recorded and find speakers from that area who will use it, or who will tell us that it has died out or is foreign to the area.

Medieval dialectologists have no such luxury. Their 'witnesses' (McIntosh et al. 1986:

86) are not really speakers as such, but documents written by a small, unrepresentative section of Older Scots society, often as a specialised, 'set-piece' type of text such as a will, a deed, a public record or a literary work. Whereas the modern dialectologist can design a questionnaire to elicit different words or pronunciations from a speaker, our object of study is purely restricted to the vocabulary present in the corpus of texts from a given area, which in turn will be heavily slanted towards registers appropriate to the functions of the text. In a world where peasants cannot read and write, it is unlikely that we will find a complete list of terms for farm implements, even traditional ones, which is often an important area of dialect vocabulary (Francis 1983; Petyt 1980), though we might know about an extensive legal or administrative vocabulary. As for pronunciations, we do not even have direct written testimony in the same sense as we do for vocabulary, morphology and syntax; we have to surmise pronunciation using a combination of assumptions and heuristics about what sounds letters and combinations of letters represent, and various reconstructive techniques. The best that we can manage is an educated guess, established as plausible by argument and devoid of most phonetic detail. Unless we are lucky enough to have a document that is definitely associated with a given place, or is dated, even the geographic and temporal provenance of a text may have to be argued for (McIntosh et al. 1986). In any case, the actual speaker behind the document remains something of an enigma, and the validity of the data cannot be checked but only corroborated as possible by usage in other texts that can be supposed to be of similar origins.

Luckily, there is at least a 200-year-old tradition of historical linguistics, and we can freely employ any of the established techniques traditionally used to interpret written data. While the values we postulate for the letter ⟨e⟩ may extend over a wide phonetic range from [æ(:)] to [i(:)], plus upgliding diphthongs like [ei] and downgliding or ingliding ones like [eə], we at least know that the symbol represents a vowel, certainly with the syllabic part front and unrounded, and with a greater likelihood than not of being low-mid or high-mid, since we know that mid front unrounded vowels of other languages, including the classical pronunciation of Latin, are generally represented by this symbol. In other cases, we cannot be sure. An ⟨ai⟩ may be a diphthong similar to the sound in *try*, but it also might be a simple long low vowel in a Scottish manuscript, especially a post-1440 one (Kniezsa 1994 and section 2.4.2 above). In some cases, too, a difference in symbol between two manuscripts of different geographical origin may not correspond to a true sound distinction at all: whether a word like *ship* starts with ⟨sh⟩ or ⟨sch⟩, and these two graphic combinations are intertwined in geographic distribution in Britain (McIntosh et al. 1986), the word almost certainly began with [ʃ], not *[sx] or *[ʃx], say. Differences in graphemes themselves may also be important clues for placement of a given manuscript (McIntosh et al. 1986), above and beyond the purely phonological value which they might have.

Since we have a poetic tradition in Older Scots, both courtly and folk (in terms of border ballads and the like), we might make use of rhyme evidence as revealing mergers and splits in the vowel systems and identity of codas. We have to be careful, though. While it seems plausible that most rhymed poetry uses exact rhymes, then as now, there are some rhymes which cannot possibly show identity of the vowels, but must show proximity instead (Johnston 1992). The fifteenth-century *St Editha*, stemming from Wiltshire, rhymes words having Middle English /i:/ as a stem vowel with Middle English /ai/, even though no dialect of English, in the south-western group or elsewhere, merges these two vowels at the present day (Anderson 1987). (However, there are dialects with partial mergers, like some town dialects of Caithnesian.) It could be, of course, that Wiltshire dialect has been restructured to restore a distinction, retained in neighbouring dialects, that had been earlier lost; but it is more likely, given that Middle English /i:/ comes out as [ɒi] and Middle English /ai/ as [æi] today, that the two diphthongs were much closer to each other then – perhaps [ëi] vs [ɛi], which the poet saw as close enough to each other to be rhymed. Since most of the 'high style' poetry comes from people based in Edinburgh and well acquainted with the English 'makars' like Chaucer, Gower and Lydgate, we cannot be sure that every rhyme represents a possible one in the poet's native dialect. Dunbar, for instance, was a Fifer, and came from an area that has kept BEAT and MEET distinct to this day, whereas that merger is solid in the Lothians. If we catch Dunbar rhyming the two classes, we have either the influence of the court dialect manifest or a near-rhyme. The more frequent the rhyme pattern is, the more likely it is to represent a real rhyme; but in any case we cannot extrapolate to talk about the rhyme patterns in Fife dialect itself here.

The discussion above suggests a third source of evidence, particularly for sound values, namely reconstruction, or at least the sort of extended reconstruction found in Macafee (1989) or Lass (1976) to deduce pathways of development. It makes use of something like the classic comparative method, heuristics about what historical statements we can make from geographical patterns in modern dialects, and our knowledge of favoured direction of sound change to 'pin down' the meaning of spelling or rhyme evidence. This is a textbook instance of 'using the present to explain the past' (Labov 1972), and has been a feature of historical linguistic argument for a long time. If conditions are right, we can even suggest a certain amount of phonetic detail (Johnston 1992), particularly if there is plentiful data and we can argue from the occurrence or non-occurrence of mergers and splits.

Since more than one source of evidence is better than only one, we should be able at least to make some hypotheses about what the dialect contained in a given text was like by combining all the above approaches. While this provides nothing like the level of accuracy in any sort of modern dialect survey, this mutual reinforcement of the methods should constrain our conclusions and should provide at least some features that could be considered diagnostic of a given area. If we then allow geographically placeable texts to serve as 'anchor texts' (Samuels 1989), and place 'unknowns' on the basis of their similarities to these, we can then build a network of localisable texts, from which we can abstract out the common features of language as traits of a given dialect or group. If there are enough texts that can be localised, such features might form the basis of a dialect breakdown similar to the ones shown in Chapter 11.

This multifaceted methodology is, indeed, what I attempt to use in this chapter, employing a mixture of the spelling evidence collected by the editors of the *Concise Scots Dictionary* (Robinson 1985), the *Scottish National Dictionary* (Grant and Murison 1931–76), the *Dictionary of the Older Scottish Tongue* (Craigie et al. 1937–) and the Scottish manuscripts in the *Linguistic Atlas of Late Medieval English* (McIntosh et al. 1986), plus rhyme evidence where relevant. While the resulting analysis will not be as detailed as that done for Modern Scots, it should at least result in a list of the most salient dialect features in each area, and a dialect breakdown showing a definite similarity to the modern one, minus the regions which, in Older Scots times, were primarily inhabited by speakers of other languages, such as the Northern Isles, which have to be counted as Norn-speaking until the very end of the period. Even in these cases, the modern reflexes of sounds and grammar should give clues about the dialect of those Scots settlers who came to Shetland and Orkney and how the dialects of today grew up as a second-language version of that variety. The task is only a little harder, largely because of unevenness of data, than trying to do the same thing for England using McIntosh et al. (1986), Kristensson (1967, 1987) and Moore et al. (1935). A number of researchers (for example, Johnston 1993, 1992) have employed this evidence to draw conclusions that the handbooks of the early twentieth century (Jordan 1934; Luick 1964; Jespersen 1914) do not always have the material to answer properly, such as clues to the early (fourteenth- and fifteenth-century) history of the Great Vowel Shift.

There are a number of things to keep in mind here that will make our task harder. First, just as Tudor English is, Scots is in the process of developing a Standard by the beginning of the sixteenth century, based on the Mid-Scots dialects spoken in Edinburgh and other important Central Belt centres. Like sixteenth-century English, there is still a large amount of variation within it, especially in the orthography, and there are no Scots grammarians or dictionary-makers to codify what is 'proper' Scots. Indeed, it is not even certain that anyone had a notion of what that would be, or even used this dialect in the spoken mode, although it certainly could have served as the sort of koiné that could be used among people of diverse origins who are thrown together, as might happen in the court, the chancery, the universities or religious houses; we do not have a Scottish Hart attempting to make the spelling system 'make sense', or a Scottish Gil railing at the *Mopsae*, or a Bullokar or Wilkins giving examples of 'vulgar' pronunciations. Before such authorities could arise, the sociolinguistic tide of Scots had changed, and the standardisation process now operated so as to install London-based norms as proper (Devitt 1989; Templeton 1973; Aitken 1973c).

This leaves us with a certain number of fourteenth- and fifteenth-century 'clues' to dialectal Scots, such as the documents and letters collected in LALME (McIntosh et al. 1986), and slips of the pen of scribes betraying their native phonologies in the sixteenth century. These exist in England too, as Orton (1933) has shown, suggesting that Scots and English were at about the same stage of standardisation. The period when Scots is being replaced by English, the late sixteenth century, is very revealing, as there seems to be a sort of hiatus in the provinces, where the pull of the Edinburgh Standard is declining and that of London not quite dominant. Scribes are very likely in these conditions to 'fill the gaps' with local forms, based on their own speech (or, in court transcripts, possibly those of the witnesses themselves). Such forms appear, in a mixed style, in records right into the early eighteenth century (Murray 1873: 96), and it might be possible, if we could collect enough letters of the bourgeois class, to extend this sort of evidence right up until 1760 or so, when Scottish Standard English (SSE) finally takes hold among them. Even then, we could probably find evidence even later among working-class semi-literates, Scots equivalents of the Geordie and Mancunian union organisers whom Thompson (1983) quotes, whose letters are as faithful representations of the local vernacular as the poems of Fergusson and Burns.

We have also to remember that we are operating with a different sort of society from a modern European one. It is true that we do not have to worry about non-Scots speakers among Lowlanders, except for recent immigrants and along the Gaelic margins. Theoretically, the king or queen can be as good an informant as to what Scots is like as the peasants who have left nothing written down for us to sift through. But we cannot guarantee that there was not any sort of sociolinguistic stratification. Certainly, there are differences in register: the 'aureate style' of a Gavin Douglas or William Dunbar is a good example of the effects of the Renaissance on Scots, with its polysyllabic Latinity well marked (Aitken 1979), just as in some registers full of 'inkhorn terms' beloved by English writers as a welcome extension of their formal styles. It is easy to see a group of high clerics or professionals with a knowledge of that sort of formality, even if those terms would be only rarely spoken; one cannot conceive of a shepherd in the Moorfoots using this sort of vocabulary, even with the more equitable system (compared to England and elsewhere) of education in Scotland. Sound changes, even if they are partly driven by natural tendencies of assimilation and dissimilation available to any speaker (Labov 1994), are usually led by a certain group, while others may resist them; there probably were conservative and innovative speakers, even if we cannot identify their social characteristics. It makes sense that those who travelled would have a 'watered-down' style to facilitate communication with speakers from other regions; and since the upper classes and professionals would do this more than others, they may have shown stylistic differentiation. It makes sense from what we know about the professional classes and their role in standardising language anyway that if anyone had a 'Standard Scots style', it would be these people (Fisher 1996; Tuchman 1978). We can surmise from what we know about late medieval bourgeoisies that their 'be true to your town' attitudes (Tuchman 1978) would have to be a sustaining force for the preservation of their vernacular; however, the town vernacular might well be different from the countryside ones just outside the walls, given that cities did tend to have a more varied population and would attract people from around their whole hinterland, which could extend over more than one dialect group. There would thus have been koinéisation, if somewhat less than we see now or than would have taken place immediately after the Industrial Revolution took hold (Macafee 1983). Putting our historical data together, we can conclude that all of Lowland Scotland was something like a Pattern I society if there was no Scottish Standard English. Local vernacular Scots was spoken by everyone in casual contexts, but some stratification *within Scots* emerged in formal ones, as people edited out their most localised forms in favour of equally Scots but more widespread forms. The dialect model which held for town and country relations was something probably more like the traditional German model: one had Scots rural *Mundarten* and urban *Stadtsdialekte* (Clyne 1984); but the latter, though somewhat koinéised, are clearly related to the former even more closely than they are now. Perhaps, as in modern Edinburgh (Johnston 1983b), the very lowest class in cities spoke something very much like the surrounding *Mundarten*, a sixteenth-century equivalent to Niddrie or Pilton Scots rather than that of Gorgie or Dalry. This speculative hypothesis becomes even more reasonable if we consider that the urban poor contained many dispossessed peasantry anyway, and the bulk of them would presumably be from nearby (Tuchman 1978).

Regrettably, such a model cannot be fully proven, because of the skewing of literacy. We can, however, postulate changes once they have been adopted by members of society who could and did read and write; and if there were no normative spoken standard, the time-lag between 'estatis' adopting a change could be very much less than now. We must take our first attestation as merely a lower limit of the dating of a change; occasionally, the way in which the changes intertwine will force such a conclusion on us (see 3.3–3.6).

The layout of topics in this chapter parallels that in Chapter 11, on Modern Scots dialectology. The next section, 3.2, gives a tentative dialect breakdown for Older Scots, based on the evidence contained in the early LALME manuscripts (McIntosh et al. 1986), knowledge of the historical record and patterns of introduction of Old Northumbrian/Early Scots and reconstructions. I shall also argue that the basic layout of dialects goes back largely to the earliest history of Scots, and that Old Northumbrian and its descendant in Scotland spread unevenly, in waves, with each push forward spawning a new dialect subgroup. I will also discuss the different linguistic mix present in the early formation of the dialects, drawing largely on the place-name evidence of Nicolaisen (1976).

The last four sections, 3.3–3.6, list the salient features of Older Scots phonology, and where possible other levels of language, as revealed by spelling, rhyme and reconstructive evidence. The sounds are divided into the front (section 3.3), back (3.4) and diphthongal vowel nuclei (3.5) and the consonant system (3.6). Reasonable hypotheses about values and developments are made in the same kind of format as characterises the corresponding sections in Chapter 11. Dialectal consonant systems are described in terms of subsystems and a list of geographically variable processes affecting them, while the vowels are defined in terms of the same word–class categories outlined at the beginning of section 3.3 and used again in Chapter 11.

3.1.2   Traits of Old Northumbrian

At this point, it might be useful to list a few of the traits that distinguished the sort of Old English spoken in Scotland, Northumberland, Durham and Cumberland. While these have left only faint traces in the modern dialects, and it is likely that the modern varieties descend from a radically restructured, Norse-influenced Northumbrian going back to the Danelaw proper as much as from the original dialects of the Berenician settlers, it is useful to list traits that a dialectologist of the eleventh century would have found. Many of the rules producing the salient differences were undone in the transformation from Old English to Early Scots/Middle English; a few more, usually of pan-Anglian distribution, became general or nearly so, spread through the old Saxon territory once Standard English, with largely Mercian roots (Samuels 1985), had come to be.

The while we have a cluster of Northumbrian documents from the seventh century – names and places in Bede's *Historia Ecclesiastica*, the *Song of Cædmon*, the *Leiden Riddle* and the *Franks Casket Inscription*, and our only Scots example, the inscription on the Ruthwell Cross – plus a smaller, later ninth- and tenth-century collection of gospels (*Lindisfarne* and the Deiran *Rushworth*), the *Durham Ritual*, and a number of glosses, giving a sort of 'before and after' temporal distribution, most of the handbooks concentrate on the earlier cluster (Luick 1964; Wyld 1937; Jespersen 1914), making it look like archaic traits are really Northumbrian ones. It is true that the past-tense ending in seventh-century *tiadæ* seems to resemble the ending of continental runic *tawido* as much as an Ælfrician **tēode*; but Northumbrian, in its late form, was a source of morphological innovation, though Norse-influenced reconstruction may have already been involved. The infinitival ending is already *-a*, rather than *-an* (Toon 1983: 432). The present-tense paradigm has already generalised *-es/-as* to all persons, provided that a pronoun does not immediately precede. While there is a tendency to use ⟨æ⟩ where West Saxon would use ⟨e⟩, this may simply have been the way of representing [ɐ] or some sort of 'lowered schwa' rather than an archaism, as it does not always stand for a West Germanic *a* or *o*. Even the *o* for final *u* is closer to the schwa that it would become than the West Saxon reflex is. Overall, Northumbrian is an innovative dialect, not a conservative one, when it comes to the development of unstressed syllables – a trend that will continue into Early Scots/Middle English as final *-e* is lost a whole century before it disappears in London (Minkova 1991).

The consonant inventory is the same in Old Northumbrian as in West Saxon, although the graphemes used to represent it may differ, as does some of the allophony. The sounds /j/ and /w/ have a tendency to be written ⟨i⟩ or ⟨ig⟩ in codas, and ⟨uu, u⟩ rather than ⟨g⟩ or ⟨w⟩, even though palatalised early Old English /ɣ/ and /j/ merge here as in other dialects (A. Campbell 1959: 24–7). The /h/ phoneme is already variably disappearing in onsets in southern dialects, but is rigorously maintained in the north, as it is in most of Scotland now

(Toon 1983: 417). This includes positions within the clusters /hn, hl, hr/ as well as /hw/ – in fact, Scots today keeps /ʍ/</hw/ separate from /w/, at least in rural varieties, and *whryne*, from Old Norse *hrína*, survived until quite recently with an apparent /ʍr/</hr/ (Robinson 1985). The phoneme /h/ is often written ⟨gh, hg⟩ as well as the customary Scots ⟨ch⟩ in codas, and the combination /xt/ may be ⟨ct⟩ suggesting at least a fortis articulation, something more than an [h] (Campbell 1959: 24). The development of /ɣ/ and the Borders diphthongisation before /h/, which goes at least as far back as our records (McIntosh et al. 1986), suggests that an *Ich/Ach* (or even *Auch*) rule was already present.

West Germanic /β/, which becomes [v] in West Saxon and is written ⟨f⟩, remains for a time in Northumbrian, as suggested by the orthography (⟨b⟩) in earlier Northumbrian manuscripts (Campbell 1959: 24): a bilabial, rather than a labiodental, strident articulation of /v/ might better explain the /v/-deletion rule operating between the time of Open Syllable Lengthening and the time that extensive records begin, as well as /v/ ~ /w/-Interchange (see section 11.3). The combination /ft/ may also have been *[ɸt], as it is written ⟨pt⟩ (Campbell 1959: 24). The phoneme /θ/ is usually written ⟨th⟩ initially but ⟨d⟩ medially; we cannot tell whether this represents [ð] or a true stop [d] in some cases, or a variable situation, making /d ð/-Interchange undatable (Campbell 1959: 25).

The vocalic inventory contained the short vowels /i e æ ɑ o u y/ and short diphthongs /æ eo iu/ (the last is represented by ⟨io⟩), but with a different lexical incidence from early West Saxon because of the more restricted operation of Breaking and the presence of Velar Umlaut. The long vowels included /i: e: æ: ɑ: o: u: ø: y: æ:ɑ e:o i:u/, with /ø:/, the *i-umlaut* of /o:/ as in Old Northumbrian *cœne*, *grœne* (West Saxon *cēne*, *grēne*), lasting until the end of the period, then apparently unrounding in parallel with /y(:)/ to /e: i: i/ as in other Anglian varieties except West Mercian (Campbell 1959: 76). The ⟨io īo: eo ēo⟩ distinction also persisted to the end of the period before resolving itself in favour of the lower pair of diphthongs, as elsewhere (> Early Scots /ɛ e:/: Campbell 1959: 124). Northern Northumbrian documents sometimes represent both /æ(:)ɑ/ and /e(:)o/ by ⟨ea⟩, but it is more likely that this represents the schwa-like quality of the V2 rather than the first element being identical. If there had been a true merger, MEET would always equal BEAT; this does indeed happen in the far north of England, southern Scotland, the East and West Mid areas and Aberdeen, but there is enough rhyme evidence from Barbour and Henryson, who came from areas that now have the merger, to suggest that the merger arose later. Even in Northumberland, there are coastal dialects where the quality of /i:/ is bipolar – with both [ɪ] and [i:] as frequent variants (Borger 1980) and in Orton and Halliday (1962), although Embleton has a slight tendency to use [ɪ] more often in BEAT words. If this is true, then the long vowel inventory is also the same as the 'handbook' one (Dobson 1957) by the twelfth century, and we cannot trace inventorial differences back to Old English times, since what differences there were became erased.

The same is true for some rules giving lexical–incidental differences between Northumbrian dialects. Like all Anglian varieties, Northumbrian has a slightly more restrictive Breaking rule than Wessex varieties, but was more sensitive to the backing influence of back vowels in succeeding unstressed syllables (Velar Umlaut). Wessex varieties broke /i(:), e(:), æ(:)/ to /i(:)u (> e(:)o), e(:)o, æ(:)ɑ/ before /w/ and /x/ alone, /rC/, and most /lC/ combinations, and all velar environments since /r l/ had velarised allophones here. Northumbrian also breaks vowels before /w x/, and /e/ > /eo/ before /rC/ if a /w/ does not precede (Campbell 1959: 55–6; Jones 1989: 33–63). However, /ærC, ælC/ retracts to /ɑrC, ɑlC/ instead of breaking, giving *ward*, *harpe* instead of *weard*, *hearpe* and *cald*, *ald* instead of *ceald, eald*. Unless a velar intervened, however, a similar diphthongisation, not found much in West Saxon, arose if the vowel in the next syllable was a back one, so that *setol* became *seotol/seatol* and *milac* became *mioloc* (Campbell 1959: 345). Another source of such diphthongs is a Palatal Diphthongisation rule like the West Saxon one, although these diphthongs were probably accented on the V2, the original vowel (Campbell 1959: 66). Yet even here, Smoothing processes at the end of the Old English period undid the diphthongisation, while the merger of /æ ɑ/ got rid of the remaining differences. At the end, the only process leaving traces was a pan-Anglian one, that /æld/ had become /ɑld/; and *all* modern reflexes of the OLD subclass derive from /ɑld/ or /ɑːld/ by Homorganic Lengthening (Jones 1989: 24–32), not just northern ones, since London and East Central Midland speech must also have had it.

Anglian dialects separate out the reflexes of West Germanic /ɑː/ which became /æː/ in West Saxon, but /eː/ in Anglian, from those of the *i-umlaut* of West Germanic /ai/, /æː/ in both dialects: *street, sheep, needle* are thus MEET words, but *clean, read, meal* ('dinner') are BEAT words. Yet this, too, is true of the ancestors of Standard English, as the orthography suggests. Furthermore, this pattern spread somewhat into southern dialects, so that forms like [streːt] do not appear if the dialect has been restructured. A similar reinforcement process led to the replacement of /yː/ forms from /iy/ = ⟨ie⟩ in West Saxon with Anglian /eː/ as the reflex of the umlaut of West Germanic /ai/, so that *hear* is now a MEET word everywhere (Campbell 1959: 76; Toon 1983: 416). As in a number of other Old English dialects (Toon 1983), /ɑ/ plus nasals became [ɒ], not [ɑ], before nasals in Northumbrian, giving *mon, hond, lond, mony* for *man, hand, land, many*. Only the last and the analogically restructured *ony* remain to testify that this change, reversed in early Middle English times, ever existed in the area north of the Lune/Humber line. The *hand*-Darkened forms like [hɔːn(d)] [ɬɔːnd] in Glaswegian and other Central Belt varieties have no connection with Old English [ɒn], which would have yielded modern *[hoːn(d), ɬon(d)] with COT vowels (Toon 1983: 416).

Anglian dialects, including Northumbrian, smoothed /eox, æɑx/ to /eːx/ (Campbell 1959: 5; Jones 1989: 58–67), and this explains the development of *heich* from *hēh* rather than *hēah*. However, Northumbrian and Scots seem to have turned at least the long vowels, as in *līoht* to /ixt/, just as West Saxon did, if a consonant followed the /x/ (Campbell 1959: 130). Northumbrian also backed a number of vowels between /w/ and a following /r/, so that /wir/ > /wur/ and /wer/ > /wor/. The form /wyr/ had apparently unrounded before the rules took effect (Campbell 1959: 57). By this rule, *wirca* 'work' > *wurca*, and *werpa* 'throw' > *worpa*, and so on. The changes affecting /wir/ are well attested in Scots and northern English dialects, but it is hard to tell if they are the result of this rule or a more general one affecting all /wiC/ by early Middle English times (Orton 1933), or even whether the retraction is due to the same rule. The stem vowel of /wer/ words like *worth, world*, oldest in Scots, though, is /ɑ/, not /o/, the same sort of change that lowers the vowel in *west*. The phoneme /o/ appears only if a labial follows, and then only if /o/ > /ɑ/ or /ʌ/ did not apply in the sixteenth century, as in *web*. It is likely that even these retractions were undone before another set applied in the early Scots period.

Similarly, Old Northumbrian developed /tʃ/ normally, as shown by a number of place-names in *-chester*, not *-caster* (Nicolaisen 1977), in Northumberland and the Scottish Borders. However, many of the words that have these sounds, like *church, churn, chaff, bridge, ridge, thatch*, have *kirk, kirn, caff, brig, rig, thack* instead. This is traditionally blamed on Old Norse influence, and the explanation seems plausible (but see Taylor 1974), as do cases with initial /g/ for /j/. These forms are still importations, however, as Norse settlers south and east of Caithness and north of the Solway could only come via secondary settlement, not as primary colonies (Nicolaisen 1977).

It seems, therefore, that very few of the salient distinctions that really separate Old Northumbrian from other dialects remained distinctive for long after the Old English period. The varieties of English spoken in Scotland – and northern England north of the Tees, for that matter – were to some extent restructured, presumably under the influence of the Norse–English contact variety common in the northern Danelaw, just as southern English dialects were later (Millar 1996). A few features remain as a token that the dialect stems from roots other than those that it seems to, but the bulk of the old distinguishing marks have been swept away in a field-of-replacement process, or generalised to other areas if they were widespread enough to begin with.

Such a phenomenon is not unusual. The process is not so different from the forces that created the lower northern dialects of the American Midwest (Carver 1989), where initial Virginian/Kentuckian settlement was overlaid by a powerful later Pennsylvanian wave of immigration, forcing the area into the linguistic north. Closer to home, the restructuring resembles that effected by Cockney speakers in southern England, or North Midland ones in the north. In exploring the roots of the dialect divisions within Scotland, one can discuss more of the ethnic and historical influences operating in the formation of Scots that the restructuring is part of. That is the goal of the next section – to reveal why the borders of language varieties are where they are and how they got there.

3.2 THE GENESIS OF THE DIALECTAL DIVISIONS OF SCOTS

3.2.1 Introduction

This analysis is based on the modern differentiating features that are attested in Older Scots times, especially in fourteenth- or fifteenth-century texts, plus a knowledge of the techniques of linguistic reconstruction and of the history and geography of Lowland Scotland and the connections of this to dialectal differentiation. The resulting map, of course, cannot possibly be as detailed as a modern one can; the sub-subdialectal and most of the subdialectal divisions are necessarily absent, partly because of the unevenness of the data, partly because of the fineness of phonetic detail that usually distinguishes such small divisions, and partly because of the opacity of the spelling system as opposed to modern phonetic transcription. However, the main North/Mid/South split is in place, and a number of types of Mid and Northern Scots can be differentiated, at least by 1600. The further extensions of the Scots area, to the Northern Isles, Caithness, Galloway, the Clyde coast and Ulster, are also in various stages of formation, so that by 1700 the modern map is virtually complete.

The map is the result of over a millennium of expansion of English-speakers (including speakers of Scots, once that had formed) proceeding in falterings and reawakenings as the speakers' military and political fortunes waxed and waned compared to the Celtic groups who were in the area before, whether these were effectively indigenous, as the Strathclyde and Rheged and Gododdin Welsh were in the south, or the Picts in the north, or whether they were fellow invaders expanding their realm in competition, as the Gaels were. The first few centuries saw English, as revealed by place-name evidence, expand into Ayrshire, Lanarkshire and even the Angus coast (Nicolaisen 1977), as well as along the Solway; the next few saw Gaelic-speaking overlords as far down as Midlothian and even Selkirkshire and Northumberland. The few after that saw the most rapid expansion, first to the Tay and Clyde and the Highland foothills, then to the Mounth, then to the Moray Firth and the opening of the Inverness area, and finally across the sea to Ireland and Shetland. With each push, there was a high-water mark created, perhaps at a natural boundary, perhaps at a boundary line belonging to a powerful enemy, which later became the basis for a dialect division, once the area beyond had been anglicised.

One can separate the areas into four zones, though these do not exactly correlate with dialect group. The southern and East Mid dialects of today stem from an Anglian core area, an area settled like England was, seized from Brythonic Celts with little future contact or bilingualism, since the people were apparently driven out. The Old Frontierland, in which small bands of Angles, in Old English times, founded villages and towns in the nooks and crannies of Welsh and/or Pictish areas, often in competition with Gaels coming from the opposite direction, constitutes the West and North Mid areas, up to the Tay and most of the Clyde coast. While it may not have been fully anglicised by David I's time, it was well on the way. Beyond lay the New Frontierland, the Gaelicised Pictish areas of the Scottish north-east, anglicised in early Scots times by the establishment and chartering of ethnically diverse burghs, with Early Scots serving (presumably) as a *lingua franca* and replacing the other tongues by 1350 or so. Finally, the extensions of the Scots heartland formed. These areas were probably bilingual throughout most or all of the Older Scots period. Some, like Galloway or Caithness, were all but totally Scots-speaking by 1600, with pockets, if that, of the old language remaining. Others, like Orkney, Shetland and Ulster, were still predominantly Norse or Celtic, and Scots functioned only as a formal language. In any case, speech habits of the former vernacular of the region helped to shape the type of Scots that replaced it, and the influence is more transparently evident than in any of the other, more established areas.

In each subsection below, the region is blocked out geographically, and the reason for the boundaries being there is outlined in terms of a history of the English/Scots-speakers and their settlement in the area. The type and depth of linguistic contacts which these speakers would have is outlined, and the earliest attested or postulated distinctive features of the dialect grouping are listed. The whole is designed to be an argument for the existence of each dialect group from the time of appearance of these features. As implied in section 3.1, one cannot easily go back into Old Northumbrian times, when the dialects of English-speaking Scotland, Cumbria and Northumberland/Durham cannot be distinguished using reconstructive methods and there are no texts – or at most, very few – until the fourteenth century that we can use for spelling evidence. It seems that our methodology runs into the brick wall of an intense period of migration and koinéisation in the late eleventh and twelfth centuries, and the earliest distinctive features that we can use to differentiate Scots dialects from each other, with one possible exception, go back only to the thirteenth century. Nevertheless, bearing in mind how (relatively) permanent the boundaries are to the features differentiated by them, we can reasonably postulate that there may have been other isoglosses at these boundaries before – the boundaries' *raison d'être* being more historical or ethnic than solely linguistic.

3.2.2   The Anglian Core: Southern and East Mid Older Scots

The natural boundary separating the southern dialects from the central ones would be the line of hills, including the Lammermuirs and the Moorfoots, that collectively are called the

Southern Uplands. From the east coast, the rough boundary line would run from Cockburnspath on the western edge of Berwickshire, through Oxton and Heriot in the Midlothian Borders, then north of Stow and Peebles to Broughton and Abington and Wanlockhead in southern Lanarkshire. Most of this line follows the modern East Mid A or West Mid and East Mid B line. Except for the Pentlands, there is no clear boundary between East Mid A and West Mid, and only the River Forth between East Mid and North Mid; there is, however, a political boundary between the Lothians and Stirlingshire defined roughly by the Avon, and between Lanarkshire and the Lothians defined by the Forth/Clyde watershed. Except for the part between the Almond and the Avon, this area constituted the Anglian core area of Scotland. Here, from the sixth or seventh century on, the majority of the population spoke English, as seen by the distribution of Anglian place-names versus Gaelic ones (Nicolaisen 1977). Only around Edinburgh and to the west is there any big concentration of Gaelic place-names, from Dalkeith and Auchendinny westwards. The names further east tend to be of English origin, and otherwise are Brythonic. Included are some very old -inghām names like *Tyningham* (pronounced with the typical Berenician [-*indʒəm*] < -*ingihām*) and *Coldingham*, as well as plain -*hāms* like *Yetholm*, *Birgham*, *Ednam*, *Oxnam* and *Hownam*, and -*ingtūns* like *Haddington*, *Upsettlington* or *Carrington*. The focus of all these names is the valley of the Tweed and its tributaries from Berwick to St Mary's Loch, with a small concentration of old Anglian names near Coldingham and on the North Berwick peninsula, and again along the Solway.

Thanks to the Welsh bard Aneurin and the Venerable Bede, we have a fairly good record of the Anglian onslaught into south-east Scotland, at least compared to other areas. The old kingdom of Berenicia had its start in the form of a tribe of Anglian sea-pirates who established a base and castle on Bamburgh rock dating supposedly from AD 558 (Duncan 1975). From there, the people pushed up the Tweed on the one hand, and up the coast on the other. The Brythonic/Welsh-speaking natives were simply pushed back in a series of advances that finally culminated in the capture of Dun Eidyn (Edinburgh) in the early seventh century (Duncan 1975). From then on, the political fortunes may have occasionally altered greatly, with periodic invasions of Strathclyde Britons, English and Viking raids, and a period of Gaelic overlordship lasting from the late ninth century to the twelfth; but the main vernacular of the territory remained English throughout, whether the region was called Berenicia, Northumbria, Lothian or Scotland. Even the Gaelic ruling classes – who often have English or Norse names (Duncan 1975) – became anglicised under Malcolm Canmore and his English-speaking queen, St Margaret, who welcomed English landholders and their tenants fleeing the Normans, largely stemming from the north. These people were really Anglo–Norse, and their dialect was probably a form of a 'creoloid' or ethnic koiné with extensive borrowings. It was they who brought the Norse element to Scots, since there was direct Norse settlement only in a section of Dumfriesshire along the Solway, as the north-western corner of the Danelaw (Nicolaisen 1977). A second influx of people, the Normans themselves with their English and Norman tenants and French and Flemish artisans and tradespeople, added the French overlay and possibly a feature or two found in the Midlands, from where many of David I's Norman followers came (Duncan 1975). One possible feature that is common to East Central Midland dialects and south-east Scotland that may be of some antiquity affects /æ:j/ words like *key*, *swey*, *wee* which have /ʌi/ as one might expect, north of the Forth, but /i:/ < /e:/ < /ei/ < /e:j/ in this region (Jordan 1934: 242).

The layout of the settlements suggests three dialects operating within this zone: one associated with the Solway/Annan settlements, one with the Tweed and its tributaries, and one with Edinburgh and the Forth coast. The last named is plainly associated with East Mid A now, although the place-name layout would lead us to assign West Lothian and western Midlothian to one of the Old Frontierland groups; the first is a Southern B-speaking bailiwick. However, the second comprises both East Mid B and Southern A-speaking areas. It is probably significant that these two dialects share the sixteenth-century Border Scots Vowel Shift and the fourteenth-century tendency to add epenthetic vowels to /Vx/ combinations, resulting in spellings of *boucht*, *soucht*, *wroucht* and so on from early times (Robinson 1985: xiv; McIntosh et al. 1986). The last-named feature differentiates dialects of the Edinburgh area from the rest very early on. East Mid B and Southern A also share a great deal of common vocabulary as against the Lothians (Mather and Speitel 1975). It is therefore quite possible that *all* the Borders, including eastern East Lothian, spoke Southern Scots in Older Scots days, and the East Mid variety, as important as it was, was confined to Midlothian and the western part of East Lothian alone.

Since Southern B today differs from Southern A mainly in what Lothian features the latter has adopted, the differences between the two were probably not very great phonologically. Lexically, it is another story: there is a group of words with a distinct south-western distribution in Scotland, and these, particularly if shared with Cumbrian, tend to divide Southern B from A clearly (Mather and Speitel 1975, 1977).

3.2.3   The 'Old Frontierland': North and West Mid Scots

Working north and west, the next sections of land to which one comes are (1) a strip traversed by the River Clyde and its tributaries, from the continuation of the Southern Upland line to the south Ayrshire coast on the south to the hills north of Glasgow that constitute the first foothills of the Highlands to the north, and (2) the Fife peninsula to the Tay and the Ochils plus the upper Forth valley and possibly the pass running north to Perth from Stirling along the Allan. North of the Tay and Perth, the main frontier is the Highland Line itself, extending from the Trossachs towards the Mounth. The first two areas, like the Lothians, were partially settled by Angles early, with an Anglian See at Abercorn established as early as the late seventh century (Duncan 1975), showing that at least the southern part of the North Mid C zone was already English-speaking; and a cluster of place-names like *Maybole*, *Prestwick* and *Symington* in the immediate vicinity of Ayr, with a thinly sprinkled scatter in Lanarkshire in between (Nicolaisen 1977). Nowhere is there anything like the dense clustering of English place-names that we find in the Borders, and often there are big gaps with none at all.

This land was evidently settled in a very different way from the south-east of Scotland, and the history books tell us the reason: the West Mid area was dominated by the Welsh-speaking kingdom of Strathclyde, with its capital at Dumbarton Rock, an intermittent power in the area until the tenth century. The Strathclyde Welsh were too strong to be simply pushed out like the Gododdin and Rheged Welsh, and from time to time they launched quite devastating (if temporary) counterpunches at the Anglian settlements to the east and south (Duncan 1975). The North Mid territory was the heartland of the Southern Picts, the Maeatae whose name is preserved in the hill of Dumyat (Dun Maeat) near Stirling. Any hope of an easy victory against them was dashed in AD 685 at Nechtansmere in Angus, halting the Anglian advance for two centuries. The place-name picture reveals the depth of settlement by Britons and Picts (Nicolaisen 1977); the Angles had to take the land they could in the nooks and crannies in between clusters of villages.

There were also the Gaels to contend with. The North Mid zone and the West Mid area down to North Ayrshire were in the main path of the Gaelic expansion from their heartland in Argyll directly eastwards down the streams that flow into the Tay, Forth and Clyde. Stronger than either the Strathclyde Welsh or the Maeatae, the Gaels arrived in profusion in the eighth and ninth centuries, founding villages whose *Auch(en)-*, *Bal-* and *Kil-* elements testify to the presence of an intensive settlement, complete with Celtic church activity. Another group of Gaels, latterly well admixed with Norse blood (Gallgaels), streamed in from Ulster into the south-west of Scotland as far as a crescent from Dumfries to Maybole, leaving similar place-names – sometimes with *Kils-* disguised as *Kirks-* from Norse (Nicolaisen 1977) – throughout the southern part of the West Mid area.

The result was a linguistic patchwork where no group had a clear majority of speakers in a given area and which, once the initial fighting had died down, we might suppose would be a multilingual and multi-ethnic area, with frequent intermarriage and much bilingualism. As in Lothian, for a time Gaelic would have been the predominant language of the upper classes – in fact, except maybe for Strathclyde, more so, since the Gaelic king of Scots moved his court to palaces like Scone, Stirling Castle and Dunfermline Castle in the heart of the northern Old Frontierland. Only slowly, and largely after St Margaret's time, would English in its Scots form replace it, once the Anglian population was fortified by the influxes of English and Anglo-Normans mentioned in section 3.2.2. All indications are, however, that except for Lennox, parts of the Clyde coast like Bute, Arran and the mainland opposite Carrick, the Ochils and the regions leading to the Highlands in north and west Perthshire, these two dialect areas were solidly Early Scots-speaking by 1250. Lennox, the Ayrshire mainland, Carrick and most of the Ochils would follow suit by the end of the period (Duncan 1975).

These dialects, therefore, would have been shaped by the speech habits of Celts, whether speakers of P- or Q-languages. Except for loanwords which are more plentiful in the regional vocabulary of the areas, especially in West Mid, it is not clear really what this would mean. The transparent characteristics – retroflex /r/'s, clear /l/'s, palatalisation of coronal consonants in the neighbourhood of front vowels, pre-aspiration – do not appear here, or, if they do, are present only in the recently won areas and districts where there has been recent Irish immigration, like Glasgow. The Celtic characteristics seem to be subtler – possibly no more than a greater degree of allophony of vowels around consonants (particularly grave ones), showing that the consonants themselves may have been velarised or palatalised at one time, and a *very* slight greater tendency towards lenition of consonants – such as /θ ð/, which turned into [hɣ] in Gaelic and may tend to [h] and [ɾ] or zero today in this area. The two areas are united by an early tendency to back or lower vowels after /w/ or before /l/ and sometimes /r/, and those rules tend to be more extended here than in the east. Thus, *two* goes back to an Older Scots /twɑ(u)/ not /twaː/; *pill* and *hill* appear with Older Scots /u/ as well as /ɪ/, and *west*, with /wɑ/, all attested from the fourteenth century on (Robinson 1991: 287). The North Mid group goes further and turns long mid vowels to diphthongs after /w/ so that *wame, weak, weave, weed* come out with /ʌɪ/ (Older Scots [ëi] or [ɛi]). Some early distinguishing characteristics may not be Celtic at all: in the manuscripts analysed by LALME in Ayrshire, OUT + alveolars is not infrequently realised as ⟨oCe⟩ or ⟨uCe⟩, while BOOT may be ⟨ow⟩. This does not show merger, as the modern reflexes are different, but it may show a near-merger, where BOOT and OUT might have contrasted as /ø(ː)·ʉ(ː)/ or the like even at this early date (McIntosh et al. 1986).

The dialect group boundaries and divisions depend as much on the early settlements as anything else. LALME manuscripts show little difference between North Mid and East Mid varieties (McIntosh et al. 1986), and it makes sense historically that there should be a close connection between the two. Differences between the various divisions of North Mid depend largely on changes belonging to the ending stages of the Great Vowel Shift, such as whether /aa ai/ is [e(:)] or [eə], and whether /au/ > [ɑː] or [ɔː]. We can postulate a reasonable unity within this group, in contrast to the present. Lexical distributions suggest that the dialect area may have extended into a great deal of West Lothian (Mather and Speitel 1975, 1977) as well as Stirlingshire.

The West Mid group originally seems to be bifocal, with Lanarkshire dialects showing more affinity with the other branches of Mid Scots than Ayrshire ones do, and there are words that have a strictly west-coast distribution, associated with Ayrshire, the Clyde coast and now Wigtownshire, but not further east. This is consistent with the history and the lie of the land and direction of travel as determined by passes; Lanarkshire can be entered directly, via either the north-east or east as well as up the Clyde from the Upper Tweed. Ayrshire must be entered (if Lanarkshire cannot be a stepping stone) from the Nith Valley and the passes leading to the west. Therefore, Lanarkshire may have taken settlers from both the Lothians and the Solway, but Ayrshire must have done so only from the Solway. The two dialects have been brought together into one group since, with the filling-in of Renfrewshire, and later, with the growth of Glasgow. This process is still going on today, as West Mid characteristics spread out from this important central city to other areas well beyond Ayrshire.

3.2.4 The Burgh-borne Dialects

North of the Tay, we reach a region where the natural boundaries are set by the Highland Line on the west, the North Sea on the east, and its arm, the Moray Firth, on the north. Technically speaking, this rolling, fertile land continues to the gates of Inverness, and if one counts the Black Isle and the mile or two of coastal plain, even further, to widen out in Caithness again in the form of flat peat bog. English/Scots-speakers reached these northern areas only late on in the period: they are therefore considered as 'extensions', and the territory covered here ends between Forres and Nairn, where the hills come down to within four miles of the coast. The region is divided in two by an extension of the first range of the Highlands, comprising the Sidlaw Hills in Angus and the easternmost extension of hillocks, the Mounth, in Kincardineshire. Even before Scots-speakers arrived, this group of hills was an ethnic boundary, dividing the Maeatae from their northern cousins, the Caledonians. The range still forms the Mid-Northern/South Northern boundary.

There was an abortive attempt by the Angles to take the Mearns, crushed by the Picts in 685 (Duncan 1975; Nicolaisen 1977). The Gaels, again pushing through the Highlands, had better luck in the next two centuries, and Pictish and Gaelic place-names are interspersed through most of the north-east, with *Aberdeen* (P-Celtic) lying not far from *Inverurie* (Q-Celtic), and *Pittulie* (P-Celtic) and *Pennan* (P-Celtic) up the coast from *Kinnaird*, *Cairnbulg* and *Inverallochy* (Q-Celtic). We do not know whether the first early Scots in the area encountered Pictish or not, because we do not know when the language finally disappeared: the names of the various earls, thanes and *murmaers* are thoroughly Gaelic (or sometimes Norse-influenced Gaelic (Duncan 1975)), but this would also be true of areas where Gaels were a thin 'overclass', and it says nothing about what peasants spoke. We do know that the area *eventually* became Gaelic-speaking by about the thirteenth century, that the political organisation was of a Gaelic type (Duncan 1975) and that, in the hilly areas, it remained so in the old Fraser, Grant and Gordon lands (to name a few) into modern times. If the substratum here was purely Gaelic, however, it makes sense to postulate a variety that was shaped by a long period (say, 750–1150) of Gaelic/Pictish bilingualism.

It is unlikely that there was any English/Early Scots spoken at all before the establishment of the north-eastern burghs under David I, when the usual potpourri of English, south-eastern Scots, Norman, Picard and Flemish settlers (possibly with a particularly large Flemish contingent) poured in. The number of English-speaking tenants no doubt increased as the land was taken away from old Gaelic noble families that had died out, or who had backed the heirs of Lalach and Macbeth against the house of Canmore and replaced them with Scoto-Normans like the Comyns (Duncan 1975). Yet there is only a single, somewhat oblique reference to the possibility of English speech north of the Tay in the twelfth century (Duncan 1975), when the Old Frontierland (and not even the North Mid A area) was becoming anglicised. It is more likely that English/Early Scots really arrived in the north-east during the very late twelfth century, with the *growth* of the burghs and infeftment of Norman nobles who had already built up estates in Scotland, especially in the Lothians. The language must have only become predominant during the thirteenth century, maybe even the early fourteenth, and even then outside many of the inland districts away from burghs. Barbour's *Brus* is therefore an incredibly early example of Northern Scots; so early, it seems, that none of its specific traits show yet, and the document could easily come from Fife, Lothian or elsewhere.

It is possible that fourteenth-century Aberdonian was as yet not fully 'crystallised', in an early state where people's speech says as much about where their parents come from as about the speech of the area, before the dialect has achieved an identity of its own. Yet there are distinctive sound changes that *must* be early, and yet are not recorded until later, like *clean-* and *stone-*Raising (Macafee 1987), the latter of which must precede the Great Vowel Shift; or /v/</w/ that arises in words likê *blaave* for *blow*, which must go back at least to a time when such words had inflectional endings, if not to a time when the /w/ would have been consonantal in all positions. The development of the vowel before it suggests that the sound had a velar component, as the (sixteenth-century?) breaking of [a: ~ æ: ~ ɛ:] < Early Scots /a:/ happens also in words like *bake*, *vaig* 'wander' and *taings* 'tongs'.

It is perhaps more likely that the north-eastern traits were present in embryo in Barbour's time, but (1) the innovations had not spread through the whole community or (2) there was already sociolinguistic pressure to adopt Central Scots traits – or a combination of both. The third alternative is perhaps the best one, as fifteenth-century burgh records begin to show typically northern traits like /xw/ > /f/ <f, ph> despite what looks like an attempt to write using Mid-Scots spelling conventions. The internal breakdown of dialects may not have been all that clear to see in Older Scots times. The present Mid-Northern/South Northern split rests on the Mounth, which is both a natural barrier and, as stated before, an old ethnic boundary. Splits between Morayshire and the rest of Mid-Northern are less easy to see, but could come about easily, given the identity of Moray as a political unit before the influx of English-speakers and the geographical clustering of burghs (Duncan 1975).

By 1400, the dialect map of Scotland would have roughly resembled the present one, minus Galloway, the Black Isle, Caithness and the Northern Isles, and with a wider Highland zone than at present. Yet the expansion of Scots was an ongoing process, and, at least in the first two areas mentioned, Scots was already making inroads on the prior language. By the end of the period, Galloway and the Black Isle were Scots-speaking *in toto*, Caithness may well have been close to it, and Orkney and Shetland were bilingual territories, already with Norn as a minority language. The present-day Gallovidian group is so integrated into the mainstream of Central and Southern Scots that it is hard to imagine that the area was one of those to which the language came after the time of David I. Anglicisation, or really Scotticisation, must have been gradual, as there are burgh records from Wigtown in Scots from the early fifteenth century – and Kirkcudbright must have preceded Wigtown in picking up the language (McIntosh et al. 1986), yet there are records of Gaelic in Carrick from the sixteenth century. The type of Scots found in the burgh records resembles that of Ayrshire most closely, but *th*-Stopping, presumably with the [t̪ d̪] present now, is well in evidence (McIntosh et al. 1986). Since this is a feature associated with a Gaelic substratum in Hiberno–English (Wells 1982: 428), this is probably true here too. The modern affinities of the dialect in the treatment of *two*, *hook* and *bite* point solely to West Mid as the source of this variety. South Mid A may have had an input from the Borders also, as *two* is [ɛ:] and *hook* is [jʉ] today.

The earliest date for any substantial anglicisation of the area is well after the establishment of the burghs – there is none that old in the area but the three county towns (Wigtown, Kirkcudbright, Dumfries) – and the area was still tied enough to Ireland and the Western Isles in the thirteenth century for the lord of the area to style himself as a king (Duncan 1975) and to try to mount a revolt to unite a number of Gaelic areas against the Crown. The native ruling house, after the second of those rebellions in 1249, was removed and replaced by the Comyns, and later on the Douglases and Hamiltons played a large political role in the area. All of these families would have imported their own tenants into their new estates, helping to anglicise the countryside at a time when the burghs were growing in importance. In this period, we can (somewhat speculatively) postulate that the absorption into the rest of Mid-Scots was partially complete, producing a sort of Mid-Scots with a Gaelic accent, rather like Ulster Scots is today. It must provisionally be called South-western Scots, as a separate group, since the differences between the already formed Mid group were fewer than today, but it is already well on the way to being just another branch of that group.

There seems to be more to the development and formation of Caithnesian than meets the eye, even if one knows the history of the area. Unlike the Black Isle, which is patently a former Gaelic-speaking area rather like the inland parts of the north-east, probably settled via maritime contact with Morayshire and derivable from the same sort of underlying phonological system, Caithness was Norse, a mainland dependency of Orkney, originally ruled by Norwegian *jarls*. The density of *-bólstaðr* and *-setr* names – both liable to come out as *-ster* – is as high as anywhere in Britain (Nicolaisen 1977), testifying to the early and complete replacement of the tribe of the Cat, the Picts who gave the area its name. The two most populous towns are *Thórs á* and *Víkr* (meaning 'bay', not 'village'). By rights, this should be an Insular Scots-speaking locality, with the same sort of Norse-influenced syntax, intonation patterns, voice quality and phonetics as the Northern Isles.

Instead, the affinities of modern Caithnesian are with the north-east coast and a *Gaelic* substratum. Given that [r] = [ɭ] in Norwegian (Haugen 1982), perhaps the retroflex /r rC/ realisations can be attributed to a Norse underlay; and clear /l/ certainly is compatible with either. The fronted /u/ realisations agree with Northern Gaelic, but short /u/ = [ɪ̈] in Icelandic and Faroese, and its long congener's reflexes go back to a /y:/ (Haugen 1982). But if all these are due to Norse influence, why are they not present in the Insular group, except for clear /l/? It seems that rather than postulating that Scots directly replaced Norse, we have to postulate a Gaelic stage in between – either by saying that the Gaelic completely replaced Norn, or, more likely, that the area for a time (most of the Older Scots period) was a *trilingual* one, that Gaels from Sutherland were penetrating the area at the same time as or slightly before Scots entered via the Moray Firth. The peasants of Caithness are still referred to as *bondi* (< Old Norse) in the thirteenth century (Duncan 1975), so Caithness is probably Norn-speaking then, though Norn's traits besides vocabulary would be more prominent if Norn had lasted as long as in the Northern Isles, into the seventeenth or maybe the eighteenth century (Barnes 1991). The likelihood is that the linguistic transfer to Gaelic and Scots happens at the latest in the late fifteenth and early sixteenth century, as no Angus/ Fife connections denoting settlement by the Angus Earls of Orkney are present: the Scots stratum is undoubtedly north-eastern.

The Scots of the Northern Isles can only be said to be in an embryonic state in the Older Scots period, though gradually there is a replacement of Norse by Scots in uses for which a standard would be appropriate, such as the law. According to Barnes (1991), the drastic decline in Norn in favour of Scots took place in the early seventeenth century, perhaps later in Shetland. We can suppose that a bilingual, somewhat diglossic situation characterised the Isles at this time, with the Scots pole being much like a North Mid variety, given the consonantal traits that are *not* Norse-like, and the general vowel layout (Catford 1957b). The colonisation came from the Earl of Angus' estates, so South Northern and North Mid speakers would predominate.

A mystery remains as to how to explain various features that are in common among all the 'extension' varieties, as widely scattered as they are. All of these dialects have *ould* forms for *old, wan* as well as other forms for *one*, a tendency to palatalise velars, to realise /l/ as [l], a tolerance for upgliding diphthongs, and to monophthongise LOUP before /p k/. Some of these could have arisen in various ways depending on area, coincidentally resulting in the same form. *Ould* could come in from Hiberno-English (explaining Galloway and the Clyde coast) or arise due to DOG-Diphthongisation in North Northern (explaining Caithness and probably the Northern Isles); but other characteristics cannot so easily be explained in this way, particularly *wan* which is ultimately a south-western English form (Robinson 1985: 769). One can get it from there to Ireland, but from Ireland to the far north is not easy.

Some of the features are attested in Early Modern Standard English varieties (Dobson 1957: 691), while others, such as the upgliding diphthongs, seem to appear first in port towns and cities (Ellis 1889; Johnston forthcoming). It is quite possible that we have the influence of a seventeenth-century koiné of some kind, possibly a maritime one which would spring up in sailor and fisher communities, the result of sailing for long periods of time with shipmates from a wide variety of dialect areas. This, however, must remain a speculative suggestion, and no more.

The classification of Older Scots dialects that seems to be most reasonable is the following: there is a Southern group of dialects, spoken in all the Marches, from Berwickshire to east Dumfriesshire, up to the Southern Upland watershed. The Mid group can be divided into an East Mid subgroup, spoken in Mid and East Lothian; a West Mid subgroup, either with the tripartite structure evident today, or with a Perthshire vs a Fife/Stirlingshire/West Lothian subdivision. The Northern group is divided as today, though North Northern is still in the process of formation. A second-language, Gaelic-influenced variety, South-western Scots, exists in Galloway, while Insular Scots is still in its 'birth stage'.

64   PAUL JOHNSTON

3.2.5   Descriptive Techniques

I have chosen, here and in Chapter 11, to organise the remaining sections by word class, adjusted for any lexically conditioned, 'one-off' developments, similar to the rhyme classes which I used as variables in Johnston (1980). Each class is denoted by a keyword standing for all its members, after the fashion of Wells (1982), and the classes are organised into subsystems based on the monophthong vs diphthong and front vs back dimensions applying to a sixteenth-century, post-Great Vowel Shift layout. Subclasses of the major classes are designated by a keyword (in lower-case small capitals), membership of which is (usually) phonetically conditioned by the factors likely to cause lexical transfer. The keywords are given under the heading of each individual vowel class, in the introduction to that subsection. Each group of vowels is listed from the highest vowel down: see Table 3.1.

Table 3.1   Word Classes for Modern Scots vowels.

Front monophthongs

Key word	Older Scots source
MEET	/eː/
BEAT	/ɛː/
MATE	/aː/
BAIT	/ai/ > sixteenth-century /ɛː/ or /aː/
BOOT	/ɔː/, /iu/ before alveolar consonants
BIT	/ɪ/
BET	/ɛ/

Back monophthongs

Key word	Older Scots source
OUT	/uː/
COAT	/ɔː/
COT	/ɔ/
CAT	/a/
CAUGHT	/au/ > sixteenth-century /aː/
CUT	/ʊ/

Diphthongs/compound sounds

Key word	Older Scots source
NEW	/iu/ in hiatus and finally
DEW	/ɛu/
BITE	/iː/ in short environments
LOIN	/ui/
LOUP	/ʌu/
VOICE	/ɔi/
TRY	/iː/ in long environments

3.3   THE FRONT VOWELS IN OLDER SCOTS

3.3.1   Introduction

According to Aitken (1977b), before the Great Vowel Shift had taken place, the Older Scots monophthongal system matched the 'Classical' (i.e. Chaucerian) Middle English system in inventorial shape and number of elements, except that the BOOT nucleus had been fronted to /ø:/, leaving a gap in the back series. Otherwise, it had a maximum of four heights in long vowels and three in short: /i: e: ɛ: a: ø: o: u: ɪ ɛ a o ʊ/. In Catfordian (1957b) terms, the system had a COT:COAT and a MEET:BEAT:MATE contrast, as well as an extra BOOT vowel; since BAIT and CAUGHT were also independent nuclei before the Great Vowel Shift, there are A1, A2, E1, E2 and Y vowels in the system. Though the supposed /o: o/ were probably low-mid rather than high-mid (see sections 3.4.4 and 3.4.5), this reconstruction otherwise seems valid, and the inventorial size adequate, given the spelling evidence. The size matches the largest system possible in Scots today, though today only a few Caithnesian dialects are isomorphous, strictly speaking.

Note that historical length was retained, at least for the greater part of the Older Scots period, though there were other early lengthening and shortening processes. For Aitken's Law to have operated, producing the modern Edinburgh or Glasgow systems, it has to have applied only after MATE and BAIT – whether merged or not – had moved to a value higher than that of BET in the Great Vowel Shift, which demands a sixteenth-century date at the earliest. Otherwise, the three nuclei would have fallen together into /ɛ/ or /e/. This, in fact, does happen in Aberdonian, but it seems that BET merged in the seventeenth century at the earliest, except where it was lengthened to equal the BAIT vowel before sonorants (see section 3.3.7). In this area, as in all other regions, Aitken's Law must therefore postdate all but the very last changes of the Great Vowel Shift, perhaps even the whole thing.

3.3.1.1 English/Scots Differences Depending on Vowel Quantity

Since we are dealing with a system with a clear long:short dichotomy in Older Scots, congruent with a peripheral:non-peripheral one, that is, long vowels were peripheral and short ones were centralised to some extent,[1] we should not be surprised to find that the Scottish and English systems operate similarly in the way in which the vowels change: the peripheral ones raise, and the non-peripheral ones lower, for the most part, as one would expect (Labov 1994; Jones 1989). There are also phonetically plausible lengthening and shortening processes which 'make sense' operating similarly in all British vernaculars.

Nevertheless, there are plentiful differences between London or London-based varieties such as Chaucerian English or the emerging Tudor Standard, or the Midland and Southern vernaculars to which they are related, and Older Scots as far as lexical incidence is concerned. It is not uncommon, for instance, to find that a Southern short vowel corresponds to a Northern long one, or vice versa, in certain words or in certain environments. Length differences like these usually go back to discrepancies in the scope of application of one of the following rules.

(a) Homorganic Lengthening

This Old English rule, some form of which applied everywhere, lengthens vowels without change in quality before clusters of consonants consisting of a nasal or liquid + a following voiced stop (or nasal) pronounced at the same place of articulation, that is, before /mb nd ng ld rd rn/. The cluster must be fully tautosyllabic for the rule to apply: if the second consonant really belongs to an onset of the next syllable, the rule is blocked. This means that the nominative of Old English *hand* 'hand' becomes /hɑ:nd/, but its genitive *handes* and other inflected forms, that are divided *han | des, han | de* and so on, stay /hɑndəs/. With the destruction of the Old English inflectional system, strong analogical pressures came to the fore, sometimes generalising the long-vowelled nominative, sometimes a form with the short vowel of the other cases, and creating a great deal of lexically conditioned variability in all dialects (Luick 1964: 476). Still, there are patterns that can be observed. Before /ld/, /eld ild/ as in *field, wild* is usually long in both north and south, but BIT forms can sometimes be observed in Scots in *wild*, and the form *chiel*, now predominantly north-eastern (and, at the other end of Britain, Devonian (Orton and Wakelin 1968), must come from a short vowel later lengthened to /i:/ rather than an Old English /ʧi:ld/. Old English *molde* (soil) survives as long in Older Scots *muil(d)* and Northern [mi:l] (Robinson 1985: 428), but forms with LOUP from the short vowel are present as well. The form /ald/ as in *old, cold* was lengthened in the south and Midlands, but the CAUGHT reflexes of most Scots and northern English dialects could result from either short or long vowels. Before /rd rn/, lengthening happens in Scots, but probably at a later point, since Old English /ord orn/ only take BOOT reflexes when a grave segment precedes, the same environments that dictate when other /orC/ and /ord orn/ words of Romance origin take COAT forms, and the lengthening of /ard arn/ as in *caird, bairn* seems rather to be part of an Early Scots lengthening of /a/ before any /rC/ cluster, homorganic or not. Homorganic Lengthening could have applied in these /rC/ clusters, but we cannot prove it.

Clusters of nasal + stop yield the clearest cases of north/south differences: /ind und/ more often than not stay long in the south and south Midlands, but have short vowels in Scots, Northern and North-east Midland English (Orton et al. 1978), and /imb/ as in *climb* shows a similar distribution. The dialects that lengthen /end/ are all south of the Humber (Orton and Wakelin 1968; Orton and Tilling 1967; Orton and Barry 1969), though Scots dialects sometimes have diphthongised BET in this position as a late rule (Robinson 1985: 35), and /eng/ raises instead (see section 3.3.7). The /aNC/ groups vary, though Scots *lang, strang* definitely come from short vowels, while the southern forms may have been lengthened and shortened early, and there are traces of length in the word *tongs* (*taings* and *tyangs* must come from /a:/), and forms like *laing* once existed (Robinson 1985: 357) and are fossilised as a surname. Generally, /and/ must have come out as the CAT vowel everywhere, although most Scots, unlike southern English dialects, has lengthened and retracted it in Early Modern times. Overall, Scots seems to have resisted generalising the long vowel to more environments than southern dialects, although there are exceptions: *thumb* is an OUT word in Scotland, but a CUT one in England, outside the far north.

(b)   Open Syllable Lengthening

In contrast to the previous rule, this thirteenth-century one is more generalised in Scotland than in southern England, both in the number of nuclei to which it applies and in the environments in which it applies. The dialects of the south and south Midlands apply this rule only to the mid and low vowels /e a o/ (or /ɛ a ɔ/), but Northern, North Midland and Scots varieties also lengthened /ɪ ʊ/ to /e: o:/ before Northern /o:/-Fronting took effect. This difference accounts for the Older Scots BOOT forms in *summer, son, sun* and the MEET vowel in *give, live*, and spellings implying the transfer are abundant in Northern LALME documents (McIntosh et al. 1986).

A distinction with even bigger effects lies in the fact that, in Scots, the Open Syllable Lengthening (OSL) rule can apply even when the next syllable ends with a consonant, though there is some variability. In the south, OSL depends very much on the syllable ending in final ⟨-e⟩ at the time of lengthening, a connection substantiated by the evidence that Minkova (1982) has collected. In other cases, lengthening is blocked. This is why *saddle, visit, summer, cousin, hammer* and most, if not all, similar disyllables have short vowels in Standard English. In Older Scots, they had long ones, and most of their descendants still belong to the same historically long classes. If the vowel is low, the lengthened form is often found in northern English vernaculars, but if it is higher, the form is purely Scots. Thus *visit, minister, decision* belong to BIT in Northumberland and Cumberland, but have belonged to *meet* since the time of the first manuscripts containing them north of the border. Perhaps fostered and 'helped along' by prestige pronunciations of French or Latin loans with /i/, the transfer even became productive, so that most Renaissance loans with short /i/ in an open syllable began to conform with the pattern already established.

The Northern and Scots varieties also seem to merge the lengthened low-mid vowels into already existing elements in the system instantly, creating a new /ɔ:/ and merging /ɛ: a:/ with the long vowels present in those slots.[2] The North Midland varieties are well known as still having a distinction between the lengthened vowels and original long ones (Anderson 1987; Orton et al. 1978), but many south-western and South Midland English vernaculars had similar distinctions until recently (Johnston forthcoming; Ellis 1889), and traces abound in *Survey of English Dialects* material (Orton et al. 1962–9), but none north of the Tees. The shortening rules, both the Old English triconsonantal and the Middle English biconsonantal type, tend to be similar in Scots to their English counterparts. However, later shortening processes may not be. Although there is a modern Northern Scots rule deperipheralising /ik/ to /ɪk/, we have to postulate long vowels in *sick, week, book, look, duck* (verb), *suck* throughout Older Scots. *Head* and the words rhyming with it never shortened before Aitken's Law took effect, though again there are modern, localised Scots analogues giving /trɛd/ for *trade*, for instance (Mather and Speitel 1986). The cluster /st/ is more clearly a lengthening group in Scots: not only is the long vowel retained in original /eːst/ cases like *breast*, but French loans like *arrest* have been transferred to BEAT traditionally. There are even traces of a general lengthening process in monosyllables before single consonants (Robinson 1985: xxvi).

(c)   Aitken's Law: The Scottish Vowel Length Rule

In the late sixteenth century, probably starting in West Mid, which has the most 'regular' system, Scottish vocalic inventories were made phonemically isochronous by the lengthening of all non-centralised vowels before voiced fricatives and /r/, and the shortening of the historical long ones in all other environments before a consonant, which, combined, comprise the Scottish Vowel Length Rule or Aitken's Law. While 'isochrony' is to some extent an idealisation, it does hold solidly for the high vowels and the diphthong resulting from Early Scots /iː/. For other vowels, some 'short' realisations before voiced consonants or voiceless fricatives are really long, and outside the focal areas, not all long vowels shorten: those from COAT, BAIT and CAUGHT, which were probably /ɔ: ɛ: ɑ:/ in most varieties at the time of application, are very resistant to shortening outside of Aberdonian and its immediate relatives, Border Scots, and the Mid dialects south of the Forth and Clyde. Even in these regions, the actual phonetic length of vowels has been adjusted by subsequent overlays such as the Glasgow Drawl and the widely spread general lengthening of low and low-mid vowels before everything but voiceless stops.

No system in England is truly isochronous, though the south-western group, which tends to lengthen all vowels under stress to some extent (Wells 1982: 345), comes close to being so, and there is generally an allophonic cline of length, with sonorant consonants and voiceless fricatives (for low vowels) tending to be lengthening, and voiceless stops forming shortening environments (Gimson 1962: 126). Only the North Midland dialects seem reasonably free of such a cline, and preserve the historical length religiously with only minor effects on the quality of the next consonant: compare Yorkshire/Lancashire *sheep* = [ʃi:p] (if monophthongal) to RP [ʃiˑp].

3.3.1.2   English/Scots Differences Depending on Vowel Quality

Differences in lexical incidence between 'Classical' Middle and Early Modern English varieties and Scots can also happen because of the differential application of various vowel-shifting rules, often linked in chains. These are responsible for many of the most salient vocalic shibboleths of Scotland and the north of England, and their boundaries are marked by lines like the *stane/stone*, *blaw/blow*, *spune/spoon* and *hoose/house* isoglosses. Most often, these lines cluster around the familiar Lune/Humber cultural boundary, though a few range further south to include Lindsey, or at least the northern half of it, and/or the region of Lancashire between the Lune and the Ribble, both of which were apparently Northern-speaking to begin with (Kristensson 1967). Few differences that affect monophthongs separate Scotland from England *per se* until the time of the Short Vowel Shifts and Aitken's Law in the sixteenth century. Rules giving birth to the salient differences include the following.

(a)   Long Low Vowel Raising

This twelfth- or thirteenth-century process (depending on area) raises one or both of the Old English nuclei /æ: ɑ:/ to low-mid level, with the latter nucleus rounding as well (Luick 1964: 359). Southern and Midland speakers implemented the change as a 'parallel' chain shift, with the two nuclei both raising the same way; Northern and Scottish speakers, however, implemented a one-sided shift, or more likely a 'series' shift, with /æ:/ > / ɛ:/ as in the south, but /ɑ:/ fronting at least at far as /a:/ to take the place of the /æ:/. Words from French [ɛ: a:], and in truly Northern/Scottish localities [ɛ: a:] arising from OSL, then merge in, giving rise to the BEAT and MATE classes. *Stone* and other words with Old English /ɑ/ thus belong to MATE in the north, but COAT in the Midlands and south. The same changes happen before a /u ~ w/, so that DEW has [ɛ:u], and *blow* [a:u] in the north, but [ɔ:u] in the south. The Southern isolative change took a century and a half to reach the North Midlands, and Kristensson's (1967) materials reveal its slow takeover of the English 'Middle North' (Trudgill 1988) up to the Lune/Humber line, though the *blaw/blow* line has traditionally followed its late thirteenth-century limit to the present day.

The change is one of several cyclical raising processes acting on long low vowels which include Anglo-Frisian Brightening, the bottom half of the Great Vowel Shift, and various modern equivalents in a number of dialects of English (Johnston 1992). Northern Scottish *stone-* and *clean*-Raising, which intervened between this cycle of raising and the Great Vowel Shift (GVS), could also be considered a conditioned version of this type of shift.

(b)   Northern /o:/-Fronting

In the late thirteenth century, once OSL had been completed but before any part of the GVS was implemented, /o:/ was fronted to /ø:/, often written ⟨u⟩ by scribes used to the French front rounded /y/. Kristensson (1967) shows this change as applying only in the old Berenician area by 1325, and while we cannot prove it, it may have actually initiated in Scotland; it soon became a defining characteristic of the whole northern English and Scots groups, and perhaps beyond, if the process giving [ʏ: ~ ɪʊ ~ ɛʊ] in the north-west Midlands and [ʊɪ] in West Yorkshire is the same change (Anderson 1987). Southern and (other) Midland dialects retain back vowels, which raised to [u:] in the GVS; examples of front rounded vowels in Norfolk, Devon and elsewhere are apparently due to later fronting.

Northumbrian does not front /o:/ when a velar, including the apparently already uvular /r/, follows. Scots fronts it in this position, as other Northern dialects do though there was early diphthongisation to /iu/ (>/ju/) before /x/; diphthongisation set in a century later before /k/. The Mid-Northern B and North Northern dialects extend this rule to pre-rhotic position also, and it is possible that /r/ was backer in some way than other Scottish /r/, whether it was retroflex (as now in Caithness and the Black Isle) or uvular (as relatively common in the north-east).

While the likely initial value after fronting was something like the [ø:] found today in Shetlandic and most Orcadian, vowel quality differed from area to area, with the north having the highest, most peripheral values, and northern English timbres apparently centring on [ʏ:] (which became [ɪʊ] in the sixteenth to nineteenth centuries).

(c)   The Great Vowel Shift

Almost all West Germanic dialects underwent some sort of massive, system-wide shifting of vowels during the middle and late medieval period (Labov 1994; Johnston 1989). Of late, the structure of the English shift, which is one of the most extensive in scope, has been re-examined, and the old notion of a unified shift starting with the movement of the top two heights has been put into question by Kubuzono (1982) and Stockwell and Minkova (1988). Proposals have been made that the shift was simply a large number of lexical transfers going back to earlier differences and dialect contact (Stockwell and Minkova's), with /a:/ perhaps being the only vowel that really raises; even Lass (1988), who otherwise is 'pro-Shift', states that only the changes involving the top two heights of monophthongs were a true chain shift. There are various counter-proposals that one might make to these suggestions (for arguments, see Johnston 1992), but it is probably true that the 'Great' Vowel Shift is really made up of smaller units. My own studies (Johnston 1989, 1992, forthcoming) of Kristensson's (1967, 1987) and LALME materials suggests that the Shift is made up of two 'halves', each smaller shift starting in its own area and at different times. At least the top half was multifocal, starting in the early fourteenth century in the north-west Midlands and south Lincolnshire, and independently in Devon. The chains comprise the raising of high-mid vowels and the diphthongisation of high ones. The contingency of the latter on the progress of the former is evident in the one-sidedness of Scots and Northern versions, where /u:/ in OUT apparently stays put because there is no /o:/ to move it, after /o:/-Fronting has occurred (to use a crude, 'billiard-ball' image for simplicity's if not accuracy's sake; Carter 1975; Lass 1976), but /i:/ diphthongises freely because /e:/ raises. In general, the form of the shift is much more conservative, at least in short environments than in England;

the predominant BITE vowel is [ɛ̆i ~ əi] rather than [ɑi], [ɒi] or [ɔi], and in both countries the values seem remarkably stable over recent centuries (Anderson 1987; Ellis 1889).

The bottom-half chain began in its 'homeland', the Plain of York or nearby, even earlier (pre-OSL), though this can only be discovered by reconstructions; ⟨e⟩ spellings for /a:/ are lacking in Yorkshire in Kristensson's (1967) data, though they are present in LALME (Johnston 1992; McIntosh et al. 1986). These changes were more truly 'localised' and spread slower, with great sociolinguistic resistance from those at the top of the social scale in London (Dobson 1957). However, the new values seem to have entered Scotland about the same time as, or even slightly before, the other changes and occasional spellings occur from about the mid-fifteenth century. The structure of this half in most Scots is similar to that of East Midland localities where whole monophthongs, and not just their first morae, were raised, so that /a: ɛ: ɔ:/ became /ɛ: e: o:/ respectively, and the front vowels often raised another height by the beginning of the sixteenth century. Southern Scots has a different structure, where MATE and COAT raise their first morae alone, resulting in down- and ingliding diphthongs, as Cumbrian and most real southern and south-west Midland English dialects do. The differences in shape are thus similar to one or another English group, though the changes were carried through much earlier in Scots than in the English Standard, and no Scottish Alexander Gil associated the new values with *Mopsae* and *mulierculae* north of the border (Dobson 1957: 148).

These 'halves' intertwined in the process of spread where the waves from different areas met, giving the appearance of unbroken large chains from their origin. Further intertwining happened in the process of koinéisation, instrumental in the formation of Standard varieties and of urban Cockney; and later, well into the modern period, systems influenced by such koinés spread through the south and Midlands of England, supplanting the results of native shifting processes. The restructuring is in progress in many Midland areas in Ellis (1889), and seems to reflect the increased mobility of people following the invention of the railway, as well as greater exposure to the Standard due to the rise of compulsory education. Scots systems were not restructured to quite the same extent, although there is certainly a tendency for forms starting in urban areas to spread.

The monophthongisations of BAIT and CAUGHT are part of the GVS too, though which half they belong to is not always clear. The changes happen so early in Scots – monophthongal spellings appear in the mid- to late fourteenth century – that they are most probably part of the bottom half, instead of (probably) the top half as in Midland England (Johnston forthcoming). The raising of the low vowel to [æ:], which must have happened early, left a big gap with room for both an /a:/ and an /ɑ:/, from BAIT and CAUGHT respectively, which then may be raised in their turn. Unlike most English shifts, Scottish (and northern English) dialects do not monophthongise LOUP except perhaps as a conditioned change before /k/ or /p/.

(d)   The Short Vowel Shifts

The non-peripheral vowels also underwent shifting in the Older Scots period about the same time as the GVS was being implemented. The top two vowels both moved down in Scotland, in contrast to the southern English shift where only the back /ʊ/ lowered when not following labials (in most cases), or the situation in northern England where there was only slight or no lowering. The bottom three vowels could shift in a counter-clockwise direction, resulting in BET lowering to [æ], CAT backing to [ɑ ~ ɒ] and COT raising to [o], as in Southern Scots and some East Mid varieties; in a clockwise direction, as in Insular Scots, so that

CAT = [æ], BET = [e ~ ei], and COT = [ɒ]; or in a combination, as in Aberdonian, where the low vowel backs as in Border Scots, but both mid vowels raise. The Shetlandic-type shift to some extent matches the southern English/RP preferred type of shift, but most English dialects of the Midlands and north do little to their short vowels isolatively.

More detailed accounts of what happens to the vowel of each word class are given in the following sections, starting with the MEET class. As in Chapter 11, the BAIT vowel is counted as front, CAUGHT as back and BITE as diphthongal, reflecting what series they belong to after 1450. At the end of each section, the most likely phonetic values about the time of Dunbar, Douglas and James IV, given the spelling and reconstructive evidence, are postulated.

3.3.2 The MEET Class in Older Scots

The vowel in MEET comes from Old English /eː/ or /eːo/ and various other close /e/ and /ø/ sounds, including the Norman /e/ corresponding to Francien French /(j)ɛ/, as in *niece, chief*. The incidence was augmented by the output of /ɪ/ when lengthened in open syllables, according to the extended, Early Scots version of the rule. Its most common spelling in Scots is ⟨eCe⟩ medially and ⟨e⟩ finally, though ⟨eeC⟩ and the Norman-influenced ⟨eiC⟩ are nearly as common from the earliest manuscripts, and even ⟨ie⟩ may appear this early in words that have this spelling now in Standard English, such as *thief, priest, field, shield, siege*, of which only the last comes from the Norman /eː/ subset (Robinson 1991: 615).

Simple ⟨eC⟩ is also found in early writings in monosyllables: some instances with this spelling are attested with shortening elsewhere in Britain, maybe even in modern Scots itself (*wet, sick, friend, fiend*), but others such as *greet* (cry), *green* or *wheel* never are (Robinson 1985: 247; Wright 1905), and it seems that this spelling, like all listed above with the possible exception of ⟨ie⟩, simply represents /eː/ also. A large number of polysyllabic words are variably spelled with both ⟨iCe⟩ and ⟨eCe⟩ not only in the fourteenth century but throughout the period, but these are the /ɪ/-lengthened group: words like *lily, villainy, pity, prison, ribald* and *sicker* ('sure') were no doubt realised with the MEET vowel then as they are in many dialects today, and apparently the KING subclass of BIT soon joined, as spellings like *tweyll, dreill, theyng* show up for *twill, drill, thing* in Northern and Mid-Scots documents. At least some of these words (no longer *thing*) can still be found with /i/.

The development of this /eː/, when isolative, to modern values ought to be simplicity itself: /eː/ raised to /iː/, which became /i(ː)/ by Aitken's Law, everywhere in Scotland. This is plainly correct: the only question is when, as there are few 'slips of the pen' made by Scots scribes. Spellings with ⟨i⟩ can be early in parts of the English Midlands in the fourteenth century (Johnston 1992), though it is not easy to distinguish them from shortenings with raising. Orton (1933: 198–9) lists a few possible Yorkshire/Lincolnshire cases from about the same time, and a great deal of them from the Durham *Cursor Mundi* written about 1400. In contrast, if we exclude the ⟨ie⟩ cases, which could be another Norman variant of /eː/, the earliest Scottish spellings including an ⟨i⟩ as the first or only grapheme date from the end of the fifteenth century: ⟨lig⟩ for ⟨league⟩, ⟨pis(e)⟩ for ⟨piece⟩, ⟨apprive⟩ for ⟨appreve⟩, a variant of ⟨approve⟩ (though this apparently is Northern, and could represent the BOOT variant too), and ⟨life⟩ for ⟨lief⟩. More of these spellings, including ⟨nidle, betwine, pipell⟩ and ⟨schip⟩ (*needle, between, people, sheep*), appear at the close of the period, when Scots spelling conventions were breaking down. However, these are accompanied by spellings still denoting a continuing /eː/ in ⟨ea⟩ (⟨pease⟩) and ⟨aCe, ai⟩ (⟨pace, shane (sheen), saige⟩) as late as the mid-sixteenth century, a date by which BITE/TRY must have been considerably diphthongised and therefore MEET already at /i/. We must conclude that there was variability in the application of the top half of the GVS, although it is not unlikely that vernaculars, as they were in England, were more innovative in applying the GVS than any Standard-in-embryo.

An interesting Scottish phenomenon, which might depend partially on this 'application lag' to begin with, is the continued pronunciation of several words with stressed /i:/ with /i/ (spelled ⟨e(e)⟩). With a few exceptions, such as *Eerisch* for *Irish* (which might go back to regular importation of the vowel in Gaelic *Eire(ann)*), these words, such as *advertise*, *exercise*, *glorify*, *private* are 'cultured' words from Latin or French, not among the stock that lower-class children might learn early, but which would have been part of the Standard. Snob value and schoolmaster pressure (at a time when Latin and Greek pronunciation models were an issue) may have contributed to the retention of /i/, which is occasionally found in London also in *oblige* (Dobson 1957: 665); /i/ forms are not found in native vocabulary with unambiguous BITE.

Northern Diphthongisation is not in evidence during the Older Scots period, but Northern Post-Velar Diphthongisation operating on the WHEEN subclass is, with the ambiguous ⟨quheyne⟩ spelling found in the late fourteenth century, and the certain ⟨quhayne⟩ one in the fifteenth (Robinson 1985: 784). The domain of this rule only makes sense if all vowels to which it applied were mid – one would expect either no effect on /i/ or a diphthongisation to something like /ui/ to high vowels – therefore, it must have applied at a very specific period in Aberdonian or in one of its close relatives, after BITE had diphthongised and MATE had raised, but before MEET had become fully high. A (probably early or mid-) fifteenth-century dating sounds reasonable. The extent of this change might have been greater than it is now: it is regular in the Mid and South Northern group, and well attested in Fife and Perthshire today, but there are traces in coastal dialects south of the Forth too, and it might have applied at least in North Berwickshire.

Pennine Diphthongisation of MEET in final position within Southern dialects must have happened late in the period, after not only MEET but also BEAT had become /i(:)/ isolatively there. The earliest date possible for this would be a sixteenth-century one. Older Scots spellings like ⟨frei, threy⟩ can be thrown out, as they occur in other areas too: they are simple ⟨ei⟩ = /i:/ spellings. However, a rash of ⟨ie⟩ spellings in this period, predominantly finally, is tantalising. It is suspicious that, except for the words spelled with ⟨ie⟩ in Modern English, these spellings really become common for both MEET and BEAT precisely in the sixteenth century and not before, and that ⟨ie⟩ at this time is a possible (if not common) spelling of BITE (Robinson 1985: 44). Again, they are not restricted to the south (J. Craigie 1950), and so these probably represent /i:/ also, perhaps influenced by the Scottish tendency to represent unstressed /i/ as in *daintie, destinie* this way. If so, Pennine Diphthongisation is probably only a Modern Scots rule from the seventeenth or eighteenth century, and all Older Scots dialects would have agreed on /i:/ as a value for final MEET.

Likely sixteenth-century values are: not after /w/ or /ʍ/, all dialects = /i:/; after /w ʍ/, Northern, North Mid and coastal Berwickshire Southern (+ some East Mid?) = /ëi/, while Insular, East and West Mid, South-western, and Inland Southern Scots = /i:/.

3.3.3 The BEAT Class in Older Scots

The BEAT class stems from the open /ɛ:/ and /æ:/ sounds of the source languages, including Old English 'umlaut' /æ:/ and /æ:ɑ/, which became low-mid in Long Low Vowel Raising.

French sources include /ɛ/ in positions where the nucleus was phonetically long, and in some cases /ɛi/ or /ai/, which were already in the process of monophthongisation in Norman (Pope 1934: 127), particularly before /n/ or /ɲ/. Finally, /ɛ/, when lengthened in open syllables in words like *eat, steal*, was added to this class, although before /r/ some varieties (especially in the south-west) merged the vowel in this subset into MEET rather than BEAT.

While the class may have had no independent existence in London English after late medieval times (Dobson 1957), this is probably not true for Scotland, even in East and West Mid, Southern Scots and Mid-Northern A, where BEAT and MEET are merged in today. It is still separate from both MEET and MATE in a few North Northern dialects, in parts of Ulster (Harris 1985) and generally in North Mid. Furthermore, although the predominant spelling, ⟨eCe⟩ medially, ⟨e⟩ finally, matches that of MEET, ⟨ei⟩ is not as common so early on, becoming so only in the course of the fifteenth century, while ⟨eeC⟩ is very rare. Instead, one finds English-like ⟨ea⟩ spellings, especially before /r/ and labials from the beginning, and ⟨aCe⟩, ⟨aiC⟩ occasionally, starting in the mid- to late fifteenth century. It seems that ⟨ee/ei⟩ spellings are therefore associated with the /e:/ value traditionally held by MEET, if not /i:/ itself; ⟨yCe⟩, ⟨iCe⟩ and ⟨ie⟩ spellings outside of Post-Velar Diphthongisation environments start appearing at the same time as they do for MEET, so the date of merger can be placed during the sixteenth century, which is confirmed by rhymes.

How do we reconcile this spelling evidence with the modern dialectal distribution? There are two areas, both focal, where MEET = BEAT in all environments, with only some cases before /r/ (a known lowering environment; see Jones 1989: 243) and a few French words which may have really belonged to MATE or BAIT (*real, seat*; words in ⟨-ceive⟩, ⟨-ceipt⟩ and so on) with /e/. The more southerly area extends to cover Cumberland and the Northumbrian-speaking area (Orton 1933; Reaney 1927) down to the Tees. In that area, ⟨ie⟩ spellings signal the achievement of either [iə] or [i:] from about 1540 on, with ⟨y⟩, presumably representing a monophthong, from the late sixteenth century (Orton 1933). This suggests a possible pathway [ɛ:] > [ɛə] > [eə] > [iə] > [i:], one step further along the same directions that MATE apparently went, and paralleled by the recent history of that nucleus in the western Borders. This could be the pathway followed in Border Scots, where ingliding diphthongs for MATE were common until the last century, but it is unlikely to have been the one of Edinburgh, Glasgow or Aberdeen, where ingliding diphthongs are recent and secondary, not noticed by earlier sources. Here, we must postulate a non-diphthongising [ɛ:] > [e:] > [i:] > [i(:)], supported by the fact that [e(:)] or [e˙(:) ~ ɪ(:)] – another intermediate possibility – surrounds these areas in Galloway, Fife/Stirlingshire, Angus and Morayshire. We can use the guide of the ⟨ei⟩ spellings to suggest that the high-mid value was reached in the late fifteenth century, possibly earlier in some environments, such as before /d/ and high consonants where these spellings appear earlier. The /i/ timbre arose during the sixteenth century, when ⟨iCe⟩ spellings and final ⟨ie⟩ start appearing, after MEET had already raised.

We can assume from the distribution of ⟨aCe⟩ or ⟨aiC⟩ spellings in the modern /e/ areas that the isolative BEAT = MATE merger (a true one where it occurs, apparently) was also reached in the late fifteenth century, about the time when BEAT is moving upwards. The merger probably occurred under [ɛ:], since it seems that the MATE vowel had already raised to [ɛ:] as early as the fourteenth century in some districts, and the WEAR and MORE subclasses probably retained [ɛ:] for a period after raising in other environments took place (hence the ⟨ea⟩ spellings), and may have actually been lower than this, given what happens to BET + /r/. The environments before velars (outside of Insular Scots) and palatals and in final position are distinguished from the rest in lacking ⟨ea⟩ and ⟨aCe⟩ spellings, except in *pacok*, which could come from a variant with the MATE vowel (or even CAUGHT, if the Dutch *pauw* influenced the first syllable). We must suppose that the vowel in these environments was raised early on in the course of the GVS to merge with MEET throughout Scotland in the fourteenth century. Analogues to this occur in the northern Home Counties (Dobson 1957: 627).

Clean-Raising, present in all dialects with /e/, and *heal*-Raising, found in many Insular Scots and Northern varieties from Morayshire northwards, however, leave scarcely any spelling evidence, with only ⟨weel⟩ 'weal' among pre-1400 spellings to show the latter, and the ambiguous ⟨queyn⟩ ('quean', not 'queen') to show the former. Nevertheless, we must postulate it as an early development, probably contemporaneous with the raisings discussed in the previous paragraph. The first is General Scots, most likely; the second must have been confined to Morayshire, and passed along to Caithness during settlement.

There is no evidence of Caithnesian [ɛi] during this period; however, *sweat* must have become something close to the pre-GVS BAIT or post-GVS BITE value in the Post-Velar Diphthongising areas by the sixteenth century, as shown by ⟨quhyte⟩ = *wheat*. The remarks about Pennine and Northern Diphthongisations in section 3.3.2 also apply here.

Likely isolative sixteenth-century values are: [eː ~ iː] in East and West Mid-Scots and Mid-Northern A; [iə] in Southern Scots; otherwise [eː]. In the CLEAN subclass, and before velars and palatals and finally, it is [iː] everywhere. In the HEAL subclass, it is as in the isolative position, except in Mid-Northern B and North Northern, where [iː] must have been present. In the WEAR subclass, if the vowel came from Open Syllable Lengthening, it is [iː]; otherwise, [ɛː]. In the SWEAT subclass, it is [ëi] in Northern, North Mid and coastal East Mid varieties; otherwise, as in the isolative position.

3.3.4 The MATE Class in Older Scots

The development of the vowel of the MATE class, the product of both original long low vowels and lengthened short ones in open syllables, is as complicated by allophony as that of BEAT. While Central Belt dialects may only show distinctive developments in the TWO and ONE subclasses, and maybe in *more* or *wame*, other dialects often reveal complex splitting patterns, with some environments joining BEAT, others BAIT, and perhaps others completely independent of both (in some forms of North Mid). The most common early spellings in Older Scots consist of ⟨aCe⟩ or the 'i-marked' ⟨ai⟩ medially, and ⟨a⟩ or ⟨ay⟩ finally. Since ⟨i⟩ can be a length diacritic, the occurrence of these spellings does not necessarily imply merger with BAIT. The spelling ⟨aC⟩ may also occur, although it could represent shortened forms, as there are words like *inflame*, *trade* which either could come from a CAT form (the former: compare *inflammable*) or may take short vowels in modern dialects (the latter: Mather and Speitel 1986). During the course of the fifteenth century, ⟨eCe⟩ and ⟨eaC⟩ before alveolar stops, nasals and liquids, and ⟨ae⟩ finally start appearing, and in the sixteenth so do ⟨ea⟩ in other positions, ⟨ei⟩ and ⟨eCC⟩ when shortened. It is plain that this change in spelling represents the workings of the GVS; and, since a few ⟨e(Ce)⟩ spellings show up early, /aː/ must have raised to merger – or near-merger – with /ɛː/ before the latter nucleus moved. The earliest (though rare) spellings are found in pre-sonorant environments: before /l n m r/, followed closely by voiced fricative ones (Robinson 1985) and, later, alveolars. Notably late environments to take such spellings are those involving labial stops, palatals and velars, though by the late sixteenth century the ⟨ei⟩ forms indicating that /eː/

had been reached are not dependent on any allophony. Since the retarding environments are those that favour raising of original /ɛ/, perhaps all that the gaps mean are that MATE did not equal BEAT, even though raising might have occurred.

To sort the situation out, we need reconstructive evidence to help us, and to approach what happened to MATE group by group, using the allophony underlying modern outcomes of lexical transfers and split distributions as our guide. Where *two*-Backing is found, there must have been a purely back allophone re-creating the Old English value [ɑː], later merging with CAUGHT. Where *stone*- or *tale*-Raising is found, involving transfer to BEAT, there must have been particularly high values, such as [æː]. Most conservative Scots dialects exhibit two developments in other cases, one leading to merger with BEAT, or at least independence, the other to merger with BAIT, perhaps an [æː] (after the mid-fourteenth century or so) and an [aː]. The conditions along which this proposed split happened vary, but there is a tendency towards lower forms in long environments and before grave segments, and higher ones before shorter, more compact consonants, as elaborated on below.

In the south away from the North Sea coast, MATE became an ingliding diphthong isolatively, separate from both BEAT and BAIT, as it did in central Northumberland, Cumberland or Durham. Allophones of MATE were transferred to BAIT before /r/ and labials, probably indicating lowering; by the sixteenth century, the [iəx] present in words like *dough* had assimilated its V2 to the back, rounded following consonant, becoming [iux] and merging with *plough*. *Two* developed normally, as in the rest of the old Anglian core, while a /j/ developed from initial or post-/h/ MATE (*one*) by the late 1500s (Robinson 1991: 13). The dating probably parallels that suggested by Orton's (1933) records for Northumbrian and Cumbrian: to [ɛː], [ɛə] or [ɛa] by the end of the fourteenth century, and [iə] by the early sixteenth, after BEAT had become [iː]. Smoothing, even in final position, only developed later.

Mid dialects raised MATE more directly, as they did BEAT. Yet, here, the evidence from Galloway suggests that this too may well have been a multi-stage process, since covered up by sixteenth-century raisings in the metropolitan dialects. Once again, there are 'retarding' environments, and /r/ is one of them, but velars and all long environments are added to the list. MATE reached [ɛː] by the late fifteenth century in non-retarding positions, staying [æː] for another half-century in the other positions before both values raised one more step. In the more innovative dialects of East and West Mid, plus a tail along the North Sea coastline extending into Northumberland, BEAT and the higher allophones of MATE did not merge, but moved upward in lockstep to [eː] and [ɛː] respectively, followed by the raising of [æː] (BAIT + the lower allophones of MATE) towards the end of the fifteenth century, and a final round of raising in the mid-sixteenth century, when ⟨ei⟩ spellings appear. The split is postulated, though there is no modern evidence, because all other Scots dialects imply it. Special developments would have occurred in *one*, though the earliest spellings, from the late sixteenth century, suggest that the /j/ in *yin* started out as prosthetic rather than developing from an /iə/; the first attested form is *yane* (Robinson 1985: 13). *Two* would have backed to [ɑː] – or not fronted from it – in the Old Frontierland and its offshoots in the south-west and the Northern Isles, but not in the Anglian core, while Post-Velar Diphthongisation would have been restricted to the Berwickshire coast and Fife, which appears as transitional to the north in this as in many other respects. The early history of MATE in Fife seems to have matched that of West Mid, but probably with no second sixteenth-century raising and immunity of the resulting [ɛː] from Aitken's Law. This nucleus must have raised to [eː] when [ɔː] became [oː], and the lateness of the raising accounts for [ɛː] in Shetlandic and Orcadian realising the lowered allophones of this class.

The pathways and dating in the north were presumably similar, with Angus and Moray/ Caithness developments resembling Fife, and Aberdeen resembling Glasgow in broad outline, with the list of late-raising environments expanding to include /f/ and all sonorants but /n l/ in the far north. However, the north is innovative in what happens to *stone*, which became transferred to BEAT at the same time as *clean* transferred to MEET in most dialects; in Angus, *stone* may have raised even earlier (late fourteenth century?), and *stone* and *clean* moved up together. Morayshire expands this early raising to include *tale*, and Caithnesian *face* also; any other allophones merge with BAIT, and raise late. A few dialects have never raised these beyond [ɛ:(ə)]. *Two* was probably back from the time of the dialects' formation, and *wame*, like *sweat* and *wheen*, diphthongises about the close of the period.

The development of MATE before velars is somewhat peculiar in the north. This is a late-raising environment, as Shetlandic/Orcadian, which have [ɛ:] here, show. However, as in the case of BOOT higher up, the velar must have exerted a backing pressure on the offglide of the vowel, resulting in breaking and backing of the V2 to [ɛɑ]; the V1 then became non-syllabic, finally giving /jɑ(:)/ in the BAKE subclass. No evidence of this value can be found before the modern period, but [ɛɑ] is a good guess as to what the vowel in sixteenth-century Aberdonian must have been like.

Likely sixteenth-century MATE value are: isolatively, Southern [eɛ ~ eə]; South-western, East and West Mid [e:]; North Mid, Northern and Insular [ɛ:].

Before velars and in other 'late-raising' environments: Southern, South-western, East and West, and North Mid [ɛ:]; South and North Northern [æ:]; Mid-Northern [ɛɑ ~ eɑ] before velars, [æ:] elsewhere; Insular [æ:].

In *tale*: as isolative, except in Insular, North Northern and Mid Northern B = [e:].

In *stone*: as isolative in Mid and Southern Scots; North Northern and Mid Northern B = [e:]; South Northern = [i:].

In *one*: no special developments initially in the North or North Mid areas; East and West Mid, and South-western [je:], Southern Scots [jĕ].

In *wame*: no special developments in East or West Mid, South-western, or Southern Scots; [ĕi] in the North.

In *two*: as isolative in East Mid east of Edinburgh, Southern Scots, and possibly Dumfries/Kirkcudbright types of South-western; otherwise [ɑ: ~ a:] = CAUGHT.

3.3.5   The BAIT Class in Older Scots

Although the vowel of BAIT was a diphthong for a great deal of the Older Scots period, it continues the development of native, Norse and French /æi ɛi/ (but not /ɛ:i/) sounds, and frequently stays a diphthong before palatal clusters and in final position. It is most frequently rendered by ⟨ai, ay⟩, which can also represent MATE, so such spellings are not useful in determining when it monophthongised. Recently, authorities such as Aitken (1977) and Kniezsa (1983c) have suggested the early sixteenth century as the date when it did so, and rhyme evidence suggests as much. However, ⟨aCe⟩ spellings suggest an earlier date, at least in certain positions; finally (with *slay*, *they*, *may* (auxiliary) and *flay* spelled with simple ⟨a⟩; Robinson 1985; 199), before /r/ in *lair*, *hair*, *despair*, and before /n/ in *vein*, *domain* and *gain* as early as the late fourteenth century (Robinson 1985: 222). A little later, /m/ is added to the list (*claim*, *acclaim*), though other environments only rarely have ⟨aCe⟩ or ⟨aC⟩ spellings (Robinson 1985: 58) in any time period. Before the palatals /ɲ/ and /ʎ/, but not palato-alveolars, the output can be the BEAT vowel as well as MATE, and modern *streen, compleen* for *strain, complain* rests on this conditioned development. The mono-phthongisation seems genuine: these environments have high sonority, making it possible for the V1 to lengthen at the expense of the V2, and monophthongisation of /ai/ in these positions is more favoured than before voiceless stops in a wide variety of English dialects, from American Southern to Yorkshire and Lancashire. However, a preceding grave consonant, in most cases (though not all), seems to have centralised the V1 if the vowel was final, giving [ɛi], signalled by ⟨ey⟩ from the late fifteenth century, and merging some time in the next century with BITE.

However, monophthongisation does not necessarily imply a merger with MATE. Except for Northern Northumbrian, Northern English varieties have ingliding diphthongs or monophthongs that have lower V1s than the MATE one: typical MATE/BAIT distinctions include [iə]/[eː ∼ eə ∼ eɛ] or [ia]/[eː ∼ ɛː] or [ɪə]/[ɛə], and patterns like this exist in Southern Scots B to this day. Although there is some neutralisation, a wide range of Scots dialects also have such a distinction: Insular Scots has [e ∼ ei] vs [ɛː]; much North Northern has [ɛi] vs [eː ∼ eːi]; South Northern and Gallovidian have [e⋅ ∼ ɪ] vs [e]. The merger is most typical of the Central Belt and Aberdeen foci, and even at the fringes of this area one still gets length distinctions, such as [e] vs [eː].

Aitken (1977b) suggests that /ai/ merged with /aː/ at the [ɛː] stage, by mutual assimilation, but this depends on a late dating of monophthongisation, with instant merger. Given the spellings, and the propensity of BAIT to merge with only the *lower* allophones of MATE, if any (except in Perthshire, where BAIT may equal BEAT and [ai] > [ɛː] is quite possible), it is more likely that BAIT monophthongised to something lower than MATE was, perhaps [aː], and raised in the front series in its wake. When MATE became [ɛː], BAIT was probably [æː], and at the close of the Older Scots period this nucleus may have been no higher than [ɛː] over large stretches of Scotland. Only in the focal areas, where BAIT was not exempt from Aitken's Law, would it have reached [eː] before the close of the sixteenth century; otherwise, it would have merged with BET, which is rare.

The pathway through /aː/ implies symmetry between the changes affecting /ai/ and those affecting /au/, the CAUGHT class, since both go to low vowels with the same backness values of the V2, joining their respective series in the vowel shift. The cause may have been the beginnings of the raising of MATE to [æː], which left the system with no long low vowels in many positions.

There is something of a tendency for BAIT to shorten at the /ɛː/ stage before /nt/, as sixteenth-century spellings like ⟨pent, plent, tent⟩ for *paint, plaint, taint* suggest (Robinson 1991: 468; Zai 1942).

Merger of *pay* with BITE or *way* with TRY (where it does this) were probably complete by the end of the sixteenth century; the change of *way* to a vowel with a backer or lower V1 is an instance of Post-Velar Dissimilation.

Likely sixteenth-century values for isolative BAIT are: Southern, South-western and North Mid [æː ∼ ɛː]; East and West Mid [ɛː]; Northern and Insular [æː], except Mid-Northern A [ɛː]. *Pay* was probably [ɛi] everywhere; *way* was the same except in North and Mid Northern dialects, with either [æi] or [əe] there.

3.3.6 The BOOT Class in Older Scots

The BOOT class, comprising those words with native or foreign /oː/ which fronted during the late thirteenth or very early fourteenth century in Scotland, is the last of the historically long front vowels treated here. A number of graphemes are used to spell the front rounded vowel of this class, including ⟨oCe⟩, ⟨uCe⟩, ⟨uC⟩ and, with ⟨i⟩ as a length diacritic, ⟨oiC⟩ and ⟨uiC⟩. In final position, any of ⟨o⟩, ⟨u⟩, ⟨ue⟩, ⟨oo⟩ and ⟨ow⟩ may appear. Towards the end of the Older Scots period, the English-influenced ⟨ooC⟩ spelling becomes a possibility medially, although there are a few rare early attestations. In West Mid or South-western manuscripts, ⟨ou⟩ is also attested, especially around /n/; these probably do not represent some kind of proto-Scottish Standard English /u/, but a recognition that the value was not far away from the fronted OUT reflex in this area. There are few patterns to what spelling goes in what environment, except that ones containing ⟨u⟩ are avoided before ⟨m, n⟩. This probably has to do more with disambiguating letter divisions in characters full of minim strokes than any height allophony.

Only a few modern dialects, notably Insular Scots, and until recently some types of North Mid and Southern, still realise BOOT as a high-mid, slightly centralised, plain rounded vowel, a little backer than French /ø/, but not unlike a German or Scandinavian one. The degree of centralisation may be slightly higher in short environments, and the vowel may be lower than high-mid in long environments (Zai 1942). The more usual realisation in Mid and Southern dialects is a centralised [ë ~ ë· ~ ɨ] in short environments, either a Y vowel or merged with BIT, and [eː] = MATE/BAIT in long ones. Fife and Tayside dialects have [e(ː)] = BEAT throughout, while most of the north (and pockets in Galloway and the Borders) have [i(ː)] = MEET. Northern [y(ː)], Fife/Tayside [ø(ː)], East and West Mid [ʏ/øː] and South-western [ü/øː] are reasonable guesses as to what the Older Scots values were like. In fact, unrounding had already begun in the north, since there are a few sixteenth-century attestations of ⟨e, ei⟩ in BOOT words, and shortened BOOT everywhere tended to unround quickly to match BIT, as Older Scots spellings like ⟨fit, pit, widd⟩ testify to (Robinson 1985: 198). Except for unrounded forms of *prove*, which probably really come from an Early Scots /preːv/, there are no other spellings implying unrounding until the rise of dialect literature.

The diphthongisation of *hook* is also attested: it occurs before /x/ as early as the late fourteenth century in *cleuch*, *heuch* and *pleuch* (although /øu/ is possible here, and certain in inflected forms: see section 3.5.1), and before /k/ in the late fifteenth century in *breuk* and *neuk* (Robinson 1985: 439). There is no sign yet of the far northern diphthongisation before /r/, which is usually spelled ⟨ure⟩ or ⟨uir⟩ everywhere. However, there may have been a difference in peripherality in the V2 between the Old Frontierland dialects and their Insular offshoots and others, since it develops like CUT, not OUT, to the modern values.

Forms suggesting northern *good*-Dissimilation show up in spellings in the seventeenth century, but must be older, as the type of dissimilation would have to precede unrounding since neither MEET nor BEAT undergoes it.

Likely sixteenth-century values for BOOT are: isolatively, Northern [iː]; Insular, North Mid and Southern [øː]; East and West Mid [ʏː] in short environments, [øː] in long ones; South-west [üː] in short environments, [øː ~ yː] in long ones.

In *hook*, Insular, North Mid and West Mid [ɪuk]; Northern, East Mid and South-western [iuk]. No special developments occur before /k/ in Southern Scots, but [øu] occurs before /x/.

In *good*, special developments occur only in Mid and South Northern to [wi].

3.3.6   The BIT Vowel in Older Scots

The BIT vowel stems from historically short sources, including the Old English and Old Norse short /i/ and /y/, shortenings in bi- and triconsonantal environments, and the checked Old French /i/, which was taken in as a short vowel. It, and its back congener, the CUT vowel, are exempt from Aitken's Law, being short even before voiced fricatives and /r/. BIT is usually spelled ⟨iCC⟩ or occasionally ⟨yCC⟩ more or less as in the present day.

In most Mid and Southern dialects today, BIT has lowered in most positions to [ɛ̈] or a similar value, lower values being found near Gaelic- or Irish-speaking areas, and higher ones in Galloway and in the western Borders, where values shade into the more typically English [ɪ]. Some Northern dialects near the Highland Line have one main allophone, but most have two: a backed, highish reflex [ɤ ~ ɨ] before voiced stops and fricatives, and sometimes around labials (in Insular Scots), and a lowered [ɛ̈] like other dialects have. The testimony of the eighteenth-century orthoepist Sylvester Douglas, from Angus, suggests that Northern Scots then had such a split distribution; and, as Insular Scots has one today, the split must go back even earlier than that (Jones 1991: 14). There is no spelling evidence of the higher allophone; however, ⟨e⟩ appears in a wide range of environments as early as the late fourteenth century, including before /ʃ/ (*wish, fish*), /g/ (*signet, big, bigg*), /n/ and /ŋ/ (*kin, blink*), and /r/ (*first*). BIT words are occasionally transferred to BET before /n/ (compare *ben, denner* for *dinner*), so some of these spellings might represent this transfer, but lowering before velars and /r/ is quite common even in SSE varieties with otherwise high BIT realisations. We can probably assume that lowering to [ɛ̈] – *High Non-peripheral Vowel Lowering* – was well advanced in innovative areas like North or West Mid this early. More conservative values could have been found in other areas.

A few special conditioned developments of BIT subclasses are also attested in medieval times. The raising to /i/ in words like *king* is reflected in spellings like *theyng, reyng* for *thing, ring* in the late fifteenth century, and the patchy peripheral modern distribution of this raising suggests that it was General Scots to begin with (Robinson 1985: 713). In the north, BIT + /k/, or after /w ʍ/, both environments involving high consonants, may also raise to /i/: *preek* for *prick* appears in the fourteenth century, but this was Old English *prician* and could have been subject to OSL. Other combinations, however, such as *quheit* for *whit*, are found in the sixteenth century (Robinson 1985: 786). Of sixteenth-century origin again is the far northern and southern diphthongisation of BIT before /x/, as *night* can be spelled ⟨neicht⟩ then (Robinson 1985: 440).

From the fifteenth century, ⟨o⟩ and ⟨u⟩ spellings, indicating retraction, appear in some WILL and PILL subclass items, particularly after /w/ (⟨wosp⟩ for ⟨wisp⟩; ⟨wonnow ~ wondow⟩ for ⟨window⟩, ⟨wull⟩ for ⟨will⟩; and, in the next century, between labials and /r/ (⟨burd⟩ for ⟨bird⟩; ⟨sworl⟩ for ⟨swirl⟩). A few occur in other grave or labial environments at this time (⟨gluff⟩ for ⟨gliff⟩; ⟨luveray⟩ for ⟨livery⟩, which could be a reverse spelling), but none in ⟨hill⟩ at this point, nor after /xw/. The retraction could have happened at any height level, but the timing suggests that the vowel was high-mid or low-mid when it was retracted.

Likely sixteenth-century isolative values are: North Mid, West Mid [ɛ̈]; East Mid, South [ë]; South-west [ɨ]; North and Insular [ɛ̈]/[ɨ] before voiced obstruents. *Girl* and *hill* develop as in the isolative position.

King is (variably?) transferred to /iː/ everywhere. *Night* = [ëi] in North Northern, Insular and Southern Scots; otherwise as isolative. *Will* is transferred to CUT everywhere; *pill* is also, in at least North Mid, West Mid and South-Western Scots; perhaps variably in Northern Scots.

3.3.7 The BET Class in Older Scots

The BET class represents the descendants of Anglian Old English /e/ and short /eo/, Old Norse /e/ and checked Old French /e/. The predominant Older Scots spelling is the same ⟨eC⟩ and ⟨eCC⟩ combination found today. At present, the isolative realisation of BET centres around the same low-mid [ɛ] values found in the rest of the English-speaking world (if a little fronter than most), but can be as low as [æ(:) ~ a(:)] in the Borders and as high as [e(:)] in the north-east, and before voiced consonants in Shetland. The 'high'-BET regions often permit diphthongised allophones, either ingliding or upgliding, before consonants like /l n/ and sometimes others.

Unconditioned deviations from /ɛ/ are associated with vowel-shifting processes affecting the short vowels at the lower end of the vowel system. The lowering of BET is apparently chained to a counter-clockwise movement of the CAT vowel to the back and the COT vowel upwards, whose geographical focus appears to be Tweeddale and Lauderdale, and, with less extreme movement of BET, the rest of the Southern Scots area. Most of the Older Scots evidence for the rest of the shift for the other two vowels is associated with the late sixteenth century, but ⟨aCC⟩ spellings for BET are occasionally found as early as the fourteenth century (Robinson 1985: 545). It is dubious, however, if they really show this lowering, as many of the words (red, ready, let, belly) could have had variants with Old English /ɛ/ or /æ/ (compare German Balg. while variants of let, red and so on with ⟨a⟩ are known from other areas; McIntosh et al. 1986), and these also could be reverse spellings reflecting the transfer of CAT items to BET before velars and alveolars/dentals, as these are well attested at the same time (see section 3.4.5). Other ⟨aCC⟩ cases occur in well-known early pan-Scots lowering environments: after /w/ in the WEB subclass,[3] and before /r/ in words of Germanic origin such as bark, carling, war and shortened forms of near, with even more words attested in the fifteenth century. The last change was apparently applied unevenly in Scotland, and is weak in the Borders (Zai 1942), but is highly widespread in English (Dobson 1957: 562).

Raised realisations of /ɛ/ are associated with one of two shifting process: (1) a Counter-clockwise Shift, associated now with the Northern Isles, in which COT is lowered and CAT (and often, CAUGHT) fronted, or (2) a process by which the mid short and mid long vowels raise in tandem, associated with the Mid-Northern area. Now, process (2) must be late, as MATE and BAIT are the classes that BET will merge with, and these only become [ɛ:] during the course of the GVS. In addition, there are north-eastern dialects that only merge BET with BAIT before /l n r/ – the sonorant environments suggest, as part of a lengthening process – and separate them as [e] vs [e:] otherwise (Mather and Speitel 1986; Dieth 1932). The raising is also in parallel to what COT and COAT do. The raising to [e(:)] must have occurred in the mid- to late sixteenth century, not before; and although there are ⟨aCe⟩ and ⟨aiC⟩ spellings in Older Scots during the fifteenth and sixteenth centuries, they mainly are associated with environments where one finds full length, by Aitken's Law (as in words like heavy; Robinson 1991: 274), or half-length, by various vowel-lengthening processes applying before single consonants (as in ⟨gled⟩ and ⟨heck⟩; Robinson 1991: 235; Zai 1942). These spellings probably denote [ɛ:], not a higher vowel. Since the other changes of the chain are attested towards the end of the sixteenth century, both the isolative lowering of Border Scots and the raising of North-eastern Scots probably date from this period also.

The Shetlandic-type raising, however, could conceivably be early, as spellings denoting the other links of the Clockwise Chain Shift can be found in the fourteenth century, and it does seem that CAT at least was quite front at this time. If this were so, the likely value would be [e], which would not necessarily show up in spellings, as the customary spelling for this sound is still ⟨e⟩, though, given the association between ⟨ei⟩ and an [e:] value, one might expect a few spellings like this. A few do occur, but only in the sixteenth century, either in *egg* words, where the diphthong [ɛi] and raised values occur, or before /ndʒ/, where ⟨i⟩ is found at an earlier date (Robinson 1985: 172).[4] These are raisings, but, alas, conditioned ones, not unconditioned. We have to suppose that, though we cannot completely exclude [e] as a value for BET in the districts with front CAT, it is more likely that the isolative vowel was low-mid everywhere. If so, only the conditioned transfers mentioned above would date back to Older Scots times.

Likely BET values in sixteenth-century Older Scots are: isolatively, [ɛ]. *Web* items would be transferred to CAT everywhere, and native *Perth* ones everywhere in Mid and Northern Scots. Northern Scots has [ɛ:] before sonorants. *Egg* was apparently [e: ∼ i:] in Insular varieties, and [ɛi] in North Northern, North Mid and Southern Scots.

3.4 THE BACK VOWELS IN OLDER SCOTS

The parent of Older Scots, Old Northumbrian, probably had the same back monophthongal inventory as any other Old English dialect (Lass and Anderson 1975: 205; Lass 1992: 33–58), with the long monophthongs /u: o: ɑ:/ and short ones /u o ɑ/. A peripheral value for the short monophthongs is suggested because of the result of Homorganic Lengthening (Jones 1989: 244–32) of /ord orn/, which must have gone to high-mid values to produce forms like *buird*, *affuird* in later times (Aitken 1977b). The rule is more restricted than in the south: /und/ does not really lengthen (compare *found* = [fʌn(d)]; *ground* = [grʌn(d)]) in any Northumbrian area, while /u:n(d)/ forms in *sound*, *hound* and so on are probably loans, and / and/ only did *late* on in some dialects (*hand*-Darkening) well after the Old English period. If /ɑrd ɑrn/ did, the rule soon extended to cover other /ɑrC/ combinations, but /urd urn/, as everywhere else, stayed short. There are some words, like *comb*, where the rule took place regularly before /ɑmb/, but the vowel in *lamb* stays short. Only traces (preserved in personal names like *Laing*) remain of any lengthening in /ɑng/ combinations, while /ung/, as elsewhere, remains short.

In the Early Scots period, first /ɑ ɑ:/ then /o:/ fronted, and the long vowels have been treated from this point of their history as the MATE (/ɑ:/) and BOOT (/o:/) classes. Before /o:/ fronted, however, the class was added to by words with /u/ lengthened by *Open Syllable Lengthening* (Jones 1989: 98–126), which usually develop to merge with BOOT (then = /o:/) or *foot* with subsequent reshortening. This change suggests that between Homorganic Lengthening and OSL, sometime towards the end of the Old English period or the beginning of the Early Scots one, the short vowels lost their peripherality and lowered slightly. The lengthening produces a reperipheralisation so that [ʊ] – that is, [ö] – became [o:] not *[u:], and [ɔ] lengthens to a presumably fully back [ɔ:]. Length interchange rules active about this time favour long rather than short outcomes, so that not all the /Vst/ combinations (like *rust*, *dust*) shorten, leading to Modern Scots /rust dust/. The OSL rule is broader in application than the one which Minkova (1982) postulates for English, really applying in all open syllables, whether the word ended in [-ɛ] or [-ɛC]. By the end of the thirteenth century, the inventory consisted of /ʊ u:/ (CUT and OUT) and /ɔ ɔ:/ (COT and

COAT). The vowel of CAT is here considered 'back' because it became back in the north, the south and many Mid dialects, and so can behave in phonological rules as a back vowel; but in Early Scots, given what happens to it when lengthened, it may really have been a front [a] or a central [ɐ].

It is often stated that the complex of shifts lumped together as the GVS did not apply in Scots (Aitken 1977b). That statement has to be strongly qualified. It is true that the 'top-half' developments were restricted to front vowels, and the explanation by Carter (1975) or Lass (1976), that /u:/ did not move because there was no /o:/ to push it, sounds mechanistic, but is at least accurate as a description of the outcome and of the interaction of the various rules in a chain shift. But the 'bottom half' did undergo change: /ɔ:/ → /o:/ or /oə/ (in the Borders), even if /ɔ/→/o/ at the same time in many localities. The other view is built on an idea that the /o/ seen today in COT words is the original Old English vowel, which is unlikely given the reflex in peripheral Scots and Northern English dialects. Furthermore, the GVS brought the CAUGHT vowel, once /au/ or /ɑu/, into the back series, and any raising of it is a late part of the GVS as well. In addition, there are a number of regional and conditioned shifts that shuffle subclasses from one back vowel class to another one, and these are analysed in more detail under the vowel classes which they affect.

3.4.1   The OUT Class: Older Scots /u:/

To recount the history of OUT in a Scots or northern English dialect, where the sound is supposed to be /u:/ in Old Northumbrian, /u:/ in Early Scots, and always and forever /u:/ – at least till it fronts – should be the easiest thing in the world, exhaustible in one sentence, with maybe another clause to tell what the usual spellings were – ⟨ou, ow⟩ with the odd ⟨u⟩ reflecting Older English practice in the earliest records. Pennine Diphthongisation of the *cow* subclass is probably not of Older Scots date, or if it is, was implemented only towards the end of the period in the sixteenth century (Orton 1933). We cannot really tell if there was an epenthetic schwa before /r l/ or not, or if it was regionalised, as *tour* and *tower* spellings are both found: in fact, there is more evidence of such a rule in England (Dobson 1957: 689), as ⟨our⟩ spellings are particularly common.

In fact, there is evidence – and very early evidence at that – for the /u:/-Fronting rule, usually felt to be so modern. The LALME manuscripts (McIntosh et al. 1986) for Ayrshire and Wigtownshire, as well as other manuscripts used by the compilers of the *Concise Scots Dictionary* – presumably western ones – show a few OUT words taking the ⟨oCe uCe⟩ of BOOT. The CSD gives examples for *brown, sprout, mould* (though ⟨muild⟩ could represent an Old English *mōlde*), *souter, house, proud, crown, gown* and *foul* (Robinson 1991: 647). LALME also supplies reverse spellings from the fifteenth century such as ⟨gowd⟩, ⟨abown⟩ for /gø:d əbø:n/ (McIntosh et al. 1986). All these words occur before an alveolar consonant, which favours a front value in modern /u:/-Fronting (Johnston 1983a), and the west is plainly one of the focal areas of the native change (Grant and Main-Dixon 1921), so its presence in Ulster Scots at least is suggestive of an early rather than a later process.

It is unlikely that OUT and BOOT ever merged, since Scots dialects today do not do this except where SSE or Highland English influence is involved (Mather and Speitel 1986). What might have happened is that /u:/ fronted to something *close* to BOOT, maybe [ʉ(:)], and the scribes had no other way of representing the vowel. Caithnesian /u:/-Fronting, if the /u:/ was equated with Gaelic /u:/ by bilinguals, might have been early as well, dating from the time of adoption, since the Gaelic sound is a front one in Northern varieties. There are also words like *cloud, ounce, poultry, mountain, couch* which may shorten with ⟨uC⟩ spellings from the sixteenth century, while in the north-east *could* and *country* are attested with ⟨qui⟩ spellings, showing the effects of an extended *good*-Dissimilation rule (Robinson 1985: 117).

Combinations of /uv/ and /ulC/ are realised as OUT words from early on, as the various consonant vocalisation rules are of fourteenth-century date (compare *scowk* for *skulk*; Robinson 1985: 589), or earlier (Robinson 1985: 589). Sixteenth-century values are: Insular, Mid and South Northern, North and East Mid and Southern /u(:)/; North Northern, West Mid and South-western /ʉ(:)/.

3.4.2 The CUT Class: Older Scots /ʊ/

The CUT class stems from Old English, Old Norse and Old French /u/ sounds. In the case of the last, only those which were the nucleus of closed syllables or before clusters of two consonants (except, sometimes, /st/) were taken in with /u/, whether they came from ⟨ou⟩ = /u/ or ⟨u⟩ = /ü, y/, as Norman French had not yet fronted original /u/ in this position at the time of the Conquest. A non-peripheral value, as opposed to a presumably more peripheral /u/ in southern and central England, is indicated by the workings of the OSL rule and, possibly, an Anglian rule that turns all /o/ between a labial – especially /w/ – and /r/ to CUT. It is this rule that is responsible for the Standard English, as well as the Scots, pronunciation(s) of *word*.

The usual spellings of the sound in Older Scots mirror the possibilities found in late Middle or Tudor English: ⟨u⟩ or ⟨v⟩ (especially initially) is the most common variant, but ⟨ou⟩ may occur in words whose French cognates have it, and ⟨o⟩ is particularly common in words where the surrounding letters are composed of minims, since a ⟨u⟩ in one of the late medieval or Early Modern hands might create a 'forest of lines' with the light cross strokes hard to see. The possibility of ⟨o⟩ or ⟨ou⟩ in this class makes it difficult to see when the usual Scots High Vowel Deperipheralisation and Lowering takes place, or any of the regional diphthongisation rules. The isolative development of /ʊ/, however, must have gone via [ö] to [ɔ̈], still found in Wigtownshire and parts of the north, Orkney and Shetland. The modern Central Scots value of [ʌ] arose through unrounding at this point, while some Northern dialects near old Gaelic areas go further, to [ɐ] or [ə~ɛ̈].

Spelling evidence is not of much use in determining the isolative development. While ⟨o⟩ and ⟨ou⟩ forms are plentiful, the bulk occur around consonants like /w m n/ which are all composed of minims. The rest, like *brokill* 'bruckle' from the fifteenth century, are quite likely to be ⟨oCe⟩ spellings indicating transfer to BOOT rather than isolative developments. However, if we assume that ⟨eC⟩ spellings for BIT are a good guide to parallel changes in the front series, we find that High Vowel Lowering began in the early sixteenth century. There does not seem to be much indication of a focal area but those regions that carried the change furthest, at least outside of labial environments, are in the Black Isle and parts of Morayshire.

A considerable number of Northern and Insular varieties take BIT reflexes in some CUT words. According to the spelling evidence, these come from two separate sources. The most widely distributed group are disyllabic or originally disyllabic items like *summer, sunder, gutter, honey* as well as *son* and *sun* in the north. These are really transfers to BOOT by Open Syllable Lengthening, which even the latter set of words would have 'qualified for' as they originally had final vowels. Spellings in ⟨oCe⟩, ⟨uCe⟩ and ⟨ui⟩ are plentiful throughout Scotland for this group from the beginning, while ⟨i⟩ spellings start appearing in the sixteenth century, the same time that the *foot*-subclass members show them, and illustrating that this group of words was highly prone to reshortening. Proof of this is found where BIT and BOOT have different vowels: these go with BIT (Robinson 1985: xxvi).

A smaller group taking BIT reflexes has only a Northern and perhaps Insular distribution: these include items in /-r/, like *worth*, *turn* and *word*, as well as *buzz*, *dust* and *hussy* (Robinson 1985: 292). The biggest component of this set has CUT in 'long environments' while no lengthening takes place; it is the same environment where BIT has high central reflexes most invariably (and voiceless fricatives are the second most likely environment to take them). This illustrates that the Northern dialects may have had a split-CUT allophonic set-up, with [ʌ] (or intermediate [ɤ]) in Older Scots confined to the same environments where BIT is mid or low. The other allophone was probably *[ö̞], parallel to [ɪ]>[ɨ] in BIT. With the unrounding of front rounded vowels, the CUT and BIT vowels fell together. *Dog*-Diphthongisation, or raising, affected CUT + /g ŋ/ and other velars only towards the end of the Older Scots period, when spellings like ⟨oogly⟩ (and ⟨dowg⟩) are found (Robinson 1985: 746) in Fife as well as Caithness, the Black Isle and Morayshire. Any other allophone is too subtle to reconstruct.

Likely sixteenth-century values are: Insular split [ʊ–ö]/[ö̞]; Northern [ɤ~ɔ]/[ö̞] and [ɔu] in *dog*, [u] in *rug* in North Northern and Morayshire; Mid [ʒ~ɤ]; South-west [ʊ]; Southern [ɤ] or [ɔ].

3.4.3 The COAT Class: Older Scots /ɔː/

The COAT class is derived only from short antecedents in open syllables, in contrast with the equivalent Southern class, which has the descendants of words with Old English and Old Norse /ɑː/ in as well. After the early Scots period, a few of these words such as *boat*, *goat*, *road* were taken in as loans, and Middle Dutch /ɔː/ also acts as a source. One word that may look surprising is *loan* for *lane*, where the apparent Northern and Southern forms are reversed; they are really not, for the alternation goes back not to /ɑː/ but to an Old English /ɒn~ɑn/ alternation. Scots had a form like /lɔnə/ before the OSL rule took effect.

The vowel in the COAT class stems largely from an Old English, Old Norse and Old French short back rounded vowel, written ⟨o⟩, and in Older Scots ⟨oCe⟩ or ⟨oi~oy⟩. The handbooks reconstruct the Middle English nucleus as a low-mid rounded [ɔː] (Luick 1964: 298; Dobson 1957: 681), and, given that one of the Southumbrian sources is the low [ɑː] of Old English and Old Norse, and that some of the orthoepic evidence points to a low-mid value in the sixteenth and early seventeenth centuries, such a reconstruction makes sense for the south and Midlands, although there might have been a period in thirteenth-century Middle English when *stone* words had [ɒː] and *coat* ones had [ɔː] (Jordan 1934: 61). However, Aitken (1977b) reconstructs a high-mid value for Older Scots, at least after BOOT-fronting. There seems to be little justification for this. In modern dialects, there are perhaps fewer dialects where COAT is lower than this height than is true for COT, but the Insular group and some Northern dialects, especially isolated ones, tend to have [ɔː] (exempt from Aitken's Law in many places), and the same value occurs again in west Cumbria outside of alveolar environments. The Southern [u(ː)~ʊ(ː)] can be proved to go back to the same [ʊə] that exists in east and central Cumbria or Yorkshire (Anderson 1987; Murray 1873: 111); and, since ⟨oa⟩ spellings are the first indicators of ingliding reflexes there in the sixteenth century (Orton 1933), and [ɔə] can be found in the far south-east of the northern English-speaking area, the likely pathway of development is [ʊə] ‹ [ɔə] ‹ [ɔː] again. If both the Northern and Southern Scots reflexes go back to a low-mid monophthong, the Mid-Scots [o(ː) ~ oː ~ oə] must also, and the spellings, including the ‹oiC ~ oyC› spellings, must indicate this. Since the raising of [ɔː] is a late part of the bottom-half vowel shift in the south of England, and the chain shifts otherwise have similar structure (if not lexical incidence), the raising is plausibly late in Scots as well, and in Central Belt dialects may even postdate Aitken's Law, since COT and COAT both come out as [o(ː)]. Alternatively, only the raising of COAT might be due to the GVS, while that of COT, though still of Older Scots date, might be associated with another shift such as the Counter-clockwise Vowel Shift shown at its fullest in Border Scots, where /ɪ ʊ ə/ shift downwards, and /a/ shifts backwards. This latter rule must precede Aitken's Law in the south of Scotland, or else long vowels would be affected; it has the advantage in that both the Mid and Southern Scots developments of COT can be covered.

Isolative COAT can be taken as [ɔː] in all areas but the south in the sixteenth century; in that area, [ɔə ~ oə] might be a good reconstruction (Orton 1933). However, there are a few conditioned developments suggested by the historical and dialectological record. COAT was not merged with COT in any dialect before Aitken's Law took effect, but there were apparently lexical transfers, in the way of shortenings before alveolars and /k/, equivalent in type to the southern English shortenings of words like *good* and *head*. Words like *throat*, *poke* (verb), *cloak*, *close* appear as early as the late fourteenth century with ‹oC› or ‹oCC› spellings, joining *yoke* and *hole*, which are probably true COT words, developing from the Old English nominatives *geoc*, *hol* rather than the oblique cases. These spellings must be separated from the late sixteenth-century ‹oCC› in *float, roast, note, poacher, thole* which occur in combination with ‹oCe› in COT items and probably do reflect merger of COT and COAT and therefore the effect of Aitken's Law. There are traces of the effect of early transfer in peripheral Mid dialects, and in Orcadian (Mather and Speitel 1986).

A preceding labial may have raised the vowel early to [oː] in some areas; where a sonorant cluster like /rC/ followed, the raising was apparently so early that it preceded BOOT-fronting, giving front rounded vowels in *board, ford, afford*, shown by ‹urd, uird› spellings (and modern reflexes in some cases) as early as the record goes back (Robinson 1985: 217). There are traces of raising after labials in those Northern dialects that still have isolative [ɔ] in other environments, though on the whole the raised forms have been receding ever since the close of the Older Scots period.

The rest of the CORN class may have taken isolative reflexes, but peripheral Mid and Northern dialects suggest that either (1) the Great Vowel Shift raising was blocked by a following /rC/ combination, or (2) there was lowering beforehand to [ɒː] in this environment. The Insular evidence suggests the latter, since Shetlandic and most Orcadian shows *corn* as one height lower than COAT is isolatively. The evidence for lowering in *thought* is less widespread, but the evidence for pre-/x/ lowering is solid along the Highland fringes and elsewhere where Gaelic played a role in dialect formation, as in Wigtown and Ulster. Otherwise, *thought* develops the same as in COAT, except in Southern areas, where an epenthetic /u/ sprang up between the vowel and /x/ as early as the fourteenth century (McIntosh et al. 1986); the lowering rule cannot be dated so precisely, but it must precede the late sixteenth century.

The north-eastern *quile, quite* forms for *coal, coat* are not attested until the eighteenth century (Robinson 1985: 105), but the two rules involved in producing these forms are both sixteenth-century rules. We therefore postulate early sixteenth-century Aberdonian [kɔːel] and so on, and late sixteenth-century [kwëil]. The rule inserting the [e] is really just an epenthetic vowel insertion, that happens before /l r/ anyway and /n/ if the vowel before is mid.

Likely sixteenth-century reflexes are: Isolative, [ɔ:] in Insular, Northern, Mid- and South-western Scots; [ɔə~oə] in Southern Scots.

Corn: [ɒ:] in Insular, Northern, Mid- and South-western Scots; [ɔ:] possibly in some urban varieties; [ɔə~oə] in Southern Scots.

Thought: [ɒ:] in North Northern, inland Mid- and South Northern, North Mid A and South-western Scots; [ɔ:] in coastal Mid- and South Northern, North Mid B and C, East Mid and West Mid Scots; [ɔu] in Southern Scots.

3.4.4 The COT Class in Older Scots

If the evidence is fairly conclusive in favour of a lower nucleus than /o:/ as the Early or Older Scots value of COAT, it is even better for postulating one for COT. Low-mid or lower forms are present in a wider variety of peripheral areas than for COAT, especially in low-sonority environments. There are traces of [ɔ] in both modern East and West Mid, and this value is the rule in Wigtownshire and Antrim. While Fife dialects tend to have high-COT, they at least separate COT from COAT, and coastal Angus dialects may have low-mid realisations. Add the usual far northern and Morayshire tendencies towards mid- and low-COT, and the fact that northern English realisations tend to be [ɒ] (Cumbrian, South Durham, Yorkshire; Orton et al. 1978) or [œ̈] < earlier [ɔ] (Northumbrian), and raising to /o/ looks distinctly like an innovation, perhaps urban in origin (since the distributions seem to be centred on the urban Central Belt and Aberdeen) and, for reasons stated below, probably datable from the very end of the Older Scots period. The history looks like simplicity itself: COT was low-mid up to the seventeenth century, high-mid afterwards where it is now, and only the conditioned developments of OFF or DOG need be explained. The spellings with ⟨oC⟩ or ⟨oCC⟩ that mark this class are perfectly consonant with this view; the few early ⟨oCe⟩ spellings – in *bonnie, body, hollin* (Robinson 1985: 295) – are the results of the extended OSL rule found in Scots, which lengthens even if the unstressed syllable is closed.

Or is it this simple? The COT vowel enters into shifts together with the other low or lowish historically short vowels, with BET and CAT, and to some extent values of one vowel tend to co-occur with values of the others. Where CAT is back, COT tends to be high, and where CAT is front, COT tends to be [ɔ] or lower. There are exceptions to this pattern, notably in the West Mid area, where, in Glasgow and the vicinity, high-COAT coexists with front-CAT, while the converse obtains in Galloway, parts of Angus and Morayshire, and, locally and conditionedly, in sections of Berwickshire. The first group of 'exceptions' lies in a region known for its Industrial Revolution-era innovations; the compactness of the geographical distribution, centred along the Clyde and in Lanarkshire, suggests that one or the other vowel has undergone recent change, probably CAT. The second group, however, is in peripheral regions. If the CAT vowel had shifted to the back, and there had been some sort of concomitant rule affecting COT, the Older Scots input must have been [ɒ] at some point. Now, this value must have, in turn, come from an even earlier [ɔ] present at the time of Open Syllable Lengthening, or the COAT vowel would have been lower; but it suggests that COT may have undergone some see-saw development as CAT is known to have done (L. Milroy 1980; Lass 1976: 105–34).

To synopsise the development that might have occurred: in Early Scots, we start out with a front-to-central vowel in CAT (see below) and a low-mid value in COT. These have previously shifted from the Old English values /a o/, and speakers carry the shift onwards after OSL had applied, adopting even fronter values for CAT and lower ones for COT. At this point, certain consonantal environments facilitate the shift in this direction more than others. From the fifteenth century on, we have transfers to BET among CAT words in what Lass (1976: 121) calls 'lingual' environments, notably before alveolars, palatals and velars in a wide variety of dialects, particularly the north and Scotland and in southern districts of England. Slightly later, COT before or around labials – our OFF subclass – starts to be spelled with ⟨a⟩, indicating unrounding to a *low* vowel (*off, shop, stop, slop, strop, pot* are so attested during the sixteenth century), though the modern forms show that the Borders are only barely affected. Similar changes are happening down in the south of England, centred around the south-west, where not only transfers are attested but also an isolative development to [ɑ] (Wells 1982: 354). The proto-Insular system, with BET = [ɛ], CAT = [a ~ æ] and COT = [ɒ], forms from Angus/Fife predecessors at this time, and similar values are imported into the Clyde coast and perhaps even Galloway, former Gaelic strongholds.

Towards the end of the sixteenth century, the 'brightening' trend reverses itself, signalled by the first indications of *hand*-Darkening in sonorant environments in the CAT class, and leading to a trend towards backer values of CAT generally, as well as towards higher values of COT. Indeed, the distribution of reflexes in long and sonorant environments in Northern and to some extent Insular Scots suggests that raising might have proceeded first in these contexts, being kept at [ɔ(:)] before /t k/ for a period (and before /r x/, for different reasons, in some Insular and East Fife varieties), before raising to [o(:)]. Unroundings after labials occur as this process is going on too, particularly in West Mid, where *bunnet, buddie* and *purritch* forms are attested from about 1650, but now result in *low-mid* vowels. The arguments for the dating of [ɒ] > [ɔ] > [o] to the late sixteenth and early seventeenth centuries are given in section 3.4.4.

Likely isolative sixteenth-century values are: early century and in Ayrshire, Galloway, Mid-Northern B, South Northern and Insular Scots throughout, [ɒ(:)]; late century elsewhere, [ɔ(:)].

OFF: Insular, Northern and Mid-Scots [a(:) ~ ɑ(:)]; Southern Scots [ɒ(:) ~ ɔ(:)].

3.4.5 The CAT Class in Older Scots

If the vowel of COT probably exhibited a see-saw development between low and high-mid values during the Early and Older Scots periods, that of CAT shows the same pattern even more clearly, and probably with more allophony. The identity of the sources, which include both front (Old English /æ æɑ/, Old French /a/ outside of nasal environments in checked position) and back (Old English /ɑ ɒ/; possibly Old Norse /ɑ/) low vowels, gives little clue of the Early Scots starting point, and the usual orthographic representation of ⟨aC aCC⟩ only suggests that the vowel was low. Yet, we know that its Middle English equivalent was front, or (at the backest) centralised front (Lass 1976: 109), and front values are found in northern England and in Insular Scots, at the two geographic extremes of Scotland. Even Caithnesian has front-to-central realisations, and in Wigtown and Northern Ireland, frontish or central realisations appear in low-sonority environments.

Closer to the centre, there are two broad bands of back-CAT, one in the north, one in the east, south and south-west, testifying to a later development to a back or centralised-back vowel, probably associated with the raising of COT and CAUGHT and, in some places, the lowering of BET. Back values seem to be associated with lengthening processes and with high-sonority developments over a wide range, even in dialects, like West Mid, that have apparently developed front isolative values again. The geographic patterning strongly suggests see-sawing over a long period of time, plus a distribution of allophones rather similar to, if less extreme than, those reported by L. Milroy (1980) in Belfast vernacular, with backer forms in high-sonority than in low-sonority environments, where nearly all modern Scots vernaculars show similar allophony to some degree.

The see-saw development can clearly be seen if we consider what happens to CAT when it is lengthened. Early lengthenings tend to be represented by ⟨ai⟩, which is a digraph frequently used for MATE, though it could represent any long low vowel also, whether or not it is the MATE reflex. In the environment /arC/, however, not only Scottish dialects but also a wide range of northern English dialects do transfer at least some words with historical CAT to MATE, proving that the lengthening must have been very early, before the Great Vowel Shift, and that CAT and MATE were similar in quality at this point. This lengthening process gives birth to the BAIRN and probably the START subclasses, and spellings are attested from the late fourteenth century (*cairn*, though this could have been taken in with MATE) and become frequent by the fifteenth (*bairn, dairt, large, Parliament, parcel, part, party, March, thar, yarn*; Robinson 1985: 27), and nearly categorical by the early sixteenth century, before which time the change had already spread across the border (Orton 1933). Any 'regularly developed' or *hand*-Darkened form must be due to loans from dialects which did not lengthen the vowel in this position this early, though there has been quite a bit of erosion of this change.

Even earlier lengthenings, the product of the Scottish, extended version of OSL, also show identity with MATE; forms like *haimmer, maiter* for *hammer, matter*, and ambiguous spellings like *apill, cradill* (and *credill*, with the raising mentioned below) and *cary*, go back nearly as far as we have records (Robinson 1985: 259). Modern descendants have MATE here. Again, a few of the words have MATE in northern England also, but the list is much larger in Scotland.

There are also apparent lengthenings – or perhaps by the mid-fifteenth century, raisings – in other positions, revealed by ⟨ai⟩ spellings. The earliest cases of these occur in what are later to become potential *hand*-Darkening settings, before nasals and /nd/ combinations in the late fourteenth century – words like *lamb, pan* and *span* are attested with ⟨aCe⟩, ⟨ai⟩ – and these could just as easily be early cases of the darkening process, representing an [ɑ:] before CAUGHT had reached that value, as mergers with MATE; in fact, spellings like *awnsweir, haun(d)* show up in the fifteenth century, especially in West and North Mid areas (Robinson 1985: 14), so this interpretation is probably supported. However, there are fifteenth-century cases of ⟨ai⟩ spellings, like *staig, craig* for *stag, crag*, and these may well indicate raised and lengthened [ɛ:], as are found in Belfast for *bag* today. The bulk of these occur before velars, especially voiced ones. The dialectology of this transfer, as revealed by modern reflexes, shows that raising before /g/ is centred around Tayside and the Glasgow area, while that before /k/ has largely a western distribution.

Raising alone happens before alveolars and palato-alveolars in a change described by Lass (1976: 121) and common in northern England also (Orton 1933). The raising really belongs to the sixteenth century, but builds upon forms that result from reshortenings of lengthened forms, particularly in /r/ + alveolar combinations and before final /r/ : the START subclass, some of which are attested as early as the turn of the fifteenth century (*car*, *heart*, *martyr*, *parcel*, *part*, *party*; Robinson 1985: 469). These early raisings could be fudged reflexes, with the quality of the lengthened forms but the quantity of unlengthened ones, or they could represent centralisation, as happens also in central Lancashire (Orton and Halliday 1962); however, they must be geographically restricted, as today a separate START subclass is predominantly confined to the Borders, the North Mid area (and Insular Scots), and to some extent in Angus and the Lothians. The later raisings are more widespread, however.

Later lengthenings back vowels, although they are not the only processes that do so. After labials, a few ⟨au, aw, al⟩ spellings are attested in the late fifteenth century (*fathom*, *pan*, *water*; Robinson 1985: 775), suggesting that the allophony observable in Central Belt and some Northern dialects goes back this far. *Hand*-Darkening proper is first attested in the sixteenth century, largely before /nd/, and to a lesser extent before /n/ alone or /n/ + other clusters. However, *hand*-Darkening before /r/ does not seem to exist before the eighteenth century. The overall conclusion is that the back allophones of CAT spread out to positions favourable to labialisation, and only later become associated with ones where lengthening is concomitant to backing. Only in the late sixteenth century do we get indications that back-CAT had become an isolative reflex, largely in the form of ⟨au⟩ spellings before alveolars, which appear about the same time as ⟨oa⟩ shows up for COAT.

Likely early sixteenth-century forms are: isolative [a(:) ~ ɐ(:)] everywhere; backer reflexes except in Galloway and Insular Scots after the late part of the century; tendency towards [æ] or [ɛ] before alveolars, and, in the west, velars. BAG has [ɛ] in Insular Scots, North and West Mid A, and possibly surrounding areas.

BAIRN: [ɛːr] in Insular, North and South Northern, Mid and Southern varieties; [eɛr] in Mid-Northern. START is similar except in Insular and North Mid dialects and a few neighbouring localities, which had [ər].

HAND: [ɑː] before /nd/ everywhere and /n/ in most areas; possibly [ɒː] in North and West Mid (see CAUGHT). The same values appear after labials in North, West and East Mid varieties, and perhaps a few Mid-Northern varieties. Towards the end of the century, backing begins to extend to other environments, notably before voiceless fricatives and /d/, but not yet /l n/ or any other high-sonority environments. The lengthening of CAT to match CAUGHT in all but /t k/, implied by Northern vernaculars today, must be of later origin.

3.4.6 The CAUGHT Class in Older Scots

The vowel of CAUGHT stems from a diphthong composed of some sort of Old English, Old Norse, or Old French low vowel + /u/, /w/, /ɣ/ or /v/ (by /v/-vocalisation, as in *hawk* from Old English *hafoc*), which became /au/ by early Middle English. The V1 might have been front or back, but a rounded V1 is precluded by the fact that Old Norse /ɒu/ = ⟨ou⟩ goes into LOUP, not CAUGHT. In the southern part of old Northumbria, it is even possible that forms from /aː/ + /u ~ w/ and /a/ + /u ~ w/ were originally separate, since words like *blow*, with the former vowel, come out as [aː], while *law*, with the latter one, has [ɔː] (Orton et al. 1978). No such distinction can be found in Scotland, even in the regions of the Scottish north-east that have apparently turned the original /w/ to /v/, since /aːw/ words like *yaave*, *blyaave* and /aw/ ones like *tyaave* (*taw* or *tew* in other dialects) share their development.

The CAUGHT class was added to in the fourteenth century, if not before, by a process inserting an epenthetic vowel between the CAT vowel and /l/ as in *old*, and in /x/, as in *laugh*; ⟨au⟩ forms date back as far as the late 1300s (*fracht*, *laughter*; *cold*). While the environments could conceivably be ones favouring retraction, true diphthongs are strongly suggested by the parallelism to rules affecting other back vowels in the same environments. The loss of /l/ unless there is a /d/ after it to protect it (a Scottish feature, since northern English dialects vocalise /l/ in *old*; Orton 1933) happened soon afterwards, apparently before consonants slightly earlier than finally (Robinson 1985: 21), and is well attested in both environments by 1425, about the same time as in northern England. *Hold* develops to /l/-less, and often shortened forms, and there are traces of /l/-less /ld/ forms in place-names like the local pronunciation of *Cumbernauld*, which is *Cummernaud*. The first could conceivably be a loan, but the second may indicate pockets where /l/-vocalisation was more generalised.

However, ⟨a⟩ spellings, revealing the next step, monophthongisation, are eighty years or so earlier than similar spellings in northern England, dating from the mid-fifteenth century. Since no ⟨o⟩ spellings are found – and indeed, they are lacking in Older Scots – the resulting vowel was presumably low, and (*pace* Aitken 1977b) there is no reason to presume that it was rounded either. Since Scottish [a:] forms, or higher front ones, are only found in areas where Clockwise Vowel Shifting has taken place, a fully front value as a result is unlikely, although the reflex could have been either central or back, and values not too far away from those of CAT or even MATE are indicated by a few ⟨aCe aiC⟩ forms before alveolars, including final /l/ – as names like *Smailholm* with [e] (⟨Old English *smæl*, namely *small*) attest to. In most cases, the ⟨ai⟩ spellings must indicate only a low vowel in general, as merger with MATE is next to unknown. Given the future developments, the backest reflexes might have been in the Old Frontierland dialects, which have low-mid or even high-mid rounded reflexes today. Given that *hand*-Darkening tends to be a rather extensive rule in these dialects, a relationship between shortness and frontness and backness and length among long vowels might well have taken hold in this area more than in others. A likely reflex here might have been the inner-rounded, fully-back and slightly raised [ɑ:] which one sees in more peripheral dialects. Outside of this region, CAUGHT was more likely to be closer to the long vowel corresponding to CAT, although it must have been a little backer in the north and in Wigtown, or else *two* and similar backed subclasses of MATE would not have joined it.

Any shortenings, as in HALF, give the CAT vowel, and presumably arose as they did in England, from an absorption of the /u/ element by the labial, resulting in *de facto* shortening. Spellings in *half* itself as *haf(f)* happen too early to be loans from Early Modern English, and must be native developments where they occur.

The *yaave* = [jɑːv] developments of the north-east suggest that the CAUGHT vowel in this position may have been fully front there in Older Scots, as the /jɑ/ results from breaking before velars in MATE words, quite probably from some sort of [æɑ] or [ɛɑ] predecessor. The /v/ is rather unusual, but may have stemmed from a /w/ still present in hiatus in Early Scots; this /w/ may have remained for a time in other dialects too, as only ⟨aw⟩, not ⟨a⟩, spellings are found until the late fifteenth century, when *ha* for *hall* first appears. The monophthongisation of CAUGHT thus appears as at first parallel in structure to that of BAIT (a preconsonantal feature), but must have been completed by the sixteenth century, by which time the ⟨au, aw⟩ graphemes were associated with low back monophthongs.

We can only guess at when /ɔ/ first arose for CAUGHT, but it is not attested in northern England before the seventeenth century, and probably postdates this, if not by too much (Jones 1996: 178).

Likely sixteenth-century values are: Insular and Northern [aː]; Northern [jaːv] finally; North Mid and West Mid [ɑ̈ː]; East, South and South-west Mid and Southern Scots [ɐː ~ ɑ̈ː].

3.5 THE DIPHTHONGS IN OLDER SCOTS

3.5.1 Introduction and Early History

At present, most Scots dialects have a phonemic inventory of four or five elements, whittled down from a 'Classical' (sixteenth-century) Older Scots system of seven: /ëi ɛi iu eu ʊi ~ oi ɔi ɔu/, representing BITE/TRY, from an earlier /i:/, and the WAY/PAY subclass of BAIT, NEW, DEW, LOIN, VOICE and LOUP respectively. Yet even this system derives from bigger ones (BAIT and LAW were diphthongs before the Great Vowel Shift), and some of the classes are the product of mergers of pre-literary date. We therefore need to talk about the early history of Scots diphthongs before tracing out the likely pathways of development of the various word classes.

As in England, the diphthongal system of Scoto-Anglian dialects underwent massive changes in typology between AD 1000 and 1200. Before that time, Old Northumbrian, like any Old English dialect, had either height-harmonic or ingliding diphthongs, short and long – the type depending upon one's interpretation of spellings like ⟨ea/ēa⟩, ⟨eo/ēo⟩, ⟨io/īo⟩ (Lass and Anderson 1975: 79; A. Campbell 1959: 50–60), and on the use of ⟨ea⟩ for historical ⟨eo⟩ in Berenician (Luick 1964: 150). By the twelfth century, unless stress shift had taken place, as in yowe < Old English eowu, these diphthongs had all been smoothed to monophthongs (⟨io⟩ having gone to ⟨eo⟩ before), adding to the CAT, BET, BIT, BEAT and MEET classes.

However, Old Northumbrian, like any Old English variety, also possessed a large number of /Vj Vw Vɣ/ combinations; and as the coda lenited, losing friction, these became new upgliding /Vi Vu/ diphthongs. The new classes were then augmented by the importation of Old Norse loans, and then by borrowing from the diphthong- and triphthong-rich systems of twelfth-century Norman and Francien French. While some adjustments in quality had probably happened in the course of language contact – for instance, Old Norse /ø ɣ/ as in deyja 'die' was certainly taken in as /ei/ by Angles who had lost their native series of front rounded vowels – the diphthong system, by 1200 or so, became especially large and full, with at least /iu ʊi ei eu ou ɛi ɛu ɔi ai ɑu/, and possibly /ɪi ʊu/ also, most of which had a limited environmental distribution, and a few of which only occurred in a handful of words. Given the intense language and dialect contact of this period and the usual simplifying tendencies that accompany such contact (Labov 1994: 391; Trudgill 1988: 59), such a large inventory would not be expected to survive, and the whittling-down of distinction must have begun nearly immediately. By the time of Barbour's Brus, the spelling system used virtually matches that of Classical Older Scots, although the GVS had not yet occurred, so that BAIT and LAW are still diphthongs, and BITE and TRY are monophthongs. However, the number of diphthongs has gone down from thirteen (or eleven) to eight.

The tiny /ɪi/ and /ʊu/ classes (which we can designate by NINE and DROWN), which stem from words with native or Norse /ij ɣj/ and /ʊɣ/ respectively, may not have existed in Scotland at all, and at least the DROWN class always takes vowels of OUT throughout Britain. We can postulate either (1) that the /ʊ/ was actually [u] everywhere, so that [uɣ] > [u:], or (2) that any [ʊu] went to [u:] very early. In Standard English, and in fact in all but some northern English dialects, words like nine, stile, tile, all with /ɪi/, take BITE reflexes, and nine at least is never attested in Scotland with anything but ⟨iCe, yCe⟩ spellings (Robinson 1985: 441), though ⟨eyC eCe⟩ are common in northern and North Midland Middle English

(McIntosh et al. 1986), and [ni:n ti:l] and the like were picked up as relics in Yorkshire, Lancashire and Cumbria (Orton and Halliday 1962). There is a Border word *steel*, used in place-names for the spur of a mountain, that derives from Old English *stigol* (Robinson 1985: 666), but otherwise no Berenician dialect has anything but BITE forms; quite possibly, this is really the reflex of a related word **stǽgel*, 'steep', which would give /i(:)/ in South Scots, and /ɹi ɷu/ either were never anything separate from /i: u:/ or were monophthongised early.

The diphthongs consisting of high-mid vowel plus high one also merged out of existence by 1300, though in a different way in the north of England and Scotland from in the south. The SPEW class, comprising words with Old English /i:w/ and Norman French /iu/ (including the royal name of Stuart, earlier Stewart < Old English *stīgweard*), never had separate ⟨iw⟩ spellings in Scotland, but only the same ⟨ew⟩, ⟨eu⟩ and, for *rule*, ⟨uCe⟩ spellings that characterise the other component of NEW, early Scots /eu/ < Old English /e:ow/ and Old English /eu/. Kristensson (1967) shows this merger as near completion in the north of England at the turn of the fourteenth century, and there is no reason to postulate any difference for Scots. The result, however, may not have been the /iu/ postulated for the handbooks (Jordan 1934: 128; see below), but something more like /ɹu/.

The /ei/ and /ou/ classes may have lasted a little longer, and the latter certainly remained separate until after Northern /o:/-Fronting had applied, as /ou/ > *[øu] is part of its pathway of development. In most modern North and North Midland traditional dialects, and in all Scots, /ei/ contained in *die, lie, fly* (noun and verb), *tie* and *eye* belongs to the MEET class unless loaning has set in. This presupposes a monophthongisation to /e:/, or a vowel shift so early that **/ei/>/i:/* would follow the raising of MEET words to [i]. The first is preferable, given the plethora of ⟨eCe⟩ spellings, even in Kristensson (1967). At the time of his manuscript evidence, Vowel Shifting was confined to the Midlands, and seems to be incipient even then (Johnston 1992). We therefore date the merger with MEET to the early fourteenth century.

There is a subclass of items, like *wee, swey*, and *key*, within the DIE class that had /æ:j/ in Old English or Old Norse. Now these could have byforms in /e:j/ quite easily, due to the workings of various raising rules, and in Mid and Southern Scots south of the Forth/Clyde line they do tend to have the same vowel as MEET. To the north, they develop like *pay* items, suggesting that they come from **/ei/. This difference is one of the earliest dialect-differentiating features within Scots, as it must go back to ways in which (umlauted) /æ:/ was pronounced in environments favouring raising.

The /ou/ diphthong, found largely in inflected forms of words like *enough, plough* and *bough*, shows up spelled ⟨ew⟩ as in *bewis*, 'boughs'. Now, nearly all of these words alternate with uninflected forms in /o:x/ > /ø:x/, and the BOOT vowel in this position diphthongises, often to the same result, but [ɪnɪəf]/[ɪnɪu] alternations are present in dialects of northern England (Orton and Halliday 1962), so the related Scots forms probably do go back to an /ou/ > /øu/ by /o:/-Fronting in the fourteenth century. The vowel /øu/ then becomes the stabler /eu/ or /iu/, merging in with NEW.

The /ɛi/ diphthong, found in words with Old English /ɛj/ and /æ:j/ in North and North Mid Scots, and in Old Norse and Old French /ɛi/, develops exactly the same as /æi/ < Old English /æj/ and Old French /ai/, allowing for position, so that the vowels of *say* (with /ɛi/) and *day* (with /ai/) are identical, not only in Scotland but in all England too. The earliest spellings in Scots have ⟨ai⟩, solid in the north of England by 1350 (McIntosh et al. 1986).

Kristensson (1967) shows the merger in progress there, so this merger probably belongs with the others as an early fourteenth-century change. Since the differences of *pay* and *way* do not correlate with what Early Scots would have, we can postulate that such differences arose from the operation of the later monophthongisation rule, not this merger. Words like *strain*, *contain*, *obtain*, with /i/, may mark either a development from an already monophthongised /ɛ:/ or an /i/ which raised to /ei/ early before the palatal [ɪ]. The effects of *clean*-Raising make it difficult to tell which, since either would result in a MEET reflex.

The Great Vowel Shift, when it happened, reduced the diphthongal system by one, since /i:/ > [ëi] or the like, but the [ai ɑu] in the Early Scots system monophthongised in most (/ai/ > /a:/) or all positions (/ɑu/ > /ɑ:/), as discussed in the previous two sections. We are then left with the 'Classical' system of seven nuclei. In the sections below, each of the nuclei is discussed under its own heading. The information gives both spelling and reconstructive evidence which may be used to derive tentative values and dialect boundaries between forms before 1700.

3.5.2 The NEW Class: Older Scots /ɪu ~ eu/

The NEW class has three main Early Scots sources: /iu/, /eu/ and French /y/. The merger between the first two belongs to pre-literary Scots and has been discussed before. The folding-in of /y/, however, was probably prone to sociolinguistic variation in Scotland and needs to be treated now. In England, at least, where a native /y/ did not exist, the foreign vowel was taken in with /iu/ in *all* positions and is separate from BOOT in all northern vernaculars with /o:/-Fronting. Whatever Richard Rolle of Hampole did or did not do (Luick 1964: 490), less literate northern English people separated NEW and BOOT as /ɪu:/ vs /y:/ (Johnston 1980), and this, barring the odd lexical transfer, is reflected in present speech.

In Scotland, French /y/ also equals NEW, and in final position it is definitely separate from BOOT: *due* is /dju ~ djy/ and *do* is /de-di ~ dø/. Before consonants, however, French /y/ and the NEW *and* BOOT vowels all fall together. Now, was this, as in England, an /iu/ which later monophthongised, or a monophthong that NEW from diphthongal sources joined? In other words, was French /y/ ever diphthongal in this position? For the most part, spelling evidence would support a negative answer: if monosyllabic, French /y/ words *only* show ⟨uCe⟩ spellings, while the few medial /iu/ items show both ⟨eu⟩ and ⟨uCe⟩ forms. One must remember, however, who is doing the writing in the fourteenth century: the clergy, who are educated in Latin *and* French, and the upper classes, predominantly of Anglo-Norman origin. It would be natural for these people to take at least a monophthong as their 'ideal', their phonetic target, since they know how the words are pronounced in the original. People who do not know French might not do this, but substitute /iu/ or /ui/, like their English equivalent. In cities, anyway, there would have been opportunities for 'weak ties' (Milroy and Milroy 1985) between the classes, and therefore for changes from above to percolate down freely, since tenements were home to both the great and the lowly of status; perhaps the presence of French merchants due to the Auld Alliance might have helped, as it certainly did with vocabulary (Murison 1979b). In any case, French /y/, and increasingly all NEW medially, since there were few other items, began to take monophthongal reflexes belonging to BOOT in this position: the final reflexes stayed diphthongal, and in the case of French /y/ became so, as the NEW class was not so overwhelmingly non-native in origin finally. The modern reflex of /iu/ type points to a value with a rounded or non-peripheral V1, such as [ɪu ~ ëu ~ øu], north of the Forth/Clyde; the border does have [iu], but had something else, written ⟨uiw⟩ in Murray's time (1873: 117), resembling the Northern/ Insular value. The ease of a stress shift to /ju:/, when it happens, and northern English reflexes (Anderson 1987), point to a long V2, giving something like [iu:] or [ëu:] as a starting point. There is very early spelling evidence for a conditioned merger between NEW and OUT after palatals and /r l/: spellings like *jow, roule, trowth* are attested in fourteenth-century sources (Robinson 1985: 738).

3.5.3 The DEW Class: Older Scots /ɛu/

The sources of the vowel in the small set of DEW words include Old English *ēaw* and Old French *eau*, both with low-mid V1. Since these triphthongs would probably have been smoothed, the handbooks are united in postulating [ɛu] (Jordan 1934: 127; Dobson 1957: 243). This value seems just as reasonable for pre-literary Scots everywhere as it does for Middle English, and the pathway of development through [eu] via the Great Vowel Shift to [iu:] and merger with NEW sounds plausible for all Mid and Southern Scots. The merger seems to be a sixteenth-century one, since it is at that time when ⟨uCe⟩ and ⟨oCe⟩ spellings proper to NEW and BOOT appear in *pewter*, and *shrew* is spelled *shrow*, probably via the /u/- (or /j/-)absorption rule mentioned above. Otherwise, the usual spelling is ⟨ew⟩.

Northern Scots dialects – and maybe more along the east coast – never merged /ɛu/ and /ɪu/. The present-day /jʌu/ values must have come about via /jɔu/, still found in very conservative Mid-Northern dialects (see section 11.6.3), which in turn must have arisen from /ɛu/, via some sort of Breaking rule parallel to the one producing *chaave, yaave* from /a:w/, which has a similar conditioning environment. Spelling evidence for this development, like so many others in the north, only appears with the birth of Buchan dialect literature in the nineteenth century, though the fact that the V2 is low-mid suggests that Breaking of this kind predates the GVS and must belong to the fifteenth century or before.

Likely sixteenth-century values are: Insular [ɪu:], North Mid and East Mid [ɪu: ~ ju:]; West Mid and South-west [ɪʉ: ~ jʉ:]; Southern [ɪu: ~ iu:]; Northern [jɔu].

3.5.4 The BITE and TRY Classes: Older Scots /ëi ~ ɛ·i/ < /i:/

The vowel of BITE and TRY is postulated to derive from both OE, ON, OF /i:/ and OE, ON /y:/, plus the NINE class mentioned above (Dobson 1957: 659). This value is fairly uncontroversial, since there are continental dialects which still retain /i:/, from Scandinavia to Switzerland (Johnston 1989), but its pathway of development in the Great Vowel Shift and how the BITE and TRY classes split – a process which involves the *pay* and *way* remnants of the diphthongal reflexes of BAIT – is, not least because there is very little spelling evidence, difficult to trace. BITE and TRY are generally represented by ⟨iCe⟩ or ⟨yCe⟩ (⟨ie, ye, iy⟩ finally), and what ⟨ey⟩ spellings occur do so in words that have some sort of variant development, often to /i:/, such as *wire* (Robinson 1985: 797). They do appear as different from *pay* and *way*, which take either ⟨ay⟩ or ⟨ey⟩, although ⟨wa⟩ may occur in *way* representing the early monophthongisation visible in *awa*. The ⟨yi⟩ word-internal spellings which start occurring in the fifteenth century may be an attempt at representing a narrow diphthong, such as [ɪi], though other spellings indicating that the top half of the GVS had taken place date only from the sixteenth century.

By reconstruction, however, we have better luck at tracing a coherent pathway of development. The most /i:/-like reflex of BITE extant is [ëi] of the western Borders and

Gallovidian; most of the rest of the country has [ëɪ] or [əɪ], with a true [ʌɪ] or [ɔɪ] restricted to the far north. This last group, however, are varieties which have shifted BEAT to [ɛɪ] – Caithnesian, Black Isle Scots – and the shift of [ɛɪ] → [əɪ] → [ʌɪ] must have been a late part of the change, too, since some Caithnesian (variably) merges BEAT and BITE under [ɛɪ]. We can conclude that this was not a focal area for diphthongisation. With the far north excluded, the North and West Mid areas, with [əɪ], look most advanced. In addition, dialects of the Borders, like Northumbrian, have less centralised BITE reflexes than others.

There also seems to be a gradation in some dialects (mostly Mid ones, though Southern ones may also have had it; see Murray 1873: 115) between less peripheral V1s before less sonorant consonants and more peripheral, fronter V1s before more sonorant consonants. If we postulate that this trend continued in Older Scots, we have a way of accounting for the BITE/TRY split that is supported by eighteenth-century evidence (Jones 1996: 185–90).

A diphthong of this type would tend to have the longest V1 in the most sonorant environment: this would also favour a peripheral realisation. Now, the association with Aitken's Law might not be original. TRY could have been confined to final position, but in any case, if BITE were [ëi] in the 'shortest' environments, it would be [e·i] in final position. A wider diphthong, which would develop as the GVS progressed, would give [ɛ·i] or [ɛ·e], the spot where sixteenth-century English BAIT may have been, and the present 'Morningside' form. It is a form like this that late sixteenth-century spellings like ⟨cray, dray⟩ for 'cry', 'dry' are trying to represent (Robinson 1985: 163). Forms before consonants that are intermediate in sonorancy would have values intermediate in peripherality, such as [ɛɪ]. In some dialects, such as the Insular ones (and their Fife/Angus ancestors?), there were fewer gradations and the 'long' forms would have apparently arisen in these 'half-long' environments. We wind up with typical Central Belt sixteenth-century realisations like [ëi~ëi] before obstruents in short environments, [ɛɪ] before nasals and laterals – and probably /r/ at this point – and [ɛ·i] before voiced fricatives and finally.

The interplay with *pay* and *way* works like this: most of the examples have a preceding grave consonant, which would tend to retract the V1 of the Early Scots diphthong, giving [ëi] before the monophthongisation of other allophones. Following palatals, as in *change, gaol, baillie*, would also tend to preserve the /i/ as a V2, and further dissimilation would likewise produce [ëi] or [ɛi]. As the allophones of BITE moved down to low-mid level, the merger took place and the BITE/TRY split arose. The [wɑ·e] forms for *way* (or *whey* or *weigh*) arise where Post-Velar Dissimilation happened to mid vowels, as /ɛ: e:/ became [ɛ·i] or [ə·i] and moved down in parallel with TRY from the sixteenth to the eighteenth century, depending on area. FIRE may have been a subclass of TRY early in the Central Belt; but, given that both Border and Northern dialects treat it under BITE, the construction of an Aitken's Law-oriented BITE/TRY split may have been due to outside influence, from Standard English.

The DIKE subclass develops normally in the Central Belt today as in Orkney, parts of northern Scotland and the Borders. It may have been a part of BITE in the Borders, but north of there *dick* forms are found in the most peripheral areas, and spellings like ⟨dick, dik, dyk⟩ occur as far back as there are records. We are probably dealing with an early shortening, maybe to a more peripheral vowel than *Dick* (the personal name) would have, such as [i] or [ɪ]. Areas with /e/ probably shortened the vowel after diphthongisation rather than before. *Wire* takes BEAT forms in North Mid and Insular Scots, and MEET ones in parts of the north. Either way, what probably happened is that the V1 of the narrow diphthong of Older Scots became absorbed by the preceding /w/, leaving the V2 as the nucleus. Its openness determined which class the word would transfer into.

Assuming that the most innovative forms were innovative in the sixteenth century, possible BITE and TRY values are the following (note that gradations in allophony are indicated under BITE with slashes): BITE: Insular [ɛ̈ɪ/ɛ·ɪ]; Caithness [ɛ̈ɪ/ɛ·ɪ]; Black Isle [ëi/æ·ɪ]; Northern [ëi/æ·ɪ]; North Mid [ëi]; East Mid [ëi]; West Mid [ëi ∼ ɛ̈i]; South-west [ɪi]: Southern-East and Central [eɪ]; West [ɪi]. TRY: Insular [ɛ·ɪ]; Caithness [ɛ·ɪ]; Black Isle, Aberdeen [æ·ɪ]; Morayshire [æ·ɪ]; Angus [ɛ·ɪ]; North Mid [ɛ·ɪ]; West Mid [ɛ·ɪ]; East Mid [æ·ɪ]; South-west [ɛ·ɪ ∼ e·ɪ]; *dike*: Insular, North and Mid [ɪ] or [i̩]; Southern [ei].

3.5.5   The LOIN Class: Older Scots [ʊi ∼ oi]

LOIN comes from a diverse group of French and Dutch diphthongs, and the variation is not easily sorted out, since the source vowels may be different in Norman and Francien (Pope 1934). For instance, the Northern *eelie in eelie-lamp* might conceivably represent the Francien /yi/ as *freet* < *fruit* does. *Point* (< Old French *point*), *boil* (< *bouillir*) and *oil* (< *huile*) all belong here, and the spelling evidence is no help in determining the starting point(s), as the customary ⟨oi, oy⟩ could stand for nearly any rounded or back mid vowel + /i/ – or /øi/ for that matter. The handbooks (Luick 1964: 482; Dobson 1957: 810) trace the two main developments in England and postulate a Middle English /ʊi/ or /ui/, with the V1 as CUT; when the CUT vowel lowers, it goes through [ɔ̈i] to [ʌi] and the merger under /əi/ found in late seventeenth-century and eighteenth-century Standard sources (Dobson 1957: 819). Modern /ɔɪ/ could happen via [ɔ̈ɪ] or, as Dobson (1957: 255) believes, by lexical transfer with words like *point* or *poison*, with Francien /ɔɪ/ (= VOICE) acting as a pivot. Such explanations could also account for the two main developments today: merger with BITE under [əi], and with VOICE under [ɔɪ ∼ oi], the last typical of Southern and South-eastern forms of Scots, of parts of Angus, and of the Insular Scots that sprang from Angus roots. There are other, conditioned developments that suggest /ʊi/ as a starting point. Before Norman /ʃ/ < /sj/ as in *bush, cushion, bushel* and so on, CUT values are found now and would have been in Older Scots also (Dobson 1957: 723; Zai 1942; Dieth 1932). In East Mid and Southern Scots, as well as Gallovidian, such developments are extended to /zj/ in *poison*, and the TRY and OUT realisations of the North and Insular groups probably also stem from /ʊi/.

But an /oi/ is implied by a fifteenth-century monophthongisation process, happening before /ʌi/ in some instances. The result might equally be spelled ⟨uCe⟩ or ⟨oCe⟩ as in ⟨june, jone⟩ for *join*, ⟨ule⟩ for *oil* and ⟨spule⟩ for *spoil*, suggesting Older Scots /øː/ = BOOT. This implies a pathway /oi/ → /øi/ (by /oː/-Fronting) → /øː/.

Northern instances of extended *good*-Dissimilation similar to that producing *quintra* from *country* could presuppose either an /ʊ/ or an /øː/ as a V1. This may happen when /k/ precedes, giving *coy* = [kwi:] and *quin(ʒ)ie* = [kwɪŋi], with spellings from the eighteenth century. The ⟨ʒie⟩ spellings in *coin, oil, spoil* could possibly be /ø·/ as well as /ʌ/. What we probably have here is a gradation in peripherality, with variation in the 'half-long' set by area, parallel to that present in BITE. Before obstruents, LOIN probably had [ɔ̈i] by the sixteenth century if the /i/ had not been absorbed. This developed to [ɔɪ] in the Mearns and Angus, and therefore the Northern Isles, and in the Borders, but otherwise became [ʌɪ] finally merging into [əɪ] in other dialects. Before sonorants, some dialects developed [oi] which became [øi] and the [ëi] or [øː] if monophthongised. The [ëi] would have merged with BITE at that point.

Possible sixteenth-century values are: Insular [ɔɪ/oi]; Northern [ɔ̈ɪ]; North Mid [ɔ̈ɪ/øː]; East and West Mid [ɔ̈ɪ]; South-west and Southern [ɔɪ/oi].

3.5.6 The VOICE Class: Older Scots /ɔɪ/

Since the usual sources of the vowel in VOICE are reconstructed as having an open V1 – Old French /ɔɪ/ = ⟨oi⟩ and Middle Dutch /ɔ:j/ = ⟨ooi⟩ (Pope 1934; van Loey 1951) – and there is a tight correlation between the quality of the V1 and the COT vowel, /ɔɪ/ is the most likely value for VOICE in Older Scots everywhere. This nucleus would have been present in the Northern dialects which have /əi/ today, since ⟨iCe⟩ spellings only appear in the nineteenth century. We therefore cannot postulate an early merger with LOIN, though true, pan-Scots transfers to that class also exist if a labial precedes, as in *buist* 'box' < Old French *boiste*, with monophthongisation to [ø:] as well.

Two special developments, now only present in relics, must be discussed here. One is a very early (late fourteenth-century) monophthongisation of /ɔɪ/ to [ɔ:] = COAT, revealed by ⟨oCe⟩ spellings in words like *choice, voice, rejoice, joyse* 'possess'/'use', *void* (Robinson 1991: 762) and *jo*, the one item that survives into modern times. Except for *jo*, all the other words show the monophthongisation in alveolar environments, especially before /s/. Now, this could be linked to the monophthongisation of /ai au/ which begins about the same time; but if so, the change is only incipient and highly conditioned and variable. The form *jo* may not even result from the same process. My own theory is that it is a back-formation, due to the reinterpretation of *joy* used as a term of endearment as containing the suffix -*ie*, as if *jo* + *ie*, which would be homophonous.

The second development, restricted to Fife and conditioned as well, results in transfers to LOUP in *loit* 'vomit', *sloit* 'amble slowly' or *stoit* 'bounce', as well as *point*. The change seems to be a sixteenth-century one. It cannot be connected with the previous monophthongisation directly, as COAT words before /t nt/ do not diphthongise to /ʌu/ in Fife, but might be indirectly if we see these as reflecting a marginal /ɔ:/:/o/ distinction which exists in some dialects with large vowel systems (Mather and Speitel 1986), though this is speculative. The /o:/ slot (and /oi/ in this position) is open in Older Scots, and in most of the attested cases a grave sound, which often triggers raising of rounded vowels, precedes. If /ɔi/ had an allophone [oi], and this monophthongised to [o], a diphthongisation to [ou ~ ɔu] = LOUP would be easy to postulate; but this is highly conjectural, and really needs more evidence to prove. Aside from this, we can say that VOICE had [ɔi] everywhere, with possible [ɵ̈i] in the north, when medial, in sixteenth-century Scots.

3.5.7 The LOUP Class: Older Scots /ɔu/

LOUP is generally considered as consisting of the COT vowel + /u/ in both Older Scots (Aitken 1977b) and Middle and Tudor English (Dobson 1957: 804), considering that its sources are Old Norse, Old French /ɔu/ and /ɔl(C)/ and sometimes /ɔv/ – and the merger of the latter is attested from the fifteenth century. This is a very good characterisation. A value of COT + /u/ is corroborated by eighteenth-century sources (Jones 1996: 190–2), and it persisted as [ɔu ~ ou] in the western Borders until recently and in the central Borders into the nineteenth century (Murray 1873: 116). Yet, the usual modern reflex today is not COT + /u/, but CUT + /u/ – if not fronted to BIT + /y/.

There are a number of dialects in Insular Scots and along the Highland Line that turn LOUP + /k/ to /ok/ in some or all words, a development not unknown in *folk, yolk* in a wide range of English dialects as well. Occasionally, such forms occur in words like *howff, dowf* as well, but many of these words started out as COAT words, and preserve in Angus and

Tayside sporadic /of/ → /ɔuf/ (Robinson 1985: 300). In either case, the forms with monophthongisation start in the sixteenth century and are more frequent in the west and south-west than elsewhere, especially in the Borders where the rule seems to be lacking.

Today, /u/ reflexes (and shortening to /ʌ/) before labials are found in Insular Scots and sometimes in the south-east. Since ⟨ow⟩ can stand for either this or the regular developments, the only spelling evidence that shows this is the anglicised ⟨oo⟩, the first cases of which are found for *roup* in the eighteenth century. We can conclude that this must have arisen before this if the /ʌ/ form in *dowf* and the like are 'shortenings' of /u/ – they must then go back to Older Scots times. Except for these developments, it can be supposed that LOUP = [ɔu] (or [ɜu]?) everywhere in Older Scots, and by the sixteenth century the forms with historical vocalised consonants were merged in.

3.6   THE CONSONANTS IN OLDER SCOTS

3.6.1   Introduction

When we look at the Older Scots consonant inventory, we find a system similar in most respects to those of other Northern dialects of English. The elements, except along the peripheries where Celtic or Norn influence is strong, are identical to most other English dialects of the time: the stops /p b t d k g/; affricates /ʧ ʤ/; fricatives /f v θ ð – s z ʃ ʒ x h/; nasals /m n ŋ/; approximants /l r j w/ and /ʍ/ in places where the original /x/ in /xw/ had been weakened to nothing more than a voiceless 'prosody' (in Firthian terms) running through the semivowel. Only two extra elements, both with distribution restricted to intervocalic position, distinguish the Scottish system from others: a palatal lateral /ʎ/ and a palatal nasal /ɲ/, present in a few words of French or Gaelic origin with these sounds in the source dialects, and written ⟨lʒ, ly, ll⟩ and ⟨nʒ, ny⟩ in words like *bailyie* 'baillie', *lunʒe* 'loin' and personal names like *MacKenzie* (compare Gaelic *Mac Coinneach*) and *Dalziel*. These segments do not occur initially in French, and the Gaelic ones tended to be taken in with simple alveolars. Nor do they occur very often finally, since the offglide on the consonant generates a prosthetic vowel except after high vowels, where other developments obtain. However, plain /n/ after /i/ in French words leading to *chain*, *drain* could also be taken in as /ɲ/, which could in turn influence the vowel before it. English dialects never had these sounds, but used simple /l n/ to represent the French palatal sonorants.

More differences may occur in peripheral areas, in some of which Scots was relatively new, spoken with an accent typical of the substratal language. The /θ ð/-Stopping shared by Galloway and Ireland is in place (see section 3.6.2), as is the Palato-Alveolar Shift, which is attested even in an Anglian core dialect like Berwickshire, though only the /ʧ/ > /ʃ/ stage shows up well out of final position (section 3.6.2). The phoneme /h/ is more fragile than it is at present, with more variability initially than one would see now, particularly in the north, over a wider area than just the Black Isle. Otherwise, the observable differences tend to involve lexical incidence more than anything else, although it should be mentioned that subtle features of phonetic realisation must be reconstructed, rather than taken from spelling evidence as a rule. However, the values suggested for /l r/ in section 3.6.4 are based on this sort of evidence.

As with the vowels, the main consonantal isoglosses distinguishing the various dialect groups of Older Scots tend to evolve slowly. Early Scots must have strongly resembled the other Northern dialects, as most of the consonantal features proper to Scots at this time seem to have a wider distribution, extending over the old Danelaw in England, or at least most of it. The line is not always easy to draw in the early days between a Scots real sound change and lexical borrowing incorporating a form from another language when discussing such diagnostic features. Forms like *kirk*, *caff*, *brig* and even *give*, *egg* do not illustrate any retention (or stopping) of West Germanic /k ɣ/ before front vowels – despite the theory of Taylor (1974) – but a patterned lexical borrowing by bilinguals who had figured out the sound correspondences between English and Norse. Nevertheless, the resulting isoglosses between places with many and with few such Anglo-Norse bilinguals prove quite diagnostic, depending on the item, in separating the north and Scotland (or the north, the Midlands and Scotland) from the rest of the British Isles.

But some borrowed forms seem to spark a real sound change by 'attracting' native words to their phonotactics. As an example of this, there are apparent interchanges between /s/ and /ʃ/ that remain to this day. One reason for this may have to do with an apico-alveolar, 'cacuminal' realisation of /s/, observable at present in a number of Scots dialects (Macafee 1983; Catford 1957b), which is acoustically intermediate between a normal 'lamino' /s/ and a palato-alveolar. But there are also individual morphemes of foreign origin where that interchange is highly regular, suggesting that the 'interchanged forms' were borrowed lexically. In words ending in *-ish* in English, Early Scots usually shows *-is* or *-eis* (Robinson 1985), with *-ish* appearing later on. This goes back to a difference in the realisation of Gallo-Latin *-isc-* in 'fourth conjugation', originally inchoative verbs in French; the northern French dialects turned this to /-isj-/ > /iʃ/, while the central ones turned them to /-is(:)-/. The English forms plainly stem from Norman (northern) originals, but the Scots forms appear to come from Francien. Now, the Auld Alliance would have kept a 'wider avenue' open for continued borrowings of lexis for a longer period when Norman was becoming a provincial dialect and Francien was in the process of forming the base of a Standard French, which such forms would be borrowed from. But purely native tendencies could have also played a role in the outcome, given that, in native words, the interchange is attested in the sixteenth century where /s/ is around high front vowels (see section 3.6.3) – or even Gaelic ones, given that that language also palatalises /s/ in this position. In fact, there are probably multiple causes of this interchange. Most of the changes present in the early Older Scots corpus (pre-1450) and stemming from the Early Scots period seem to be similar.

However, by the sixteenth century, real native sound changes, localised now as they were then, begin to show up in spellings. The Northern change of /xw/ > /f/ dates from this point, as does the simplification of /ld nd/, which separates the north and west from the rest; /xt/ takes a number of spellings besides ⟨cht⟩ or ⟨ght⟩ such as ⟨tht⟩, ⟨th⟩, which may be merely scribal, but might also designate the change to /θ/ attested in north-eastern *Survey of English Dialects* materials, Mutschmann (1908) and Dieth (1932) in *nought*, *might* and *daughter*. The phonemes /d/ and /ð/ begin to alternate medially, with a preference for the latter in the south and the former in the north. By the end of the period, although there is not yet any evidence for glottalisation and only the restricted /r/-Vocalisation found in Morayshire, most of the diagnostic traits defining major dialect groups within Scots (as well as Scots as a whole!) are in place, and the consonant systems resemble the present ones.

In the material below, I provide sections on stops and affricates (3.6.2), fricatives (3.6.3) and sonorants (3.6.4). Characteristics typical of any division of Scots, Scots *in toto*, or wider divisions including Scots are all included, with the changes listed under the segment that did the changing first. Thus, the simplification of /ld nd/ is treated under the stops, the same way as that of /pt kt st/ is, while a discussion of /v/ ~ /w/-Interchange goes under the fricatives.

3.6.2   The Stops and Affricates in Older Scots

All Older Scots dialects exhibit the same basic inventory of stop-like sounds as any other dialect of English: true stops /p b t d k g/ and affricates /ʧ ʤ/ are present. The lexical incidence of these words may differ from Southern or Midland English, particularly in forms like *birk, brig, kirk, pik, rig, thack, reik, sik* and *streke*, where, even in fourteenth-century sources, velars appear instead of Southern palato-alveolars (Robinson 1985: 678). It is likely that this is due to Norse lexical influence rather than retention of an originally Northumbrian conservative feature – but see Taylor (1974) – as place-names in *-chester* instead of *-caster* predominate north of the Tees, and other native words have the initial affricates. Otherwise, the most likely reflexes of the stops would be something much like the values they have in a conservative modern Scots dialect; voiceless unaspirated stops in the /p t k/ series, and voiced stops with a tendency to devoice partially when final.

It is noteworthy how few of the dialectally diagnostic processes affecting modern Scots stop systems are present before 1700 in any large-scale capacity. There are no forms implying Glottalling before the eighteenth century, and little evidence of medial voicing unless lexical analogical pressure existed, as in *cannobie* for *canopy*, evidently influenced by the name of the Dumfriesshire town of *Canonbie*, which is sometimes pronounced that way (Robinson 1985: 82), and *ankersaidil*, influenced by *saddle* rather than *settle*. The Caithnesian voicing of stops in codas of unstressed syllables is of substratal origin, and could have been present, but the evidence only goes back as far as modern Caithnesian dialect literature does, to the nineteenth century. Further south, there is a sixteenth-century spelling of *packed* for *packet*, but this is not necessarily indicative of a regular, non-analogical voicing process, as it comes at a time when native *-it* and English *-ed* are beginning to vary with each other as a past-tense suffix. Otherwise, only *id* (or *'d*) for *(h)it* with spellings like *ford* for *for it* and *beid* for *be it*, with an eastern distribution as early as the fifteenth century (Robinson 1985: 33), testify to any tendency towards voicing, and even this is lexically conditioned, though it is today diagnostic of Fife and Tayside as well as Orkney.

T-Flapping is only attested at the very end of the period, in *carritches* for *catechis(m)* and *orra* from *odd* (Robinson 1985: 455); and, in contrast to the modern distribution of the rule, both of these terms have a mainly northern distribution. The flapping in *parritch* and its variants is more or less General British.

The modern replacement of /x/ by /k/ is only exemplified by *selkie*, which should be *selchie*, from Old English *seolh* 'seal'. There may be analogical influence here of native double diminutives in *-ockie* or even of originally Flemish *-ke*. The apparent simplification of /ks/ to /s/ in *oussen, aneist, assletree* is really probably a simplification of the original Old English cluster /xs/, and is attested from the fifteenth century, though it could have happened at any time before this point (Robinson 1985: 18). The clusters /kl gl/ are not attested with /tl dl/, though when evidence (in reverse spellings or hypercorrections like *wheegle, hankle*) finally comes it has a predictably Gallovidian and western Border distribution. We are left with only a few changes involving stops or affricates in any capacity to deal with: (1) simplifications of clusters like /ft st xt kt pt ld nd/, ending with an alveolar stop; (2) the simplification of /xt/ > /θ/, associated with Northern Scots; (3) the interchange of /d/ and /ð/, and to a lesser extent /t/ and /θ/; and (4) Palato-Alveolar Shift. Of these, the first five changes listed under (1), though common in Scots as a whole, are not uncommon elsewhere and have no regional provenance within Scotland. To some extent, this also holds for (3), with some regions preferring a fricative and others a stop output, though this is no more than a tendency.

3.6.2.1 Alveolar Cluster Simplification

A number of clusters ending in /t d/ lose their second element when they appear at the end of a syllable. Such a development is a natural one throughout English when a consonant begins the next word; Scots carries it further into citation forms, so that the coda consists of the consonant that preceded the alveolar. The effect seems to appear first in clusters of /kt/ and, to a lesser extent, /xt/ and /st/, with spellings like *contrak, prefec, suspeck, deiching* (< *dichting*) and *cassen* already in evidence in the late fourteenth century. These changes appear not to be localised within Scotland, though /xt/ > /x/ had to compete with /xt/ > /θ/ in Fife and even Edinburgh, and it is exceedingly hard to tell what happens to these clusters, as <ch, cht, th, tht> appear interchangeable, leading some authorities to conclude that they are just graphical variants. The clusters /pt/ and /ft/ join the list of permissible inputs for this rule, also non-localisedly in the mid-fifteenth century, with the hypercorrect *clift* for *cliff, transsump, excep, interrup, accep* all attested by 1500 (Robinson 1991: 181). Towards the end of the period, a tendency to restore the /t/ in /st xt ft/ starts to work (Romaine 1982b), leading to forms with 'excrescent /t/' as well as restored forms, which now can be observed in many non-standard dialects today in England, Ireland and America, as well as Scotland (Romaine 1982b).

Unlike the clusters involving /t/, those involving /d/ have localisable distributions within Scotland, much as they do today. Final /ld/ clusters tend to be simplified, starting in the last decades of the fifteenth century in the north, west and south-west, including the Southern Scots-speaking parts of Dumfriesshire, while medial ones are only simplified in the north, starting in the sixteenth century, with spellings much less frequent. In Older Scots, the simplifying area extends well to the east of where /l/ appears regularly today to cover most of Stirlingshire, Perthshire, the western Lothians and even Edinburgh, as spellings like *wile* 'wild' and *yeel* 'yield' appear during the sixteenth century even in 'standardised' documents.

The simplification of homorganic /NC/ sequences varies quite widely in geographic extent. In the labial series, /mb/ > /m/ finally everywhere, with examples such as *dum, kame, lam* even in the earliest manuscripts (Robinson 1985: 355). Scots, like all Northern dialects, has a distinct preference for simplification in the sequences /mbl mbr/, and examples like *tummle, tymmer* are attested in the fifteenth century (Robinson 1985: 745), though it should be pointed out that the /b/ was often originally excrescent anyway, and may have only been variably inserted to begin with. One cannot ascertain by spellings when /ŋg/ simplified, but it must have done so before the fourteenth century, or the interchange between /n/ and /ŋ/ in the suffix *-ing* could not have happened this early. We can, likewise, only guess when medial /ŋg/ was simplified; but, as the simplified reflex covers an intermediate area compared to /mb/ on one hand and /nd/ on the other, an intermediate dating to the late fourteenth century sounds reasonable. Like the equivalent rule affecting /ld/, /nd/-Simplification primarily divides the west and north of Scotland from the rest; again, however, the rule must have applied further east, with only Tayside, the eastern regions of Fife and the eastern Borders not taking part. The medial application of the rule is categorical in many northern English dialects of the old Danelaw as well, even if it is only variable within Northumbrian (Orton 1933; Reaney 1927). As with the other cases of simplification, /nd/ > /n/ finally in the fourteenth century, at least in the heart of the simplifying area (*lan* and *len* appear by then; Robinson 1985: 355), while medial /n/ is attested from the fifteenth century in *winnow/wonnow* for *window* (Robinson 1985: 796). The Edinburgh street-name *Lawnmarket*, originally where *land* was sold, stands as testimony that the rule was once common in this city, though it is still somewhat variably applied in Edinburgh Scots.

3.6.2.2   /xt/-Dentalisation

From about the late fifteenth century on, ⟨th⟩ instead of ⟨ch⟩ appears for /xt/, mostly after mid or high back vowels. The change seems rather odd, but can be viewed as a sort of mutual assimilation, whereby the result takes on the flat fricative quality of the /x/ and the nearest place of articulation to the /t/ where flat, rather than grooved, sibilant fricatives are normal. While the rule has British if not Gaelic parallels, the date of first appearance is probably too late to tie it to the Pictish that was once spoken in Fife and the north-east. Most of the words showing this form in the Older Scots period – *dother*, *noth*, *drouth* – are words that have been recorded with /θ/ in South and Mid Northern, but *broth* for *brought* also appears on the list (Robinson 1985: 65).

3.6.2.3   /t d/–/θ ð/-Interchange

The process that underlies /θ ð/-Stopping, the difference between Northern *idder* and Mid Scots *ither*, and perhaps even the Glaswegian /ð/-Rhotacisation rule, has its roots deep in the Older Scots period, and in part may even go back into Old Northumbrian. Most northern English dialects have a tendency to neutralise alveolar stops and dental fricatives in environments where an /r/ follows in the next syllable, or in /Cr/ clusters. In Hackness, Lorton, Dentdale, Kendal, Penrith and Byers Green, there is a tendency to merge /ð/ and /d/ before an underlying /-r/, with the outcome being a dental stop or affricate in the Norse Crescent dialects (Reaney 1927; Cowling 1915; Hirst 1913; Brilioth 1913) and a dental fricative in the Northumbrian ones (Orton 1933). That tendency was present in Older Scots as well, at first favouring some sort of stop realisation, which could have been dental; this became more and more the tendency of northern dialects in most items (Robinson 1985). In the Central Belt, fricatives predominate, but there is more variability than in England, since forms in *ther* (in *either*, *nether*, *father* and even *fother* from *fodder*) alternate with /d/ forms towards the end of the period. Except for western Gallovidian, and possibly some Clyde coast dialects, which have always had Stopping, the fricatives become more common the further south one goes, forming a continuum with the north-eastern English dialects. By the late fifteenth century, the same interchange, with roughly the same output, is happening where the next syllable contains /n/ as well: *Suethin*, *tythand* appears early for *Sweden*, *tiding* (Robinson 1985: 721), indicating that the fricative was at first favoured here, but before the sixteenth century one begins to find frequent stops also in *idand* (originally with /ð/), *widdie* for *withy*, and *smiddy* for *smithy* (Robinson 1985: 635), especially in the north and far south-west.

The interchange is not common for /t/ in the same position, and true /θ/-Stopping is rare even in Wigtown (McIntosh et al. 1986), but there are two environments where /t/ is often spelled ⟨th⟩ from the fifteenth century on. Initial position is one, with forms like *tholl* for *toll* and *thwa* for *twa* attested, particularly in the late sixteenth century; and since this is a time when English spelling habits are being learned, this could reflect a writer's hypercorrection of Stopping. The other environment is in final /nt rt/ clusters, with *dynmonth* for *dynmont*, *wanskoth* for *wainscot*, and *airth* for *airt*. At least the last one is attested in several peripheral Northern and Western Scots dialects (Mather and Speitel 1986).

3.6.2.4 Palato–Alveolar Shift

The processes by which the palato–alveolar phonemic inventory are simplified to an affricate /ʧ/ and a fricative /ʃ/, as found today in Insular and North Northern Scots, are not unknown in Early Scots times, even though most of the shifting dialects formed late in original Gaelic- or Norn-speaking districts. Indeed, the older shift may not be the same process at all, but reflects the outcome in nineteenth-century Berwickshire and Border dialects, as the environments where shifting is favoured match these varieties better than the north. There is no trace of initial /ʤ/ devoicing, the most widespread feature of the Northern rule. However, there are plenty of ⟨sch⟩ spellings for historical initial /ʧ/, and conversely ⟨ch⟩ for /ʃ/, with the latter dating from the fifteenth century and the former becoming more common in the sixteenth. Forms like *shill, shimley, shire* (for 'chair') visible in manuscripts from the East Mid and Southern areas therefore probably reflect the same change that is now recessive in the eastern Borders (Wettstein 1942) in pronunciations like *Shirset, Shillinjum, Shatton* for *Chirnside, Chillingham, Chatton*. The change also goes through in final position, in *dispasch* 'despatch', *fesh* 'fetch' and *flech* 'flesh', all sixteenth-century spellings (Robinson 1985: 201), and, as a General Scots feature, finally after /r l n/, with *munsh* for *munch* being the earliest (sixteenth-century) instance in this environment, and more frequent spellings in the seventeenth century (Robinson 1985).

Devoicing of /ʤ/ is rare outside of final position, though there are spellings reflecting it there, as in the north-eastern *careache* or *grutch* (Robinson 1985: 249). One cannot rule out the possibility of the influence of the *-age* suffix in some words ending in historical voiceless affricates, as in *elrage* for *el(d)ritch* (Robinson 1985: 173), so one-off lexical transfers and folk etymologies may play a part in the shift, but it is attested widely in *parritch*, *carritch* in a large variety of Scots dialects.

There is only one example of devoicing of the rare /ʒ/ sound; *Scherand* (Robinson 1985: 586) is a kind of wine from the *Gironde* in Bordeaux. Given that neither Scots nor English possessed this sound at that time, to take it in with its voiceless counterpart makes perfect sense.

There are even examples where the shift intertwines with /ʃ/–/s/-Interchange, so that /s/ results from historical affricates, as in *challance* for *challenge* or *ersedene* for *archdean*, or *oblis* for *oblige*. In many of these cases, which tend to be much earlier than the others mentioned above, there appears to be lexical repatterning; *oblige* has been treated as if it were a typical French *-iss-* verb, like *finish*. It is unlikely that these alternations reflect a regular sound change.

3.6.3 The Fricatives in Older Scots

3.6.3.1 Introduction and Widespread Changes

The section of the consonant system where Older Scots differed from London Middle English was the fricatives. All varieties of English shared the voiceless phonemes /f θ s ʃ x/, the last of which had an initial allophone [h] from which stemmed the modern /h/. All dialects, too, vocalised the common Old English velar voiced fricative [ɣ] (probably best counted as an allophone of /g/) that appeared in *dragan* 'draw', *fugol* 'fowl' and so on, and lacked the palato-alveolar /ʒ/ (see above), which did not arise until later, and is quite marginal in Scots when it does. This leaves /v ð z/ to deal with; these were originally allophones of their voiceless equivalents, and in Old English they were restricted to medial position around voiced sounds. Certainly, at least, some sort of distribution like this characterises the Midland dialects, and even some South-west/Midland transition dialects (Ellis 1889), and London English. This account obscures a regular dialectal progression in the treatment of these fricatives, at least in native words. Before the Battle of Hastings, or at least before significant loaning from French took place, the West Saxon dialects had already voiced the initial voiceless fricatives (Wakelin 1972), which accounts for the fact that native words have voicing but Norman loans do not. As we go north, voiceless forms are more resistant to being replaced by voiced ones, especially finally; this accounts for why *wise* in Scots (< Old English *wis*) has a voiceless, not a voiced final consonant, and originally *five* did also (Robinson 1985: 797). For the most part, the medial allophones are voiced in Scots and Northern dialects, but the rarity of voiced fricatives in other parts of the word creates anomalies; the relatively non-strident labiodental and dental fricatives tend to disappear, while the strident /z/ tends to devoice. Furthermore, in Scots the final /v/ that is quite common in French loans after the loss of final -*e* also tends to be restructured to /f/. None of these features is characteristic of areas within Scots, though the devoicing of /v/ and deletion of /θ/ does seem to be diagnostic of Scots as a whole, and the deletion of medial /v/ in certain contexts (when the next syllable ends with a sonorant) defines all North Britain from the North Midlands up (McIntosh et al. 1986). These changes are early ones wherever they occur; forms like *deil* for *devil*, *fleur* for *flavour*, *gayle* for *gable* 'gavel' and *leful* for *leveful* are found even in fourteenth-century Scots manuscripts (Robinson 1985: 140), and final /v/ is almost always represented by ⟨f⟩, or the giveaway sign of voicelessness, ⟨ff⟩. The extension to contexts after a consonant, as in *ser* for *serve*, *sel* for *self*, *hairst* for *harvest*, arises later, in the late fifteenth century (Robinson 1985: 260), and is by no means universally shown even in sixteenth-century writing, but occurs over the whole area. The deletion of /ð/, which appears to occur in the same environments that /v/-deletion does, is contemporaneous with the other changes: *birn* for *burden* (Old English *byrðen*) and *unschait* for *unscathed* date from the fourteenth century, and forms like *mow* for *mouth* start appearing a century later.

Initial /z/, which occurs in only a few items, holds its own, but ⟨ss⟩ spellings reveal devoicing in words like *cussing* for *cousin*, *wissen* for *weasand* and *vissie* for *visit* (Robinson 1985: 759). The examples belong mostly to the sixteenth century, but there are a few older forms.

However, there is no trace in Older Scots manuscripts of spellings suggesting that voiceless fricatives are being lenited; the combination /θr/, in Northern Scots, may result in ⟨fr⟩, as in *freid* for *thread*, but there is no ⟨hr⟩ or ⟨rh⟩ spelling illustrating the modern Mid-Scots outcome of [çr ~ hr]. The initial consonant of *th*- pronouns and articles may be Stopped in some localities, but there is no evidence of deletion, even in the Mid-Northern area, until the nineteenth century.

Scots retains medial /x/ in a few words like *aicher*, *techyr* (Robinson 1985: 705) intervocalically, where it was lost very early in the Old English period in the south (these two words are the same as *ear* (of corn) and *tear* (noun), and has a tendency to have taken in French loans in -*ée* < -*eðe* as -*eth* in *dainteth*, *cuntrith*, *moneth* more often than English does.

3.6.3.2   /h/-Deletion

One does not usually think of the deletion of initial /h/ as having anything to do with Scots, though it does occur as nearby as Cumberland, as well as in the Black Isle. Indeed, there are far fewer spellings implying deletion of /h/ or insertion of an unetymological /h/ in Scotland than anywhere else in Britain. Many of the examples that do exist are of Romance words, which lost their Latin /h/ on the way to French, and this perhaps explains such late fourteenth-century forms as *eritage*, *ost* and *aubirchoun* (for *haubergeon*), and the later *onhabill* for *unable*, given Latin *habilis* (Robinson 1985: 747). However, in Northern Scots manuscripts – and Mid-Northern ones at that – starting in the fifteenth century, the same phenomenon happens in native words also, in *haith* for *oath*, *appin* for *happen* and so on. It seems that /h/-Deletion was once more widespread in Scotland, or at least the north, than it is now, and has receded to the Black Isle since.

3.6.3.3   /s/ ~ /ʃ/-Interchange

Although it is not tied to any one dialect area, one of the more salient features of Older Scots phonology is the presence of /s/ where one would expect /ʃ/ and vice versa. One must distinguish between several types of this interchange, as they seem to occur in different groups of words. The earliest-attested type, in fact, may not be true examples of a sound change producing alveolars from palato-alveolars but a lexical phenomenon: forms in French loans that correspond to English *-ish* which have Scots *-is* or *-eis*. These, presumably, represent the Central French (Francien) /s/ forms rather than Norman or Picard /ʃ/ (Pope 1934), and occur in words with the same ⟨ss⟩ in other cases also: in *parish* from Old French *pareisse*, in *brush* from *broisse*; in *push* from *pouss-* and so on. The same forms occur for the native suffix *-ish* (as in *Scottis*, *Inglis*) and other words with /ʃ/ (*wiss*, *ass*), but these may reflect an Early Scots simplification of an original /sk/ cluster rather than involving a /ʃ/ stage. Since we know so little about Old Northumbrian, it may have even developed directly from an /sx/ < /sk/, much as the Dutch /s/ in *vis* did. Still, except for the one item *shall* > *sal* and its forms, this interchange is confined to final position.

The converse change is sporadic in the oldest manuscripts, but becomes significantly more common as time goes on, and spreads to final position about the same time as the other changes involving fricatives occur. It remains most common initially, however; and, although some items (mostly involving a French /sj/, like *schir* for French *sieur*) are found anywhere, the change is more common in the north than the rest of the country. Here, one finds forms like *schervice*, *schervitour*, *schunder* 'cinder', *schon* 'son' in sixteenth-century works, and in some cases, notably forms of *cinder* and *soon*, /ʃ/ forms are still quite common there (Speitel and Mather 1968). This may well have its roots in the cacuminal pronunciation of /s/, which does sound acoustically something like /ʃ/, and could reflect a sound change; it could have also been reinforced by Gaelic, since most of the examples occur around front vowels, and the Gaelic palatalised sibilant that occurs there is palato-alveolar (Borgstrom 1940).

3.6.3.4   Dental/Labiodental Interchange

In a number of dialects of English, especially Cockney, the dental fricatives /θ ð/ are replaced by /f v/ in all positions. It is doubtful that this replacement ever applied across the board in Scotland, but there is at least evidence in the north of Scotland that this interchange 'nearly made it' as a sound change. The Norse item *Furisday* (modern *Feersday*) meaning 'Thursday' is still current and dates back as far as the late fourteenth century (Robinson 1985: 217); the native place–name element *hive*, originally the same word as the last syllable of the English *hithe*, is not attested until the very close of this period, but underlies the native pronunciation of *Stonehaven* as [stinhaev].

3.6.4　The Sonorant Consonants in Older Scots

3.6.4.1　The Nasals

All Older Scots dialects shared an inventory of a bilabial /m/, an alveolar or perhaps more often dental /n/, and two other phonemes of restricted distribution, the palatal /ɲ/ mentioned at the beginning of this section, and the familiar velar /ŋ/ from an Early Scots /nK/ (where /K/ = any velar consonant) where the nasal was assimilated to the following consonant. One must assume that the phonology of these nasals – their allophones and phonotactics – was in large part the same as any English dialects, for the restrictions on the nasals' appearing in onsets (only alone or preceded by /s/ for /m n/; no appearance for the others), and in coda clusters (that they must be followed by a homorganic sound within a morpheme; no clustering for palatals) are what you find everywhere. The favouring of /N(ə)l N(ə)r/ over forms with epenthetic stops /ND(ə)l ND(ə)r/, shared with all northern British varieties, and the tendency of northern and western varieties to simplify final /ND/ regardless of the place of articulation, has already been discussed (section 3.6.2). There are only a few other changes – or in one case, probably a borrowed 'pseudo–change' – that need to be discussed here, though most of these are of General Scots or wider distribution, and most affect comparatively few words.

(a)　The Palatal Nasal /ɲ/

There seems to be no question that /ɲ/, taken in from French or Gaelic, survived at least before original or prosthetic /ə/ > /i/ all across Scotland throughout the period, as spellings implying /n/ only start appearing after the Scottish standard variety was in process of being replaced by the English one, and ⟨ny⟩ and ⟨nz⟩ spellings (though the last could be spelling pronunciations) survive in *cunyie, linyie, minyie* into the nineteenth, if not the twentieth century (Robinson 1985: 128). In final position after high vowels, the native development was to /ŋ/, possibly through a palatalised velar the same way as Gaelic /ŋj/ (written -*inn*) developed, with *benign, condign, malign, reign, sign* all being spelled with -*ing* as early as the fifteenth century. These forms were later replaced by /n/ forms from English (Murray 1873: 124; Zai 1942), but were probably General Scots in earlier times. Those items that do not take /n/ or /nz/ spelling pronunciations today now have /ŋ/, such as *ingan, Menzies* (as if *Mingis*); spellings implying this development also date from the fifteenth century.

(b)　Clustering with Nasals

The sequences /mpt nkt/ have a tendency to be simplified to /nt/, in both French words (*cont* ⟨ *compt*; compare English *(ac)count*) and native ones (*blent* ⟨ *blinkit*). Examples are found from the earliest manuscripts (Robinson 1985: 48), although it should be mentioned that such changes partially parallel French developments, so that Norman pronunciation habits may have influenced the development. On the other hand, the interlude /mn/, as in *condemn(it)* and so forth, becomes realised in spelling as ⟨mpn⟩. The insertion of a voiceless oral obstruent between two nasals hardly makes sense finally, although spellings like *dampn* are attested (Robinson 1985: 134); but something like a glottal stop conceivably could have arisen at a syllable boundary, as when a suffix was present. Such spellings are found throughout the Older Scots period, though modern vernaculars have nothing but /m/ in *damn, condemn, hymn* or *damage* (which gets drawn in to this set), and /mn/ in *damnable*.

In Older Scots, the native present participial suffix *-and* tends to be confused with both the suffix *-ing*, with spellings dating from the late fifteenth century, and the borrowed French suffix *-ant*, which was already beginning to lose its /t/ at the time of borrowing in French (Pope 1934). This, in turn, leads to a certain amount of interplay between final /nt/ and /n/, though this is confined to this suffix until the very end of the period, when spellings like *yont, ident* appear largely in dialects that simplify /nd/ (Robinson 1985: 812). This foreshadows a much larger interplay between /nd/ and /nt/ (in *ayont, behint* and so on) extant in the eighteenth century. Due to these developments, the participial and gerundive forms could fall together if not distinguished by the prior vowel, and spellings implying this are amply attested, joined by other words such as *cusing* for *cousin* in the fourteenth century, and others like *elsing/elshion, herin/herring, mornin/morning* in the fifteenth. While the adoption of /n/ in both is pan-Scots in vernaculars (and pan-British, ultimately, too), only a few Central Belt dialects may have completely lacked traces of a vocalic distinction, whereby original *-ing* = [-ɪn] or [-in] as opposed to the [-ən ~ -n] of *-and*, since non-Mid dialects still have the distinction today.

The combination /ln/ > /l/ in *mill* throughout English (except for the name *Milne*) but also happens in *kiln* over most of northern Britain. If *selvin* really represents [sɛln], with /v/-deletion, this too would have gone to /l/, just as the uninflected *self* would; the north-east Midland assimilation to /n/ (Orton et al. 1978) is lacking in Scotland.

3.6.4.2 The Laterals

Scots seems to have adopted an allophony of /l/ whereby the realisation was a true clear /l/ (as in peripheral dialects like Wigtownshire, Insular Scots and Caithnesian) as well as northern England) in onsets and in codas after front vowels, but after back vowels was a dark [ɫ]. This set-up was probably not the original Northumbrian situation, since if it were, Old English Breaking would have happened over a wider range of environments than just /lx/ codas. However, it does resemble the modern RP (originally of Midland or Southern type) distribution except that there, velarised [ɫ] is found in all codas. It could therefore have been a historical compromise, adopted as Midlanders moved up to south-eastern Scotland after the Norman conquest. Alternatively, it could reflect a compromise with the Old Norman system, which must have had the identical rule, considering what happened to French /V(u)lC/ combinations in words like *chevaulx, cheveulx, doulce* and so on. In any case, a starting-point system like this would be the prerequisite for the Northern and North Midland form of /l/-vocalisation that begins in the fourteenth and early fifteenth centuries (Orton 1933). Scots adds a twist to this; the alveolarity of /d/ (but not the voiceless /t/) appears to have attracted the /l/ before it to that position early on even if a back vowel precedes, so that vocalisation does not generally happen in words like *old*, as it does in northern England, though there may have been some lexical variability, which led to *hold* developing as it does south of the border. Before a consonant, vocalisation appears to have happened in all other back vowel + /l/ + C cases about the same time, with not much of a conditioning effect of the height of the vowel; apparent exceptions, as in early examples of *faut*, *sauce*, say, could reflect borrowing of innovative French (Francien) forms already without /l/ (Robinson 1985: 189). The combination /ul/ + word boundary shows vocalisation (in *fow* for *full* for instance) as early as the late fourteenth century, while the earliest attestations of /ɔl/ or /al/ > /ɔu au/ finally (*bowster*; *aw*, *forestaw*) occur only in the fifteenth, if necessarily earlier than the monophthongisation of CAUGHT.

No-one can indicate when the remaining /l/ realisations became dark in turn in Mid dialects, but it may well have been late rather than early, as even early twentieth-century researchers uncovered traces of Mid-Northern clear /l/, and Murray's (1873: 123) remarks about central Borders /l/, as well as even earlier commentators in the Central Belt (Jones 1996: 211–13), appear to suggest that /l/ was clear at least in middle-class speech even in Central Belt centres. While the darkening of /l/ could have been present in working-class focal areas by 1700, we cannot prove this, and thus we could take either (or both) values as possible in East, West or North Mid. Other dialects probably had [l], like Early Scots must have done.

The phenomenon of /ld/-Simplification has been discussed in section 3.4.2.

The palatal lateral /ʎ/ occurred in the same positions where /ɲ/ is possible. Since spellings (again, possibly spelling pronunciations) like *bailzie*, *culzie*, *fulzie*, *ulyie*, *tailyour* can be found in this century, there was probably a palatal realisation throughout the Older Scots period in all Scots varieties. Unlike /ɲ/, /ʎ/ never occurs finally, but generates a prosthetic vowel after it.

3.6.4.3   The Phoneme /r/

Old English breaking rules suggest that /r/, too, had a 'strong'/'weak' allophony present, with the 'weak' allophone, restricted to codas before a consonant, being velarised as it 'breaks' or diphthongises preceding front vowels. Again, Northern dialects have a more restricted form of this rule, sensitive to what the vowel actually is, with /a/ often retracting instead of breaking. Modern-day rhotic Midland English dialects, such as those of central Lancashire, give clues as to what this allophony might have become in much Middle English: onsets, including clusters ending in /r/ and intervocalic /r/, have a tap [ɾ], while in codas, /r/ is realised as a liquid [ɻ]. In the far south of England, as in American dialects, there was a tendency to extend the weak allophone to all positions; but in the north, if anything, the strong allophone was extended, except possibly along the boundary line with Gaelic. There is thus little trace of /r/-vocalisation or deletion except sporadically in unstressed syllables before /d t/: *placad*, *orchat* for *placard*, *orchard* in the late sixteenth century, and more regularly in Northern Scots before /s/ from the late fifteenth century: *hace* for *hoarse*, *eschip* for *heirship* (Robinson 1985: 280). This Scots equivalent of the same change that produces *hoss* for *horse* still survives in Moray Scots, and may have its roots in a Gaelic or Norse collapsing of retroflex /r/ + alveolar to simple retroflexes (Borgstrom 1940; Haugen 1982). The /r/-deletion in other coda positions is nowhere to be seen until the modern period.

There does seem to be a General Scots change of /rd/ to /rt/ in words ending in *-ward* (*towart*, *upwart* are attested from the fourteenth century, *awkwart* from the fifteenth; Robinson 1985: 23), which later in the fifteenth century extends to other words like *mustard*, *bastard, orchard* (Robinson 1985: 453). By the sixteenth century, /rd/ can simplify to /r/ sporadically, especially in the north (*mustar* by the seventeenth century; Robinson 1991: 431) in a parallel fashion to /ld nd/ > /l n/, though at least in most of the cases lexical confusion with words in *-er* (Scots *-ar*) such as *muster* might have helped the process along.

Our postulation of the position of /v/ ~ /w/-Interchange governs the most likely value of initial /wr-/. However, the /w/ was almost certainly present in some form, as no spellings suggesting simplification to /r/ appears before the nineteenth century, at which time the south, like the north, still had /wr/ (Murray 1873: 131). The pronunciation [wr-] seems reasonable at least for all groups but the north, since it was the form exported to Insular Scots and which is attested in Murray, and since /vr/ spellings are lacking even in the north-east until later. Unless /w/ = /v/ this early, the north-east probably lacked a labiodental fricative in this position. However, there is nothing preventing there being something like a bilabial fricative from the sixteenth century on, especially since it is this region that shows /v/ ~ /w/-Interchange and turns voiceless /ʍ/ to /f/, presumably through [ɸ]. The one case of retained /hr/, *whrine*, is spelled *quhrine* in this period, suggesting that it had become a cluster of /ʍ/ + /r/ (Robinson 1985).

3.6.4.4 The Unrounded Semivowel /j/

The phoneme /j/, restricted to onsets after the Old English period, appears to have been a simple palatal semivowel then as now, though it is possible, if unprovable, that Early Scots may have had fricative realisations. The /j/-insertion which is seen in words of the ONE group starts to appear in that word in the late sixteenth century, and becomes found in other words in the seventeenth, and the spelling *yield* for *eild*, if the other item *yield* is not responsible for this, may indicate that Northern Scots sometimes deleted initial /j/ before /i/. There is no special development of /hj/ observable in spellings, and words like *Hugh, human* probably had [hiu-] here anyway (see section 3.5.1).

3.6.4.5 The Rounded Semivowels /w/ and /ʍ/

The Northumbrian /w/ is, at first, represented by ⟨u, uu⟩, with no tendency towards minority or sporadic forms with ⟨f, b⟩, so there is no difficulty with postulating a simple labiovelar approximant, much as one has now. Even the Norse ⟨v⟩ was probably a /w/ (Haugen 1982), and that this was true in the Norn spoken in Scotland is confirmed by early Norse loans like *uinneog* < Old Norse *vindauga* and place names like *Uig* < *Vikr*. Anything more fricative than [w] would presumably have been represented by ⟨bh⟩, or even ⟨f⟩, the realisation of Proto-Celtic */w/ (compare Latin *uir, uinum* with Gaelic *fir, fion*). There plainly was no ancient /v/ ~ /w/-Interchange. Nor would French influence have caused the interchange, or at least Norman would not have; /w/ exists in Norman, Picard and Walloon in words like *warder, werre* (hence *ward, war*), and even Germanic *west* was taken in with and remains *ouest*.

The Francien substitution for /w/ was, like most Romance dialects, /gw/, not /v/, though there is sixteenth-century evidence that French speakers may have used /v/ for /w/ at that time. Examples of the interchange, however, as shown above, do occur in Older Scots, but are over 5:1 in favour of ⟨w⟩ spellings for /v/ rather than the other way around (Robinson 1985), suggesting that the reverse spellings are just that: hyperdialectal spellings really reflecting the lenition of /v/. Furthermore, this substitution would make sense, given that

Old English (and Old Norse) lacked initial /v/ this far north. However, older /w/ was not affected in onsets, except maybe in Northern Scots when in clusters, given the eventual outcome of /wr/ as /vr/ and /xw/ as /f/ – attested plainly by forms like *for* for *where* and *phingear* for *whinger* in sixteenth-century texts from Aberdeen (Robinson 1985: 788). This Northern Scots stereotype was therefore already in place, even if Barbour presumably still had unlenited, unchanged /xw/. Even the lenition of /xw/ to /ʍ/ or even /w/ is suggested by fifteenth-century Edinburgh *alwair* for the more usual *alquhare* ('everywhere'; Robinson 1985: 23) and reverse spelling *quharm* for *warm*. But this change adds to the number of words with /w/, rather than subtracts from it. There are the usual deletions of /w/ in clusters that give English dialectal *forrard* and even standard *Warwick* with /r/ – *chessel* was originally *cheese-well* (Robinson 1985: 94) – but absolutely no other conditioned changes to suggest /v/, barring reverse spellings, except for one: one of the great mysteries of Scots phonology.

Where does the /v/ in Northern Scots *b(l)yauve, yaave, tyaave* come from? Only *yaave* of the whole set of words is actually attested (in the form *ave*) as early as the late sixteenth century (Robinson 1985: 807), with all other words having to wait until the rise of Buchan dialect literature for their attestation. These words plainly had Old English /w/, but so did *new, dew, stow* which do not come out today as *neeve, dave* (or *deeve*, or *dyauve*), *stove* (or *steeve*, with Early Scots /θ:/). The vowel before was either Early Scots /a/ or /a:/. Now, there must have been something more than a simple /u/ at the end in Older Scots. Otherwise, *all*, which becomes /au/ after /l/-deletion, should give **/a:v/, not /a:/. Furthermore, whatever was after the vowel must have had a velar component to it. The vowel is not simple [a:], but [ju:], and this only develops from earlier [a:] by Breaking (as in *byaak* for *bake*) before velars, not labials. Modern /v/ is thus ruled out at the time of Breaking, the late fifteenth century. However, [w] would not be. We are forced to conclude that final consonantal /w/ was in fact retained at least in the first half of the Older Scots area in this highly peripheral area alone, and that this lone exception to the general English constraint that true semivowels do not appear in codas was 'regularised' by the stage /w/ > /v/ in this position during the sixteenth century. As with /vr/, a bilabial fricative is possible as a midway point, but this must have been doubly articulated as late as the time of the Breaking rule if we postulate one.

The Older Scots systems, as a whole, seem more close to each other than modern ones, although the Northern group already shows some independence from the rest, as early as the sixteenth century, and the Border varieties form a clearer transition zone with England than they do now. It is clear, however, that the germs of difference between the groups of Scots dialects were already planted before 1700, though much more has to be done in localising what manuscripts have been handed down to us before the definitive dialectology of Older Scots is written.

NOTES

1. One *can* have peripheral and non-peripheral high-mid and low-mid vowels, despite the accepted 'tense/lax' distinction of Chomsky and Halle (1968). For the high-mid vowels, the IPA has separate symbols already: [ɪ ʊ] as opposed to [e o], although these have to do double duty as the 'lax' high vowels. In fact, the usual 'General' RP vowels (and the American and Scottish Standard English equivalents) are most likely high-mid (Gimson 1962: 38–45).

   For low-mid vowels, there are no separate symbols (though there should be). However, one can call the RP monophthong in *law* decidedly more peripheral than, say, the Philadelphia one – to pick an American dialect with a low-mid monophthong. This difference is perhaps responsible for the discrepancies encountered in measuring tenseness by bioelectric activity in the oral cavity muscles between American and British researchers (Catford 1977). 'Tense', peripheral /ɛ/ types are found in old-fashioned RP, in the Newcastle monophthong of words like *air*, and in much Scottish Standard English, particularly among East Central speakers; non-peripheral ones in some General RP, north English and North American dialects. I get a better approximation to the pre-Second World War RP BET vowel if I push my tongue forwards from my native 'lax' /ɛ/ position than if I raise it, which gives something like the Australian /ɛ/ instead. The old-fashioned RP /æ/ in CAT is likewise peripheral, as are some 'corrected' /æ/ types in Chicago English.

2. An exception is on the Plain of York, where the lengthened /a:/ (apparently /a:/) is distinct from Old English /a:/, which is higher, and must have already been /æ:/ by the time of lengthening (Johnston 1992).

3. *Wob* and *wub* forms in this word are not attested in Older Scots, but *wab* is (Robinson 1985: 764). We cannot tell whether or not these existed this early as conditioned variants depending on the following labial, but the well-known process of *off*-Lowering apparently did not apply to it.

4. BET plus /n/ was already transferred to BIT in Early Scots times, parallel to its development in any other form of English, as spellings from the fourteenth century like *hing*, *Inglis* (Robinson 1985: 315) show.

4

The Syntax of Older Scots

Lilo Moessner

4.1 INTRODUCTION

The ancestor of the Scots language is the Northumbrian dialect of Old English. In the history of Scots, it plays the same role as the West Saxon dialect in the history of English. Strictly speaking, the runic inscription which is known as *The Dream of the Rood* on the Ruthwell Cross in Dumfries is the first Scots written document; it dates from the eighth century. Yet the texts which we usually associate with the beginning of Scots were written in the second half of the fourteenth century (e.g., John Barbour, *The Bruce*, *The Craft of Deying*), but the manuscripts in which they have come down to us are unfortunately about 100 years younger.

The database[1] for this study includes prose and verse texts from the very beginnings up to 1700. The focus, however, is on the sixteenth century, because this is linguistically the most interesting period. Scotland had become an independent national state with a language which was clearly distinct from that of its southern neighbours. This was already noted by contemporary observers. Don Pedro de Ayala, the Spanish ambassador at the court of James IV, wrote in a letter to Ferdinand and Isabella in 1498 that the language of the Scottish king was as different from English as Aragonese from Castilian (Watt 1920: 158).

Under the growing influence of the English court after the Union of the Crowns in 1603, the Scots adapted their native language more and more to the southern prestige variety. As syntactic structures are notoriously slow to change, the increasing anglicisation is most prominent in spelling and morphology. It reached its climax at the beginning of the eighteenth century with the Union of the Parliaments in 1707. This historical event is therefore an appropriate endpoint of the first part of the history of the Scots language.

In a publication which covers several centuries of linguistic development in one volume, it is quite natural that the description of the syntactic structure cannot be exhaustive. The aspects which are selected will necessarily reflect the author's own research interests. Therefore some readers will look in vain for such sections as word order, number concord, or negation. It is hoped, however, that at least the basic syntactic structures of Older Scots are included. The description proceeds from the simpler to the more complex structures. It starts with syntagms which in their most reduced form consist of one word only, the verbal and the nominal syntagms. Here the stress is on their constituent structure. Then the basic clause constituents, subject and predicate, are treated. In the section about the predicate, different types of verbal complementation are distinguished, and their realisation possibilities are outlined. The last part deals with constituents of the complex sentence. Each pattern is described with respect to its constituent structure and to the functions which it can realise in a larger context.

4.2   VERBAL SYNTAGMS

The only compulsory constituent of an Older Scots clause is a predicate. Its nucleus is realised by a verbal syntagm, which can but need not be complemented. Three types of verbal syntagms have to be distinguished; they will be called the active verbal syntagm, the copulative syntagm, and the passive syntagm. This distinction is appropriate, because these syntagms have different syntactic properties. Only the copulative syntagm can govern an adjectival syntagm, which denotes a quality of the person or object denoted by the subject. Only the passive syntagm can govern a prepositional syntagm which denotes the agent of the activity or state which is expressed in the predicate.

4.2.1   The Active Verbal Syntagm

The nucleus of the active verbal syntagm consists of a lexical verb; it can but it need not be expanded. If it is not expanded, the nucleus is realised as an inflected verb form: *the deuil tempis a man* (DE 43).[2] One possible expansion is by a modal auxiliary, e.g. *can*, *couth*, *may*, *mycht*, *sall*, *suld*, *will*, *wald*, *dar*, *durst*, *man/mone* 'must', *mote* 'may', *thar* 'need'. In texts of the seventeenth century, we find additionally the forms *must*, *need*, and *dought* 'could'. If a modal auxiliary is the only expansion, it is followed by the infinitive of the lexical verb:

> *thai mone dee* (DE 175)
> *whan he fand me lying Sick, At Gogor Bridge, and dought not speak* (WAT 62.653f.) '[I] could not speak'

Although Brown and Miller (1982: 12) claim that the combination of two modal auxiliaries 'is not a new feature of the language', I could not find one single instance of this construction.

Another expansion is realised by a form of *have* or *be* to express pastness. It conditions the following element in the past-participle form. The tense marker *be* expands verbs of motion, but these can also be expanded by *have*:

> *he Wes cummyn [. . .] Neir to the place* (BRU XII.3ff.)
> *jhesus [. . .] has cummyn jn this waurld* (WIS 17.20ff.)

The third possible expansion resembles the English progressive aspect. It is realised by a form of *be* and followed by a present participle. An aspectual meaning can, however, not be established; this is why I will call this expansion type 'pseudo-progressive': *ve haue fled fast fra oure enemeis, quhen ther vas nocht mony of them perseuuand vs* (COM 29.6f.).

Finally, a causative expansion is realised by the verb *ger/gar*. Like the modal auxiliaries, it conditions the following element to occur in the infinitive: *the merschale Gart bring watter* (OWL 678f.).

Several expansion types can be combined in front of the same lexical verb. A modal auxiliary can be combined with an expansion either by a tense marker, by a pseudo-progressive expansion, or by a causative expansion. The combinations are realised in this order with modal auxiliaries and the causative expansion conditioning the next element to be in the infinitive, the tense marker conditioning the verb to be in the past participle, and the pseudo-progressive marker conditioning the verb to be in the present participle:

> *na man wald haif had suspicioun* (BELL 98.1)
> *there sal be no man follouuand ʒou* (COM 24.27f.)
> *ʒe sall ger mak [yow] tharof king* (BRU I.491)

When the tense marker and the causative expansion co-occur, they follow each other in this sequence with the causative verb in the past-participle form and the lexical verb in the infinitive: *men has gert ʒow wndirstand* (BRU II.102). A combination of the causative with the pseudo-progressive expansion is not attested in the database, and the earliest examples of the combination of a tense marker and a pseudo-progressive marker date from the middle of the sixteenth century:

> *thai hed bene dansand* (COM 55.6)
> *as plutois paleis hed been birnand* (COM 42.20)

Whereas the expansions described above show various combination possibilities, there are some which do not combine at all. They are followed by the bare infinitive or by the infinitive preceded by *to*.

Modal auxiliaries which are followed by the infinitive with *to* are *aw/aucht* and *be*:

> *man aw to part with thir gudis glaidly* (DE 194f.)
> *few nobillis or prudent men wer to geif him counsale* (BELL 88.25f.) 'could advise him'

This list is expanded in the sixteenth century by *vsit*, in the seventeenth century by *need* and *vse*:

> *[seruandis] berijt it in þe myddis on þe samyn, quhair þe streme vsit to pas* (BELL 96.25f.)
> *Vse often to pray* (DOR 39.17)
> *He needed not to bid me twice* (WAT 13.60)

An expansion by *gin* (present) or *gan* (past) can be followed by the bare infinitive or by the *to*-infinitive. Although formally similar to the expansion by a modal auxiliary, it is syntactically and semantically different; syntactically, because it does not combine with other expansions, semantically, because *gin/gan* does not add a modal component. Expansions by *gin/gan* occur mainly in verse texts, where they are used for metrical reasons, providing an extra syllable or allowing the shift of a desired rhyme word to the end of the line:

> *And to the wyndow gan I walk in hye* (KI 207)
> *The marschell till the hall gan ga* (BRU II.10)
> *Esperus his lampis gan to light* (KI 502)

Causative expansions which are not attested in combination with other expansions are realised by *do*, *make* and *cause*. The causative verb *do* is followed by the bare infinitive, *make* by the infinitive with *to*, and *cause* occurs with either:

> *warldly wight that dooth me sike* (KI 304)
> *sum twig may wag and mak hir to wake* (KI 420)
> *god causis ws to haue þe gret gift of pite* (WIS 4f.)
> *Your Page it will cause disappear* (WAT 15.141)

The periphrastic auxiliary *do*, which is always followed by the bare infinitive, is absent from the early texts. It begins to appear in the sixteenth century in affirmative statements. Here my findings are in line with those of Meurman-Solin (1993a: 263), who claims that 'the device seems to have been introduced into Scottish prose as late as in the 1550s'. I also agree that 'it may be necessary to look at some more material' (1993a: 211), because the inclusion or non-inclusion of text passages can have a considerable effect on our results. Meurman-Solin's extract of *The Complaynt of Scotland* contains no evidence of periphrastic *do*; since I included the whole text, I counted at least seven unambiguous examples:

> *i did spaceir vp and doune* (COM 38.3f.)
> *baytht horse & meyris did fast nee* (COM 39.3f.)

The first occurrences of periphrastic *do* in verse texts date from the same time, i.e., the middle of the sixteenth century. Like *gin*, it is a convenient means to provide an extra syllable or allow the lexical verb to be shifted into rhyme position:

> *Quhen he in Carthage did arryue*
> *And did the seige of Troy discryue* (MEL 877f.)

The functionless, automatic element *do* which characterises negative statements and questions in Modern Scots, is the exception rather than the rule in Older Scots:

> *Gyf thou obeyis nocht the voce to the lorde thy gode* (COM 24.2f.)
> *I do not care for Feid or Favour* (WAT 30.180)
> *Seis thou noght hir that sittis thee besyde* (KI 376)

4.2.2 The Copulative Syntagm

The structure of the copulative syntagm resembles that of the active verbal syntagm, but it is much simpler. It has a linking verb as its nucleus, i.e. a verb which can govern a substantival, an adjectival, or a prepositional syntagm. The most common linking verb is *be*; others are *worth*, *becum* 'become' and *seem*. The nucleus can be expanded by a modal auxiliary and by a tense marker. Both expansions can be combined in this order. The usual tense marker in the copulative syntagm is *have*; occasionally the nucleus *becum* is expanded by *be*. The inventory of modal auxiliaries is the same as in the active verbal syntagm. High-frequency modal auxiliaries in the copulative syntagm are *sall*, *suld*, *may*, *mycht*, *can*, and *wald*:

(a) expansion = modal auxiliary

he wald in his chambre be (BRU II.7)

Several modal auxiliaries can be linked by *and* or *or*:

he is mare besy fore our gud than we our self can ore may be (DE 32f.)

(b) expansion = tense marker

we þat has bene maid haly jn þe bapteme (WIS 35.25f.)
i am be cum ane begger (COM 123.17) 'have become'

(c) expansion = modal + tense

it mycht haf beyne Cauß of thair tynsale (BRU XII.94f.)

The only modal auxiliary which conditions the *to*-infinitive of the linking verb is *aucht*:

we, [. . .], aucht till be Worthy (BRU XII.231ff.)

4.2.3   The Passive Syntagm

The passive syntagm is the verbal syntagm of passive sentences. Its nucleus is complex; it consists of the past participle of a lexical verb and a form of either *be* or *becum*. This complex nucleus can be expanded by a modal auxiliary, by a tense marker, or by a causative expansion. It is to be assumed that the tense marker can be realised by *have* or *be*, but since the database contains no examples with *become* as a constituent of the nucleus of the passive syntagm, only the tense marker *have* is attested. The most frequent modal auxiliaries in passive syntagms are *may, mycht, sal, suld, mot,* and *mon.* Expansions by a modal auxiliary and by a tense marker can co-occur. The causative expansion does not combine with any other expansion:

(a) modal expansion

jt mone be fulfillit (WIS 38.24)

(b) tense expansion

That [. . .] had noght bene sene (KI 339)

(c) causative expansion

The pepill, [. . .], gart all þe wiches be brynt (BELL 95.18ff.)

(d) modal + tense expansion

Thai mycht nocht haiff beyn tane throw mycht (BRU I.527)

The modal auxiliary *be*, which does not combine with another expansion, conditions the *to*-infinitive of the nucleus of the passive syntagm. In texts of the seventeenth century, we find the modal auxiliary *vse* with the same properties:

> *this lytill trety, [. . .], is to be notyde* (DE 4f.)
> *the doctryne of the euangelistis is nocht to be kepit be cristin men* (COM 31.4f.) 'need not be respected'
> *two diseases, wherewith it vseth oft to be infected* (DOR 43.25f.)

In a special type of passive construction, the passive syntagm consists of a form of *have* or *get* and the past participle of a lexical verb. As a rule, the passive syntagm in this construction type is realised as a discontinuous constituent (for a detailed description of this type of passive construction, see section 4.4.3):

> *King Athelstane [. . .] gatt all municionis, strenthis and townis randrit to him at his plesir* (BELL 88.15ff.)
> *þai suld [. . .] haif [. . .] þair realme defendit fra þair inymyis* (BELL 92.29ff.)

4.3 NOMINAL SYNTAGMS

Nominal syntagms have a substantive, an adjective, or a pronoun as their nucleus. All three types can function as complements of verbal syntagms; substantival and pronominal syntagms can also function as subjects and as complements of prepositions, substantival syntagms additionally as adverbial complements. They are established as different types of nominal syntagms not only because they realise different syntactic functions, but also because of their different constituent structure.

4.3.1 The Substantival Syntagm

The most striking feature of this syntagm is the variability in the arrangement of its constituents. Its nucleus is a substantive, which can be expanded. But even the so-called countable substantives occur with and without determiner:

> *i sau ane erb callit barba aaron, quhilk vas gude remeid for emoroyades of the fundament* (COM 67.2f.) [without determiner]
> *i sau the vattir lille, qhilk is ane remeid contrar gomoria* (COM 67.6ff.) [with determiner]

On the basis of the position of the expansions with respect to the nucleus, we distinguish premodifiers, and postmodifiers. Premodifiers are subdivided into predeterminers, determiners, postdeterminers and modifiers. They follow each other in this order. Among the expansion types which always follow the nucleus are relative clauses, infinitive constructions, conjunctional clauses, participle constructions, adverbs and *thairof* 'of it'.

4.3.1.1 Premodification

Predeterminers are *all* and *bayth*. They can be combined with elements in all other premodification positions apart from the indefinite article and indefinite pronouns:

(a) predeterminer + determiner

> *all this caβ* (BRU I.563)
> *baytht thir documentis* (COM 130.7)

(b) predeterminer + postdeterminer

> *all vthire thingis* (WIS 32.2)

(c) predeterminer + modifier

> *all gud werk* (DE 9)

The most frequent elements in determiner position are possessive adjectives, demonstrative adjectives, the definite and the indefinite article, the inflected form *quhois/quhais* of the relative pronoun *quha* as well as some indefinite pronouns like *sum*, and substantival syntagms themselves. Some determiners can be expanded themselves, e.g. possessive adjectives by the intensifier *awn*, demonstrative adjectives by the intensifiers *ilk* and *self*, the definite article by the intensifier *same*:

(a) determiner = possessive adjective

> *my quorroll* (MEL 1273)
> *our awne land* (BRU XII.239)

(b) determiner = demonstrative adjective

> *ʒon man* (BRU II.105)
> *that ilk nycht* (BRU I.512) 'that same night'
> *that self tyme* (BRU XII.2)

(c) determiner = definite article

> *the ded* (DE 18) 'the death'
> *þe sammyn gud lord* (WIS 38.3f.)

(d) determiner = indefinite article

> *ane baitt* (BELL 34.15) 'a boat'

(e) determiner = *quhois/quhais*

> *quhois penance* (KI 487)

(f) determiner = indefinite pronoun

> *sum bird* (KI 409)
> *ilk temporall man* (DE 48) 'every temporal man'

(g) determiner = substantival syntagm

Substantival syntagms in determiner position express the semantic relation of possession. Their nucleus, which can also be premodified, is usually marked by a genitive ending. The only postmodifier of such a nucleus is *awn*:

> *The pure howlatis appele* (OWL 850) 'the poor owl's appeal'
> *god Cupidis owin princesse* (KI 295)

In the following examples, the genitive of the substantive in determiner position is unmarked:

> *the kyng of ingland saue conduct* (COM 107.32f.) 'the King of England's safe conduct'
> *his systir son* (BRU I.557) 'the son of his sister'

Occasionally, we find a 'split genitive', i.e., a genitive determiner which is realised as a discontinuous constituent:

> *the kyngis dochtir of vest mure land* (COM 63.20f.) 'the King of Westmorland's daughter'
> *þe nobillis childeryn of France* (BELL 26.32f.) 'the children of the French noblemen'

As a rule, the nucleus of a substantival syntagm can only be premodified by one element in determiner position. Very rarely, one finds the combination of a demonstrative and a possessive adjective, of a demonstrative adjective and a substantival syntagm, or the combination of a substantival syntagm and a possessive adjective in front of the same nucleus. In the latter combination, the possessive adjective is usually interpreted as genitive marker:

> *that his service* (LAU 209.4)
> *this the said patrikis ansuer* (GG 233.1)
> *that gud his grace* (OWL 86) 'the good one's grace'
> *this present Dutches hir body* (LAU 208.20)

Elements which realise the position postdeterminer are numerals, ordinals, and *vther* 'other'; numerals and *vther* can co-occur:

> *the vij hevinly wertuis* (WIS 18.24)
> *the fyften day* (BRU II.17) 'the fifteenth day'
> *vthire haly men* (DE 55)
> *vthir tua heydis* (COM 161.14) 'two more heads'

The most frequent expansion in modifier position is by adjectival syntagms, i.e. by adjectives with or without modifier. Other elements in the same position are present and past participles:

> *A weill gret quhile* (BRU II.8)

зon othir ioly rout (BRU XII.180)
euill disponit persounis (WIS 39.2)
quaking spangis (KI 323) 'trembling spangles'

Several adjectives can be simply juxtaposed or linked by *and* in the modifier position:

this sueit, nobile and hevinly affeccioune (WIS 38.8)
The scharp[e] grene suete ienepere (KI 221)

Adjectival syntagms are most variable with respect to their position. They can either precede the nucleus of a substantival syntagm or follow it, or partly precede and partly follow it:

ane bailfull bikker (MEL 1122) 'a dire encounter'
wandis long and small (KI 213)
his blisfull grace benigne (KI 270)
Hir fair fresche face, as quhite as ony snawe (KI 465)

In an even more complex combination of premodification and postmodification, the second adjective is preceded by *and* and optionally by the indefinite article:

his naturale sone & eternale (WIS 25.19)
ane gud knycht and hardy (BRU XII.30)

Adjectival syntagms of a complex constituent structure follow the nucleus:

This gardyn full of flouris (KI 299)
all thingis necessare for our saluacioune (WIS 18.15f.)

Most premodifiers can also occur after the substantive, even such unexpected elements as numerals, ordinals, and *all*. This strange position of these expansions is mostly found in verse texts for the usual reasons of rhyme and rhythm. In this case, other postmodifiers are excluded:

(a) postmodifying predeterminer

my wittis all (KI 282)

(b) postmodifying postdeterminer

yeris twise nyne (KI 173)
the copill next (KI 230)

In the following example, the expansion of the substantival nucleus is realised as a discontinuous constituent; the numeral follows the nucleus, and the restrictive modifier of the numeral, *onely*, precedes it:

onely wommen tueyne (KI 291)

4.3.1.2   Postmodification

Structurally simple postmodifiers are adverbials and *thairof: a lyf without* (KI 223) 'a creature outside'; *þe inhabitantis þerof* (BELL 35.1). The other postmodifiers are structurally complex, i.e. relative clauses, participle constructions, conjunctional clauses and infinitive constructions (for their constituent structure, see sections 4.6.1 and 4.6.3–4.6.5):

(a) relative clause

> *þis hevinly Orisoune, þat he has teichit ws* (WIS 18.19)
> *darius kyng of perse, quha hed euer ane ardant desyir to conqueis greice* (COM 87.20f.)
> *a gude ende, the quhilk makis al werk perfyte* (DE 8)
> *the freschest yong[e] floure That euer I sawe, me thoght, before that houre* (KI 277f.)

(b) participle construction

> *that sanct, walking in the schade* (KI 432)
> *The apostile writtand to þe pepil of Ephis* (WIS 25.11)
> *þe airis maill gottin betuix þame* (BELL 86.19)

(c) conjunctional clause

Postmodifying conjunctional clauses, also known as appositive clauses, are introduced by *that/at*, *gif/if* or *quhethir* 'whether'. They have to be distinguished from relative clauses introduced by *that/at*. The nuclei which are modified by appositive clauses are abstract, often deverbal substantives:

> *confidence, at oure peticioune and prayere be hard & grauntit be the hie grace and maieste*
>   *of the fadere* (WIS 29.8f.)
> *a takyne at thai luf hyme nocht* (DE 122f.)

(d) infinitive construction

There are two types of infinitive constructions, which postmodify nuclei of substantival syntagms. One type corresponds to relative clauses, the other to appositive clauses:

> *a warldly creature, On quhom to rest myn eye* (KI 352f.)
> *mony threatningis to haue the said patrikis lyff* (GG 233.17f.)

A syntagm, which usually follows the nucleus of a substantival syntagm, but which can also precede it, is the prepositional syntagm. The most frequent preposition is *of*, but other prepositions occur as well:

> *The fyrst day off thar assemble* (BRU I.600)
> *off hevyn king* (BRU II.144)
> *a man in his deing* (DE 43)
> *to the erll of Herfurd cosyne* (BRU XII.31) 'a cousin of the Earl of Hereford'

Apart from adverbs and *thairof*, which are not attested in combination with any other type of postmodification, postmodifiers can either be juxtaposed after the same nucleus, or they can be linked by *and*:

(a) prepositional syntagm + participle construction

> *the distructione of the superb troy, exsecutit be the princis of greice* (COM 25.16f.)

(b) participle construction + relative clause

> *thir mecanyc pepil heffand superflu prosperite, that refusis the genoligie of there fathere ande mothere* (COM 142.28ff.)

(c) infinitive construction + conjunctional clause

> *confidence to pray to him and þat our prayere be admittit* (WIS 30.20f.).

4.3.2 The Adjectival Syntagm

The nucleus of an adjectival syntagm is an adjective, which can be expanded. As in the substantival syntagm, expansions can precede or follow the nucleus. Intensifying adverbs usually precede it, e.g. *all, full, ouer, richt, sa*; only *inewch* follows it:

> *oure vit is ouer febil, oure ingyne ouer harde, oure thochtis ouer vollage, and oure ʒeiris ouer schort* (COM 22.2ff.)
> *to be inducit and ourecummyn js richt euill and miserabile* (WIS 23.2f.)
> *a full hevy byrdinge* (DE 19) 'a very heavy burden'
> *he wes traist inewch* (BRU I.627) 'sufficiently trustworthy'

The postmodifiers in the adjectival syntagm are comparable to those in the substantival syntagm, but the variety in the latter is greater. Shared postmodifiers are prepositional syntagms, infinitive constructions, and conjunctional clauses:

(a) prepositional syntagm

> *þis haly Orisoune js full of humilite* (WIS 20.12f.)
> *he that is ferme in the faithe* (DE 59)

(b) infinitive construction

> *worthy to have thaim to thare bruþir, redemar & helpare* (DE 85f.)
> *boune [. . .] To tak with him the gud and ill* (BRU II.160f.)
> *Than wes the Squyer diligent To declair monie sindrie storie* (MEL 1032f.)

(c) conjunctional clause

> *full blyth, That he had gottyn that respyt* (BRU II.2f.)
> *gyf he be blyth at he deis in the faith of crist and of haly kirk* (DE 217f.)

Prepositional syntagms and infinitive constructions can also precede the nucleus. Yet this position is found only in verse texts:

> *that we To meit our fais [ay] be boune* (BRU XII.326f.)
> *I am not in Lufe expart* (MEL 1157)
> *He wes off his eschap sary* (BRU II.65)

The morphologically composite postmodifier *tharto* is parallel to the postmodifier *thairof* in the substantival syntagm: *nan was worthy þarto* (DE 71f.)

A complex type of modification is given when an adjective forms part of a comparison construction. Two types of comparison constructions have to be distinguished, comparisons of equivalence and comparisons of non-equivalence. In the former, the quality denoted by the adjective is attributed in the same degree, in the latter in different degrees. Comparisons of equivalence are expressed by *as . . . as*: *Hir fair fresche face, as quhite as ony snawe* (KI 465). In comparisons of non-equivalence, the adjective is in the comparative, either formed by an ending or by the preposed comparative element *mair/more*. The part of the expansion which follows the adjective can be introduced by different elements. The most frequent comparative element is *then/than*, which is attested in the whole period. In the very early prose texts *The Craft of Deying* and *The Meroure of Wiβdome*, we find additionally *na*, and from the mid-sixteenth century *nor* can be used in verse and in prose texts:

> *he is mare besy for our gud than we our self can ore may be* (DE 32f.)
> *he Suld pas to mare Ioy na fore* (DE 169f.)
> *thir tua doctours, agustin & lactantius, var mair expert in theologie nor thai var in*
>   *cosmographie* (COM 51.11ff.)
> *þai come in þe Firth of Taye, quhar þai fand litill bettir fortoun þan afoir* (BELL 92.15f.)

4.3.3 The Pronominal Syntagm

Although interrogative pronouns and relative pronouns function also as nuclei of pronominal syntagms, they need no special attention here, because their constituent structure is very simple. If they are expanded at all, they are postmodified by a prepositional syntagm. Structurally more complex are pronominal syntagms whose nucleus is realised by a personal, a demonstrative, or an indefinite pronoun. Premodifiers are rare in these pronominal syntagms, too; *all* is attested in front of personal and demonstrative pronouns, *ouer* as a premodifier of *mony*:

> *al them that ar of his companye* (COM 159.20)
> *ouer mony that beleuis in the opinione of Scocrates* (COM 35.12f.)

Apart from conjunctional clauses and *thairof*, personal, demonstrative and indefinite pronouns have the same postmodifiers as substantival syntagms, namely relative clauses, participle constructions, infinitive constructions, prepositional syntagms, and adverbs:

> *all þai quhilkis wer of þis opinioun* (BELL 38.16)
> *mony that knauis the cause of thir mutations* (COM 21.34)

he, not being content with this the said patrikis ansuer (GG 232.32ff.)
to be one of tho Him trewly for to serue in wele and wo (KI 272f.)
ilkane of þir twa pepill (BELL 34.9)
Then slayn wes mony thowsand Of thaim withowt (BRU I.524f.) 'those outside'

4.4   TYPES OF VERB COMPLEMENTATION

Depending on the type of verbal syntagm by which the nucleus of a predicate is realised, it contains up to two non-verbal complements. They are governed by the nucleus.

4.4.1   Complements of Copulative Syntagms

Copulative syntagms may, but need not govern a non-verbal syntagm. It has been argued for several languages that copulative syntagms must be complemented (Strang 1968: 203 for Present-day English), that otherwise a verb with a different meaning was involved. This argument is valid neither for Present-day English nor for Older Scots: *j say þat god is, and þat he js in hevin* (WIS 31.16). In the first clause, the copulative syntagm *is* is not complemented, in the second clause it governs the complement *in hevin*. The paraphrase 'exists', which may be suggested for the first occurrence of *is*, can also be used for its second occurrence. Those who insist that there is a meaning difference between the two items *is* should also postulate a meaning difference between the two occurrences of *hear* in the following example, where nobody would claim that two different verbs *hear* are involved:

> *The byschop hard, and had pite* (BRU II.113)
> *quhen the Bruce had herd his will* (BRU II.162)

There is as much less information in the predicate *hard* than in the predicate *had herd his will* as there is in the predicate *is* than in the predicate *js in hevin*. A description which postulated two verbs *be* would also have to postulate two verbs *hear*, and such a description would not only be inadequate but also unnecessarily complex.

The syntagm which is governed by the copulative syntagm will be called copulative complement. Its most frequent realisations are by a substantival, an adjectival, and a prepositional syntagm. Usually the copulative complement follows the copulative syntagm, but especially in verse texts, it can also precede it.

(a) copulative complement = substantival syntagm

> *we ar his creaturys and handewerkis* (DE 34)
> *they wer euer Luiferis fo* (MEL 1188) 'lovers' enemy'
> *Gif ye a goddess be* (KI 302)

(b) copulative complement = adjectival syntagm

> *he yong was* (OWL 602)
> *þe pane js gret* (WIS 49.27f.)
> *He wes angry out of mesur* (BRU I.570)

(c) copulative complement = prepositional syntagm

> *My seyle is nocht all tyme with me* (BRU I.616)
> *he wes of þair blude* (BELL 91.20)
> *þai wer of sik pyssance and multitude* (BELL 88.8)

Prepositional syntagms in this function often denote the place where the subject is located (compare BRU I.616), but other semantic relations are also possible (compare BELL 91.20). In the following example several prepositional syntagms are coordinated; they stand in different semantic relations to the subject: *The tothir monstour wes in Northumberland, of manis figure, with ane wame fra þe navill doun* (BELL 88.37ff.)

Other, less frequent realisations of the copulative complement are primary adverbs, conjunctional clauses, nominal relative clauses, and infinitive constructions:

(d) copulative complement = primary adverb

> *This Squyer and the Ladie trew Was thair* (MEL 1213f.)

(e) copulative complement = conjunctional clause

> *The first is, that we haf the richt* (BRU XII.235)
> *the thrid thing requirit jn oure part þat þis peticioune be grauntit to us js, þat we forgif oure nychtbouris þe offensis and trespassis done agane us* (WIS 50.8ff.)

(f) copulative complement = nominal relative clause

> *J am at j am* (WIS 31.22)

(g) copulative complement = infinitive construction

> *in-paciens or vntholmudnes, the quhilk is nocht to luf god abwne al thinge* (DE 108f.)
> *the onely way to bring you to this knowledge, is diligently to reade his word, and earnestly to pray for the right vnderstanding therof* (DOR 29.7ff.)

Beside the copulative complement, the copulative syntagm can also govern an additional non-verbal complement, which expresses the beneficiary. It will be called object, and it is realised by a pronominal or a prepositional syntagm. If the nucleus of the pronominal syntagm is a personal pronoun, it is in object case:

> *all that was vs necessarye* (KI 155)
> *the passage of this vrechit warlde, [. . .], semys harde, perelus ande rycht horrebile to mony men* (DE 1ff.)
> *temptacione Is rycht prophetable tyll ws* (DE 209f.)

4.4.2 Complements of Active Verbal Syntagms

Depending on the nucleus of the active verbal syntagm, it governs either one or two non-verbal syntagms, or it is the only constituent of the predicate. The latter type of predicate will be called intransitive:

> *he chapyt wes* (BRU II.24)
> *The lordis leuch* (OWL 828) 'the lords laughed'

All other types of predicate will be called non-intransitive. In those with one complement, this complement will be called object. Two basic realisations of this object have to be distinguished, namely that by a substantival or pronominal syntagm on the one, and by a prepositional syntagm or an adverb on the other hand. Predicates with objects realised by substantival or pronominal syntagms often have passive counterparts. Predicates with objects realised by prepositional syntagms or adverbs are not passivisable. Without making any claims about passivisability, I will refer to the first kind of objects as direct and to the second as prepositional objects. Many of the verbs which govern prepositional objects denote a movement to or from a place.

(a) direct object = substantival syntagm

> *na thing mycht brek his invincibill curage* (BELL 266.1)
> *the king saw the endentur* (BRU I.569)
> *we desyre the stat of beatitud* (WIS 42.28)

(b) direct object = pronominal syntagm

> *he him thankit humyly* (BRU I.578)
> *thay tak me* (MEL 1247)
> *I neede not to delate them* (DOR 31.15f.)

When the direct object is realised by a personal or a demonstrative pronoun, this pronoun usually refers back to a substantive mentioned before, as in the following example where *it* refers back to *seyle* 'seal' in the line before: *Ik have ane othir it to ber* (BRU I.617).

When such a definite reference is not possible, the situation is similar to that of so-called impersonal subjects (see section 4.5.1). They will analogically be called grammatical objects. Like grammatical subjects, they can be followed by lexical objects, which are realised by complex structures, preferably by conjunctional clauses:

> *They did bot kis, as I suppois it* (MEL 1154)
> *I trow, and knawis it all cleirly, That mony ane hart sall vaverand be* (BRU XII.185)

(c) prepositional object

> *on the morn to court he went* (BRU I.601)
> *I raikit till ane reveir* (OWL 12)
> *Sum [. . .] on the Squyer followit fast* (MEL 1232f.)
> *Thir twa brethir succedit to þair faderis landis* (BELL 87.3f.)
> *gyf he wylfully consent thar-to* (DE 62)

More complex realisations of the direct object include infinitive constructions, participle constructions, conjunctional clauses, simple clauses, and nominal relative clauses (for their constituent structure, see sections 4.6.1–4.6.5):

(a) direct object = infinitive construction

> *al men that [. . .] suld leir to de* (DE 34f.) 'should learn to die'
> *the Erle off Carryk Clamys to govern the kynryk* (BRU II.103f.)
> *The pape commandit [. . .] to wryte in all landis* (OWL 131)
> *thai will nocht here spek at thai suld de* (DE 202) 'they do not want to hear somebody say that they should die'
> *ik herd neuir in romanys tell Off man sa hard [sted] as wes he* (BRU II.46f.)
> *this lustie ʒoung Squyar Saw this Ladie [. . .] Cum to his Chalmer* (MEL 940ff.)
> *thai hard nane mak ansuar* (BRU II.60)
> *The Denys, [. . .], belevitt grete felicite [. . .] to cum to þame* (BELL 87.14f.)
> *Vtheris, quhilkis traistit be deth of King Edward Langschankis grete alteracioun and troubill to follow* (BELL 268.18f.)

(b) direct object = participle construction

> *I sawe, walking [. . .] The fairest or the freschest yong[e] floure That euer I sawe* (KI 275ff.)
> *This Ladie [. . .] hard the Squyer [. . .] makand his mone* (MEL 917ff.)
> *scho [. . .] fand hir madinnis [. . .] Sleipand full sound* (MEL 1107ff.)
> *They left him lyand thair for deid* (MEL 1362)
> *he beheld it birnand* (COM 25.26)

(c) direct object = conjunctional clause

> *þe deuill assais gif he can gare ony man vare in the treuth* (DE 45)
> *The king [. . .] askyt, gyff it enselyt he* (BRU I.610ff.)
> *we desire þat his will be done* (WIS 41.3)
> *He [. . .] swour that he suld wengeance ta* (BRU I.570f.)

(d) direct object = simple clause

> *he saw thar wes na rede* (BRU I.546)
> *King Malcolme ansuerit, [. . .], he wes content to haif peace* (BELL 89.3ff.)
> *I beleue scho said not nay* (MEL 998)
> *The lord the Brwiβ [. . .] wend he spak bot suthfast thing* (BRU I.503f.) 'the lord Bruce thought he [=John Cumyn] spoke nothing but the truth'

(e) direct object = nominal relative clause

> *quhat sa euyr maid the debate [. . .] weill I wat* (BRU II.41f.)
> *To maynteym that he had begunnyn* (BRU II.189)
> *He sall haf that he wonnyn has* (BRU XII.129)

Very rarely, the direct object is realised by a complex sentence, e.g. a combination of a main and a subordinate clause: *to remembre, gif þai schew þame self wailȝeand for ane houre or twa, þai suld possede infinitte gudis and riches* (BELL 275.17f.). Here the conditional clause *gif þai [. . .] for ane houre or twa* is embedded as an adverbial complement in the matrix clause *þai suld possede [. . .] riches*. This complex sentence functions as the direct object of *remembre*.

A complex realisation of the prepositional object is by a nominal relative clause: *leit the laif gang quhair they pleisit* (MEL 1144) '[the squire] let the rest go where they pleased'.

Predicates with more than one complement contain a direct object and another non-verbal syntagm. Several construction types have to be distinguished. In one of them, the semantic relation between the direct object and the other complement is the same as that between the subject and the copulative complement. The other complement will therefore analogically be called verbal complement. Its most frequent realisations are substantival, adjectival, and prepositional syntagms as well as primary adverbs. When a verbal complement is present, the structure of the direct object is usually very simple; it is realised by a substantival or a pronominal syntagm.

(a) verbal complement = substantival syntagm

> *Arthur, that throw chevalry Maid Bretane maistres & lady Off twelf kin[rykis]* (BRU I.549ff.)
> *une that I think Flour of all* (MEL 910)
> *He tuik the Tyrane presonar* (MEL 1421)

(b) verbal complement = adjectival syntagm

> *a gude ende, the quhilk makis al werk perfyte* (DE 8)
> *a verray penytent man thinkis al his seknes lytill* (DE 128)
> *laboure to keepe sounde this conscience* (DOR 43.23)

(c) verbal complement = prepositional syntagm

> *Gif he micht find him in that hald* (MEL 1070)
> *Keepe God more sparingly in your mouth, but aboundantly in your hart* (DOR 51.13f.)

(d) verbal complement = adverb

> *he fand þame awaye* (BELL 277.27f.)

When the constituent following the direct object is realised by a past participle, it seems doubtful whether it should be analysed as a verbal complement. The test of the required semantic relation between the direct object and this constituent yields a construction which is structurally ambiguous. It can be interpreted as a copulative or as a passive construction. The analysis of the past participle as a verbal complement seems, however, more adequate because of the static meaning of the paraphrase. The past participle in this context has a more adjectival and less verbal character:

(e) verbal complement = past participle

> *hors and men slayn left thai thar* (BRU XII.136)
> *swa trowblyt the folk saw he* (BRU I.479)
> *quhen the deuill fyndis a man wexit and torment with seknes* (DE 76f.)

A similar analysis of present participles following the direct object is not possible. Therefore such constructions have to be analysed as complex direct objects realised by a participle construction with subject, e.g. *Quhen this gude Knicht the Squyer saw, Thus lyand in till his deid thraw* (MEL 1391f.) (for a more detailed description, see section 4.6.5).

Another construction type is given when the direct object is followed by a prepositional syntagm or an adverb which cannot be analysed as verbal complements. Here the second complement is a prepositional object; it often denotes a direction:

(a) prepositional object = prepositional syntagm

> *he hint hir in his armes* (MEL 960)
> *Thow dang seir Sutheroun to the ground* (MEL 1406) 'you struck many southerners
>   down'
> *he [. . .] suld [. . .] conferme his wyll to the wyll of gode* (DE 27f.)
> *to thank hyme of al his sayndis and gyftis* (DE 109f.)

(b) prepositional object = adverb

> *myn eye [. . .] adoun I kest* (KI 367f.)
> *thiddir somownys he [. . .] The barownys of his reawte* (BRU I.592f.)
> *he thankis hyme thar-of* (DE 222f.)

A more complex realisation of the prepositional object is by a conjunctional clause: *if my conscience had not resolued me, that all my Religion presently professed by me and my kingdome, was grounded vpon the plaine wordes of the Scripture* (DOR 31.20ff.)

In a last construction type, the active verbal syntagm governs two complements, one of which realises the semantic role of beneficiary or recipient. It will be called indirect object. The indirect object is usually realised by the object case of a personal pronoun, by a substantival or by a prepositional syntagm. In this construction type, the simplest realisation of the direct object is a pronominal or a substantival syntagm.

(a) indirect object = personal pronoun

> *he gaif hir ane lufe drowrie* (MEL 1003)
> *Makfagon [. . .] nouther left her kow nor hors* (MEL 1055ff.)

(b) indirect object = substantival syntagm

> *so mich gude It did my wofull hert* (KI 353f.)

(c) indirect object = prepositional syntagm

> *he gaif to the maist synare maist mercy and grace* (DE 103f.)
> *our fader of hevin prouid to us temporale sustinaunce* (WIS 44.9f.)
> *That he ma till his men gud cher* (BRU II.6)

More complex realisations of the direct object include conjunctional clauses, infinitive constructions and nominal relative clauses:

(a) direct object = conjunctional clause

> *I ȝow pray, That ilk man for his awne honour Purvay hym a gud baneour* (BRU XII.218ff.)
> *i exort the that thou cause al thy membris concur to gyddir* (COM 161.24f.)

(b) direct object = infinitive construction

> *god hes permittit the inglis men to scurge vs* (COM 27.5)
> *oure lord jhesu biddis ws demand at oure fadere of hevin oure necessare thingis* (WIS 45.17f.)
> *gif God me had deuisit To lyve my lyf in thraldome* (KI 190f.)
> *Who [. . .] Requested him right earnestly To send the silly Beast Supply* (WAT 51.331ff.)

(c) direct object = nominal relative clause

> *he thame gaif quhat they wald haue* (MEL 1442)

The following examples show that different realisations of the direct object can be combined in one single sentence: *he than urgeid the said mr williame to go with him to rothemay, and that he sould tak on with him and that he sould decyde his querrell with the said mr william and his bruther* (GG 237.6ff.); *He [. . .] tauld him haly all his state, & quhat he was, & als how-gat The Clyffurd held his heritage: And that he come to mak homage Till him* (BRU II.153ff.)

4.4.3 Complements of Passive Syntagms

As passive constructions are related to their active counterparts such that the direct objects of the active constructions function as subjects in the passive, we can expect that passive syntagms can govern the same constituents as active verbal syntagms except direct objects, i.e. verbal complements, prepositional objects, and indirect objects.

(a) verbal complement

> *sic folkis suld erar be callyt bestis vnraconable than man rasonable* (DE 183f.)
> *the toune hes bein called Desertum* (LAU 207.24f.)
> *I am formed so fowle* (OWL 102)
> *Sa wes his matter left vndrest* (MEL 1492)

(b) prepositional object

> *the Brwce to dede war brocht* (BRU I.581)
> *thir temptacions at will be put to hyme* (DE 216)

(c) indirect object

> *there is an expresse and most notable exhortation and commandement giuen them* (DOR 29.17ff.)
> *2 were brought him* (LAU 205.16)

A comparison between the passage *the Bruce to dede war brocht* (BRU I.581; under (b) above) and the last example might suggest an analysis of *him* as a prepositional object, because the same verb is involved. This analysis must be rejected, because *him* denotes the person who profited from the act of bringing, i.e. the beneficiary, not a direction.

In passive counterparts of active predicates with a direct and an indirect object, the passive syntagm can also govern a direct object. In this case, the indirect object of the active construction corresponds to the subject in the passive construction.

(a) direct object = infinitive construction

> *the grite toune of Babillon vas permittit be gode to scurge the pepil of israel* (COM 27.36f.)

(b) direct object = conjunctional clause

> *he suld be demandyt, Fyrst, gyf he be blyth at he deis in the faith of crist and of haly kirk* (DE 216ff.)

In a special type of passive construction, which does not occur before the sixteenth century, the passive syntagm is realised by a form of *have* or *get* and the past participle of a lexical verb. It always governs a direct object. In passive constructions of this type, the subject denotes not the agent of the action but a person who is affected by it. Sometimes, but not always, the subject initiates the action which is expressed by the passive syntagm. The direct object, which is placed between the two constituents of the passive syntagm, is usually realised by a personal pronoun in object case or by a substantival syntagm of a simple structure:

> *þai had wapynnis hyd in sum quiete place* (BELL 33.4f.)
> *Calene, quhilk was Thayn of Anguse and had vij sonnys slayne with King Donald in þis last batall* (BELL 58.23f.)

When such a passive construction corresponds to an active construction with a predicate containing a direct and an indirect object, the passive predicate governs also an indirect object. It is realised by a prepositional syntagm introduced by *to*:

> *he gatt þe crovn of Scotland tailʒeitt to him and his airis maill* (BELL 278.24f.)
> *thai gatt ane place gevin to þame be þe King in Pareiβ* (BELL 26.30f.)

The agent of the action denoted by the passive syntagm is an optional constituent of Older Scots passive constructions. It is not governed by the passive syntagm, but it expands the whole passive predicate. Therefore it is only for completeness' sake that its realisations are described here. It is realised by a prepositional syntagm; the usual preposition is *be*, but others occur as well, e.g. *of*, *with*, *throw*:

> *proffit þat may be desirit be mortale creature* (WIS 31.14f.)
> *Of inymyis takin and led away We weren all* (KI 166f.)
> *he with his fair Ladie Ressauit wes full plesantlie* (MEL 1149f.)
> *ane Petir Vaston þat was haittit nocht onlie with Inglißmen bot als with Scottis* (BELL 268.21f.)
> *in hys capitole wes he, Throw thaim of his consaill priue, Slayne* (BRU I.543f.)

4.5   SUBJECTS

The basic constituents of Older Scots clauses are the predicate and the subject. Whereas the predicate is an obligatory constituent, the subject is not. Subjectless clauses are more frequent in earlier than in later texts: *gyf It be his fre consent and be in his rycht mynde* (DE 205f.). Here two clauses with copulative predicates are linked by *and*; the subject of the first clause is *It*, the second clause has no subject. If the passage is to be translated into a language with a compulsory subject, a subject must be recovered from the context, e.g. 'if it is his free will, and he is in his right mind'.

Some occurrences of subjectless clauses can be accounted for by the text type. They are typical of the less explicit style of diaries and household books: *Having past over to Fyffe about the latter end of August 1671, I went to Leslie. Saw by the way Finglassie and Kinglassy and Caskieberry, bought by a German who came heir about 60 or 70 years ago, and professed medicine: was called Shoneir* (LAU 205.1ff.) In a more explicit style, we could expect a subject *I* in front of *saw*, and a subject *he* in front of *was called Shoneir*.

4.5.1   Simple Realisations

In its simplest form, the subject is realised by a substantival or a pronominal syntagm:

(a) subject = substantival syntagm

> *the body of King Duffus wes brocht with hye solempnite to Colmkill* (BELL 98.26f.)
> *This worthie Squyer courageous Micht be compairit to Tydeus* (MEL 1,309f.)

When a copulative syntagm is combined with one substantival syntagm only, the construction is syntactically ambiguous:

> *part of pepill are þat confidis and traistis oure mekile in thare strenthe and wertu* (WIS 47.4f.)
> *Sum persounis are, þat of þar syn and trespaß has pennaunce & forthinkinge* (WIS 52.1f.)

The syntagms *part of pepill [. . .] þat confidis and traistis oure mekile in thare strenthe and wertu* and *Sum persounis [. . .], þat of þar syn and trespaß has pennaunce & forthinkinge* can be analysed either as subjects or as copulative complements. The position of the nucleus of the substantival syntagm in front of the verb is an argument in favour of the analysis as subject.

(b) subject = pronominal syntagm

> *he forthinkis his mysdedis* (DE 219f.)
> *this is a perelus temptacione* (DE 86f.)
> *it aperit to be perdurabil ande inuyncibil* (COM 20.24)

Usually pronouns refer back to a substantive mentioned before; *he* in (DE 219f.) refers back to *the dear* 'the dyer', *this* in (DE 86f.) to *the topir temptacioune that the deuill tempis a man with*, and *it* in (COM 20.24) to *the grite tour of babilone*. Sometimes such a clear reference is not given, the pronominal subject cannot be substituted by a substantival syntagm:

> *With this Squyer it stude not so* (MEL 1328) 'for this squire it was not so'
> *all this is bot feynyt fantasye* (KI 259) 'all this is only false imagining'

In these passages, *it* and *all this* refer not to a particular syntagm, but to a whole situation. Although grammatically these subjects do not differ from other subjects, they are usually called 'impersonal subjects', and the verbs with which they combine 'impersonal verbs'. When 'impersonal subjects' combine with passive predicates, these constructions are called 'impersonal passive constructions':

> *it wes cruelly fochtin* (BELL 88.1)
> *it is befor rehersit* (COM 29.4)

The terms 'impersonal subject' and 'impersonal verb' will not be used here for the following reasons. First, the same syntagms can be used as 'personal subjects' and as 'impersonal subjects'. The only difference is that as 'personal subjects' they have a lexical meaning, as 'impersonal subjects' they have not a lexical but a grammatical meaning. They will therefore be called grammatical subjects. In most contexts, a special name for 'personal subjects' is not necessary; where they have to be distinguished from grammatical subjects, they will be called lexical subjects. Second, there are no verbs which only combine with grammatical subjects. Some verbs combine preferably with person-denoting, others with object-denoting subjects; similarly, some verbs combine preferably with grammatical, others with lexical subjects. Third, the same verb can combine with a grammatical and with a lexical subject in the same sentence.

In contexts where one would expect a grammatical subject, this can be lacking in the same way as a lexical subject: *wele were him that now were in thy plyte* (KI 371). This happens often in clauses of comparison introduced by *as*:

> *as lykis the best* (OWL 249)
> *as oft occurris* (BELL 87.23)
> *as said is* (BELL 98.15)

4.5.2   Complex Realisations

Subjects can also be structurally more complex; they can be realised by infinitive constructions, conjunctional clauses, and nominal relative clauses:

(a) subject = infinitive construction

> *to have pryd of his gud dedis is a temptacione* (DE 159f.)
> *for to lende by that laike thocht me levar* (OWL 19) 'I preferred to linger near that lake'
> *Us help the behufis* (OWL 754)
> *happyn thame [. . .] Till fynd fantiß in-till our deid* (BRU XII.255) 'should it happen that they find weakness in our actions'

(b) subject = conjunctional clause

> *na merwell js, that we call him oure fadere* (WIS 24.10f.)
> *necessare js þat men obey to god* (WIS 38.24)
> *happin that his halynace Throw prayer may purchace To reforme my foule face* (OWL 75ff.)
> *gyf ȝe think spedfull that we Fecht* (BRU XII.194f.)

It must be admitted that the analysis of the conjunctional clause *that we call him oure fadere* in the first example as the subject of the sentence is arbitrary; it could also be analysed as the copulative complement. An argument in favour of the latter analysis is the word order. That this argument is not conclusive, however, becomes evident in the second example, which is taken from the same text. Here the conjunctional clause must be analysed as the subject, because the other nominal constituent is realised by an adjective, and subjects are not realised by adjectives. Further support of the analysis as the subject comes from parallel constructions with an additional grammatical subject (cf. BELL 92.25f.; cf. p. 136).

(c) subject = nominal relative clause

> *come that bur office* (OWL 196) 'those that bore office arrived'
> *that ve cal vniuersal is ane vthir thyng* (COM 32.33f.)

A further type of complex subject is restricted to passive sentences. It has the same structure as complex direct objects in active sentences:

> *myddis euery herber myght be sene The scharp[e] grene suete ienepere, Growing so fair with branchis here and there* (KI 220ff.).

Here the subject *The scharp[e] grene suete ienepere, Growing so fair with branchis here and there* functions as the direct object in the corresponding active construction. It is realised by a participle construction with its own subject.

> *be I seyne in thar sicht To luke out on day licht* (OWL 62f.)

In this example, the subject *I [. . .] To luke out on day licht*, which is realised as a discontinuous constituent, corresponds to a direct object which is realised by an infinitive construction with a subject of its own. In the active construction, this subject is a personal pronoun in object case; in the passive construction, it is a personal pronoun in subject case. Additionally, the verb *see* governs an infinitive construction without preposition in the active; in the corresponding passive construction, the infinitive construction is preceded by *to*.

4.5.3 Multiple Realisations

As a rule, the subject is expressed once. But multiple realisation of the subject is possible, too. One type of multiple realisation of the subject is given, when a grammatical and a lexical subject are combined. The following pair of examples shows that even the same verb occurs either with a combination of a grammatical and a lexical subject or with a lexical subject alone:

> *Sa fell it in the samyn tid, That at Dumfreß, [. . .], Schir Ihone the Cumyn soiornyng maid* (BRU II.25f.)
> *in that self tyme fell, throu caß, That the kyng of England, [. . .], gert arest all his batalle* (BRU XII.2ff.)

When grammatical subjects occur together with lexical subjects, they follow each other in this order, and the lexical subject is realised by an infinitive construction, a clause, a conjunctional clause, or by a substantival syntagm:

(a) grammatical subject + infinitive construction

> *to þaim ande to al vthire folk It may awaill rycht mekile till have a gude ende* (DE 7f.)
> *it wes the ladyis will to mak a testament for the weele of hir oyis* (GG 232.26f.)
> *gif it happynit þame to be invadit* (BELL 91.29f.)
> *that were ouer vnmanerly a presumption, to striue to be further vpon Gods secreats, then he hath will ye be* (DOR 37.18ff.)
> *to luke it did me gude* (KI 210)

The exceptional arrangement of the lexical in front of the grammatical subject in the last example is due to rhyme requirements.

(b) grammatical subject + clause

> *It is said, [. . .], ʒite his body wes als fresche of coloure and hyde as þe first houre it wes hyd* (BELL 98.28ff.)
> *It wes ansuerit be þe nobillis, [. . .] God wes sa commovitt at þe slauchter of þe nobill King Duffus* (BELL 97.19ff.)

(c) grammatical subject + conjunctional clause

> *jt apperis þat he prayis agane himself* (WIS 50.16f.)

it follouis nocht that god vil tyne vs perpetualye (COM 27.6f.)

it wes na litill signe of victory þat þai wer to fecht aganis þe residew of þair inymyis (BELL 92.25f.)

that follouis nocht that hyr ȝouthed is ane plage (COM 29.36f.)

þat Is a takyne at thai luf hyme nocht (DE 122f.)

this is ane generall prouerb, that syne noyis nocht that is sufficiandly for-thocht (DE 97f.)

Conjunctional clauses in this function are always introduced by *that*.

The following pair of examples shows that the same verb can be combined with a grammatical subject and different realisations of the lexical subject: *it pleased God of his infinite wisdome and goodnesse, to incarnate his only Sonne in our nature* (DOR 33.25f.); *it pleaseth me, my Body be solemnously Laid in that place with Honesty* (WAT 56.473ff.).

(d) grammatical subject + substantival syntagm

it did approch the nicht (MEL 857)
It is vritin in the thrid cheptor of esaye thir vordis (COM 25.6f.)

This is probably the most striking realisation; it is attested with active verbal and with passive syntagms. Its occurrence in a prose text shows that it is not conditioned by metrical or rhyme requirements. The singular form *is* in COM 25.6f. is no valid argument against the analysis of *thir vordis* as subject, because the same form of the passive syntagm occurs in a parallel passage on the next page, where *thir vordis* is the only subject: *as is vrityn in the xxvi. cheptor of leuitic thir vordis* (COM 26.14f.). This realisation type is of low frequency, and it probably died out after the end of the period to be described here.[3] On the other hand, a similar construction type became very productive, namely the combination of the grammatical subject *there* with a lexical subject realised by a substantival or pronominal syntagm:

there is an expresse and most notable exhortation and commandement giuen them (DOR 29.17ff.)
there sal be no man follouuand ȝou (COM 24.27f.)
ther vas nocht mony of them perseuuand vs (COM 29.7)
on ilk side, thair wes men slane (MEL 1124)

A second type of multiple realisation of the subject is given, when two lexical subjects are combined. The most obvious reason for a second realisation of the subject is a big distance between the subject and the predicate. Then the substantival syntagm expressing the subject is taken up again in the form of a corresponding personal pronoun: *The Presbyterians at that tyme, hearing of the Indulgence given to some ministers in Scotland, they offer to the King to pay all his debt* (LAU 233.16ff.); *ane ox that regungnis the brod of his hird, he gettis doubil broddis* (COM 28.20f.).

In the following passages, which are taken from a report given before the Privy Council, the multiple expression of the subject is a characteristic feature of oral style. The subject, once expressed by a personal pronoun, seems to be repeated at random: *he persaueing the said patrik walking some space asyde with the minister of rothemay, he brak at him in a grite raige and furie* (GG 234.8ff.); *he resolueing to tak some advantage of thame at that tyme, he, accumpaneid with george craufurd, william prat in monkishill, Johnne Abirnethie, his servitor, and williame essillis in fettircarne, with vtheris his compliceis, bodin in feir of weir, with pistolletis prohibite to be worne as said is, come vpoun the sext day of Maij last to the said place of Rothemay* (GG 233.26ff.). At first glance the two examples are of a similar structure with the first occurrence of the personal pronoun *he* far away from the verbal syntagm. Yet in the second passage the second occurrence of *he* is also far away from the verbal syntagm, but it is not taken up again. So we must conclude that the repetition of the subject is at the speaker's discretion.

When this construction type occurs in verse texts, more often than not it can be explained by requirements of metre and rhyme:

> *The bird, the best, the fisch eke in the see,*
> *They lyve in fredome, euerich in his kynd* (KI 183f.)
> *That little man he is right wise* (WAT 15.125)
> *Now who shall play, the day it daws?*
> *Or hunt up, when the Cock he craws?* (WAT 32.7f.)

In terms of discourse analysis, it can also be explained as a focusing device: *The pape and the patriarkis, the prelatis ilkane, Thus pray thay as penitentis* (OWL 865f.); *Aulus he pretended, Decreets must not be given out at Randum* (WAT 22.38f.).

4.6 CONSTITUENTS OF COMPLEX SENTENCES

Simple sentences consist of one clause only, i.e., they contain only one verbal syntagm. Complex sentences contain at least two. The constructions involved are either joined by a linking element, or one is embedded in the other. They belong to the construction types conjunctional clause, clause, relative clause, infinitive and participle construction. Embedding of these will be treated in this order; where relevant, remarks on linking will be added.

4.6.1   Conjunctional Clauses

They consist of a conjunction followed by a complete clause, and they can function as postmodifiers in substantival and (more rarely) in adjectival syntagms, as subjects, copulative complements, direct objects, and adverbial complements. In the first four functions, two forms can be distinguished, namely *that*-clauses, i.e., clauses introduced by the conjunction *that/at*, and indirect yes/no–questions, i.e. clauses introduced by *gif/if* or *quhethir*.

(a) conjunctional clause = postmodifier

> *sampill [. . .] That pryde never yet left His feir but a fall* (OWL 960ff.) 'an example that pride never yet left his companion without a fall'
> *the fame, That Squyer Meldrum wes cum hame* (MEL 849f.)
> *full blyth, That he had gottyn that respyt* (BRU II.2f.)

(b) conjunctional clause = subject

> *happin that his halynace Throw prayer may purchace To reforme my foule face* (OWL 75ff.)

As was pointed out in the section about subjects, conjunctional clauses can also form part of complex subjects, which consist of a grammatical and a lexical subject. In this case, the conjunctional clause is the lexical subject:

> *Of warldlie Ioy it is weill kend, That sorrow bene the fatall end* (MEL 1183f.)
> *it wes aganis hir hart That scho did from hir Lufe depart* (MEL 1475f.)
> *it was belevitt þat þai war angellis* (BELL 277.29f.)

(c) conjunctional clause = copulative complement

> *The ferd js þat god of his mercy and grace deliuer ws fra syn and perdicioune of oure saule* (WIS 21.6f.)
> *The sext js, þat he of his mercy deliuer ws fra pane eternall of hell* (WIS 21.11f.)

(d) conjunctional clause = direct object

This realisation of the direct object is especially frequent, when the predicate contains no other non-verbal constituent. Depending on the verb by which object clauses are governed, the verbal syntagm is in the indicative or in the subjunctive. Verbs which express a wish, a request, or a command are usually followed by the subjunctive.

> *we desyre at þat be Completit in ws* (WIS 42.3)
> *I wate that I have rycht* (BRU I.509)
> *Iudge ʒe gif he hir schankis shed* (MEL 994)
> *We can nocht declair quhethir þis nerracioun be ane trew history or ane fabill* (BELL 268.6f.)

The next two examples illustrate conjunctional clauses as direct objects in predicates which contain also a verbal complement or an indirect object:

> *Hys brodir Eduuard [. . .] That thocht ferly, [. . .], That thai come hame sa priuely* (BRU II.19ff.) [*ferly* = verbal complement] 'his brother Edward who considered it a miracle that they came home so secretly'
> *þe haly spireit of jhesu teichis us, [. . .] that we do nocht oure awine will, bot the will of god* (WIS 41.8ff.) [*us* = indirect object]

(e) conjunctional clause = adverbial complement

The most characteristic function of conjunctional clauses is that of adverbial complement. Traditionally adverbial conjunctional clauses are classified on the basis of the semantic relation which holds between them and the matrix clause. The most important relations are time, condition, concession, reason, purpose, result, similarity and comparison. They will be treated in this order.

Clauses of time: Conjunctions which are attested in adverbial clauses of time are *or, or ever, afoir/afore* 'before', *till, quhil/quhill* 'until', *quhen, fra/fra tyme that/frae this time, as* 'when', *since* 'since', *alsone as/sae soon's/sae soon as, be* 'as soon as', *efter* 'after'. With the exception of the complex conjunctions with the meaning 'as soon as', all others can be expanded by *that* without change of meaning or function. Especially in some texts of the seventeenth century, the conjunctions occur in an anglicised form, e.g. *ere, before, while, when, after*. Examples are:

> *or he deit, his land delt he* (BRU I.535)
> *childir [. . .] grouis & incressis quhil thai be ascendit to the perfyit stryntht of men* (COM 20.7f.)
> *Fra his body come abufe þe erd, þe weddir chengit to grete serenite* (BELL 98.30f.)
> *as it did approch the nicht, Of ane Castell he gat ane sicht* (MEL 857f.)
> *Since first he laid his Fang on me My self from him I dought ne're draw* (WAT 11.3f.)
> *be he had endid this word, He drew ane lang twa handit sword* (MEL 1253f.)
> *eftir the dear be informyt of thir temptacions at will be put to hyme, he suld be demandyt, [. . .], gyf he be blyth* (DE 216ff.)

In the following example the complex conjunction *till that* is realised as a discontinuous constituent: *swa gat all the nycht baid thai Till on the morn that it wes day* (BRU XII.333f.). The conjunction *quhil/quhill* is used not only in clauses denoting an action which occurs after the action denoted by the matrix clause (meaning: 'until'), but also in clauses denoting an action co-occurring with that of the matrix clause (meaning: 'as long as'): *quhill that I may indure, I vow to be ʒour seruiture* (MEL 979f.); *while we haue leasure & are heere, we may remember to amende* (DOR 43.19f.). The second example shows quite clearly how eager printers were in the seventeenth century to anglicise their texts. The corresponding passage in King James's autograph (MS ROYAL 18.B.xv) reads as follows: *quhill ue haue laiser & are heir ue maye remember to amende*.

Clauses of condition: They are introduced by the conjunctions *and, geve/gif, gif that, in caß* 'if', *vnles, were nocht/were nocht that, quhil, without/without that, bot* 'unless, if not'. For more anglicised texts, this list must be supplemented by *provydeing* 'provided'. Verbs in conditional clauses tend to be in the subjunctive; unambiguous cases of the indicative are only attested after *gif* and *were nocht*:

> *and he de as he Suld de, he suld think that he suld pas to mare Ioy* (DE 168f.)
> *geve þou sais this orisoune jn þi awine name and behalf, beand jn syn, jt helpis þe nocht ore litile* (WIS 22.33ff.) [indicative]
> *gif that he Be lord, [. . .], Than wold I pray his blisfull grace benigne To hable me vnto his seruice digne* (KI 267ff.) [subjunctive]
> *in caß he mend of that seknes, [. . .] he sal neuir wylfully syne* (DE 258f.)
> *he sould cleive him to the harne pan, vnles he causit the said testament ather to be nullit or reformit* (GG 233.5ff.)
> *all creaturis [. . .] wauld turne jn noucht, were nocht that he sustenis þaim throu his wertu* (WIS 31.35ff.) [indicative]
> *þou art nocht deliuerit of þi syn quhil þou restore wrangwiß gud, [. . .], or haue werray purpoß to restore* (WIS 44.22ff.) 'unless you restore wrongful goods'
> *Without ʒe mak me sum remeid, Withouttin dout I am bot deid* (MEL 957f.)
> *Bot thow reule the richtwis, thi roume sall orere* (OWL 984) 'unless you govern yourself rightly, your place will go back'
> *they offer to the King to pay all his debt, [. . .], provydeing the same liberty be granted them* (LAU 233.17ff.)

When two conditional clauses are linked by *and*, the second clause can be introduced by *that/at*:

> *Gif ye a goddess be, and that ye like To do me payne, I may it noght astert* (KI 302f.)
> *quhat temptacioune at euir the deuill putis to man sal nocht noy hyme bot gyf he wylfully consent thar-to, and at he be in his rycht mynd* (DE 60ff.)

Conditional clauses need not be introduced by a conjunction; condition can also be indicated by the inversion of subject and the inflected form of the verbal syntagm. In this construction type, too, the verb form is in the subjunctive mood: *Chaip he away, we ar eschamit* (MEL 1339) 'if he escapes'; *þe will of god js sa stark, þat, will we ore nocht, jt mone be fulfillit* (WIS 38.23f.) 'whether we like it or not'.

A special case of conditional clause is given, when instead of one condition, a choice of several conditions is expressed. In their description of Present-day English, Quirk et al. (1985: 15.42) call these clauses 'universal conditional–concessive clauses'. They are introduced by *how . . . at euir*: *the dede of gude men, how soding or terreble at euir It be, is gude & precious before gode* (DE 16f.); *how wyolently at euir thai dee, thai Suld nocht dreid thare ded* (DE 26f.). The anglicised form of this conjunction is *howe . . . soever*: *forgette it not in your bed howe oft soeuer ye doe it at other times* (DOR 39.17f.)

Conjunctional clauses which are introduced by *except*, *bot* or *bot gyf/but gyf that* are not pure conditional clauses; they combine negative condition and exception:

> *Except the Lorde build the house, they laboure in vaine that builde it* (DOR 25.17f.)
> *bote is none, bot Venus of hir grace Will schape remede or do my spirit pace* (KI 482f.) 'there is no remedy, unless/except that Venus . . .'
> *bot gyf þai be cumyne to the natural cours of eilde [. . .], thir men [. . .] ar laith to de* (DE 111ff.) [I follow the editor's suggestion to emend *or* to *ar*] 'these people are loath to die, unless/except they have grown old naturally'
> *the diuyne indignatione had decretit ane extreme ruuyne on oure realme; but gyf that ve retere fra oure vice* (COM 23.29ff.) 'unless/except that we abstain from our vice'

Clauses of concession: The following introductory conjunctions are used: *albeit, howbeit/quhou be it that, thocht/althogh, nochtwithstanding* 'though, although'. Only the conjunction *thocht* invariably governs the subjunctive; the other conjunctions occur with either mood:

> *albeit the beiring and weiring of hagbutis and pistolletis hes bene oftymes prohibite* (GG 231.6f.)
> *quhou be it that the pepil knauis thir mutations to be of verite* (COM 21.32f.) [indicative]
> *quhou beit that the thretnyng of gode contrar vs be verray seueir ande extreme* (COM 26.8f.) [subjunctive]
> *nochwithstanding þe half of his army wes lost, King Malcolm, [. . .], commandit all his prelaittis be generall processionis to geif thankis to God* (BELL 89.26ff.)
> *thair fayis [weill] soyn [sall] be Discumfyt throu thar awn mycht, Thouch no man help thaim for to ficht* (BRU XII.116ff.)
> *þocht he gowerne all creaturis, ʒit þe laif he gouernis generaly as seruaundis* (WIS 24.15f.)

> *althogh this conscience be a great torture to the wicked, yet is it as great a comforte to the godlie* (DOR 43.12f.)

Very rarely, the conjunction *as* is used to introduce adverbial clauses of concession. It conditions the fronting of a constituent of the predicate: *deuise and laboure as he list* (DOR 25.15).

Clauses of reason: The list of conjunctions which denote this semantic relationship is quite long; it comprises the following elements: *sen/since/since that, for/for that, forquhy, because/be cause that, in respect, as, be rason that, in sa far as.* The mood of the verb form in clauses of reason is the indicative:

> *The king thocht he wes traist inewch, Sen he in bowrch hys landis drewch* (BRU I.627f.)
>
> *since that ye withoutten Swither, To Visit me are come down hither, Be blyth, and let us drink together* (WAT 66.765f.)
>
> *thai had gret abaysing; And specialy for that the king So smertly that gud knycht had slayne* (BRU XII.70f.)
>
> *becauβ þai fand þair gude moder participant with þe samyn, þai gart hir sitt nakitt in ane cauld stedy* (BELL 87.5ff.)
>
> *so much the fitter ar they for you, then for the common sorte, in respect the composer thereof was a King* (DOR 39.12ff.)
>
> *Indulphus, [. . .], went throw þe campe with ane sobyr cumpany, as na danger mycht occur be þe samyn* (BELL 93.6ff.)
>
> *ther is nocht mony that knauis the cause of thir mutations, be rason that the iugement of gode [. . .] is ane profound onknauen deipnes* (COM 21.33ff.)
>
> *it is bot ane corrupit poison, in sa far as ve can nocht serue gode ande it to gyddir* (COM 32.1ff.)

Clauses of purpose and result: Conjunctional clauses which express these two semantic relations are treated together, because it is often a matter of interpretation whether the action denoted in the conjunctional clause is an intended result (= purpose) or an achieved result (= result proper). Additionally, there are conjunctions which can denote either relationship. The conjunctions *to that end that* and *lest* denote purpose only, while the conjunctions *that/at, so/sae . . . that* and *so/sa . . . as* occur in both contexts:

> *he suld pray mekil til god to gif hyme grace till haf knawleg of the synis that he haβ forȝet, to that end that he may the bettir mak amendis þarof* (DE 255ff.) [purpose]
>
> *I ordain my Executours, To gang amang my Creditours, [. . .], And [. . .] Content them a' with Honesty, lest afterward they wearie me* (WAT 58.534ff.) [purpose]
>
> *he suld brynge to his mynd his Ill dedis, at thai ma law hyme and bryng hyme to knaw his fragelyte* (DE 156) [purpose]
>
> *Than was he [. . .] So clene and so colourlyke That no bird was him lyke* (OWL 891ff.) [result]
>
> *he thow pasis to, & thow [sa weill all tyme may] do, That ȝe ȝow fra ȝowr fayis defend* (BRU II.127ff.) [purpose/result]
>
> *he wald quite his pairt of the said testament for ane plak, so as he micht haue his releif of twa thowsand merkis* (GG 232.29ff.) [purpose]

he wes so fer distemperit and careyed with a cruell purpois of revenge as he could tak no rest
(GG 237.16ff.) [result]

Clauses of similarity and comparison: Although they are structurally similar to comparative constructions, which expand the nucleus of adjectival syntagms, they are to be distinguished from them. They are introduced by *as* or *as gif*. The first conjunction is used to express a real or a pretended similarity, while *as gif* is only used in the second case:

> *and he de as he Suld de* (DE 158f.) [real similarity] 'if he dies as he should die'
> *I had bene with the, As thow in France was anis with me* (MEL 1395f.) [real similarity]
> *liuing euerie day as it were your last* (DOR 45.30) [pretended similarity]
> *Tak him as off thine awyne [heid], As I had gevyn thar-to na reid* (BRU II.121f.)
>   [pretended similarity]
> *he [. . .] quarrellit the said patrik for suffering hir to mak ony testament, as gif it had lyne*
>   *in his pouer to haue stayed hir* (GG 232.18ff.) [pretended similarity]

When the adverbial clause precedes the matrix clause, the comparison can be expressed by the correlative pair *as . . . so*: *as in dignitie he hath erected you aboue others, so ought ye in thankfulnesse towardes him, goe as farre beyond all others* (DOR 25.26ff.) [real similarity].

Stanza 41 of *The Kingis Quair* shows that several conjunctional clauses can be embedded in one matrix clause. Each of them functions as an adverbial complement. The conjunctional clause introduced by *forquhy* serves as a matrix clause itself; it contains another conjunctional clause (introduced by *That*) as an adverbial complement, and finally it, too, contains an embedded conjunctional clause (introduced by *for*):

> *And though I stude abaisit tho a lyte,*
> *No wonder was: forquhy my wittis all*
> *Were so ouercom with plesance and delyte,*
> *Onely thou latting of myn eyen fall,*
> *That sudaynly my hert became hir thrall*
> *For euer, of free wyll − for of manace*
> *There was no takyn in hir suete face.*
> 'And although I was confused for a while, that was not surprising because I was so overwhelmed with pleasure and delight − I had only looked down at her − that suddenly my heart became spontaneously and for ever her servant, because there was no sign of menace in her sweet face.'

4.6.2 Clauses

Clauses which are embedded in matrix clauses can only realise one function, namely that of the direct object. Verbs which can govern *that*-clauses as direct objects can usually also govern simple clauses with this function. The distribution of indicative and subjunctive follows the same rule as in conjunctional clauses:

> *ȝe sall vnderstand þai ar þe refuse of all realmes* (BELL 274.35f.)
> *I beleue scho said not nay* (MEL 998)
> *The king thocht he wes traist inewch* (BRU I.627)
> *God geif þai be soddin or brynt in hell* (BELL 83.1f.)

4.6.3 Relative Clauses

Relative clauses are introduced by a relative marker, i.e., a relative pronoun or a relative adverb. They have basically two functions; they are either postmodifiers in substantival and pronominal syntagms, or they realise one of the functions which can also be realised by substantival syntagms. In the first case they are called attributive relative clauses, in the second nominal relative clauses. The syntagms which are modified by attributive relative clauses are also called their antecedents. The following aspects will be considered here: the antecedent, the relative marker, the function of the relative clause, and the function of the relative marker.

The most frequent realisation of the antecedents of relative clauses is by the nucleus of a substantival or a pronominal syntagm. More interesting are relative constructions which do not occur in Modern Scots. Here the antecedent is a determiner in a substantival syntagm, realised either by a possessive adjective or by the genitive of a substantive:

(a) antecedent = substantive

> *Iulius Cesar als, that wan Bretane and Fraunce* (BRU I.537f.)
> *ver that full of vertu is and gude* (KI 134)

(b) antecedent = personal pronoun

> *jt þat he will and ordanis* (WIS 41.21)
> *We, quhilkis has bene als oft victorious on Scottis as vincust be þame* (BELL 43.28f.)
> *þame quhilkis gevis occasioun of batall* (BELL 85.16)

(c) antecedent = demonstrative pronoun

> *that which they behoved to get notice of* (LAU 233.14f.)
> *those that are somewhat difficile* (DOR 37.15)

(d) antecedent = indefinite pronoun

> *nane, To whom that I can mak my Mane* (WAT 50.305f.)
> *nane þat was ouretakin* (BELL 37.35)
> *nocht [. . .] quhilk nature has producit for þe wele of man* (BELL 27.16f.)

(e) antecedent = possessive adjective

> *ʒour name þat sendis me* (WIS 31.21) 'the name of you who sends me'
> *thair avise that had of me the cure* (KI 153) 'the advice of those who . . .'
> *her Love And Kindness which I fectlie fand* (WAT 14.101f.) 'the love and kindness of her whom I found efficient'
> *his opinione that conquesis the victore* (COM 181.15) 'the opinion of him who wins the victory'

(f) antecedent = genitive of a substantive

> *þe Kingis hattrent, quhilk commandit to puneiβ him for his cruelte* (BELL 285.29f.) 'the cruelty of the king, who commanded to punish him . . .'

From the very earliest text, the relative pronoun *that/at* occurs side by side with relative pronouns with initial *quh-* (on their distribution cf. Caldwell 1974; Romaine 1980). The relative pronoun *quhilk* can be preceded by the definite article *the*, and it is inflected for number; its plural form is *quhilkis*. The inflected form occurs after a plural antecedent. Whereas the relative pronouns *that/at* and *(the) quhilk(is)* are used with animate and inanimate antecedents, animate antecedents can also be referred to by the relative pronoun *quha*. Its inflected forms are *quhais/quhois* and *quhom*. The first occurrences of the subject form *quha* date from the middle of the sixteenth century. A further possibility which must be mentioned is the introduction by a zero relative marker. It is attested already in the earliest texts with animate and inanimate antecedents.

Relative clauses cannot only be introduced by relative pronouns, but also by the relative adverbs *quhar/quhair, quhen, how (that)* and *quarfor* or *quhy*. Additionally, there is the possibility of a complex relative marker consisting of *quar/qhair* as a first and a preposition as a second element (e.g. *quairto, quairat,* etc.) . Depending on their function, relative adverbs and complex relative markers commute with the relative pronoun *that/at* and the combinations of a preposition with one of the relative pronouns *(the) quhilk(is)* or *that/at*. There is a tendency for the prepositions to precede *(the) quhilk(is)* and to follow *that/at*.

(a) relative pronoun = *that/at*

> *the wnknawlage at thai have thare-of* (DE 3f.)
> *the Lad that was Skipper himsell* (WAT 9.52)
> *Beatrice, þat wes gevin in mariage to Cithrik* (BELL 90.22)

(b) relative pronoun = *(the) quhilk(is)*

> *this lytill trety, the quhilk is callyt the craft of deyng* (DE 4f.)
> *the notis of the philomene Quhilkis sche sang* (KI 428)
> *Beatrice, quhilk wes gevin to Cithrik in mariage* (BELL 86.30f.) [animate antecedent + *quhilk*]

(c) relative pronoun = *quha/quhom/quhais*

> *the lacedemoniens, quha var mortal enemes to the atheniens* (COM 87.30f.)
> *ther vmquhile subiectis [. . .] quhome of be for thai commandit be autorite* (COM 19.9ff.)
> *your man Quhois seruice is yit vncouth vnto yow* (KI 435f.)

(d) relative marker = zero

> *al [0] he has tane wrangwysly* (DE 265)
> *Thys lord the Brwyβ, [0] I spak of ayr* (BRU I.477)
> *to here the mirth [0] was tham amang* (KI 423)

(e) relative marker = relative adverb

> *the place, [. . .] Quhar Scottis men arayit war* (BRU XII.5f.)
> *That time quhen done wes the outrage* (MEL 1390)
> *mony causis quharfor we call þe hie god aboue oure fadere* (WIS 24.6f.)
> *The second ressoune quhy we call him oure fadere* (WIS 24.14)
> *will ȝe nocht se How that governyt is this countre* (BRU I.485f.)

(f) complex relative marker

> *rothemay, quhairvnto the said mr william had reteirit him selff* (GG 238.19f.)
> *A gudely cheyne [. . .] Quhareby there hang a ruby* (KI 331f.)

All examples quoted so far belong to the category attributive relative clause. They realise the function postmodifier in a substantival or pronominal syntagm. Nominal relative clauses can realise the functions subject, copulative complement, direct object, prepositional object, and adverbial complement. The inventory of relative markers differs only little from that of attributive relative clauses. The relative pronoun *that/at* occurs only in the very early texts, whereas in later texts only *quh*-forms are found. The latter include *quhat*, a pronoun which cannot be used in attributive relative clauses. The relative pronouns of generalising relative clauses are expanded by *(sae, that/at) evir*.

(a) relative clause = subject

> *quhat temptacioune at euir the deuill putis to a man sal nocht noy hyme* (DE 60ff.)
> *come that bur office* (OWL 196) 'those that bore office arrived'

As with other realisations of the subject, a nominal relative clause as subject can be taken up by a personal or a demonstrative pronoun:

> *quha euyr hed gottyn it, he suld haue been able to do mekil displeseir til his enemeis* (COM 176.18ff.)
> *Quhome euer he hit, [. . .], Thay did him na mair deir, that day* (MEL 1287f.)

(b) relative clause = copulative complement

> *Ĵ am at j am* (WIS 31.22)

(c) relative clause = direct object

> *To maynteym that he had begunnyn* (BRU II.189)
> *he thame gaif quhat they wald haue* (MEL 1442)
> *to se quhare þe Scottis war* (BELL 287.36)
> *I sall ȝow tell, How that he seigit ane Castell* (MEL 1051f.)

(d) relative clause = prepositional object

Prepositional objects which denote a direction can be realised by nominal relative clauses introduced by a relative adverb. In other prepositional objects, only the constituent following the preposition can be realised by a nominal relative clause, which is then introduced by a relative pronoun.

> *leit the laif gang quhair they pleisit* (MEL 1144) 'he let the rest go where they pleased'
> *he tuk alsua full gud hed To that the byschop had said* (BRU II.94f.) 'he also paid heed to what the bishop had said'

(e) relative clause = adverbial complement

> *I will [. . .] begyn quhar I left* (OWL 632f.)
> *He purpoisit him to repois, Quhair ilk man did of him rejois* (MEL 861f.) 'he intended to rest where everybody was joyful on his account'

In the following, rare example, the nominal relative clause functions as the addressee of an imperative: *Awake [. . .] that haue your hevynnis wonne* (KI 236).

The introductory elements of relative clauses have the function to indicate that what follows is a dependent clause. In this respect, they are comparable to the introductory elements of conjunctional clauses. They differ from them in that relative markers have an additional function in the relative clause itself. This double function will be called functional amalgamation: *þe gret mercy and gentrice þat jhesus the blist sone of god omnipotent has schawin to ws miserabile and wrechit persounis and creaturis* (WIS 17.19ff.). Here the relative marker *þat* indicates that a relative clause follows, and it functions as the direct object in the relative clause.

The individual relative markers can realise different functions in relative clauses. The following functions are involved: determiner in a substantival syntagm, subject, copulative complement, direct object, prepositional object, indirect object, adverbial complement, and complement of a preposition.

(a) relative marker = determiner

This is the only function of the inflected relative pronoun *quhais/quhois* and one of the functions of *(the) quhilk(is)*. In the latter case, the nucleus of the substantival syntagm is the same as the antecedent:

> *Tantalus [. . .], quhois penance is an hell* (KI 484ff.)
> *Culyne [. . .] quhais cuming maid þe Murrayis richt effrayitt* (BELL 97.23ff.)
> *ane hauy melancolius dreyme [. . .], the quilk dreyme i sal reherse* (COM 68.9ff.)[4]
> *the space of tua houris [. . .], during the quhilk haill space the said mr williame euir expectit that he sould have put violent handis in his persone* (GG 236.28ff.)

(b) relative marker = subject

This function can be realised by the relative pronouns *that/at*, *quha*, and *(the) quhilk(is)* as well as by zero:

> *Alexander the conqueroure, That conqueryt Babilonys tour* (BRU I.529f.)
> *Ninus kyng of the assiriens, quha vas nocht contentit vitht his auen cuntre* (COM 166.36f.)

Thomas Randall, quilk was Erle of Murraye (BELL 278.30f.)
Was nevir leid saw thaim lauch (OWL 188)
Wes neuer man, with sword nor knyfe, Micht saif their honour and thair lyfe (MEL 1511f.)

(c) relative marker = copulative complement

Since copulative complements are realised not only by substantival and adjectival but also by prepositional syntagms, it follows that beside the relative pronoun *that/at* we also find relative adverbs and combinations of a preposition and a relative pronoun with this function:

J am at j am (WIS 31.22)
William Sinclair, [. . .], nochtþeles brocht him agane quhair þe Inglismen war (BELL 280.29ff.)
oure necessite that we are dayly jn (WIS 22.17f.)
þis hill quhilk þai war last on (BELL 288.14f.) [preposition following the relative pronoun *quhilk*]
grete men [. . .], amang quhom war þe Murrayis (BELL 94.24f.)

(d) relative marker = direct object

This function can be realised by the relative pronouns *that/at*, *(the) quhilk(is)*, and *quhom* as well as by zero:

the mekill ill That thai and tharis has done vs till (BRU XII.227f.)
hir richt hand gluif, The quhilk he on his basnet bure (MEL 1076f.)
dame Natur [. . .] Quhom thai ressaif with reverens (OWL 867ff.)
the behest he hecht to the king (OWL 470) 'the promise that he gave to the king'

(e) relative marker = prepositional object

Prepositional objects are realised by the combination of a preposition and a relative pronoun, by a relative adverb, or by a complex relative marker consisting of a relative adverb and a preposition:

the toþir temptacioune that the deuill tempis a man with (DE 75f.)
vij wellis of grace, cleire and nete, fra þe quhilk passis furthe the sevin Riueris of hevinly werkis (WIS 18.29f.)
our heynd Squyar, Of quhome we can not speik bot gude (MEL 1425f.)
all partis quhare þai come (BELL 287.28f.)
that mater quhairwith he burdynit him (GG 236.13f.)

(f) relative marker = indirect object

Since the indirect object denotes a person, it is not surprising to find only the inflected form *quhom* of the relative pronoun which refers only to animate antecedents in this function. It is preceded by or combined with the preposition *to*:

> *O Venus clere, [. . .], To quhom I yelde homage and sacrifise* (KI 358f.)
> *that God, whome-to ye haue a double obligation* (DOR 25.23f.)

(g) relative marker = adverbial complement

This function can be realised by the relative pronoun *that/at*, by zero, by a combination of a preposition and the relative pronouns *that/at* and *(the) quhilk(is)* as well as by a relative adverb. The antecedent often denotes the place, time, reason, or manner of the action denoted by the verbal syntagm of the relative clause:

> *the Time and Year, And Day, that e'er I found you* (WAT 56.471f.)
> *the cause that he [me] more comprisit Than othir folk to lyve in suich ruyne* (KI 192f.)
> *þe first houre it wes hyd* (BELL 98.30)
> *þe samyn croce þat þe Apostill deit on* (BELL 29.6)
> *The thrid way and manere þat we haue confidence throu* (WIS 30.4f.)
> *ane counsale [. . .], in þe quhilk be generall counsale of þe þre estatis he gatt þe crovn of Scotland tailʒeitt to him and his aires maill* (BELL 278.23ff.)
> *þe nixt kyrk, quhair he was berijt* (BELL 29.36)
> *that vnknyghtly dede Quhare was fro thee bereft thy maidenhede* (KI 385)

(h) relative marker = complement of preposition

Prepositional syntagms occur as copulative complements, prepositional objects, and adverbial complements. Relative markers as constituents of such prepositional syntagms were dealt with under the respective headings. Two more functions of prepositional syntagms must be mentioned, in which relative markers realise the complement. One function is that of modifier in a substantival syntagm, the other is that of the agent in passive constructions:

> *thai cluddis, fra the forse of the quhilk there cummis fyir and ane grit sound* (COM 59.29ff.)
> *the oreginall syne at thai ware fylyt with* (DE 69) 'the original sin by which they were corrupted'
> *ane Inglisman, [. . .], be quhom it was deliueritt* (BELL 281.16f.)

In a complex type of relative construction, the relative marker functions as a nominal constituent of a clause, a conjunctional clause, an infinitive or participle construction which is embedded in the relative clause. As the functions involved are realised on a lower structural level, the relative marker will be called relative push-down element in these constructions:

> *the vailʒeant actis that ther prince hes knauen them til haue committit* (COM 148.21f.).

The verbal syntagm of the relative clause is *hes knauen*. Its object is an embedded infinitive construction with subject. The relative pronoun *that* functions as the object in this infinitive construction.

> *King Robert, quhilk ʒe may evill suffir to be novmerit with thir twa first campionis* (BELL 291.11f.).

The active verbal syntagm *may [. . .] suffir* governs an embedded infinitive construction as object. The subject of this infinitive construction is realised by the relative pronoun *quhilk*:

> *that ending That thai think it sall cum to* (BRU I.584f.).

The verbal syntagm *think* in the relative clause governs an object which is realised by a clause. The relative pronoun *that* is a constituent of the prepositional object in this clause.

> *al the vicis that oure cupidite prouokis vs to commit* (COM 35.2f.).

The verbal syntagm of the relative clause is *prouokis*. It governs the direct object *vs* and a further object, which is realised by an embedded infinitive construction without subject. The relative pronoun *that* realises the object in this infinitive construction.

Although functional amalgamation is the rule for Older Scots relative clauses, a less frequent form occurs without functional amalgamation: *his faythtful natyue natural leigis and inhabitaris of his realme, of the quhilk ther vas sum of them that var of his kyn and blude* (COM 162.30ff.). The relative clause in question is *of the quhilk ther vas sum of them*. In a relative clause with functional amalgamation, the modifier of the nucleus *sum* of the lexical subject would be realised by the syntagm containing the relative pronoun (= *of the quhilk*). Here it is realised by the prepositional syntagm *of them*.

John Smith [. . .], Wha sae soon as he came her till, Into his Arms he caught her (WAT 65.734ff.). In this example the relative clause is a complex sentence with a conjunctional clause embedded in the matrix clause as an adverbial complement. The subject of the matrix clause and that of the embedded conjunctional clause (introduced by *sae soon as*) is realised by the personal pronoun *he*. So the only function of the relative pronoun *Wha* is to indicate that what follows is a dependent clause (here a postmodifier of *John Smith*).

There are clauses which superficially resemble relative clauses in that they are introduced by the same elements as relative clauses. But they have neither an antecedent nor are they embedded in other clauses. Their introductory elements have the same syntactic function and the same semantic role as determiners or demonstrative pronouns. They establish a semantic link between the clause which they introduce and the preceding text: *The nobillis condiscendit wele to þe samyn, traisting all thingis gevin to þe kirk tynt na leβ þan it war fallin in herschip to þair inymyis; quhilk wes cauβ eftir þat þair realme wes brocht to vtter exterminioun* (BELL 30.26f.). The sentence introduced by *quhilk* is not a relative clause, but an independent sentence with the subject *quhilk*. This subject establishes a semantic link with the preceding text. The same analysis is also possible for clauses with initial *(the) quhilk(is)*, which functions as a determiner: *The quhilk opinioune apperandly arestotill held* (WIS 31.3f.)

Often these constructions are introduced by a prepositional syntagm, one constituent of which is realised by one of the elements which also introduce relative clauses: *[. . .]; on quhom followitt Scottis with incredibill hatrent* (BELL 42.4f.); *[. . .]; be quhayis sicht þe Scottis war sa effrayit* (BELL 37.29f.)

Quite naturally, constructions with initial *that* are not mentioned in this context, because nobody would assume that it could be analysed as anything else but a determiner or a demonstrative pronoun in this position. But it is probably due to the overlap in the inventories of determiners/demonstrative pronouns on the one and relative pronouns on the other hand that the relative pronouns *(the) quhilk(is)*, *quhais/quhois* and *quhome* started commuting with the former in clause-initial position.

4.6.4   Infinitive Constructions

Infinitive constructions consist of a predicate with an infinitive as its nucleus. Usually this nucleus is of the type active verbal syntagm, i.e., the infinitive of a lexical verb. More complex realisations are by a perfect infinitive (*have* + past participle) and the infinitive of a passive syntagm (*be* + past participle). Infinitive constructions can but need not be preceded by the prepositions *tae/to*, *till*, or *for to*. Depending on their function, they occur with or without a subject of their own. This subject is realised by a substantival or pronominal syntagm.

The functions of infinitive constructions are the same as those of conjunctional clauses, i.e. postmodifier in nominal syntagms, subject, copulative complement, direct object, and adverbial complement.

(a) infinitive construction = postmodifier

Like conjunctional clauses, infinitive constructions expand substantival syntagms. Yet, the other nominal syntagm which they modify is not the adjectival but the pronominal syntagm. As postmodifiers, infinitive constructions are always preceded by a preposition:

> *ane instrument to file doune yrn* (COM 28.7)
> *sic mischance, To be subject or seruiture Till ane quhilk takis of me na cure* (MEL 914ff.)
> *Ik have ane othir it to ber* (BRU I.617)

(b) infinitive construction = subject

As a rule, infinitive constructions as subjects are preceded by a preposition. This is not the case when they combine with a predicate with the nucleus *behufe* 'to behove':

> *Perforce behuifit him, than, fall doun* (MEL 1356)
> *vs behwys all de o neid* (DE 28f.)
> *To se his dede wes gret pite* (BRU I.536)
> *apon Natur to pleyne it is perell* (OWL 119) 'to blame it on Nature is dangerous'
> *to be inducit and ourecummyn js richt euill and miserabile* (WIS 23.2f.)

Infinitive constructions as subjects are often combined with a grammatical subject in initial position: *it war syn to leiß his priß, That of sa souerane bounte is* (BRU XII.125f.). When infinitive constructions realise the subjects in passive sentences, they have a separate subject. If its nucleus is a personal pronoun, it is in subject case: *he wes desyrit be Avalassus, [. . .], to raiß his ordinance* (BELL 90.28f.).

(c) infinitive construction = copulative complement

In this function, infinitive constructions are always preceded by a preposition:

> *vntholmudnes, the quhilk is nocht to luf god abwne al thinge, & to thank hyme of al his sayndis and gyftes* (DE 108f.)
> *My purpos is nocht to speik of this material varld* (COM 33.16f.)

In a fossilised form the construction is found in the set phrase *that is to saye*: *that is to saye, he distroyt assure the kyng of the assirriens* (COM 27.33f.).

(d) infinitive construction = direct object

When infinitive constructions realise the function of direct object in predicates which contain no other non-verbal constituent, they occur with and without preposition, with and without a subject of their own. If the subject of the infinitive construction is a personal pronoun, it is in object case. The presence or absence of the preposition depends on the verb which governs the infinitive construction.

> (1) without subject, without preposition:
> *thai will nocht here spek at thai suld de* (DE 202) 'they do not want to hear somebody say that they should die'

> (2) with subject, without preposition:
> *ye hard me say* (BRU II.70)
> *the kyngis men [. . .] Saw him [. . .] [Have] slayn ane knycht* (BRU XII.62ff.) [perfect infinitive]
> *quhen the gud king can thaim se Befor him swa assemblit be* (BRU XII.165f.) [passive infinitive]

> (3) without subject, with preposition:
> *I trast, and trowis sekirly, To haue playne victor in this ficht* (BRU XII.294f.)
> *resolueing, [. . .], to have slane them at that same instant* (GG 235.23f.) [perfect infinitive]

> (4) with subject, with preposition:
> *the pepil knauis thir mutations to be of verite* (COM 21.33)
> *he commandit fyfty barnis [. . .] to be slayn* (BELL 268.10f.) [passive infinitive]

When infinitive constructions realise the function direct object in predicates which contain an additional indirect object, they have no subject of their own, but they are preceded by a preposition: *jhesus [. . .] prait his fader of hevin for to remyt þame þar fautis and synnys* (WIS 50.32ff.).

(e) infinitive construction = adverbial complement

Infinitive constructions in this function are preceded by a preposition. The only semantic relations which hold between them and their matrix clauses are those of purpose and result:

> *The erll, [. . .], And his men als [. . .], Hynt of thair basnetis in-till hy Till avent thame* (BRU XII.142ff.) [purpose]
> *quhat haue I gilt, to faille My fredome in this warld and my plesance* (KI 178f.) [result]

Sometimes it is difficult to decide which semantic relation is implied. No ambiguity arises with more complex prepositions like *with purpoß to*: *King Edward, [. . .] invadit oure realme and pepill with purpoβ to reiff sindry landis fra þe samyn be wrangwis batall* (BELL 85.11ff.); *sa departit, blyith and mirrie, With purpois to pas ouir the Ferrie* (MEL 1223f.).

4.6.5 Participle Constructions

Like infinitive constructions, participle constructions contain a predicate with a non-finite verb form. As there are two participles, namely present and past, two classes of participle constructions have to be distinguished.

Constructions with a present participle will be dealt with first. They function as modifiers in substantival and pronominal syntagms, as adverbial complements, subjects, direct objects, and as complements of conjunctions. Only as modifiers can they have no subject of their own.

(a) present participle construction = modifier

> *This Edward, following his faderis fute steppis, maid ane conuencioun of all þe nobillis of Scotland* (BELL 268.14f.)
> *he hange þarone, Inclynand the hed to the heryng* (DE 99f.)

(b) present participle construction = adverbial complement

In this function, present participle constructions occur with and without a subject of their own. The participle of the lexical verb can also be expanded by the present participle *being*:

> *thus a man suld with al his hart conforme hyme to haf paciens, thankand god without murmur of that payne* (DE 141f.)
> *King Robert [. . .] enterit twiβ in Ingland, putting þe landis and pepil þerof to herschip and slauchter* (BELL 269.18ff.)
> *he being walking in quiet maner afore the ʒet, he was almoist surprysit of him* (GG 237.28ff.)
> *the said mr williame being sitting at his denner, he rais presentlie frome the table* (GG 235.28ff.)

Often it is difficult to decide whether a present participle construction functions as adverbial complement or as modifier. We tend to interpret it as a modifier when it follows the potential nucleus directly, otherwise as an adverbial complement:

> *King Robert, seying þame proceding forthwert, send Erle Thomas Randaill* (BELL 272.30f.) [postmodifier]
> *þe castell was nocht only strang be wallis, bot als richt strenthy be nature of þe crag, standing on ane hye moitt* (BELL 270.15ff.) [adverbial complement]

(c) present participle construction = subject

Present participle constructions in this function are rare. They occur in passive sentences, in which they correspond to the direct object in the corresponding active predicate (see section 4.5.2): *myddis euery herber myght be sene The scharp[e] grene suete ienepere, Growing so fair with branchis here and there* (KI 220ff.)

(d) present participle construction = direct object

Objects can only be realised by present participle constructions with subject. This construction type is not very frequent, and it occurs only from the sixteenth century onwards. After the verbs *see* and *hear*, which characteristically govern it, it commutes with the infinitive construction with subject and without preposition:

> *he [. . .] saw þe victory inclynand to him* (BELL 273.3f.)
> *I sawe, walking vnder the tour, [. . .], The fairest or the freschest yong[e] floure* (KI 275ff.)

(e) present participle construction = complement of conjunction

Here the present participle construction has the same function as the clause in adverbial conjunctional clauses. As in these, the conjunction establishes a semantic link between the embedded construction and the matrix clause. It is probably by accident that so far only examples with subject have been found:

> *King Robert eftir sindry chancis of batall succeding to him with grete felicite on þis maner enterit in Ergyle with ane strang army* (BELL 269.4ff.) [relation of time]
> *sindry Scottis men quhilkis for felicite succeding to Inglismen tuke þair part þis tyme contrair þair native prince* (BELL 271.23f.) [relation of cause]

In the participle constructions described above, the participle has only verbal properties, e.g., it can govern an object, and it can combine with a subject. In a different type of participle construction, the present participle has the properties of a substantive e.g., it can be premodified by a determiner and postmodified by a prepositional syntagm. Present participle constructions of this type occur with the same functions as substantival syntagms, subject, copulative complement, direct object, and complement of a preposition in a prepositional object:

> *belongeth the reading thereof vnto Kings* (DOR 29.14f.)
> *þis js the fud and werray nurising of the saule* (WIS 45.28f.)
> *he, that had na persawyng Off the tresoun* (BRU I.596f.)
> *he that baide the cumyne of his frend* (DE 37f.)
> *thaim that ar put in the fechinge of dede* (DE 5f.)

Past participle constructions occur only as modifiers and as adverbial complements. As modifiers they have no subject. When the past participle has an active meaning, it is expanded by *having*; when it has a passive meaning, it is sometimes expanded by *being*. In the first case, it can govern the same complements as an active verbal syntagm, in the second, those of a passive syntagm. Past participle constructions as adverbial complements occur with and without subject.

(a) past participle construction = modifier

> *al tormentis and passionys done to thaim* (DE 56f.)
> *this hevinly Orisoune teichit and gevin be the blist sone of god jhesus* (WIS 24.1f.)

(b) past participle construction = adverbial complement

> *Being thus advis'd away to Pete I trudge* (WAT 21.7) [without subject]
> *the said patrik haueing verie modestlie and soberlie ansuerit him [. . .], he, [. . .] burst*
>   *furth in moist bitter and passionat speetcheis aganis him* (GG 232.24ff.)
> *The Speech thus ended, she sat down* (WAT 67.785)
> *þe vangard of Ingliſßmen being disconnfist, þe Danis & Scottis fell to spoulʒe* (BELL 88.2f.)

As with present participle constructions, there is a structural ambiguity when a subject is lacking: *missing him thair, being informed that he wes riddin to the place of tullidone to the baptisme of his susteris bairne, he addrest him selff with all speid and come to the said place* (GG 231.22ff.). Here the clause-initial position of the two participle constructions suggests an analysis as adverbial complements.

NOTES

1. Database

BELL: *The Chronicles of Scotland. Compiled by Hector Boece. Translated into Scots by John Bellenden 1531*, 2 vols, ed. R. W. Chambers and Edith C. Batho (Edinburgh and London: William Blackwood, 1938 and 1941).

BRU: *The Bruce or The Book of the Most Excellent and Noble Prince Robert de Broyss, King of Scots. Compiled by Master John Barbour*, 2 vols, ed. Walter W. Skeat (Edinburgh and London: William Blackwood, 1894; repr. 1966).

COM: *The Complaynt of Scotlande wyth ane Exortatione to the Thre Estaits to be vigilante in the Deffens of their Public veil. 1549*, ed. James A. H. Murray (London: Trübner, 1872).

DE: 'The Craft of Deyng', *Ratis Raving and Other Early Scots Poems on Morals*, ed. R. Girvan (Edinburgh and London: William Blackwood, 1939), pp. 166–74.

DOR: *The Basilicon Doron of King James VI*, 2 vols, ed. James Craigie (Edinburgh and London: Blackwood, 1944 and 1950).

GG: 'Register of the Privy Council (1618). The Story of Gordon of Gicht', in Gregory G. Smith, *Specimens of Middle Scots* (Edinburgh and London: William Blackwood, 1902), pp. 231–8.

KI: *James I of Scotland. The Kingis Quhair*, ed. John Norton-Smith (Oxford: Clarendon Press, 1971).

LAU: *Journals of Sir John Lauder Lord Fountainhall with his Observations on Public Affairs and Other Memoranda 1665–1676*, ed. Donald Crawford (Edinburgh: The Scottish History Society, 1900).

MEL: 'The Historie of ane Nobil and Wailʒeand Squyer, William Meldrum', *The Works of Sir David Lindsay of the Mount 1490–1555*, vol. 1, ed. Douglas Hamer (Edinburgh and London: William Blackwood, 1931), pp. 146–88.

OWL: 'The Buke of the Howlat', *Longer Scottish Poems: Volume One 1375–1650*, ed. Priscilla Bawcutt and Felicity Riddy (Edinburgh: Scottish Academic Press, 1987), pp. 46–84.

WAT: *James Watson's Choice Collection of Comic and Serious Scots Poems*, vol. 1, ed. Harriet Harvey Wood (Edinburgh: The Scottish Text Society, 1977). [The following poems are included in the database: 'The Blythsome Wedding'; 'The Banishment of Poverty'; 'The Poor Client's

Complaint'; 'The Speech of a Fife Laird, Newly come from the Grave'; 'The Life and Death of the Piper of Kilbarchan'; 'The Mare of Collingtoun Newly Revived'; 'The Last Dying Words of Bonny Heck, A Famous Grey-Hound in the Shire of Fife'; 'William Lithgow, Writer in Edinburgh, his Epitaph'.]

WIS: *The Meroure of Wyβdome Composed for the Use of James IV, King of Scots A.D. 1490 by Johannes de Irlandia*, ed. Charles Macpherson (Edinburgh and London: William Blackwood, 1926).

2. Texts are quoted by page and line number. Where it was thought helpful, English translations of the examples are added in inverted commas.
3. The construction is still current in Modern German, where it varies freely with the construction without an initial grammatical subject, e.g. *es kam ein heftiger Wind auf – ein heftiger Wind kam auf*. If the lexical subject is a plural, it governs a plural verb form, e.g., *es ereigneten sich viele Unfälle*.
4. For an alternative analysis of this construction, compare p. 149.

5

The Inflectional Morphology of Older Scots

Anne King

5.1 INTRODUCTION

5.1.1 Pre-literary Scots: Reconstruction and Linguistic Influences

This chapter deals with the inflectional morphology of Older Scots, conventionally that period in the history of Scots from 1100 to 1700. Both topic and time are particularly fascinating because these six centuries witness the transformation of Scots on several different, but interrelated, linguistic and sociolinguistic levels. The language started out as the most northerly branch of the Northumbrian dialect of Old English, which reached Scotland as a result of northward raiding and then conquest by Bernicians and Deirans in the seventh and eighth centuries (on the historical and archaeological evidence, see, for instance, Yorke 1990: chapter 5). Analysis and interpretation of those 'Anglian' place-names which indicate Northumbrian settlement in various areas of southern Scotland, mainly the south-east, from the late seventh century onwards allow the assumption to be made that some form of Northumbrian Old English – which developed into Pre-literary Scots (c. 1100 to c. 1375) – was spoken to some extent in this region from at least this time on (see the account in Nicolaisen 1976: chapter 5; and articles as relevant in McNeill and Nicholson 1975).

We have very little written evidence of the kind of evolutionary or stylistic intralinguistic variation that must have existed and is to be found in later periods of Scots until the Older Scots period proper (c. 1375 to c. 1700) is under way. It is only at the very end of the aptly named Pre-literary Scots period that we find the first written records of Scots. No records survive from before the twelfth century, and even those from it and the next century tend to be confined to glosses in Latin charters translating personal and place-names. But, from these meagre resources, it is still possible to glean some evidence of the inflectional morphology of nouns and adjectives in twelfth- and thirteenth-century Scots which helps us to reconstruct developments that had occurred since the tenth century – see W. A. Craigie (1925) and sections 5.2.4, 5.2.5 and 5.2.11.1 below. However, as Macafee (1992–3: §1.4) points out, 'Fortunately, Scots can more or less be identified [linguistically] with Northern Middle English in the early Middle English period'. This is not only to be expected in view of the shared origins of both Scots and Northern English, but it is also very welcome: although early Northern Middle English writings are relatively rare until the thirteenth century and there exists a gap between them and extant tenth-century late

Northumbrian Old English texts (see section 5.2.7.2 below), they do provide data from the thirteenth century which help us to reconstruct the changes that took place in the inflectional morphology (and, of course, other levels of the language) until our earliest substantial Scots texts in the late fourteenth century.

Furthermore, the linguistic similarity between Scots and Northern English must have increased, or at least been fostered, as a result of the direct linguistic contact into which both were brought by the external historical events of the eleventh and twelfth centuries which saw the reform of the Scottish church and the introduction and establishment in Scotland of the feudal and burgh systems along the lines of their English models (for details, see for instance Lynch 1992: chapters 5, 7 and 10; Dickinson 1961: chapters 9–15). These institutions and systems were begun and staffed mainly by emigrants from the north of England, some of whom were Anglo-Norman noblemen or Anglo-Norse by descent (Murison 1974) on the personal-name evidence from witnesses' lists in contemporary charters. Most of these émigrés were, however, natives who spoke (and wrote) a Northern English dialect influenced by Old Norse and Norman French. So, not only was Pre-literary Scots exposed to, and affected by, this Northern English, but it was at the same time indirectly influenced by these other languages too, as will emerge from the morphological evidence presented below.

5.1.2 Older Scots: Textual Evidence

From its beginnings as a somewhat isolated linguistic offshoot of Northern English, Scots passed through the period of strongest Northern English influence just described and, by the midpoint of the Middle Scots period (c. 1450 to c. 1550), had established itself as a standard written language, independent of the burgeoning Southern English one. This was the result of various language-internal developments which marked it off from the non-Northern Englishes contemporary with it, as well as the functional elaboration, with concomitant stylistic variation in language, necessary for the establishment of a standard language (Meurman-Solin 1993a).

Agutter (1989b) makes a plausible case for the completion, so far as Middle Scots is concerned, of the first two stages – selection and acceptance – in the process of standardisation (Leith 1983: 38–57, and, on Scots, 153–64). Her evidence for the completion of the third stage – elaboration – is not, however, quite so convincing, since she concentrates only on a few aspects of stylistic variation in literary texts, with the result that she examines only a small portion of the existing evidence. From the Early Scots period on, the range, quantity and subject matter of extant texts in Scots is impressively large. Text types belong to the 'public' domains of law, government, scholarship, education, religion and literature, as well as 'private' ones like travelogues. From the Early Scots period on, Scots was the medium of, for instance, charters, indentures, Acts of Parliament, burgh records, the Laws of Scotland, diplomatic letters, trials, histories, treatises (on, for instance, chivalry or morality), handbooks (on topography, kingship, theology), diaries and private letters, as well as a vast body of literature encompassing the whole stylistic range from courtly lyric and epic to flyting and drama (Slater 1952; MacRae 1975; Jack 1988; Meurman-Solin 1993a; King forthcoming). All in all, the evidence points to 'Scots having been a multi-purpose language which developed into a . . . national standard' (Meurman-Solin 1993a: 41).

By the end of our time-span, Scots was changing yet again as a result of the beginnings of a restandardisation process which Meurman–Solin (1993a: 41) very nicely describes as Scots 'gradually los[ing] its multiple functions and merg[ing] into a closely related language'. The linguistic evidence at this time therefore has to do with co-variation between Scots and English, as well as the effects of late Middle Scots diachronic change. Both of these led ultimately to the present-day situation in Lowland Scotland whereby a Scottish form of 'Standard' English exists alongside the eight or so regional dialect descendants of Older Scots.

5.1.3   Older Scots Inflectional Morphology

Older Scots was affected by the same sort of fundamental linguistic restructuring undergone by English in its transition from Old to Middle and Early Modern English. Where inflectional morphology is concerned, this restructuring often involved the same processes, for example analogy, extension and levelling. Sometimes these produced identical results in Scots and English, such as the reduction in number of vowel grades per verb or the introduction of a new periphrastic type of genitive. However, the Scots and/or Northern linguistic input often differed from that of Midland, Southern and South-eastern dialects of early Middle English; and, moreover, divergent developments occurred in Scots, so that features specifically characteristic of Scots emerged as the outcome. The description and discussion of these processes and their results, and their interplay with the standardisation and restandardisation factors outlined earlier, will form the basis of the rest of this chapter.

As Lass (1992: 91) points out, 'morphology is [. . .] something of a "bridge" or interface between phonology and syntax [which] in any significant sense really exists only via a complex of dependencies and realisations involving not only syntax and phonology, but semantics as well'. The material which follows, therefore, is structured so as to reflect these interdependencies. Where reference is made to 'English' or 'Englishes' henceforward, all English dialects, Northern and Southern is the meaning intended; 'the north' refers to Lowland Scotland and England north of the Humber, while 'Northern' refers to Lowland Scots and Northern English; 'Scots' is Older Scots, unless otherwise specified.

5.2   THE NOUN PHRASE

Under this heading fall four major word classes relevant to Older Scots, each of which will be examined in turn: nouns; determiners (articles, deictics, numerals and some quantifiers); pronouns (personal, relative and interrogative) and adjectives – see, for instance, McArthur (1992: 287–8); Greenbaum and Quirk (1990: §§5.3–5.10); Burton-Roberts (1986: chapter 7).

5.2.1   Nouns and Morphosyntactic Categories

The Old English division of nouns into strong or weak declensions no longer pertains by the time of Older Scots, and, of the three morphosyntactic categories, gender, number and case, expressed in the inflectional morphology of nouns in Old English, only two – number and case – survive. Gender, number and case concord between noun-phrase constituents is greatly modified.

The shift, complete in Middle English by the end of the thirteenth century, from the grammatical gender which characterised Old English[1] to the natural gender with which we are familiar now, had taken place also in Scots by the Early Scots period. This move away from grammatical gender marking in nouns (and their modifiers and anaphors) in the earliest Scots texts should come as no surprise given that this simplification began in the north in late Northumbrian Old English texts like the *Glosses* to the *Lindisfarne Gospels* or the *Durham Ritual* (Jones 1988: chapters 2 and 3; Lass 1992; Traugott 1992). In the former text, fluctuations occur involving traditionally masculine nouns, such as *stān* (masculine) appearing as both masculine and neuter, or *lofsong* 'hymn' (masculine) appearing not with the expected masculine demonstrative but with a neuter one in accordance with its natural gender (or rather, absence of animacy).

Number and case, as stated above, remain as categories expressed in Older Scots, but are simplified along lines similar to the Englishes contemporary with it. Singular or plural number marking on nouns continues (on dual number, see section 5.2.8), but case marking is eroded, largely by the twelfth century, resulting in accusative and dative merging to produce one, oblique case. This happens partly as a result of its being, like gender, what Lass (1992: 105–6) calls a 'covert noun category' – neither case nor gender in Old English being clearly and unambiguously indicated in the inflexions added to the noun itself. Because the domain of these categories is the noun phrase, the forms of determiners, pronouns and the endings on strong adjectives (to which the noun was related via concord or anaphora) had to provide the necessary distinctive and overt expression of this grammatical information. Erosion of the case system was also a by-product of the restructuring of the noun declension system itself (its membership and paradigm types) producing a general type following the pattern of the commonest Old English noun type: strong masculine *a*-stems, as in Table 5.1. When this paradigm is compared with its Older Scots descendant (see Table 5.2), it can be seen that only the two parameters of singular vs plural and non-genitive vs genitive were normally expressed in the noun, and these, where the general declension class is concerned (see section 5.2.3.1 below), by means of only one inflection -{S}, spelled ⟨is⟩ contrasting with the two ⟨es⟩ (genitive singular) and ⟨as⟩ (nominative/accusative plural) encountered in Old English. The extension of this paradigm – which Lass (1992: 109) accurately calls 'the target for analogical modification of other declensions' – took place first and most quickly in the north. Many nouns originally of other declensions had gone over to this strong masculine *a*-stem declension in late North-umbrian (see Strang 1970: §165). The evolution of the ⟨is⟩ inflection, whether nominal, as here, or verbal (see sections 5.3.2.1–5.3.2.2 below), and the realisations of inflections (whether nominal or verbal) containing the unstressed vowel spelt ⟨i⟩ and the consonant spelt ⟨s⟩, will now be considered.

Table 5.1

	Singular	Plural
Nominative	*cyning* ø	*cyning*as
Accusative	*cyning* ø	*cyning*as
Genitive	*cyning*es	*cyning*a
Dative	*cyning*e	*cyning*um

Table 5.2

	Singular	Plural
Nominative/oblique	*king* ø	*king*is
Genitive	*king*is	*king*is

5.2.2 The Realisations of Inflections Containing ⟨i⟩

5.2.2.1 The ⟨i⟩ Graph in Inflectional Syllables

The paradigm illustrated in Table 5.2 shows the use in Older Scots of the ⟨i⟩ graph (⟨y⟩, its graphic equivalent appears too, but less persistently, and mainly in earlier texts; wherever ⟨i⟩ is cited below in inflections, ⟨y⟩ is a possible graphic alternant) in the unstressed vowel position of nominal inflections (as here, or in the gerundive inflection ⟨ing⟩) and verbal ones like ⟨is⟩, ⟨it⟩, ⟨id⟩ or ⟨in⟩ – see sections 5.3.2.1 and 5.3.5.3 below. From the late thirteenth century onwards, this ⟨i⟩ is found in Northern English texts too, as Kristensson (1967: 182–8) describes. There, however, its occurrence was much less regular than in Scots or than the ⟨e⟩ spelling with which it co-occurred and which was common in this unstressed final syllable position in all Middle English dialect texts. Indeed, ⟨e⟩ is the very earliest spelling that we find in inflections in Scots too, a usage which Slater (1952) attributes to English scribal influence. Given the linguistic contact between Northern English and Pre-literary and Early Scots speakers and writers, this usage, as well as the introduction of ⟨i⟩ as a replacement, may well have Northern English scribal practice as their source.

However, while there may well be something in Slater's claim, it is equally or more likely that both spelling usages have a phonetic basis. A. Campbell (1959: §§369, 373–80) gives an account of the confusion and gradual disappearance during the tenth century of distinctive spellings for what had been a variety of unstressed front and back vowel qualities in inflectional syllables in earlier Old English (that is, excluding the high front vowel /i/ found in derivational suffixes like *-ic*, *-isc*, *-ing*, *-ig*, *-lic* and so on which has tended to retain its ⟨i⟩ spelling in the Modern English reflexes of these Old English suffixes right up to the present day (Campbell 1959: §371). Free variation of ⟨e⟩, ⟨a⟩, ⟨æ⟩, ⟨o⟩ and ⟨u⟩ spellings for the vowel(s) in inflectional syllables gives way to a predominant ⟨e⟩ spelling in late Old English which, Campbell suggests, represents a reduction to one unstressed vowel quality, normally interpreted as /ə/. Or, to put it another way, as does Minkova (1991: 89):

> after the beginning of the eleventh century, more and more graphemic differences begin to disappear, a fact suggesting progressive neutralisation of phonemes occurring in this position. The lack of phonemic distinctiveness apparently underlies the replacement of the old graphemes by ⟨e⟩. The appearance of this grapheme in practically all post-tonic positions is interpreted as a graphic reflex of what, in phonetic terms, would be a reduction of the respective vowels, and in phonemic terms – a structure determined neutralisation – a case of suspended opposition due to lack of stress. Thus English sees the advent of the schwa, the reduced, . . . indeterminate . . . vowel.

The evidence just presented reinforces such statements in Middle English grammars as: '[i]n a weakly stressed position Middle English [including Northern varieties] had two phonemes, /i/ and /ə/' (Fisiak 1968: 46). As to how the ⟨i⟩ spellings which develop in Northern and Scots texts relate to these vowel qualities, Minkova (1991: 121) proposes that they might represent the output of a raising of schwa in some environments, for example, 'before nasals and dentals'. While there is nothing to indicate that the consonants represented by ⟨s⟩, ⟨t⟩ or ⟨d⟩ (for verbal forms) in Older Scots inflections were dental (they are usually thought to have been alveolar), this does not present a problem. Lass, for instance, includes alveolars with dentals as a vowel-raising 'agent' in his rule for Middle English pre-dental raising (1976: 79, 185), Minkova's suggestion is therefore a perfectly acceptable one. She goes on to say (1991: 122):

> It would be reasonable to interpret [the ⟨i⟩ spellings] as an attempt at a more rigorous phonetic representation of the raised unstressed vowels, for which there are no adequate symbols in the graphemic system. This would account for the use of the same graphemes for the high vowels in stressed as in unstressed position.

The vowel in the Older Scots ⟨is⟩ nominal inflection therefore represents a reduction to /ə/ of the various unstressed vowels seen in the ⟨s⟩ forms of the Old English paradigm in Table 5.1, followed by a raising to /i/ in Northern Middle English varieties (which of course include Scots) in the context of a following 'dental' or nasal consonant, in turn reflected by the choice of ⟨i⟩ (or ⟨y⟩) in spelling. Scots apparently generalised /i/ (though /ə/ remained part of the unstressed vowel system) while Northern English, on the evidence of ⟨e⟩ and ⟨i⟩ usage (see section 5.3.2.1), used both /ə/ and /i/ interchangeably.

5.2.2.2 The Realisation of the Consonant in the ⟨is⟩ Inflection

The morpheme {S} is spelled either ⟨i/ys⟩ or, where the stem ends in a vowel graph (for example, *buke* 'book') by ⟨s⟩ alone. Assuming that the same morphophonological rules apply as for {S} in modern Standard English, ⟨(i)s⟩ was, we could posit, realised in Older Scots as:

1. [iz] after sibilant or affricate consonants, for example ⟨hous*is*⟩ [hu:siz];
2. [s] (sometimes [is] in poetry if the metre requires a syllabic pronunciation), after other voiceless consonants, for example ⟨catt*is*⟩ 'cats' or 'cat's' [kɑts];
3. [z] (or [iz]; compare preceding) after other voiced consonants, for example ⟨dogg*is*⟩ 'dogs' or 'dog's' [dɔgz].

However, realisations of [iz] and [z] with the voiceless fricative [s] rather than its voiced counterpart [z] – that is [is] and [s] respectively – are certainly a possibility in the Older Scots period in view of the apparent Scots preference in syllable-final position (whether the syllables are stems or inflections) for the voiceless rather than the voiced congener of pairs like [s, z], [f, v] and [t, d]. This can be seen in, for example, Older Scots *haif* 'have' or *luf(e)* 'love', where ⟨f⟩ apparently represents voiceless [f] and not the expected [v] (which would be spelled ⟨u⟩, ⟨v⟩ or ⟨w⟩ in Older Scots). Jordan and Crook (1974: §214) ascribe this phenomenon to a devoicing in the north of /v/ to /f/, following final schwa loss. Kristensson (1967: 235–6) also presents Northern English data from the thirteenth and fourteenth centuries in support of Jordan and Crook's claim.

According to the spelling evidence, the voiceless [(i)t] ⟨(i)t⟩ inflection for the past tense and past participle in weak verbs is preferred in Scots over the voiced [(i)d] ⟨(i)d⟩ option (see section 5.3.2.2 for verbs). It is also a feature of Modern Scots: see, for instance, Jones (1996: 77–8) for eighteenth-century data, and Macafee (n.d. 19–22) for a description of twentieth-century mainland Scots dialect characteristics like the occurrence of the [-t] ⟨it⟩ form of weak verb past-tense inflection showing a voiceless [t] even after voiced non-sibilants or non-affricates where Standard English would have voiced [d], such as [g] in *biggit* 'built' or [v] in *screivit* 'written', or the occurrence of the [t] ⟨t⟩ form as against Standard English [d] following nasals and liquids, for example *earn't* 'earned', *flutter't* 'fluttered' or *killt* 'killed'.

Where [s] and [z] are concerned, evidence is harder to come by since normally only the graph ⟨s⟩ (or sometimes ⟨ss⟩) is used in Older Scots to represent either consonant; ⟨z⟩ occasionally occurs, but only in words of Greek origin, such as *zeill, baptize* (Kuipers 1964a: 82). Jordan and Crook (1974: §208) claim in relation to the ⟨is⟩ inflection that '*s* must have become voiced before the disappearance of the vowel [presumably schwa]'. They present no evidence to support this claim, however. On the contrary, they adduce rather a lot of evidence for either the retention of voiceless [s] or the devoicing of [z] to [s]. For instance, they cite Murray (1873: 126) as 'show[ing]' [s] in the words *(h)is, was, has* in the sixteenth century and go on to claim that schwa loss in hiatus or in weakly accented words before the occurrence of the [s] to [z] voicing which he describes (1873: 153–4) meant that [s] remained voiceless, though there is no evidence of this in spelling until the Modern English period when ⟨ce⟩ is used to represent [s], for example Middle English *trews, twis, pens* or *whens* vs their Modern English forms *truce, twice, pence* and *whence*. In addition, in their next paragraph (§209), Jordan and Crook describe the Northern devoicing of intervocalic [z] to [s] when it becomes syllable-final as a result of schwa loss (compare the analogous [v] to [f] development described earlier).

Jordan and Crook, then, present no evidence synchronic with Older Scots which would count against an [s] realisation rather than, or as a possible alternative to an [z] one. In addition, there is ample evidence above of the Scots preference for voiceless realisations of the labiodental, dental and alveolar fricatives (whether this is phonologically or morphologically motivated, see section 5.2.3.6) where other varieties have the voiced realisations. There seems no reason in principle, therefore, to discard the possibility of a Scots preference for the voiceless rather than the voiced realisation of the ⟨(i)s⟩ inflection on nouns, as here, or on verbs. Furthermore, there is the evidence of the behaviour in Scots of the minor class of nouns described at section 5.2.3.6 below which arose in the Middle English period and which give further support to the claim being made here.

5.2.3 Noun Classes and their Membership

There are four main noun declensions in Older Scots, classified according to the way in which plural number is expressed: general, weak, mutative and invariant, together with a few minor types such as those showing *r*-plurals. In this respect, Scots does not differ significantly from the Englishes contemporary with it. Noun–class membership did, however, show some variation, as will emerge.

5.2.3.1 The General Class

As in Modern Scots and English, most nouns in Older Scots belong to the general class, descended, as pointed out earlier, from the Old English strong *a*-stem masculine type. The paradigm in Table 5.2 is typical of general-class inflections – indeed, of those of all noun classes, except where the marking of non-genitive plural (and the occasional genitive plural; see further below) is concerned.

5.2.3.2 Weak Plurals

A small number of nouns in Older Scots continue as members of what had been the weak -*an*-inflected class in Old English. The Scots plural inflections are in ⟨(i)n⟩. Membership of this class remained slightly larger in Scots than in non-Northern English, for example *ox* 'ox' (which remained a weak plural in English too with the inflection ⟨(e)n⟩), plural *oxin* (with a mixed, root-modified plus {N}-inflected variant *oussin*), plus *e(y)* 'eye', plural *eyn* and, from the thirteenth century, *scho* 'shoe', plural *scho(y)ne*. The latter exemplifies the shifting between declensions that occurred in Scots (as in English): *shoe*, for instance, had been a strong *a*-stem noun in Old English (indeed, an ⟨s⟩ form – *schoys* – of this noun continued in use in Scots).

5.2.3.3 Mutative Plurals

The membership of this class – characterised by modification in the plural of the root vowel seen in the singular (the result of *i-umlaut* in Pre- Old English) rather than the addition of an inflection – decreases quite significantly between Old English and Early Scots (for example *buke* 'book', *nut* 'nut', *ake* 'oak', all of which go over to the general class). On the other hand, a fair number survive, such as *fute* 'foot' with /øː/, (compare plural *fete* with /iː/), *mous/mys* and *cow/ky*. The plural form *brether* 'brothers' continues, just as it had in Old English, to be uninflected, but the mutated root vowel (compare singular *brother*) has been extended from the Old English dative singular. The forms *ky* and *brether* are distinctive to Scots in that Southern English had the mixed forms *kine* and *breth(e)ren* with vowel mutation simultaneous with weak noun inflections.

5.2.3.4 ø-plurals

As in English, this class was much larger in Older Scots than at present. A significant number of the nouns in this class are descended from the strong neuters with a ø-plural in Old English, for instance *deir* 'deer' (singular and plural), *schepe* 'sheep', *swine* 'swine', *hors* 'horse'. Bird and fish referents like these animal ones existed too: *foul* 'fowl' or *fisch* 'fish' (see, for example, Ekwall 1975: §192) for examples applicable to Scots and English). The last two examples illustrate the noun class switching from the -*as* plural of Old English to the ø-plural. This switching was not complete, however, as forms in {S} continued side by side with those with no plural inflection mark.

Nouns expressing quantity, extent or measurement belong in this class in Older (and sometimes still in Modern) Scots, showing ø-plural forms in the following: *pund* 'pounds', *mile* 'miles', *yere* 'years', *nicht* 'nights' (an Old English mutative noun) or *monith* 'months'. Only some of these nouns had no plural inflection in Old English, such as *yere* or, sometimes, *monith*, and the lack of plural inflection on the others may be explicable simply in terms of the reduction to schwa and subsequent schwa loss of Old English nominative/ accusative plural inflections. Such would be the case for *mile*, which was an Old English weak feminine noun with nominative/accusative plural in -*an*. As Campbell (1959: §617) points out, in late Northumbrian Old English (from which Scots is, of course, descended), final -*n* was always lost. The development of the remaining [ɑ] vowel would be as outlined above, producing the ø-plural which we find in Older Scots. An alternative explanation, deriving from the use of such nouns most commonly in expressions of quantity, is given below in section 5.2.4.1.

Also belonging here, at least for the north, are nouns denoting rank, for instance *duke* 'duke', and miscellaneous words like *thing* 'thing' or *fowk* 'folk' (both long-stemmed strong neuter nouns with ø-plurals in nominative/accusative in Old English) as well as Old French loanwords with stem-final consonant [s] themselves uninflected for plural in French, remaining thus in early Middle English and Scots, for example *case* 'case/s', *vers* 'verse/s', *sense* 'sense/s', *cors* (later *corps*) 'corpse'. Alongside a number of these ø-plurals, regular {S} forms existed too during the Older Scots period, and such doublets can for the most part still be found in Modern Scots.

5.2.3.5   *r*-plurals

A few *r*-plurals survive from the Old English paradigm containing -*ru* plural inflections, for example *caur* 'calves', the plural of *calf* with /v/-deletion (a general class variant existed too – *kavis*). Another instance is the plural form *childer* 'children' (compare English mixed *children* with {R} and weak {N}). This may derive from an early Old English (West Saxon) nominative plural form *cilderu* (Campbell 1959: §635). The more usual Scots lexeme for 'child', however, is *ba(i)rn* with the {S} general class plural inflection.

5.2.3.6   Plurals with Voicing + {S} Inflection

A small class of nouns arose in the Middle English period displaying morphophonemic voicing alternations in the stem, that is, voicing of voiceless fricatives in conjunction with the adding of the {S} plural morpheme typical of general class nouns. Most of these survive into Modern Standard English and include (in Modern English forms) the following singular/plural, voiceless/voiced fricative alternants: *elf/elves*, *dwarf/dwarves*, *roof/roofs*, *wife/wives*, *house/houses*, *mouth/mouths*, *path/paths*, *bath/baths*, *youth/youths*.

This noun class tends not to exist in Modern Scots, as Macafee (n.d.: 32) points out. She cites the forms *houses* with stem-final [s] and *wifes* 'wives' with stem-final [f]. What generally happens is that the voiceless fricative of the singular stem does not become voiced in the plural, as a result of which the voiceless realisation [s] of the {S} plural morpheme is triggered. In Standard English, the modified, voiced stem-final consonant triggers the voiced [z] allomorph of {S}. Morphophonologically, then, nouns like Modern Scots *knife*, *wife* or *mooth* 'mouth' behave exactly like general class nouns, and, in so doing, they evince once again the Scots tendency noted earlier to select a voiceless over the voiced alternative in syllable-final contexts.

Because our primary source of evidence for Older Scots phonology is its spelling, and since only with [f] and [v] are voiceless ~ voiced alternations likely to show up in ⟨f⟩ ~ ⟨u/ v/w⟩ spelling alternations, this set is the only one to which we can turn for information on the existence or not in Older Scots of this class of noun plurals with voicing + {S}. The available data, however, suggest that the situation in Older Scots was not so stable as the Modern Scots one seems to be: variation between ⟨f(f)⟩ and ⟨v⟩ forms appears to be the norm; for example, *wyvis* 'women/wives' occurs as well as *wyfis*, *neves* 'fists' alongside *neif(f)is*, *elffis* 'elves', *calfis/calfis/kavis* 'calves', *lyvis/lyfis* 'lives'. This class of nouns may or may not, therefore, have existed in Older Scots.

5.2.4 The Expression of Genitive Case

There are traces in the very earliest records of Scots (W. A. Craigie 1925: 64) of the survival into the twelfth century of genitive plural inflections of the Old English type, for example *munkeford* 'monk's ford', where the ⟨e⟩ graph represents schwa, the reduction of the [ɑ] vowel which in Old English expressed genitive plural in the strong masculine *a*-stem class to which *munuc* 'monk' belonged. Apart from rare relic forms like this, however, ⟨(i)s⟩ seems very quickly to have replaced the paradigm-specific type of inflection seen in Old English (indeed, the form just discussed appears in Early Scots charters as ⟨monkisford⟩) and to have become the regular inflection in Older Scots for the genitive case. This applied to all classes of noun and for singular and plural, as the examples in Table 5.3 show.

Table 5.3

Class	Genitive singular	Genitive plural
General	*dogg*is	*dogg*is
Weak	*ox*is	*oxin*is
Mutative	*cow*is/*ku*is	*ky*is
Invariant	*nicht*is	*nicht*is
r-plurals	*cauf*is	*caur*is

5.2.4.1 ø-genitives

There exist in Older Scots two small noun subclasses which remain uninflected for genitive case. The first of these is an example of the limited survival in Scots of the ø-morpheme for genitive singular found in nouns of relationship in Old English (Campbell 1959: §629). Instances of this are: *sistir son* 'sister's son' ('nephew on the sister's side'), or *brothir/brodir dochtir* 'brother's daughter' ('niece on the brother's side'). With such nouns, uninflected genitive plural forms may also occasionally surface, such as *bredir barnys* 'brothers' children'. Some examples of this continue to exist in Modern Scots, such as *mither side*, *sister bairn* or *sister son* (the latter two from Shetland and Orkney respectively). These forms are, however, probably only fossilised remains; this genitive marking seems no longer to be productive. Analogous to this usage in the sense that it defines one's place in society (compare one's place in the family, above) is the ø-genitive singular which can occur in nouns which are expressions of rank or office, for example *duke*, *friar* and so on.

The second subclass exhibiting ø-genitives, this time in the plural, is certain ø-plural nouns of quantity, extent or measurement, like *pund*, *mile*, *nicht* discussed in section 5.2.3.4. This usage is probably a continuation of the measuring, partitive and adverbial functions of the genitive case in Old English (Quirk and Wrenn 1957: §§101–2), marked in strong nouns by the ⟨a⟩ inflection. This, following reduction of the [ɑ] to schwa and then loss of final schwa, produced the ø-inflection which we have here; as hinted at in section 2.3.4, this might also be the source of the pattern, for some ø-plural nouns of quantity and the like, of the non-marking of nominative/oblique plurals. Examples include: *xx chalder aits, j fute & vi inch of clath*, *alkynd fruyt and grayn* and *ii pund of buttir*.

5.2.4.2   Periphrastic Genitive Expression

A new analytic genitive using the preposition *of*, for example *ye seel of ye saide katerine* 'the said Katherine's seal', becomes in the course of Older Scots a strong alternative to the synthetic ⟨(i)s⟩ expression. This usage, favoured particularly in prose at first, may, at least partially, as Macafee (1992–3: §3.10) suggests, have been due to the influence of Old French and Medieval Latin, both of which had periphrasis with *de* as the normal expression of genitive. This type of genitive had a parenthetic or split variant, as in *ye kingis docher of England* 'the King of England's daughter'.

5.2.5   The Expression of Dative Case

As already pointed out with regard to the genitive, vestiges of the Old English synthetic marking of the dative case on nouns can be found in the earliest Scots texts. Craigie (1925: 64) cites, among others, the form *hale* 'haugh/river-meadow land', which retains the Old English dative singular inflection ⟨e⟩, in comparison with the uninflected nominative form *halch*. However, such forms very soon give way to the more usual Scots periphrastic expression using prepositions like *to* and *for* with uninflected nouns, for example *to the forsaid Alexander*.

In Early Scots, synthetic and analytic expressions of what had been in Old English the adverbial function of the dative case could co-occur, as in *for ye terme of hir lyfe*, where *term* is marked with ⟨e⟩ (the reflex of the Old English dative singular ⟨e⟩), as well as occurring in the prepositional phrase with adverbial function. After this transitional period, inflectional marking of the dative case in nouns largely disappears and, like the object dative function, is expressed only periphrastically with prepositions and nouns unmarked for dative. A few instances of dative plural-inflected forms become fossilised in Older Scots and English and function as adverbs, so: *quhilom* 'at times/sometimes' (compare Old English *hwilum*) and *seldom*, a form altered on analogy with *quhilom* from its Old English form *seldan*. These adverbial forms therefore stand apart from the usual ones which are inflected in ⟨ly⟩ or (less commonly) ⟨li⟩, though forms do occur which add this suffix to a former strong dative singular form of the adjective, such as *gretumly* 'greatly'.

5.2.6   Articles

5.2.6.1   The Indefinite Article

The split in function of the Old English cardinal numeral *ān* into two, the numeral *one* and the indefinite article *a(n)* (which function was shared in a sense with *sum*), was embryonic in late Old English, but *an* was established as the indefinite article by the Middle English period, with the form *a* appearing also in the twelfth century (Strang 1970: §151; Jordan and Crook 1974: §§150, 170, 172). In Scots, three forms occur: *a*, *an* and *ane*, and their usage varies according to date and whether the article preceded a word beginning with a vowel, a consonant or ⟨h⟩.

Table 5.4

Early Scots (late 1300s)	Middle Scots (late 1400s)
a + vowel or + consonant	*an* + vowel only
an + consonant or + ⟨h⟩	*ane* + vowel or + consonant or + ⟨h⟩
(not pronounced in French loans)	(not pronounced in French loans)
ane + vowel	

From Table 5.4, it is clear that only the 'inflected' form of the indefinite article was used by the Middle Scots period: *ane* was the most usual form, and it occurred before consonants as well as before vowels and silent ⟨h⟩; so, for example, *ane buke, ane egg, ane herb*. We cannot be certain whether final [n] of *ane* was pronounced or not before a consonant (other than that spelt ⟨h⟩), but there is no evidence from Modern Scots to suggest that this was the case. *Ane* continued in use also as a cardinal numeral, where it probably had the pronunciation [e(:)n], with a short [e(n)] or even an unstressed [ə(n)] pronunciation for the indefinite article form.

5.2.6.2 The Definite Article

The definite article *the* (spelt ⟨þe⟩ in preference to ⟨the⟩ in Early Scots) is indeclinable and is the sole form used in this function. This contrasts with the nearest equivalent to the definite article in Old English, which is classified and which functioned also as a demonstrative pronoun, and which was fully inflected and marked for case, number and gender as in Table 5.5. As Lass (1992: 112) points out, there is no form in this paradigm which seems a likely ancestor for *the*. He rejects the idea that the Old English indeclinable relative particle ⟨þe⟩ could have been the source, and suggests instead analogical levelling of initial ⟨þ⟩ throughout the paradigm, aided by the fact that only the masculine and feminine nominative singular have forms with initial ⟨s⟩. A form ⟨þe⟩ appeared in the tenth century (co-varying with ⟨se⟩) in Mercian and Northumbrian texts, and this is the probable source of the form ⟨þe⟩/⟨the⟩ – invariable apart from merely orthographic changes, exemplified in the forms which follow – which is encountered first in the north and so in Scots texts, as Early Scots ⟨y(h)e⟩/⟨þe⟩, giving way to ⟨the⟩ from the 1300s onwards.

Table 5.5

	Singular Masculine	Feminine	Neuter	Plural All genders
Nominative	se	seo	þæt	þa
Accusative	þone	þa	þæt	þa
Genitive	þæs	þære	þæs	þara
Dative	þæm	þære	þæm	þæm

It is worth also remarking upon the use – distinctively Scots, in the Older Scots period and still in Modern Scots – of *the* with indefinite sense, as in the following examples:

1. *and crose your corps from* the *top to tay*
2. *and he sat doun to say* the *spynning*
3. *quhair he hapnit for the tyme to be at* the *ewinsong*
4. *xv li* ye *tovn of bourdoux wyne*.

In example 1, *the* is used where English would have the ø article; in 2, *the* is used before a non-count/mass noun; example 3 exemplifies *the* usage for a regular activity; in 4, *the* is used in a quantifying, partitive sense where English would probably have the indefinite article or a universal determiner like *each*. Other uses of *the* also occur in Older Scots shared with contemporary English, for instance *Robert* the *Brus* (compare French *X le Y*) to indicate the head of a family, or, 'ye *crag*, ye *ester wele of Sanct Johnnis*' in place-names.

5.2.7 Demonstratives/Deictics

5.2.7.1 The Older Scots System of Demonstratives/Deictics

The paradigm for this category is as in Table 5.6. Old English did not have a grammaticalised proximal vs distal (speaker-centred vs non-speaker-centred contrast): both the *se* paradigm set out above and its *þes* 'this' paradigm (Campbell 1959: §711) had specifying and loosely deictic functions (see Quirk and Wrenn 1957: §120 for examples). This overlap of function meant that while the *þes* paradigm provided the singular proximal *this* (originally a neuter nominative singular form appearing at first only in the north and the East Midlands, the south having opted for the masculine shape *þes*), it was the *se* paradigm which provided the singular distal *that* (from the neuter nominative singular *þæt*), as well as the Northern plural distal *thai* (from the nominative/accusative all-gender plural ⟨*þa*⟩). *Yon*, indicating something more distant than the distal *that* and neither speaker- nor non-speaker-centred, derives from an Old English adjective **ʒeon* (which is not attested in this form, but only as early West Saxon feminine dative singular *ʒeonre*). It is found as a demonstrative/deictic in Middle and Early Modern English too, only becoming characteristic of Scots in the Modern period.

Table 5.6

	Singular	Plural
Proximal	this	thir
Distal	that	thai
More distal	yon	yon

5.2.7.2 *Thir*

The origins of *thir* are generally held to be obscure. The nominative all-gender plural was *þas* (from the *þes* paradigm), and this is the source of Modern English *those*. According to Strang (1970: §148), this form went out of use in the north before 1200. *Thir* is recorded in

Northern English from the thirteenth century, in Scots from the fourteenth. However, from the mid-tenth century (as exemplified in the Northumbrian Old English Glosses to the *Lindisfarne Gospels*, *Rushworth 2* and *The Durham Ritual*) up to the late thirteenth century, we have very few extant Northern texts. Given this gap in our surviving written sources for the north, we have no means of telling what plural demonstrative/proximal deictic usage was in this area, for instance, for how long ⟨þæs⟩ continued in use, or *if* it did, or when it was replaced by *thir*.

The profound linguistic impact of Scandinavian in the north from the late Old English and into the Middle English period, and its effects on the open and, especially, closed class systems of all the Englishes, is well attested: see Strang (1970: §139), for instance, on the former and Samuels (1989) on the latter, as exemplified in the personal pronouns *they* and *their*. Bearing this in mind and considering it together with the recently-mentioned gap in our written evidence, a very likely source of the plural demonstrative *thir* in the north would seem to be Old Norse þeir or þeir(r)a (the forms which provided the English third person personal pronouns *they* and *their*).

In Old Norse (Gordon 1957: §§109, 111), the paradigms for the third person personal and the demonstrative pronouns were identical in the plural because, as Gordon says, 'the plu[rals] [of the third person personal pronouns in Old Norse were] originally [and continued in use as] demonstrative pronouns'. The Old Norse third person plural forms meaning 'they' and 'their', therefore, functioned also as the plural demonstrative 'those'. Borrowing of these forms as pronouns and demonstratives in the north to produce Northern *thir* is, then, a distinct possibility. Furthermore, identical and near-identical forms (allowing for the usual interchange of ⟨y⟩, ⟨þ⟩ and ⟨th⟩ as graphemic representatives of /ð/) for both *their* and *thir* are found in the north; see *their* and *those* in LALME (vol. 4, 1986), where recorded forms include *their/thir*, *their(e)/yeir(e)*, *thair(e)/yar(e)/yair(e)*, *ther/þer*.

5.2.8 Personal Pronouns

The personal pronoun system was greatly simplified during the Middle English period, but the parameters of the Old English system – person, number, gender and case – are generally preserved (Strang 1970: §§143–6; Lass 1992: 116–21). In outline, the changes that occurred between the Old English and late Middle English/Early Scots period were that (following Lass 1992: 117): (1) the dual number in the first and second person pronouns was lost; (2) the dative and accusative cases had generally merged, usually to the dative form, so that the case distinctions were reduced from the four in Old English to three – nominative, genitive and oblique/'objective'; (3) the feminine nominative singular pronoun found in Old English *heo* had been replaced in the north by *scho* – see Lass (1992: 118–19) for a précis and Britton (1991); (4) the Old English third person plural forms in *h-* gave way to Scandinavian-derived forms in *þ/th-*; (5) new genitive forms arose. Only (2), (4) and (5) will concern us here.

5.2.8.1 The Personal Pronoun System

The paradigm that resulted from these changes by the Middle Scots period was as in Table 5.7. The forms in ⟨th⟩ could also be spelt with ⟨þ⟩, though this latter usage tends to occur in Early Scots; ⟨y⟩ in the paradigm in Table 5.7 could co-occur with ⟨ȝ⟩, and these usages correspond respectively to Early Scots ⟨yh⟩ or ⟨ȝh⟩.

Table 5.7

	Singular					Plural		
	1	2	3			1	2	3
			Masc.	Fem.	Neut.			All Genders
Nom.	I	thou	he	scho	(h)it	we	ye	thai
'Obj.'	me	the	him	hir	(h)it	us	you	thaim
Gen.	my(n)	thy(n)	his	hi	–	our	your	thair

5.2.8.2   Oblique/'Objective' Case

Apart from the retention and use, alongside the more usual *it*, of the Old English-derived neuter personal pronoun *(h)it* (which survives into Modern Scots), the main point of note with regard to the 'objective' case is the merger of the dative and accusative cases. This resulted in, for instance, impersonal verb constructions (involving verbs like *think* 'seem', *need, like, (be)fall, forthink* 'regret', *happin, list, worth* 'be necessary'), which in Old English had taken a dative object, now taking as their object an accusative form (with the exception of *behufe* which occurs in Middle Scots mainly with the nominative); so, for instance:

> *likit yhu to wit yat* 'may it please you'
> *For me list with na Inglis buikis to flyte* 'for it pleases me'
> *me thocht fresche may befoir my bed vpstude* 'it seemed to me'
> *sa yat hym nedit nocht in tyme to cum* 'it was not necessary for him.'

The Old English use of a dative form of the personal pronoun to express reflexivity continues commonly in Older Scots (though with the derived 'oblique/objective' form), for example *I obliss me and myn airis* 'I pledge myself and my heirs'. As in Old English, *-self* could also be suffixed to this 'objective' base to give a pronoun reflexive in form, as in *himsel(f), hirsel(f)*. In a new development, the genitive, and not the 'objective', form was used as a base for the first and second person reflexive pronoun forms, so: *mysel(f), thysel(f), oursel(f)(is), yoursel(f)(is)*.

5.2.8.3   Genitive Case

In line with English developments, the genitive forms of the personal pronouns came to function more as possessive adjectives than had been the case in Old English; they no longer occurred as partitives or as the obligatory case-form objects of verbs which took the genitive (Quirk and Wrenn 1957: §§101, 103; Lass 1992: 119). It can be seen from the personal pronoun paradigm set out above that there is no neuter singular genitive form corresponding to Modern English *its*. In Southern 'Standard' English, such a form does not develop until the end of the sixteenth century, so its absence in Scots is not unexpected. Since gender marking now conformed with natural rather than grammatical gender so that neuter referred to inanimate objects, perhaps, as Macafee (1992–3: §2.3) suggests, there is no *its* form because 'the idea of possession does not apply in the same way to inanimates [as to animates]'. In the absence of *its*, possession was expressed by a variety of constructions such as the periphrastic possessive *of it*, but more commonly *thareof* and *of the sam(yn)*.

Beginning in the north and north-west Midlands in the late twelfth to early thirteenth century, a new predicative genitive type arose with suffixed {S}, for example *hirs*, *thairs*.

5.2.8.4 First and Second Person Pronouns

While the singular and plural forms of the second person pronouns functioned as regular singular and plural, their use was also sociolinguistically or stylistically governed. Like the Modern French *tu ~ vous*, the Scots singular *thou* (and so on) was used as a familiar, warm or patronising form of address and plural *ye* (and so on) as the polite, deferential, distant one. The second person system was later reduced by the falling into disuse of the singular forms (though they were retained in religious contexts and apparently were still in widespread use in Scots and Northern English until the eighteenth century). After *thou* forms were lost, this left only *you* to function in contexts requiring singular and plural reference. This loss of number distinction has been made good in Modern Scots by the forming of a new plural form *yous(e)*.

The forms *my* and *thy* evolved from the Old English *min* and *þin* at first in a sandhi development before words beginning with a vowel or ⟨h⟩ leading to loss of final -*n*. The distribution of *my* and *myn(e)* was as follows: in the Early Scots period, *myne* tended to be restricted to contexts where the word following began with a consonant; after the fifteenth century, however, it occurs only before vowels or ⟨h⟩ (compare *an(e)* in section 5.2.6.1), for example *myne airis* 'my heirs'. The form *my* is more common before consonants, for example *my seyll* 'my seal', but does early on occur before vowels, for example *in the absense of my auwyn seale*. The form *myn(e)* could be used attributively (as in modern predicative usage), for example *To this myn present assignatione*.

5.2.8.5 Third Person Pronouns

The Old English third person plural pronoun forms in ⟨h-⟩ were replaced uniformly by ⟨þ-⟩ or ⟨th-⟩ forms derived from Old Norse *þeir*, *þeirra*, *þeim* (for nominative, genitive and oblique cases respectively). This innovation took place first in the north and spread to the south from there, though it was not until the beginning of the sixteenth century that the full paradigm was completely established. It is, therefore, evidenced in Scots from our earliest texts onwards.

5.2.9 Relative and Interrogative Pronouns

Two relatives, or relative types, existed in Older Scots: *that* and *at* on the one hand, and *quh*-forms on the other. A ø-relative, in subject position, could also occur (a feature which is typical today of colloquial varieties and is therefore found in Modern Scots too). The first type is exemplified in *Here bene the princis, ø faucht the grete batailis . . . Here bene the poetis, ø the sciencis knew*.

5.2.9.1 *That, at*

The Old English relative pronouns were the indeclinable *þe*, alongside other forms, as context required, taken from the *se* paradigm (see sections 5.2.6.2 and 5.2.7.2 above). *That*, sourced in the Old English neuter nominative/accusative demonstrative *þæt*, is the indeclinable Older Scots relative pronoun. It occurs in texts of all stylistic registers, unlike *at* which tends to be a colloquial form found most often in low/informal-style texts. The latter pronoun, derived probably from Old Norse *at* 'who/that', is recorded like *that*, from the Early Scots period on, though *that* becomes, by the Middle Scots period, the more usual form. *That* occurred with human, non-human or inanimate antecedents and functioned as a relativiser in non-restrictive as well as restrictive clauses (see Macafee 1992–3: 31 for examples).

5.2.9.2 *Quh*-forms

These correlate orthographically with present-day ⟨wh-⟩ forms. The form *quhilk* is thought to have descended from Old English *hwelc/hwylc*, an interrogative pronoun meaning 'which (of many)'. These forms would, however, normally retain the palato-alveolar /ʧ/, seen word-finally in Modern English *which* (this had developed in West Saxon Old English when word-final /k/ followed a front vowel; see Campbell 1959: §428). Since the Northern *quhilk* forms have final velar /k/ instead, alternative derivations might be the Old English dative form *hwelcum* in which /k/ is not word-final and would not therefore be expected to have palatalised, or the Old Norse cognate *hvillikr*. Either way, this relative form, unlike *that*, could be marked for case and also be inflected for plural number (see subsection (b) below).

(a) Case-marked Forms

Case-marked forms are regularly descended from their Old English equivalents, though as with the personal pronoun, accusative and dative cases merge in the one 'objective' form derived from the Old English dative. So, Old English masculine/feminine (which were not distinguished) nominative singular *hwa* yielded Scots *quha*; this form, however, functioned solely as an interrogative at first, *quhilk* fulfilling a subject-relative function until the late sixteenth century, from which date on *quha* supersedes it. The Old English dative *hwæm* produces Scots *quham*, which usually refers to human antecedents and which is often the object of a preposition which follows rather than precedes it, such as *quham to* 'to whom' or *quham fra* 'from whom'. Scots genitive *quhase/quhais* derives from the Old English genitive *hwæs* and exists side by side with the periphrastic construction *of (the) quhilk*. As just seen with the 'objective' form *quham*, the preposition may in the case of the genitive also be postposed, when, as Macafee (1992–3: 32) points out, a 'shadow pronoun' – *it* in the following example – is usual, for instance, *þe scharp croun of throne, þe quhilk wes horabill and terrabill to behald the scharp lang pikes of it*.

(b) Forms and Use of quh- Relatives

Perhaps in order to distinguish it from interrogative use, *quhilk* occurs in the definite form *the quhilk* (with the usual orthographic variants, such as ⟨th⟩ ~ ⟨y⟩, ⟨u⟩ ~ ⟨v⟩ ~ ⟨w⟩); compare the possible model of Old French *liquels* from the fourteenth century onwards, for example *ye qvylk thyng* 'which thing'. An inflected plural form – *(the) quhilkis* – occurs, in which the inflection ⟨is⟩ may represent a replacement of the usual Middle English/Pre-literary Scots descendant [ə] of the Old English nominative/accusative plurals *-e* and *-a*. Alternatively, French or Latin influence may be the source of the usage (see section 5.2.11).

Quh- pronouns occur, like *that*, with human, non-human and inanimate antecedents (with the exception, already cited, of *quham*). They may also be used as adjectives, with a determining function, as in the example cited by Macafee (1992–3: 32): *þe gret straik þat wes gevin to ȝow before Annas . . . throu þe quhilk straik. Quhilk* could also be found functioning as a conjunction: *þat merciless her servand be nocht slane, Quhilk and scho do.* Finally, it could take as its antecedent a whole preceding clause (this, incidentally, is the only use of *which* found in Modern Scots); again, see Macafee (1992–3: 32) for an example of this.

5.2.10 Numerals

In Scots, the cardinal series of numbers (*ane, twa, thre* and so on) are sometimes used where ordinals (*first, secund, thrid* and so on) might be expected. Ordinal forms in -*t*, derived directly from Old English, such as *fifta, siexta, ellefta* 'fifth', 'sixth', eleventh', as well as one borrowed from Old Norse (*aucht* 'eighth'), led to the generalisation of this suffix so that forms such as *fourt* occur alongside *ferde* 'fourth', or *nynt* as well as *nynd* 'ninth'.

Tens followed by units is the usual ordering in composite numbers between twenty-one and ninety-nine (compare the contemporary Middle English where the order is reversed), for example *[f]ourty and acht yheris* 'forty-eight years'.

5.2.11 Adjectives

5.2.11.1 Adjectival Inflections

As might be expected in view of the general decay of case, gender and number inflections by the Middle English period, the only sign in Pre-literary Scots of the two distinct fully inflected adjective declensions – strong and weak – of Old English is vestigial final ⟨e⟩ inflections on adjectives which in an Old English context would have been declined weak. In such instances, the ⟨e⟩ represents the reflex schwa of the Old English nominative singular endings like masculine -*a* and feminine/neuter -*e*. Craigie (1925: 64) cites place-name forms like *blake burne, brade wude, kalde strem* which occur in documents written predominantly in Latin and which are preceded by the French definite article *le*. This is exactly the defining sort of context – definite article/demonstrative plus attributive adjective – in which the weak forms of adjectives would occur in Old English, that is, when the adjective followed a determiner (primarily the definite article/demonstrative). These same forms, or near-forms, occur in later documents without the final ⟨e⟩, thus: *blacburn, bradfurde, caldwelle* in line with the general loss of adjective inflections. Variation between adjectival forms with and without ⟨e⟩ is found, however, in the same syntactic contexts, even within the same text throughout the fourteenth century in Scots (as in English) texts, for example *the forsayde land*, compared with *the forsaid Jonkyne*. What this suggests is that by this time the final ⟨e⟩ on adjectives no longer served any grammatical purpose.

Forms of adjectives inflected in ⟨is⟩ for plural number are sometimes found in Older Scots; the same phenomenon occurs in late Middle English (with the ⟨(e)s⟩ inflection), but there, claims Lass (1992: 116), it is found most often on postposed adjectives of Romance origin, since both the addition of an ending and the word order of the construction reflect a French pattern. Postposed adjectives, with or without plural inflection, are a feature of Older Scots too, but plural marking does not seem to be confined to adjectives in this position, as the following examples of (1) preposed inflected and (2) postposed uninflected adjectives illustrate: (1) *the foresaidis lordis; our belwiffitis friendis; with othiris divers; thir our presentis lettres*; and (2) *in tyme bipast; air male; maitteris debatable*. Nor is the addition of a plural inflection confined to postposed adjectives of Romance origin, as for example *bipast* in (2) above shows. The situation in Older Scots seems therefore to be very variable with regard to plural inflection (see also subsection 5.2.9.2 (b) above for *quhilk*).

5.2.11.2   Comparison

Both synthetic and analytic means are used in Older Scots to form comparative and superlative forms of adjectives (and adverbs). In the former, the inflection *-ir* (though not in irregular comparative forms like *bettir* 'better') indicates comparative, and *-ist* superlative. Analytic-type expression involves, as in English, the use of *ma(re)* 'more' and *maist* 'most', though unlike *myn(e)* and *my* or *an(e)* and *a* examined earlier, *ma* and *mare* have two different sources in Old English: *ma* 'more in number' and *mara* 'greater'. This seems to be reflected in the Older Scots usage whereby *ma* occurs to express number in count nouns, for example *ma persones* or *ma men*, and *mare* to express quantity in mass nouns, so: *A mar sowme of ane hundredth merkis* 'a larger/greater sum of one hundred marks'.

The present-day pattern whereby polysyllabic adjectives take analytic comparison only began to be established by the mid-fifteenth century, with the result that we find a fair amount of variation all through the Older Scots period as seen in, for example, *mair sueit* (a monosyllabic adjective with analytic comparison) or *perfectir* (a polysyllabic adjective with synthetic comparison). Instances of double comparison also occur for adjectives, for example *mair lichtir* 'lighter', or *mair bettir* where the irregular comparative of *gude* has not been recognised as such (incidentally, this feature is found in adverbs too, such as *planerly* 'more plainly', *alanerly* 'uniquely').

5.3   THE VERB PHRASE

5.3.1   Verbs and Morphosyntactic Categories

In common with Middle and Early Modern English, and in line with the morphological evolutionary trends already witnessed in the noun phrase and its constituents, developments in the Older Scots verb system, when compared with the complexities of the Old English one, exhibit the same simplifying traits and tendencies towards the favouring of particular grammatical categories at the expense of others. With regard to these – tense, number, person and mood – the Older Scots and late Middle English situations are broadly comparable. Lass (1992: 139) states:

> Aside from later stabilisations and reductions, Late Middle English had clearly reached a point at which marking for person and number (and even mood) was becoming rather marginal; tense was the one obligatory category, with person second in importance, but only in the singular.

While in one sense Lass's remarks certainly apply to Scots (with the exception of 'but only in the singular'), in another, as will emerge from the discussion below, Scots (and Northern English) developments with regard to person and number were well ahead of those in the south and diverged fairly markedly from them.

5.3.2 Tense and Number

5.3.2.1 Present Tense

The usual Older Scots present tense paradigm was as in Table 5.8 (with the contemporary Northern and Southern 'Standard' English ones set beside it for comparison). It will be recalled from section 5.2.2.1 that in the very earliest Scots, forms in ⟨e-⟩ can occur, but these soon give way to ⟨i⟩ as the regular spelling. The Northern paradigm is the source of the third person singular inflection which spread in the course of Middle English to other English dialects (compare present-day Standard English {S}; see for example McIntosh 1983; Lass 1992: 138–9; Schendl 1996). Alongside this paradigm, another one operated in Scots and the north (and still does to some extent in Modern Scots) according to what is known as the 'Northern Present Tense Rule' (NPTR) – this is a rather more accurate name for it than the conventional 'Northern Personal Pronoun Rule' (on the NPTR see, for instance, Meurman-Solin 1992; Montgomery 1994a). This describes Subject–Verb concord and states that when the *subject is an immediately adjacent personal pronoun* (either preceding or following the verb) which is *first person singular, or first, second or third person plural,* then the verb has no ending (see Table 5.9). The examples which follow illustrate the workings of the NPTR.

Table 5.8

		Older Scots	Southern 'Standard' English	Northern English
Singular	1st	-(i)s	-ø	-(i)s/-(e)s
	2nd	-(i)s	-(e)st	-(i)s/-(e)s
	3rd	-(i)s	-(e)th/-(e)s	-(i)s/-(e)s
Plural	All	-(i)s	-ø/-(e)n	-(i)s/-(e)s

Table 5.9

		Older Scots	Southern 'Standard' English	Northern English
Singular	1st	-ø	-ø	-ø
	2nd	-(i)s	-(e)st	-(i)s/-(e)s
	3rd	-(i)s	-(e)th/-(e)s	-(i)s/-(e)s
Plural	All	-ø	-ø/-(e)n	-ø

I grant and alsa bindis and oblisis me
It obscuris and diminucis
ye burn yat rynnis
quhen he desiris
We requir yhu
Sum swallis suan sum swallis duik | and j stand fastand jn ane nuik
Gefe j ore yai yus warnyt comperis no[ch]t . . .

(a) Present-tense inflections

When the paradigms in Table 5.9 are compared with each other, it can be seen that the Northern system of inflections is much more innovative than that of the south. In it we see the collapse of second and third persons singular under one form and the collapse of this with the plural. Only one inflection in ⟨(i/e)s⟩ was used for all persons and numbers. These developments seem less surprising if we consider the evidence of Northumbrian Old English. Its present tense paradigm was extremely innovative when set beside the other Old English dialects and was probably Scandinavian-influenced. Campbell (1959: §§735, 752) cites early and late Northumbrian variant verb forms, and it is possible from these to reconstruct the basic paradigm type from which the Northern one developed:

Singular	1st	-o/-e
	2nd	-as
	3rd	-as/-es
Plural	All	-as/-es

With the collapse of the unstressed vowels in schwa (or loss, as in the first person singular above) and the development to /i/ in Scots and the north (with schwa remaining as a possible realisation; see section 5.2.2.1 above), as well as the generalisation of {S} to the first person singular, the paradigm in Table 5.9 is the result.

(b) The Northern Present Tense Rule

Macafee (1992–3: 21) states '[i]t is unclear how this double system of concord arose'. Two tendencies seem to be at work: where non-prominal subjects are concerned, the verbal ⟨(i)s⟩ inflection is generalised throughout. This happens at the expense of the expression of the category of number; singular cannot be distinguished from plural. Yet where pronominal subjects are concerned, the opposite tendency seems to be at work: zero-marking on verbs with plural pronoun subjects serves to highlight the category of number. The traditional inclusion in the NPTR paradigm of one singular pronoun (the first person) as a zero-morpheme trigger for an adjacent verb not only blurs this highlighting but also produces an odd imbalance in the paradigm, whereby this one singular form is aligned not with the other singulars but with the plurals. Given that the development of the first person singular verb form, with final-schwa loss, would normally produce a -ø inflection, it could be that the first singular -ø inflection with first person singular pronoun subject has been mistakenly attributed to the operation of the NPTR with which it may in fact have nothing at all to do, being merely the normally developed form. If this is the case, and the first person singular were removed from the equation, then not only would the paradigmatic imbalance disappear, but also the apparent flagging (by means of the NPTR) of the saliency of the singular vs plural number distinction – clearly and directly expressed by means of the respective presence vs absence of the ⟨(i)s⟩ inflection – would become more obvious.

As to the question of why the NPTR forms arose (1) despite the resultant loss of distinction of person marking on the verb and (2) only with personal pronominal subjects, some kind of precedent may be seen in Old English usages like that described by Campbell (1959: §730): '[w]hen a pronoun of the 1st or 2nd pers[on] follows [a strong verb] the pl[ural] endings -aþ, -on, -en can be reduced to -e, e.g. ride we, ge'.[2] As a result of this reduction, verb forms with this ⟨e⟩ (presumably representing schwa) would cease to be distinctive for person in the present tense or for mood, since both singular and plural forms in the subjunctive would become identical in ⟨e⟩. Less distinctive tense marking would also result (the second person singular past tense form, while it has a short /i/ (compare the /i:/ of the present) took the inflection ⟨e⟩ too). By the time the NPTR had been established in the north, however, indicative vs subjunctive mood distinctions had apparently broken down – at least formally – and reduction of the number of vowel grades per strong verb had (see section 5.3.4) produced new past tense singular forms, so these sorts of considerations no longer applied. Where loss of person marking in verbs is concerned, in both the Old and Middle English periods (especially for the latter in the north), the forms of most of the personal pronouns were distinct enough from each other to supply any 'missing' information on person.

5.3.2.2   Past Tense

The expression of tense in verbs is traditionally the criterion used in their classification. As in English, the majority of main verbs in Older Scots fall into one of four conjugations or classes, the largest of which is weak verbs. These formed their past tense and past participle by affixation: adding the inflection ⟨(i)t⟩ or ⟨(i)d⟩ (regularly descended from late Northumbrian *-(a)de* and *-(e)de*). The same considerations apply here as to the ⟨(i)s⟩ inflection discussed earlier in sections 5.2.2.1–5.2.2.2, so these inflections were probably, when syllabic, pronounced /it/ and /id/ respectively; the Modern Scots reflexes /ɪt/ and /ɪd/ or [t] and [d] would support the pronunciations suggested here. The inflection ⟨d⟩, /d/ also occurs after stems ending in a vowel.

Strong verbs signal past tense by modifying the root vowel of the present tense; the past participle can have yet another vowel. In Older Scots, the number of vowel grades per verb had reduced by comparison with Old English, with the previously different vowels of past-tense singular and past tense plural often levelling under the vowel of the singular. Yet another class of verbs – suppletive – shows past tense by changing form completely (consider Modern English *go* ~ *went*). There seem to be no suppletive verbs in Scots, unless *be* is classified as one. In the final class of verbs are placed, for example, *be* and *have*, conventionally described as anomalous verbs.

5.3.3   Verb Conjugations and their Membership

5.3.3.1   Weak Verbs

This conjugation grew in size in the Englishes of the period as a result, for instance, of strong verbs changing conjugation type or the borrowing of foreign verbs into this – the numerically largest – conjugation. What had been three classes of weak verb in Old English were generally restructured and merged into one.

Verbs such as *beseik* 'beseech' with past *besocht* 'besought', *think* ~ *thocht* and *bring* ~ *brocht*, all have the characteristic ⟨t⟩ inflection signifying membership of the weak class. They do, however, display root-vowel modification as well because of *i-umlaut* having affected the present-tense root vowel in Germanic, but not the past. These verbs probably merit being grouped together into a subclass of weak verbs. The verb *bring* in Scots has a distinctive past participle form *brung* which is regularly descended from an Old English form *brungen* found only in poetry.

Some differences in form and classification between the English and Scots systems exist. The verbs *tell* and *give* are good examples. *Tell* originally belonged to the subgroup just discussed, as its past form was *ta(u)ld* until the late sixteenth century. From then on, however, forms appear which level the vowel of the present tense to the past, thus producing the now usual Scots wholly weak past *tel(l)t*. *Give*, derived from Northumbrian *gifan* – a strong verb of class V – remained strong in Older Scots, but from the eighteenth century written forms like *gied* are attested (with no ⟨v⟩ – the /v/ had been lost in the fourteenth century). *Gi(v)e* has remained in the weak class in Scots (though a strong past-participle form *gien* alongside the weak one testifies to its origins). The verb *ga* 'go' in Older Scots behaves like a weak verb, taking ⟨(i)d⟩ for past tense and past participle. It derives from an Old English anomalous verb *ga(e)/æ* (late Northumbrian infinitive form, minus final *-n*), with suppletive past *eode* and past participle *gega(n)*; see Campbell (1959: §768(c)). In the north, however, a new suppletive past *wente* (originally the past of *wendan* 'to turn') developed and spread south in the thirteenth and fourteenth centuries, replacing *yede/yode*, the reflexes of Old English *eode*. The preferred form in Scots is, however, *gaid/geid*.

5.3.3.2 Strong Verbs

These exhibit in Scots, as in English, a great deal of flux, with three major trends, begun in the north, operating simultaneously and variably. The first is that many strong verbs move completely or partly into the weak conjugation: for example *help* (Old English class II with past singular *healp*) levels the present vowel, producing past *helpit* and past participle *helpin* (this form, however, retains the strong verb past participle inflection); *crepe* 'creep' (Old English strong class II) has both strong (*crap(e)*) and weak (*creipt*) past forms, but a strong past participle *cropyn*.

The second trend restricted the complexity and variety of vowel alternations by, for instance, levelling past plural forms under the vowel of the singular, as in *drive* with singular and plural past *drafe/drave* (compare Old English *draf*, *drifon*). Consonant variations were subject to this process too, for example *choose*: Old English *ceosan*, *ceas*, *curon*, *(ge)coren*, with /r/ in past plural and participle; compare Older Scots *chese*, *chesit* (for singular and plural), *chosyn* with levelling of /s/ to all forms (and weak past, but strong past participle).

Hybridisation is the third trend, being the transfer of forms from one strong class to another: for example *speke* 'speak', the Old English class V verb, takes on the vocalism of class IV in its past participle, producing *spokin* rather than the expected **spekin*.

5.3.3.3 Anomalous Verbs

As indicated earlier, there are two of these in Older Scots – *be* and *have* – and they could make use of different forms to reflect the operation of the NPTR (this could apply, oddly enough, in the past tense too, though not consistently: Meurman-Solin 1993a; Montgomery 1994a). Distinct second person singular forms occur when the NPTR operates in the present tense. The three different Old English paradigms – *eom* (first person singular; an infinitive is not recorded), *beon* and *wesan* (Campbell 1959: §§762, 768) – contribute the different NPTR-reflecting forms. The paradigms are as in Table 5.10.

Table 5.10

Be:		Present		Past	
		Adjacent pronoun	Other	Adjacent pronoun	Other
Singular	1st	am	is/be	was	wes
	2nd	art	is/be/beis	was	wes
	3rd	is	is/be/beis	wes	wes
Plural	All	ar(e)	is/be/beis	wer	wes

Have:		Present	
		Adjacent pronoun	Other
Singular	1st	have (haf/hef)	has/hes
	2nd	haist/has (hes)	has/hes
	3rd	has/hes	has/hes
Plural	All	hav(e)/haif has/hes	

5.3.4 Mood

In Older Scots, indicative, subjunctive and imperative continued as for Old English. Where the subjunctive is concerned, however, apart from the use of special forms of the verbs *be* and *have* (*be* or *beis* and *haf* or *have*), verbs in Scots are uninflected: the ⟨e⟩ inflection seen in late Southern Middle English does not seem to occur even in Early Scots, perhaps reflecting the early Northern loss of schwa in final position (the Old English inflection had been ⟨e⟩). Subjunctive mood could, however, be said to be indirectly indicated in Scots and in the north in contexts where an indicative inflection would normally occur owing to the operation of the NPTR, but as an expression of subjunctive mood a ø-morpheme is found instead: for example, *yat ye forsayde Alayne delyuer* (-ø); *y[a]t thou kepe* (-ø)*jt secretely*.

The subjunctive tended to be expressed by the use of modal auxiliary verbs such as *can* ∼ *couth*, *may* ∼ *micht*, *sall* ∼ *suld*, *will* ∼ *wald*, *ma(u)n* (present tense only, a loan from Old Norse with a Northern distribution), *mot* (present tense only, 'must') and so on. As just illustrated, most of these had each only one present and one 'past' (past in form only; past tense is not expressed in these forms, as today); a few occurred only in a present tense form. They were normally followed by a main verb, except when this was the infinitive of a verb of motion and the modal was *will* or *ma(u)n*, for example *And I will* (-ø) *to my pleuch . . .* (*ga* omitted).

The imperative is usually unmarked, but in Early and early Middle Scots texts, verbs may be inflected in ⟨(i)s⟩ for plural, for example *kepys [y]ow fra disparying*.

5.3.5 The Infinitive, Gerund and Present Participle

5.3.5.1 The Infinitive

Apart from some relics of final schwa in very early Scots, the infinitive was unmarked in Older Scots. It was usually introduced by the infinitive marker *to* – before a consonant – or *til* (borrowed from Old Norse; a preposition *til* does occur in Northumbrian Old English, but means 'for' or 'as') before a vowel or ⟨h⟩ (compare *a/an(e)* in section 5.2.6.1). *For to/til* 'in order to' also occur as infinitive markers which carry a meaning of purpose or intention. Forms without any preposition can be found after causative verbs like *gar*.

5.3.5.2   The Gerund

The intertwined development of the gerund and the present participle is described in Lass (1992: 144–6). In Scots, as in English, this is straightforwardly marked in ⟨ing⟩ (or in Early Scots ⟨yn(g)⟩). Unlike English, though, there is no identity of form (until the late Middle Scots period; see section 5.4) between the present participle (see section 5.3.5.3) and the gerund.

5.3.5.3   The Present Participle

This carries the inflection ⟨and⟩ in Older Scots and the north, and reflects a borrowing of the Old Norse present participle ending *-andi*. It was probably pronounced /ən/.

5.4   LATE MIDDLE SCOTS MORPHOLOGICAL CHANGES

From around the time of the late sixteenth century, the language of Scots texts changed fairly rapidly. All of these changes were apparently in the direction of the written Southern English standard. Where morphology is concerned, for instance, we find changes like ⟨es⟩ as the inflection on nouns and verbs for the {S} morpheme, ⟨(e)th⟩ rather than ⟨(i)s⟩ for third person singular present tense, ⟨ed⟩ for the weak verb past tense and past participle forms and relative pronoun variants of non-Northern ⟨which⟩, rather than ⟨quhilk⟩, and so on (Agutter 1989b; Devitt 1989; Meurman–Solin 1993a: passim, but especially 48–54, 132, 137–48, 232–57).

Such changes have traditionally been interpreted as deliberate anglicisations (Bald 1926) in view of the external historical circumstances (like the Reformation, the Union of the Crowns and so on) which encouraged greater linguistic contact between speakers, and writers, in Scotland and the south of England. However, from the evidence presented in sections 5.2 and 5.3 above, it should be clear that where ⟨es⟩ or ⟨ed⟩ spellings for inflections are concerned, while Scots did favour ⟨i⟩ spellings, the ⟨e⟩ graph, representing schwa, was familiar not just from the contemporary Southern English but also from the Early Scots period and from Northern English usage. Recall also the suggestion (in section 5.2.2.1) that Scots retained the schwa vowel in its unstressed vowel system alongside the favoured /i/. It is possible that this change in orthographic practice – which is by no means universal – simply reflects the alternative available allomorph schwa.

Similarly, the change in form of the present participle ending from ⟨and⟩ to ⟨in(g)⟩ (occasional ⟨ing⟩ forms for the present participle occurred from the early fifteenth century onwards) may simply be a reflection of the probable pronunciation /ən/ suggested in section 5.3.5.3. This pronunciation seems the most likely one, given that the loss in syllable-final position of the final consonant of a voiced or a voiceless cluster is well attested from the fifteenth century on in forms like *excep* for *except*, *han* for *hand* and so on. Back-spellings, such as ⟨Latyng⟩ for ⟨Latin⟩ (Macafee 1992–3: 23; Agutter 1989b: 4–5), and inflectional ⟨in⟩ and ⟨an⟩ forms seem to support this. This evidence, together with that provided by Modern Scots pronunciations of ⟨ing⟩ as /ən/ and the fact that the forms occur in informal as well as formal texts (anglicisation is conventionally held to be particularly common in formal texts), suggests that the most likely explanation of this change is a phonological one – the falling-together of the present participle and gerund endings in /ən/.

Changes in usage like ⟨(e)th⟩ third person singular present tense inflections and ⟨wh⟩ forms for the relative pronoun differ, however, from the rest. These are clearly imported Southern usages. The ⟨(e)th⟩ shape appears most often in the forms *hath*, *doth* and *saith* (Meurman-Solin 1993a: 250–2), which may point to the influence of Biblical Southern English. Its use decreases towards the end of the seventeenth century, in line with Southern developments, while the {S} third person singular present tense (original to the north), which had continued in use in Scots (as did the Northern Present Tense Rule), reasserts itself, probably assisted by its now being standard in the south. While ⟨wh⟩ relatives gradually replaced ⟨quh⟩-spelled forms, it should be remembered that the neutral *that* remained as the relative pronoun predominantly used in Scots.

Contemporary linguistic attitudes, the influence of printing and its Southern English models on the linguistic forms found in texts and other factors all contributed of course to the changes that affected Scots at this time. They seem largely not to have been deliberate (except when, for example, an English market was intended for writings by Scots (M. Robinson 1983: 59–78)). When the evidence of the morphological changes just considered is viewed in tandem with these factors, they point to a process of restandardisation – where writing is concerned – in the direction of the Southern standard and, where speech is concerned, merger of two closely related linguistic varieties, which produced the present linguistic state of affairs whereby Scottish 'Standard' English coexists with the Scots dialects directly descended from Older Scots (King forthcoming).

NOTES

1. Gender did not operate, or does not seem to have been thought of, wholly grammatically in Old English (that is, as a classifying device that predicted concord). Cases of conflict between grammatical and natural gender occurred, as, for instance, Lass (1992: 106–8) points out: *stān* 'stone' (masculine), *duru* 'door' (feminine) and *cild* (neuter) were classified according to grammatical gender, while nouns like *cyning* 'king', *cwen* 'queen' and *scip* 'ship', masculine, feminine and neuter respectively, or *lufiend* (masculine) and *lufestre* (female) to denote 'male lover' and 'female lover', had classifications that accorded with their natural gender (or, as Lass expresses it, their 'sex in the real world'). Further, Traugott (1992: 177–8) describes a tendency towards preference for natural over grammatical gender in reference to humans where an anaphoric pronoun is separated from its antecedent: for example, *ænne wifman* [masculine] . . . *heo* [feminine] 'a woman . . . she'.

2. I am indebted to Derek Britton for having 'a vague recollection of a usage like this from somewhere', as well as for several fruitful and encouraging discussions which we had on Middle English and Scots morphology.

6

Older Scots Lexis

C. I. Macafee

6.1 INTRODUCTION

Ane argwnde thaim, as thai throuch the toun,
The starkast man that Hesylryg than knew,
And als he had of lychly wordis ynew.
He salust thaim, as it war bot in scorn;
'Dewgar, gud day, bone Senʒhour, and gud morn!'
'Quhom scornys thow?' quod Wallace, 'quha lerd thc?'
'Quhy, schir,' he said, 'come yhe nocht new our se?'
Pardown mc than, for I wend ye had beyne
And inbasset to bryng ane wncouth queyne.'
Wallace ansuerd; 'Sic pardoune as we haiff
In oys to gyff, thi part thow sall nocht craiff.'
'Sen ye are Scottis, ʒeit salust sall ye be;
Gud deyn, dawch Lard, bach lowch banʒoch a de.'
Ma Sotheroune men to thaim assemblit ner. . . .

　　　(*The Actis and Deidis of the Illustrere and Vailzeand Campioun Schir Wiliam,
Wallace, Knicht of Ellerslie by Henry the Minstrel*, ed. J. Moir 1889, VI: 128–41).[1]

The study of vocabulary is the domain of lexicography. Any generalisations that can be made about the wordstock depend on this prior work. Only with individual lexical items identified, catalogued and given an etymological pedigree can we begin to search for regularities and trends in the lexicon. Scots has fortunately been well served by lexicographers, and the main outlines of the history of the language have been clear since the nineteenth century. However, much of the detail remains to be filled in, and for Older Scots this is the task of *A Dictionary of the Older Scottish Tongue* (DOST: Craigie et al. 1937–).

　　Like the *Scottish National Dictionary* (SND: Grant and Murison 1931–76) and the *Middle English Dictionary* (MED: Kurath and Kuhn 1954–), DOST was conceived as a supplement to the *Oxford English Dictionary* (OED: Murray 1989), whose coverage of Older Scots texts is quite respectable but is confined to the major writers in the editions then available. DOST is based on an enormously larger and more varied corpus, particularly from the letter H onwards. This is the result of a new reading programme initiated by A. J. Aitken in the 1950s. Until DOST is completed, there can be no definitive study of the structure of the

Older Scots lexicon. There will be interesting work for future generations of scholars to do. The full potential of the completed dictionary will be realisable when it is available to researchers as a computerised database, and this is a goal that the scholarly community should hold in view.

6.2 ABOUT DOST

The basis of a historical dictionary is a collection of citation slips, from which the editors select representative and interesting examples for quotation in the dictionary. Aitken (1988) estimated that there were about 300,000 illustrative quotations in DOST up to the letter Q. Once sorted into separate entries under a headword, the citations are grouped so as to trace the shifts of meaning across time. The definitions are then written. Dictionary definitions are described by Aitken as merely helpful 'sign-posts' (1978a: 29); for serious study of the language, they are less important than the citations that they attempt to encapsulate. In concise dictionaries, such as *The Concise Scots Dictionary* (CSD: Robinson 1985), it is of course only the definitions that are given, but a full-scale historical dictionary

> may be regarded as primarily a large and ordered selection of citations from and references to the original source-texts of the language and period embraced by the dictionary. These dictionaries present a representative selection of citations assembled by the editors so as to display at first hand the forms, applications and habitual collocations of each of the words entered and the distributions of each of these features in time, region, and register or genre. (Aitken 1978a: 29)

Lexicographers often have the problem of deciding whether two bundles of citations (that is, two senses) are sufficiently closely related to be treated as a single dictionary entry (that is, one word), or whether one group must be treated as separate, in which case an alternative etymology must be sought. For instance, OED distinguishes two verbs, *found v^2* and *found v^3*. *Found v^2* 'to establish on a firm basis' is traced to Old French *fonder*, ultimately from Latin *fundare*, based on *fundus* 'bottom'. *Found v^3* 'to melt metal for casting in a mould' is traced to Old French *fondre* from Latin *fundere* and ultimately an Indo-European stem reconstructed as *$gh(e)ud$-, which actually had an Old English reflex *ʒeotan*. (This latter gives Scots *yet* 'to found'.) Both OED and DOST have a third *found v^1* 'to go', a native word (< Old English *fundian*) surviving in Older Scots poetic diction.

It is not always easy to distinguish homonyms in this way, as words that are the same in form and similar or overlapping in meaning tend to become entangled with each other. In Scots, the sense of melting and casting metal is recorded only as a noun in the idiom *of found* 'made of cast metal'. This distinctively Scots use is traced to a French noun *fonte*, although the pronunciation suggests a close link to the verb. It is therefore said to have become assimilated to the verb *fondre*. Nor are the workings of coincidence to be underestimated. For instance, there was a unit of land, the *markland*, in 'the Highlands and Islands and the West, South-west and South' (DOST *markland n^1*), which had an annual rental value of one mark. Coincidentally, Orkney and Shetland had a *markland* which was a land measure, possibly originally 'land valued at a purchase price or capital value of one mark of pure silver' (DOST *markland n^2*).

Multiple etymologies, reflecting the complex interactions among the source languages, are not uncommon. For example, *mair* (the same word as English *mayor*, but in Scots referring usually to an officer of the law) comes ultimately from Latin *mājōr*, but reaches

Scots both through Gaelic *maor* (resulting also in Scottish Medieval Latin *marus*), from which it takes its sense, and through Old French *maire*. Cases of this kind ('multiple etymologies') account for about 1 per cent of the words sampled below, excluding those where the possible sources are closely related (such as Latin or Old French; Middle Dutch, Flemish or Low German). The editors of a historical dictionary have also to establish the range of phonological variants that can be counted as the same word – a task requiring a systematic reconstruction of the history of sounds. This philological work was largely done in the nineteenth century for the Indo-European language family, including Scots and English, but the picture for Scots in particular has been refined and modified in DOST and SND.

The dictionary editors have to decide how to handle variant forms of the same word, which are very common in unstandardised languages and dialects and thus in the early period.[2] The variants can automatically be conflated if the same range of senses and grammatical use is recorded for all variants, but this is not usually the case. Variants used alongside each other in a language have the potential to become specialised into distinct lines of development. A striking example is *laird* and *lord*, both from Old English *hlaford* (see below). *Lord* replaced *laird* with reference to the higher nobility, as opposed to the smaller landowners (who remained *lairds*). Similarly, in *law*, *laich*, *lauch*, we have three forms from the same etymon, Old Norse *lágr* 'low', which show only a partial overlap in their range of senses and usages (see Table 6.1), though it can be seen that *lauch* (the least frequent form) tends to agree with *laich*. Another case is the Old English word *ȝenog* 'enough', which gives two main forms in Scots, *eneuch* and *enew*, the latter from the plural form *ȝenoge*. In Older Scots, *enew* was used as the adjective with countable nouns, *eneuch* with mass nouns.

So as not to conflate distinct lines of development, the dictionaries tend to separate the more important variants of words, and this is particularly true of DOST. This can be a problem for the dictionary user trying to obtain an overall impression of a lexical item and its variants. Recognising the problem, the present editorial team is following a policy of combining variants much more than was previously the case. Dareau et al. (1987) discuss the DOST entries for the variants *gef*, *gefe*, *geve*, *gif* and *give* (all forms of 'give'). They re-edit *gif* to show how it would be treated according to the practices now followed, gathering the five entries into one. The reader wishing to have a full picture of a word in Scots must very often follow up cross-references and read several entries as a group. Perfect cross-referencing is not to be expected in a work of this kind compiled over several generations, particularly in a forward direction. In this respect, we are of course hampered also by the fact that the dictionary is still in progress, having reached *s(c)hake* at the time of writing. Furthermore, both DOST and SND must be used to complete the picture chronologically. The spelling practices are very different in the periods covered by the two dictionaries, and not standardised in either period, so CSD is a useful bridge, also collecting together variants more than do the parent dictionaries.

A further serious obstacle to the user of DOST stems from a decision that must have been made by William Craigie, the first editor, at a time when the range of works cited in the dictionary was expected to be rather small: the citations from many works are undated. The reader must refer to 'The combined register of titles of works quoted' at the start of volume 3, with additions in later volumes. Fortunately, the DOST lists are highly reliable. If the user of DOST is interested in the dates of the citations, it is very helpful to have an idea of the chronology of the main Older Scots writers. R. Watson (1984) is useful for this.

Table 6.1 Variant lexical forms in Older Scots.

Sense	Form		
	law	laich	lauch
Low in stature	*	*	*
Phrase: *to lede/bear ane/the lawar saill*	*		
Not tall		*	*
Flat		*	
Narrow (of lace)		*	
Lower (steeple)		*	
Occupying a low position	*	*	
Low in position		*	*
Deep in situation	*	*	
Low-lying	*	*	
Phrase: *the law cuntrey* Lowlands	*		
Low (Germany/countries)	*	*	
Compound: *law watter*	*		
Phrase: *fra the hiest (stane) of the hill to the lawest (stane) of the eb*	*		
Occupying a low situation in a building		*	*
Situated in the lower part of a building		*	
Ground floor or basement (room)		*	
Compound: *laich hous/lauche hous*		*	*
Denoting the lower part of a specific building		*	
On the floor of a church as distinct from a loft		*	
A lower building attached to a principal building of several storeys		*	
Phrase: *heich and laich*		*	
Not loud	*	*	
Low in pitch	*		
Of a colour: dull	*		
Of a coat: long		*	
Of a person: of low birth/rank	*	*	
Of low condition	*	*	
Junior (class in a college/school)	*	*	
Of birth or rank: low	*	*	
Low in order of seniority		*	
Of condition/quality/degree: inferior	*		
Minor (office)		*	
Low in amount	*		
Phrase: *hie and/or law* of less consequence, (minor) office	*		
Applied to certain churches in contradistinction to the high or principal churches of these towns		*	

In what follows, when etymologies are mentioned, I will usually state that a Scots word simply *is* derived either from an earlier native form or from a cognate word in some other language. The dictionaries are not so categorical. They give cognates where these are known, leaving it to the reader to infer the route by which a word has been borrowed (except in difficult cases, where the etymology may be discussed at some length). It is very important, therefore, for the dictionary user to have a sound outline knowledge of the sources of the vocabulary and the historical circumstances of borrowing.

Often, too, the dictionaries cite parallels in other languages that are not to be understood as sources. The Scots dictionaries generally cite parallels in Middle English (c. 1150 to c. 1500) and Early Modern English (c. 1500 to c. 1700).[3] Information about Middle English is valuable because it helps to fill in the gap in the record of Scots between Old Northumbrian and the literary corpus beginning in the late fourteenth century. For words of Old English origin, the Middle English forms and sometimes sense developments are of interest too.[4] DOST will sometimes appeal also to Modern Scots where a word is rare in the earlier period: for example *schakarstane*, an unidentified bird, in a single citation, is referred to the Modern Scots *stane-cha(c)ker* 'the stone-chat, the wheatear or the whin-chat'. *Hettell*, cited once (from Kirkcaldy in 1676), is 'also in the mod[ern] dial[ect] of Caithness and the Firth of Forth as *hettle*, *hattle*'. The definition is quoted from SND: 'A name given by fishermen to the rough stony sea-bottom some distance from the shore beyond the area covered with seaweed'.

For loanwords, it is useful to know the period in which the word first enters the dictionary record of English. This might be influential in weighing possible etymologies – putative loans from Old Norse, for instance, would probably already be recorded in Middle English. So would those from Anglo-Norman, whereas loans from French as a literary language continue over a much longer period.

Most words of Old English origin are part of a common West Germanic wordstock, in which case there will be parallels in German as well as Dutch, and perhaps also in the North Germanic (Scandinavian) languages and the extinct East Germanic branch represented by Gothic. For those belonging to the common stock of Indo-European words, there will also be parallels in other Indo-European language families, and in OED Latin, Greek and Sanskrit forms may be cited (these languages being well documented from an early period), and perhaps even Old Irish and Old Slavonic. The Scots dictionaries are to some extent dependent on OED, having been conceived (along with the *Middle English Dictionary* and other period dictionaries) as specialised supplementary projects to OED. For those words that are shared with English, we turn to OED for the fullest etymological information. We would not discover from DOST, for instance, that *richtis* (if it is to be identified as a form of *rickets*) is from Greek, or that *saffroune* 'saffron' is ultimately Arabic.

However, the distinctively Scots material is covered in much greater width and depth than in OED:

> The figures are something like this: the Oxford Dictionary's cohort of readers examined some 16,000 titles, over the whole range of English. Of these I estimate some six or seven hundred as Scottish works and the *English Dialect Dictionary* adds about another 600. In contrast, the two modern Scottish Dictionaries between them draw on upwards of 8000 volumes for a total of one and a half to two million quotations. This covers virtually everything of consequence so far in print and also some hundreds of manuscript volumes which were read for the *Dictionary of the Older Scottish Tongue*, whereas the *Oxford Dictionary* relied exclusively on printed editions . . . [The Scottish Dictionaries] . . . are far ahead in their coverage of the more obscure literary works and also of a great variety of official and private record sources such as the parliamentary and legal records, local records such as burgh court books and kirk session records from every corner of the land, the account books of, for example, coal-mine managers, skippers and farmers, and such things as private correspondence, wills and diaries. (Aitken 1964: 132–3)

For example, OED gives *lade-gallon* as one of several compounds s.v. *lade v* 8, collectively defined as 'names of vessels used in lading [that is, bailing out water]', the earliest citation being a Scots one of c. 1575. DOST, on the other hand, gives *lade-gallone* a separate entry, describing the object in some detail as

> a kind of vessel used for ladling and carrying liquids. ? Generally, or ? always, one of cooper's work, appar. a kind of wooden pail with a handle. Appar. orig. applied only to a large ladle of this sort used in brewing, but also latterly used for various other purposes.

It gives twelve citations, of which the first is an earlier (1421) version of the same Scots law cited by OED. Similarly, for the Scots material, the Scots dictionaries can very often improve on the OED etymologies (and it is to be hoped that a future edition of OED will incorporate the many improvements made by the supplementary dictionaries). An example is *jackteleg* (OED *jockteleg*) 'a clasp-knife'. The dictionaries agree in rejecting an eighteenth-century suggestion that Jacques de Liège was a famous cutler whose knives were well known throughout Europe. It is left to DOST, however, to cite the result of more recent scholarship:

> that *jackteleg*, like the 17th c. F. (1622–) and mod. dial. F. *jambette* (dim. of *jambe* leg) a clasp-knife, may contain an allusion to the leg-like shape of the hafts of early knives of this kind.

To give another example, OED describes *murgeon* (DOST *mudgeoune*) 'a grimace' as 'of obscure origin'. DOST, however, identifies it as a form of *motioun*.

In the early letters of the alphabet, DOST is less comprehensive in its treatment, and it is frequently necessary to use OED or MED to supply etymologies. These sideways moves will be successful more often than working forwards in time to SND, which does give etymologies but only includes words not found, or no longer found, in Standard English.[5] For those items introduced into the language up to 1600, DOST's treatment is comprehensive. Thereafter (that is, 1600–1700), because of the large volume of loans from English, a selective treatment is applied, including only items recorded earlier in Scots than in English.[6]

For those who have not used DOST before, several 'tours' of the dictionary are suggested below:

1. COINAGE. See *money* and follow up the cross-references given there. Search the quotations of each new item for further names of coins. See OED and CSD for later letters of the alphabet (*teston, turner, yokindale*). For the etymology of *bodle*, see also SND, and compare *bawbe* and *achesone*. See the appendix to CSD for a table of the native Scots currency. Notice how often the currency was *cryit doun*, and compare *cruikie* in SND.

2. FABRICS. Look up *demigrane, demi-ostage, nane-so-prettie, hardin, hunscott, ley, birges, contrick, cristigray, damacella, lillikins, pleismadame, fleming, grof, deroy, drop wecht*. Notice how these tend to reflect patterns of Scottish trade.

3. FEUDALISM. Look up *cuddeich, ladle, cumerlach, (out-)multure, casualty, ayre*, and see CSD for *sucken* and *soum*. See also *landimer, baillie, dean of guild, deacon, farthingman, bludewite, hamesukkin, assith, herezeld, infangthefe*.

4. STURDY BEGGARS. See *guberlungy* (SND *gaberlunzie*), *halland-schaiker, blewgown, bareman, dyvour, custron, culroun, loun*, and CSD for *smaik, sorner* and *thigger*.

DOST is a work by several hands, and the editors differ in the precise emphasis which they give to various types of optional editorial comment. However, one of the senior editors, A. J.

Aitken, has described the policies and practices of DOST in some detail (Aitken 1964, 1971b, 1973a, 1973b, 1977a, 1978a, 1981b, 1988). Some of the examples above and below are ones given in various places by Aitken.

Serious users of the dictionary are expected to read the citations. In doing so, they may observe that the word, or a particular sense, is restricted in its occurrence, either stylistically or geographically. *Mow*, the reduced form of *mouth*, is cited largely from low-style verse, including a flyting. A large majority of the citations for *roy* 'a king' are from alliterative contexts in verse. *Davach* 'a measure of land, commonly explained as equivalent to four ploughgates' is cited from Acts of Parliament, but otherwise overwhelmingly from Aberdeen northwards (it is a loan from Gaelic). The DOST editors often draw attention to such restrictions on the distribution of words:

> Any apparent or certain restrictions in the external distributions of words or senses which are not self-evident in the lay-out of the citations themselves may call for an explicit mention either as part of the definition or in an appended note. In effect this means that regional restrictions of distribution of frequently occurring items almost always require such mention, though chronological distributions seldom do. As for stylistic restrictions of distribution, these are often too uncertain for explicit notice, so with these we must leave the reader to shift for himself. Where we do feel confident enough to mention these explicitly, this is done by some suitable *ad hoc* label like 'chiefly in Chaucerian verse', 'only in abusive contexts', or 'only in (a particular author or work)'. (Aitken 1973a: 263)

Further regional examples (some from the supplements to volumes 1–3) include: Orkney and Shetland: *austercope, ayr, callow, haifreis-dyk, hailye, helmein, quoy n*^{2}; Caithness: *hasty*; Easter Ross: *schafe*; North-eastern: *marschall n 7b*; Central: *halfe-gavill, husband-land, kirkman n 2, marschall n 7b*; South-western: *half-manure, half-net, heft, kirkman n 1c*; Southern: *lokman.*[7] The *mait* form of *mete* is 'appar[ently] chiefly eastern in provenance, north of the Forth'. Occasionally, the regional origins of individual writers are pinpointed: for example under *lowand-ill* 'a disease of cattle characterized by prolonged or continuous lowing or bellowing', we learn that this word is '[f]ound only in Knox and in the Haddington records'. We learn also that the more widespread term is *rowting-evil*. Under *idy*, we find that this is a word of Scandinavian origin, later recorded only in Orkney and Shetland, and found in Older Scots only in Holland's *The Buke of the Howlat*. We are also given the very interesting information that this is not the only Orkney word in Holland, another being located at *lang reid*.

Typical DOST comments on style identify literary or formal words such as *pas* 'to go'; words found only in verse, such as *rubeatour* 'a scoundrel' (a flyting term of unknown origin); and words confined to Chaucerian verse, such as *lite* 'little', or to alliterative verse, such as *mold n*^{1} 2. The peculiarities of individuals' vocabularies are also identified, and Douglas frequently figures, particularly where the exigencies of translation in the *Aeneid* have led him into *ad hoc* borrowing from Latin, as for example the sense 'blade of an oar' for *palme* (though this is also found in the Middle Dutch, as DOST notes s.v. *palme n 4a*).

Another type of editorial comment is concerned with phonology. Minor sound changes confined to small groups of words are the subject of cross-references: for example, at *mow* 'mouth' we are told 'For the loss of *-th*, cf. *uncow* beside UNCOUTH'. Where the pronunciation is uncertain, rhyme evidence may be adduced in citations, and is sometimes explicitly commented upon. Rhyme and metre can both help to clarify stress placement: for example, the stress is seen to fall on the second syllable of *maner* 'manner', and likewise in early use on the second syllable of *river*, which rhymes, we are told, with '*chere, dere* (= deer), *fere, nere* and *stere*'. For *mischevous*, '[i]n verse the main stress generally falls on the second syllable'.

DOST also contains a wealth of information about the grammatical behaviour of individual words; and, of course, closed-class items such as pronouns, prepositions, conjunctions and auxiliary verbs are treated in full. Changes over time are illustrated by the citations: for instance, after the fifteenth century, the original form *mine* of the possessive pronoun occurs only before vowels and /h/ in attributive use. As I have said elsewhere (Macafee 1992–3), a fairly comprehensive grammar of Older Scots is implicit in DOST, though some aspects of syntax, obviously, are not amenable to alphabetic treatment.

6.3 THE COMPOSITION OF OLDER SCOTS LEXIS

Macafee and Anderson (forthcoming) present the results of a random sampling of one word in forty from the published volumes of DOST, giving 868 items and 983 etymologies.[8] The data are divided into three categories:

1. Originals (occurring in Old English or in source languages).
2. Derived forms (created in Older Scots by affixation, change of word class, or other processes of word-formation). If the affix (for example) was already present in Old English or in the source language, the item was counted instead as 'original'.
3. Compounds (created in Older Scots). If the compounding was already present in Old English or in the source language, the item was counted instead as 'original'. Compounds are a difficult category in historical lexicography, as there is no clear boundary between compounds and collocations. The identification of an item as a compound depends very much on editorial judgement.

Figures are also given separately for 'more frequent' and 'less frequent' items, based on the editors' use of large or small type for the headwords in the dictionary (see Tables 6.2a and 6.2b). Entries for cross-references, erroneous forms and variant forms were excluded from the sample. It can be seen that the proportion of Romance loanwords is remarkably high (nearly half of the total), while the proportion of Old English words is just over a third, and that this relationship persists even when we look only at the 'more frequent' category. This high proportion of words of Romance origin is also found in English, with over 50 per cent of the vocabulary in the *Shorter Oxford English Dictionary* being of Romance origin (Finkenstaedt and Wolff 1973: 119). In English, the proportion of Latin is almost identical to that of French, whereas in the DOST sample, loans from Latin are considerably less numerous. This is probably only partly due to Macafee and Anderson's category of indeterminate French/Latin loans.

Table 6.2a Proportions of more and less frequent items by originals, derivatives and compounds.

	Originals		Derivatives		Compounds		Total	
	no.	%	no.	%	no.	%	no.	%
More frequent	242	55.9	112	33.5	40	39.6	394	45.4
Less frequent	191	44.1	222	66.5	61	60.4	474	54.6
Total	433	100.0	334	100.0	101	100.0	868	100.0

χ^2 = 39.56, df = 2, p < 0.001

Table 6.2b Sources of the vocabulary of Older Scots (based on Macafee and Anderson forthcoming: Table 4).

	All no.	All %	More frequent no.	More frequent %	Less frequent no.	Less frequent %	Originals no.	Originals %	Derivatives* no.	Derivatives* %	Compounds* no.	Compounds* %
Old English	340	34.6	171	39.0	169	31.1	103	23.8	102	29.7	135	65.5
French	271	27.6	119	27.2	152	27.9	137	31.6	116	33.8	18	8.7
French/Latin	105	10.7	47	10.7	58	10.7	53	12.2	46	13.4	6	2.9
French/Italian	1	0.1	1	0.2	0	0.0	1	0.2	0	0.0	0	0.0
Latin	82	8.4	25	5.7	57	10.5	48	11.1	30	8.7	4	1.9
Total Romance	459	46.7	192	43.8	267	49.1	239	55.2	192	56.0	28	13.6
Scandinavian	82	8.4	46	10.5	36	6.6	29	6.7	29	8.5	24	11.7
Flemish/Dutch/LG	22	2.2	6	1.4	16	2.9	13	3.0	6	1.7	3	1.5
Gaelic	6	0.6	5	1.1	1	0.2	6	1.4	0	0.0	0	0.0
Celtic	2	0.2	1	0.2	1	0.2	0	0.0	1	0.3	1	0.5
Total Celtic	8	0.8	6	1.4	2	0.4	6	1.4	1	0.3	1	0.5
Greek	1	0.1	0	0.0	1	0.2	1	0.2	0	0.0	0	0.0
Anglicised	3	0.3	0	0.0	3	0.6	2	0.5	0	0.0	1	0.5
Multiple	9	0.9	5	1.1	4	0.7	5	1.2	1	0.3	3	1.5
Onomatopoeic	7	0.7	2	0.5	5	0.9	3	0.7	3	0.9	1	0.5
Proper names	8	0.8	3	0.7	5	0.9	4	0.9	1	0.3	3	1.5
Unknown	43	4.4	7	1.6	36	6.6	28	6.5	8	2.3	7	3.4
Grand total	982	100.0	438	100.0	544	100.0	433	100.0	343	100.0	206	100.0

* Excludes words subject to derivation or compounding in Old English or before borrowing into Scots. Percentages are rounded to the first decimal place.

In the DOST sample, Old Norse and Flemish/Dutch/Low German are also quite numerous, but the contribution from the Celtic languages is very small. The category of 'multiple etymologies' is necessary for the small body of loans whose possible sources cross the boundaries of the named etymological groupings. Words of unknown origin are also quite a substantial component.

Comparing the 'more frequent' and 'less frequent' categories, we find that Old English, Old Norse, Gaelic and the 'multiples' are similar in having a higher proportion of 'more frequent' than 'less frequent' words in the sample. Surprisingly, the Flemish/Dutch/Low German language group does not share in this pattern, although it is, like Old Norse and Gaelic, a contributor to the everyday vocabulary. The Romance words maintain their position in the derivatives category. However, the proportion of compounds formed on Romance roots is considerably smaller. Old English and Old Norse again behave similarly in having higher proportions of the compounds than of the originals. A high proportion (40.9 per cent) of *hapax legomena* are of unknown origin, while 43.2 per cent are of Romance origin, including 25 per cent from Latin, indicating a high degree of *ad hoc* borrowing from Latin by individual writers. Table 6.3 compares the sources of loanwords in the DOST sample with Barber's (1976) figures for Early Modern English (1500–1700) based on a 2 per cent sample from OED. The 'other' category includes various *ad hoc* alterations of words of Old English origin, which form a higher proportion of the DOST sample, perhaps just indicating a higher proportion of oddities and erroneous forms in DOST's more intensive coverage. Both Scandinavia and the Low Countries appear to be more important to the

Scots vocabulary, while the Spanish/Portuguese element is more important for OED, reflecting contacts between English and Spanish/Portuguese in the New World.

The most striking contrast, however, is the reversal of the positions of Latin and French in the two samples, even allowing for the indeterminate French/Latin category being larger in the DOST sample. This tends to confirm the impression of W. A. Craigie (1935), who thought that he detected a preference for French rather than Latin forms in Older Scots. This difference may suggest that the Scots were less preoccupied than their English contemporaries with 'inkhorn' terms and the self-conscious elaboration of the vocabulary. It is probably not simply an effect of DOST's less full coverage for the period 1600–1700, as the falling-away of the Latin contribution is apparent before 1600 in the DOST sample.

Table 6.3 Comparison of neologisms, 1500–1700, in DOST and OED* (based on Macafee and Anderson forthcoming: Table 6).

	OED no.	OED % of originals		DOST no.	DOST % of originals
Originals					
Latin	393	55.4		33	17.8
French/Latin	20	2.8		19	10.3
French	121	17.0		62	33.5
Greek	35	4.9		1	0.5
Italian	16	2.3	French/Italian	1	0.5
Spanish/Portuguese	16	2.3		0	0.0
German/LG/Dutch	9	1.3	Flemish/LG/Dutch	9	4.9
			Old Norse/Scand.	11	
			Gaelic/Celtic	2	
Other languages	15	2.1	Total	13	7.0
Onomatopoeic	9	1.3		3	1.6
Proper names	1	0.1		3	1.6
Unknown	63	8.9		19	10.3
Other	12	1.7		22	11.9
Total	710	100.0		185	100.0

* OED figures based on Barber (1976: 167, 194–5).

When the Latin and French loans are subdivided into nouns, verbs, adjectives and adverbs, the DOST figures for French are very similar to Barber's OED figures, with nouns forming by far the highest proportion and adverbs by far the smallest proportion. However, the figures for Latin are significantly different between the two dictionary samples, with verbs outnumbering nouns in the DOST sample (Macafee and Anderson forthcoming: Table 10; Barber 1976: 173; 176).

Many of the dates used in the study are approximations, so the figures must be treated with caution. Where the date of a citation was expressed as a date-range, the figure used was the midpoint. In rare cases where a text was only dated to a particular century, the midpoint of the century was taken. C[irca] and a[nte] in dates were ignored. The first appearance of an item in the dictionary record is only a *terminus post quem*, a point after which the word is known to be in the language. Many, especially those that were part of the popular (as opposed to learned) vocabulary, must have been in the language long before they were first recorded. Any word correctly identified as Old English or Old Norse must have been in the language before Scots as such begins, and the period of borrowing from Anglo-Norman (or 'Anglo-French', as DOST prefers to call it) also predates all but the earliest documentary witnesses of Scots. The large peak in the last quarter of the fourteenth century is to a large extent an artefact of the documentary record, marking the beginning of the corpus of literature in Scots with Barbour's *Bruce* and *Legends of the Saints*. The age of the makars and the beginnings of prose in Scots show up as another surge of new vocabulary from the late fifteenth century to the late sixteenth century.

As we would expect, the 'more frequent' items tend to enter the dictionary record earlier. After 1475, they are overtaken by the 'less frequent' items and rapidly fall away to zero. Figure 6.1 shows the dates of first citation for originals, derivatives and compounds. Derivatives show a second, larger, peak in the period 1550–74. Compounds show no marked peak but a fairly constant low level. Old English, Old Norse and Romance all show the initial late fourteenth-century peak, high levels in the late fifteenth to the late sixteenth centuries and a falling-away thereafter, in line with the overall pattern (Figure 6.2). However, if we separate the French, French/Latin and Latin contributions in the sample (Figure 6.3), we see that Latin does not show the first peak, and falls away early (from 1575 on). These patterns for French and Latin contrast with Barber's (1976: 86) findings:

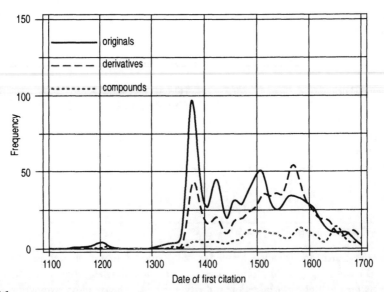

Figure 6.1

> ME loans are predominantly from French, with a minority from Latin; in the fifteenth century the number of Latin loans increases; and in the eModE period the loans are mainly from Latin, with a minority from French.

Barber found that the highest rate of borrowing from Latin in Early Modern English was between 1591 and 1660 (1976: 161). His median date for Latin loans is estimated to be approximately 1636, whereas that for the DOST sample is more than eighty years earlier, at 1550 (Macafee and Anderson forthcoming). Since the medians for French are much closer (1555 and 1565 respectively), it seems unlikely that the difference in the figures for Latin is merely an artefact of DOST's less full treatment of the period 1600–1700.

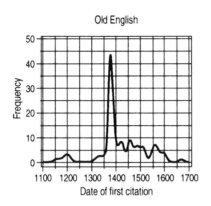

Old English

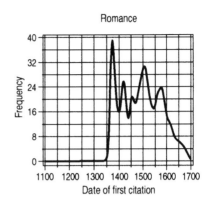

Romance

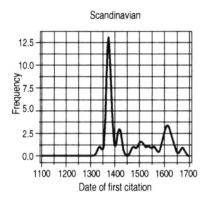

Scandinavian

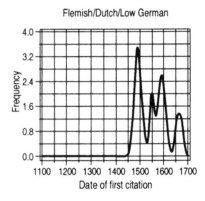

Flemish/Dutch/Low German

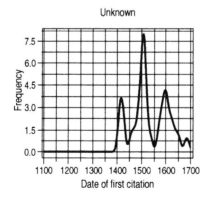

Unknown

Figure 6.2

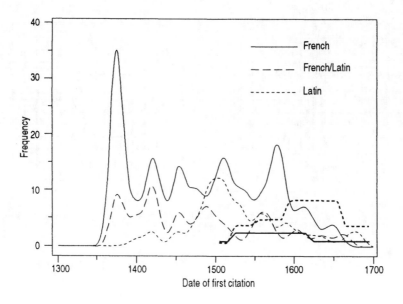

Figure 6.3

Finkenstaedt and Wolff (1973: 88) point out that the reshaping of the English vocabulary in the Early Modern period (particularly 1520–1620) was fundamental to the character of Modern English, adding about 15 per cent of the core vocabulary of the modern language. The Early Modern English expansion in the vocabulary was accompanied after a delay of twenty to fifty years by an increase in the rate of vocabulary loss. The fact that Scots lost its independence precisely during this period of enormous lexical change was critical for the future development of the language.

In Barber's sample, the peak period for affixation is 1591–1660, and this again was not evidenced in the DOST sample. In the DOST sample, the productivity of affixes of Old English origin was not so constrained by time as those of Romance origin, the interquartile spread of the Latin affixes being particularly narrow and concentrated in the late sixteenth century.

It is not uncommon for words to exhibit a change of affix. The etymologically related forms of the ending of the *nomina agentis* are frequently confused: *-er* from Old English and Anglo Norman, *-ar* from Latin, *-our* from French. Pairs of similar-sounding unstressed affixes are also confused, for example *-it* and *-ate* and the prefixes *im-* and *em-*. Metathesis gives such forms as *perfound* for *profound*. As in Barber's OED sample, change of word class was an important method of word-creation, particularly of verbs and nouns. Other types of word-formation exemplified in the DOST sample were: (1) aphetic forms, such as *fect* ‹ *effect*; (2) reductions, for example *monzie* 'a disparaging term for a Frenchman' is a clipped form of *monsieur*, with *-ie* added, while *kent n^2* appears to be short for *Kentschyre claith*; (3) back-formation, such as *grede* ‹ *gredy*; (4) metanalysis, for example *nother* from the wrong division of *ane other*; (5) false etymology, for example *forfaltour* is based on *forfat*, *forfet* 'forfeit' with influence from *forfalt* 'to commit a fault'.

6.4 SOURCES OF THE VOCABULARY

In this section, we look at the main sources of the vocabulary in more detail, and in historical context. In the discussion below, words surviving into Modern Scots are given in their more familiar modern spellings.

6.4.1 Native Vocabulary

A major part of the vocabulary of Scots is, naturally, of Old English origin, namely from the Northumbrian dialect of the Anglian dialect group. Much of this vocabulary is, of course, shared with Standard English, but with forms and senses independently developed. There are a few differences in word form between Scots and Standard English arising from Old English dialect differences, such as *grieve* 'an overseer' (< Old Northumbrian *græfa* = West Saxon *ȝeréfa*, which gives *reeve*), *moch* 'moth' (< Old Northumbrian *mohðe* = West Saxon *moþþe*) and *aicher* or *icker* 'ear (of corn)' (< Old Northumbrian *eher* = West Saxon *ēar*). Southern Scots *ticher* 'a weeping sore' is from Old Northumbrian *tēhr* = West Saxon *tēar*, which gives English *tear(drop)*.

Most of the Old English documents that survive are West Saxon, and the forms that are cited in dictionary etymologies are the better-attested West Saxon forms unless specifically labelled otherwise. Neither Scots nor Standard English is descended from West Saxon. Scots descends from the Northumbrian, and Standard English from the Mercian dialect of Anglian Old English.[9] Reliance on the well-documented West Saxon forms can sometimes obscure the phonological development. The word *bairn* 'child', for instance, develops regularly from Anglian *barn*. The West Saxon form cited by most dictionaries, including CSD, has *ea* as the result of West Saxon 'breaking' or 'fracture' (diphthongisation). This sometimes leads to the word being mistakenly treated as a loan from Old Norse. Scots *daur* and Standard English *dare*, Scots *swallie* and Standard English *swallow* are all from similar, unfractured Anglian forms.

However, dictionaries do usually give the Anglian *ald* forms that are the precursors of both Scots *auld*, *cauld* and so on, and the Standard English equivalents *old*, *cold* and so on, where West Saxon again has *ea*. Where West Saxon has *ǣ* from West Germanic *ā*, Anglian has raised *ǣ* from this source further to *ē*, giving Modern Scots /i/, regardless of the development of other Old English *ǣ*. Examples include *neep* 'turnip', *sweer* 'reluctant', *eeran* 'errand', *dreed* 'dread', *breer* 'briar', *bleeze* 'blaze'. Curiously, some of the main features of Northumbrian are not represented in Scots, lending weight to Aitken's (CSD) suggestion that Scots may not go back to the Old English spoken in the south-east of Scotland, but rather to the language of a population moving in subsequently from the north (or north Midlands) of England. W. A. Craigie (1925), however, suggested that the explanation might be variation within Northumbrian. One feature whose reflex is found is the rounding of *e* after *w*, thus Northumbrian *uoe*, Modern South-eastern Scots *oo* 'we'. However, the confusion of *ea* and *eo* that is found especially in the tenth-century texts is not represented in Scots, where their reflexes are distinct.

There are a few loans from East Midland English (the incipient standard) into Scots, identifiable by their word form, that are well established, independently of anglicisation as a general process. These include *boat*, alongside *bate* from the late fifteenth century, and *drove(road)*, the only form used in Scots, not **drave*. The *o* in *lord*, however, may be a native development. This form already existed in Scots in the fourteenth century, and is paralleled by *or* 'ere, before' from Old Norse *ár* (DOST s.v. *or conj*[1]).

A substantial part of the native vocabulary has dropped out of the language since the Old English period, often replaced by Old Norse or Old French loans, but it sometimes happens that a native word lost in Standard English has been retained in Scots (or in non-standard dialects in England). Görlach (1987) lists 100 such words in Scots.[10] His list includes *attercap* 'spider', literally 'poison head' (< *attorcoppe*); *bannock* (< *bannuc*); *ben* 'inwards' (< *binnan*); *bield* 'shelter' (< Anglian *beldo*); *fey* 'doomed' (< *fǣʒe*); *foumart* 'polecat', literally 'foul marten' (< *fūl mearþ*); *fremit* 'foreign' (< *fremede*); *harns* 'brains' (< *hærn*); *kythe* 'make known' (< *cȳþan*); *leid* 'language' (< *lēod*); *neb* 'beak, nose' (< *nebb*); *ream* 'cream' (< *rēam*); *smeddum* 'pith, spirit' (< *smed(e)ma*); *soutar* 'cobbler' (< *sutere*); *speir* 'ask' (< *spyrian*); *stey* 'steep' (< *stǣʒe*); *thairm* 'intestine' (< *þearm*); *threip* 'argue, rebuke' (< *þrēapian*); *wyte n* 'blame' (< *wītan*).

Some Old English survivals in Scotland and the north of England may have been reinforced by their Old Norse cognates. Examples include *bairn* 'child' (< Old Northumbrian and Old Norse *barn*; see above); *hause* earlier *hals* 'the neck' (< Old English and Old Norse *hals*); *deave* 'deafen, annoy' (< Old English *dēafian* and Old Norse *deyfa*); *drite* 'to shit' (< Old English *drītan* and Old Norse *dríta*) and *thole* 'endure' (< Old English *þolian* and Old Norse *þola*). Björkman (1900) considers that the frequentative suffix *-le* (as in *smittle* 'infectious') became more common in Middle English under Scandinavian influence. The Low German language group is also a source, for example *sprittled* 'speckled'.

6.4.2 Loanwords

Loanwords in Scots and in Standard English come largely from the same range of contacts, chiefly in the medieval period: Latin, with loans entering the language at every stage from the Germanic ancestor of Old English to modern scientific terminology; the Celtic languages; Old Norse – in some dialects more than others, but a considerable influence even in Standard English; French, especially the Anglo–Norman dialect, but later Standard French (the Central dialect), especially for learned loanwords; and the language group consisting of Flemish, Low German and Middle Dutch.

For a significant proportion of the vocabulary, no etymology has been ascertained. Almost certainly, some of these words have precursors, either in Old English or in the languages from which Scots borrowed, but these have gone unrecorded. Others are *ad hoc* coinages – we can be fairly certain of this when some identifiable principle of word-formation is at work. Another clue is the stylistic restriction of coinages in the early part of their history, when they are often treated as slang (appearing only in 'low-life' texts such as the Middle Scots flytings). If they become established in the language, this wears off, and they are assimilated to the everyday vocabulary, for example *gully* 'a large knife', *bonny* 'pretty' and *glower* 'scowl'.

6.4.2.1 Latin

In the Older Scots period, Latin influence is generally mediated by French. Sometimes a loan could equally well be from either language (hence the use of the convenient term 'Romance loanwords'), but often the pronunciation (as indicated by spelling and rhyme) and the inflectional endings are French. However, one word with ecclesiastical associations that is habitually latinised in spelling in Older Scots is *sanct*. This was actually the Old

English form, but it was early superseded by Old French *saint* (itself < Latin *sanctus* 'holy'), at least in the written record. CSD offers the pronunciation [saŋkt] for the Older Scots spelling, but with a question mark.

Even in Early Scots, the influence of formal Latin prose is very marked. As Scots begins to be used for official purposes, Latinate stylistic traits (mainly tending to complexity in sentence construction) are carried over into the vernacular. Individual items of learned vocabulary are also carried over, extending the range of expression of Scots. Romance loanwords continue to be borrowed in large numbers in Middle Scots prose. Also, in poetry, alongside the native poetic diction, an 'aureate', Romance-based poetic diction appears in Middle Scots. This fashion was initiated by Chaucer and followed by Lydgate and other English poets. The Scots poets who contribute most notably to the genre are James I, Henryson and Dunbar, sometimes known as the 'Scottish Chaucerians', although the aureate style is only one style in their repertoires. Dunbar's *Ane Ballat of Our Lady*, seven stanzas of variations on the *Ave Maria*, takes the aureate style to its apogee. It relies on Romance loanwords and *ad hoc* forms of Latin words for the rhymes in six of the seven stanzas. An examination of a stanza will help to illustrate the poet's relationship with the Latin language.

> Hale, sterne superne! Hale, in eterne,
>   In Godis sicht to schyne!
> Lucerne in derne for to discerne
>   Be glory and grace devyne;
> Hodiern, modern, sempitern,
>   Angelicall regyne!
> Our tern inferne for to dispern
>   Helpe, rialest rosyne.
>   *Ave Maria, gracia plena!*
>   Haile, fresche floure femynyne!
> ȝerne us, guberne, virgin matern,
>   Of reuth baith rute and ryne.
>
>   (*The Poems of William Dunbar*, ed. W. Mackay Mackenzie,
>   London: Faber and Faber, 1932).[11]

Here we find numerous examples of Latin loans. *Eterne* (first in Chaucer), *discerne*, *modern* (occurring in Scots earlier than in English), *sempitern* (first in Gower), *angelicall* and *femynyne* are all simultaneously from Old French and Latin. *Superne* (first in Henryson), *inferne* (only here) and *matern* (first here) we can take as Latin, since French does not show forms without *-al*. *Hodiern* (< Latin *hodiernus*) and *regyne* (< Latin *rēgīna*) are likewise recorded only here. *Lucerne* (< Latin *lucerna* 'a lamp') was used earlier by Henryson. *Dispern* 'disperse' (< Latin *dispernere*, *dispersus*) is first used here. *Guberne* (first in Henryson, < Latin *gubernare*) is equivalent to *govern* from the Old French cognate *governer*. *Rosyne* 'rose' is an *ad hoc* alteration (for the rhyme) of Latin *rosa*. Here we see that Dunbar's relationship with Latin is at some points direct, at others mediated by the shared literary tradition of Scotland and England. This is generally the case, and the result is that different variants were not infrequently borrowed on different occasions. A similar case to *dispern* (above) is *dispone* 'dispose' (a Scots law term): both are from Latin infinitives rather than past participles. Conversely, *appense* 'append' is from the past participle (or from Old French *appenser*). Kuipers (1964a: 92), writing about French and Latin loans in

Middle Scots, notes that 'there was considerable freedom' in the choice of infinitive or participial forms, and writes of 'a vague preference for non-English forms'.

Apart from Scots legal terms, most Latin loans into Scots are also attested in some form in Middle English or Early Modern English, whether before or after their appearance in Scots. Dost has numerous predatings in comparison with the dictionary record for England, for example *commiseration, emendation, immediate, intricate, location, metonymical, occur* and *pagan* (Aitken 1981b). Two well-known words, *allocate* and *narrative*, are so well established in Scots before their first appearance in texts from England that they should probably be regarded as loans from Scots into English.

Past participles borrowed from Latin most often end in /t/, and the native *-it* ending was often omitted in these words in Older Scots (and likewise in Middle English). These forms have been more persistent in Scots, for example *(weel)-educate* and *intimate*.

Loans from Latin, directly or via French, in the Older Scots period are mainly literary rather than popular. They are characteristic, as we have seen, of formal prose and of the aureate style of Middle Scots verse. The subsequent loss of status of Scots means that the aureate style is rather a dead end in Scottish literature. The tradition that continues into the modern period is the tradition of poetry and song in the native plain style, which remains close to the spoken language. Accordingly, only a small body of distinctive Latin loans survives in Modern Scots, based as it is on the colloquial and plain registers of the language. The surviving Latin component in the vocabulary is chiefly associated with Scots law.

6.1.2.2 British and Pictish

British place-names – Nicolaisen (1976) prefers the term *Cumbric* – are common in Scotland as in England, but only a handful of words were taken into Old English. These include *brock* 'a badger' (< *brokkos), *brat* 'cloak' (in Modern Scots mainly 'a coarse apron') and *cam* 'crooked' (< *kambos). These words are treated as British simply because they occur in England (where they cannot be Gaelic), but Old Irish etymons also exist. *Cam-* is productive as a prefix in Scots and was probably at least reinforced by Gaelic. Other British loans include *bodkin, cobble* 'a type of boat' and, Dost suggests, *lum* 'a chimney' (compare obsolete Welsh *llumon* in the same sense). In England and south-east Scotland, the British were subjugated by the Anglians, who would consequently have little occasion to learn their language, rather the reverse, so that British is not such an important source of loanwords as we might expect, although it may have had some subtle syntactical influences (Hamp 1975–6: 73, addendum; Mustanoja 1960: 590).

In the rest of Scotland, British and Pictish tribes came under Gaelic domination. Gaelic would tend to mask any loans from British that might be peculiar to Scots. Outside of the south-east, the British and certainly the Pictish tribes were already strongly Gaelicised before the Angles had much contact with them. Nevertheless, one word, *peat*, has been suggested as a Pictish loan (SND; Murison 1974). It appears first in a Scottish Latin context as *peta*. Another may be *month* (A. J. Aitken, personal communication). This term is applied to 'the mountains of the eastern Highlands' (in modern usage, *the Mounth*) and to 'any stretch of hilly, barren country or high ground'. The word is found in Scottish Gaelic, as *monadh*, but not in Irish Gaelic, so that it may have been borrowed into Scottish Gaelic from P-Celtic. It appears in Welsh as *mynydd*. The fact that the Scots word's place-name reference, and most of the citations for its more general application, are located north of the Tay suggests that the source may have been Pictish.

6.4.2.3 Gaelic

As we have seen, the proportion of loans from Gaelic in Macafee and Anderson's DOST sample is very small. As Aitken (1954) notes, there are very few Gaelic loans in the Early Scots texts, despite the conditions for borrowing being 'most favourable and the population most linguistically intermingled' in the eleventh and twelfth centuries. This is another reason to suspect that the rural Anglian population of the south-east was less important to the eventual form of Scots than the Anglo-Danes who were to form part of the population of the early burghs.

The interaction between Gaelic and Scots is described in Chapter 13 by Ó Baoill. The low status of Gaelic would not have encouraged much borrowing. Nevertheless, the numerical superiority of the Gaels over the Anglians, Anglo-Danes and other Germanic-speaking groups might have overcome this factor (as in Ireland). It may be (as suggested in Macafee and Ó Baoill forthcoming) that the prolonged period of contact allowed Gaelic-speakers to acquire perfect Scots, with less substratum effect as a consequence.

While burghs sprang up in the Lowlands, Gaelic remained very much a rural language, and contact with it was at a popular level within the receding band of Gaelic–Scots bilingualism. Up to the late eighteenth century, Gaelic came right to the fringes of the more densely populated Lowland zone. Withers (1984: 40) hints that an enclave of Gaelic speech may have persisted in south-west Scotland beyond the seventeenth century, but for the most part Scots probably replaced Gaelic in the south-west by the sixteenth century (Speitel and Mather 1968). The Scots-speaking fishing villages west of Nairn and up the coast to Helmsdale date from the seventeenth century or later.[12]

The late persistence of Gaelic in many areas probably meant a correspondingly late influx of Gaelic loans as the language was abandoned: more detailed study of the Modern Scots dialects, following up McClure (1986), is needed to confirm the geographical distribution of loans. If Gaelic loans were entering Scots in the late Middle Scots period mainly in the more peripheral dialect areas, then the written corpus is probably a particularly poor guide to this body of loanwords. Pődőr's (1995–6) work on Gaelic loanwords suggests, on sound philological grounds, that some loans must have been in Scots for several centuries before their appearance in the dictionary record. For instance *culrath* 'the surety given on removing a case from one court to another', although not attested in Scots until the fifteenth century, contains the phoneme /θ/, which was apparently lost in Gaelic in the thirteenth century. In *bladdoch* 'buttermilk', the same sound appears as /d/, although this word is not recorded in Scots until the late sixteenth century. Many of these apparently early loans have to do with Celtic law and society, and it is possible that some were transmitted via Scottish Medieval Latin (Pődőr 1995–6: 177; DOST s.v. *cateran*).

There are also, as suggested above, popular loanwords, for example *car-* as in *car-handit*, *corrie-fistit* and so on 'left-handed' (< *ceàrr*); *mant* 'to have an impediment in one's speech' (< *manntach* 'stammering'); *ingle* 'an ordinary domestic fire' (< *aingeal*); *ganʒe* 'an arrow or (crossbow) bolt' (< *gàinne*); *partan* 'a crab' (< *partan*); and *o* 'a grand-child' (< *ogha*). There may also be considerable, subtle, influence on the semantic development of Scots lexis. By its nature, this would be difficult to detect, and research in this area must await the publication of *The Historical Dictionary of Scottish Gaelic*.

Various influences on phonology have been suggested (Macafee and Ó Baoill forth-coming), of which the most convincing is the Northern Scots /f/ for /ʍ/ (evidenced from the sixteenth century on). Gaelic may also have influenced the retention in Older Scots of the

French consonants /ʎ/ and /ɲ/, which also occur in Gaelic and in Gaelic-derived names, for example *Menzies* (now /'mɪŋɪs/) and *Culzean* (now /kʌ'len/).[13] The change of /ɲ/ to /ŋ/, which occurs in several Scots words, most notably *ingan* 'onion', is also found in some Gaelic dialects, especially Eastern dialects (Seumas Grannd, personal communication).

6.4.2.4 Old Norse

Old Norse appears to have had a considerable influence on late Old English, especially on the grammatical system. It has been suggested that the close relationship between these two Germanic languages quite possibly made them mutually intelligible at this time. The relationship was appreciated by contemporary observers:

> Englishmen write English with Latin letters such as represent the sound correctly. . . .
> Following their example, since we are of one language, although the one may have changed
> greatly, or each of them to some extent . . . I have framed an alphabet for us Icelanders . . .
> (c. 1150, quoted in translation by Skeat 1887: 455)

Although they disagreed on many of the details of inflectional endings, much of the core vocabulary of everyday peasant life was the same (or obviously cognate, as with *kirk* = *church*, *kirn* = *churn* and so on). It was probably at least partly as a result of Old Norse influence that English grammar underwent a radical simplification, after which we speak of Middle English. New forms can be seen to spread southwards in the English texts of the twelfth to fifteenth centuries. They include *th*- forms of the third person plural personal pronouns (*they*, *them*, *their* corresponding to Older Scots *thai*, *thaim*, *thair*), replacing Old English *h*- forms; and *s(c)h*- forms of the third person singular nominative feminine personal pronoun (*she* – Older Scots *scho*), replacing Old English *hēo*.

The Old Norse component in General Scots is surprisingly large, just as the Gaelic component is surprisingly small, hence the suggestion that Lowland Scots should be traced to the Scandinavian-influenced dialects of the north of England, sometimes called Anglo-Danish (although clearly more Anglian than Danish). Unfortunately, the lack of Scottish texts between early Old English and the fourteenth century, apart from occasional words in Latin documents, makes it impossible to trace the transition from Old English to Older Scots in detail. When the written record of Scots really begins again, in the fourteenth century, we find that it shares in the Old Norse influence. For instance, in *The Scone Gloss* (W. G. Craig 1935, vol. 2, no. 19), an interlinear gloss written before c. 1360 in a Latin lease, the present-participle ending is already the Old Norse -*and*, not the native Old English -*ende*; and we even find the Old Norse -*and* ending of the ordinal numeral: *the four and tuentiand fat* 'the four and twentieth vat'.

The quantity of loanwords from Old Norse in Standard English is very large, but it is larger still in the dialects of the north of England, and it is with these that Scots must be compared. A 'Scandinavian belt' can be observed in the dialects of Middle English (Samuels 1985; McIntosh et al. 1986), and this is still visible in the modern dialect atlases. A typical example is the word for 'anvil'. In the Scandinavian belt, this is *stithy* (< Old Norse *steði*). In what was English Northumbria, north of the main concentration of Old Norse settlement, there is a gap in the distribution, where the only word used by dialect-speakers is *anvil* (< Old English *anfilte*). This is the case with many words, for instance *cush*, a call to cows to come in (< ON *kussa*); *dike* 'hedge' (< ON *dík*); *addle* 'earn'

(< ON *oðla*); *gimmer* 'ewe-lamb' (< ON **gymbr*); *lake* 'play' (< ON *leika*); *stee* 'ladder' (< ON *stige*) (Orton and Wright 1974). The same applies to word forms, for instance *heng* or *hing* 'hang' (< ON *hengja*); *gesling* 'gosling' (< ON *gæslingr*); *lig* 'lie' (verb) (Orton et al. 1978); *kern* 'churn'; *birk* 'birch' (Kolb 1964). However, in other cases, the Old Norse loan has spread right over this area, filling in the 'gap', for instance *clipping* 'shearing' (< ON *klippa*); *throng* 'busy' (< ON *þrǫngr*); *ewer* 'udder' (< ON *júðr*); *gilt* 'young sow' (< ON *gyltr*) (Orton and Wright 1974); *frae* 'from' (< ON *fra*) (Orton et al. 1978); *rig* 'ridge'; *flik* 'flitch' (Kolb 1964).

The remarkable thing is that on the other side of the border (which the Survey of English Dialects unfortunately did not cross), the Scots word is likewise often the Old Norse form – *stithy* or *studdy*, *gimmer*, *hing* or *heng*, *gaisling*, *big*, *thrang*, *gilt*, *frae* – although other evidence suggests that Old Norse settlement was minimal in Scottish Northumbria.[14]

It would seem that the Old Norse element in Scots (apart from the dialects of Caithness, Orkney and Shetland, where the influence was direct) must be attributed to population movements of Anglo-Danes from England before and during the feudal period. English prisoners were brought back from campaigns against Northumbria by Malcolm III (1058–93), and English clergymen and the households of Anglo-Norman barons settled in the country in the process of reorganising church and state on the feudal model. There is a brief period c. 1100 when men with Norse names like Thor, Cnut and Swein figure as witnesses to feudal charters in south-east Scotland (Murison 1974). Such names appear also in occasional place-names in the south-east, but mostly with Old English or Gaelic generic elements, for example *Dolphinston* and similar place-names containing the personal name *Dólgfinnr*, suggesting people of Scandinavian descent, though not necessarily Old Norse speakers (Nicolaisen 1976). Aitken (1954) makes the important point that the Old Norse loans found in Scots (again leaving aside Caithness and the Northern Isles) are almost all found likewise in the dialects of the north of England. This is in contrast to direct borrowing from other languages such as Middle Dutch and Anglo-Norman, where the loans into Scots are independent of the influence of these languages in England. In the Introduction to CSD, Aitken goes so far as to suggest that the contribution of Anglo-Danish to Scots is even greater than that of the Old English of south-east Scotland. Thomason and Kaufman (1988) have similarly suggested that Old Northumbrian is not the principal ancestor of the dialects of the north of England, so there appears to be a measure of agreement that Anglo-Danish has exerted a considerable influence on the language to the north of the Danelaw.

Orkney and Shetland were added to Scotland only in 1472, and their Scandinavian language, Norn, was gradually absorbed into Scots. We must distinguish between the loans from Norn on the one hand, into Orkney, Shetland and to a lesser extent Caithness dialect, and, on the other, the loans from Old Norse that Scots inherits from late Old English. Scandinavian material that is peculiar to the Norn-influenced dialects we can take to be from Norn. Melchers (1980) also makes the reasonable assumption that any Shetland word that can be traced to Norn should be, even though the word may occur also in General Scots, for example *grice* 'pig, piglet' (< Old Norse *griss*). The Scots word would then be seen as merely reinforcing the local word.

The common wordstock of Old English and Old Norse included such fundamental concepts as *man, wife, folk, house, under, mine* and *thine*. A number of basic vocabulary items have been influenced or replaced by their Old Norse cognates, even in Standard English, for example *sister* (< ON *systir* = OE *sweostor*); *egg* (< ON *egg*, compare ME *ey* < OE *æʒ*). Such words are much more numerous in Northern English dialects and in Scots. For instance, the word *ken* 'know' takes its sense from *kenna* rather than Old English *cennan* 'make known', and *stot* 'a bullock' from Old Norse *stútr* 'an ox' rather than Old English *stott* 'a poor horse', though closer in form to the latter.

It is possible that there are lost native sources for some words. The two languages being very close, there would generally be an Old Norse cognate of any such unrecorded native word. Wall (1898) suggests that *lowe* 'a flame' may be native, since it occurs in Frisian (the nearest relative of Scots and English) as well as in Old Norse and Middle Dutch. It is also suggested that *nieve*, *lug*, *muck* 'dung' (compare Old Norse *myki*), *ding* 'beat, strike' (compare Old Norse *dengja* 'to hammer') and others may really be native words because of their wide (though sometimes scattered) distribution in the modern English dialects (Wall 1898; Wakelin 1972). Given that geographical distributions ebb and flow, it is the distribution in earlier periods of the language which is of most interest here. In support of an Old Norse derivation, *The Oxford Dictionary of English Etymology* (Onions 1966) notes that *muck* occurs earliest in eastern parts of England, while *lug* is earliest in Scots, one of the very few Scandinavian loans in Scots not traceable to Anglo–Danish (Aitken 1954). Where an Old Norse etymon is not known, a word may nevertheless be identified as Scandinavian by the discovery of parallels in the modern Scandinavian languages and dialects. Examples include *titlin* 'the meadow pipit', recorded from the sixteenth century and paralleled by Faroese *titlingur* ('the pipit', in Icelandic 'the sparrow'); and *flan* 'a gust of wind', recorded from the late fifteenth century and with parallels in Icelandic and Norwegian dialects.

We should perhaps assume that most such words were borrowed during the period of contact with Old Norse, but we cannot discount the possibility of continuing Scandinavian influence through trade and general sea-faring contacts with the Northern Isles and the Scandinavian countries. For instance, the distributions of the word *sill* 'the fry of fish, especially of herring', found mainly in Shetland and Fife, and its derivative *sillock* 'saithe in its first year', found in Orkney and Shetland, Caithness and Moray, suggest the southward spread of fishing terms from the Norn areas. *Sill* is parallel to Swedish dialectal *sil*. The phonology is indicative here: the earlier borrowing of Old Norse *síld* 'herring' gives the usual Scots form *sile*. Susanne Kries (personal communication) notes that while a number of semantic fields are already in evidence in the fourteenth century – administration, law, agriculture, ships and shipbuilding – words in the semantic field 'trade' appear somewhat later (fifteenth or sixteenth century), reflecting later trading links with the Scandinavian countries, particularly Norway. Words for fauna also tend to appear in the fifteenth century.

Examples of Scandinavian word forms substituted for Old English ones include *drucken* 'drunken' (< ON *drukkinn* = OE *druncen*); *strae* 'straw' (< ON *strá* = OE *streaw*); *ain* 'own' (< ON *eiginn* = OE *āʒen* > *awn* 'own'); *gowk* 'the cuckoo' (< ON *gaukr* = OE *ʒēac*); *coup* 'buy, barter' (< ON *kaupa* = OE *ceapian* 'trade, bargain' > *cheap*); *nowt* 'cattle' (< ON *naut* = OE *nēat* as in the place-name *Nitshill* outside Glasgow); *gleg* 'keen in perception' (< ON *gleggr* = OE *glēaw*); *trig* 'nimble, neat in figure' (< ON *tryggr* 'faithful, secure' = OE *trēowe* > *true*); *lig* 'lie, recline' (< ON *liggia* = OE *liʒ* > *lie*).[15] It will be observed that there is a degree of regularity in the correspondence of forms in the two languages. Old Norse /g/ = Old English /j/ in *garth* 'yard' (< ON *garðr* = OE *ʒeard*)[16] and other examples of /g/ for /j/ occur in Scots, but there are also native /j/ forms. For instance, we have /g/ in *gif* 'give' (see above), but also in Older Scots the native form *ʒif*. The /g/ in English *gate* may be from the native Old English plural *gatu* (but compare Old Norse *gat*), while the singular *ʒeat* gives Scots *yett* (Scots *gate* meaning 'road, way' is from another word, Old Norse *gata*).

The form *she* (Older Scots *scho*) for the third person singular feminine personal pronoun, Old English *hēo*, is traced by Dieth (1955) to a dialectal Old Norse sound change [hj] > [ç] >

[ʃ]. The same development is seen in Northern English *shoops* or *choops* = *(rose)-hips* (< Old English *hēope*). *Choops* is also found in the south-west and south of Scotland (SND; and compare Mather and Speitel 1977: Map 18).[17]

Old Norse appears to have actually reversed, in the Northern English dialects and Scots, a group of native sound changes (with a few Scandinavian forms also penetrating Standard English). The Old English sound changes are referred to as 'palatalisation', because they involved moving the place of articulation of certain consonants from the velum to the palate when followed by certain other sounds. However, subsequent developments mean that the native reflexes are, in fact, no longer palatal. Old Norse preserved the original Germanic /k, sk, g/ sounds where native changes give /ʧ, ʃ, ʤ/.[18]

Examples include: (1) /k/ = /ʧ/ in *dyke* (< ON *díki* = OE *dīc* > *ditch*); *carl* 'churl'; *kist* 'chest, box' (< ON *kista* = OE *cist*); *birk* 'birch' (< ON *bjǫrk* and OE *birce* – the vowel apparently being from the native form); *muckle* 'much' (< ON *mikill* = OE *micel, mycel*). The phoneme /k/ is likewise Scandinavian in such loans as *sark, serk* 'shirt' (< ON *serkr* = OE *serce*); *reek* 'smoke' (< ON *reykr*, with the vowel of OE *rēc* which also gives English dialectal *reech*). However, the /k/ of *sic*, earlier *swik, swilk* is thought to be from the Old English dative *swilcum, swylcum*; while other parts of *swilc, swylc* give Standard English *such*. Other examples include: (2) /g/ = /ʤ/ in *brig* 'bridge' (< ON *bryggja* = OE *brycg*); these forms are less numerous, but the other common word showing this is *rig* 'ridge' (< ON *hryggr* = OE *hrycg*).[19] Also, (3) /sk/ = /ʃ/ in *skirt* (< ON *skyrta* = OE *scyrte* > *shirt*, the garment originally hanging from the shoulders to the knees); the suffix *-skep* '-ship' (< ON *-skapr* = OE *-scipe*) in *hussyskep* 'housewifery'; *mask* 'brew' (compare Swedish dialectal *mask* 'draff', that is dregs in beer manufacture = *mash* < OE *masc*); *skemmel* 'bench' and *skemmels* 'slaughter house' (< ON *skemill* 'footstool' = OE *sc(e)amul* > *shambles*, both < Latin *scamellum* 'small bench'). In *shairn* 'cow dung' (< OE *scearn*), Scots has the native form, while *scarn* (< ON *skarn*) is found in the north of England (J. Wright 1905; Mather and Speitel 1975: Map 60).

When /sk/ is final in a word, it is sometimes reduced to /s/, as in *ass* 'ash' (sixteenth-century *Ask Wednesday*) (< ON *aska* = OE *æsce*); *Pace, Pask* 'Passover, Easter' (Icelandic *paskar* < ecclesiastical Latin *pascha* > ME *pasch*); *mense, mensk* 'honour, dignity, common sense' (< ON *mennska* = OE *mennisc* 'human'). In some cases, there is no Scandinavian etymon to explain the 'non-palatalised' forms. Original Germanic /k/ is perhaps restored from Dutch in *caff* 'chaff' (Middle Dutch *kaf* = OE *ceaf, cæf*) and *streek* (Middle Dutch *strecken* = OE *streccan* > *streetch* = *stretch*). Latin may have influenced the retention of /k/ in *pik* 'pitch' and *cauk* 'chalk'.

Others remain unaccounted for, such as *merse, mersk* 'marsh' (< OE *mersc*). There is some doubt about whether the sound changes were complete in Old English. Research in sociolinguistics supports the view that sound changes spread quite gradually through the vocabulary and through geographical and social space, so that residues (appearing as exceptions to 'sound laws') are to be expected. In particular, linguists have been reluctant to believe that the hundreds of *sk-* and especially *skr-* words in Scots and English could all be the result of Old Norse influence reversing a native sound change (OED s.v. *scr-*), and not all have Old Norse cognates, for example *screw* 'shrew'. It is possible that to some extent Old Norse influence worked upon a basis of native residues. But certainly palatalisation did take place in the north. In early Scots place-names, the palatalised form *chirche* is found, replaced by *kirk* only in the thirteenth century (DOST s.v. *kirk*).

The process of analogy may also be involved. That is, we suppose that an awareness of the correspondence between the native and Scandinavian forms led to speakers altering other words to fit the pattern. This type of argumentation is difficult to sustain, being essentially speculative, and has been challenged in principle (Lass 1980). However, Trudgill (1986) shows that in situations of abrupt dialect mixture, a few unetymological forms typically do occur. He terms mixed forms (like *stot*, *birk* and *reek*) interdialect forms, and analogical forms (like *screw*) hyperdialectisms. Such forms could have arisen between Old English and Old Norse, or between more and less Scandinavian-influenced English dialects.[20]

To turn now to loanwords at large, these are numerous, and extend to basic, everyday vocabulary. The verb *tak* = *take* (< *taka*) replaces Old English *niman*, while *anger* (< *angra* 'to grieve') replaces a range of native near-synonyms, and *leg* (< *leggr*) joins native *shank*. Another very common word is *gar*, *ger* 'cause (something to be done), make (a person do something' (< *gera*). Sandred (1987) discusses in detail four words of Scandinavian origin that concern measurement by the hand: *gowpen* 'a double handful' (< *gaupn*); *luif-fu* 'palmful' (< *lófi*); *nievefu* 'fistful' (< *hnefi*); *starn* 'a star', figuratively 'a pinch' (< *stjarna* 'a star'). In general, Aitken (1954) gives as his impression of the Scandinavian loanwords in Scots the observation that 'they reflect the interests and activities of a farming people living an outdoor life without much in the way of aristocratic or civilised luxuries or much interest in intellectual pursuits'. The Scandinavians did however contribute to Scots and English terminology in the area of law (in its pre-feudal, customary phase), including the word *law* itself (< **lagu*). *Hamesucken* 'an assault upon a person in his own dwelling', now only Scots, may be from Old Norse *heimsokn*. Old Norse loans also figure in the poetic diction of Older Scots, for example *boune* 'ready' (< *bún-*); *fere* 'companion'; *brathely* 'fiercely' (< *bráðr* 'fierce'). But the bias of the contact towards everyday life and colloquial speech appears again in the Old Norse contribution to 'low' diction in Older Scots, for example *gyre* 'female monster', now only Shetland (< *gygr*), and *lug* 'ear', literally 'a flap' (compare Swedish *lugga* 'to tug at one's hair' and *lugg* 'forelock').

The Old Norse influence is remarkable for its pervasiveness in the Scots and English linguistic systems. It is quite easy for languages to borrow items of vocabulary from each other, since vocabulary is relatively open-ended and atomistic. Loanwords may affect the semantics (organisation of meaning) of the borrowing language, as with *ken* and *stot* (above). If borrowing is extensive, it may even affect the phonological system (as also with French influence). But it is much rarer for the morphological systems to be affected, because morphological structures are relatively closed and tight-knit. The influence of Latin on Scots and English grammar, for instance, is peripheral, and was long confined to certain prose registers, where the vernacular replaced Latin, taking over functions in the process. Old Norse influence on the grammar, in contrast, affects the language in its entirety, not only special registers. As we have seen, the native forms of the third person plural personal pronouns (Old English *hīe*, *hire*, *him*) were superseded by Scandinavian *th-* forms. The form *though* is Scandinavian, replacing Old English *þeah*. Other grammatical words borrowed in Scots are *at* 'that', *frae* = *fro* 'from' and *maun* 'must' (< *man*). The *-and* inflection of the present participle (= Middle English *-ende*) is likewise from Old Norse.[21]

6.4.2.5 Middle Dutch

The Low German language group is differentiated into Flemish, Dutch and the Low German dialects of German itself. However, these form a continuum, and are identical at many points, so that the precise source of a loan may be unclear, although the assumption is

that the earliest loans are from the Flemish spoken by immigrants to the Lowlands, and the
later loans mainly from Dutch. Both of these are sometimes termed Middle Dutch.

The Dutch or Flemish element in the Scots lexicon is the subject of a comprehensive
article by Murison (1971). The Flemish presence in Scotland dates from at least the twelfth
century, and includes refugees expelled from England in 1155. Right up to the sixteenth
century, Flemish craftsmen were encouraged to immigrate, and they formed small enclaves
(seen in such place-names as Flemington, of which there are four in Scotland) or settled in
the burghs, where they played a prominent part in public life. Some were recruited from
Flemish colonies in England. The constitutions of the burghs were probably modelled on
those of the Low Countries. Linguistic influence is reflected in burghal terminology. For
instance, the word *guild* (in Scots also *guildry*) is from *gilde*. *Kirkmaister* (pre-Reformation,
'a burgh official responsible for the upkeep of the church fabric') appears to be a calque on
kercmeester.

The early date of many loans from this source is shown by the fact that they participate in
the fronting of $\bar{o}$ to /ø:/. Examples include *bucht* 'sheep-pen' (< Flemish *bocht*); *cuit* 'ankle'
(< Middle Dutch *cote*); *smuir* 'suffocate' (< Middle Dutch *smoren* = Old English *smorian* >
smore); *yeuk* 'to itch' (< Middle Dutch *joken*); and *crune* 'bellow' (< Middle Dutch *kronen*,
kreunen), still found in the west and south-west of Scotland and in the north-west of
England for 'bellow' (Mather and Speitel 1977: Map 48). This has been taken into Standard
English as *croon*. The Low Countries were important trading partners, and the only
Scottish staple port abroad was maintained in different places in the Low Countries from
the thirteenth to the eighteenth century. Shetland continued to experience Dutch influence
even after trade waned, because of its use as a base by Dutch fishing vessels. Scottish
merchants were also involved further afield with the Hanseatic towns of the Baltic, Low
German-speaking at this time. Murison suggests that as the first occurrence of *galya* 'safe-
conduct' refers to Gdansk, it is more likely to be from Low German or even Danish than
Dutch, the original being *geleide* 'escort' in either case.

The close relationship between Scots and Dutch would facilitate loan-translations of
compounds such as *kirkmaister* (above), *landwart* 'rural' (Middle Dutch *te land(e)waert(s)*)
and perhaps *wappenshaw* (Dutch *wapenschowe*) (Murison 1971), though the possibility
always exists of the compounds having been created independently. Flemish speakers in the
early Scottish burghs would have added their weight to the restoration of non-palatalised
forms of words like *kirk*. These languages are themselves sources of non-palatalised /k/, /g/
and /sk/, for example *kink* 'choke, including choke with laughter; an irrepressible fit of
laughter' (< Low German *kinken* = Old English *cincian*); *kinken* 'keg, firkin' (< *kinnekijn*);
seg 'sedge' (< Low German *segge* = Old English *secg*); *arscap*, later remodelled as *heirskap*
'heirship' (< Middle Low German *arfskap*); *skaillie* 'slate (pencil)' (< *schalie*) and *skink*
'shin' (< Middle Dutch *schenke*). *Kink* 'twist in a rope' (< *kinke*), however, has a palatalised
Scots variant *kinch*, apparently by analogy.

In some cases, a loan might be from either Scandinavian or Dutch, such as *galya* (above);
grue 'shudder' (compare Middle Swedish *grwa*, Dutch *gruwen*); *knick* 'make a clicking
sound, especially with the fingers', clearly imitative, and recorded only from the eighteenth
century, but perhaps borrowed, nevertheless, from Middle Low German *knicken*, Dutch
knikken (and compare Norwegian *knekkja*). *Knack* 'make a cracking sound, especially by
snapping the fingers' has the same range of parallels. *Kip* 'a bundle, to parcel into bundles'
(< Middle Dutch, Middle Low German *kip* and the verb *kippen*) is paralleled by Old Norse
kippi 'a bundle', but first appears only in the fifteenth century, and first as a verb.

Loans from this source, especially from the earliest period, range over the vocabulary of everyday life. Some examples are *craig* 'the neck' (< Middle Dutch *craghe*, Middle Low German *krage*); *spean* 'wean' (< Middle Dutch, Middle Low German *spenen*); *golf*, the game (< Middle Dutch *kolf* 'a club', *kolven* 'a game with clubs'); *redd* 'to clear up, clear out' (< Middle Dutch, Middle Low German *reden* = OE *rǣdan* 'put in order' > *rede*). Murison (1971) treats the Middle Dutch element, by the century of first recording in Scots, under topic headings. Cloth is a prominent category, as for English generally, as this was the chief commodity of the Netherlands in the Middle Ages. Examples include *dornick* 'tablecloth linen' (< *Doornik*) and *camrick* = *cambric* (< *Kamerijk* 'Cambrai'). The Scots surname *Bremner* or *Brebner* is Middle Dutch *Brabander* 'native of Brabant', also in Older Scots as *brabanar* 'weaver'.

Sea-faring is another important area of borrowing. Scots examples include *dworce* 'athwart' (< Dutch *dwars*); *reid* 'a roadstead', that is, a place where ships can ride at anchor (< Dutch *reede*, Low German *rêde*). Weights and measures are mostly now obsolete, except perhaps *mutchkin* 'three-quarters of a pint' (< Dutch *mudseken*), and the same is true of coins. General trade terminology includes *coft* 'bought' (< Middle Dutch *cofte*) and *copar* 'dealer'. The verb *cope* (< *copen*) did not become established in Scots in its own right, although it appears briefly; compare *coup* from the Old Norse cognate (above). *Calland* 'customer', hence 'fellow', is from Flemish *caland*, or directly from the Northern French word that is in turn its source.

The nature of the contact with Flemish and Dutch means that the loans are of a colloquial kind, extending to pejorative words, such as *swinger* 'scoundrel' (perhaps <Middle Dutch, Middle Low German *swentzen* 'roam about'); *loun* 'fellow' (< Dutch *loen* 'a fool'). In the ameliorated sense 'boy', *loun* is a stereotype of modern North-eastern Scots. Other examples include *doup*, *dub*, *fozie* and *scone*. Middle Dutch is the source of the diminutive suffix *-kin*, as in *kinken* and *mutchkin* above, and *lillikins* 'a type of lace' (possibly from Early Modern Dutch *leliekijn* 'lily of the valley'). The diminutive suffix *-ie* may have been reinforced by Dutch *-je*, which became common about the same time, the seventeenth century, in the Protestant Netherlands (Murison 1971). It has even been suggested that this diminutive ending, which appears in Scots earlier than in English, is of Dutch origin (Partridge 1966).

6.4.2.6   Old French

Borrowing from Old French occurred in two overlapping phases. In the first, loans of a popular kind were taken into Scots speech, largely from Anglo-Norman (DOST's 'Anglo-French').[22] In the second, literary loans were borrowed from Standard (that is, Central) French, either directly or through English poets such as Chaucer. We know less about the use and ultimate decline of Anglo-Norman in Scotland than in England. Fewer documents survive and there is less contemporary comment. As in England, the important state and chancery documents continued to be in Latin; but whereas in England Anglo-Norman documents concerned with other legal business and government administration proliferate from the mid-twelfth century, in Scotland it is the late thirteenth century before we find French documents in any quantity at all.[23] Eventually, the Anglo-Norman families, forced by wars to choose among and divide their possessions in three countries, became nativised, and French ceased to be spoken as an everyday language in Britain. The appearance in Scotland of vernacular official documents in Scots in the second half of the fourteenth century is associated with the abandonment of French. George Dunbar, 'Le Count de la Marche d'Escoce', for instance, writes in Scots ('englis') to his distant cousin, Henry IV of

England, c. 1400: 'And noble Prynce, mervaile yhe nocht þat I write my lettres in englis / fore þat ys mare clere to myne vnderstandyng than latyne ore Fraunche' (W. G. Craig 1935, vol. 2, no. 53).

In the past, the Auld Alliance has sometimes been emphasised at the expense of the Norman presence nearer home (Michel 1882). Franco–Scottish alliances go back to the twelfth century, and the two countries were continuously allied from 1295 (when John Baliol, during his brief reign and in the face of England's interference in Scottish affairs, made a treaty with England's enemy, France) up to the Reformation of 1560. French troops were present at various times, and a large force garrisoned Scotland during the minority and reign of Mary, from 1542 up to 1560. Likewise, Scottish troops fought in France in the Hundred Years' War with England (1337–1453), and Scotsmen often studied at the universities of Paris or Orleans. Murison is prepared to credit the Auld Alliance with 'the bulk of French words which are not found at all in English, Standard or dialect' (1979b: 7), but there seems no inherent reason why the Scots should not have borrowed a distinctive body of words earlier from Anglo–Norman. We are on safer ground if we regard the Auld Alliance as prolonging the phase of popular borrowing. This is not to say that popular loans did not continue also in England, to some extent; and some of the examples below are found also in Early Modern English.

Popular loans first appearing in the dictionary record as late as the sixteenth or seventeenth centuries include: *fash* 'annoy, trouble oneself' (< *fascher*); *tass(ie)* 'goblet' (< *tasse*); *vivers* 'victuals' (< *vivres*); *gardyloo* the cry when chamber pots were emptied from the windows of Edinburgh tenements (< *prenez garde à l'eau* or *gardez-vous de l'eau*); *bejan* 'first-year student', now only at St Andrews University (< *béjaune, bec jaune* 'young bird, callow youth'); *howtowdie* 'a chicken for the pot' (< *hétoudeau*). Their non-literary character is confirmed when the source is dialectal French, for example *Hogmanay* 'New Year's Eve' (< Old Northern French *hoguinané* 'a gift on New Year's Eve, the word shouted by guisers asking for this'); *suggeroun* 'a kind of oats' (compare north-eastern French dialect *soco(u)ran*). Also in Early Modern English, and still in Scots, are *gigot* 'leg of lamb' (< *gigot*); *gean* 'wild cherry' (< *guigne*); *groser* (Scots also *groset* or *grosell*) 'gooseberry' (< *groselle*); *dams* 'draughts', the game (< *dames* 'ladies'); *jalouse* 'suspect' (< *jalouser*, related to *jaloux*, of which the earlier form *gelos* > Standard English *jealous*) (Murison 1979b; SND).

Most of the popular loans in Scots must nevertheless have been taken over from Anglo–Norman when it was a spoken language among the feudal ruling caste. Some writers, for instance Görlach (1987: 4), have doubted whether Norman influence could have been as strong in Scotland, where there was no Norman Conquest as such. However, the French influence is already considerable when Scots emerges as a literary language in the late fourteenth century. Evidence on Scots is lacking for the crucial period when Anglo–Norman was actually spoken in Scotland, so we must look at the form of the loanwords themselves for some indication as to whether they were borrowed from Anglo–Norman or from continental French. It can be shown that there are indeed distinctively (Anglo–)Norman forms among the French loans in Scots.

Unfortunately, there are few features that are unique to Anglo–Norman. Most of its characteristics are shared by the dialects of the continental areas from which the Norman invaders came. The Normans were originally Norsemen, who had seized what is now Normandy in the tenth century. Upper, or North, Normandy is part of the Northern French dialect area, while Lower, or South, Normandy is part of the (North-)Western dialect area. References to Old Northern French in etymologies can be taken as referring to either or both parts of Normandy. William also brought with him adventurers from Picardy (Northern dialect) and others from Norman-controlled Brittany. The influence of the Western dialect was strengthened in England in the late twelfth century, when the Norman royal house was joined to that of Anjou, and Henry II (1154–89) inherited both territories, while his marriage to Eleanor of Aquitaine extended the Angevin Empire to the Pyrenees. Although the other continental territories were lost, Gascony remained Norman until 1453. We should probably regard Anglo-Norman in Scotland as basically a northerly extension of Anglo-Norman in England. The Normans in Scotland were a small group who often continued to hold lands in England.

Central French would have been encountered by Scottish students abroad, but Scottish trade links were mainly with northern France. Leaving Northern French aside, therefore, it is the Anglo-Norman peculiarities and the Western elements in Scots that most unequivocally attest Anglo-Norman influence.[24] Western and Anglo-Norman give, for instance: (1) *leal* and *rial* (corresponding to *loyal* and *royal* from Northern and Central French), and *receipt* (Scots also *ressait*) rather than a form answering to *recoite*; but Scots has *moyen* (Northern or Central) as well as *mean(s)*; (2) *ui*, giving Modern Scots /ʌɪ/; this has usually been replaced by Central *oi* in English, but remains distinct in Scots, *pint = point*, *bile = boil*, *jine = join*, *poison* /pʌɪzɪn/; (3) *floor* (*= flower*), *oor* (*= hour*), in contrast to Standard French *fleur* and *heure*; (4) final /θ/ in certain words, thus *puirtith* 'poverty', *daintith* 'a dainty', *idelteth* 'idleness'.

Anglo-Norman criteria include: *aun* and *aum* for *ãn*, *ãm*, for example *chaunt = chant*, *chaunce = chance*, *graunt = grant*, *chaumer = chamber*, *daunger*, *braunche*, *enchauntement*, *launce*.[25] Other peculiarities of Anglo-Norman (Pope 1934) lie mainly in its conservatism in relation to continental French: first, /kw/ remained where continental French gave /k/ in such words as *quit*, *squar = square*. The late borrowing *quart d'écu*, a coin first struck in 1580, by contrast, normally gives *cardicue* (though there are also spellings in ⟨qu⟩). Spellings suggesting variants in /k/ for the earlier loans are however found in Older Scots as in Middle English, such as *cartane = quartane*, *corum = quorum*, *cote = quot* 'quota'. It is the predominant /kw/ forms that survive into Modern Scots, reinforced by the Latinate ⟨qu⟩ spelling. An exception is *corter* 'a quarter of an oatcake'.[26] Second, /dʒ/ remains, for example in *gentle*, *justice*, whereas it is altered to /ʒ/ in thirteenth-century French; likewise /tʃ/ rather than /ʃ/ in *chanoun* and so on (if not Northern /k/; see footnote above). Third, *-ary*, *-ory*, *-ery* are the borrowed endings from disyllabic Anglo-Norman forms corresponding to French *-aire*, *-oire*, *-ère*. Early Scots has, for instance, *contrary* though also *contraire*; *historie* though also *histo(i)r*.

On the whole, the mixture of Northern and Western characteristics is comparable to that in Middle English, and consistent with Anglo-Norman influence. The extent of Norman influence is less surprising when we remember how much the spread of Lowland Scots depended upon the spread of the feudal system and the reorganisation of the church. Dickinson quotes Walter of Coventry, writing in the late thirteenth century: 'the more recent kings of Scots profess themselves to be rather Frenchmen, both in race and in manners, language, and culture; and, after reducing the Scots [that is, Gaels] to utter servitude, they admit only Frenchmen to their friendship and service' (1977:83). Extensive bilingualism is suggested by the fact that French vowels and consonants were introduced into Scots. The diphthongs *ọi* (Modern Scots [oe], as in *noise*) and *ui* (Modern Scots [ʌɪ], as in *jine = join*) were borrowed, and also the consonants [ʃ] and [ɲ], perhaps reinforced by Gaelic, for example *feingie*, *feinʒie = feign*; *ingan*, *inʒane = onion*; *assoilʒe = assoil* 'absolve'; *bailie*, *balʒe*.

Variation among French dialects and between Latin and French gives rise to variation both within and among dialects of Scots and English. The French development of Latin /mn/ to /mpn/ is reflected in occasional Older Scots variants such as *impnis* = *hymns* and *autumpnal* = *autumnal*. On the other hand, Latinate spellings were favoured in French itself. A late thirteenth-century treatise written in England recommends: 'quelibet diccio gallica concordans latino in quantum poterit debet sequi scriptura latini' (quoted by Pope 1934: § 1,218). Thus spellings such as *doubt* (Old French *duter*, Latin *dubitāre*) are found alongside *dout*, and *recept* or *receipt* (Anglo-Norman *receite*, Medieval Latin *recepta*) alongside *ressait*. *Paroche* = *parish* is from a Latinate variant of *paroisse*, and occurred in Scots alongside *parise* and *pairish*. French silent *h* tends to be restored from Latin, and this is another source of variation, for example *able* and Scots also *hable* (< Old French *able* < Latin *habilis*); *heritage* and Scots also *eritage* (< Old French *(h)eritage* < ecclesiastical Latin *hērēditāre*).

Turning to grammar, French influence supports the Latinate use of the interrogative pronouns as relative pronouns (the *quh-* relatives). French also supplies models for certain periphrastic constructions, which became more common as Scots and English moved from being synthetic to being analytic languages. These include comparatives and superlatives with *mair* = *more* and *maist* = *most* (compare *plus* and *le plus*); possibly the periphrastic possessive with *of* (compare *de*); and individual prepositional phrases. Phrases sometimes coalesce in popular borrowings, encouraged by the blurring of word boundaries in colloquial French, for example *amagger o* or *maugre* 'in spite of' (< *maugre, à mal gré*); *allevolie* 'at random' (< *à la volée*); and compare also *ava* = *of all* (calqued on *du tout*).

French words are borrowed in the same spheres as in English. Anglo-Norman loans include much of the terminology of feudalism and its attendant social relations. Popular loans in general range over everyday life, for example *cummer* 'female crony' (< *commère* 'fellow godmother'; compare the similar sense development of *gossip*); *murdris* 'murder' (< *murdriss-, murdrir*); *plenis, plenish* 'furnish, stock' (< *pleniss-, plenir*); *corbie* 'raven' (< *corbe*); and *turkas* 'smith's pliers' (< *turcaise*).

6.5 CONCLUSION

This chapter has given an overview of Older Scots lexis, and has looked in more detail at the main etymological sources. The abundance of Old Norse loans is one very striking characteristic of Older Scots. Coupled with the relative paucity of Celtic loans, this lends support to the view that Scots is descended from Anglo-Danish more than from the language of the original Anglian settlements in the south-east. In comparison with Early Modern English, Middle Scots is not particularly rich in Latin loans, lending support to the view that French was, and remained, more important than Latin as a source of loanwords. This chapter has attempted to refute the view that Anglo-Norman was lacking as an influence on Older Scots.

A great deal of work remains to be done on individual sources of Older Scots lexis. There are detailed studies of the Flemish/Middle Dutch/Low German group (Murison 1971), of early Gaelic loans (Pödör 1995–6) and of reduplicative words (Thun 1963). All of these could usefully be supplemented, and their arguments strengthened, by a comprehensive examination of DOST. Enough of the alphabet has already been published to allow an ambitious study by Kries (H. Berlins Ph.D. in progress) of the Scandinavian element in the vocabulary. This will surely be followed by other similar studies. Whether or not they will confirm the tentative findings of this chapter remains to be seen.

NOTES

1. 'Someone accosted them as they [went] through the town, the strongest man that Hesilrig then knew, and also he had plenty of slighting words. He saluted them, as if merely in scorn, "God save you, good day, good sir, and good morning!" "Whom do you scorn?" said Wallace [notice the condescending *thou*]. "Who taught ['instructed'] you?" "Why sir" he said, "have you not just come over the sea? Pardon me, then, because I thought you were an embassy to bring a strange queen!" Wallace answered, "Such pardon as we usually give, you will not go without on your part." "Since you are Scots, you will still be saluted: good day, bonnet laird, herdsman, God's blessing." More Englishmen drew in around them . . .'

   I am grateful to A. J. Aitken, Sonja Cameron, Susanne Kries, David Murison and Colm Ó Baoill for comments on various parts of this chapter.

2. OED sometimes resorts to constructing what the modern Standard English form *would* have been: for example, **victorage* is the headword for Older Scots *wictorag* 'victory' (with normal Older Scots ⟨w⟩ for ⟨v⟩); **uncunyed* for Older Scots *un-*, *oncunȝeit* (Martin 1979: 34).

3. Although some writers use the term Middle English to include contemporary Scots, in the dictionaries it is intended to contrast with Older Scots.

4. The late appearance of the corpus of Older Scots is the reason why many words in CSD, even words of Old English origin, are dated 'la14–' 'late fourteenth century on'. Only a few words are recorded as Scots from an earlier date, mainly place-name elements such as *tod* 'fox', 'in place-names la13–' (CSD).

5. A second opinion is worth having when the etymology is difficult. In this connection, it may be useful to know that SND is subsequent to DOST in the letters B and C, but ahead of it elsewhere.

6. This policy has been changed by the present editorial team, but the effects have yet to be seen in print.

7. Further examples can be found in Aitken (1971b: note 8).

8. The number of etymologies is larger because of compounds.

9. However, some Old Northumbrian words and forms have entered Standard English, for example *whisper* and *little*.

10. The article in general is, however, rather misconceived, and should be read sceptically.

11. Translation: 'Hail, supernal star! Hail, in eternity, in God's sight to shine! A lamp in darkness to discern by glory and divine grace; daily, of this time, eternal, angelical queen! Our infernal darkness to disperse, help, royalest rose. Hail, Mary, full of grace! Hail, fresh feminine flower! Diligently govern us, maternal virgin, both root and rind of compassion.'

12. The distinct separation of fishing and agricultural communities that allows these to remain enclaves within Gaelic (latterly Highland English) territory is quite characteristic.

13. Spelling pronunciations are established for the names *Cockenzie*, *Mackenzie* and *Menzies*. In Middle Scots handwriting, the rare letter ⟨z⟩ is indistinguishable from yogh ⟨ȝ⟩. Conversely, both were printed as ⟨z⟩.

14. The sense 'hedge' of *dyke* is recorded in the south-west of Scotland in the twentieth century; *ure* or *yower* 'udder' from the late eighteenth century in Dumfriesshire and Roxburghshire. These forms may have spread from England in modern times, or they may have been in the dialects, unattested.

15. *Licgan*, the Old English infinitive, should have given **lidge*.

16. Old Norse /ð/ corresponds to Old English /d/ in such words as Old English *mōdor* > *mother* (Scots *mither*) and Old English *fæder* > *father* (Scots *faither*), but the /ð/ forms are the result of a fifteenth-century native sound change (Jordan and Crook 1974: §298).

17. In the name *Shetland* (Old Norse *Hjaltland*), a different dialectal development of /j/ gives the variant *ȝetland* (also spelled and consequently pronounced *Zetland*).

18. Before the migration from the continent, the Anglo-Saxons fronted the pronunciation of Germanic *k* before vowels, before *j* (as in the infinitive ending), and word-finally after *i* and *ī*.

Jordan and Crook (1974: §177) reconstruct the sequence phonetically as [k] > [kç] > [tç] > [ʃ]. Since the spelling remains ⟨c⟩, the chronology is unclear, but the difference becomes phonemic when new front vowels arise after *k* as a result of *i-umlaut* (crudely, the fronting and raising of vowels when *i* or *j* followed in the next syllable) early in the Old English period.

Germanic *sk* became palatal in almost all environments in Old English, perhaps as [sk] > [sç] > [ʃ]. The cluster /skr/, however, may actually have remained in the south-west of England, the north Midlands and the north (ibid: §181).

Some Old English inflectional endings had a front and some a back vowel, thus creating different phonetic environments in different forms of the same word, either directly or because of the influence of the vowel of the inflection upon the vowel of the root in earlier sound changes. The variants are usually levelled by analogy, though dialects may disagree on which variant to favour, so that we find native doublets such as *sic* and *such*, *gate* and *yett*.

Old English /j/ and /w/ from Germanic ȝ and *ww* correspond to Scandinavian /gg/. In early Middle English, the semivowels /j/ and /w/ were absorbed into any preceding vowel, hence *ey* 'egg', *true* and so on (ibid: §§189, 190).

Whey (<Old English *hweȝ*) has a Scots form *whig*, apparently by analogy with forms like *egg*. Likewise *fleg* appears alongside *fley* 'frighten' (< Old Norse *fleygia* 'let fly' – the sense is closer to that of Old English *āfliezan* 'put to flight'). The late appearance of these forms (seventeenth century) makes the derivation problematic.

19. When West Germanic *g* was followed by *j*, this 'lengthened gg' gave /ʤ/, written ⟨cg⟩ in late Old English (see Jordan and Crook 1974: §192).

20. Other phonological influences from Old Norse have been suggested. Baugh and Cable (1982: 96) maintain the view that /e/ in words like *hale* = *whole*, *gait* = *goat* is to be traced not to Old English *ā* but to Old Norse *ei* via Middle English *ai*. Although there are Middle English spellings that suggest *ei* in a few words such as *goat* (Jordan and Crook 1974: §130), this is not tenable as a general explanation of the development north of the Humber, in view of the systematic nature of the fronting and raising of *ā* in the north, from every etymological source, and regardless of whether there is an Old Norse cognate. Also, there are separate reflexes of *ai* in some Modern English and Scots dialects.

Samuels (1985) revives the hypothesis of Scandinavian influence on *ā* in another guise, suggesting that sociolinguistic forces within the mixed Anglo-Danish population may have precipitated the change of *ā* from a back to a front vowel, and likewise the fronting of *ō* to *ū*/ø:.

21. The form *are* of the verb *be* is often seen as influenced by Old Norse (reinforcing Anglian *aron*), but the form within the Scandinavian belt is *er(e)* (Samuels 1985). In dialects of the north of England, Old Norse *at* is found before infinitives (instead of *to*). In Scots, as in Standard English, this occurs only in one or two fixed collocations, notably *adae* = *ado* (< *at* + *dae*/*do*).

22. From the thirteenth century, the dialect of Paris, namely Central French, was increasingly influential as a literary standard within France, and this led to Central French influence on Anglo-Norman. It is this later, more standardised, dialect that most dictionaries (apart from DOST) are referring to when they use the term 'Anglo-French'.

23. A curious macaronic habit in the Latin documents of medieval Scotland is the use of the French definite article before vernacular names, not only French names but also Scots ones, for example *Ad crucem ligneam que vulgariter dicitur ly girthtcorse* (1440) (DOST s.v. *le article*). In the form *lie*, this French definite article continued to be used in certain Scottish records in Latin until 1897 (DOST ibid.). Likewise in the Middle Ages the names of nobles regularly appear in Latin and English contexts with *de*, for example *Robertus de Bruce*.

24. We also find, as in England, a large Northern component. Northern are, for instance: (1) /w/ rather than /gw/ (later French /g/), for example *weir* = *war* (compare Standard French *guerre*), and *wardon* = *guerdon* 'reward'; (2) /g/ before *a* rather than /ʤ/ (later French /ʒ/), for example *garden*. Likewise /k/ rather than /ʧ/ (later French /ʃ/), for example *kinch* = *chance*, 'the fall of the dice'; *campioun* = *champion*. However, Lower Norman also had /ʤ/ and /ʧ/: 'such forms therefore may

not simply be designated as Central French' (Jordan and Crook 1974: §223). In Scots, /ʧ/ also occurs, for example *eschape* = *escape*; *roche* = *rock*; *chanoun* = *canon*, and *chanonry* in place-names; similarly inconsistent are Northern /ʧ/ forms for Western and Central /s/ in words like *hurcheon* 'hedgehog' (< *herichon*); but /s/ in such words as *civil*, *city* and Scots *sybow* 'spring onion' (< *ciboule* = Old Northern French *chiboule* > English dialectal *chibol*). Northern or Central are for example, *appreve* 'approve' and *prieve* 'prove' (later *pree*). These have the same vowel as for example *beef*. Northern, Western and Anglo-Norman is the retention of *ẽn*, separate from *ãn*, giving for example *gentle*, *amend*, *defend*.

25. It has been suggested that Anglo-Norman *a* > *au* was influenced by the English development (south of the Humber) of *ā* to *ō* in words like *home* (Old English *hām*) (Pope 1934: §1,152).

26. Peculiar to Older Scots are reverse spellings such as *quomon* for *commoun*, *quonciens* for *conscience*, *quottar* for *cottar*.

7

The Language of Literary Materials: Origins to 1700

Ronald D. S. Jack

7.1 WAYS AND MEANS

Textually, the journey proposed in this chapter is an ambitious one. It begins with John Barbour's historical Romance, the *Bruce*, composed in the mid-1370s, and reaches its highpoint at the turn of the sixteenth century with the verse of Robert Henryson, William Dunbar and Gavin Douglas. It continues with what, for most literary critics, is a qualitative descent from David Lindsay through the Marian and Jacobean writers into a virtually ignored seventeenth century.

The diachronic, text-centred approach advocated in these volumes is not now favoured among literary critics. The use of modern theories to explicate texts is generally preferred. The effect of this is to ask students first to understand the code and then to view the poem or play from that perspective. As many of these systems are themselves extremely sophisticated, the advantages which they hold out for the specialist may be gained at the expense of the student, who is expected to master Derrida or Kristeva before *King Lear*. More pertinently, neither the placing of theory before text nor the synchronic methodology were the way of either the medieval or the Renaissance writer or critic. If modern literature is likely to be amenable to contemporary theorising, ancient literature warrants consideration of the critical frameworks of its own time as well.

In those days, antiquity and authority were revered. Medieval commentators followed their classical predecessors in linking the skills of poetry to those of persuasive oratory. In his *Art of Rhetoric*, Aristotle had warned against over-complex theorising because the verbal persuader's realm was, in part, a popular one. Like dialectic, it 'treat[s] of such things as are in a way common for all to grasp' (Lawson–Tancred 1965: 66). Indeed, the art of persuasion is only a discipline in a limited sense. 'The *proofs* alone are intrinsic to the art and all other features merely ancillary' (1,354a). Only when measuring eloquence is the literary critic on home ground: 'Its [Rhetoric's] function is not persuasion. It is the *detection of the persuasive aspects of each matter*' (1,355b).

Language's ability to convey ideas and emotions is not called into question. Nowadays, attention moves pessimistically away from meaning to the circle of language signing itself. Such ideas are discussed by classical writers and will be highlighted in the Middle Ages; but language's power to sign meaningfully, if imperfectly, cannot be absolutely challenged without destroying the premises of effective persuasion on which the entire discipline rests.

And the focus for poet and critic alike, as the highlighting in the manuscript reveals, remains the individual work. '*Let rhetoric be the power to observe the persuasiveness of which any particular matter admits*' (1,355b).

Even less would the peripatetic school have favoured the importation of ideas from other disciplines as a means of explaining the text. The critic has to know 'something about the subject matter' in order to assess the best means of persuasion, but that subject matter is 'extraneous to the business' (1,354b). That is, while the rhetorician will have his own views on the ethical or political content of the arguments he is assessing, his special expertise equips him only to evaluate the ways in which language is employed. Listening to a discussion, he may believe that a stoic's arguments hold greater truth yet award rhetoric's prize to a hedonist because the latter's case is more persuasively presented. This is because rhetoric is a contingent art, opening out its findings to other disciplines with different criteria of judgment. Where his outlook differs most clearly from our own days is in his acceptance that there are 'truths'. It follows that 'in all cases the true and naturally superior position . . . is more easily argued' (1,355b). But the defining area of rhetorical concern and therefore any theorising concerning that discipline lies within the verbal matrix. Further distinctions define the forensic method as against the poetic, while accepting their many shared features.

It has been necessary to begin an essay on the Scottish literary language in this way, not to decry the synchronic and theoretical bias of literary criticism today but to maintain the value of the alternative diachronic approach when assessing earlier writers, who composed according to its principles. Aristotelian and Neoplatonic aesthetics, as refined first by the Scholastic thinkers of the Middle Ages and then by the humanists of the Renaissance, provided European poets and dramatists with a way of viewing and describing their art. The critic who does not understand the conventions governing their thought is in constant danger of blaming them for doing badly what they were not trying to achieve at all.

To place Scottish literature and Scottish language within these broader critical currents will introduce additional problems centred on the ethnic adjective. Is there such a thing as a specifically Scottish literary language or a Scottish nation? These questions will be introduced with ever greater precision as the discussion progresses, but the next section will primarily explore the ways in which authors who happened to be Scots thought about their art and language.

7.2 MAKING, MOVING AND MEMORISING: EARLY SCOTS LITERATURE (c. 1375 TO c. 1455)

A. J. Aitken (1977b: 2) defines the Early Scots period as stretching from c. 1375 to c. 1450. That covers a long and varied historical time from the early days of Robert II's reign to James II's troubles with the Douglas family. Yet, the three major writers chosen to represent it were all well-educated men connected with the court, and so they approach these varied times from similar educational and sociological perspectives. John Barbour (c. 1320–95) studied in Paris before becoming an archdeacon and historiographer in Robert II's court. James I (1394–1437) received the thorough education appropriate for a monarch during the eighteen years of his youthful captivity in England. Richard Holland (c. 1420 to c. 1495) was secretary to the Earl of Moray in his early years and rector of various churches in the Caithness area.

Linguistically, there is also variety. James I's long imprisonment in England results in an unusual vocabulary range in which Scots forms mingle with those drawn from the English dialects of the south and midlands. But he is still recognisably an Early Scots poet. That is the broad 'kind' to which the language of all the poems in this section belongs. Although the manuscripts in which they are preserved postdate composition, the scribes transmit this earliest stage of Scots with enough accuracy to sustain the validity of that grouping.

All the evidence is poetic because verse was then the favoured mode, but the poems chosen span a wide range of literary forms and stylistic modes. Barbour's *Bruce* (McDiarmid and Stevenson 1981–5) is a twenty-book Romance composed in the mid-1370s. It is written in couplet form, and its martial story retraces the entire history of the Early Scots period. Indeed, although the Scottish Wars of Liberty in the early fourteenth century are its major theme, they are introduced with reference to the even earlier succession problems following the death of Malcolm III in 1093. The heroism of Bruce and Douglas is then 'prophetically' linked to a second Golden Age, heralded by the accession of Barbour's own monarch, Robert II.

James I's *Kingis Quair* was written about sixty years later, c. 1425 (McDiarmid 1973). It uses the seven-line rhyming stanza employed by Chaucer for *Troilus and Criseyde* to tell of the king's youthful imprisonment and first experience of romantic love. The poet links his own early bad fortune and the metaphysical questions arising from it to the imprisonment and philosophical worries expressed by his major authority, Boethius, in the *Consolation of Philosophy*. A mixture of romantic biography, spiritual journey and pagan dream vision, the *Quair* is not easily categorised.

No easier to define is Richard Holland's *Buke of the Howlat* (Amours 1896). Written c. 1452 in a thirteen-line, alliterating, bob-and-wheel stanza, it tells of a bird parliament convened by the Pope to judge the owl's complaint against Nature. Borrowed feathers beautify the bird whose emergent pride results in it being stripped of that plumage. Leitmotiv images drawn from nature and heraldry suggest variations on a theme of conflict, death and rebirth as translated in terms of current Scottish and European politics, transcended by God and contained within His cosmic signing system.

In order to fulfil the interrelated aims discussed in section 7.1, it will be helpful to pinpoint those broad attitudes to literature, language and interpretation shared by these authors and then to identify where these differ from modern presumptions. As both Aristotle and later medieval commentators advocated the syllogism and the analogic method as especially appropriate for the craft of poetry, comparisons between that art and other activities will be an appropriate starting point for the search.

When Barbour introduces the *Bruce*, he refers to it as a 'made' work, dealing with the 'stalwart folk' of Scotland (I. 33):

Off thaim I thynk this buk to ma.

James, at the start of the *Quair*, lies awake regretting the lack of 'craft' (12), which prevents him from composing. When he picks up the *Consolation*, he refers enviously to the way in which Boethius had *set awerk* his *pen*. Holland establishes his craftsmanship as a shadow of Nature's *making* (72) *in whose care all shaping lies* (110–11). In the mid-1470s, the author of the *Wallace* (McDiarmid 1959–60) will still describe his Early Scots predecessors as *gud makaris* (XII: 1,453).

This analogy between poetic composition and making or building reflects the way in which medieval writers and critics thought about literature, language and interpretation.

First, the twentieth-century distinction which places creative artists above manual labourers is not shared. The perspective is the pragmatic one anticipated by Aristotle: *Rhetoric is a useful skill* (1,355a).

Secondly, imaginative composition is not a natural activity but a skill to be mastered. Modern ideas of spontaneous creativity were not highly valued in the Middle Ages. Nor were theories of art for art's sake. The supposition that one should strive to imitate actual life so closely that naive listeners or readers might mistake the contrived for the real was seen as superficial artifice supporting a dubious end. The medieval poet rejoiced as much in the mastery of difficult construction as the medieval builder in planning a cathedral.

If poetry is the natural medium for the word–builder precisely because it is a non–natural form, it follows that literary language must also be crafted. While colloquial or 'low style' literary Scots, with its greater proportion of Anglo-Saxon vocabulary items and loanwords from Old Norse and Middle Dutch, is closer to the spoken language than the more ornate and Latinate rhythms of the 'high style', both are part of an essentially artificial language. If the artificiality of the Early Scots poetic language provides the first piece of evidence which can only be diachronically uncovered, the mode in which it was transmitted provides the second. Most Early Scots verse was performed – read aloud from a manuscript copy for students or recited in performance at court. The oral dimension of early literary evidence constitutes the most basic division between our experience of literary language and the way in which it was received and understood before the invention of the printing press.

Crucially, this reminds us that what we now think of as written literature was then conceived of as, primarily, a branch of persuasive oratory. That assumption, in its simplest form, holds for learned and unlearned throughout Western Europe. The early Scottish writers being well educated, it is possible in their case to be more specific about the way in which rhetoric influenced both their critical thinking and their creative practice.

Preparing his audience for a story based on the fourteenth-century Wars of Independence and centred on Robert I, Barbour outlines his own views on art's function (I.1–7):

> Storys to rede ar delitabill
> Suppos that thai be nocht bot fabill,
> Than suld storys that suthfast were
> And thai war said on gud maner
> Have doubill plesance in heryng.
> The first plesance is the carpyng,
> And the tother the suthfastnes.

He writes these words down but thinks of them as sounds to be voiced aloud. In the activities of *carpyng* (speaking) and recreating historical *suthfastnes* (truth) lies the poet's dual claim to please and to teach. More pertinently, the orator-poet has to cater for the fallibilities of human memory. Stylistically, he will repeat keywords such as *suthfastnes* over and over again. To the modern reader, accustomed to the printed word, this seems a crude technique. To the poet-craftsman in the days of manuscript and evaluating usefully, it is the most effective method of oral persuasion. 'Memorability' is added to 'making' as an important criterion for critical assessment (Carruthers 1990).

Barbour values the written word more highly than the spoken for two 'memorial' reasons. The existence of his poem in manuscript form makes his tale accessible to memorising in future ages. The deeds of Bruce may *lest ay furth in memory* (I.14). Equally, while a written text is held in the memory by both eye and ear, speech commands the latter alone. The immediate audience in Robert II's court will only hear these lines once, and so the poet-bard uses stylistic techniques which will counteract the fallibility of human memory. Holland also composes as an orator whose words will sound out fleetingly for most of his audience: *And ye sall heir in schort space* (310). Even his fullest poetic description of the different skills of bard, scribe and orator – *It war tyrefull to tell, dyte or address* (421) – accepts all three as complementary activities.

James I, whose poem is at once the most personal and the most overtly philosophical, outdoes the others in his specific references to the written word. He profits from *the writing* of Boethius, as produced by his *flourit pen*. His own difficulties in writing end with a decision to take his *pen in hand* and make the mark of a cross (97–8). Even in bed, when trying to induce sleep, he pictures himself reading aloud from the text (28–9):

> And there to here this worthy lord and clerk
> His metir swete, full of moralitee.

Private recitation was the accepted equivalent of public performance at that time. As a consequence, James is concerned with the fleeting and therefore inadequate nature of sound-signs, verbal and otherwise. When he hears the matins bell apparently telling him to write, he is wary even of his own ability to interpret sense impressions (79–82):

> It is no lyf that spekis unto me;
> It is a bell or that impressiounes
> Off my thoght causith this illusioune,
> That doth me think so nycely in this wise.

This pessimistic emphasis on the word as sign introduces another area in which modern assumptions are necessarily divorced from medieval experience. Most twentieth-century people can read effortlessly, in the many printed texts available, the agreed visual coding of their long-established vernacular tongue. This combination of factors deadens them to the immediacy of the word and forces modern authors into finding new means of recreating its power. In a mainly illiterate society, language's living mystery in strangeness still dominated. Only a chosen few could translate spoken sounds into significant marks on vellum. Words still had a magical aura surrounding them.

Further, for the Early Scots writer, composing at a time of early Christian certainty, word-signs existed at the lowest level of a comprehensive signing system extending downwards from God as Word. This final optimism has been anticipated by Holland's view of his making under Christ, the shaper of all. No age – not even our own in its postmodernist and deconstructionist phase – has cast its heuristic system so thoroughly in terms of signs. For medieval thinkers, the entire world was God's book. If his artifice, Nature, was the macro-code in which he had signified his intentions, so the makar in his micro-code, signified his. If medieval listeners were expected to break the conventions of these codes and read their 'dark' figurings, modern readers can hardly expect to understand easily now what was laboriously crafted then.

Any critic who wishes to understand this significant, recited code must necessarily pay as much attention to the role of the author/performer as to the text itself. Most medieval teachers follow Conrad of Hirsau in recommending their pupils to ask first 'Who the author is'. Only once that has been established along with the motivations for composition does the scholar move to language ('Whether it is in prose or verse') and theme ('What the subject matter is'). Even then, the interpreter's task remains incomplete. The pragmatic aim of all verbal 'making' is persuasion. Considerations of audience and effective exhortation ('What end the composition has in view') become the final aim of critical enquiry (Huygens 1970).

In seeking to establish how medieval writers evaluated their 'making', it is sensible to follow their own methodological line. In beginning this study of the literary language with questions concerning the creative process, we have begun that procedure. Before looking in detail at the position of Early Scots itself, the role of the Scottish word-maker warrants further attention.

If a poem is modestly 'made' as part of a craft, the author by extension becomes the 'maker' or builder. Modesty reigns in this area of analogic transference also, for if modern critics like to think of the death of the author, medieval poets thought of themselves as relegated under God. The concluding lines of the first three verse paragraphs of the *Bruce* respectively place the book's completion in the hands of the first creator (I.34–6), submit the outcome of Scotland's history to divine prescience (I.131–4) and attribute the overthrow of Edward I's tyranny to God's omnipotence (I.177–8). As the Scots are a favoured race, this implies that Bruce's victory exists complete within the Word before Barbour has begun verbally to recount that hero's first battles.

James I opens his *Quair* with an image of God's perfect dwelling place in the 'hevynnis figure circulere' (1). Beneath that perfect sign ('figure'), he detects the secondary semiotic code of Nature. Natural harmony signifies to him a benevolently intended world, from which his own misery distances him. His attempts at poetry, like Barbour's, exist at the lowest level of verbal sign-making within this hierarchy as a *craft in erth* (12).

Of the three authors chosen, it is Holland who considers in most detail the possible roles of the relegated author. The *Howlat* opens with Spring and rebirth controlled *be Dame Natur, that noble mastress* (32) as a sign of *the greable gift of . . . Godhed* (8). If this confirms the hierarchical system within which relegated authorship is sited, the text of the *Howlat* further distinguishes the four grades of creativity available to the poetic craftsman. The lowest level of efficient making is that of the *scriptor*, who merely copies down the words of his authority. In the Asloan MS, Asloan notes that he is Holland's scriptor, having copied the text by hand: *Scriptum per manum M Joannis Asloan*. Holland, at times, reduces himself to this level, seeking only to copy or report (507) *as tellis the writ*. More often, he places himself on the next grade as *compilator* with the power to rearrange or excise passages. When his author describes in full the armorial bearings of those who come to judge the Owl, he feels that the long list will bore his audience, so decides (622–3) *I durst nocht kytth to copy,/All other armes thar by'*. Even more specifically, he argues that, having heard the overall intention of his author expressed, it is unnecessary to realise it in fastidious detail (692): *I press nocht all to report; ʒe hard thaim expremit.*

Sometimes, he decides to move even higher in the authorial hierarchy, reserving the right to assume the glossing powers of the *commentator* (33–7):

> Bot all thar names to nevyn as now it nocht neid is,
> It war prolixt and lang, and lenthing of space,
> And I have mekle matir in metir to gloss
> Of ane nothir sentence,
> And waike is my eloquence.

Although in broad terms he follows the French 'reverdie' form, Holland claims the highest freedom of the four authorial categories, the inventive originality of the *'auctor'*.

Authorship in this sense is still relegated under God as first cause and dependent on the example of earlier written authorities. The medieval makar, as efficient cause, builds upon past literary examples by remodelling them. Barbour relies on Latin and vernacular chronicles; Holland opens in a highly conventional 'reverdie' form. Both are also anxious to stress that they have been authorised in another sense; *asked* to write by a patron. This not only prevents any personal charge of pride or self-interest being levelled against them, it also gives the poetic building a firm foundation in authority.

Although James I's kingship made the latter type of authorisation inappropriate, it is the *Quair* which provides the fullest evidence on literary authorities. The king, writing in what he knew was an English dialect, admits his debt to earlier English poets, especially Gower and Chaucer (1,368–9). His major authority, however, is Boethius' *Consolation of Philosophy*. Although this Latin dialogue in prose and verse was composed in the early sixth century, its Christianity and range of philosophical reference made it popular throughout the Middle Ages. In it, Dame Philosophy chides Boethius for spending too much time on imaginative compositions. If, instead, he had studied philosophy, he could have conquered the despair which his adverse fortune has induced.

James reads this book, uses it as his first authority, and stresses the parallels between his biography and that of Boethius. But his invention makes poetic rather than philosophical inadequacy the source of his problem. Unlike his distinguished predecessor, the king already has a mature philosophy, capable of defeating Fortune (70–5):

> Among thir thoughtis rolling to and fro,
> Fell me to mynd of my fortune and ure:
> In tender youth how sche was first my fo
> And eft my frende, and how I gat recure
> Off my distresse.

What he lacks are the rhetorical skills, which Boethius had, in the opinion of Dame Philosophy, mastered too well. The medieval author may found his 'making' on the works of others and defer ultimately to God. But a true 'auctor' as opposed to a 'scriptor' or even a 'commentator' must produce a recognisably new house, as James does at the outset of his *Quair*.

The historical approach has so far revealed medieval writers approaching the creative process as craftsmen rather than artists; as the efficient rather than the original causes of their own work. These attitudes in turn affect the way in which the language of poetry is conceived. Artificial in form, drawing in coinages and archaisms from other tongues and earlier writings, it is written with the sound of the speaking voice in mind, in close alliance with the practical rules governing persuasive oratory. When critical attention moves along the interpretive line from questions of authorship and 'how' language is used to the words themselves and 'what' form of language is employed, further gaps open up between modern assumptions and medieval practice.

Many critics wrongly assume that Early Scots was the only literary language available for expression of nationalist feeling. Within a poetics aimed at the widest possible imaginative presentation of ideas, Latin had many claims to be the most suitable language in which to praise Scottish achievements. Not only was it the subtlest tongue, it was also the language of scholarship throughout Europe. To choose the 'young' and 'rough' Scots vernacular against such competition implied, in terms of the building image, the knowing acceptance of fewer, more roughly hewn bricks than those elsewhere available.

James I admits this, when comparing Boethius' Latin to his own proposed medium (50–3):

> With mony a noble resoune, as him likit,
> Enditing in his fairë Latyne tong,
> So full of fruyte and rethorikly pykit,
> Quhich to declare my scole is ouer ȝong.

Nonetheless, he decides to *lat pas* Latin and *procede* to the task of conveying his theme (*sentence*) in his own *tong*.

If Latin was the preferred 'artistic' choice for poets, fourteenth-century patriots should really have chosen Gaelic, had their views on patriotism, language and literature been similar to those prevailing today. The policies of Malcolm Canmore and David I had resulted in a situation where, 'By the end of the 13th century, the English vernacular had driven Gaelic back to (virtually) the present highland line – except for Galloway and parts of Aberdeenshire' (Templeton 1973). Barbour and James knew this, but their pragmatism prevented them from attempts to divert the normal processes of language. Holland (794–800), indeed, mocks Gaelic:

> Sa come the Ruke with a rerd and a rane roch,
> A bard out of irland with Banachadee!
> Said: 'Gluntow guk dynyd dach hala michy doch;
> Raike hir a rug of the rost, or scho sall ryive the.
> Mich macmory ach mach mometir moch loch;
> Set hir downe, gif hir drink; quaht Dele alis she?'
> O Deremyne, O Donnall, O Dochardy droch.

The tone is playful rather than biting. But if James thought Early Scots uncouth when compared to Latin subtlety, Holland views Gaelic as rough, even in comparison to the *young tongue*.

The French language as spoken in Scotland had several distinctive features and offered a third possible literary path. As all three poets were composing works with a nationalist theme and wished to present them to a reasonably wide audience, however, the French of Scotland would have been at once inappropriate and restrictive. It was seldom used in other than macaronic contexts.

Clearly, however, with a greater variety of tongues to choose from, the emergence of Early Scots even as the chosen vernacular tongue was, in the early stages, slow and fraught with difficulties. Literary Early Scots with its desire for crafted fullness was particularly subject to the influence of Latin, French and the Southern English of Chaucer and Gower.

But the major problem with assuming Early Scots to be the necessary linguistic sign of national identity lies in the history of that language itself. When Early Scots poets refer to it as *Inglis*, they are doing no more than stating the truth. In the twentieth century, when a Scottish poet chooses to write in Scots, that choice is made against the current English norm. To make the same nationalistically significant point against the linguistic current in the fourteenth or fifteenth century, a Scottish makar would have had to use Gaelic. Early Scots emerged from the Northumbrian dialect, having been encouraged by Scottish monarchs in a bid to facilitate political relations with England. This issue is not addressed either by Barbour or James. The diachronic approach has been necessary to uncover the two reasons for that silence. The Scots language is a dialect of English, and the end of literature prescribed in those days transcends national concerns to teach ethical lessons. When historical research enables the student to clarify problems of interpretation in this manner, the extra effort involved in recovering past attitudes is justified.

So far, study of authorship and language has resolved apparent oddities in each of these areas. Understanding of the oral means of transmission has also revealed why medieval critics discuss the form of a text (*causa formalis*) only after questions of authorship (*causa efficiens*) under God (*causa originalis*), and grammar (*causa materialis*), have been fully considered. Having ourselves reached this third stage of enquiry, it is appropriate to ask whether an understanding of the rules of rhetoric helps a modern reader to break the structural as well as the creative and linguistic coding of Early Scots texts?

For example, why does James I apologise for the quality of his language at the opening of the *Quair* (stanza 7) and for the quality of his entire *tretise* finally (stanzas 194–5)? More pertinently, why does he raise the question of failed *eloquens* within stanzas which are among the most carefully crafted in the entire work? The ornateness of stanza 195 (1,365–71) will focus attention on this issue.

> Allace! and gif thou cum in the presence
> Quhare as of blame faynest thou wald be quite,
> To here thy rude and crukit eloquens,
> Quho sal be thare to pray for thy remyt?
> No wicht, bot geve hir merci will admytt
> The for gud will, that is thy gyd and stere,
> To quhame for me thou pitously requere.

A complex, Latinate question is followed by a dramatic pause and contrastingly brief reply – *No wicht*. Only then are the complexities and concessions drawn in. Throughout, syntactic parallelism guides the reader or listener. *Quhare*, *Quho* and *To quhame* respectively announce rhetorical questions at the start of lines two, four and seven. Similarly, the doublet *rude and crukit* is balanced by *gyd and stere*. More subtly, the surface message conveys a proper sense of inferiority before Latin but uses Latinate grammar to boost Scots into a position of rivalry rather than simple homage.

Why apologise for lack of craftsmanship when advertising it so obviously? As a branch of dialectics, poetry followed set rules of argument. James I, in humbly apologising for his lack of art, is employing one of these set arguments or topoi and so, covertly, proving the very skills which he seems to deny. Those who know the code are alerted to the tension by the complex style. This is, specifically, a modesty topos, which should come at the start or conclusion of a poem (Trask 1994). James chooses to make a double plea, using both recommended structural placings. In so doing, he helpfully 'signs' his awareness of the proper rules of 'making'. Holland apologises for his *waike . . . eloquence* initially, as does Barbour. They also employ the location, style and form of the modesty topos to convey artistically a hidden sense at odds with the overt sense, yet signed by it.

Once the rules have been learned, many apparent strangenesses become, themselves, the benevolent textual equivalents of God's hidden yet revealed signs in nature. Christian aesthetics demand this. The text must conceal but not unfairly. To those willing to work at its artifice, useful teachings should emerge. Dante expresses the two sides of this equation clearly. In the *Divine Comedy*, he warns his readers repeatedly that his method is allegorical. That is, the surface story conceals other ideas. If they are to find the spiritual meaning, they must therefore *whet their wits* on the poetic evidence ('Piglia/quel ch'io ti dicerò, se vuo' saziarti;/ed intorno da esso t'assotiglia': *Paradiso* XXVIII, 61–3). Only in that way will they note *the teaching hidden under the veil of the strange lines* ('O voi ch'avete li 'ntelletti sani,/ mirate la dottrina che s'asconde/ sotto 'l velame de li versi strani': *Inferno*, ll. 61–3). Yet, Dante also commits himself to the traditional 'end' (*causa finalis*) of the Aristotelian hermeneutic line: *It may be stated briefly that the aim of the whole and of the part is to remove those living in this life from a state of misery, and to bring them to a state of happiness* (Minnis 1991: 460).

The fact that he refers to the individual members (*those*) of his audience reveals his Christian modification of the classical definition. As the Christian God had an individual bond with each individual soul, Boethius and other medieval commentators believed that the text must offer a fair interpretive test to each unique member of any given audience within the intellectual parameters of that audience as conceived by the author. How, then, within the line of the text can a medieval author helpfully sign his intention? And how can study of medieval aesthetics resuscitate the fairness of the test being set? I shall first consider significant persuasion and then significant teaching, as the poetic ideal at that time sought at once to persuade and to illuminate.

Nowadays, we think of literary genres on the classical model. Medieval thinkers preferred organic images, sustaining their sense of a semiotic hierarchy, connecting divine, natural and verbal on an overlapping principle. They, therefore, referred to different 'kinds' of literature. Given the oral basis of composition, they also spoke of different 'voices'. These terms substitute openness for generic closure and are consistent with the ideas of disciplinary harmony, interrelationship and transference, which form the centre of medieval thinking on aesthetics. While verse is the preferred mode for literary artifice, therefore, it may variously take on a narrative, lyrical or dramatic voice. The mode of transmission reinforces this blurring of neat distinctions among poetry, prose and drama. When a bard relates his tales as part of a performance, he becomes narrator, poet and player at once.

As a result, the medieval audience was accustomed to listen for obvious changes in stylistic mode, when seeking guidance from one section of recitation to another. Of the three poems chosen, the *Bruce* is the most sustained piece of narrative. Barbour's principal aim is to narrate the history of Scotland clearly, and so he seldom resorts to melodrama. Robert Bruce's address before the Battle of Bannockburn, histrionically translated by Robert Burns in *Scots Wha Hae*, had been much less passionately reported by Barbour (XI. 404–12) in indirect speech:

> And syne gert cry our-all on hycht
> That quha-sa-ever he war that fand
> Hys hart nocht sekyr for to stand
> To wyn all or dey with honur
> For to maynteyne that stalwart stour
> That he betyme suld hald his way,
> And suld dwell with him bot thai
> That wald stand with him to the end
> And tak the ure that God wald send.

By sustaining the narrative voice, Barbour ensures that any changes into the lyrical or dramatic mode will attract the audience's attention. For example, when he wishes emotively to announce the theme of political freedom, he does so in a style which contrasts markedly with his prosaic norm (I.225–8):

A! fredome is a noble thing!
Fredome mays man to haiff liking,
Fredome all solace to man giffis,
He levys at es that frely levys.

The succession of staccato exclamations breaks in on the audience's attention every bit as
effectively as the direct bardic formula *Lordingis, quha likis for till her*, which he will employ
200 lines later.

James I and Holland move from one mode to another – narrative to dramatic; dramatic to
lyrical – with greater regularity. When the king wishes to emphasise the autobiographical
voice, he prefers short exclamations and questions broken up by dramatic pauses. This takes
over from the more fluent descriptive style which he uses for narrative. These two styles
coexist in stanza 54. The king imagines himself turning to address the nightingale, which
has ceased singing after the appearance of the lady in the garden (372–8):

Ane othir quhile the lytill nyghtingale
That sat apon the twiggis wold I chide,
And say ryght thus: 'Quhare ar thy notis smale,
That thou of love has song this morowe tyde?
Seis thou nought hire that sittis the besyde?
For Venus sake, the blisfull goddesse clere,
Sing on agane and mak my lady chere!'

If this signs a change from narrative voice to dramatic for the attentive listener, both James
and Holland are equally adept at highlighting lyrical set-pieces stylistically. The song of the
birds in stanza 34 of the *Quair*, beginning *Worschippe, ye that loveris bene this May*, is only
the first of many in that poem. Holland follows the method in the *Howlat*. Here, for
example, is the song to Mary sung reverently by his choir of birds (716–26):

And thair notis anone, gif I richt nevyne,
War of Mary the myld, this maner I wiss.
Haile temple of the Trinite, crownit in hevin!
Haile moder of our maker, and medicyn of myss!
Haile succour and salf for the synnis sevyne!
Haile grane full of grace that growis so evyn!
Haile lady of all ladyis, lichtest of leme!
Haile chalmer of chastite!
Haile charbunkle of charite!
Haile! blissit mot thow be
For thi barne time.

Syntactic parallelism was accepted in the game of rhetoric as signing high seriousness. In
the devout Middle Ages, Mary especially warranted this sign as Queen of Heaven. Holland,
therefore, moves from narrative mode to lyrical while granting the Virgin her decorous due.

In Early Scots, transitions away from the bardic style to lyrical or dramatic set-pieces are
primarily signed by stylistic changes rather than by the introduction of different
vocabulary. The opportunity to denote thematic or tonal change by introducing either
the Latinate forms or archaisms of the high style is not entirely bypassed, but its fuller
development awaits the greater vocabulary range of Middle Scots. If modal changes mark

out different types of persuasion, the way in which a medieval author orders his material is one of the most significant signs of his teaching aims. How do the rules on ordering relate to use of the literary language in the late fourteenth and early fifteenth centuries? The major relevant divergences in expectation can be summed up as follows. Early Scots poets saw the literary language as an artificial set of oral signs designed to teach allegorically; modern readers assume a natural set of written signs without allegorical intent.

Artificial orderings of the story line are, therefore, encouraged by medieval teachers. Geoffrey of Vinsauf urges the skilful 'maker' against following *Nature's smooth road* in which 'things' and 'words' follow the same sequence, and the order of discourse does not depart from the order of occurrence. The poem travels the pathway of art if a more effective order is attempted (Nims 1967: 14). Practically, Vinsauf favours the *ordo artificialis* because it is more *effective* and more *prolific in its branches*. But the form chosen may also signify the theme.

Circular structurings, in which the last words of a poem echo the first, are often favoured because the circle was the sign of God's infinity, the mystic Word within which all verbal signing was conducted. Dante works within this tradition and so, in the final canto of the *Paradiso*, uses images which relate both language and action to these ultimate mysteries. The divine purpose is revealed as a book bound by love ('egato con amore in un volume': XXXIII, 86). The feebleness of the poet's words as well as mankind's actions is likened to squaring the divine circle (XXXIII, 137–8): 'veder volea come si convenne/l'imago al cerchio'.

Orality provides the idea of words moving through the air as sounds. In *The House of Fame*, Chaucer relates the new ideas of Dante and the Scholastics to Aristotle's theories of movement (compare St Thomas Aquinas, *Summa Theologica*, Pt. 1–11, Q 8: 'Of that which moves the Will'). Words (*every speche that ys spoken*), like all else in the sub-lunar world, are on a constant journey. Rest exists only after death in Heaven. Until then, *every thyng/ Thorgh his kyndely enclynyng/Moveth*. This encourages the idea of the storyline, within the analogic semiotic pattern, as a verbal journey. As Nature (*kynde*) moves us towards death within linear time, so the poem as line of sounds necessarily journeys from beginning to end.

But natural line and movement exist within the artificial structures of the poet-maker. Emblematically, this represents man's lifeline within God's purpose; persuasively, the pleasant story must be adapted to the aim of teaching ethically helpful ideas. There must, therefore, be inbuilt tensions between the natural line of sounds and the artificial, significant ordering of the material. Hugh of St Victor uses the building image to explain this. Just as the builder's wall rises from its foundation, so the word-wall rises from the 'literal sense'. The story words are 'the bases from which spring' the audience's under-standing of any allegorical sense – moral, spiritual or mysterious – of the poetic structure. But the artist in his words, like the mason with his file, must skilfully shape the 'course' to fit that 'superstructure' (Minnis 1991: 78).

The gap between medieval and modern linguistic conventions is a large one. Does mastery of what a medieval teacher might have summed up as 'making, memorising and moving' help us to bridge it? To try to answer this question, the ordering of the storyline in each of the three Early Scots poems will be examined in turn. The critical dilemmas faced by those who expect Vinsauf's natural ordering will then be described and an alternative, diachronic interpretation offered. This is not an attempt to reclaim exactly the views of past audiences – a self-evidently impossible task. The aim is to employ Derrida's idea of *différance* historically in order to establish the broad intentional parameters of authorship outwith which unnecessary critical obtuseness resides.

The most obvious allegorical use of the traditional journey motif to sustain the storyline is to be found in the *Quair*. The king's actual journey from Leith becomes the spiritual journey of all men in stanza 16 (*Quhen stereles to travaile I begouth/ Amang the wavis of this warld to drive*) and then an emblem of the poet's verbal journey in stanzas 17–18. The start of the ship's journey becomes the difficulty experienced in beginning the poem. The lack of wind is James's lack of inspiration, and the black rocks in the open sea are identified with the difficulty of composing allegorically (*the prolixitee of doubilnesse*).

The poem's first modern editor, W. W. Skeat, thought of the king whiling away his time in prison by writing the poem. This theory he adduced in order to account for the 'haphazard' and poorly constructed storyline, with its many false starts. For Skeat, James's poem deals in unconnected fashion first with Boethius, then with his own romance, before turning into a dream vision peopled by pagan gods. Only by positing an unskilled artist writing for therapeutic purposes over a long period of time can he 'excuse' James (Skeat 1884: 547). What signs might have led him to view the order differently? First, the two modesty topoi, earlier noted, stand in their traditional placings within the opening and concluding sections. Second, the narrator clearly states that the poem has a 'double' allegorical meaning, referring overtly to his authorial difficulties in coping with the *prolixitee/Of doubilnesse* (18: 1–2). If this evidence leads to re-examination of the storyline, it soon becomes clear that the poem is written after the imprisonment in maturity. James, as early as stanza 10 (10: 3–4), thinks of Fortune, remembering *In tender youth how sche was first my fo/And eft my frende*. Vinsauf had recommended retrospective structuring to the ambitious poet.

Nor is the Boethian material irrelevant. Skeat thinks biographically and sees the long discussion of the senator's life as an artless extension of the king's proper citing of his authorities. But the medieval poet was taught to use the opening to announce his theme. Sententially, Boethius's life anticipates the broad movement from personal misery to metaphysical contemplation and so to theological resolution, which characterises James's own youthful predicament. It also confirms the spiritual journey motif while permitting poetic invention to highlight any variations on the shared pattern.

Principal among those inventions is the very problem which first caused Skeat to question the king's artistry. Where Boethius convicted himself of philosophical naivety, James substitutes poetic naivety. Skeat is correct in noting the narrator's difficulty in getting his verbal journey started. Apart from stanza 1, there are new openings in stanzas 7, 13 and 18. Indeed, the really odd thing is the very obvious and personal way in which the audience's attention is directed to this dilemma. The medieval vision of relegated authorship encouraged self-effacement, yet James uses the first person pronoun on seventy-nine occasions in the first nineteen stanzas. Working on the naturalist assumptions that the poem is 'made' on a single level and follows the linear movement of life, Skeat does not see the proper significance of the very oddities he has defined. As he also ignores the oral dimension of the poem and so does not seek stylistic clues in relation to 'memorising', he fails subsequently to correct his initial impression that this is a poorly constructed work.

If, instead, one isolates the most distinctive linguistic sign of performance poetry of that day, repetition, and relates it to the poem's proposed theme, reassuring circles at once emerge around the broken line of cancelled openings. The largest of these contains the entire poem, save the final stanza with its expression of James's literary debts. The *Quair* opens (1:1) *Heigh in the hevynnis figure circulere*. It ends (196: 1) *Hich in the hevynnis figure circulere*. James opens by calling attention to the heavenly symbol ('figure') which at once justifies his poem's message and describes its major structuring principle.

The opening passage, which so offended Skeat, is full of smaller circles, signed by images or the echoing of words and ideas. The cycles of the solar year and of night becoming day are evoked in stanza 1 and completed in stanza 20. The poet's thoughts are represented as circling, *in my mind rolling* (stanza 8). The topic of Fortune is also introduced at this point through its emblem of the revolving wheel. The significant 'figure' of the circle is, therefore, traced from macrocosm to microcosm at the outset.

Historians are agreed that James I was imbued with self-confidence. The king would, I am sure, have been astounded to discover that his *Quair* could be read as a modestly artless statement of youthful insecurity. He would have assumed that the frequent reopenings of his story would have called attention to its unusual autobiographical form. That would have led a medieval audience to think of the poetic opening according to the conventional critical procedures of the causal line. James had planned his work artfully under these headings of authorship, intention, language, structure and persuasive intent.

Parallelism and variation emphasise the maturity of his philosophy through an authorial comparison with Boethius. The decorous high style of the first modesty topos and the allegorical poem-journey stridently contradict any apparent literary humility. The retrospective and circular structurings formally translate the skilfulness of his thought and verse. Persuasively, only the echoing of the first line at the end of the poem will complete the figure of man's broken journey into the circle of rest. But all the apparent strangenesses of the opening section have anticipated this sophisticated patterning for those who understand the king's artifice. For them, the multi-openings in their apparent humility would already suggest a supremely self-confident authorial voice, ready to guide its audience through the broken journeyings of life into the *figure circulere* of pre-planned intentionality artistic and divine.

The narrative line of the *Howlat* also looks disordered. Opening with a natural description, Holland introduces a bird parliament which appears to move associatively into the broad European issues raised by the Council of Trent and then narrow to consideration of the Douglas family via study of its escutcheon. Towards the conclusion, the bird parliament and the owl's tale hold central focus again. Early critics were puzzled by this chaotic story. Some highlighted only one political line. Pinkerton, for example, tried to force the evidence into a consistent satire on James II. Walter Scott, in a letter to the poem's first editor, came to precisely the opposite conclusion, denying any reference *to local or national politics*. Anticipating Skeat on the *Quair*, Scott accounted for the episodic form by positing an unprofessional poet and haphazard composition over a long period of time: *Holland amused his leisure at Ternaway by compiling a poetic apologue upon a plan used not only by Chaucer but by many of the French minstrels* (Amours 1896: xxxii).

In seeking first to define the poetic mode, Scott shows his awareness that the art of the 'makars' involves studying the precise conventions chosen for a particular artifice. In citing Chaucer and the French poets, he thinks correctly of bird allegory, *reverdie* and *chanson d'aventure*. These are, indeed, the poetic kinds invoked by Holland. As in Chaucer's *Parlement of Foules*, there is likely to be a hidden theme. The lyrical modes suggest that this topic must be one which is suitably set within the natural cycles of birth, death and rebirth. If, thematically, a proud owl and the deliberations of the Council of Trent seem far apart, they are formally set within a suitably broad European tradition of love allegory. Holland's invention has added at once a more specifically Scottish topic (the fate of the Douglas family) and associations with a more local poetic mode. Stanzaically and stylistically, the *Howlat* derives from the alliterative Romance form. This was enjoying a major revival in northern England and in Scotland.

The idea of the spiritual journey is also more thoroughly developed in Holland's poem. The narrator enters his own allegory as (43) *a wretche in this warld, wilsome of wane*. This gravity of the confused pilgrim evokes *Piers Plowman* and the *Pearl* rather than the love lyric. Indeed, a comparison with the *Pearl* dreamer will help to underline the mysteriousness with which Holland endows his narrator and his vision. The *Pearl* dreamer was an old man who, in a dream, saw his dead daughter at the far side of the river of death and grace. He was taught by her and finally was granted a 'received vision' as a sign of his spiritual advancement. Holland's narrator is associated with birth rather than age, *Blyth of the birth* (25) at *the prime of the day* (40). He moves from rest, *Thus sat I in solace, sekerly and sure* (22) and a clear vision of Nature as *the greable gift of . . . Godhed* (8) into movement. It is as if he were descending from birth into the misery which defines life. In this sense, he begins in the same position of transcendent innocence as the maiden in *Pearl*, only later taking on her father's role. Consequently, his received vision is given to him immediately without the need for dreaming. A river *ryally apperd* (13). Only when he is 'moved' in two senses into the owl's world – *I herd ane petuoss appele . . . Nerar that noyss in nest I nechit* (41, 47) – does he become part of that world and its worries.

Holland, like James I, sets this journey through mutable nature within the harmony of the spheres (31–2): *Under the Cirkill solar, thir savoruss seidis/War nurist*. The ending of the *Howlat* returns us to the same season, the same images and some of the same phrases with which the poem opened. Affectively, it moves us after our own battle of interpretation into the restfulness of heaven and *the sanctis so sere* (988). The penitential Owl advises us to follow his example in late humility and accept faithfully the *gret micht* of God (986).

Approaching the *Howlat* through careful study of literary conventions and artificial ordering will not 'explain' the poem's meaning. But it does replace an apparently unconnected line of events with a structure, using harmony and counterpoint to suggest different perspectives on the cycles of life. These are most mysteriously introduced through the narrator, who appears to issue from birth into the conflict of the poem and then depart beyond life into death. The rebirth of nature into spring after the death of winter is dramatised through the reverdie and bird parliament. These in turn contextualise the rise and fall of man on the wheel of fortune. That form of birth and death is variously translated on a broad and spiritual stage (Council of Trent), within domestic politics (the Douglas family) or personally, as man tries to defeat the devil within him (Owl).

Although this interpretation is, inevitably, a personal evaluation, the fact remains that a return to the modes of thought favoured at the time of composition resolves in 'artificial' terms the major critical dilemmas which, on naturalist assumptions, remain insuperable. 'Variations on a theme' provides a more promising critical starting point for discovering why an owl with stolen feathers shares a poem with the schisms of the Catholic church and the escutcheon of the Douglases than the task of explaining them as causal links within a story-chain.

The *Bruce* provides a fitting final test for the methodology. Its twenty books follow historical chronology quite closely. Given the frequent promises of *suthfastnes* noted earlier, this is unsurprising. At the same time, as James I's many cancelled openings and frequent use of the first person pronoun proved, when an early poet 'protests too much' initially, these are very often the 'difficult lines' to which Dante refers. The bard voices the keywords often to give listeners the opportunity to identify the interpretive area in which they are being tested. Certainly, this is true of the *Bruce*. Barbour appears stridently to offer the truth of chronicles; but, in every area of poetic ordering, the nature of that truthfulness is called into question. Although, he does trace faithfully the history of the Wars of Liberty from the days of Alexander III until Bannockburn, a series of apparent errors historical and literary continues to worry critics.

Of these, the one most often cited concerns Robert I himself. Why did Barbour, the genealogist of the Stewarts, open his *suthfast* poem by erasing his major hero's earlier life and substituting the life of his grandfather, Bruce the Competitor? 'The Bruce of whom he is going to speak is the hero of the poem (I.477), but the Bruce of whom he has already spoken (I.67, 153) is that hero's grandfather' (Skeat 1896: 547). As the titles granted to Bruce's father are also attributed to the grandfather (I. 66–7), Barbour claims to write of one man but actually presents his audience with a family hero, three-in-one. Many of his listeners could still remember that time and would have noticed so obvious an error.

Barbour, however, promises historical truthfulness only within specific literary conventions, as the bardic formula announces (I.446):

Lordingis, quha likis for till her,
The Romanys now begynnys her.

The fact that this Bruce *is* a literary, Romantic figure is underlined very thoroughly. The family hero three-in-one of the opening Book is regularly associated with the three 'Matters of Romance': Rome, France and England. He and Douglas are also compared to the Nine Worthies of Romance, themselves divided into three groups of three: Jewish, Classical and Christian. In the opening Book, when the technique is being underlined, the Scottish king's fate is linked with that of Alexander, Caesar and Arthur, Douglas's with Hector of Troy. In addition, the alliterative repetition of the words *wys and wicht* in that book (I.22, 401, 518) measures Bruce and Douglas against the Epic criteria of bravery and wisdom. Established by Homer, these evaluative criteria continued into the historical Romance form. To these, the third Virgilian criterion of 'pietas' is added. Barbour does this by playing on the Scots word *pite*, using it to mean either 'pity' or 'piety', but sometimes combining both senses.

That Barbour's *Bruce* exists within the rules of fiction could not, therefore, be missed; that a hero three-in-one was being associated with the trinary patternings of Romantic heroism and judged by the trinary criteria of classical epic was made as evident as possible. An imaginative discipline had the right to simplify memorably in order to teach more effectively. These criteria, related to the poem's proposed topic of political freedom, provide another – even more important – reason for denying the 'faith of chronicles'. In fact, most of Robert I's early life had been spent opportunistically serving the poem's major villain, Edward I, and attacking the estates of his co-hero Douglas (Nicholson 1974: 70). Substituting his grandfather's patriotic battles may be anachronistic, but it makes the persuasive model clearer.

If the characterisation of Barbour's hero raises questions about Barbour's ordering of history which can only be explained by redefining literary *suthfastnes*, the characterisation of his major villain raises questions about the literary ordering which can only be explained by redefining historical *suthfastnes*. It is Edward I, returning from an entirely imagined crusade (I. 135–48; McDiarmid 1973: 68), who first holds the attention of Barbour's courtly audience. If it is difficult to understand why an enemy and another obvious historical invention should open the *Bruce*, it seems equally strange to many that the crucial martial victory of Bannockburn does not end it. Instead, Edward Bruce's unsuccessful campaigns in Ireland and Douglas's heroism in Spain (Books XIV–XX) seem to divert attention away from Robert I's glorious victory.

Historically, the parallel between Scotland's tale and the fate of the Maccabees (I. 464–76) signs the reconfiguration of truthfulness, necessary to explain Barbour's chosen ordering. The poem imitates not the line of chronicle but the patterning of Scotland's mythic history. The comparison with the Maccabees had recently been used in an earlier, political plea for national liberty, the Declaration of Arbroath. There, mythic history had been used to reassure Scotland that it was a chosen nation. Just as the Maccabees had been victorious against the odds, so would the Scots, both victories being guaranteed by God.

Only if one thinks of Bruce as the poem's hero and the inculcation of martial values as its highest pedagogic aim does the later movement of the action to Ireland and Spain seem anticlimactic. But the hero of the poem is not Bruce but Scotland. What the poem's ordering accurately traces is Scotland's emergence from and return to its mythic origins. To complete the latter movement, the Irish campaign and Douglas in Seville on a holy war are necessary. Nor does Bannockburn lose its structural importance. It holds the key central position within this poetic circle (Books X–XIII).

Edward I's crusade is invented so that the poem may begin and end with holy wars. Temporal battles, however worthy, are framed within two pilgrimages. As Augustine (Tasker 1967: 1) had taught in *The City of God*, the virtuous journey on earth as *a pilgrim among the wicked*. Our true end lies in *That most glorious society and celestial city of God's faithful*. Emblematically, the structure of the *Bruce* contains Scotland's martial journey towards freedom within two such pilgrimages. Edward's fictive crusade in Book I is balanced by Douglas's historical crusade carrying the Bruce's heart in Book XX. In this case, however, the frame also sets English villainy against Scottish holiness and so underlines the poem's patriotic theme. If, in Book I, Edward I abandons penance because he wishes to increase his temporal power, so in Book XX Robert I altruistically sends his heart on that same journey in the name of patriotism and love.

Numerological symbolism confirms the circular patterning. Book I and Book XX each have the same number of lines – 630, the multiple of three fortunate numbers 9 (3×3), 7 and 10. The overarching pilgrimage structure, which opened with three successive invocations of the deity in Book I (34–6, 131–4, 177–8), closes in Book XX with the explicit hope that the Trinity guide us out of life's journey into divine rest (628–30):

Quhar afauld God in trinyte
Bring us hey till his mekill blis
Quhar alwayis lestand liking is.

If a God, three-in-one, is the divine end of the *Bruce*, a king three-in-one shows us the practical means by which that end may be attained. The immediate political purpose of Barbour's poem is to encourage the weak nobles of Robert II's day to imitate their courageous ancestors under Robert I. Writing with the value of hindsight, Barbour uses Book XX to 'prophesy' the complex succession situation which would lead to a second Robert ascending the throne (XX. 131–54). A Golden Age will emerge in those days, *ordained* (XX. 132) by Bruce as well as God – but only if all levels of Scottish society learn the lessons of that earlier age as recounted by the bard. The romantic mode and divine teachings of the *Bruce* do not prevent the poem from having a down-to-earth political purpose.

What, then, has been the effect of using Early Scots verse to assess the value of a diachronic, linguistic approach to literary evidence? In broad aesthetic terms, a return to medieval hermeneutics under the broad headings of 'making', 'memorising' and 'moving' has revealed in each case supreme craftsmanship. There is no need to apologise for Early Scots poetry as the necessarily haphazard and artless beginnings of Scottish literature. *Bruce*, *Quair* and *Howlat* in very different ways, appropriate to their different literary modes, use artificial orderings of the storyline to sign hidden meaning and test the wits of their audience.

More specifically, how is the literary language viewed? It is distinguished from the spoken tongue as the necessarily artificial medium out of which the makar's word-structures are compiled. Yet, like the spoken tongue, it is thought of primarily as a sound system designed to persuade and communicate with specific audiences. It is also overtly viewed as part of a living semiotic system. When medieval people looked at the heavens, they beheld the origins of a significantly ordered system. When they looked out at nature, they saw signs, and when they listened to words they heard signs. Early Scots, in these terms, was the social means of explaining the Word Divine through the Book of Nature.

The significance which it did not have is the ethnic one, usually assumed by critics when seeking to establish a 'Scottish tradition in literature'. Early Scots historically is a branch of Inglis. Early literary Scots is assessed by poets only in terms of its capacity to persuade effectively and subtly. Within the brotherhood of scholars, Latin still remains the ideal choice from that point of view. Within the European brotherhood of poets, no nationalistic qualms prevent Scottish makars from echoing Chaucer or making the aureate style also the most linguistically cosmopolitan. Rhetoric and decorum rule rather than geographical boundaries at a time when language's mystery is causally related to its divine origins and Dante can use Scots–English rivalry to exemplify mankind's failure to accept his puny place 'sub specie aeternitatis':

> Lì si vedrà la superbia ch'asseta,
> che fa lo Scotto e l'Inghilese folle,
> sì che non può soffrir dentra a sua meta.
>   (*Paradiso* XIX, 121–3)

> ['There shall be seen the pride that makes men thirst and so maddens the Scot and the Englishman that neither can keep within his bounds.']

As Early Scots developed into Middle Scots, did literary use of the vernacular become more closely identified with Scotland and its national identity, or did the definition of 'making' continue to withstand such an easy equation?

7.3 WORKING, PLAYING AND *ANE MANER OF TRANSLATIOUN*: MIDDLE SCOTS LITERATURE (c. 1455 TO c. 1555)

This section celebrates four of the finest writers that Scotland has produced. Robert Henryson (c. 1420 to c. 1490), William Dunbar (1460 to c. 1513), Gavin Douglas (1476–1522) and Sir David Lindsay (c. 1486–1555) all have worldwide reputations. They also belong to a later period in time, poised uneasily between Middle Ages and Renaissance, scholasticism and humanism. When these poets used Scots, did they think of it in the same way as we do now? That is, did their literary use of the vernacular necessarily imply a desire to be thought of as distinctively Scottish writers? The question is of crucial importance because most modern critics, intent on establishing a Scottish tradition in literature, not only make this assumption but also use it to determine canonical selection for all literary periods (Henderson 1900; Speirs 1940; Wittig 1958; R. Watson 1984.) On these grounds, it becomes much easier for writers who use Scots to be accepted within the parameters of Scottish literature than those who do not.

From a twentieth-century perspective, this seems sensible. In the present political and linguistic context, use of Scots dialectal forms usually does signify a desire to be known as a specifically Scottish writer. But no allowance is made by those critics intent on creating a separate Scottish literary 'tradition' for the possibility that linguistic patriotism may have expressed itself differently in the earlier periods. The Early Scots evidence has provided a series of warnings – linguistic, aesthetic and ontological – against oversimplifying in this way. Linguistically, the Scots dialect is a kind of English. Unsurprisingly, there is no evident poetic desire to escape from that fact. In those days, Scotland was a nation. Writers prior to the Unions of Crown and Parliament are inevitably less sensitive to linguistic signing of nationhood than those who compose after that status has been politically forfeited.

Aesthetically, the idea of a European brotherhood of poets was a more powerful influence on Barbour, James I and Holland than that of political identity. The vernacular was the appropriate medium for patriotic tales, but that was also true for history. The distinctive features which made literature more philosophical than chronicle were also those which transcended politics and nationalism. The makar distanced himself from lived reality by creating artificial structures under the rules of rhetoric. He used images and particular tales but did so in order to teach concepts across the range of potentiality.

Theologically, the particular and the patriotic were submerged within the mysteries of origin. To the European poetic brotherhood of the Middle Ages must be added the universal brotherhood of the fallen. So far, the positive side of Christian mythology has been stressed in terms of language's inclusion within the Word's benevolently intended signing system. The idea of the relegated author has inevitably a darker side, especially when composition and evaluation are thought of in relation to art as oratory and performance. Medieval commentators began by considering how the work was delivered and by whom. In so doing, they accepted *a priori* St Paul's view (1 Corinthians 13:12) that all human authors, as fallen creatures, saw life and ideas *through a glass darkly*.

To discover how these different views of language developed within the Middle Scots period, I shall first examine the views of the two earlier makars, Henryson and Dunbar. In so doing, I stress that I am searching for literary signs of Scottishness through differentiations within the literary discipline itself at different stages of its aesthetic development. I do so as an alternative to creating a pattern of literary Scottishness by using modern linguistic distinctions as the internal criterion for selection in alliance with political, sociological and even psychological paradigms of Scottishness, externally and retrospectively applied.

In many ways, Robert Henryson and William Dunbar differ. Henryson is the more learned, holding university degrees and becoming headmaster of the Abbey School in Dunfermline during the 1470s. As John MacQueen has demonstrated, he benefited from the greater educational opportunities available in an age when higher education flourished (MacQueen 1967: 1–23). He is best known for his long narrative poems, *Orpheus and Eurydice* and *The Testament of Cresseid*. These, along with his collection of *Morall Fabillis*, are written within the erudite 'moralising' tradition. While his comic and tragic tales offer much enjoyment in and for themselves, Henryson clearly expects the serious reader to seek out deeper meanings.

If Henryson is a teacher in the country, Dunbar is *maister poete* at the dazzling court of James IV, whose pageantry and liberality are fully documented. Preferring shorter lyrical forms and speaking with an array of voices from the sycophantic to the downright scurrilous, he advertises the new-found range of Middle Scots as 'medium' more dramatically than any other makar. Although some of his work provides the form of allegorical challenge regularly set up by Henryson, more often the modern reader will be tested by the surface brilliance of his verse. While Henryson asks the reader to solve problems of intepretation from his knowledge of philosophy or theology, Dunbar tests understanding by pushing poetry to the extremes of stylistic virtuosity. A dictionary of Middle Scots will be of more use to the student of Dunbar than the *twenty bookes, clad in blak or reed, of Aristotle* so much cherished by Chaucer's Clerk.

When they wrote, the Scots vernacular had become much more clearly differentiated from Northumbrian English than Early Scots had been. Years of usage, colloquial and literary, had also made it a *subtell dyte*, capable of expressing meaning across a wide range from invective to panegyric. When Hugh MacDiarmid looks back to this period as the Golden Age of the Scots language, he is not romanticising. Why had the vernacular developed so rapidly? Politically, the Scotland of the later fifteenth century saw government strengthened and centralised. A new system of law courts, lay and clerical, was established. As these were institutions procedurally distinct from their English equivalents, a specifically Scottish vocabulary was developed to describe them. Scots also became a richer language than Northumbrian at this time, largely because that area lacked an equivalent group of institutions. Northumbrian would slowly assimilate southwards towards the dialect of Chaucer, as the south-east of England was gaining a similar form of institutionally based predominance south of the Tweed. Meanwhile, Middle Scots assumed lordship in its own realm.

All the major religious orders were also represented in the Scotland of the late fifteenth century. In their scriptoria, the practice of copying and glossing manuscripts continued apace. This encouraged the transmission of texts, many of which were written in the vernacular. Meanwhile, improved trade routes brought Scots into closer contact with merchants as well as noblemen. Dutch in particular began to influence Middle Scots, its social origins being mercantile.

Although all these forces made Middle Scots the accepted national vernacular, neither Henryson nor Dunbar, when discussing the use of literary Middle Scots, value it as a distinctive means of patriotic expression. In *The Goldyn Targe* (253–61), Dunbar describes himself as sharing the *Inglisch* literary language with Chaucer and Gower (Kinsley 1979: 37):

> O reverend Chaucere, rose of rethoris all,
> As in oure tong ane flour imperiall
> That raise in Britane, evir quho redis rycht,
> Thou beris of makaris the tryumph riall;
> Thy fresch anamalit termes celicall
> This mater coud illumynit have full brycht:
> Was thou nocht of oure Inglisch all the lycht,
> Surmounting eviry tong terrestriall
> Alls fer as Mayes morow dois mydnycht.

Henryson, in *The Testament of Cresseid* (Fox 1981: 113; ll. 57–60), places himself within the same literary tradition. The primary source of his poem is the English poet's *Troilus and Criseyde*:

> Of his distres me neidis nocht reheirs,
> For worthie Chauceir in the samin buik,
> In gudelie termis and in joly veirs,
> Compylit hes his cairis, quha will luik.

Neither writer is troubled by thoughts of possible linguistic treachery in aligning himself with the English language or the English literary tradition. Both think linguistically of Scots as a branch of English and aesthetically of the brotherhood of poets.

If one looks in more detail at what does concern them, the continued influence of classical rhetoric as redefined by Christian thought is revealed. Dunbar values Chaucer primarily for his rhetorical skills within the high style. In so doing, he reconfirms the traditional Scholastic view that the aureate style is especially to be encouraged. It at once celebrates art's artifice most clearly and is most fitted to illuminate mankind's quest for wisdom through eloquence. Henryson is more searching. One can hear in his lines the new learning. In probing the question of literary authority, however, he confines himself to means rather than ends. Far from casting doubt upon the need for sources *per se* or on God's status as author of all, *The Testament* will enact the value of the first and moralise upon the fideistic and penitential truths implied by the second. What Henryson does question is the degree to which poetic evidence can be relied upon as a true basis for literal truthfulness. *Quha wait gif all that Chauceir wrait was trew?* (64). If poetry is, by definition, imaginative, Chaucer's own evidence is unlikely to be literally accurate. As each poet builds on earlier 'invented' sources, that grounding in truth may become less rather than more secure as one *quair* after another is consulted.

While the Scots language was developing as the accepted vernacular in national terms, humanist influences in the late fifteenth century were also refining the rhetorical approach to the literary language in particular. As Robert Kindrick has thoroughly illustrated, the availability of Horace's *Ars Poetica* and the rediscovery of the complete text of Quintilian's *Institutio Oratoria* permitted the traditions of Christian rhetoric to be 'reintegrated into a more comprehensive and synthetic study' (Kindrick 1993: 8–9). Henryson, who had trained as a lawyer, was particularly well equipped to adapt the *artes* of Ciceronian spoken discourse to Christian poetic practice. These were, however, old 'new' texts and the major result for the Scottish poets of the later fifteenth century was a systematising of earlier practice rather than a radical challenge to the principles on which it was based.

The *Prologue* to Henryson's *Morall Fabillis* is the first piece of overt poetic 'theory' preserved in Scots. Stanza 2 demonstrates the truth of Kindrick's contentions (9–15):

> In lyke maner as throw a bustious eird,
> Swa it be laubourit with grit diligence,
> Springis the flouris and the corne abreird,
> Hailsum and gude to mannis sustenance;
> Sa springis thair ane morall sweit sentence
> Oute of the subtell dyte of poetry,
> To gude purpos, quha culd it weill apply.

The image which dominates the early stanzas of the *Prologue* is that of labouring; breaking up the soil of the text. This confirms the connection between poetic 'making' and manual work. The immediately relevant modal question is why any labour at all is needed for the beast-fable form in particular. In the normal medieval league table of allegorical seriousness, this mode was placed at the bottom, precisely because it did not need much interpretive labouring. The moral confirmed what the fable had enacted; the audience listened to a pleasant tale whose moral was then explained for them. Henryson's answer in stanza 2 follows the causal line of medieval criticism.

Authorially (*causa efficiens*), even in a simple form such as this, the poet must work imaginatively. His first task, therefore, is to transform his material analogically so that an audience may be drawn easily and pleasurably into the discussion. Labouring the soil is itself an analogy (*In lyke maner . . . swa*), and as such announces the methodology appropriate to the craft. Verbally (*causa materialis*), the task is to provide a *subtell dyte*. The codes of grammar are not those of life, only attempts to imitate them. Poetic composition must use words as subtly as possible because the poet strives, through verbal signs, to translate an infinitely more complex divine signing system; that of nature. Almost all of Henryson's images of labouring in the *Prologue* are themselves fittingly drawn from nature – nurturing flowers, ploughing cornfields, breaking the shell of a nut.

The argument for artifice follows classical and Scholastic practice in moving from significant words to significant arguments; from rhetoric to dialectic. In stanza 6 (36–8), a modesty topos disclaims artifice to prove it:

> In hamelie language and in termes rude
> Me neidis wryte, for quhy of eloquence
> Nor rethorike, I never understude.

The balanced phrases of the first line lead by way of enjambement into hyperbaton. Once more, words convey subtly as a sign of craftsmanship.

Each of these acts of labouring further distances poetic practice from life. This is because Henryson has set himself the task of explaining why a factual lie – speaking animals – may convey poetic truth. The purpose of an imaginative discipline, he states, is to use imagery and analogy to teach practical ethics, *ane morall sweit sentence*. The fable form itself (*causa formalis*) is an image of this more serious mimetic aim. Like the logician, he argues in stanza 7, the fabulist proposes *ane sillogisme* (46), an *exempill and similitude* (47) for a higher purpose. Poetic labour involves using the particular and the sensual to explore ideas. Poetic practice is, therefore, closer to that of the philosopher than the chronicler, and the issue of poetic 'truth' should, therefore, be weighed – in Aristotelian rather than Platonic terms – against conceptual criteria. 'Do these talking animals effectively convey truths about the human state?' is the relevant question, when considering poetic 'lies', not 'Do animals talk?' This is because the latter question ignores all the labour which separates art from life. In Henryson's case, talking animals will be used to warn men against acting bestially (*operatioun*) by counterpointing the rational part of their *conditioun* against their instinctive desires (47, 48).

This leaves the audience, whose effective persuasion (*causa finalis*) is the justification of the poetic 'lie', with at least one labouring task of their own. First, they must break the earth of the narrative to find the hidden *morall sweit sentence*. Stanza 3 of the *Prologue* offers a second, supportive analogy. The hard textual surface of the storyline has to be cracked like a nut's shell in order to reveal the *frute* of it (17). Once more, the ancient voices of the Aristotelian and Christian commentating traditions sound through. Even Aquinas, in his aesthetic conservatism-cum-condescension, could not have disagreed with this.

When considering the status of the literary language in Scotland at this time, it is important to realise that the movement of Middle Scots towards acceptance as the national vernacular was accompanied by a refinement of the rhetorical guidelines governing imaginative writing. The former was part of a natural linguistic development and unconsciously assimilated at a time when nationhood was taken for granted. The latter, by providing a self-conscious critical account of authorship, artifice and allegory, explains why Henryson and Dunbar, on their own evidence, think of themselves as part of a European community of philosophical poets and only secondly as Scots within a specific nation state.

The third, mysterious definition of language is also evident in the *Prologue* (55–6). When concluding his poetic self-justification, Henryson defines his persuasive purpose as the inculcation of practical Christian ethics. The mind must control the passions, as the alternative course leads to evil and, ultimately, to hell:

> Syne in the mynd sa fast is radicate
> That he in brutal beist is transformate.

This is scarcely surprising, as the *Prologue* (1–7) opens by relating all imaginative writing to the account of creation in Genesis:

> Thocht fein3eit fabils of ald poetre
> Be not al grunded vpon truth, yit than,
> Thair polite termes of sweit rhetore
> Richt plesand ar vnto the eir of man;
> And als the caus quhy thay first began
> Wes to repreif the of thi misleving,
> O man, be figure of ane vther thing.

Rhetoric's sweetness and its figural approach were unnecessary before man sinned. Only when the Fall distanced him from God was poetic 'reproof' needed to guide the lost pilgrim on earth back to his heavenly home. *Misleving*, therefore, accounts for rhetoric as means, origin and end.

Only those who simplistically assume a sudden movement from faith to humanism, equating one with the Middle Ages and the other with the Renaissance, will find it strange that Henryson relates his artistic toil in this way to the six days of divine labour figured in the Biblical account of origin. As Stephen L. Collins notes, the hierarchically ordered pattern for existence derived from Christian belief 'remained a dynamic concept capable of explaining various changing social attitudes without necessitating a self-conscious value re-assessment . . . until the end of the sixteenth century' (Collins 1989: 15). In 1559, when John Aylmer (Sig. C3) wrote that *Nature is nothynge else but God himselfe, or a divine order spred throughout the whole world and ingrafte in every part of it*, he was still expressing a conventional metaphysical viewpoint. Henryson, in the 1480s, would have been well in advance of his time had he posited an alternative causal scheme for authorship.

How did the idea of the Fall influence understanding of the literary language? This question returns us to James I's pessimistic refusal in the *Quair* to accept his own ability to understand sounds or words. When he reduces the voice which he hears within the tolling of the matins bell to an *impressioune off my thought* within an *illusioune*, he is simply taking the implications of Genesis to their logical conclusion. If mankind sees only darkly, all interpretation must be misinterpretation.

In his fable, *The Preiching of the Swallow*, Henryson also describes the counterbalance between nature's positive semiotic power and mankind's darkened vision under God (1,643–6):

> For God is in his power infinite,
> And mannis saull is febill and ouer small,
> Off understanding waik and unperfite
> To comprehend him that contenis all.

The perspective and intentions of author and of literary persona were especially emphasised within the Christian version of the causal line. Poetry as performed oratory demanded that the critic discuss delivery; poetry as a vehicle for Christian ethics demanded consideration of the deliverer's moral position.

If failure to understand nature's signing system was due to humanity's darkened vision, inability to communicate with words was due to inadequacies within the verbal signing system itself. God as Word, having *spoken* the universe into existence in Genesis, substituted a single holy language for perfect, wordless communication after the Fall. Additional linguistic confusion was introduced as a punishment for continued *misleving* at Babel. As Dante explains in the *De Vulgaria Eloquentia*: 'We maintain that a particular form of speech was created by God with and for the first soul . . . and this form would be used by every speaking tongue still had it not been broken up and scattered by human presumption . . . [At Babel] as many types of work as there were, so many different languages now separated the human race.' More sanguine views of language development within a benevolent metaphysics prevented early writers from becoming as morosely absolutist about language's inadequacies as postmodernists. But, following St Augustine's lead, they did introduce a triadic relationship involving adding to sign and referent the interpreter, who gives the sign meaning. They also distinguished between natural signs which relate to objects in nature as against conventional signs, which only indicate operations of the mind (Markus 1972: 74).

With similar subtlety, Henryson often opens the moral section of a fable by reminding his audience that it is only a series of images; *figurall* (1,099). Although these may, in a general sense, enable those who *tak heid* to *find . . . ane gude moralitie* (365), ultimately they are just the signs used by fallen authors in a fallen language, creating other images in other fallen minds. These ideas are summed up in the moral of *The Cock and the Fox* (592–8):

> Now worthie folk, suppose this be ane fabill,
> And ouerheillit wyth typis figurall,
> Zit may ye find ane sentence richt agreabill
> Under thir fenƷeit termis textuall.
> To our purpose this cok weill may we call
> Nyse proud men, woid and vaneglorious
> Of kin and blude, quhilk is presumpteous.

'This is an imagined story', the narrator explains. 'It is addressed to individuals in an audience. It seeks to teach a message by means of the allegoric method. What, if anything, you as an individual may make of these non-existent word-people and word-ideas will depend on how you relate the images and types of the tale to its moral message. As author [having translated the tale from my sources], I now propose to slant it towards one of many possible teaching functions. I choose to show how it may exhort us to avoid pride'. The fact that Henryson may assume a community of understanding (*to our purpose*) reminds us that what may seem complex to a later age would have been clear to most people living at the period whose mythology – in this case Biblical – is being described. Few in Henryson's audience could have quoted St Augustine on semiotics; practically all would have understood the broad movement of his argument and the theological beliefs which sustained it.

How does this evidence affect the definition of Scottish literature promulgated by the 'Tradition' critics? From their point of view, not at all. For Kurt Wittig (1958: 3), Scottish literature can be defined through a series of distinctive tales and topics. He is aware of the isolationist tendencies implied by this methodology but plays them down: 'I am not surreptitiously attempting to . . . isolate Scottish Literature from the larger world to which it belongs'. He is even conscious of where the most complete breach may open up: 'In Scotland a different set of traditions has created a society which in many respects (though not all) is very different from that which exists in England'. But he is content to use the method, relying on his own sensitivity to detect which ideas are canonically relevant. 'In compounding these values I have picked out the ones *which seem to me* to be specifically Scottish and have largely ignored the rest' (1958: 4).

The distinctive traditions which create this 'Scottish Tradition in Literature' are, therefore, drawn from disciplines other than literature. A medieval commentator, observing Wittig at work, might describe his canonical method as one which employs psychological, sociological and political criteria as they appear to a twentieth-century mind conditioned by Romantic and post-Romantic thought. Such a retrospective, extra-disciplinary definition of Scottish literature is not concerned with any of Henryson's literary theory because its canonical logic bypasses *all* literary and linguistic theorising, let alone diachronic study of changing attitudes to language and aesthetics. Wittig foreseeably welcomes Henryson's *Fabillis* especially. The animals depicted in them are usually distinctively Scottish fifteenth-century beasts, living in the newly established burghs, suffering under the Scottish law system and commenting on life under James III. This patriotic thematic passport permits the quality of Henryson's poetry to be assessed. High critical evaluation, in turn, allows the non-Scottish verse (*Orpheus* and the *Testament*) to enter the canon and be fully treated.

This is rather like a doctor who accidentally offers the correct medicine after wholly misinterpreting his patient's symptoms. The direct representations of Scottish life, which Wittig so values, are only the husk of a literary shell whose fruit is the inculcation of ethically relevant teachings for Henryson. They are universally applicable and exist as examples at the simpler, story level of allegorical narrative, shared with chronicle. They do so within a discipline definitively justified by its power to rise above this level imaginatively within the broader, more philosophically testing range of potentiality. They are composed in literary Middle Scots at a time when that tongue was still viewed historically as a branch of English, rhetorically as an artificial language, poetically as part of a British quest for mimetic subtlety and ontologically as a branch of one of the seventy-two languages of Babel. This is a good distance from Wittig's assumption that, if Scots is the linguistic sign of national pride today, Middle Scots must have had the same significance for the late medieval makars.

To state that Henryson enters Wittig's traditional canon accidentally is a twofold truth. The themes and tales which he sympathetically analyses are, for his author, the accidentals of the discipline; its 'trivial' means rather than its philosophical end. But his lack of critical understanding also results in misinterpretation of the means itself. Important arguments are highlighted on mistaken, naturalist assumptions. The two kinds of accident conjoin when he highlights the crucially important opening line of the *Testament*, with its sententially significant matching of *ane doolie sessoun to ane cairfull dyte* as a sign that there are especially cold springs in Scotland.

In fact, this cold spring must be unusual, even in Scotland, if the seasonal image is to 'correspond and be equivalent' (Wittig 1958: 2) to the poem's tragic account of personal disorder within a chaotic world. It is consciously invoked as a sign in nature of Cresseid's sinful blasting of her own youthful spring. If this divine sign is to work effectively, its audience must not assume that this 'weather forecast' represents the Scottish norm. Wittig's value scheme correctly highlights these important lines but for the wrong reasons.

As Hugh of St Victor's building image suggested, a critic ignores the foundation level of narrative at his peril. But the image is a comprehensive one, relating that level to all the upper courses of the entire structure in prose or verse. To draw the themes and values which determine the Scottish literary paradigm from this foundation level is, therefore, fair so long as they are not claimed as the poet's only or principal topic. Such an approach dislocates them from the entire metaphysical and aesthetic framework within which Christian rhetoric works.

The hermeneutic dangers of building the larger critical artefact called Scottish literature from themes or values defined outside the discipline and detected naturalistically at the surface level within it are many. The most perverse canonical implications are, however, accidentally concealed within the Early Scots and Middle Scots periods. They will be discussed in full at the stage of literary development where they first emerge – Late Middle Scots. If the labouring analogy in Henryson's *Prologue* warns his fifteenth-century audience to relate the fable to its allegoric framework, another image warns that the story is also subject to rules. The narrator sets the idea of 'play' or 'game' against that of labour. Games, however, only provide pleasure to those willing to learn their sporting code (*Prologue*: 19–25):

> And clerkis sayis, it is richt profitabill
> Amangis ernist to ming ane merie sport,
> To blyth the spreit and gar the tyme be schort.
> For as we se, ane bow that ay is bent
> Worthis unsmart and dullis on the string;
> Sa dois the mynd that is ay diligent
> In ernistfull thochtis and in studying.

This image of the bowstring was used in Scholastic thought to refer to the pleasurable side of the teaching/pleasing equation with which Henryson's *Prologue* had opened. Aquinas employs it in his *Summa Theologica*, attributing the advice to St John. Asked to justify the disciples playing together, John enquired whether the questioner could continue plying his bow without breaking the string. Getting a denial, 'the Blessed John drew the inference that in like manner man's mind would break if its tension were never relaxed' (*Summa Theologica*: II–II, q. 168, a. 2). Interestingly, this argument is an analogic one, used to record a parable, by a writer who found in analogy the justification for tale-telling. St Thomas introduces the anecdote to prove that game-playing may be a virtuous form of action.

Henryson's 'playing' analogy advises his audience to approach the story with care, as an artefact. Henryson's proud town mouse, who was *gild brother and made ane fre burges* (172), is, therefore, correctly analysed as a specifically Scottish creation by 'traditionalist' critics. But her outlook and self-justification derive specifically from the conditions laid down by the beast-fable in the late fifteenth century. Mice talk because the mode so demands; the town mouse boasts of her property because the fifteenth century saw the emergence of the burgh in Scotland. The critic who does not know that a burgher had to build his own house within a year and a day, for example, will miss one of the important details, which lie at the base of all comedy.

But this is a game within a game. 'Playing', for Henryson, derives not only from sounds which are *plesand unto the eir of man* (4); these sounds exist under the *polite termes of sweit rhetore* (3) as ethical means to a divine end. That mouse is also a group of Middle Scots sound-signs, guiding us to the *gude moralitie* (366) that *blissed be sempill lyfe withoutin dreid* (373) so that we all may share her company as *pure* 'poor' *pylgryme[s]* (181), through life's exile into the bosom of God. The various analogies teach exactly this. We can only be 'moved' effectively by the pleasurable word-journey if we share the 'maker's' 'labour' under the rules of this 'game' and apply our understanding, through 'memory', at all stages of our own lived pilgrimage.

The idea of play ranges over all these areas but is primarily focused on the rhetorical rules governing significant use of language. These derive from the classical concept of decorum. Henryson was acquainted with Horace's *Art of Poetry*, which provided a much fuller account of this hierarchical system of differentiated styles than any textbook available to the Early Scots poets (Kindrick 1993: 8, 12, 60). Broadly, serious and noble topics and the eulogistic mode were marked by Latinate vocabulary and the sonorous, Ciceronian rhythms of the high style. A fall into staccato rhythms, heavy alliteration and colloquial language signified low life, low themes and satire. Dutch and Old Norse loanwords tend to dominate. The use of Scots forms beside their English equivalents, which Aitken notes as a sign of Middle Scots' progression towards expressive fullness, was particularly characteristic of the middle style.

Henryson, even in the *Morall Fabillis*, does make significant decorous transitions from one style to another (MacQueen 1967: 106–7; Kindrick 1993: 57–9). But as a teacher, he generally prefers the middle style for its ease and clarity. It is Dunbar who is the virtuoso word-player. In his verse, all the joys and strictures of the decorous word-game are to be found. After all, this poet defines himself as a professional entertainer. Only when a headache prevents his enjoyment is he loath to leap out of bed, *for mirth, for menstrallie and play, for din nor danceing nor deray*. At the same time, as master poet he knows that he is paid as the finest 'wordsmith' at court.

As such, he is grateful that Middle Scots already provides a wide range of vocabulary. He not only admires Chaucer's example in *The Goldyn Targe*; as a disciple, he follows it. He seeks to engraft as many new words and coinages as possible into the literary form of that dialect. Now, he can play the game of art within a 'subtle dyte', worthy even of the Virgin:

> Empryce of prys, imperatrice,
> Bricht polist precious stane;
> Victrice of vyce, hie genitrice
> Of Jhesu lord soverayne;
> Our wys pavys fro enemys
> Agane the Feyndis trayne;
> Oratrice, mediatrice, salvatrice,

To God gret suffragane;
Ave Maria, gracia plena:
Haile, sterne meridiane;
Spyce, flour delice of paradys
That baire the gloryus grayne.

This extract comes from *Ane Ballat of Our Lady* (61–72). Given its divine theme and addressee, it is appropriately cast in the high style at its most ornate. Each of the lyric's seven stanzas 'adores' Mary in the same complex rhyme scheme with variations upon a set of key images. The liturgical Latin salutation is set within five lines rhyming three times on the one sound, counterpointed by six lines rhyming on another. Alliteration and the heavily Latinate vocabulary remain constant throughout the poem's eighty-four lines.

In terms of the 'game' analogy, Dunbar is a word-player of genius, not content to practise a limited range of skills but anxious to demonstrate the entire range permitted by the rulebook. Although he was probably in religious orders and certainly was used as a mouthpiece for James IV's political policies, his first and last love was words. His stylistic range may economically be demonstrated by contrasting *Ane Ballat of Our Lady* with a stanza drawn from *The Flyting of Dunbar and Kennedie* (49–56):

Iersche brybour baird, vyle beggar with thy brattis,
Cuntbittin crawdoun Kennedy, coward of kynd;
Evill farit and dryit as Denseman on the rattis,
Lyk as the gleddis had on thy gulesnowt dynd;
Mismaid monstour, ilk mone owt of thy mynd,
Renunce, rebald, thy rymyng; thow bot royis;
Thy trechour tung hes tane ane heland strynd –
Ane lawland ers wald mak a bettir noyis.

The contrasts between this extract and Dunbar's Marian lyric are striking. Instead of high-style Latinate praise, the master poet mocks Kennedy in low style, relying on a vocabulary drawn mainly from Old English and Old Norse sources. The staccato rhythms and heavy alliteration also characterise that style.

But the flyting stanza, which continues the anti-Gaelic strains of the *Howlat*, is not an attempt factually to imitate the way in which a fifteenth-century Lowland Scot might have insulted a Highland contemporary. It is as highly crafted as *Ane Ballat of Our Lady*, albeit in satiric mode. In a staged flyting, such as this one, two poets would indulge in a verbal battle for the amusement of the court. The winner was the one adjudged to have shown greater verbal skill and ingenuity. In matching himself against Kennedy in this courtly game, Dunbar, like a boxer, is motivated by the desire to display his skills and be rewarded for victory rather than by malevolence towards his opponent.

To that end, he is as ambitious in his alliterative denunciation of Kennedy as in his internally rhymed praise for the Virgin. His vocabulary is as full of recent coinages. The difference lies in the decorous choice of these compounds. *Gulesnowt*, for example, gives Kennedy a very lower-class yellow nose by way of Old Norse *gul-r* and Middle English *snute*. *Cuntbittin* joins Middle English *cunte*/Old Norse *kunta* to Old English *bitan*. When languages, unfavoured in the lower mode, provide the vocabulary, they are part of Dunbar's attempt to puncture Kennedy's pretentiousness. As rascal poet or *brybour baird* (Anglo-Norman *brybour* + Gaelic *bard*), Kennedy attempts to set himself above other vernacular poets. The falsity of that position is linguistically mirrored by contrasting loanwords drawn from those traditions against the low-style norm.

While Dunbar's colloquial verse is not usually so highly crafted, earthy poems – such as *The Turnament* and *Ane Dance in the Quenis Chalmer* – are still part of a courtly game played out according to the rules of art. The many textbooks of rhetoric with their detailed discussions of literary decorum in its social and thematic context enabled authors in the late fifteenth century to assume that, when a particular stylistic register was announced, their audience would expect the associated tones and topics to follow. A high-style Ciceronian opening, for example, should lead into a serious discussion among noble characters. Dunbar used this rhetorical sophistication to frustrate audience expectations as well as to fulfil them.

In *The Tretis of the Twa Mariit Wemen and the Wedo*, a satire on the evils of medieval marriage, he clothes his three 'heroines' elegantly and places them within an idealised pastoral setting. One recognises the French *chanson d'aventure* mode and settles down for a noble tale of courtly love. Linguistically, these anticipations are reconfirmed. The high style decorously describes *the sugurat sound of hir sang*. Its *hautand wordis* are even referred to directly. The poet's style, like the women's clothes, *glitterit as the gold*; even the *gressis* of the pastoral setting *gleme*. Nobility and aureation rule.

But as Dunbar 'pans in' to focus on this supposedly ethereal trio, they appear to be quaffing their wine with an enthusiasm unknown in the rarefied world of the *chanson d'aventure*. Characteristically, he marks the comic transition by describing not only action but also speech (39–40):

> They wauchtit at the wicht wyne and waris out wourdis
> And syn thai spak more spedelie and sparit no matiris.

This is a fine description-cum-enactment of the low style's staccato rhythms. It warns correctly of a poem in which the drama will encompass all 'matters' and so embrace all styles. It is decorously marked off by a transition to the middle style and psychologically justified by the power of drink to loosen tongues.

It remains doubtful whether even these rhetorical warnings would have prepared the *maister poete*'s courtly audience for the comically vicious low-style indictments of men and marriage which the three ladies subsequently offer. When the widow asks the first wife her opinion of marriage, she enthusiastically launches into the low style to describe her aged husband's ugliness and impotence (89–96):

> I have ane wallidrag, ane worme, ane auld wobat carle,
> A waistit wolroun na worth bot wourdis to clatter,
> Ane bumbart, ane dron bee, ane bag full of flewme,
> Ane scabbit skarth, ane scorpioun, ane scutarde behind.
> To se him scart his awin skyn grit scunner I think.
> Quhen kissis me that carybald, than kyndillis all my sorow –
> As birs of ane brym bair his berd is als stif,
> Bot soft and soupill as the silk is his sary lume.

The heavy alliteration is reminiscent of flyting techniques, but this vicious invective is viciously invented. Bestial imagery is used to demean her ancient partner mentally and physically. Close observation of him scratching himself opens up a line of visualised repulsiveness, more usually associated with death lyrics. The husband's embraces are those of a *glowrand gaist* whose *grym ene ar gladderit all about/And gorgeit lyk tua gutaris, that ar with glar stoppit*.

This manipulation of high and low styles assumes an audience, aware of the rules governing the poetic game. Arguably, it is easier for the professional makar to advertise his rhetorical skills at the extremes of virtuosity in this way than to turn the more ordinary middle style into verse whose emotive power is difficult to account for analytically. The actor Richard Burton, when offered the opportunity to read aloud his three favourite lyrics, chose one by Dunbar. It is in the middle-style range, and, of its twenty-five stanzas, nineteen are essentially a roll-call of those whom death has summoned while so far leaving the poet alive. To make a list so dramatically poignant that it appeals to an actor is Dunbar's triumph. But it is also a sign of Middle Scots' new expressive fullness.

Commonly known as *The Lament for the Makaris*, its stanza form is simple (1–4):

> I that in heill wes and gladnes
> Am trublit now with gret seiknes
> And feblit with infermite:
> *Timor mortis conturbat me.*

Personal fears of illness lead the poet first into a more general consideration of death as leveller, then into the roll-call of poets. The Latin refrain, drawn from the liturgical *Office of the Dead*, sounds out like a drumbeat. The effect is cumulative and quietly expressive of the melancholy, penitential spirit of the age (45–52):

> I se that makaris amang the laif
> Playis heir ther pageant, syne gois to graif;
> Sparit is nought ther faculte:
> *Timor mortis conturbat me.*
>
> He hes done petuously devour
> The noble Chaucer of makaris flour,
> The monk of Bery, and Gower, all thre:
> *Timor mortis conturbat me.*

English poets give way to Scots with the geographical change of location noted but the shared status of verbal making still dominant. Death has destroyed Early Scots writers, including Barbour and Holland (61), into his ghostly band. As the process draws nearer to Dunbar's own time, he employs images recalling the devil's action in Eden and Judas's in the garden of Gethsemane, to introduce the summoning of his near-contemporaries. Death has whispered in the ear of Henryson and embraced John Ross (81–4):

> In Dunfermelyne he hes done roune
> With maister Robert Henrisoun;
> Schir Johne the Ros enbrast has he:
> *Timor mortis conturbat me.*

Slight changes in perspective, tone and rhetorical technique satisfy the listener's desire for variety. But the verse list with its repeated liturgical refrain carries the heaviest emotive power. It imitates the inevitable rhythms of life and death, coming ever closer to the poet. With the memory that his flyting opponent, Walter Kennedy, *in poynte of dede lyis veraly*,

Dunbar returns to the case with which he had begun – his own. *On forse I man his* (death's) *nyxt pray be* (95). The last stanza is set apart tonally. But reflective self-pity does not, conventionally, turn into joyous acceptance of heaven. Dunbar clearly covets life's pleasures too much. He turns to God stoically as a last resort (97–100):

> Sen for the ded remeid is none
> Best is that we for dede dispone
> Eftir our deid that life may we:
> *Timor mortis conturbat me.*

As a trained actor, Burton 'heard' this list within the performance mode for which it was intended. The dramatic player recognised a verbal player of equal genius, able to demonstrate the skills of the word-game even when most constrained by its rules.

Henryson's *Prologue* uses the analogies of work and play to release helpful lines of enquiry within the potential meaning of the text, in the manner encouraged by medieval commentators. In that sense, a third image drawn from the same source may, literally, 'carry us across' time into the days of Gavin Douglas (1476–1522) and David Lindsay (c. 1486–1555). Referring to his authorities, the Dunfermline poet claims (32) *to mak ane maner of translatioun*. That is, he will 'carry across' meaning from his Latin source into Scots, allowing the uneducated in his own land to benefit from classical wisdom.

Ane maner of reminds that audience of another fact. Literary transference may take many forms. Henryson's reinvention of Aesop is derived from Latin fables within the Aesopic tradition. It is a very free reworking of source material. Gavin Douglas's *Eneados* will claim a much closer relationship with its original, Virgil's *Aeneid*. More generally, the 'maners' of literary transference ease the development of the history of ideas from one period's major concerns to another. These three modes of 'translation' – authoritative, ideological and linguistic – will mark out the route of argument through a particularly dramatic period in Scotland's history.

Inevitably, in a study of the Scots language, the journey begins with 'authorities' and Douglas. The first recorded references to the literary language as *Scottis* rather than *Inglis* appear in the *Eneados*. Douglas not only claims to compose in *Scottis*; he stresses that this is the *langage of Scottish natioun* (Coldwell 1950–6: ll. 103, 108). His Middle Scots version of Virgil is a much finer work than Caxton's earlier attempt in the *sudron, Inglyss* tongue. Unsurprisingly, this early anticipation of Hugh MacDiarmid's competitive, nationalistic view of Scots is regarded by many critics as a sign that Renaissance humanism had finally rescued the Scots vernacular from the more comprehensive linguistic viewpoint of rhetorical theory. Now, they argue, it is Scots alone; a national standard for a unique nation state.

Two words of warning are properly sounded before such claims are tested against Douglas's detailed statement of intent. The first stems from biographical evidence. The poet's life does not reveal a man usually given to Anglophobic pronouncements. Douglas had, in his youth, been a courtier at the court of James IV. He attended the University of St Andrews and chose to become a cleric. He quickly gained recognition and eventually became Bishop of Dunkeld. On the occasions when James V called upon him to advise or negotiate, he proved himself anxious to draw Scottish and English interests into closer harmony (McClure 1988: 13).

The *Eneados*, completed in 1513, is his major work. Along with the earlier *Palice of*

Honour (c. 1501), it reveals his humanist interests. His wide reading in the classics included the most recently discovered texts and their modern commentators. But his clerical position guaranteed that humanist learning did not imply a non-Christian viewpoint. Indeed, his flyting against Caxton uses St Bernard as the arch-arbiter on translation (Prol. I, 139). It culminates with a comparison likening the truth of the English translator's version to the devil's in opposition to St Augustine (Prol. I, 143).

The second caveat is linguistic. As McClure (1988: 13) comments, '[although] it was in the late fifteenth century that the practice of calling the language by the national adjective arose . . . it did not, and indeed never has, become universal'. The ethnically specific definition of Scots did not at once arise and erase other attitudes to the vernacular. Why, then, did it take a bishop with known English sympathies in the early sixteenth century to voice the nationalist view of the Scots vernacular?

The Prologue to *Eneados*, Book I (109–24), describes Douglas's authorial position fully:

> And ʒit forsuyth I set my bissy pane
> As that I couth to mak it braid and plane,
> Kepand na sudron bot our awyn langage,
> And spekis as I lernyt quhen I was page.
> Nor ʒit sa cleyn all sudron I refuss,
> Bot sum word I pronunce as nyghtbouris doys:
> Lyke as in Latyn beyn grew termys sum,
> So me behufyt quhilum or than be dum
> Sum bastard Latyn, French or Inglyss oyss
> Quhar scant was Scottis – I had nane other choys.
> Nocht for our tong is in the selwyn skant
> But for that I the fowth of langage want
> Quhar as the cullour of his properte
> To kepe the sentens tharto constrenyt me,
> Or than to mak my sayng schort sum tyme,
> Mair compendyus, or to lykly my ryme.

The portions of this quotation which most neatly fit the criteria usually employed in establishing a Scottish literary tradition are 'Scottis' in line 118 and the claim for simplicity ('mak it braid and playne') in line 110. They are critically extrapolated to prove that Douglas supports Scots against English linguistically and sociologically. In the twentieth century, Scottish literature claims to distinguish itself from English in just these ways – through the use of Scots and through a more democratic spirit expressed unpretentiously. Douglas is, therefore, heralded as the prophet of this movement. But does his own evidence support him in that role?

Certainly, the bishop is proud of Middle Scots as a vehicle for literary expression (*fowth of langage*). At the same time, the case which he argues is modally delimited to the 'maner of (close) translation', which he and Caxton claim to emulate. This recontextualises the apparent evidence in a variety of ways. In terms of intent, the activity of translation was closely associated with Renaissance nationalism. In those days, the translator saw his 'work as an act of patriotism' (Matthiessen 1931: 3). It is, therefore, significant that Douglas only uses the word *Scottis* to distinguish the language from *Inglis* when he is involved in a literary activity thus defined. Neither the distinction nor the word *Scottis* appears in *The Palice of Honour*.

To argue *Scottis* against *Inglis* was seen by Douglas as appropriate to a specific poetic challenge thrown down to a particular English rival within one rhetorical mode. As a Scot, he is proud to have introduced his fellow countrymen to Virgil more accurately, more poetically and more judiciously *in the langage of Scottis natioun* (103) than Caxton, as representative *of Inglis natioun* (138). But he quickly warns his readers against wider analogic assumptions. The dismissive, nationalistic tone is justified on literary criteria related to the act of translating. It embraces neither English poetry nor scholarship generally, *For me lyst with nane Inglis bukis flyte* (Prol. I, 272). There, *throu Albion iland braid* (Prol. I, 343), Chaucer remains *the principal poet but peir* (Prol. I, 339).

The argument of the Prologue is also couched in contingent and comparative terms. Douglas does not say that he will always imitate the plain spoken tongue of his childhood. He says that he will use it as the norm for his verse, moving to other stylistic registers when necessary. His literary Middle Scots will incorporate Southern forms. It must also admit inferiority to Latin. Measured against the language of classical Rome, Scots remains a 'bad harsk speche', a *lewit barbour tong* (Prol. I, 21).

Clearly, Douglas is still influenced by rhetorical views of the literary language. He accepts Scots as his national vernacular but within the wider harmony of European poetic practice. A translator, especially, cannot avoid confronting the greater *fowth* of the Roman tongue:

> For thar be Latyn wordis mony ane
> That in our leyd ganand translatioun hass nane
> Less than we mynyss thar sentens and gravyte.
> (Prol. I, 363–5)

> Betweyn 'genus,' 'sexus' and 'species'
> Diuersyte in our leid I cess.
> (Prol. 371–2)

The critic who understands the co-presence of rhetorical and nationalist approaches to translation can face with equanimity Bruce Dearing's valid objection that the *Eneados*, far from offering only *braid and plane* Scots, often presents the reader with a particularly 'thorny . . . blend of Scots, Latin, French and Sudroun' (Dearing 1951: 845). At times, this may even be a more difficult language to understand than that of Dunbar, who does not make any claims to be *plane*. Why is this the case?

The first answer relates to decorum. On Douglas's own evidence, the *Aeneid* transmits a highly serious message:

> The hie wysdome and maist profund engyne
> Of myne author Virgile, poet dyvyne,
> To comprehend makis me almaist forway,
> So crafty hys wark is, lyne by lyne.
> (Prol. V, 27–30)

Decorously, *hie* and complex wisdom demands the high style. Although the length of Virgil's epic implies the dramatic use of aureation for local effects rather than setting the entire poem in a style equivalent to Dunbar's *Goldyn Targe*, many lengthy passages witness Douglas's acceptance of the rhetorical principle that *the authouris word* must *baith accord and bene convenient* with its theme.

As a result, as Bawcutt (1976: 45–9) and others have proved, the *Eneados* is replete with ornate rhetorical figures. Expansive strategies such as *repetitio*, *circuitio*, parallel constructions and alliterative doublets are at once stylistically appropriate and sententially necessary. Archaisms characterise this high style and punctuate Douglas's translation. Many of these, such as the past participle with the *y* prefix (*ybaik*; *yfettyrit*) and *bene* for Scots *ar* for the present indicative plural, resurrect specifically Southern forms.

The second reason for linguistic complexity vying with plainer Scots derives from the practical persuasive aims of Douglas's verse. The causal line of Aristotelian oratory still broadly governs the *Eneados*, whose author regularly refers to God as 'my makar' and 'our makar'. If this implies authorial humility at one end of the causal line, it involves due consideration of the practical needs of his audience at the other. He thinks of his text being privately or publicly read aloud, referring consistently to the spoken word – *spekis*, *pronunce*. He admits that he has often introduced English forms simply to provide the necessary visual rhyme. The Scots *a* and *ai* form, for example, will alternate with English *o*, giving sometimes *ane*, sometimes *one*, sometimes *hait*, sometimes *hote*. To facilitate rhythm, he is equally pliable, giving the Scots *is* ending its full two syllables when that serves, but changing to *s* and one syllable if the metre so demands. As he presumes that the text will be 'heard' in a Scots accent, the evidence of the eye will be translated by the voice and so concerns him less than it might a modern linguist searching a printed text for dialectal variations. He has decided, in obedience to Horace's commands, not to translate line by line. The clear transmission of ideas is his principal concern:

> And to the sammyn purpos we may apply
> Horatius in hys Art of Poetry:
> 'Press nocht,' says he 'thou traste intepreter,
> Word eftir word to translait thi mater'.
> (Prol. I, 399–402)

Pedagogically, he chooses the role of 'commentator' and so commits himself to glosses and paraphrases. These vary in nature: sometimes they may be advanced in plain Middle Scots, sometimes they must match the Latin poet in erudition. In the latter case, new coinages and aureation may be brought into play.

The range of styles and fullness of vocabulary are anyway already present in the Latin of the *Aeneid*. Virgil's narrator

> altyrris his style sa mony way,
> Now dreid, now stryfe, now lyfe, now wa, now play,
> Langeir in murnyng, now in melody,
> To satisfy ilk wightis fantasy.
> (Prol. V, 33–6)

A dedicated translator has no choice but to follow that example. This quotation provides a third, mimetic reason for Douglas's linguistic range to add to the decorous and persuasive arguments earlier advanced. The translator imitates a text. If that text employs the entire gamut of styles within its own language, the vernacular chosen to represent it should also be exhaustive, verbally and stylistically.

Despite the modally specific, contingent and comparative basis on which Douglas made his claim for Middle Scots as the literary language of Scotland, the fact that he did so at all does mark a new stage within the developing history of the literary language in Scotland. Time and poetic practice have now given Middle Scots a vocabulary capable of rivalling other European vernaculars. Scotland's status nationally and institutionally has drawn that vocabulary sufficiently far away from any of the English dialects to give it a distinctive status.

But can the works of Henryson, Dunbar and Douglas be regarded as constituting a National Standard? This is, in part, a terminological rather than a substantive issue, well addressed by Aitken (1971a: 177–209), who shows how particular analysis reveals a good deal of variation, regionally and scribally. In concluding that 'the old concept of Middle Scots as an "artificial" and highly uniform language should now be discarded', Aitken does not embrace the antithesis of denying any artifice or uniformity. The authoritative array of specific variants which he assembles is designed to overthrow the simplicity of the myth rather than the facts and tendencies which underlie it. Those specifics confirm the continued presence of self-conscious artistry inherent in the idea of 'making'. They demonstrate a movement towards but not the attainment of National Standard status.

The idea of a National Standard is, anyway, in itself a theoretical extrapolation from the specifics of a language. Given that language is constantly changing, it is helpful to imagine it 'held' at one moment in time and to define it through the evidence drawn from perceived majority practice. Pedagogically, this may be a valuable strategy. Empirically, the claim for Scots is based on accurately perceived trends and biases. But they are not 'suthfast' in the literal sense. Aitken (1971: 198) sums up the situation nicely: 'If we assume that it was writers like these royal and literary clerks who were likely to have set the standards of spelling and other literary usages, then we may regard this limited majority practice as the "standard" form of written Middle Scots'.

Douglas would certainly have supported this view of language. His major source, Horace (Dorsch 1965: 80), had strenuously maintained the ever-changing nature of verbal communication in both its spoken and written forms:

> If it happens that you have to invent new terms for the discussion of abstruse topics, you will have a chance to coin words that were unknown to earlier generations of Romans, and no one will object to your doing this, as long as you do it with discretion . . . Why should I be grudged the right to add a few words to the stock if I can, when the language of Cato and Ennuis has enriched our native speech by the introduction of new terms? . . . As the words change their foliage with the decline of each year, and the earliest leaves fall, so words die out with old age; and the newly born ones thrive and prosper just like human beings in the vigour of youth.

Continuity of linguistic process is also implicit in Henryson's view of literary invention as *ane maner of translatioun*; an unbroken 'carrying across' of literary authority from one source, one language and one age into one's own texts, terms and times. Both he and Dunbar, like James I before them, view this form of continuity, however, within an English literary and dialectal process stretching from Chaucer through *morall* Gower to Lydgate *laureate*.

To carry a discussion on Scottish language and literature across the years separating Douglas's *Eneados* of 1513 from the 1552 Cupar performance of Sir David Lindsay's *Ane Satyre of the Thrie Estaitis* may not seem a massive task until one contemplates the intervening historical events more closely. Douglas's translation was completed well before Luther's Wittenberg challenge to the Catholic faith (1520), before Calvin's state of presbyters (1541) and before the martyrdom of the Scottish reformers Hamilton (1528) and Wishart (1546). Lindsay writes as a Scottish courtier who had lived through the Reformation. Although in an early poem, *The Dreme* (358), he claims *that the trew Kirk can no way erre at all*, he was an Episcopalian whose later writings argue a Protestant position.

Henryson's second 'maner of translatioun' provides guidance. For him, literature is primarily concerned with ideas. The 'conditioun' of his imagined *beistis* acts as a universal *exempill* for behaviour. His first animal, the cock, significantly represents knowledge being brought down from the heights of contemplation to influence the active life.

> Quha can governe ane realme, cietie, or hous
> Without science?
> *(Cok and Jasp*, 136–7)

From Augustine onwards, this view of art's purpose dominated. The allegory of the poets, as defined by Dante in the *Convivium* (Tract II, Chapter 1), held the literal, historical sense to be figurative. In non-scriptural texts, such as the *Morall Fabillis*, only the allegorical, conceptual sense is true.

In the Renaissance, the influences of Bacon and of Neoplatonism began to blur or even reverse this prioritisation. This process in Scottish literature begins with Douglas and gains momentum with Lindsay. Neither denies God's signing system nor the allegorical method premised by it, but both emphasise historical actuality within that model.

Of the two, Bishop Douglas is, predictably, the more conservative. As noted earlier, he claims that his translation seeks primarily to transmit ideas. He chooses Virgil on strictly medieval grounds – as a pagan who prophesied Christian truths *under the clowds of dyrk poecy* (Prol. I, 191–8). Allegorically, he sets the story of the *Aeneid* within the traditional moralised scheme of Bernardus Sylvestris (Jones and Jones 1977). The first six books represent the six ages of man; Aeneas becomes an image of Everyman; classical history shadows the pilgrimage of life:

> In all his warkis Virgil doith discrive
> The stait of man, gif thou list understand,
> Baith lif and ded in thir fyrst bukis fyve;
> And now, intil this saxt, we have on hand,
> Eftir thar deth, in quhat ply saulis sal stand.
> He writis lyke a philosophour naturall;
> Tuichand our faith mony causis he fand
> Quhilk beyn conform, or than collaterall.
> (Prol. VI, 33–40)

But Douglas, in his commentary on the text, also claims to have chosen the *Eneados* for its political relevance: *Bot ye sall know that the principall entent of Virgill was to extoll the Romanys.* The literal level of the text in this case presents its own truths, allowing Douglas to ally himself with Valla, Landino and the new line of Neoplatonic thought as Bawcutt (1976: 32–3) claims. It also permits him to resume his challenge – begun in *The Palice of Honour* – to the more sterile aspects of Scholastic-Aristotelian aesthetics, while working within that system's causal and allegorical framework.

Lindsay's concern is more overtly political. *Ane Satyre* is the first extant example of Scottish drama. It is written for a popular audience within the conventions of the later Morality. Earlier plays within this form had sought to explore the divine mysteries. In the later sixteenth century, the state of the nation rather than the state of the soul stood at the centre of the morality stage. Lindsay's title with its reference to government and the body politic confirms his sympathy with that definition of persuasive focus. The case of the lower classes is represented by Pauper and John the Commonweil using the powerful audience-involvement techniques of theatre in the round. In the Cupar performance, John sat and commented from a position among the audience on the hill. He only entered the playing area by jumping across the burn which bounded it when fair government had been promised. This does give him representative status but in sociological terms as a representative of the fourth estate rather than Everyman. In accordance with the traditions of the touring morality, the names of local towns and dignitaries were introduced into the script to localise it even more narrowly.

It is no coincidence that this play assumed major popularity after the Union of the Crowns, for it tells a patriotic Scottish tale from a democratic viewpoint with a satiric directness, demanding little interpretive 'labour' from the audience. It also favours France against England (Lyall 1989: 161; ll. 4,599–602):

> Quhat cummer have ye had in Scotland
> Be our auld enemies of Ingland?
> Had nocht bene the support of France,
> We had been brocht to great mischance.

Post-Union audiences, conscious that their nationhood had been sold 'for English gold', read Lindsay's Anglophobic lines enthusiastically as a new form of political correctness, born of political frustration and guilt by association.

It is important not to oversimplify. Lindsay does not forsake the allegoric high ground entirely. *Ane Satyre* may be, chronologically, the first Scottish literary text which is amenable to the literal, even Realist, approach of most literary historians, but it is still set within the Christian mystery. Allegory, artifice and language as sign do not disappear; they are simply subsumed. The critic must still be aware of this older order and of when the conventions appropriate to it are being invoked. The opposition to England voiced above is, for example, spoken by Folie within the conventions of the French *sottie* form. The seriousness of the point is guaranteed by that artifice, which marked out the inverted world of chaos by giving to madness the words of truth.

Ane Satyre opens and closes with God; a specifically Christian order is achieved for Scotland by a king called Humanitie rather than James V. The just man's achievement pales before the mysterious embrace of the four daughters of God; his end is defined in the words of St Matthew, *Beati qui esuriunt et sitiunt Justitiam* (5:6). Man's body as microcosm shadows the body politic with the king as head, which in turn shadows the divinity. John the Commonweil only returns to Scotland when virtue rules. As a sign of his faith, he recites the creed and so accepts for himself and Lindsay the role of efficient author under the maker of all: *I belief in God, that all hes wrocht, and creat everie thing of nocht* (3,022). Latin and not Scots moves the audience away from play to worship finally (4,672–3):

> Rex sibi eterne Deus genitorque benigne,
> Sit tibi perpetuo gloria, laus et honor.

But *Ane Satyre* could not have gained its iconic status within Scottish literary history had it not been composed in powerful Middle Scots. Linguistically, it shows few signs of those anglicising forces which were already at work at this time and will be discussed in the final section (although some anglicised forms are to be found in the printed edition of 1602). Stylistically, the most noticeable feature in the drama corresponds to Lindsay's prioritising of the particular over the conceptual. Douglas may have begun the movement away from a prosody mirroring moral distinctions to one determined by immediate rhetorical effects; Lindsay – as McGavin has demonstrated (1993: 39–66) – skilfully develops the strategies of localised decorum in *Ane Satyre*.

Rime couée, characteristically a low-style form, is used for a variety of different local effects. These include the general court business of the Parliament and the pardoning of misguided courtiers (1,785–860). The form is even employed by Divyne Correctioun to give a powerful warning to King Humanitie (1,761–8):

> Now, Sir, tak tent quhat I will say:
> Observe thir same baith nicht and day,
> And let them never part ȝow fray;
> Or els withoutin doubt,
> Turne ye to Sensualitie,
> To vicious lyfe and rebaldrie,
> Out of your realme richt schamefullie
> Ye sall be ruttit out.

Ballat royal is predominantly used for high moral purposes, but the length of *Ane Satyre* militates against one consistent prosodic strategy. The normal 'high' stanza as well as the 'low' is subject to a freer system of decorum, derived from immediate persuasive needs.

If *Ane Satyre* continues the Middle Scots artistry of Henryson, Dunbar and Douglas, it is possible to hear bleaker warnings for the future within it. As MacQueen (1970: xvi) points out, Lady Sensualitie may use the rhetorical device of *descriptio* with as much confidence as any contemporary love lyricist (279–82):

> Behauld my heid, behauld my gay attyre,
> Behauld my halse, lusum and lilie-quhite;
> Behauld my visage, flammand as the fyre;
> Behauld my papis of portratour perfyte.

But she does so as a vicious force, whose sensuous songs and erotic imagery are then rejected. The major nurturing force for literary Middle Scots had been the court. Lindsay's drama sings the very love songs which his Protestant Parliament rejects, and so gets the best of both worlds. Soon, in the 1560s, Maitland of Lethington would be lamenting the actual results of King Humanitie's fictive reforms (*Satire on the Age*, 1–4):

> Quhair is the blythnes that hes bein
> Bayth in burgh and landwart sein,
> Amang lordis and ladyis schein
> Daunsing, singing, game and play?

Were the literary delights of the poetic Golden Age of Middle Scots to give way antithetically to a Dark Age characterised by explicit verse sermons written in English, as an imposed, 'foreign' tongue? The fact that the next period in Scottish literature, from the reign of Mary Queen of Scots until the Union of the Parliaments, is practically erased from most anthologies and literary histories suggests that Maitland may not be overstating his case.

7.4   THE LOST YEARS: LATE MIDDLE SCOTS AND SCOTS-ENGLISH LITERATURE (c. 1555–1700)

To assert that practically all histories and anthologies of Scottish literature 'erase' the period between 1555 and 1700 is only a slight exaggeration. The most recent critic to have compiled both history and anthology is Roderick Watson (1959, 1984). In *The Literature of Scotland*, only fifteen pages are reserved for literature from the Castalians in 1580 until the Union of Parliaments in 1707. His anthology, *The Poetry of Scotland: Gaelic, Scots and English* (1959), gives eleven pages out of 711 to the Marian and Castalian periods from 1560 to 1603. Courtly poetry in Anglo-Scots throughout the seventeenth century is not represented at all.

Watson is a good critic, who has the support of traditional practice behind him. It is strange, however, that the period including the Union of the Crowns and leading to the Union of the Parliaments is so superficially treated in a discipline described as 'Scottish'. It is, of course, possible that this is a valid critical reaction to a poor period qualitatively. Scotland is a small country, and the highest standards of creativity may not have been sustained. Before addressing such questions, however, one has to be convinced what the criteria being employed for evaluation are. A brief recapitulation of the conclusions reached so far in this area reveals that entry into the Scottish canon does not only, or even primarily, depend on literary quality. A simplified list of the primary 'entrance' criteria might read:

1. Writing in Scots.
2. Writing on Scottish themes.
3. Writing well.

This ordering reflects first the necessary definition in difference, which, on a more mundane level, relates the Swiss nation to clocks and the Scots to bagpipes. When patriotic differentiation is the prime canonical concern, the danger arises that linguistic (1) and thematic (2) 'correctness' may determine choice. Evaluative literary judgements (3) are only applied to the chosen texts, thus creating a form of cultural antinomianism.

The political dimension of the discipline provides additional criteria. They do not guarantee canonical admission on their own, but may ease acceptance for those authors who do not clearly fulfil the primary demands.

4. (a) Writing in a down-to-earth, direct manner.
   (b) Writing in a politically democratic manner.
   (c) Writing when Scottish literature bears comparison, qualitatively, with English.

Early Scottish writers would have found the demand for directness (4a), which is based on current views of the Scottish psyche and the political desire for clarity, aesthetically baffling. For them, the more complex and indirect the poetic artifice was, the more it justified the makar in the specifics of his craft. Democracy (4b), despite some levelling in the Renaissance, was not the pattern of society suggested by the theology or sociology of their hierarchical times. Nonetheless, as a system of checks and balances, applied when Scotland's nationhood was secure, the methodology embraces Barbour and his successors until Lindsay.

Why, then, does it 'reject' the Scottish Renaissance? Essentially, this is because those writers, who might make a claim on grounds of quality in this period, appear to satisfy none of the other criteria at all. Interpretation at the literal level of 'things' according to realist principles in an age which, aesthetically, prioritised concepts, had welcomed most of the earlier writers by hermeneutic accident. The particular tales, which were the early writer's exemplary means, are the political critic's end. So long as they are drawn from a confident nation's patriotic vision of itself, these features will guarantee acceptance. The latent misdirections will emerge only when the sociolinguistic situation changes. This occurs in the later sixteenth century. Late Middle Scots and Anglo-Scots literature appears to tell an unpatriotic 'tale' of surrendered nationhood, linguistically mirrored by the surrender of Scots to English.

To the mannerism and courtliness, shared with their Early Scots and Middle Scots predecessors, the writers of the later sixteenth century and the seventeenth are also unfortunate enough to compose in rivalry with England's Golden Age of Shakespeare and Milton (4c). These competitive models are founded on twentieth-century views of nationhood and art to which they did not subscribe.

A truly ridiculous situation emerges. The Scottish court poets of the later sixteenth and the seventeenth centuries are condemned by those intent on charting Scottish literary history, yet accepted into the British canon in competition with the finest English writers. Most judges rank such courtly poets as Alexander Scott (c. 1515–83), Alexander Montgomerie (c. 1545–97) and William Drummond (1585–1649) as strong writers of the second rank. Some accord to the first fictive prose writer in Scotland, Sir Thomas Urquhart (1611–60), the status of wayward genius. These authors are less highly regarded within Scottish literary histories because their names are associated with anglicisation. In *The New Oxford Book of Seventeenth-Century Verse*, twenty-seven of Drummond's works are included. In the period of Donne, the Scottish courtly writers, who are almost entirely obliterated in most Scottish anthologies, warrant thirty-four pages in competition with Shakespeare and Jonson (Fowler 1991).

Modern assumptions about the proper patriotic language for literary expressions are the major reason for this state of affairs. If one assumes that writing in Scots is the only linguistic sign of patriotic intent, then Drummond has scant claim to be regarded as a Scottish writer (G. Simpson 1975: 41). Anglicisers, on this view, must be literary traitors, the cultural equivalents of Burns's *parcel o' rogues in a nation*, selling out to England. But this is to assume that the same sociolinguistic pressures, the same nationalist concerns and the same hierarchy of aesthetic values pertain then as now. They do not. Nor does Dunbar write from the same linguistic, political and artistic viewpoint as James VI. What modifications and warnings does diachronic study offer to those who wish to canonise or ostracise by Scots alone?

The traditional principles for canonical selection challenge the critic to consider carefully the linguistic, thematic and aesthetic grounds on which such judgements are based.

1. Writing in Scots invites discussion on the literary language. This discussion will focus on the two 'villains' of the period, John Knox (c. 1513–72) and King James VI (1566–1625).

2. Writing on Scots themes relates that linguistic definition to the imaginative expression of specifically 'Scottish' themes and concerns. Drummond and the Latin writers will be the centre of this examination.

3. Writing well involves defining an interpretive procedure based on these findings, which works in sympathy with the aesthetic priorities of the time. The verse of Montgomerie and John Stewart of Baldynneis (c. 1550 to c. 1605) as well as the prose of Urquhart will test the range of issues implied under that heading.

The aim is not to replace the 'political' canon but to urge that critics state clearly their own evaluative priorities. This is the carefulness urged by Boethius. In Book 5 of the *Consolation*, he stressed the importance of defining 'how' one perceived before examining 'what' was being viewed. Such a strategy, in this case, reveals the degree to which critical evaluations and the canon emerging from them will vary, depending on how the proper literary language or languages of Scotland is or are defined and on whether a synchronic or diachronic approach is adopted.

7.5 LINGUISTIC ISSUES: JOHN KNOX AND JAMES VI

The dual assumption made by most Scottish literary historians is that Middle Scots represents an achieved *state* of the literary language and that an author who uses Scots is making an ethnically significant move. Diachronic study of Scots as *process* has revealed that it emerges historically as an English dialect and is constantly redefined by changing social pressures. The first literary suggestion that use of Scots is a reliable sign of patriotic intent occurs in the sixteenth century with Douglas. In that case, the nationalist argument is modally confined to translation, and plain Scots emerges as the middle style within a decorously comprehensive vision of language. How does this view of language as decorous process modify the popular view that Knox and James VI sold their Middle Scots inheritance for English?

For the earlier period and Knox, the most important sociolinguistic change is the invention of the printing press. As most printing was done in London or abroad, this further destabilised all modes of written Middle Scots (G. Simpson 1975: 41). So, when the reformer appears to anglicise in the Geneva edition of *The First Blast of the Trumpet against the Monstruous Regiment of Women*, it is quite possible that some or all of the changes are made in the printing house (Jack 1981: 239–51):

> For this present, I say, that the erecting of a Woman to that honor is not onely to invert the ordre which God hath established, but also it is to defile, pollute, and prophane (so farre as in man lieth) the throne and seat of God, whiche he hath sanctified, and apointed for man onely, in the course of this wretched life, to occupie and possesse as his ministre and lieutenant, secluding from the same all women, as before is expressed. (*First Blast*, IV. 397).

Morphologically, English forms dominate. English *-(e)th* third person singular present tense is preferred to Scots *-is* in 'hath' and 'lieth'. The English past participle in *-ed* is regularly employed rather than Scots *-it*. *Secluding* has the English present participle inflection *-ing* instead of Scots *-and*. Orthography and lexis also show an English bias, with the digraph ⟨ea⟩ preferred to Scots ⟨ei, ey⟩.

Knox had spent part of his life in England, so his Scots may naturally have a hybrid form, analogous to James I's. As a letter to an English correspondent confirms, he also regarded himself as writing more naturally in Scots than in English: *I wryte to ʒou my mynd in Latin, for I am nocht acquyntit with ʒour Southeron*. In the same letter, he notes that the spoken language in Scotland is moving towards English. Scots now is not the same as *the auld plane Scottis* which his mother had taught him (Templeton 1973: 7). Decorously and pragmatically, Knox wished to convey religious truths in the high style to as many people as possible. Anglicised Scots is the appropriate choice on either logic. The Scottish reformer's practice does not, therefore, seem at odds with the rhetorical and persuasive norms of his day. Equally consistent is his more regular employment of Scots forms in his unprinted sermons, where no audience other than Scots is contemplated. It is not, therefore, valid to compare Knox's *Regiment* with, say, Dunbar's *Tretis*, and then equate the reformer's more anglicised language with literary treachery. The changing nature of spoken Scots, the issue of textual transmission, the author's upbringing and decorous propriety are all relevant.

Decorous criteria also encourage a comparison between his historical prose and his religious tracts. Unsurprisingly, different styles emerge, with the 'lower' topic inviting a racier prose. In Knox's *Historie of the Reformation*, he regularly uses Scots words and idioms (Lyall 1988: 146):

> so that from glowmyng thei come to schouldering; frome schouldering, thei go to buffettis, and from dry blawes, by neffis and neffeling; and then for cheriteis saik, thei cry '*Dispersit, dedit pauperibus*', and assayis quhilk of the croces war fynast mettall.

This mixture of forms may be thought of as prefiguring the precariously balanced fate of Late Middle Scots. Seemingly secure in its aesthetic and ethnic dimensions, having reached new heights of literary excellence in the hands of the four great makars, Scots faced the later years of the sixteenth century within a cultural scene every bit as troubled as its political equivalent.

James VI is, for the 'traditionalists', Knox's successor in cultural villainy. For Henderson, whose influence on MacDiarmid and the Scottish literary/critical Renaissance of the 1950s cannot be overestimated, 'Scottish vernacular prose as well as poetry virtually terminates with James VI'. Henderson (1900) assumes that Middle Scots represents an attained linguistic state and measures any 'fall' patriotically against it. James VI, according to this view, wrote in anglicised Scots at the Edinburgh court prior to the Union of the Crowns. He then went south, taking many Scottish writers with him. They submitted their work to an even more stringent system of anglicisation. Scottish literature, therefore, became English throughout the seventeenth century and was only rescued from this fate by Burns and the Vernacular Revival. Not only Watson's anthology but also *The Oxford Book of Scottish Verse* translates this opinion canonically. There, the court poets after the Union are covered within seven pages. The finest poet of the seventeenth century, William Drummond, is represented by a single sonnet, *To Sleepe* (MacQueen and Scott 1966; compare Fowler 1991).

What are the facts? When James assumed the reins of power, the anglicising pressures experienced by Knox had intensified. By a Scottish law of 1579, every householder with 300 merks had to possess a Bible and a psalmbook *in vulgare langage*. Scottish homes contained the English version of the 1561 Geneva Bible. English literature was also very popular in Scotland at that time, while the London base for the printing industry resulted in Scots texts being 'corrected' (anglicised) in the printing house.

As the likelihood of Union speeded up, so did the anglicising pressures. As Jespersen (1946: 52) notes, 'It is self-evident that . . . under a single government, the chances of a common language being evolved are so much the better. The court, the government have occasion for a language which will carry its message to all the inhabitants of the country'. James was aware of the insecurity of the Scots vernacular. In 1584, he composed Scotland's first treatise on literary theory, *The Reulis and Cautelis to be observit and eschewit in Scottis poesie*. This presented a more radical case for Scots as ethnic tongue than Douglas's. Douglas had not sought to stem a linguistic tide moving in the other direction. James opens the *Reulis* by noting that the standard of Scots poetry has fallen. This he relates to the changing characteristics of literature and language, *as the tyme is changeit sensyne, sa is the ordour of Poesie* (Gregory Smith 1904: 208–25). The rise of competitive vernacular movements strengthens the need to define literature in these terms. His critical treatise is, therefore, the answer to Du Bellay, Gascoigne and others. Its purpose is to provide the impetus for a Scottish Renaissance by maintaining the distinctive strengths of that nation's literary language:

> The uther cause is that as for thame that hes written in it of late, there hes never ane of thame written in our language. For albeit sindrie hes written of it in English, quhilk is lykest to our language, yit we differ from thame in sindrie reulis of poesie, as ye will find be experience.

Historically, it is this literary 'villain' who first uses the traditionalists' own argument patriotically to stem the linguistic tide.

As patron of his Castalian band of poets and musicians, James used the *Reulis* to push Scottish writing in certain ethnically distinctive directions. Linguistically, he urged his poets to use heavy alliteration, as Scots was richer in voiced consonants than English. By using the term *literall* (French *lettrisé*) for alliteration, he encouraged another distinguishing tendency. Comparatively, Scottish literature would prefer the Pléiade and French sources at a time when English literature was Italianate. Modally, his most ambitious suggestion was for a unique sonnet form, which would challenge love's thematic dominance and instead employ the quatrain/couplet or octet/sestet division for *ony argumentis . . . quhair sindrie sentences and change of purposeis are requyrit*. He also encouraged translation, the mode for which Douglas had first stated the nationalist view of Scots. One Castalian, Thomas Hudson, records that his version of Du Bartas' *Judith* had been 'assigned' to him in conversation with the king, who found it 'an agreable Subiect' (Craigie 1941b: 4).

The *Reulis* were first printed in Edinburgh rather than London under James's supervision. But does this evidence, seldom mentioned by Scottish literary historians, not make the king's subsequent anglicisation (literary and geographic) even more self-consciously perfidious? The first resolution of this apparent paradox involves contextualising the nationalist line within the *Reulis*. The *Preface*, insofar as it is a political statement, urges distinctiveness; insofar as it is a literary statement, it does so securely within the rules of decorum. Nationalistically, James may set himself against Du Bellay and Gascoigne; in championing the vernacular, he may throw down the gauntlet to his own classical education. But he does so in a treatise which borrows extensively from the very French and English writers whom he identifies as his rivals. Classical sources, most notably Horace's *Art of Poetry*, influence an argument against reliance on classical models.

There is no conflict here. Nationalist rivalry in the real world does not cancel the rules governing imitation and invention within the game of art. Indeed, James's study of Horace influences his account of decorum, making it one of the most innovative sections of the king's brief tract. He accuses Puttenham of conservatism in holding rigidly to the three levels of style as sociologically defined. In the Scottish Renaissance, a much more adventurous programme will be followed. Hybrid levels will be added and the principle extended to cover modes and moods of argument. As a practical piece of exhortation, the *Reulis* are addressed to apprentice poets in the Edinburgh court of the 1580s. This pragmatism can be shown at its most specific by reconsidering the case of Hudson. He is asked to translate the *Judith* not into Scots but into English, because he is an English member of the band. Politically, the emphasis on French sources over Italian is appropriate for a time when the alliance with France was particularly strong.

The conclusion that James's Renaissance is at once nationalistically and rhetorically defined has far-reaching effects. Specifically, it reminds James's readers that neither he nor the Castalians would necessarily feel themselves bound by the principles of the *Reulis* after the Union. A new political situation and a wider audience might dictate different persuasive means and ends for the patriotic 'makar'. Even the supposition that James and his followers anglicised their work entirely proves false. Here is a Scots manuscript quatrain written by Sir Robert Ayton before the Union (Gullans 1955: 138–9; 11. 1–4):

> My captive thocht's perhap's
>   might be redeem'd from pane,
> And thois my mutineris malecontent's
>   mycht freind's with hoip agane.
>   (Ayton, *Will thow remorsles fair*)

This is already an anglicised medium if compared to Middle Scots. Scots *mycht* alternates with English *might*; *hoip* retains its Scots form, *bloode* and *redeem'd* do not. The post-1603 revision continues the process, but not rigorously (Gullans 1955: 139; 11. 1–4):

> My Captive thoughts perchance
>   Had been redeem'd from paine,
> And those my Mutinous discontents
>   Made freinds with hope againe.

Thoughts, *perchance*, *paine*, *mutinous* and *hope* are all anglicising alterations, as is the loss of the apostrophe signing the Scots *-is* form for plural nouns. The preservation of *freinds* could be variously viewed. The form is uncommon in English at this time but not unknown. Alternatively, Ayton might wish to sign a specifically Scottish friendship by imitating Scots pronunciation. This would be consistent with James's own policy, as recorded by Charles I, of retaining Scotticisms in specific, rhetorically justifiable situations.

7.6 LANGUAGE AND THEMES: THE LATIN AND SCOTS-ENGLISH TRADITIONS

Seventeenth-century Scottish court poets unashamedly revised their older verse in this way but did so in a paternalist spirit. With Scots as an additional decorous level in their literary armoury, they saw themselves following a conquering peacemaker-king who would enlighten war-weary England like Apollo. Soon, those who went south were to discover themselves to be victims of their own optimistic mythologising; but most would stay to contribute within the richness of the London-based Renaissance. Literary allegiance rather than national identity dictated alliances. Drummond corresponded with Drayton while Ayton preferred Jonson or Donne. Another group, including Alexander Craig of Rosecraig (c. 1567–1627), returned to rejoin the north-eastern group of Scottish poets whose literary language remained closer to Scots. Homebound poets, including Drummond, regretted this loss of Edinburgh's cultural centrality (Shire 1969). They corresponded regularly with Scottish and English writers in London as a means of keeping up to date.

However, most of the evidence on this varied linguistic picture is to be found in the Latin and Anglo-Scots writings of the period. There, consistent with the principles of decorum, as argued in the *Reulis*, the use of the subtlest available language fittingly 'signs' the high seriousness accorded to patriotic topics. James, with a mixture of political astuteness and rhetorical propriety, had warned the inexperienced vernacular writers addressed in his critical treatise to avoid *wryting any thing of materis of commoun weill* or, indeed, *uther sic grave sene subjectis*.

This was a humanist age, and Scotland's classical scholars were pre-eminent. The two large volumes of the *Delitae Poetarum Scotorum* confirm that Latin remained 'the language of scholarly Scotland'. James's own tutor, George Buchanan, had celebrated the marriage of the king's mother with as much fervent patriotism as Barbour in the *Bruce*. Referring to the race as having endured in common all fortune's setbacks (*tulit haec communiter omnes/ Fortunae gens una vices*), he imagines the 'savage Dutchman' and the 'warmongering Englishman' marvelling at the greatness of the Auld Alliance (MacQueen 1988: 213–26).

Drummond of Hawthornden, writing in English, has no doubt either that the Scots king has been divinely appointed to bring peace to England and so create a Golden Age: *So ever Gold and Bayes Thy Browes adorne, . . . So may Thy high Exploits at last make even/With Earth thy Empyre, Glorie with the Heaven* (*Forth Feasting*, 401, 407–8; Kastner 1912). In Latin, the lengthy titles spelling out James's newly gained power are the clearest evidence of this optimism. One eulogy, for example, hails the king as *Genethliacum Serenissimi Scotiae, Angliae et Hiberniae Principis Jacobi VI*.

Those who remain in Scotland mingle pride with a sense of loss – *Jacobo Magnae Britanniae, Franciae et Hiberniae Regi Valedicens*. Arthur Johnston, appointed *medicus regius* by James, views the loss of a Scottish cultural centre seriously but not pessimistically. His context is consistently European; his mood is that of stoical optimism. 'Scotland loses its best to make the world better', he claims. If Drummond places the nation's immediate loss within a political Golden Age, Johnston moves even higher into cosmological Scottishness. Praising Scot of Scotstarvet in *Ad Eundem* for keeping the muses in Scotland healthy, he gives to Euterpe the positive vision which he will reiterate for Charles I and others (7–12):

> Euterpe: Hic Scoti congesta manu Fergusia cernis
>   Sidera, quae tenebris mersa fuere prius.
>   Tota micat stellis pars caeli dextra, sub illa
>   Sideribus pariter Scotia tota nitet.
>   Sidera sideribus confer: non emnibus illa
>   Astra Caledoniae gentis ubique micant.

'Here you see the stars of Fergus amassed by the hand of Scott, stars which were previously submerged in darkness. The whole part of the sky to the right is flashing with stars. Likewise beneath it the whole of Scotland shines starrily. Compare these stars: the stars of heaven are not for all men; the stars of the Caledonian race shine everywhere' (MacQueen 1988: 213–26).

T. F. Henderson (1900: 268) fended off Latin poetry canonically: 'With this artificial phase of poetry we have no concern'. Since then, there have been few attempts to reverse that view. As a result, the evidence of Scotland's scholarly language is excluded when creating the nation's literary history. Buchanan's drama and Arthur Johnston's verse are only highpoints in an area where Scottish verse enjoyed a deserved European reputation. Johnston's satiric pen-portraits, 'Nosey with the huge nose' or 'A defence of the midwife Iris', for example, bear comparison with the best work in that mode by Dunbar or Allan Ramsay.

The mood of conquering condescension did not last. James remained in England until 1617. When he did return, a dramatised panegyric was read aloud at one of the welcoming ceremonies. While duly noting his political achievements, a Scottish poet, in English, lamented Scotland's sense of betrayal. The voice of the River Tweed makes the appeal:

> Ah! why should Isis only see Thee shine?
> Is not thy FORTH as well as *Isis* Thine?
> (*Forth Feasting*, 383–4)

This patriotic writer is none other than the arch-angliciser, Drummond of Hawthornden. He makes the patriotic appeal in English because, like all writers at this time, he thought of language choice decorously rather than politically.

If the failure to judge against rhetorical criteria results in one form of misinterpretation, the failure to think of literature as a branch of oratory produces another. Drummond's *Forth Feasting* was part of a public performance, while his lyrics and madrigals were composed to be sung. Thus, while a song may look English:

> Like the Idalian Queene
> Her haire about her Eyne,
> With Necke and Brests ripe Apples to be seene,
> At first Glance of the Morne

pronounced by a Scottish voice it would have sounded rather differently:

> Like the Idawlyan Queen
> Hir hair aboot hir Een
> Wi Neck an Breists ripe Epples tae be seen,
> At first Glence o the Morn.

James VI and Drummond cooperated poetically during the British half of the king's reign. They disagreed on many poetic matters, but James's critical emphasis on voiced rhythms in the *Reulis* was enthusiastically supported by the Hawthornden poet.

Another distinguished Castalian, Sir William Alexander, had earlier been chastised by the king on rhythmic and phonetic grounds for writing *harshe vearses after the Inglishe fasone* (J. Craigie 1948–58; II, 114). In the *Reulis*, the king had been especially concerned with the sound of Scottish verse. The technical word which he used to explain this rhythmical dimension of his cultural programme was *flowing*. Alexander must work on this. *Bewray there* (that is, English) *harsh hard trotting tumbling vayne . . . Our songs ar fil'd with smoothly flowing fire*.

After the Union, he would prove that he had taken the royal advice to heart. Introducing his Senecan tragedy, *Darius*, to a British audience, he accepts that some may find his language, *mixt of the English and Scottish Dialects, strange*. To English readers, he asserts his need *to retaine some badge of mine, by using sometime wordes that are peculiar thereunto*. To the Scot, he argues that English is now the more expressive tongue. To both, he urges the value of a unified approach to literary language (Kastner and Charlton 1921, 1929: cxcvi). Later revisions of *Darius* are, orthographically, more thoroughly anglicised. Read the text aloud, however, and sometimes a Scots pronunciation is still assumed. The original line, *Them to out-goe, that nearer wayes would rin* is rewritten with the verb in the English form *runne*. But it still rhymes with *gathered in*. Written signing may aid an English eye, but the piece, in performance, 'flows' best for a Scottish ear.

7.7 LANGUAGE AND AESTHETICS: CASTALIAN VERSE AND POETIC PROSE

Once a decorous view of language has widened the field within which Scottishness may be detected, only one further adjustment remains. The synchronic, political view of Scottish literature naturally seeks to counterbalance that country's currently fragile claims on nationhood by seeking a clear pattern of things which make Scotland distinctive, especially from England. But this not only starts from a different political perspective to the one prevalent before 1707, it also gives canonical priority to the types of writing which were then judged inferior – prose and realism. Poetic indirectness and the crafts of mannerism were the skills valued by the 'makar', not direct representation of lived reality.

As Ortega Y Gasset has argued, in epochs with two different types of art, one for minorities and one for majorities, the latter has always been realistic (Weyl 1948: 12). This is because, in order to judge, say, a soap opera, one only needs to have lived. To judge, by way of contrast, a painting by Picasso, one has to know in addition about art and the means by which the known has been retranslated. To the degree to which Scottish literature is seen as serving a wide clientèle drawn from different disciplines for an essentially political end, to that degree realist art and criteria for judgement will dominate it. The trouble remains that neither the root problem nor the realist/popular view of art existed during this period.

The fact that the first piece of fictive prose written by a Scot does not appear until 1652 supports this view. That its fiery patriotism is expressed unapologetically in aureate English and that its author outdoes Donne in poetic ingenuity is also relevant. Before looking at Urquhart's *Jewel*, however, I shall use two Castalian poets to introduce the critical dilemma. The first quotation is a stanza drawn from one of Montgomerie's religious songs (Cranstoun 1887: 238; 11. 1–10):

> Come, my Children dere, drau neir me,
> To my Love when that I sing;
> Mak your ears and hairts to heir me,
> For it is no eirthly thing,
> Bot a love
> Far above
> Other loves all, I say,
> Which is sure
> To indure
> When as all things sall decay.

This not only looks like a stylised hymn; it *is* a stylised hymn. Yet, in three ways at least, it follows the Castalian *reulis* for a specifically Scottish poetic revival.

First, it is a song. One of James VI's revivalist strategies was to reopen the *sang sculis*, closed throughout his minority by the Protestant government. Second, folk song as well as *musick fyne* influenced the Castalian muse (Shire 1969: 55–66, 139–69). The setting for *Come, my Children dere* is heavily indebted to folk song. Musical considerations led Scottish lyricists to simplify their metres and shorten line lengths; to favour lilting rhythms with short–long line alternations. Third, Montgomerie is also writing in the middle style on a divine topic. James VI's Scottish poetics had suggested a more liberal form of decorum than that proposed for English verse by Puttenham. By not simply equating godly topics with the high style but instead choosing the straightforward middle style as more appropriate for an audience of children, Montgomerie lyrically confirms one of the king's *reulis*. If patriotic intent is to be limited to themes, then *Come, my Children* will not impress. Specific literary contextualisation, however, at once reveals its centrality to the first consciously organised Scots vernacular revival and significantly modifies the oft-repeated charge that courtly literature despised popular influences.

Positive signs may not only be missed; they may be negatively interpreted. The extreme mannerism of James's most faithful poetic disciple, John Stewart of Baldynneis (c. 1550 to c. 1605), is often cited as an example of the court's unhealthy concern with form rather than content. Virtuoso efforts such as his *Literall Sonnet*, in which every line alliterates on a single sound, are used to force home the point (Jack 1978: 142; 11. 1–4):

> Dull dolor dalie dois delyt destroy,
> Will wantith wit waist worn with wickit wo,
> Cair cankert causith confortles convoy,
> Seveir sad sorrow scharplie schoris so.

This particular piece of apparently trivial word-play shows Stewart to be obeying his monarch-patron's 'rule' that the Scots vernacular should emphasise those 'figures of rhetorique and dialectique' which most lend themselves to its peculiar sounds and rhythms. Alliteration, as before noted, was foremost among these.

The Horatian view that literature is not life but language – 'the form of art which uses language alone' – is, however, most spectacularly translated by Scotland's first literary prose writer. For Sir Thomas Urquhart of Cromarty, the 'game' of language is the beginning and the end of the literary endeavour. To suppose that language is a clear mimetic glass on Victorian Realist criteria is, for Urquhart, so obviously fallacious that both the idea and the evaluative method employed to reach it become the target for his wit. Having described the lovemaking of hero and heroine in his romance, *The Jewel*, he defends himself against the anti-pornography lobby of his day by stressing the distance separating the categories of grammar and those of life (Jack and Lyall 1983: 124):

> To speak of her hirquitalliency at the elevation of the pole of his microcosme or of his luxuriousness to erect a gnomon on her horizontal dyal, will perhaps be held by some to be expressions full of obscoeness and offensive to the purity of chaste ears; yet seeing she was to be his wife and that she could not be such without consummation of marriage, which signifieth the same thing in effect, it may be thought, as *definitiones logicae verificantur in rebus*, if the exerced act be lawful, that the diction which suppones it can be of no great transgression, unless you would call it a solaecisme or that vice in grammar which imports the copulating of the masculine with the feminine gender.

Language, being a sign system, is distinct from the objects or ideas which it seeks to 'translate'. 'Words are the signes of things, it being to signifie that they were instituted at first', he notes in the first of a long, itemised list of the attributes possessed by his own universal language, an advertisement for which precedes the romance proper (Jack and Lyall 1983: 62; l. 1).

He identifies the prime purpose of verbal signing as the transmission of concepts and Platonic ideas rather than particulars. 'There is no word spoken which to the conceit of man is not able to represent more individuals than one, be it sun, moon, Phoenix or what you will' (Jack and Lyall 1983: 69; l. 54). The 'labour'-in-frustration of the author involves narrowing the inevitable gap between grammatical and natural categories. As all languages 'since the deluge' (p. 65; l. 18) are fallen media, even the most subtle at its most aureate level is inadequate (p. 67; ll. 29–30). What is needed is a new start working logically with these 'philosophical quiddities' in mind (p. 67; l. 27). Such a perfect language is the one proffered by Urquhart.

The Jewel, by exemplifying in extreme form the different linguistic, thematic and aesthetic criteria adhered to in those days, conveniently ends our own verbal 'journey'. The work was composed and offered to Cromwell after the Battle of Worcester in 1651. Urquhart, a staunch royalist, had been imprisoned. It is, of course, his use of mannerised English prose which sends out the wrong signs to those whose linguistic criteria are ethnic and realistic. Why does Urquhart consider this an appropriate medium? Why does he begin not with the story but with his Universal Language? Why is the creation of such a language an invention of so much importance that Sir Thomas thinks that Cromwell may release him from prison and return him to Cromarty on the grounds of an outline alone? The answers to these questions return us to a definition of literary language grounded on ideas of 'making', 'memorising' and 'moving'.

Within the craft of persuasion, it is the intention of the author which first determines perspective. Urquhart, whose favoured mode is irony, uses the modesty topos to deny patriotic intent. That the author 'is a Scot he denieth not; but that he thereby meriteth to be either praised or dispraised is utterly to be disavowed' (p. 87). This modesty topos introduces a sustained panegyric on Urquhart's genius and Scotland's tendency to produce more heroes per head of population than any other country under the sun.

The major purpose of language is not, however, to transmit particular patriotic claims. That may be the chosen means, but it would never make *The Jewel* worthy of Cromwell's attention. In explaining this, Urquhart anticipates the central argument of this chapter (p. 68; l. 32):

> I must acknowledge my aviseness of opinion from those who are so superstitiously addicted to these languages, that they account it learning enough to speak them although they know nothing else; which is an error worthy rebuke, seeing *philosophia sunt res, non verba* and that whatever the signes be, the things by them signified ought still to be greater worth.

In a period which prioritised concepts and still felt the magical power of words, the literary language is essentially a philosophical instrument, designed to explore ideas. However modern critics choose to organise their own accounts of Scottishness, this was the understanding of all writers before the Union of Parliaments.

Urquhart's pride in having invented the subtlest means 'for futherance of philosophy and other disciplines' (p. 61; l. 71) follows from this rhetorical, 'trivial' perspective. While he does defend the power of individual dialects, his vision remains comprehensive. 'The

French, Spanish and Italians are but dialects of the Latine, as the English is of the Saxon tongue' (p. 65; l. 21). The best language will, therefore, be the subtlest and the most comprehensive. It is that language which Sir Thomas claims to have 'made' (p. 61):

> The Universal Language; wherein whatever is uttered in other languages hath signification in it, whilst it affordeth expressions both for copiousness, variety and conciseness in all manner of subjects, which no language else is able to reach unto: most fit for such as would with ease attaine to a most expedite facilitie of expressing themselves in all the learned sciences, faculties, arts, disciplines, mechanick trades and all other discourses whatsoever, whether serious or recreative.

Poetic, aureate English is the best medium currently available to translate that intention. It would be replaced by Urquhart's new tongue, which must now justify itself in terms of greater linguistic flexibility.

Specifically, as his numbered list explains, it will have more grammatical categories. For example, four numbers, eleven genders and ten verbal tenses lurk in the lexicon which Urquhart withholds pending his release. Will it not, then, be too complex? On the contrary, the logical matching of grammar's categories to nature's has been thought out 'memorably'. As language is still thought of aurally, it is crucial that key images enable the student to retrieve the model. Before creating the lexicon, he has constructed its organisational principle. Instead of the limited image of the tree with its 'two and hundred prime radices', he has made 'use of another allegory', that of the city. This can be subdivided into streets, lanes, houses, storeys and rooms. The procedure has been worked out 'so methodically' that it will be easier to recall than other, accidentally created languages.

Such 'memorable making' applies to language; compare Vinsauf's broader organisational advice to poets that they work out a structure first and develop it in a way that listeners will understand. But the end of the endeavour is, for both, effective 'moving'. Urquhart is, in practical terms, trying to persuade an audience of one. Although he was not successful in blackmailing Cromwell into returning him to his estates, it was not for want of rhetorical exhortation. At the highest level, Urquhart claims to offer the subtlest of verbal signing systems. This form of linguistic patriotism offers a language whose grammatical niceties and verbal profusion will, in the first instance, be available to the best minds in Britain alone. Cromwell's nation will, therefore, be able to resolve divine mysteries and philosophical conundrums first. That is why his complex language has been 'made'.

It has been made 'memorably' because the most accurate transmission of ideas to the maximal number of people is another necessary function of language. As an educational instrument, its easily memorised structure will result in a 'saving of two yeers' charges to scholars' (p. 86). Pragmatic as well as idealistic exhortations are directed at the Lord Protector. Urquhart was not alone in searching for a universal language. Francis Bacon explored the idea; Francis Lodwick's *A Common Reader* (1647) and Cave Beck's *The Universal Character* (1657) are less ambitious attempts. Utopian these efforts may seem, but they do emerge as the logical conclusion of contemporary attitudes to the literary language, its transmission, nature and function.

In asking those whose perspective comes from later periods to think carefully when assessing earlier literature, I am aware of the necessary constraints under which the twinning of 'Scottish' with 'literature' places them. But the vastness of the presumptive gulf separating Urquhart's view of literature, life and language from the traditionalist line makes the *cautel* necessary.

The poets of the so-called 'Vernacular Revival' in the eighteenth century did not perceive the problem facing Scots in defensive, nationalist terms. What concerned them about seventeenth-century practice was the loss of decorous flexibility implied if Scots were to become a proscribed literary option. Correctly, they saw that poetic strengths had been confirmed rather than threatened by the non-establishment, up until that point in time, of one national language for Scottish writers. They did not, therefore, dismiss English language and literature on nationalist grounds. What they were concerned to re-establish was a full variety of stylistic levels within which Scots would resume its full role and govern the narrowing of choice implied by the weakening roles of Gaelic and Latin, the increasing domination of English and printing's adverse influence on the Scottish 'voice' of the aural tradition. That is why Ramsay claims a double heritage from Gavin Douglas *as well as* Isaac Bickerstaff (Ramsay 1944–74: vol. 28). Burns, who praised Murdoch for giving him a full training in rhetoric, will welcome his *Vision* of Scotia and her bards in high-style English, use Anglo–Scots as his linguistic norm but modulate into middle high-style English when moralising or overtly poeticising. Thick Scots and the low style he usually reserves for vituperative comedy in the manner of *Willie Wassle dwalt on Tweed*. This gave Scots writers a potentially wider stylistic range than their English counterparts (Jack 1994: 150–66). Anyone who adopts the same 'decorous' approach when assessing Scottish language and literature before Ramsay will see a continuous, varied and consistently patriotic Scottish literary history emerging to replace the broken line of heroes and villains produced when those 'makars' are assessed retrospectively against criteria that they did not themselves recognise.

Part 2

1700 to the Present Day

8

Phonology

Charles Jones

8.1 AN ENGLISH NATIONAL LANGUAGE

One of the defining characteristics of the Enlightenment lay in its sustained and persistent attempt to achieve a state of national linguistic hegemony. Regional and socially unacceptable forms of pronunciation, and indeed grammatical forms in general, were proscribed, and every possible effort was made to establish linguistic uniformity and conformity. This was to be based upon what was condescendingly (we might even say provincially) seen as the standard metropolitan London norm, itself characterised by the language of the professional and court classes of the capital. Even the Scottish divine George Campbell in his *The Philosophy of Rhetoric* (1776) claims that what he considers to be 'Reputable Use' is represented by the 'conversation of men of rank and eminence', and is to be seen as a national, not regional phenomenon since 'National language' is 'found current, especially in the upper and the middle ranks, over the whole British empire' (1776: 133):

> Thus, though in every province they ridicule the idiom of every other province, they all vail to the English idiom, and scruple not to acknowledge its superiority over their own. For example, in some parts of Wales, (if we may credit Shakespeare) the common people say *goot* for *good*: in the South of Scotland they say *gude*, and in the North *gueed*. Whenever one of these pronunciations prevails, you will never hear from a native either of the other two; but the word *good* is to be heard every where from natives as well as strangers. The provincials may not understand one another, but they all understand one who speaks properly.

At the same time, it was argued that a national linguistic hegemony would bring with it an end to linguistic evolution itself, leaving the standard 'pure' language free from what were considered to be the corrupting effects of innovation and change. The eighteenth-century predilection for 'scientific' attempts at linguistic normalisation and conservation resulted in various (ultimately unsuccessful) endeavours to set up an English Academy on the model of those in France and Italy (Monroe 1910; Freeman 1924; Emerson 1921; Read 1938). Jonathan Swift's *A Proposal for Correcting, Improving, and Ascertaining the English Tongue* – described in his famous letter to Lord Oxford of 1712 – was one of several of Addison's suggestions on the same topic in his *Spectator* (no. 135) article of the same year. The proposal for the establishment of an English Academy Sheridan refers to as 'so noble a work' (1762: xvi), while Elphinston too (1786: vi–vii) embraces the idea wholeheartedly for the opportunities which he thinks it would bring for the establishment of orthographic homogeneity. A fixing of the spelling would, in its turn, be the means whereby further linguistic change (to his mind 'corruption') would best be resisted:

> Dhe Italian Acaddemiscians had set dhe exampel; and rendered dhe eldest daughter ov dhe Lattin tung, consistent and communicative az her parent. Dhey fixed her Orthoggraphy, beyond dhe power ov chainge; and went immediately fardher, dhen even dhe French hav yet been abel to follow. Inglish Orthoggraphy must pas like firy trial.

Other, home-based, Scottish writers of the period also saw the advantage of an Academy model for orthographic and pronunciation regularisation, notably Sylvester Douglas (Jones 1991: 109): 'Indeed the numerous and judicious alterations which have been made from time to time in Italian and French orthography, by the Academia della Crusca, and the French Academy, are sufficient to demonstrate that such improvements are both practical and advisable'.

But it is Sheridan in his *Heads of a Plan for the Improvement of Elocution and for the Promoting of the Study of the English Language* (the sequel to his *Two Dissertations on the State of the Language in Different Nations*) who pleads most eloquently for the establishment of public and private institutions whose function it would be to proselytise the best kind of English pronunciation. Not only do the English lag behind continental European countries in this area, but he also observes how even England's close neighbours have already set up such institutions: 'This practice, which was first begun in Ireland, and soon adopted by the sharp-sighted people of Scotland, in both which kingdoms most excellent effects have been produced from it'. Sheridan argues that the function of these institutions is to improve the general level of reading and writing skills among the young and to provide a model of pronunciation for prestigious social groups, in particular those encompassing the legal profession, the clergy and politicians. The 'excellent consequences' and 'good effects' which would result from the establishment of such language-monitoring institutions, he asserts (1762: 205–6), would be:

> I The establishment of an uniformity of pronunciation throughout all his Majesty's British dominions.
> II The facilitating the acquirement of a just, proper delivery, to such as shall apply to it; and the enabling all such as are to speak in public, to deliver their sentiments with due grace and force, in proportion to their talents for elocution.
> LASTLY, the refining, ascertaining, and establishing the English language on a durable basis.

Attitudes of this kind led to an officially held perception that the unimproved variety of English spoken in Scotland in the eighteenth century was, at best, stigmatised and if possible best eradicated and replaced by some southern, metropolitan linguistic model of propriety. Many Scots writers had considerable sympathy with such views and attitudes. That archetypal Enlightened Scot, Sir John Sinclair (1782: 4), relegates Scots to a subsidiary status, seeing 'the Scotch dialect' as merely 'a dialect of the Saxon or Old English, with some trifling variations' and, while recognising the 'quaintness' of Scotch, not hesitating to recommend its abandonment in the cause of the political and economic advantage of a 'national language' (1782: 1–2):

> To many it seems of no importance, whether this or that word expresses, with the greater purity, a particular idea; and, perhaps, it is of little consequence to any individual, who lives in a retired

or distant corner of the country, in what stile his sentiments are given. His highest ambition generally is to be understood, not to please his hearers. But such as wish to mix with the world, and particularly those whose object it is to have some share in the administration of national affairs, are under the necessity of conforming to the taste, the manners, and the language of the Public. Old things must then be done away – new manners must be assumed, and a new language adopted. Nor does this observation apply to Scotchmen only: the same remark may be extended to the Irish, to the Welsh, and to the inhabitants of several districts in England; all of whom have many words and phrases peculiar to themselves, which are unintelligible, in the senate-house, and in the capital.

Throughout the eighteenth century, attitudes to the Scots language, from Scottish as well as English writers, range from the downright condemnatory, advocating eradication, to the patronising. Quite typically, Buchanan (1757: xv) describes 'Scotch' as 'that rough and uncouth brogue which is so harsh and unpleasant to an English ear', pontificating on the enduring 'foreign-ness' of its users, despite the otherwise civilising advantages of a long-established political and economic union:

> The people of North Britain seem, in general, to be almost at as great a loss for proper accent and just pronunciation as foreigners. And it would be surprising to find them writing English in the same manner, and some of them to as great perfection as any native of England, and yet pronouncing after a different, and for the most part unintelligible manner, did we not know, that they never had any proper guide or direction for that purpose.

For a certain school of eighteenth-century linguistic observer, the speech of the Lowland Scot is generally characterised as containing 'errors' which require correction, or, at worst (and it usually is at worst), as the repository of 'barbarisms and vulgarities'. It is only occasionally that we find appeals for tolerance from a sophisticated observer like Beattie (1788: 91) in the face of a culture which seems totally dedicated to linguistic sameness:

> we may learn, that, as every nation and province has a particular accent, and as no man can speak intelligibly without one, we ought not to take offence at the tones of a stranger, nor give him any grounds to suspect, that we are displeased with, or even sensible of them. However disagreeable his accent may be to us, ours, it is likely, is equally so to him. The common rule of equity, therefore, will recommend mutual forbearance in this matter. To speak with the English, or with the Scotch, accent, is no more praiseworthy, or blameable, than to be born in England, or Scotland: a circumstance, which, though the ringleaders of sedition, or narrow-minded bigots, may applaud or censure, no person of sense, or common honesty, will ever consider as imputable to any man.

Yet even Beattie persists in recommending as the 'standard of the English tongue' what he characterises as 'The language . . . of the most learned and polite persons in London, and the neighbouring Universities of Oxford and Cambridge'. Even so, such an apparently contra-dictory stance serves to remind us that alongside the doctrine of 'Reputable Use' there was also a recognition by many eighteenth-century scholars of the existence of other widely spoken social, regional and stylistic varieties, and of the fact that even the standard language could itself be irresistibly open to temporal change. Recall Buchanan's (1762: 58–9) comment:

> In the English Tongue, as in all living Languages, there is a double Pronunciation; one cursory and colloquial, the other regular and solemn. The cursory Pronunciation, as the learned Mr Samuel Johnson observes, is always vague and uncertain, being made different in different

Mouths by Negligence, Unskilfulness, or Affectation. The solemn Pronunciation, though by no
Means immutable and permanent, is yet less remote from the Orthography, and less liable to
capricious Innovation. We shall observe, however, that although the best Speakers deviate least
from the written Words, yet the more precise and severe Part of the solemn Pronunciation is
seldom used in ordinary Conversation: For what may be suitable and becoming in a Pulpit,
Desk, or on the Stage, or in other public Declamations, would often be exploded as formal and
pedantic in common Discourse.

We can see in this statement a recognition of the fact that linguistic innovation is
unstoppable and that a single prescriptive variety can compromise speakers in certain
social contexts. Even Sheridan (1762: 30), promoting the pronunciation norm 'which
prevails at court, the source of fashion of all kinds', and who sets out 'the difficulties of those
who endeavour to cure themselves of a provincial or vicious pronunciation', nevertheless in
his attitude to non-metropolitan varieties (albeit those of the upper classes) can be
surprisingly tolerant (1762: 34): 'With respect to the rustic pronunciation, prevailing in
the several counties, I mean amongst the gentry, and such as have a liberal education, there
does not seem to be any general errour of this sort'. It is not necessarily the inherent
vulgarity or lack of aesthetic expression perceived in Scots pronunciation which forms the
basis of its condemnation in the period; rather – and this is in particular true of the Scottish
observers themselves – what is stressed is the socioeconomic disadvantage under which a
Scots speaker will find himself (and, we shall see, herself) when unable to produce a
pronunciation acceptable to an English audience. Typically, Sinclair (1782: 9–10) claims:

During the reign of James the First, the Scotch and English dialects, so far as we can judge by
comparing the language of the writers who flourished at that time, were not so dissimilar as they
are at present. Time, however, and commerce, joined to the efforts of many ingenious men, have
since introduced various alterations and improvements into the English language, which, from
ignorance, inattention, or national prejudices, have not always penetrated into the north. But the
time, it is hoped, will soon arrive, when a difference, so obvious to the meanest capacity, shall no
longer exist between two countries by nature so intimately connected. In garb, in manners, in
government, we are the same; and if the same language were spoken on both sides of the Tweed,
some small diversity in our laws and ecclesiastical establishments excepted, no striking mark of
distinction would remain between the sons of England and Caledonia.

Particularly worth noting in this context too are the remarks of Sylvester Douglas, a native
of Ellon, Aberdeenshire, who as a KC at Lincoln's Inn rose to the heights of late eighteenth-
century London society (Bickley 1928):

There are, I believe, few natives of North-Britain, who have had occasion either to visit or reside
in this country, that have not learned by experience the disadvantages which accompany their
idiom and pronounciation [sic]. I appeal especially to those whose professions or situations
oblige them to speak in public. In the pulpit, at the bar, or in parliament, a provincial phrase
sullies the lustre of the brightest eloquence, and the most forceful reasoning loses half its effect
when disguised in the awkwardness of a provincial dress. (Jones 1991: 99)

This point of view is almost exactly mirrored by Buchanan (1757: xv) on the people of
North Britain: 'Their acquiring a proper accent and graceful pronunciation, would
embellish and set off to far greater advantage the many excellent and rhetorical speeches
delivered by the learned both from the pulpit and at the bar'.

Rectification of the perceived defects of Scots pronunciation became a very public and even a political issue in the late eighteenth and early nineteenth century in Scotland. The principal thrust of this corrective movement took two main and interconnected forms. In the first place, there was a serious attempt made to set up what was in effect a Scottish Academy having powers to encourage and facilitate a knowledge and use of some kind of Reputable Speech; as a result of this foundation, there appeared a whole set of pedagogic establishments, set up in several of the main conurbations in the country but most particularly in Edinburgh and to a lesser extent in Glasgow, in which 'proper' English pronunciation could be profitably (in every sense) brought to the attention of those who were socially aspirant. Almost certainly as a direct result of a set of high-profile lectures delivered in Edinburgh in 1761 by Thomas Sheridan and the interest which these engendered in many of Edinburgh's middle and upper classes, the *Scots Magazine* (July 1761, vol. 23: 390) records that 'Notice was given in the Edinburgh papers of July 27, that on the Tuesday following, the plan of a new establishment for carrying on, in that country, the study of the English tongue, in a regular and proper manner, was to be laid before the Select Society. Mention was made of this by Mr Sheridan, on the Friday before, in the last lecture of his first concourses' (McElroy 1969). The Select Society of Edinburgh is described by Henry Mackenzie (H. W. Thomson 1927: 40) as

> A literary, or properly speaking a philosophic society, for they discussed all manner of subjects; initiated and supported by the principal literary men of Edinburgh. The regulations were like those of other debating societies: a subject was given out; if a question of doubt arose, a supporter and impunger were appointed who opened the discussion, and then the members and the few strangers admitted spoke at their discretion.

In 1761 we find the publication in Edinburgh by the Select Society of a special set of *Regulations* 'for promoting the reading and speaking of the English Language in Scotland':

> As the intercourse between this part of GREAT-BRITAIN and the Capital daily increases, both on account of business and amusement, and must still go on increasing, gentlemen educated in SCOTLAND have long been sensible of the disadvantages under which they labour, from their imperfect knowledge of the ENGLISH TONGUE, and the impropriety with which they speak it.
> Experience hath convinced SCOTSMEN, that it is not impossible for persons born and educated in this country, to acquire such knowledge of the ENGLISH TONGUE, as to write it with some tolerable purity.
> But, with regard to the other point, that of speaking with propriety, as little has been hitherto attempted, it has generally been taken for granted, that there was no prospect of attempting any thing with a probability of success; though, at the same time, it is allowed to be an accomplishment, more important, and more universally useful, than the former.

Among its members, the Select Society included such worthies as Hugh Blair, William Robertson, John Adams, Adam Ferguson and Lord Alemoor, of whom Sheridan (1781: 142) rather condescendingly observes:

> And yet there was still a more extraordinary instance which I met with at Edinburgh, in a Lord of Session (Lord Aylmoor), who, though he had never been out of Scotland, yet merely by his own pains, without rule or method, only conversing much with such English men as happened to be there, and reading regularly with some of the principal actors, arrived even at an accuracy of pronunciation, and had not the least tincture of the Scottish intonation.

Nevertheless, some forty years later, the author of *The Vulgarities of Speech Corrected* confidently asserts (Anon. 1826: 224) that 'the English accent can never be acquired; the attempt is hopeless. Scotsmen indeed, who vainly endeavour to attain the English, almost uniformly fall into the Irish accent . . . Accent then must be abandoned as impossible, and English must, by all Scotsmen, be pronounced with the Scots accent'. The Edinburgh Select Society initiative may have been the closest realisation of Sheridan and Swift's scheme to establish in Britain a society for the 'refinement and establishment of the English Language' (Sheridan 1781: 229).

An important part of the Select Society's aim was to ensure that

> a proper number of persons from ENGLAND, duly qualified to instruct gentlemen in the knowledge of the ENGLISH TONGUE, the manner of pronouncing it with purity, and the art of public speaking, were settled in EDINBURGH: And if, at the same time, a proper number of masters, from the same country, duly qualified for teaching children the reading of ENGLISH, should open schools in EDINBURGH for that purpose.

In these aims the Society was largely successful, and numerous pedagogical establishments were set up not only in the capital but also in Glasgow, Dundee and Aberdeen (Law 1965: 144–92). Their existence was widely advertised in the press of the day, testified by the following extract from the *Edinburgh Evening Courant* for 10 November 1781, on behalf of William Scott, author of *A Short System of English Grammar* (1793), *A New Spelling and Pronouncing Dictionary* (1807) and *An Introduction to Reading and Spelling* (1796):

ENGLISH LANGUAGE

> Mr Scott proposes next week, to open the following CLASSES: – A Class for Gentlemen attending the UNIVERSITY – Another for young Gentlemen attending the HIGH SCHOOL – and a third for Young Ladies – The terms of admission will be moderate, and may be known by enquiring at Mr Scott's house, in the Trunk Close, any day between 11 and 12, Saturdays excepted – PRIVATE TEACHING as usual.
> ☞ Mr Scott intends to begin a COURSE OF LECTURES on ELOCUTION, in St Mary's Chapel, Niddry's Wynd, on *Monday the 26th current*, at 7 in the evening. – The number of lectures will be SIX; one lecture to be delivered each Monday till the course be concluded. – Tickets of admittance to the *whole* course, 5s. each Lady and Gentleman; to a *single* lecture, 2s.

In the same newspaper for 12 May 1781, the entrepreneurial Scott assures his potential clients that

> The very great encouragement which Mr Scott has met with in the teaching of English, has determined him to attend more particularly to that branch of education in future; on which account he will give up his *public writing school* the beginning of next August. – Young Ladies and Gentlemen are instructed in a just and graceful pronunciation, at his own house, in separate classes; and, in boarding-schools and private families, he continues to teach English, writing, and accounts.

Proselytisers of the Scots language saw in the foundation in 1780 of the Society of Antiquaries of Scotland (a 'Temple of Caledonian Virtue') another mechanism through which the language's cause could be furthered. Callander of Craigforth (1782: 16) concludes his *Preface* with the following remarks:

We cannot conclude these cursory remarks without congratulating our readers on the establishment of a Society, which promises to revive a taste for the study of national antiquity. The
worthy nobleman [the eleventh Earl of Buchan] to whose truly patriotic spirit it owes its
institution, and the gentlemen associated for so laudable a purpose, it is hoped, will look with
indulgence upon this poor attempt to second their endeavours, in restoring and explaining the
ancient language of Scotland.

8.2 THE NATIONALIST BACKLASH

We should not underestimate the extent to which there was resistance to and even
resentment of the sustained attempt to 'purify' Scots pronunciation from its many
perceived 'vulgarities' throughout the eighteenth and nineteenth centuries. There was a
strong sense in Scottish intellectual circles that Lowland Scots had a long and respectable
historical pedigree and that it had produced an outstanding literary tradition. At the same
time, there was a related perception that there already existed a recognisable, refined and
prestigious version of the Scots language spoken by what might be generally described as
the Scottish upper social classes, a status speech form which was not, as we shall see,
associated in a systematic way with any ongoing tendency to Anglicisation. Many writers in
the period protest that had Scots been left to its own linguistic devices – in a political
environment where Union with England had not occurred – and been unaffected by the
consequent and what they see as the misguided attempts to anglicise it, then it would have
developed along the lines of a classical dialect, with its own linguistic and literary integrity.
Sylvester Douglas stands out as one of the most enthusiastic espousers of this position. He
asserts that the fact that Edinburgh, the 'Capital of the Kingdom . . . After the Union . . .
sunk from that distinction, and became, at most, the first provincial town of Great Britain',
is to be seen as the chief cause 'which completely established the English dialect of our
language as the standard of what is considered as classical' (Jones 1991: 98). However, 'If
the two kingdoms had continued as distinct, as they had been until the death of Queen
Elizabeth, it has been thought probable, that two dialects might gradually have been
formed, bearing that sort of relation to each other which subsisted between those of ancient
Greece: that we might have possessed classical authors in both'. Such a view is still to be
heard at the end of the century: 'Had we retained a Court and Parliament of our own, the
tongue of the two sister kingdoms would, indeed, have differed like the Castilian and the
Portuguese; but each would have had its own classics, not in a single branch, but in the
whole circle of literature' (James Ramsey of Ochtertyre, 1800; see Allardyce 1888: 74).
Alexander Geddes (1792: 404) takes a similar position: 'if the Scots, remaining a separate
nation, with a King and court residing among them, had continued to improve and
embellish their own dialect, instead of servilely aping the English, they would at present be
possessed of a language in many points superior to the English'; and again (1792: 448):

> Had Jammie never seen the Thames,
> Nor chang't the Abbey for St James',
> Edina's Court had nou been fund in
> As geud a plight, as that of Lundin:
> And nowther PIT or FOX had been
> Politer speakers than MACQUEEN.

Clearly, such a position is in direct contrast to that of Sinclair and his promotion of the
benefits of a 'national language'. It contrasts sharply too with the philosophy of Elphinston,

who sees even the English language itself to have suffered a 'corrupcion in her verry vitals', a corruption only to be cleansed by the adoption of his *Inglish Truith*, a representational system to preserve the integrity of the standard and which, if the conditions were propitious and the natives willing, might just also assist non-standard speakers to achieve a linguistic purity (1786: xiii):

> Hwile all endowed widh speech, ar dhus interested in propriety; such members ov dhe Metropolis, az hav had dhe good-fortune, (hweddher from dellicate edducacion, or from incorruptibel taste) ov keeping equally free from grocenes, and from affectacion; hav doutles a chance, if stil but a chance, for purity. But dhe distant hav no possibel chance, unless from repprezantacion.

There can be no doubt that there was another side to the somewhat stereotypical view that even educated Scots themselves considered their usage to be simultaneously im-propitious and vulgar, requiring refinement by some kind of accommodation to a self-proclaimed English metropolitan norm. In the first place, there is some evidence to suggest that what was being advocated by several of the most important pronouncing dictionary-type publications produced by Scottish authors in the eighteenth century was not any wholesale abandonment of Scots language characteristics by the socially aspirant, but rather that such speakers should adopt a type of contemporary 'Standard Scots' based perhaps upon the language of the legal, clerical and academic professions in Edinburgh, or even other large Scottish conurbations (Jones 1993). Indeed, the evidence from James Robert-son's *A Ladies Help to Spelling*, published in Glasgow in 1722, suggests that, even in the early part of the eighteenth century, some writers were prepared to advocate for emulation the prestigious version of Scots pronunciation found in a city like Glasgow (Jones forthcoming). It is interesting to record as well that Sylvester Douglas appears to admit that variation can exist between different kinds of Scots speakers dependent upon the degree of exposure that they have had to 'polite' varieties (Jones 1991: 101):

> Let it be understood however that it is by no means my intention to observe upon all the grosser barbarisms of the vulgar Scotch jargon. This would be an useless and an endless labour. I only mean to treat expressly of the impurities which generally stick with those whose language has already been in a great degree refined from the provincial dross, by frequenting English company, and studying the great masters of the English tongue in their writings: Of those *vestigia ruris* which are apt to remain so long; which scarce any of our most admired authors are entirely free from in their compositions; which, after the age of manhood, only one person in my experience has so got rid of in speech that the most critical ear cannot discover his country from his expression or pronounciation [sic].

Much the same kind of note is struck nearly fifty years later by the author of *The Vulgarities of Speech Corrected* in a section dealing with *Provincial Scotch Vulgarities* (1826: 222–3):

> Many well educated Scotsmen, who move in polite circles in their own country, take a pride in speaking the Scots dialect blended with English, and when this is not done from affectation, and a love of singularity, it can scarcely be reckoned vulgar, though it must require great attention to avoid low and unseemly expressions. It is not with this class of persons, however, that I am at present concerned, but with natives of Scotland, who endeavour to speak English, without any mixture of the Doric dialect of Scotland, as written by Ramsay, Burns, Sir Walter Scott, Alan Cunningham, Galt, and other modern authors; and who in such endeavours mistake errors for excellence

perhaps the group whom the author characterises as the 'vulgar genteel' (1826: 228).

In both the eighteenth and nineteenth centuries, negative perceptions of Lowland Scots were by no means the order of the day, and there were groups of individuals who, far from being apologetic for any perceived 'impropriety' or 'impurity' in Scots, vigorously and chauvinistically advocated its use, promoted its survival and pointed to its long and legitimate historical pedigree. John Callander of Craigforth, in the *Preface* to his *Two Ancient Scots Poems* (1782: 12), commenting on the necessity of producing a comparative Germanic-language dictionary, observes: 'It is high time that something of this kind were attempted to be done, before the present English, which has now for many years been the written language of this country, shall banish our Scottish tongue entirely out of the world'. Like several other contemporary Scots language apologists, Callander appeals to what he sees as the language's pristine state of preservation and originality (1782: 8–9):

> Our language, as it is at present spoken by the common people in the Lowlands, has maintained its ground much longer than in England, and in much greater purity. This must be owing to the later cultivation of this part of the island, and its less frequent communication with strangers . . . we, in Scotland, have preserved the original tongue, while it has been mangled, and almost defaced, by our southern neighbours.

Two scholars in particular stand out among the Scots language chauvinists, both Roman Catholic clergymen, one an Englishman turned Scotophile, the other a native born of Buchan stock – James Adams and Alexander Geddes – both of whose lives spanned the period 1737–1802. In 1792, the members of the Society of Antiquaries of Scotland saw published in their *Transactions* a long essay by the Reverend Alexander Geddes, L.l.D., entitled *Three Scottish Poems, with a Previous Dissertation on the Scoto-Saxon Dialect*. The *Dissertation* is a long justification and history of what Geddes describes as the 'Scoto-Saxon Dialect' (the somewhat similar term *Scoto-English* was used by Zacharaias Collin in 1862), followed by an energetically chauvinistic *Epistle* extolling the virtues of the same. Geddes' outspoken support for Scots is everywhere evident in *Three Scottish Poems*, and he takes the customary anti-provincial argument, turning it against the English language itself (1792: 447):

> Let bragart England in disdain
> Ha'd ilka lingo, but her a'in:
> Her a'in, we war, say what she can,
> Is like her true-born Englishman,
> A vile promiscuous mungrel seed
> Of Danish, Dutch, an' Norman breed,
> An' prostituted, since, to a'
> The jargons on this earthly ba'!

The Scoto-Saxon dialect was until recent times, Geddes claims (1792: 402), 'the general language of the low-lands of North Britain, and is still prevalent among the people of the north east provinces'. He attempts to justify the linguistic integrity of Scots by referring to its possession in equal measure with English of what he sees as the linguistically advantageous 'properties' of *richness*, *energy* and *harmony*. With respect to the first two of these, he demonstrates that his contemporary Scots shows as complex and various a lexical inventory and morphological structure as its English cousin, although it has to be admitted that some of his observations are somewhat fanciful (1792: 420):

The superior ENERGY of a language (independent of peculiarity of stile) seems to consist in this, that it can express the same sentiments in fewer words, and with fewer symbols, than any other, and this, I apprehend, is the just boast of the English. Our numerous monosyllables, rough, rigid, and inflexible as our oaks, are capable of supporting any burthen; whilst the polysyllables of our southern neighbours, tall, smooth, and slender, like the Lombardy poplar, bend under the smallest weight. From this, no doubt, arises the confessed superiority of our poetry; especially of the higher kinds, the *epic* and *tragic*. This, also, gives a peculiar strength to our apophthegms, and to every sort of composition, where strength is a chief ingredient.

Geddes' interest in Scots is not antiquarian or sentimental, but centres on the spoken language itself, disdaining attempts at artificial creation and maintenance (1792: 403):

> Thus, to write Scottish poetry . . . nothing more was deemed necessary than to interlard the composition with a number of words and trite proverbial phrases, in common use among the illiterate; and the more anomalous and farther removed from the polite usage those words and phrases were, so much the more apposite and eligible they were accounted. It was enough that they were not found in an English lexicon to give them a preference in the Scottish glossary

– an observation which might apply today to some groups of Scots language apologists.

It is the English Jesuit James Adams, a native of Bury St Edmunds, who provides the most powerful antidote to the 'pure' English language school. Written in 1799 while enjoying 'the summer's recess at Musselburgh', his *Pronunciation of the English Language* – especially its *Appendix* on *The Dialects of all Languages and Vindication of that of Scotland* – provides a powerful rationale for the preservation of 'non-standard', regional varieties (especially that of Scotland, 'which is so remarkable and original') in the face of the normative, standardising culture of the period. It is difficult to find in the period an Englishman more admiring of what he himself describes as the 'noble race' of Scotland. Following the example of Geddes – a 'learned and reverend Friend' (1799: 162) – in referring to Scots as the 'Scoto–Saxon', which 'triumphs, to the present day, in its contrast with our Anglo–Saxon', James Adams is one of the very few commentators in the eighteenth century who actively argues against the abandonment of provincial speech habits in favour of some metropolitan standard (1799: 159):

> For, if the fair daughters of Scotia laid aside all distinction of accent, and wholly adopted our refined sounds, they would frequently, both at home and abroad, be challenged for natives of our South. How ready are Englishmen to claim every affinitive perfection for their own; and how ready is a Scotchman to give up what genuinely appears not to be his own.

All this in a context where 'the Scotch accent yields in the Capital, and in Universities, to refined English' (1799: 148). Adams' appeal for the retention in Scotland of a recognisably distinct regional usage is persistent and uncompromising (1799: 157):

> The sight of the Highland kelt, the flowing plaid, the buskin'd leg, provokes my antagonist to laugh! Is this dress ridiculous in the eyes of reason and common sense? No: nor is the dialect of speech: both are characteristic and national distinctions. National character and distinction are respectable. Then is the adopted mode of oral language sanctioned by peculiar reasons, and is not the result of chance, contemptible vulgarity, mere ignorance and rustic habit.

Doubtless his insistence on the importance of and need to recognise the status of regional language (especially where it brings with it some kind of claim to nationhood) would have caused English contemporaries such as Kenrick, Sheridan and Dr Johnson (although perhaps not Thomas Spence of Newcastle) to shudder with apprehension. Adams asserts that not only is regional variation of value in its own right, its destruction or even modification under the dictates of a 'national language' is physically impossible (1799: 161):

> The learned, even in remoter days, yielded to the impulse of literary conformity, and now honour the classical English, and perfect it by their writings; but mere local dialectal sound *never should, never will, never can be*, totally removed; the effort would be as vain, and the prejudice is as unjust, as to attempt to change the green colour of the eye in the natives of the Orknies.

Perhaps one of the most important messages to be derived from Adams' writings is his consciousness of the existence of a prestigious form of Scots itself in the eighteenth century (possibly one which was Edinburgh-based), some kind of *regional Scottish standard*, not a 'refined' London form of speech which many Scottish grammarians (and, we must assume, most schoolteachers) were promoting. Adams himself is quite explicit on this matter. While asserting that the 'broad dialect rises above reproach, scorn and laughter', he emphasises (1799: 157) that there is another form of the Scots language, its 'tempered medium' which is 'entitled to all the vindication, personal and local congruity can inforce, by the principles of reason, national honour, and native dignity'. About Scotland, he argues (1799: 158) that 'refined English is neither the received standard of that country, and its most eminent scholars designedly retain the variation; retain it with dignity, subject to no real diminution of personal or national merit'. Adams argues that the Scots 'dialect manifests itself by two extremes. The one is found in the native broad and manly sounds of the Scoto-Saxon-English; the terms of coarse and harsh are more commonly employed. The other is that of a tempered medium, generally used by the polished class of society' (1799: 156–7). The implication of these statements is that the importation of a London standard to Scotland is pointless – even unnecessary – since its own prestigious native norm is already flourishing, Adams claims (1799: 160), in particular among the members of the Scottish Bar:

> The manly eloquence of the Scotch bar affords a singular pleasure to the candid English hearer, and gives merit and dignity to the noble speakers who retain so much of their own dialect, and tempered propriety of English sounds, that they may be emphatically named *British Orators*. In fine, there is a limited conformity in the present union of heart and interest of the two great kingdoms, beyond which total similarity of sounds would not be desirable, and dissonance itself has characteristic merit.

Adams is almost unique for his time in recognising that a 'polite and mitigated [Scots] dialect' and the 'common and broad mode of speaking' the Scots language 'both have their merit, and give room for fair vindication'. Yet his justification and support are primarily based on patriotic feeling and some sentimentality, since (1799: 159) 'every liberal and well educated observer will admit that there is something pleasing in the tempered dialect of the Scotch; that it is graceful and sweet in a well tuned female voice: that it would be a pity, nay an injury, to local merit, wholly to forgo it'. Indeed, not at all unlike Sylvester Douglas, he is willing to recognise that some 'provincial sins' are worse than others (1799: 154): 'every word has some particular twang, or twist discordant with received classical English sounds, and that there is a dialect of dialect in different quarters, and it is this kind of local dialect alone that locally sinks into vulgarity among the illiterate Scotch, and may rank with our provincial corruptions'. This distinction of a 'vulgar/genteel' Scots is also recognised by

Henry Mackenzie (Thomson 1927: 15): 'There was a pure classical *Scots* spoken by genteel people, which I thought very agreeable; it had nothing of the coarseness of the vulgar *patois* of the lower orders of the people'. Interesting too in this context are the remarks by Walter Scott in his letter of 25 February 1822 to Archibald Constable of Castlebeare Park, Ealing, Middlesex:

> By the way did you ever see such vulgar trash as certain imitators wish to pass on the world for Scotch. It makes me think myself in company with Lothian Coal carters – And yet Scotch was a language which we have heard spoken by the learned and the wise and witty and the accomplished and which had not a trace of vulgarity in it, but on the contrary sounded rather graceful and genteel. You remember how well Mrs Murray Keith – the late Lady Dumfries – my poor mother and other ladies of that day spoke their native language – it was different from English as the Venetian is from the Tuscan dialect of Italy but it never occurd to anyone that the Scotish [sic] any more than the Venetian was more vulgar than those who spoke the purer and more classical – But that is all gone and the remembrance will be drownd with us the elders of this existing generation and our Edinburgh – I can no longer say our Scottish gentry – will with some study speak rather a worse dialect than the Newcastle and Sheffield riders. So glides the world away.

It is interesting to record too that this ambivalent attitude to Scots pronunciation is to be found even in works whose principal intention was the eradication of the non-standard. Nearly thirty years after Adams' treatise, we find delivered in the popular *Vulgarities of Speech Corrected* (1826: 222–3) the usual negative view of what it sees as *Provincial Scotch Vulgarities*:

> No Scotsman, therefore, who is above the age of fifteen, or perhaps eighteen, ought ever to attempt to speak with the English accent; for if he do, he is almost certain of going into ludicrous affectation; examples of which are numerous at the Scotch Bar, and among Scotsmen who reside in England. In this way the original native accent may be caricatured, or spoiled, but the English accent can never be acquired; the attempt is hopeless.

Yet at the same time its author recognises the status of a 'non-vulgar' (if hybrid) variety of Scots:

> Many well-educated Scotsmen, who move in the most polite circles in their own country, take a pride in speaking the Scots dialect blended with English, and when this is not done from affectation, and a love of singularity, it can scarcely be reckoned vulgar, though it must require great attention to avoid low and unseemly expressions.

8.3   SOURCES FOR SCOTS PRONUNCIATION: THE EIGHTEENTH CENTURY

We might reasonably expect that the kind of information to be gleaned from eighteenth- and nineteenth-century observers who, by and large, were prescriptive and normative in orientation, would not be of a type directly illustrative of contemporary Scots usage. Such a marked regional form would be automatically treated as 'vulgar' or 'low' and therefore not be seen to warrant a record. Indeed, in the terms of the grammatical tradition of both centuries, we would expect any Scots language materials to arise by default, detailing the kind of usage deemed best to be avoided, with the bulk of the materials selected for the efficacy with which they supported their authors' prejudices and the extent to which they provided models against which forms considered to be correct, elegant and standard could be set. In consequence, we might expect such Scots exemplars as arise to have no more than anecdotal or stereotypical status and to be of very limited use as an accurate guide to actual contemporary usage; our anxieties in this regard being justly heightened given the fact that data are usually provided by non-Scottish observers, or by Scots who saw themselves already 'cleansed' of the worst idiosyncrasies of their North British dialect. We shall see in what follows that such assumptions are only partly true. While it is certainly the case that many English observers are content to illustrate Scots phonetic characteristics through sets of examples which may have no independent status in actual usage, there are nevertheless a great many eighteenth-century source materials which provide an accurate and detailed picture of contemporary Scots phonology. Indeed, in several cases, even where such sources themselves are heavily prescriptive and normative in tone, the pronunciation which they recommend and describe is of a Scottish type – a prestigious Scots usage, the speech of the educated 'middle' classes of the day.

It is useful to divide the evidence-providing materials into six main types, although within these there are overlaps as well as clear subdivisions:

1. short lists and catalogues of Scots pronunciation characteristics, constructed mainly to highlight their alleged shortcomings in comparison with some standard, usually London metropolitan, norm;
2. specialised, innovative orthographies attempting to capture specifically Scottish pronunciation characteristics;
3. spelling books, usually aimed at an audience of schoolchildren;
4. pronouncing dictionaries;
5. grammar books and treatises on grammar;
6. general essays on the nature of language.

8.3.1 Short Lists and Catalogues

Under this heading we can include those sets of brief, anecdotal and often stereotyped lists of Scots pronunciation characteristics, mainly of the kind indicative of where Scottish speakers are 'prone to err'. Although some of these accounts are fairly detailed, others are tantalisingly brief, notably the one provided by the northern Englishman Nares (1784: 212):

> Mistakes in quantity are not uncommon, and indeed a very principal error in the pronunciation of our northern neighbours is that of lengthening the vowels which we pronounce short, and of shortening those which we make long: thus for *heăd*, they say in Scotland, *hēde* or *heēd*, for *tāke tak*, etc.

Perhaps the best known of the more extensive summaries of this kind is John Walker's 'Rules to be Observed by the Natives of Scotland for attaining a just Pronunciation of English', featured in his *A Critical Pronouncing Dictionary* (1791: xi–xii):

> That pronunciation which distinguishes the inhabitants of Scotland is of a very different kind from that of Ireland, and may be divided into the quantity, quality, and accentuation of the vowels. With respect to quantity, it may be observed that the Scotch pronounce almost all their accented vowels long. Thus, if I am not mistaken, they would pronounce *habit*, *hay-bit*; *tepid*, *tee-pid*; *sinner*, *see-ner*; *conscious*, *cone-shus*; and *subject*, *soob-ject*.

Despite the limitations of Walker's respelling system and descriptive terminology, his observations are not without merit and are considerably more informative than the parallel section in Sheridan's *Appendix* to his *A General Dictionary of the English Language* (1780: 61):

> With regard to the natives of SCOTLAND – as their dialect differs more, and in a greater number of points, from the English, than that of any others who speak that language, it will require a greater number of rules, and more pains to correct it. The most material difference in point of pronunciation, and which pervades their whole speech, is that of always laying the accent on the vowel, in words where it ought to be on the consonant . . . for it is in this that the chief difference between the Scotch and English pronunciation consists.

By far the most informative list of North British 'vulgarities' is to be found in the anonymous *A Spelling-Book upon a New Plan*, whose author proclaims (1796: vii) that 'It may not be improper here to set down a few of those words in which the Natives of North Britain are most apt to err, in order that the teacher may be particularly on his guard to prevent the . . . children from falling into these common errors'. Some examples of this observer's perceptions of what constitutes 'Common' versus 'True' pronunciations are set out in Table 8.1. In the course of what is one of the most full and detailed surveys of eighteenth-century Scots phonetic characteristics – the second volume of James Elphinston's *Propriety Ascertained in her Picture* in a section entitled *Anallysis ov dhe Scottish Dialect* (1787: 1–35) – we find a summary (under DHE CONSEQUENT CONFUZION) of what are perceived by its author to be the most salient of Scots speech habits (1787: 11–12):

> Infinite must be dhe confuzion from dhe Scottish interchainge (or coincidence) ov different or even oppozite vowels; dhe interchainge ov *pike* and *pic*, *titel* and *tittel*, az ov *duke* and *duc*; dhe coincidence ov *wake* and *walk*; *walks*, *wakes* and *wax*; *take*, and *tac*, almoast widh *talk*; *bade* and *bad*, almoast with *bawd*; *scarc* [sic] with *scar*, boath uttered *scaur*; *hope* and *hop*, *sope* and *sop*, *note*, *knot*, and *not*; *coat* and *cot*, *rode*, *road*, and *rod*, *toad* and *tod*, *cloke* and *cloc*, or dhe like; dhe vocal gradacion ov *peat*, *pit*, *pet*, *pat*; into' *pit*, *pet*, *pat*, *pot*: like dhe Inglish jargonnic *sat out* for *set out*; or interchainge ov *set* and *sit*, *lay* and *ly*. If *came* and *cam* be equally distinct from *calm*; dhe last, prolonging *a* slender shut, cannot also prolong *a* broad, more dhan can *a* slender open be interchainged widh *a* slender shut prolonged. *Calm* cannot dhen be *caum*, *psalm* cannot chime widh *shawm*, nor *alms* and *aums* coincide. *Salvacion* similarly can no more be strained into' *salvahcion*, dhan into' *salvaucion*.

Elphinston even attempts to provide 'A faithfool specimen ov Scottish colloquial iddiom' (1787: 119–20), what he describes as 'dhe old dialect' (1787: 80) or 'true (dhat iz, braud) Scotch': *Ye'r aw wrang: he's up e' dhe buckel (or weel at hemsal). But I dread he'l gae af at dhe nail wih hemsal: I wos he mayna faw awstaps, or gang a gray gate. He leves on nae deaf nets: he fists at hac an mainger, ev no on wein an wastels. Aw dhes'l coast hem monny a saut tear, though he let na on, an kens I hev sin hez hairt gret afore noo. Its el yoor comon to' spic sae: ev he be en sec a tacking, he spoails (or speils) good (u French) leikly. Bat deed, he woz ey a spelt bairn: nabody cud tal hwat he wod baut, or thought he sud be last at hiz ain haund.* Utilising his own specialised orthographic system, Elphinston asserts that this specimen, 'may run into' Inglish dhus: "Yoo ar all in dhe wrong: he iz wel to' pas, or in good condiscion. But I dred hiz running riot: I wish he may not fall to' pieces, or go to' pot. He livs on no hollow nuts: he feasts at rac and mainger, if not on wine and walnuts. All dhis wil cost him manny a briny tear, dho he poots a good face on it, hwile he knows I hav seen hiz hart redy to' burst before

Table 8.1

Spelling	Commonly pronounced	True pronunciation
Act	Ack	Act
and	ånd	ănd
arm	ārm	àrm
art	ārt	àrt
base	bāze	băce
beau	bew	bō
beaux	beux	boze
card	cărd	càrd
charge	*chārge*	*chàrge*
corps	corpse	cōre
cough	coch	còff
dost	dōst	dŭst
doth	dōth	dŏth
fact	fack	făct
guard	*guārd*	*guàrd*
has	hās	hăz
him	hum	hīm
his	huz	hīz
in	un	īn
it	ut	īt
juice	*joice*	*jûce*
large	*lārge*	*làrge*
laugh	lach	lăff
mourn	mŭrn	mōrn

now. It il becoms yoo to' talk so. If he be in such a case (or such a taking), he belies hiz appearance. But indeed, he waz always a spoil'd child: noboddy cood tel hwat he wood be at; or thaught he shood be left at hiz own dispozal." '

Given his well-attested anti-Scottish bias, Kenrick's (1784: ii) rendering of a passage from Johnson's *Idler*, translated by 'an essayist [who] must be a North-Briton, and not a native of England', must surely smart of parody:

Eezy poeetry iz that in wheetsh nateuril thots air expressed without violins too the langwidsh. Thee diskriminaiting karitir ov eez konsists principilly in the dikshun, for awl trew poeetry reequirs that thee sentimints be nateuril. Langwidsh suffirs violinss by harsh or by dairing figurs, by unshootibl transpozeeshun, by uneuzyl akseptaishuns ov wurdz, and any lisins wheetsh wood bee avoided by a ritir ov proz.

In this genre too can be included the summation of Scotch characteristics found in Fulton and Knight in a section dealing with the *Principles of English Pronunciation* in their very popular and influential *A General Pronouncing and Explanatory Dictionary of the English Language* (1813: xi):

The Scots confound the sounds of the vowels in almost every instance. Instead of Rāce rēed rōad rûde, they say Ràce, rèed, ròad rŭde; and instead of Hat hem hĭll hog, they say HÅt ham hell hòg. This remark, however, applies only to the retainers of their native dialect, for many of the Scots (as well as of the Irish and Provincial English) can pronounce the language as correctly as the most cultivated inhabitants of London.

This probably echoes the earlier list of 'The common and striking differences between the Scotch and English accent' (again containing some of the descriptive ambiguities of Walker and Sheridan) in the anonymous *A General View of English Pronunciation: to which are added EASY LESSONS for the use of the English Class* (1784: 11–12) – ascribed probably wrongly by Alston to William Scott – to which we shall have cause to return below.

Not unlike this too are the comments of one of the most influential of the Scottish grammarians in the century, James Buchanan. In his *A Plan for an English Grammar-School Education* (1770: 44), Buchanan shares the recurring concern of many contemporary commentators for what was claimed as the significance of differences in the 'length' or 'quantity' of vowel segments as a means of distinguishing the idiosyncratic nature of contemporary Scots. Asserting how 'Quantity is the measure of sounds, and determines them to be long or short', he continues:

> I shall adduce but a few examples, out of a multitude, to shew how North-Britons destroy just quantity, by expressing the long sound for the short, and the short for the long; as abhōr for abhŏr, abhōrrence for abhŏrrence, abōlish for abŏlish, thrōn for thrōne [sic], munt for mount, muntain for mountain, funtain for fountain, amunt for amount, tўp for tўpe, cairy for cărry, mairy for mărry, apostateeze for apostatīze, sympatheeze for sympathīze, ceevil for cīvil, civileeze for cīvilīze, cōmfōrt for cŭmfŭrt, eetem for ītem, eer for īre, leer for lўre, breer for brīar, deemond for dīamond, maijesty for mājesty, &c, &c.

Brief and usually anecdotal descriptions of Scots usage and the prevalent attitudes towards it are often to be found too in letters addressed to the editors of periodicals such as *The Gentleman's Magazine*, *The Scots Magazine* and *The Weekly Magazine*, reminiscent of a practice still common in the letters pages of the modern *Scotsman* and *Herald*. It is unfortunate that such eighteenth-century materials have never been fully investigated, since they appear to contain a rich collection of interesting (if biased) data.

8.3.2   Specialised Orthographies

Eighteenth-century writers on Scots pronunciation did not in general develop the innovative phonetic-alphabet type of representation in the earlier tradition of John Hart, Richard Hodges or John Wilkins. With the notable exception of the *New Alphabet* proposed by Thomas Spence of Newcastle in his *The Grand Repository of the English Language* (1775), most eighteenth-century orthographic innovations were not of the type where idiosyncratic and innovative graphic usage were to the fore. In general, most commentators in the century are content to use occasional (standard alphabet-based) 'respellings' which have only very limited value for consistent and accurate phonetic representation. A typical example can be seen in James Dun's manipulation of conventional orthography throughout his *The Best Method of Teaching* (1766). However, there are at least two sustained attempts at modification to and manipulation of the existing orthographic set (introducing a minimum of 'new' symbols) in an attempt to represent (and hence 'fix') the spoken word in a phonetic form. The best known of these (perhaps emulating the anonymous *The Needful Attempt to Make Language and Divinity Plain and Easy* of 1711) is to be found in James Elphinston's two-part *Propriety Ascertained in her Picture, or Inglish Speech and Spelling Rendered Mutual Guides, Secure Alike from Distant, and from Domestic, Error* (1786, 1787), while there is also the lesser-known (but in some ways more phonetically revealing) orthographic method invented by the Scotsman Alexander Scot and illustrated in his *The Contrast* of 1779 (Jones 1993):

> Oy haiv bin cradeblay enfoarmed, thaut noat lass auz foartay amenant samenaurays oaf lairnen enstruck cheldren en ainay laungage boot thaut whoch auloanne ez nidful, aund nurter tham en ainay haibet oonlass thaut oaf civeeletay. Oy haiv massalf tnoan dip–lairned professours oaf fowr destengueshed oonavarsetays, caupable oaf coamoonicatten airts aund sheences auss w–al auz laungages auncient oar moadarn, yet endefferent auboot, aund froam thance oonauquant woth thaut sengle launge whoch ez auboov ainay laungage alz; aund en whoch auloanne these maisters ware tow empairt tnoalege. Foar moy share, oy moast aunoalege oy caunnoat winder ev Cauladoneaun paurents sand cheldren tow Yoarksheir foar leeberaul adecatione, aund paur-teekelarlay foar thaut poalisht *lengo*, whoch ez noat spoc en Scoatlaund.

Not all contemporary grammarians were enamoured of such orthographic 'rescramblings', mainly for what they saw as the adverse effect that these would have in the school classroom. The Scotophobe, William Kenrick (1784: iii–iv), warns that

> this method of disfiguring the orthography is very prejudicial to the learner; who, in thus being taught to speak and read, will forget, or never learn, how to write: an accurate method of spelling words being attained chiefly by reading books correctly printed; in which the word is literally presented in its due proportion of number and character to the eye . . . The celebrated Mr Sheridan has avoided falling into this erroneous practice, and very judiciously proposes to distinguish the sound of words by certain typographical marks to be placed over particular syllables.

8.3.3 Spelling Books

There can be little doubt that spelling and writing textbooks provide one of the major sources of evidence – at least in terms of the quantity of surviving materials – for eighteenth-century speech habits (and the attitudes towards them). Extremely popular in England, the Spelling Book genre is typically exemplified in Thomas Tuite's *The Oxford Spelling-Book (Being a Complete Introduction to English Orthography)* of 1726. It shows sections on the letters of the alphabet, vowel, diphthongal and consonantal sounds, division of syllables, lists of words *Alike in Sound but Different in Spelling and Signification*, and rules for points and abbreviations, the whole illustrated by moral and religious exercises. Although in most instances derivative of English models, the tradition of Spelling Book and Spelling Catechism production in Scotland (and particularly in Edinburgh) was an especially strong one. The contents of these works were often tailored specifically for the instruction of schoolchildren in both private and public educational establishments; as we have already seen, some of these were set up in response to the pedagogic aims of the Select Society (Law 1965: 148–61). Yet, that the tradition was not entirely recent is evidenced by the sustained popularity in the early eighteenth century of James Porterfield's *Edinburghs English School-Master (Being the easiest way to Spell and Read either in English or Latine, that ever was publickly known to this Day)*, first published in 1695.

Not all of the Scottish Spelling Books had Scotsmen as authors, nor were they always specifically describing Scots usage, but it is very often possible to deduce features of contemporary Scots pronunciation from the (often negative) comments which they contain. Spelling and Writing Guides were produced in considerable quantities and from a range of publishing houses throughout Scotland; their popularity (Lennie's *Principles of English Grammar*, first published at the beginning of the nineteenth century, saw an eighty-fifth edition in 1886) and their daily use in the classroom are testified by their scarcity today. The consequences of their prevalence in Scotland itself are highlighted by Buchanan (1757: 6–7) who, after criticising teachers of English south of the border – where 'Great numbers set up for Teachers of English (when they fail in the business they were brought up to) without a preparative education, or being the least qualified for the execution of such an important trust' – proceeds to rhapsodise on the advantages of the Scottish educational system: 'Let us but travel North of the Tweed, and we will find these grand errors in a very great measure repudiated as scandalous'.

As sources for contemporary pronunciation, Spelling Books vary enormously. The kinds of information which they provide can range from the level of the almost insignificant – for instance, James Gray's *A Concise Spelling Book for the Use of Children* (1794) – to one where there is detailed description of phonetic segments, sometimes even in a specifically Scots context, perhaps most notably in *A Spelling-Book upon a New Plan* (Anon. 1796) and *A New Spelling-Book: In which the Rules of Spelling and Pronouncing the English Language are Exemplified and Explained* by William Adie, Schoolmaster in Paisley, published there in 1769. Some of these books make little pretence at providing any significant level of linguistic information, notably the Aberdeen-published *The Child's Guide* (1795) – 'by a Lover of Children' – which is replete with religious materials, prayers and proverbs, a short catechism, graces, psalms, a history of the Bible, Solomon's *Precepts*, a young man's library, examples of the punishments for breaking the Ten Commandments, lessons in arithmetic and a Latin glossary. In his *A Spelling Book*, Warden is unrepentant of this heavy emphasis on Christian materials (1753: xv): 'The *Mohametans* carefully preserve every piece, every loose bit of paper of their *Alcoran*, and why should we be behind hand with these infidels, in shewing a veneration for that book which God himself has penned?' Typical of the more general observations found in the Spelling Book genre is the following from William Scott's *A Short System of English Grammar* (1793: Lesson xvi):

The Little Prat-A-Pace
Leonora was a little girl of quick parts and vivacity. At only six years old, she could both work and handle her scissars [sic] with much dexterity, and her mamma's pincushions and huswifes were all of her making. She could read, with ease and readiness, any book that was put into her hand; She could also write very prettily, and she never put large letters in the middle of a word, nor scrawled all awry, from corner to corner of her paper. Neither were her strokes so sprawling, that five or six words would fill a whole sheet from the top to the bottom; as I have known to be the case with some other little girls of the same age.

Alexander Barrie's otherwise useful *A Spelling and Pronouncing Catechism* published in Edinburgh in 1796 is prefaced by almost thirty pages of religious catechism exercises, containing no fewer than 195 questions and answers of the type: 'Q. "What is the chief end of man?" A. "Man's chief end is to glorify God, and to enjoy him for ever"'. Perhaps not unexpectedly – since it was commissioned by the Scottish Society for the Propagation of Christian Knowledge – James Gray's *A Concise Spelling Book for the Use of Children* (1794) is given over largely to religious materials. Many of the lessons selected for pronunciation and spelling practice have a strong religious flavour, and many pages are devoted to hymns and prayers in this most extensive of all the Scottish Spelling Books.

Instructions to the teacher on the use of the Spelling Book are not, in general, particularly common or helpful, a notable exception being Barrie who, in his *The Tyro's Guide to Wisdom and Wealth with Exercises in Spelling* (1800b: 4), gives detailed instructions to the schoolteacher as how best to use the work in a practical situation:

> After the scholar is well acquainted with the above key, together with the directions prefixed, the teacher may select a few words out of every lesson, as he goes along, and order the scholar to spell them, to point out the number of syllables, and where the accent is placed; to mention the number of vowels, and their respective sounds, according to the key; to point out the diphthongs, where they occur, whether proper or improper, and to give the reason why they are said to be so. Take, for example, the word *Reason. Teacher.* Spell reason. *Scholar.* r, e, a, *rea*, s, o, n. *son.* How many syllables are in it? *Two, rea, son.* Which is the accented syllable? *rea.* How do you know the accent is upon *rea*? Because it is most forcibly uttered in pronouncing the word. How many vowels are in it? *Three.* Point them out; *e, a,* in *rea,* and *o* in *son.* How do you know there are only *two syllables* when there are *three* vowels in it? Because *ea* is a diphthong, or double vowel. What kind of diphthong is *ea*? An improper diphthong. How do you know that it is improper? Because only one of the vowels is sounded. Which of them is it? *e.* What does *e* in *rea* sound like? *e* in *these.* What does *o* in *son* sound like? It is indistinctly sounded, like *e* in *able*.

In much the same vein, James Dun's *The Best Method of Teaching to Read and Spell English,* published in Edinburgh in 1766, provides what, for the genre, is a wealth of information to the prospective teacher on how to instruct the child according to the method proposed by the writer (1766: x):

> The Method I would observe in teaching this little Book is this, I would begin with the Vowels, and teach them by themselves, then the consonants by themselves, that the Child may the sooner know what Letters are Vowels, and what Consonants, and understand, when he is told, there can be no Syllable or perfect Sound without a Vowel.

The author of *A Spelling-Book upon a New Plan* has a thoroughly pragmatic outlook on the role of the teacher (1796: 6):

> In teaching the lessons at the end of the spelling columns, much useful and important information may be communicated to the children, by catechising them upon the facts contained in the individual lessons, as they go along; but this must be left to the discretion and good sense of the teacher.

The importance placed upon the skill and professionalism of the instructor is very clear from Buchanan's (1757: 7) observation of how

> It is common with the vulgar and illiterate to imagine, that any one who can read tolerably well, is surely a person proper enough to teach little children. But the learned and more judicious part of mankind know better; and that it requires the utmost skill and ability in a teacher, to lay the foundation of a child's education, as it is then, the dawning genius can be either strengthened, and properly cultivated, or enervated and utterly marred.

His pedagogic methodology too appears to be enlightened (1770: 30):

> Children should be taught the alphabet, and the combination of letters into syllables, as it were
> by way of diversion; and, in all their progress in syllabification, in order to preserve the genuine
> sweetness and benignity of their dispositions, the teacher will put on the vowels of a parent, and
> instruct them with the utmost mildness, benevolence, and affability.

In general, the intentions of the authors of these Spelling and Writing manuals appear to
have been centred around the enhancement of the linguistic skills and abilities of
schoolchildren, attributes which were themselves perceived as the most appropriate route
to a way of life which was virtuous and God-fearing. Typical are the sentiments of William
Scott in the *Advertisement* to his *An Introduction to Reading and Spelling* (1796): 'the
compiler hopes it will be found particularly well-adapted to initiate young people in the
Knowledge of the English Language, and at the same time to form their minds to the love of
learning and virtue'. But it is in the *Preface* to what is surely the technically best developed
of all the Scots Spelling Books – *A Spelling-Book upon a New Plan*, published in Edinburgh
in 1796 – where we find the educational ideal of the genre expressed:

> The Design of this Book is, to render the teaching and acquiring of the English Language easy
> and agreeable, both to teachers and taught; and to introduce an uniformity of pronunciation into
> the different parts of the country where it may be used, in a manner never before attempted. The
> importance of such an object will be allowed by all. – How far the following Treatise is calculated
> to accomplish it, time alone can tell; – sure it is, however, that the right pronunciation of a word
> is easily learned by a child, as a wrong one: and upon that principle this book proceeds.

It is, of course, tempting to see the underlying intention of the authors of these Spelling
Books as promoting conformity in matters religious and linguistic (recall Perry's stated
intention in the dedication to *The Only Sure Guide to the English Tongue* (1776) that 'the
following Spelling Book [is] intended to fix a standard for the pronunciation of the English
language, conformable to the practice of polite speakers in the city of London'). Nonetheless, there was at the same time a strong sense of the practical social and economic
benefits to be gained from the acquisition of enhanced linguistic skills. After all, it was Perry
who composed *The Man of Business and Gentleman's Assistant* (1774) with advice on book-
keeping, accounts and general business management techniques, a work heavily subscribed
to by the landholding and business community around Kelso and beyond. However, it is
perhaps Buchanan (1757: xii), in his *Linguae Britannicae Vera Pronuntiatio*, who sees most
clearly the social advantage in rectifying non-standard pronunciation at the earliest possible
age:

> It ought to be, indispensably, the care of every Teacher of English, not to suffer children to
> pronounce according to the dialect of that place of the country where they were born or reside, if
> it happens to be vicious. For, if they are suffered to proceed in it, and be habituated to an
> uncouth pronunciation in their youth, it will most likely remain with them all their days. And
> those gentlemen who are so captivated with the prejudice of inveterate custom, as not to teach to
> read by the powers of the sounds, ought in duty, at least, to make their scholars masters of the
> various formations of the vowels and diphthongs, and of the natural sounds, or simple contacts
> of the consonants both single and double, whereby they may form the various configurations of
> the parts of the mouth, and properly apply the several organs of speech in order to speak with

ease and propriety. And as children do not commence scholars so soon as their capacities admit, or often on account of their speaking but badly, if they were taught the mute sounds or simple contacts of the consonants, it would immediately enable them to pronounce with a peculiar distinctness. I had a child lately under my care, of about nine years of age, whose speech from the beginning was unintelligible to all, but those who were acquainted with her manner of expression. After I had taught her the sounds of the consonants, and the proper motions that were formed by these contacts both in her own, and by looking at my mouth, I brought her by a few lessons to pronounce any word whatsoever. And by a short practice, she spoke with perfect elocution. This method effectually cuts stammering or hesitation in speech, either in young or old; especially if a grown person be taught to speak for some time with great deliberation.

The general shape of the eighteenth-century Spelling Book follows a fairly standard pattern. There is normally a *Preface* or *Introduction* setting out the author's intentions and any claims for innovation in presentation and methodology. Here, too, we normally find exemplification of the letters of the alphabet and how they should be pronounced; arguments in favour of and opposing VC and CV alphabet pronunciations are often set out at some length and justified on historical, educational and mnemonic criteria. In his discussion of the teaching of the consonantal components of the alphabet, Telfair, in recommending *eb*, *ec*, *ed* and so on rather than *bee*, *cee*, *dee*, comments (1775: 2):

> Others there are who make the Scholars mouth (as they call it) all the consonants, and pronounce them as much as possible without either a vowel before or after them. This is a very trifling bad innovation: it is a method no ways easier for the Scholars than that of putting the vowel before the consonant; and by making children force out the sounds too hard, it becomes sometimes a cause of stammering.

The bulk of many Spelling Books is otherwise dedicated to lists of lexical items (some invented especially as illustrative material) which purport to demonstrate the syllabic, morphophonemic and accentual characteristics of the language. Nearly all authors, but notably William Scott (*An Introduction to Reading and Spelling* (1796)), the anonymous authors of *A Spelling-Book upon a New Plan* (1796) and *The Instructor* (1798), as well as Gray (*A Concise Spelling Book for the Use of Children* (1794)), begin their handbooks with an illustration of the various syllable combinations which the language allows in monosyllabic words: VC, CV, VCV; this is followed by lists of lexical items (and often ingeniously devised prose *Lessons*) illustrating the same, with the recommendation that these be read aloud by the pupil.

It is in all probability such 'long and useless tables of words' which Telfair criticises so strongly (1775: 2) and which arouse the concern of Warden (1753: vii), who condemns 'the present spelling books, I mean, the tabular part of them' as 'nothing but a confused heap of words'. Perhaps the classic shape of the eighteenth-century Spelling Book can best be seen from a perusal of the *Contents* list of James Robertson's *The Ladies Help to Spelling*, published in Glasgow in 1722. Robertson, 'School-Master at Glasgow', informs us that the 'Contents are taught to Ladies and Gentlewomen by the Author, in *Gibson's Close* in the *Salt-Mercat*, betwixt the Hours of 4. and 6. at Night':

> Of the Various Sounds of the Letters with their Exceptions; Of Right Dividing of Words by Syllables; The Use of Capital Letters; Abbreviations; Numeral Letters; Of Stops and Points; Notes of Direction; A Catalogue of Words, almost equal in Sound, but very much different in

sense and Spelling; Of Missive Letters; How to Write to Persons of all Ranks; How to begin
Letters upon any Subject; How to end Letters upon any Subject; Of Folding Letters upon any
Subject; Of Directing Letters; Of Sealing Letters; A Catalogue of the Proper Names in the
Bible.

The Ladies Help – perhaps a response to the establishment in Edinburgh in 1720 of the all-
female Fair Intellectuals Club (Jones forthcoming) – takes the form of 'A Dialogue betwixt
a Young Lady and her School-Master Concerning Orthography; or the Art of Spelling, &c'
(1722: 2–3):

> *Master*: 'I suppose you can Read well enough'; *Lady*: 'It's but a supposition, for I Read by
> Chance, or like a Parrot – pronouncing words, not knowing, whether the Letters be right or
> wrong plac'd'.
> *Master*: 'You ought to know the different sounds of the Letters, Especially the Vowels'. *Lady*:
> 'That's my great trouble, for sometimes I find the Letters sounding one way, and sometimes
> another, as *tion* frequently sounds *shon*: *tial* as *shall*, *can* as *kan*: These, and many others, are so
> uncertain in their pronounciation [sic], that in Writing, I know not what to Write'.

8.3.4 Pronouncing Dictionaries

Scottish-produced or -published Pronouncing Dictionaries range from those in which there
is provided a minimal degree of phonetic information, almost none of it showing any direct
evidence for contemporary pronunciation, to those where not only is the information
provided specifically in a Scots context, but it is also couched in considerable phonetic detail
and descriptive sophistication. In the first category falls the *Linguae Britannicae Vera
Pronunciatio* or *An English Pocket Dictionary* written by James Buchanan in 1757, while
more reliable and systematically presented phonetic description is to be found in William
Angus' *A Pronouncing Vocabulary of the English Language* (1800a) which includes lists of
'words similar in Orthoepy, but different in Orthography and Signification', such as *adds*,
adze; *burrow*, *borough*; *soared*, *sword* and so on (1800a: 112–14). The bulk of this work
consists of an alphabetically arranged list of words ('which frequently occur') in two
columns, one representing *Orthography*, the other *Orthoepy*, with the phonetic significance
of the symbols in the latter explained in the *Key to the Sounds* (1800a: 7), so that we find
entries such as:

Orthography	*Orthoepy*
abstemiousness	ab-stĕ'mĕ-us-ness
shrewdly	shrûd'lĕ

Barrie's *A Spelling and Pronouncing Dictionary of the English Language for the Use of Schools*
(1794) follows a very similar pattern, with long lists of words arranged under o^1, o^2, a^3 (and
so on) headings, a representational system which he later abandoned in favour of
superscripted accents, acutes, graves and macrons in *The Tyro's Guide* (1800b) and *A
Spelling and Pronouncing Catechism* (1796, 1799).

John Burn's *A Pronouncing Dictionary of the English Language*, published in Glasgow in
1796, is set out in a much more conventional dictionary format, heavily influenced by the
approach taken by William Johnston's *A Spelling and Pronouncing Dictionary* (1764), Kenrick
and Buchanan. His 'characteristical figures' refer to no fewer than seventeen numerical

superscripts denoting vowel quality (set out in his table entitled *Of the Vocal or Vowel Sounds in the English Language* (*Introduction*: v)), placed at the end of the word (in the case of monosyllables and disyllabic words) or at the end of syllables in polysyllabic items, thus: 'Bèat[14] *n* to strike, knock, conquer, rouse, throb' and 'Be[15]lèa[14]guer[1], *v*, to besiege, block up'.

James Douglas' *Treatise on English Pronunciation* (c. 1740; see Holmberg 1956) might also be treated as a type of Pronouncing Dictionary to the extent that it is set out in a fashion which could enable the reader to find examples of the pronunciation of individual vowels, diphthongs and consonants, all alphabetically arranged. The entire *Treatise* is structured on a question/answer-routine basis. For instance (Holmberg 1956: 141),

> How is the Vowel *E* Sounded in the first Syllable of a Word? I The Vowel *E* is Sounded Long in the first Syllable of a Word. 1. When *E* final follows a Single Consonant in Words of one Syllable, as GLĒBE, GLĒDE, HĒRE, MĒTE, THĒSE, SCĒNE, RĒRE, THĒME, BĒDE, VĒRE. *Except* WĔRE which is sounded short. 2. When the Vowel *E* terminates the first Syllable, as, BĒSOM, MĒDIATE, PĒTER, FĒVER, FRĒQUENT, RĒCENT, VĒNAL.

But by far the most sophisticated example of the Pronouncing Dictionary in eighteenth-century Scotland is to be found in *A Treatise on the Provincial Dialect of Scotland* (1779; see Jones 1991) by Sylvester Douglas (Lord Glenbervie). This insightful work has three initial chapters dealing in turn with the nature of sounds and their orthographic representation, the pronunciation of the sounds represented by the letters of the alphabet and a long discussion on the nature of rhyme. However, the section which has the greatest interest for the student of late eighteenth-century Scots pronunciation lies at the heart of the *Treatise: A Table of Words Improperly Pronounced by the Scotch, Showing their True English Pronunciation* [sic] (Jones 1991: 158–233). This alphabetical list of items is unique in the eighteenth century for the way in which it reveals specifically Scots pronunciations, albeit to point out how 'improper' they are, and for the detail of phonetic description and social comment which it incorporates. Consider the following typical entry as an instance of Douglas' pronunciation recommendations:

> ALMOST
> Here the *a* has its long broad open sound, as in *all*, or like the *aw* in *awl*, which two words are to the ear entirely the same. Most good speakers sound the *l* in *almost*. In familiar conversation there are some who do not. The *o* has its long close sound, like the *oa* in *coast, toast*. Of words of this termination some are by the English pronounced in the manner I have just described; some with the short open *o*, as for example, *lost, cost, frost*. The bent of the Scotch pronunciation [sic] is to give both to the *o*, and *oa*, this last mentioned sound, in all cases. I believe the *oa* has constantly the long close sound in England whatever consonant follows. In *cloak, boar* &c as well as in *coast*. This general rule, and some few others in the course of this catalogue, I will venture to hazard, though I have already declared how dangerous I think general rules in every thing relative to English pronunciation. *Cost, frost, lost* are the only words I now recollect terminating like *almost*, where the *o* is short, unless you reckon *crost, tost*, and participles of that sort. But they ought to be written *crosst, tosst*, or rather *cross'd, toss'd*. *Dost* the abbreviated participle of the verb *to do*, is pronounced like *dust*.

8.3.5 Grammar Books and General Essays on Language

There are extant at least three major grammar books composed by Scottish writers in the eighteenth century, works whose primary aim it is to provide an analysis and categorisation of the main features of English syntax (and occasionally morphology) based mostly upon Latin stereotypes (Michael 1970: 9–23). Probably the most important of these was James Buchanan's *The British Grammar* published anonymously (Kennedy 1926) in 1762, written, its advertisement boasts, 'towards Speaking and Writing the English Language Grammatically, and Inditing Elegantly'. The bulk of this work is a treatise on the syntax of English, with lengthy sections on noun and verb structure, including discussions upon case, gender, tense and modality. Rules for concord are set out, and the whole is concluded with extensive exercises upon False Syntax. However, the work has some interest for the historical phonologist in that its *Introduction* contains a discussion of the language's sound system, in a format very similar to that of the Spelling and Writing Books. Buchanan begins with a description of the alphabet symbols and proceeds to examine the various 'powers' of these symbols as vowels, diphthongs, triphthongs and consonants. There is a discussion of syllabicity and the principles of syllable division, concluded by a section on prosodic structure. This overall model is followed too by William McIllquam in his *A Comprehensive Grammar*, published in Glasgow, in 1781 and republished as *A Compendious Grammar* (1789, 1797, 1802). These grammar books are intended 'for the Use of Schools', and attempt to cover much of the ground normally associated with Spelling Books. McIllquam's work is exceptional, however, for its attention to vowel quantity, emphasis and cadence and for its attempts at a derivational morphology together with its detailed examples of the parsing technique.

General treatises on the nature of language are, of course, the hallmark of the eighteenth-century Enlightenment (Dwyer 1987; Michael 1970), and there were several notable Scottish contributors to the type. Not all of these have direct interest for the student of contemporary Scots phonology (Monboddo 1774). But *The Theory of Language* (1788) by James Beattie, Professor of Moral Philosophy and Logick in the Marischal College and University, Aberdeen, contains much sophisticated information on matters relating to pronunciation, syllabification, prosody and linguistic standards.

8.3.6 Miscellaneous Sources

Information concerning matters phonological and phonetic can be found too in the pages of 'near alike' lists and catalogues of Scotticisms, as well as in other, often anecdotal and indirect contexts. Perhaps the best instance of the last is the anecdote by James Adams concerning contemporary habits of Latin pronunciation. Commenting upon the pronunciation *ankshus* for *anxious*, he recounts (1799: 115–16):

> This hissing English contraction extended to Latin words, shews another absurdity in our pronunciation of Latin. In the year 1755, I attended a public Disputation in a foreign University, when at least 400 Frenchmen literally hissed a grave and learned Doctor (Mr Banister) not by way of insult, but irresistibly provoked by the quaintness of the repetition of *sh*. The Thesis was the concurrence of God in *actionibus viciosis*: the whole hall resounded with the hissing cry of *sh* (*shi, shi, shi*) on its continual occurrence in *actio, actione, vicios – ac-shi-o, vi-shi-osa*. Strange, that our great Schools will not adopt the laudable precedent of the Scotch; for we render all the vowels, syllables and words absolutely unintelligible, exemplified in this phrase: *Amabo, Domine refer mihi quae curatio dari possit huic aegro uti cito sanetur, – emebo, Dâm-ine reefur meihei quee curaisho heic eegro dairei pawssit yutei ceito sai-neetur*. This pronunciation would make a French Doctor think the address was abusive, Hebrew, or High Dutch; the first hearing would go far to puzzle the ablest Latin scholar in Scotland, the eminent Doctor Gregory.

The French may laugh at us, not so much indeed on account of the singularity of native pronunciation, as our want of good sense in not imitating their example of tempering the sounds of their own tongue in speaking Latin; for any Latin phrase, articulated by the strict laws of French nasal sounds, monotonous, and final accent, would be equally unintelligible to Italians, Spaniards, Germans, English and Scotch Literati.

A 'Scotch' pronunciation of *sanetur* as what Adams' 'respelling' suggests is [senitur] highlights (as we shall see in detail below) two of the most typical features of Scots eighteenth-century vowel phonology, the raising of [a] and [e] to [e] and [i] respectively.

Many authors of Spelling Books include lists of lexical items which are homophonous or near-homophonous under general titles such as *Words nearly the same in sound; but different in signification and spelling* (*A Spelling-Book upon a New Plan*, 1796); *Words the same in Sound, or nearly so, but different in Spelling and Signification* (Barrie 1794); *Words the same in Sound, but different in Spelling and Signification* (William Scott 1793). In particular, Robertson's *The Ladies Help to Spelling* (1722: 41–62), with 'near alikes' such as *Bruise/Bruce; Bread/Breed/Bred; Brow/Brew*, is especially insightful in terms of contemporary Scots pronunciation and its relationship to a perceived standard (Jones forthcoming).

8.4 THE NINETEENTH CENTURY TO THE PRESENT DAY

The continuation of Scottish grammar book, linguistic treatise and schoolbook writing into the nineteenth and twentieth centuries means that we have a ready source of materials to turn to for evidence of contemporary pronunciation as well as phonological change. At the same time, we have in these centuries too a rich literary heritage in which we can view the perceptions of authors concerning the phonetics of their imaginary Scottish characters. However, direct and professional observation is plentiful and is especially useful in the shape of general treatises, most notably those of James Murray (1873), *The Dialect of the Southern Counties of Scotland*, James Wilson (1915, 1926), *Lowland Scotch as Spoken in the Lower Strathearn District of Perthshire* and *The Dialects of Central Scotland*, William Grant and James Main Dixon (1921), *A Manual of Modern Scots*, William Grant (1913), *The Pronunciation of English in Scotland*, William Grant and Elizabeth H. A. Robson (1926), *Speech Training for Scottish Students*, and A. J. Ellis (1889), *On Early English Pronunciation*, volume 5. Throughout the nineteenth century in particular, the tradition of writing and publishing grammars of all kinds persisted in Scotland, producing reprints and revisions of important eighteenth-century works as well as innovative nineteenth-century ones. In the former category, we have versions of William Angus' *An Abridgement of Angus' Grammar* between 1809 and 1822; his *English Pronouncing Vocabulary on a New Plan* (1805 through 1851); William Barrie's *The Tyro's Guide* (1807, 1815, 1818); and William Perry's *The Only Sure Guide to the English Tongue* (1802) among several others. The doyen of the new Scottish grammarians seems to have been William Lennie, a teacher of English in Edinburgh, who wrote enormously popular works such as *The Child's Ladder* and *The Principles of English Grammar*, the former going through twenty-one editions by 1851 (Volker Mohr: personal communication). Although mainly dealing with syntax and morphology and not always providing direct comment on matters phonological, other important Scottish grammar-book writers in the nineteenth century include Thomas Ewing (1856), *Principles of Elocution*, Alexander Bain (1877), *English Composition and Rhetoric*, Matthew Graham (1826), *The Instructor*, Rosaline Masson (1896), *Elements of English*

Composition, and Alexander Reid (1872), *Rudiments of Grammar*, in addition to works by a number of anonymous writers.

Important evidence is provided too from a group of sources of a type which are recommendatory or even cautionary in their linguistic intention. In particular, we have already had occasion to mention those sections dealing with 'Provincial Scotch Vulgarities' (including the 'vulgar genteel') in the anonymous *The Vulgarities of Speech Corrected* (1826: 222–43), together with the phonetic information to be gleaned from the (mainly lexically oriented) lists of *Scotticisms*. Continuing the tradition established by David Hume's *Political Discourses* (1752), James Beattie's *A List of Two Hundred Scotticisms* (1779) and Hugh Mitchell's *Scotticisms, Vulgar Anglicisms, and Grammatical Improprieties Corrected* (1799), the extremely popular lists of 'Scotticisms' in the period (Basker 1993; Rogers 1991) seem most often to have been the product of abashment at provinciality, many writers systematically expurgating their writings of any trace of what were perceived as Scots characteristics of syntax, morphology or vocabulary. However, the lists themselves provide us with some phonological information, notably in the areas of the suprasegmental (metathesis phenomena) and at the phonology/morphology interface. Notable among the later lists of *Scotticisms* are Cleishbotham the Younger (1858), *Handbook of the Scottish Language* and Alexander Mackie (1881), *Scotticisms Arranged and Corrected, Solecisms Corrected*, together with the various lists to be found in *Blackwood's Edinburgh Magazine* (1817) and *Chambers' Edinburgh Journal* (1847) (D. Hewitt 1987).

The nineteenth and twentieth centuries have also seen the continuation (and revival) of the great Scottish dictionary-compiling tradition (Murison 1972), important source materials being found in the pages of the *Scottish National Dictionary*, Jamieson's *Etymological Dictionary* (1808) and the *Concise Scots Dictionary* (Robinson 1985) as well as *Chambers' Scots Dialect Dictionary* (Warrack 1911), *A Dictionary of Lowland Scotch* (C. Mackay 1888). It is, however, more difficult to assess the linguistic value of the large number of Scots materials which emanate from the late nineteenth and early twentieth-century Scots 'vernacular revival' tradition, in particular the popular journalistic writings found in the *People's Journal* edited by writers such as William Duncan Latto between 1861 and 1898 under his pen-name 'Tammas Bodkin', William Alexander the novelist and contributor to the *Aberdeen Weekly Free Press* and, in the early twentieth century, James Leatham, the 'Airchie Tait' of the *Peterhead Sentinel* and *A Socialist Weekly*. Research needs to be done to determine the extent to which materials such as these (in common with other literary and quasi-literary sources) can be said accurately to represent contemporary regional and social usage, rather than what might be the stereotypical perceptions of their authors as to what that usage might be or even ought to be (Donaldson 1986, 1989). Perhaps in this category too we might include the attempts to represent contemporary speech (*On Som Differences between the Speech ov Edinboro and London*) by the use of specialised phonetic alphabets, for instance Ellis' 'glossic' spelling, although some less systematic attempts (*Scots Magazine*, new series, 88 (1821)) clearly aroused some suspicion (Sprague 1881):

LETTER IN THE AYRSHIRE DIALECT

We hope our readers will be able to make out the sense of the following letter in the Ayrshire dialect better than we can do – a shameful confession, we own, for the Editor of the Scots Magazine. Yet we suspect this will puzzle Dr Jamieson himself.

MAISTER GOLLIZCLYPE

Wow! but I was fain whan I gat a glyff o' your auld-fawsont letter, an' muckle mervait what kin'
o' birkle ye ware ava that cou'd write sae pithily in auld braid Scotch . . .

8.4.1 The Sound System: Vowel Sounds

Using the kinds of source materials outlined in section 8.3, the aim of the following sections
will be to provide a general overview of what were perceived to be the most salient Scots
features of vowel and consonantal production between 1700 and the present day, stressing
the continuity of development which has occurred in the period and, wherever appropriate,
relating innovations in the phonology to the kinds of ongoing changes in the modern
language described in Chapter 12 Our main concerns will be (1) to record those
phonological innovations which characterise the language in the period, notably the ways
in which major vowel processes such as the Great Vowel Shift are manifested; (2) to isolate
the limited sociophonetic information relating to such innovations which are provided by
the sources in the epoch under consideration; and (3) to identify those features and of the
phonology and phonetics of Scots which might be considered as identifying the evolution of
a *standard* Scottish pronunciation type.

For the pre-twentieth-century materials, we are all too obviously constrained by the
quantity, quality and integrity of the data which our source materials provide. For instance,
we do not have access to the types of data which would enable us to distinguish between the
'tempered medium' in Adams' sense and a 'vulgar', more broad variety of the type of which
Sylvester Douglas attempts to rid his readers. The evidence from English observers is
particularly difficult to interpret in this respect, since many grammarians from south of the
border are unable systematically to distinguish regional and social variation in Scots
pronunciation, treating everything as a homogenous 'Scotch'. Probably the best observers
among the Scots in the eighteenth century – especially when it comes to a differentiation
between sociolinguistic and geographic variance – are Geddes, Elphinston, Sylvester
Douglas and Alexander Scot, but even they show gaps which we are only able to fill
with considerable speculative effort. As we have already shown, most of the extant sources
provide general overviews (perhaps stereotypical overviews) of the traits of Scots pronunciation in the eighteenth and (to a lesser extent) nineteenth centuries, notably Walker,
Sheridan and the anonymous author of *A Spelling-Book upon a New Plan* (1796). One of the
few which lists Scots characteristics without subjective comment is the anonymous
Edinburgh-published *A General View of English Pronunciation: to which are added EASY
LESSONS for the Use of the English Class* of 1784, to which we have already referred
above. Using the representational scheme of superscripted numerals so popular in the
century, the author fairly typically provides an exemplar (Table 8.2) for what he sees as the
vowel sounds of English.

In a set of *Remarks*, the author makes two observations upon the idiosyncrasies of spoken
Scots usage:

Remark. The difference between the Scotch and English, in the sound of these vowels, lies
chiefly in this, – that the former confound the $\underline{a}^1$ with $\underline{e}^1$, as $b\underline{a}^1d$ for $b\underline{e}^1d$, and back again, as
$h\underline{e}^1b$-it, for $h\underline{a}^1b$-it; $\underline{e}^1$ with $\underline{i}^1$, as $f\underline{e}^1t$ for $f\underline{i}^1t$; $bl\underline{i}^1ss$ (made a verb) for $bl\underline{e}^1ss$, $r\underline{i}^1d$ for $r\underline{e}^1d$: – o^1
short with o^2 long, as $l\underline{o}^2ng$ for $l\underline{o}^1ng$, and $m\underline{o}^1st$ for $m\underline{o}^2st$.
Remark: The common and striking differences between the Scotch and English accent, is in the

former generally making short syllables long, as bo^2-nd for bo^{1}nd, pri^2-vy for pri^{1}v-y; ta^2-lent for ta^{1}l-ent; te^3-pid for te^{1}p-id: and long syllables short, as po^{1}st for po^{2}st; no^{1}t-ice for no^2-tice; cra^{1}dle for cra^2-dle; ca^{1}d-ence for ca^2-dence.

Table 8.2

	1	2	3
a	hat	hate	hall
e	bet	bear	beer
i	fit	fine	field
o	not	note	noose
u	but	bush	cure
y	lovely	fly	

These statements point to six major and apparently salient characteristics of Scots pronunciation in the last quarter of the eighteenth century, although we shall show that they are all prevalent in the first quarter of the century as well, some indeed 'surviving' into the nineteenth century and even in certain manifestations of the modern language. The alternations in question appear to be between [a]/[ɛ], [ɛ]/[ɪ], [ɔ]/[o], [ɛ]/[i], [e]/[a] and [i]/ [aɪ]. The last would seem to represent what for the moment we might see as an 'advanced' version of the Great Vowel Shift, with diphthongisation of a pure palatal [i] vowel not found in an item like *privy* in the modern standard language (Jones 1989: 281–91). The remaining five alternations all appear to represent height contrasts, not unlike those characteristic of the Great Vowel Shift process itself, but in contexts where the affected vowels do not appear to meet the expected (and necessary) extended length criterion so intimately associated with it. We should bear in mind that for eighteenth- and nineteenth-century observers the descriptive terms 'long' and 'short' do not invariably and simply refer to relative durational characteristics of vowels; certainly the notion of 'long/short syllable' appears to have little correspondence with durational phenomena.

8.4.1.1   Low and Mid Vowel Alternations and Mergers

(a)   The [e]/[a] Merger

One of the major characteristics of what we might describe as 'polite' Scots usage in the eighteenth century – in what Alexander Scot calls the language of the 'College, the Pulpit and the Bar' – was its tendency to show raised (palatalised) versions of front vowels (apparently both long and short), such that we find alternations like [a]/[e], [a]/[ɛ] and [ɛ]/ [e]. Several writers attest such alterations, perhaps most notably Sylvester Douglas in his *A Treatise on the Provincial Dialect of Scotland* (Jones 1991). His entries for the items DRAGON and DRAMA (Jones 1991: 189) are illustrative:

DRAGON
The *a* as in *drag, brag, wagon*. The Scotch, when they aim at propriety of pronounciation are apt to sound it as in *plague*.

DRAMA
The *a* short as in *manna*. The Scotch, in aiming at propriety, are apt to pronounce it as in *same*.

Douglas' pronouncing manual is not aimed at those of his contemporaries who use 'the vulgar Scotch jargon', rather at 'those whose language has already been in a great degree refined from the provincial dross' (Jones 1991: 101). His assertion that speakers use the raised form of the vowel when 'aiming at propriety' is indicative of the sociolinguistic status in an educated and polite Scots context of the [e] vowel; a vowel which is probably one of the most salient characteristics of the speech of those Scots who endeavour to produce the 'tempered medium'. In much the same fashion, Douglas asserts that although the stressed vowels in items like *Saturday* and *Saturn* are to rhyme with the vowel in *share*, which he characterises as [ɛɛ], they are also likened to the vowel in *state*, pointing to realisations like [setərn] and [setərde]. Douglas' uncertainty over the precise phonetic value of the 'raised' [æ]/[ɑ] stressed vowels (whether to [ɛɛ] or to [ee]) as they appear in Scots can be sensed in his NAPKIN entry where, although the rhyme model is given as *Neptune* (possibly with [ɛ]), Douglas in his Signet Library revision of the Advocates Library version of the *Treatise* has scored through rhyming model entries like *nape, cape, rape*, the last unambiguously marked as [ee] (under STAPLE) in the *Table*. Consider data like those in Table 8.3, in which items marked * represent those which Douglas specifically refers to as long, and where items in upper case denote the rhyming exemplars which he suggests.

Table 8.3

Pure dialect	Scotch
[ɑ]/[æ]	[e]/[ee]
dragon	PLAGUE
*Danish	FAME
*famine	GAME
*have	SAVE
pageant	PAGE
camel	FAME
patent	PATE
*plaid	PLAY'D
rather	RATE
ravish	PAPE, RAVE
*statue	STATE
talent	TALE
drama	SAME
garden	CAVE

It is important to observe as well how Douglas describes many of the Scottish vernacular [e]/[ee] versions, notably *dragon, Danish, camel, famine* and *drama* as characteristic of the usage of those Scottish speakers who 'aim at propriety', 'try to catch the right pronuncia- tion [sic]' or are 'aiming at the improvement of their pronunciation'. Elphinston's (1787: 14) record of Scotch *mak, tak, brak, mappel, apel, craddel* and *sadel* forms against English *make, take, mapel, appel, cradle* and *saddel* also seems to point to some kind of low/mid vowel alternation, as do his *garden/gairden, yard/yaird, dazzel/dazel, stag/staig* and *nag/naig* contrasts, among others. John Warden's *A Spelling Book* (1753) probably contains the greatest number of instances of what appear to be [e] for [a] stressed and unstressed vowel forms. His long list of words in Section VI of his *Preface* contains many instances of his three kinds of *a* sound, his sub- and superscripted a^1, a^2 and a^3, stereotypically exemplified by *place*, *and* and *all* respectively. Listed with a^1 we find *era₁dicate*, *ta₁lents*, *a₁bundance*, *va₁lue*, *a₁re*, *na¹tional*, *necessa₁ry*, *a¹bsurd*, *a¹mong*, *era₁dicate*. An [e]/[a] (or occasionally [ɛ]/[a]) merger may be what supports some of James Robertson's (possibly Glaswegian) 'sounding alikes' in his *The Ladies Help to Spelling* (1722), especially in instances like *vann* 'of the army'/*vane/vein*, *said/sad*, *plain/plane/plan*, *grace/graze/grass*, *lace/lash*, *lamb/lame*, *made/mad*, *quack/quake*, *ass/ash/ace*, *add/aid*, *barley/barely*, *cain/can/cane*, *damn/dam/dame*; in this context as well, we should note Cortez Telfair's *waistcoat* and *plaintif* with a recommended [a] pronunciation. However, there is some ambiguity, in the eighteenth century at least, with regard to the social consequences of this [a]/[e] merger. Alexander Scot records this Scots tendency in his renderings like *haibit* 'habit', *pairts* 'parts', *airts* 'arts' – where his ⟨ai⟩ represents [ɛ·] – as instances of the 'present Caledonian English of the college, the pulpit and the bar' (Jones 1991: 102). Other writers regard the usage as vulgar, notably Sylvester Douglas under his entry for ART, ARTIST (Jones 1991: 164–5):

> Pronounce the *a* short and open, as in *start*. The Scotch commonly give it its long slender sound [[ɛɛ]]; As in *fared*, *pared*. They commit the same error in most other words of this sort; as *cart*, *dart*, *hart*, *part*, *party*, *smart*. In avoiding this false pronounciation [sic], care must be taken not to substitute the long open *a* as the inhabitants of the north of England particularly do, in the word *cart*.

In much the same fashion, the anonymous author of *A Spelling-Book upon a New Plan* (1796) records *ārt* 'art' and *cārd* 'card' with possible [ee] or [ɛɛ] as 'Commonly Pronounced'. A Scots [a]/[ɛ] merger is the stuff of much nineteenth-century comment as well, the author of *The Vulgarities of Speech Corrected* (1826: 225) highlighting the phenomenon as a prominent 'Scotch Vulgarity' and, paradoxically, as an affectation of those Scots who endeavour to speak after the English fashion:

> In the long open sound of 'a', as in the word *fare*, similar mistakes are committed, by giving it where it ought not, and altering it where it ought to be. *Latin*, for instance, is pronounced *Laytin*, instead of *Lattin*, *satin* – *saytin*, *habit* – *haybit*, *sacrament* – *saycrament* . . .

(b) The [a]/[ɛ] and [e]/[ɛ] Mergers

However, there is evidence from the period which suggests that the palatalisation of the [a] vowel was constrained as far as [ɛ]. Compare Douglas' APPLE and HARRY entries:

> APPLE
> The *a* must be pronounced short and open as in *tap*, *rap*, *happen*. By the common Scotch pronounciation [sic] this word would rhyme to *Keppel*. According to the proper sound it rhymes to *grapple*.

> HARRY
> The short open *a*, as in *parry*, *tarry*. The Scotch generally pronounce it in all these words with the slender *a* as in *pare*, but shorter.

Here, his 'slender *a*' is [ɛɛ]. Robertson provides only a few instances of this alternation, showing *cattle/kettle*, *vassal/vessel*, *ketch/catch*. By the first quarter of the nineteenth century, such raised values for the historical low mid vowel were clearly viewed as stigmatised, a fact vividly recorded by the author of *The Vulgarities of Speech Corrected* (1826: 226–7):

> The letter *a*, for example, when pronounced short, has properly a sound intermediate between *e* in *fell*, and *a* in *fall*, but a Scotsman endeavouring to speak English almost uniformly mistakes it for the first, and pronounces *bad – bed, tax – tex, lamb – lemb, black – bleck, hand – hend, back – beck, fat – fet, cattle – kettle.* This is miserable and disgusting affectation.

But note that here again (as with the [e] pronunciations discussed in the previous section), for the Scots speaker these raised, 'anglicised' forms are clearly regarded as prestigious, while for the English observer they are 'vulgar'.

Just such an [a]/[ɛ] type alternation is very much a characteristic of many modern Scots regional and especially social dialects. In a recent survey of Edinburgh usage, Johnston (1983a) investigated the speech habits of some ninety-one informants (forty-five males and forty-six females) ranging in age between 17 and 79 and belonging to a cross-section of socioeconomic types. Johnston showed that for these speakers there was a tendency for women of all social classes to lead a change towards a more fronted vowel in items like *cat*, while males of the working and lower working classes tended to realise pure sonorant [ɑ] type vowels. However, in what Johnston calls Localised Edinburgh Scots (as distinct from Standard Scottish English) a raised [ɛ] vowel could also be found (although perhaps restricted to a set of lexical items). Interestingly, these [ɛ] forms – typically seen as upper-class 'Morningside' manifestations – are rarely used by male speakers under 60 years of age and are even avoided by females (with whom the form is usually associated) under 50 years of age. It appears that younger middle-class women are eager to avoid the raised form since it is locally regarded as 'too affected' or at least too much associated with an older generation of female middle-class speakers and thus too stereotypical of a particular social group. A similar situation appears to apply in prestigious Glaswegian pronunciation, where [ɛ] for [a] forms are regarded as 'over-refined' (Johnston 1985a). Although they do so without sociolinguistic comment, Grant and Main Dixon (1921: 44) record [a]/[ɛ]/[ɑ] alternations in items like *glass* and *brass* with an [ɛ] vowel, while *arm, harm, sharp* and *yard* they record with [e]. For the sociolinguistic distribution of this variable among twentieth-century speakers in Ayr, see Macaulay (1991: 44–9).

In the late eighteenth and early nineteenth centuries, we can also find many instances of what appears to be an [ɛɛ]/[ee] merger in Scots. For instance, many of the examples cited by Alexander Geddes as instances of the Edinburgh dialect show ⟨â⟩ (his [ɛɛ]) in stressed-vowel space which we might expect to be [ee] in contemporary polite London English. This ⟨â⟩ Geddes characterises as '*a* slender, as in *fate, nation;* This is plainly a simple sound, and would better be represented by the Greek η. I believe the Scots have but lately adopted it from the English' (Jones 1994: 92), assigning its value to items like *admirâshon, agân, bâr* 'bare', *domân* 'domain', *fâr* 'fair', *fâr* 'fare', *gâ* 'gave', *kâr* 'care', *kâr't* 'cared', *mâd* 'made', *nât* 'native' (but note *náti* 'native'), *plân* 'plain', *rârli* 'rarely', *remân* 'remain', *shâdan* 'shading', *suâin* 'swain', *suzurâshons, tânt* 'taint', *ungrâtfu*' 'ungrateful'. Indeed, he shows more instances of this [ɛɛ] value for standard [e(e)] shapes than he does with those derived from low mid values. Alexander Scot as well gives *adecation* 'education', *trad* 'trade', *laddy* 'lady' spellings where his *a* is most likely to represent some kind of [ɛ·] segment (Jones 1993: 119). In similar vein, we recall Douglas' entry for THAMES (Jones 1991: 227):

The *th* has the sound of *t*. The Scotch, following the analogy of other words spelt in this manner, as *lame, same, blames*, pronounce the *a* long and slender [[ee]]. They make *Thames*, and *tames*, (*Mansue facit*) the same word, to the ear. But in England the *a* is short, and has the same sound with *e* in *ten, hem, pen*.

It is in his CLEMENCY entry that Sylvester Douglas shows most forthrightly the salience of a Scotch predilection for using an [e] vowel in contexts where low front mid vowels might be expected:

The *e* is short, and as in *pen, hen, Pembroke*. The Scotch pronounce it long, and like their sound to the Greek ε; or like the English pronunciation [sic] of *ay*, in *pay, say, a* in *phrase*, and *eigh* in *weigh*. In *delicate, delicacy, indelicacy*, &c there is the same difference between the Scotch and English pronunciations of the *e*. This particularity, like the Scotch manner of pronouncing *bought, sought*, &c, is among the things which are most striking to an English ear, and are generally laid hold of in 'taking off the Scotch dialect,' as the phrase is.

The very fact that Douglas sets aside such a long entry for this word attests to the 'Scotchness' of the stressed high mid vowel in this item, as does the fact that he equates it – as a marker of regional salientness – with those two other peculiarly Scots manifestations: the high back mid [o] in *bought* and the idiosyncratically Scots 'short obscure *i*' in *will, ill* (perhaps, as we shall argue below, some kind of [ɛ̆] segment) in reference to which he writes (Jones 1991: 26): 'It is, however, so sensible to the English, that when they mean to ridicule the Scotch dialect they frequently lay hold of this circumstance, at the same time with the provincial sound of the *ou* in *bought* and *sought*, and of the *e* in *clemency, memory, echo* &c'. Other items which Douglas records with an [e]-type vowel, or one which we may speculate is nearer [ɛ·], include *Helen, jealousy, pedant*. The JEALOUSY entry is particularly interesting, since Douglas observes that 'The Scotch pronounce it as they often do in *death* and as they sound the *e* in *clemency*' (Jones 1991: 203). Since his analysis of the stressed vowel in the former suggests [ɛ], the fact that he appears to equate that segment here with the peculiarly Scots rendering of *clemency* might point to an interpretation of the stressed vowel in the latter as some kind of raised low mid front [ɛ·].

The sociophonetic implications of this Scots high mid usage are hard to assess with certainty from Douglas' comments, although he does rather pointedly comment under his HELEN entry that 'the Scotch do not sound the *h*. And are apt, when they mean to speak correctly, to sound the *e* as they do in *clemency*' (Jones 1991: 201). Such a mid front vowel alternation is also well attested early in the eighteenth century in James Robertson's 'sounding alike' list in his *The Ladies Help to Spelling* (1722), where we find pairs such as *age/edge, abate/abett* and *bacon/beckon*. Elphinston (1787: 3) comments also: 'Hwile *defference* retained dhe false face ov *deference*, no wonder dhe Scots, insted of opening dhe apparently open Inglish *e*, (hwich dhey knew not) called in the French *é* to' dheir *déference*'. Among the *Provincial Scotch Vulgarities* in *The Vulgarities of Speech Corrected* is the observation that words with the ⟨ea⟩ digraph represent 'a great puzzle to natives of Scotland' (1826: 226), who, it is claimed, produce *dayth, bayrd, ayrly, paysant, zaylous* for 'death', 'beard', 'early', 'peasant' and 'zealous'. The author of this highly condescending work is at great pains to describe what is seen as a general Scots inability to handle low front mid vowels at all (1826: 226): 'The short *e* has, in some words, the sound prolonged till it can no longer be recognised by an English ear. A Scotsman will not, indeed, readily mistake this sound in the words *beg*, or *fell*, but he will seldom pronounce the words *bed, leg*, without drawling.'

(c)   The [ɛ]/[i] Merger

Well attested for eighteenth- and nineteenth-century Scots is the still current (though universally stigmatised) palatalisation as far as [i] of front mid vowel segments, Elphinston (1787: 2) decrying the fact that the Scots pronounce *mare* as *mere*, *blaze* as *bleze*, *complain* as *compleen*, *entertain* as *enterteen*. Robertson (1722) provides many instances of this development, notably in the pairs *hare/here*, *chair/cheer*, *bacon/beckon/beacon*, *fair/fare/fear*, *shave/sheaf*, *wane/wean* and even, perhaps with non-diphthongisation through failure of the vowel shift of [ii], in instances such as *lice/least/less*, *nay/neigh/nigh*. This saliently Scots short [ɛ] to [i] raising is also witnessed by Robertson in *beast/best*, *bread/breed/bred*, *breadth/breath*, *dread/dryed* 'with heat', *red/read*, *ear/err*, *heal/hell* and *dead/deed* nearalikes. Douglas (Jones 1991: 28) claims Scots high front vowels for items like *bear*, *chair*, *mare*, *ne'er*, *pear*, *bread*, *breast*, *friend*, *head* and several others, commenting under BEAR how

> this word, to the ear, is, in both senses, exactly the same sound with *bare* [his [ɛɛ]]. The Scotch generally pronounce it like *beer* . . . Many who correct themselves in some words, retain the improper sound in others, and, as there is no rule to go by, they often in trying to shun their vernacular sound, where it is improper, introduce the other, in words in which (like *spear*) the English sound the *ea* in the Scotch manner. (Jones 1991: 173)

This might suggest that [i] for mid vowel pronunciations was a stigmatised feature of eighteenth-century Scots as well, or that it was a regional variant; commenting on CHAIR, Douglas opines: 'Rhymes to *fair*, *care*, *air*. In many parts of Scotland, and by some vulgar persons in England, it is pronounced *cheer*.' It is interesting to bear in mind, however, that on the whole, writers like Douglas and Robertson appear to attach no stigma to [i] for mid vowel pronunciations in items like *bread*, of which the former is content merely to observe that 'The *ea* in *Bear*, but short. The Scotch pronounce it as *breed*.' Adams (1799: 152–3) contends that, in the Scots dialect, a palatalisation of [ɛ] to some kind of [i] occurs, especially in pre-nasal contexts, thus he represents *send* and *end* by ⟨seend⟩ and ⟨eend⟩.

8.4.1.2   Lowering and Centring of High Front Vowels

One of the most widely and regularly observed features of eighteenth-century Scots pronunciation is the tendency to realise stressed high front vowels like [i] and [ɪ] as segments which are more central and somewhat lower. Although we do not have the kind of data to enable us to make a precise phonetic identification, this lowering and centring perhaps resulted in a sound not so palatal as [i̵] and yet not so sonorant as [ə], some more central [i̵] or even [ə], a mid central unrounded vowel. Alternatively, as we shall argue below, it is possible that some kind of [ɛ] segment may be involved (Jones 1996: 121). It is under his FILL entry (Jones 1991: 193–4) that Sylvester Douglas makes the important observation that

> As there is only a slight shade, or gradation, between the Scotch method of sounding the *i*, in *fill*, *fit*, *wit* &c and the English, the difference generally escapes the attention of Scotchmen who are endeavouring to mend their pronunciation [sic]. It is however so sensible to the English, that when they mean to ridicule the Scotch dialect they frequently lay hold of this circumstance. . . . Indeed, as caricature adds to the ridicule in all sorts of mimicry the English in their imitation

exaggerate the Scotch pronounciation of the short *i*, and turn it into the obscure *u* or *a*. '*What's your wull?*' '*You have a great deal of wat*'. (Jones 1991: 194)

Perhaps it is some lowered/centred value which is referred to in the 'Commonly Pronounced' *hum, hus, un, uz* and *ut* respellings for the 'True' *hĭm, hĭz, ĭn, ĭz* and *ĭt* in the list of 'those words in which the Natives of North Britain are most apt to err' of *A Spelling-Book upon a New Plan* (1796: vii). Perhaps, too, it is the same phenomenon which is the subject of Elphinston's comment on the vagaries of what he calls the 'Scotch interchainge' (1787: 3): 'Evvery sound becoms dhus anoddher (almoast anny oddher) sound: *hwip* hwop; *lodge* ludge; *trudge*, trodge; *joggel*, juggel or shuggel; *jostel*, justel; *rustel*, ristel; *summer* and *winter*, semmer and wonter . . .'. The lowered/centralised variant is in fact attested by the majority of observers in the eighteenth century, with, for example, Adams (1799: 152) noting Scots '*Hell, mell, tell*; and *hull, mull, tull . . . fust*' matching what he calls his English short *i*² types such as '*still, mill . . . mist, fist*'. Robertson's (1722: 41ff.) near-homophonous group: *tip* 'the End'/*type* 'Figure'/*tup* 'a Ram'; *Bill/bell/bull*; *treble/ trouble/triple*; *sin/sons/sun*; *big/beg* and *quince/quench* might with some justification be interpreted as instances where the [ɪ] has been lowered and centralised. It is interesting to notice how the lowered/centralised version of [ɪ] was still seen as a peculiarly Scottish phenomenon in the nineteenth century and discussed in terms not unlike those of Douglas a century earlier. Recall Murray's (1873: 108) observations:

> Many years ago I read some remarks, by a southern critic, on the pulpit oratory of the late Dr Chalmers, in which the pronunciation of that divine was given as 'Let *hum* that is *fulthy* be *fulthy stull*.' With my Scotch value of *u*, I read the words italicised, as (Hɜm, fɜlthi, stɜl), and knowing that this was *not* the pronunciation of Dr Chalmers, I resented the caricature as a libel upon my native tongue. Acquaintance with southern English habits of utterance has since shewn me that the London critic attached a different meaning to his spelling from that which I did, and only intended to give the Scottish pronunciation, as (Həm, fəlthi, stəl), which he perhaps heard. Even if the sound really given were (hem, felth*i*, stel), with a 'Scotch accent', it would be so far from the English (Hĭm, fĭlth*i*, st*i*l) as to seem to a Londoner more like his *hum, fulthy, stull*, than anything else.

Since such a lowered/centralised vowel was such an extremely salient Scots form, it may also have been the case that it had come to be considered in Scotland itself as in some way stigmatised. A pronunciation guide for young ladies of social standing like Robertson's may well have sought to avoid such a shape, recommending instead forms which, although purely Scots, were regarded as acceptable and even standard for certain social groups. Consequently, we might speculate that the [ɪ] segment, rather than become lowered/ centralised, might – in certain contexts and with particular lexical items – undergo some kind of hypercorrection to be raised and fronted. A phenomenon like this might be what Walker describes in his 'Rules to be Observed by the Natives of Scotland for attaining a just Pronunciation of English' in his *A Critical Pronouncing Dictionary* (1791: xi–xii): 'if I am not mistaken, they would pronounce . . . *sinner, see-ner*'. Buchanan (1770: 45) too criticises Scots pronunciation in the way that it 'confuses' short for long, and vice versa: 'I shall adduce but a few examples, out of a multitude, to shew how North-Britons destroy just quantity, by expressing the long sound for the short, and the short for the long; . . . as *ceevil* for *cĭvil*'. At the same time, Sylvester Douglas' HIS entry (Jones 1991: 202) suggests a similar close-to-pure palatal realisation of the item's vowel space: 'At Edinburgh, and in the adjoining counties, this pronoun instead of being made to rhyme to *is*, is pronounced as if written *hees'*. The tendency of Scots to raise and front the [ɪ] segment is noted too by Murray (1873: 104); commenting on the pronunciation in Southern Scots of the 'High Front Wide' (Paleotype *i*) [an [ɪ] sound], he asserts:

> In deference to the opinions of Mr Ellis and Mr Melville Bell, I identify the unaccented *ie*, *i*, in bònni*e*, marri*e*t, fytti*t*, lassi*s*, lassi*e*s, with the English short *i*, *y*, in man*y*, marri*e*d, benef*i*t, Harr*i*s, merce*i*s. My own appreciation of the sound would lead me to refer it rather to the short of No. 1, the French *i* in fi*ni*, and the Scotch *ei* in fe*i*t. At least when the sound is emphasised or artificially prolonged, it seems to become pure *ee*, as *cun-tree* in singing, which is different from the English cun-try; and I think the Southern Scotch sound must at least be considered a closer or less 'wide' variety of *(i)* than the English *i* in *it*.

This [i]/[ɪ] alternation is one of the most common Scotticisms observed by Sylvester Douglas, although often characterised as 'vernacular' rather than 'vulgar', suggesting that it has sociolinguistic prestige in a Scottish context. His LIBERTY entry recommends an '*i* short', with 'The Scotch are apt to give it the long vocal sound of *e*, or *ee* as in *leer*, *leave*; *sieve* rhymes to *give*. This is the vernacular Scotch pronunciation [sic]; but many people make it rhyme to *receive*'. So too under SICK: 'The *i* has its short obscure sound as in *thick*. The Scotch make this the same word, to the ear, with *seek*'; WHIM: 'In this word and in *swim*, the Scotch give the *i* its long vocal sound like the *ee* in *seem*. But it should be pronounced short as in *him*'; WICK: 'pronounce like *lick*. The Scotch make this, to the ear, the same word with *week*'. Robertson too seems to have been aware of this phenomenon, treating as showing similar vowels such items as: *red/rid/read/reed* 'for weavers'; *itch/each*; *pick/pique*; *deep/dip*; *green/grin*, *tith/teeth*. An [ɪ] → [i] raising is, of course, still a characteristic of Modern Scots, although its sociophonetic distribution has yet to be fully investigated (Murray 1873: 94; Grant and Main Dixon 1921: 40–1). However, the salientness and social significance of the palatal vowel alternations at the beginning of the nineteenth century are well captured in *The Vulgarities of Speech Corrected* (1826: 228):

> The short sound of *i*, however, is much more difficult than the long sound to Scotsmen, who can seldom acquire it after the most careful trials, because they are almost certain of verging to the long sound of *ee* or the short sound of *u*. Thus we may hear *een*, *en*, or *un* for 'in'. The short sound is the pedantic or vulgar-genteel, the long sound is universal, and both are bad. As examples I may mention *wheech*, or *whuch* for 'which', *veesion*, or *vesion*, for 'vision', *deceesion* or *decesion* for 'decision', *eedea* sometimes *yedea* for 'idea', *deeameter* sometimes *day-ameter* for 'diameter'.

An alternation between [ɪ] and its lowered/centred variants is well documented in the modern language and points to interesting sociophonetic contrasts involving age, sex and social class as well as providing evidence for phonological change in action. In their Glasgow study, which involved a sample of some 130 male and female informants across wide social, age and occupational categories, Macaulay and Trevelyan (1977: 35) found that speakers in the city produced several outputs (involving lowering, retraction and rounding) of the [ɪ] vowel, including [ɛ· ɛˑ ɜ· ʌ ɪ]. Their study showed that there were clear differences in the use of this variable corresponding to social contrasts in the city. Social classes 2 and 3 (perhaps best described as upper and lower working class, corresponding approximately to skilled and semi-skilled manual workers) showed the greatest preference in the sample for lowered and centralised forms, but it is interesting to note how even professional, upper middle-class speakers in Class 1 also used the 'stigmatised' form to a measurable extent. Distributional characteristics of this variable become clearer when the sex and age of the speakers, as well as their social class, were considered. While again there exists a sharp difference between Class 1 and Class 2/3 speakers in their use of the centralised form, the overall appearance of the stigmatised variant is less frequent with female speakers as a whole and with Class 2 females in particular, suggesting that this group are targeting their speech towards that of Class 1 speakers in the city. Interesting too is the sharp division between Class 1 boys and Class 1 girls, the former showing a greater tendency to use stigmatised variants despite their middle-class status, a phenomenon paralleled in several other studies (Chambers 1995: chapter 3), and partly at any rate explained by the tendency of young males in general to use more 'macho' and correspondingly more highly socially stigmatised forms of speech.

Rather similar results were recorded in Johnston's Edinburgh survey (Johnston 1983a: 14–15) where variants of [ɪ] included retracted, centralised and lowered forms such as [ə] and [ʌ], but especially [ë] and [ɛ̈]. Johnston showed that in formal speech all social groups tended towards the [ɪ], while the lowered forms surfaced whenever the level of formality in the speech style decreased. However, most notable was the tendency for the [ɛ̈] variable, primarily a working-class output, to spread to the speech of the middle classes in Edinburgh. Indeed, this ongoing 'change from below' appeared to be mainly spread by middle-class women in the community.

8.4.1.3 The [o]/[ɔ] Alternation

From the eighteenth century onwards, perhaps the most frequently commented-upon feature of pronunciation considered to be overtly Scots is the merger of the [o]/[ɔ] (high/low mid back) vowels. The subject of much anecdotal illustration among eighteenth-century observers in particular, there is nevertheless some considerable doubt about the socio-phonetic status of the alternation in Scotland itself both in that and the following century. Sylvester Douglas' observations seem to suggest that the substitution of a high back for a mid back vowel was, to English ears, a characteristic Scots 'vulgarism', since under his COAST, COAT, COX entry (Jones 1991: 185) he comments:

> COAST, COAT, COAX
> The *oa* as in *boat*. Not long ago, a Scotch Gentleman, in a debate in the House of Commons upon the Affairs of America, began a speech, in which he proposed to examine whether it would be more advisable to adopt compulsive, or soothing measures towards the colonies. Unfortunately instead of *soothe*, *coax* was the word that had presented itself to his mind. And he pronounced it as if written *cox*. This, added to several other peculiarities of manner and dialect, tickled the House extremely, and produced a general laugh. The Gentleman was unconscious of the false pronounciation [sic] into which he had fallen. His speech had been premeditated, and *coax* was, it seems, a sort of cue, or catch word. Every time therefore that the silence of his hearers permitted him to resume his harangue, he began by repeating this unlucky word. But every fresh repetition of it occasioning a louder burst of laughter, he was obliged at last fairly to give the matter up. And break off his oration in the middle.

On the other hand, however, James Adams' (1794: 21) observations on the reaction of what we can only assume was an educated (perhaps conservative) Scots-speaker to an anglicised use of a low mid back vowel in the item *body* might suggest that for certain types of Scottish speakers the high version was an acceptable, even a prestigious output:

> In 1775 I lived in the Scotch College of Doway in Flanders, having learnt as good English and Latin as St Omers afforded to moderate proficients. The old Scotch gentlemen soon began to fear I should spoil the accent of their pupils, who endeavoured to imitate my pronunciation. Our table wanted not the better store and seasoning of instructive reading during meals. A young reader (Chearly Câmeron) lighting on these words, *the body of his father*, read them according to the English way, upon which the presiding old Gentleman's ears being shocked, he cleared his mouth as fast as possible, and dropping his spoon and hands on the table, made him repeat the words several times, and spell them again and again. Still the youth read *bâddy*; then the old gentleman ordered each letter to be named and counted, which being done, and repeated again and again, he fixed his eyes on me, and with triumphant smile, mixed with a good Scotch grin, rebuked the reader sharply for spoiling the *a*, and introducing a second *d*, then ordered him to sound it *bô-dy*.

It has to be admitted, though, that nearly all the prescriptive Scottish observers in the eighteenth century predominantly discourage this 'Scotticism'. Buchanan's list of eminent Scotticisms includes 'confusions' of long and short vowels, such that 'North-Britons destroy just quantity, by expressing the long sound for the short, and the short for the long; as *abhōr* for *abhŏr*, *abhōrrence* for *abhŏrrence*, *abōlish* for *abŏlish*, *thrōn* for *thrōne* [sic]'. William Scott (1807: xxvi), under his 'list of words in which the Natives of Scotland are very apt to err', tells us that 'These two sounds of the vowel [represented by ⟨o⟩ – probably his [o] and [ɔ]/[ɒ]] are particularly difficult to North Britons when occurring in the same word or near one another; as in *post-office, coach-box, a long story, I thought so, not only, go on*, &c'. Sylvester Douglas too, under his BOUGHT entry (Jones 1991: 47), perhaps paints the clearest picture of all his contemporaries of the significance of this variable:

> In this and similar words, as *sought, thought, fought, drought*. The *ough* has the long open sound of the *o* in *corn*, or of *oa* in *broad*. This sound, if at all, is but just distinguishable from the long broad *a* in *all, malt* or *au* in *Paul*. Some writers on pronounciation [sic] consider them as entirely the same. They are generally made to rhyme with such words as *taught*, and *fraught*, but that is no proof that their sound is exactly the same.
>
>> If e'er one vision touch'd thy infant thought
>> Of all the nurse, and all the priest e'er taught.
>
> The Scotch, after they get rid of the more barbarous pronounciation in which the *gh* is pronounced as a strong guttural, generally fall into the mistake of using the long close sound of *o*, and making (for instance) *bought*, and *boat*, the same word to the ear. And this they do so generally that in endeavouring to mimic the Scotch pronounciation I have observed that the English are apt to hit upon this particular way of sounding this class of words. Yet this, in truth, is not part of the vernacular pronounciation of Scotland.

One problem here is to determine what Douglas means by 'vernacular' in this context. He states quite categorically in his *Treatise* that

> it is by no means my intention to observe upon all the grosser barbarisms of the vulgar Scotch jargon. This would be an useless and an endless labour. I only mean to treat expressly of the

impurities which generally stick with those whose language has already been in a great degree
refined from the provincial dross, by frequenting English company, and studying the great
masters of the English tongue in their writings: Of those *vestigia ruris* which are apt to remain so
long; which scarce any of our most admired authors are entirely free from in their compositions;
which, after the age of manhood, only one person in my experience has so got rid of in speech
that the most critical ear cannot discover his country from his expression or pronounciation [sic].
(Jones 1991: 101)

If we interpret his 'vernacular' as some kind of regional Scots (perhaps Edinburgh) standard
or even an eighteenth-century version of some type of 'Standard' Scots, he seems to be
suggesting that in that (formal) context the merger of the two mid back vowels has not taken
place.

However, the evidence provided by Alexander Scot's *The Contrast*, an attempt to portray
the presumably prestigious language of 'the present Caledonian English of the college, the
pulpit and the bar' (Jones 1993: 102), seems to offer some support for an interpretation of
the Scots [ɔ]/[o] alternation as having sociophonetic significance. Using an ⟨oa⟩ digraph to
characterise [ɔ]-type pronunciations, we find Scot realising *poalesh* 'polish', *proaper*
'proper', *Scoat* 'Scot', *foar* 'for', *noat* 'not', *bayoand* 'beyond', *aupoastles* 'apostles', *foarty*
'forty', *oad* 'odd', *oar* 'or', *poands* 'ponds', *poassebly* 'possibly', *froam* 'from'. Using ⟨o⟩ for
[o(o)], he includes: *those*, *notted* 'noted', *spoc* 'spoke', *premoted* 'promoted', *hopful*,
pronunsatione, *obadiant*. However, there are four (and only four) instances where ⟨oa⟩
is used where etymologically a high mid vowel might be expected: *soajurner* 'sojourner',
auloanne 'alone', *tnoan* 'known' and *prevoack* 'provoke'. While we should be cautious in
placing too much significance upon such sparse evidence, it might just be possible to
conclude in this case that so stigmatised was the substitution of [o] for [ɔ] for certain groups
of speakers, that a limited 'hypercorrect' accommodation to stressed [ɔ] vowels in some
items with etymological [o] is to be expected. But the overall picture is far from clear, and
there is some evidence to suggest that several of the Scottish observers reject 'best English
practice' by assigning values to ⟨o⟩, ⟨ou⟩, ⟨ow⟩ and ⟨oa⟩ which are often difficult to
equate with 'standard' London-based usage: Angus (1800a) recommends [oo] values to ⟨o⟩
in items like *chronology*, *decorate*, *comedian*, *coquetry*, *dissoluble*, *solemn*; Warden (1753)
shows [oo] in *solemnity*, *solid*, *monument*, *moderate*, *constant*, *provident*; Barrie has [oo] for
corn, *cord*, *sort*, *cost*, *sloth*; Burn shows [oo] in *acknowledgement*, *fought*, *brought*, *George*,
Georgics, *lord* with [ɔ(ɔ)] for ⟨ow⟩ in *fellow*, *follow*, *meadow*. The anonymous author of *A
Spelling-Book upon a New Plan* has [oo] in items like *glossary*, *florid*, *homage*, *oven*, *evolve*,
resolve, *border*, as well as in the first ⟨o⟩ in *colonnade*, *colossus*, *columnar*, while low mid
values are assigned to *arrogant*, *revolt*, *brocade* and *glorify*.

While we still lack a quantitative analysis of both urban and rural usage, there is
considerable evidence that the low mid/high mid back vowel alternation is prominent in
nineteenth-century Scots and is, indeed, still active. Grant and Main Dixon (1921: 50–1)
record 'Scots' [o] vowels in items like *corn*, *horn*, while earlier Murray (1873: 111) describes
how

If the English vowel [*ou*] be pronounced pure without the terminal ŏŏ, into which it glides, it will
be nearly the Scotch *o*, the difference between the 'mid back round' (*o*) and mid back wide round
(*o*) not being great. This vowel occurs long in *noa*, *doar*, *loard*. *God* is also pronounced in the
same way, *Goad* (*noo*, *door*, *loord*, *good*); short, but unchanged in quality, in *lot*, *dot*, *scon*, which
must be carefully distinguished alike from the long *lōte*, *dōle*, *scōne*, and the English *lot*, *doll*,

sconn, where the *o* represents, not the short quality of long *o*, which English has not, but the short 'wide' sound of *au* or *aw* in *laud*, *law*.

Interestingly too, in the Edinburgh sample set out in Ellis' *On Early English Pronunciation* (1889: 35–6), considerable evidence for this variant is shown. Ellis' informant was the sister-in-law of James Murray – Mrs Charles A. Murray – who was by all accounts 'an educated bi-lingual Edinburgh speaker' probably at home both in Scottish Standard English of the period and in a local Edinburgh dialect (Speitel 1969). Mrs Murray regularly appears to use an [o] or its raised [o·] version in items like *Jock*, *yonder*, *corner*, *body* and *daughter*, while a lower back mid [ɔ] segment appears in *old*, *going*, *crow*. Obviously, since we do not have a detailed description of the everyday language of the informant or of the conditions under which the sampling was made, we have to treat these data with some caution. But they do seem to suggest that, even for educated speakers in the late nineteenth century, this alternation was operative in a somewhat different form from current usage which, if anything especially among educated Edinburgh females, tends to see the abandonment of [bodɪ] for *body* realisations, instead seeming to hypercorrect an [ɔ] vowel in contexts where [o] might etymologically be expected: compare [fɔrd] for *Ford* pronunciations.

8.4.1.4 Labial Vowel Sounds

This is a particularly complex area of the vowel space to interpret with any precision from the historical record, not least because of the availability of such a relatively large amount of contemporary comment, much of which is difficult to analyse in a wholly satisfactory way. There appears to be some evidence from the eighteenth- and nineteenth-century materials that Scots high mid back [o] vowels (especially in those contexts where they were perceived to be long) tended to be realised near the pure labial end of the spectrum (that is, with lowered F_2 configurations) as something corresponding to [o·]. Sylvester Douglas (Jones 1991: 133) suggests as much when he claims that 'The close *o* verges toward the vowel represented by *oo*' (his [u] or [ω]), although he does not inform us whether this is a particularly Scotch feature. Robertson, however, describing what may be a peculiarly Glaswegian version of early eighteenth-century Scots, seems to go out of his way to show a raised value for [o], as in his 'sounding alike' examples: *boar/bore/boor*, *booth/both*, *boots/boats*, *door/doer*, *whom/home*, *shoe/sew*, *stole/stool*, *tone/tune*, *who/woe*. Indeed, Robertson's data appear to suggest an overall tendency for Scots speakers to realise mid and even centralised back vowels which are close to pure labial values. This tendency is explicitly to be seen under Sylvester Douglas' ABOVE entry (Jones 1991: 159):

> The *o* has the second or short sound of *u*, exactly as in *rub*, *sunk*. The Scotch are very often apt to sound it like the long vocal *u* or *oo*; so as to make *above*, rhyme to *groove*. There are a considerable number of words of this termination, and they are pronounced in three different ways. Some of them in the manner we have just described. In some, as *strove*, *rove*, *grove*, the *o* has its long close sound as in *abode*. And in some, as *move*, *prove*, it is sounded in the manner in which the Scotch pronounce it in *above*. As these 3 sounds are generally confounded in Scotland, so that the words pronounced in England in one way, are, in that country, pronounced in an other, it will be useful to attend to the following lists, where they are arranged according to their true pronunciation [sic] *Love* which they sound properly, and which rhymes to the true pronunciation of *above* will serve as the leading word in the first list. *Move* which rhymes to *groove* in the second. and *Jove* (which is also properly pronounced by the Scotch) in the third.

1. *Love, above* (pronounced by the Scotch like *move*) *dove* (by the Scotch like *Jove*) *shove*, noun and verb (by the Scotch like *Jove*) *glove, True-love*.

2. *Move, amove, approve, behoove, disapprove, improve, prove, (remove, reprove)* All often pronounced by Scotch like *love*.

3. *Jove, alcove, cove, clove* (verb and noun,) *drove* (verb and noun,) *grove, hove, rove, strove* verb and noun, *throve, wove*. The following is a perfect rhyme

O! witness earth beneath, and heav'n above;
For can I hide it? I am sick of love.

Douglas seems to suggest three main phonetic manifestations for labial vowel space: [u], [ʌ] and [ɤ]; from the detailed description which he provides (Jones 1991: 14–22), the third of these, his 'short sound of *u*', is some kind of unrounded and possibly lowered version of [u], perhaps a [ɤ] (or even a [ə]) vowel and characteristic of words like *love, dove, glove* contrasted against a 'long' version in items such as *groove*. His observations under ABOVE (together with comments from other parts of his *Treatise*) might be summarised as in Table 8.4.

Table 8.4

	Scotch [uu]	Scotch [oˑ]	Scotch [ɤ]/[ʌ]
London standard [uu]			*move* *improve* *prove*
London standard [ʌ]	*above*	*dove* *shove* *covet* *oven*	

Data like these suggest that late eighteenth-century Scots vernacular (but not vulgar) speakers could substitute a lowered [ɤ] in place of a London standard lengthened [u] and a raised, rounded [u] (perhaps [oˑ]) for London standard [ʌ]. The former tendency of Scots speakers is recorded by Sylvester Douglas in many places, notably under FOOT where 'The Scotch, Irish, and Northern English, pronounce the *oo* like the *u* in *shut, hut, cut*. It should be pronounced as in *fool*, and so the *oo* is to be sounded in all other words of this termination. Some few English people who speak well pronounce it in *soot* as the *u* in *shut*' (Jones 1991: 197). Under his FULL entry, too, we find: 'The *u* has its distinct vocal sound like *oo* in *foot, fool* but shorter. In Scotland and in the North of England it is pronounced as in *dull*' (Jones 1991: 198). Indeed, the high sociophonetic status of the centralised vowel pronunciation for Scots speakers is highlighted by Douglas under his BUSINESS, BUSY entry where, despite the idiosyncratic [ɪ] stressed vowel realisation so assiduously recorded by almost all eighteenth-century observers, he is careful to point out that the Scots too 'in their vernacular pronounciation [sic] . . . sound it nearly in this manner, but they often when they *aim at speaking well* [my italics] give the *u* the sound it has in *guzzle, puzzle*' (Jones 1991: 179). Sentiments like these recur in the following century too: the anonymous author of *The Vulgarities of Speech*

Corrected (1826: 228–9) in several places notes the Scots non-standard usage in this area of the phonology, of which

> The most decidedly vulgar, because it is always affected, is that of sounding the words *door* and *floor*, as they are spelled, so as to rhyme with 'poor', instead of the broad Scots 'dore', which in this case is right, though not in 'flore', that sounds precisely the same. In many of the words in which the *o* ought to sound like *u* in 'but' Scotsmen sound it long, as in *among* for 'amung', *comefort* for 'cumfort' . . .

It is in the eighteenth century in particular that we begin to find extensive comment upon the shape of those labial vowels which owe their origin either to the Great Vowel Shift of an earlier [oo] or to a diphthongal [iu] (Wells 1982: 147); these labial vowels often appear in varieties of Modern English as [ju(u)]. While we shall discuss in section 8.4.2.5 the Scots diphthong/monophthong distribution in such items, there are in the period other important manifestations of these labials (expressive of sociophonetic contrasts), many of which are still apparent in Modern Scots. Sylvester Douglas comments on several occasions upon what he perceives to be the standard shape in the southern Scottish vernacular of the vowel which in the 'pure' London dialect appears as a [ju] diphthong. Under his discussion of BURIAL, BURY, he observes that while 'these words are a great stumbling block to many a Scotchman . . . The true provincial sound of the *u* in the southern counties [of Scotland], both in these and a great many others, is like the French *u*'. While we must be cautious of attaching too much significance to the accuracy of this observation, and at the same time be conscious of the difficulty in reconstructing a precise value for late eighteenth-century French *u*, it might not be unreasonable to interpret such a segment as some kind of [ʉ] or [ɯ], a high central rounded or high back unrounded vowel shape. Douglas' observations appear to be an echo of those of Buchanan (1757: 29), who quite confidently states that 'In other tongues there may be simple vowel sounds quite different from ours. Such is that of the French *u*; which is not heard in England, or in the North of Scotland; but in all the lowland provinces of North Britain, from the Grampian mountains to the Tweed, is still in very frequent use'. Elphinston too makes a similar comment: 'Against the English *oo* . . . dhe Soddhern Scots hav garded dheir dialect widh *u* . . . French; hwich dhe nordhern [Scots] found as forrain, az did the Inglish' (1787: 4, 10), observing that

> *duke* retains dhe licquid in *dyuc*; hwen he plays not hiz parent, dhe French *duc*. Dhus ar dhe Inglish *duke* and *duc* Scottishly interchainged . . . Dhe Scots, naming dhe vowel forrainly *oo*, nevver prefix dhe licquefier, but hware dhey shood not. Hence *book* iz *byook*, *byuc*, or (Frenchly) *buc*; and *rebuke*, *rebook*, *rebyuc*, or (French-like) *rebuc*. No wonder dhe soddhern Scots adopt dhe French vowel in *cure* and *curious*, if so manny Inglish provincials drop dhe licquefaccion in dhe blunt *coor* and *coorious*, or even *coorous*. If dhe Inglish hav hiddherto' expected *coosshon*, or *coossion*, from *cushion*; dheir neighbors may az wel (but alas! no better) think to' bring dhe town ov *Coopar*, from *Cupar* . . .

Further evidence for the value which we have ascribed to the French *u* once more comes from Sylvester Douglas' important BURIAL entry, where we are told that speakers in the north of Scotland realise the vowel by what Douglas represents as *beerial*, *beery*, perhaps a pure palatal [i]/[ii] sound or (more likely) a high central unrounded [ɨ] vowel. Elphinston too tells us that in Edinburgh *shoe* is '*chu* Frenchly' and *rude* '*rude* French'; on the other hand, for Aberdeen speakers he cites *shee* for 'shoe' and *rid* or *reed* for 'rude' (1787: 4).

Perhaps something like this [ɨ]-type vowel is referred to by Adams in his description of the *Scotch Dialect* (1799: 153) when he suggests as Scotch variants of *soon* and *moon* realisations rendered as *sain*, *main*, where he uses ⟨ai⟩ as a symbol for [e], perhaps perceived by him as being phonetically close to [ɨ]. Among his labial vowel sounds, Alexander Geddes recognises a *û* '*u* English as in *pure*' (1792: 432), observing on it that

> This is really a compound of *e* and *u*. It is, however, to be observed, that it is not sounded exactly in the same manner by the Scots and English. In the mouths of the latter it seems to be composed of *i* and *eù*; while the former pronounce it more like the French *u* or *eu*, in the word *peur*.

He appears to suggest that for standard English speakers there exists a genuine [ju] diphthongal segment, which some speakers of Scots are liable to interpret, at least on occasion, as monophthongal and approximating to a 'French' probably fronted labial segment of the type we have tentatively suggested. Perhaps it is this fronted *u* sound which is attested in the late nineteenth century by Murray as well (1873: 112–13):

> The 'Mid Front round' vowel . . . which, following the usual spelling, is here represented by *ui*, has very different values in different Scottish dialects, ranging almost from the French *eu* in *peu* to the German provincial *ü* in *übel*, and the English *ee* in *Dee*; a common form in the north being also the 'high mixed wide', identified by Mr. Ellis with the Welsh *u*, and almost the Slavonic *y*. Thus Aberdeenshire *muin*, *ruit*, *tuip*, are (myn, ryt, typ), that is, nearly *mìn*, *rìt*, *tìp*; *puir*, *dui*, are indistinguishable from *peer*, *dee*. The Southern Counties' *ui* is one of the openest, being equal to the French *eu* in *peu*, nearly the German *ö* in *löcke*. It is long in *dui*, *puir*, *bruise*, stopped in *buit*, *cuit*, *fuil*, *duin*. This vowel seems to be eminently a restless and unsettled one, and in almost all languages gradually gravitates to rest in *ee*.

The degree of centring and fronting of the labial vowel is a very active sociophonetic indicator in the modern language. In their Glasgow survey, for instance, Macaulay and Trevelyan (1977: 47–51) record the vowel showing values such as [u], [ü], [ʉ] and [ɯ]. The distribution of the level of fronting was clearly shown to be a function of social class: the lower the social class of the informant, the higher the level of fronting occurrence was likely to be. When the sample is broken down to reflect sex and age differences, there is seen to be a reluctance on the part of Class 1 female speakers to use the stigmatised fronted version of the vowel, although Class 3 females are as much likely to use it as their male peers. Indeed, even Class 1 males have a tendency to use the fronted versions a great deal of the time, perhaps attesting to a phonological change 'from below'. Johnston's (1983a: 15–17) survey for Edinburgh informants showed a very similar picture, although there the height of the fronted form was a significant factor as well, with Class 3 speakers (especially males) using a lower reflex than those of Class 1. Class 3 males also tended to show very highly rounded variants in [ø]. In his Ayr study, Macaulay (1991: 39) records lower–class speakers as showing an unrounded high front [ɪ] segment for the Standard Scots [u] in a restricted lexical set like *afternoon*, *foot*, *football*, *good*, *school*, *soon*, *wood*, *wooden*.

8.4.2   The Diphthongs

8.4.2.1   The [au]/[u] Alternation

The failure of pure labial vowels to diphthongise in the Northern English and Scots versions of the Great Vowel Shift is one of its best-attested characteristics. The Scots and

Northumbrian [hüs]/[hɑus] alternation is probably one of the most widely commented-upon characteristics of British English phonological phenomena (Wells 1982: chapter 5). Many explanations have been offered to account for this failure, one of the most common centring around the Great Vowel Shift as a Push-chain phenomenon, whereby the introduction of new low segments into the phonological system results in a general raising of all other vowels, a process driven by a constraint in the system which avoids vowel mergers. Vowels which are already high, the argument goes, are required to diphthongise to avoid merging with lower segments which 'encroach' on their vowel space. In Northern Middle English, high mid back vowels like [oo] did not undergo this raising, centring instead to some kind of [œœ] or [øø] segment. This failure to raise left the pure palatal vowel space unencroached upon, so that it had no need to diphthongise in order to avoid merger with a raised [oo] (Lass 1984: 126ff.; Jespersen 1949; Labov 1994: 115–54), the result of a 'no raising – no diphthongisation' stratagem. Undiphthongised Scots pure labial forms are regularly recorded in both the eighteenth and nineteenth centuries, contrasting with London standard forms which show a mid to high diphthongal transition [ou] (Jones 1991: 59–60) and, in the nineteenth century, with 'southern Scots' [ʌu] shapes (Murray 1873: 117): 'So the Central Scotch *soo, doo, hoo, yoo, foo, noo*, are in the South [of Scotland], *suw, duw, huw, yuw, fuw, nuw*'. Murray certainly sees a phonetic difference in the expression of this diphthong when it arises from non-Great Vowel Shift sources, for instance through [l]-vocalisation, or pre-[r] Breaking:

> The diphthong *òw, owe* differs but little from the long *o* in *no, road*, as pronounced in the south of England, *no°°, rō°°d*, the terminal *oo* being more distinct. In the Southern Scottish dialect it occurs final in *howe*, 'a hollow', *knowe*, 'a knoll', *growe, yowe*, 'a ewe', etc., which, in other Scottish dialects, have the next diphthong, *huw, knuw, yuw*. So also it is used in this dialect for the *uw* of the other Scots before a voiced consonant, liquid or nasal, especially *l* and *r*, as *buwl, gluwr, fuwr,*

a contextual distinction also noted by Alexander Geddes in the late eighteenth century (Jones 1994: 86).

However, it is worth noting that there is not as much comment from eighteenth-century observers as we might expect upon the sociophonetic value of the diphthongal/non-diphthongal contrast. There is indeed some evidence to suggest that undiphthongised forms had something of their present-day low-prestige status – the *Spelling-Book upon a New Plan*, for instance, assigning (under its list of 'those words in which the Natives of North Britain are most apt to err') *oor* and *oot* realisations of 'our' and 'out' to the 'Commonly Pronounced' category (Anon. 1796: vii). This fact might lead us to anticipate evidence in favour of hypercorrection in the direction of diphthongal outputs. Sylvester Douglas, for instance, records the Scottish dialect as showing a diphthongal stressed vowel space in the item SHOULDER (an item with the long close *o* sound in the London standard): 'The Scotch are apt (when they aim at propriety) to give it the diphthongal sound as in *foul*' (Jones 1991: 223). Again, under his the item TOUCH (Jones 1991: 229),

> The Scotch in general, pronounce this word properly, so as to rhyme to *such, much*. But I know a Scotchman who from the rule of analogy has persuaded himself that it should be pronounced so as to rhyme to *crouch, pouch*: and constantly did pronounce it in that manner. The reader will judge of the ridicule this necessarily brought upon him.

Yet there is some evidence which suggests that non-diphthongal forms (perhaps confined to specific lexical items) were regarded as acceptable and even prestigious in some surprisingly formal Scottish sociophonetic contexts. For instance, Alexander Scot's characterisation of prestigious Scottish English pronunciation – 'the present Caledonian English of the college, the pulpit and the bar' – has the items 'round', 'about' and 'however' represented as *roond*, *aboot*, *whoever*, all showing a non-Great Vowel Shift monophthongal [u] stressed vowel shape, rather than some expected [ɑu] type (Jones 1996: 193). Even early in the eighteenth century, we see Robertson recommending equivalencies such as *flower/ floor*, *foul/fowl/fool/full*, *hoar/hour/whore*, *muse/mouse*, *power/pure*, *sound/swoon*, *brow/brew*, *shout/shut/shoot* where monophthongal labial outputs for the stressed vowels in *foul*, *mouse* and so on appear to be a possible interpretation; such equivalencies, recall, Robertson was recommending to the socially aspirant young ladies of Glasgow.

There is, too, some suggestion of lexical diffusion as a basis for the selection of diphthongal/monophthongal vowel shapes. For instance, Sylvester Douglas claims that a [bou] pronunciation for *bow* is restricted to a 'to bend' interpretation, while the [boo] shape is associated specifically with 'arcus' (Jones 1991: 177): 'But Scotchmen, who have acquired a good and ready pronounciation [sic] in other respects, often find themselves puzzled and confounded between the different pronounciations of this word'. The 'true provincial' pronunciation, he asserts, is [buu], to which if the Scotch speaker does not aspire, then [bou] is the favoured alternative, with [boo] the least preferred (and by implication the least prestigious) in the Scotch vernacular. Such a tendency in the late eighteenth-century London standard dialect to differentiate phonetically between lexical contrasts is also noted by Douglas for the item sow; when referring to a female pig, the pure dialect realises an [ou] vowel, in the 'act of sowing' an [oo], while Scots speakers pronounce the latter, he claims, as [suu] (to rhyme to *shoe*), but they 'often pronounce it with the diphthongal sound so as to rhyme to *Now*, *cow*'. In the same way, *bowl* 'a basin' and *bowl* 'ball in the game of bowling' are distinguished as [bool] and [boul] respectively; only the Scots pronunciation of the former as [boul] is recorded by Douglas.

The distribution of the [au]/[u] alternation in modern Scots has been the subject of several studies. All show a strong correlation between social class, age and sex for the variable as well as with the formality of the discourse during which data-gathering took place (Macaulay and Trevelyan 1977: 52ff.; Macaulay 1991: 41ff.; Johnston 1983a: 22ff.). The Macaulay and Trevelyan Glasgow survey showed a not unexpected increase in monophthongal scores from social class 1 (professional) through social class 3 (unskilled manual) for both male and female informants. However, it is worth noting again how relatively frequently the 'stigmatised' version occurred even among Class 1 informants, notably male speakers, especially younger male speakers, once more suggesting a 'change from below' scenario. But this survey suggested too that even younger female speakers are also using the monophthongal form, notably among the Class 2a (upper middle-class) informants, hinting that the adoption of non-standard forms is not the preserve of 'macho' male speakers alone. Johnston's (1983a) Edinburgh survey showed that young women from the lower social groups tended to confine the monophthongal output to a limited set of lexical items, in particular *about*, *down*, *out*, *around*, while male speakers showed it in a much wider lexical range. The common theme of these surveys is the extreme sensitivity of the alternation to stylistic considerations. Speakers of all social classes, ages and sexes produced a lower tendency to monophthongal forms when they were in a formal interview situation. Indeed, in Macaulay's Ayr study (1991: 42), there was even a difference in response between different points in the interview situation. Near the beginning of the interview (and perhaps in response to the fact that the interviewer has a high proportion of diphthongal forms), informants tended to avoid a [u] output, but the frequency of this increased as the interview progressed, suggesting that informants were becoming more relaxed and producing more unconscious vernacular speech.

8.4.2.2 The [ai]/[ii] Alternation

Eighteenth-century grammatical and orthoepistic Scottish sources quite regularly record the failure of high front palatal [i]-type vowels to appear as diphthongs, as might be expected under the effect of the Great Vowel Shift. Conversely, Scots speakers in the period can produce an [aɪ]-type diphthong in environments where a standard metropolitan dialect would realise [ii]; that is, the vowel-shift diphthongising mechanism would act upon long high front vowels which, for a variety of reasons – including those associated with lexical diffusion – were left unaffected by it at an earlier date. An excellent example appears in the list of 'those words in which the Natives of North Britain are most apt to err, in order that the teacher may be particularly on his guard to prevent the children from falling into these common errors' set out in the anonymous *A Spelling-Book upon a New Plan* (1796: vii). There we see the items *reprieve* and *retrieve* rendered for 'Common' and 'True' pronunciations respectively as follows: *reprîve/repreeve, retrîv/retreeve*, with the ⟨î⟩ symbol representing for the stigmatised dialect what looks like diphthongal stressed vowel space, the palatal monophthong recorded for the standard context. This distribution is also echoed in Sylvester Douglas (Jones 1991: 219) under his REPRIEVE entry:

> The *ie* here, as in *field, mien*, &c has the long vocal sound of *e*, or *ee*, or the second sound of *i*, or that of *ea* in *appear*; which are all one and the same. The Scotch in this word give it the diphthongal sound of *i*, so as to make *reprieve*, and *thrive* form a perfect rhyme.

In this context too, we might include Elphinston's (1787: 7) observation that the vowels in *rip* and *sip* 'open Scottishly' as *ripe, sipe* (together with his *Aprile/April* and *fifeteen/fifteen* contrasts). However, Douglas' BEDIZEN entry shows how Scots speakers are just as likely to resist such a diphthongisation: 'In this word, and its original (*dizen*) the Scotch pronounce the *i* short, and as in *phiz, mizzen*. In both it should have its long diphthongal sound, as in *wise, miser*.' Nonetheless, Douglas' observations on the Scots pronunciation of VICAR seem to suggest that Scots speakers emulating the most propitious pronunciation are liable to realise the diphthong: 'The short obscure *i* as in *victory*. The Scotch, when they aim at the English pronounciation [sic], are apt to give it the diphthongal sound as in *vice*.'

While we labour under the uncertainty of how to equate Robertson's presentational sequence with any model for a recommended pronunciation, it seems that he is suggesting pure palatal (monophthongal) vowel space in the following, where a diphthongal form might be expected in the contemporary London (or even Lowland Scots) standard: *career/crier, lees* ('dregs of wine')*/lies* ('untruth'), *niece/nice, peal/pile, steel/style, teal/tile, wield/wild, wheat/white/wight*. On the other hand, we might be less confident that the non-head items in the following sets would be recommended a diphthongal output in the Glaswegian of the early eighteenth century: *dryed* ('withered')*/dread* ('terror'), *find/fined/fiend, fry/fray/free, rhyme/ream, lice/least/less*. Yet that some of these front mid vowel/diphthongal alternations were a genuine and socially sensitive characteristic of eighteenth-century Scots vernacular appears to be justified from Sylvester Douglas' WEIGH entry (Jones 1991: 231–2):

The vernacular Scotch pronounciation [sic] makes this word rhyme to *eye*, *try*, *high*. Those who endeavour to speak with more propriety make it rhyme to *see*, *pea*. But the true pronounciation is with the thin slender sound of *a* or *ay*, in *pay*. Or as the second sound of *ne*, or *nae*, in the vulgar Scotch dialect, when used instead of *no*.

Diphthongal alternation with pure palatal standard English [ii] was certainly a characteristic of regional Scots in the nineteenth century and is still prevalent today. Murray (1873: 115) records Lothian *dee* 'die' as Teviotdale *dey* – where his ⟨ey⟩ digraph represents a diphthong 'composed of the *y* in *hyll*, or *e* in *yet*, and *ĕĕ*. As a rule it represents the long English ī before a consonant, *e.g. pipe, fire, time* . . .' It is a mono/diphthongal contrast like this, Murray claims, which differentiates Southern Counties Scotch – 'the language of yuw and mey' – from that of central Scotland. Likewise, Grant and Main Dixon observe (1921: 57): 'ɛi is heard in Southern Scots in final position, where i is the rule in Mid. Sc., e.g. *bee, free, he, me, pea, we, dee* (die), *flee* (fly), *lee* (a lie) are the Sth. Sc. bɛi, frɛi, hɛi, mɛi, etc.'

8.4.2.3   Other Great Vowel Shift Anomalies: Front Mid/High Alternations

The eighteenth-century records give evidence for Scottish (as well as English) speakers showing [e(e)] stressed vowels (in a 'retarded' Great Vowel Shift manner) in contexts where the London Court dialect produces pure palatal [ii] vowels. Consider, as an example, the data (in Table 8.5) provided by Sylvester Douglas, although he claims that the [kreem] pronunciation only occurs 'sometimes', while the [tee] version is specifically associated with 'the North of Scotland', perhaps suggesting that the 'unshifted' [ee] was infrequently used by Scots speakers at the close of the eighteenth century (Jones 1991: 226–7):

> TEA
> In the North of Scotland, they pronounce the *ea* as the English do the *ay*, in *day*, *Tay*, the *ey* in *obey*, or the *a* in *tale*. That is, with the second, or thin sound of the slender *a*. According to the English pronounciation [sic] of *obey* and the Scotch pronounciation of *tea*, the following is a perfect rhyme.
>
> Here thou, great Anna! whom three realms *obey*
> Dost sometimes counsel take, and sometimes *tea*.
>
> But the English now (whatever may have been the case when the *Rape of the Lock* was written) pronounce *tea* as in *appear*.

Table 8.5

Pure dialect	Scotch
[ii]	[e]/[ee]
recent	[resənt]
cream	[kreem]
tea	[tee]

Several examples of this phenomenon are cited by Adams (1799: 152–3), who represents as Scots the pronunciation of the items *decent, thee, me, be* by *dai-cent, thai, mai, bai*, his ⟨ai⟩ digraph representing in this case an [e]-type vowel. Robertson shows the item *earth* with some kind of pure palatal and suggests that *beat/bait, chair/cheer, shave/sheaf, bleed/blade, vail/veal* and *spare/spear*, among several others, are to be considered as 'sounding alike'. Once more, Sylvester Douglas' description of Scottish vernacular low mid front [ɛ]/[ɛɛ] stressed vowel shapes suggests that, for some lexical items at least, the result of the vowel shift was a 'retarded' one for these too, as in Table 8.6. From data like these, it would appear that the Scottish vernacular *neat, retreat* (and so on) items have failed to undergo Great Vowel Shifting of [ɛɛ] to the more palatal [ee]/[ii]. But it has to be stressed that the vernacular Scottish situation reveals lexical diffusion and sociophonetic alternation in this area of the phonology. Under his SPEAR entry, Douglas comments (Jones 1991: 224): 'The *ea* as in *appear*. The Scotch often sound it as in *bear*. Tho' the other is their vernacular pronounciation [sic]', suggesting a polite vernacular [spiir] with a less acceptable, vowel-shift-retarded [spɛɛr] variant. Retarded vowel-shifting may also underlie Telfair's recommendation of a low mid front vowel (*e* as in *end*) in items such as *clearly, leap, seamstress, yeast* and *lieve*, while Dun also recommends *e* short in *fierce, tierce, piece, pierce*. Nevertheless, we should always bear in mind the possibility, suggested by Scot's description, that '*e* short' vowel types may represent some kind of palatality-heightened version of [ɛ], such as [ɛ˖] or [e˕], thus making their 'conflation' with pure palatals something of a near rather than a complete merger (Harris 1985; Jones 1989: 288).

Table 8.6

Pure	Scotch
[ii]	[ɛ]/[ɛɛ]
neat	BEAR
retreat	BEAR
spear	BEAR
deal	BREAST
idea	PEN

8.4.2.4   The [ɔɪ] and [ɑɪ] Alternation

> Boath master and scollar had herd, no les dhan seen, dhe difference between *oil* and *isle*, az boath doutles painted our *ile*: for dhe good rezon, dhat French (our parents and parragons) had not entirely cesed so to' paint dheir *île*. Yet nedher harmonist had conceived dhe suspiscion dhat won dipthong might not chime widh anoddher, compozed ov so cognate partikels.

Observant as ever, Elphinston (1786: 279) here captures two of the most discussed characteristics of Scots and English eighteenth-century diphthongal phonology – the apparent merger of [ɔɪ] and [ɑɪ] diphthongs and the nature of the former transition's terminal points. Almost all observers in the century comment on what they see as the undesirable practice of conflating [ɔɪ] and [ɑɪ] diphthongs. Typically, Kenrick (1784: 61) declares that

> *oil, toil*, are frequently pronounced exactly like *isle, tile*. This is a fault which the Poets are inexcusable for promoting, by making such words rhime to each other. And yet there are some

words so written, which by long use, have almost lost their true sound, such are *boil*, *join*, and many others; which it would not appear affectation to pronounce otherwise than *bile*, *jine*. We find, indeed, that this mode of pronunciation becomes every day more general.

Scottish observers too note this tendency in their native speech, and generally condemn it. Yet Robertson – recommending what must surely be a prestigious form of speech for his young Glasgow ladies – appears to suggest a total merger of the two diphthongs in his dialect, citing as 'alike' *high/hoy*, *I'll/isle/oyl*, *kind/coyned*, *line/loyn/Lyon*, *mighty/moiety*, *tye/toy*, *vice/voice*. While the [ɑɪ] shape predominates among his headed entries, we also find *boil/bile*, *imploy/imply*, *voil/vial/vile*, *point/pint*. It is, of course, important not to attach too much significance to the relative order of Robertson's examples, given that he himself makes no mention of how we are to interpret the way in which he presents his list. Yet, so common in the eighteenth-century literature is the condemnation of the *boil/bile* conflation under the latter, that we might just interpret the prominence given to *boil* in Robertson's list as a sign of a hypercorrection away from the [ʌɪ] pronunciation in at least a limited set of lexical items, arguing for a local standard pronunciation of *bile* as [bɔɪl].

Late nineteenth- and twentieth-century observers in general also record this diphthongal merger, although a detailed sociophonetic study of its distribution is awaited. Grant and Main Dixon claim a merger under [əi] in items such as *white* and *boil*, while Murray (1873: 116), noting, like most observers in the previous century, the high mid starting point of the *boil* diphthong, describes its regional distribution at the end of the nineteenth century as:

> In the central and north-east districts of Scotland this diphthong, when medial, is pronounced exactly like No. 2 ['Composed of the *y* in hyll, or *e* in yet, and ёё'] in the same dialects, *boil*, *point*, *quoit*, becoming *buyl*, *puynt*, *kuyte*, or *beyle*, *peynt*, *keyte*. So a *collier* is in Dalkeith called a *keyler*, i.e. *coiller* (compare *Rauf Coilzear*), which rhymes with *teyler*, tailor. In Roxb. the two words are far apart, *cuollier* and *teallier*, with liquid ll, Old Sc. *coilzear*, *tailzeour*. This substitution of *ey*, *uy*, for *oy*, was all but universal in English a century ago. The borderers who laugh at the *peynts* and *jeynings* of their northern neighbours, pride themselves upon their well-rounded *oy*, although a false etymology confounds one word, *beyle*, i.e. a boil, with *beyle*, bile.

Ellis' 1873 Edinburgh informant (1889: 35–6) also shows some evidence for this variant. Recall that Ellis' informant was 'an educated bilingual Edinburgh speaker' probably at home both in the Scottish Standard English of the period and in a local Edinburgh dialect (Speitel 1969). The data from this informant show that she distinguishes three shapes for the [ɑɪ] diphthong: before voiceless obstruents it is [əɪ], as in [ləɪk] 'like', [ləɪklɪ] 'likely', while before a vowel it is [aɪ], [kwaeət] 'quiet' and before a nasal sonorant and voiceless fricative is [ʌɪ], as in [nʌɪn] 'nine', [wʌɪf] 'wife', [tʌɪmz] 'times'. However, this speaker conflates the [əɪ] diphthong with the etymological [ɔɪ], producing [vəɪs] 'voice', [pəɪnt] 'point' and [bəɪln] 'boiling'. Speitel's modern informant – 'a native Edinburgh speaker' – produces two forms of the diphthong only: an [ae] in the pre-vowel 'quiet' instance, in all other contexts realising [ɛɪ], thus [lɛɪk], [nɛɪn], [vɛɪs] and [bɛɪlɪn].

The Scots Vowel Length Rule affects both stressed vowel and diphthongal length and quality (Aitken 1981a; MacMahon 1991; Wells 1982: 400–2). This rule captures the fact that contemporary Scots diphthongs appear to show a durationally extended first element (some kind of [ɑ'e] shape is claimed) before voiced fricatives, [r] and word boundaries (as in *rise*, *ties*, *tie*, *tire*). On the other hand, a short and qualitatively different transition (usually [ʌɪ]) will appear before voiced obstruents and [l], thus *ride*, *tide*, *tile*. In the same way, this [ɑ·e]/[ʌɪ] alternation is sensitive to morpheme- and word-boundary contexts, as the pairs [tʰɑ·ed]/[tʰʌɪd] *tied/tide* demonstrate (Aitken 1981a). Sylvester Douglas (Jones 1991: 108) gives an interesting description of the [ɑɪ] diphthong, seeing in it a long/short contrast. This 'length' contrast is perhaps best interpreted as referring to diphthongal complexes with different starting and finishing points rather than to any inherent durational characteristics of their composite vowels. That Douglas describes the first element of the 'long' version as 'short open *a*', his [æ], implies that the complex is [æɪ], while the short version, we might argue showing a lesser degree of travel, may represent some kind of [ɛɪ] (or even [eɪ]) shape. From the evidence which he cites, there appears also to be some Standard London/Scots alternation between the two diphthongal types: in general the London [ɛɪ] items with syllable-final [s] (*ice, nice, twice, thrice, entice, precise*) are realised in the Scots dialect with [æɪ]; however, in the context of preceding a syllable-final voiced segment, the Scots *precise* rhymes to *wise*. Douglas notes too (Jones 1991: 130) the similar German diphthong in items like *eis, Rhein*; but, where the diphthong is 'composed of the short slender, instead of the open, *a*, and the first sound of *e*. Many Scotch people pronounce the diphthongal *i*, exactly like the German *ei*', arguing for a Scotch realisation like [ɛɪ] or [æ·ɪ]. But whatever their exact phonetic characteristics, Douglas' short and long diphthongal types seem to correspond well both in contextual preference and F_2 transition curve with their modern [ae] and [ʌɪ] congeners. A distinction like this is also attested by Alexander Scot in his *The Contrast* (Jones 1993: 103), where we find ⟨ei⟩ and ⟨oy⟩ spellings in items like *oys* 'eyes', *moy* 'my' contrasting with ⟨ei⟩ digraphs in *Cleid* 'Clyde' and *mein* 'mine'. Yet Robertson's lists of words which are 'equal in sound' show no such distinction, and he presents pairs such as *spies* 'lookers on'/*spice* 'pepper', *price/prize, rice/rise, advice* 'councel [sic]'/*advise* 'I councel you'; *device* 'contrivance'/*devise* 'cheat'; *I'll/Isle* and even *tide* 'the flux and reflux of the sea'/*tied* 'bound' where the Scots Vowel Length Rule would predict a [tʰɑ·ed]/[tʰʌɪd] distinction in the morphologically sensitive context. There might be two conclusions to be drawn from Robertson's anomalous data: first, that his ear was not sufficiently sensitive to the diphthongal degree of travel distinction in such pairs; or second, and perhaps more likely, he is recording a genuine feature of early eighteenth-century Glasgow polite speech, namely a complete merger between the 'short' and 'long' [ɑɪ] diphthong types, possibly under some kind of [ɛ̆ɪ] ('narrow travel') kind.

We must beware of accepting uncritically the predictive power of a model like the Scots Vowel Length Rule, since actual observation shows that speakers do not always conveniently conform to such a 'rule'; the two Edinburgh speakers sampled by Lodge (1984: 88–9) appear to interchange somewhat randomly the two diphthongal types in identical contexts: [ʌɪ] 'I', [baɪ] 'by', [sʌɪd] as well as [saed] 'side'. Indeed, Lodge's data show that increase in vowel duration is just as likely to occur in non-'Aitken's Law' contexts: [ðaat aaksɛnt] 'that accent', [baad] 'bad', [ɬaaft] 'laughed'. Nevertheless, the salientness of the Scots treatment of the Standard English [ɑɪ] diphthong is regularly observed in the nineteenth century and attested in *The Vulgarities of Speech Corrected* (1826: 227):

> the sound 'i' when long, as in 'fire' and 'fine', seems to be very hard for the natives of Scotland, not so much from the difficulty of the sound itself as from habit. It ought always to sound exactly like 'y' in the word 'my', but the Scotch sound is very different, as any Scotsman may at once perceive by trying to pronounce 'child', 'mild', 'wild' &c. The peculiarity, however, is not universal, and in some words, such as 'fire', pronounced *feire*, is confined to the eastern counties, as near Edinburgh . . . Throughout Scotland, it is nearly universal to sound 'I', like 'a' in

'father', as 'A did not intend to go', for 'I did not intend to go'; and even the most careful speakers, are apt to fall into this vulgarity.

8.4.2.5   The [ju]/[u] Alternation

Despite the fact that the distinction seems particularly salient to the Scottish observers in the period, the distributional characteristics of the [ju]/[u] alternation throughout the eighteenth and nineteenth centuries are far from transparent. Although readily admitting that with respect to this alternation even 'good speakers among the English differ', Sylvester Douglas almost everywhere treats as offences against propriety the Scottish rising diphthongal [ju] for a [u] vowel in items such as *blue* and *pursue* where the '*ue* represents the first sound of *u* where the Scotch give it the diphthongal sound'. Under BUILD, he informs us that 'Many Scotch people sound the *ui* like the diphthongal *u* in *mule*', while the others sound it 'like the long first sound of *e*, or *ee*; so as to make *build* and *steel'd* or *wield* rhyme together. Both these methods are erroneous' (Jones 1991: 178). Again, under LUXURY there is the strong injunction: 'the second *u* has not the diphthongal sound which some Scotch people give it; but the same short, close vocal sound, as the first, or as it has in the words *stuck*, *luck*, but more obscure' (Jones 1991: 207). Other authorities too suggest that there was a predilection among many Scots speakers for the monophthongal form. Alexander Geddes (1792: 432) describes his third *u* sound – represented by the graph ⟨û⟩ – as:

> *u* English as in *pure*; This is really a compound of *e* and *u*. It is, however, to be observed, that it is not sounded exactly in the same manner by the Scots and English. In the mouths of the latter it seems to be composed of *i* and *eù*; while the former pronounce it more like the French *u* or *eu*, in the word *peur*.

He thus appears to infer that for Standard English speakers there exists a genuine [ju] diphthongal segment, which some speakers of Scots are liable to interpret, at least on occasion, as monophthongal and approximating to the kind of 'French', probably fronted labial segment, discussed above. Examples which Geddes cites for the Edinburgh dialect include *abûn* 'above', *attûn* 'attune', *brûz*, *brûzan* 'browsing', *bûs* 'bows', *dû* 'due', *enûkh* 'enough', *fûl* 'fool', *imbû* 'imbue', *lûk't* 'looked', *mûs* 'muse', *nû* 'new', *refûs*, *sûner* 'sooner', *tûn* 'tune'.

We should not be surprised by the fact that speakers should perceive [ju] as something approximating to [ü]. Rather than interpret the [ju] signal as comprising a palatal/labial *sequence*, listeners hear it as a complex or *internally mixed* phonetic segment made up *simultaneously* of a labial (prominent) and palatal (subordinate) segment; the surface manifestation of such a mixture being perceived as [ü] or [ɯ] (Anderson and Ewen 1987: 212–14). This 'reinterpretation' of linear segments in terms of simultaneously expressed internal components of a single, complex segment also appears to lie behind the well-known English and Scots diphthongal [au] to monophthongal [ɔ] change in the history of words such as *law* and *bought*. In this case, the [a] > [u] elements in a linear sonorant/labial diphthongal sequence are perceived as the simultaneous internal components of a mixed and complex segment like [ɔ] (Jones 1989: 260).

Elphinston claims that '*duke* retains dhe licquid in *dyuc*; hwen he plays not hiz parent, dhe French *duc*. Dhus ar dhe Inglish *duke* and *duc* Scottishly interchainged', while Robertson's evidence might be interpreted (if we take his first mentioned item as the 'head' form) as pointing to a preference among Glaswegian speakers for the diphthongal variant: *Adieu/adoe* 'bustle', *dew/due/dove/do*, *duke/duck*, *savour/saviour/saver*, *sugar/sucker*, *us/use/ewes*. In this context, we recall Walter Scott's well-known anecdote in *Heart of Midlothian* (Parker 1971: 207): summoned before the House of Lords, the Edinburgh Provost's language might be expected to be of the formal variety, a variety which, under conditions of hypercorrection, could well produce a [ju] diphthong where Scots speakers in the late eighteenth century might informally pronounce the stressed vowel in an item like *duck* as a centralised [ɤ] shape:

> The Magistrates were closely interrogated before the House of Peers, concerning the particulars of the Mob, and the *patois* in which these functionaries made their answers, sounded strange in the ears of the Southern nobles. The Duke of Newcastle having demanded to know with what kind of shot the guard which Porteous commanded had loaded their muskets, was answered naively: 'Ow, just sic as ane shoots *dukes* and *fools* with.' This reply was considered as a contempt of the House of Lords, and the Provost would have suffered accordingly, but that the Duke of Argyle explained, that the expression, properly rendered into English, meant *ducks and water-fowl*.

There is evidence from the eighteenth century too that the [ju]/[u] alternation could also, especially in the Buchan dialect, include the pure palatal [i(i)]. Recorded mainly by Geddes, expressed by his ⟨è⟩ symbol, we find examples such as: *bèth* 'both', *brèm-hill* 'broom-hill', *fèls* 'fools', *flèds* 'floods', *frèt* 'fruit', *ghè* 'you', *lè-lorn* 'love lorn', *lèv* 'love', *Mèses* 'Muses', *nèn* 'noon', *sèn* 'soon', *sèth* 'sooth', *shèt* 'shoot', *snèd* 'snood', *unmèvt* 'unmoved', while Elphinston (1787: 4) comments:

> Against dhe Inglish *oo* (hweddher simpel, or licquidly articculated in *u*) and *a* slender, dhe soddhern Scots hav garded dheir dialect widh *u* and *é*, equally French; dhe former of hwich dhe nordhern sound az forrain, az did dhe Inglish. Hwile Eddinburrough, dherfore, uttered boath *shoo* and *she*, Frenchly *chu*; Abberdeen joined Ingland to' prezerv dhem; dho vulgarly emitting boath, *shee*: won pronouncing dhus, *rood* and *rude*, alike *rude* French; dhe oddher, like *rid* or *reed* Inglish.

Yet the very existence of [ju] diphthongal types in the phonology of prestigious contemporary Scots appears to be denied by one of the eighteenth century's most careful observers of prestigious Scots usage, Alexander Scot (Jones 1993: 102). Consider the data (Table 8.7) from his *The Contrast*, where he shows only a simple orthographic contrast between ⟨u⟩ (some kind of [u] vowel) and ⟨oo⟩ (some kind of [ɤ]). The absence of [ju] diphthongal types is puzzling, but in the light of Sylvester Douglas' injunctions against the use of the diphthong in provincial Scots, we might interpret Alexander Scot's reticence to record it as a signal of its stigmatised status with his Standard Scots speaking informants. Yet Adams (although possibly describing a more 'broad' version of Scots) uses the ⟨ú⟩ symbol, his *yu* as in *Duke*, ⟨diuuk⟩, for the Scotch rendering of *poor*, *door* and *moor*.

The current regional distribution pattern of [j]-adding and dropping is discussed in Chapter 11, section 11.6.2. Recording the usage of 'older' speakers, Wilson (1926: 18, 1915: 47) claims [j]-less pronunciations for items in Lothian and Fife such as *creature*, *picture*, *venture* and in general 'Lowland' Scots for *natural* as well as *use*, *refuse*, *excuse*. On the other hand, [j]-adding is attested by Wilson for Lothian and Fife (1926: 20) for items such as *hook*, *tough*, *enough*, and it is not uncommon to hear Standard Scottish English speakers produce

Table 8.7

Modern Standard Scots	Modern Standard Scots
SHOULD/BUT	NEW
[ü]/[ʌ]	[jü]

Scot's spelling:	Scot's spelling:
⟨u⟩	⟨u⟩
⟨shud⟩ *should*	⟨graitetud⟩ *gratitude*
⟨buke⟩ *book*	⟨curaoozetays⟩ *curiosities*
⟨ful⟩ *full*	⟨excuze⟩ *excuse*
⟨much⟩ *much*	⟨oapoartunetay⟩ *opportunity*

Eighteenth-century Scottish Standard [u]/[uu]

Scot's spelling:	Scot's spelling:
⟨oo⟩	⟨oo⟩
⟨wood⟩ *would*	⟨rabook⟩ *rebuke*
⟨boot⟩ *but*	⟨oonavarsetays⟩ *universities*
⟨cood⟩ *could*	⟨coamoonicatten⟩ *communicating*
⟨auboov⟩ *above*	⟨maunoofaucters⟩ *manufactures*
⟨oonless⟩ *unless*	⟨amoolatione⟩ *emulation*

Eighteenth-century Scottish Standard [ɤ]

forms like [dɛvəljuʃən] 'devolution' and [pɔljuʃən] 'pollution'. Palatalisation in the [j] environment is a common feature of the modern language too, Lodge (1984: 92) attesting [aktʃəlë] 'actually', [ɛdʒükeʃn] 'education', [ʌnjüʒɫ] 'unusual' and [aʔtʃəɫɨ] 'actually', although his informants also produce shapes like [ɨntɹədjüst] 'introduced' and [wəz jʌŋ] 'was young' (see section 8.4.3.3).

8.4.3   Consonantal Sounds

With the exception of a few important instances, the majority of consonantal alternations and innovations to be found in Scots over the past 200 years or so are still to be found active in the modern language and, indeed, represent features associated with consonantal change in the general history of English. However, although many of the consonantal variations which we shall describe can be classified as historically recurrent, there can be little doubt that they enjoyed a regional and social distribution in many ways different from that in the modern language. While a more detailed account of the regional and social mapping of consonantal variants in this late period will be found in the appropriate sections in this volume (notably in Chapter 11, section 11.7), we shall wherever possible recount contemporary attitudes to them (in however banal a fashion these might be expressed) and discuss how their modern implementation might add to our knowledge of general phonological change and its lexical transmission.

8.4.3.1   The Lateral Sonorant [l]

This segment shows variation along at least two parameters. On the one hand there is (a usually phonetically conditioned) variation between dental and palatal [l] sounds – the 'bright' and 'dark' [l] and [ɫ]. It is extremely difficult to glean any precise information from the eighteenth- and nineteenth-century source materials as to either the existence of such a contrast (although, as we shall see, evidence from vocalisation is indicative here) or what kind of sociophonetic distribution in the language it may have shown. Eighteenth-century Scots commentators rarely appear to distinguish between fronted and retracted [l] sounds. Buchanan describes the segment merely as 'a palatal' (1762: 21), while there might just be a hint of the contrast in what Holmberg (1956: 107) describes as 'a distinction in quality between initial and final *l* in [James Douglas'] language, the latter being transcribed *El*'. Nineteenth-century observers like Murray make little of the distinction socially, historically or regionally. Yet in the modern language it has been shown (Johnston 1983a: 23–5) how among Edinburgh speakers front forms are a marker of prestige speech, while retracted laterals mark working-class usage. However, although the situation is a complex one, Johnston records how in the city the dark, retracted lateral appears to be spreading up the social scale and is coming to be the prestige form, particularly among lower middle-class men. Certainly this spread of the 'dark' form is particularly noticeable among young speakers of all social classes in the city, even for female speakers.

One of the most common and historically recurrent features of English and Scots phonology involves the effacement of syllable-final lateral sonorants, a phenomenon of [l]-vocalisation. With their relatively low F_2 frequency and highly periodic shape (well-defined formant structure), [l] segments in general show acoustic fingerprints which are often perceived as if they were 'full' vowels, and full labial vowels at that; hence the common modern Glaswegian realisation of items like 'Channel Tunnel' and 'well' as [ʧænoʷ tʌnoʷ] and [wɛoʷ]. Under his section dealing with L MELTED OR DROPT (1787: 34), Elphinston describes the effect of this 'licquid meltabel' in his contemporary Scots: '*l* final, sometimes medial, melts in dhe Scottish dialect. Dhus *ball* and *boll*, *pool* and *fool* (boath short) *bulk* and *sculk*, *allum* and *Allardice*, wer *bow* and *bow* (dipthong), *poo* and *foo*, *book* and *scoog*, *awm* and *Airdice*: *all won woll*, *aw*, *é*, *oo*, a figgurative Scotticism for *All won thing*'. Adams (1799: 152–3) asserts somewhat tortuously that 'When coalescing consonants preserve the long, or broad sound of preceding vowels, then the vowel is changed, or the double consonant vanishes or receives the guttural sound, if combination admit it', listing as Scots usage *caw*, *saw*, or *cá*, *sá* for English *câll*, *fâll*, where it is possible that his ⟨aw⟩ symbol represents [ɔ] or [ɒ] rather than a diphthong, while ⟨á⟩ probably realises [ɑ]. Sylvester Douglas remarks how [l], 'This semivowel and liquid' which he regards as 'the most pleasing to the ear of all consonants' (Jones 1991: 132), appears 'mute' in items like *half*, *walk*, *stalk*, *talk*, *salmon*, *psalm*, while it is 'generally sounded' in the 'standard' London dialect in *scalp*, *calm*, *balm* and *psalmody* (Jones 1991: 221).

Although straightforward effacement of syllable-final [l] is fairly well recorded by Scots writers in the eighteenth century, commentators are rarely specific concerning the degree of 'residue' left behind as a result of the sonorant's vocalisation; perhaps what Elphinston intends by [l] sounds being 'meltabel . . . into cognate effisience'. Of the Scots observers, it is Drummond who (if only to disown it) most explicitly points to a genuine vocalisation of (what would be a retracted) lateral sonorant in syllable-rhyme position (1767: 23): 'some pronounce this letter [⟨o⟩] like the diphthong *ou* in *croud*, in the words *old*, *cold*, *scold*, *hold*, *molt*, *bolt*, *colt*, a practice not general, and therefore not to be imitated'. Given the prevalence of [l]-vocalisation among present-day Glaswegian and West of Scotland speakers of almost all social classes, it is disappointing (and perhaps significant) that there are so few instances recorded in Robertson's lists: *could/cool'd/cud* ('chewed by cattle'), *Dauphine/Dolphin*. Wilson (1915) records many instances of the vocalisation in his Perthshire informants, a phenomenon he asserts to be especially common in post-back-vowel and mid-back-vowel contexts, thus his *aw* 'all', *waw* 'wall', *row* 'row', *maut* 'malt', *book* 'bulk', *goup* 'gulp' and many others. Murray (1873: 123) also notes how 'After *o*, L is also often dropped, making the diphthong *owe*: *powe*, *knowe*, *rowe*, *bowe*, *howe*, *cowt*, *yowk* = English poll, knoll, roll, boll, hollow, colt, yolk'. While Wilson too (1915: 21) attests the intervocalic [l]-vocalisation in an item like *how* 'hollow', he also notes the existence among his speakers of a syllable-initial [l]-vocalisation (presumably a fronted [l] sound) in the item *cloak* which he represents as *kyuk*, some kind of [kjuk] pronunciation.

Although his data sample is limited, Lodge's two modern Edinburgh speakers show an interesting contrast in the extent to which they vocalise syllable-final [l]. While both speakers appear to realise a 'dark' [ɫ] in all vowel contexts, the younger speaker is much less likely to vocalise the sonorant, producing [oɫd] 'old', [skuɫ] 'school', while the older speaker regularly alternates vocalised and non-vocalised forms: [ʧëɔd] 'child', [skuö] 'school' and [səbstaanʃəö] 'substantial', alongside [stiɫ] 'still' and [wɛɫ] 'well'. Macaulay's Ayr study (1991) suggested that the full/vocalised lateral alternation was primarily lexically determined (restricted in the main to items such as *all*, *hold*, *roll*, *pull*, *soldier* and *fault*, with vocalisation rarely, if ever, occurring in *always*, *bald*, *cold*, *doll* and *haul*), although there is a hint of some phonetic conditioning as well. However, the frequency of the vocalisation seems to correspond with lower-class social status in the town.

Elphinston (along with several others) records (the still current) [n] ∼ [l] alternation in the item *chimney*, where 'Vulgar Inglish turns . . . *chimney*, into . . . *chimley*' (1786: 19), while Sylvester Douglas states (Jones 1991: 182): 'This word by many vulgar people both Scotch and English is pronounced (very unaccountably) as if written *chimley*' (Jones 1989: 123ff.). Note too Beattie's (1788: 33) comments on this kind of phenomenon:

> The liquids L and R are acknowledged by Wallis to be anomalous. He is inclined to derive them from D and N. He mentions a tribe of American Indians adjoining to New England, who cannot articulate R or L; but when they attempt either, fall into N, and instead of *lobster* say *nobsten*: I have met two persons, natives of Scotland, who did the same.

In his list of 'Words like in Sound but different in Spelling', Robertson (1722: 62) has as homophones *appear/appeal* and *ail/aim*.

8.4.3.2   [r] Segments

The [r] segment is the object of much phonaesthetic description in both historical English and Scots grammatical traditions. It is often described as the 'harsh guttural', the 'canine guttural'. Elphinston (1766: 136, 284) typically sees the sound produced by it as the consequence of an 'irritated throat' and having an effect on the ear which is 'rough, harsh, horrid and grating' (1766: 302). No less an observer than Buchanan (1762: 22) comments: '*R*, a palatal; it is expressed by a Concussion, or Quivering of the Extremity of the Tongue, which beating against the Breath as it goes out, produces this horrid dog-like Sound'.

Indeed, for Elphinston one of the virtues of his contemporary prestigious pronunciation lies in the fact that 'dhe old aspirate ov R' has been replaced (1795: 29):

> Som Greeks, followed by som Lattins, fancied to' ad rufnes to' dhe licquid *R*, or to' paint its innate rufnes more foarcibly, by subjoining aspiracion . . . til at length harmonious *rezon* introduced *rime*, boath into' French and Inglish . . . Dhe very *rinosceros* disdains now alike to' ruffen hiz horn widh adscitious snorting, and to' stifel even hiz moddern sibbilacion.

Commentators in the early part of our period appear to recognise several different phonetic shapes for the segment. Sylvester Douglas' comment that the English pronounce this sound 'the harshest of all letters . . . more softly' than the Scots (Jones 1991: 135) might be an indication of obstruency versus (mainly affricative) continuancy: thus we might see the two [r] sounds, one a 'hard' obstruent like [r], the other the alveolar voiced frictionless continuant [ɹ] (Laver 1994: 263–4).

In his *Observations* to the *Table*, Alexander Geddes (1792: 423) comments that 'In some parts of Scotland this letter is pronounced with an aspiration, though not so hard as that of Northumberland. The Greeks seem to have given it the same sound'; such a description we might consider appropriate to a description of some kind of frictioned, uvular [ʁ], perhaps exemplified through his *trhein* spelling for 'train'. The fact that some kind of [ʁ] or perhaps [ʀ] segment is also recognised by Sylvester Douglas in the contemporary language seems clear from his statement (Jones 1991: 134) that 'What by the French is termed *grassayment*, in England the *burr*, and by the Scotch a *rattle* proceeds from pronouncing the *r* in the throat, without applying the tongue to the upper jaw, as must be done in the proper pronounciation [sic]. This guttural *r* it is that resembles the snarl of a dog.' Nineteenth-century descriptions vary in their detail, Murray (1873: 120) perhaps suggesting the prevalence of tapped forms over what might be frictionless continuants:

> R is in Scotch always a consonant, and in all positions trilled sharply with the point of the tongue, and never smoothly *buzzed* or burred, or converted into a mere glide as in English, nor *rolled* with the whole length of the tongue as in Irish, nor roughly *burred* with the pharynx as in Northumberland, in France and Germany. Even the initial English *r*, in *road*, *rung*, is softer and more gliding than the Scotch, which is used with equal sharpness before or after a vowel, as in *rare*, *roar*, *rayther*, *roarer*. In the south of England, its subsidence after a vowel into a mere glide renders it impossible to distinguish, in the utterance of some speakers, between *law*, *lore*; *lord*; *laud*; *gutta*, *gutter*; *Emma*, *hemmer*. Hence, when these words are used with a following vowel, a hiatus is avoided by saying draw-*r*-ing, Sarah-*r*-Anne, Maida-*r*-ill, idea-*r* of things, law-*r* of England, phrases of which even educated men are not ashamed, or not conscious, of uttering. No such liberties are allowable with the Scotch *r*, which is always truly consonantal.

Much after the same fashion, Wilson (1915:16) claims that the sound is 'pronounced in Scotch differently from the English *r*, being always given a distinct trill, whether at the beginning or end of a word, and it does not, as often in English, alter the pronunciation of a preceding vowel sound'. The Murray/Ellis Edinburgh specimen of 1873 appears not to differentiate between [r] types at all, merely indicating that there was no deletion of the segment post vocalically.

Indeed, loss of syllable-final [r] appears to be recorded only intermittently throughout the eighteenth- and nineteenth-century record, and all the available evidence points to Scots being then, as now, universally rhotic. Walker's (1791: 50) comment on its (partial) effacement in London speech is well known:

In England, and particularly in London, the *r* in *bard, lard, card, regard*, &c is pronounced so much in the throat as to be little more than the middle or Italian *a*, lengthened into *baa, baad, caad, regaad* . . . But if this letter is too forcibly pronounced in Ireland, it is often too feebly sounded in England, and particularly in London, where it is sometimes entirely sunk.

Sylvester Douglas rarely comments directly upon the possible effacement of syllable-final [r] in the London prestige dialect; the only lexical context where he seems to recognise the potential for postvocalic [r]-effacement (albeit by 'the English' only) appears under his unsmiling observations on the item ASS (Jones 1991: 165):

> This word is not inserted on account of any provincial manner of pronouncing it, but to illustrate the pronounciation [sic] of another, which the English sound so very like this, as to give occasion to numerous ambiguities of a very coarse nature. I remember a popular ballad several years ago, which was in great vogue for some time in the streets of all the great towns of the kingdom, and which was not deficient in humour. The burthen of it was this word *Ass*. But it was only used for the sake of an indecent equivocation in the sense, by its similarity in point of sound to the other word to which I allude. In Scotland, where I then happened to be, the joke was scarcely understood, because in that country, the sounds of the two words differ nearly as much as those of *pass*, and *pairs*.

Elphinston (1786: 141) notes syllable-final [r]-effacement (perhaps accompanied by vocalisation producing some kind of [ɑu] diphthong) only for the item *Marlborough*: 'Nay *marl* wood yield to *maul* . . . and show herself onnestly *Maulburrough*; but for fear ov dhe learned laffers ov London, hoo so duly decide in difficult cases'. Other evidence for the effacement of [r] is difficult to come by: George Fisher's *The Instructor or Young Man's Best Companion* (1789: 12ff.), under his list of 'Words of the Same Sound', records *Harsh* 'sever'/ *Hash* 'minced meat', *Marsh* 'low ground'/*Mash* 'for a horse'/*Mesh* 'of a net', while Robertson (1722: 47) has the pair *Torn* 'rent'/*Tun* 'of wine'.

Data from twentieth-century surveys show Scots speakers using both frictionless continuant [ɹ] and flaps, while only Grant (1913: 35) seems to show evidence for [r]-dropping and then only in 'some dialects of the North East, [where] *r* is regularly dropped before *s* as *purse, horsie*, pʌs, hɔsɪ'. Lodge (1984: 89) notes vocalisation, deletion and lenition to a frictionless continuant of the flap in syllable-final position, citing cases like [mʌɹtʃənt] 'merchant', [koət] 'court', [bʌdz] 'birds', [fʌʌst] 'first'. Romaine (1978: 148ff.) has shown that, for Edinburgh speakers at least, a phonetic variation involving [r] (trilled point), [ɾ] (single tap), [ɹ] (voiced frictionless continuant) and non-realisation is not without socio-phonetic significance, her study showing how males tend to prefer tap and non-realisation, while female speakers consistently produce the frictionless continuant shape and 'they are almost always rhotic'.

8.4.3.3 Fricativising and Voicing Contrasts

The eighteenth-century record shows evidence for the reduction in vocality of the palatal vowel in *-ium* terminations in items like *medium* to some kind of [j] palatal semivowel, thus Cortez Telfair (1775: 127): 'In such words as *medium, genius, Indian, i* may either make a diphthong with the next vowel or not, in poetry; But in prose, it makes always a diphthong; and then those words are pronounced as if written *meed-yum, geen-yus, Ind-yun*'. The author of *A Spelling-Book upon a New Plan* (1796: 26) makes a similar observation: 'The vowel *u*, in the terminations *ure* and *ute*, though marked with a circumflex accent, has not exactly the same sound as *ew*: – it sounds rather like *yŭ*, as, *creature*, (creatyŭr); *leisure* (leisyŭr), &c'; and commenting on his *lenient* (lēni̯ĕnt) entry, he states:

> Though *i*, in the terminations beginning with a consonant and in *ia* or *ie*, is marked as silent [italicised], it is not *wholly* so: – its effect is twofold. 1. It carries the preceding consonant, by a soft, and almost imperceptible transition, to the following vowel. 2. it affects the sound of the preceding consonant, if it be *d*, *l*, *n*, *s*, or *t*; making *d* to sound somewhat like soft *g*, as in *sol-dier* (sol-g*i*er); *In-dia*, (In-g*ia*): it makes the sound of *l* and *n* more liquid, as val*i*ant, len*i*ent; gives *s* a kind of musical sound, between that of *z* and hissing *s*, as in trans*i*ent; and makes *t* soft like *sh*, as in quot*i*ent, part*i*al: But a good teacher would do more to describe its power by one word of his mouth, than five pages in writing.

He seems to be suggesting pronunciations like [soldʒər], [ɪndʒə], [valjənt], [linjənt], [tranʒənt], [kwošənt] and [paršəl].

Adams (1799: 114–15) delimits the operation of the continuancy shifting of voiceless dentals to those instances where he claims the [t] to be part of the inherent structure of the lexical item:

> *T* preserves its sound when it forms a radical syllable, for, on examination, it will appear not to be part of an expletive: as – *bast-ion*, *combust-ion*, *christ-ian*, *fust-tian*: Hence by strict rule (contradicted by use) *Egyp-tian* should be sounded, *Egypt-ian*, because the root *Egypt* is closed by *t*, and *ian* is the expletive; custom has made it yield to the rule of finals, *teon*, *tian*, *sion*, &c. which the above and similar words do not so readily admit, on account of a singular harshness they would thus produce.

Adams, in a typical anecdote, goes on to illustrate the English tendency to fricativise the [t] obstruent in such contexts through what he sees as its almost parodied use in Latin pronunciation:

> This hissing English contraction extended to Latin words, shews another absurdity in our pronunciation of Latin. In the year 1755, I attended a public Disputation in a foreign University, when at least 400 Frenchmen literally hissed a grave and learned English Doctor (Mr Banister) not by way of insult, but irresistibly provoked by the quaintness of the repetition of *sh*. The Thesis was the concurrence of God in *actionibus viciosis*: the whole hall resounded with the hissing cry of *sh* (*shi*, *shi*, *shi*) on its continual occurrence in *actio*, *actione*, *viciosia* – *ac-shio*, *vi-shi-osa*.

Present-day speakers of Scots can be heard to alternate for *media* pronunciations like [midɪə]/[midʒə]/[midjə].

Walker discusses at some length the possibility of palatalisation of [t] in pre-palatal vowel and semivowel contexts, relating its occurrence to the placement of the accent: 'This pronunciation of *t* extends to every word where the diphthong or diphthongal sound commences with *i* or *e*. Thus *bestial*, *beauteous*, *righteous*, *frontier*, &c, are pronounced as if written *best-cheal*, *beaut-cheous*, *right-cheous*, *frontchier*, &c', although he roundly criticises Sheridan for generalising the phenomenon to 'non-accented' contexts:

> he has extended the change of *t* into *tch*, or *tsh*, to the word *tune* and its compounds, *tutor*, *tutoress*, *tutorage*, *tutelar*, *tutelary*, &c. *tumult*, *tumour*, &c. which he spells *tshoon*, *tshoon-able*, &c.

tshoo-tur, tshoo-tris . . . the words ought to be pronounced as if written *tewtor, tewmult, tewmour,* &c. and neither *tshootur, tshoomult, tshoomour,* as Mr Sheridan writes them, nor *tootor, toomult, toomour,* as they are often pronounced by vulgar speakers.

The phenomenon is much commented upon too by the Scots observers, notably Barrie (1796: 3–5), who asserts that 'Italic *e* and *i* sound like initial *y*, as in hid*e*ous, fil*i*al, while Italic *ce, ci, cy, si,* and *ti* sound *sh*, as in o*ce*an, so*ci*al, hal*cy*on, pen*si*on, a*cti*on; Roman si sounds *zh* as in conclusion, also Italic *s* before *u*, as in plea*s*ure'. McIllquam (1781: 118) refines this generalisation: 'T, when followed by *i* and another vowel, sounds as *sh* as; *nation, motion, satiate, satiety*; except when it is preceded by *s* or *x*, and derivatives from words ending in *ty*: as *suggestion, commixtion, mighty, mightier*'. Drummond (1767: 66) and Burn (1766: 13) hear terminations in *-tion, -tial* and so on as monosyllabic, the latter representing *condition, partial, tertian, Grecian, coercion, halcyon* and *division* as [condishun], [parshal], [tershan], [Greshan], [coershun], [halshun] and [divishun], as does Buchanan (1757: 13): 'Observe, that (si) before (on) at the end of words, takes the sound of (sh); as *division, occasion, evasion, mission,* &c. read *divishun, occashun,* &c. so that the terminations *sion* and *tion* have generally the same sound, *viz, shun* or *shon,* and are always, as they ought to be, pronounced as one syllable'. Elphinston (1786: 45–6) in his customary fashion is expansive on the issue:

Into' won absurdity, however, dhe French hav not led us; nor hav dhey led us into' manny, or evver committed won equal to' dhat (we hav hiddherto' practised) ov prezenting before dhe aspirate licquefaccion, *i* occularly (az ettymolodgically) open, for *i* really (az auriccularly) shut! True It Iz dhat, before *tl* belyIng *si*, or *ci*, no shutting dubbler cood be vizzibel; an irretfragabel argument, wer dhare no odher, against any such substitucion. Dhus dubbly impossibel iz dhe continnuance ov anny such picture az *ambition, ambitious; propitious, propitiate, propitiation; initial, initiate, initiation;* or az *Titian, Politian, Domitian,* or *Domitius;* for (dhe indispensabel az unexcepcionabel) *ambiscion, ambiscious; propiscious, propisciate, propisciacion; iniscial, inisciate, inisciacion;* hware dhe preceding *ci* remains dhe simpel sibbilant, articulating dhe febel vowel. Nor iz *inisciate* more clearlly a word ov three syllabels, *i-nis-ciate;* dhan *inisciacion,* ov five: *i-nis-ci-a-cion:* dhe last being vertually *shate* and *shon.*

Some of the Scots consonantal alternations most regularly commented upon by contemporary observers are those which involve voicing and fricativising contrasts. Commentators from both sides of the border regularly note the way in which Scots speakers tend to devoice obstruents and voice those which are devoiced in the 'standard' language. Sylvester Douglas, for instance, observes how Scots vernacular speakers use [s] fricatives in items like *damsel, resign, possess, preside, president, residence,* while voiced [z] fricatives are regularly produced in *debase, rase, erase, place, base, precise, profuse, design, nuisance.* Robertson too bears witness to this tendency in his pairs: *arrows/arose, arrass/harrows, bruise/Bruce, cease/seas, deseased/deceased, Jews/juice* and many others. Likewise, [k]/[g] and [f]/[v] voicing alternations are evidenced in pairs like *creek/Greek, sugar/sucker, disgust/discussed, contend/content, extend/extent, parasite/paraside/patricide.*

Douglas also records a [ʃ]/[ʒ] contrast under his discussion of the ASIA item, where the pure dialect is said to realise the former, as in *nation* and *Dacia,* the Scots producing [ʒ] as in *pleasure* or as the French ⟨j⟩ in *ajouter,* a usage that Walker (1791: 54) identifies as Scots 'when . . . it ought undoubtedly to be pronounced *Azhia* . . . This is the Scotch pronunciation of this word, and unquestionably the true one: but if I mistake not, *Persia* is pronounced in Scotland with the same aspiration of *s*, and as if written *Perzhia'*. Elphinston (Rohlfing 1984: 280ff.) fires a general broadside against Scots voicing habits:

> Notthing can be more dialectally incident, dhan dhe interchainge ov direct and depressive. If, from unmodelled, or unmoddulated moudhs, may be stil herd ar London *padrole*, *pardner*, *prizes*, for *patrole*, *partner*, *prices*, and dhe like; it cannot surprize, if dhe same rank in Scotland guiv *blash*, *barley*, *cabtain*, *luvtennant*, *steve*, *boddom*, *gowk*, *baggabag*; *Zion*, *uz*, *elz*, *caze*, *baze*, *rize*, *doze*, *excuze*, *moroze*, *precize* (if not *preceze*) *dezign*; *choiz*, *rejoiz*, *Nanzy*, *Dezember*, *Prezentor*, *egzit*; for *plash*, *parley*, *captain*, *lieftennant*, *stif*, *bottom*, *coocoo*, *buccabac*; *Sion*, *us*, *else*, *case*, *base*, *rise*, *dose*, *excuse*, *morose*, *precise*, *design*; *choice*, *rejoice*, *Nancy*, *December*, *Precentor*, *exit*, dhat is *ecsit*. But dhe direct sinks not oftener into' dhe depressive, dhan dhe depressive rizes into' dhe direct, particcularly in Scotland az in Wales, in dhe Celtic or Gaulic manner. Az *Taffy Etwarts*, and *Tonnel Tingwall*, for *Davy Edwards*, and *Donnald* (or *Donnel*) *Dingwal*.

Perhaps the most widely commented-upon of all lenition processes in the period is that typified by Sylvester Douglas' comments under the entry for the items CALF'S, WIFE'S, KNIFE'S (Jones 1991: 180), where he notes: 'The genetives of *calf*, *wife*, *knife* are pronounced by most English people like the plurals of the same words, i.e. as if written, *Calves*, *wives*, *knives*. The Scotch, and some English people, retain in the genetive the same hard sound of the *f* as in the nominative.' Likewise, under his HOUSES (THE PLURAL OF HOUSE) entry he claims (Jones 1991: 202) that 'The Scotch, and some provincials in England, pronounce the *s* hard in the plural, as it is in the singular; but it ought to be soft as in the verb to *house*; and in the singular and plural both, of *spouse*, *spouses*'. Elphinston notes too for him as Scottish those alternations, whereby 'Affinity ov articulacion, accounts ezily for dhe chainge ov *us* to' *uz*, *az* to' *as*, *if* to' *of* (1787: 22–3). Wilson (1926: 28) claims, among others, *shufful*, *neffay*, *weifs*, *tneifs*, *loafs*, *haafs* as representative of 'shovel', 'nephew', 'wives', 'knives', 'loaves' and 'halves', while Murray (1873: 122) states: '*F* of the Old Scotch, still retained in the more northern dialects, is in the south often *v*; not only in plurals, as *weyves*, *thieves*, for wyffis, theiffis, but in some singulars, as *neive*, *caave*, for neif, calf or chaff, and sometimes *staave*, *scheive*, for staff, sheaf. *Grave* is *graaf* (older) and *greave*.' Lodge's (1984: 90) informants appear to show devoicing of both [r] and fricatives even in phonetic contexts which might be considered to be strongly voiced, notably before other voiced sounds word-finally: [wəʐ wɪð̥ ðæt] 'was with that'; [ʍɛðəɾ wɪð̥ ð̥ɛ̈] 'whether with the'; [ɬɨɣ ðɛɾ] 'live there'.

Of the set of possible Scots consonantal alternations in evidence over the past 300 years, one of the most salient is the tendency to change obstruency value, either in the direction of or away from relatively vocalic continuancy. The majority of instances seem to occur where obstruent consonants come to be realised as noisy fricative continuants, although there are a few cases where the opposite process is recorded. An alternation involving [d]/[ð], notably in intervocalic environments, can still be attested in regional Scots usage, and is highlighted at the end of the nineteenth century in the southern counties by Murray (1873: 121), who points to 'a confusion between *d* and the voiced *th* (dh)', citing an intervocalic voiced dental fricative in items such as *adder*, *bladder*, *ladder*, while the voiced dental obstruent is used, he claims, in *bother*, *fathom* and *worthy*, while found alongside each other are continuant and non-continuant alternants for 'shoulder' – *shoodder/shoother*; 'powder' – *pooder/poother* and some others. In the previous century, Alexander Geddes observes (1792: 423): 'The sound which we now express by *th*, and which almost all other nations, except the Spaniards, in vain attempt to utter, was changed by the Scots into *d* or *dd*, to speak more properly, they retained the ancient Saxon and Teutonic sound and symbol *d*, which the English have changed into *th*, as *fader, moder, broder, hidder, quhidder*'; and, while it is once more difficult to be sure of the 'directionality' of Robertson's pairs, we find him advocating as sounding alike *either/adder, Forth/fourth/Foord* ('a shallow'), *lethargy/liturgy*.

The historical evidence for a [p]/[f] alternation is also strong, Elphinston (1787: 26–7) noting (alongside [ð]/[θ] – [d]/[t] alternations): 'dhan for dhe Inglish *gahp, flap, skip, stripping, chop, trump; chub, gabel, caldron, Lauder, ladder, udder, consider* . . . to' becom dhe Scotch *gahph* or *gahf, flaf, skif, striffin, chost, trumph, chuf, gavel . . . caudhron, laudher, laddher, uddher, considdher*', although he is careful to say that the obstruentising of the fricative is not just a Scots characteristic, since 'dhe Inglish vulgar say *farden* . . . for *fardhing*' (Rohlfing 1984: 242). Sylvester Douglas as well claims that the voiceless obstruent [p] in the pure dialect item *trumps* is made continuant (more vowel-like) in the Scots version, pronounced 'as if written *trumphs*' (Jones 1991: 230).

Intervocalic [ʧ]/[k]/[ç] alternations are also well recorded throughout our period. Wilson (1926: 23) claims Lothian and Fife pronunciations of *steek, larrik, streek* for 'stitch', 'larch' and 'stretch' and, in Lower Strathearn (1915: 28), *rigg, brigg* and *segg* for 'ridge', 'bridge' and 'sedge', with Murray (1873: 122) pontificating:

> K or hard C of the Anglo-Saxon is, as is well known, preserved in the northern dialect, where the southern has developed the palatalised form of CH. Thus we have *kyrk, kyrn, cairl, kyst* . . . *larick, raaks, ylk, quhylk, syc, gowd-spink*, corresponding to the English *church, churn, churl, chest* . . . *larch, reach, each, which, such, gold finch*.

Sylvester Douglas, under his RACHEL entry (Jones 1991: 218), comments: 'The *a* as in *race*, the *ch* as in *Chester, church*. Many Scotch people substitute, in this word, for their vernacular and guttural sound of the *ch*, that of *k*'. Elphinston (1787: 27–8) is quite positive in this area:

> dhe Scotch stil loves even dhe simpel guttural, much beyond dhe moddern aspirate: retaining dhus *mac, thac* or *thic, sic, birk, kest, caf, cart, calk, streek; rig, brig, fike, dog;* for *match, thatch, such, birch, chest, chaf, chart, chalk, stretch; ridge, bridge, fidget,* and *dodge*. *Mac* may be less recogniz'd a match, remaining onely in such old phraze az *I nevver kenn'd (or kent) hiz mac:* I never knew hiz fellow.

Throughout the eighteenth century, there appears to have been an alternation, especially word-initially, between the less and more noisy fricatives [s] and [š], Walker (1791: 54) criticising Sheridan (1780) for recommending pronunciations of *suicide, presume* and *resume* 'as if written *shoo-icide, pre-zhoom, re-zhoom*', with Elphinston (1787: 26) noting that the contrary interchange is a characteristic of Scots: '*shal, shood, wish, Scotch fasshion*, (or *fassion*), to' be herd Scottishly . . . *sal, sood* (or *sud*), *was, Scots fasson*, dropping onely dhe nazallity ov dhe French *façon*', and again (1787: 23): 'Hence dhe Scottish *offisher* for *officer*, and *sal* for *shal*; . . . *plezer* for *plezzure*, and dhe like'. This general Scots characteristic is recorded by Robertson in such pairs as *ass/ash, shoe/sew, quince/quench, lace/lash, cruse/cruise/crush, kiss/kish*.

8.4.3.4 Cluster Simplifications

(a) Syllable-final

Comments on cluster simplification in Scots in the period are extensive (Jones 1996: 220), Alexander Geddes (1792: 423) observing that Scots shows 'fewer harsh combinations of consonants' than Metropolitan Court English, rendering *neglect, self, twelve, precinct, decerpt, tempt* and *kiln* by what he represents as *neglek, sel', twel, precink, decep, temp, kil.* The anonymous writer of *A Spelling-Book upon a New Plan* (1796) condemns as 'Commonly Pronounced' Scotticisms such as *fack* 'fact', *canle* 'candle' and *suttle* 'subtle'. Yet such a sociophonetic judgement needs to be considered in the light of the fact that Alexander Scot (1779) records realisations like *aicsap* 'except', *enstruck* 'instruct', *raspacks* 'respects' and *affack* 'effect' in *The Contrast* which – he explicitly states – represents a form of prestigious Edinburgh usage appropriate to 'the college, the pulpit and the bar'. The fact that Robertson's list contains examples such as *acts/axe/ask, temper/tempter, mind/mine*, and *presence/presents* might just suggest that the 'reduced' forms were acceptable enough to recommend to socially aspirant young ladies in Glasgow. That the social distribution of these cluster reductions is complex is suggested too by the fact that Scot represents 'acknowledge' by *aunoalege*, while Sylvester Douglas reserves his severest strictures for such a pronunciation of the word (Jones 1991: 158):

ACKNOWLEDGE
As Scotchmen soon learn that the *k* is mute in *knowledge* and other words wherein it is followed by an *n*, they, for the most part, fall into the error of suppressing the *c* likewise in *acknowledge*, and pronounce it as if it were written *anowledge*, or *aknowledge*. But the English give this *c* its hard sound, and utter it distinctly . . .

Elphinston (1787: 17–18) too notes how

Dhe Scotch doo indeed, az littel az dhe French, lov clustering consonants in dhe cloze. Peculiarly ar dhey dherfore apt to' drop dhe final dental, after a shutting consonant: saying *ac, corrup, temp; acs, corrups, temps*; for *act, corrupt, tempt* (hwich can be but *temt*); for *acts, corrupts, tempts*, and dhe like . . . after *l*, or *n*, dhe nordhern Scots drop *d* final; saying *aul commauns* for *old commands*. Dhey dhus call dheir *boddhy*, or littel *boodh*, sometimes a *shiel* for a *shield*; and say *Dunkel* (strong on dhe latter), hware dhey see *Dunkeld*. . . . and dhe Scots say, in dhe North, *cenner* or *thunner*; and evverihware, *temmer, nummer, tummel, sooroc*, for *cinder, thunder, timber, number, tumbel, sourdoc*, or dhe like . . . Simmilarly ezy, and totally French, iz dhe Scotch rejeccion ov dhe braud licquefier in dhe *lang-or* ov *lang-age*, for dhe *laguor* ov *language* (vertually, dhe *langgwor* ov *langgwage*).

That Elphinston sees such deletions as phonaesthetically motivated is clear from his claim that 'From ruf, dhe organs run to' smoodh; not from smoodh to' ruf. Hence dhe Inglish tendency to' dilate *Henry* into' *Hennery*; and dhe Scotch inscercion ov dhe dental, hwich harmoniously dividing, unites dhe licquids, in *Hendry* hwence *Henderson*' (1787: 20). Lodge's modern Edinburgh informants (1984: 92) produce reduced syllable-final clusters in shapes such as: [fʌɹs θɹi] 'first three', [is sæɪd] 'east side', [dɪstɹɪks] 'districts', [fɹɛnz] 'friends'. Half a century earlier, Wilson (1926: 16–17) records *brammul* 'bramble', *rummul* 'rumble', *hawn* 'hand', *ack* 'act', *empay* 'empty' and so on, similar observations being made by Murray (1873: 120–1): 'B is usually dropped in pronunciation after M in the accented or any following syllable', and he goes on to record *thymle, rumle, noomer*.

There is some evidence to suggest that consonantal cluster simplifications were subject to considerable lexical diffusion; for instance, while Sylvester Douglas records that in items like *tremble* and *humble* 'the Scotch are apt to suppress the *b* in this and other words ending in *ble*', yet 'in *member* . . . the *b* is to be sounded, both in this, and all other words of the same kind' (Jones 1991: 229). Again, under his LONDON entry we find the observation that: 'The formal way of pronouncing this word, is to sound the *d*. The more usual and familiar method is to suppress it. Both are countenanced by the example of good, and unaffected speakers' (Jones 1991: 206).

Syllable-final [ŋ]/[ŋg] alternants in Scots are well attested throughout our period. Sylvester Douglas makes the claim that late eighteenth-century Scotch vernacular usage was such that 'In almost all cases where *ng* is found in the middle of a word, the Scotch sound it as in *singer*. Thus they make *finger* and *singer* a perfect rhyme, and *anger* and *hanger*' (Jones 1991: 163). Likewise, he claims that in the Scotch vernacular *longer* is pronounced as the London standard *singer*, that is, with [ŋ], not [ŋg] (Jones 1991: 207). James Douglas (Holmberg 1956: 269) asserts that 'When *G* follows *N* at yᵉ end of a Word it is always hard, as, BANG, HANG, RANG . . . CLING, STRING, SONG . . . LONGEST, BRING-ING', where his 'hard *g*' represents a voiced obstruent; Elphinston also records [ŋg] in *hanger, singer, longer, hanging, longing* in contemporary polite London speech (Rohlfing 1984: 329). Nares' account (1784: 113–14) claims: 'In some provincial dialects, this final *g* is more distinctly spoken than it is among correct speakers; which mode of pronunciation sounds as if the *g* were doubled, thus, *sing-g, bring-g*'. Yet the devocalising of the nasal in the morphological ⟨ing⟩ to [n] as a Scottish characteristic is also prominent in the contemporary literature: '*G* . . . is often dropped in the termination *ing*, as *hearing, speaking, working, smelling* whereby they are liable to be mistaken for *here in, speak in, work in, smell in*' (McIllquam 1781: 16); and Elphinston's (1787: 41) 'az in dhe addage *A wollen meddher maks a daw dochter*: A willing (or An active) moddher makes a lazy daughter'. In the nineteenth century, Murray (1873: 124) witnesses this characteristic in Southern Scots as well: 'NG in the middle of a word always retains its simple final sound, as in *sing, long*. In English, on the contrary, it usually takes an additional *g* in pronunciation, as *sing-gle, long-ger, fing-ger, hung-gry, young-gest, Eng-glish*, which in Scotland and North England are *syng-'l, lang-er, fyng-er, hung-rie, yung-est, Ing-lish*', while for the early twentieth century we find: '*ng* in the middle of a word is a simple sound – no *g* follows it; hence we say – *sing-l, lang-er, hung-ry*, just as in Standard English we pronounce *sing-er*' (Grant and Main Dixon 1921: xiv).

There is considerable reference throughout our period to the still common Scots habit of realising a dental nasal in rhymes terminating in fricative consonants, as [lɛnθ] 'length' and [strɛnθ] 'strength' (Murray 1873: 124). Grant (1913: 32) avers that these 'are probably derived from Scotch dialect and should be avoided'. Over 100 years earlier, under his discussion of the LENGTH, LENGTHEN items, Sylvester Douglas too observes an [ŋ]/[n] contrast. The standard London dialect he records as showing [ŋ], but the Scots 'and inaccurate speakers among the English sound both words as if written *lenth, strenth*' (Jones 1991: 205). Elphinston (1787: 15–16) waxes quite lyrical on this Scots habit:

> Dhe Scots must howevver be owned inclinabel to' suppres dhe guttural after dhe dental, and so to' simplify away dhe nazal sound. Dhus hear we *Launton* and *Monton* (*Munton*) for *Langton* and *Monkton*; *moarnen* and *murnen*, for *morning* and *moarning*: hwence dhe Scottish Shibboleth ov *lenth* and *strenth*, for *length* and *strength*. Nor can aught proov more sallutary to' Caledonians, boath for sense and for sound, dhan dhe frequent and attentive reppeticion ov dhe awfool cupplet: *Dhe yong diseze, dhat must subdue at length,/Grows widh our growth, and strengthens widh our strength.*

(b)   Syllable-initial

Eighteenth- and nineteenth-century Scots materials witness the continuing demise of syllable-initial [k] and [g] segments in [kn] and [gn] clusters, although Murray (1873: 122) attests their survival (albeit in some kind of syllabified [kən] shape) late in the nineteenth century: 'K is still pronounced before N by old people, as *k'neyfe*, *k'nowe*, *k'neycht*; but the habit of suppressing it in the English taught at school has led the rising generation to drop it also in the vernacular. In the north-east of Scotland it remains in regular use.' However, there is some evidence to suggest that in certain instances the effacement of the palatal obstruent in the pre-nasal context was neither immediate nor total; some degree of obstruency may have been perceptible syllable-initially, perhaps in the shape of some level of glottal reinforcement. The phenomenon is recorded in the eighteenth century principally in Alexander Scot's rather odd-looking spellings for *known* and *knowledge* which appear in *The Contrast* text: ⟨tnoan⟩, ⟨tnoalege⟩. What may be a similar phenomenon is recorded by Drummond (1767: 26) under his *Rules for Pronouncing the Consonants*: 'C – sounds his first sound before *a*, *o*, *u*, his second before *e*, *i*, *y*, his third before *i*, and another vowel. In some counties they pronounce *t*, for *c*, before *l*, as *tlear*, *tlay*, *tlout*, for *clear*, *clay*, *clout*, a dialect not to be imitated'. Grant and Main Dixon (1921: 8) record an identical usage: 'In Forfar and East Perth, *t* takes the place of *k* before *n* as

Scots	Phonetics	English
knee	tni:	knee
knife	tnəif	knife
knock	tnɔk	clock
knowe	tnʌu	knoll'

while Wilson (1926: 25) records *tnee*, *tneif*, *tnoack*, *tnoab* for 'knee', 'knife', 'knock' and 'knob', a phenomenon perhaps related to his ('children's games') instances of *kwaw* 'two', *kwaal* 'twelve', *kwintee* 'twenty', *akween* 'between' (Melchers 1981).

8.4.3.5 Glottalisation

Despite the fact that the glottalisation of voiceless obstruents is such a common feature of modern English in general and some varieties of Scots in particular, it is difficult to find evidence for the phenomenon in either the eighteenth- or the nineteenth-century source materials. Such a dearth of evidence does not mean, of course, that the phenomenon did not occur in the period; it may have been the case that such glottalisation was regarded as too 'vulgar' to be recorded, or – perhaps equally likely – observers found it difficult to produce an appropriate orthographic mark for the feature. It may be the case too that glottalisation of syllable-final voiceless obstruents is a twentieth-century innovation. Certainly it is observed by Wilson (1926: 44), but only in intervocalic contexts: 'The glottal catch in place of *t* between two vowels is more common in Fife than in the other three dialects. It is also characteristic of Glasgow, e.g. *be'ur* "better", *bu'ur*, "butter", *taw'ay*, "potato", *gi'in* "getting", *boa'ul* "bottle" ', and again: 'The glottal catch in place of *t* between two vowels, e.g. in *butter*, *water*, is rarely heard in Lothian, but is common in Fife' (1926: 17). Recent studies of the phenomenon as it occurs in urban situations – Macaulay and Trevelyan (1977), Macaulay (1991), Johnston (1983a) suggest that incidence of glottalisation varies with phonetic context in the discourse, being perhaps most common in pre-pausal environments. The voiceless obstruent/glottal stop variable is also one which is extremely sensitive to general situational conditioning, especially formality level of the discourse, social class and sex of speaker, most surveys suggesting that in general glottalisation becomes more common with diminution of social status, with middle-class females especially likely to avoid the use of the glottalised shape. Yet glottalisation tends to increase among younger speakers, even among young females of the middle classes, although for the latter group an aspirated [tʰ] form is also used in competition with it.

8.4.3.6   The [ʍ]/[w] Alternation

There is little doubt that, as in the modern language, the Scots of the eighteenth and nineteenth centuries showed a [ʍ]/[w] word-initial alternation. Scots-speakers still tend to realise word-initial [w] as the voiceless labial velar fricative [ʍ]; compare Standard RP [waɪt] 'white' with colloquial Scots [ʍʌɪʔ]. Murray (1873: 118) stresses the distinction: 'Wh has in most parts of England so degenerated as not to be distinguished from W, and the pairs *when wen*, *whale wail*, *while wile*, are pronounced in the south exactly alike . . . We require a spelling to show that the corresponding Scotch words must not be so treated'. While asserting that the inhabitants of Fife and the Lothians universally pronounce syllable-initial *hw-* with 'both sounds being distinctly uttered' – perhaps suggesting [hw] rather than [ʍ] – Wilson claims that 'curiously enough, the Newhaven fisher-folk often drop the sound of *h* before *w* in such words, as in southern English, e.g. *wun* "when", *wit*, *wut* "what", *wawr* "where", *wail* "whale", *wup* "whip", *wuskay* "whisky"' (1926: 19). There is much comment in the eighteenth century too on this [w]/[ʍ] alternation. What seem to be [hw] or [ʍ] syllable onsets appear universally in Alexander Scot's *The Contrast* in items such as *whoch* 'which', *whother* 'whether', *whey* 'why' and *whoa* 'who' – forms which, we recall, Wilson claims to be typical of prestige Edinburgh speech of his time. Indeed, there is evidence that Scot's ⟨wh-⟩ digraph might even represent a more highly fricativised onset – some kind of [x]/[ç] – suggested by the 'Commonly Pronounced' *chot* 'what' and *chuen* 'when' for the 'True Pronunciation' ⟨whàt⟩ ⟨whĕn⟩ – where italicised ⟨h⟩ signifies non-realisation – of *A Spelling-Book upon a New Plan* (1796). Sylvester Douglas observes too how: 'The Scotch pronounce the *wh* like their guttural *ch* followed in like manner by a *u*, losing itself in the succeeding vowel. When they endeavour to correct this fault they are apt to omit the *h*, so as to pronounce *whit*, and *wit*, *whig* and *wig* in the very same manner', this perhaps in imitation of upper-class London usage, as noted by Walker (1791: 46): 'This letter [that is, h] is often sunk after *w*, particularly in the capital, where we do not find the least distinction of sound between *while* and *wile*, *whet* and *wet*, *where* and *were*. Trifling as this difference may appear at first sight, it tends greatly to weaken and impoverish the pronunciation, as well as sometimes to confound words of a very different meaning.' Indeed, it has recently been suggested that throughout the eighteenth and nineteenth centuries, [hw]/[ʍ] rather than [w]-initial forms 'appear in the context of discussions of the greater proprieties (and greater femininity) which the Proper Lady manifested in her speech' (Mugglestone 1995: 206).

The characteristic modern Scots habit of realising a voiceless labial velar fricative onset in items like *why* and *where* seems to be typical of the usage recommended by Alexander Geddes, as is suggested by his spellings like *huyl* 'while', *hua* 'who', *huilk* 'which' and many others. Elphinston spells *hwich*, *hwat* and *hwen* throughout, commenting on such items: 'That the *w* was subjunctively aspirated in them at all . . . appears not only from the surviving pictures, but from the real aspirations being yet preserved by the ancient Britons, the Welch, Scotch and Irish; who, later in receiving, must be later in refining, the English articulations; while the language of London (in general the best) has lost the power with the practise' (Rohlfing 1984: 339). Robertson's evidence is ambiguous. His 'sounding alike' pairs show 'head' words in the lists commencing in etymological [w] segments including *wail/wale/whale, wet/whet/what, way/why/whey*, while those with etymological [ʍ] are *while/ wile, whore/woer, white/Wight, who/woe*. It is difficult to imagine [ʍ] onsets in items like *woe, woer* and *wile*. We might therefore tentatively suggest that voiceless labial velar fricative onsets are what is being recommended by Robertson to the young ladies of Glasgow, a female usage directly opposed to that (we have suggested above) of London. Since [ʍ] forms were regarded as peculiarly Scottish (especially their 'Commonly Pronounced' *chot* 'what' and *chuen* 'when' types with their syllable initiating [x]/[ç]), then their replacement by [w] might be expected in a work recommending at least local prestige usage.

Surprisingly, there is little record in the eighteenth-century source materials of the current Northern Scots use of the bilabial fricative [β]/[f] for [ʍ] or [hw], with the exception of Sylvester Douglas (Jones 1991: 141): 'In the North of Scotland *wh* is pronounced like *f*; so that *what*, and *fat*, *why*, and *fie*, form to the ear in that part of the Island, the very same words', while Elphinston (1787: 32) comments on the [v]/[w] interchange: 'If Londoners be liabel to' interchainge *wile* and *vile*; no wonder Abberdeens-men, to' prezerv dhe aspiracion (hwich Londoners often looz) shood be apt to' say *file* for *hwile*. More pardonabel iz *furl* for *hwirl*, dhan *worse* for *verse*.'

8.5 STRESS AND STRESS PLACEMENT

The bulk of what passes for discussion on matters relating to phonological suprasegmentals in the eighteenth and nineteenth centuries is centred on the nature of the syllable, and many schoolbooks and grammar books are replete with lists of words of one-, two- and three-syllable structures. However, descriptions of stress and stress placement are frequent in the works of both Scottish and English writers, and there is important discussion upon the best method of formulating stress-placement rules and of regional variation in stress placement itself. For Walker (1791: 59), the notion of stress is often associated with both accent and emphasis:

> Accent, in its very nature, implies a comparison with other syllables less forcible; hence, we may conclude, that monosyllables, properly speaking, have no accent: when they are combined with other monosyllables and form a phrase, the stress which is laid upon one, in preference to others, is called emphasis . . . the accent always dwells with greatest force on that part of the word which, from its importance, the hearer has always the greatest occasion to observe; and this is necessarily the root, or body of the word.

He is careful to note too that while such a situation holds rather well for lexical items of native origin, it often fails with those derived from Romance sources, so that 'Accent . . . seems to be regulated, in a great measure by etymology'. Yet many of the descriptions of word and syllable stress are confusing and appear to be underpinned by notions of long and short syllables: for Sheridan (1781: 88), stress, or accent, is 'a particular manner of distinguishing one syllable from another, either by dwelling longer upon it as, *móment, músic, tríal*; or pronouncing it quicker, as in *mánner, présent, sýstem*'. But some observers see a multiplicity of features characterising the stress phenomenon, notably Buchanan (1766: 50), who sees an inter-connection between stress, intonation, amplitude and vowel quantity:

> Accent is the elevation and inflexion of the voice upon a certain syllable in a word. The syllable, therefore, which takes the accent is both louder and longer than the rest; as in the noun *tórment*,

the first syllable (*tor*) is louder and longer than the second (*ment*), thus *tŏrmènt*. So in the word *reconcíling*, the third syllable (*cil*) which takes the accent, is louder and longer than any of the rest, thus, *reconcīling*; it is louder by the accent, that is, the elevation of the voice; and longer by quantity, that is, the inflexion of the voice.

Although several other Scottish writers note the stress alternation between verbal and nominal types as in *óbject/to objéct, férment/to fermént, pérmit/to permít* and so on, it is only Dun who attempts to formulate phonologically based principles for the assignment of stress in lexical items, based mainly upon syllable length and combinatorial characteristics, especially as regards termination type, despite his assertion (1766: 137) that 'it is natural for one to pronounce one Syllable of a Word with a louder and stronger sound than another Syllable of the same Word, the accent is somewhat natural, and consequently will come easy . . .'. Dun's main concern is to provide rules – his 'general directions' – for stress placement in those nouns and adjectives which are characterised by showing certain types of 'terminations'. Thus nouns and adjectives with endings such as *ial* and *ion* will show penultimate stress placement, as in *mansion, jealous* and so on, while if the terminations are disyllabic, such as *uous*, then the stress is placed on the antepenult. Verbs terminating in *ise*, it is claimed, always show syllable-final stress placement, thus *surmíse, surpríse, naturalíse*. Compound words and derivatives (especially of non-Romance origin) show the same stress patterning as their 'Principles'. Syllable length is also an important determining criterion for Dun, and he claims that the greater the number of syllables in a word, the less likely is the stress to fall on the 'right-hand' syllables, tending instead to be placed near the beginning of the word, thus *céremony, élegancy, abóminable*. On the other hand, disyllabic words tend to show stress on the first syllable rather than the second, save when they are 'compounds': *compléte, contríte* (Giegerich 1992: 183ff.).

Only a few eighteenth-century observers, notably Buchanan and Elphinston, highlight regional (and particularly Scots) variation in stress placement. Elphinston (1787: 47) confidently states: 'az evvery word, in proparcion to' its number ov syllabels, iz liabel to' just so manny (at least possibel) vaarriacions ov ennergy; in notthing can distant dialects be suppozed more to' disagree'. Buchanan (1770: 51–2) seems to regret the inconsistencies of Scots stress placement, giving examples of this 'false accent' so common among his North British contemporaries:

> It is remarkable, that though the pronunciation throughout the several counties of England differs more or less from the purity of the best speakers; yet the accent is uniform overall. Hence arises another great disadvantage in speaking or reading, to which North-Britons, in general, subject themselves, namely, false accent. I shall here contrast a few examples. North Britons lay the accent wrong in the following words, and say

áccess	for	accéss
súccess		succéss
áffĩance		affĩance
aliénate		álienate
alíenable		álienable
apostateéze		apóstatize
dífficult		dífficult
difficulty		dífficulty
chórography		chorógraphy
cósmography		cosmógraphy

démocracy	for	demócracy
excéllency		éxcellency
haráss		hárass
embarráss		embárrass
inexórable		inéxorable
intellígible		intélligible
unintellígibly		unintélligibly
irrevócable		irrévocable

while an even more extensive list of stress-placement contrasts is provided by a letter in the *Edinburgh Magazine* of 1722 from a reader signing himself as Philo-Orthologie (Jones 1996: 259–61). Several of the examples provided by these sources suggest that eighteenth-century Scots speakers rely more on end-stress than their English contemporaries (the *access* instance, for example), a phenomenon not unknown in modern Scots as well, thus *novél*, *mischíef* (Grant and Main Dixon 1921: 62). Elphinston too (1787: 51) stresses the fact that Scots speakers are inclined to favour end-stressing (at least in a limited lexical set), regardless of syntactic category:

> Dhe Scots, perceiving dhat raddical verbs natturally emphatticize dheir ending; and dhat sevveral nouns beccomming verbs, invert dheir stres accordingly; hav imadgined dhemselvs authorized to' uze dhe same fredom widh *bias, canvas, silence, sentence, triumph, comfort* and *sollace*; az in dhe North, widh *seccond*: much more widh dhe oridginal verbs *construe, rescue*, (resscue), *respite* or *respit* (resspit); *govvern, harras, ransac* and *cancel*; all Inglishly invariabel in prior strength: az iz *perfet* in evvery capacity, dho dhe Scotch hold it *perfite*, a rival to' dhe Inglish *polite*. Obzerving *practice* so nicely distinguished from *practise*, dhey cood not fancy dhe verb and noun (az dhey ar to' dhe Inglish ear) indiscrimminabel.

8.6   INTONATION

Many of the grammarians associated with Scotland in the eighteenth century have something to say about intonation (which they often refer to as Accent or Emphasis), yet their observations are too imprecise and vague to make it possible for us to trace an evolutionary phonological pathway between the usage which they observe and the complex picture which exists in the current language (Macaulay and Trevelyan 1977: 240; Brown 1979; Kenworthy 1978: 267–82; Currie 1979; McClure 1980b; Macafee 1983: 236). Indeed, none of the Scottish observers achieves a degree of sophisticated description like that found in the musical notation of Joshua Steele's *An Essay towards Establishing the Melody and Measure of Speech* (1775). Beattie (1788: 91) regrets that this is a work which is unread by him: 'An attempt has lately been made by Mr Steele, to express certain accents of the English tongue by a new invented sort of written characters. This work, I hear, is very ingenious; but, as I have not seen it, I can say nothing more about it.' Emphasising that 'every nation and province has a particular accent' and stressing that different accents must be treated with 'forbearance', he points out that 'of all the peculiarities of a foreign tongue, accent is the most difficult for a grown person to acquire . . . Scotch men have lived forty years in London without entirely losing their native tone':

> Mr Sheridan, in those elegant Lectures which I heard him deliver at Edinburgh about twenty years ago, distinguished (if I rightly remember) the English interrogatory accent from the Irish and the Scotch, in this manner. His example was: 'How have you been this great while? – in pronouncing which, he observed, that towards the end of the sentence an Englishman lets his

voice fall, an Irishman raises his, and a Scotchman makes his voice first fall and then rise. The
remark is well founded; but it is difficult to express in unexceptionable terms a matter of so great
nicety. I shall only add, that what is here said of the Scotch accent, though it may hold true of the
more southerly provinces, is by no means applicable to the dialects that prevail in Aberdeenshire, and other parts of the north: where the voice of the common people, in concluding a clause
or sentence, rises into a very shrill and sharp tone without any previous fall. 'You bark in your
speech' says a man from Edinburgh to one of Aberdeen: 'and you growl and grumble in yours'
replies the Aberdonian. In Inverness-shire and the western parts of Moray, the accents become
totally different, and resemble the tones and aspirations of the Erse. (1788: 90)

But, on the whole, comment upon and definition of intonational phenomena are rare and
not particularly enlightening or terminologically consistent; fairly typical is McIllquam
(1781: 22):

> What is meant by Emphasis and Cadence? A proper modulation of the voice in reading; thus,
> emphasis raises the voice, and cadence lowers it on certain words of a sentence. – Emphasis and
> Cadence, or the proper rising and falling of the voice, are best attained by practice, and careful
> attention to those who read or speak well.

On other occasions, intonation is seen as inherently associated with vowel length, as for
Buchanan (1770: 46):

> Quantity regulates the tone of voice in words, as emphasis does in sentences. So that the voice of
> a North-Briton is easily distinguished from that of a South-Briton, though we do not see the
> persons nay, though we do not hear a word either of them says, the very tone will discover the
> country. The one of the former, though often rough with guttural sounds, is weaker, flatter, and
> less animating and approaches too much to a monotony. The tone of the latter is more grand and
> elevated, by the various sounds being uttered according to just quantity and accent; long or
> short, loud or low, grave or acute. There are Scotch gentlemen indeed in London, whose
> pronunciation, and consequently tone of voice, cannot be distinguished from natives of the
> place: but then they applied themselves rigorously to the study of it under the best masters, and
> with the advantage of not imbibing the least tincture of the provincial dialects, to which the
> generality of South-Britons are subjected.

Obviously, for Buchanan, being a North Briton had at least, albeit occasionally, some
advantages. It is probably true to say that most observers in the period see the same physical
correlates underlying the perception of both word-stress placement and intonational
patterning: 'What is meant by accent? Accent [ˇ] is the raising of the Voice upon a Syllable
in a Word; or, it is a remarkable Stress of the Voice upon a Syllable in a Word. What is
Emphasis? Emphasis is the raising or depressing of the Voice upon a Word, or Words, in a
Sentence' (Gray 1794: 102). Beattie, again probably following Sheridan, equates emphasis not
only with stress marking in words but also with the intonation shifts in sentences whereby
changes in topic are identified (1788: 59): 'Emphasis, which is a stronger exertion of the voice
upon some words and syllables than upon others, is necessary to give spirit and propriety to
pronunciation, by marking, first, the most important words in a sentence; and, secondly, those
syllables in a word, which custom may have distinguished by a more forcible utterance'. He
proceeds to illustrate through the sentence Do you walk to town today? the various
topicalisation possibilities: 'If we exert our voice upon the pronoun, and say, "Do you
walk to town today?" the answer might be, "No, but my servant does", and so on, applying in
turn differential intonation to the verb and adverb in the sentence.

9

Syntax and Morphology

Joan Beal

9.1 INTRODUCTION

Given that the period covered by this chapter begins at the point of the Act of Union (1707), we might expect a history of Scots syntax and morphology in this era to document a process of attrition, of the progressive replacement of the older 'Scots' features discussed in Chapters 4 and 5 by 'English' ones. Romaine (1982b: 59) suggests that this is the case:

> As anglicization took place, the grammatical system was first to conform to English patterns in the written language, and by 1700, only a few distinctive parts of Scots grammar remained.

If we were to take this statement seriously at face value, then this chapter would be very short indeed, starting as it does at the very point at which, according to Romaine, distinctively Scots features of syntax and morphology disappear. However, accounts of present-day 'non-standard' Scots such as Miller (1993) tell a different story, not only documenting the survival of many features which eighteenth-century anglicisers listed as Scotticisms to be avoided, but also pointing out innovations, for instance in the urban Scots of Glasgow, which are proof of the regenerative power of Scots. Even the English of the middle classes in Scotland, Scottish Standard English, is, according to Aitken (1979: 105), 'rather more Scottish in its grammar than has hitherto been realised'.

If we look more closely at these apparently contradictory statements, we shall see that the distinctively Scottish features referred to by such as Romaine and Aitken are rather different: Romaine, like Görlach (1985b), is referring to the disappearance of those features, such as the *-is* noun plural morpheme, the *-it* past-tense morpheme, and the distinction between the *-and* ending for present participles and the *-ing* ending for gerunds, which distinguished the older standard Scots from the standard English of the same period. Aitken and Miller, on the other hand, are referring to those features of present-day Scots, both standard and non-standard, which distinguish those varieties, particularly from Standard (English) English, but also from most other dialects of British English.[1] Such features may not have been distinctive or even present in older Scots: some, like the 'double modal' construction in *He'll can do that*, for example, were once found in Standard English and have become 'distinctively Scottish' by virtue of their disappearance from Southumbrian dialects. Others, such as the comparatively recent use of *yin* for the older a body, may have originated as anglicisms, but are now perceived as salient features of urban Scots; yet other features, such as the second person plural pronouns *yiz, youse* and so on, appear to have been introduced into urban Scots from Hiberno-English. I intend, as far as possible, to chart both the demise of older Scots features of syntax and morphology and the rise of the newer ones. I shall take as a starting point accounts of what was perceived to be distinctively Scottish in the eighteenth century and as an end point accounts of present-day Scots such as those of Miller (1993) and Macaulay (1991). By examining a range of materials in and about Scots from the eighteenth, nineteenth and early twentieth centuries, I hope to shed some light on the evolution of Scots syntax and morphology in the modern period.

9.2   SOURCES OF INFORMATION

In undertaking such a task, I realise that I am venturing into uncharted waters, or at least waters for which only charts of the 'here be dragons' variety exist. As the first seven chapters of this *History* demonstrate, older Scots has received and is still receiving a healthy amount of scholarly attention; and, indeed, works such as Romaine (1982a) and Devitt (1989) provide a useful backdrop to this chapter, charting as they do the development of features such as relative pronouns up to the end of the older Scots period. The availability of the *Helsinki Corpus of Older Scots* has provided a stimulus to research on this earlier period of Scots. With regard to the history of modern Scots, though, and especially its syntax and morphology, the following statement made by Donaldson (1989: 9), regarding the study of Scottish culture and literature, rings true:

> There is a yawning gulf in the textbooks between James VI and Allan Ramsay. And another nearly as big between Scott and MacDiarmid. Two whole centuries of the post-Reformation period lie virtually unexplored.

The first 'gulf' has, of course, been breached by the provision of the *Helsinki Corpus*, but the second remains, although Donaldson himself has made available a whole body of invaluable material from the nineteenth century, which I shall use as evidence here. Nothing like the *Helsinki Corpus* exists for the modern period of Scots, so I have had to use a range of such resources as are available in compiling this chapter. Each of these sources of evidence has its limitations, and it is certainly not possible at this stage to produce the kind of quantitative sociohistorical study undertaken by, for example, Romaine (1982a). All that I can hope to achieve here is to give an account of such restricted evidence as is available, which I hope will provide a stimulus to research in this comparatively neglected area of Scots studies.

The first, and, indeed, the earliest evidence to be considered here is that provided by the grammarians of the eighteenth century, and more specifically by those who saw fit to provide for their compatriots useful lists of those 'Scotticisms' which should be avoided by those wishing to speak and write what was deemed to be 'correct' English. The Act of Union of 1707 came just at the time when 'Augustan' adherence to what Leonard (1929) termed 'the doctrine of correctness' was gaining momentum. Exposed to what was by then almost universally acknowledged to be the 'correct' usage of educated Londoners, middle-class Scots became almost obsessed with the notion that any deviation from the London norm must be eradicated from their language. Leonard (1929) notes that half the grammars which he studied for his eponymous work on the 'doctrine of correctness' were written by and for Scots and other 'provincials', while Crowley (1991: 73) points out with regard to two of the foremost elocutionists of the age:

Sheridan was Irish, Buchanan was a Scot; it is no small irony that it is from the edges of the dominant culture that these two prominent elocution masters arrive with their prescriptions for 'proper English'.

Although the most pressing concern was with 'correct' pronunciation, respected authors such as David Hume and James Beattie were sufficiently concerned about their written English to compile their own lists of such Scotticisms as should be avoided. Hume's is the earliest of these lists, appearing first in 1752 and then in the *Scots Magazine* of 1760. Hume's concern about the 'correctness' of his language is often expressed in his correspondence: in a letter to Gilbert Elliot in 1757, he states that he and his fellow Scots 'speak a very corrupt Dialect of the Tongue which we make use of' (Greig 1932: II, 154). His list of Scotticisms consists largely of lexical and idiomatic usages, such as *part with child* which, according to Hume, should be *miscarry*, but there are a few indications of syntactic and morphological variants which were considered to be Scottish and therefore incorrect. The list in the *Scots Magazine* begins with an account of the 'correct', that is, English, rules for the use of *shall* and *will*, *would* and *should* and *these* and *those*, which, as we shall see, were all vexed issues at the time, but gives no indication of the ways in which Scots usage deviated from these norms. The only morphological Scotticisms mentioned by Hume are various preterite and past-participle forms: *proven*, *improven*, *approven* for English *proved* and so on, and *drunk*, *run* for *drank*, *ran*, while in the area of syntax he notes that *to be angry at* should be *angry with*, and *hinder to do* is a Scotticism, the 'correct' English phrase being *hinder from doing*. This latter usage seems to have been something of an obsession with Hume: in a letter to Thomas Reid in 1763, he writes (Greig 1932: I, 375–6):

> As I was desirous to be of some use to you, I kept a watchful eye all along over your style, but it is really so correct, and so good English, that I found not anything worth the remarking. There is only one passage in this chapter, where you make use of the phrase *hinder to do* instead of *hinder from doing*, which is the English one; but I could not find the passage when I sought for it.

This, like all the Scotticisms in Hume's list, is repeated in the more comprehensive accounts of Sinclair (1782), Beattie (1787) and Mitchell (1799), but whether this was ever a specifically Scots usage is open to question: the OED records the feature as *obs.* or *rare*, but not as Scottish. It is possible that a usage which was becoming 'old-fashioned' in London might still be current in Scotland, but the same could be said of any 'provincial' area in the late eighteenth century. What is more likely is that writers such as Hume were so acutely aware of the differences between Standard English and Scots that, living as they did in such a normative age, they would assume any variation from London usage to be a Scotticism. This tendency to err on the side of caution is confessed by Beattie, who writes in his *Introduction* (1787: 3):

> It is possible I may have marked as improper some words for which good authority might be produced. But, where the purity of language is concerned, it is, in *my* opinion, more safe to be too scrupulous, than too little so.

These lists of Scotticisms provide a useful starting point for this survey, providing as they do an insight into what was *considered* to be distinctively Scots usage at the time; but, where no other or later evidence exists that a particular variant was confined to Scotland, we must treat lists such as Hume's and Beattie's with caution. Nevertheless, as we shall see, the fuller lists of Beattie and Sinclair do provide us with a wealth of information corroborated elsewhere.

The purpose of these lists of Scotticisms was, of course, to eradicate such features at least from the written language of educated Scots. Fortunately for our purposes, Scots continued in use in informal, and particularly spoken, registers even among the educated upper and middle classes, and the eighteenth century saw a revival of poetry in Scots. The latter might appear remarkable in the light of the widespread condemnation of Scots usage at that time, but M. Robinson (1973: 42) points out:

> In these circumstances it is perhaps rather remarkable that anyone should have bothered to write in Scots at all. The so-called revival of Scottish poetry in the eighteenth century was in fact largely caused by the Act of Union. For as Scotland was finally stripped of its separate identity, there was a simultaneous back-lash of patriotic nostalgia which found an outlet in antiquarianism.

There is, therefore, written evidence of Scots usage from the eighteenth century in the poetry of such as Allan Ramsay, Fergusson and, of course, Burns. Robinson herself provides useful examples, and I shall include quotations from these poets as evidence for continuing usage of Scots features in this chapter. We must bear in mind, though, that such usage, however 'authentic', is still poetic. In areas of syntax such as the relative clause, in which, as Romaine (1982a) has demonstrated, more formal variants, in this case the wh-relatives, had already entered the written language by the end of the older Scots period, it is difficult to tell whether the occurrence of such 'formal' variants in Scots poetry represents a failure of 'authenticity' on the poet's part. Robinson, for instance, asserts that 'the relative pronoun . . . in Scots is not who, which, but that' (1973: 43), but makes no comment on the use of wh- relatives by poets, Burns' Scots wha hae wi' Wallace bled being a famous case in point. Where other evidence for Scots usage in a particular period is scant, we simply cannot afford to dismiss literary materials, but we must bear in mind that, however 'authentic' such materials might appear to be, they are unlikely to provide a range of usage identical to that of informal speech, so that, in comparing the language of, say, Tam o' Shanter with the spoken language of present-day Ayrshire as represented in Macaulay (1985, 1991), we are clearly not always comparing like with like.

On the other hand, we must be wary of dismissing variation between what appear to be 'Scots' and 'English' features as evidence of non-authenticity. McClure (1983: 131) notes with regard to Scots and English that

> when the two languages came to be spoken in the same country and by the same people a mixed dialect would arise, tending towards sometimes a Scots and sometimes an English pole depending on the circumstances of the speaker.

He goes on to point out:

> Some writers, particularly in the present century, have seemingly assumed – erroneously, of course – that no word which a monolingual Englishman would understand can be accepted as Scots.

We shall see in the discussion of particular syntactic and morphological features that, at least in literature, even of the most 'popular' kind exemplified in Donaldson (1986, 1989), such variability is the norm, and, far from being the result of the author's failure to produce authentic Scots untainted by anglicisms, probably gives a fairly true picture of the variability present in Scots itself in the modern period, the equivalent in written, literary usage of the sociolinguistic variation found in studies such as Macaulay (1991).

Regard for 'authenticity' and 'purity' of language is perhaps nowhere more obvious than in the works of traditional dialectologists: witness, for example, the mission of the *Survey of English Dialects* to collect only 'traditional vernacular, genuine and old' (Orton 1960: 332). Another aspect of the antiquarian backlash referred to by Robinson, along with the interest aroused by the works of Indo-European scholars and, later, the Neogrammarians, was the appearance in the nineteenth and early twentieth centuries of 'grammars' of Scots dialects. The turning point here is the publication of Jamieson's *Etymological Dictionary of the Scottish Language* (1808), in the *Preface* of which he makes the following assertion (1808: iv):

> I do not hesitate to call that the Scottish *Language*, which has generally been considered in no other light than as merely on a level with the different provincial dialects of the English. Without entering at present into the origin of the former, I am bold to affirm, that it has as just a claim to the designation of a peculiar language as most of the other languages of Europe.

Jamieson goes on to accuse those 'not only in the higher, but even in the middle ranks of life', who go out of their way to avoid Scotticisms, of 'childish fastidiousness', and produces a forty-six-page dissertation on the origin of the Scottish language to justify the point made in the above quotation. Jamieson was not the first to assert that Scots was equal in status to Standard English: James Adams (1799: 155) asserting that 'an Englishman has no right to censure and laugh at his Northern brother's language, till he has spent two months on the north of the Tweed, and then he will begin to think his own native words are as just a subject of laugh and censure to a Scotchman'.

However, it is the publication of Jamieson's dictionary which marks the first really scholarly attempt to justify Scots as 'grammatical' in its own terms. Charles Mackay, in his *Dictionary of Lowland Scotch* (1888), goes further than Jamieson in singling out certain features of Scots morphology as 'superior' to English: he cites the productive use of the -*ie* suffix in diminutives such as *laddie, wifie* as 'another source of the superior euphony of the Scoto-Teutonic'[2] (1888: xiii) and, far from condemning as, for example Beattie did, 'irregular' preterite and past-participle forms such as *I hurted myself* or *I have putten on my coat* as 'incorrect', he asserts (1888: xiv) that 'the retention of the old and strong inflexions of verbs, that are wrongfully called irregular, contributes very much to its force and harmony, giving it at the same time a superiority over the modern English, which has consented to allow many useful preterites and past-participles to perish altogether'. Perhaps the most extensive and significant of these nineteenth-century works on Scots is James Murray's *Dialect of the Southern Counties of Scotland* (1873). Murray, like Jamieson before him, justifies the claim of these dialects to be equal in status to Standard English by the use of scholarly arguments. He produces 'rules' for usages that have previously (and, indeed, subsequently) been condemned as 'incorrect' and often strengthens his argument by comparisons with other languages such as French and Hebrew. For instance, Beattie condemned as a Scotticism *Him and me set out together*, pointing out that the correct usage was *He and I*. Murray, however, writes (1873: 187):

> The usage of the Personal Pronouns in the current Scottish dialects differs from that of Standard English, being in most respects identical with the French. There is a *direct* or proper *Nominative* and a *direct Objective* as well as an *indirect* case, used like the French *moi, toi, lui, eux* for both Nominative and Objective in certain positions.

He goes on to give a list of six rules for the use of the indirect form for the nominative, with examples of usage in each case. For the first five of these, he adds 'so in French', and gives a corresponding example in French. Rule 5 covers exactly the usage objected to by Beattie 'when two or more nominatives form the subject of the same Verb', as in *Yuw an' mey'll gang ower the field* (1873: 190). Murray thus provides a wealth of information on the syntax and morphology of Southern Scots in the nineteenth century, especially in his examples, but in defending these dialects as 'rule-based' and 'grammatical' he may well tend to overstate their regularity. His rules for the allomorphic variation in weak verb preterites (1873: 199) are very clear, but, as we shall see in the discussion of this area of morphology below, they seem not to be followed consistently by any writer in Scots of Murray's time or later.

Murray's work is in many respects seminal, and certainly provides extensive coverage of all the areas of syntax and morphology to be discussed here, but we must be careful not to judge more literary sources from the nineteenth century, such as the novels of Scott (Tulloch: 1980) or even the more 'popular' literature collected in Donaldson (1986, 1989), as 'inconsistent' or 'inauthentic' because the authors fail to apply Murray's rules consistently. Other works which provide useful information about Scots in the earlier twentieth century are Grant and Main Dixon (1921), Wilson (1926) and Dieth (1932). More recent works such as the publications of the *Survey of Scottish Dialects* and sociolinguistic surveys such as that carried out by Macaulay (1991), are discussed in Chapter 12 but I shall refer to them insofar as they provide evidence of change in progress in the syntax and morphology of Scots. Works such as these and, for example, Macafee (1983) are particularly useful in providing examples of urban Scots as a counterbalance to the rural nature of earlier dialect works. Macaulay's work is also valuable in that it highlights the importance of discourse markers such as initial *see*, used to extract and foreground the theme of a sentence, as in *See him, he canny drive* (*Concise Scots Dictionary* (CSD), Robinson 1991: 597). These are features not noted by earlier commentators, and CSD, for instance, gives this usage as 'late 20c', but it may be the case that they occur only in the most informal speech and so have not been noticed earlier.

Tracing the history of Scots syntax and morphology in the modern period has of necessity entailed using an assortment of resources, most of which have their limitations as outlined above. In the following account, I have chosen to concentrate on those areas of syntax and morphology for which there is a reasonable amount of evidence rather than attempt to give a complete account of the 'grammar' of Scots through this period.

9.3 MORPHOLOGY

9.3.1 Noun Inflections

We have already noted Romaine's (1982b: 60) assertion that the 'regular' *-is* plural inflection of nouns is 'a trait that disappeared from the written language in the eighteenth century'. This is confirmed by L. E. C. MacQueen (1957: 131), whose study of letters and public records between 1700 and 1750 shows that the *-is* inflection by that time no longer appears in national and Kirk Session records and only appears sporadically in some local records, the latest examples being *expensis, spadis, spoussis* from 1716–17. Murray (1873: 155) suggests that the reduction of this ending to *-s* occurred first in speech:

> In the end of the 15th and beginning of the 16th century, the *-is*, although still generally making an independent syllable in monosyllables, or after a final accent, had quite sunk into *-s* in other words of two or more syllables. Even in writing, *-s* alone began to appear.

He goes on to suggest a transition period in the seventeenth century, when variation occurs:

> In Scottish prose, the spelling *-is* long survived the pronunciation. In the dialect of Teviotdale the *Annals of Hawick* show it in full use in 1600, by 1640 forms in *-es* and *-s* become equally frequent, the same document shewing *personnis, personnes* and *persons, utheris* and *uthers, mindes* and *minds, quhilkis* and *quhilks*; the forms in *-is* finally disappear about 1660.

Although Murray's date for the final disappearance of the *-is* ending seems a little early in the light of MacQueen's findings, his account of the manner of its disappearance is wholly plausible. Once Scots ceased to be a standard language, the constraints against the reduction of [ɪs] to [əs] and then to [s] in speech would be removed. Since the resulting *-s* ending would be identical with that of Standard English, anglicisation would speed up the process of reduction in the written language, but a transition stage characterised by the kind of variability illustrated by Murray would be typical when a change such as this is in progress. That the *-is* ending had disappeared from Scots by the beginning of the eighteenth century is confirmed by the lack of any reference to this ending in the lists of Scotticisms produced by such as Hume, Beattie and Sinclair. Nor do we find it in the literary Scots of writers such as Burns and Scott.

Where 'irregular' plural inflections are concerned, distinctively Scots forms seem to survive longer. Grant and Main Dixon (1921: 79) give, as examples of plurals in *-en*, *een* 'eyes', *shoon, shuin, shaen* 'shoes', *hosen* 'stockings', *owsen* 'oxen', *treen* 'trees', *turven* 'turfs', and *breeken* 'breeches'. They provide citations from literature of the nineteenth and early twentieth centuries for some of these forms:

> Can this be you, Jenny? – a sight o' you's gude for sair *een*, lass. (Scott, *Antiquary*, chapter 26)

> I ate the half o' 't mysel, and rubbet the ither half into ma *shaen*. (*The Scottish Review*, 1908: 545)

Tulloch (1980: 268) confirms that *shoon, een* and *owsen* are the only examples of this *-en* ending found in Scott's writings. Because this ending had long ceased to be productive in Scots and in Northern English generally, 'double plural' forms are found: Tulloch cites *breekens*, while Grant and Main Dixon also give *shins* 'shoes' as an example of this. Although neither CSD nor SND suggests an end-date for these *-en* plurals, Miller (1993: 107) suggests that they belong to 'earlier stages of Broad Scots' and are therefore tending to die out in the later twentieth century. The same could be said of the few examples of *-er* plurals found in Scots but not in Standard English, which appear to be even rarer: Tulloch (1980) does not mention these as occurring in Scott, and there are no examples in J. B. Reid's (1889) concordance of Burns. Grant and Main Dixon (1921) suggest that *kaur* 'calves' and *breer* 'eyebrows, eyelashes' are localised, *kaur* occurring in the dialects of Aberdeenshire, Perthshire, west Forfarshire and Renfrewshire, and *breer* in those of Aberdeenshire and Banffshire. Dieth suggests that by the early twentieth century these *-er* plurals were dying out in Aberdeenshire, or at least in the dialect of Buchan which is the subject of his monograph. He writes of the '*r*-pl.' (1932: 137, author's emphasis):

> It lives on in kɑːr . . . and in the unhistorical and double pl. briːrz . . . The former is the only form a genuine speaker would use . . . the latter is ousted in everyday speech by the regular ibruːz, but it remains in the saying hiz hɪŋɪn 'ɛn bɪ ðə 'briːrz oz 'in 'he's doing his utmost'.

Grant and Main Dixon write of *childer* that it 'is almost never heard now in Scotland', and Dieth states that while this form is found in Barbour's *Bruce* 'and in present day Yorkshire and Perthshire', in Buchan it 'can no longer be ascertained'.

Such 'non-standard' plurals as persist in Scots in any numbers and with any frequency are those such as *knifes, wifes, lifes, leafs, thiefs, loafs* and *wolfs*, in which the regular -*s* inflection is used, but the voicing of [f] to [v] found in Standard English does not occur. This is mentioned by Miller (1993) and could be a relatively recent phenomenon. Sylvester Douglas, writing in 1779, notes (Jones 1991: 180):

> The genetives [sic] of *calf, wife, knife*, are pronounced by most English people like the plurals of the same words, i.e. as if written, *Calves, wives, knives*. The Scotch, and some English people, retain in the genetive the same hard sound of the *f* as in the nominative.

Douglas would seem to suggest here that the Scots plural was pronounced with [v] at the time, but the genitive with [f]. It would be highly likely that the analogical process would spread to the plural in due course, especially since this appears not to have been stigmatised. Miller suggests that speakers are more aware of non-standard verb inflections as shibboleths than non-standard noun plurals such as these, and that the latter are used in speech even by educated speakers. Certainly, there is no reference to them as a Scotticism in the eighteenth century, suggesting either that they did not exist at this point or that they were not sufficiently stigmatised to be of note.

One aspect of noun inflection which eighteenth-century writers such as Beattie do notice and condemn is the use of uninflected plurals. Beattie (1787: 23, 45) notes the following as Scotticisms: *A bunch of candle; a coach and six horse*, both of which examples are also cited in Mitchell (1799: 26, 46). Sinclair also cites as a Scotticism *Three sheet of paper* (1782: 58). On the other hand, Beattie (1787: 9) gives as an example of the incorrect use of *altogether* for *in all*: *Of money and moveables I lost altogether about fifty pound* without any adverse comment about the uninflected *pound*. This would suggest that uninflected plurals of certain categories of noun were probably fairly common in eighteenth-century Scots usage, but were only sporadically noted as Scotticisms. Tulloch (1980: 269) notes that Scott uses uninflected plurals for nouns of money and measurement such as *pund, merk* 'marks', *mile* and *year*, while Reid's concordance of Burns (Reid 1889: 304, 313) shows evidence of variation between inflected and uninflected plurals for most of these words: for *mark* we find *He gied me thee, o' tocher clear, An' fifty mark (A Guid New Year)*; *My daddy says, gin I'll forsake him, He'll gie me gude hunder marks ten (Tam Glen)*. For *mile*, there is also variation: *But sax Scotch mile, thou try't their mettle (A Guid New Year)*; *We think na on the lang Scots miles (Tam o' Shanter)*.

It would appear that variation such as this was normal by the mid-eighteenth century. MacQueen (1957: 131) notes instances of uninflected plurals in records with the dates as follows: *eighteen horse*[3] (1701); *the price of candle, many candle* (1736); *nineteen unce, fourteen drop* (1716); *8 drop* (1730). However, she points out that 'inflected plurals of the same words are also found throughout, the Scottish variants being very occasional'. Murray gives a more detailed and characteristically rule-based account both of the categories of nouns which have uninflected plurals in Scots and of the nature of the variation with inflected forms of the same words. He points out (1873: 161) that some animals retain a singular form, and as an example quotes 'D.C.', in the *Athenaeum* of 27 February 1869, as stating that *gaitt* for 'goats' 'is in familiar use in the north-east of Perthshire'. Murray goes on to provide the following rule to explain variation:

> Most nouns of time, space, quantity, weight, measure and number remain unchanged in the plural when used collectively, or with a numeral that already indicates plurality . . . But when used *severally*, or not preceded by a numeral, they are made plural in the usual way.

Some of the examples given to illustrate this variation are: *Hey has eacres an' eacres, aa s' warrant ye a thoosant eacre; Hoo monie dyzzen hae ye? Aa dynna coont be dyzzens.*

Grant and Main Dixon (1921: 80) simply state that 'such nouns, when immediately preceded by a cardinal numeral, are frequently used without any plural sign in Sc. dialect'. Their use of the word *frequently* implies variation, but they do not attempt to provide a 'rule' for this. Indeed, Murray may well have been exaggerating the regularity of this variation: the examples from Burns quoted above seem to follow Murray's rule in the case of *mile(s)* but not *mark(s)*. What is more likely is that the variation which is present, as we have seen, at least from the beginning of the eighteenth century marks a stage in the decline of these unmarked plurals as features of Scots. Later evidence would seem to support this: the extracts from popular literature of the nineteenth century provided in Donaldson (1986, 1989) have many instances of inflected plurals for these nouns in passages which have many other distinctively Scottish features of syntax and morphology. Examples are: *The loch is aboot four miles lang*; *The sum total o' my expenses were . . . just twenty-twa shillins an' sevenpence (The People's Journal*, 4 September 1858; Donaldson 1989: 42, 46); *For the last twa twalmonths he has keepit barkin' awa at the heels o' the Rooshian Bear (The People's Journal*, 28 November 1878; Donaldson 1989: 66).

Macaulay confirms that uninflected plurals are, in fact, found much less frequently in Scots than in English dialects today, and that the variation between inflected and uninflected forms may be lexically determined. He writes (1991: 110), of nouns of measurement and quantity used in the interviews conducted with lower-class informants in Ayr: 'There are 90 examples, and 41 (46%) have an inflected plural. *Minute, day, week, shilling, inch* and *yard* are always inflected. The percentage of inflected plurals for the other nouns of measurement and quantity are as follows: *pound* (both money and weight) 89%, *month* 86%, *year* 68%, *ton* 50% and *mile* 17%.' He notes that these findings contradict the assertion of Trudgill et al. (1983: 32) that in British dialects 'it is an almost universal rule that, after numerals, nouns of measurement and quantity retain their singular form'. In Scots, it would appear that this rule has been becoming progressively less 'universal' since the beginning of the eighteenth century.

A feature which is in some ways the converse of the uninflected plurals discussed above is the use of some singular nouns as plurals. These nouns all refer to foods, mostly of a semi-liquid nature, such as *brose, broth, porridge, pudding*. This feature is noted as a Scotticism by Sinclair (1782: 61), who gives as an example *The broth are very good* and notes: 'It is a common error in Scotland to suppose that *broth, cabbage, spinnage* and *potage* or *porridge*, are in the plural number'. This feature is not noted in the shorter lists of Hume, Beattie or

Mitchell, however. Tulloch (1980: 269) records two examples of the plural use of *parritch*, *porridge* in Scott; and, while Reid (1889: 61) has no examples from Burns of this noun as a plural, there is one example for *brose*. Murray (1873: 162) explains the phenomenon as follows: 'Collective nouns being in Scotch usually construed as plural, several preparations of food, considered as collective nouns, are spoken of as *thay, thaim, monie, meae* or *fewer*. Such are *bruose, porritch, sowers, keale, broth, cruds*.' Grant and Main Dixon (1921: 80) note that these words 'take plural pronouns and verbs north of the Humber', and indeed they are still used in this way on Tyneside.[4] Whether these, like the singular forms of nouns of measurement and so on, are becoming rarer in Scots is hard to tell, as there is little discussion of the matter in more recent literature.

9.3.2 Pronouns

There have been several developments in the personal pronouns of Scots in the modern period, some of which are fairly recent. Murray (1873: 188) gives *us* as an alternative to *me* for the first person singular object case and suggests that, at the time of writing, it was a recent innovation:

> Where an old person would say 'hey tælld-mă, gi'-mă', the present generation say, 'hey tælld-us, gie 's or gie z' *in the singular* as in the plural. The same usage prevails over the English part of Bernicia.[5]

There is certainly no mention of this in the eighteenth-century texts, and Aitken (1979: 69) lists it as one of a number of 'shibboleths of Central Scots urban working-class speech, apparently mostly of comparatively recent origin'. Grant and Main Dixon (1921: 95) note that 'the accusative "me" is colloquially *us* or *'s*' and provide the following examples from literature: '*Will ye hae's, Bell?*', *demanded Sam'l, glaring at her sheepishly* (J. M. Barrie, *Auld Licht Idylls*, chapter 8); '*Will ye no gie's a kiss, Dand?*', *she said* (R. L. Stevenson, *Weir of Hermiston*, chapter 6). The lack of any reference to this use of *us* for the first person singular in the eighteenth-century lists of Scotticisms, and its absence from eighteenth- and early nineteenth-century Scots literature, would appear to confirm Murray's statement that this is an innovation of the later nineteenth century. Murray does not suggest that this is particularly stigmatised, or confined to urban usage at the time, although Grant and Main Dixon's use of the term *colloquially* suggests that it is more usual in informal speech in the early twentieth century. Miller (1993: 108) points out that *us* is used most frequently in collocation with certain verbs, for example *give, show, lend* (as the examples from Grant and Main Dixon above demonstrate), and that 'this usage can be found among educated speakers in informal situations'.

Another of the 'shibboleths' of urban working-class Scots listed by Aitken is the use of *yous* as the second person plural pronoun. Macafee (1982: 45) considers this to have originated in Glasgow as a result of borrowing from Hiberno-English and to be 'now general in Glasgow dialect and apparently spreading from there into other Central dialects'. According to both SND and CSD, the use of *yous* and similar second person plural forms such as *yiz, yaes, yeez* first appear in Scots in the twentieth century: the former states that 'in the past fifty years distinctive plural forms . . . have spread, especially in illiterate use in modern Scots from Ir. influence' and gives the first dated example from 'wm. Sc. 1921', while CSD marks the forms *ye(e)z, yiz, yaes, youz(e)* as 'c. 20' and 'only Sc.'. There seems to be agreement therefore, if not much in the way of proof, that forms like *yous* do not appear in Scots until the twentieth century, that they appear first in west central Scots and more specifically in Glasgow, and that they were introduced there as a result of Irish immigration. Given the long history of migration back and forth between the north of Ireland and the western central areas of Scotland, it is sometimes hard to tell where features found in the dialects of these two areas originated. James Milroy (1982) has shown, for instance, that phonological features found both in Galloway and Ulster originated in the former. However, in the case of *yous*, there is more evidence to support an Irish origin. Wright's *English Dialect Dictionary* (henceforth EDD) (1905) does not give any indication that *yous* is used in Scotland at that stage, but has entries for both *yees* and *yous*. Under *yees*, Wright (1905: 574) has the following entry:

> YEES. pron Irel. Also written *yez, yiz* [jīz; jiz].
> You; used when speaking to more than one person. Cf *yous*.

Wright (1905: 590) goes on to give examples of usage, the earliest of which is dated 1842, from both southern and northern Hiberno-English. Under *yous* he writes:

> YOUS. pron. Irel Amer. Aus. Also in forms *youse*. Amer. Aus. *yowz* Don. You, used when speaking to more than one person. cf YEES.
> Ir. Boys, boys – look yous at that. BARLOW, *Lisconnel* (1895) 225.
> Don. Done! An yows, boys, are all witnesses in this. *Pearson's Mag.* (July 1900).
> Amer. Youse fellys is gettin' that mule all excited. LLOYD. *Chronic Loafer* (1901) 57.
> Aus. We can wait till Hamlet comes, if youse fellows are game. *Longman's Mag.* (Aug. 1901) 301.

According to Wright's evidence, then, *yous, yees* forms of the second person plural are found in Hiberno-English from the mid-nineteenth century, and appear in American and Australian English at the very beginning of the twentieth century. That he has no reference to these forms appearing in Scots dialects at this time may be an oversight on Wright's part due to a tendency to concentrate on traditional rather than urban dialects. On the other hand, *yous* is not mentioned as a feature of what Trotter (1901: 23–4) calls the 'Glasgow Irish', which, according to him, 'originated in Glasgow about sixty years ago' (that is, 1840) and was spreading rapidly among young people everywhere in Scotland 'except, perhaps, the villages of the East Coast'. Trotter mentions as characteristics of what he considers a 'corrupt' dialect threatening to oust the 'true Scotch', phonological features such as glottalisation ('the "T"s' and "D"s" in the middle of words are never sounded' (1901: 24)); but as far as morphology is concerned, the only 'Glasgow Irish' feature mentioned is 'the invariable use of the past participle of the verb for the past tense indicative, and *vice versa*'. Had *yous* been common in Glasgow by 1901, Trotter would almost certainly have seized upon the opportunity of condemning it. Since neither Wright nor Trotter mentions *yous* as occurring in Scotland in the early twentieth century, and nor, for that matter, is it mentioned by either Murray or Grant and Main Dixon, we can probably assume that SND and CSD are right to assign it to the twentieth century.

However, CSD's marking of these second person plural forms as 'only Sc.' would appear to be inaccurate: before they even appeared in Scots, forms like *yous, yeez, yiz* and so on had become established in Hiberno-English and appeared in America and Australia, where they are still to be found, particularly in lower–class urban speech. Moreover, these forms can be found today in several urban English dialects, most notably those of Liverpool and

Tyneside, and appear to be spreading to other urban centres: Cheshire et al. (1993: 81), for instance, note that, in responses to their survey of English dialect grammar, 'schools in the core of the Manchester metropolitan region consistently reported the occurrence of the pronoun *youse*, whereas schools elsewhere in the region did not'. The history of *yous* and related forms is clearly a subject on which further research needs to be carried out, but if we ask ourselves what America, Australia, Glasgow, Liverpool and Tyneside have in common, one obvious answer is a high level of Irish immigration in the late nineteenth and early twentieth centuries: *yous* could well be a trace of the Irish diaspora. In Scotland, as in parts of England, *yous* and related forms have spread in the course of the twentieth century from the point of entry, in this case Glasgow, to other urban areas and have become, as Aitken notes, a 'shibboleth' of lower-class urban Scots, at least throughout the Central Scots area. Miller (1993: 108) observes that *yous* is 'very frequent and assiduously avoided by educated speakers even in informal situations'. Macaulay (1991), whose data were collected in Ayr in 1978–9, found that *youse* appeared only in lower-class interviews, and was not used at all by his two oldest informants (78 and 70 at the time of the survey). Although, as Macaulay points out, examples of *youse* appeared only sporadically in his data because a second person plural pronoun was unlikely to arise in the course of a dyadic interview, such information as he provides does seem to confirm that these second person plural forms are of recent introduction (his two oldest informants would have reached adulthood round about 1920), have spread beyond Glasgow to Ayr, and are associated with lower-class speech.

Of course, in those varieties of Scots in which it occurs, *yous* performs the function of distinguishing the second person plural from the singular. In older Scots, and in some traditional dialects still, this function is performed by distinct second person singular forms such as *tu, thou*. These seem to have been dying out in Southern dialects before the advent of *yous* and so on, for Murray (1873: 187) has *thou* marked as 'obsolete' in his table of personal pronouns. Grant and Main Dixon (1921: 96–7) note that 'the colloquial use of *tu*, tu; *tou*, tu; *thoo*, ðu; *thee*, ði; *thou*, ðʌu, is a distinctive mark of Paisley', and that 'in north-east Aberdeenshire, *thoo* was once in common use, and may still be heard occasionally among old people', while 'in the Sc. dialect of the Black Isle, Easter Ross, and in the Canonbie dialect of the Sth. Counties, *thoo* and *thee* are still in use'. This would suggest that *thou* forms were already recessive in the early twentieth century; and, indeed, Dieth (1932: 152) notes in his study of the Buchan dialect that he 'never heard' *thou*. The use of forms like *tu* in Paisley seems to have persisted as a stereotype into the twentieth century: the phrase *seestu* used as a discourse marker became a shibboleth of Paisley speech to such an extent that it was used as a designation for the town itself. However, like most stereotypes, the use of *seestu* as a name for Paisley probably outlived its actual use by the inhabitants of that town.

Donaldson (1986: 58) notes that one of the popular comic papers which appeared in Paisley in the 1880s was actually called *Seestu*, yet in the very pages of this publication:

> Neither of the correspondents uses the characteristic dental plosive 'tu/tat', and the inference would be that by the early 1880s this was a decaying feature. One writer spoke of his mother using it when he was a boy, with the implication that even then it was considered rather archaic: 'Ma mither's auld-fashion'd way o' speakin' was a rale trate. She had the Paisley language at her fingers' [end] . . . and the lasses used tae staun and draw her oot, as she wad say in rale Paisley Scotch: "Weel na, Seestu tat, and what is't tu wants!"

Donaldson here focused on the phonological characteristic of the [t] for [ð], but it is clear from other extracts from *Seestu* quoted here that the *thou/ tu* form of the pronoun itself was no longer current. If the *thou* form had been in use, we might expect to find it used between sweethearts, yet the extracts quoted by Donaldson (1986: 56) from a 'set of spoof love letters' – in which 'the conventions of the written language are ruthlessly undermined and the rhythms of the spoken vernacular hold absolute and riotous sway' – use the forms *ye* and *yer* throughout. It would appear that, at least in Southern and Central dialects, *thou* forms were on the decline by the end of the nineteenth century, leaving a functional gap which the newly imported *yous* could fill in the twentieth. I venture this functional explanation tentatively, but the loss of *thou* as a distinct second person singular marker, in Scots as in English dialects, might be one factor which facilitated the adoption of *yous* from Hiberno-English and its relatively rapid spread in urban areas in the twentieth century.[6]

Another personal pronoun which is of relatively recent origin is the possessive *mines*. This is almost certainly an analogical formation on the pattern of Standard English *yours, hers, theirs, ours*. Aitken (1979: 105) includes this in a list of distinctively Scots forms used even by educated middle-class Scots, and Miller (1993: 108) simply states that 'the first person singular possessive pronoun is *mines* (not *mine*) when it is the complement of the sentence', making no comment as to its social distribution. This usage is older and therefore perhaps more established than that of *yous*: it is mentioned by Murray (1873: 192), who writes: 'The form *meynes* . . . often heard in South Scottish vernacular. "Aa'll gi'ye yoors, quhan ye bryng mey meynes" '. Grant and Main Dixon (1921: 95) state that ' "Mine" takes the form *mines* or *mine's*', and provide the following examples: *Mines is no to be mentioned wi' it* (R. L. Stevenson, *Weir of Hermiston*, chapter 5); *Keep your min' easy; mine's is a clipper* (D. Gilmour, *Gordon's Loan*, p. 8). This would suggest that use of *mines* is well established by the early twentieth century. Although *mines* does not appear in eighteenth-century lists of Scotticisms or in the works of Burns or Scott, according to CSD it is found from the seventeenth century onwards, while SND has as the earliest citation: 'Sc. 1789. *Shepherd's Wedding*, 8. *She sall be mines in less than half-a-year.*' *Mines* would appear to be older and more established than singular *us* or plural *yous*, more widespread both geographically and socially, and less stigmatised. Unlike *yous* and *us*, it would also appear to be exclusively Scots.

I have already mentioned, as an example of the change of attitudes to Scots between the eighteenth and nineteenth centuries, the use of what Murray calls the 'indirect case' for the nominative, as in *Him and me set out together*. This is by no means exclusive to Scots (see, for instance, Beal 1993: 190), but is interesting as a feature which was so strongly defended as 'grammatical' and 'Pure Scotch' by the likes of Murray and Trotter (1901). Murray (1873: 190) sets out clear rules for the use of this 'indirect case':

The Indirect form is used for the Nominative:
1. When the verb is not expressed as in answer to a question: *Q. Wheae was here? A. Mey.*
2. When the Nominative is separated from the Verb by a Relative or Relative clause, a numeral or substantive. *Mey at haes been theare.*
3. As the second Nominative (predicate) after the verb to be etc. *It wasna mey.*
4. When the Nominative is repeated for the sake of emphasis, the added Nominative being put in the indirect case. *Mey, aa canna gang.*
5. When two or more nominatives form the subject of the same verb. *Yuw an' mey'll gang ower the field.*
6. With a participle as the absolute case. *Hym beyin sae heyrie.*

Trotter (1901: 26) cites something very similar to Murray's rule 5 as an example of the 'Scotch' which he contrasts with the 'corrupt' 'Glasgow Irish': 'When two or more words are joined by a conjunction, both words are put in the objective, as, *Him an' me*; *You an' her*; *Us an' them*; *Tam an' us*; *Pate an' Jock*; *an' them or him*; *Me or you*; *She's auler nor him.*

This feature is mentioned little in later literature, possibly because by then it is recognised as not being exclusively Scots. Dieth (1932: 152) only mentions in a note that 'the accented obj. form is also that of the absolute usage'; and in later works such as Macaulay (1991), it is of interest not so much because of the fact that the pronoun is in the object case form, but by virtue of the discourse features such as clefting and right-dislocation, with which it is associated. We shall deal with these discourse features later, but examples from Macaulay (1991: 120, 121) with the 'object' pronoun are: *he was some man him*; *that was him idle*; *it was him that led the band.* These are given as examples of right-dislocation, demonstrative focusing and clefting respectively, but in terms of the *him* form, all conform to Murray's rules 3 and 4, quoted above. It would appear that despite the efforts of the eighteenth-century anglicisers like Beattie, who saw *Him and me* as a Scotticism to be eradicated, this use of the 'indirect' pronoun is still an integral part of the grammar of Scots, as of non-standard dialects of (English) English.

In Scots, as in many non-standard dialects of English, reflexive pronouns have been regularised so that they all have the possessive form of the pronoun followed by *-sel* or *-sels*. Thus, where Standard English has *myself* but *himself*, Scots has *mysel*, *hissel* and so on. This feature is not mentioned as a Scotticism in the eighteenth century, and, indeed, Reid (1889: 234) lists only *himsel* with no examples of *hissel* from Burns. The usage must have been well established before the end of the nineteenth century, though, for the forms with *his*, *their* are listed by Murray (1873: 197), and Grant and Main Dixon give examples from the 1860s. Macaulay (1991: 77) shows that the *hissel*, *theirsels* forms are found in lower-class speech today: in his lower-class interviews, only one instance of *themselves* occurred and this was followed immediately by *theirself*, but in the middle-class interviews, only *himself* and *themselves* occurred. Macaulay (1991: 77) also points out that the use of *myself* and so on without a coreferential noun phrase in the same clause occurs only in lower-class interviews, an example being *there was only mysel aboot this place.*

As Tulloch (1980: 273) points out, such a usage is found in Scott: 'The use of the *-self* pronouns as the independent subject of a sentence and not merely in apposition to another pronoun . . . seems . . . to survive in Scots: *Mysell am not clear to trinquet and traffic wi' courts o' justice, as they are now constituted* (*Heart of Midlothian*, p. 283)'. Murray (1873) points out that *itsel* may be replaced by *the sel o't*, confirmed by Tulloch as occurring in Scott. The example cited by Tulloch and also in Grant and Main Dixon (1921: 99) is: *Kirkaldy, the sell o't, is langer than ony town in England* (*Rob Roy*, p. 196). Possibly this periphrasis was used particularly with *it* because of the relatively late introduction of *its*; as Murray (1873: 192) observes: 'The word *hyts* is, as in English, of very recent formation, and but little used. Instead of *yts heid*, *yts han'le*, *yts ayn*, are generally used *the heid o'd*, *the han'le o'd*, *the ayn o'd* or *ayn o't.*' The pattern of *the sell o't* and *the heid o't* suggest that, in Scots, *sel(l)* is perceived as a separate word, and *mysel* and so on as compounds. Such an interpretation is confirmed by the continuing existence of constructions such as *Me and Jimmy are on on Monday our two selves* (Miller 1993: 108).

Another area of change in the pronoun system of modern Scots has been that of the indefinite pronoun. In present-day urban Scots particularly, the indefinite pronoun is *yin*, but in earlier Scots and to some extent still in traditional dialects, *a body* or *a buddie* is used.

Robinson (1973: 53) comments on the following line from Hugh MacDiarmid's *A Drunk Man Looks at the Thistle*: *Yin canna thow the cockles o' yin's hert*, suggests that *yin* is 'one example of an anglicism which has been in Scots since the eighteenth century', and goes on to explain:

> In Middle Scots *ane* is found as a pronoun meaning 'a certain person' = French *quelqu'un*, but this use of it = French *on* has certainly been taken over from the English *one*. The native Scots would be *a body* as in *Comin' thro' the Rye*.

In fact, as Robinson herself points out, *ane* has been in competition with *a body* at least since the eighteenth century: even in *Comin' thro' the Rye* with its repetition of *a body* we find the line: *Ilka body has a body, ne'r a ane hae I*. Grant and Main Dixon (1921: 103–4) give both *ane* and *a body* as indefinite pronouns. They give [jɪn] as one of the pronunciations of *ane* and provide the following example from Scott: *Ane canna expect to carry about the Saut Market at his tail* (*Rob Roy*, chapter 34). However, they go on to note that 'the common indefinite term is *a body*' and provide an example from Alexander: *Weel, weel, a body canna help a bit idle thocht rinnin i' their heid* (*Johnny Gibb* (1884), chapter 47).

Tulloch (1980: 274) gives no examples of *a body* from Scott, but points out that the use of *ane* meaning 'someone', as in *there's ane coming down the crag e'en now* (*The Antiquary*, p. 91) or *there's ane frae Cumberland been waiting here for ye* (*Black Dwarf*, p. 426), is 'obsolete in Standard English . . . the last OED citation for this meaning of *one* is dated 1759'. If, as Tulloch suggests, this use of *ane* was already distinct from English *one* by the later eighteenth century, it is hard to see any justification for calling it an anglicism. To insist, as Robinson does, that only *a body* qualifies as 'native Scots' would be to fossilise the language. Today, both the distribution of *yin* and its characteristically Scots spelling and pronunciation render it distinct from the English *one* and *anybody*, and certainly it is perceived by all but purists as distinctively Scots.[7] Macaulay's survey of speakers in Ayr would appear to confirm this: we might expect *a body* to survive here, in the birthplace of Burns, if anywhere; yet, while Wilson (1923: 58–9) suggested that *a buddie* was then the usual form of the indefinite pronoun in Ayrshire, Macaulay found only one example of this in data collected approximately fifty years later. This was used, significantly, by the oldest of Macaulay's informants, who was 78 at the time of the interview and therefore of the generation whose speech had been described by Wilson. Furthermore, as Macaulay (1991: 74–6) points out, *a body* occurs in 'what is almost a formulaic expression': *I don't think it did a body ony herm*. *A body* would appear to have been fossilised in the Ayrshire speech of the present day. Its place has been taken by *yin*, *wan* and forms like *anybody*, *nobody*, *somebody* and so on. Of these, *yin* and *wan* are the 'vernacular' forms used in lower-class interviews and, as Macaulay points out, they are used in different contexts: only *yin* occurs with adjectives (*a big yin*); with determiners other than *the* alone (*this yin, the next yin*); in the plural (*some of the young yins*); in the idiomatic phrase *to be yin for*; whereas both *wan* and *yin* occur as the head of a relative clause (*the yin that we were getting, the wan that's going that road*); with *thing* (*that's yin thing, that was wan thing*); and as numerals (*twenty-wan, twenty-yin*). *Wan* alone occurs with *the* alone when not the head of a relative clause (*I got her over on tae the wan*); and before a noun other than *thing* (*wan depreciation I dae see*). Macaulay's findings here suggest that in the grammar of present-day Scots, at least in Ayr, *a body* survives as a relic feature in formulaic expressions, with *wan* and *yin* having a rule-based distribution. Middle-class speakers whose grammar is more anglicised tend to use forms like *anybody*, *somebody* and so on.

9.3.3 Demonstratives

As pointed out in section 9.2, one of the features first seized upon as a Scotticism by the likes of Hume and Beattie was the 'failure' on the part of Scots to observe the English rules for the use of *those* and *these*. Hume (1760) goes no further than providing the 'correct' English rules, but Beattie (1788: 92–3) explains the problem more fully:

> *These* is the plural of *this* and *those* of *that*. The Scots often use *these* very improperly for *those*, and as the plural of *that*; but the rule is clear and admits of no exception . . . They who speak any of the dialects of the south of Scotland will be pleased to observe that *these* is of the same import with the Scotch *thir* and *those* the same with the Scotch *thay*. In the north of Scotland, *thay* and *thir* are not used; and the vulgar say, *this things* and *that things*, as if *this* and *that* had no plural form.

Here, Beattie somewhat uncharacteristically appears to give preference to the southern dialects, presumably because they make what he sees as a rule-based distinction which he thinks should be easily 'translated' into English. The northern dialects are condemned for having no distinct plural determiners, as is the speech of other 'Scots', who, according to Beattie, simply use the English determiners incorrectly. The last group are probably the educated middle–class Scots at whom Beattie's tract is directed, and their usage was perhaps hypercorrect. Wilson (1923: 54) confirms that the tendency to use *these* where Standard English would have *those* persists into the twentieth century, at least in the phrase *in these days*, referring to the distant past, where Standard English would have *in those days*, and Macaulay (1991: 72) confirms that this usage persists, at least in the language of lower–class speakers. Grant and Main Dixon (1921: 106) confirm the other usages mentioned by Beattie as still occurring in various dialects of Scots: they give as examples of 'modern use in the N.E.' *I'll knock aff some o' that loons' heids*; *This twa three notes* (Greig, *Main's Wooing*), and they go on to state:

> 'These' is *thir* (O.N. ðeir; found in M.E. as ðir, ðer): . . . '*Thir kittle times will drive the wisest o' us daft*, said Neil Blane' (Scott, *Old Mortality*, chapter 19). But 'these' is sometimes *thae*: '*They hae been a sad changed family since thae rough times began*' (Scott, *Old Mortality*, chapter 36).

For *those*, Grant and Main Dixon give *thae* as the norm in Scots, providing the following examples from nineteenth–century literature: '*Upon my conscience, Rose,*' *ejaculated the Baron*, '*the gratitude o' thae dumb brutes, and of that puir innocent, brings the tears into my auld een*' (Scott, *Waverley*, II, chapter 35); '*Are there really folk that do thae kind o' jobs for siller?*' (Galt, *Sir A Wylie*, I, chapter 30). They go on to cite *that* for plural *those* as 'a North country idiom' in line with Beattie's observations. They then conclude that *those* takes the form *them* when used pronominally, and give as an example: *Them that buys beef buys banes, as the aul' by-word says* (Alexander, *Johnny Gibb*, chapter 25).

The use of *them* as a demonstrative is now common in most non-standard dialects of English (Cheshire et al. 1993) but is generally viewed as a relatively recent anglicism in Scots. Macafee (1983: 51) notes that '*them* as a deictic determiner occurs as early as 1935 in the West of Scotland'. To be fair, Macafee is here attempting to counter claims that non-standard features of Glaswegian English are recent innovations, but this use of *them* is far older than she suggests. It is noted as a widespread non-standard feature by Beattie and Mitchell: the former gives the example *I mind none of them things* as 'Scot. and barbarous

English' (1787: 95), while the latter (1799: 83) designates the same example as 'Irish and vulgar English'. It is most likely that this use of *them* was just beginning to be stigmatised in the eighteenth century: Beattie may here be wrong to include this use of *them* as a Scotticism, but Grant and Main Dixon's example shows that it was at least perceived as a Scots usage by one nineteenth-century author. Macaulay found that, in his survey, 'one of the more salient markers of social class differences is the use of *thae* and *them* by lower-class speakers where middle-class speakers usually use *those*'. He also found that *thae* was used almost exclusively by three speakers, two of whom were the oldest in his sample, which 'suggests that *them* may be replacing the older term *thae*'. As with the case of *a body/yin* discussed above, we have here a case of an older Scots form being replaced by another non-standard form in Scots vernacular usage. Since demonstrative *them* is, and has been since the eighteenth century, widespread in non-standard varieties of English, it is perhaps easier to view this development as leading to a diminution of the 'distinctively Scottish' element in the modern vernacular.

Like several dialects of English, Scots retains the remnants of an older, three-term deictic system, in which *this* refers to objects close to the speaker, *that* to objects further away, and *thon*, *yon* to objects even further away, or 'over there'. Murray (1873: 179) sets out the rule for the use of these terms in Scots with characteristic clarity: 'When several objects are under consideration: *Thys* is used to identify the object nearest to the speaker; *That* is used to identify the object nearest to the person spoken to; *Thon* or *yon* is used to identify an object remote from both'. Murray goes on to state that '*yon* . . . is constantly used in Scotch, in referring to things remote in place or time, where the English would generally use *that*' and gives as an example to illustrate the use of the three terms in Scots: '*Thys* is meyne, *that's* yours, but quhae's aucht *thon*' (1873: 186). Wilson then goes on to claim of *thon* that it 'is probably a corruption of *yon*, developed by analogy of *thys*, *that*, to render it more significantly demonstrative. It is in regular use in all parts of Scotland, in Northumberland, about Shields, and as far south as Teesdale.' Grant and Main Dixon (1921: 107) fail to note the significance of the three-term deictic system, simply stating: '*That* is yon, thon'. More recent studies show that *thon* and *yon* are falling out of use in Scots, as in the other dialects mentioned by Murray, Macaulay finding 'only three examples of *yon* and two of *thon*', suggesting that this feature is recessive in Scots.

9.3.4 Verb Inflections

The regular past-tense morpheme of Older Scots was *-it*, and the use of this morpheme in written Scots of the sixteenth century is one of the main factors noted by such as Görlach (1991) as distinguishing Scots from English. The loss of this feature is likewise viewed as one of the main symptoms of anglicisation of the written language (Görlach 1985; Romaine 1982b). As far as official records and letters are concerned, MacQueen (1957: 138) found that 'the older Scottish *-it* of the weak past participle (and past tense) has almost entirely anglicised by 1700'. These authors are, however, referring to the 'official' language, which ceases to be recognisably Scots by this time. As far as the spoken language and the Scots of literature are concerned, the picture is more complex. Murray (1873: 199) acknowledges that the past-tense morpheme has changed from 'the old Scotch', but views this not as a process of loss or anglicisation but rather as the result of a set of regular, conditioned sound changes. His 'rules' for these changes are worth quoting in full:

In the modern dialect this full form [-*it*] undergoes certain euphonic changes in accordance with the character of the preceding letter or syllable.

1. The full form is retained only by verbs ending in a shut consonant (k, t, p, g, d, b), e.g. *lyckit, teastit, slyppit, ruggit, bendit, rubbit.*

2. After any other consonant, except a liquid or nasal, the vowel is elided and -*t* retained, as *snuff, snuff't; ax, ax't.* Also a liquid or nasal preceded by another consonant: *turn, turn't* etc. This rule, moreover, includes all words of more than one syllable unaccented on the last, except such as fall under rule 1, e.g. *honour, honour't.*

3. After a liquid or a nasal or a vowel in a monosyllable or accented syllable, the connecting vowel is elided and -*t* becomes -*d* as *taell, taell'd; deem, deem'd; steane, steaned; belang, belang'd; stay, stay'd.*

A condensed account of these rules is presented by Grant and Main Dixon (1921: 113 n. 1): 'The connecting vowel is dropped when the verb ends in any consonant except t, p, k, d, b, g. After an accented vowel d (instead of t) is more common in the Mid and Sth. dialects as also after a liquid or nasal', while Dieth (1932: 139) gives the rule as follows:

This dental ending . . . appears

(I) after non-stop consonants	as	[t]
(II) after stops	as	[it], [ɪt], [ɛt]
(III) after vowels	as	[t], [d].

He then goes on to give as exceptions to rule 1: [hard] 'heard', [he:vd] 'lifted' and [ʃe:vd] 'shaved'. The rules referred to by Murray, Grant and Main Dixon and Dieth are morphophonemic: in the written language, as MacQueen shows, the ending would be written ⟨ed⟩ from the eighteenth century onwards, except where the writer is deliberately attempting to reproduce the sound of Scots. The main difference between the three sets of rules concerns verbs ending in a liquid or a nasal: Murray's rules predict the ending [d], as in his example *taell'd*; Grant and Main Dixon's would give [t] but [d] in middle and southern dialects; while Dieth, who is describing a northern dialect, would have [t] here. There is not necessarily any contradiction here: Murray's work is, after all, a grammar of the southern dialects, so Grant and Main Dixon's variation between [t] and [d] could simply represent a stage in the loss of this voicing rule in southern dialects by the twentieth century. However, Tulloch's (1980: 288) examination of the preterite endings used by Scott suggests that the rules given by Murray were never 'as strict as he would make them out to be'. Tulloch finds examples in Scott which conform to Murray's rule: *belang'd, caa'd, gae'd, kamed, kend, sell'd*, but also others which do not: *kent, selt, hangit*.

Tulloch goes on to discuss Scott's general reluctance to use the -*t* ending, quoting, for instance, an -*ed* suffix surfacing between two -*it* endings in the phrase *tuggit and rived and ruggit* (*Rob Roy*, p. 199), where Murray's rule 2 would predict a -*t* ending for the second verb. In cases like this, as in other instances where Scott has variation between -*it* and -*ed* endings for the same verb on the same page, what we may have is simply a mixture of 'Scots' and 'English' forms, but this cannot be the case with the -*t* ending for such as *selt*; in this instance, it is more likely that Scott is attempting to represent a variant he had actually heard, or actually used himself. Certainly, in present-day Scots, forms like *tellt, selt, killt* and so on are so common, contrasting with Standard English *told, sold, killed* and so on, that

Miller (1993: 106) is able to state categorically that '*sellt* is simply *sell* + *ed*, *ed* being realised as *t* in Scottish English'. This is to some extent confirmed by Macaulay's findings: in his data, *tellt*, *sellt* are socially salient variables occurring in the speech of some of his lower-class informants. The alternative forms used by his other informants are not, as Murray's rule 3 would predict, *tell'd* and *sell'd*, but the Standard English forms *told* and *sold*. If Murray's rule 3 was ever consistently adhered to even in the south of Scotland (and Tulloch's findings suggest that it was not), it would appear that it no longer operates. Instead, the Scots preterite forms of verbs ending in [l] and possibly [n] have the ending *-t* and contrast with Standard English forms with *-ed* as well as, in the case of *told*, *sold*, an internal vowel change.

The viability of Murray's rules 1 and 2 is difficult to ascertain from written sources because, as we saw from the discussion of Tulloch's findings above, literary Scots often shows variation between *-it* and *-ed* which may represent variation between Scots and English forms, or even a failure of consistency on the author's part, rather than reflecting any true variation within Scots itself. On the other hand, an attempt on the author's part to restore 'true' Scots forms might lead to overuse of the Older Scots *-it* ending. One example of variation between *-it* and *-ed* endings for preterites (and, for that matter, past participles) can be found in Donaldson's (1989: 30–4) collection of popular literature from the nineteenth century. One of the extracts from *The North Briton*, published in Edinburgh between 1857 and 1859, is in the form of a letter from the Scots-speaking persona 'Mr. M'Korkindale' to Napoleon (20 March 1858). In this letter, there is considerable variation between *-ed* and *-it*, *-et*, *-t*, but the *-ed* forms are more numerous (forty-two instances as against twenty-two of *-it*, *-et*, *-t*). The only verbs which appear with different endings are *ken*, which has three instances of *kent* and one of *kenned*, and *follow*, which appears once as *follow't* and once as *followed*. Verbs ending in stops which appear with *-ed* (in violation of Murray's rule 1) are *needed*, *demanded*, *invited*, *indicated*, *awarded*, *committed*, *prosecuted*, *intended*, *extended* and *uplifted*, while those conforming to Murray's rule 1 are *intendit*, *conneckit*, *markit*, *unexpecket*, *stabbit*, *widet*, *eleckit*, *winket*, *colleckit*, *askit*, *attempit* and *expeckit*.

Kent, of course, conforms not to Murray's rule 3, but to Dieth's rule I, and shows the same pattern noted by Miller for verbs ending in [l]. If this letter represents the spoken Scots of Edinburgh in 1858, then our scepticism about the hard-and-fast nature of Murray's rules is borne out. There is thus a tendency for verbs ending in stops to have the *-it* ending, but many do not, and rule 3 is not followed in *kent* (although it might be in *kenned* if the ⟨e⟩ is silent). On the other hand, the diversity in this letter may to a large extent represent not variability in Scots *per se* so much as a tendency on the author's part to adopt English forms when the verb concerned is of a more learned nature. A glance at the list of verbs with *-ed* suggests that this may go some way towards explaining the variation, but, there again, the form *eleckit* occurs six times in the repeated phrase *eleckit by universal suffrage*. This kind of variation between 'Scots' and 'English' forms in Scots literature is discussed in Chapter 7 for the early period; here, I draw attention to it merely to suggest that the rules given by Murray probably never applied as consistently as he seems to suggest. On the other hand, forms in *-it* do still occur in Scots: Macafee (1983: 49) tells us that 'in Glasgow, /ɪt/ is heard only after plosives, e.g. *landit*, *likit*, *skelpit* "spanked". /t/ is heard after /l/, /r/ and nasals, e.g. *killt*, *battert*, *kent* "knew". Otherwise the form is /t/ or /d/ depending on the voicing of the preceding segment, as in Standard English.' McClure (1983: 6) notes that features such as 'the past tense ending of *dippit*, *helpit* . . . are general in Scots dialects' and provides examples in extracts from contemporary Scots literature, but his extracts from literature in urban Scots (Kelman, Banks) show either no -*it* forms (Kelman) or variation between -*it* and -*ed* (the extract from Banks showing *ejucatit* but *expected*, both past participles). This would suggest that the use of -*it* after plosives and -*t* after /l/, /r/ and nasals is still current in Scots, but not used categorically by all speakers.

This morphophonemic variation in the 'regular' (weak) preterite and past-participle forms, which, as we have seen, generated so much interest among dialectologists like Murray and Dieth, is not mentioned at all in eighteenth-century lists of Scotticisms. This is probably because, as MacQueen notes, -*ed* is the norm in written usage by then. When it comes to 'irregular' or strong preterites and past participles, though, eighteenth-century authors such as Beattie have a great deal to say. Hume (1760: 686) mentions several of these in his list of Scotticisms: *proven*, *improven*, *approven* for English *proved* and so on, and *drunk*, *run* for English *drank*, *ran*. The first three are examples of Scots use of the -*en* ending, while the latter two show a tendency to level the preterite and participle in strong verbs. Sinclair (1782), Beattie (1787) and Mitchell (1799) all note *proven* and *improven* as Scotticisms. Sinclair (1782: 69) comments that of the 'many false formations in the Scottish dialect, which ought to be avoided', many are preterite forms and he lists, as well as *proven* and *improven*: *keept*, *sweept*, *keeped*, *pled*, *catched*, *teach't*, *run* and *drunk*. It is noteworthy, in the light of our discussion of -*it* forms above, that Sinclair has *keept* and *keeped* as Scotticisms, but not *keepit*. It is possible that his primary concern is the failure of the Scots forms to conform with English usage in changing the vowel to [ɛ] in the preterite. Beattie and Murray's examples of 'incorrect' preterites and past participles are fewer, but Beattie (1787: 33) cites past participles *broke* and *wrote* as in *the glass is broke*, while both he and Mitchell (1799: 46) cite *eat* used as preterite and past participle, as in *you eat little yesterday and have eat nothing today*. In both these instances, Beattie notes that the 'incorrect' usage is not exclusively Scots, but that 'this is not always attended to, even by English writers'. Beattie is referring here to a general tendency towards what Aitken (1979: 109) terms the 'syncretism of past tense and past participle', which, as Aitken points out, is a 'shibboleth' of modern urban Scots, but which is common to all non-standard Englishes, even to modern standard English where, for example, earlier *holpen* has been replaced by *helped* as a past participle. Beattie and Mitchell also note *hurted*, *pleaded* and *seed* for *hurt*, *pled* and *saw*, all of which involve extension of the 'regular', weak, -*ed* ending to 'irregular' verbs.

Of the forms noted as Scotticisms in the eighteenth century, only *proven*, *improven*, *approven* are distinctively Scottish: the others exemplify the kind of analogical levelling which was occurring and continues to occur in all non-standard dialects. Murray (1873: 203) notes the differences between Scots and 'literary English' as follows:

> Several verbs, which in the Literary English have a new weak form, retain in Scotch the strong form of the Anglo-Saxon and Old English; and conversely, a few verbs which retain in English the old strong forms, have in Scotch adopted a new weak one. But many weak verbs, which are in English contracted or otherwise divergent, are in Scotch full and regular.

Here, as with the 'weak' past-tense endings discussed above, Murray perhaps over-emphasises the 'regularity' of Scots, implying that it is superior to 'literary English' in this respect. As already noted, Mackay (1888: xiv) makes the same point about strong verbs, and asserts that 'the Scottish language . . . has retained all the ancient forms of (these) verbs, and can say "I *cast*, I *coost*, and I have *casten*, a stane", or "I *put*, I *pat* or I have *putten* on my coat", "I *hurt*, I *hurted* or I have *hurten* myself" and "I *let*, I *loot*, or I have *letten* or *looten* fa' my tears", etc.' Both Murray and Grant and Main Dixon give large tables of verb forms, showing both verbs that are 'strong' in Scots but 'weak' in English and vice versa, stretching to six pages in Murray's case (1873: 203–9) and seven in Grant and Main Dixon's (1921: 126–32). Examples from the latter list of the *-en* past participles of which Mackay is so proud are: *baken* 'baked', *bursten* 'burst', *cruppen* 'crept', *comen* 'come', *fochten* 'fought', *gatten* 'got', *gruppen* 'gripped', *hauden, hadden* 'held', *hutten*, 'hit', *leughen* 'laughed', *luppen* 'leapt', *pitten, putten* 'put', *proven* 'proved', *sputten* 'spat', *wooshen* 'washed' and *wutten* 'wet'. It is worth pointing out, though, that some of these are given with alternative forms in Grant and Main Dixon: for instance, alongside *comen* as a past-participle form, *come* and *comed* also appear, showing that both a 'weak' form, and a form identical to the Standard English past participle, existed alongside the strong past participle. Moreover, weak forms are given as alternatives even in some cases where the Standard English past participle is strong, for example *choosed* alongside *chosen*. This suggests that the retention of 'older' strong verb patterns, at least by the early twentieth century, was not as widespread as Murray and Mackay made out half a century earlier. Some of the strong past participles were still used in the nineteenth century, for Tulloch (1980: 291–2) gives the following examples from Scott: *cruppen, gotten, hadden, letten, luppen, putten* and *stooden*. There has certainly been a reduction in the number of 'strong' preterites and past participles in Scots since the eighteenth century, but some are still used today. Aitken (1979: 96) suggests that 'the past-participle form *proven*' is one of a number of Scotticisms 'which seem to have been successfully eliminated', but this surely persists in the uniquely Scottish legal term *not proven* as well as in the sense 'put to the test'. If anything, this use of *proven* is spreading into English usage: Collins' *Softback English Dictionary* (1992) gives as a definition of *proven*: '1. a past participle of *prove*. 2. See *not proven*. – adj. 3. tried, tested: *a proven method*'. The form is not marked as Scottish.

In modern urban Scots, such strong forms would appear to be giving way to weak and/or syncretised forms: neither Macafee (1983) nor Miller (1993) makes any reference to forms like *putten*, while Macaulay (1991: 109) cites only one isolated example of *gotten*. What is more noticeable today, according to both Miller and Macaulay, as well as Macafee, is the tendency to regularise the paradigm by using the same form for the preterite and past participle. This was noted by Trotter (1901: 24), who considers the 'chief characteristic' of the 'Glasgow-Irish' dialect, which he compares so unfavourably with 'Scotch', to be 'the invariable use of the past participle of the verb for the past tense indicative, and *vice versa*'. Trotter goes on to give as examples of this 'Glasgow-Irish' usage: 'As *we was goin* dinn the street *we seen* Toamie Tode, an if he *hadnae went* awoe when *he seed us he wad hae fell* into the syvor, or *he wad been* cleverer *as* he looked'. Apart from *he wad been*, which Trotter presumably considers incorrect because of the omission of *have*, and the use of *as* for *than*, all the forms which he italicised are past tenses or participles. Although these particular forms were not mentioned by the eighteenth-century authors cited above, Trotter is not necessarily right to suppose that they are 'Glasgow-Irish' and therefore of relatively recent introduction: Miller (1993: 107) points out that '*went* as a past participle has a long history, occurring in Dunbar's poem *Celebrations*' (end of the fifteenth century). Certainly, the use of all these forms, and others such as *come*, *done* and *run* used as preterites, is common in lower-class Scots speech today, as Macaulay's survey shows. What makes Trotter, and many Scots today, reluctant to consider these syncretised preterite and past-participle forms as 'good Scots' in the sense used by Aitken (1982) is the fact that they can also be found in many non-standard dialects in England, and so are not considered to be 'pure' Scots. Furthermore, they constitute a simplification of the grammar, and so are seen as slovenly, while the strong verb forms in Scots of which Murray and Mackay were so proud, and which are found much less frequently in modern Scots, keep the grammar more complex. However, as Aitken points out, English has been simplifying verbal paradigms in this way since the Old English period, and Scots, like any living language, will continue to do so.

One feature of Older Scots which is generally agreed to have been dying out in the course of the Modern Scots period is the distinction between the present participle, ending in -and, and the gerund, ending in -ing. From the time the language ceased to be used in official documents, the standardising forces that kept these two endings distinct in writing would be considerably weakened. MacQueen concluded from her study of official records written in the first half of the eighteenth century that 'the -and of the present participle was . . . practically obsolete in 1700' (1957: 141). Murray (1873: 210) explains the loss of this distinction as follows:

> In the sixteenth century, the dialect of Central Scotland, and the literary Middle Scotch founded upon it, lost the distinction between the participle and gerund, apparently on account of the final consonants becoming mute, and the vowels being then confounded, so that both forms were written -ing, -in.

He goes on to claim that, in the Southern dialects, the two forms are still kept distinct, despite the final consonants being 'mute'. Indeed, he goes so far as to make the following assertion (1873: 211).

> It is as absurd to a Southern Scot to hear eating used for both his eiting and eatand, as it is to an Englishman to hear will used for both will and shall. When he is told that 'John was eating', he is strongly tempted to ask what kind of eating he proved to be.

Romaine (1982b: 60) suggests that the distinction is maintained in pronunciation, [kʌmən] being used for the participle 'he is coming' and [kʌmɪn] for the gerund 'the Second Coming'. This point is also made by Grant and Main Dixon, who, like Murray, claim that the distinction is maintained only in certain dialects, namely those of the south and Caithness. Dieth (1932: 140) confirms that the endings of the present participle and gerund have fallen together in the dialect of Buchan in the north-east. This distinction between present-participle and gerund forms would appear to be increasingly recessive: it is certainly not mentioned by Macaulay (1991), Miller (1993) or Macafee (1983) as occurring in modern urban dialects of Scots.

Görlach (1985: 29) notes that '-s is a Scots marker for "present" with all persons (unless pronoun preceded)'. He is referring here to the Scots of the sixteenth century, but the tendency to use the -s inflection for the present tense, particularly with third person plural subjects, persists throughout our period. MacQueen finds this feature still occasionally used in eighteenth-century records, examples being the great loss the poor sustains (1732); They . . . statute and enact . . . and prohibit and discharge . . . and appoints this prohibition (Dundee Burgh, 1772) (1957: 137).

This feature is not mentioned as a Scotticism in the eighteenth-century lists, but it was used by Scott, as Tulloch (1980: 287) points out:

When the subject is something other than a personal pronoun (e.g. a noun, adjective or relative), or when the pronoun is separated from the verb, the third person singular form may be used for all persons . . . the -s inflection of the third person is, however, used in all cases, even with the pronoun adjacent to the verb, when the tense is the historic present used for the past.

Examples provided by Tulloch include the following: *It's gude ale, though I shouldna say sae that brews it* (*Old Mortality*, pp. 487–8); *So there's hope Plainstanes may be hanged, as many has for a less matter* (*Redgauntlet*, p. 209); *In troth, says I to him, an' that be the case, Davie, I am misdoubting* (*The Antiquary*, p. 81). Murray (1873: 212) sets out the same rules as Tulloch for the use of the -s ending of the present tense, and sees the use of this ending as rule-based, insisting that 'such expressions as *the men syts* are not vulgar corruptions, but strictly grammatical in the Northern dialect'. That this usage was not stigmatised is confirmed by Trotter, who, as we have seen with regard to the syncretised past-participle and preterite forms, was quick to criticise the corruptions of the 'Glasgow-Irish', including this use of the -s ending in his list of true 'Scotch' features. Like Murray, Trotter (1901: 26) describes this usage as rule-based and therefore respectable:

> In Scotch there is one singular and two plurals – the singular the same as in English, and one of the plurals the same as the singular. This plural is used for all plural nouns, and where two or more pronouns, singular or plural, or one or more pronouns, singular or plural, join with one or more nouns, singular or plural, to form a compound nominative, as *Tam an' Dick hates you; Dick an' me hates you; Him an' me hates you; Tam an' Dick an' him an' us hates him; The verra dogs hates him, an' the horses an' kye hates him too.*

In the same fashion, Grant and Main Dixon (1921: 112) point out that 'in ordinary speech the termination -s is sometimes added to the 1st pers. sing., especially of habitual action: or when the present is used for a dramatic past: or when a relative pronoun is the subject of the verb' and that 'with noun subjects, not pronouns, the verb has -s in the plural pres. indic.'. These rules for the use of the present-tense -s ending still operate in vernacular Scots, although they are no longer perceived as features of 'good Scots'. Miller (1993: 109) notes the use of *is* and *was* with plural nouns, as in *the windies wiz aw broken, the lambs is oot the field*, but tells us that this construction 'is avoided by educated speakers'. The latter do, however, use *is* and *was* with plural nouns after existential *there*, as in *is there any biscuits left?* Macafee (1983: 49–50) notes that, in Glasgow, -s endings for the present tense are used with noun phrases and with all types of subject in narratives. Macaulay, likewise, finds that, in lower-class speech, the -s inflection is used particularly after a relative, as in *some of the girls that was in it*, and with plural noun phrases, such as *my brothers was aw working*. Again, the fact that this feature is not used by middle-class speakers confirms that it is no longer viewed as 'good Scots'. Macaulay also provides a good deal of evidence that the -s inflection is used with all persons in what is a genuine narrative tense in Scots. This is used mainly by the lower-class speakers in his sample, but one of his middle-class speakers shows variation between *I say* and *I says* which is genuinely rule-based. Macaulay notes of this speaker (1991: 161–2):

> There is an interesting contrast between his use of *I says* in a narrative context in (22) and his use of *I say* in a reminiscence in (23):
> (22) he says 'What are you doing?' I *says* 'I'm doing nothing.' He says 'Would you like to work?' I *say* 'Of course I would like to work.'

In (22) [the speaker] is referring to a particular occasion that is part of a narrative that also
includes the exchange, and *says* has a specific time-reference. In example (23) he is not talking
about a specific occasion but about something that frequently occurs:

(23) but as I *say* often to people – New Zealanders when they come in 'Oh you're New
Zealanders which part North or South?' 'Oh we're from the North' and I *say* 'Oh you're not you
North people you're not so hot. I like the South.'

In (23) [the speaker] is not referring to a particular occasion, and the verb *say* does not refer to a
specific time but is instead a habitual tense.

Macaulay's survey thus shows that the rules set out by Tulloch for Scott's use of the -*s*
ending are still in operation in Scots today: it is used with noun phrases, when the
pronominal subject is separated from the verb (by a relative) and as the 'historic present' of
narrative. All that has changed is that this usage, like that of the syncretised past participles
and preterites discussed above, has become stigmatised, regarded as 'bad Scots' and so
tends to be used more in lower-class speech.

9.4   SYNTAX

9.4.1   The Noun Phrase

9.4.1.1   Relative Clauses

One area of Scots syntax which has received a comparatively large amount of scholarly
attention is that of relative clauses. The introduction of *wh*- relatives into Older Scots has
been discussed in Caldwell (1974), Romaine (1982b) and in Chapter 4 above. Romaine
(1982a: 60) sums up her findings as follows:

> It appears that WH-marked relative clauses entered the language and spread from more formal to
> less formal styles and from less frequently relativized syntactic positions (e.g. genitive) to more
> frequently relativized ones (e.g. subject) gradually displacing *that* as a relative clause marker.
> While the modern written language shows WH-forms in nearly all styles and all syntactic
> positions, there remains a significant residue of *that* forms in the spoken language.

This dichotomy between written and spoken usage in Scotland seems to have been
established before the beginning of our period. Perhaps this is why there is little mention
of Scotticisms involving relative clauses in the eighteenth-century lists that I have
examined, concerned as they are mainly with written usage. There are a few references
to the 'incorrect' use of relatives, but this matter is not given anything like the same
prominence as, for example, use of *shall* and *will*. The only reference made by Beattie
(1787: 104), in fact, suggests that *wh*- forms *are* being used by Scots, but not correctly: 'Do
you know *who* you speak to. *whom*. Scot and vulg. Eng. *Who* is often used ungrammatically
for *whom*, especially in conversation. But, in elegant writing, this impropriety must always
be avoided.' The same point is also made by Mitchell (1799: 72), who also notes the
incorrect use of *as* for *in which* in *In the order, as they lie in the preface*, which, he says, should
be *In the order, in which*; and, in another case, he corrects the use of *that* in a sentence
without commenting on it (1799: 62): 'The works of the Lord are great, sought out of all
them that have pleasure therein. Sought out by all those who have pleasure in them. *Of* in
good English, never means *by*.'
   Here, Mitchell corrects *them that* to *those who*, but only makes explicit comment on the

use of the preposition. It is perhaps worth noting here that Mitchell's is the latest of the lists of Scotticisms that I have examined, indicating perhaps that consciousness of 'incorrect' Scots usage in relative clauses increases towards the end of the eighteenth century. On the other hand, the examples of 'incorrect' usage cited here are not particularly Scottish: Mitchell could be taking his cue from English grammarians like Lowth.[8] It would certainly appear that use of *that* rather than *wh-* forms persisted in Scots, at least in speech, but that this usage was not so heavily stigmatised as to attract the censure of the likes of Hume and Beattie. Murray goes so far as to state that 'the simple relative of the Scottish and Northern English dialects is *ăt'* (1873: 194, 196). He goes on to claim that *who (quheae, quha)* is not used as a relative in 'spoken Scotch' and that *which (quhilk)* 'is used in the spoken dialect as a compound relative, when the antecedent is a sentence or clause' as in '*Hey said 'at they maet us onna the muir, quhilk wasna the case*'. Murray defends the use in Scots of *that (at)* + possessive pronoun rather than Standard English *whose*, as in *the man at hys weyfe's deid*, pointing out that the same construction is used in Hebrew and Anglo-Saxon and is therefore perfectly grammatical. He also notes (1873: 97) that the omission of the relative is common 'especially where it is the object of a verb or preposition, or a nominative in verbs beginning with *there is, there was* etc.'. Grant and Main Dixon (1921: 102) give an account of relatives in Scots almost identical to Murray's: 'the idiomatic relative pronoun in Sc. is *that*, taking the forms '*at, 't* and often being omitted even when nominative of a clause'. On the last issue, they do not make the point about omission after existential *there* explicitly, but their example is: *There's no mair than twa acre seen the ploo.* They make the point that the *wh-* pronouns are not 'modernisms', being found in Middle Scots, but that they have never passed into popular speech, and that the 'oblique cases *whase, wham* are found in poetry and prose, especially where tinctured by biblical phraseology'. Grant and Main Dixon thus confirm Romaine's findings quoted above: *wh-* relatives enter Scots in more formal styles and in 'oblique cases' first, and have never really filtered down into colloquial usage. In the nineteenth and early twentieth centuries, they are common in literary Scots but not in everyday speech. Tulloch (1980: 275) takes issue with Murray on this point, because he finds many examples in Scott's representation of informal speech, both of *whae* and of *whilk*, with nouns as antecedents. Examples of these are, respectively: *The Hieland lairds whae hae deil a boddle o' siller* (*Rob Roy*, p. 364); *The breath of man, whilk is in his nostrils* (*The Antiquary*, p. 272).

Tulloch (1980: 276) goes on to argue:

> Murray's firm assertion [that only *that* is used in spoken Scots] is hard to accept unless we apply it only to very informal speech. With the example of written Scots and English before them it is surely likely that Scots-speakers, even in only slightly formal speech, would occasionally use *wha* and *whilk*. Rather than see Scott's use of these pronouns in dialogue as a literary convention, we might see them as a realistic representation of the tendency of the spoken and written forms of the language to interact and influence each other, especially in any speech which has even a small degree of formality.

Of course, what Scott produces is by definition literature and is a *representation* of spoken Scots, not spoken Scots itself, but his representation of the vernacular is generally agreed to be authentic: Murison (1970: 220), for instance, writes 'that he knew his Scots thoroughly and could reproduce its idioms and cadences perfectly is obvious to anyone who is a native speaker himself'. Perhaps the key point here is that made at the end of the passage from Tulloch quoted above: Scott uses *wh-* forms to signal that the speech has some degree of formality, indicating that, by the nineteenth century, these forms had infiltrated Scots further, moving from written usage to the more formal end of the spectrum of spoken usage. Certainly, Scott shows elsewhere that he is capable of using the full range of options with regard to relative clauses: for instance, *that* is used with human antecedents, as cited by Murison (1970: 217): *If folk have ony thing to write to me about, they may gie the letter to John Hislop, the carrier, that has used the road these forty years* (*St Ronan's Well*, chapter 2).

Tulloch points out that Scott even uses *that* in non-restrictive clauses, a usage not found even in informal Standard English: *When Sanders Aikwood, that was a forester in thae days, . . . was gaun a daundering about the wood* (*The Antiquary*, p. 271); *That it may be a lesson to you, that are but a young thoughtless chap, wha ye draw up wi' on a lonely road* (*Redgauntlet*, p. 150). Scott also puts the relative *as*, which was objected to by Mitchell, into the mouth of a character who is said to speak 'broad Scots of the most vulgar description' (*Waverley*, p. 359). The example given by Tulloch here is: *the aits will be got bravely in . . . and the cornmongers will make the auld price gude against them as has horses till keep* (*Waverley*, p. 360, quoted in Tulloch 1980: 277).

This would suggest that Scott was aware of, and exploited, the full range of options available in the Scots of the early nineteenth century, from the use of *wh-* forms in more formal speech, through to the use of *that* in less formal spoken Scots, to the 'vulgar' *as* of Broad Scots. As with the case of the preterite verb endings discussed above, Murray may have been overemphasising the predominance of *that* in spoken Scots in order to give a picture of a regular, 'pure' vernacular. On the other hand, all accounts of present-day spoken Scots confirm that *that*, rather than *wh-* forms, is the norm, at least in lower-class usage. Macafee (1983: 52) states that 'Scottish speakers commonly use the relativiser *that* with personal antecedents . . . *that* also occurs in non-restrictive clauses' and 'Scottish speakers use *which* almost exclusively in non-restrictive relative clauses with sentential antecedents'. As we have seen, this last point was made by Murray but denied by Tulloch. Miller (1993: 111) confirms the widespread use in Scots of *which* with sentential antecedents, or what he calls 'event relative clauses', but does not go so far as to suggest that this is the *only* use of *which*. Miller also notes that *that* is used in restrictive relative clauses and *that* + possessive pronoun is preferred to *whose*, while Macaulay (1991) found that *wh-* forms were less frequent (but not non-existent) in the speech of lower-class informants. Yet while Macafee notes the use of *that* in non-restrictive relative clauses, Miller (1993: 112) observes that such clauses are very rare, and that usually coordinate structures occur instead, as in: *the boy I was talking to last night – and he actually works in the yard – was saying it's going to be closed down*. This point is also made by Macaulay, who shows how the lower-class speakers in his sample use non-restrictive relatives less frequently than those from the middle class. All this seems to suggest that *wh-* forms have made further inroads into Scots usage in the course of the modern period: they are used in written Scots, where they have distinctively Scots spellings such as *wha, whilk*, and in certain dialects *fa* and so on, but they are also used in more formal spoken Scots and in more informal speech by educated, middle–class Scots. In 'vernacular' Scots, that is, the informal, spoken usage of the lower classes, *that* still holds sway as the most frequently used relative, but Macaulay's results suggest that *wh-* forms are infrequent rather than non-existent.

Murray noted that in Scots the relative could be omitted where it was the object, or the subject in an existential sentence. Tulloch (1980: 277) gives several examples from Scott of subject relatives omitted in non-existential sentences, such as *it was about a bit grey cowt*, *wasna worth ten punds sterling* (*Heart of Midlothian*, p. 369). Macafee, likewise, shows that the omission of subject relatives is not restricted to existential sentences in Glasgow speech, but states that it is more common in such sentences. Miller, on the other hand, simply states that '*that* (as a subject relative pronoun) can be omitted in existential constructions', and goes on to point out that such usage is not uniquely Scots, but can be found even in informal Standard English. Macaulay finds that 'zero subject markers' are used by both lower-class and middle-class speakers, but the latter use them much less frequently, and that most, but not all of these occur in existential sentences.

Macaulay's findings with regard to relative constructions, displaying as they do a certain degree of social stratification, would suggest that this is an area of Scots in which change is still in progress. *Wh-* forms first infiltrated the written language in formal styles in the Older Scots period, moving into more formal spoken Scots, and then into the less formal spoken usage of the middle classes. Categorical statements about the absence of *wh-* forms from Scots usage such as that made by Murray are no longer valid, if they ever were: these forms are part of the repertoire of Scots, available for more formal and literary styles, throughout the Modern Scots period.

9.4.1.2 Use of the Definite Article

Miller (1993: 128) notes that 'a well-known characteristic of Scottish English is the use of *the* with nouns denoting institutions, certain illnesses, certain periods of time and with quantifiers such as *both* and *all*'. This use of the definite article where it would not appear in Standard English is well represented in the eighteenth-century lists of Scotticisms, but seems not to have died out in present-day Scots, despite the strictures of Beattie and his fellows. Beattie (1787: 53, 87, 90, 91, 95) lists as Scotticisms:

1. the morrow's morning, the morn's night for English tomorrow's in both cases
2. he was born in the forty-five for in forty-five or 1745
3. The sugar is cheaper but the rum as dear as ever; five shillings the piece
4. He has studied every part of natural history except the botany
5. I shall see you in the summer, the harvest, the winter
6. He has got the cold; the fever
7. say the grace, go to the school, the church.

These examples are all used by either Sinclair (1782) or Mitchell (1799), or, in most cases, both. It is worth noting that not all these eighteenth-century examples fit into the categories given by Miller: (1), (2) and (5) possibly all fit in with Miller's category 'certain periods of time', but the only examples of this given by Miller are all of the type found in (1); (7) corresponds with Miller's category of 'institutions', and his examples are similar; (6) corresponds to Miller's category of illnesses, and his examples are only different because we have more and different names for illnesses today.[9] The examples given by Beattie, Sinclair and Mitchell which have no counterpart in Miller's list are those under (3) and (4) above. These could perhaps be taken together as a 'generic' use of the definite article: Beattie is careful to note that his *the sugar* and *the rum* refer to these commodities generally and that if one were referring to a particular example of these, as in *This shop sells rum and sugar. The rum is excellent, but the sugar is poor* (my example), then the use of the article would be quite correct. It would be tempting to look at the disparity in size between Miller's list of Scots uses of the definite article and Beattie's and conclude that the range of uses has become restricted over the last 200 years, but it may be the case that different scholars notice different usages. Tulloch, for instance, finds examples in Scott of *the day, the night* ((1) in my list) and comments, on the usage listed as (2) above, that the use of a definite article with a numeral could simply mean 'the year', as in the following quote from a letter to Boswell from his father: *If you fall on any of the very old editions before the 1500* (Pottle 1952: 106, quoted in Tulloch 1980: 278).

Tulloch goes on to add that in Scott's time, as today, this use of the definite article was mainly employed with reference to the years of the two Jacobite rebellions: *And is it so singular that a man should have been out in the forty five . . . your father, I think, Mr Foxley, was out with Derwentwater in the fifteen?* (*Redgauntlet*, p. 308). In this case, these two years have become so important in Scottish history that a Scots use of the definite article with numbers of years has become fossilised with reference to them. Tulloch goes on to discuss an interesting example of a use of the definite article which has been extended as a result of Scott's influence. In Lowland dialects, Tulloch says, it was usual in Scott's day to use the definite article with a family name, as in: *Can I not frame a fever'd dream/But still the Douglas is the theme?* (*Lady of the Lake*, vol. 1, p. xxxv). Tulloch goes on to point out that Scott 'went further and applied the idiom to Highland names, so that the wife of Rob Roy, head of the outlawed MacGregor clan, refers to him as *the MacGregor* (*Rob Roy*, p. 442). This usage, incorrect when applied to a Highlander, was picked up by Scott's readers and is now regularly employed to denote the chief of a Scottish clan.'

Thus, Scots has actually gained one more application of the definite article since 1700! Grant and Main Dixon (1921) note all the uses listed above except (2) and (3), but also note examples where Standard English would use a possessive pronoun (*the hat, the wife*), and names of trades (*the carpenterin'*), which perhaps should fall into category (4) as an area of expertise. Grant and Main Dixon also list 'names of sciences or departments of learning' (*the chemistry, the Latin*), and list, along with 'institutions' like *the church, the school*, meals such as *the tea*, and, as a separate category, *the now*. They point out that the usual pronunciation of this is [ðə nu:] and that 'genteel Scots' is [ðə naʊ]. That some of these expressions with definite articles survive today even in 'genteel Scots' is confirmed by Aitken (1979: 106), who tells us that 'to take *the* 'flu, go to *the* church or *the* school' are 'examples of what we might call covert (or "unmarked") Scotticisms'. By this, he means usages which are more or less uniquely Scottish but which are not stigmatised within Scotland because most speakers are unaware that these usages are definitively Scottish. This would suggest that the efforts of Beattie, Sinclair and Mitchell were in vain in the case of uses of the definite article, as they certainly took pains to point out that these usages were Scotticisms to be avoided.

However, it may be the case that employment of the full range of uses of the definite article outlined above is no longer as common in present-day Scots. Macaulay found that some uses of the definite article were employed by all classes of speaker, while others occurred only in lower-class speech. The former set comprise time expressions, for example *the day's paper* ('today's'), *the night, the noo, the morn, On the Sunday night* ('every Sunday'), *the August* ((1) and (5) in my list); and institutions, for example *the school, the church, the hospital* ((7) in my list). In addition to these, lower-class speakers also used *the* with games (*at the football, to the bingo*), expressions of quantity (*the half, the maist, the one*), directions (*back the way, up the stairs*) and generic expressions (*the holidays, that's the tractors for you, the folk, the buttermilk*; this last corresponds to (3) in my list). All we can conclude about the history of these uses of the definite article is that some – those with time expressions and institutions – remain extremely common in Scots, and others, notably the use with years, are now fossilised, while many others, possibly more than have been listed here, remain in lower-class speech. The range of uses of the definite article surviving, at least in lower-class Scots speech, would suggest that this part of speech may have a different function in Scots from in Standard English: this is an area of syntax in which further research, of both a synchronic and a diachronic nature, needs to be carried out.

9.4.1.3 Use of Possessive Pronouns

The use of possessive pronouns in Scots is linked to that of the definite article. In some of the examples cited in the previous section, Standard English would use a possessive pronoun where Scots has *the*, notably *the hat, the wife*. There are also instances in Scots of a possessive pronoun being used where Standard English would have neither pronoun nor article: examples provided by Aitken (1979: 106) as further instances of 'covert Scotticisms' are *I'm away to my bed, What would you like for your Christmas?* (In both these cases, Scots can also use *the*, but with a different meaning.) Like those of the definite article, this use of the possessive was noted as a Scotticism by Beattie (1787: 57) and Mitchell (1799: 56), who record that *I am going to my bed, my dinner* would be better as simply *to bed, to dinner*. Perhaps the fact that they criticise this usage mildly, only stating that the English form would be 'better', accounts for the survival of this idiom even in middle-class Scots. This function of the possessive pronoun is not mentioned by Murray (1873), Grant and Main Dixon (1921) or Dieth (1932), perhaps suggesting that they failed to recognise it as a Scotticism, for it must have existed then as it does today. Macaulay (1991: 71) observes how 'possessive pronouns are sometimes used by lower-class speakers in place of another determiner (including zero)' and gives the examples: *we were in for wer lunch*; *for that pool you could buy your pint of beer your stout or a strong ale or that*; *to get her wee blether*; *by the time you got up and got your breakfast*; *that spent her couple of oors up there*; *you had your singsong*; *they finally gave us oor notice*; and a similar range is noted by Miller (1993: 129). The fact that Macaulay found this use of the possessive only in lower-class speech would appear to contradict Aitken's assertion that it is a 'covert Scotticism' characteristic of middle-class Scots, but what has probably happened is that, as with the uses of *the* discussed above, the possessive is used in a narrower range of contexts by the middle-class group. Certainly *I'm away to my bed* is a phrase that I have heard often from middle-class Scots residing on Tyneside: perhaps this usage has become fossilised as an idiom in middle-class speakers, whereas in lower-class 'vernacular' Scots the possessive, like the definite article, has a more productive role in the grammar.

9.4.1.4 Measure Phrases

In section 9.3.1 we highlighted the tendency in Scots for nouns of measure or quantity not to realise a plural inflection after a numeral, such as *three year old, five mile long*. In phrases with certain nouns of measure, *of* would be used in Standard English, but not in Scots. Miller (1993: 109) gives the examples *a bit paper, a bit steel, a drop water* and points out that 'these constructions are typically Germanic and correspond to the standard German *zwei Meter lang* ("two metres long"), *ein Stück Papier* ("a piece of paper")'. This usage was noted as a Scotticism by Beattie (1787: 73) and Mitchell (1799: 68). Beattie points out that *A piece cheese, bread etc.* should be *A piece of, or a bit of, cheese, bread etc.* Tulloch (1980: 285) notes how *of* is omitted after nouns such as *bit*, *hantle* ('a considerable quantity'), *pickle* ('a small quantity') and *wheen* ('a small number') in Scott's works, as in: *their bit cauld meat* (*St Ronan's Well*, p. 16); *a hantle bogles* (*Guy Mannering*, p. 7); *a pickle ait-meal* (*The Antiquary*, p. 270); *the wee pickle sense he had* (*Old Mortality*, p. 92); *a wheen duddie bairns* (*Heart of Midlothian*, p. 449). Tulloch does not tell us whether the omission of *of* after these nouns was categorical in Scott's usage, but in the popular literature from the second half of the nineteenth century collected by Donaldson (1986, 1989), there is evidence of variability. The following extract is taken from the Dundee *People's Journal* for 5 June 1858, and written by William D. Latto, who, according to Donaldson (1986: 39, 44), was 'the greatest exponent of epistolary vernacular prose in Victorian Scotland'. The italicised phrases show that there was, even in what is acknowledged to be an authentic representation of the vernacular, variation with regard to the omission of *of*:

> 'I think I could save ye a gude *hantle o' trouble* as weel as travel, Mrs McBean', said my father, wi' a consideration for her auld Heilan' shanks that I couldna approve o'; 'I've a *bit callant* o' my ain to spare, joost a wee thocht ootheady an' rebellious in his natur' – Gude be thankit for the aflictions as well as for the manifold mercies that he sends us – but gin ye haud the stap gaen on'm wi' reasonable vigour, I've nae doot but he'll grow main complowsible under the visitation. Wadna this *bit callant* suit your purpose, d'ye think?

The variation is not lexically determined, for elsewhere in the same passage *bit* is used with *of* in *bit o' meat* on two occasions. More likely, with *callant* the word *bit* is acting adjectivally, in the meaning 'little', so that *of* would not be needed anyway. If this passage is as authentic as Donaldson suggests it is, and certainly there are many other features of Scots syntax and morphology to be found in it, such as the *-it* ending on *thankit*, the use of *that*, as a relative, and the cliticised negative on *wadna*, then it would appear that this omission of *of* after nouns of measure was no longer categorical in the Scots of the late nineteenth century, if indeed it ever was. This usage is also recorded by Grant and Main Dixon, who state that *of* or *o* is omitted after nouns of quantity like *wheen*, *piece*, *bit*, *drap* and so on, but is not mentioned by either Macafee (1983) or Macaulay (1991). This is not to deny that Miller's statement, quoted above, is correct, for he does cite actual instances of usage omitting *of*, but simply to question whether this particular 'Scotticism' is, or has ever been, categorical even in lower-class usage.

9.4.1.5   Order of Direct and Indirect Object

Another syntactic Scotticism noted by Beattie, Mitchell and Sinclair in the eighteenth century is the placing of the indirect object pronoun before the direct object, as in *give me it*. Beattie simply points out that this should be *give it me* (1787: 54), but Mitchell (1799: 54) goes on to explain 'the former is Scotch, the latter English. The French and English constructions of these phrases is the same. The French say "Donnez le moi, montrez le moi."' Murray (1873: 191) too comments: 'After the verbs *give*, *tell*, *send*, *bring*, *sell* etc. in such sentences as *Give them to me*, *He told it to them*, the order of the pronouns is reversed in Scotch, that expressing the Dative relation being put first, without a preposition thus *gie mey them*, *he toeld them't*'. Grant and Main Dixon, on the other hand, state the opposite: 'Note that the order of pronominal objects, direct and indirect, when used consecutively, often differs in Sc. from St., the direct object coming first. *I'll show it ye some of thir days if ye're good*' (R. L. Stevenson, *Weir of Hermiston*, chapter 5) (1921: 98).

Now, it may be that Stevenson's representation of Scots is less than authentic, but this does not alter the fact that the serial ordering which Grant and Main Dixon perceive as Standard, Murray and the eighteenth-century authors consider a Scotticism. More recent works such as Miller (1993), Macaulay (1991) and Macafee (1983) make no mention of either word order as a Scots feature, but there is some indication as to what might have been happening to the serialisation of indirect and direct objects in the course of the Modern Scots period in Cheshire et al. (1993: 74). They point out that, in English, '*give me it* is a more recent construction than *give it me*, which in turn is a more recent construction than *give it to me*, where the prepositional group *to me* reflects the function of the Old English dative case'. They report that Hughes and Trudgill (1987) give the order *give me it* as that most usually cited in descriptions of present-day standard English, but they also state that the reverse order is common among educated speakers in the north of England and is acceptable to many southern English speakers as well. This would suggest that not only does variability exist on a wide scale throughout England today, but that the order condemned as a Scotticism by Beattie, Mitchell and Sinclair in the eighteenth century, *give me it*, is gradually taking over from *give it me* and the even older *give it to me*. No dates are given here for the introduction of the newer word order in England, but it would appear that Beattie and his fellows objected to *give me it* because it was an innovation rather than, or as well as, because it was a Scotticism.

Possibly, Scots was in the vanguard with regard to the use of this serial order, but English dialects, and especially Standard English, have now caught up, so that the word sequence once viewed as a Scotticism is no longer marked. The complete turnaround between Murray (1873) and Grant and Main Dixon (1921) would suggest that, in the course of the intervening half-century, *give me it* had at least been introduced as an alternative to *give it me* in Standard English. Since Grant and Main Dixon's comment and evidence on this point are not extensive, they could simply be assuming that anything different from the current Standard English norm was a Scotticism.

Murray's examples of the indirect and direct order do, however, point to another feature of this phrase structure which perhaps has a better claim to the title of Scotticism: the cliticisation of one of the pronouns in *he told them't*. This cliticisation certainly persists in present-day urban Scots, but the indirect object pronoun is the one cliticised, as in [giːz ɪt] *gie's it* for *give me it*.

9.4.2 The Verb Phrase

9.4.2.1 Modal Verbs

Miller (1993: 116) states that the area of modal verbs is 'one . . . in which Scottish English is massively different from standard English'. Some of these differences were noticed by eighteenth-century writers such as Hume, Beattie, Mitchell and Sinclair, who all gave prominence to the area of modal verbs in their lists of Scotticisms. Sinclair (1782: 72) notes that 'there is nothing that the inhabitants of Scotland are so apt to err in, as in the use they make of *shall* and *will*, *should* and *would*, *these* and *those*'. The use of the demonstrative has already been discussed, but the issue of when to use *shall* rather than *will*, or *should* rather than *would* was an equally vexed one for educated Scots in the eighteenth century. Hume's (1760) list of Scotticisms begins not with an indication of where the Scots go wrong, but simply with a statement of the 'correct' English rules for the use of these two pairs of modals. However, Sinclair, Beattie and Mitchell are more explicit in their condemnation of Scots practice, particularly the use in Scots of *will* where standard English would have *shall*. Sinclair, Beattie and Mitchell all give as examples of Scotticism *I will be drowned* for *I shall be drowned*, but only Sinclair (1782: 73–4) elaborates on this by relating what was to become a common joke at the expense of both the Scots and the Irish in eighteenth- and nineteenth-century grammars of English:

> As an instance of the different manner in which the Scots and English use *shall* and *will* in the first person singular, a story is told of a Scotchman, who having fallen into a river in England, had almost perished in it, in consequence of his calling out, *I will* for *I shall be drowned*, the spectators having for some time hesitated, whether they should venture their own lives for the safety of one, who, as they were led to imagine, was determined to make away with himself.

Beattie (1787: 111) notes on this point that 'the Scots are more apt to misapply *will* than *shall*, especially in the first person singular and plural', while Sinclair (1782: 76) sees a parallel between these two verbs and *would* and *should*: 'it is also in the first persons singular and plural that the Scots are most apt to err in the use they make of *should* and *would*'. What Beattie and Sinclair are probably referring to here is the absence of *shall* and *should* from Scots, as it is only in the first person that *shall/should* are 'unmarked', according to the traditional 'rules' for these verbs, first laid out by John Wallis in his *Grammatica Linguae Anglicanae* of 1653. By all accounts, the efforts of Hume, Sinclair, Beattie, Mitchell and many other grammarians of the eighteenth and nineteenth centuries[10] were in vain, for, according to Aitken (1979: 105), 'Scottish eschewing of . . . *shall* . . . *will* or '*ll* replacing the *shall* of other English' is one of a number of Scots features that persist at least in the spoken usage of middle-class Scots today. That the crucial feature here is the 'eschewing of *shall*' is confirmed by Murray, who states of the Southern dialects that *shall* 'is almost out of use', and by Dieth, who tells us that in the north-eastern dialect of Buchan too, '[ʃɑl] is obsolete' (1932: 175). Although both Aitken and Miller (1993: 116) note the avoidance of *shall* as a Scots feature, the fact is that it is no longer distinctively Scots, because other dialects of English, including informal Standard English, have 'caught up' with Scots in this respect. The SND entry for WILL is enlightening on this issue:

> The distinctions between the Sc. and Eng. uses of *shall* and *will*, so frequently noted by 18th and 19thc. writers have become less marked owing to the fact that the prescriptive rules in St Eng. are becoming less and less adhered to, esp. in colloq. speech. The usages of *shall* and *will* which were established in Mid. Eng. in the 14th and 15thc. became blurred in Sc. and dial. Eng. early on, with *will* gradually encroaching on the province of *shall*, and Modern St. Eng. is now following this development, already well established in Irish, and U.S.A, as well as Sc.

The only construction in which *shall* (or *should*) rather than *will* remains categorical in Standard English is the first-person question, for example *Shall I put the kettle on?* However, the use of *will* even in this context was noted as a Scotticism in the eighteenth century, Sinclair (1782: 74) observing that *Will I do this or that?* for *shall I?* is not unusual in Scotland. Beattie (1787: 107) gives the example *Will I help you to a bit of beef?* and corrects it to *shall I help you?*, noting that '*Will I help?* means, 'Am I willing to help?' Mitchell comments that 'no colloquial idiom in Scotland is more common than *Will I?* instead of *Shall I?*' (1799: 95). Murray (1873: 220) confirms that, a century later, *will I?* is the norm, when he writes: 'the interrogative form *sal* is quite obsolete, and a Scotchman says *wul aa?*

where an Englishman says *shall I?*, *will* having almost lost in Scotch its sense of volition, and become a mere sign of futurity'.

Murray's last point here is perhaps a moot one with regard to the survival, in Standard English, of *shall* in first-person questions: if in any dialect *will* retains a sense of volition, then its use in first-person questions would be inappropriate, as Beattie suggests, for how can the interlocutor know whether the speaker is willing to do something? In dialects, like those of Scots and, indeed, Northumberland and Tyneside, where *will* has lost its sense of volition, there is no bar to its use in first-person questions. As far as the use of *will* for Standard English *shall* (and, to a certain extent, *would* for *should*) is concerned, then, there has been little change in Scots use over the last 300 years. If the Scots use of *will* seems less marked today, it is because, except in the case of first-person questions, Standard English has finally caught up with Scots.

Both Aitken and Miller also draw attention to the avoidance of *may* in present-day Scots, its place in the sense of permission being taken by *can* and *get to*, as in Miller's (1993: 117) examples: *you can have this afternoon off; the pupils get to come inside in rainy weather*. This goes unnoticed as a Scotticism by those eighteenth-century authors who had so much to say on the matter of *will* and *shall*, nor is there any comment on the use of *can* for permission by either Murray (1873) or Grant and Main Dixon (1921). It is possible, of course, that this use of *can* is relatively recent in Scots, but it could also be the case that it had not been noticed to the same extent as *will*. In any case, the use of *can* for permission is no longer a Scotticism: *may* is increasingly confined to more formal usage in standard English and has long been 'eschewed' by most non-standard dialects of English.[11] The entry for *may* in Collins' *Softback English Dictionary* (1992) is helpful on this point:

> In careful written usage, *may* is used rather than *can* when reference is made to permission rather than capability. *He may do it* is, for this reason, more appropriate than *he can do it* when the desired sense is *he is allowed to do it*. In spoken English, however, *can* is often used where the correct use of *may* results in forms that are considered to be awkward. *Can't I?* is preferred on this ground to *mayn't I?* in speech.

This is a conservative appraisal of the use of *can* and *may* in Standard English: I would say that *may*, in speech, sounds affected today. However, it does show that, if ever the use of *can* for permission was a Scotticism, Standard English here, as in the case of *will*, is catching up.

The one place where *may* is used in Scots more than in Standard English is as part of the word *maybe*, in which, of course, it no longer acts as a modal verb, but has become lexicalised as an adverb. Although *maybe* is perfectly acceptable in Standard English, it does not occur so frequently there as in Scots. The fact that *maybe* has long been acceptable to Standard English speakers perhaps explains why it is not mentioned as a Scotticism in the eighteenth century. The first authors to note this use of *maybe* are Grant and Main Dixon (1921: 142), who simply record that it is used for *perhaps*, while Dieth (1932: 175) observes under *may* that 'the present is commonly used in ['mebɪ] "perhaps". That it is the relative frequency of *maybe* in Scots that distinguishes its use from that of Standard English is confirmed by Macaulay (1991: 134 n. 2). He found that 'one curious feature of the evidential adverbs' was 'the preference for *maybe* over *perhaps* . . . the reverse of the situation in most written English'. He goes on to report that he looked up instances of *maybe* and *perhaps* in concordances of several British and American authors; these all showed an overwhelming preponderance of *perhaps*, with three exceptions: Burns, Langston Hughes and Yeats. Burns had four instances of *maybe* and none of *perhaps*, suggesting that a preference for *maybe* in Scots was established by the eighteenth century. Because the difference between Scots and Standard English is one of frequency, the Scots use of *maybe* has never been stigmatised, and so it remains as perhaps the least obtrusive of all Scotticisms.

Miller (1993: 120) makes the interesting observation that, in Scots, *might* appears to be 'developing into an adverb, syntactically equivalent to *maybe*'. This is because, in Scots, or at least in what Miller calls 'Broad Scots', each member of the following pairs of sentences would have the same meaning:

(1) They might could be working in the shop.
(2) They maybe could be working in the shop.
(1a) She might can get away early.
(2a) She maybe can get away early.

The only difference between the (1) and (2) sentences is that the former would be more overtly Scottish, because, if *might* is perceived as a modal verb, as it is by Standard English speakers and indeed speakers of most English dialects, then the (1) instances contain two modal verbs. Such 'double modal' constructions occur with other combinations of verbs in Scots as well, so here the grammaticality of sentences like those marked (1) above is not dependent on *might* becoming an adverb. It is more likely that *might* is becoming perceived as an adverb because of its syntactic equivalence with *maybe* in Scots.

Other examples of 'double modal' constructions given by Miller (1993: 119–20) are:

(3) He'll can help us the morn.
(4) You might would like to come with us.
(5) You might should claim your expenses.

Miller points out that sentences like (1), (1a) and (3) – that is, those with *can* or *could* as the second modal – are more common in Scots than those like (4) and (5) with other combinations. 'Double modal' constructions have been ungrammatical in Standard English since the Early Modern period, because of radical changes in the English auxiliary verb system which effectively outlawed any non-finite forms of modal verbs.[12] Since modals are followed by infinitives, the second modal in a 'double modal' is an infinitive, and so such constructions are ungrammatical in Standard English. Strangely enough, there is no mention of the 'double modal' construction in eighteenth-century lists of Scotticisms, although it must by that time have appeared outlandish to Standard English speakers. Visser (1973: 2,404) notes of these constructions that they, 'having been in frequent occurrence in Middle English, became obsolete by the beginning of the Modern Period, except in Scottish dialects where clusters with *can* in central position survived'. This implies that there has been a continuous presence of these constructions in Scots, yet while the latest English example given by Visser is from Caxton in 1489, the earliest Scots example is from Scott in 1816. It is highly unlikely that a feature which died out of Standard English by the sixteenth century should suddenly appear in Scots more than 200 years later, yet SND also gives no citations of 'double modals' from earlier than the nineteenth century, while CSD gives the construction *nae doot ye'll can* as occurring from the late eighteenth century.

That there appears to be no evidence of 'double modal' constructions from earlier than this may simply be an accident: they must certainly have been well established in spoken Scots by the beginning of the nineteenth century for Scott to employ them. According to Miller, sequences other than *will can* appear to be even more recent in origin 'but the general construction, far from being the whim of urban dwellers, dates from at least the last century and is widespread in the southern United States and in northern England'. He goes on to suggest that, if the appearance of this construction was taken to the southern USA by 'Scotch-Irish immigrants', then it must be much older. The history of these constructions is obviously an area in which much useful research could be done.

That there is more and earlier evidence for 'double modals' with *can* or *could* as the second 'modal' than with any other of these verbs is perhaps due to the uncertain status of these verbs as modals in Scots. Even in Standard English, they fail one of the defining tests of modals, for, unlike *shall* and *should*, *can* and *could* sometimes act as present and past tense respectively, thus:

Today I can swim twenty lengths.
Yesterday, I could only swim ten lengths.
Tomorrow, I shall swim twenty lengths.
* Yesterday, I should swim twenty lengths.

In Scots, *can* appears not only as the second verb in 'double modals', but also in other non-finite forms. Murray (1873: 216) gives examples of *could* used as a past participle in *thay haena cuid geat eane* 'They had not been able to get one', and *cannin'* as a present participle in *wi' hym no cannin' fynd them* as well as 'double modal' constructions such as *ye'll can cum neist weik*. Trotter (1901: 26) justifies the use of these constructions, which, according to him, occur in 'Scotch' rather than 'Glasgow-Irish', in terms implying that *can* has a different status in Scots and English: 'There are many minor differences [between "Scotch" and English"], such as . . . the peculiar use of the auxiliary verb *To can*, which is unknown in English – as *He'll no can do that*, instead of *He wil not be able to do that*, *He micht 'a' could dune that yince*, for *He may have been able to do that at one time*. That Trotter sees this as only a 'minor difference' seems strange, but Aitken (1979: 105) confirms that sentences like *They'll can see to it* or *I'd could have done it* persist in middle-class Scots usage, at least in speech. Although Trotter here treats *can* as a verb with non-finite forms, he does not mention any of these except the infinitive and past participle. The present participle form *cannin'*, cited from Murray, above, seems not to be mentioned in any twentieth-century source except SND, which gives both this as *cannan'* and a gerund *cannin'*. The citation for the gerund *cannin'* is: '*Wi him no cannin' wun hyim wi' the railway strike* (Rxb 1923)'.

The existence of 'double modal' constructions and non-finite forms of the verb *can*, at least from the late eighteenth century, suggests that the modal system of Scots is different from that of Standard English. Were it not for the continued existence of constructions with other combinations of modals, as shown by Miller (1993), then we could explain this by suggesting that *can* (and therefore *could* as its preterite and past participle) is not really a modal in Scots, and *might* is becoming an adverb. These constructions do not always appear in interviews or corpora: Macaulay (1991), for instance, makes no mention of them, but they are still attested as occurring in Scots, and sequences like *He'll can do that* are found even in educated middle-class usage. Their relative infrequency, rather than non-occurrence, might account for the lack of evidence for these constructions pre-1800. Another construction involving modal verbs which is recognised as distinctively Scottish, but is not mentioned in eighteenth-century lists of Scotticisms, is the omission of *have* between a modal and past participle. Tulloch (1980: 298) notes examples of this construction in Scott and Burns: *The tythe o' what ye waste at cartes/Wad stow'd his pantry* (*To William Simpson, Ochiltree*, ll. 19–20), where *wad* equals English *would* with the typical Scots omission after it of *hae* 'have'. Tulloch (1980: 299) goes on to give the following examples from Scott: *I hae kend the day when less wad ser'd him, the oe of a Campvere skipper* (*Heart of Midlothian*, p. 270); *I wad likeit weel just to hae come in at the clipping-time* (*The Antiquary*, p. 286).

Robinson (1973: 43) points out another example in Burns' *The Twa Dogs* (ll. 20–2): *But he wad stan't, as glad to see him,/An' stroan't on stanes an' hillocks wi' him*. She goes on to state that 'Scots omits the auxiliary *have* after a modal. This usage survives most frequently when the verb is made negative with *-na*, as *I wadna dune it*.' Since this omission of *have* is not mentioned by Miller (1993) or Macaulay (1991), perhaps it is no longer as current as it was in the time of Burns and Scott. Robinson's statement that the omission is more frequent after a cliticised negative is similar to that made by Grant and Main Dixon (1921: 120): '*Have* (*hae, 'a*) is constantly dropped after the auxiliaries *would, should*, etc. especially when followed by *-na*'. What strikes me here is that the 'omission' after *-na* may have survived longer and/or may be found more frequently in modern Scots, because it can be analysed as having the *hae* in its unstressed form *'a*, assimilated into the *-na* rather than omitted.

9.2.2   Negation

In Standard English, negation takes the form of a clitic *-n't* attached to an auxiliary, as in *he won't come, he didn't come* or, in emphatic use, *not* after an auxiliary, as in *he will not come, he did not come*. In earlier English, *not* was formerly used after verbs other than auxiliaries, for example *but saw not Betty* (Pepys, *Diary* VIII 514.2 (1 Nov.), quoted in Denison 1993: 450), but, except with a small number of verbs such as *know, doubt, see, say, mistake, matter* and so on, this had died out by the beginning of the eighteenth century. The introduction and regulation of *do* as an operator in English negatives has, like the modal verbs, been a subject of a great deal of research and debate (Denison 1993: 448–71). In Scots, too, *dae* has been introduced as an operator, and carries the Scots negative clitic *na*. This negative clitic, like English *-n't*, is attached mainly to modal and auxiliary verbs today, but cliticised negatives of other verbs seem to survive longer in Scots than the 'main verb + *not*' construction in English. This development of *dae* as the operator in Scots is probably, like the introduction of *wh-* forms of relative pronouns, not so much due to influence from English as such, but to a parallel development in two closely related languages. Aitken (1979: 88) states that 'in part this internal history proceeded on lines common to all varieties of English, including *he cums nocht* becoming *he's no cumin, he cam nocht* becoming *he didna cum*'.

The use of *no* in negation as opposed to English *not* is included in eighteenth-century lists of Scotticisms. Sinclair (1782: 136) notes that '*no* is sometimes used for *not*', Beattie (1787: 59) gives the example *This is no a good day*, corrected to *Not a good day*, and Mitchell (1799: 60) tells us that '*no* instead of *not* is, in familiar discourse, very commonly used by all ranks of people in Scotland' and gives, as well as the example cited by Beattie, *I have walked forty miles, and yet am no wearied*. Tulloch (1980: 295) notes that *no*, rather than the clitic *-na*, is used in Scott as a more emphatic negator and gives the examples: *This is no it* (*Heart of Midlothian*, p. 178); *It's no a Scots tune, but it passes for ane* (*Redgauntlet*, p. 139). Murray (1873: 216), likewise, points out that this construction is the 'negative emphatic – a strong negation, or re-denial, of a statement asserted, formed in auxiliaries by the full form with the adverb *no* or *not*'. It is worth noting that, while Mitchell in 1799 saw *no* as 'very commonly used by all ranks of people, in Scotland', Murray suggests that it varies with *not*. In present-day Scots, *no* is no longer used by 'all ranks of people', for Macaulay finds the variation between *no* and *not*, and, for that matter, between cliticised negatives like *he willna* and cliticised subject + *not*, as in *he'll not*, to be socially stratified. He found that middle-class speakers used the *he'll not* pattern, and avoided cliticised negatives even where cliticisation of the subject is not possible, as in *Largs is not so far away* (1991: 51). Lower-class speakers, on the other hand, tended to use the cliticised negative pattern as in *he willna* and, in cases where they did cliticise the subject, used *no* rather than *not* as the negative particle. This suggests that both the cliticised negative with *-na* and the Scots emphatic negator *no* are becoming less common in middle-class Scots, but both persist in the 'broader' Scots of the lower classes.

In Scots, as in English, the cliticised negative now tends to be used only with modal and auxiliary verbs. Up until relatively recently, though, other verbs were found with the cliticised negative. Tulloch (1980: 295) lists the following as all occurring in Scott: *kenna*, *carena*, *doubtna*, *it maksna*, while Murray (1873: 216) notes that 'in some verbs, the custom is retained of adding *-na* as in auxiliaries, as *aa cayrna*, *hey geadna*'.[13] Grant and Main Dixon (1921: 115) give a list of verbs with *-na* of which only *comesna* and the marginal modal *daurna* (compare English *daren't*) are not modals or auxiliaries, but elsewhere (1921: 133), discussing the order of words in interrogatives, give the nineteenth-century example *Sawna ye nae appearance o' the fishers getting the muckle boats built doon to the water?* (Alexander, *Johnny Gibb* (1884, chapter 6)). It would appear that the *-na* clitic is now, like *-n't* in English, confined to modal and auxiliary verbs, for neither Miller (1993) nor Macaulay (1991) gives any examples with other verbs.

Other features which were noted as Scotticisms in the eighteenth century are, and have long been, also found in all non-standard dialects of English. Multiple negation was a favourite shibboleth of English as well as Scots grammarians. It is not mentioned by Sinclair or Beattie, but Mitchell (1799: 26–7) writes: '*I cannot walk no further, I cannot eat no more* are phrases very common among the lower class of people in Scotland . . . In the English language, two negatives make an affirmative'. It is interesting to note that, unlike *no*, which was used by 'all ranks', multiple negation in Scots, as in English, was confined to lower-class use by the eighteenth century. Tulloch (1980: 295) gives two examples from Scott and comments that 'the double negative is allowable in Scots', but does not comment on the social class of the characters concerned. It is certainly the case today that multiple negation is, as Aitken (1979: 69) puts it, 'one of the shibboleths of Central Scots urban working-class speech'. Yet Trotter (1901: 26), who is so scathing about the 'Glasgow-Irish', seeks to justify this as grammatical in 'Scotch': 'In English, a double negative amounts to an affirmative; but in Scotch a double or even a triple negative is simply an intensification of a single one, as *Had he nae hair on his heed? He hadna nae hair on his heed*.'

While this is a fair analysis of the function of multiple negation, it is almost certain that this construction was stigmatised among Scottish speakers by the beginning of the twentieth century. Macaulay (1991: 54–5) finds that examples of multiple negation are confined to lower-class speakers in his sample, and even there they are rare. He goes on to state that 'the low frequency of multiple negative concord suggests that it is not the preferred form for lower-class speakers, and it does not appear to be used for special emphasis or rhetorical effect'. On the other hand, Macafee (1983: 47) notes that, in

Glasgow, 'multiple negation, where the negative particle is semantically reinforced by the negative determiner and its compounds, is common'. However, Macafee's account is not based on a corpus as Macaulay's is, and so it is hard to tell just how 'common' multiple negation is in Glasgow. I would suggest that here, as elsewhere in Britain, it is probably stigmatised and so largely confined to lower-class usage.

Mitchell (1799: 58) also notes, not as a Scotticism but as a usage common 'in the north of Ireland', the use of *never* instead of *not*. Whether this, like *yous* (see above, pp. 344–6), was actually imported from Northern Ireland is impossible to say without further research, but the use of *never* as a non-emphatic negator is certainly common in Scots today. Miller (1993: 115) notes that 'in Broad Scots the normal negative with past tense verbs is *never*' and that 'this use of *never* is found in the speech of many educated people . . . it has not made its way into formal writing, although it occurs in essays by some secondary school pupils'. The example that he gives, *I sat down to that . . . essay at 7 o' clock. I never got it started till nine*, was, he says, 'uttered by a university undergraduate'. Miller goes on to suggest that *never* is taking over from *not* with past-tense verbs in Scots, so that 'on no occasion' has to be expressed as *never ever*. Macaulay (1991: 55–6), too, finds that *never* is more frequent in lower-class interviews and suggests that it therefore has 'a wider meaning than in the middle-class interviews' and that in most cases 'the substitution of a simple negative would change the meaning little, if at all'. Although *never* as a negator of the past tense is common at least in lower-class Scots, it is not a distinctively Scottish feature, for, as Cheshire et al. report (1993: 67), it is widespread in all dialects of English. However, the sentence type which 85 per cent of the schools taking part in their survey reported to have heard was *No, I never broke that*, in which *never* is clearly emphatic. Unfortunately, they did not include a sentence like that reported by Miller above, so it is difficult to tell whether the more neutral use of *never* as equivalent to *not* is more prevalent in Scots than in English dialects. More research is needed on this area, which seems to involve a change in progress, but I have the impression that this use of *never* is also taking over from *not* in many English dialects.

9.2.3   Use of the Progressive

We have already discussed the form of the present participle in Scots, and the fact that it is no longer differentiated from the gerund, except perhaps in writing in literary Scots. Nevertheless, the present participle in Scots is still distinctive from that of English in terms of its range of use in the progressive. This phenomenon was noted by Mitchell (1799: 79), who writes that '*I'm thinking* instead of *I suppose*, *I conjecture*, is very common in Scotland. *He is not at home, I'm thinking.*' Tulloch confirms that this usage was common in Scott's time, particularly with the verbs *think* and *doubt*. The examples which he cites are as follows: *sae me and my mither yielded oursells prisoners. I'm thinking we wad hae been letten slip awa, but Kettledrummle was taen near us* (*Old Mortality*, p. 201); *an unco cockernony she had busked on her head at the kirk last Sunday, I am doubting that there will be news o' a' these braws* (*Old Mortality*, p. 61) (1980: 296). Tulloch goes on to explain that *I'm thinking* corresponds to Standard English *I imagine* and *I'm doubting* to *I'm afraid*. These are the verbs which most frequently occur in the progressive where this form would not be used in Standard English, but it is also to be found with other verbs. Examples from Scott where the simple present or past would be used in Standard English are: *Sae, I'll een pit on my boots the morn, and be jogging ower Drymen-Muir wi' Mr Frank here* (*Rob Roy*, p. 367); *And ae day at the spaw well . . . she was seeing a very bonny family of bairns . . . and she broke out:*

'Is it not an odd-like thing that ilka waf carle in the country has a son and heir, and that the house of Ellangowan is without succession? (*Guy Mannering*, pp. 390–1); *ye wad rather hear ae twalpenny clink against another, than have a spring from Rory Dall, if he was coming alive again* (*Redgauntlet*, p. 144).

Grant and Main Dixon (1921: 114) also note that the progressive form 'is used colloquially in making deliberate statements, where the standard usage employs the simple verb'. However, the only examples given are with *think* and *doubt*. Trotter (1901: 26), on the other hand, notes 'the habitual use of the progressive voice of the verb in Scotch' and gives as examples *As A wus gaun* for English *As I went*, *A'm thinkin* for *I think*, and *Whaur'll ye be bidin?* for *Where do you live?* That this use of the progressive is still common today, if not more common, is confirmed by Miller (1993: 121–2) who notes that, whereas in Standard English 'stative' verbs such as *like* and *know* never occur, and others, such as *see* and *hear*, rarely occur in the progressive, these restrictions do not apply in Scots. Moreover, he cites instances of the progressive where Standard English requires the simple form, taken from undergraduate essays: *Thus the nominal construction is denoting a process; although 'coffee' and 'black' are occurring together as a unit, it is not grammatical; It seems that Extraposition is conforming to two conditions.* Miller goes on to report that 'various native speakers, Scots and Non-Scots, have expressed unhappiness with the above examples'. The existence of these progressives in educated written usage, presumably of young people, would suggest that the progressive is gaining ground in Scots and increasingly occurs with a larger number of verbs than in Standard English. That this is likely to be an innovation of the modern period is suggested by Strang's (1982: 429) observation that the progressive is not grammaticised in Standard English until the eighteenth century.

9.4.3 *For to* + Infinitive

In Standard English, *for to* introducing an infinitive is, according to the OED, archaic or vulgar in the sense 'in order to' and obsolete as a neutral introduction to the infinitive (last citation 1674). In Scots, however, this usage persists. It is noted as a Scotticism by Sinclair (1782: 66), who cites *I love for to do good.* However, his censure of this form is tempered by his acknowledgement that '*For to*, at the same time, is in the English version of the Bible'. Grant and Main Dixon (1921: 156) make the same point: 'An intrusive *fur* or *for* is common before infinitives, as in archaic English', and cite the Biblical *What went ye out for to see?* (Matthew 3: 13, *Authorised Version*) as well as the Scots *Ay, an he begood fur to greet* (J. J. Bell, *Wee MacGregor*, chapter 12). Macaulay (1991: 106) suggests that this use of *for to* may be dying out in Scots: it is used only in lower-class speech in his sample and, while the two oldest speakers in this class use it most frequently, the two youngest do not use it at all. As Macaulay states, this 'suggests that this construction may be about to disappear from Ayr speech'.

9.4.4 Prepositions and Conjunctions

Among the features noted as Scotticisms in the eighteenth century, there are several cases involving different prepositions or conjunctions. Both Sinclair (1782: 54) and Beattie (1787: 8) state that *more as that* should be *more than that* and *I would rather go as stay* should be *rather go than stay*. According to the OED, this use of *as* is now obsolete in English except in dialects, the last English citation being from 1568. Tulloch (1980: 286) notes this usage in

Scott: *she doesna value a Cawmil mair as a Cowan* (*Rob Roy*, p. 406), and goes on to state that 'the present-day meaning of *as* here will not fit the context'. This usage has perhaps become obsolete now in Scots as in Standard English, since there is no mention of it in Grant and Main Dixon (1921) or in more recent works such as Macaulay (1991) and Miller (1993).

Beattie and Sinclair both mention the use of *at* rather than *with* as a Scotticism, when used in phrases like *angry at him*. Beattie points out that 'one is angry *at a thing* but *with a person*' but hints that this usage may not be exclusively Scottish by adding 'but this is not uniformly attended to, even by the best writers'. Sinclair, likewise, concedes that *at* was formerly used in this way by respected English writers: '*angry at* may be found in *Spectator* No 197 *in fine*, but it is at present confined to Scotland'. This is not mentioned in later works, and indeed was probably never a Scotticism: the OED does not mark this use obsolete or archaic, although the last quote is from Richardson (1742). It is possible that there has long been variation between *at* and *with* in this context, and that Beattie and Sinclair were simply noting a trend in the direction of *with*. Beattie (1787: 9) and Sinclair (1782: 28) also note that *I asked at him* should be *I asked him*, *I asked of him*. In this case, they were more accurate in their diagnosis, for the OED records this use of *at* as obsolete or dialectal. On the other hand, the OED has quotes from English writers up to 1883 for this usage, so the obsolescence must be recent in both English and Scots.

Another prepositional use which was probably not a true Scotticism is the use of *among* in *I stuck among the snow*, *among the clay*. Beattie writes that this should be *in the snow*, *in the clay* and explains that '*among* in English has reference to that which may be numbered'. Mitchell (1799: 17) reproduces this more or less word for word. There is no mention of this use of *among* in the OED, and I would guess that, rather than being a Scotticism, this was once more merely a solecism which offended against Beattie's sense of 'correctness'.

Both Beattie (1787: 54) and Mitchell (1799: 53) mention the Scots use of *married on* for English *married to*. The OED does not mention *marry on* but does give *marry upon* as Scots, citing Drummond of Hawthornden (1639). That Beattie and Mitchell were correct in identifying this usage as a Scotticism is confirmed by Miller (1993: 132), who cites *married on someone* as still occurring in Scots. Beattie, but not Sinclair or Mitchell, notes that *I will wait of you* is 'Scots and vulgar English' and should be *wait on* or *upon you* (1787: 64). The OED confirms that this use of *wait of* is dialectal, but does not give *wait on* in this sense at all. According to Miller, *wait on* is now the Scots usage for Standard English *wait for*. In Standard English, *wait on* is, of course, used only to mean 'serve'.

Yet another conjunction proscribed by Beattie is *without* in the sentence *I will not go without I am paid for it* (1787: 101). Tulloch notes this, and gives the following quote from Scott to confirm that this was indeed a Scotticism: *thae corbies dinna gather without they smell carrion* (*Rob Roy*, p. 255). Grant and Main Dixon (1921: 167) have a section on Scottish forms and uses of *without*, but in their case it is noted only as a preposition. Their examples seem to me not to differ from Standard English (at least, in the use of *without*): *Some fowk cudna ca' the niz o' their face their nain withoot speirin' leave* (Alexander, *Johnny Gibb*, chapter 45); *Wi-oot ony thing to weet them, their dooms dry* (G. Macdonald, *Alec Forbes*, chapter 26). The OED states that the use of *without* as a conjunction was 'formerly common in literary use . . . later *colloq.*' and cites Dr Johnson (1755) 'not in use, except in conversation'. Beattie's observation that this was 'Scot. and obsolete vulgar English' was probably pretty near the mark for 1787. If *without* survives as a Scotticism, it is not exclusively such, but continues in general non-standard use throughout Britain.

One conjunction mentioned by Beattie is *whenever*. He notes as a Scotticism: *I rose whenever I heard the clock strike eight* in which *whenever* means *when, as soon as*. Beattie (1787: 107) explains that in 'correct' usage '*whenever* is *at whatever time*: as, whenever you awake me, I shall arise'. Apart from Mitchell (1799), this is not mentioned elsewhere as a Scotticism, but Harris (1993: 165) tells us that this usage is 'characteristically northern Irish English', giving the example, recorded from a Belfast speaker: *My husband died whenever I was living in New Lodge Road*. This would appear, like *yous*, to be yet another example of the mutual influence between Scots and northern Irish English. From which direction the usage came is impossible to say without further research.

The prepositions and conjunctions noted as Scotticisms in the eighteenth century were in many cases simply usages that were falling out of favour, but might be found in non-standard or colloquial English anywhere. Some, however, such as *married on*, survive as Scotticisms. There are many other prepositions and conjunctions which are used differently in Scots and Standard English: as Miller (1993: 131) notes, 'the prepositional system of Broad Scots has yet to be studied in detail'. The examples given by Miller, *from, frae, off* and *with* rather than *by* with passive agents, as in *she was attacked with a labrador, ah'm gonna get kilt fae ma maw*, are not mentioned in earlier works, but whether this means that they are innovations, or simply have not been noticed before, is difficult to tell without further research.

9.4.5 Discourse Features

All recent surveys of Scots point out that it is in the organisation of discourse that Scots, and particularly lower-class urban Central Scots, reveals some of its most distinctive features. Because discourse analysis is a relatively new discipline, traditional dialectologists like Murray, Grant and Main Dixon and Dieth paid little attention to it as such, and, since its characterising features are used mainly in informal spoken discourse, there is little evidence of them from literary sources. Whether these features are new to Scots, or whether they have simply been overlooked so far, is impossible to judge at this stage, but I feel that it is appropriate to end this chapter by discussing some of the most interesting features of the present-day vernacular.

Macaulay (1991: 138–76) examines the use of what he calls *discourse markers* in the speech of his interviewees. By discourse markers, he means items such as *oh, well, (you) see, I mean, you know, (you) ken, (of) course, anyway, in fact, now, here* and *mind you*. Although not all of these are peculiar to Scots, Macaulay (1991: 142) found a difference in the overall use of such features between his middle-class and lower-class interviewees to the extent that they were 'more than twice as numerous and frequent' in the speech of the latter. Of these discourse markers, *(you) see* and *(you) ken* were the most salient, so we shall discuss these in more detail.

Both features are mentioned by Aitken (1979: 69) as 'shibboleths of Central Scots urban working-class speech'. *Ken*, of course, is a Scots lexical item of ancient pedigree: it is the use of *(you) ken* as a discourse marker which is characteristic of the urban vernacular, and therefore stigmatised. Miller (1993: 135–6) explains its use in Broad Scots as follows:

> *Ken* can introduce items into a discourse, or a complete new topic of conversation. It never combines with *you* or *ye* in this construction. Examples are . . .
> (a) ken John Ewan – he breeds spaniels
> (b) the estate up at Macmerry – ken there's a big estate there – it's got a gamekeeper

(c) (after a long pause in the conversation) ken this wee lassie comes in with tea towels at ten to seven and I washed them – ken I'm wanting them boiled so they take a wee while you know. The second *ken* in (c) illustrates another use of KEN – to introduce a proposition by way of explanation.

His example (c) also illustrates that the Scots use of *ken* is not the same as the English *you know*, although it can be used as a tag in final position as well, as we see from the following quote from Iain Banks' *The Bridge* (1986: 78), quoted in McClure (1983: 18): *Enyway, like I say, I've dun alright sinse it took up with me an its taut me a load a new wurds an that, so am a bit mair ejucatit these days ken*. McClure goes on to point out that this 'sentence-final *ken* . . . is . . . a passing request for confirmation of the hearer's understanding'.

Macafee (1983: 19) notes the use of *see* in Glasgow speech:

> In Central urban Scotland, the word *see* is used to isolate the theme of a sentence on first mention. The subject noun phrase is extracted from the main clause to stand as the object of *see*, its place being filled by an appropriate personal pronoun. This structure perhaps originates with asyndeton of *(do you see* – Noun Phrase – Recapitulatory pronoun).

She goes on to provide an example which proves beyond doubt that *see* is not being used in a literal sense in this construction: *See the smell aff it when it's jist been laid!* These uses of *ken* and *see* are, as I have already suggested, not mentioned in earlier works on Scots. This could mean that they are of very recent introduction: CSD has, under SEE 3: '*vt, introducing a person or thing about to be discussed, la20c–, "see him, he canny drive"*'. However, if Macafee's suggestion that this is a contraction of *do you see* is correct, then could this usage in Central Scots not have developed from the earlier *seestu*, which, as we have seen (above, p. 346) was a stereotypical Paisley usage up until the nineteenth century? This is perhaps a fanciful conjecture, but one which might be worth taking seriously as a starting point for further research. To discover whether *ken* and *see* might have been used as discourse markers in earlier Scots, I looked up both words in Reid's (1889) concordance of Burns. There were many entries with *see* at the beginning of a line, but, in such as *See him, the poor man's friend in need* (*To Rev. J. McMath*), this could simply be a rhetorical, poetic device, and there were no examples of the construction reported by Macafee of *see* + noun phrase + coreferential preposition. With *ken*, though, the results were more promising. I found the following lines in which *you ken* seems to act as a discourse marker: *In Tarbolton, ye ken, there are proper young men* (*Ronalds of Bennals*); *And lassie, ye're but young, ye ken* (*In simmer when*). These appear similar in function to the sentence-final *ken* noted by McClure above: perhaps both *ken* and *see* have been around as discourse markers for longer than we realise, but have dropped the *you* relatively recently.

It is perhaps appropriate that this chapter should end on a speculative note, since it has become evident at several points that there is a great deal of research still to be done on the history of Scots syntax and morphology in the modern period. What I hope to have demonstrated is that, despite the demise of Older Scots features such as the distinction between the present participle and gerund, and in the face of the proscriptions of eighteenth-century anglicisers like Beattie, Mitchell and Sinclair, much that is distinctively Scots remains. Indeed, if we put aside the notion that Scots should be kept in a kind of cryogenic stasis, we can appreciate that innovations such as plural *youse*, *yin* for older *a body* and the discourse features discussed in the last section testify to the continuing viability and vitality of Scots.

NOTES

1. I say *most* varieties of British English because almost all the 'distinctively Scottish' features of syntax and morphology discussed in this chapter can also be heard in the English counties of Tyne and Wear and Northumberland. See Beal (1993) for a discussion of this.

2. This feature was also mentioned approvingly by Adams (1799: 155), who pointed out that diminutives 'express what we often want in English, and is so abundant, in Italic and Scotch and has sometimes a pretty effect'.

3. In the case of *horse*, the uninflected plural was found even in standard English at this time with the meaning 'cavalry', for example *a regiment of horse*. As Beattie points out, it is only the extension of this to non-military contexts that was viewed as a Scotticism.

4. I have, for instance, heard the catering assistant in the Newcastle University Senior Common Room ask: *How many soup?*

5. By 'the English part of Bernicia', Murray presumably means Northumberland. See Beal (1993: 205).

6. Obviously, more research is needed into the present-day distribution of *yous* and *thou*, but I would strongly suspect that this distribution would turn out to be complementary. In Tyne and Wear, for instance, *yous* is now heard from middle-class adolescents on Tyneside, while *thou* is a residual feature of older speakers on Wearside.

7. The use of the name *The Big Yin* by so stereotypically Glaswegian a figure as Billy Connolly would appear to confirm this.

8. Elsewhere (1799: 46), Mitchell cites Lowth in a footnote to support his view that *had rather* should be *would rather*. This is not a Scotticism, so it would appear that Mitchell did take some non-standard forms from Lowth, whether they were Scottish or not.

9. The definite article is employed in a similar range of circumstances in Tyneside English. I have heard from my daughters the following clapping rhyme:

   > The dog's got the measles,
   > The cat's got the 'flu
   > The chicken's got the chicken pox
   > And so have you.

10. Leonard (1929: 178–9) points out that 'no discussion of the *shall* and *will* matter in the latter part of the eighteenth century or later, could get under way without condemnation of the Scotch and Irish for their misuses'.

11. Many people of my generation retain painful memories of being humiliated by a teacher who, on being asked the question 'Can I go to the toilet, miss?', gave the withering reply 'Well, I'm sure you are capable, my dear!'

12. The syntactic changes concerned have been the subject of much research and debate: see Denison (1993: 229–39) for a summary of the various arguments.

13. It is perhaps worth pointing out that the verbs which retain *-na* longest in Scots are precisely those which continue to occur without *do* as an operator in English.

10

Lexis

Graham Tulloch

10.1 INTRODUCTION

Lexis is a very large subject, indeed a dauntingly large one. The ten-volume *Scottish National Dictionary*, entirely devoted to presenting the vocabulary of Scots since 1700, reminds us how large the topic is. At the same time, it is precisely because we have SND as well as *The Dictionary of the Older Scottish Tongue*, *The Oxford English Dictionary* and the very useful synopsis provided by *The Concise Scots Dictionary* that writing on the vocabulary of Scots since 1700 becomes possible.[1]

We must begin with a question: what qualifies as the vocabulary of Scots? There is an apparently straightforward, though awkwardly expressed answer – that the vocabulary of Scots is the vocabulary used when Scots is used. But the straightforwardness of this disappears on further examination, the main difficulty being that the identity of Scots is by no means clear-cut. As A. J. Aitken (1981c, 1982) has argued, it is very hard, in the period covered by this chapter, to define an identity for Scots which is totally distinct from Scottish English. It could well be claimed that, ever since Scots began to develop a separate identity from English, this identity has been under threat from the tendency to mix Scots and English vocabulary, grammar and spelling or pronunciation. From the start, the two languages have shared a vast body of vocabulary. In speech or writing, it is very natural for writers and speakers to feel that all the resources of *both* languages are available for use alongside this common core. In speech, it must be unusual to find 'pure' forms of either language: are there any speakers of Standard English in Scotland who never use Scottish pronunciations, idioms or vocabulary? And what speaker of Scots is there, however rural, who is totally unaware of the English language of education, the media and bureaucracy and never makes use of it? In writing, there may be more clear-cut cases: works like Lorimer's translation of the New Testament or Milne's *Eppie Elrick* are conscious attempts to write in a language which is, wherever possible, distinctively Scottish; but they are exceptions, and we would certainly not want to limit Scots vocabulary to words appearing in such texts.

Since it is virtually impossible to draw clear boundaries around Scots and English which keep them separate from each other, we are forced for practical reasons for the purposes of this chapter to adopt another definition of Scots vocabulary – as the distinctively Scottish elements of the vocabulary of Scots and English speech and writing in Scotland or, more precisely, the elements in Scots and English in Scotland which are not shared with English Standard English. (This includes some words which are not exclusive to Scotland, such as words shared with northern English dialects.) This is effectively the definition used in SND (Grant 1931: xlv) and CSD (Robinson 1985: xvii). It is both broader and narrower than the first definition suggested above, broader in including elements of Scottish Standard English which may not be used in Scots and narrower in excluding words shared with English unless they have different forms or meanings in Scotland. It also includes words or meanings of words which died out in English but continued to be used in Scotland.

The inclusion of Scottish Standard English vocabulary is not a serious problem. There may be some Scotticisms that are, for sociolinguistic reasons, common in middle-class Scottish Standard English speech but generally not found in working-class broad Scots speech, but it must be unlikely that they are never used in broad Scots and it would, in any case, be very hard to identify them. Similarly, there are certainly some kinds of Scottish vocabulary, such as legal terms and the terms of local and church administration (*provost, region, district*; *General Assembly, kirk session, moderator*) which are more likely when written and spoken to appear in a context of Scottish Standard English, but they are certainly available to both speakers and writers of Scots and would certainly be considered Scots when surrounded by other Scots terms.

This suggests that we should apply one other criterion as well: whether a word is likely to appear in a Scots context. While it is not possible to absolutely separate Scots and English, the mass of evidence assembled in SND allows us on occasions to identify words which seem to be fairly unlikely to turn up in Scots contexts: for instance, *some* of the Gaelic terms included in SND do not seem to have entered either popular spoken Scots or literary Scots. They are used in texts concerned with the Highlands or Highlanders to add authenticity to the setting. Such seems to be the case with the group of words concerned with what is more commonly referred to as second sight. *Taisch* (Gaelic *taibhse*) meaning 'a vision seen by second sight', *taishatar* (Gaelic *taibhsdear*) 'a second-sighted person' and *taishataragh* (Gaelic *taibhsdearach*) 'the faculty of second sight' achieved a reasonable currency in late eighteenth- and earlier nineteenth-century Scottish texts written in English and were used by Scott but do not appear to have been taken into Scots, perhaps because the alternative term *second-sicht* had been established in Scots usage since the sixteenth century. Here we appear to have a fairly clear-cut case of terms that should not be considered as Scots. However, such cases are exceptional.

I will, then, be dealing here with distinctively Scottish words that occur in both Scots and Scottish Standard English contexts, but I will try to avoid any items which, on the basis of whatever evidence is available, seem to be confined to Scottish Standard English.

The exclusion of words or meanings of words that are shared with English (words like *aunt, bide, big, brain, brave, claw, clean, clearance, crack, cranny, crave, deliverance, delve, exercise* and so on) is theoretically a more serious problem but it can be justified, indeed can *only* be justified, on practical grounds. Dictionaries of Scots exclude such words (unless the time-span of their use in Scots differs from that in English) both because they are more than adequately covered in dictionaries of English and because the person who picks up a dictionary of Scots is likely to be looking for distinctively Scottish words or meanings of words. Likewise, in practical terms, the interest in a history of Scots vocabulary lies in the distinctively Scottish elements, the elements which make it possible, as regards vocabulary, to think of Scots as a separate language or dialect even if the boundaries with English are not in all respects clearly defined. In practice, too, while meanings which are shared with English are not generally discussed here, the words may still appear if they have other meanings not shared with English (as is the case with the words listed above).

It will be noted that, in defining my subject, I have throughout referred to both spoken and written Scots. I see no justification for the view that only spoken Scots is real Scots and that all literature which is not a representation of spoken usage is artificial and not to be counted as evidence for the 'real' language. Spoken and written forms of all languages diverge from each other (where both forms exist), but this does not make one 'real' and the other 'artificial'. Written Scots is an important part of Scots; indeed it is the presence of such a large body of written texts that makes Scots so different from all other strongly marked dialectal forms of English. At the same time, in looking at the vocabulary of Scots we should certainly be aware of the different registers and especially of the divergence between the written and spoken forms of the language. In section 10.3, on additions to Scots vocabulary, I have included discussion of literary texts which do not confine themselves to representing current Scots speech but actively search out old words, create new ones or borrow them from other languages. It is instructive to see to what extent these literary additions to the vocabulary parallel or diverge from other additions to the vocabulary.

So far, we have looked at this question in relation to the practicalities of identifying what vocabulary is to be considered as Scots given that Scots and English are closely inter-connected. There is, however, another way of looking at it which must not be neglected. The definition of modern Scots cannot be separated from its history. While the history of the use of Scots in speech and writing since 1700 is considered elsewhere in this volume, a short summary provides essential background to a study of the development of the vocabulary.

While it seems probable that in 1700 Scots was still spoken by the majority of the population in Lowland Scotland, over the next three centuries the Scots-speaking community has narrowed to the working classes in the cities and country. By 1700, some upper class Scots would have adopted the speech of England, and during the eighteenth century middle-class Scots began to adopt English as their language. Nowadays, middle-class Scots do not generally speak Scots, although they speak Scottish Standard English with a distinctively Scottish accent and some Scottish vocabulary and grammar. This reduction of speakers of Scots has naturally entailed a reduction in the sorts of occasions on which Scots is used. It is very unlikely, for example, that Scots will nowadays be used for formal speeches, although this may occasionally be done for special reasons. Spoken Scots has thus been largely redefined over the last three centuries as an informal language, so that the strongest elements in present-day spoken Scots tend to be colloquial.

In 1700, Scots had a very diminished role in writing compared to, for instance, the earlier sixteenth century. Printed books were in English, although Lilian MacQueen's (1957: 124–7) detailed examination of handwritten records of the first half of the eighteenth century has shown that they were less thoroughly anglicised than were books; indeed they 'contain a strong element of Scots vocabulary, much of which persists to the middle of the century', as well as Scots forms, spelling and grammar, and a slow but steady process of anglicisation was underway. This would eventually leave little beyond legal and administrative terms that was distinctively Scots in such records. However, early in the eighteenth century, Allan Ramsay established a role for Scots in comic, satiric and sentimental poetry which it has never since lost and also used it for verse pastoral drama. In the early nineteenth century, Scott and other writers added another function to Scots, its extensive use in the dialogue of novels and this proved to be a very productive area for Scots throughout the next century or more, with some narratives also appearing in Scots where they could be presented as speech. At about the same time, James Hogg experimented with antique Scots as a way of providing a register for serious Scots verse, but he had no followers. Towards the end of the nineteenth century, the role of Scots in prose was further expanded with its use in Bible translation. This represents an incursion into an area which had for a long time been the domain of English and specifically of the *Authorised Version*. In the 1920s Hugh MacDiarmid and others enriched the vocabulary and tried to break out of the confines of the established genres of the comic, satiric and sentimental verse. Later in the twentieth century, Scots was extended to drama (where it had not been used seriously since Ramsay), both original works and translations, and into the new prose domain of autobiography. Meanwhile, the journal *Lallans* has been, since 1973, a centre for experiment in the use of Scots for a variety of different purposes.

Overall, then, the fortunes of written and spoken Scots over the last three centuries have apparently moved in contrary directions. Scots speech has become more restricted in the community, while Scots writing has extended progressively into more and more fields. In fact, this impression is somewhat misleading. While written Scots has expanded into new domains, they are all within the general field of creative writing or such closely related areas as autobiography. Scots is not used in writing about science and technology or the social sciences, it is not used in journalism, in history, in government documents or in the operations of business and industry. Scots as it has developed could be used for certain kinds of journalism where a colloquial style is appropriate, but is ill-equipped for use in functional formal prose where neither a colloquial style nor an elevated literary style is required. As a result, what we see in the history of Scots since 1700 is great strength in the development of colloquial vocabulary and of certain kinds of literary vocabulary but a marked decline in general formal vocabulary, an area where English has established itself as the norm. The vocabulary of Scots law is one partial exception to the decline of formal diction, but even there the normal surrounding medium is Scottish Standard English. Scots legal language may seem to have very little to do with the racy, colloquial Scots of the city but when we consider the two of them as both arising out of an earlier unified but multi-registered Scots, then it makes a lot more sense to consider them as part of the one language.

The roles that Scots has played over the last three centuries are reflected in the areas covered by *The Scots Thesaurus* (Macleod et al. 1990). Areas of everyday life are well covered in the categories of *Life Cycle, Family, Physical States, Food and Drink* and *Character, Emotions, Social Behaviour*, the last section occupying 106 of the 476 pages of the actual thesaurus. These are areas in which everyday spoken Scots is necessarily strong. The physical world and the plants and animals in it are also well covered; the surviving strength of rural dialects helps explain this. Certain traditional occupations such as farming, fishing, mining, weaving and building figure fairly prominently too. The section on *War, Fighting, Violence* includes a high number of obsolete terms and does not include the language of modern warfare. Among the professions, the law figures most prominently, then religion, then education, while medicine has only a relatively small section. Notable by their absence are politics, science, modern technology and modern manufacturing. Overall, the areas represented most strongly are those which one would expect for a language whose two great areas of strength are everyday, informal speech and creative writing. It is important to note that *The Scots Thesaurus* does not aim to cover the whole of the vocabulary in the *Concise Scots Dictionary*, on which it is based. Nevertheless, the areas chosen for coverage in *The Scots Thesaurus* do seem to reflect the particular strengths (and weaknesses) of modern Scots vocabulary. This chapter will deal firstly and briefly with continuity, secondly and at greater length with changes, both additions and losses, and finally in less detail with the geographical distribution of Scots vocabulary in this period.

10.2 CONTINUITY IN VOCABULARY

As part of a history, this chapter will be particularly concerned with change. But, clearly, not everything has changed in Scots. Even leaving aside words shared with English (which are reinforced by the presence of English in Scotland), there are many Scots terms that were current in 1700 and remain current today. A grand overview of the extent to which the vocabulary of Scots in 1700 survives today and what percentage of the current vocabulary it constitutes is beyond the scope of this discussion. In any case, the fate of a single very common word might be of more significance than the fates of unusual ones. Or one unusual word taken up by a major poet may be more important than twenty more common ones. Instead, I want to consider briefly two short poems, one at the beginning of our period and one at the end, to see how much of the Scots vocabulary they use has been stable since 1700. Obviously, we have to use written texts since there are no tape-recordings of Scots speech in 1700, and we cannot use prose texts since there are no prose passages from 1700 which can be compared with prose material belonging to a similar genre today. The most common modern prose Scots texts are in the dialogue of novels and plays, and no similar texts exist in 1700. Poetry, then, provides us with the best opportunity for finding somewhat comparable texts, and I believe that the poems which I have chosen provide a reasonable comparison. Both are written in what one might call a colloquial literary register, where the poet makes use of everyday colloquial language but moulds it into a literary medium which is different from everyday speech. To my necessarily subjective judgement, neither appears to be particularly straining to include or avoid unusual Scots language. They are both also in the voices of people who live in an urban setting. Obviously it would be absurd to claim that either of the texts could be considered typical of the whole language of each period. The most that might be claimed is that they are not totally atypical for each period of the genre to which they belong.

Let us begin by considering the first forty-two lines of Allan Ramsay's *Elegy on Maggy Johnston* (Martin 1945–74, vol. 1: 10–13), of which the first recorded printed edition was in 1718. Some of Ramsay's language is now obsolete, both words like *bedeen* 'at once' and *swash* 'fuddled with drink' and meanings like *bend* 'drink hard', *cant* 'tell stories', *mistak* 'make an error in counting', *scuds* 'foaming beer' and *Tippony* 'weak beer sold at twopence a Scots pint'. *Gamester* 'a player in a game' (in this case it is golf) was still in use in English at the time, but the last OED quotation is 1775. It lasted somewhat later in Scotland but is now entirely obsolete. However, alongside these are a number of terms still current in Scots though perhaps not all as common as they once were: *blyth* 'happy', *braw* 'excellent', *fou* 'drunk', *gaunt* 'yawn', *howff* 'favourite haunt', *maunt* 'stammer', *syne* 'next' and *true* 'believe'. Others like *bang* 'a crowd', *dowff* 'melancholy', *fouth* 'abundance', *pike* 'pick', *rung* 'a cudgel', *thrang* 'crowded' and *yowff* 'a sharp blow' are still in use but only in parts of Scotland, not including Edinburgh where Ramsay was writing. *Yesk* 'belch' is probably now obsolete, although it was known in the form *isk* meaning 'sob' in Caithness in the mid-twentieth century. Further terms no longer strike us as Scots because they have since entered Standard English, like *glower* and the exclamation *wow*. The *Hy-jinks* Ramsay refers to was a drinking game. A version of its complicated rules is described in Scott's *Guy Mannering* (Lang 1898–9, vol. 2: 345) which brought the term to the notice of non-Scots; the rules have been forgotten and only the general sense of 'high-spirited merrymaking' now survives in both Scots and English. In this poem, Ramsay makes no use of archaisms. Thus in a work written just after the beginning of our period, we have a significant number of items of Scots vocabulary, some of which are still in normal use, some in more restricted use, some now part of Standard English and some obsolete.

The element that is necessarily absent is words added to the language since 1700. That element can be considered by looking at a modern poem published in 1971, Stephen Mulrine's *Nostalgie* (Macafee 1983: 134). Mulrine's (1985) comments on Glasgow dialect poetry show that he is, like Ramsay, interested in using Scots as a literary language and in drawing on the resources of everyday speech in his poetry. Mulrine's Scots, like Ramsay's, is the Scots of his own time without archaisms. It is also specifically Glasgow Scots. Much of Mulrine's contemporary Scots has come into the language since 1700: in the later eighteenth century, the noun *scunner* developed the sense 'disgusting person', the nineteenth century saw the appearance of the words *chuckie* 'pebble' and *wheech* 'snatch away', and the extension of the verb *plank* to mean 'hide away' and the twentieth century has produced the words *broo* 'unemployment benefit office' and *Clenny* 'Corporation Cleansing Department' as well as the meanings 'something of value found among rubbish' for *luckie*, 'spoil' for *waste* and 'piece of fun' for *tear* and the figurative use of the phrase *put the hems on* to mean 'restrain'. Mulrine also uses *cowp* in the sense of 'fill up by dumping (something) in it', an extension of a meaning, 'dump a load of rubbish', which had established itself in the later nineteenth century (D. Donaldson 1887: s.v. *coup*). This is perhaps Mulrine's own innovation, as may be *slevvery* which I take to mean either literally 'covered in saliva' or more loosely 'slimy, slippery'. (Even though SND does not give either of these senses for *slevvery*, they are are natural ones to develop from *slaver* 'saliva' which is used in some parts of the country to mean 'slime'.) Likewise, Mulrine uses *easy-osying* 'ambling' which is a development from the nineteenth-century noun and adjective. At the same time, the poem contains quite a lot of vocabulary which was already in Scots in 1700, the exclamation *ach*, *bailie* 'town councillor', *glaur* 'slimy mud', *howk* 'dig', *tim* 'empty', *wean* 'child' and *wee* 'little', along with *toonheid* 'the upper end of a town', here preserved as a place-name. Furthermore, *cowp*, *hems* and *scunner* had been in use before 1700 although with different senses. *Wizzent* was also in use in Scots before 1700 but entered Standard English in the course of the nineteenth century; only the *t* ending identifies it here as distinctively Scots. Altogether the poem contains a good deal of post-1700 Scots vocabulary, as we might expect, but also a significant element of pre-1700 vocabulary. Moreover, the element of surviving older Scots is not bolstered by the revival of obsolete terms; all the Scots used is current in contemporary Glasgow speech. Thus even a poem in contemporary language contains a good deal of long-standing, even pre-1700, vocabulary. While these two poems cannot be called on to represent the whole of Scots vocabulary in 1718 and 1971, we can perhaps go as far as saying that in the Scots vocabulary of certain kinds of poetry there has been considerable continuity as well as considerable change.

Two other aspects of the vocabulary of these poems call for comment. Firstly, both have traces of Standard English poetic diction. Ramsay's first line urges Edinburgh in true elegaic style to *Mourn with sable hue*, but the way in which Edinburgh has already been addressed in the first two words as *Auld Reeky* marks this a comic rather than serious elegy. Mulrine has a mock-serious reference to *Monklan's purlin stream*. Thus both poems remind us that Scots poets have always been aware of the work, and specifically the diction, of English poets and can expect their audience to pick up references to English poetic vocabulary. This means it is unlikely that Scots poetry will preserve a purely Scots diction. Secondly, both poems include some general British slang. Ramsay has *bumper* 'full glass', a term only recently arrived in English and still looking very much like slang, *duds* 'clothes' and *cant* 'tell stories'. Mulrine has *breezin alang*, *hell-bent*, *non-runners*, *nutter* and *stchumers*. These words sit easily beside the highly colloquial Scots diction and do not prevent us from classifying the whole passage as Scots since both passages also contain plenty of Scots pronunciation and grammar – for instance, Mulrine has *pit*, *aff*, *oot*, *aw*, *ye*, *isnae* and *the rats is shootin the craw*. Because Scots is particularly strong in its colloquial register, it will always have strong connections with colloquial and slang English. What is important to realise is that this incursion of English slang and colloquialisms is not something that has only affected Glasgow speech in the twentieth century but has been occurring since at least Ramsay's time, if not before.

10.3 CHANGES IN VOCABULARY: ADDITIONS

The question of whether or nor a dialect will survive raises powerful emotions. Pessimism and despair are often the result. They are not necessarily justified. It is easy to see the history of Scots vocabulary over the last three centuries as one of increasing capitulation to encroaching English and to believe that Scots has been in decline throughout this period. As A. J. Aitken (1981c: 80–2) has pointed out, a long line of commentators since at least the later eighteenth century have been claiming that Scots is dying out, yet it seems not to have done so yet. In fact, Scots has been very creative in this period, and it would be quite misleading to think of the history of this period as overwhelmingly a history of loss.

10.3.1 Loanwords

Though not so important perhaps as in earlier centuries in providing new words, loanwords are still a significant element in the development of Scots since 1700.

10.3.1.1 Gaelic

Already by 1700, Scots had borrowed from Gaelic such words as *caird*, *cairn*, *clachan*, *coronach*, *ingle*, *messan*, *partan*, *quaich*, *raith*, *spreath* and *tocher*. In subsequent centuries, there has been a continuing influx of Gaelic words reflecting various kinds of contact between Scots- and Gaelic-speakers (McClure 1986). The eighteenth century saw an awakening of interest by Lowlanders in the culture of the Highlands. The Highlanders' very different clothing and arms were of particular interest. Travellers made terms like *claymore*, *fillebeg*, *skene-dhu* and *sporran* known outside the Highlands, but their accounts were written in English not Scots. For the words to enter Scots and move beyond areas of English discourse, such as travel writing and social studies, their referents had to become well known in popular Scottish culture, a domain of the Scots language. The claymore ceased to be a common item of Highland dress, and *fillebeg*, though used by Burns and Scott, lost the contest with its synonym *kilt*, a word of Scandinavian origins, which developed this sense about the same time as *fillebeg* entered the language, having been earlier in use as a verb to describe the action of a woman tucking up her skirts to leave her legs free. On the other hand, both the concept of and the Gaelic term for the *sporran* and *sgian dubh* (as it is now generally spelt) are well established in the Lowland consciousness and appear in Scots-language contexts.

One group of Highlanders who were well known in the Lowlands were the drovers, and it is probably from them that Scots took the adjective *gaidhealach*, meaning 'of the Highlands,

Gaelic' and applied it, in the form *kyloe*, to a breed of small Highland cattle. The greater interest in the Highland culture also manifests itself in the reappearance in Lowland speech, about the middle of the century, of the related noun *Gaelic* from *Gàidhlig*, the Highlanders' own name for their language. (It had surfaced in the sixteenth century in forms like *Gaelig* and *Gathelik* but then disappeared.) By the middle of the next century, *Gaelic* had ousted *Erse*, the name by which the Gaelic language had been known in the Lowlands, and had become the normal English and Scots name for the language. On the other hand, *Gael*, from Gaelic *Gaidheal* and meaning 'a Highlander', which also appears in English in the eighteenth century, seems never to have entered popular Scots usage and to have remained a somewhat self-conscious literary and historical term in Standard English. Not all eighteenth-century borrowings are of this self-conscious kind; *clyack* 'the last sheaf of corn of the harvest dressed as a girl' comes from Gaelic *caileag* meaning 'a girl' and is followed in the next century by *cailleach*, which appears with the same application to the last sheaf of corn in the twentieth century but retains when first borrowed its basic Gaelic meaning of 'old woman'. Burns provides the first SND citation for another Gaelic borrowing, *glaum* 'to grab', and it has been widely used since both as verb and noun.

Another source of information about Gaelic culture was Macpherson's *Ossian*, interest in which was fuelled by the controversy surrounding it. At the head of the two sections of *The Vision*, Burns placed the words *Duan First* and *Duan Second*, explaining in a footnote that it was 'a term of Ossian's for the different divisions of a digressive Poem'. Burns, however, did not start a fashion – no one followed his lead in using the word in Scots contexts.

As Gaelic speech receded in the nineteenth century, more Gaelic terms were transferred into Scots, many of them with only very localised use, like *galat* a term of endearment applied to a young girl in the north-east and Argyll, and *shannack* or *sownack* 'a (Hallowe'en) bonfire', common in Perthshire and also found in Fife and Aberdeenshire. *Scattan* 'herring' occurs, as SND notes, 'Only in areas such as the Moray Firth and the Firth of Clyde where there has been contact with Gaelic-speaking fishermen'. More widespread is *fank* 'a sheep-fold' which entered Highland use from Gaelic as sheep spread out to replace men in the Highlands but then came to be used in other parts of Scotland as well. *Kailie*, another nineteenth-century borrowing, was originally similarly restricted to rural localities at the edge of the Gaelic-speaking areas (including Ulster), but since about the 1930s has spread throughout Scotland and now appears with its Gaelic spelling *ceilidh*. However, the ceilidh as we know it is very much a modern invention, and its name is a Scots extension of the Gaelic meaning of the word, which is 'gossiping' or 'visiting'. Another but more geographically restricted term for a ceilidh or more generally for a wild party is *horoyally*. Taken from a meaningless refrain found in some Gaelic songs, it is largely confined to Argyll. By contrast to these terms originally of the Celtic borderlands, the term *keelie*, applied to a rough male living in a city, first appeared in Glasgow and no doubt reflects another kind of contact between Scots- and Gaelic-speakers, that caused by the migration of many Highlanders to the big city. It derives from Gaelic *gille* 'a lad' and had earlier been borrowed in the form *gillie*. *Gillie*, in its nineteenth-century development of the meaning 'sportsman's attendant', preserves, but with much less exalted connotations, something of the other Gaelic meaning, 'a servant or attendant of a chief'. The combined history of these two separate borrowings of the same word nicely reflects some of the ways in which Highland culture has often been modified and downgraded in its transit to the English- and Scots-speaking world.

In the twentieth century, very localised borrowings continue, as with *biach*, a colloquial form of address found in Caithness and Ross, *shangan* 'an ant' confined to Caithness, *smiach* 'a slight sound, a whisper' appearing in Caithness, Ross, Inverness-shire and Perthshire, *tuchin* 'a hoarse cough', used in Inverness-shire and Moray while, on the other side of the country, *garlach* 'a little rascal, a dwarf' is found in Argyll. *Cuttag*, a Caithness term applied to a middle-sized, sturdy woman and also used as a term of abuse for a girl, has the extra interest that it was itself originally borrowed into Gaelic from Scots. However, there is wider use of the term *teuchter* which was originally applied pejoratively to a Highlander and later to anyone uncouth. Its origins are much disputed, but there is a strong possibility that the ending is borrowed from Gaelic occupation names ending in *-dair*, and one explanation of the first element derives it from the Gaelic *tuath* 'countryfolk'.

We have already noticed the twice-over borrowing of *Gaelig/Gaelic* and *gillie/keelie*. The local term *gronach* meaning 'to grumble' is a similar case, having been taken, along with some influence from the English word *groan*, from the same Gaelic word as *coronach* 'a funeral lament' which was first borrowed in the sixteenth century and then revived and popularised by Scott in the nineteenth. *Scronach* 'a shrill cry; to shriek' is yet another form of the same word, the initial *s* having intensive force. *Greeschoch*, a widespread term attested from the first years of the nineteenth century and no doubt borrowed earlier, and the north-eastern Scots *drieshach* also found from the early nineteenth century, are both from the Gaelic *griosach* and keep its meaning of 'the glowing embers of a peat fire'. In Banffshire, there appeared yet another form of the word, *gleeshach* meaning 'a large bright fire'. Another double borrowing is represented by the pair *usquebae* and *whisky*. The earlier form, first found in the sixteenth century, derived from the full Gaelic term *uisge beatha*, literally 'water of life', while the name that we now use, which first appears in Scots in the eighteenth century and is soon adopted into Standard English, derives only from its first element. On the other hand, shared elements but different meanings are evident in *deoch-an-dorus* 'a stirrup cup', borrowed in the late seventeenth century, and *deochray* 'sowans', borrowed in the eighteenth. In each, the first element is the *deoch* meaning 'a drink', but Gaelic *an-doruis* means 'at the door' and *rèith* 'prepared'.

In selecting the words discussed so far, I have made use of examples where there is some evidence, such as change of form or number of attestations, that the word was fully acclimatised in Scots although sometimes only in one small region. However, as McClure (1986: 94–6) has pointed out, SND has quite a few instances of words of Gaelic origin known to only one of SND's correspondents (for example, *blianach* 'a pithless man', an East Ross-shire word reported by W. J. Watson of Edinburgh in 1927, *drollan* 'a half-witted person' given on the authority of R. J. G. Millar, the editor of the *John o' Groats Journal* in Wick, as in use about 1920, and *drooach* 'a small quantity of liquid', supplied by L. McInnes of Campbeltown in 1935); others are found only in Jamieson's *Etymological Dictionary of the Scottish Language* (such as *delgin* or *dalgan*, defined by Jamieson as 'the stick used in binding sheaves', *mirran* 'a carrot' and *mollachon* 'a small cheese').[2] Yet others are only used by one author (like *drimindo* or *drimindu*, Gaelic *drioman-dubh* 'a black cow with a white back', found in poems by Robert Tannahill (1774–1810), *juskal* 'tale', a corruption of Gaelic *ur-sgeal* used in John Mackay Wilson's (n.d., vol. 2: 26) story *The Outlaw, or The Maiden of Lednick* in 1836, Neil Munro's (1898: 10) *braddan* 'salmon' from his *John Splendid* of 1898, or *ballachan* 'a young lad' cited solely from the *Argyllshire Herald* of 3 June 1882). One might add to this list words which are only found in Mactaggart's (1824) *Gallovidian Encyclopedia*, like *loddan* 'a pool'. The status of such words is very doubtful. Are these solitary appearances an indication that the terms were in current use in Scots at the time, or are they merely memories of Gaelic usage wrongly identified as Scots – it is noticeable that many of these words come from Gaelic-speaking areas or their near surrounds – or, in the case of writers, are they deliberate insertions of Gaelic terms into Scots (or English) contexts?

The difficulties can be seen by taking just the literary examples: Tannahill writes in English, using the word in one poem with an indeterminate (presumably Scottish) setting (*The Poor Man's Lament for the Death of his Cow*, line 4) and another poem called *The Irish Farmer* (line 19); Munro writes in English about the Highlands, and the word may be intended to reflect the hero's ability to speak Gaelic although it is not in italics, unlike other Gaelic words in the novel; and Wilson's story is set in Perthshire on the edge of the Highlands with Scots-speaking characters. In such contexts, it is hard to be certain whether the words function as Gaelic (Scots or Irish) or Scots. Occasionally, one may feel reasonably confident that the term has not transferred to Scots; for instance, SND contains some terms, so far excluded from my discussion, which are reported by scholars or visitors writing about the Hebrides but not otherwise attested and unlikely ever to have been part of Scots speech. *Struan* 'a special cake baked on Michelmas Eve' and the St Kilda word *lavie* 'guillemot or razorbill' are instances of this. But what is one to make of cases like *cairban*? Patrick Neill (1808–10: 550–1), in a list of fishes, noted that the basking shark was on the west coast 'well known by the name of *sail-fish* and *cairban*' but in the north called '*pricker*, and *brigdie*'. *Cairban* also appears in Jamieson's supplement, but the supplement is evidently relying on Neill (who is quoted under *brigdie*), so Neill is our only real source: does he mean that in the west *sail-fish* is the Scots or English term and *cairban* the Gaelic one, or does he mean that *cairban* has been borrowed into Scots and English usage? And does any of this apply to Scots or only to the English of the Highlands and Islands? We are unlikely ever to determine the status of individual terms like *cairban*, *drimindu* and *braddan*, but what we can say is that, among the large list found by McClure in a 'quick skim' (1986: 85) of SND and other words which he passed over, there must be some that were naturalised in Scots even if only used in a limited area. Furthermore, a knowledge of Gaelic has clearly lain in the background and provided Scots-speakers with a continuing resource for enriching their vocabulary even if their borrowings were not always permanently adopted.

Attitudes to Gaelic have changed and it is no longer seen, as some Lowlanders once saw it, as the barbarous tongue of a barbarous people. The greater respect for Gaelic is visible in a slight tendency to move towards Gaelic spellings of loanwords rather than the phonetic (in Scots/English terms) ones that once prevailed. We have noted the change of *kailie* to *ceilidh* and of Scott's incorrectly Gaelicised *skene-dhu* to *sgian dubh*. In like fashion, the name of the dance *shantrews* which appears in Scots from the eighteenth century is now more commonly spelt *seann triubhas*. Such evidence of respect for the integrity of Gaelic is welcome but brings with it one problem: the imposition of the very different rules of Gaelic spelling has the effect of denaturalising long-standing loanwords and reassigning them to foreign status. It would be a pity if respect for Gaelic spelling, the end result of a learned interest in Gaelic which began by giving many Gaelic words to Scots and English, ended up inhibiting the free borrowing of its words or, where they are borrowed, preventing them from being recognised as fully naturalised Scots terms.

10.3.1.2 Irish

Of the Celtic languages, it is naturally Scottish Gaelic which is the biggest source of loanwords in Scots, although in many cases Scottish and Irish Gaelic are identical and, with both the Highlanders and the Irish migrating in great numbers to Glasgow, both languages may have contributed to the appearance of words like *keelie*. Sometimes there is reason to believe that Irish is the main or only source. Galloway was an area particularly subject to Irish influence. Gaelic had died out there in the late seventeenth century, but in the mid-eighteenth century the Irish began to come to Galloway. Some would have been Scots-speakers from parts of Ulster, others Gaelic-speakers (Riach 1979). The Galloway *callan* which confusingly means 'a girl', unlike the much more common general Scots *callan* (derived from Northern French or Dutch) which is applied to men, is first recorded around 1800 after this influx of Irish immigrants had begun, and Jamieson was soon to suggest that the word was from Irish. The dating makes this probable although the word has the same form, *cailin*, in both Scots and Irish Gaelic. In Irish English, it appears in the form *colleen*. Similarly limited, within Scotland, to Galloway is the term *spalpean* meaning 'a naughty child', cited by Riach (1988) in *A Galloway Glossary*. This suggests a borrowing from Irish Gaelic *spailpín* meaning 'a labourer' or, as a term of abuse, 'a bold boy, a worthless fellow' or Irish English *spalpeen* 'a labourer, a mean fellow, a boy' rather than the related Scots Gaelic. One might further wonder if the already mentioned Galloway use of *loddan* 'a pool' is from Irish rather than Scots Gaelic. A derivation from both Irish and Scots Gaelic *cutharlan* is probable in the case of *curluns* or *gourlins* 'the earth-nut', a word used in Galloway but also appearing in the form *gowlins* (possibly an error) in Inverness-shire. Ulster is also, obviously, exposed to the influence of the Irish language. There we find terms like *gomach*, meaning 'a fool', attested since the nineteenth century, which appears to be related to the Irish Gaelic *gamach* and the modern Irish dialect word *goamie* and *glaiks* (found also in the south-west of Scotland) meaning both 'a lever attached to a churn staff' and 'an instrument for twisting straw into ropes', which derives from Irish *glac* 'a handle'.

10.3.1.3 Welsh

While the Brythonic language originally spoken in parts of Scotland may have survived as late as the eleventh century, it clearly did not survive long enough to directly influence the Scots of our period, and any direct influence must come from its close relative, modern Welsh. Brythonic influence of some kind is in evidence in two counting sequences found in recent Scots: *zeendi, teendi, taedhaer, mundheri, baombe, hecturi, zecturi, aover, daover, dek* is a sequence used by shepherds in the hill districts of Dumfriesshire (published in the 1920s) and is clearly related to a children's counting-out rhyme appearing as *eendy, beendy, bambor, eendy, over, dover, dick* recorded in the 1880s in Moray and to *eenty, teenty, tethery, methery, banful, eetful, over, dover* in use in Edinburgh early in the twentieth century (see SND s.vv. *baombe, eendy, methery*). Although the earliest record is from the nineteenth century, these sequences could have been in Scotland for much longer, especially given the conservatism of the language of children's play, but since we do not know how long, we cannot be sure of their source. In these circumstances, the increasing circumspection of SND over the years of its publication between 1931 and 1976 is no doubt appropriate. While in the first volume under *baombe* the editor is willing to claim that this is a corrupted form 'of the numerals once used by the shepherds of the hill districts of the old Cymric kingdom of Strathclyde', by the time it has reached *dek*, in a volume dated 1952, the primitive origins have been abandoned in favour of the claim that 'S.Sc. usage derives from Welsh shepherds in N.Eng. *a.* 1600', and in the last volume under *zeendi* we find the very cautious 'Gen. ascribed to Welsh influence, of uncertain date and provenance, in S.W. Scot.' Indeed, all that can be said with certainty is that these sequences are first recorded in Scotland in the later nineteenth century and that they show influence from Welsh or another Brythonic language. It is therefore certainly possible that they represent a Welsh borrowing within our period.

In the written language, Bible translators add another Welsh term. Both Waddell (1879) in his Isaiah (36.7) and Cameron (1921) in his Genesis (22.9), wanting a word for the concept of an altar, use the Welsh word *cromlech*, a name given to various prehistoric structures found in the British Isles consisting of a horizontal stone supported by three vertical ones. In a Scots text, however, the Gaelic form *cromleac* might have been more appropriate.

10.3.1.4 English and Irish Dialects

The direction of borrowing between dialects is often hard to establish, given the inadequacy of records, but sometimes we can be fairly certain of Scots being the borrower rather than the lender. For instance, as SND points out, the phonology of *goam* 'pay attention', which has been found in central and southern Scots since the late eighteenth century, shows that it has been borrowed from northern English dialects, although ultimately it is from Old Norse *gaumr*. Its derivative *goamless* or *gaumless* is a more recent borrowing, having entered Scots in the twentieth century. *Jonick* 'genuine' is also a recent arrival: SND's first quotation is from 1887, and in the 1950s it was known in the north-east and nearby areas, but the OED under *jannock*, in a section prepared by December 1900, while noting that it was used from 'Northumberland to Hampshire, Norfolk to Cornwall', specifically marked it as 'Not *Sc.*'.

Graphite was found in reasonable quantities in Cumberland and was originally imported from there although small deposits were later found in Scotland. Because of this, two Scots words for graphite pencils are of Cumberland origin. The better known, *keelivine*, was actually borrowed in the seventeenth century and seems to derive in some uncertain fashion from a Cumberland word for graphite, *killow*. The other Cumberland word for graphite is *wad* and appears in Scots from the eighteenth century, originally applied to graphite but later to a pencil as well. *Keelivine* is widespread in Scotland but, according to *The Linguistic Atlas of Scotland* (Mather and Speitel 1975: Map 27; 206–7), *wad* seems to be confined to the southern and south-western counties. Another import from northern England but of much more limited geographical range in Scotland is *bait* in the sense of 'a snack a man takes to work'. In most of Scotland this is called a *piece*, although in Shetland it is called a *fairdiemaet* and in Angus and Perthshire a *mid yokin*. *Bait* is the normal term in Cumberland and Northumberland and widely used in other parts of England, but in Scotland it occurs only in the counties bordering with England (Mather and Speitel 1977: Map 34; 135–6). *Playgins* 'broken pieces of china' comes from Northumberland dialect and occurs only in Roxburghshire, Berwickshire, Selkirkshire and East Lothian (Mather and Speitel 1975: Map 31; 214–16).

Apart from northern England, the nearest other English-speaking area to Scotland is Ireland. Galloway, subject as we have noticed to Irish Gaelic influence, is also affected by Irish dialects of English; the first SND citation for *malvader* 'stun with a blow', derived from Irish dialect *malvather* 'confuse, bamboozle', is from Mactaggart's *Gallovidian Encyclopedia* of 1824. Of somewhat wider currency is *dudgeon* or *dudyen* 'a short clay pipe' which is from Hibernian English *dudyen* or *dudeen*, itself from Irish Gaelic *dúidín*. It is found in the West Central Scots area, where Irish immigrants were numerous, and (less explicably) in Perthshire.

10.3.1.5   Romany

There have been gipsies in Scotland since at least the fifteenth century, but their language remained for a long time very much their own possession and has made only a small contribution to Scots. However, that small contribution is worth mentioning as a case, like Gaelic loanwords, of borrowing from a language spoken within Scotland. *Barrie*, an adjective expressing strong approval, was first recorded in Roxburghshire earlier in the twentieth century and comes from gipsy speech in that area but, according to Stevenson and Macleod, is 'now common especially among the under-15s in Lothian and Fife'. They also discuss *chore* 'to steal', which first appeared in the same area and from the same source as *barrie*, then spread as far as Aberdeen and continues in localised use today (1989: 17, 215). From the same area, too, comes *gadgie* 'a man', a term from Romany originally applied to a non-gipsy which has spread to various parts of Scotland, while *curdie* 'a very small coin, a farthing', found in Scots from the late nineteenth century, may come from Scottish gipsy speech where it means 'a halfpenny'. *Chore* and *gadgie* have entered thieves' cant in the twentieth century, and this provides another possible route into Scots.

10.3.1.6   Latin

The consequences of the loss of a formal prose register for Scots can be seen in the sorts of words borrowed from Latin in this period. Whereas earlier Scots borrowed extensively from Latin in a relatively wide range of areas, loans in the last three centuries have been less frequent and in more limited areas. It is particularly in law (including church law), a domain of Scots terms though not of a fully developed Scots language, that we find borrowings. Potentially literary Scots, especially in the twentieth century with its desire to create a formal register, could have been another area where Latin terms might have been borrowed, but there is little to be found apart from the occasional piece of aureate diction introduced in imitation of the Middle Scots makars, like Lewis Spence's *vivand* in his *Portrait of Mary Stuart, Holyrood*. Even this word could be considered, in its particular context, as more a tribute to Mary's French upbringing than a Latinism, derivation from either French or Latin being equally possible. Underlying the reluctance to draw on Latin may be an ideological commitment to a view of Scots as essentially a Germanic language (with some Gaelic and French influence). Such is certainly the case with Waddell (1871 and 1879) in the innovative language which he uses in his translations of the Psalms and Isaiah. In a lecture on Burns (Waddell 1859: 5), he makes it clear that the Germanic origins of Scots are particularly important to him but describes Latin terms as 'absolutely foreign' to Scots. His efforts to replace even well-established, but Latin-derived, religious terms such as *salvation* with terms of Germanic origin will be discussed later.

Even when we turn to the one register that does borrow quite strongly from Latin in this period, the law, we can sense a reluctance to adopt Latin terms in a fully naturalised form. Much of the Latin which SND records as having come into Scottish legal usage since 1700 takes the form of phrases which retain their full unassimilated Latin form: *cessio bonorum*, *delectus personae, dominus litis, invecta et illata, nobile officium, quadriennium utile, ultima haeres* and *vergens ad inopiam* to cite a few. Even individual words often retain their full Latin form: *mora, praecipium, subsidiarie* (although this is also generally true of English borrowings of the same period). Does this influx of Latin phrases reflect a desire to bolster the status of a legal system which still uses a lot of diction derived from a variety of language which no longer carried prestige? Could it be that the lawyers are willing to use unambiguously Latin words and phrases but are not willing to be seen as using 'bad English', which might be the result of using newly assimilated Latin loanwords? By contrast to earlier Scots, I have found very few examples of assimilated loanwords. One is *consanguinean*, which in the strict legal sense means 'having the same father but not the same mother' but which is also used by Scott in the looser sense of 'related by blood'.

Most legal language remains restricted to the courts and legal documents, but some terms gain a wider currency. Of the word *locus*, used in referring to the site of significant events, including 'the scene of the crime', Gibb (1946: 32) wrote that it was 'beloved of the police and certain lawyers' and from there the transition to newspapers (and perhaps to wider general use) is natural. If SND's suggested derivation from an unrecorded *locus strae* is correct, *locus* also occurs in *lockerstrae*, a word found in the north-east from the 1820s for about a century. It means a straw (*strae*) or other marker used in pointing out the place (*locus*) when teaching children to read or when reading a book. As we might expect, church law follows state law in the use of Latin phrases: *fama clamosa* denotes a widespread rumour about scandalous behaviour by a church member, especially a minister, and appears from the earlier eighteenth century, while a parish which is *quoad sacra* (literally 'as regards sacred matters') is one which has been separated off from the rest of the parish for religious purposes only but remains part of the original parish for purposes of civil administration; a parish combining both functions is called *quoad omnia*.

Courts using a system of Roman law had a natural connection with Latin but the connection was even stronger in the case of schools where, for generations of students, education and learning Latin were inseparable. One symptom of this is one of the best-known and most fully acclimatised Latin borrowings in Scots, *dominie*. The Latin *dominus* 'master' had been used in its vocative form *domine* in addressing teachers and clergy in England since the sixteenth century. In the partially Shakespearean *Two Noble Kinsmen* it also appears as a normal noun, but it was perhaps the Scots in the eighteenth century who were the first to use it on a regular basis as an ordinary word for a schoolmaster. The actual practices used in teaching Latin gave rise to another term, *maxie*, short for *maximus error*, a name given to the worst kind of mistakes in a Latin translation. In Aberdeen in the early twentieth century, a *maxie* led to the loss of four marks whereas a less serious mistake, a *medie*, cost two marks. However, in Crockett's (1904: 19) Kirkcudbright, the result was physical punishment, a *palmie*, that is a hit on the palm of the hand with a cane or strap, and there were different names for the lesser mistakes: 'Yae palmie for a *minie*, twa for a *majie*, an' three for a *maxie*'. *Palmie* derives either from the word *palm* or, more probably, from the Latin *pande palmam* 'hold out your palm'. This phrase was strongly imprinted on students' minds, and its first word yielded *pandie*, another term for the same punishment. *Palmie* is first attested in SND in 1787 and *pandie* in 1808, and both were widely used, but in 1931 an article in the *Aberdeen Press and Journal* of 15 January reported that '*Pawmies* was not in ordinary use, though it was known to the older generation; we loons occasionally spoke of *pandies*, but more often of *licks wi' the tag*', and The Linguistic Atlas of Scotland shows *pandie* as more common in North-eastern Scots and parts of Southern Scots and *palmie* as predominant in Central Scots. (This is somewhat simplifying a rather complicated picture; see Mather and Speitel 1975: Maps 30 and 30A; 211–14.) Outside the classroom, Latin left its mark in the schoolyard in two names of games, both using the Latin word for 'king': *rex* (or *rax*) uses the nominative form of the word and *regibus* the dative or ablative. The first was played in Inverness-shire and Banffshire, while the second was apparently used for two quite different games played by boys in the north-east.

Further on in the education system, Latin seems a natural choice for naming university administrators, so that at St Andrews University the chief financial officer was called a *quaestor* from the name given to public officials in charge of revenue in ancient Rome. Likewise, when a systematic way of giving plants a scientific name was developed, the use of Latin terms as a basis was equally natural. Familiar plants continued to have their familiar names, but new ones might well be introduced under their Latin names. The beginning of the eighteenth century saw the first extensive forestry plantations in Scotland and the planting of new species of trees, like the larch, which was known both by this, its German name, and by its Latin name *laryx*. Once established in speech, the Latin was liable to be misunderstood as a plural, and by the nineteenth century we find references to a *larick*. In this form, the Latin origin of the word is no longer immediately obvious, as is also the case with *loorach* which reaches Scots via Gaelic during this period. With a variety of meanings from 'rag' through to 'trailing garment' and 'anything messy', it derives through Gaelic from Latin *lorica* 'coat of mail'.

10.3.1.7 French

French was an important source of older Scots vocabulary but is less important after 1700 for several reasons. There was no longer any special political connection with France, and French language and literature stood for the very opposite of the down-to-earth vigour that was seen as one of the essential qualities of writing in Scots. Where the makars would draw on French to enhance an elevated register of Scots, modern writers, with some exceptions, look for words which will suit a more colloquial register. Nevertheless, we do find some loanwords from French in this period. The continuing export of French wines directly to Scotland may explain the appearance in the later eighteenth century in Scotland, but not in England, of the word *gardevine* 'wine or spirit bottle, chest for storing wine-bottles'; admiration for French cooking perhaps led to the borrowing of *howtowdie* 'young chicken for the pot; young unmarried woman', which is apparently derived from Old French *hétoudeau* 'young capon', and of *padovie* 'minced beef pie or patty' if it is indeed a corruption of French *godiveau* 'kind of sausage filled with minced meat'. The French variety of pear known as *cuisse-madame*, literally 'lady's thighs', was evidently introduced in Scotland by its enthusiastic gardeners, leading Andrew Fairservice in *Rob Roy* to speak of a *queez-maddam* (Lang 1898–9, vol. 4: 282). Some clothing terms also come from French: the woman's short jacket or gown called a *cartoush* or *cuttoush* (also shortened to *toush*) takes its name from French *courthousse*, and the kind of cloak known as a *rokelay* is named after the Duc de Roquelaure (1656–1738) who brought it into fashion. As usual, exact dating of borrowing is not possible, but the duke's dates suggest that his word, for which the earliest SND citation is dated 1720, was indeed borrowed within our period or only shortly before. On the other hand, the name of another item of clothing, a *biggin* or linen cap, could just as easily have survived in Scots from its earlier English usage rather than being borrowed anew from French *beguin*, and the same applies to *skelet* 'a skeleton'.

10.3.1.8 Scandinavian Languages

When thinking of the substantial body of words of Scandinavian origin in Scots (Murison 1979a; J. J. Smith 1994), it is well to begin by remembering that the English-speaking areas of Scotland were not part of the area settled by the Danish and Norwegian invaders in the later Old English period. The influence of these settlers on the English, later to become Scots, language of Scotland was thus indirect, but it was all the same considerable. Contact between the areas of Scandinavian settlement and the rest of English-speaking Britain led in the course of time to the adoption of many Norse words outside the original Danelaw areas; this was particularly brought about in Scotland by an influx of immigrants from the northern and midland counties of England in the twelfth and thirteenth centuries. Norse words adopted into Middle English appear, then, in Older Scots and include some of the most widespread and familiar terms in Scots such as *big* 'build', *gowk* 'cuckoo', *graith* 'prepare; equipment', *lowp* 'leap', *maun* 'must', *nieve* 'fist', *skelp* 'hit', *skirl* 'scream' and *wale* 'choose'.

The influx of words of Norse origin continues after 1700, although it must be said that, despite the enormous resource which we have in DOST and SND, the dating of these borrowings is not entirely certain. For instance, SND's first citation for *gizzen* 'shrink, warp, leak' is in Allan Ramsay's *An Ode to Mr Forbes* (line 5) of 1721, but the word seems to be already well and widely established in the eighteenth century and could well have been in use before 1700. Even more unlikely to be a recent borrowing at the time of its first SND citation is *scrae* 'stunted or shrivelled person, animal or object', since that first citation is from Kelly's collection of proverbs, published in 1721. A different argument but the same possibility applies to *ure* 'udder', which is first recorded in the later eighteenth century in SND but is found in Middle English and northern English dialects and may well have been one of the original group of borrowings reaching Scots via northern Middle English.

Bearing this caveat in mind and excluding words which are well established in northern English dialects, we nevertheless find a sufficiently large number of possible post-1700 Scandinavian borrowings into general Scots usage to make it likely that some at least do indeed belong to this period. For instance, in the eighteenth century we have *braise* 'roach', *scour* 'shower', *skair* 'slanting cut or notch for joining one piece of wood to another' and *taupie* 'giddy, scatterbrained, awkward or untidy person', while in the nineteenth century we find *brainyell* 'break out; outburst', *cair* 'stir, scrape', *cleester* 'smear; glutinous mass', *dorro* 'a trailing fishing line', *lunt* 'walk with a springy step', *skrink* 'shrivelled up person' and *ure* 'damp mist'. These words are not found in northern English dialects and presumably arise from peaceful contact across the North Sea, with words like *brase* and *dorro* apparently reflecting the specific influence of contact with Scandinavian fishermen. The speakers of Scandinavian languages with whom the Scots had contact did not represent a ruling class like the medieval French-speakers or a learned class like the Latin-speakers, and these words noticeably denote familiar and everyday things, as is the tradition with borrowings from Norse into English. There is also the possibility of continuing influence from northern English dialects; it is quite likely that a word like *skime* 'glance, gleam' (noun and verb), which is well established in the north of England but is not recorded in Scots before 1700, could have been borrowed into Scots from northern English dialects even at that late date. On the other hand, as with *ure* 'udder', it could be a case of a word borrowed at an earlier stage but not caught by the written record.

With the exception of *lunt* which is found only in Southern Scots and Galloway, these words have widespread use. The case of words confined to Northern and Insular (Shetland and Orkney) Scots warrants separate discussion. These areas are not only more likely to have direct contact with speakers from Scandinavia, but they are also, in the case of the islands and Caithness, areas where a variety of Norse known in the islands from at least the late fifteenth century as Norn continued to be spoken for a long time (A. Fenton 1978: 616–22; Barnes 1984). Its replacement by Scots was not sudden, nor are the dates at which it happened entirely certain, but Norn perhaps continued until the fifteenth century in Caithness, the late eighteenth in Orkney and the early nineteenth in Shetland. At the same time, Scots was in use in the islands for centuries before the final disappearance of Norn. Even when the full Norn language, Norse in grammar and pronunciation as well as vocabulary, finally disappeared, the Scots which replaced it borrowed much of its vocabulary from the superseded language. Unfortunately, the information that we have about the original Norn is very scanty, and it is not usually possible to relate an individual word in the later Norn-influenced Scots to a recorded instance of the word in Norn (Melchers 1986). We can, however, say in general terms that many of the words peculiar to Shetland and/or Orkney dialect in recent times are of Norse origin, either survivals of Norn or the result of contact with Scandinavians (Shetland, for instance, is only about 270 kilometres from Norway) or both.

Words confined to the islands include such terms as *frush* 'splutter', *hunse* 'search for', *skimp* 'poke fun at', *skoot* 'project; a projection' and *upspraet* 'thread'. Other terms also extend to Caithness as well, like the synonyms *roog* and *roo* (found in Caithness in the diminutive form *rooag*), meaning 'a heap or pile, especially one of peats', *hookers* 'haunches', and *eem* which means 'condensation' in Caithness and 'a hot foetid smell' in Caithness and Orkney. Given the length of time since Norn was spoken in Caithness, these words are perhaps more likely to have been borrowed from Insular Scots into Caithness usage or to have been independently borrowed from Scandinavia than to have survived from Caithness Norn, although in the case of *roo* the route may be via Gaelic *rugh*. This route was clearly followed by *trosk*, a Caithness word meaning 'a silly, oafish or slow-witted person' adopted from Gaelic *trosg* but ultimately from Norse *þorskr*. Indeed, Caithness seems in general to show a great deal of influence from Gaelic. *Oam*, clearly related to *eem*, and meaning, among other things, 'steam' and 'a warm, stuffy atmosphere', extends further south, into the Scots of the north-east; it may well have started as an Insular Scots term and spread south, as SND believes happened with *upslaag* 'a change in weather' which is recorded in Shetland in this form and in North-east Scots in the forms *upslay* and *upsilly*. Sometimes the dates strongly suggest such a case: *rakki* 'parrel' is recorded in Shetland before 1838 but first appears in the mainland (in Kincardineshire) in 1910. However, not all words follow such a neat pattern of dates. This may be significant or it may simply be that the written record is deficient as a record of spoken usage. Other words which could have followed the same path into Northern Scots are *brath* 'weave (straw ropes) around a stack', *glamse* 'snap' (noun and verb) and *scorie* 'young seagull'.

Words like these, then, raise the possibility of a pattern of borrowing of items of Scandinavian origin from Insular into Northern Scots. However, direct Scandinavian import into Northern Scots is also clearly possible and may explain the North-east Scots *floan*, a disapproving verb used of a woman showing overt affection for a man, which probably has Scandinavian origins, as well as the Caithness use of *struie* meaning 'sweep threshed straw aside with the flail', a word clearly related to Norwegian dialect *strøya* 'sweep aside'. Similarly, the North-east *fuggle* 'small truss or bundle' (apparently a diminutive form of unattested *fug*) may arise from the borrowing of Norwegian dialect *fugge* which has the same meaning.

In a more literary register, Scott has apparently borrowed the word *langspiel* in the Shetland setting of *The Pirate* (Lang 1898–9, vol. 8: 237) to denote some kind of stringed instrument. Perhaps he heard the word used in the Northern Isles or took either the Norwegian dialect *langspel* or the Old Danish *langspil* from some unidentified source. In *The Pirate*, it does not function as a Scots word but becomes one when adopted by Waddell in his Scots Psalms (57:8, 92:3) to render the word which the *Authorised Version* translates as *psaltery*.

10.3.1.9 Dutch and Flemish

Direct contact between Scotland and the Low Countries was strong and continuous for many centuries; it is only in the last two centuries or so that there has been any weakening of this link. Trade contacts across the North Sea were always strong, particularly with the small ports in the East Neuk of Fife, and the Scots had a staple, a specially authorised place of trade, at Campvere (now known as Veere) in Zeeland until 1799; hence Meg Murdockson's slighting reference to Bailie Middleburgh in *The Heart of MidLothian* as 'the oe [grandson] of a Campvere skipper' (Lang 1898–9, vol. 6: 270). In the seventeenth century, many Scots went to the Netherlands to serve as soldiers, and in the later seventeenth and earlier eighteenth century prospective ministers and lawyers studied theology and Roman law there. The linguistic influence on Scots of the closely related languages of the Low Countries, Dutch and Flemish and the nearby Low German dialects was profound, and continued after 1700 although with a noticeable waning in the twentieth century.

Dutch, Flemish and Low German are so closely related that they are best dealt with here as one group; they also have many similarities with Scandinavian languages, and some Scots words could equally well have come from the Low Countries or Scandinavia or both. With the verb *knip*, it may be possible to separate the two influences, though it could also be a home-grown onomatopoeic term. It first appears in the sixteenth century applied to animals cropping grass, a meaning close to that of the Dutch and Low German *knippen* 'clip, snip', and then apparently falls out of use only to reappear in the twentieth century in Shetland and the north-east with the meaning 'pull to pieces, snap', a meaning rather more akin to the Norwegian dialect *knippa* 'snap'. With English also being a closely related language, uncertainty can also extend as to whether English or Dutch is the source: is *glimp* 'a glimpse' a back-formation from *glimpse*, of presumed Old English origins, or is it from the cognate Dutch *glimp* which has the same meaning?

As with Scandinavian words, the dating of the entry of these words into Scots is uncertain. For instance, regarding *spiel* 'a game, especially a curling match', SND notes that 'The phonology suggests early borrowing, though evidence is not available': the first use recorded in SND is in 1789. Nevertheless, SND does record quite a few Dutch/Low German loans as appearing in Scots after 1700 which do not appear in DOST or the OED before that date, and there is no reason why borrowing should not have taken place in this period. For the eighteenth century, we have *cookie* 'plain bun', *cowk* 'retch, vomit', *cud* 'cudgel', *doss* 'tobacco or snuff box', *haar* 'cold easterly wind; cold mist or fog', *knoll* 'large piece or lump', *knoost* 'large lump, hunk', *scranch* 'crunch', *skellum* 'rogue, scroundrel', *wintle* 'stagger, tumble' and *winze* 'curse'. *Cookie* is, of course, also found in the USA and South Africa, which are subject to separate influence from Dutch, and refers to different things in different countries. Another apparently eighteenth-century arrival is *matkie* 'a young maiden herring with the roe not fully developed'. This, or *matkiss*, is the normal eighteenth-century form and apparently derives from Middle Low German *madikes-*

herink. After the nineteenth century, the form is normally *mattie* or *matie* until the appearance in twentieth-century Aberdeen of *madgie*, a form clearly influenced by the pronunciation of the Dutch *maatjes haring*. Also in the eighteenth century, we first find the very common word *fozie* meaning 'soft and spongy' when applied to vegetables and 'flabby' or 'unintelligent' when applied to people. This has developed from Dutch *voos* 'spongy, porous' but exists in Scots only as a derivative. In the nineteenth century, we find *besle* 'to talk without proper thought', *bum* 'kind of broad and shallow fishing boat', *cran* 'a tap', *scow* 'flat-bottomed boat, such as a barge' and *strule* 'stream or steady trickle of liquid' from a Dutch verb meaning 'urinate'. Once again, one of these, *scow*, is found in the USA under separate Dutch influence. In the twentieth century, however, the influence of Dutch seems to be seriously weakened, and I have only found the one example, *faan* 'weather vane'; for this, SND cites only one authority, but it is no less a one than David Murison himself.

The kind of influence which leads to borrowing is not usually a one-off thing; reborrowing if a word dies out or further influence of its meaning is quite likely to occur if the language contact continues. *Track*, from Dutch *trekken* 'draw, pull, tow, make (tea)', is used by Scottish writers in the eighteenth century in the sense 'tow'. From the later nineteenth century and only in Shetland it is applied to making tea. This would suggest that *track-pot* 'teapot', found in Scots since the early eighteenth century, is a separate borrowing of Dutch *trekpot* rather than a native-born compound. It spawned the now-obsolescent diminutive *trackie*, allowing the development of the jocular phrase *to saiddle the trackie* meaning 'to make tea', recorded in the 1960s in Aberdeen. *Prink* 'to make smart or pretty, to deck out' comes to Scots by the nineteenth century via English where it appears from the sixteenth century as a variant of *prank*, itself apparently a borrowing from Dutch *pronken* 'to show off', but the form *prunk* found in Shetland may be a separate borrowing from the Dutch or from the German *prunken*. That there was a separate influence of Dutch in Shetland – where Dutch was widely spoken in the later seventeenth century, and probably afterwards (Sibbald 1845: 16) – is beyond doubt: as Murison (1971) notes, there are a number of words of Dutch origin found in Shetland and not in the rest of Scotland like *dulhoit* 'stupor, lethargy', *leppel* 'horn spoon' and *pram* 'press, squeeze, stuff', to cite a few of his examples. Dutch words, like Scandinavian words, generally denote everyday things; a more specific influence from the contact with Dutchmen in the small vessels which crossed the North Sea for fishing and trade can be seen in borrowings like *bum*, *mattie* and *scow*, while the informality of much of the language is exhibited in a borrowing like *skellum*.

Not surprisingly, since the language has never been extensively studied in Scotland, Dutch is not a major source of literary borrowings. However, Waddell (1871 and 1879), in this as in many things an innovator, draws on Dutch for his language in his translations of the Psalms and Isaiah. The reason for this is very clear: Waddell believed that Scots was an essentially Germanic language, claiming that 'the vernacular of Scotland . . . adheres more perfectly in its root to the old Teutonic than the English does', so that he looks to 'the old Teutonic homestead that is across the sea' (Waddell 1859: 7) and, as I have shown elsewhere (Tulloch 1989: 42–3), avoids romance diction in his translations. Dutch *rechter* 'a judge' appears unchanged (Ps. 7:11), and he refashions Dutch *toorn* 'anger' as *torne* 'anger' (Ps. 6:1), although influence from German *Zorn* is also possible. Dutch *toevlucht* or German *Zuflucht* are evidently his source for *to-flight* 'refuge' (Ps. 62:8).

10.3.10 German

In contrast with this substantial borrowing from Dutch and Low German, there is very little that is of distinctively High German origin in spoken Scots, no doubt because areas speaking High German had much less direct contact with Scotland. One possible case is *doudle*, a verb used to describe playing a bagpipe or other wind instrument. It apparently comes from German *dudeln* 'play the bagpipes', itself of Polish origin. In keeping with what has been said above about Waddell's Dutch borrowings, he also takes *righter* 'judge' from German *Richter* and *wuth* 'anger' from German *Wut*. While many of his innovations remain peculiar to him, *wuth* was taken up by H. P. Cameron in his Genesis (27:45). In a post-Hitlerian world, Waddell's enthusiasm for pure Germanic roots is tinged with the irony of history, and it is unlikely that he would have applied the German-influenced *fuhre* 'lead' (Ps. 78:52) to the actions of the Lord if he had been writing in 1971 rather than 1871.[3] In the twentieth century, Douglas Young (1950) has drawn on German for calques such as *owreset* 'translate' (*Epilogue to Theokritos*, line 2) from German *übersetzen* rather than straight loanwords.

10.3.2 Formation of New Words

So far, we have dealt with the introduction of new words through borrowing. This is in many ways the most interesting aspect of additions to the vocabulary, because the words borrowed often reflect recognisable cultural influences. Nevertheless, loanwords are not in our period the most common way of adding to the vocabulary of Scots. Numerically much more important is expansion of the vocabulary by building on the existing lexis of Scots whether by extending the meaning of existing words, creating new words by compounding, derivation and reduction, or adding together words to produce new phrases. The special status of Scots as a widely used literary and spoken language with no agreed standard vocabulary made it particularly open to innovation. In the absence of a dictionary of contemporary usage, writers and speakers clearly felt free to make new words, being assured that they could not be accused of using words which were 'not in the dictionary'. Even when Jamieson (1808) and SND were available, only some writers would want to confine themselves purely to words found in dictionaries with such a heavy orientation towards the historical.

McClure has suggested one index of the linguistic inventiveness at work in Scots, the 'astonishing number of words, some extremely imaginative, which have been attested once or twice only'. McClure (1981: 97) makes this point with a list of *ma-* words, but the same point can obviously be made from other parts of the dictionary. The *ga-* section of SND, including its supplement, yields the following selective list of words attested only once or twice: *gaabril* 'ill-natured and ugly person', *gaberosie* 'a kiss', *gabiator* 'gourmandiser' (from John Wilson's *Noctes Ambrosianae* 1855–6, vol. 3: 135), *gabsie* 'talkative person', *gaffie* 'grandfather', *gaggers* exclamation of disgust, *gainter* 'use conceited airs and gestures', *gairy* 'whim' (Hogg, *Connel of Dee*, line 38), *galdroch* 'greedy, long-necked, ill-shaped person', *galimavis* 'stupid person', *gall-flower* 'bedeguar', *Galliceer* 'Highlander', *galligaskin* 'goose-berry', *gallion* 'lean horse', *gally-gander* 'a fight with knives', *galorem* 'in abundance', *gameracus* 'clown or clumsy fellow', *gamfelet* 'gad about', *gammar* 'babble', *garhashloch* 'wet, windy and cold' (of weather), *gashie-wife* 'kind of shell', *gateless* 'pathless' (Waddell 1871: Ps. 78:40), *gaugnet* 'needle fish' and *gazzard* 'gossip'. There are many different kinds of words here – derivatives, compounds, fanciful variations on existing words, blends – and they come both from writers (some of whom I have listed) and from speakers (attested to in dictionaries and word-lists). The perceived right to create has clearly been exercised.

10.3.2.1 Compounds and Phrases

Compounding has been an important source of new words in English, particularly in the Old English and Modern English periods, as has the very similar process of forming new phrases. Scots is in this no exception. A cursory glance through CSD will immediately reveal that the reason why many of the longest entries are so long is precisely that they contain numerous compounds and phrases: the entry for *hand*, for instance, lists twenty-three compounds and thirty-eight phrases (of which thirteen and sixteen respectively first appeared after 1700). Some nouns were more productive before 1700, like *burgh*, *land* and *lord*; some, like *hand*, *hill*, *heid*, *kirk* and *water*, have always been productive; others have been particularly productive since 1700, like *craw*, *hen* and *hert*, or are in fact, like *sweetie*, only found in this period. The largest contribution to the vocabulary from nouns takes the form of compounds, but some nouns, for example *wey*, produce more phrases than compounds, and it is reasonable to consider phrases like the following as contributions to the lexis of Scots: *a' wey* 'everywhere', *aye the ae wey* 'always the same', *all weys* 'in every way', *by his wey o't* 'according to him', *in a dreedfu' way* 'in a state of distress', *be in the way of* 'have a habit of', *nae weys* 'in no way', *say ae wye* 'agree', *some ither way* 'somewhere else', *the wey that* 'because of the way in which', *the wey o* 'in the direction of', *wey o daein* 'means of livelihood' and *what wey* 'why' and 'how' (as in *What way is she?*). All of these are first attested after 1700.

The relevant parts of the CSD entry for *hen* provide a convenient example of compounds: the eighteenth century sees the arrival of *hen-bauk* 'tie-beam in cottage (where hens sit)' and *hen-hertit* 'cowardly', the nineteenth of *hen-aipple* 'fruit of the service tree', *hen-broth* 'chicken-broth', *hen's flesh* 'goose-flesh', *hen's gerse* 'enough grass to feed a hen' and figuratively 'a trifle', *hen-laft* 'hen-roost', *hen-pen* 'droppings of fowls used as manure', *hen's taes* 'scrawls' and *hen-ware* 'an edible seaweed', and the twentieth of *hen-crae* 'hen-coop', *hen's croft* 'part of field frequented by fowls', *hen's errand* 'fool's errand', *hen picks* or *hen-plooks* 'gooseflesh', *hen-ree* hen-run', *hen-taed* 'pigeon-toed' and *hen taes* 'crowfoot'. Furthermore, the long-established *hen-wife* 'a woman dealing with poultry' has extended to cover 'a man who concerns himself with what are seen as women's matters'. These Scots compounds are not without parallels in English, and there may well have been productive interaction between the two languages: as SND points out, *hen* often takes in Scots the role of *chicken*, as in *hen-broth* and *hen-hertit*, and this extends to the use of *hen* as a verb for English 'chicken out'. We might also note the way in which it fulfils the role of English *fool*, *goose*, *pigeon* and *crow* in, respectively, *hen's erran*, *hen's flesh*, *hen-taed* and *hen taes*. *Hen-hertit*, *hen's erran* and the phrase *to have a memory like a hen* applied to a forgetful person imply that hens are not held in high regard, but *hen* has also been used in Scots as a familiar way of addressing a girl or woman since the later eighteenth century, no doubt reflecting the affection in which farmyard fowls are often held. (Compare English *chickabiddy* used as an affectionate address to a child.) Thus one small word has produced a host of compounds, some purely functional, others more imaginative. However, it is worth noting that, with the exception of *hen-broth* and *hen-hertit*, these usages are geographically limited within Scotland, reminding us that much of the creativity in modern Scots is at local dialect level.

Turning to adjectives and adverbs, *auld, gray, half, hard, heich, ill, lang, muckle, reid, sair, wee, weel* and others have provided many new compounds since 1700. With verbs, most of the activity lies with the formation of phrases, particularly of the verb–particle kind. For example, *haud* has combined with *(a)back, aff, again, awa, awa frae, by, for, forrit, in, in about, in with, out, till, to, up, up to, up wi* and *wi*, with many of these phrases first appearing in our period. Some of these in their turn generate noun compounds like *haud-again* 'opposition, hindrance', a nineteenth-century creation, and *haud-doon* 'a handicap', a twentieth-century one. Verbs productive after 1700 include *ca, come, gae, gang, lat, lay, lie* and *tak*. Some of the verb-particle phrases are replicated in English, but they have different meanings, and it seems highly likely that we are dealing with separate creations in Scots, rather than borrowings from English. Moreover, as with *chicken* and *hen* discussed above, Scots often uses a different verb in creating equivalent phrases: *haud* sometimes performs the role of English *keep*, as in *haud at* and *haud up wi*, and *win* corresponds to English *get*, as in *win aff* and *win out*. In Scots as in English, verb-particle phrases generally belong to an informal register where they fulfil the role that foreign borrowings like *persist* (*haud at*) and *escape* (*win out*) have in more formal language. Their proliferation in Modern Scots has made a large contribution to the vigour of its colloquial register.

In English, phrasal verbs date from the later thirteenth century and have become increasingly common. The earlier practice, dating back to Old English and only gradually displaced, is the use of the particle as the first element in a compound to form both verbs and nouns. Earlier Scots has plenty of examples of this, some shared with English, others, such as *outgang, outquit, outreik, outrig, outwale, upbiggit, upheeze* and the noun *owercome*, limited to Scots. All of these except *outquit* and *upheeze* (which was revived in the nineteenth century) continued in use after 1700 and in some cases added new meanings. In more recent times, Scots seems to be more open than English to the creation of such compounds, although they are nowhere near as common as the phrasal verbs and nouns. Murison (1971: 172) has suggested that 'the influence of Flemings in Scotland' may have helped bring about greater use of these compounds in Older Scots, since they are common in Flemish and Dutch, and it is further possible that the ongoing influence of Dutch encouraged their continued creation at a later period. Certainly, the last three centuries have seen the arrival of *outding* 'surpass', *owercoup* 'overturn', *upget* 'get up', *uplook* 'respite' and *upredd* 'tidy; cleaning up' (verb and noun) as well as such derivatives as *upmade* 'pleased' or 'elated', used in Southern Scots. The greater willingness of Scots to generate these forms is evident in *upsticken* or *upstuck* meaning 'conceited', which is first attested in the nineteenth century and corresponds exactly to English *stuck up* just as the nonce-word *upbuckled* (1873) parallels English *buckled up*. In each case, the English equivalents (which occur earlier) probably inspired the Scots compounds, but it is the Scots writers who find it natural to create the forms with prefixed particle. Nouns, too, have been created on this model such as, in the nineteenth century, *ongang* 'starting up machinery; rowdy behaviour' and, in the twentieth, *onhing* 'waiting around'.

Many, probably the majority, of these compounds denote everyday things, activities, emotions and attitudes applying in a broad sphere of life, but certain specific phrases also show the language responding to particular changes in society. With industrialisation came factory workers or *mill-yins* (a twentieth-century coinage) who might in the nineteenth century become sick with *mill-fever* from working in overcrowded factories or with *milk-reek* caused by the poisonous fumes of lead-smelting furnaces. Motherwell became a centre of steel-making, and its football team was nicknamed *the Steelmen*. Mechanisation spread to agriculture, where a steam threshing mill, often a travelling one, was known as a *steam-mill*. As people moved to the expanding cities, many new things were needed, including public toilets. In the men's toilet, one might find the kind of urinal known in Glasgow as a *wally waw*, literally 'porcelain wall'. Almost all forms of activity have changed in some way; as it became easier to travel around the country and compete away from home, the old rough and ready sport of curling became more sophisticated and regulated, and with this came a whole set of new terms including compounds like *inring*, *outring*, *inwick* and *outwick*.

Compounds are a natural and obvious resource for writers of synthetic Scots[4] who want to enlarge the vocabulary at their command, but some are more willing than others to use it. Sydney Goodsir Smith has *ayebidan* 'everlasting' (*The Grace of God and the Meth-Drinker*, line 42) and, from the same poem, *fozie-fousome* (line 5) and *scheer-bricht* (line 27), in each of which he combines an archaic word or meaning of a word (*fousome* 'filthy' and *scheer* 'bright') with a still current term – *fozie* here means 'ragged'. Similarly, Douglas Young in the title of his poem *Ice-Flumes Owregie their Lades* creates a word for 'glacier' by combining *ice* with the archaic *flume* 'river', and his adverb–verb combination *owregie* is a revival of an obsolete term meaning 'surrender'. However, *dounpitten* 'put down, paid' (*Thonder They Ligg*, line 36) is his own creation. The word that MacDiarmid used for the title of his first collection of Scots poems, *Sangschaw*, was not his own, but it was a recent creation. From the sixteenth century on a *wappenshaw* (literally 'weaponshow') was, as all readers of *Old Mortality* will know, a review of the men under arms in a particular district or lordship, but in the nineteenth century it came, usually with the spelling *wapinschaw*, to be applied to a rifle-shooting competition. Early in the twentieth century, *sangschaw* was suggested as the name for a singing competition (SND, s.r. *sang* n., 1 (iv)). That earlier synthesiser Waddell has a large number of compounds, some specifically religious, others of more general use. Thus we find *blythe-bid* 'bless' (Ps. 28:9), *erran-rinner* 'angel' (Ps. 34:7), *furth-tell* 'declare' (Ps. 18:1), *in-win* 'breaking in' (Ps. 144:14), *kith-gettin* 'generation' (Ps. 10:6), *out-bide* 'someone who lives out of doors' (Is. 16:3) and *Quattin Day* 'Sabbath' (Heading to Ps. 93). Waddell's already-mentioned reliance on German is in evidence here as well: his *heal-ha'din* 'salvation' (Ps. 3:8) is influenced by German *Heil* 'salvation', although *heal* was used in earlier Scots in the sense 'salvation'.

Another common form of compounding is with place-names, often with jocular intent. In the eighteenth and nineteenth centuries, *Lammermuir lion* is used as a jocular name for a sheep, the Lammermuir Hills being sheep country, and in the nineteenth century we find a reference to *Paisley mittens* meaning 'trouser pockets' with the implication that laziness is a characteristic of *Paisley bodies* (a slightly derogatory term first found in the seventeenth century). Similarly, *Paisley Play* is a simple way of playing whist. The only consolation to those suffering from these unjust suggestions is that they are freely applied elsewhere as well: a synonym for *Paisley mittens* is *Kilmarnock mittens*, found right at the end of the nineteenth century, just as in the twentieth century a hammer is both a *Paisley screwdriver* and a *Glesca screwdriver*. Kilmarnock is further maligned in the twentieth century with *Kilmarnock shot*, a term applied to various kinds of play which are considered to be unsporting, but it is also associated with serious compounds like *Kilmarnock bonnet* 'broad, flat woollen bonnet' and *Kilmarnock hood* 'woollen conical skull-cap', both often shortened simply to *Kilmarnock*. Personal names can only be used in compounds: a very localised case is *Swankie's doo* or *Swankie's hen*, a jocular name for a sea gull – *Swankie* is a common surname in the fishing town of Arbroath. In the field of literature, Allan Ramsay coined the name *Standard Habbie* for the stanzaic form used in the seventeenth-century poem *The Life and Death of Habbie Simpson, the Piper of Kilbarchan* and imitated by Ramsay himself, Burns, Fergusson and others.

10.3.2.2   Blends

Blends represent another way of bringing together two separate words as one new word. Although they can often be very suggestive, as Lewis Carroll's *slithy* shows, they are often less immediately intelligible than compounds and are much less frequent. A blend seems almost inevitable where there are two words of similar form and meaning; thus the later twentieth-century Scots *skintie*, also found in northern English dialects, is a conflation of *skimpy* and *scanty* and has much the same meaning. On the other hand, *mirligoes* 'dizziness' is a blend of quite unrelated words, *mirl* 'to speckle', referring to the sensation of seeing spots in front of one's eyes, and *vertigo*, while the rare and now obsolete *cantation* 'conversation' could be seen as a blend of the verb *cant* 'talk' and *conversation*. Among literary nonce-blends, one might note John Wilson's already-mentioned *gabiator* 'gourmandiser' (from *gab* plus *gladiator*; but compare Scots *rabiator* 'a villain') and Douglas Young's *flather* 'flurry' (applied to the frothing of waves; *Requiem*, line 2), which could be seen as a blend of *fluther* 'hurry, bustle' (a word which Jamieson suggested was primarily concerned with the rushing of water) and *lather*.

Acronyms are in a way a more drastic kind of blend. They have been a very popular source of new words in recent English, and Scots has some of its own. At the end of the nineteenth century, the term *paf* came into use as a convenient way of referring to herrings from the three major selling points of *P*eterhead, *A*berdeen and *F*raserburgh.

10.3.2.3   Derivation

Derivatives, formed by adding affixes of various kinds to existing words, are probably numerically somewhat fewer in Scots dictionaries than compounds and phrases but they include many very common words, as will be obvious if we merely take such diminutives as *mannie, wifie, lassie* and *laddie*. The suffix *-ie* is particularly flexible, forming adjectives from nouns (*goskie* 'luxuriant' from *gosk* 'coarse, rank grass produced by cattle droppings') and from verbs (*grippie* 'avaricious'); making nouns from verbs (*winnie* 'a marbles game in which the winner keeps his gains' and *plottie* 'a hot drink' from *plot* 'scald'); allowing one noun to give rise to another (*batchie* 'baker', from *batch of bread*, and *steamie* 'public washhouse'). As a diminutive, *-ie* has a rival in *-ock* which gives us *devilock* and *Sannock*, an alternative to *Sandie*, and also appears in *mealock* 'crumb' derived from *meal* 'crumble'. *Mealock* gives rise in its turn to a double diminutive form *meelackie*, recorded by Jamieson in 1808 and still known in the north-east in the 1960s. Whether or not the *ock* in *haddock* is of the same origin is uncertain – the origin of the whole word is obscure – but the very common Scots alternative *haddie* could have arisen by replacing one perceived diminutive with another.

Some of the words formed with *-ie* or *-y* are themselves productive with proliferating meanings and compounds. A good example of this is *cutty*, a seventeenth-century creation with many post-1700 compounds. Some of these compounds are shortened back to *cutty*, thus adding to *cutty's* meanings. As an adjective, *cutty* means 'short, stumpy' and (less commonly) 'short-tempered' and as a noun 'a short dumpy girl or a mischievous one', 'a hare' and 'the black guillemot'; even, in Caithness and Orkney, 'a small oatcake, often with a hole in the centre'. It is used affectionately to a child and contemptuously of a woman, in the latter case perhaps as a development from the compound *cutty quean*, a disparaging term applied to a woman but first attested applied jocularly to a wren, itself quite often called a *cutty-wran*. Two further compounds, *cutty-pipe* and *cutty-spoon*, are both shortened to *cutty* and give it the meanings 'a short pipe' and 'a short-handled spoon', and from the latter meaning develops the verb 'eat greedily' as well as the new compounds *cutty-basket* 'basket for holding cutties' and *cutty-free* 'able to take one's food', each of which is attested only once. Alternative names for the pipe are *cutty-clay* and *cutty-gun*, while the best-known compounds are probably *cutty-stool* applied to a low stool, especially the one used in church as a stool of repentance, and *cutty-sark* 'a short chemise', its fame established by Burns in *Tam o' Shanter* (line 201) and renewed as the name of an exceptionally fast sailing ship built on the Clyde in 1869, now open to public exhibition in Greenwich.

A *cutty-stoup* is defined by Jamieson in his *Supplement* as 'a pewter vessel containing the eighth part of a chopin or quart', and a *cutty-mun* is 'a short-hafted, small-mouthed spoon', although in Ramsay's addition to *Christ's Kirk on the Green* 'Cuttymun and Treladle' seems to be the name of a dance tune. *Cutty-gun*, *cutty-stoup* and *cutty-mun* are all open to somewhat different interpretation in the poem *Andrew and his Cuttie Gun* from *The Merry Muses of Caledonia* (Barke and Goodsir Smith 1965: 147–8). Finally, one must mention two contributions peculiar to Mactaggart's (1824) *Gallovidian Encyclopedia*: he notes the application of *cutty-mun* to 'A short person, with an extremely small face' and is the only source for 'Cutty-Glies – A little squat-made female, extremely fond of the male creation, and good at winking or *glying*'. Apart from *cutty* itself in the sense of 'spoon' and the compound *cutty-spoon*, all of these are only attested after 1700. Some have been more widely used than others, some are now obsolete; *cutty* is evidently past its prime as a stimulus for new words, but it has obviously been a most productive word. It also illustrates that word-formation is not a simple progression, for example from stem to derivative to compound, but an interactive process in which a compound can transfer its meaning to one of its elements (itself a derivative of another word) and give rise to new compounds, or the presence of one compound can apparently stimulate the creation of another.

The ending *-ie* or *-y* is used as a suffix in other varieties of English, but Scots has some of its own distinctive suffixes, such as the versatile *rife* which has been particularly active as a component in new words since 1700. It can be added to nouns and verbs with the sense of 'liable to', as in *flichtrife* 'unsteady, fickle' and *mockrife* 'mocking', or to adjectives with intensive force as in *coolrife* and *wildrife*. Such words are a useful model for the creativity of writers, such as in Hogg's nonce-word *steelrife* which could mean either 'steely, hard' or 'violent' (Mack 1976: 94).

In the group of words *docus*, *gawpus*, *govus*, *gropus* and *gumpus*, applied variously to someone who is foolish or stupid or simple-minded, we find a suffix of a more indeterminate nature. It has been added to *gaup* and *gove* which mean 'stare' and *gumph* which means 'fool'; *gropus* may be a corruption of *gawpus*, and the first element of *docus* has not been identified. The ending has taken on what SND calls 'slightly disparaging force, connoting smallness, dullness or stupidity' and functions effectively in creating new words despite the vagueness of its meaning. Three *-us* words of uncertain meaning occur in a children's rhyme recorded by Robert Chambers (1870: 113), which SND conjectures may have originated in a parody of the Latin of scholars and churchmen:

> The gray cat o' grapus
> Is up the steps o' fundus
> Wi' montapus on her tail.

An extended form appears in *luckiedaicus* 'a rough old woman' and *pilliedacus*, used in the phrase *the heid pilliedacus* 'the boss'.

Suffixes are also added to place-names. For example, in the nineteenth century there appear two terms uncomplimentary to the people of Fife – *Fifer* is an inhabitant of Fife often with implications of greed and cunning, and *Fifish* means 'eccentric'. Twentieth-century additions are more neutral in tone: a *fifie* is a kind of fishing boat, and *Fifer* extends to cover a kind of marble.

Derivation by prefixes is similarly productive. The reversive prefix *mis-* provides words which are either unknown in English, like *mislikely* 'make unlikely, smirch', *misliken* 'speak ill of', *mismarrow* 'mismatch' and *misrestit* 'suffering from loss of sleep', or used with a different meaning, like *misfit* 'displease'. To these we can add the synthetic Scots of Waddell's creations *mislooin* 'displeasure' (Ps. 2:5) and *misgate* 'transgression' (Ps. 25:7). In *misguggle* 'spoil with rough handling' and *mismaggle* 'disarrange', *mis-* has intensive force; these words derive from the verbs *guggle* 'soil' and *maggle* 'spoil, mangle'. *Misanswer* is found in fifteenth- and sixteenth-century English but is created anew in the twentieth century in Ulster, where it means 'give a rude answer'. In the north-east it means 'disobey', building on the local use of *answer* to mean 'obey', also apparently a twentieth-century development. *Misbelieve* in the sense of 'disbelieve' is found in Middle Scots and revived in the nineteenth century. Likewise *disconvenient* and *disconvenience*: their earlier use, in English or Scots, is probably a borrowing from Latin *disconveniens* but, given the rarity of borrowings from Latin into Scots in the nineteenth century, their appearance then may be more plausibly explained as a use of the prefix *dis-* which also appears in *dispeace*, *dishealth* and the nonce-word *discompliment*.

Scots has, of course, its own reversing prefix *wan-*, also appearing as a separate word meaning 'lacking'. Found in Old English but dying out in southern England before the end of the Middle English period, it was used in a number of words in the Older Scots period, some of which survive into our period like *wanchance*, *wanhap* and *wanluck*, all meaning 'misfortune', and *wanwordy* 'unworthy, worthless'. From these come some simple derivatives or back-formations like *wanchancy* 'unlucky' and *wanworth* 'something worthless'. *Wanchancy* may also have been modelled on the existing *unchancy* as *wansonsy* probably is on *unsonsy*. Riddell's Psalms of 1857 are SND's only source for *wanhonor* 'dishonour' (Ps. 69:16), *wantimely* 'untimely' (Ps. 58:8) and the verb *wanrest* in the meaning of 'to upset' (Ps. 42:5), and they may be purely literary creations since Riddell (1857) is patently not a guide to contemporary spoken usage. On the other hand, *wan-* or *wun-* is the Southern Scots pronunciation of *un-* (described by Murray (1873: 131) as 'disappearing' but not, apparently, obsolete), and these may simply be representations of Southern Scots pronunciations of *un-* forms of these words. In Shetland and Orkney, the use of *wan-* was probably reinforced by the exactly parallel Scandinavian *van-*, but words like *wanfine* 'an unprofitable ending', *wanjoy* 'sorrow' and *wanpeace* 'strife' which combine *wan-* with words of Romance origin are clearly new creations and not borrowings from a Scandinavian source. Further *wan-* words appearing after 1700 are either merely Scotticisations of English words like *wanbritherly*, *wanearthly* and *wantidy* or rather self-conscious literary creations used by only one author, like *wanbod* 'damaging report' (based on an obsolete sense of *bode* 'news') and *wanliesum* 'unlovely'.

A further Scots prefix, of less straightforward origin and meaning, is *cur* or *currie*; in Older Scots it only appears in the word *curfuffle* (now found in English), but in the later period it forms a part of many words, some of which, however, are not all that common. As

SND notes, in most words its force is intensive, in others the implied meaning is 'awry' or 'closely'. Nor are the elements with which it combines always easily identifiable: the origins of the second elements in *curcuddoch* 'intimate, good-humoured', *curjute* 'overwhelm' and *curmud* 'close, intimate' are uncertain, but in *curgellit* 'shocked', *curmurring* 'a low rumbling, a cat's purring etc.' and *curnab* 'grab' they have been identified as *geal* 'freeze', *murr* 'purr, murmur' and the English slang *nab*. *Currie-* appears in *currieboram*, *curriebuction* and *curriemushel*, all of which have much the same meaning of 'a confused crowd of people', and in *currieshang* (or *collieshangie*) and *curriewurrie* which mean 'a violent quarrel'. *Cur-* takes other forms as well: *gar-* in the rare *gargrugous* 'austere and frightening' and probably *gil-* in *gilravage* meaning 'feast riotously, make merry noisily, rove about, devour' as a verb and with similar meanings as a noun.

Another such rather ill-defined but nevertheless forceful prefix is *ram-* (or *rum-*), used, as SND notes, 'with intensive force before words which gen[erally] imply something forcible, vigorous or disorderly'. Its origin is uncertain, but in some cases its use may be influenced by the popular notion of a ram (the male sheep) as a headstrong and violent animal. If this implication was not originally present, it was subsequently understood through folk etymology as when Mactaggart, after glossing *skerie* as 'somewhat restive', defines *ramskerie* as 'very restive and lustful; of the nature of a ram'. Some of these words are quite rare, like *ramskerie* and *ramskittle* 'set about with violence', but *ramfeezle* 'muddle, confuse' has achieved some popularity, no doubt because it occurs in Burns (in his second *Epistle to J. Lapraik*, line 13) and was indeed apparently his creation. The presence of the *ram-* prefix has both affected the form of other words – *robust* is altered, rather appropriately, to *rambust* – and perhaps encouraged the use of the English word *ramshackle*. *Ramshackle* has then taken on new meanings (for example 'a thoughtless fellow') in Scots and influenced the formation of the nonce-word *ramsheuchet* 'dishevelled' from *sheuch* 'distort'. *Cur-* and *ram-* words are quite numerous though not all widely used; the popularity of such formations suggests that the presence of such vaguely defined prefixes constitutes an irresistible invitation to use them, especially in a strongly colloquial context where innovation in language is especially welcomed. Moreover, the abrupt sounds of *cur*, *ga*, *gil* and *ram* produce some of those words with strong phonetic impact which have been seen as peculiarly characteristic of Scots: to quote McClure (1990: 138), 'No other European language, it is safe to say, can compete with Scots for the wealth of words in which a powerful semantic force is accompanied by a distinctive and striking phonological shape'.

10.3.2.4   Reduplication

In English, the kind of reduplication found in *curriewurrie* is a feature of both very informal language and the language used by and to children. Likewise in Scots, it appears in the children's counting-out rhyme *Eetle, ottle, black bottle, Eetle, ottle, out*, as the name for blind-man's buff, *glim-glam* (from *glaum* 'an unsuccessful snatch at something'), and in a children's game where the key question is *Eetie ottie for a tottie, where shall this boy go?* In adult language, *equal* has been transformed into *eeksie-peeksie* meaning 'on an equality, much alike', and *row* has been expanded to *towrow* meaning 'an uproar'. *Ramstam* 'headstrong' (also used as an adverb, noun and verb) is a slightly different case in that it is not an entirely arbitrary expansion of *stam* 'stamp along, blunder onwards, stagger'; its first element is, or can be identified with, the prefix *ram-*. From their very structure, such reduplicated forms have a natural forcefulness, and their popularity has extended to the modern writers of synthetic Scots, with MacDiarmid, for instance, having *heich-skeich* (*A Drunk Man Looks at the Thistle*, line 424) and Sydney Goodsir Smith *hidderie-hetterie* (*The Grace of God and the Meth-Drinker*, line 15).

10.3.2.5   Clipping

This same colloquial vigour which encourages the formation of the *cur-* compounds ensures the presence of another common feature of colloquial language, clipping. When clipped, words often develop a different meaning: *mineer* is a clipped form of *domineer* appearing in the later nineteenth century but means 'make a din', and in the twentieth century has also become a noun. One cause of clipping is misunderstanding of a word's make-up. Nouns beginning with an *a* or *n* are liable to lose it when it is wrongly thought to be the indefinite article or part of it. Thus *peaser* 'a drink of liquor, especially whisky' is shortened from *appeaser*, and in the north-east *ation* or *etion* has been formed from *nation* and incidentally in this form has preserved a meaning found in earlier Scots and English, 'stock, breed'. *Stupe* 'a fool', on the other hand, is a back-formation from *stupid*.

Often a diminutive ending is added to a clipping: in the nineteenth century, *Episcopalian* is clipped at both ends to give *Piskie*, and *Prodistan*, a form of *Protestant*, gives *Proddie*. A Roman Catholic is a *Pape*, shortened from *Papist*. *Scavenger* is shortened to *scaffie* and takes the meaning 'a street-sweeper, a refuse-collector'; a refuse-collector's truck can be a *scaffie-cairt*. In the twentieth century, *gutties*, a name given in Glasgow and surrounding areas to gymshoes, is from a shortening of *gutta-percha*, a material used in making the soles, and the alternative name *sannies* is from *sandshoes*, *airie* is short for *airieplane* a Glasgow pronunciation of *aeroplane*, while *Accies* serves as a nickname generally for a group of students of an Academy and specifically for the Hamilton Academicals football team. The Aberdeen football team also has a clipped name, *the Dons*, if it is short for *Aberdonians*, but popular etymology explains the name as referring to the team's being founded by teachers. Perhaps we should think of both origins as functioning here: right from the beginning, the word could have been intended to convey both implications, and the two possible explanations can operate simultaneously to reinforce the perceived appropriateness of the name.

Personal names are regularly clipped and equally regularly have diminutive endings added. These diminutive forms then develop new meanings, one of the more sinister being *shusy* (from *Susie*) which came to mean a corpse used in anatomy lessons and very often stolen from the grave. As one might expect, female names are also used as derogatory terms for effeminate males; this happens with *jenny*, *jessie*, *katie* and *teenie*, all in the twentieth century. *Jenny Wullock* 'a hermaphrodite' fittingly combines male and female names, *Wullock* being a diminutive of *William*. *Teenie* (from *Christina*) also means a domestic servant; an earlier term was *Girzie* (from a metathesised form of *Grizzel*, itself from *Griselda*). *Jenny*, *Johnnie*, *Tammie* and *Willie* all combine with *a'thing* to mean a male or female owner of a general store, and *Jimmie*, now most familiar as a way of addressing a man, especially a stranger, also means a white pudding or an oatmeal pudding, otherwise known as a *mealie-jimmie*.

10.3.3   Variant Forms and Popular Etymology

Some Scots terms are simply variant forms of other Scots or English terms, but they often develop new meanings. *Hemmel* is apparently a metathesised form of *helm* but has come to mean 'a shed and attached open area used for housing cattle', and *rickmatick* is a variant of *arithmetic* but in the common phrase *the hale rickmatick* means 'the whole caboodle'. Words like *rickmatick* and *audiscence* 'attention, encouragement to speak', a corruption of *audience*, are evidence of a spoken language free from the constraints imposed on written language by the norms of spelling. In these circumstances, folk etymologies can flourish. Sometimes one case of folk etymology leads to another. When English *trullibubs* 'entrails' was changed in Scots to *trollie-bags* by folk etymology, the meaningful element was clearly *bags*. It seems likely that *trollie* was then related to either *troll* 'a slovenly person' or *trollop* 'an ungainly person' and, with further interpretation of *bags*, the meaning 'fat, unshapely person' emerged for *trollie-bags* in the latter part of the twentieth century as the original meaning died out. Folk etymology has also been at work in the case of the late nineteenth-century creation *joskin* which means 'a country bumpkin'. It would appear that *bumpkin* has been wrongly perceived as derived from *bump* and a new word created by replacing *bump* with *joss* 'jostle'. It is not, of course, only the 'folk' who can make mistakes about etymology. Scott's respelling of the word *hallockit* as *hellicat* and the way in which Cuddie uses it to describe 'that hellicat trooper, Tam Halliday' in *Old Mortality* (Lang 1898–9, vol. 5: 202) strongly suggests that Scott saw it a variant of *hellcat* whereas it actually derives from the verb *hallock* 'to behave in a crazy, half-witted, noisy manner'. Hogg, Barrie and James Lorimer subsequently use *hellicat* as a noun with very much the connotations suggested by Scott's spelling.

10.3.4   Extension and Transfer of Meaning

Although some developments will always be resisted, English is very open to the process by which the vocabulary of a language is enlarged through the extension or transfer of a word to cover new meanings, but Scots is perhaps even more open than English since the absence of an agreed standard of Scots makes innovation easier, as we have already noted. As so often in Scots, we face problems of dating in this area. The meanings attached to the word *souch* provide a necessary caution in this context. The layout of the CSD entry for the noun, which is more or less chronological, seems to show a logical sequence of development. Consider first the noun:[5]

> 1 the sound of the wind *esp* when long-drawn-out *16-*. 2 the rushing, roaring or murmuring of water *la18-*. 3 a rustling or whizzing sound, as of an object moving rapidly through the air; a whizzing blow *la18-*. 4 (1) a deep sigh or gasp, heavy breathing, panting *la18-*. (2) heavy breathing in sleep; a snooze *19-*. 5 a song, tune, melody *19-*. 6 (1) the sound or timbre of a voice, an accent, way of speaking *la18-*. (2) *specif* a high-pitched, nasal way of speaking, a whine, *esp* in preaching *18-e20*. 7 general feeling or opinion, attitude, style *18-*. 8 gossip, rumour, scandal *19-*. 9 an uproar, fuss *la19-*.

Allowing for the likelihood that meanings attested later in the eighteenth century were present earlier in the century, the sequence suggested here is that the word begins with a specific meaning, 'the sound of the wind', is extended to the sound of moving water and then generalised to cover any kind of similar sound. At the same time, new specific senses relating to the sound of a person's breath develop and these are extended to include the sound of a speaking voice. From 'the sound of a voice' to 'opinion' is a natural step and the meanings 'gossip' and then 'fuss, uproar' follow on. By this account, sense 5 'a song' is misplaced and is a development from the meaning 'sound of a voice'. The neatness and apparent logicality of this sequence seems to support the dating – until we look at the meanings of the verb:

> 1 *vi, of objects moving through the air* whizz, buss, drone, flap, whirr *la15-*. 2 *of leaves etc* rustle, whisper; *of water* ripple, gurgle, make a slapping sound *16-*. 3 *of wind* make a rushing, moaning, murmuring sound *la18-*. 4 breathe heavily, sigh, wheeze, splutter, gurgle *18-*. 5 **souch awa** breathe one's last *la18-*. 6 *vti* sing softly, hum, whistle *18-*. 7 *vi of music* sound, waft *19-*.

Here a quite different sequence is suggested. The verb starts with a general meaning applied to any object moving through the air. This is then specialised to refer to the wind, water and a person's breath. *Souch awa* 'breathe one's last' is a further specialisation of the application to a person's breath, as is 'sing softly, hum', and from this last sense (but with perhaps some influence from the original general meaning) develops the application to music wafting through the air. Thus the noun meanings suggest broadening from a specific application, while the verbs suggest that the broad meaning was there at the beginning, although both agree in suggesting that the specific application to breath, voice and song is a later development. We might further note that *swogan*, the Old English verb from which this derives, had the meaning 'make a sound, move with noise, rush, roar' or figuratively 'move with violence, enter with force, invade' (Bosworth 1882–98: s.v. *swogan*). It is of course perfectly possible for a verb meaning to exist while the corresponding noun does not have the corresponding sense; but, given the incompleteness of our record of Scots, we might wonder whether the noun also had the general application to things passing through the air at an earlier stage than the later eighteenth century. The possibility that noun or verb senses developed not from other meanings of their own part of speech but by conversion from the other part of speech must be taken into account. All this provides an illustration of a well-recognised fact, that it is hard to trace with any certainty the exact path of a word's semantic development, but more pertinently in this context it reminds us to be wary in accepting the dating of developments derived from the DOST (or in this case the OED) and SND citations. At the same time, DOST, the OED and SND do provide a remarkably full, though not complete, record and it would be silly to throw our hands up in the air and say that no generalised comments are possible.

With this proviso in mind, we can see that many words do seem to have developed substantial new senses since 1700. This process is, of course, by no means limited to the last three centuries, and a verb like *set* will provide us with an example of semantic extension both before and after 1700. Its meanings as recorded in CSD are set out in Table 10.1 illustrating the period over which they were in use. In the first place, it can be seen that the process has been going on throughout the history of Scots, and secondly that it has been especially productive since 1700 although many of the senses have been limited to only part of the country. This verb is perhaps atypical in that there are no cases of loss of meaning in the last three centuries, but it certainly makes clear how much, without adding any new words, Scots has been able to expand the range of referents covered by existing individual words. Of course, in some cases alternative words exist in the Scots lexis for the various referents covered here, but, if nothing else, the range of choice is expanded.

Extension of meaning is one of a number of ways of naming new things and actions. Thus *stance*, which already meant generally 'a standing place' and specifically, among other things, 'a place for a drove of cattle to stop overnight', came in the twentieth century to refer first to a place where buses or taxis stand waiting for passengers and then to any bus-stop,

Table 10.1

Century:	14	15	16	17	18	19	20
1 = set	*	**	**	**	**	**	**
2 (1) *vtr* cause or make to sit, seat, place on a seat	*				*	**	**
2 (2) *vt* cause (an assembly etc) to sit	*	**	**				
3 *vi* sit, be seated	*				**	**	**
4 stack peats in rickles to dry							**
5 dislocate (one's neck)							**
6 bring (a mill) to a stop by turning off the water from the wheel					**	**	**
7 *vi and in passive, of plants and animals* stop growing, have the growth checked						**	**
8 *vt* disgust, nauseate						**	**
9 *vi, of a horse* jib, become restive, refuse to obey the rider or driver						*	**
10 (1) start off, set out, make one's way				**	**	**	**
10 (2) *vt* direct or guide in a certain course						**	**
10 (3) cause to go, send (a person or thing)					*	**	**
10 (4) accompany, escort, convey (a person home *etc*)					**	**	**
11 leave (milk) standing for the cream to rise							**
12 (1) let by contract, lease		**	**	**	**	**	**
12 (2) *vi* be leased, hired out, fetch a rent					**	**	**
13 apply oneself (to do something)			*				
14 sight or make (land)				*			
15 *law* reject, set aside				*			
16 (1) *freq impersonal, with infin, of a thing or action, now sometimes ironic* be seemly or suitable for, become, suit	*	**	**	**	**	**	**
16 (2) *of a person* look becoming in						**	**

whether or not the bus regularly waits there. The action of switching off an electrical appliance is now covered in parts of Scotland by the verbal phrase *sneck off*, an extension of the meaning of a verb meaning 'to fasten with a latch'; and *lum*, a traditional word for a chimney, is now used to refer to the funnel on a locomotive or a steamship. (It also, from the similarity of shape, came to refer in the later nineteenth century to a top hat.) The arrival of an organised police force is another kind of innovation which took place within our period. The normal term for the police is the one shared with English, although in Central and Southern Scots the word is pronounced with the stress on the first syllable and hence regularly spelt *polis*, but they and their activities can also be referred to by extending the meaning of existing words. *Lift* in the twentieth century takes on the meaning of 'arrest', rather at odds with the earlier application to the stealing of cattle, and a detective or policeman is referred to in various localities as a *snout*. Yet another innovation is the health visitor, known in Glasgow as a *green lady*, from the colour of the uniform worn, but the name continues though the uniform has gone. This looks at first to be simply an innocent, newly created compound but may well be a case of rather cunning transfer of meaning – well before health visitors appeared on the scene, Glasgow children were already playing a game in which a child calls others up a dark stair with the words 'Green Lady, Green Lady, come up for your tea'. Originally the green lady was a ghost, green being associated with death in folklore.

Sometimes a word can be transferred to refer to something which is quite different in physical form but serves the same function. *Wall*, the Scots equivalent to English *well*, has in both of the two forms extended its range to cover first from the sixteenth century a drinking fountain, then from the nineteenth century a stand-pump and finally in the twentieth century a cold-water tap at a sink. Interestingly, Macafee reports continuing use in Glasgow of *well* in this last sense (*wall* was unknown to the younger speakers and stigmatised by some of the older ones) but also records that some speakers feel it is inappropriate to transfer it further to the kind of taps found in modern houses (Macafee 1994a: 108–10). Perhaps this adaptable word is about to hit the limits of its adaptability. Similarly, as the population has moved from the country to cities and as sanitation has improved, the meaning of *midden* has extended from the original sense of 'a dung-heap' to cover more generally a compost-heap or a place to put household rubbish until it has finally come to mean 'a dustbin' – in Glasgow also referred to as a *midgie*. Once again the word may have reached the limits of its adaptability: Macafee (1994a: 100) records that in Glasgow 'The term *midden* or *midgie* is still applied to various refuse collection arrangements (frequently a semi-covered "bin area"), but not to the disposal chutes found in some high-rises'. *Midgie* in its turn forms part of compounds to denote associated aspects of modern life – the dustman is a *midgie-man* (also known as a *binnie*) and his lorry is a *midgie-motor*.

As one might expect, *midden* has also become a term of abuse, another common way in which a word's meaning may be extended. The use of the word *bun* as a term of abuse for a woman is puzzling if we are thinking of the normal English meaning of the word, especially as Macafee (1994a: 144) describes it as 'pretty well a swear word' in Glasgow. In fact it appears to be a development of a later nineteenth-century colloquial meaning 'a young woman', although by at least 1934 it had come in Glasgow to mean 'a whore' (Partridge 1984: s.v. *bun*). Another Glasgow term is *keech*, which M. Munro (1985: 58) notes is 'Sometimes used as a term for a despicable person'. Its normal meaning is 'excrement' or 'filth', and in origin it is a child's variant form of *cach*, itself a variant of the more widely, known *cack*. Other abusive terms are milder in their tone: in the later twentieth century, *heifer* 'a young cow' has been applied in the north-east, Fife and Midlothian to a big, awkward, clumsy person, usually a woman, while since the eighteenth century *messan*, which originally meant 'a small pet dog' and then derogatively 'a mongrel', has come into use as a contemptuous term for people but, according to Munro's (1985: 45) account of Glasgow usage, it is 'used as a mildly insulting name, of the kind adults might use for a child: *Get out of that bunker ye dirty wee messin*'. The sense development is clear enough here, but sometimes the appropriateness of an abusive term is less obvious; for example, in the nineteenth century, *aumry*, a long-standing but now obsolete term for a cupboard or larder, came to be used for a stupid and clumsy person.

Although opposite in intention to terms of abuse, terms of endearment also obviously involve transfer of meaning. Some such terms appear incongruous to non-speakers of the language; generations of English-speaking schoolchildren have found amusement in the French *mon chou*. The same can apply to English-speakers encountering Scots terms, although Scots does share with English such long-established usages as *hinnie* (English *honey*) and *doo* (English *dove*). In the case of *worm*, however, Scots usage diverges from English. While it is not exactly a term of endearment, it can be used in Shetland and Angus without the full contemptuous force that it has in English but 'rather indicating commiseration or good-natured banter', as SND puts it. We have already noted the Scots use of *hen* as an affectionate form of address to a young girl, which may seem quaint to non-Scots. Its future life may be limited, to judge by an older speaker's comment reported by Macafee (1994a: 189): 'Ah remember Ah sayed tae ma wee granddaughter, *Com oan, hen. I'm not a hen.* Ah says, *Ah better watch what Ah'm sayin here.*' A similar development of meaning has taken place with *pout* which means 'a young fowl'; in its diminutive form, *poutie* (as well as being a term for a small haddock) was used affectionately in addressing a young girl or sweetheart from the eighteenth century, though this sense is perhaps now obsolete. More straightforwardly appropriate is the nineteenth-century adoption of *posy* for the same purpose, a usage which still survives.

Terms of abuse and endearment like these are essentially metaphors, and metaphor underlies many other extensions. Thus in the eighteenth century *wersh*, a word used to describe tasteless food or drink, was applied to various kinds of discourse, as when Patrick Walker in the 1720s speaks of 'wisned, warsh, coldrife formal sermons' (Hay Fleming 1901, vol. 1: 157). In the nineteenth century, *kinch* 'a kink in a rope' developed the meaning 'a tight corner, a predicament' and *thrum* 'a scrap of waste thread' came to mean 'a whim', while in the twentieth century *tunkit*, literally 'having lost all one's marbles in a game', took on the sense 'bankrupt'. Sometimes the figurative meaning ousts the original, literal one. In the nineteenth century, *kell* 'a woman's hairnet or cap' came to mean 'an incrustation of scabs or dirt on the head or face', and by the end of the century the original meaning had gone out of use.

Needless to say, such extensions can also take place with words shared with English. For instance, in the nineteenth century *key* comes to be applied figuratively from its musical use to 'a mood', *kick* comes to mean 'a dismissal' and *scent* takes on the extra meaning 'a small quantity'. One rather sad historical reminder is supplied by *tanyard* which, after the Poor Law Act of 1845, was applied in Caithness to the poorhouse, an extension of its earlier meaning of 'a place for worn-out horses to be disposed of'. Transfer of meaning can also take place when one element of a combination is dropped and the remaining element takes up the full meaning; thus the word *whisky* was soon dropped from the phrase *peat-reek whisky*, leaving *peat-reek* alone to find considerable use as a synonym for *whisky*. This may rather be a case of direct transference of meaning (as CSD treats it), but the phrase *peat-reek whisky* precedes (by a narrow margin) the first unambiguous use of *peat-reek* alone in this sense. Continuing the subject of drink, the very common use of *mortal* to mean 'extremely drunk' arises from dropping the second element of the phrases *mortal drunk* or *mortal fou* where *mortal* is an intensive adverb; a modern Glasgow variation is *mortalled*. In calling the hero of his poem *Tam o' Shanter* and describing him as wearing 'his guid blue bonnet' (line 91), the normal headwear at the time of Scottish peasants, Burns set in train a double process of transference. First of all, in the nineteenth century, the name of the character was transferred to his cap, and then in the twentieth century his Christian name alone, in its diminutive form *Tammie*, took on that meaning.

Rhyming slang is also open to this process; indeed, one of its attractions for its users lies in deliberately dropping the rhyming element and leaving a word which has no apparent connection at all with the word which it replaces. Glasgow speech is rich in such usages, and this must be recognised as one of the very productive areas of lexical growth in twentieth-century Glasgow; but, given the popularity of rhyming slang in other parts of the English-speaking world, it is not always easy to be certain that they originated in Scotland. Macafee's (1994a: 155–60) long list of rhyming slang recorded in Glasgow provides the following examples: *chorus and verse = erse* (arse), *chuckie stanes = weans*, *cornbeef = deef* (deaf), *winners and losers = troosers* (trousers) among many others. These are manifestly Scots in origin, either because Scots pronunciation is needed to produce the rhyme or because the words involved are already Scots words. No doubt at some time all have been shortened to the first element; certainly Munro (1985: 81) records the use of *corny* for 'deaf', and Clifford Hanley (1958: 58) uses *chuckies* for 'weans', two clear cases of the transference of a word's meaning to another quite unrelated word. Euphemism can have the same effect: in such phrases as *Praise be blest*, found since the eighteenth century, *praise* euphemistically substitutes for *God* or *the Lord*, and *guid* has the same function in a number of contexts from at least as early as Burns' 'Gude forgie me' (*Epistle to J. Lapraik, An Auld Scots Bard*, line 98). The Devil also must have his due share of euphemisms like *sorra*, found from the eighteenth century and still in some use, and *the bad man*, used especially by children in the later nineteenth and earlier twentieth centuries.

Through various associations, both place and personal names are liable to take on extended meaning. Kelton in Kirkcudbrightshire and Kirdamdie in Ayrshire (locally pronounced with an *n* for the *m*) figure in two terms for 'a rumpus', *Kelton Hill Fair* and *kirdandy*; but *dundee* (or *dindee*) which has a similar meaning and thus looks like a parallel case is not derived from the place-name but from *din* and *adae* 'to do'. Surnames provide us with *shankie* 'a lavatory', easily recognisable as derived from the very well-known name of Shanks & Co., makers of lavatories, and *macallum* 'a raspberry-flavoured ice-cream' for which the origin is not so obvious. SND at first speculated that it was a pun on *mak, caul(d)* and *em'*, but the Supplement records an 'unconfirmed explanation' that it commemorates John McCallum of Bridgeton, a football player and later Provost of Rutherglen. McCallum was a popular figure in the 1880s, but the term was still known in the Central and Southern Scots areas eighty years later. Christian names give us, in Glasgow and its surroundings, two names for 'a Roman Catholic' *Dan* and *Tim*, with the latter giving rise to the rhyming slang *Jungle Jim*. A Protestant is a *Billy* with reference to William III.

Naturally, literary Scots makes use of similar processes but perhaps more self-consciously. In Waddell's Psalms, *halirude* (Ps. 78:54) or *haly-rood* (Ps. 150:1) serves as a translation of a Hebrew word which the *Authorised Version* renders as *sanctuary*. Presumably this is because Holyrood Abbey was a sanctuary; I know of no other such use of the term. As a translator of a fixed text dealing with certain key concepts and set in a distant time and place, Waddell was obliged to come up with words for such diverse things as 'an offering', 'sin' and 'a tent'. These things are traditionally referred to in Scotland with words shared with English, but Waddell looks for a distinctively Scots diction. He shows some ingenuity in using *shielin* (normally 'a temporary shelter used at a place of summer grazing') and *hansel* (normally 'a gift to bring good luck to something new') for 'tent' (Ps. 18:4) and 'offering' (Ps. 40:6), but *misfaur* for 'sin' (Ps. 109:14) is probably best looked on as a new compound rather than as an extension of the meaning of the existing *misfare* 'misfortune'. *Deray* for 'assembly' is less satisfactory, with its radical departure from the word's normal meaning of 'disturbance, disorderly revelry'.

The twentieth-century Scots Renaissance poets also practise some manipulation of the meaning of existing words, often ones found in Jamieson's dictionary. It is worth looking at an individual case as an example. In *The Drunk Man Looks at the Thistle* (lines 2,336–8), MacDiarmid asks:

> is this fratt upon the air the ply
> O' cross-brath'd cordage that in gloffs and gowls
> Breaks up the vision o' the warld's bricht gy?

Gowl comes from Jamieson, who glosses it as 'A Hollow between hills'. As hollows are the opposite of hills, so MacDiarmid uses *gowl* as the opposite of *gloff*. *Gloff* is also from Jamieson, who explains it as 'A sudden, partial and transitory change of the atmosphere, surrounding a person; caused by a change in the undulation' and adds, as another meaning, 'It is also applied to darkness, when occasionally it appears denser to the eye than in other parts of the atmosphere'. In both cases, he ascribes the usage to Ettrick Forest. Taken together, these two definitions sound very much like a gloss on the word's use by James Hogg, the 'Ettrick Shepherd', in the song *The Witch of Fife* from *The Queen's Wake* (lines 37–8):

> And aye we raide, and se merrily we raide,
> Throw the merkist gloffis of the night.

This is SND's only citation of the word in this sense, which it glosses 'A sudden variation in the density of darkness'. Thus *gloffs and gowls* (following Buthlay 1987: 168) seems to mean 'darker and lighter patches in the sky or the surrounding air'. To produce this striking phrase, MacDiarmid has picked up a unusual sense of *gloff* apparently only attested in Hogg and combined it with another word pushed to the very limits of its meaning. Compared to the creative audacity of this phrase, some of his other extensions are tame: for instance, he takes *eel-ark* 'a box in lakes and ponds used for catching eels' from Jamieson (1808: s.v. *ark*) but extends it to cover a breeding ground for eels (*A Drunk Man Looks at the Thistle*, line 887). Turning to another practitioner of synthetic Scots, Douglas Young, like Waddell, exhibits considerable resourcefulness in finding language for topics which have not traditionally been dealt with in Scots. McClure (1981: 95) takes as an example the word *gaig*, defined by Mactaggart (1824) as 'A rend or crack in flesh brought on with dry weather', a definition repeated in Jamieson, and applies it to the fissures in a glacier (*Ice-Flumes Owergie their Lades*, line 33).

As words take on new meanings, their associations often improve or worsen. For instance, English *fracas* 'a noisy quarrel' appears in Scots as *fraca* with the slightly ameliorated sense 'a fuss' in the earlier nineteenth century[6] and then later in the century considerably improves its associations by taking on the meaning 'warm affection' or 'intimate friendship' still current in parts of Scotland in the middle of the twentieth century. Similarly, *cowshus* (a Scots form of *cautious*) takes on the meaning 'considerate'. By contrast, *vision* has arguably deteriorated in being used from the nineteenth century for 'a person or animal who is puny or wasting away' and then for 'an insignificant, characterless person'. The distance that a word can move from its original meaning is well illustrated in *smeddum*. Ultimately deriving from the Old English *smedema* 'fine flour', it continued to be used in Scots of various kinds of finely ground material well into the nineteenth century. From this it developed the sense 'pith, essence' and then finally 'spirit, energy, drive, spunk', shading into 'common sense and resourcefulness'.

10.3.5 Conversion

Conversion (functional shift) is not always easy to identify. Has a verb extended to cover new meanings or has the parallel noun shifted function to cover those meanings? Where a verb and noun pair have a large range of meanings, such questions are not easily answered, although with words with fewer meanings the case may be clearer. Thus in the nineteenth century the noun *college* developed a verbal meaning 'to educate at a university' in keeping with the Scottish use of *the college* to mean 'university', and *divert* and *exclaim* came into use as nouns, if the noun *exclaim* is interpreted as a new case of conversion rather than as a revival of the earlier English meaning which Dr Johnson had described as 'now disused'. In English, *have* has been used as a noun as in the phrase *the haves and the have-nots*, and in early Middle English had the meaning 'possession, having'; but in Scots it has developed other noun meanings, 'property', mainly in the phrase *hae and heal* 'health and wealth', and used in contrast with *want*, 'possession of something'. Furthermore, the phrase *hae't* (literally 'have it', as used in various phrases such as *deil hae't*) was construed as a noun. This led to such phrases as *deil a haet* 'devil a bit' and the use of *haet* alone meaning 'a minute particle'. If these phrases and usages have an old-fashioned ring to them, then another case of conversion is very much a contemporary term. The adjective *gallus*, as it is now generally spelt, derives from the noun *gallows* and its earlier uses had a corresponding meaning, 'villainous', but later uses have weakened senses, 'wild, unmanageable, reckless, impudent', which shade imperceptibly into more positive meanings like 'bold, high-spirited'. The qualities and behaviour associated with this word can be criticised from one point of view and admired from another. In Glasgow, as Macafee (1994a: 128–31) reports, the word has undergone even greater amelioration and 'can be a general term of approval' with some speakers, although with other speakers the negative associations prevail – for them, 'In a man, a gallus character is a certain toughness, a flashy self-importance associated with an insecure and shady way of life, or with teenage bravado', while 'A gallus female would be forward, brazen, common, a *herry*'. In *herry* we have another case of functional shift, the use of the adjective *hairy* as a noun. Originally a Glasgow usage, it meant 'a woman slum-dweller' but deteriorated to mean 'a woman of loose morals' and specifically 'a prostitute', its current Glasgow meaning. However, the useful word *wee* can mitigate its effect so that it has a rather less derogatory tone when applied to a young woman in the phrase *a wee hairy*.

Complete phrases can also become different parts of speech, generally nouns and adjectives. *Kill-the-cairter* is a name for strong whisky, and a *cheat-the-wuddie* is a rogue – *wuddie* means 'hangman's noose' – while *loup-the-dyke* means 'undisciplined', *loup-the-coonter* is a contemptuous name for a male shop assistant and *loup-the-cuddy* is leap-frog. As in English, verb-particle phrases are readily converted into nouns: *ca-through* came to be used for 'drive, energy' and 'a disturbance' in the nineteenth century and 'a preliminary washing of clothes' and 'a search' in the twentieth. Conversion can be another of the ways in which writers of synthetic Scots push words to their limits. In *A Drunk Man Looks at the Thistle*, MacDiarmid's *airgh* takes a variant form of *ergh* 'scanty' given by Jamieson as an adjective 'used when anything is wanting to make up the level' and gives it the role of a noun meaning 'gap' (line 1,022), while his *crottle* employs a noun meaning 'fragment, crumb' as a verb meaning 'crumble' (line 1,918).

10.3.6 Revivals and Literary Allusions

The practice of reviving old words is a recognised aspect of the work of the Scots Renaissance poets of the twentieth century, but has in fact been going on for much longer than that in literary Scots. In the eighteenth century the emphasis, it is true, is on contemporary language, but the nineteenth-century literary scene in general, both English and Scottish, favours a greater interest in archaic language, and this carries over into the writing of Scots.

Most of Scott's archaic language came from English, but he did revive a few obsolete Scots terms in Scottish novels set in the more distant past. In *The Monastery* we find him using *black-jack* 'a doublet quilted with iron' (Lang 1898–9, vol. 10: 169), *jackman* 'a soldier' (95) and *pedder-coffe* 'pedlar' (486); likewise in *The Abbot* we find *pilgrimer* 'pilgrim' (Lang 1898–9, vol. 11: 203) and *vasquine* 'a kind of gown' (496). These words were introduced as appropriate to the medieval and Renaissance settings of these novels and have had little currency, if any, since Scott. Novels with later settings also have archaisms, some of which have been used by other writers. For instance, *unfriend*, which appears in English and especially Scottish writers until the end of the seventeenth century, was taken up after Scott's use of it (for example, *Waverley*: Lang 1898–9, vol. 1: 134) by a number of later Scottish writers including Stevenson and Neil Munro, perhaps because Scott seems generally to use it without any particular archaic flavour. Another word adopted by later authors is *peat*, a term of obloquy for a woman, used especially in the phrase *proud peat*. Before Scott, the word was not used in this sense in Scots; in English it was only found in Elizabethan drama. Scott uses it as an archaism in *The Fair Maid of Perth* (Lang 1898–9, vol. 21: 333), but Scottish writers have adopted it from Scott's archaic language and brought it into modern Scots, extending it to cover men. Scott further revived a specifically Scottish sense of *peat*, 'a judge's protégé', as well as the derivative *peatship* (*Redgauntlet*, Lang 1898–9, vol. 18: 199) but these did not return to normal currency after him.

Wandering Willie's Tale in *Redgauntlet* reflects its narrator's sense of history in many ways, including by his use of archaisms. For instance, in saying that Steenie followed Sir Robert in 'hunting and hosting' (152), Willie draws on the obsolete verb *host* 'to follow one's feudal superior to war or on a foray' not found in Scots after the earlier eighteenth century. Willie speaks too of 'dancing and deray' (164). This comes from *Christ's Kirk on the Green*, an early poem which was quite well known in the nineteenth century, partly because Allan Ramsay had published an edition of it with a continuation of his own. It begins with the words *Was never in Scotland hard nor sene | Sic dansing nor deray*. *Deray* 'disorderly revelry' has been picked up by a number of subsequent writers. From the same poem (line 100), or from Jamieson, John Mackay Wilson took the obscure term *hensour* which probably means 'a swaggering young fellow' and used it in his *Tales of the Borders* (Wilson n.d., vol. 4: 7; vol. 5: 65) while in *Papistry Storm'd* William Tennant formed the verb *outbock* 'vomit forth' (iii: 193) on the basis of the poem's use of the phrase *out bokkit* (line 177). Elsewhere in *Papistry Storm'd*, Tennant revived a number of other obsolete terms such as *sacrify* 'to consecrate' (v: 363), *furth-shaw* 'show, reveal' (v: 550), *rambarre* 'to repulse' (v: 323) and *sailzie* 'to assail' (i: 413). SND records no writers following him in using *sacrify* and *rambarre*, but the other two terms do reappear, *furth-schaw* in Waddell's translation of the Psalms (19:1) and *sailyie* in Cameron's translation of *The Imitation of Christ* (1913: 31). Waddell (1871) also revived such terms as *lawtie* 'loyalty' (Ps. 21:5) and *stith* in the sense of 'unshakeable' (Ps. 31:4), while Cameron (1921) in his translation of Genesis brings back the Middle Scots terms *mawngery* 'feast' (26:30) and *waithman* 'hunter' (10:9). Cameron cites various authors in his glossary to Genesis as authorities for items of his vocabulary, but he obviously used Jamieson as well. For instance, Cameron's *skultie* 'naked' (Genesis 2:25) is not attested in any way before him except in Longmuir and Donaldson's 1879–82 edition of Jamieson. The penalty for using a dictionary is that one perpetuates the dictionary's mistakes: Cameron's Genesis, for instance, contains the word *smewy* 'savoury' (27:4), which Jamieson had taken from the glossary to Shirrefs' poems where it is a misprint for *smervy*.

From its first appearance in 1808, Jamieson's *Etymological Dictionary of the Scottish*

Language played a crucial role in facilitating revivals. Its store of attractive words, long and interesting illustrative quotations and fascinating (though sometimes inaccurate) information about etymology was a goldmine that no author wanting to enrich his vocabulary with rare and obsolete words could afford to ignore. But the relationship between Jamieson and literary texts was an interactive one. Jamieson himself often draws on literary texts as his source of information just as they drew on him. The original 1808 edition of Jamieson includes the phrase *schore chiftane*, explained as 'high chieftain'. Jamieson quotes his source, the fifteenth-century poem *Golagros and Gawane* where, to quote SND, 'the meaning is uncertain and the text may be corrupt' (s.v. *schore*). It seems that Galt found the word in Jamieson and then used the phrase *hieland* or *Highland schore* in *Ringan Gilhaize* (1984: 11) and *The Spaewife*, both published in 1823, where *schore* appears to mean 'chief' (Galt 1823, vol. 1: 54, 144). In his 1825 Supplement, Jamieson included *schore* by itself, giving Galt's *The Spaewife* as the source but expressing some uncertainty as to its meaning in this context. Subsequently, in some later abridged editions of Jamieson, *schore* appears with the definition 'A man of high rank' with *The Spaewife* named, but not quoted, as the source. It seems that Jamieson's original dubious adjective has been converted by Galt into a noun, which Jamieson's later editors admit as a full word although Jamieson himself merely cautiously quoted Galt.

Various writers had demonstrated the value of Jamieson's dictionary as a resource for writers of Scots, and the appearance of Cameron's *Genesis in Scots* in 1921 further reinforced this; but this resource was about to be exploited by a far more important and influential writer. At just about this time, Hugh MacDiarmid began to work on poems in synthetic Scots – the first to be published, *The Watergaw*, appeared in 1922 (anonymously in the *Dunfermline Press* on 30 September and then in the October issue of *The Scottish Chapbook*). As is well known, this and other poems, collected in *Sangschaw* (1925) and subsequent volumes (Weston 1967), contain a number of revived words (Murison 1980: 83–99). Indeed, the very first line of poetry in *Sangschaw* contains the word *crammasy* 'crimson' or 'crimson cloth', which MacDiarmid had found in Jamieson. The word seems to have been very rare since the early eighteenth century, but had been used by Waddell in the compound *cramosie-red* (Is. 1:18).[7] After MacDiarmid, it became a favourite word with Sydney Goodsir Smith. Terms which are rare, even only once attested, figure prominently among MacDiarmid's revivals. *In the Pantry* starts off with a reference to 'Knedneuch land', making metaphorical use of a term hitherto only found in Jamieson with the meaning 'A peculiar taste or smell; chiefly applied to old meat or musty bread'. *The Eemis Stane* contains in its title another revival, *eemis* or *immis*, here meaning 'insecurely placed'. Applied in various senses to the weather, it is attested from the early nineteenth century to the mid-twentieth, but the sense used here is recorded only in Jamieson before its use by MacDiarmid. The first line of the same poem contains yet another term almost certainly gleaned by MacDiarmid from Jamieson, *how-dumb-deid* 'the depths, the darkest point'. In 1820, Thomas Gillespie used the phrase 'in the *how-dumb-dead* o' a caul' ha'rst night' in a piece in *Blackwood's Magazine* (vol. 8, 1820: 197–203; for attribution of authorship, see Strout 1959: 73), and in 1825 Jamieson included *how-dumb-dead* in his Supplement quoting a short passage from Gillespie. Apart from its subsequent appearance in Wilson's *Early Recollections of a Son of the Hills* (Wilson n.d., vol. 4: 290), where it no doubt derives from Jamieson, the word remained unused until MacDiarmid made the whole phrase into the first line of his poem. This rare but expressive compound was too attractive for MacDiarmid to resist and also appealed to William Soutar (*Wintry Boughs*, line 5) and to Douglas Young who incorporated it into a further compound, the paradoxical *howedumbdeidsuinsheen* (*For a Wife in Jizzen*, line 17). Similarly, after MacDiarmid had found *spatrils* 'musical notes in printed music' in Jamieson and used it, in *Ex Verminibus* (line 5), 'to denote visual effects of a bird singing' (to quote the Glossary to *Sangschaw*), it was then used by William Soutar (1935: *The Auld Tree* (*For Hugh M'Diarmid*), lines 125–6). Jamieson, in including *spatrils* in this sense, cites only the 1805 *Poems* of the Roxburghshire poet Andrew Scott and gives Roxburghshire as the only place where the usage occurs. Scott's usage is rare or unique, but once it had been incorporated in Jamieson it had the authority of a dictionary word and was available to be taken up by later writers like MacDiarmid, who then could be imitated by other writers. Through Jamieson, a minor poet like Andrew Scott could reach forwards and influence more than one important poet in the twentieth century. As Douglas Young (1950) put it, 'Frae Jamieson's muckle buik the words tak wing' (*Thesaurus Paleo-Scoticus*, line 12).

Jamieson's intermediary influence is not needed, however, to explain how certain of Burns' words have been taken up by later writers. Burns' own popularity is sufficient to explain this, although it did not render him immune from being misinterpreted. Indeed, several terms arise from misreading him. For instance, the frequently used *willie-waught* 'a hearty swig' comes from a wrong division of the words *We'll tak a right guid willie waught* in his most widely known poem, *Auld Lang Syne* (line 19) – the phrase should properly be understood as made up of *guid-willie* 'generous, hearty' and *waucht* 'swig'; the less common *gizz* 'face' probably derives from his *Address to the Deil* (line 98) where the word, which actually means 'wig', could easily be so misunderstood. Burns seems to have invented *moistify* 'moisten', applied by him and other writers to drinkers; and, though he did not invent *howdie* 'midwife' which had earlier appeared in Ramsay and was apparently a piece of cant or a nickname used in Edinburgh, his use of it brought it into much wider circulation. At least two nicknames for football teams are owed to Burns: *Killie* (from several poems) and *the Honest Men* (from *Tam o' Shanter*) refer to Kilmarnock and Ayr United. *Mailie* is a pet form of the name *Mary* but, used by Burns in *The Death and Dying Words of Poor Mailie, the Author's Only Pet Yowe*, it came to be used as a general term for a ewe.

The extent of Burns' influence is rivalled only by that of Scott – some of the terms derived from him have already been mentioned – but some lesser writers have also made a contribution. The name of a character in Elizabeth Hamilton's *The Cottagers of Glenburnie* (1808) gave rise to the term *Mrs MacClarty* (with its pun on *clarty* 'dirty') for a slovenly housewife, and the phrase *lad o' pairts* derives from the first chapter-title in the story *Domsie* in Ian Maclaren's immensely popular *Beside the Bonnie Brier Bush* (1894), *lass o' pairts* being a later development.

There is, however, one text that has been read even more widely than any of these and that is the Authorised Version of the Bible. Biblical language is, of course, an important part of Scottish discourse, but its lexis is not distinctively Scots. However, a few items, notably proper names, have specifically Scottish meanings in our period. *Goshen*, the name of the fertile land assigned to the Israelites in Egypt, takes in early Modern English the generalised meaning of 'a place of plenty', but in Scotland in the late nineteenth century it further develops, in the plural form *goshens*, the meaning 'abundance'. *Nabal* was used in seventeenth-century English to mean 'a mean and miserly person' with reference to the person mentioned in I Samuel 25, but survived much longer in Scotland than in England, so that in our period the usage becomes distinctively Scottish. From the nineteenth century it also functions as an adjective, but was already showing signs of obsolescence at the time of

SND's usage survey in 1963. It might be expected to disappear as knowledge of the Old Testament diminishes, except that spellings like *nabble* suggest that the word may be more strongly connected in some speakers' minds with the verb *nab* than with the Bible. The curious use in the nineteenth century of *timothy* to mean 'a drink of liquor' may also have Biblical origins if SND is correct in surmising some allusion to I Timothy 5:23: 'Drink no longer water but use a little wine for thy stomach's sake and thine often infirmities'.

10.3.7 Survivals

Apart from being from the Bible, *nabal* brings us into another group of words, not numerous but nevertheless significant in the relationship between Scots and Standard English. Some words or senses of words become Scots by default when they cease to be used in English but survive in Scots. *Nabal*, as we have seen, is such a case. So is *strute* 'crammed full', which is found in Early Modern English in the form *strut* but from the eighteenth century is found only in Scots. The word *brogue* meaning 'a hoax, a trick' has a similar history, but the other word *brogue* meaning 'a rough shoe' has followed the opposite path; originally it was a Scottish and Irish term but has now entered Standard English. As regards meanings of words, examples are *decay* in the sense of 'a decline in health, especially from tuberculosis' which died out in English in the eighteenth century but survived in Scots until the early twentieth century; likewise the continuing Scots use of *doubt* in the sense 'fear, suspect', which has died out in English.

These were, of course, Scots words beforehand; all that has happened is that they have ceased to be shared with English. Nevertheless, this does change their status; they become active markers of distinctively Scots speech. Being Scots by default, they form a rather unfitting ending to this section which has, by contrast, shown Scots over the last three centuries as very active in creating new words and meanings of words, and by no means reliant on conservatism in charting a separate path with its lexis.

10.4   CHANGES IN VOCABULARY: LOSSES

There must always be questions about the dating of the disappearance of a word from a language as there are about the dating of a word's arrival. Any linguist is familiar with the situation of believing that a word is no longer in use or no longer used in a particular way and then hearing or seeing someone use it within a few days or weeks. Indeed, no word can ever be definitely labelled obsolete, since there is always the possibility of its being revived. This is even more the case with Scots, which has a particularly strong tradition of the revival of obsolete terms, at least in writing. Moreover, very extensive and useful tools exist for any writer wanting to do this. What Jamieson did for earlier generations, the monumental DOST and SND can do, and do more completely, for succeeding generations. The extensive quotations in both those dictionaries also allow modern writers to get close to the exact meanings and nuances of the past. The potential for the revival of any obsolete word or meaning is thus very high. At the same time, anyone looking at SND must recognise that it does contain a very large number of words that seem to be obsolete and must conclude that it is unlikely that all of them will be revived. There is a large amount of language that has been lost, and we must find some way of discussing it.

With any wide-ranging study like this, the main source of information has to be SND. It is the only work which has attempted anything like a complete survey of usage. There are

smaller studies which have looked at the knowledge of certain Scots terms in the second half
of the twentieth century, but none of them offers the comprehensive coverage attempted by
SND. Apart from examining extensive written sources, the SND editors sent out a series of
word-lists and included among their instructions to respondents: 'If you know the word in
the meaning printed, please underline it. If in any other meaning, please add this in the
space at the right or on a separate sheet of paper' (*Scottish National Dictionary Questionnaire*
– WE–ZEBRA: 1973). Thus respondents were asked whether they knew the word rather than
whether it was still in current use, and this should be borne in mind in considering SND's
data. At the same time, the importance of the distinction between knowing and using a word
can be overemphasised. There are plenty of words which we as English-speakers know and
would freely use when we needed to but which may not occur in our conversations for
months or even years. If asked whether we used them, we might well answer no. All the
same, if a word is known but not used, this may well be evidence of obsolescence, so that the
distinction remains potentially of some significance. These are important theoretical
considerations, but in practical terms we have no choice but to interpret the SND material
as it stands and decide whether or not, and since when, a word is obsolete.[8]

Loss can involve all the senses of a word or merely some of them. By the eighteenth
century, the following words seem to have become totally obsolete: *auchteen* the numeral
meaning 'eighth' (of Old Norse origin and distinct from the numeral meaning 'eighteen'
which is identical in form but derived from Old English), *flighter* 'to pinion', *gardnerie*
'employment as a gardener', *pairty* 'to take sides with', *peatch* 'an arcade' (from Italian
piazza; the meaning was found in English but not this form) and *stake* 'to be sufficient for'.
By the end of the nineteenth century, the same fate overtook *flaunter* 'quiver, waver in
speech, prevaricate', *lax* 'salmon', *nibbit* 'an oatcake sandwich', *pechan* 'stomach, belly' (the
word having been kept alive until the end of the century by recollection of its use in Burns),
skeldock 'wild mustard', *skelet* 'skeleton' and *strute* 'crammed full'. The pace of loss perhaps
quickened in the earlier twentieth century, with no lack of examples of words becoming
obsolete by the middle of the century such as *aumeril* 'an awkward, stupid fellow', *bever*
'shake, tremble', *clem* 'mean; queer', *crame* 'merchant's booth' (the derivatives *cramer* and
cramery had already died out in the eighteenth century), *gabbart* 'lighter, barge', *killywimple*
'trill or affectation in singing', *nig nay* 'trifle' (noun and verb), *ramiegeister* 'sharp blow' and
wees't 'depressed'. In the later twentieth century, further words have become obsolete or are
obsolescent, like *flary* 'gaudy', *haivel* 'conger eel', *killiecoup* 'tumble head over heels',
killyvie 'a fuss', *plainen* 'coarse linen', *rambust* 'robust', *skathie* 'rough shelter' and *weebie*
'common ragwort'.

Of the words mentioned so far, *aumeril*, *clem*, *flary*, *flaunter*, *killiecoup*, *killyvie*,
killywimple, *nibbit*, *pechan*, *plainen*, *rambust*, *ramiegeister*, *skaithie*, *weebie* and *wees't* had
all entered Scots since 1700. The principle of 'last in, first out' seems to operate here to
some degree, perhaps because the longer a word has to establish a number of meanings and/
or derivatives, the less likely it is to entirely disappear. Where a word forms part of a
complex of related words, the individual word may disappear while something closely
related remains. *Bravity* 'splendour, elegance in dress' went out of use earlier in the
twentieth century, but the adjective from which it derives, *brave*, remains with its Scots
sense, often used ironically, of 'splendid, fine', as does the adverb *bravely*. Likewise, *helplie*
'helpful' became obsolete about the same time but *help* remains. With compounds, one or
both of the components can remain but the compound be lost: *weel-farrant*, *weel-faurdly*,
weel-hained, *weel-hertit*, *weel-natured*, *weel-willed* and *weel-willie* are not recorded in use

after the end of the nineteenth century. Alternatively, a compound can survive when one of its components is obsolete: *mantie-maker* 'dress-maker' was still known in Shetland, the north-east and Selkirk in 1962 at a time when the original meaning of *mantie* on which it is based, 'a loose flowing gown', was apparently obsolete. Similarly, the nouns *etter* or *atter* 'corrupt matter, pus', the verb *etter* 'fester' and the derived adjectives *ettery*, *attery* and *ettersome* are all obsolete in the second half of the twentieth century but *ettercop*, *nettercop* (from wrong division of *an ettercop*) and perhaps *attercop*, all meaning 'spider', survive. The connection between the two sets of words goes back to Old English *attor* 'poison' but was no longer evident in Scots as *etter* had lost this sense. Consequently, we see the appearance of the forms *eddercap* and *addercap* where folk etymology has presumed a connection with *edder* 'adder'.

Where a word has a number of senses, it may lose some but not all of them. This is a common process. To choose examples of meanings which became obsolete by the end of the nineteenth century, this process applies both to peculiarly Scottish words like *cleuch* meaning 'crag', *fang* as a noun meaning 'predicament' and *feck* 'value', and to distinctively Scots senses of words shared with English: *fa* (*fall*) as a noun meaning 'share' and 'fate', *fair* (with the infinitive) 'likely, ready', *panel* 'dock in court' and *queer* 'amusing'. Loss of distinctively Scots meanings may leave a word with only the meanings shared with English, as has happened with *sermon*. From the late sixteenth century to the end of the nineteenth, it was used (without the article) for the whole service of worship, a reflection of the importance given in Presbyterian churches to preaching. When this usage died out, *sermon* ceased to have any distinctively Scots meanings.

Sometimes losing some senses can result in a substantial shift in the meaning of the word. Consider the verb *bicker*, the semantic development of which can be set out schematically as in Table 10.2. In both English and Scots, the original meaning of the word *bicker* was 'to make an attack, to fight', and in both languages this meaning has been lost. In English, new figurative senses developed, of which the most important are its application to a verbal fight, the sound of a stream and the flickering of a flame. Scots added to these a specific sense of 'engage in a street fight', extended the sense of rapid and noisy movement of water to boiling water and to the movement of human beings, created the sense 'pelt' (used both transitively and intransitively) and developed the meaning 'to laugh'. By the middle of the nineteenth century, the senses to do with physical fighting had become obsolete, and today the only senses which might still be in use are the application to boiling water (known in Aberdeenshire and Banffshire in 1975 both with the verb and with the noun) and possibly, in Morayshire and Banffshire, 'to laugh'. The verb has thus come a long way from its original application to fighting. It has also become much more geographically restricted. Another traditional Scots term which is now both semantically and geographically restricted, if it survives at all,[9] is *bield*, noun and verb, meaning 'protect(ion), shelter'. It perhaps survives in Banffshire as a noun, and in the south the derived adjective *beildy* 'cosy' may also still be in use. *Stripe* reverses the situation with *bicker* by retaining its original meaning of 'a small stream' and losing its extended meaning of 'a street gutter'.

When some senses survive and others are lost, the overall associations of the word may improve or worsen. Starting off with neutral associations, the adjective *tight* developed in Scots and English both positive and negative meanings when applied to people. On the one hand it came to mean 'competent, skilful; shapely; neat in appearance' and on the other, somewhat later, 'avaricious'. The positive senses lasted somewhat longer in Scots than in English, but their disappearance by the middle of the twentieth century left the word with predominantly negative associations as applied to people. By contrast, *loon* has lost much of its negative meaning and gained some new positive or, at least, neutral ones. Before 1700 it had ceased to mean 'a dishonest rascal' or 'a robber'. Over the last three centuries it has lost its application to a despised member of the lower classes and a whore, while the more general meaning of 'a worthless person' has become restricted to localised use in East Central and Ulster Scots; meanwhile it gained the sense 'a young farm worker' and 'a male child' in the nineteenth century and added the function of being a nickname applied to a native of Forfar or a member of the Forfar Athletic football team in the twentieth. Especially in the north, where the only remaining negative meaning is the mild one, 'a young scamp', the word has considerably ameliorated.

Table 10.2

	Century:	14	15	16	17	18	19	20
1 *vt* attack with arrows, stones etc		*	**	**	**	**	**	
2 *vi* fight with arrows, stones, or other weapons; make skirmishing attacks; engage in (street) fights			**	**	**	**	*	
3 (1) *of water in gen* move quickly and noisily; *of rain* pelt, patter; *of boiling water* bubble quickly						*	**	**
3 (2) *of living creatures* move quickly and noisily, rush							**	*
4 *of light, fire etc* gleam, flicker, sparkle							*	
5 laugh heartily								**

So far, we have dealt with words or meanings which appear to have gone totally out of use. However, there are various kinds of half-life in which words can exist. We have already considered in theoretical terms the category of words which are known but not used. With users of Scots who build their Scots vocabulary on the language, that they hear around them, one would assume that these words will eventually cease to be held in the collective memory. However, if some words are known but not used because of some perceived barrier to their use (the language is not seen as respectable or is seen as inappropriately old-fashioned), they might come back into use if that perceived barrier were seen to be removed – for instance if the speakers began to see the old-fashioned as having a higher status than before (Macafee 1994a: 174–212). On the other hand, those who are well acquainted with literary texts in Scots may well know many words which they never use, and this situation could continue indefinitely. Middle-class speakers of Scottish Standard English are likely to have read Burns and perhaps other writers and to understand the Scots vocabulary used in those writings and yet never actually use much of it in speech or writing.

Another kind of half-life is where a word is only now used in a fossilised phrase and not any longer as a general term. It cannot be said to function as a full word and, if the phrase is figurative in origin, it may not even be understood in its original meaning. For instance, Macafee (1994a: 149) found that, in her sample of Glasgow speakers, most over 26 years old knew and many used the phrase *to put the hems on* (meaning 'to curb'), but 'the imagery was opaque to my interviewees'. This is not surprising, since *hems* is literally 'a draught-horse's collar'. However, this does not stop the phrase being used or its meaning extended. Munro (1985: 33) lists the phrase in the sense 'restrain' and remarks that it is 'also used when something is ruled out or made impossible: *There's the snow on again. I doubt that's put the hems on the game the morra.*' The phrase is also used in Jamie Stuart's (1992: 33) recent *Glasgow Gospel: There'll be a right stushie and the Romans will pit the hems oan us aw!*

The names of features of the landscape can have another kind of half-life. *Inver* meaning 'a confluence of streams' and 'the mouth of a river' no longer functions as an independent word, but place-names containing this element are still in use. *Drum*, like *inver*, is a word of Gaelic origin and still found in place-names. Jamieson in 1808 recorded that it was 'applied to little hills, which rise as backs or ridge above the level of the adjacent ground' in the north (a meaning known to one of SND's Perthshire correspondents in 1950), while Mactaggart gives it in the plural as meaning 'Curved wet land' (likewise known to only one SND correspondent, in Kirkcudbrightshire in 1940). Judging by SND, one would expect it by now to be obsolete, but Riach's (1988) survey of Galloway dialect found the word to be known in three parishes in the sense 'a small rectangular hillock' and 'a field sloping on all sides' in one, so it would seem to be not quite dead. Moreover, the derivative *drumlin* has entered Standard English as a geological term meaning 'a long whaleback mound of glacial deposit'. *Weem*, though obsolete in the sense 'a cave', also shows a little life beyond place-names as a technical historical term for an underground dwelling and with just one attestation of it in the sense of 'cellar' in Midlothian in 1958. Other terms which are now obsolete or geographically restricted in use but which survive in place-names are *kippie* 'a small hill', *month* 'hill, stretch of hilly ground' and *slack*, *slock* and *swire* all meaning 'hollow between hills'. Even where the word is in some use, it is unlikely that all those who use the place-names always recognise their meaning, but the place-names do serve to keep the words in one sense alive.

When we turn to the referents of these obsolete words, it is natural to seek words for obsolete things since their disappearance is self-explanatory. In fact, obsolescence of the thing denoted is not the primary cause of words going out of use. Words denoting human attributes and activities, plants, animals, birds and fish can all become obsolete without any disappearance of their referents. To take just one example, the following bird-names have apparently disappeared by the late twentieth century but presumably not the birds: *gorcock* 'male of red grouse' (known to only one SND respondent in 1955; last previous attestation 1903), *gormaw* 'cormorant', *killieleepie* 'sandpiper' and *mitten* 'male hen-harrier'. The same can be said about the following fish names: *goukmey* and *goupney-fish* 'grey gurnard', *haivel* 'conger eel', *lax* 'salmon', *nine-eyed eel* and *ramper eel* 'lamprey', *plash-fluke* 'plaice' and *skelly* 'chubb'. Even where something does become obsolete, the word denoting it may remain in use for some time. Macafee (1994a: 62–4) found that the phrase *two bob* 'two shillings' was still well known among the 10–15-year-old group in her sample of Glasgow speakers, being applied to its decimal equivalent, ten pence, although decimal currency was introduced in 1971 before they were born. It was also well used among the 16–25-year-old group, most of whom could not have remembered using shilling or two-shilling coins. Earlier coin-names had a similar, and longer, survival. A *plack* was a small coin valued at four pennies Scots and issued until the Union of the Crowns. A separate Scottish currency was abolished by the Act of Union (by which time a Scots penny had depreciated in value to one twelfth of an English one), yet the term was still in use in the first half of the eighteenth century with specific reference to four pence Scots or one third of an English penny. As time went on, the specific sense was superseded by the general sense of 'a very small amount of money'. A similar fate befell the *bawbee*, a coin worth six pence Scots, and the *bodle*, worth two pence Scots, which were struck until the reign of William III. These terms continued to be used through the eighteenth century and beyond. Some sense of their relative value survived even as late as 1871, when the phrase *to make your plack a bawbee* meaning 'to improve one's situation' appeared in Alexander's *Johnny Gibb of Gushetneuk* (1884 edn: 118).

Yet, having said all that, there are certainly cases of terms which have become obsolete along with what they denoted. Until the abolition of heritable jurisdictions in Scotland in 1747, the office of Sheriff in a county was usually hereditary in a family, and the sheriff had a deputy to carry out the judicial functions known as the *sheriff-depute*. After 1747, the sheriff-depute took over as sheriff although the word *depute* was not officially removed from his title until the 1820s. At the centre of the judicial system, the Court of Session's judges were known as *the Feifteen*. The number of judges was reduced to thirteen in 1830, although the old phrase was used for most of the century and *the thirteen* never took on the same meaning. More recently, the reforms of local government in Scotland in 1975 removed some long-standing traditional terms from all but historical use. In the seventeenth century, because weights and measures were not standard throughout the country, it was decided to place exemplars of standard measures in the care of certain burghs: for lineal measure in Edinburgh, for liquid capacity in Stirling, for dry capacity in Linlithgow and for weight in Lanark. This led to the use of such phrases as *Linlithgow measure* and *Lanark weight* alongside such terms as *Scots mile* and *Scots pint*. Despite the attempts to standardise, local measures continued, like the so-called *Nithsdale measure* used in Dumfriesshire and east Kirkcudbrightshire in the eighteenth and early nineteenth centuries. Local weights (which continued in use though officially abolished) were referred to as *Tron weight*, a tron being a weighing machine set up in a burgh for public use. Most of the names of measures were shared with English (though the measures were different, for instance one inch according to the standard of Edinburgh equalled 1.0016 inches in the imperial measure), but some names for dry measure were peculiar to Scotland, like *lippie*, *forpet* and *firlot*, or found in Scotland and the north of England, like *boll* and *chalder* (introduced from the north into southern English usage as a measure for coal). In 1824, the separate Scottish standards were abolished and replaced by imperial weights and measures. Over time, imperial standards prevailed and references to *Lanark weight* and *Linlithgow measure* disappeared, but some of the individual terms continued in use. *Lippie*, for instance, was still widely known in 1961 but as a measure for potatoes, barley and oats when sold by weight, being equivalent to one eighth of an imperial stone.

The disappearance of certain customs and beliefs likewise leads to the obsolescence of vocabulary. With the end to public executions, it was no longer the practice to give the magistrates of a burgh a dinner after an execution. This was known in the earlier nineteenth century as a *deid-chack*. The same term is recorded earlier in the twentieth century for food asked for by dying people and for the sound made by the death-watch beetle, which was regarded as an omen of death. The word is obsolete. A waning of superstition may also have something to do with the disuse of the term *weird* for 'a prophecy' and 'someone with supernatural skill'. Along with public executions, one would hope that the practice of punishing someone by bumping their buttocks against a wall or caning the soles of their feet has likewise disappeared – certainly this meaning of the verb *ram* seems to have passed out of use. The public executioner was formerly known as a *dempster* because he often combined this role with another one, abolished in 1773, that of the officer who pronounced the sentence (*doom*) of a court.

On another front, the change to large flour mills rather than small local ones means that it was no longer possible to oblige tenants on an estate to use a particular mill. This obligation was known as *sucken*, as were the lands of an estate where a sucken applied. Around this developed a set of now obsolete terms. Someone who came from outside a sucken was an *outsuckiner* and was obliged to pay an *outsucken multure* (a proportion of the grain) for use of the mill as opposed to the *insucken multure* paid by someone from inside the sucken. The tenant's obligation to use a particular mill is also called *thirlage*, and such a tenant was said to be *thirled* to that mill. *Thirlage* is now obsolete, as is *thirled* in this sense, though it can still be used in a more general sense of being bound in certain ways. A more recently obsolete practice was authorised by the Glasgow Police Act of 1866. The Town Council placed an official notice on the door of a house stating how many people were allowed to spend the night in it. Such a house was said to be *ticketed*. Beside these legally authorised customs existed social customs like that of asking for a *beverage*, that is, a fine demanded from someone wearing something new.

Sometimes it is obvious that some other term has for some reason overtaken a word or phrase. Thus it has become normal for us to refer to the two Jacobite risings of 1715 and 1745 as *the Fifteen* and *the Forty-five*. It has an appealing neatness about it and is perhaps subconsciously reinforced by forty-five being a multiple of fifteen. In the process, *the Fifteen* has completely ousted an earlier name, *Mar's Year*, given to it because the rebellion was led by the Earl of Mar, for which the last SND quotation is dated 1845. The terms *the Fifteen* and *the Forty-five* have now been inseparably linked with the two Jacobite rebellions because we have forgotten that this usage arises from an earlier general usage in which any year could be referred to in this way, as by Hogg when he writes that 'in the saxteen and seventeen the scourge fell on our flocks and herds. Then in the aughteen and nineteen, it fell on the weavers' (*The Shepherd's Calendar*, Hogg 1865, vol. 1: 292–3).

Thus words can become obsolete for no obvious reason or because the thing that they denote becomes obsolete or because some other term becomes popular for some reason. In the case of the loss of a significant body of Scots formal diction over the last three centuries, a different explanation applies. Rather, as we have noted before, the whole drift of the development of Scots over the eighteenth and nineteenth centuries and, to some extent, the twentieth has been towards the definition of Scots as an essentially informal language used generally for informal purposes such as colloquial speech, comic verse, satire and sentimental poetry. Even in the twentieth century, there have been only limited (although individually important) attempts to revive a register for serious, formal written prose. In 1700 the Scots language contained a considerable body of distinctive formal Latinate diction which it did not share with English. In a few cases, the word was entirely or almost entirely unknown in English, like *necessar* 'necessary', *notour* 'notorious' and *repone* 'restore'. Other words had been used in earlier English but were now confined to Scots, like *calcul* 'calculation', *compesce* 'restrain', *decrete* 'decree' (noun and verb) and *propale* 'make public'. Yet others were known in English but had distinctive senses now or always confined to Scotland, like *decern* in the sense of 'decree', *deduce* in the sense of 'substract' and *excrescence* in the sense of 'excess amount'. As we would expect, with English increasingly taking over the role of the formal register in Scotland, in the course of the next three centuries most of this has been lost. Nevertheless, some of the distinctively Scots formal diction was surprisingly resilient in a context of increasing anglicisation of formal registers, especially when one considers that figures as important as David Hume and James Beattie added their weight to attempts to proscribe these and other Scotticisms. Hume and Beattie's concern was with the writing of normal English prose, and with the lapse of time some of the results which they wanted have come to pass in the context of functional everyday prose, though not with creative writing, where Scots still has a strong foothold even in texts that are mostly written in Standard English.

All the same, the process of removing these words took some time and is not yet complete. One possible reason why Scottish writers were willing to retain certain Scotticisms while aiming to write like Englishmen is that they could be seen as more 'correctly' or 'logically' derived from their Latin roots. There is a certain illogicality about the way verbs like *deduct, dismiss, exempt, insert, oppose, promote* and *situate* are formed in English – they derive from the stem of the Latin past participle, whereas logically one would expect them to be derived from the stem of the infinitive or the present tense, since we add our own endings to them to make them into past tenses and past participles. Of course, language is not logical in this way, but its users often want it to be, and Scottish writers may have continued to use *deduce* meaning 'subtract', *dimit* (usually spelt *demit*) meaning 'dismiss', *exeme, oppone* and *promove* because they derive ultimately from the infinitive stem and can thus be seen as more 'logical' and 'correct'. Meanwhile, achieving the same end by different means, they continued to use *insert* and *situate* as past participles, contrary to English usage, which has never treated *insert* as a past participle and has given up so treating *situate*. Thus, in these various ways, what might be seen as more etymologically appropriate derived forms of Latin verbs survived in Scots.

There was also another factor working to preserve some of the older Scots formal diction. Some words had developed or were to develop specific meanings in Scots law: *cognosce* 'investigate judicially', *decern* 'pronounce judicially', *decrete* 'judicial decree', *dispone* 'make over, convey', *homologate* 'ratify', *mortify* and *mortification* 'assign land, property or money to a body in perpetuity' and 'whatever is so assigned', *notour* 'commonly known', *oppone* 'advance arguments or evidence against', *propone* 'advance arguments in a court of law', *repone* 'restore to a defender his right to defend a case', *subject* 'a piece of heritable property'. Once these became legal terms, there was another sense in which they could be seen as the 'correct' terms, and most of them have survived with these meanings at least into the first part of the twentieth century, *oppone* and *cognosce*, which died out earlier, being exceptions. Finally, a small group of terms objected to by Beattie such as *compete* and *narrate* have survived in Scottish Standard English for a quite different reason – they are now accepted as part of international Standard English usage.

For all this, there has been a steady erosion of the store of distinctively Scots formal diction. This is unfortunate because it makes it difficult to maintain any sense of a formal register of Scots separate from English. The bulk of formal diction always would be identical to English because it draws on the same major source, Latin loanwords. But so long as it was possible to sprinkle that shared diction with a number of purely Scots forms, it made more apparent sense to claim the whole vocabulary as part of Scots. Without this, the shared diction was much more likely to be seen as purely English, and thus the notion of a Scots formal diction was seriously undercut. By the end of the eighteenth century, these words had ceased to be used in Scots: *calcul* 'calculation', *compone* 'come to an agreement regarding payment', *deduce* 'subtract', *excrescence* 'excess amount', *exerce* 'perform (an act); act (in a particular capacity)', *notar* 'notary' and *oppone* 'oppose by argument'. By the end of the nineteenth century, they were followed by *cognosce* 'investigate judicially, examine' (SND describes it as 'Now *rare*' but has no citations after 1823), *compesce* 'restrain', *difficulted* 'place in a difficulty' (not a case of functional shift but borrowed from medieval Latin), *evert* 'overthrow in an argument', *exeem* 'exempt', *propale* 'make public' and *superplus* 'surplus' (from medieval Latin), while by the middle of the twentieth century *decrete* 'judicial decree' and *depone* 'declare on oath' had gone out of use. The result is that Scots today preserves very little of this body of Latinate formal diction apart from a few isolated words like *evite* 'avoid', *-ar* alternatives to English *-ary* words like *necessar* 'necessary' and *ordinar* 'ordinary' and some of the past-participle forms like *situate* and *insert*. A modern writer of literary prose who wishes to use a formal register in Scots containing distinctively Scots terms will need to revive some obsolete terms. Scots law provides an exception to this. Legal language is by its nature both formal and conservative. Some Scots legal terms have gone out of use but many remain. It is true that these words mainly occur nowadays in a Scottish Standard English context, but they are available to any writer for use in Scots contexts where appropriate.

Our discussion so far has been based on the material in SND. It remains the largest single survey of Scots lexis in the twentieth century, but some of its information is now out of date and it is a survey of knowledge of lexis rather than active use. The next largest survey is that undertaken for *The Linguistic Atlas of Scotland*, but this was particularly concerned with variation within Scotland and will be considered in that context. In the second half of the twentieth century, there have also been a number of smaller-scale examinations of Scots lexis concerned with particular areas or places and based on questionnaires or interviews. These include Agutter and Cowan (1981) on Larbert, Macaulay and Trevelyan's (1977) and Macafee's (1994a) separate studies of Glasgow, Pollner (1985b) on Livingston, Riach (1979–82, 1984) on Galloway and Wickens (1980, 1981) on Caithness. All of these studies, except Macaulay's, are concerned at least in part with lexis that has been recorded as used in the particular localities.[10] They use different methodologies and investigate different areas of lexis, but they all provide us with relatively recent and detailed information about Scots vocabulary in those different places. What they do not do is provide a comprehensive picture of the present state of Scots vocabulary either across Scotland or in those particular localities, so that, neither from SND nor with the additional help of these other studies, can we answer questions like these: what percentage of the Scots vocabulary in use in 1700 is in use today? Is the vocabulary of Scots larger or smaller today than it was in 1700 (or 1800 or 1900 for that matter)? Indeed, these questions, though they naturally come into the minds of anyone concerned about the survival of Scots, are not really valid questions anyway. They assume that there is, or has been, at some time one entity, Scots vocabulary, whereas throughout the whole period since 1700 Scots has been divided both in its spoken and written forms into a number of dialects which share many features in common but also have many individual features. It would be hard to answer these questions about even just one of these dialects since, apart from the absence of full information, one would immediately run into problems of how to define the dialect area, what constitutes 'use' of vocabulary, whether or not to include both speech and writing, whether or not to include urban areas and so on.

A complete picture is impossible; nevertheless, certain recurrent features emerge from taking these studies together despite their different methodologies and their concern with different localities. Most importantly, perhaps, the picture that emerges is not one of total decay. Some words are known to the informants, some are not. Some are known to older people and not known, or not as widely known, to younger people. Some were almost equally known to both age-groups. In some studies, some words are better known to younger people. It would seem that some traditional Scots vocabulary still has strong currency and is presumably likely to survive into future generations. Even where terms are not known or are not widely known to the younger informants, this does not mean that the word is obsolescent. As Agutter and Cowan (1981: 52) point out, the fact that a word is not known to some or all younger informants can have various explanations. For instance, it may simply be 'because the informant is too young to have any use for such a word – e.g. few twelve-year-olds would have any word for the concepts *pigeon-toed* . . . or *co-habitee* (bide-ye-in)'. At the same time, their study and Macafee's (1994a: 61–2) provide evidence of new vocabulary arriving on the scene. In the case of Glasgow, this picture of lexical innovation is supported and supplemented by such informal studies as Munro (1985, 1988). Provided that we do not deny the name 'Scots' to such urban dialects, it is very obvious that there is innovation in Scots lexis in our time.

Even when a Scots word disappears, this does not mean that it has been replaced by a Standard English one – it may have given way to a new Scots term. On the other hand, there may already be an existing alternative Scots term or, where the usage is a local one, a term from another Scots dialect may be imported (Agutter and Cowan 1981: 52). There is no way of determining the relative frequency of these processes. There is also no way of knowing whether it is more common for new words to be created or for new meanings to be assigned to existing words. If distinctively Scots words were regularly replaced by new meanings of existing words (especially words shared with English), then the degree to which Scots was obviously different from English would be reduced even though there was no replacement of Scots with Standard English. What is very evident is that concentrating only on losses will not give us an adequate picture of what is happening to Scots today.

To sum up, these studies, combined with the SND data, do not suggest the imminent demise of Scots. At the same time, they are not totally reassuring for anyone concerned to see Scots survive. Many words and meanings of words have disappeared, and there is no way of knowing whether an equal number of words and meanings have been created to replace them. Furthermore, qualitative studies such as Macafee's provide us with further evidence of attitudes to Scots which do not seem likely to enhance its chances of survival. Macafee (1994a: 97) describes 'the self-deprecating tendency, especially amongst younger people, to refer to their language as *slang*' and contrasts this with older people's use of the term *Scotch* with its more positive associations. Even if, as Macafee says, '*Slang* . . . and *patter* are apparently neutral terms' (1994a: 209), labelling Scots as slang removes its significant role as an indicator of Scottish identity and associates it with a class of ephemeral language. Macafee goes on to show that attitudes to Scots are complex and in particular discusses a distinction between ordinary language and colourful language; colourful language 'includes what is usually termed *slang*', and by older speakers 'it could be regarded as rough to use some of this material inappropriately' (1994a: 207). If Scots lexis comes in time to be identified by all speakers as slang, it runs the danger of being seen as 'rough' and thus not acceptable to many speakers. She concludes her discussion (1994a: 211) with the suggestion that 'If the older way of talking and thinking about the vernacular is dying out, then there is a danger that many traditional Scots words – those that have passed from active everyday use into passive knowledge – will come to be seen as simply the colourful language of an older generation, subject to changes in fashion'. If lexical innovation is one way of compensating for lexical loss, it must not take place in such a way and at such a pace as to undermine the sense of Scots as tied to a particular place (whether the whole country of Scotland or a particular place like Glasgow) and thus redefine it as just a register of ephemeral, non-regional slang.

10.5 GEOGRAPHICAL DISTRIBUTION

As is abundantly evident from our discussion so far, not all Scots lexis is used throughout Scotland. Scots is not one dialect, even in its written form, but a group of dialects. The previous discussion has already referred to such local features as Norse words in Shetland and Orkney, Gaelic words in Caithness, Irish words in Galloway and Ulster and rhyming slang in Glasgow, as well as constant references to the geographical limitations of the use of individual words.

SND identifies a number of major dialect divisions, and these divisions are repeated in CSD although with slightly different names. The basic divisions were those described by Murray (1873: 78), who characterises them as 'founded solely upon internal characteristics of pronunciation, grammar, and vocabulary'. However, his later description of their main characteristics (apart from Southern Scots with which most of the book is concerned) is largely in terms of sounds; and the boundaries, while they work reasonably well for some sounds, are less satisfactory for lexical distribution. Words cross boundaries, and even a quick glance at *The Linguistic Atlas of Scotland* will show that the distribution of words, where there is variation within Scotland, rarely falls neatly within the boundaries of Northern, East Central, West Central, South-west Central and Southern Scots. Take, for instance, the LAS map for words for *Triticum repens* or 'couch grass' (Mather and Speitel 1975: Map 87). This shows *knap grass, knot grass, string grass* and *lonach* confined to Northern Scots, *wrack (grass)* found only in East Central and Southern Scots except for a small area of West Central Scots, *felt (grass)* and *purl (grass)* only in West Central Scots and *scutch grass* only in Ulster. But such a neat picture can only be arrived at by omitting certain elements from the map. In fact, *couchgrass* occurs in parts of both West Central and Northern Scots, and, most importantly, *quickens* occurs somewhere in each of these dialect areas (often overlapping with other words) and is the only word mapped for South Central Scots. Furthermore, the LAS only maps the dominant terms, and its lists of respondents' returns show scattered occurrences of some of these terms outside these areas as well as the use of extra terms like *remmick(s)*. Another complication is that *knot grass* is used in Orkney and Northern and Central Scots for various other grasses. Even if we treat each county as a separate dialect area, we cannot produce a neat pattern; in every county a variety of terms occurs.

As a way of describing the distribution of vocabulary, the boundaries work best if taken in their broadest categories, Insular, Northern, Central, Southern and Ulster. Even then, the pattern is often one similar to that outlined for 'couch grass', where one or two terms are found throughout most of the Scots-speaking area but local terms prevail in certain parts. One set of words that can be reasonably easily described in terms of the full set of SND divisions is that for 'broken pieces of china' (Mather and Speitel 1975: Map 31; 214–16), but there is still some overlap of words within dialect areas. It is best to consider individual referents one by one, as the LAS does, and then one becomes quickly aware of the diversity of patterns of distribution.

Over time, the distribution of individual words has changed, as we can see by taking the LAS maps in conjunction with DOST and SND. Of the terms for 'couch grass' (Mather and Speitel 1975: Map 87; 322–3), *quickens* is the earliest attested in Scotland, being first recorded in 1661; it derives from northern Middle English *quik* which corresponds to southern English *quitch* of which *couch* is a variant. *Couchgrass*, being the Standard English term, would have been introduced later, and it is perhaps direct from Standard English that it has come into use in the area west and north of Inverness which was not traditionally Scots-speaking. A number of the other terms mentioned seem to have developed since 1700 and become common in certain areas without entirely ousting *quickens*: according to SND, *felt (grass)*, *wrack (grass)* and *lonnach* appeared in the eighteenth century, *pirl-grass* in the nineteenth and *knap grass* and *string grass* in the twentieth.

A somewhat similar situation applies with words for 'a seagull' (Mather and Speitel 1975: Map 74; 297–8). *(Sea)gull* has been recorded in Scots since the fifteenth century and *(sea)gow* since the seventeenth; it is used throughout Scotland except in Caithness, Orkney and Shetland and is the dominant term in some areas. *Maw*, ultimately derived from Old Norse and attested in Scots from the sixteenth century, is also widespread (*white ma* being the Orkney form and *pick(ie) maw* the southern one) though it is unknown in Ulster. In Shetland, Caithness and Aberdeenshire, *maw* coexists with another word of Scandinavian origin, *scorie* or *scurrie*, and in Banff and Buchan with *(sea) peul*, but in Kincardineshire *maw* has been supplanted by *plingie*, although *(sea)gull* is even more common there. Thus once again, more modern terms, in this case the nineteenth-century arrivals *peul* and *plingie* based on the bird's cry, have in some areas established themselves in strong competition with the older terms. Words for the wild bee present a similar picture (Mather and Speitel 1975: Maps 77 and 77A; 302–4). The earliest of the terms now in use seems to have been *bumble bee*, found in English from the sixteenth century and occurring throughout nearly the whole of Scotland. *Bumbard* occurs from the sixteenth century and is perhaps the origin of *bumber* in Ross and Cromarty and Inverness-shire. It is followed by *bumbee*, attested in figurative use in the mid-seventeenth century and in literal use in the early eighteenth, and still common in Central and Ulster Scots and in parts of the north-east. Other related terms like *bummer*, *bummle* and *bummlie bee* prevail in other areas. Later, new terms developed like *foggie (bee)* and *foggie toddler* based on *foggie* meaning 'mossy'. They are first attested in the nineteenth century and now widely used alongside the *bum-* group. However, *baker* and *cannie nannie* which are first attested in the twentieth century are more geographically restricted.

Other words not covered by *The Linguistic Atlas of Scotland* have also undergone geographical expansion and contraction, as the pages of SND amply show. For instance, the noun *flaucht* has been used in Scots since the fifteenth century in the sense of 'a burst of flame, a flash of lightning', but SND's entry shows it now confined to the north-east and Shetland, although in the nineteenth century it was established in Central, Southern and Ulster Scots. A second sense, 'a flake', was known to SND's correspondents only in Shetland, yet it had been used in at least the north-east and North-east Central areas in the nineteenth century. A less common third sense, 'a tuft of wool or hair', has disappeared entirely. Similarly, *fire-flaucht* 'lightning, a flash of lightning' is now more geographically restricted than it was. As a transitive verb meaning 'tingle' or 'prickle', *prinkle* occurred in Central, Southern and North-eastern Scots in the nineteenth century but was not known to correspondents in the Central area in 1962. The corresponding transitive sense has also contracted, and the senses 'twinkle' and 'simmer' have gone out of use. *Goller* in the sense 'make a gurgling sound' (also applied to a turkey's goggling) has even more markedly contracted to dialects on the periphery – Shetland, Roxburghshire and Wigtownshire – and ceased to be used in Central and North-eastern Scots where it was formerly strong, while *rame* in the sense of 'drone on' is now confined to Ulster. Some pet names for cows seem also to have become less widely used than they once were: *Brandie*, *Brockie*, *Fleckie* and *Hawkie* are names given to cows which were respectively brindled, with a black and white face, spotted and with a white face. Many other cases of contraction could be cited.

The contrasting process of expansion is illustrated in a very well-known word, *wean*, pronounced [wen]. In origin a compound of *wee* and *ane*, it began in West Central Scots in the seventeenth century but has moved west and east, largely replacing but not totally ousting the older term *bairn* (for maps illustrating the distribution of *wean* and *bairn*, see Catford 1957c). However, it still remains very uncommon in Southern Scots, just as Murray (1873: 77–8) reported it to be. It also occurs in other dialects but is there still thought of as two separate words. From the same region comes *cludgie* 'toilet'. Originally a Glasgow term, it had spread by the mid-1970s to Edinburgh and Fife where it competes with the term *yuffie*.

The various words used around the country reflect some of the diversity of sources for new words which we have already considered in relation to additions to Scots in this period. The words for 'a hen-coop' are a case in point. *Hen-coop* itself is shared with English and is found in all areas except Shetland. *Coop* occurs in this sense in English from the fifteenth century, although the earliest recorded Scottish uses are in the sense of 'a basket for catching salmon'. *Hen-house* is the normal term alongside *hen-coop* in Ulster and the north-east, common in parts of the Central Scots area and virtually unrivalled in Shetland. It is such an obvious compound that it may have been created separately in various areas. The Orkney form is *hennie-house*. *Cavie*, strong in Central and Southern Scots and found less frequently in Northern Scots as far north as Moray, is of Flemish origin and first appears in Scots in the sixteenth century. *Cray*, used mainly in Ayrshire, Renfrewshire and Dunbartonshire, is a specific use of a more general term meaning an animal pen or fold and derives from Gaelic, while *crib* is a nineteenth-century extension of the meaning of the English and Scots word and is found from Caithness to Fife especially in the southern part of that area. Thus two compounds shared with English, a Scottish sense of a word and Flemish and Gaelic loanwords come together to provide some of the variety of terms used through the country. Different parts of the country provide a like diversity of sources for words for 'caterpillar': compounds like *kail worm* and *hairy worm*, the Gaelic borrowing *brottag* (found in Caithness), two Christian names in *hairy Wullie* and *hairy Mary*, the Middle English *wolbode*, appearing in modern Scots as *oobit*, and the transferred use of *granny*. This variety of sources should by now be familiar, since our earlier discussion of Gaelic, Scandinavian and Dutch loanwords and of extension, conversion and compounds included many examples of local words of diverse origins.

The subject can also be looked at by considering not individual referents, but individual dialects. Some of the greatest differences lie perhaps at the two ends of the Scots-speaking area, in Ulster and Insular Scots with their very different special influences, but even two geographically closer dialects like Aberdeenshire and Glasgow Scots have developed new and distinctive features in our period. The inventiveness and innovations of Glasgow Scots are well known, but in Aberdeenshire we find, for instance, in the twentieth century, the new compound *bidie-in* 'an unmarried live-in partner' (an appealing term that has now spread elsewhere) and a new onomatopoeic word *gramsh* 'grit (one's teeth), crunch' in the nineteenth century. There is also the extension of the adjective *ramsh*, previously used of rank or coarse food, to people in the sense of 'brusque, testy' and the arrival of *kim*, a word of unknown origin meaning 'spirited' or 'spruce'. Likewise, phrases can be of very local currency: *as hard as Henderson's erse* and its more polite truncated form *as hard as Henderson* occur only in Aberdeenshire and Angus. On the other hand, *to gie somebody rhubarb* meaning 'to give somebody a thrashing' was perhaps originally an Aberdeen phrase, being recorded there in 1930, but by 1968 had spread to Glasgow and Wigtownshire as well.

A colourful phrase like this would have found ready acceptance in Glasgow, where such language flourishes. Munro (1985) records a number, some with specifically local reference, as in the similes *like Sauchiehall Street* (said of a busy place) and *a mouth like the Clyde Tunnel* and others with more general applicability like *screw the heid* or *screw the nut* which means metaphorically 'keep calm'. A lot of the current terms recorded by writers like Munro are very recent and have not been included in surveys for SND or the LAS, so it is not always easy to know how far they are confined to Glasgow. Some terms may have always been more widely used, others may have spread out from Glasgow. Certainly Munro (1988: viii) believes that 'it could be argued that Glasgow speech is spreading in a kind of imperialistic way, at the expense of other dialects of Scots. I would attribute this to the perception of Glasgow language by young people all over Scotland as being attractive, even glamorous.' Terms strongly associated with Glasgow if not perhaps exclusive to it include new compounds like *sody-heidit* 'stupid' (*sody* being the Scots form of *soda*) and *bampot* 'a fool', derivatives like *riddy* 'a face red from embarrassment' also applied to the cause of the embarrassment, new meanings of words like *ginger* 'any kind of fizzy soft drink' and *wee barra* used as a form of address to a small person. We also find clippings like *photie* 'photograph' and a perhaps ephemeral shortening of *remedial* (as in the *remedial classes* held for children with learning difficulties) to *remmy* 'a stupid person'; this last may disappear as this use of the term *remedial* goes out of fashion or it may survive the disappearance of its source. The Gaelic borrowing *keelie* which first appeared in Glasgow has already been discussed and to it can be added *clappydoo*, an Argyllshire word of probable Gaelic origin now established in Glasgow. It is the name given to a kind of large black mussel. In the twentieth century, loans have come from different sources, such as the gangster slang noun and verb *chiv* 'knife' which takes the form *chib* in Glasgow and seems to have moved out of a purely underworld context there.

Some terms are necessarily local because they refer to local conditions. For example, *sma shot* is a strengthening thread in Paisley shawls and *sma shot day* is a Paisley holiday, originally for weavers, held on the first Saturday of July. It is necessarily a Renfrewshire term. Likewise, *Mochrum elder* or *Mochrum laird* functions as a name for the cormorant only in Galloway, where it is recognisable as referring to a coastal village near which they congregated. However, most terms do not build in such local references. Local innovation has been a powerful force in Scots in recent centuries and has helped to strengthen the geographical diversity of the language. It remains to be seen whether this centrifugal force will be counteracted in the future. If a dialect or dialects were to attract special prestige, they might begin to affect speakers of other dialects (as Munro (1988) believes may already be happening with Glasgow Scots), and linguistic diversity across the country might reduce. If it does, there is a long way to go before the strongly local character of Scots vocabulary which has developed over the centuries is overturned.

10.6 CONCLUSION

From what I have written above, it will be clear that there are a variety of reasons for what I began this chapter by noting, the enormous size of the vocabulary of Scots since 1700. While there has certainly been loss, Scots in this period has also had all the vigour and creativity of a strongly colloquial tongue, and, if there has been continuing geographical fragmentation, this has been seized as an opportunity for local innovation. At the same time, writers, unconstrained by any agreed standard of written Scots, have employed many means to enrich the vocabulary at their disposal and expand the expressive capabilities of the language. Since 1700 the vocabulary of Scots has lost a lot, retained a lot and gained a lot.

NOTES

1. My debt to SND, DOST, OED and CSD is enormous. Apart from providing me with the basic information needed to write this chapter, I have also constantly drawn on these works, particularly SND and CSD, for the definitions of Scots words used here.
2. John Jamieson, *An Etymological Dictionary of the Scottish Language*, 2 vols (Edinburgh: Creech, 1808) and *A Supplement to the Etymological Dictionary of the Scottish Language*, 2 vols (Edinburgh: Tait, 1825). Unless otherwise stated, references to Jamieson refer to material in the original edition and the supplement. Later editions included much extra material by his editors. Of these, the most important are a large four-volume edition which appeared between 1879 and 1882 with a supplement (Donaldson) in 1887 and a hefty one-volume abridgement of 1912.
3. The spelling strongly suggests borrowing from German *führen*, and Luther (whom Waddell consulted) uses this verb later in this same verse and with this same sense. On the other hand, Jamieson gives *fure* in the sense 'conduct, lead', quoting a passage from Bellenden. However, DOST glosses Bellenden's use of *fure* as 'bring, carry, bear'.
4. I use this term as a convenient name for a particular kind of literary Scots prominent in the Scots Renaissance but also found with other earlier writers where the accepted vocabulary of Scots is expanded by taking words from dictionaries and other sources. In using it, I do not intend to suggest that such Scots is not 'real'.
5. In this and subsequent entries quoted from CSD, material not relevant to the current discussion (such as notes on geographical range) has been omitted. I have drawn my examples from CSD because it covers the period both before and after 1700 and presents the material in a neatly summarised form.
6. The earliest SND quotation for this sense is dated 1836, but it could well be argued that Burns' *raise a fracas* in the first line of *Scotch Drink* means no more than 'make a fuss', although there the rhyme shows that the final -*s* is pronounced.
7. MacDiarmid could be using either the adjective or the noun (the line reads 'Mars is braw in crammasy'), but follows the spelling which Jamieson cites for the adjective. Apart from giving the Jamieson reference (which seems to refer only to obsolete usage – he cites Douglas's *Virgil* as his source for the noun and a sixteenth-century inventory for the adjective and uses the past tense in his comments) and Waddell (who probably took the word from Jamieson), SND cites only a 1940 comment by the Aberdeen poet and folklorist David Rorie that it was 'used rarely by old folks about forty years ago'. The SND Supplement adds an 1824 example with the spelling *crimsie*.
8. This is largely what CSD does, and it thus provides us with a neat summary of what the SND data suggest except that it omits some words and ignores some recognised users of archaisms like Waddell. See Robinson (1991: xvii, xxx), but note also M. Robinson (1987: 59–72). It is worth noting that it is naturally difficult to make a distinction between words which have become obsolete in the course of the second half of the twentieth century and those which are obsolescent, and this is reflected in CSD's use of the notation -*20* to mean 'recently obsolete or known to be obsolescent' (Robinson 1991: xxx).
9. The latest dating provided by SND and its Supplement is Banffshire 1933 for the noun and Southern Scots in the same year for *beildy*, but this derives from a fascicle published in the 1930s. One hesitates with a formerly common word like this, used by Scott and Burns, to label it obsolete since it is likely to be revived in writing.
10. Macaulay (1977: 55–6) checked his informants' knowledge of ten 'old Scots words' all of which

have been recorded in West Central Scots, although he does not specifically mention this. He also listed the words which arose spontaneously in the interviews. (The list aims to be complete, but the next paragraph, as well as referring to younger informants' use of the intensifier *dead*, includes two locutions in quotations (*slippy* and *our bit*) which could also be considered as 'local or Scots dialect words'). Pollner has a special problem; because Livingston is a New Town, its inhabitants do not really belong to the dialect area surrounding them. Recognising this problem, he uses a mixture of general Scots terms and words recorded for the area in *The Linguistic Atlas of Scotland*.

11

Regional Variation

Paul Johnston

11.1 THE LANGUAGE ECOLOGY OF CONTEMPORARY SCOTLAND

Whether the dialectological picture of contemporary Scotland differs vastly or mainly in detail from that of the Older Scots period depends on what one is looking at. If one concentrates on geography alone, the dominant pattern within Modern Scots dialectology reflects a definite continuity with that of the Older Scots period, as outlined in Chapter 3. The most salient geographical boundaries – the Highland Line, the Mid/North Line, the Scottish/English linguistic border – are still roughly where they were three centuries ago. Furthermore, as the relevant features in subsequent sections will show, many major dialect differentiae are old, continuations of the same differences found in Older Scots. There are a few qualifications that need to be added to this picture of cosy continuity, however. First, there are a few dialects of Scots that were only in the early stages of their formation in the Older period. In the Northern Isles, a new dialect type, Insular Scots, has arisen from a second-language variety with Angus and Fife roots (Catford 1957b). Scots was also exported to Northern Ireland in the seventeenth century as a colonial dialect, and a separate South-west branch of Mid-Scots, with affinities to West Mid, Gallovidian and Southern Scots, formed there (G. B. Adams 1986: 24–5; Gregg 1985: 7–10). Small parts of the Highlands, notably Speyside, the Black Isle, Bute and parts of Arran and Argyll, have also been added in recent years (Macafee 1989: 431).

There have also been a few dialect realignments. Gallovidian has lost its 'second-language'-like characteristics and is no longer distinct enough from the rest of Mid-Scots to be more than a subdialect, called South Mid in the terminology of the *Scottish National Dictionary* (Grant 1931: xxviii). Southern dialects have been losing their traditional characteristics for a long time, and are being 'captured' by neighbouring speech communities with greater cachet and influence, as a comparison of Sir James Murray's (1873) account of Central Roxburghshire dialect with Zai's (1942) material from Morebattle, or my own (Johnston 1980) Hawick or Yetholm data, would reveal. It seems only a matter of time before Central Border dialects become fully-fledged East Mid ones, much like Berwickshire or Tweeddale in character. West Dumfriesshire dialect is undergoing a similar absorption into West Mid; a comparison of the West Mid/Gallovidian line in SND (Grant 1931: xxiv–xxv) with the one in Map 11.1 shows that the modern line lies considerably to the south of where it used to be. Recent Mid-Scots innovations, such as OUT-Fronting, /t/-Glottalling and /r/-Vocalisation no longer stop at the dialectal border in the way that earlier Central

Map 11.1 Dialect map of Scotland.

Belt changes sometimes did (Johnston 1985b); instead, they often expand both northwards and southwards, making further realignments possible as Mid-Scots influence increases on nearby areas.

There are also a few cases where forms of Scots face imminent 'dialect death'. Black Isle dialects of Scots are eroding and being transformed into 'Broad Invernesian', a locally accented form of Highland English, while in Ulster, only three centuries after its formation, Scots as a linguistic system in much of Antrim, Down, Derry and Donegal is similarly prone to replacement by Mid-Ulster dialects related to Belfast vernacular, which is of Hiberno-English origin (Harris 1985: 139), but thoroughly influenced by forms of Ulster Scots in most aspects of the language (Adams 1986: 25; Harris 1985: 140).

The cause of all these developments has been the same: a trend towards increasing ease of travel and communications, making it possible for much more social interplay between large cities and their expanding hinterlands than was available before (Macafee 1994d: 69). This results in the spread of forms from the centres as rural people come into first-hand contact with city residents, speaking forms of Urban Scots that carry connotations of modernity and a measure of 'street-smarts', though not overt prestige (Pollner 1985b: 60–75; Sandred 1983: 16–19).

Yet, such a strictly geographical account gives only a small glimpse of the extent of change. The 'language ecology' of modern Scotland and the sociolinguistic status of Scots is very different from what it was in 1500 or even 1700, and, because of this, we even have to redefine what Scots is. It is not a mere *patois*, as the English vernaculars are, but has a special status, as a language of a nation, and, at least, the best example of a *dialecte* in English. The phonology of modern Scots, except in certain areas in Ulster and the Black Isle, also remains essentially native despite a certain amount of word-by-word 'dialect drain', including non-Standard restructurings (like Central Belt *bought* [bo?]) of some items due to Scottish Standard English influence (Macafee 1994a: 222–35). There exists relatively little trace yet of the North Midlandisation that is spreading diphthongal reflexes in *out*, *house*, back rounded ones in *no*, *stone*, and /u:/ values in *moon*, *do* throughout the north of England. One main effect of the wave of modernisation associated with urbanisation in the nineteenth and early twentieth centuries has been to harden the Scottish/English linguistic border, as Glasgow and Edinburgh forms – linguistically further from Northumbrian and Cumbrian than the Southern Scots ones which they are replacing – have seeped into the border country just when the English Border dialects were becoming more influenced by Newcastle (South Northumbrian) speech in the east, and Lancastrian (never mind Carlisle) varieties in the west (Johnston 1980: 181, 210, 213, 217, 229). This creates the linguistic conditions for reinforcement of the persistent sense of cultural uniqueness which most Scots feel (Macafee 1985: 7), aiding the further preservation of Scots forms, in a feedback loop.

Whether this will remain the case in the future remains to be seen. Our prognosis depends heavily on our definition of Scots. If we take a phonology- or syntax-based definition, and count it as comprising the localised English dialects of Scotland while allowing lexical turnover, one could consider it the 'healthiest' traditional dialect in Britain, and accord it a rosy future. If however, we define it mainly in terms of its traditional lexis, there is another, less optimistic viewpoint tenable (Macafee 1994a: 31–3). The conclusion which we must draw is this: at least for the present, the dialect boundaries within Scots seem to remain roughly constant, with the exceptions mentioned above, although the characteristics delineating these boundaries may be transitory, particularly in the lexical sphere. It therefore makes sense to define as Scots such dialect features as are localisable and present, and to use these, not obsolete items, as our diagnostic characteristics. This view reflects a cautious optimism about the future of a distinctive Scots dialect group.[1]

11.1.1 Outline

In the next section, I define the geolinguistic divisions of Scots, based on a modified version of the analysis used in the *Scottish National Dictionary* (Grant and Murison 1931–76). While Grant based his breakdown on a Neogrammarian *Stammbaum* framework, the analysis used here, while keeping alive the notion of dialect group and subgroup, reflects more of a wave or gravity model (Chambers and Trudgill 1980: 189–202). Each dialect is considered in the core or periphery of several 'influence zones' based on Glasgow, Aberdeen, Belfast, Newcastle, Kirkwall and Lerwick, so that one can see clearly which regions are focal, transitional or relic areas. I also present a model for discussing the sociolinguistic characteristics of those who use Scots in each area so that the dialects may be placed in their proper social context.

Sections 11.4 through 11.7 each concentrate on the internal definition of Scots, delineating the different types of Scots from each other, one facet of their phonology at a time. Section 11.7 concentrates on consonantal features, and 11.4, 11.5 and 11.6 respectively on the front, back and diphthongal vowel classes in Older Scots, the extra space needed to define these being necessary because of the plethora of vocalic changes that may serve as important dialect differentiae.

In the consonantal section, characteristics of the stop/affricate, fricative and sonorant systems are described in terms of the geographical distribution of specific rules or processes of change affecting each system or its members. These rules may belong to layers necessary for external definition as mentioned above, or may serve to differentiate units within Scots of varying sizes. They may produce splits, mergers and phonemic transfers of any kind, or simply might change phonetic realisations of consonant phonemes across the board or in specific environments.

The vowels are treated in a different way. In each section, an introductory discussion compares the inventories of different Scots front, back and diphthongal phonemic systems respectively, clearly indicating the possibilities for the shape of the systems using the framework developed in Catford (1957b). The following subsections describe the results of each Older Scots vowel class in turn, outlining the distribution and timbre of isolative reflexes, the allophony patterns, and special developments of subclasses transferred to other classes since the Older Scots period, so that the reader can trace the historical development of each sound.

11.2 THE GEOGRAPHICAL BREAKDOWN OF MODERN SCOTS DIALECTS

11.2.1 The Classification of Scots Dialects

To analyse the dialectology of Modern Scots, one must first develop some sort of classification of Scots varieties, so that the similarities and differences between them may be enumerated and geolinguistic patterns discovered. Second, one must define the social characteristics and the linguistic attitudes of Scots speakers towards their language, giving a sociolinguistic profile of each region.

The most accepted classification (Robinson 1985: xxxi) was developed by Grant (1931: xxv–xli) in the introduction to the *Scottish National Dictionary*. This, in turn, was a refinement of an earlier classification developed by Ellis (1889: 709–820) with Murray's help, as part of a wider classification of English dialects. In Grant's scheme, Scots was divided into four main dialect groups, each with several subdivisions: (1) *Insular Scots*, comprising Shetlandic (Insular B) and Orcadian (Insular A); (2) *Northern Scots*, consisting of the dialects of Angus and the Mearns (South Northern), Buchan/Aberdeen and Morayshire (Mid Northern A and B) and the Black Isle and Caithness (North Northern A and B); (3) *Mid Scots*, comprising Clydesdale/Glaswegian (West Mid), Gallovidian (South Mid), Fife/Perthshire, and Edinburgh and the Eastern Borders (East Mid A and B respectively); and (4) *Southern Scots*, encompassing the dialects of the Western and Central Borders.

Except for the omission of Ulster Scots, which probably should be treated as a separate Mid-Scots variety,[2] Grant's classification still seems accurate in broad outline, allowing for the static, *Stammbaum*-based arrangement that he uses (Petyt 1980). Nowadays, we recognise that contact and interplay between adjacent dialects is normal, and that boundaries between regional forms of language are rarely sharp (Trudgill 1986). Modern sociolinguists adopt a dynamic version of the wave model of linguistic spread (Trudgill 1986; Petyt 1980), by which innovations spread out from centres like waves from a pool via weak social ties (L. Milroy 1994: 136–8), or even better, the 'gravity model' of Chambers and Trudgill (1980), which incorporates the finding that innovations seem to spread from large city to large city before affecting smaller places in between. This latter model works very well for Scots, since many recent innovations, anyway, are first attested in centres such as Glasgow or Aberdeen, and spread out from there (Macafee 1983: 42).[3]

While I do not wish to depart too much from tradition in this account, and therefore keep most of the traditional names and classifications, I have superimposed another level of analysis upon it based on this idea of dynamic spread. In this model, the Scottish Lowlands are divided into spheres of influence: (1) a Central Belt sphere of influence, where the focal areas are the cities of Glasgow and Edinburgh; (2) a north-eastern sphere, where Aberdeen is the focus; and (3) similar spheres based on non-Scots-speaking towns such as Belfast and Newcastle, and tiny, Insular Scots spheres based on Kirkwall and Lerwick. Each of these is composed of an *inner core*, dialects within the actual focal area of the sphere; an *outer core*, areas affected by most of the innovations (if not all) spreading from the inner core; and a *periphery*, which receives only some new features. Spheres of influence can overlap, and location in a *transition zone* is defined by belonging to two at once, as Angus dialects do, being probably best characterised as part of the Aberdonian outer core and the Central Belt periphery (Perthshire dialects would have the converse relationship). *Relic areas* such as Insular Scots are characterised as peripheral (here, to Aberdeen) and in no major region's core.[4]

It follows that we can make some predictions about what features a given dialect is going to possess. For instance, the relative linguistic distance to a Central Belt inner core would be reflected in the number of speakers possessing such Glasgow-based or amplified innovations as /t/-Glottalling and /r/-Vocalisation. We can probably predict that inner core dialects like West Mid might have a higher vowel in CAUGHT than Lothian dialects do, and these, in turn, will be closer to [ɔ:] than the equivalent vowel in Central or Eastern Border Scots, Gallovidian or Ulster Scots, or that Aberdonian has a rule changing /xw/ → /f/ with fewer exceptions than other Northern dialects, or has more Post-Velar Dissimilations (turning *guid* to *gweed*, *wame* to *wyme*, and *coal* to *quile*) than Angus, Morayshire or Caithness. Where we cannot predict the frequency this way, as with *wear/care/air*-Lowering, which is at least as old in Ulster Scots as in Glasgow (Macafee 1994a: 225–37), or Northern Diphthongisation, which is as common in north Banffshire as in Aberdeen (Johnston 1985b: 31), the innovation stems from somewhere else in the area.

The finer points of Grant's classification also need to be revised, partially because some linguistic features used as diagnostic criteria have spread or receded since his time, but also because the linguistic distance between his subvarieties is sometimes as great as between those accorded full varietal status. A case can be made, for instance, for renaming East Mid A as North Mid, since Fife and Perthshire dialects appear to share some Northern features with Angus varieties, such as the *wame* > *wyme* part of Post-Velar Dissimilation, final /ʌi/ for earlier /e/, low CAUGHT[5] reflexes in Perthshire, and so on (Macafee 1989). These make the linguistic difference from Lothian dialects (Grant's East Mid B) about as great as that between West and East Mid. The diversity of the North Mid group also merits a further division into Perthshire and Kinross (North Mid A), North, East and Central Fife (North Mid B), and South-west Fife, Clackmannan and possibly Stirling (North Mid C), with the first shading into Angus and the last into Lothian and Lanarkshire varieties.

Grant's East Mid B could easily be split into Lothian Scots and Eastern Border Scots (a putative new East Mid A vs B distinction), based on the former's lacking a merger between CAT and CAUGHT vowels, and recent innovations, such as extensive /t/-Glottalling, /u/-Fronting and /r/-Vocalisation, which are well established in the Lothians but new in the eastern Borders.

Southern Scots, treated as a unit by Grant (1931: xxviii–xxxii), probably once exhibited a much closer unity than it does today, due to the differential effects of Central Belt influence. It can now be split into the Southern A of the Central Borders and Teviotdale, open to influences from Mid Scots in the merger of COT/COAT (Older Scots /ɔ/:/ɔ:/) and MATE/BAIT (Older Scots /a:/:/ai/); in the unrounding of the first element of NEW and LOUP (Older Scots /iu/ and /ʌu/) and the whole of BOOT (Older Scots /ø:/); and the Southern B of the western Borders, which preserves the ancestral features more faithfully. South Mid also can be split into at least two dialects, that of Wigtownshire and of West Dumfriesshire and Kirkcudbrightshire, again based on a better-preserved BEAT/MATE/BAIT distinction, rounded CUT vowel and CAT/CAUGHT distinction in the former. I have therefore split South Mid into A and B subdivisions in my breakdown.[6]

11.2.2   The Sociolinguistic Characterisation of Scots

Scots, of course, does not only vary geographically; it varies socially as well, since different types of people use it in different regions, depending on many factors such as the size of town and distance from major cities, the social class and social network make-up of the locality, the proportion of natives in a given community's population, and socially held and personally held attitudes towards the language. While in a sense, every town in the Scottish Lowlands uses Scots in its own way, and there is ample scope for individuals to differ from the rest of the community, my own experience suggests that many patterns predominating in a given town fall into one of four major patterns. In Pattern I, localised Scots is used by nearly all natives, of whatever social class or educational attainment, with hardly any Scottish Standard English (SSE) devoid of marked Scotticisms in use at all, even in speech to outsiders. In these communities, style-shifting may nevertheless be present, due to the importance of an ingroup/outgroup distinction, since local networks are generally strong in such areas. There may be some class-tying in formal styles, but generally class variation is an unimportant determiner of dialect, particularly compared to identity of the interlocutor.

In Pattern II communities, like Pattern I ones, virtually everyone uses Scots to fellow ingroup members. Such native speakers of SSE that exist are statusful, but marginal to the tight networks within the community – the local schoolteacher, possibly the preacher, or local gentry, if any. However, marked class-tying appears in speech to outgroup members, or when distancing ingroup members, treating them as 'honorary' outgroup members. Middle-class residents of such a community can often perform prodigious feats of code-switching, from very localised Scots to pure, even sometimes RP-influenced SSE, depending on the setting, situation and participants in the conversation. Working-class members may code-switch similarly, if they are not members of tight social networks, but if they are network members they generally code-switch only partially, editing out only some Scotticisms, especially lexical and syntactic ones. The result is a mixed dialect. Many dialect monographs (Hettinga 1981; Wettstein 1942; Zai 1942; Dieth 1932; Mutschmann 1908) conducted outside the urban Central Belt seem to describe communities like this.

Pattern III communities, at first glance, appear to use language like Pattern II ones. Scots speakers are plentiful up and down the social scale, many upper middle-class members code-switch radically, and class-tying is in evidence in formal styles, so that a Labovian sociolinguistic survey would find regular variation patterns for most variables (Johnston 1980). Close examination, though, would uncover a few native-born SSE monodialectals, mostly middle-class children of middle-class parents, as well as those who, for personal or background reasons, disparage the local form of Scots or are not members of any tight local networks. Pattern III communities tend to be small towns or villages, where, often, most inhabitants are working-class members and code-drift between Scots and mixed styles as in Pattern II areas.[7]

Pattern IV most closely approaches the 'classic' Labovian pattern seen in English and American communities (Trudgill 1974; Labov 1966), where Scots is a working-class vernacular. Here, the middle classes are nearly exclusively composed of SSE monolinguals, though they may use bits and pieces of Scots as 'set pieces' within an otherwise Standard matrix, and may retain a mixed style in their most casual styles if they used Scots extensively in their youth. The true code-switchers in Pattern IV are upper working-class and perhaps lower middle-class members, together with members of less statusful groups who do not belong to tight social networks similar to those described by L. Milroy (1980). As in other communities, network members drift between more-or-less localised Scots and mixed varieties, depending on the usual stylistic and interlocutory factors. This is the pattern exhibited in major Scottish urban centres in the Central Belt (Macafee 1994a; Johnston 1983a; Macaulay and Trevelyan 1977).

While I cannot prove this, the 'nested' geographical distribution of these patterns seems to suggest that something like Pattern IV evolved through stages resembling Patterns II and III from something like the Pattern I Older Scots set-up, as IV does seem to be associated with the major centres of innovation (except for Aberdeen) and the lower-numbered patterns with more peripheral communities. There are also correlates of some aspects of linguistic attitudes with type of pattern. We might speculate, for instance, that someone from a Pattern IV community, on average, would be less likely to regard Scots as a separate language from English, and would be more likely to either disparage or romanticise it (Macafee 1985: 13). Having said this, however, there are differences which do not correlate so well. Pattern III communities exist in both the Borders and the north-east, but the north-eastern speakers seem to regard their variety as Scots-*par-excellence* (or, to use their terminology, *Doric*), and the Borderers regard theirs with far more localism – Hawick, Jedburgh, or Galashiels first and Scots second (if Scots is not only a literary language to them). These differences have to do with the individual social history of the region, and sometimes the community in question, as shown below.

In the following descriptions, information on what patterns are found is worked into the rest of the layout of the geography. Statements made on this matter should be taken as tentative, as it is often based on anecdotal information and personal observation, the usually scanty (and ancient!) accounts of dialect monographs (Zai 1942; Wettstein 1942; Dieth 1932; Wilson 1915, 1923; Mutschmann 1908), if also the much more current and complete information found in sociolinguistic works (Macafee 1983, 1994a; Pollner 1985c; Melchers 1985; Hettinga 1981; J. Milroy 1981; Johnston 1980, 1983a, 1983b, 1985a; Reid 1978; Romaine 1978; Douglas-Cowie 1978; Macaulay and Trevelyan 1977), which, however, is biased towards Pattern IV communities and neglects the Northern and South Mid groups.

11.2.3 Mid-Scots

Dialects belonging to the Mid-Scots group are spoken over a wide area south of the Highland Line, centred around the Forth and Clyde estuaries but extending from the north shore of the Tay to the Cheviots on the eastern side and from the Highland Line to the Solway Firth, and beyond to the Glens of Antrim and the Ards Peninsula, and even to Derry and Donegal on the western side. The area thus includes every major conurbation in Scotland except Aberdeen and Inverness, and the majority of Scots speakers live in it.

The *West Mid* group is the best known of any of the Mid-Scots – or any Scots – dialects to outsiders, as it includes both the dialect of Glasgow, the largest city in Scotland, made familiar throughout the world by entertainers from Stanley Baxter and Rikki Fulton to Billy Connolly, and the Ayrshire dialect, which forms the primary base of Robert Burns' poetic Scots. West Mid dialects extend eastwards to the present Lothian/Strathclyde border, where the boundary is rather sharp. A few West Lothian and Peeblesshire communities like Fauldhouse and Biggar probably belong here, however. On the south side, West Mid shades gradually into South Mid, and, although south Lanarkshire down to the Moorfoots has always been assigned to this area, Grant (1931: xxiv–xxv) and others following him (Robinson 1985: xxxi) have generally assigned Carrick in Ayrshire to Gallovidian. Based on the findings in Mather and Speitel (1986: 122–6), Carrick dialects down to Ballantrae are better counted as West Mid, although they do exhibit transitional character in their back reflexes of the vowel of CAT and low ones in the CAUGHT class. On the other hand, though dialects of West Dumfriesshire and Nithsdale have small West-Mid-like vowel systems, they are still South Mid lexically, and are better treated under the latter division. The southern boundary of West Mid, therefore, follows the crest of the Moorfoots, then crosses over the southern extremity of Ayrshire.

On the north and west, West Mid is bounded by the Highland line, and the area includes all Dunbartonshire and Bute on the Lowland side, and even East Arran and Campbeltown in Argyll as an enclave[8] (Grant 1931: xxvii–xxviii). On the north-east side, the West Mid/ North Mid line seems even harder to define than the Gallovidian boundary. Even Grant (1931: xxvii) did not really know where to put Stirlingshire. West Stirlingshire communities as far as Denny and Larbert mostly use forms shared with Glasgow and Airdrie, but the dialects of Stirling and Falkirk could equally well be put here, into East Mid, or into North Mid. The last-mentioned is proposed in this chapter on lexical grounds, but one must remember that East Stirlingshire dialects are transitional to all three groups both lexically and phonologically.

There is more uniformity within West Mid than most other dialect groups, but subtypes can be enumerated as: (1) Glaswegian itself, spoken in Rutherglen, Clydebank, Paisley and Renfrew as well as in the city; (2) a closely allied east Lanarkshire type (Motherwell, Hamilton, Wishaw, Strathaven, Airdrie, Coatbridge, Cumbernauld, Denny); (3) a more conservative Clyde mouth type, near the Highland Line (Greenock, Gourock, Rothesay, Dumbarton, probably Campbeltown); (4) an Ayrshire type (Kilmarnock, Irvine, Prestwick, Ayr) and (5) the transition dialects to South Mid A in Lanarkshire (Lanark, Carnwath, Carstairs, Leadhills) and to South Mid B in Ayrshire (Maybole, Barrhead).

As the West Mid group is to Glasgow, so East Mid is to Edinburgh. However, this group is far less uniform, and is best divided into A and B varieties. Lothian dialect proper, East Mid A, is spoken over most of the present-day region of that name, except East Lothian east of Dunbar. Subtypes include (1) a West Lothian variety, with a heavy influence of West Mid on vocabulary (Linlithgow, Bathgate, West Calder, Livingston), (2) a Midlothian variety, including Edinburgh vernacular (Edinburgh, Dalkeith, Penicuik, Bonnyrigg) and a closely-related East Lothian type (Tranent, Haddington, North Berwick, Dunbar). The boundary with East Mid B is semi-circular, roughly following the watershed between the Forth and Tweed, curving up through the Lammermuirs to Dunbar. The North Mid boundary lies at the Forth, though it is more gradual than the width of the Firth of Forth would suggest; the North Mid C dialects of South Fife are transitional to East Mid, and Forthside communities such as Leith or North Berwick traditionally have a North Mid feature or two (Mather and Speitel 1986: 136–7; 140–5).

Eastern Border Scots (East Mid B) covers a more strictly rural area, with few major towns, in the Lammermuirs, Berwickshire and Tweeddale, extending south to the border as far as the Cheviot, then following a line just south of the Tweed and Yarrow west to just past Selkirk; the boundary then curves north to west Peeblesshire. Coastal (Cockburnspath, Burnmouth,[9] Ayton), central Berwickshire/east Tweeddale (Duns, Coldstream, Kelso, Yetholm) and west Tweeddale (Galashiels, Selkirk, Melrose, Earlston) types can be differentiated, with the last two mentioned shading into Southern Scots, to which much of the area apparently once belonged (Zai 1942: 5).

North of the Forth/Clyde line lie the North Mid dialects, which exhibit similarities in lexicon and phonology with all their neighbours, even while maintaining a distinctive character all their own. The area covered is large, taking in all of the 'Wee Kingdom of Fife', plus Clackmannanshire, east Stirlingshire and Kinross, a corner of west Angus, and the Tay Valley from Dundee and Tayport as far north as Blair Atholl and Pitlochry. The large number of centres in this district (Stirling, Dunfermline, Kirkcaldy, Perth, St Andrews and Dundee) and the diversity typical of transition zones (Trudgill 1986: 52–62) ensures a large amount of internal variability, so that *three* major varieties have to be postulated within this area.

North Mid A is the Perthshire dialect, to which west Angus, Dundee and Kinross have affinities, with many ingliding mid vowels, a COT/COAT contrast, back reflexes of the vowel in CAT, and low ones in CAUGHT. Subtypes include North-eastern (Coupar Angus), Highland Line (Pitlochry, Blair Atholl, Dunkeld), central Tayside (Perth, Kinross, Comrie) and Dundonian proper. The last two types shade into North Mid C and B respectively to some extent.

North Mid B is historically centred around Cupar and St Andrews, and is spoken over all of central (Auchtermuchty, Cupar) and east Fife (St Andrews), including the conservative East Neuk (Crail, Pittenweem). These dialects often have COT/COAT and BEAT–BOOT/MATE– BAIT contrasts and [ɔ:] in CAUGHT.

The Fife coalfields and the heavily industrialised lands in the Dunfermline area and along the Forth are the heartland of North Mid C, which can be separated into west Fife (Dunfermline, Cowdenbeath) and Stirlingshire (Stirling, Falkirk, Alloa, Clackmannan) subtypes. These dialects must have been much more like A and B ancestrally, but now are subject to influence from East and West Mid, so that the COT:COAT and BIT:BOOT–BEAT contrasts are being realigned.

The South Mid (Gallovidian) dialects are also quite diverse, but their conservatism is more pronounced, as the area is largely a rural one, with Dumfries and Stranraer as the only towns with over 10,000 inhabitants (*Book of British Towns* 1982: 126–27, 377). The boundary line with Southern Scots is abrupt, cutting between Annandale and Nithsdale as far north as Lochmaben, then across to the old Dumfriesshire/Selkirkshire boundary to end at St Mary's Loch; but, as discussed before, there is a gradual shade-in to West Mid from there to Ballantrae.

East Gallovidian (South Mid A) is associated with the old counties of Dumfriesshire and Kirkcudbright, and like its neighbours to the east has no or restricted contrast between CAT:CAUGHT, an unrounded CUT vowel, and, in the Dumfriesshire type (Moffat, Dumfries), a small vowel system. Dumfries dialects are prone to pick up West Mid innovations, being on the main communication routes from Glasgow to England. The Kirkcudbrightshire type (Castle Douglas, Kirkcudbright, Gatehouse of Fleet, Dalbeattie), which extends over the Solway Firth coastline as far as the Nith, keeps more of the ancestral distinctions.

South Mid B, the Wigtownshire dialect, is the most conservative of the group, and still accords reasonably well with the description of Gallovidian given in Grant (1931: xxviii). There are Rinns (Stranraer, Ballantrae) and Machars (Whithorn) subtypes associated with the two peninsulas that make up Wigtownshire, but the differences between them are minor.

Across the Irish Sea, settlers from Ayrshire, Galloway and the Borders planted Ulster Scots, *South-west Mid*. According to Gregg (1985: 11–14), Ulster Scots once extended over a wide area, including the Ards Peninsula, north and central Antrim and Derry, and parts of Donegal near the mouth of the Boyne, and was once spoken in centres like Coleraine, Ballymena and Derry City, at least by the Protestant population. The modern evidence suggests that there were Western (in Derry and Donegal), Central (in Antrim) and Eastern (in the Ards) subtypes (Mather and Speitel 1986: 192–203; Gregg 1985: 11–17), but all but the dialects of north Antrim and the Ards were already eroding by the time the Linguistic Survey of Scotland came through, and the whole group is apparently gradually turning into a new North Ulster Hiberno-English prone to Belfast influence. Phonologically, Antrim dialects resemble South Mid (as did Derry ones) and Down varieties resemble West Mid, but all have the same Gaelic substratal characteristics present that characterize all Ulster (and to a lesser extent, Wigtown) varieties: a tendency to palatalise /k g/ before front vowels, a retroflex /r/ and clear or doubly articulated /l/, variable /θ ð/-Stopping, and so on.

In the Central Belt, which forms the core of the Mid-Scots area, Pattern IV prevails both in the large centres and small towns, many of which have added city residents due to Glasgow, and to a much lesser extent Edinburgh, overspill. In this area, Mid-Scots today is generally considered a true vernacular in the sense of L. Milroy (1980: 19), the property of the working classes, whether we mean by that a rural set of smallholders, farm workers and miners or fishers, or an urban one of factory workers, labourers and the chronically poor. As all sociolinguistic studies have shown, these people are generally speakers of modern, non-traditional Scots, even if they have partial or total command of SSE, in a highly accented form in their formal styles (Pollner 1985c; Macafee 1983, 1994a; Johnston 1980, 1983b; Reid 1978; Romaine 1978; Macaulay and Trevelyan 1977). Middle-class members are primarily SSE monolinguals, although, as stated above, they may borrow from Scots in certain contexts.

However, Patterns II or III obtain, or did until recently, in small localities on the periphery of Mid Scots, in the North Mid A and B, South Mid and East Mid B-speaking areas. Here, traditional forms are retained to a greater extent (Mather and Speitel 1986: 88–90, 92–7, 106–10, 141–51, 160–4, 170–90; Hettinga 1981) and are thus a closer approximation to the sociolinguistic situation of older times. Scottish Standard English monolinguals are rare here, first, because small towns and villages characterising these localities often have large working classes (who would use Scots anyway) and tight village social networks; and second, because people of middle-class parentage often move away, finding their fortunes (and social networks) elsewhere. Those who stay are marginal to the networks of the community, though they may be fully tolerated as peripheral members. Working-class members speak a more conservative Scots than their equivalent in the cities, but drift or switch in the same way. Since Pattern III is sustained by a largely locally born populace and the presence of the sort of traditional networks characteristic of villages, it remains to be seen whether this pattern will remain intact in the future.

In Central Scotland, the difference from northern English sociolinguistic patterns lies less in who uses the vernacular as what it is associated with – class/network identity and localism in both cases, although there is at least an overtone of an association with a true ethnicity, which helps to keep Scots registers alive (Aitken 1979: 106–8). Now, as Macafee (1985) has stated, a sense of Scottish ethnicity and nationalism does not need to be mobilised using Scots, and it does seem that urban speakers of Mid-Scots varieties do not feel the linkage of their ethnicity with language as overtly as north easterners or Borderers do (Johnston 1983b), and even seem torn about whether their 'patter' is real Scots (Sandred 1983: 25), but the link to Scottish pride seems to be at least covert (Macafee 1994a: 197).

Innovations within Mid-Scots are spread from or via Glasgow and Edinburgh, often up the railway lines and main roads, though spreading evenly around the cities' immediate hinterlands. The Glasgow–Edinburgh, Glasgow–Stirling–Perth–Dundee, Glasgow–Ayr and Glasgow–Carlisle corridors are especially likely to be regions of rapid spread of innovations, while areas away from these 'nerve centres' are the most conservative areas. New towns like Cumbernauld, Livingston, Glenrothes and West Kilbride have a large urban-born contingent and pick up innovations early (Pollner 1985b, 1985c), although not without koinéisation. They are probably close enough to major centres to participate in the early spread anyway.

11.2.4 Southern Scots

At one time (Murray 1873: 84), Southern Scots varieties, growing out of an old Scots/English transition zone, occupied the whole of what is now the border region from central Berwickshire west to east Dumfriesshire. The dialect group is now found no further east than central Roxburghshire, although the Dumfriesshire boundary has not receded.

Western Border Scots (Southern B), spoken along the Solway Firth, in Annandale, Eskdale and Liddesdale, as well as the old Debatable Land in Cumbria, is the only variety to have retained such ancestral Southern features as the MATE/BAIT and COT/COAT contrasts, and Rounded-LOUP reflexes that were once found as far east as Morebattle in East Roxburghshire (Zai 1942: 5). Subvarieties include Liddesdale dialect (Langholm, Newcastleton), east Dumfriesshire/north Cumberland (Longtown) and Annandale/Eskdale (Annan, Canonbie, Lockerbie), with the last two strongly shading into varieties of Cumbrian both lexically and phonologically.

Southern A, to the north and east, still has the distinctive diphthongisation of final MEET/BEAT and OUT (a version of Pennine Diphthongisation, usually associated with northern England) and an extreme Ich/Ach rule (in so far as /x/ is present), as well as the Border Scots Vowel Shift (Lass 1976: 121). The size and configuration of the vowel inventory, however, resembles an East Mid B variety, and East Mid innovations penetrate the area freely, which does not bode well for the dialect's distinctiveness in the future. There are Jedwater (Jedburgh, Newtown St Boswells) and Teviotdale subvarieties (Hawick, Oxnam), with only minor phonetic differences between them. In contrast to the gentle boundary with English varieties along the Cumbrian coast, differentiation from west and north Northumbrian is sharp, although a few Scots characteristics extend into Glendale and Berwick to the east (Glauser 1974).

The whole of Southern Scots seems to be associated with archetypal Pattern III communities (Johnston 1980), where middle-class but upwardly mobile speakers retain a Scots register for use with family and friends. There is still a strong sense of locality, and a penchant for tight networks among locals dating back to reiving-family days. Central Borderers (Johnston 1980: 39) have a pride in their towns still reinforced by rugby loyalties and old festivals based historically on the guarding of the town limits, and a pride in their local vernacular goes with the territory. The dialect is felt to be 'Hawick' or 'Selkirk' or 'Jedburgh' more than it is perceived as Scots, which is more likely to refer to the traditional language of Burns. Borderers regard it even more as a coherent system than speakers in the most peripheral Mid Scots localities do. My impression is that Southern Scots speakers may have a different set of language attitudes from even Berwickshire ones, or at least from the East Mid B speakers whom I interviewed in Yetholm. These latter people asserted that they spoke Scots; the only thing distinctively 'Yetholm' about their dialect was the eastern Border layer of words of Romany origin like *joogal* 'dog', *barriegadgee* 'man', *barriemanishee* 'woman' and *chorry* 'to steal' (Grant 1931: xxvi), reflecting the village's settlement by Romany travellers under the Faa kings. For the Hawick informants, on the other hand, their vernacular is first and foremost local. There is no question to them that it is not 'English', which subsumes both the dialects of England and SSE here, and for most, that neither 'Hawick' nor 'Scots' is English either. Some speakers can translate from 'Hawick' or other local vernaculars to 'English' and back again, regarding such code-switching as evidence of bilingualism.

There is only a small native SSE-speaking contingent, mainly middle-class children of middle-class parents, often from other areas. The class-consciousness of most informants is much less strong than that of Edinburgh ones, and what really dictates the choice of variety seems to be primarily whether their interlocutor is a member of the same network (or a similar one) or not, and only secondarily, other factors. This ingroup/outgroup sense, of course, underlies other distinctions anyway. If Southern Scots becomes recessive, it will be due to societal trends of a post-industrial nature, which greatly reduce the importance of locality, combined with increased ease of access to and from major cities. Twentieth-century immigration from the Central Belt has not helped the dialect's survival at all (Johnston 1980: 12–13). Whether the Borderer's local pride will keep any variety of this type of Scots alive will be a fruitful topic of future study.

11.2.5 Northern Scots

The Northern group constitutes the dialects of the Scottish mainland north of the Tay Valley and east of the Highland Line. This is the land of the Aberdonian sphere of influence, the second biggest in Scotland. These varieties occupy a rather peripheral position not only relative to English dialects as a whole, but also with respect to Mid-Scots. The Northern group has therefore developed a large component of its own vocabulary and its own sets of phonological changes. However, as in the Borders, the language of the Scottish north and north-east has been associated traditionally with rural lifestyles, which usually correlates with cultural and linguistic conservatism. Even Aberdeen took most of its people from its own immediate hinterland until the recent oil boom, so that there was no need for the extent of koinéisation that affected Glasgow until the last few decades or so.

Nowadays, while one can easily go up the east coast or through the Mearns to Aberdeen, and from there further into other Northern Scots centres such as Fraserburgh, Peterhead, Banff or Elgin, the routes are rather restricted, as the Grampian range forms a formidable barrier to direct north-south penetration. All routes to the west of these mountains go through traditionally Gaelic-speaking Highland areas. This makes the North Northern dialects true geographic isolates, separated from the rest of Scots by all land routes. Yet maritime connections have historically been strong between the fishing cultures that extend from John o' Groats down to Fife's East Neuk, and these links seem much more important than land connections from the Moray Firth northwards. Each fishing town seems to have its own vernacular, with grouping rather loose (Dieth 1932: xvii). Since the farming districts inland have their own versions of Northern Scots, spread over wide areas as West Mid Scots dialects are, all divisions of this group have inland and coastal subtypes. The relative isolation and geographic semi-independence from the rest of Scots has assured a strong linguistic identity, and for many north-easterners their 'Doric' *is* Scots, and the fact that strict class-tying is either lacking or a recent consequence of the oil boom helps to assure the vitality of the dialect.

Geographically, the South Northern dialects occupy a wedge-shaped area between the part of the Highland Line roughly following the old northern boundary of Angus and the sea, from the rolling countryside just north of the Tay alluvial plain and the Dundee conurbation to the range of small hills called the Mounth, reaching the sea south of Stonehaven. While there exists the usual heightened amount of variability in this area typical of a transition zone, one can separate out coastal (Arbroath, Montrose), central Mearns (Brechin, Forfar) and north Angus/Kincardine subtypes, with the last shading into North Mid A. Since the South Northern area lies between Dundee and Aberdeen, it is prone to linguistic influence from both cities, but at the moment the Dundonian influence is stronger, so that Mid features tend to be dominant and Northern ones recessive. Recent Glasgow-based sound changes such as OUT-Fronting, extensive Glottalling and even /r/-vocalisation have made it to the Mearns towns, where they are combined with older Northern features like /xw/-Labialisation in *wh*-pronouns and Post-Velar and Post-/w/ Dissimilations, and uniquely Angus ones like Scottish COAT-Fronting. Vowel systems tend to be large.

Further north than these are the Mid-Northern dialects belonging to the 'heartland' of Northern Scots, exhibiting the most extensive panoply of Northern features. Grant (1931: xxxiv–xxxvi) divides this area into two main dialects, Mid-Northern A, containing the most typical north-eastern varieties ('Buchan' – taking in Mar and Formartine as well – and Aberdonian), and Mid-Northern B, associated with the Laigh of Moray and the Elgin area. Central and south Banffshire are considered as B dialects by Grant (1931: xxiv–xxv), though the first occupies the same sort of transitional status as Stirlingshire has in the Mid group, and is here assigned to A. Mid-Northern A has as small a vowel system as the West Mid group, with a tendency to get rid of /ɛ/ entirely, though there may be a partial COT:COAT distinction in back vowels. The latter has the lost distinctions, but primarily in restricted environments, resulting in a larger system before /t k/ than before sonorants or fricatives. Morayshire varieties also exhibit features (such as diphthongisation of /ɛ, ɔ, ʌ/ before /g ŋ/, so called *Dog*-Diphthongisation, which exists in Banffshire and north Aberdeenshire also) in common with North Northern, which historically stems from this area. Both subgroups show a strong coastal/inland internal division, representing the importance of the fisher links along the Moray Firth and the separation of fishers from the agricultural, rural base of the rest of the area, which is suitable for arable as well as pastoral farming. The dialects of fisher towns exhibit their own lexis in some cases, and tend to be conservative phonemically but innovative phonetically. The various Dissimilation rules seem to have their roots along the coast (Macafee 1989). The inland dialects within a group are surprisingly uniform, although within Mid-Northern A one can distinguish a central Banffshire/west Aberdeenshire variety transitional in some respect to B (Keith, Huntly, Rhynie) and a central Aberdeenshire (Turriff, Inverurie) inland type, typically 'Buchan' to the outsider. The urban dialect of Aberdeen is a separate division of Mid-Northern A with ties to both Buchan and the coastal dialects of north Kincardineshire, and is more likely to accommodate OUT-Fronting and Mid-Scots-type Glottalling than any other Mid-Northern A dialect.

Within inland types of Mid-Northern B, one can likewise separate out a mainstream Laigh of Moray variant, centred around Elgin (and Lossiemouth!), from a more conservative Speyside one, hard against the Highland Line, spoken in all the 'whisky glens' such as Glenlivet as well as in Grantown-on-Spey and Dufftown. Like Arran and Bute, this area is one that has been reclaimed from Gaelic since the Highland Clearances (Durkacz 1983: 137–8).

Coastal North-eastern dialects form a cline connecting Aberdeen and north Kincardine dialect with North Northern, and the differences between A and B are less profound than further inland. On the 'A' side of the line are an 'east coast' type associated with Peterhead and nearby villages; a 'corner' type, with Fraserburgh and extending westwards to just short of Pennan; and a 'north-west' type associated with a wide range of ports, from the Spey to Gardenstown (Buckie, Banff, Macduff). On the 'B' side, the inland Laigh of Moray type takes over at the Spey to just west of Lossiemouth, and again near the Highland boundary at Findhorn, but Hopeman and Burghead speak a separate, strongly innovative type of Mid-Northern B, with strong affinities with Black Isle speech.

The North Northern dialects occupy the territory to the west and north of where the Highland Line comes to the Moray Firth, at Nairn, forming islets of Scots in a Highland English sea. The North Northern A dialects are, or were, found in northern Nairnshire, at least according to Mather and Speitel (1986: 47–9), and across the end of the Moray Firth on the eastern end of the Black Isle peninsula in such towns as Avoch and Cromarty. Since the whole area is within the bailiwick of Inverness, the dialect is prone to be replaced by the same locally accented SSE that characterises that town.

On the other hand, Caithnesian (North Northern B) is still very much alive, and its varieties occupy the greater part of the old county of Caithness. Here, the existence of centres like Thurso and Wick and the pervasiveness of a Scots-speaking fishing culture and strong networks separating it traditionally from the *Gaidhealteachd* has protected this distinctive form of speech from extinction. Caithnesian carries tendencies like Northern Diphthongisation and the Northern form of Glottalling to its extreme, and adds features, such as early and pervasive OUT-Fronting and retroflexion of /r/, that probably reflect substratal effects of Northern dialects of Gaelic (David Clements, personal communication) more than from the Norn once present. The result sounds not unlike a Belfast person attempting to speak a Mid-Northern variety, such as a Morayshire fisherman's dialect. Within Caithnesian, one can distinguish an east-coast type (John o'Groats, Keiss, Stroma, Wick) and a north-coast one (Thurso, Dounreay), with south and west Caithness speaking a mixed dialect, with Scots and SSE features variably coexisting (Mather and Speitel 1986: 34–5; 37–40).

While no sociolinguistic projects have yet been completed on northern soil,[10] the anecdotal information that I can gather seems to suggest that northern Scotland consists of a patchwork of Pattern II and III localities. Pattern II seems to be the traditional set-up (Dieth 1932: vi, xix) and characterises Buchan and Banffshire as well as most fisher speech communities. Even Aberdeen seems to have been a Pattern II community, since speakers of any class born before 1950 or so seem to use Scots quite frequently to fellow Aberdonians in casual contexts. However, places near the Highland Line, such as Caithnesian market towns, Elgin and Lossiemouth, as well as Angus localities, seem (at first impression) to be Pattern III communities rather than II, as there seems to be a rather larger group of SSE monolinguals. Perhaps the influx of English and other speakers into the area of Lossiemouth Air Force Base or Dounreay nuclear power plant or of incomers from the nearby Highland English-speaking communities or from the Central Belt has had some effect on who uses Scots.

11.2.6 Insular Scots

The Insular Scots dialects, taken together, are the best examples of a relic speech form in Scotland. The vowel system of Insular Scots is large and roughly isomorphic with both the typical vowel systems of Angus and other peripheral Northern dialects – not surprising since Scots was brought from there in the sixteenth century (Catford 1957b: 73–5) – and not that different from Older Scots itself. Yet both Orcadian (Insular A) and Shetlandic (Insular B) are not totally conservative: they are better described as going their own way relative to the rest of Scots, adopting sometimes striking but highly localised innovations including an extensive Clockwise Vowel Shift, far-reaching diphthongisation, a consonant system recast to match the inventory of the Norn that was spoken alongside of Scots, and a strongly Norse-influenced vocabulary and syntax scattered among the archaic features in the linguistic system. Scandinavian influence also seems to have been responsible for the prevalence of consonantal changes such as /kw xw/ confusion (with both /kw/-lenition and /xw/-fortition present and competing) and /θ ð/-Stopping, which are well attested in Scandinavian (Haugen 1982: 66) and the reinforcement of the Scots retention of /øː/, the palato-alveolar shift, and /k g/-palatalisation (Haugen 1982: 65). Insular Scots, therefore, still has some sort of a 'Scandinavian accent' to go with its Norse lexis; even the voice quality seems to be atypical of Scots, with less pharyngealisation and raised larynx setting than most, and strong dentalisation (Barnes 1991: 438; Esling 1978).

Since the eighteenth century, some forms from Caithnesian have crept into Orcadian and from Aberdonian into Shetlandic as an overlay, but the dialect boundary within the Pentland Firth remains a sharp one to the present, with South Ronaldsay and Stroma, near Caithness, as different as Border Scots and Northumbrian.

The great geographical divide between Insular A and B is just as straightforward. It is safe to say that any island in the Orkney archipelago speaks Orcadian, and any in Shetland, plus Foula and Fair Isle, speaks Shetlandic. Yet both groups contain a high level of diversity, and the internal divisions do not always correlate with island boundaries. For instance, Unst, Yell and the north mainland of Shetland down to Nesting and Voe all speak an Eastern subdivision of Shetlandic, but the rest of the mainland is divided between a Western type (around Walls) and a Southern type (around Cunningsburgh), with Lerwick town and Scalloway, the only true villages in Shetland, occupying a transitional position between all. Nor does isolation matter much: Foula, according to Mather and Speitel (1986: 6–7), though quite far west of the Shetland 'mainland', fits in nicely into a simple west Shetlandic pattern, but Whalsay, just off the east coast, is as different from central mainland dialects as Fair Isle is. Both could be lumped together and called 'outlying Shetlandic'.

Orcadian has a similar internal structure. Again, the 'mainland', Pomona, is divided, this time into three parts, but each of these subdialects extends over adjacent islands: an east (or south-east) type based on Kirkwall extends into South Ronaldsay; a western type, common around Stromness and central parishes like Stenness, is also found on Hoy; and Birsay, once the seat of the Earls of Orkney, stands alone on Pomona, but the dialect has affinities with next-door Rousay and Stronsay (and Soay?). The remaining islands, Westray, Sanday and North Ronaldsay, each have their own subvariety, but only the last-mentioned is as distant phonologically from Orcadian mainland varieties as Whalsay or Fair Isle are from mainland Shetlandic.

The occurrence of the same innovation in several different places makes it hard to talk about foci and relic areas within Insular Scots itself. It is plain, however, that the 'weird' varieties, the ones that go their own way the most, come from the most tight-knit communities, perhaps consisting of only one social network. According to local lore (Brian Smith, personal communication), the Whalsay dialect was shaped by the speech habits of a single family, to whom everyone on the island is related. While such explanations usually can be dismissed as smacking of myth, it may be true in the particular case of such tiny island communities. It would be interesting to see if Fair Isle or North Ronaldsay has similar types of networks.

The Norse and Scots settlers of the Northern Isles had developed a farming and fishing economy similar to that on the northern mainland of Scotland, and though the towns of Kirkwall, Stromness, Birsay and Lerwick had been important local centres and, in the case of Kirkwall, a fully-fledged cathedral town, even in medieval times, a rural way of life predominated in the past and still does to a large extent now. The inhabitants are still likely to live in loosely-scattered farmsteads near the coasts, rather than in true villages, and to farm small parcels of land in widely-scattered areas, relics of the old runrig system. Agriculture and fishing are done by the same people at different seasons on both archipelagoes, but on fertile, low-lying Orkney there is more arable farming done than on rugged Shetland. This, and the presence of many small harbours, favours a greater emphasis on fishing on the more northerly island group. (It is often said by the locals that Shetlanders are fishers first and farmers second, while Orcadians are the opposite.) Boys in both island groups are still encouraged to do a stint at sea, whether it be as a fisher, a Navy man or a merchant sailor, while Shetland and Orkney women, who traditionally filled their time with crafts while waiting for their husbands to come back from the boats, still hand down the traditions of knitting patterns that may have been in their mothers' families for centuries. The juxtaposition of features of a traditional lifestyle among all the recently arrived modern technology found in any other area of Western Europe is remarkable. Even the large influx of outsiders on Shetland due to the oil boom is felt to be something temporary, which will leave a more modernised and prosperous but essentially locally oriented region in its wake. In an atmosphere like this, it is clear that the associations of the Insular Scots dialects, as local identity markers and real media of communication, not just a source of interesting words, remain largely intact. The word 'local' here must be emphasised: since each parish and each outlying island has its own form of Orcadian or Shetlandic Scots, even the subvarieties may function as potent identity markers.

This intensely insular way of life has helped the communities to preserve their Pattern I way of using Scots. There is only a tiny minority of native SSE speakers among the upper middle class in the Orkney towns, and next to no such speakers who are Shetland-born and -raised. Even university graduates have their local village dialect as the main part of their repertoire, and may not be 'pure' SSE speakers in any style. Localised dialect is thus used by nearly everyone to insiders, and mixed lects to outsiders, with the proportion of SSE forms increasing with greater formality and among higher-status speakers. Class differences, however, are much less important in determining what variety is employed than the ingroup/outgroup distinction, a situation that one would expect in a community with such tight networks and historical isolation (Melchers 1985: 98).

11.3 INTRODUCTION TO THE ANALYSIS OF SCOTS VOWEL SYSTEMS

While differences in consonant systems can define dialect groups quite well, dialectologists and historical linguists working with English have traditionally focused on the vowels (Trudgill 1990; Wells 1982; Dobson 1957). Within the especially large systems character-istic of English (and Germanic as a whole: see Johnston 1989; Lass 1984: 144–6; Lass 1976: 51–102), vowel systems change readily, participating in shifts that may vary by dialect area. Even such a large-scale process as the complex of small shifts traditionally entitled the Great Vowel Shift[11] (Johnston 1992; Kubuzono 1982) is prone to much regional variation, and the more we know about it, the more heterogeneous and intricate the shift looks (Johnston 1989, 1992; Lass 1988, 1990; Stockwell and Minkova 1988, 1990; Kubuzono 1982). The same is true for smaller shifting processes such as the series of changes in Shetlandic and Orcadian that change Older Scots /a/ to [æ], /ɛ/ to [e] or [ei], /ɑ:/ to [a: ~ æ:], /ɔ/ and /ɔ:/ to [ɒ(:)], here entitled the Insular Clockwise Vowel Shift, from the direction in which the nuclei move from the point of view of a conventional vowel chart; or a similar but counter-clockwise-moving process in the Borders, by which /ɪ ʊ/ lower to [ɛ̈], /ɛ/ goes down to [æ ~ a], /a/ goes back to [ɑ ~ ɒ ~ ʌ·], and /ɔ ɔ:/ go up to [o] (the Border Scots Counter-clockwise Vowel Shift. Not only are shifts like these highly regionalised, but they are also 'detachable'. Parts of them, but not others, may be shared by neighbouring dialects, producing variants of the original processes in each region. For instance, most East Mid A and South Mid A varieties have all the Border shifts except the lowering of /ɛ/, and West Mid and some North Mid types may lack the backing of /a/ as well. Mid-Northern dialects have a similar shift, but /ɛ/ goes up instead of down, and so on. The differences in shift structure produce highly diagnostic realisation patterns that one can use to classify dialects.

Dialectologists as far back as Catford (1957b) have also successfully used vocalic inventorial characteristics to classify the divisions within Scots. Catford, looking at monophthongal vowel contrasts before /t/, catalogued the type and number of distinctions that existed in each Scots dialect subgroup, discovering in the process the presence of major focal areas in the north-east and the western Central Belt possessing especially small vowel systems, the result of mergers taking place in these dialects in early modern times. He was also able to characterise the systems as containing a 'basic' vowel system of nuclei, shared by Scots dialects as a whole, /i e ɛ[12] a o u~y ɪ ʌ/, with several optional extra elements serving as important diagnostic features. Dialects could have up to two extra vowels in the low or low-mid back region ('A vowels'), one front rounded or unrounded non-peripheral nucleus (a 'Y vowel'), and one extra nucleus in the mid front region (an 'E vowel'), for a maximum of thirteen contrastive monophthongs before /t/ (Catford 1957b: 73–4). One could also extend his model to diphthongs (see section 11.6) and to other environments. Since his methodology simplifies the analysis of vocalic inventories, I have employed a variant of it here. However, because of the nature of my sources, especially the third volume of the *Linguistic Survey of Scotland*, conclusions about inventory must be taken as tentative, and a slight methodological diversion, serving as an explanation, is necessary.

My sources on information about vocalic characteristics are quite varied, including (1) early, complete dialect surveys (Wright 1905; Ellis 1889); (2) dialect monographs and similar works, mostly of pre-1960 origin (Gregg 1985; Borger 1980; Glauser 1974; Stursberg 1969; Zai 1942; Wettstein 1942; Dieth 1932; Wilson 1915, 1923; Mutschmann 1908; Murray 1873); (3) the introduction to SND (Grant 1931); (4) post-1970 sociolinguistic works and articles taken from areal studies of this nature (Melchers 1985; Shuken 1985; Macafee 1983, 1987, 1988, 1994a; Hettinga 1981; L. Milroy 1980; Johnston 1980, 1983a; Macaulay 1991; Macaulay and Trevelyan 1977); (5) my own observations from travels throughout Scotland, especially those gathered as part of a study financed by the Nuffield Foundation to collect dialect material for teaching purposes (Johnston 1985b); and (6) last, but most, Mather and Speitel's (1986) *Linguistic Survey of Scotland* phonology volume, in which an extensive structural treatment of vocalic systems forms the core.

Now, one would think that LSS vol. 3 could serve as the *Survey of English Dialects* (Orton et al. 1962–9) has done in accounts of traditional English dialects (Trudgill 1990; Wells 1982; Wakelin 1972; though see Trudgill 1983: 31–52), as *the* source *par excellence* on matters about vocalic systems. The Catford-like structural organisation of the material should only simplify matters. It does not. While I have made more use of the LSS than of any of my other sources, its framework and analysis are by turns awe-inspiring and infuriating. It is plain, by comparing the material with that of the other sources, that the LSS 'phonemes' are not phonemes at all, but phonetic realisations of some type that have undergone some (probably slight) degree of regularisation. I can only make a hypothesis here, but my guess is that they are something like frequent phonetic variants of vocalic variable classes, and these *classes* are what really correspond to phonemes. It is thus necessary to do a further round of analysis on the data before using them to say anything about inventory (or any other vocalic matters), since many supposed 'phonemic distinctions' most probably reflect simple subphonemic variability, as the systems of LSS vol. 3 are often too big compared to other sources. To pick just one example of many in an area familiar to me: compare the layout of reflexes of words containing Older Scots /ɛːr aːr air ɛr/ for Newhaven, Midlothian (Mather and Speitel 1986: 137), where *five* 'phonemes' are given for what is almost certainly a modern two-phoneme distinction /er ɛr/ (Johnston 1983a: 149–50), with variability in /er/ realisation.

In 'boiling down' LSS vol. 3 data, I first made the assumption mentioned above (which may be disputable, but seems intuitively correct) that the 'phonemes' are somewhat regularised phonetic reflexes, and belong to vocalic variables corresponding to the word classes mentioned below. I then sorted out the words by their Older Scots ancestral vowels, and by the following (and sometimes preceding) consonantal environment, resulting in several cells. Each cell was then treated as a 'micro-variable', with its own variation pattern (Thelander 1979). I took the most frequent form in each cell as the genuine majority reflex of the Older Scots ancestral vowels in that environment, treated minority forms which equalled majority forms for other Older Scots vowel classes in that environment as reflecting genuine 'one-off' lexical transfers, and ignored rarer variants as simple minority realisations of variables, rather than reflecting phonemic splits. I did take cases in which there were *two* frequent reflexes and no transfers as genuine splits, listing both reflexes as separate phonemes.

I then put the modern phonemic classes back together again by listing the majority forms in the different environments and combining those that were in complementary distribution. Where there was more than one way of combining, the source vowel in Older Scots decided which forms were to be lumped together. The result was a phonemic inventory, with detailed information on major allophonic variation, which accorded much more closely with inventories given in the other surveys[13] in the overwhelming majority of the cases.

Now, it is likely that even *this* represents only an approximation to a true phonemic analysis, since apparent 'allophonic rules' may really reflect variability also (see below), but the information on inventory seems accurate enough to form the basis of any further remarks, if one combines this with other sources.

There remain a few interesting disparities, however. These often involve vowel distinctions in very restricted, low-sonority environments in transition zones and relic areas. One can nearly always explain the transition-zone cases as interactional, as comparison with adjacent dialects will reveal. There is a group on one side of the transition zone with a solid distinction not shared by the group on the other. The intermediate varieties have variability (in Chambers and Trudgill's (1980: 132–3) sense, they are *mixed lects*), which is at least partially phonetically weighted due to the workings of lexical diffusion, producing the marginal distinction. As an example, take the CAT:CAUGHT distinction in East Mid B. Where it exists, it is spotty in LSS vol. 3 data, though there is a trend for it to be firmer before voiceless obstruents than elsewhere (Mather and Speitel 1986: 145–8). The most likely interpretation is that this situation represents a compromise, probably a constantly changing one, between Southern dialects with merger and Mid- and West Lothian ones with no merger. If we postulate, that as often happens, the merger takes place by the replacement of short or non-peripheral CAT forms by long or peripheral CAUGHT ones, the weighting makes sense, as vowels are longer and/or more peripheral in high-sonority environments (Jones 1989).

The rarer cases in relic areas probably represent the last dying stages of an earlier distinction. Again, this is due to interaction; the merger is most frequently coming in from dialects nearer to a major centre, and often there the distinction is more solid the further away from the centre one goes. Remnants of COT:COAT contrasts in Morayshire and

Banffshire show this; the further away from Aberdeen or subsidiary centres like Elgin one goes, the more likely there is a marginal distinction, and there are even cases in remote districts, such as Upper Cabrach, Banffshire (Mather and Speitel 1986: 63–4) – really a type of Mid-Northern B – where the merger is entirely absent. Again, there is phonetic weighting, with the merger more common in environments where the vowel is likely to be long or half-long rather than short.

However, there are also tantalising distinctions in some LSS vol. 3 data (Mather and Speitel 1986: 84, 86–92, 94, 97–8, 103–6, 110–11) that may be real unreported near-mergers, Scottish equivalents of the phenomena reported by Labov (1994: 349–90). For instance, Grant (1931: xxi) asserted that COT = COAT in Mid-Scots, presumably including North Mid, and there are spots, like Kippen, Stirlingshire, where this is uncontroversial. Most of the rest of the area, however, has a distinction in at least some, and sometimes most, environments, of the type of [ö]/[ö:(ə)] or [ö]/[o:]. These represent subtle differences, but their consistency throughout the area and their presence in several different fieldworkers' corpora suggest that the distinction is a real one. In these cases, I have reported these as genuine distinctions, and added an extra A vowel to the putative inventory accordingly. More work needs to be done, however, to show whether this distinction is receding or remaining stable in the light of increasing influence from major centres that may be spreading merger patterns.

Given that the Older Scots ancestral form plays such an important role in this analysis, I have chosen (as in Chapter 3) to organise the remaining sections of the chapter by word class, which really stands for putative vowel in Older Scots, adjusted for any lexically conditioned, 'one-off' developments, similar to the rhyme classes which I used as variables in Johnston (1980). Each class is denoted by a keyword standing for all its members, after the fashion of Wells (1982), and the classes are organised into subsystems based on the monophthong vs diphthong and front vs back dimensions, applying to a sixteenth-century, post-Great Vowel Shift layout. Each group of vowels has its own section devoted to it – front monophthongs (11.4), back monophthongs (11.5), and diphthongs (11.6) – and is listed from the highest vowel down.

This framework allows for differences in phonemic inventory to be analysed easily. However, inventory is only one diagnostic criterion. Lexical incidence, which here would involve matters resulting from conditioned splits and lexical transfers, is also important. For instance, the important *twa(w):twae* distinction, resting on the process backing an early /a:/ to /ɑ:/ in all varieties except East Mid, South Mid A and Southern Scots, and the most widespread of the Post-Velar Dissimilation rules, produces lexical-incidental differences. So does the more northerly post-velar change diphthongising MATE and BEAT vowels after /w/, so that *wame > wyme* and *sweat > swyte*, which originally must have extended down to the Forth/Clyde line (Macafee 1989). Since Scots vowels are particularly sensitive to environment by English standards, such transfers are common. Differences such as these are handled by setting up subclasses of the major classes, also designated by a keyword (in lower-case small capitals), membership in which is (usually) phonetically conditioned by the factors likely to cause lexical transfer. The keywords are given under the heading of each individual vowel class, in the introduction to that subsection.

Simple phonetic realisation may also be an important diagnostic criterion. The method of description here again uses keywords as well as IPA symbols, so that dialects that have [a(:) ~ ɐ(:) ~ æ(:) ~ ɛ(:) ~ ɑ(:) ~ ɒ(:)] in words with apparent Older Scots /a/ (the CAT class) are called Front-, Central, Raised-, Mid-, Back- and Rounded-CAT dialects respectively, thus streamlining descriptions and providing the reader with a catchy mnemonic.

Except for very general inventorial matters, characteristics are treated by major dialect within Scots, except with the MEET class, which shows very little difference in development over Scots, and with certain diphthongal classes of low functional load. In these cases, one can usually cover the existing differences quickly in a few paragraphs.

Table 11.1 Word classes for Modern Scots vowels.

Front monophthongs	
Keyword	Older Scots source
MEET	/e:/
BEAT	/ɛ:/
MATE	/a:/
BAIT	/ai/ > sixteenth-century/ɛ:/ or /a:/
BOOT	/ɔ:/, /iu/ before alveolar consonants
BIT	/ɪ/
BET	/ɛ/

Back monophthongs	
Keyword	Older Scots source
OUT	/u:/
COAT	/ɔ:/
COT	/ɔ/
CAT	/ɑ/
CAUGHT	/ɑu/ > sixteenth-century /ɑ:/
CUT	/ʊ/

Diphthongs/compound sounds	
Keyword	Older Scots source
NEW	/iu/ in hiatus and finally
DEW	/ɛu/
BITE	/i:/ in short environments
LOIN	/ui/
LOUP	/ɔu/
VOICE	/ɔi/
TRY	/i:/ in long environments

11.4 THE DIALECTOLOGY OF SCOTS FRONT VOWEL SYSTEMS

11.4.1 Introduction and Inventorial Shape

Except for the descendants of pre-Great Vowel Shift /i:/, the BITE and TRY classes, which diphthongised in all dialects, Older Scots possessed seven front vowel phonemes. In the long series, there was (1) an /e:/ in MEET which underwent a shift to /i:/ in the top half of the Great Vowel Shift in all Scots and nearly all English dialects (Johnston 1992); (2) an /ɛ:/ in BEAT, usually raised in this position by the bottom half of the vowel shift; (3) an /a:/ or /æ:/ in MATE, which may have been shifted to /ɛ:/ at the same time, or slightly before BEAT was raised; (4) the descendant of an Early Older Scots /ai/ in BAIT, which monophthongised either to /a: ~ æ:/ or to /ɛ:/ before consonants (Kniezsa 1994); and (5) an /ø:/ in BOOT, the result of Early /o:/-Fronting, which had applied in Scotland in the late thirteenth or early fourteenth century (Luick 1964: 426–9).

In the short series, there were two other front nuclei, a putative /ɪ/ in BIT and similar words, and an /ɛ/ in BET, corresponding to similar values in England (Aitken 1977b).

The effects of monophthongisation of /ai/, the bottom-half vowel shift, and BOOT-unrounding, which is attested in the north-east in Older Scots times (Dieth 1932: 8) but is mostly a modern change in other varieties (Grant 1931: xix), usually create at least one merger, so that all but a small handful of dialects now have fewer than seven front monophthongs. One possible merger might be caused by the unrounding of BOOT to merge with some other vowel in the system, often MEET (Mid- and North Northern dialects, and Northern Northumbrian), BEAT (South Northern and North Mid), MATE (in most North Mid and in long environments in most other Mid and Southern varieties), or BIT (in East and West Mid, and Southern Scots in short environments). Where BOOT stays a front rounded vowel as in Insular Scots, or (until recently) conservative types of Angus, Perthshire and Border dialects; or where it does unround, but to a non-peripheral nucleus higher than the present BIT vowel, as in the South Mid group and some other Mid and Southern varieties, there is a Y vowel, one of the optional elements which Catford (1957b) mentions.

The interaction of BAIT and BEAT vowels with other nuclei in the front series can give rise to a number of configurations, since either of these may be separate or merged in with something else, reflecting differences in the ordering of bottom-half Great Vowel Shift raisings versus the monophthongisation of /ai/. If there are enough mergers, the set of MEET, BEAT, MATE, BAIT and BET can be reduced to only two nuclei, as in most Aberdeenshire speech, where /i/ results from the first two classes and /e/ from the next three. This, however, is exceptional; the more usual 'basic' system has an /i e/ and /ɛ/, the last one most often resulting from BET alone, though the incidence of the other two classes may vary. As a rule, MEET has /i/ and MATE/BAIT /e/ in these systems; BEAT can go into either phoneme. The 'classic' Glasgow and Edinburgh systems have shapes like this, with MEET = BEAT; they are similar to English systems like the RP one in their front vowel merger patterns.

Bigger systems than this have what Catford (1957b: 71–5) calls an E vowel, and they reflect one fewer of the requisite mergers. If there is only one E vowel, as is most often the case, it can reflect an independent BEAT class, separate from both a merged MATE/BAIT and MEET, a very common configuration in North Mid B and C and in parts of Galloway and Caithness. Alternatively, BEAT and MATE may be merged together, and BAIT is separate, as in other types of Caithnesian and in Insular Scots. If BEAT, MATE and BAIT stay separate, and MEET and BET undergo no further mergers, there are two E vowels, which I entitle E1 (usually a long or diphthongised peripheral one) and E2 (a non-peripheral, highish one, like a Y vowel). E2s may also arise if there is a phonemic split in BIT interacting with conditioned developments of other nuclei, usually BITE before /k/, as in *dike*, so that a *dike: Dick* contrast is produced, with each word having pronunciations that are allophones of BIT in other positions. This is rare, but can be found in some types of outlying Northern dialects. In any case, E2s, in contrast to E1s, usually have very restricted distribution.

11.4.2   The MEET Class: The Descendants of Older Scots /e:/

The nucleus of MEET, Early Older Scots /e:/, was raised one height throughout Scotland in the top half of the Great Vowel Shift (Aitken 1977b). The isolative vowel has since undergone little change in most dialects. One can therefore speak about a 'normal' reflex of MEET: a highly 'tense', height-peripheral [i(:)] (Normal-MEET), strictly following Aitken's Law as to length. In a part of the Northern Diphthongisation rule, MEET may undergo some diphthongisation to [ɪi] (Diphthongised-MEET) in North and Mid-Northern localities, but the wide, extensive diphthongisation present in the south and Midlands of England has not penetrated Scotland yet.

Except in words from Early Older Scots /e:x/ > /ei/, like *die* and *high*, MEET has high front [i:] in SSE.

Words like *city, pity, vision*, where an Early Older Scots /ɪ/ became /e:/ by Open Syllable Lengthening, still have /ɪ/ in the Standard accents, since this nucleus did not often lengthen in ancestors of RP, and seemingly only did so at all when the next syllable contained a final schwa (compare *week* < Middle English *wike*: Minkova 1982).

Although the MEET and BEAT classes have been merged in the Standard dialects, they can usually be told apart easily by the spelling – the ⟨ee⟩ of this class usually gives the membership away; words from Old English 'Germanic' /æ:/, like *needle*, also go here, and in some dialects, like Gallovidian, so does Early Older Scots /e/ lengthened in open syllables (Mather and Speitel 1986: 160–3, 170–92). These words, usually considered part of BEAT, may be spelled ⟨ea⟩ or ⟨eCe⟩. Otherwise, MEET words include *creep, sheep, creeper; meet, greet, pity; week, leek, weekend, sick; leech, speech; need, heed, seedy; beef, chief; Keith; piece, niece; wheech, dreich, high; live; seethe; breeze, seize, visit; vision; seem, teem; green, seen; peel, keel; beer, tear* (noun), *speir, cheer*.

Two subclasses must be mentioned: (1) the WHEEN group (*wet, weep, wheel, wheen, queen*), containing a prior /w/ or /ʍ/, which can thus undergo Northern Post-/w/ Dissimilation; and (2) the TREE set (*bee, free, fee, see, tree, three, agree; die, lie, fly; key*) having final MEET, an input of Restricted Pennine Diphthongisation. In either case, the result is usually upgliding diphthongisation and transfer to the BITE class.

Since isolative MEET is nearly always [i] (though there are some cases of unraised [e] before labials in the northernmost dialects of Shetland; Mather and Speitel 1986: 1), all that needs to be discussed are the cases of Northern Diphthongisation, conditioned developments before /r l/, and in *wheen* and *tree*.

Full-blown Northern Diphthongisation, affecting high and mid vowels, is largely restricted to the North Northern group, but a more restricted version of the rule applies to /i u/ alone in scattered Mid-Northern communities also. It is particularly frequent in Caithnesian, where MEET becomes [ɪi] and OUT [ʏy ~ øy] (Mather and Speitel 1986: 29, 35–6). It is phonetically unconditioned, unlike the parallel Pennine Diphthongisation process in the Borders, and resembles slight diphthongisations found in some types of American English (Wells 1982: 487) more than it does the Pennine process.

Epenthetic schwa is common after MEET, as with any high or high-mid nucleus, before liquids, especially /r/, in a wide range of dialects from Orkney to the eastern Borders and Galloway. It occasionally results in truly disyllabic forms, especially in Aberdeenshire and parts of the Borders. Schwa-Insertion precedes /r/-vocalisation, so Mid-Scots groups with that rule insert schwa and the rule is becoming more common as vocalisation spreads. The most exceptionless rules are present in West Mid and Mid-Northern varieties.

Epenthetic schwa before /l/ is less common. Mather and Speitel (1986: 88–9, 92–3, 96–8, 100, 110–15, 140, 146–7, 149–53) shows it in a few pockets only, mostly in North Mid territory and in Tweeddale, but I have observed it commonly in the Lothians and central Borders also, and it is not unknown in either Dundee or Aberdeen.

The diphthongisation of MEET to merge with BITE after /w ʍ/, so that *wheen* becomes *fyne*, is the most restricted of the various Post-Velar Diphthongisation rules affecting front vowel classes in the north-east. Lss vol. 3 shows it in *weed* in some north-eastern localities near the Highland Line (Migvie and Kirriemuir, Angus; Upper Cabrach, Banffshire; Dallas, Morayshire) and in a few scattered coastal villages (Keiss, Caithness; Findhorn, Morayshire), so it is probably a relic feature, once widely spread in Northern Scots (Mather and Speitel 1986: 33–4, 54–5, 56–7, 63–4, 82–3, 86–7). It is also absent from Perthshire and Fife, unlike the parallel diphthongisations of BEAT and MATE.

Pennine Diphthongisation is well established in all positions in parts of Cumbria (Reaney 1927: 19) and South Durham (Orton 1933: 58–60), but the only unconditioned example of it in the sources is at Gretna Green, right at the Cumbrian border (Mather and Speitel 1986: 168–9). Elsewhere in the Borders, it is restricted to final position, where it leads to *tree* taking BITE reflexes. This feature was once found in eastern Roxburghshire (Zai 1942: 70), and maybe once existed in Tweeddale, as OUT diphthongises here (Mather and Speitel 1986: 143–6, 148–51), but is receding towards Teviotdale and the western Borders. My investigation in the Hawick area showed that *tree* = [trɛ̆ɪ] was still current, in fact a local stereotype there, but it was reportedly recessive at Jedburgh (Johnston 1980: 166, 309). It apparently survives in Southern B, though the quality may be different, usually [ë̆i ~ ei] (Mather and Speitel 1986: 159, 165–70). Northern Northumbrian may undergo the same change, but generally diphthongises final MEET only as far as [ë̆ɪ] (Johnston 1980: 172–7).

11.4.3   The BEAT Class: The Descendants of Older Scots /ɛ./

The bottom half of the Great Vowel Shift applied to BEAT to varying degrees, resulting in a wide range of reflexes, from Standard-like [i(:)] (High-BEAT) to [e·(:) ~ ι(:)], [e(:)] or [ɛ(:)] (Raised-, Mid- and Low-BEAT types respectively), diphthongs like [ɛɪ] or [eɪ] (Diphthongised-BEAT), usually resulting from Northern Diphthongisation, and even [e·ə ~ eə] (Ingliding-BEAT), from either a form of vowel shift allowing raising of the first element alone, or Late Mid Vowel Ingliding, common in North Mid A and sporadically elsewhere. A merger with MEET, MATE, BAIT and BOOT, or any combination of the last three, is possible. The most frequent reflex is a Raised or Mid type obeying Aitken's Law and merged with MATE, closely followed by High types merged with MEET.

BEAT, usually spelled <ea> or <eCe> (where <C> is a consonant symbol), has been merged with MEET in Scottish Standard English under [i(:)], reflecting an RP merger present since the early eighteenth century. According to Dobson (1957: 607–12), this merger is an importation from a south eastern English vernacular. This was most probably Cockney, or a far south eastern dialect, a descendant of a Kentish variety with Middle English /e:/ instead of /ɛ:/. Its adoption into SSE was probably helped by the presence of the same merger, only naturally developed, in both Edinburgh and Glasgow Scots vernaculars. A sample of BEAT items would include *beat, heat, peaty; bead, head, leader; heap, leap, reaper; leak, beak, beaker; beach; league; deaf, deafen; death; breath;*[14] *lease, feast, beast; creash; leave, seven; breathe; ease, please, easy; meal, seal; tear, fear, beard; steam, team.* Words like *real, seat* or verbs in *–ceive* and their derivatives generally do not go here, but are MATE words, like the usual set of *steak, great* and so on; every dialect seems to have its own list of such early transfers. *Break* is highly idiosyncratic and may go here or in a number of other classes, including BET and BIT, and even CAT.

Finally, /w/ + BEAT and final BEAT are subject to the same diphthongisation processes that MEET words in the same positions are, even, in the first case, in varieties without MEET/ BEAT merger; there are thus analogous subclasses to WHEEN and TREE, namely SWEAT (*sweat, wheat, weave*) and TEA (*tea, sea*). A following /n/, as in the CLEAN subclass (*clean, lean, wean* (verb), *scene, Jean, dean, mean, chain, drain*), led to raising (*clean*-Raising) before the vowel shift in most Scots (Mather and Speitel 1986), producing an early transfer to MEET, and a few dialects extend the raising process to the HEAL subclass (*heal, beal, steal; steam, team*), which contain BEAT + /l m/. Words containing an Early Older Scots /er/ in an open syllable, the WEAR set (*wear, swear, tear* (verb), *pear, mare*) have MEET forms in several varieties, but possibly for a different reason; it could equally be the case that merger with other BEAT + /r/ forms never took place, and that the output of Open Syllable Lengthening did not involve stepdown in this environment.

11.4.3.1 BEAT in Insular Scots

Although SND (Grant 1931: xl) mentions Insular Scots BEAT as taking variable reflexes depending on area, [e(:)~i⸱(:)~i:], LSS vol. 3 shows BEAT to be isolatively merged with MATE under /e/ throughout the whole of the Northern Isles, although there are phonetically conditioned transfers of both classes to /i/ due to *clean*- and *stone*- (and, in outlying varieties, *heal*- and *tale*-) Raising. The phoneme /i/ is also general in *tea* and, of course, may occur in any BEAT word due to SEE influence. The phonetic realisation is generally a Mid [e(:)], perhaps slightly retracted in Shetlandic to a close Raised [ɪ(:)] in short environments or, in the north and central sections of the mainland of Shetland, Upgliding reflexes like [eⁱ]. In Orcadian, only monophthongs are found, however. The realisation [ɛ:] is typical before /k/ in both divisions of Insular Scots; these represent the merger of all the 'e'-vowels under what are isolatively BAIT reflexes.

11.4.3.2 BEAT in Northern Scots

The North Northern dialects are set apart from the other branches of Northern Scots by having isolative Upgliding [ɛi], which must be counted as an E1 vowel here. It is often, although not always, separate from BITE reflexes, which may have a backer or lower first element. Morayshire dialects tend to have Mid reflexes such as [e(:)], and Angus ones some sort of Raised-to-Mid reflex like [ɪ ~ e] in short environments and [e:] in long ones. In both these cases, BEAT = MATE. In Mid Northern A, however, MATE is separate, and BEAT instead merges with MEET as [i(:)], though traces of /e/ before /t/ can be found all over coastal Banffshire and north coast Aberdeenshire, and in Kincardineshire.

The path of development seems to have been the same everywhere as far as the [e:] stage, with both [ɛi] (< *[ei]) and [i(:)] developing from that. The raising to /i/ at first sight seems unconnected to the similar change in the Central Belt, southern Scotland and the northern counties of England, though it could conceivably be a result of centre-to-centre spread as Aberdeen does seem to be the focus, and there seems to be conditioned raising to /i/ in more and more environments as one approaches the city.

Even where the isolative development is /e/ or /ɛi/, /i/ is found in *clean* and before palatals throughout the Northern group. The phoneme /i/ once also appeared before *heal* in North Northern and Mid-Northern B varieties, but it has been replaced since by regularly developed forms (Grant 1931: xl; Mather and Speitel 1986: 27–57). Raising before velars produces /i/ in Northern dialects as far north and west as Nairn and west Morayshire, and voiced fricatives cause raising even beyond this, into southern Caithness. Even final position is a raising environment, as it is in Insular Scots, so that *tea* has /i/ in Caithnesian on the one hand and Kincardineshire, Angus and, of course, the Mid-Northern A area on the other. Words like *death* and *breath*, however, have /e/ everywhere in the group.

While originally long /ɛ:r/ usually develops to an invariable /er/, *wear* takes the usual BEAT reflexes of each division, suggesting that the first group of /ɛ:r/ words in fact had Older Scots /a:r/ here.

Sweat undergoes diphthongisation to /ei/ in all Northern Scots, merging with BITE, as *wame* does in the whole group, and *wheen* in Mid-Northern.

11.4.3.3 BEAT in Mid and Southern Scots

East Mid, West Mid and South Mid A varieties, as well as Southern Scots, have High-BEAT [i(:)], and thus an isolative merger with MEET under /i/, except in *death*, *breath* and the /ɛ:r/ words that do not belong to *wear*. *Tea* undergoes the same Pennine Diphthongisation process in the central and western Borders as *tree* does, and epenthetic schwa is quite common before /r/ in almost all Mid and Southern areas, whatever the realisation of the vowel before it or /r/ after it.

North Mid A and B act like peripheral Northern dialects, with some sort of Mid reflex as an isolative form. Perthshire dialects merge BEAT and MATE, at least conditionedly; the eastern varieties either have the same [e˕] forms that South Northern dialects do or Ingliding forms like [eə], but Central Perthshire dialects only have [e(:)], partially distinct from an [e:] used in BAIT, and MATE words transferred to that class. Fife dialects tend either to have a three-way merger of MATE, BAIT and BEAT under [e(:)] or a contrast of BEAT with a merged MATE/BAIT by length in short environments. North Mid C dialects mostly have [i(:)] now, but there are enough traces of prior /e ~ e˕ə/ to postulate that they were once like others in this group. As in Northern dialects, *sweat* has [ĕɪ] = BITE, and raising to /i/ takes place in *clean*, *tea* and before high consonants (palatals and at least /x/ in the velar series), with /k g/ added in west Fife and Stirlingshire (Mather and Speitel 1986: 109–16).

South Mid B (Wigtownshire) has a Raised [e˕] (to my ears, sounding a lot like an old-fashioned RP [ɪ]) as the isolative form. As in other dialects with mid vowels for BEAT, /i/ is found in *clean*, *tea* and frequently before voiced fricatives. Ulster Scots dialects mostly have /i/ in the LSS vol. 3 materials, but there are enough examples of an earlier /e/ (Mather and Speitel 1986: 192–204) to suggest that this was the original form, whether or not it was merged with MATE (compare Harris 1985) or was separate.

The sequence /er/ from this or any other source undergoes Pre-Rhotic Vowel Lowering to /ɛr/ in Ulster Scots and Glaswegian, and sporadically elsewhere; the /r/ is [ɹ] in the Irish case and a pharyngealised vowel in the Scottish one, either one of which could conceivably foster lowering.

The overall reflex patterns imply that /ɛ:/ may have become /e:/ early before high consonants and /n/ over all of Scotland, and word-finally and before voiced fricatives over large stretches. In the vowel shift, the remaining cases of BEAT raised one height everywhere, but only raised two in the far north of England down to the Tees Valley and Cumbrian border (Orton 1978: 72–81), the Borders and the Central Belt south of the Forth/Clyde line, and in Aberdeenshire and Buchan. That second raising is now extending over many of the remaining /e/ areas, due to either SSE influence, the influence of large urban varieties, or both, since these prestigious varieties have it.

11.4.4 The MATE Class: The Descendants of Older Scots /a:/

The bottom half of the Great Vowel Shift likewise applied to MATE, producing a wide range of isolative modern reflexes. Most of these are mentioned under BEAT also. These include upgliding diphthongs of the [eɪ ~ ɛɪ] type (Upgliding-MATE); ingliding diphthongs like [ɛə ~ eə ~ ʉə ~ iə] (Ingliding-MATE); and, more commonly, monophthongs such as [i(:)] (High-MATE), [ɪ(:) ~ e·(:)] (Raised-MATE), [e(:) ~ e·(:)] (Mid-MATE) or [ɛ(:)] (Low-MATE). The monophthongs usually obey Aitken's Law, and Mid types are by far the most frequent across Scotland. Merger with BAIT, BEAT or both in different environments is common, with BET, BOOT (in short environments) or MEET possible but exceptional. Most of the variation results from different 'potencies' of Great Vowel Shift raising rules and different orderings with respect to /ai/-Monophthongisation in Older Scots. Isolative High types, however, are the result of Border Area Smoothing, succeeding an [iə] attested in the nineteenth century (Murray 1873: 104–6).

The Standard correlates to MATE fall into two groups, according to their pre-Middle English/Older Scots sources (Luick 1964: 358–64). The words with an original long Old English/Old Norse /ɑ:/ now possess SSE /o/ isolatively (= coat), and usually /or/ (RP /ɔ:/) before /r/, and those with /a:/ derived from Old English/Old Norse/Old French low vowels lengthened in open syllables are represented by SSE /e/. This division reflects the South-umbrian developments of these nuclei, where the first group had /ɔ:/ in Middle English, and the second /a:/. These sets are usually spelled with ⟨oa⟩ or ⟨oCe⟩ and ⟨aCe⟩ respectively. MATE words include: mate, rate, later; load, made, shading; rope, soap, apple; babe, baby; sake, rake; vague; age; safe, chafe, wafer; save, rave, shaver; loath; bathe; laich; lame, foam; toe, so.

Allophony in Older Scots times has led to considerable splitting within this phonemic class, resulting in many conditioned subclasses. Some of these are quite parallel to special developments of BEAT. For instance, Post-Velar (including Post-/w/) Diphthongisation can set in if the following consonant is sonorant, in the WAME set (wame, claes, great), resulting in transfer to bite, just as with SWEAT and WHEEN. Early, pre-Great Vowel Shift raising and merger with BEAT (stone-Raising) may happen before /n/ (the STONE subclass: stone, bone, alone, moan, none) or /l/ (the TALE subclass: tale, kale, scale, dale, sale, stale, whole) and, more rarely, /s/ (the FACE subclass: face, taste, lace, pace), just as with CLEAN or HEAL. A following /r/ (more: more, sore, bare, fare, there, dare, share, care, blare, flare) might provoke Pre-Rhotic Mid-Vowel Lowering, resulting in merger with BET or with a pre-existing BAIT class, as with WEAR. However, there are also developments unique to this class. A preceding /w/ might cause retraction if there is no following sonorant, and so the TWO subclass (two, who, away, waken) can join the CAUGHT lexical set. The MATE vowel is also prone to dissimilation initially, and sometimes after /h/, in the ONE subclass (oak, one, oats, oaths; home, whole), resulting in clusters beginning with /j/ plus a front mid element, usually identical to BIT or BOOT in Scotland (Johnston 1980: 110; Zai 1942: 62–3). Finally, a somewhat similar dissimilation happens in a few Northern dialects between grave consonants, especially before /v k/ in the tiny bake group of words (bake, cake), resulting in /j/ + the CAT vowel, presumably the outcome of an Older Scots allophone *[ɛæ ~ ɛɑ] or the like.

11.4.4.1 MATE in Insular Scots

In Insular Scots, as in the more peripheral Northern dialects, MATE undergoes a split development. In most environments, it takes the same Mid [e(:) ~ e·(:)] or Upgliding [e¹] forms that BEAT does, with the latter more or less restricted to eastern and southern Shetlandic and the dialect of Lerwick town before consonants, and the Shetlandic mainland finally.[15] Before or after velars or /r/, forms belonging to BAIT occur instead, usually [ɛː] (North Ronaldsay [eː]) = Catford's E1. This means that the vowels in words like *gate*, *great* differ from those in *late*, *mate* (Mather and Speitel 1986: 1–2, 4, 6, 8, 10–21, 24–5). In Orcadian and north Shetlandic, BET merges in also, due to lengthening. *More* falls together with *wear* and *air* as [ɛːᵊ ~ eːᵊ] and Fair Isle even has [iːə]; all of these go back to an underlying /eːr/ or /ɛːr/. The result is generally higher than *Perth* or *heart*. Otherwise, long MATE is most often [eː].

The raising of *stone* to /i/, a result of pre-vowel shift changes of /aːn/ to /ɛːn/ present in the Angus source dialects (Macafee 1989), applies throughout the group, although for *one*, both *een* and *wan* = [wæn] coexist. In most of the outer islands of both archipelagoes, including Yell, Fair Isle and Whalsay within Shetland, and Westray, Rousay and Stronsay in Orkney, as well as the Kirkwall area, the raising applies to *tale* also. The peripheral position of these dialects argues for the extended rule once being more widespread, and Grant's (1931: xl) remarks may confirm this.

While *sweat* = [swɛɪt] and *wame* = [wɛɪm] are attested in at least some Insular dialects (Mather and Speitel 1986: 1, 4, 7, 12, 26),[16] other words within these subclasses do not generally undergo any special developments. *Two*, however, is transferred to CAUGHT, as in everywhere else north of the Forth/Clyde line.

11.4.4.2   MATE in Northern Scots

The most typical Mid-Northern A reflex of MATE is a Mid, sometimes slightly lowered [e(ː)] that merges in most environments with both BAIT and BET (Dieth 1932: 20; Mutschmann 1908: 42–5). In north Banffshire and north west Aberdeenshire, one might get ingliding realisations instead, such as [eɛ], but the same merger patterns are present. As one approaches the Mid Northern B border, however, there is a cline towards a split distribution similar to that found in Insular Scots, and the possibility of a MATE:BAIT distinction becomes more likely. Here, the merged MATE/BEAT nucleus, usually [e(ː)], undergoes Aitken's Law but BAIT may not, and in addition might be lower or ingliding.

Caithnesian dialects are divided in what their isolative realisation of MATE is. Around Thurso and Wick, the same [ɛɪ] that is found for BEAT predominates, except around velars, or /r/, or before voiced obstruents. In these environments, a constantly Long or Upgliding [eː ~ eːⁱ] (= BAIT) is usual. In the rest of Caithness, as in the Black Isle, the diphthongisation to [ɛɪ] is a conditioned change, restricted to *stone*, *face*, and maybe *tale*, and the Long reflex has to be taken as the isolative one. This realisation usually implies that MATE = BAIT in the relevant positions, though there are dialects in Caithness which keep all mid-front vowels distinct, and have a length distinction between the two classes (Mather and Speitel 1986: 27).

Angus varieties also exhibit a split development, with MATE = BEAT in most environments, usually as a Raised vowel [ɪ(ː) ~ e·(ː)], and a Long [eː] or Ingliding [eɛ] found before velars, /f/ and all sonorants, except where *stone*-Raising takes place. As in Caithness, this latter allophone often stands for BAIT also, but need not; in Kincardineshire and north Angus, BEAT = [e], MATE = [eː] and BAIT = [ɛː]. Forfar has only an [ɪ]/[eɛ ~ eː] contrast.

Since some form of split is common to the whole north except the Aberdeen focal area, with traces even in the North Mid dialects, it is likely that it goes back to late Older Scots times, to some sort of lowering rule around grave sounds, maybe from an [ɛː] to something like *[æː ~ εˑ], which sporadically appears in Insular Scots even today, and which equalled BAIT. The environments were generalised in Angus (and Perthshire/Fife) by the addition of a later lengthening rule before sonorants, at a point when the higher nucleus had developed to [e(ː)] and the lower one to [eː ~ εː]. Only Aberdonian applied Aitken's Law to the second nucleus.

Aberdonian may have had its own rule, affecting MATE between grave sounds, especially velars, however, as in BAKE. This subclass has /j/ followed by the vowel in CAUGHT = [jɑː]. These go back to the same lowered [æː] as the other reflexes do, but with a rule which I entitle Aberdonian Breaking, which assimilates the second element to the following velar. The resulting [æɑ] then undergoes stress shift, possibly after the V1 was raised to something like [e] > [jɑː]. This rule type is attested in other dialects of English, even in less favourable environments, and may underlie the *yutt* forms for *eat* and similar BEAT words in the south west of England (Wakelin 1972: 95).

Before the Great Vowel Shift ever took place, *stone* and *one* had already merged with BEAT, possibly in tandem with the more widespread *clean*-Raising discussed above (Macafee 1989). Where BEAT is [i(ː)] as in Aberdeen, you get *steen* and *een*. Where it is not, you get [e(ː) ~ ει], the first in Moray and Nairn, the last in Caithness and the Black Isle. The Angus [i(ː)] forms may be loans, or may simply show that here, raising of *stone* preceded that of *clean* so that the first Raising rule feeds the second one. *One* can be *een* in addition to the regularly-derived form anywhere in the north (Mather and Speitel 1986: 28–30, 32–3, 36–7, 40, 46, 80, 82–9; Johnston 1985b: 25, 29, 33, 39; Grant 1931: xxxii), though the irregular *wan* variant (from Highland English?) is restricted to North Northern.

Wame undergoes Post-Velar Dissimilation quite regularly, with little lexical conditioning, resulting in transfer to BITE. In Mid-Northern dialects, and especially Mid-Northern A, other consonants besides a preceding /w/ can trigger the change, including a dark /l/, so that *clothes* is [klɛ̈ιz ~ kləιz ~ klʌιz]. It is likely that North Aberdeenshire is the focal area of this type of diphthong formation, as it affects, after /w/ anyway, all the front vowels, with the short ones backing and the historical long ones diphthongising with fewer exceptions than elsewhere (Macafee 1989). The change is quite natural given that /w/ and /l/ have low second formants, which would tend to lead to some sort of backing, especially of the first mora of the vowel next to it. Second elements away from it would tend to front, leading to a mutual dissimilation or 'disproportionation' to which the Northern group is especially prone, as the Breaking rule above and *good*-Dissimilation below corroborate.

More shows few special developments, with Lowering mainly in North Northern, where /r/ is a retroflex approximant. Lowering may happen in Aberdeenshire, but here the /εr/ form varies with often disyllabic /er/ reflexes like [ejë̞ɾ]. *Two* is backed regularly to [ɑː].

11.4.4.3 MATE in Mid-Scots

The typical MATE realisation over a wide range of Mid-Scots dialects is a 'normal' Mid [e(ː)], perhaps a little raised in the east and lowered in the west, obeying Aitken's Law. Like any non-high vowel, it becomes fully long in tonic syllables in the 'Glasgow drawl' area, which extends over most of Lanarkshire, Renfrewshire, Stirlingshire and north Ayrshire, plus the Perth and Dundee areas and parts of adjacent counties (Mather and Speitel 1986: 117–18, 131–4). In the typical Mid dialect, MATE = BAIT, not BEAT, and there are few conditioned developments besides epenthetic schwa-insertion before /r/, and possibly /l n/, Pre-Rhotic Lowering in Glasgow and north Lanarkshire and pockets elsewhere (Macafee 1994:

225–32), and *twaw* or *twa* forms (= CAUGHT) in *two* in all North and West Mid, South Mid B and South-west Mid (Grant 1931: xxv, xxvii–xxviii). These realisations may also be found in some Lothian speech, especially around Linlithgow and in coastal communities, including Leith and North Berwick. Edinburgh has both *twaw* and the more typically Lothian *twae* with isolative reflexes, which also appears in most of the rest of East Mid and South Mid A.

A few of the more peripheral Mid varieties have an underlying split like the north does. North Mid varieties are always transitional, and the more northerly North Mid A and Tayside dialects may have a Raised reflex resembling [ɪ] here isolatively, but [e: ~ eə] in *bake* and before voiced stops. Otherwise, only [e(:)] (North Mid B, central Perthshire), Ingliding [eə ~ ɪə] (south Perthshire, west Fife), or Drawled [e:] (Stirlingshire) is found, usually = BAIT. *Two* has the vowel of CAUGHT, and some *wame* items including the keyword itself have a restricted form of the Northern Post-Velar Dissimilation rule, with vowels merging with BITE. Though epenthetic schwa is common before /l r/, Pre-Rhotic Lowering is not.

A salient difference between the North Mid group and the rest is the development of *one*, especially the item itself and its derivatives. North of the Forth/Clyde line, these words develop normally to /en/. South of it, including in Glasgow and Edinburgh, *yin* forms, historically associated with the Borders, become the rule. As one goes south and closer to the Borders, more and more items in the subclass are affected, and in the transitional East Mid B, /ha:/ words like *home* are variably affected as well (Wettstein 1942: 40). *Yin* is now spreading northwards; even Mather and Speitel (1986: 113–15) show it as normal in North Mid C, alongside *wan*, spread from Irish English through Glaswegian (which uses both) to other urban varieties. Each of these has a tendency to replace *ane*, which is recessive.

East Wigtownshire and Ulster dialects (except for Belfast city and most of Scots-speaking Down) also have a split. MATE takes the usual BEAT reflex in most environments ([ɪ] for the Machars of Wigtown, [e] in Antrim) in most environments, but the normal BAIT form before /d/ and all velars, and in long environments ([e:] and [ɛ:] respectively). In Rinns dialects, however, [ɪ(:)] is extended to all environments, and in Down, [e(:)] is found everywhere but before /r/ and finally, where the original BAIT form [ɛ:] appears (Mather and Speitel 1986: 180–204). This, of course, is also an extended Pre-Rhotic Lowering Rule, and it is conjectured that this rule entered Glaswegian from Northern Irish varieties (Macafee 1994: 225–32). In any case, whereas the lowered form is not endangered, the [e] is being replaced by Belfast vernacular [ɪə]. South and South-west Mid dialects have both *yin* and *wan* for *one*, and *twa* for *two*.

11.4.4.4　MATE in Southern Scots

The predominant form in this class in Southern A today is the same Mid [e(:)] that appears in Edinburgh, with only the extension of the typical development of *one* to cover /ha:/ sequences also to show that this is a separate dialect group. Ingliding forms are sporadic, and occur in the same environments that they do in the Lothians (Johnston 1980: 110). This was not always the case (Zai 1942: 57–8; Murray 1873: 104–5). Except before /r/, the usual realisation in this class was an Ingliding diphthong similar to what one finds in the Border Northumbrian dialects, though it might have been [ɪɪ ~ ɪɛ̆] rather than [ɪɛ̆]. These nuclei, sometimes disyllabic, survive in Southern B, and are not found in BAIT. BAIT-like [eə ~ e: ~ ɛ:] do arise before labials and pre-rhotically, implying a similar split to the north. In other long environments, the Ingliding forms have been Smoothed to High [i:], a development hinted at by Murray (1873: 104), who mentions how short and fleeting the offglide is (Mather and Speitel 1986: 164–9). English Border dialects, until very recently, only smoothed their Ingliding realisations in final position, where it has been [i: ~ ëi] since 1700 (Orton 1933: 212), but Longtown, Cumbria has [i(:)] throughout (Stursberg 1969: 60). Northern Northumbrian has a range of realisations before consonants, with [e:], [i:] and [iɛ] all possible (Johnston 1980: 112), but Tynedale and most Cumbrian has the ingliding diphthong as the broadest form (Johnston 1980: 112; Stursberg 1969: 169–71, 253–5). *Two* is *twae* throughout the Scottish Borders (Zai 1942: 94–101).

11.4.5 The BAIT Class: The Descendants of Older Scots /ai/

BAIT stems from an Older Scots /ai/, which monophthongised isolatively before all consonants but palatals (Kniezsa 1994). A diphthong was retained at the end of words, especially if grave consonants precede. The monophthongisation was somewhat variable in this position, but did tend to go through after alveolars (see *day*, *say*). BAIT merges with MATE (Northern Mid Vowel Merger) in at least some positions in most Scots, as mentioned above, and in the focal areas this happens in all places where monophthongisation took place, but monophthongisation probably preceded merger, as both to the north of the Tay and in Galloway, the Borders and northern England, it is realised as either a lower or a longer nucleus, indicating that it probably slipped into the Older Scots monophthong system as a vowel one height below MATE, and merged during the course of the vowel shift. In either case, the most common reflex is an [e(:)] (Mid-BAIT) if merged, and [e:] (Long-BAIT) or [ɛ:] (Low-BAIT) if separate from MATE. Any MATE realisation but the High and Raised types can also be a BAIT reflex – Ingliding [ɛə ~ eə ~ ɪə], Low [ɛ:] and, more rarely, Upgliding [eɪ ~ ɛɪ] types. Merger with BEAT rather than MATE, typical of parts of the Midlands of England and Devon (Anderson 1987: 88), is rare in Scotland, but is attested in Perthshire (Mather and Speitel 1986: 94–5).

The BAIT nucleus is the most common source of E1 vowels in systems, and in one case, that of Stroma (Mather and Speitel 1986: 27) has generated an E2 vowel.

Long Mid Merger of MATE/BAIT (Wells 1982: 192–4) applies in SSE as in RP, so that this class has the same isolative SSE [e(:)] that the words with /a:/ lengthened by Open Syllable Lengthening have. They can often be told by their spelling, however, which tends to be ⟨ai, ay, ei, ey⟩ rather than ⟨aCe⟩, as *aim*; *bait*, *wait*; *laid*, *said*; *waif*, *faith*; *plaice*; *raise*; *raik*; *Haig*; *Tay*, *say*, *day*, *slay* do.

BAIT has considerably fewer subclasses than MATE does, though one can isolate the position before /l n/, which can undergo ingliding diphthongisation (the RAIN subclass: *rain*, *brain*, *main*, *pain*, *vain*, *gain*, and the TAIL subclass: *tail*, *pail*, *bail*, *sail*, *wail*, *rail*) and BAIT + /r/ (the AIR subclass: *air*, *hair*, *pair*, *prayer*, *stair*, *fair*, *chair*, *lair*, *Claire*), which undergoes the same sort of developments as *wear* and *more*, with which it is nearly always merged. The words with final Older Scots /ai/ that do not monophthongise transfer to BITE or TRY; these can be considered a PAY subclass (*ay*, *may*, *pay*, *gey*, *hay*, *clay*, *stay*; *change*, *chain*; *baillie*, *tailor*, *gaol*). Within this subclass, other special developments might happen before palatals (*change*) or after /w/ (WAY: *way*, *whey*, *weigh*).

11.4.5.1 BAIT in Insular Scots

In the Northern Isles, BAIT takes the E1 vowel /ɛ:/, generally a Low form [ɛ:(ᵊ) ~ e:(ᵊ)], with or without a following schwa offglide. On the west side of the Shetlandic mainland, [e:] may appear instead, while the Outlying varieties' reflexes range from [ɛ:ˡ] (Whalsay) to [e:ˡ] (Fair Isle), involving an extended form of a diphthongisation rule affecting all final /e/-like sounds. Even forms as low as [æ:] may occasionally result before voiceless stops in Orcadian, but whatever the vowel is, it can be considered a consistently-long version of the BET nucleus.

The neutralisation of MATE and BAIT before velars and /r/, where the reflex originally belonging to the latter class stands for both, has already been discussed. Before /s/, the two classes are again merged, but under the MATE form [e(:)], and in some Shetlandic and south Orcadian, the same is also true before all voiced sounds, revealing a late application of the Clockwise Vowel Shift. *Rain* and sometimes *tail* have ingliding [ɛ:ᵊ]. Finally, BAIT = MATE as [e:] in Orcadian and north Shetlandic, or [ei ~ əi] elsewhere, while *pay/way* has a distinctive [ɛɪ] in all Insular Scots (Mather and Speitel 1986: 1–27).

11.4.5.2 BAIT in Northern Scots

As mentioned under MATE, the more peripheral a Northern dialect is, the more environments a separate BAIT reflex appears in. In Buchan and Aberdeen, the isolative realisation is the same [e(:)] as for MATE; the distinction appears only in *rain*, and possibly *tail*, where an [e(:)ᵉ] appears that is also used for a merged *wear/more/air* class (Dieth 1932:22–5). In Banffshire and Morayshire, the merger has not gone through in as many positions, and a Long, Low, or Ingliding nucleus [ɛ: ~ e: ~ ɛ:ᵊ] persists in a number of low-sonority environments, though [e(:)] again appears for BAIT + /s/; the E1 vowel functions as the reflex in long environments for a combined MATE/BAIT class. While *pay* proper takes BITE realisations, as elsewhere in Scotland, *change* tends to have /i/, and all *way* items have [ɑˑe ~ ɑˑɛ], the vowel of TRY, in yet another manifestation of Post-Velar Dissimilation throughout Mid-Northern (Mather and Speitel 1986: 51–2, 54–79, 82–6; Dieth 1932: 54).

The Angus pattern resembles the Morayshire one. The isolative reflex is Long, and sometimes Low [e: ~ ɛ:], which is often ingliding among younger speakers to something like [e:ɛ]; the same neutralisations take place as in Mid-Northern. While a subsequent /l n/ often promotes ingliding, it does not have to, and *rain* and *tail* have Long monophthongs in great swaths of Kincardineshire and north Angus. *Air* has [e:ə] down to Montrose on the coast, [e:] below that, and historically, short [e] in inland Angus, though such forms seem recessive in modern Forfar dialect (Johnston 1985b: 25).

Pay and *change* develop as in Mid-Northern, though *way* varies. Merger with TRY extends into South Northern as far down as the Esk, but below that, *way* merges with BITE just as *pay* does, as in Mid Scots.

North Northern dialects traditionally have isolative [e:] in the Black Isle and [e:] or [e:ˡ] in Caithness, though the [ɛɪ] that usually stands for MATE/BEAT is coming in among younger speakers, especially before anterior sounds (including *tail*, *rain*) and a nearly-completed three-way merger under this value is characteristic of Thurso fishers (Mather and Speitel 1986: 31). *Air* develops like *more*, while *pay* generally has the vowel of BEAT. *Way, whey* and *weigh* all tend to have different vowels: [e:], [äe] and [ɛɪ] respectively.

11.4.5.3 BAIT in Mid and Southern Scots

Except for a few traces of an isolative [e:] in Berwickshire (Mather and Speitel 1986: 142–3), and the transfer of *pay*, *change* and *way* to BITE,[17] the Mid-Vowel Merger goes through fully in East and West Mid, South Mid A and., more recently, Southern A as well. From this core area, with support from SSE, the Merger is spreading out in all directions, so that any distinction is a relic where it exists at all, usually restricted to low-sonority, anterior environments. North Mid varieties may have a residual distinction of the form of [ɪə ~ e·ᵊ]/ [eᵊ] in North Mid A and C and [e(:)]/[e:] in B, or may show a pattern where MATE/BAIT take the lower and longer reflexes and BEAT/BOOT the higher and shorter ones, which seems transitional between Northern and Central Belt patterns. In any case, any such distinction is increasingly tenuous in North Mid C and in market towns in Fife and Clackmannanshire – Cupar, for instance, nowadays only has a clear distinction in *tail* and *rain*, much as in Aberdeen, allowing for the lack of *stone*-raising (Johnston 1985b: 4; Mather and Speitel (1986: 103) has a more conservative pattern). *Air* merges with *more*, and *pay* is transferred to BITE, though the odd TRY form appears for *way* occasionally.

Wigtownshire Scots patterns like a peripheral Northern, or even an Insular dialect, with a Lowered isolative form like [e·(:)] contrasting with the [e·(:)] of BEAT/MATE in at least some environments, such as before /t/. The conditioned merger under the lower form has already been mentioned under the treatment of MATE, but there is also a merger under the higher reflex before /s/ and possibly /p/, as in Insular Scots. Ulster Scots has only traces of a distinction, with the merger having gone through in most positions, but the original [ɛ:] of this class is retained as the usual reflex of the merged MATE/BAIT in pre-rhotic and final position. *Pay* and *way* both have [ɛə] (Mather and Speitel 1986: 152–8).

Western Border Scots distinguishes BAIT from MATE in a similar manner to the dialects of Cumbria and most of Northumberland. The vowel used in this class has a lower V1, and is Inglided in most but not all communities, so that [eə ~ e: ~ ɛ: ~ ɛə] are all possible variants (Mather and Speitel 1986: 159, 165–70), the lower variants being used nearer the border. There is no Smoothing in final position, in contrast to MATE. Most *pay* items stay diphthongal, as in the rest of Scots, but monophthongisation is common in more items as one approaches the border.

The overall pattern suggests that BAIT may have monophthongised to a nucleus lower than the vowel of MATE in most regions, though there was certainly interplay with some of the allophones of the monophthongal class. In the focal areas, it developed via raising to the same vowel that MATE had at the time, probably [ɛ:] (Aitken 1977), but in other dialects, it only moved higher than [æ(:)] once MATE had raised to [e(:)]. The result is that most of the conservative varieties of Scots have an E1 vowel, though, looking at the recessiveness of separate BAIT realisations in Fife and similar places, this may not be true for too much longer.

11.4.6 The BOOT Class: The Descendants of Older Scots /øː/

BOOT stems from either an Older Scots /øː/ < /oː/, or /iu/ before consonants, which merge together in one of the earliest distinctively Scots changes (Aitken 1977b). Given the range of realisations, there must have been substantial variation in the pronunciation of this vowel, but it had a tendency to unround (about 1530 in Aberdeenshire, and in the eighteenth century in Mid-Scots: see Dieth (1932: 8) and Wilson (1923)), particularly in long environments. Surviving Rounded types point to a value of [ø: ~ ö:] in earlier stages of Scots, plain to slightly under-rounded, never over-rounded. When this vowel unrounds, it often merges with an already existing front mid unrounded vowel, especially in long environments, where forms usually equal MEET, BEAT or MATE. If there is no merger, the dialect has a Y vowel, usually a high to high-mid centralised front or central monophthong. The most common pattern involves a split, whereby BOOT unrounds to [ë ~ ë] in short environments but [e:] in long ones; the first may merge with BIT or be separate, but the second always equals another class. Other possible realisations include [e(:)] in all positions (Mid-BOOT), [e·(:)] (Raised-BOOT), [ɟ(:)] (Central-BOOT) and [i(:)] (High-BOOT), from either an earlier /y:/ or /iə/ via Smoothing (Orton 1933: 68–9).

BOOT items are usually spelled with ⟨oo⟩, though ⟨o⟩, ⟨u⟩, ⟨uCe⟩ or ⟨ui⟩ occur in a few individual instances. Words in this lexical set include *loop, tuip; loom, tuim; boot, suit, shoot, fruit; food, mood, hood; goose; tune, June, moon; fool, pool;* and in long environments, *move, prove; smooth, soothe; use* (verb), *confuse; do, to, too, shoe.*

Scottish Standard English has /u/ in this class, realised as whatever the local form of OUT is in low-status varieties, but tending toward backer variants in many high-status types (Johnston 1983a: 155; Johnston 1980: 204, 209–15; Macaulay and Trevelyan 1977: 38–40). Such pronunciations are slowly replacing original BOOT reflexes on a piecemeal basis in all but the most common words, and though it is hard to tell how far this 'bleeding' has actually gone in the various districts, it appears to be highly advanced in parts of the western Borders, in Ulster and along the Highland Line. Before /v ð/ and /z/ except for *use* and *confuse*, the regular development is hardly found any more in any district, though it did appear in early twentieth-century monographs (Zai 1942: 90; Wettstein 1942: 42; Dieth 1932: 8). We can probably consider *move, prove, smooth* as totally transferred to OUT, and *bruise* is not far behind in the north.

Since Pre-Rhotic Mid Vowel Lowering follows BOOT-Unrounding in the dialects that have it, the POOR subclass (*poor, floor, moor, sure*) may have the same vowel as BET just as *wear, more* and *air* do. In other traditional dialects, the vowel in these words may dissimilate to /jur/, a development more commonly associated with BOOT followed by velars (the HOOK subclass: *duck* (noun), *book, hook, cook; leuch, sheuch, enough, tough*). In recent times, the /j/ in *hook* or *poor* has often been absorbed, resulting in just plain /u/ or /ʌ/. BOOT preceded by a velar, similarly, may dissimilate to /wi/ in dialects that had Older Scots /y:/ in a rule called *good-* Dissimilation here (in *good, cuit, cool, school*). There is also a Scots analogue to Wells's (1982: 132–3) *foot* set, whereby the vowel shortened and unrounded early to merge with BIT over all of Scotland, although it has different membership from the Southern subgroup (*foot, good, mother, other, brother, summer*). Many of these words, though not all, are disyllabic.

11.4.6.1   BOOT in Insular Scots

Most Insular dialects have a Rounded Y vowel in BOOT such as [ø(:) ~ Y(:)], the last in west Shetlandic (Mather and Speitel 1986: 1–27). There is often little allophony, although south Shetlandic may have central rather than front realisations in long environments, and lower the vowel of *poor* to [œ: ~ ɞ:]. Unrounding to a Split pattern like that of Mid Scots ([ɪ] short/[e:] long) is only characteristic of Stronsay, Orkney (Mather and Speitel 1986: 17–19). However, SSE loans with /u/ can occur for any word in this set, especially in Orcadian (Mather and Speitel 1986: 12–27).

Boot takes /u/ before /p/, and increasingly before /k/, replacing earlier /ju/ in the latter case (Mather and Speitel 1986: 14, 15, 17–18, 22, 24–6). There is evidence of /ʌ/ in some south Orcadian varieties in *hook* (ibid.: 23).

11.4.6.2   BOOT in Northern Scots

Mid- and North Northern Scots varieties have had High-BOOT for years, usually in the form of [i(:)], and thus have no Y vowel. This may undergo Northern Diphthongisation where MEET does (Mather and Speitel 1986: 27–79; Dieth 1932: 8). In east Angus, and increasingly the whole county, the reflex tends to be Raised [e·(:) ~ e·ə] = BEAT isolatively, but west Angus, at the time of LSS vol. 3 (Mather and Speitel 1986: 82–4, 86), retained [ø(:)] as Shetland does. *Hook* and *poor* in traditional Morayshire and North Northern dialects both dissimilate to /ju/, although in recent years the /j/ has been increasingly dropped, or loans with /u/ have come in via SSE except in a few items (Mather and Speitel 1986: 51–6; Grant 1931: xxxiv, xxxvi–xxxvii). *Good*-Dissimilation applies in that subclass in South and Mid Northern, so that *gweed* results, but North Northern has regularly derived *geed* instead (Grant 1931: xxxiv, xxxvi). *Foot* takes BIT realisations throughout the region.

11.4.6.3   BOOT in Mid- and Southern Scots

For the most part, the North Mid developments of this nucleus continue the developments of the varieties' neighbours. Like west Angus, Perthshire dialects retained Rounded [ø(:) ~ Y(:)] in at least short environments, but is now tending toward a Split pattern reminiscent of dialects further south, with [e:] in long and [ë ~ ɛ̈], which may be a separate Y vowel or be merged with BIT, in short environments. North Mid C has the same pattern, but with a greater frequency of BIT/BOOT merger. However, there are traces of an earlier pattern, with a Mid [e(:) ~ eə] in all positions, equal to BEAT; this is what is usual in North Mid B, although the Split pattern is becoming more frequent in this part of Fife also (Mather and Speitel 1986: 101–2, 104–10). *Foot* always merges with BIT, *poor* with *more* and *air*, but *hook*, traditionally, has a distinctive [jʌk], shared only with West Mid, and stemming probably from a non-peripheral Older Scots *[Y:k] via dissimilation and lowering of the [ʊ] > [ʌ] (Mather and Speitel 1986: 94, 98–105, 108–11, 114–35; Grant 1931: xxv).

South of the Forth/Clyde line, the Split pattern prevails everywhere, except in traditional Borders varieties, which used the old Rounded reflex [ø(:)] even in *hook*, which as late as 1942 extended into east Roxburghshire (Zai 1942: 88–9, though /jux/ appears in words like *enough*). Increasingly, the short reflex is merged with BIT, and the long one with whatever nucleus is in the /e/ slot. The fully developed pattern was already established throughout most of West Mid and East Mid A as far as Edinburgh, and has spread considerably since then, already affecting East Mid B and Border varieties (Johnston 1980: 204) The older situation was to have some kind of Y vowel in short environments that was higher than the reflex of BIT, such as [ë] in most of the East Mid area, Peeblesshire and variably in south Lanarkshire; [ɪ] in the southern Lammermuirs, Tweeddale and north Dumfriesshire, and [ɨ] in all Galloway. Centralised forms may even appear before voiced fricatives in some localities to this day, and used to be more widespread (Wettstein 1942: 42). *Poor* develops like other /e:r/ nuclei, undergoing lowering where *more/air* do (Macafee 1994: 225–32), while, within the Mid dialects, *hook* had [jʌk] in West Mid and [juk] in the rest. This form is losing its /j/ in many localities, giving rise to sse-like forms or *huck* forms (Mather and Speitel 1986: 114–35).

Western Border dialects tend not to adopt the West Mid patterns, but 'bleed out' BOOT as a class, directly adopting SSE loans with /u/, as northern English dialects do. The same thing happens in Ulster, where /y/ = OUT replaces [i(:)], [e(:)] and [ɨ ~ e:] patterns (Gregg 1985). The replacement was already in evidence in Mather and Speitel (1986: 164–9) and must be more or less complete by now, constituting an important step in the anglicisation of Ulster Scots phonology.

11.4.7 The BIT Class: The Descendants of Older Scots /ɪ/

The BIT class contained one of only two non-peripheral vowels in Older Scots, both of which are immune from lengthening by Aitken's Law. The /ɪ/ is generally a good deal lower in Scots than in English dialects, due to Non-Peripheral Vowel Lowering, which affects BIT and CUT alike. The most common reflex overall, and one that is increasing in frequency, is [ɛ] (Mid-BIT), although higher centralised front realisations closer to high-status SSE and RP such as [ë ~ ɪ] (High-BIT) are far from rare. Less commonly, and more localisedly, even lower BIT types such as [æ ~ ä] (Low-BIT) may occur, as may backed types such as [ə ~ ɜ] (Central-BIT), [ʌ] (Dark-BIT) or [ɨ ~ ɤ] (Backed-BIT), any of which may overlap with CUT. Some Northern and Insular varieties even exhibit a split, with backed types in some environments and Mid ones in others. If something else merges with one of these allophones, the split becomes phonemic, producing an E2 vowel if there is no Y vowel that these allophones can merge with. BIT words are most often spelled with ⟨iC⟩ or ⟨yC⟩, although other graphemes may occur in individual lexical items. The set includes *ship, lip, dipper; kit, split, kitten; lick, tick, sticky; itch, stitch, Mitchell; rib, chib; kid, lid; big, rig, bigger; stiff, lift; this, kiss, mist, lisp, risk; wish, pish; light, bright, sight; sieve; his, Liz; dim, Jim, Jimmy; skin, thin, hint, inch, India, dinner; thing, ink, English.*

SSE and RP are usually represented in sources as sharing an [ɪ] for BIT, though the usual high-status SSE reflex is in fact a slightly lower [ë] outside of older or elocuted varieties such as Morningside or Panloaf (Johnston 1983a: 155). Before /r/, SSE may have /ɪr/, /ɛr/, /ʌr/ or an in-between /ər/ (the latter two involving merger with CUT, and the second, frequently with BET), with the last-mentioned the most RP-like.

Systematic transfers of BIT items often result in a merger with CUT, MEET or a separate BOOT, if there is one. BIT-Retraction, which can transfer items to CUT, may apply in various environments, usually involving consonant gravity in some way. The most widespread environment is (1) a preceding /w ʍ/ (the WIND subclass: *win, wit, what, Wick, whisky, whiff*), followed in frequency by (2) any labial, usually with a following /l/ (the PILL subclass: *pill, bill, will, fill, mill, Willie, miller*), or (3) simply the following /l/ (the HILL subclass: *hill, kill, chill, till, killer, silly*), or (4), /r/, which may also cause lowering (the GIRL subclass: *girl, kirk, kirn, fir; spirit, mirror*). High consonants around BIT can raise the vowel to /i/, though this rule is always somewhat lexically conditioned where it exists (the KING subclass: *kick, king, wig, whip, swim*).

11.4.7.1 BIT in Insular Scots

Shetlandic and north Orcadian show their north-eastern heritage in that they have some sort of Split-BIT pattern (Mather and Speitel 1986: 1–27; Johnston 1985b: 43, 47). One allophone is a fairly normal Mid-to-High [ë ~ ë], short in all positions, and perhaps slightly retracted in Shetlandic and slightly fronted in Orcadian.[18] There is little distinctive about it, as it is close to realisations of BIT in any conservative Scots dialect. The second allophone, however, is a backed [ï], unique to the Northern Isles. It probably derives from an earlier [ë], as it is associated with grave environments, and backing in such a setting would make sense (Lass 1976: 204). Most mainland Shetlandic, including that of Lerwick, has it before both labials and velars, but the other dialects only have it before labials, with velars being a raising environment, favouring [ɪ]. Central and south Orcadian have [ë] in all positions.

Pill/hill tends strongly towards Central BIT, [ɜ] in Shetlandic, and a quite peripheral [ɛ] in Orcadian, but the effects of a preceding /w/ are not profound – some dialects even have the normal, unbacked form after /w/. *Girl* also tends to be regularly developed, with no 'Abercrombie vowel' present in words like *earth*.

High consonants may peripheralise BIT to /i/, as is typical in *swim*, *king* and fairly frequent in *kick* also (Mather and Speitel 1986: 1–26). High fricatives such as /ʃ/ or even more commonly /x/ tend to diphthongise and dissimilate the vowel, so that *fish* and *night* often have [ɜi ~ ɛi] = BITE. If there is an E2 vowel, it most often results from Central or Backed allophones of BIT overlapping with those of CUT, so that [ɜ] contrasts with /ɪ/ in some environments and /ʌ/ in others.

11.4.7.2 BIT in Northern Scots

The typical Mid-Northern pattern of BIT realisations is a split distribution. In Buchan dialects, [ɪ ~ ɨ] appears before voiced stops and fricatives, before voiced velars and possibly /k/, and Mid [ë] appears elsewhere (Mather and Speitel 1986: 64–76; Dieth 1932: 39–47). In Morayshire, this sort of distribution is on the increase, replacing a set-up where [ɜ] is common in most positions (Mather and Speitel 1986: 56; Johnston 1985b: 34). The whole set of *king* items except *kick* takes /i/, as throughout the north. Backing in *hill/pill* is not very important or marked around Aberdeen (though *wind* is generally backed to match CUT; Dieth 1932: 50), but in the north and west of Aberdeenshire, Banffshire and Morayshire, these subclasses are transferred to CUT, and in west Morayshire, BIT develops to [ʌ̈] before labials also.

Black Isle speech has isolative Central [ɜ] for BIT, with [ë] only as a conditioned form before voiceless fricatives. Low-BIT [æ], showing overlap with CUT, occurs inconsistently before /d n/ and variably in long environments. *Swim* and *king* are transferred to /i/, though *night* develops normally. *Girl* is retracted only in Nairn, but stays separate from *turn* in the Black Isle proper.

Caithnesian has isolative Mid [ë], perhaps a little fronter than the Central Belt reflex. A following /x/ causes diphthongisation, as in Insular Scots; there is the usual transfer of *swim/king* to /i/, and *girl* merges with *turn* and, more recently, *Perth* (Johnston 1985b: 39–40), no doubt due to the retroflex quality of the following [ɹ].

There is much variability in South Northern, but it exhibits similarities to both the Central Belt dialects and the rest of the north. The usual reflex varies, but is most frequently [ë]; [ɜ] becomes more common near the Perthshire border. The high reflex of Mid Northern shows up in some Mearns dialects before velars, while backing to [ʌ] is usual in *hill*, *pill*, *wind* and before labials, much as in those Mid-Scots varieties adjoining the Highland Line. No special developments happen for *girl* (Mather and Speitel 1986: 51–79; Johnston 1985b: 26).

11.4.7.3   BIT in Mid and Southern Scots

Most North Mid varieties have isolative Mid [ë] for BIT, though near the Highland Line the reflexes are considerably backer, and in fact BIT is in a near-merger relationship with CUT in west Perthshire (Mather and Speitel 1986:94). In Fife as in the Lothians, backing only occurs in *wind*, *pill*, but as one goes west or north, the number of backing environments increases until they match the array found in Angus varieties on Tayside and in Perthshire. No other special developments are extant, though at one time *king* had /i/ and *wig* had /ëi/ (Grant 1931: xxv).

The Mid dialects south of the Forth/Clyde line develop BIT similarly, with [ë] the usual isolative form in the Central Belt and higher forms in peripheral regions: [ɪ ~ ë] is typical of Berwickshire and Wigtownshire for instance (Mather and Speitel 1986: 143–4, 146, 183–4), and peripheral [ɛ], contrasting by length with BET, may also occur in parts of the Borders (Zai 1942: 41–2; Wettstein 1942: 43). Central [ɜ] or Low [æ] is typical of Ulster Scots (Mather and Speitel 1986: 192–202). Southern Scots shows a gradual shade in from Mid forms to High, RP-like ones, though even Border Northumbrian tends to have [ë] (Mather and Speitel 1986: 164–9). Higher forms than this are found in Cumbrian, Tyneside and Coalfield varieties.

All Mid- and Southern Scots dialects transfer the vowel to CUT in *wind* and *pill*. The West Mid group, and neighbouring West Lothian and Stirlingshire, add *hill* and, increasingly, *girl* to this transfer list, and tendencies to do so are increasing over time, spreading eastwards and southwards (Johnston 1985b: 7). *King* now has /i/ in a westerly distribution (Ayrshire, Galloway and Ulster; compare Wilson 1923: 21), but *wig* has it in only a few Forthside communities (Mather and Speitel 1986: 109, 139–41). *Swim* has [swim] in Ulster Scots, but otherwise the /wi/ is assimilated to /ʉ/ throughout both Mid and Southern Scots, just as in *sweep* and, in the Borders (on both sides), *we* = [ʉ].

11.4.8   The BET Class: The Descendants of Older Scots /ɛ/

Words such as *step, kept, reputation; bet, set, better; neck, cheque, chequers; etch, fetch, lecher; ebb; bed, led, shredder; edge, swedger; Jeff, left, after; Beth, meths, method; mess, grass, best, desk, lesser, jester; ash, mesh; sever, Kevin; blether, tether; fez; hem, stem, lemming; men, dent, fend, fence, tenner, spending; bell, spell, melt, held, else, hellish; merry, Kerry, carry* containing the descendants of Older Scots /ɛ/ comprise the BET class. As the list above shows, the most common spelling of this group is ⟨eC⟩. The vowel in this class, as in other parts of the English-speaking world, is most commonly [ɛ(ː)] (Mid-BET), although the Scottish version may be slightly more peripheral or higher than a typical English or American BET form. It may also have been shifted, up or down, in the course of Clockwise and Counter-clockwise shifts, or even, as in Aberdeen, raised in the Great Vowel Shift bottom half if Aitken's Law applied early enough. Realisations range from a Low-BET [æ(ː)] to a High-BET [e(ː)]. Both Ingliding [ɛə ~ eə] and Upgliding [ɛɪ ~ eɪ] are occasionally attested, usually as concomitants to raising shifts. Split distributions are possible as well, as BET is quite responsive to the conditioning effects of surrounding sounds.

In SSE, BET results in /ɛ/ except in early Northern transfers like *after, grass*. Standard varieties generally share the local Scots vowel unless it is particularly far away from a Mid value. Before /r/, high-status types may sometimes have [ə] after the model of RP [ɜː], either merged with both *girl* and *turn*, or with *girl* alone. Words such as *dead, head, red, deaf*, which have BET forms in the Standard reflecting Southern and Midland developments, do not belong here, but are best treated as normal BEAT items in Scots.

Subclasses of BET are rather plentiful. A preceding /w/ (*web*: *web, west, well* (noun), *work* (noun) or original /wr/ (*wretch*: *wretch, wren, wrestle*) may 'darken' – lower, back and/or round – BET realisations, and transfers to CAT, CUT or COT are quite frequent. A following /r/ may also cause retraction or lowering. In some words, such as *dark, far, war, farm, heart*, /ɛr/ lowered in Middle English, though tended not to in Older Scots. The variability of this group, where each word more or less has its own distribution between BET and CAT or CAUGHT reflexes, makes it hard to talk about a true subclass, but individual items can be alluded to. If this group is excluded, the ones that remain (*Perth*: *Perth, kerb, pert, third, terse, perfect, jerk, earn, earn, term, Kerr*) form a true subclass, in which the vowel may be retracted and merged with BIT, especially in dialects with a retroflex /r/ = [ɹ]. A similar development may happen in the so-called 'Abercrombie vowel' (Abercrombie 1979: 74) set (*never*: *ever, never, heaven, twenty, next, dress; earth*), where the original /ɛ/ was raised to /ɪ/ in most, though not all, Scots and English vernaculars. While the independence of this set as an E2 vowel is not really characteristic of vernaculars but of certain SSE varieties (Johnston 1983b), they may still take either BET or BIT forms, and in the case of *twenty* an underlying *twinty* can be assimilated to [tʉnʔe], as in East Mid B (and some A) and Southern varieties. The vowel here is the same as OUT.

The height of following velar consonants such as /g/ (*egg*: *egg, leg, beg, keg*) or /x/ (*eight*: *pech; straight, eight, weight, fight*) may have a raising or a diphthongising effect, resulting in transfer to BITE, MEET, BEAT or BIT.

11.4.8.1   BET in Insular Scots

BET is realised as a Mid-to-Low [ɛ(:) ~ æ(:)] before voiceless sounds in most Insular Scots localities (Johnston 1985b: 43, 47); the vowel, as is typical of dialects of the east-coast source dialects and eastern Lothians and Borders, is often no shorter than half-long in any environment, and may be fully-long. Before /k/, especially in Shetlandic, one can even get a BET/BEAT/MATE/BAIT four-way merger, and lengthening is frequent before voiceless fricatives also (Mather and Speitel 1986: 1–12). Before voiced sounds, the action of the Clockwise Vowel Shift may raise BET to [e(:) ~ ɛ·(:)], and can even form Upgliding diphthongs here; the [ɛ·ɪ] of words like *Ed, men* in central and south Shetlandic can be quite striking, and BAIT and BET can be contrasted by type of offglide rather than by length. Outer islands like Whalsay can go further, producing [ɟi]. Orcadian reflexes tend to be either monophthongal or ingliding rather than upgliding like this.

Eight develops much as BET does before voiced sounds, to upgliding diphthongs (= BITE and *night*) in Shetlandic, but isolative reflexes in Orcadian (Mather and Speitel 1986: 1–27). *Perth* and *heart* have [ɛ:] in both dialects, and are kept separate from the higher *wear/more/ air* complex. *Egg* most often develops regularly now, but this is a recent replacement of /i/, still present in Fair Isle and in the far north of Shetland (Mather and Speitel 1986: 1, 12).

Around Kirkwall, a following /l/ raises BET to [e:], and North Ronaldsay has central [ɜ] in this position, but all other dialects develop BET normally. A preceding /w/ as in *web* transfers the vowel to CAT, however.

11.4.8.2 BET in Northern Scots

BET exhibits one of two developments in the north of Scotland. In the Mid-Northern A focal region, the typical form is the same [e(:) ~ e˕(:)] found for the merged MATE/BAIT class. As with BAIT, lengthened and ingliding reflexes are frequent before sonorants, especially /l n r/, and such forms have a tendency to spread to other environments (Mather and Speitel 1986: 59–61, 63–70, 73, 76–9; Johnston 1985b: 30). Presumably, Aitken's Law applied early here, merging BET together with the nuclei that were then in the [ɛ:] slot, and, as in the back series, the low-mid vowels raised to high mid.

Outside this area, in North Northern, Mid-Northern B and South Northern, BET stayed separate, resulting usually in an [ɛ(:)] that (*pace* LSS vol. 3) is often higher and more peripheral than most English reflexes, and is quite easily lengthened and even diphthon-gised to Ingliding [e(:)ɛ], especially in high-sonority settings in Angus, Kincardineshire and Moray (Mather and Speitel 1986: 51–2, 54–7, 78–80, 86–9), though monophthongs prevail in North Northern (Mather and Speitel 1986: 28–32, 35, 37; Johnston 1985b: 40).

Special developments are common. *Wretch*, most *web* items, and words with the BET vowel between palatals and /l/ (*shell, yellow*) are mostly transferred to CAT, though *web* itself tends either to have regular developments or backs and rounds to transfer to COT, and may even subsequently diphthongise and take LOUP forms in coastal communities like Hope-man, Morayshire (Mather and Speitel 1986: 52).

Perth and *heart* develop as other BET items in a high-sonority setting do, though in North Northern (Johnston 1985b: 40) the vowel here has been quite recently retracted to [ɜ], merging with *girl* and *turn* in a chain shift that involves lowering of *wear/more/air* to [ɐ(:)]. Where BET – [e(:)], epenthetic vowels are common before /r/, often in the form of [ɛ̆]. Although *straight* is usually a CAT word here, and, in the heart of the Northern area, so is *eight*, other items take normally developed reflexes unless the /x/ is strongly palatal, as in Thurso. In this case, diphthongisation to [ɛɪ] and resultant transfer to BEAT sets in. *Egg* is also frequently transferred to BITE by diphthongisation, particularly in coastal communities, although the geographical distribution is wider, affecting towns as far south as Fraserburgh, and may have receded from being general north of the Mounth (Mather and Speitel 1986: 31–8, 46, 48, 51–2, 58, 63–5, 69; Grant 1931: xxv).

11.4.8.3 BET in Mid- and Southern Scots

While a handful of dialects in the southern part of the Lothians may merge BET with MATE/BAIT (Speitel 1969), the more usual pattern is for some sort of Mid-BET realisation, often half-long or longer (even outside the Glasgow Drawl area), and is often raised to [ɛ˔(:)], especially in North and East Mid A areas (Johnston 1985b: 4, 7). This vowel was shifted downwards in the Border Scots Counter-clockwise Vowel Shift, so that Southern dialects tend to have Low-BET [æ(:)] (Mather and Speitel 1986: 154–60, 164–9; Zai 1942: 33–4) and the lowest forms of all are found in Tweeddale and central and south-western Berwickshire, where [a(:)] results (Mather and Speitel 1986: 151; Wettstein 1942: 44). Ulster Scots, koinéised as it is, has a split development, with [æ] before voiceless sounds or clusters containing them, and long [ɛ˔:(ə)], reminiscent of Gallovidian, elsewhere. However, the lowering rules are becoming undone, as Raised reflexes are coming in, leading to a more Central Belt-like system (L. Milroy 1994: 138).

Perth is generally regularly developed, but may be /er/ in districts adjoining the north and in Galloway, where it takes BAIT reflexes, while Ulster Scots has [ʒ] = *girl*, as in other districts with [ɹ] (Mather and Speitel 1986: 88, 90–7, 182–4, 186–9, 194, 196, 198). Diphthongs for *egg*, mentioned by Grant (1931: xxv) as typical of several North Mid and Border varieties, are rare and recessive, but *igg* forms may be found, especially in east Fife (Mather and Speitel 1986: 101, 104–7, 109). *Eight* is, similarly, most often the BET isolative realisation + /x/, but Border Scots has [æɪç], which does not equal *night*, with the epenthetic high vowel creeping in because of the *Ich* allophone of /x/ being so far front.

A separate 'Abercrombie vowel' does not generally appear to be a trait of vernaculars, though speakers may have one in formal styles. Most of these words are transferred to BIT, though the /ɛv/ words in the set remain in BET in the Borders. The English–Scottish border contains sharp isoglosses where BET is concerned, though both lowered and raised forms may be found sporadically in Border Northumbrian. Originally, *Perth* (and *girl*) was separate from *turn* in these dialects as [aːᵏ]/[ɔːᵏ] (Orton and Halliday 1962), but they are now fully merged under the latter value. Cumbrian has [ɜː].

11.5   THE DIALECTOLOGY OF SCOTS BACK VOWEL SYSTEMS

11.5.1   Introduction and Inventorial Shape

Older Scots possessed at least four back vowel phonemes: (1) an /uː/ in words of the OUT class, equivalent to Middle English /uː/; (2) an /ʊ ~ ʒ ~ ɤ/ in words of the CUT class; (3) a long mid vowel, probably /ɔː/ (though /oː/ is traditionally generally chosen to represent it; see Aitken 1977b) in COAT;[19] and (4) its short congener, probably /ɔ/ (or /o/) in COT. In addition, there were two low vowels, the /a ~ ɑ/ of CAT, and the /aː ~ ɑ/ (traditional /ɒ/) of CAUGHT, resulting from the monophthongisation of an earlier /au/ or /ɑu/. Since they often pattern like back vowels in conditioning consonantal allophones, they are treated here.

In Catford's (1957b) schema, Scots dialects either have the whole set of six vocalic nuclei, with no mergers reducing the inventory; five, with one; or four, with two mergers. The most frequent mergers are the widespread union of COT:COAT, and either a COT:CAUGHT or a CAT-CAUGHT merger. The first is frequent in SSE varieties, but rare in localised vernaculars, while the second is more common. If a system has both COT = COAT and CAT = CAUGHT, the way that Border Scots does, for example, it has a basic system, consisting of /u ~ ʉ ~ y ʌ o ɔ/. So do the North and West Mid varieties with COT = COAT = CAUGHT but a separate CAT. Varieties where CAUGHT does not either equal COAT or CAT have an extra back vowel, usually rounded and low-mid or low [ɔ(ː) ~ ɒ(ː)], which Catford calls an A vowel. Likewise, if COT does not equal COAT or CAT, any [ɔ(ː)] or [ö(ː)] realisation can be considered another type of A vowel. I have disambiguated these types by calling the first A vowel an A1 and the second an A2. Generally, A1s are lower and less likely to obey Aitken's Law than A2s, and there is nothing preventing both from being in the system.

In a few cases, Mather and Speitel (1986: 70, 73–4, 76, 88, 97, 98, 101–2, 105, 107–9), but no other sources, show that a separate A1 or A2 vowel phoneme exists, but marginally, only in a few environments, often before /t k/. Because of the way in which the survey is organised, it is not easy to see what is going on, though it is unlikely that the distinction is an innovation. For instance, COT words may take [ö(ː)], but COAT [oː], before /t k/, but both classes have [o(ː)] in other environments. In some of these cases, it is probably best to postulate either a true near-merger (Labov 1994: 349–90) or a merger nearing completion, with any residual distinction having been unreported by previous researchers because of its subtlety and/or restriction of its occurrence. Another interpretation might be that, because LSS vol. 3 involved minimal pairs, the speaker, who ordinarily merges COT and COAT, but is aware of spelling differences, gives one possible phonetic variant in cases of COT, but another one, belonging to the same variable, in the case of COAT. He/she has then made an artificial distinction, depending only on the format of the questionnaire. If variability is present across environments, as is often true, determining the true situation becomes highly problematic – in fact, impossible without a second study focusing on this very matter.

Still, cases like the latter would presumably be in the minority, well outweighed by the near and partial mergers. If the distinction were false, why would the tendency to make one be restricted to one or two environments, when spelling differences that could trigger false distinctions exist in others also? Why distinguish *cot* from *coat* but not *cod* from *code*? Why are *back* and *balk* different but not *pal* and *Paul*, unless there is a real live distinction, albeit a restricted and conditioned one?

I have decided to treat such cases as representing distinct phonemes, if *marginally* so, unless it is plain that one of the two reflexes may occur for members of both classes. In other words, if COT words are always [ö(:)], never [o(:)], before /t k/, and COAT words the opposite, I treat this as a real near-merger situation. If there is any phonemic overlap so that there are COT words taking [o(:)] or COAT words [ö(:)] in this environment, I interpret the data as reflecting a combined [ö(:) ~ o(:)] merged class. Doing this does result in some discrepancy between SND's phonemic breakdowns and those used here. However, this should be taken as an invitation to further researchers to investigate the authenticity of this putative near-merger and its status, using the methodology employed by Labov (1994: 403–18) in Philadelphia, for example.

11.5.2   The OUT Class: The Descendants of Older Scots /u:/

In Northern Britain, /u:/ did not diphthongise in the Great Vowel Shift, so that the modern isolative reflexes of OUT are retained as high monophthongs obeying Aitken's Law in Scots, unless the words have been transferred by lexical erosion to the LOUP class under SSE influence (Grant 1931: xx). The segment /u:/ may remain as a back vowel [u(:)] (Back-OUT), although this is no longer the most common reflex, since OUT-Fronting is widespread, producing anything from [u(:)] through [ʉ(:) ~ ɵ(:)] (Central-OUT) to [y(:) ~ ʏ(:) ~ ø(:)] (Front-OUT). Such fronted forms can be under-rounded or over-rounded, depending on the articulatory setting of the dialect. Diphthongal [ʊu ~ ʊʉ ~ øy] (Diphthongised-OUT) reflexes occur occasionally in the dialects that do the same to MEET, via Northern Diphthongisation or, on the Cumbrian Border, Pennine Diphthongisation word-internally.

Members of the OUT class include *south, mouth; house, mouse; out, about; crowd, loud; crown, down; booze; couch; scrounge; power, sour, flower.* The usual spellings include ⟨ou⟩ and ⟨ow⟩, though the same graphemes also designate LOUP and so cannot be used as an infallible guide to membership. SSE has a diphthong /ʌu/ in OUT realised as whatever the local Scots vowel in LOUP is, and immune from Aitken's Law. Since LOUP may be affected by OUT-Fronting just as much as OUT itself is, forms such as [ëü] are quire common, and are becoming more so.

The same Pennine Diphthongisation that may affect Southern Scots *tree* applies to final OUT also in words of the COW subclass (*cow, how, now, bow* (verb), *sow, full, pull*), and either allophonic backing and diphthongisation may apply to /l/ in the FOUL subset (*foul, cowl, towel*). There are otherwise no other distinctive subclasses.

11.5.2.1   OUT in Insular Scots

In Insular varieties, the usual isolative reflex of the OUT class (Back-OUT) may be slightly lowered or centralised from Cardinal 8 – that is, [u(:)] to [u˕(:)], but is fronted only sporadically. It obeys Aitken's Law strictly, and stays monophthongal in all environments, although an epenthetic schwa may appear before /r/ (Mather and Speitel 1986: 2, 11, 13–14, 17–23).

11.5.2.2   OUT in Northern Scots

Northern Scots dialects are divided between those that front OUT and those that do not, though the frontings in Angus and in Caithness are not exactly the same process. All speakers of Caithnesian, even old ones, front OUT markedly to [ʉ], [ʏ] or even [ø]. SND recorded a central value (Grant 1931: xxxviii) at a time when the typical modern Mid-Scots /u/-fronting had barely spread into the Lothians, so it must be independent of the Central Belt developments. The reflexes sound nearly exactly like Ulster Scots (or Belfast) /y/ forms (Wells 1982: 441), and the only allophony noticed at Wick was a slight tendency towards diphthongisation to [ʏy] word-finally, and low-mid [œ:ᵊ] pre-rhotically, both of which are also reminiscent of Belfast vernacular. According to Mather and Speitel (1986: 27–40), Caithnesian fronting is most advanced around the north and east coasts of Caithness, and is lacking entirely in the south of the county.

At the other end of the Northern Scots area, in Angus, OUT-fronting takes place as a continuation of the process extant in Mid-Scots. Mather and Speitel (1986: 77–87) find little fronting north of Arbroath in the South Northern area, but I found that speakers born about 1920 at Forfar had front-to-central, mildly over-rounded [ʉ(:) ~ ʏ(:) ~ ø(:)] reflexes matching possible Fife or Perthshire forms, and that [ʉ(:)] can occur as far north as Aberdeen and Deeside among younger speakers (Johnston 1985b: 31). In the rest of North and Mid-Northern A and B, there exists little tendency for the OUT vowel to front. It generally remains [u(:) ~ ü(:)], though lowering might take place before velars, and sometimes elsewhere, to [ʊ], and in some Mid-Northern areas Northern Diphthongisation may apply in *cow*, producing [ʊu]. Epenthetic schwa is common before /r/ (Dieth 1932: 36; Mutschmann 1908: 53).

11.5.2.3   OUT in Mid and Southern Scots

In contrast to the north, most Mid-Scots dialects today generally exhibit OUT-Fronting in most or all environments, with over-rounded reflexes (particularly over-rounded [ʉ(:) ~ ø(:)], which sound considerably higher than they are) characterising North and East Mid dialects, and under-rounded varieties of the same vowels occurring in West Mid and South Mid A. Sporadically, even [ɨ] may be present in words like *down* in Glaswegian and North Lanarkshire dialects (Macafee 1983). Plain [ʏ(:)] typifies Wigtown and Ulster Scots, and the fact that these dialects have, on average, the frontest realisations of all discloses that OUT-Fronting is probably not Glaswegian, but South-west Scots in origin, though Glasgow may have served to 'amplify' the change (but see Grant 1931: xxvii, who noticed the Mid-Scots change only in Glasgow). Fronting is, at present, spreading into Dumfriesshire and the eastern Borders, though some tendencies are already evident in Tweeddale varieties in Mather and Speitel (1986: 138, 144–6, 149, 151; Johnston 1980:

214); it has reached completion quite recently in the East Neuk and central Fife also, though in all these areas young speakers have markedly fronted forms (Hettinga 1981). There is weak allophony, with pre-alveolar environments favouring fronter reflexes than elsewhere (Mather and Speitel 1986: 101, 104–5, 138, 144–6). Epenthetic schwa is common before /r/ in most Mid dialects with fronting.

East Mid B dialects, especially in central and southern Berwickshire, may have diphthongs like [ʌu ~ əʉ] (=LOUP) for *cow* and *foul* (Mather and Speitel 1986: 143–52). In the case of *cow*, the diphthongs are probably old, exhibiting the last traces of specifically Southern Scots traits in varieties that have been transferred to the Mid group. While the diphthongisation of *tree* and *tea* has been reversed, that of *cow* has not been, since it is supported by SSE. Southern dialects, like East Mid B ones, traditionally lack OUT-Fronting. However, in recent years, Fronting, entering from the Mid dialects, is on the increase, particularly in central Border dialects (Johnston 1980: 210). It is favoured in the shortest environments, before voiceless sounds. *Cow* and often *foul* undergo diphthongisation, both where SSE agrees as in *now, how, foul, towel* and where it does not, as in *you* (Zai 1942: 99–102; Murray 1873: 117).

OUT is slowly gaining members from BOOT, but losing them to LOUP where SSE-influenced restructuring is taking place (Macafee 1994: 229).

11.5.3   The CUT Class: The Descendants of Older Scots /ʊ/

The vowel of the CUT lexical set, Older Scots /ʊ/, not only deperipheralised early, but underwent Non-Peripheral Vowel Lowering in a parallel fashion to BIT, unrounding and lowering to [ʌ ~ ʌ] (Normal-CUT). More fronted variants, such as very low [æ ~ ä] (Low-CUT) or [ɛ̈] (Front-CUT), are also attested. The lowering and unrounding processes could apply in either order, so that both intermediate types, with lowering only ([ö ~ ɔ ~ ɒ], Rounded-CUT), or unrounding only ([ɤ], High-CUT) exist. Fronted-CUT ([ɵ]) can be found in the areas where Backed-BIT is normal, often before the same consonants. The class is generally spelled ⟨uC⟩ (sometimes ⟨ouC, oC, ooC⟩), and contains *cup, up, upper; cub, rub, rubber; come, lum, rummy; huff, suffer; love; Guthrie, but, hut, stutter; thud, bud, study; fuss, must, lusty; buzz, buzzer; run, stun, scunner; much, crutch, Hutchinson; budge, judge, judging; rush, hushing; muck, ruck, lucky; dull, duller; front, hunt, lump.*

Isolative CUT also results in /ʌ/ in SSE. The BULL subclass (*bull, pull, bulk, wool*) has /ʊ/ in RP (that is, it is in Wells's (1982: 132–3) FOOT class), but has /u/ in SSE, merging with BOOT. Before /r/, all but the very highest-status SSE has a separate /ʌr/.

As with other originally short mid vowels, a following voiced velar such as /g ŋ/ (*rug: rug, lug; tongue, sung, rung, trunk, drunk*) or /x/ (*rough: rough, brough, bucht*) may trigger raising or diphthongisation in much the same way as with *egg, log* or *eight, loch*. CUT + /r/ (*turn: hurt, lurk, work, slurp, lurch, purse, turf, curb, curve, bird, burn, urge, burst, burnt, murder*) may be fronted somewhat, and may even merge with *girl* in some Scots, if not as commonly as in English dialects. This merger correlates highly with the use of approximants for /r/ rather than taps.

11.5.3.1   CUT in Insular Scots

The isolative Insular Scots CUT realisation tends to be a Rounded one of some type. In Shetland, the prevailing form is the same one as in Hiberno-English (Wells 1982: 422), [ɔ] (which Mather and Speitel (1986) call [ɔ·], though it is usually quite centralised). Orkney, too, may share this realisation, though the rounding is more variable, and Normal-CUT is more common. Lowering to /ɒ/ results from CUT + /f/ in some Orkney communities, like Birsay (Mather and Speitel 1986: 20).

Before other grave sounds, CUT usually undergoes no special developments, but Fair Isle Shetlandic and South Ronaldsay Orcadian have Fronted or Central [ö~ɵ~ɜ] before labials, and transfer CUT before /k/ to COT = [ɒ(:)] so that *luck = lock* (Grant 1931: xl). In some central Shetlandic, CUT diphthongises to [ɔ·u] = LOUP before all velars, not just /g/ (Mather and Speitel 1986: 3).

Not much effect of /l/ is recorded for CUT, although there may be some centralisation to [ɜ] in south and Fair Isle Shetlandic, parallel to that observed for COT in these varieties (Mather and Speitel 1986: 9–11). CUT + /z/ is transferred to BIT in Shetlandic. There may be some centralisation to [ɵ] before /v/ over most of the mainland, and again on South Ronaldsay in Orkney, but otherwise no special developments occur in this position (Mather and Speitel 1986: 8, 25–6). *Turn* shows a tendency to centralise to [ɜ] outside of the central and south mainland of Shetland. There may be variable merger with *girl*, though generally speaking *girl* has higher and fronter forms.

11.5.3.2   CUT in Northern Scots

Isolative Northern Scots CUT forms reveal quite a bit of variety, although generally speaking Mid-Northern A and South Northern tend to have Normal [ʌ] reflexes, and Mid-Northern B and North Northern, Low [ɐ~ä~æ] or Central-to-Front [ɜ~ɛ̈] forms, with considerable allophony. While Rounded [ɔ~ɒ] reflexes are quite common around grave sounds generally, and sometimes before voiceless fricatives, they may be isolative reflexes in north Banffshire and north-west Aberdeenshire, around Aberdeen city and along the Kincardineshire and Angus coasts (Mather and Speitel 1986: 57, 61–2, 64, 75, 78, 84; Johnston 1985b: 31, 34).

Most North Northern, coastal Morayshire and west Banffshire dialects exhibit diphthongisation and transfer to LOUP in the RUG subclasses, a process called *dog*-Diphthongisation, as this is one of the lexical items affected, as are words like *tongue* and *drunk* (Mather and Speitel 1986: 28–34, 36–7, 43, 48, 51–5, 58–9, 64, 66, 68). In *rug, lug*, Caithnesian has /y/ (= OUT) instead, but has diphthongs in the other items (Johnston 1985b: 40; Grant 1931: xxxviii). East Banffshire and some Angus varieties may have rounding here, but other varieties do not exhibit special developments in *rug*.

CUT + /x/ does not diphthongise, although some *rough* words (like *rough* itself) tend to take COT reflexes, and others, like *bucht*, may shift to BIT in some varieties (Mather and Speitel 1986: 78–9, 86). Indeed, there is a set of words like *sun, son, wonder* and so on that quite routinely is transferred to BIT in Northern Scots (Dieth 1932: 45; Grant 1931: xxi). While the great majority of these involve words that were disyllabic before the loss of Old English *-e*, and it is possible that these are really members of the FOOT subclass of BOOT, items like *word*, which had no second syllable, also go here. However, in contradiction to the usual Scots trend, Older Scots /wʊ/ > /wʌ/ in this group as a rule anyway, so it is most likely that this set represents a mixture of words undergoing fronting rules and *foot* forms.

The effect of high-sonority following consonants is to lower or centralise CUT vowels in North Northern, but there is little effect in Mid- or South Northern, unless there are lexically conditioned transfers to BIT probably resting on early lengthening and reshortening; words like *glove* and *buzz* may do this readily (Mather and Speitel 1986: 52–3, 56, 63–4, 66–70, 72, 76–9, 82–3). *Turn* has [ɜ] and merges with *girl* in North Northern, as is usual in dialects with [ɹ] as the usual /r/ realisation (Mather and Speitel 1986: 30–1, 34, 37; Johnston 1985b: 40).

11.5.3.3 CUT in Mid- and Southern Scots

Unlike dialects of Scots further north, Mid-Scots and Southern Scots varieties exhibit little allophony in their CUT realisations, which depart only in Galloway and perhaps Ulster Scots from Normal types (Johnston 1985b: 15; Wells 1982: 442). These exhibit stages on the way from [ʊ] to [ʌ], with south Ayrshire and central Kirkcudbrightshire having High [ɤ], and Wigtownshire Rounded [ö～ɵ], even before /r/ (Mather and Speitel 1986: 126, 173, 176–8, 181–9; Johnston 1985b: 15). Ulster Scots generally has [ʌ～Ä], but Rounded types shared with Hiberno-English may occur variably and since, as in the far north, /r/ = [ɹ], and *turn* = *girl* = [ɜ]. In the East Mid B and Southern regions, Pre-/x/ Diphthongisation applies, at least variably, to *rough*, producing /ʌux/ forms, in parallel to what happens with other /Vx/ combinations (Mather and Speitel 1986: 148–56, 158, 160; Zai 1942: 55).

The /ʌ/ region originally extended into Northern Northumbrian, separating the northern frontier from the rest of the county, with [ɤ～ʊ] (Ellis 1889: 638). Nowadays, [ɤ] is the normal reflex, although [ʌ] is plentiful as a Standard form. Cumbrian has [ʊ], like the rest of the north of England (Stursberg 1969: 47, 135, 220; Reaney 1927: 41). *Turn* is a strongly uvularised [ɔˠ:] in Northumbrian (equalling *north*, and among most speakers, *force*) as well (Orton et al. 1978: 58–9), and appears either as [ɜ:] or [ʊr] in Cumbrian (Stursberg 1969: 47, 136, 220).

The distribution of innovative CUT forms, and the link between lowering of CUT with that of the BIT class, suggests that the focus of Non-Peripheral Vowel Lowering, which may have already been in progress in the Older Scots period, lies in the vicinity of the Highland Line. This, in turn, would at first seem to suggest that Gaelic influence may have had something to do with this change. However, this is unlikely, since (1) lowering of CUT is as advanced in London as in Morayshire or Nairn (Wells 1982: 305), and (2) Gaelic possesses no [ë], and [ʌ] is a rare, conditioned variant of /a/ (Borgstrom 1940). It is true that Brythonic deperipheralised short /i u/ early, and in Modern Welsh the first eventually becomes [ʌ], but the second stays instead of lowering (Schrijver 1995: 25). It is more likely that the rule is native than the result of anything Celtic.

11.5.4 The COAT Class: The Descendants of Older Scots /ɔ:/

COAT, from a presumed Older Scots /ɔ:/ (but compare Aitken 1977b), underwent the bottom-half Great Vowel Shift late in most Scots dialects,[20] so that Aitken's Law, and thus a merger with COT, preceded raising. It is most often realised as [o(:)] (Mid-COAT), though in some regions it may become consistently long, peripheral [o:] (Long-COAT), even if merged with COT. However, the shift did not apply in all dialects in the back series, so that Low-COAT [ɒ～ɔ], sometimes confined to short environments, may survive in peripheral areas. Diphthongisation to [ou] (Upgliding-COAT) is much rarer than in England, and is only present in dialects that diphthongise high and high-mid vowels this way, such as Caithnesian and Ulster Scots; that to [oə～ʊə] (Ingliding-COAT) is more widespread. A High-COAT type [ʊ～u:] (High-COAT) descends from Ingliding forms via Border Area

Smoothing, and COAT reflexes are fronted to [ɵ:] or even [ø:] (Fronted-COAT) in a few districts. Lexis in this class, with the distinctive ⟨oa, oCe⟩ spelling, includes *hope, Pope; robe; oaf, cove, drove; loam, gloaming; coach; smoke, joke, yoke; rogue*.

SSE possesses back rounded monophthongs or diphthongs for COAT, with /or/ in /r/-combinations. These are identical to the reflexes of Old English /oː/ listed under MATE above, reflecting a Southumbrian merger between this vowel and /ɔ/ lengthened in open syllables.

Special developments of COAT are about as common as those of BEAT. A following /r/ in words belonging to the CORN subclass (*bore, lore, tore, shore; born, corn, shorn, forlorn; board, cord, hoard, afford; storm; force*) may trigger a form of Pre-Rhotic Vowel Lowering, and may result in merger with COT or CAUGHT. A following /x/, as in *thought* words (*thought, brought, bought, wrought*) may either lower a preceding COAT vowel or diphthongise it, a process that leads to transfer to LOUP. In dialects that have *good*-Dissimilation, a somewhat similar process affects Older Scots /kɔː/, which comes out as [kwɛ̈i] in modern speech in words like *coat, coal* (the COAL subclass), probably via a /kɔe/ stage, as in parts of the north Midlands of England (Macafee 1989). In others, Ingliding reflexes develop before all alveolars, usually subphonemically, in words of the *road* group (*code, rode, road, mode; coat, boat, goat, moat; cone, zone; close, toast, boast; close* (verb), *froze, hose*). There is also the possibility of transfer to a separate COT class through lexically conditioned shortening, quite common in items like *close, road* or *yoke*.

11.5.4.1   COAT in Insular Scots

It appears that COT and COAT were originally merged throughout the Insular Scots area, as a Low vowel, [ɒ(ː)], often a little centralised and lengthened (Grant 1931: xl). Higher allophones, [ɔ(ː)] in Shetland and [o(ː)] in Orkney, appear in long and voiced environments non-contrastively in words that are not loans from SSE. However, in most areas, because of length interchange rules and the importation from SSE of loans with /o/, there are now separate /ɒ/ and /o/ phonemes, with minimal pairs like *for: (a)fore* and near-minimal ones like *coal: foal*, even though one can still say that the majority of COAT items have the low vowel before voiceless sounds as well as /l n/ (Mather and Speitel 1986: 1–13).

The /o/ phoneme has a Mid realisation, and is often long [oː]. *Road*-diphthongisation may occur before /t d/; rarely before /n/, except in formal styles, since only /ɒ/ is found here. All low vowels are lengthened variably before at least /f s k/, making possible a neutralisation between COT/COAT as [ɒ(ː)] before /s k/. Before /x/, CUT/COT/COAT/CAUGHT all fall together into [ɒ(ː)] ([ɒː] on Fair Isle).

The vowel in COAT is often raised before voiced sounds, especially in Orcadian, where there are COT/COAT contrasts before /g/, because the COT vowel lengthens but does not raise. Both classes have /o/ before /l/. In Shetlandic, raising of COT/COAT (and CAUGHT, which is merged in) before /b d/ results in low-mid [ɔ] allophones, and /o/ is only found for COAT + /g/. Before /l/, there is a distinction between the two classes as [ɔl]: [oː(ᵊ)l] or the like. In long environments, COAT is [oː] in the overwhelming majority of Insular dialects, although slightly lowered allophones may occur around Lerwick, and the Shetlandic varieties that diphthongise /e/ to [ei] may have upgliding diphthongs for final COAT. High-mid realisations in *corn* (with epenthetic schwa before /r/) are restricted to final position in north and central Orcadian. Here, some form of Pre-Rhotic Vowel Lowering to [ɒː] (north) or [ɔː] (central) applies medially, and this is extended to all positions (> [ɔː]) in Shetlandic and south Orcadian, where *corn* and *north* are distinguished.

11.5.4.2   COAT in Northern Scots

The North Northern dialects tend to have a Long-COAT [oː] realisation isolatively. In western Caithness near the Highland Line, and in fisher districts, this vowel is diphthongised to [ou]. There may be transfers to COT before /d/ or /n/, and both *thought* and *corn* words, at least before a following consonant, have lowered [ɔː] in both Black Isle Scots and Caithnesian, and a consequent merger with *loch* and *north*, the equivalent classes of COT.

Mid-Northern A dialects most often have a normal [o(ː)] realisation obeying Aitken's Law, though Lowered reflexes [ɔ‧(ː)] also occur on Deeside, around Aberdeen, and in the Peterhead and Fraserburgh areas. Whether high- or low-mid, the possibility of a merger with COT becomes greater as one approaches the heart of the Mid-Northern A area. Morayshire varieties keep at least a partial /ɔ/ COT: /o/ COAT distinction, with merger most advanced before /x/ (where it is general Northern Scots), before /rC/, and often before other voiceless fricatives. Kincardineshire dialects also have an /ɔ(ː)/:/o(ː)/ distinction, in fact more solid than any other in Northern Scots.

Special developments are plentiful in the north-east. Lowering in *thought* is not usual except in Kincardineshire, but lowering in *corn* before a consonant is usual, although in some areas a preceding labial can raise the vowel to [oː] even if followed by /rC/. *Corn* itself thus tends to have [ɔː], though *bore* has [oː], and *born* varies. In coastal Banffshire and north-west Aberdeenshire, *dog*-Diphthongisation, which normally applies to COT and/or CUT, is extended to this vowel before /b g/ and, in some words, notably *hope*, to /p/ as well. Hopeman, Morayshire, is always [hɔupmən] to natives, for instance (Mather and Speitel 1986: 52–3).

In Mid-Northern A, though rarely in B, *good*-Dissimilation is extended to words like *coat*, *coal* which result in [kwɛɪ? ~ kwɛ̈ɪ̯]. COAT + /n r/ diphthongises differently to forms like [oːɛ] (Dieth 1932: 70–2). Though *road*-Diphthongisation is fairly frequent here, the V2 of the resulting diphthong tends to be backer than this before /d t z/, about [ʌ]. Angus dialects exhibit a number of isolative reflexes, including [o ~ ö] as well as Fronted [ɵ] or even [ø] realisations, as in Northumbrian. Fronted forms are recorded only for Arbroath in Mather and Speitel (1986: 90–1), but I have observed them as well from natives of Forfar and Montrose, and Scottish /o/-Fronting might be common to all the Mearns by now. Merger with COT is variable, but favoured in high-sonority environments and sometimes before voiceless fricatives. The ROAD subclass routinely has ingliding reflexes such as [oʌ], [ɵə] or even [oɑ] (Johnston 1985b: 26). There may be a *north*/*corn* distinction in coastal dialects (as /ɔr: or/), but both have /or/ in the Mearns (Mather and Speitel 1986: 82–91).

11.5.4.3   COAT in Mid- and Southern Scots

Within Mid-Scots, high-mid reflexes of some type are the norm, although North Mid A and C, and East Mid reflexes often have centralised [ö(ː)], and as usual, the Drawling areas have long, drawled [oː] in most or all positions. Merger with COT is more or less complete in vernacular Scots, except in Argyll, Bute and adjacent parts of north Ayrshire, extreme south Ayrshire, Wigtownshire and Ulster on one side, and central Perthshire, north central Fife and parts of Berwickshire on the other. In the North Mid cases, it appears that there is at least a near-merger with older speakers, and a variable true merger with the young (Mather and Speitel 1986: 88–9, 92, 94, 97, 98, 100, 101, 103–5, 112–15, 116–17, 128–9, 181–205). There is little allophony, but *road* in most areas can have ingliding [oᵊ ~ öˣ] reflexes. *Bought* may undergo transfer to CAUGHT, as in Galloway, Ulster and sections of Perth and Fife, or be diphthongised to [ʌu] = LOUP in parts of Berwickshire next to the Borders (Grant 1931: xxiv).

Lowering of *corn* before consonants is less typical here than in the north, but can occur in east Fife and Galloway. It may have once been a widely distributed form (Mather and Speitel 1986: 104–5, 108, 160, 170–8, 180–9). Southern Scots once had [uə] or [oə], separate from COT and equalling the usual reflex in Carlisle, as an isolative realisation (Stursberg 1969: 187–9, 261–2; Murray 1873: 111–12). This can still be found in Liddesdale and in the Debatable Land to some extent (Mather and Speitel 1986: 159, 164; Stursberg 1969: 79). However, it has either been Smoothed in most western Border localities to [u: ~ ʊ:], with absorption of the V2, or been replaced by the Lothian reflex [o(:) ~ ö(:)], which used to stand only for the COT vowel in Murray (1873: 111). Southern A has taken the replacement route, as with other vowel changes, and increasingly these forms are characteristic of the whole Border region. *Road* or *corn* may have epenthetic schwa after the main nucleus. *Thought* words have [ʌu], the same as LOUP (Zai 1942: 51–2).

Initial COAT or /h/ + COAT had /wʌ/ in words like *hope, hole; open, orchard* in Murray's (1873: 111–12) time. Such forms are now highly recessive. The process is the back series analogue to the development of *ane* to *yin* and *hame* to *hyimm*.

11.5.5   The COT Class: The Descendants of Older Scots /ɔ/

The vowel of COT is always isolatively round in Scots, and in most dialects it is high-mid [o(:)] (High-COT), producing merger with COAT if the two classes are not distinguished by length or peripherality. Low-COT forms, however, with [ɔ(:)] or even [ɒ(:)] are plentiful, though even here, a full or partial merger with COAT or CAUGHT is not precluded. Fronted-COT forms of the [œ(:) ~ ɵ(:) ~ ø(:)] type are found in the same dialects which front COAT reflexes, and the same Upgliding and Ingliding forms exist also, if rarely. This class comprises items like *hop, rob, bomb, hopper, robber, bomber; pot, cod, con, grotty, coddle, bonnie; sock, hockey, box; cough, croft, profit; boss, frost, crossing; posh; romp, font, fond; doll, solve, collie; orange, horror*, which for the most part are spelled with ⟨oC⟩ combinations.

SSE generally merges COT with CAUGHT under /ɔ(:)/, although some high-status varieties not only distinguish the two classes as /ɒ(:)/ vs /ɔ(:)/, but also transfer a number of original COT words, mostly belonging to Wells's (1982: 136–7) CLOTH class, to CAUGHT. Before /r/ (Wells's 1982: 159–60) NORTH class), SSE possesses /ɔr/, different from COAT except in the most statusful varieties.

The most widespread special development of COT results from an Older Scots lowering and unrounding of /ɔ/ to /a/ before labials, and resultant merger with CAT. This change has exceptions, but applies fairly regularly except in the Borders before /p f m/, and less so before /b/. The class of words undergoing it can be designated by *off* (*off, soft, loft, croft; Tom; top, stop; stob, Rob, sob*). A following /g/ (*log: dog; frog, hog, log*) or /x/ (*loch: loch, trough, daughter, bought, fought, wrought*) may cause diphthongisation and transfer to LOUP, or, more rarely, raising or unrounding (in *log*), or lowering (mostly in *loch*). There are also lexically conditioned transfers to CUT (*dog; bonnet*). COT + /r/ (*north: or, for; Thorpe, sort, short, stork, torch, horse, absorb, Geordie, gorge, corpse, mortal, border, organ, corner, aura, borrow*) may transfer to COAT even where this merger is not usual in other positions.

Since the developments of COT are so intertwined with those of COAT, and much of the analysis of COAT had to do with whether or not there were mergers between these two classes in specific positions, I will concentrate on the points of difference between the classes in the analysis below.

11.5.5.1   COT in Insular Scots

The isolative reflex of COT in the great majority of Insular dialects, as stated before, is a weakly rounded, centralised Low [ɒ(:)], with fully central or even front allophones possible in south Shetlandic. It is merged with COAT before all stops but /g/ (in Shetlandic), before /l r/, and in a few central and southern Shetlandic and central Orcadian varieties, before /n/. Before /l/ and /n/, low values are found in the more northerly Shetlandic varieties, but centralised [ɔ̈(:)~ɞ(:)~œ̈(:)] in the other dialects distinguishing COT and COAT. *North* tends to have [ɒ(:)] throughout most of both archipelagoes.

Dog-Diphthongisation is nowhere as common as within Northern Scots, but it does occur in north and central Shetlandic dialects, and on South Ronaldsay. Otherwise, the development is either the same as isolatively (if lengthened) as in Orcadian, [ɔg], as in south Shetlandic, or [ʌ̈g], as in west Shetlandic. The usual transfer of *off* to CAT holds for all of Insular Scots (Grant 1931: xl).

11.5.5.2   COT in Northern Scots

There is quite a lot of variation in the isolative Northern Scots COT realisation. The more peripheral dialects, such as Caithnesian and Black Isle Scots, inland Moray varieties and coastal Angus ones most commonly have [ɔ:], long in North Northern, but obeying Aitken's Law in the rest (Grant 1931: xxi, xxxvii) Near the Highland Line in west and south Caithnesian, Low [ɒ(:)] prevails. Even in Mid-Northern A, where the isolative reflexes are higher than low-mid = [ɔ̩(:)~o(:)], there may be a distinction with COAT before /t k/ and sometimes in other velar contexts even in Mid-Northern A varieties (Mather and Speitel 1986: 57–62, 66–7, 72, 75; Dieth 1932: 34–6). However, COT is fully merged with COAT in many Mearns dialects. The presence of a *north/corn* distinction parallels the isolative distinction, though in some Caithnesian the two are merged only before a consonant.

In Caithness, *Dog*-Diphthongisation has transferred COT + /g/ to LOUP, with the pathway being /ɔu/ > [ʌu] > [ɛy] (Grant 1931: xxviii). It also applies in coastal dialects throughout the area, extending as far east as north-west Aberdeenshire (Mather and Speitel 1986: 68), though without the diagnostic Caithnesian fronting.

A number of dialects, including northern Caithnesian and Morayshire Scots, with isolative low-mid /ɔ(:)/ nevertheless have [o] before /n/. *Off*-unrounding and transfer to CAT applies throughout the whole area with the single exception of Black Isle Scots, where Highland English influence has probably affected the outcome.

11.5.5.3   COT in Mid- and Southern Scots

As discussed under COAT, the Central Belt Mid dialects tend to have a merger of the two '/o/'s' under [o(:)], though of course SSE influence can always restore an [ɔ(:)] value, even in those North and West Mid dialects which have a 'supermerger', with CAUGHT also = [o(:)]. Among dialects north of the Forth/Clyde line, dialects in or near large centres such as Perth or Dundee, south-west Angus and the whole North Mid C region tend to have a fairly solid merger, which suggests that High-COT is, in origin, an urban innovation that spread from the Central Belt at some point in the fairly recent past, possibly the eighteenth century, since CAUGHT becomes involved where its reflexes raised early.

High reflexes are also presently characteristic of most peripheral Mid varieties: those of inland Berwickshire, the Southern Uplands from Peeblesshire to south Ayrshire, and Nithsdale and west Dumfriesshire. Most recently, the merger has spread to Southern A varieties, which had not yet experienced it in Murray's (1873: 111) time. The reflex is often somewhat centralised (especially in North and East Mid: Mather and Speitel 1986: 88–9, 93, 95–7, 103, 109–11, 114, 138–9, 151), and may be realised as an ingliding diphthong, particularly before /t d n l z/ (*road*) and under emphasis (Macafee 1983: 35, 37; Johnston 1980: 116–17).

However, there are dialects on all four sides of the Central Belt which still keep the distinction intact and have an A2 vowel. To the north, in North Mid A and B, there is the possibility of either a residual /o/: /o:/ distinction, as in north central and east Fife, or /ö/: /o:(ᵊ)/, as in most of Perthshire. Lowering to [ɔ(:)] in *north* or *loch* is variable, and tends to be east coastal in distribution. *Off*-unrounding is extended here to words with preceding labials, like *pot*, a development that must have been more widespread at one time (Mather and Speitel 1986: 117–22, 129–33).

To the west, in Argyll and the Clyde coastal dialects, COAT has [o], and COT [ɔ], merging with CAUGHT, much as in SSE. These are next door to dialects along the lower Clyde that have the three-way COAT/COT/CAUGHT supermerger (Mather and Speitel 1986: 116–17, 128). To the east, there are traces of [ɔ] around St Abbs' Head and in Coldstream (Mather and Speitel 1986: 143, 147). Otherwise, East Mid A and B is a fairly solid merger area. Only in some forms of Edinburgh speech, where SSE influence is strong, and in these Berwickshire dialects is there any tendency towards lowering in *north*.

In the south-west, in Galloway and Ulster, there is a trend towards lower and lower isolative forms as one moves away from the Central Belt, and, thus, a decreased likelihood of the COT/COAT merger. North Dumfries dialects have High-COT and the merger, as south Lanarkshire West Mid does. South Dumfriesshire still has the merger, but under a lowered [o̞(:)]. In the rest of Gallovidian, and in most Antrim dialects, Mid [ɔ(:)] is the rule, without merger except before /x/ and final /r/, as in Caithness. In County Down, [ɒ(:)] is the majority form except pre-rhotically, and unrounded low [ä(:) ~ ɑ̈(:)] becomes regular, not somewhat lexically conditioned as in the rest of Scots, around labials. The forms approach the usual Hiberno-English [ɑ(:)] (Wells 1982: 419) as one goes southwards. There is something of a tendency to have raising to /o/ before /g n ŋ/, and for [ɔ:] to appear as the reflex of both COT and COAT before /k x/ in Gallovidian and Ulster Scots.

Mid dialects share the transfer of *off* to CAT, and most often *dog* to CUT, whether they merge COT/COAT or not; the latter development was originally a Clydeside/Stirlingshire one, and was common around labials where *off*-Unrounding did not apply (Grant 1931: xxviii). In Southern Scots, the usual realisation is High [o(:) ~ ö(:)], with slightly lowered forms possible in the western Borders. In Southern B, this contrasts with the [ʊ(:) ~ ʊə ~ u(:)] of COAT, shading into a Cumbrian pattern (Mather and Speitel 1986: 159, 164–70). While forms this high are occasionally found in Wooler and Berwick as minority realisations, North Northumbrian tends to have [œ(:)] and Cumbrian [ɒ] (Orton and Halliday 1962). There is only a restricted *off*-Unrounding rule, extending into Northumbrian Tweeddale (Mather and Speitel 1986: 192). Teviotdale and the western borders have isolative developments in *off* (Grant 1931: xxx), and no dialects in this group have special treatment of *dog*, although *loch* may diphthongise to [ʌu], the same way as *rough* and *bought* do, in the Borders from Hawick eastwards.

11.5.6   The CAT Class: The Descendants of Older Scots /a/

The vowel in words of the CAT class is well known as having undergone a certain amount of
see-saw development between raised front and low back realisations (L. Milroy 1994: 138;
Lass 1976: 104–28), such as those brought about by processes like Insular Clockwise and
Border Scots Counter-clockwise Short Vowel Shifts. It is hard to tell a true conservative
dialect from one that has 'gotten back' to a putative Older Scots [a(:)] via other values, since
both the most peripheral dialects and the most innovative tend to have Front-CAT [a(:)] and
even Raised-CAT [æ(:)] values. If one excludes the Northern Isles, backer forms like [ɑ(:)]
(Back-CAT) or [ɒ(:)] (Rounded-CAT) are common in relic areas – but in Aberdeen and
Edinburgh as well. Extreme values like [ɛ(:)] (Mid-CAT) or [ɔˑ(:) ~ ʌˑ(:)] (Mid-Back-CAT)
exist too, but more often as conditioned developments. Merger with CAUGHT can occur
under any value but [ɛ(:)], and is more frequent the backer the CAT vowel is. Partial mergers
with BET, COT or CUT occur rarely. The usual spelling of CAT is ⟨aC⟩, as shown in *cap, tap,
happy; cat, rat, batter; back, rack, blacker; batch, match, Thatcher; cab, tab, rabbit; mad, sad,
laddie; bag, rag, Maggie; badge, cadge, badger; staff, draft, crafty; bath, path,*[21] *Kathy; class,
mast, mask, asp, lassie, bastard; ach, Bach; ham, palm,*[22] *hammer; can, grant, demand, dance,
branch, dandy, fancy; bang, long, banger, banker; Al, shall, Allan; star, hard, harp, hark, tart,
arrow, narrow; ma, pa, spa.*[23]

Most words in this class have SSE /a/ and RP /æ/, and belong to Wells's TRAP set (1982:
129–30), but Wells's (1982: 132–6, 142–4, 157–9) BATH, most of PALM and, because of
rhoticity, START sets, all with RP /ɑ:/, also belong here. All of these sets have forms equal to
CAT in low-status SSE, though the high-status varieties have a back vowel where RP has one,
separate from the [a(:)] or [æ(:)] used in other cases of CAT.

Special developments of CAT words tend to be full of exceptions: as in England, there are
lengthening processes applying at various times. Some words with older /ar/, such as *airt,
bairn, arm* (and often *part*), lengthened so early that the words are better considered to be
normal MATE words (Grant 1931: xxi). Others resisted lengthening at this stage, but
participated in some varieties in a pre-sonorant lengthening-and-backing process later on
entitled *hand*-Darkening, here especially common before /r rC l/ and /nd/ (not usually
simple /n/, although /nt/ may be affected); this happened after CAUGHT had become
monophthongised to /ɑ:/ but before any raising took place, so that this set (*hand: band,
hand, land, sand, Andrew; pal; car, bar, dark, tar, waur*) is transferred to that class.[24] In still other
words, /ar/ was raised to /ɛr/ in some varieties as part of a general tendency of raising before
alveolars (Lass 1976: 176–84), intersecting with original BET items in complicated, dialect-
specific ways (*start: start, arse, card, scarf, starve, farm, charge*). They may come out with the
typical reflexes of either class, or of MATE. A following /ŋ/, as in *long* words (*long, song, strong,
wrong, thrang; tang, gang, Lang*) may retract the CAT realisation or raise it, depending on whether
the assimilation is to the backness or height of the following velar, while a preceding /w/, as in
the WANT subclass (*want, wash, watch, quart, quarry, quarrel*), may do the same.

Common words with restressable weak forms like *have* or *what* may develop highly
idiosyncratically, and are best treated under other classes than this one.

11.5.6.1   CAT in Insular Scots

The CAT:CAUGHT contrast is usually solid in Insular Scots. If there is no A1 vowel, the
reason is not that CAUGHT = CAT, but that CAUGHT = COT (and mostly, COAT), as in south

Shetland and on Fair Isle. CAT tends to have Front [a(:)] realisations (often a little raised or centralised, possibly as far as [æ̈(:)]) in both subdialects before voiceless sounds, and even higher Raised allophones like [æ(:)] before many voiced obstruents. This vowel, like other Older Scots low and low-mid nuclei, is affected by the Insular Scots Clockwise Vowel Shift, whereby the low front vowels raise normally, pulling the CAT and maybe the CAUGHT vowel forwards, and then the merged COT/COAT vowel down to the low back position, where CAT and CAUGHT were. The process was favoured in voiced contexts, allowing for further developments in the same direction.

CAT lengthens before /p k/ in Fair Isle and the far north and south of Orkney; the change may have formerly been more widespread. Although CAT merges with CAUGHT in this position, very front reflexes of CAT such as [æ: ~ ɛ:] are a possibility here.

The environment before voiced stops may favour raising of CAT, which takes [æ(:)] allophones, especially before /b d/, though there are regional differences. Higher reflexes than this ([ɛ:]) are routinely found in outlying dialects such as Fair Isle, and may occur elsewhere, leading to some phonemic overlap with BET allophones. The raising is extended to *bag* items in western Shetlandic, Fair Isle speech and central and south Orcadian. North Ronaldsay is rather unusual in that CAT is backed before /b d/ to [ɒ], leading to overlap with COT/COAT, but raises normally in *bag* words to [ɛ:] in a pattern reminiscent of some forms of Belfast vernacular (L. Milroy 1994: 138).

Before /nd/ and /l r/, *hand*-Darkening takes place, so that CAT and CAUGHT usually merge. Reflexes centre around [ɑ:], though more centralised forms do exist. Since the /d/ in /-nd/ is often lost, the distinction between *ban* and *band* is transferred to the vowel. The sharing of *hand*-Darkening with the source dialects testifies to its antiquity, which must date to a time after the top half of the Great Vowel Shift had been completed, but before Aitken's Law took effect. The usual transfers before /r/ are found: *bairn* goes with MATE and *start* with BET. Forms with [æ:r], which are present in all Insular dialects, must be taken as variants of /ɛr/. Words like *far*, *warn*, *war*, which tend to have this vowel, therefore develop from Older Scots *fer*, *wern*, *werre* rather than /ar/ variants.

11.5.6.2   CAT in Northern Scots

Although isolative CAT reflexes vary considerably over the Northern Scots region, the merger situation with CAUGHT is not unlike that of COT/COAT. Before sonorants, and often before voiceless fricatives, the two vowels are generally merged due to transfer of the originally monomoric to the bimoric class via *hand*-Darkening and similar retraction and lengthening processes, but they tend to be separate, distinguished by length alone in some areas, and by length and quantity in others before stops, especially voiceless ones. The separation appears in more environments the further away one goes from Aberdeen and the Mid-Northern A area, where the distinction is only solid before /t/ and possibly /k/ (Dieth 1932: 29–34). Urban dialects tend to have the two classes separate in fewer environments than rural ones, even within the same division of Northern Scots.

Most areas outside of north Caithness show merger by equalisation of length before voiceless fricatives, with a phonetically long result in the majority of cases; lengthening is also quite common before velars of any kind, although there may still be a CAT:CAUGHT distinction shown by quantity here. There is at best variable merger before any sort of stop outside of Aberdeen.

In Caithness, CAT is most often a Front-to-Central [ä(:) ~ ɐ(:)], much fronter than in

Mid-Northern dialects, except after labials, and before /l n r/, where it is back [ɑ(:)]. Black Isle dialects shade into Mid-Northern by having Back reflexes. Any tendency towards merger with CAUGHT appears to be a fairly recent innovation within North Northern, strongest in market towns like Thurso and Wick, especially in fisher varieties, and in the Black Isle. Lengthening generally does not necessarily imply retraction, but [aː] is usual before /l r x nd/ outside of the north coast, as well as after labials around the Black Isle and Nairn. *Long* has COT reflexes near the Highland Line, probably due to SSE influence. As usual in North Northern, *bairn* and *start* are both transferred to MATE, if they do not take SSE /aː/ (Mather and Speitel 1986: 27–37, 46).

The whole of Mid-Northern has back realisations isolatively; any distinction from CAUGHT consists only in a length contrast. There are few special developments in either Morayshire or Aberdeen/Buchan types, but lengthening before /l n/, and sometimes before voiceless fricatives may be present, and in coastal varieties in both divisions the CAT vowel is slightly fronted around labials in a dissimilation process among older speakers. Speakers in Gardenstown and Aberdeen were found who used inner-rounded [ä˕] variants before grave sounds, much as in the Lothians and Borders (Johnston 1985b: 14, 31). *Bairn* and *start* again share MATE reflexes (Mather and Speitel 1986: 51–90).

Angus dialects distinguish CAT and CAUGHT at least before stops, most often by quantity alone as Back [ɑ(:) ~ ɒ(:) ~ ɔ(:)/ɑ: ~ ɒ: ~ ɔ:]. Only the Dundee suburbs and south-west Angus have a shaky distinction. Lengthening in high-sonority environments is possible, though more typical of the west of the area, across the North/Mid line. The Dundee suburbs up to Arbroath have a distinctive fronting to BET before /b g/, so that *bag* = *beg*. As in Mid Scots, *bair* most often gets transferred to MATE, but *start* may be transferred to BET. In some dialects, this is a moot point, as either class comes out as [ɛ:] due to Pre-Rhotic Lowering (Mather and Speitel 1986: 82, 88).

11.5.6.3   CAT in Mid- and Southern Scots

Mid-Scots varieties are split between Front-CAT varieties with isolative [a(:) ~ ä(:)], like North Mid B and C, most of West Mid and Antrim South-west Mid, and Back-CAT ones like North Mid A, East Mid, South Mid and the dialects of the Moorfoots and Dumfriesshire, which have [ɑ(:) ~ ä(:) ~ ɒ(:)] (Grant 1931: xxv–xxvi). Merger with CAUGHT is generally confined to those varieties adjoining the linguistic north or south, such as Tayside, most of the eastern and northern Borders, the Moorfoots and east Galloway. Northern-style near-mergers, with the environment before /t k/ excepted, prevail in County Down and the west coast from Wigtownshire up to around Maybole, Ayrshire (Mather and Speitel 1986: 123–7, 181–204). Elsewhere, there is usually a contrast of the type of /a ~ ɑ/ vs /ɔ/, with suspension before all labials, as well as /l n/ in Wigtownshire. There are usually at least two allophones, a somewhat centralised one that is the real isolative reflex and a Darkened one in *hand* and other words in high-sonority environments. In Central Belt vernaculars, *hand* is Darkened to merge with CAUGHT, so that *hand* rhymes with *sawn* and *pal* with *Paul*, though this is somewhat recessive in Edinburgh speech. Outside the Central Belt, where CAT and CAUGHT vowels are closer together, and sometimes even within it in East Mid, there may be instead a fully back, raised, strongly velarised or uvularised [ɑ˖:] that does not quite match CAUGHT.

The CAT vowel appears to be fronting at the moment within North Mid. The data in LSS vol. 3 report a centralised back [ä] in this class, except in north and east Fife, where [a], or perhaps long [aː], is common (Mather and Speitel 1986: 92, 98–103, 105–7). At Cupar, front [a] can be found except around labials or velars, or, often, before /t d/ (Johnston 1985b: 5), where forms agreeing with the *Survey* were found. Lss vol. 3 corroborates similar allophony in most areas of Fife, which is becoming more pronounced as [ä(ː)] becomes more common, except where *hand*-Darkening (to /ɔ∼o/) has taken place; this change applies here to positions before /l n/, but not /r/. *Bairn* belongs to MATE, while *start* usually goes in the BET class; in north and east Fife, this really may only be true of *heart*, and the rest are MATE items. Otherwise, /ar/ is front only in north Fife, east Fife, and in Stirling among the old, but is spreading to other parts of North Mid. A preceding /w/ backs the reflex, but produces no merger with CAUGHT.

West Mid has similar centralised Front or Central-CAT [ä∼ɐ] type isolatively in CAT. Among Drawling speakers, this vowel is often long in all positions (Mather and Speitel 1986: 129–34). There is considerable allophony, however. Fronter reflexes than normal, even as front as [æ], may occur before velars (Macafee 1983: 34–5), while, outside of the transition zone varieties in the south of the area, the HAND subclass is often Darkened to merge with CAUGHT, reflecting pre-Great Vowel Shift lengthening before high-sonority environments such as /nd/ or /r(C)/ to /ɔː/. There is considerable lexical conditioning of this change, however, especially in /ar/ combinations, where *dark, park* can take /ɔ/, but not *lark, wark* ('work' noun); *card* but not *hard*; *bar* (tavern) but not *bar* (law profession). *Bair* and *start* take /e/ except in Greater Glasgow, where Lowering to /ɛ/ is found, as in other /er/ combinations.

The Lothians are still a Back-CAT area, though upper working-class speakers often have front realisations. The usual form in Edinburgh is a slightly centralised [ɑ̈(ː)] isolatively, with a strongly back and somewhat raised and/or slightly rounded [ɑ̣(ː)] appearing around grave consonants or before /l n/. Eastern Border dialects have even backer values, with only the barest traces of a quantity-based CAT:CAUGHT distinction before /t d/. In most cases, the two vowel classes are merged under some sort of fully back vowel, sometimes the same one as the Edinburgh darkened one, but possibly Rounded [ɒ(ː)∼ɔ(ː)] in Tweeddale, the Lammermuirs and a good deal of Berwickshire (Wettstein 1942: 44). Extreme east Roxburghshire south of Kelso has [ɑ̣(ː)] (Mather and Speitel 1986: 153–4). Both *bairn* and *start* tend to have /er/, except in Edinburgh itself, where either /er/ or /ɛr/ may be found in the latter.

Within South Mid and the West Mid dialects transitional to it, the reflex is usually Back [ɑ(ː)] in most environments. However, before /t/ and velars, South Mid B varieties and those Kirkcudbright and Ayrshire ones adjoining them have central, raised variants like [ɐ] which may be so centralised as to be merged with CUT in a few dialects. Rounded forms, too, may occur in some Moorfoots dialects. There is backing, but no rounding or raising, in *hand* and in high-sonority positions generally. All *bairn* and *start* words take MATE reflexes except *heart*, but the realisation may be lowered slightly from /e/.

Southwest Mid varies a great deal, but generally Antrim dialects have isolative [a], and Down ones [ɑ]. There is a tendency to back and lengthen the CAT vowel before voiced sounds, nasals, /l r/ and, in Down, voiceless fricatives, rather as in some types of Belfast vernacular (L. Milroy 1994: 138). Some very front reflexes of the [æ∼ɛ] type can occur before velars, and in *bag* they are lengthened to [ɛː] in Down and south Antrim (Milroy 1994: 139). Diphthongs of the [æi∼ai] type can occur in BAG also. *Bairn* has [ɛːə], which matches MATE + /r/, while *start* varies, with the same vowel in Down, but [ɜɪ] in Antrim (Mather and Speitel 1986: 192–209).

Southern Scots varieties have fully back isolative forms – the product of the Border Scots Counter-clockwise Shift, which raises the vowel in COT and lowers that of BET and BIT (Lass 1976: 120–2; Zai 1942: 23–33). The Central Borders forms are quite similar to the adjacent eastern Borders forms, with raised, rounded realisations like [ɒ(:)] on the south side of the Tweed, and unrounded [ɑ‧(:)] or [ʌ‧(:)] further west, much like Lothian Darkened forms. Eskdale dialects within western Border Scots have [ɑ:], but Annandale reflexes are slightly centralised. Except for unrounded allophones before labials and the usual effects of Aitken's Law, there is little allophonic variation, though Front forms may be found in some younger people's speech, owing to the influence of SSE, Glaswegian or the neighbouring northern English dialects, which all have Front-to-Central CAT.

The designation of Older Scots CAT as front or back is problematic, but on balance, the dialectal evidence probably favours a front value. Insular Scots front values might be explained away as being due to the workings of vowel shifting, and the backings that develop after /w/ could support a back value (the /w/ protects /a/ from undergoing a putative fronting rule) as well as a front one (the /w/ causes backing). It is also plain that the West Mid/North Mid /a/ forms, sandwiched as they are between regions of back vowels, are innovations. But what about *hand*-Darkening? There is nothing particularly favouring a 'protection' hypothesis with this development, where reflexes are 'darker' – backer, rounder – than normal. High-sonority environments like these tend to *lengthen* vowels; /n/ has no 'back vowel' resonance, unlike /w/. But long low vowels in English (except maybe for the south-west of England; Lass 1976: 118) do tend to back in post-medieval times, and England across the border only has vowels going back to a Middle English /a/ (Lass 1976: 105–28). The same arguments from Open Syllable Lengthening developments would hold for Scots, as for English. I therefore postulate an Older Scots /a/, although I do concede that it might have backed in a wide variety of Scottish dialects early in the Modern period.

11.5.7   The CAUGHT Class: The Descendants of Older Scots /a:/ < /au/

CAUGHT, from Older Scots /au/, has a wide range of isolative realisations within Scotland, ranging from high-mid [o(:)], through low-mid [ɔ(:)] (Raised-CAUGHT), [ɑ(:)] (Low Rounded-CAUGHT) and [ɒ(:)] (Low-CAUGHT) to [a: ~ æ:] (Front-CAUGHT), depending on the workings of the bottom half of the Great Vowel Shift, which probably monophthong-ised this nucleus. Low-mid and low unrounded forms are the most common. This vowel may merge with CAT or COT (and COAT), or contrast with one of these nuclei in terms of length alone, as it does not always obey Aitken's Law.

CAUGHT words consist of items like *scaup, scalp; fault, caught; fraud, applaud; walk, talk; false; cause; Walsh; drawn, lawn, dawn, known; drawl, Paul; fall, call, ball; law, jaw, saw, Shaw, know, blow, crow, sow, row* (noun), generally with spellings like ⟨al, au, aw, ow, ol⟩. In words from Old English /ɑ:w/ like *blow, flow, know*, or /ɑ:ld/ like *old, cold, hold, fold*, SSE has the same [o(:)] vowel as COAT and LOUP, reflecting the Southumbrian /ɔ:/ or /ɔu/ reflexes which these words had in Middle English. In other items, the Standard has [ɔ(:)].

Only two subclasses need be mentioned: a small set of CAUGHT words before labials or /x/, the HALF subset (*half, calf, laugh; halve, calve; calm, balm, palm*), which may undergo unrounding to forms equalling CAT, and words containing Older Scots /auld/ (the OLD subclass: *old, cold, hold, fold, bold*), which may take LOUP reflexes, either through Hiberno-English influence, where this is the usual outcome due to the North Midland input in the formation of this colonial dialect (Gregg 1985), or as part of a diphthongisation process related to those affecting *log*, *thought* or *loch*.

11.5.7.1 CAUGHT in Insular Scots

CAUGHT varies widely in Insular Scots, and is often variable within each community. It may be Front [a:], Back [ɑ:], or an intermediate value in mainstream Insular Scots as an isolative reflex, but unusual values such as [ɛ:] (North Ronaldsay, Orkney), [æ:] (Sanday, Orkney) or [ɒ(:)] (south Shetland) are attested (Mather and Speitel 1986: 9–12, 14–15; Grant 1931: xl). In southern Shetland and on Fair Isle, CAUGHT = COT and COAT. These, and Orcadian CAUGHT forms, are generally back, except in the more northerly outlying islands, which have the extremely fronted values, due to the advanced version of the Clockwise Shift.

Before /x/, CUT/COT/COAT/CAUGHT all fall together into [ɔ(:)] ([ɒ:] on Fair Isle). *Old* words may have [ɑ:], as is often the case before /l/, or take LOUP reflexes, with *ould* forms common throughout the Isles (Grant 1931: xl). These may result from early raising of a retracted /ɑld/ to /ɔld/ in Older Scots days, or be loans from North Northern. Before voiced fricatives, CAUGHT exhibits fronted and raised allophones in most Shetlandic ([æ: ~ a:]) and on North Ronaldsay ([ɛ:]).

11.5.7.2 CAUGHT in Northern Scots

In most Northern Scots, including the Mid-Northern varieties, the CAT/CAUGHT distinction is neutralised, usually under CAUGHT, in high-sonority environments, and contrasts often by length with CAT in other environments. The most frequent form is Low [ɑ:], with little tendency to round, except in some Kincardineshire dialects (Mather and Speitel 1986: 78–9; Grant 1931: xxxii, xxxvi–xxxviii). Angus reflexes are also [ɒ:] or [ɑ· ~ ɒ:], exempt from Aitken's Law, though North Mid B /ɔ/ is creeping into west Angus and the Dundee area, and, in any case, is supported by the local variety of SSE. *Half* usually equals CAT, but there is no special development of *old*.

Most varieties of Caithnesian, in environments where it is separate from CAT, realise CAUGHT as Front-to-Central [a:] (Grant 1931: xxxviii), though, as with CAT, back [ɑ:] is frequent after labials, before /l n r/, and in final position. Black Isle has backer reflexes like [ɑ: ~ ɒ:], distinguished only by length, if at all, from CAT, as in Mid-Northern.

Old generally takes /ʌu ~ ɛy/ in all North Northern, but it is not clear what connections, if any, there are with Glaswegian, Gallovidian or Irish *ould* forms (Grant 1931: xxxviii). This may be a native change, somehow connected with the diphthongisations before voiced velars, despite the fact that /l/ is clear here, since /l/ is dark in Morayshire dialects, from which more northerly dialects originate. *Half* is transferred to CAT, due to lengthening of that class before voiceless fricatives.

11.5.7.3 CAUGHT in Mid- and Southern Scots

North Mid-Scots has quite a range of isolative CAUGHT realisations, ranging from Northern-like [ɑ:] in parts of Perthshire, to [o(:)], merging with COAT, in parts of west Fife, Clackmannanshire and Stirlingshire. A Mid [ɔ:], exempt from Aitken's Law in North Mid A and B, but obeying it in C, is the most common form, and one that is beginning to characterise the whole area, including Perthshire, among the young (Grant 1931: xxv).

There is a tendency for [ɑ(:)] to occur before labials, including *half*, in what might be considered an extended *off*-Unrounding process, and *ould* forms may occasionally occur in urban dialects. They are more frequent in North Mid C, the most urbanised division and the one closest to Glasgow, than the other two.

As in North Mid, the East Mid division shades from Mid [ɔ(:)] reflexes in West Lothian, nearest to Glasgow, through [ɒ(:)] in Midlothian and parts of Berwickshire, to [ɑ:] in most of the rest of the East Mid area. In the south of the area, near Tweeddale and in south-west Berwickshire, Rounded and Mid reflexes occur again, as they do for CAT. In the whole area, [ɔ(:)] is increasing in frequency under a combination of influence from the west and from SSE, and it seems only a matter of time before it becomes the usual East Mid form. All reflexes obey Aitken's Law. *Half* usually takes regular CAUGHT forms, which equal those in CAT only if there is an isolative merger. *Old* generally undergoes the regular development, though forms with [əʉ] are not unknown in Edinburgh or West Lothian, and even sometimes in the eastern Borders.

CAUGHT realisations vary considerably across the West Mid area, though Glaswegian tends to have a slightly raised low-mid [ɔ(:)], obeying Aitken's Law normally. However, Mather and Speitel (1986: 116) found /o/-forms, equalling COT/COAT, in Bute, and the West/ South Mid transition dialects have /ɑ~ɒ/, which merges with CAT, especially in south Lanarkshire and north Dumfriesshire. The HALF subclass develops normally, although forms with /a/ are normal in *calm*, *palm*, but the OLD subclass, particularly *old* itself, may take LOUP reflexes and come out as [əʉl]. Such forms may be found over the whole West Mid region, but are especially common where the connections with Ireland are close – in Glasgow and the vicinity, along the Clyde coast, near Wigtownshire and in Argyll (Grant 1931: xxviii). There can be no doubt that in this area, these forms are an importation from Hiberno-English, in contrast to the Northern forms. West Mid probably serves as the conduit of such forms to the rest of the Central Belt.

In South Mid A, CAUGHT merges with CAT, and the [ɑ(:) ~ ä(:)] reflexes have already been described. The same sound serves as the isolative realisation in Wigtownshire, where the two classes are separate before non-labial voiceless sounds. The realisation [ɒ(:)], mentioned as the usual vowel in Grant (1931: xxviii), occurs also, but only as a minor variant, while [ɔ(:)] is increasing in frequency. *Ould* forms are quite common in Wigtownshire (much less so in Kirkcudbrightshire, and *half* is transferred to CAT. Roughly the same forms are extant in Ulster Scots, with the most common forms being Down [ɒ(:)] and Antrim [ɑ:]; there is a tendency for [ɔ:] to occur as a conditioned development before /d l/, and perhaps other voiced sounds, while, according to Mather and Speitel (1986: 192, 194–8, 200–3), final CAUGHT comes out as a diphthongal [ɒɔ ~ äɔ]. This could represent the last traces of a final /au/, presumably the value of the nucleus that was present before the Great Vowel Shift, but is more likely to represent a secondary diphthongisation, similar to the one that happens in some Upper and Lower Southern American English in words of the same class (Wells 1982: 540). Transfer to LOUP is regular in words of the OLD subclass, as in all of Ireland; this form may go back to North Midland forms with historical /ɔuld/, as part of the Hibernian settlement from England came from areas with this reflex (Gregg 1985). In Southern dialects, CAUGHT = CAT = [ɑ(:)] for the most part. Where the two reflexes are distinct, they are only differentiated by length before /t/ or /d/, and *old* and *half* develop regularly.

The vowel which Aitken (1977b) suggests for CAUGHT is a rounded but low [ɒ:]; while this might possibly have arisen in places where the present reflex is rounded, it seems evident that roundness is an innovation, as it is confined to the Central Belt, between areas with [ɑ(ː) ~ ɒː] on both sides. Therefore, the Older Scots form is likely to have been low and *un*rounded. Backness is suggested by the merger of *two* and, in many places, *hand* into this class; the first involves a vowel in an environment likely to cause backness, the second suggests a backer allophone than the isolative front reflex of CAT. If the monophthongisations of BAIT and CAUGHT are related, as may well be the case in North British dialects as a whole (Johnston forthcoming), a change /ai au/ > /aː ɑː/ would be symmetrical. While allowing that fronter or rounded reflexes might have resulted in certain areas, the Older Scots reflex of CAUGHT after 1400 or so was probably near or at [ɑː].

11.6   THE DIALECTOLOGY OF SCOTS DIPHTHONG SYSTEMS

11.6.1   Introduction and Inventorial Shape

Since Early Scots /ai au/ (the BAIT and CAUGHT classes, treated above) were monophthongised in most or all positions throughout Scots as part of the Great Vowel Shift, and, conversely, the descendants of Early Scots /iː/ (the BITE and TRY classes, in Aitken's short and long environments respectively) became diphthongal at the same time or slightly before, the nuclei treated as diphthongal here consist of BITE and TRY (sixteenth-century /ëi/), and the descendants of Older Scots /iu ɛu ɔu ɔi ʊi ~ oi/ (respectively, the DEW, NEW, LOUP, VOICE and LOIN classes). Owing to mergers, no living Scots dialect retains all these as separate. DEW either falls together with NEW or breaks to /jʌu/, with the nucleus the same as the LOUP class, while LOIN may merge with either BITE or VOICE. This leaves a maximum of five diphthongal phonemes, though most Scots dialects only have four, with one or two being of restricted environmental distribution.

Although Catford (1957b) did not treat diphthongs before /t/ as part of his schema, and at least TRY never occurs in this environmental frame anyway, one can easily extend his analysis to this sort of nucleus. All Scots systems include (1) a diphthong conventionally represented as /ʌi/ (Abercrombie 1979: 72; though, in most varieties, calling it /ɛi/ or /əi/ would make more sense phonetically[25]), occurring in short environments and word-finally; (2) an /ʌu/ of nearly unrestricted distribution; (3) an /oe/, in some varieties unrestricted in distribution, in others restricted to long environments or to final position; and (4) an /ae/, found at least word-finally, and most often appearing in other long environments. The only modification to this is that in some (usually eastern) Orcadian, in western Border Scots, and sporadically among older speakers in central Border varieties, an extra /iu/ (perhaps better represented as /ʏu/ in some regions) may occur syllable-finally in words of the NEW or DEW classes. This extra diphthongal phoneme is highly recessive, but it survives better in western Border speech than elsewhere. It is also recessive in northern England (Johnston 1980: 278). Except for this /iu/, all Scots shares the same diphthongal inventory.

11.6.2   The NEW Class: The Descendants of Older Scots /iu/

Except in the areas where true diphthongs of the [ɪu ~ ʏu ~ øu] (Diphthongal-NEW) type can be encountered, the first element of Older Scots /iu/ was desyllabicised to a /j/ followed by /u/, as happens in many English dialects; if there is an alveolar before it, the /j/ combines with it to form a palato-alveolar (Wells 1982; but see Johnston 1979: 311), and /hj/ may go to [ç] or [ʃ]. The mnemonics Front-, Central- or Back-NEW therefore refer to the frontness of the syllabic nuclei, which front parallel to OUT values, with possible slight extra fronting due to the influence of the preceding palatal. NEW now includes many words which had medial /iu/, recent loans from SSE; originally, these words would have belonged to the BOOT class. There are no subclasses, and the spelling may be ⟨ew⟩, ⟨uCe⟩ or, more rarely, ⟨ue⟩ and ⟨ui⟩. The class comprises items such as *new, pew, imbue, flue, blue, brew, spew, stew, skew, pursue, sue; dupe, mute, duke, cube, rude, fugue, huge, plume, tune, mule, duty, pupil, student, feud, human*. SSE has similar reflexes to Scots, namely /(j)u:/, with a tendency for the amount of fronting to be less the further up the social scale one goes (Johnston 1983a: 135). Older speakers also have backer values in most localities where variation exists.

Except for the eastern and south-eastern Orcadian dialects with final [ʏu ∼ əu ∼ ɿu] in NEW, Insular Scots varieties have Back [ju(:)], possibly slightly lowered or centralised, but otherwise with the nucleus not appreciably fronted beyond [ü]. Generally, words like *tune, use, fruit* and so on take regular BOOT reflexes, and have not been added to this class (Grant 1931: xx).

Northern Scots shows the same three-way geographical split in NEW that holds for OUT. Caithnesian has very Front [jy(:) ∼ jÿ(:)] reflexes if /j/ precedes; Angus dialects also have Fronted forms, though here Central-NEW with plain-to-over-rounded [jʉ(:)] predominates, with traces of this development as far north as Aberdeen, where younger speakers are beginning to adopt it. Between these two Fronting areas, from southern Caithness to north Kincardineshire, NEW is generally Back /ju/ with only traces of Fronting possible (Mather and Speitel 1986: 37–74, 76–8).

Tune, and *use* (noun) take BOOT forms in south Northern and Mid-Northern A, with *use* = /i/ in Caithnesian and Morayshire also. The realisation /e/ in *fruit* is now restricted to Angus within the north. Otherwise, this word is usually realised as /u/, evidently a recent loan from SSE, replacing /i ∼ e/ (Mather and Speitel 1986: 27–33, 34–78; Dieth 1932: 8; Mutschmann 1908: 52).

Most Mid-Scots varieties have Front- or Central-NEW reflexes, centring around [jʉ(:) ∼ jʉ(:)]. Just as with OUT, under-rounding is prevalent in West Mid and South-west Mid, and over-rounding in North and East Mid varieties. The frontest reflexes are found (1) in Ulster and Wigtown; (2) near Glasgow, Edinburgh and Dundee; and (3) in the Glasgow–Perth and Glasgow–Dundee corridors within the North Mid area, all areas where OUT is quite front also. The backest forms are found in the eastern Borders, where older speakers still have [ju(:)] (Johnston 1980: 267–75; Wettstein 1942: 44; Zai 1942: 112–14). Even here, Central-NEW forms are used by the young. South Mid A, the Midlothian Borders, Tweeddale and parts of Fife also have Central forms. *Tune, use* and the like tend traditionally to have BOOT developments, except in Ulster, but SSE loans are increasingly common; the regular developments in *fruit* south of the Forth/Clyde line are slowly receding (Mather and Speitel 1986: 117, 121–2, 126, 131, 135, 140, 144, 146, 160–2, 170–1, 175, 178–9, 181–3, 186–7).

Southern dialects retain more preconsonantal realisations identical to BOOT than most varieties, traditionally; this is true not only of *tune, use* and *fruit*, but also regularly in NEW preceding a /k/, as in *duke* or *duck* (Mather and Speitel 1986: 153–60, 167–8; Zai 1942: 115). These are all in the process of being transferred together to the OUT class. In other positions, the usual realisation was once [iu ∼ iʉ ∼ ijʉ], which still can be found sporadically from older speakers (Johnston 1980: 278). Younger speakers have adopted Back or Central-NEW, a loan from Mid-Scots. It seems only a matter of time before the traditional diphthongs disappear, and since similar developments are going on in northern England, if at a slower pace (Johnston 1980: 267), there is no geographical support for them in any neighbouring dialect either.

11.6.3 The DEW Class: The Descendants of Older Scots /ɛu/

This tiny class, which has *newt, lewd, beauty, dew* and *few* among its members, was merged with NEW almost everywhere in Scotland (and in England outside Lancashire and the south-west; Orton et al. 1978: 178–9), since the first element raised as part of the Great Vowel Shift parallel to /ɛ:/ (Dobson 1957: 798–9). In regions where it does not undergo this merger, the first element dissimilated ('broke') into a non-syllabic /j/ and a backer new first element /ʌ/ = /j/ + the LOUP nucleus. It thus never constitutes an independent vowel class in Scotland, and there are no subclasses. Standard varieties all merge DEW and NEW. DEW can be taken to be equal to NEW except in the Northern Scots area, where DEW-Breaking, as described above, took place; even here, Caithnesian generally lacks it, although this may be due to SSE influence through Highland English, as Mather and Speitel (1986: 33) collected an unbroken but separate [ɛy] (=LOUP) in Keiss. DEW-Breaking is solid in the north-east and on the Black Isle (Grant 1931: xxxiv), but variable in Nairn, Moray and Angus, dropping off in incidence as the Mid/Northern and Highland English lines are approached. There were once traces of DEW-Breaking in Berwickshire (Robinson 1985: 144).

11.6.4 The BITE Class: The Descendants of Older Scots /ëi/ in Short Environments

Early during the top half of the Great Vowel Shift, the diphthongal descendant of Early Scots /i:/, [ëi], underwent a split distributed along Aitken's Law environments in the Berenician area (Orton et al. 1978: 103–11). The main effect seems to have been that the first element was lengthened, as other vowels were; however, a lengthened non-peripheral vowel tends to sink in height (Labov 1994: 116), so that the 'long' diphthong soon developed a lower but, eventually, probably more peripheral V1 than the 'short' one did. When the PAY subclass of BAIT fell in with the short diphthong, the split between BITE and TRY became phonemic.

In Scots, forms with low V1s (Low-BITE) are rare, and usually due only to conditioned developments. Most dialects have either [ɛi ~ ëi] (Front-BITE) or [əi] (Mid-BITE), usually distinct from all other diphthongs, but, in some Caithnesian, merging in some environments with /ɛi/ = E1 (from BEAT or MATE). Forms with back V1s, such as [ʌi] or even [ɔi] (Back-BITE), are not unknown in Scotland, but are most often found in specific environments favourable to backing, such as post-labially (the WIDE subclass: *wide, white, mice, pipe, imbibe, bide, wife, bike, while, wine*) or after /r/ (the RIDE subclass: *write, ride, rice, ripe, bribe, Rhine, rifle, pricing*). Other members include *type, hype, viper; kite, site, inviting; tyke, hike, liking; hide, tide, tidy; tiger; life, knife; Smythe* (if it ends with [θ]); *dice, lice, slicing; time, lime, chiming*. The usual spellings include ⟨i(Ce), y(Ce), ie⟩. Merger with *pay* is inevitable, and with LOIN is very common indeed.

All except the most high-status SSE varieties have diphthongs similar to the local Scots form or slightly backer, with [əi] forms the most common. Old-fashioned high-status varieties heavily influenced by RP have forms of the TRY class in BITE, usually [ae], though occasionally forms with [æ] as a V1 occur, and are stereotypical in elocuted or 'Hyper' varieties, such as Morningside/Kelvinside (Johnston 1985a: 41).

Besides *wide* and *ride*, two environments may show special developments. Before sonorants and possibly all voiced sounds (the LINE subclass: *mile, tile, mild, wilder; fine, kine, kind, line, lining*), dialects with Mid-BITE may take Front-BITE realisations. Before /k/, the DIKE subclass (*like, dike*) may lose the second element and shorten the first to a vowel like [e ~ ë], which may be separate from BIT. It is the usual source of E2 phonemicisation, as minimal pairs of the *dike:Dick* type may result, and there is usually some interplay with Split-BIT developments.

11.6.4.1   BITE in Insular Scots

In Insular Scots, the /əi ae/ distinction is 'softer' and more variable than in most other dialects. Shetlandic at least has something of a clear distinction between the usual isolative BITE reflex [ɜi] and TRY, which tends towards [ai], with a low, front V1, distributed by Aitken's Law environment, like elsewhere in Scots (Mather and Speitel 1986: 1–12). However, the 'long' vowel may occur variably in short environments also, even if the *pay: pie* distinction is often secure.

Orcadian goes further. In this variety, while BITE usually takes Front forms like [ɛi], the 'long' form [æi] occurs regularly before /d l n/, and the 'short' form is usual before /r/. A possible variant of final TRY is [ə·e], closer to the usual form of BITE than what LSS vol. 3 shows (Johnston 1985b: 43). There is only the slightest tendency to front /əi/ to [ɛi] in *mile*. *Dike* in Shetlandic usually has [ë], going in with either /ɪ/ or /e/ as in South Northern (but usually not an E2), while Orcadian develops *dike* normally.

11.6.4.1   BITE in Northern Scots

Northern Scots shows a patchwork of reflexes. In Caithnesian, the most common reflex is generally a very distinctive [ʌi], with a back first element. In the WIDE subclass, this becomes [ɔi], which is spreading to all positions (Mather and Speitel 1986: 27, 30–3, 35, 39; Johnston 1985b: 40; *pace* Grant 1931: xxxiv, who saw it as used by 'old people'). LSS vol. 3, however, shows Front forms merged with the usual vowel of BEAT and MATE as common before /t/ and voiceless fricatives (Mather and Speitel 1986: 27–8, 32). *Dyke* quite commonly has [ɛː], merging with BET.

The Black Isle has [ɛɪ] isolatively, with low-BITE [aɪ ~ æɪ] before voiced sounds, while [əi] predominates in rural mid-Northern A and [ɛ̈i] in Morayshire, Angus and Aberdeen city itself. In the WIDE subclass, there is generally backing of the V1 one degree to [əi], and, where the first element is already central, to [ʌi ~ ɔi], especially in coastal varieties (Grant 1931: xxxiv). *Mile* may be fronter than usual, especially around Aberdeen, while *dike* may be realised as /e/ in the northern Mearns and in Kincardineshire, and is frequently an E2, not really merged with any other class. If it does go into a vowel class, it merges with BEAT (Mather and Speitel 1986: 43–87).

11.6.4.3   BITE in Mid- and Southern Scots

Mid-Scots realisations centre around [ë̃i], which is the usual isolative reflex in Fife, Perthshire, the Stirling area, Edinburgh and much of the eastern Borders and south Kirkcudbrightshire. While LSS vol. 3 shows the Glasgow and West Mid reflex as [əi] (Mather and Speitel 1986: 116–36), I hear no difference between this area and the others, except a slight drawl on both elements in the Glasgow Drawl area (but see Macaulay 1991: 41). An uncentralised [ɛi] is common in parts of Fife, Wigtownshire, Ulster and the

Tweeddale area as an isolative form, and occurs over a very wide extent, including the whole Central Belt, in *mile*, *line* and *ride*. There may be backing to [ʌi] in *wide* as well as before labials in parts of North and East Mid (Mather and Speitel 1986: 100–4). Reflexes very close to the postulated Older Scots form, [ëi], exist in parts of Galloway, in the Moorfoots and the western Borders (Mather and Speitel 1986: 159, 163, 167–9, 171–4, 179).

Dike usually develops normally, but south Argyll, and more rarely Gallovidian, is reputed to have /e/ = MATE/BAIT (Grant 1931: xxviii). Southern A generally shares East Mid forms of BITE, but Liddesdale and western Borders speech may have uncentralised [ɛi] or [ei]; the first occurs variably in Teviotdale, and is the usual Border Northumbrian and Cumbrian reflex.

11.6.5   The LOIN Class: The Descendants of Older Scots /oi ~ ui/

This small lexical set, usually from French or Dutch sources, comprises items like *coin, join, loin*; *oil, boil, spoil, toil*; *anoint*; *poison*; *hoist, joist*, and is spelled ⟨oi⟩. There is no way to tell this class apart from VOICE by spelling, since ⟨oi, oy⟩ has been the representation of both since Norman times. It merges with either the BITE class under [ɛi ~ ɛ̈ɩ ~ əɩ ~ ʌ̈ɩ] or the VOICE class as [ɔɩ ~ oɩ ~ oˑe]. In SSE, /ui/ has been levelled with VOICE under /ɔɩ, although merger under BITE was common in the seventeenth and eighteenth centuries in the English model for SSE (Dobson 1957: 823–6).

There are no subclasses, although certain members undergo lexically specific transfers; *poison*, for instance, may be a CUT (in East, South or South-west Mid, and Southern Scots), BOOT (in North Mid), TRY (around Aberdeen) or OUT word (in Insular Scots, the far north and parts of Angus and Perthshire). Since the LOIN class is so small, it is hard to establish exactly what the isolative developments are, and what is due to lexical conditioning. LOIN merges into the VOICE class in both extremes of the country: in Insular Scots varieties on the one hand, and Southern, Gallovidian, Ulster Scots and East Mid B varieties as far up as southern Midlothian and East Lothian on the other. The merger is also attested in Angus. The southern developments agree with the usual English outcome, carrying the merger into Scotland. In other areas, LOIN generally merges with BITE, though in Mid-Northern Scots in short environments there is a three-way BITE/LOIN/VOICE merger (Mather and Speitel 1986: 52–64, 67–9, 73–4, 76–8; Mutschmann 1908: 32).

11.6.6   The VOICE Class: The Descendants of Older Scots /ɔi/

This class, continuing Older Scots /ɔi/ in words spelled with ⟨oi, oy⟩, like *boy, toy, joy, annoy*; *noise, voice, choice, Joyce, void, Boyd, moist*, consists of the COT vowel + [ɩ ~ e], and one usually finds Low-, Mid- and High-VOICE areas in the same places where equivalent values appear for isolative COT. Occasionally, however, VOICE merges in partially or totally with BITE (or, more likely historically, LOIN) or TRY (Mather and Speitel 1986: 30, 36, 46–7, 51–64, 67–9, 73–4, 76–8). SSE has /ɔɩ/ in this class most often, though [oˑe] is quite common in low-status SSE, if this is the local Scots reflex.

VOICE has the COT vowel + /i/ in Insular Scots, so the most common reflex is [ɒi] in both island groups, with the slightly more raised Mid-VOICE [ɔ̈i] in central and south Shetland in all positions. Most Orcadian has a second High allophone, [oi], appearing at the end of words and before /l n/ and possibly /d/, in parallel to the allophony that COT/COAT has. The V1 may be fronted also.

In Northern Scots, VOICE usually merges into BITE and LOIN in short environments, but has /oe/ types in long ones (Mather and Speitel 1986: 51–78). The centre for the three-way merger is probably Aberdeen, as it is solid in that area. It is only variable in Caithnesian, and lacking in Angus and the Mearns, where 'long' /oe/ reflexes are extended into 'short' position, continuing the usual Mid-Scots separation of VOICE and LOIN. Phonetic forms of /oe/ generally match up with COT nicely. Low-VOICE [ɒi] characterises most Caithnesian and areas near the Highland Line. Mid-VOICE [ɔi ~ ɔe] types are found in eastern Moray, south Banffshire, Aberdeenshire, the Mearns and Angus, while the Moray Firth coast from Cromarty to Gardenstown has [oe].

In Mid-Scots, VOICE is generally separate from BITE, except for some coastal Fife speech and some types of Glasgow speech (Mather and Speitel 1986: 105–6, 108). The most common reflex is High-VOICE [oe ~ öe], matching the usual COT reflex in quality, but opener diphthongs than this are quite common in Fife, Stirling and the Lothians, and are usual in Wigtownshire. Low-VOICE is confined to Ulster, where it is quite common (Mather and Speitel 1986: 192–204).

Southern dialects have [oe ~ oi], with the latter characteristic of the western Borders (Mather and Speitel 1986: 164–9), though I have interviewed speakers who have short [ɔi]/ long [ö·e] at Hawick (Johnston 1980: 292). High-VOICE realisations extend into England at Berwick, and sporadically around Glendale in Northern Northumberland, but otherwise Northumbrian has [œɪ], and Cumbrian [ɒɪ] (Johnston 1980: 293–5; Orton and Halliday 1962: V.2.13; Orton 1933: 90).

11.6.7   The TRY Class: Reflexes of Classic Older Scots /ëi/ in Long Environments

TRY words comprise descendants of Older Scots /ii/ in long environments like *try, pie, sly, fry, kye, tied, shied; fire, tyre, mire, dire, Biro, tiring, prior; drive, five, hive, alive, ivy; Blyth, lithe, writhing; rise, size, analyse*, and are nearly always realised as a diphthong of the CAT vowel + /e/. TRY has Raised-, Front-, Back- and Rounded- types as CAT does, although there are a few dialects with monophthongal forms like [ɑ:] or [ɛ:] (Mather and Speitel 1986: 114). Since Back-CAT dialects predominate in Scotland, Back-TRY forms do also. Spellings and RP forms are the same as for BITE, while SSE often has [a·e].

In some peripheral areas, one may find BITE reflexes on either side of /r/, because the lowering that followed Aitken's Law was restrained by the centralising effect of the /r/. One can therefore delineate FIRE and DRIVE subclasses, with following and preceding /r/ respectively. *Wire* is transferred to the BEAT class in Northern and Insular Scots. Here, the first element of Older Scots [əɪ ~ ëɪ] was 'swallowed up' by the preceding /w/, leaving the original second element intact.

As stated under BITE, Insular Scots comes closer to merging BITE and TRY (or not having a split here) than any other variety.[26] Shetlandic uses ordinary Front [ai] in long environments, though it may also occur before /d l n/ and voiceless fricatives, and in-between [æi] is not unknown in a number of environments. Orcadian has varied realisations from [ɛi] through [æi ~ ai] to a very distinctive Raised [ə·e], and there is much variability especially before voiced consonants (Mather and Speitel 1986: 12–27).

In Northern Scots, Back-TRY realisations of the [ɑ·e] type predominate, although this is not so true of North Northern, where Front-to-Central [ä·e ~ ɐ·e] forms are the traditional reflexes and backer forms are recent innovations. Such forms can be occasionally encountered, too, in Arbroath and along the Angus coast, continuing the patterns of

Fife dialects. North Northern also differs from the rest of the group in that TRY has its 'classic' distribution found in SSE, while other varieties of Northern Scots have BITE forms in *fire* and *drive*.

Mid-Scots varieties show a tight parallelism between CAT and TRY. As a rule, front-CAT dialects like Fife, Stirling, Glasgow, Ayrshire and Ulster Scots have [aˑe~äˑe], and, with the support of both Glaswegian and SSE, these forms are spreading to other areas, such as the Lothians. Ulster Scots may even have fronter forms such as [æˑe]. But Perthshire, the Lothians and eastern Borders, and Galloway more often have [ɑˑe] or [ɐˑe], with the backest reflexes in the southernmost and northernmost of these dialects. *Drive* often takes BITE realisations, with regular TRY forms for this subclass restricted to the urban Central Belt and eastern Galloway, but BITE forms for *fire* are restricted to the most peripheral areas within Mid-Scots, namely the eastern Borders and Perthshire, where the dialects continue Southern and South Northern patterns respectively.

Monophthongs for TRY are found in a few North Mid A and C localities, mostly in south-west Fife or Clackmannanshire, but [ɛ:] in *pie* and so on is a stereotype of urban Dundonian. Southern Scots often shows very Back reflexes of TRY, just as for CAT, with typical forms like [ɑˑe~ɒˑe]. Tweeddale dialects have rounded and raised this nucleus further to [ɔˑe], while the Hawick area has a very distinctive [ʌˑe] (Johnston 1980: 184). Traditionally, both *fire* and *drive* took BITE reflexes, and this was still elicited in my Hawick (and Yetholm) material (Johnston 1980: 184), just as in northern English dialects (though TRY = [aˑe~aɪ] there). However, the regular TRY reflexes are becoming more common in these subclasses throughout the border area.

11.6.8 The LOUP Class: The Descendants of Older Scots /ɔu/

Older Scots /ɔu/ was one of the few bimoric nuclei not to undergo the Great Vowel Shift in northern English and Scots dialects, and the LOUP class contains items like *coup, loup; golf, howff, dowf; colt, nowt; gold; loose; lowse, dowse; through;*[27] *roll, toll, poll; four,*[28] *glour, stour; grow, glow, hoe, knowe*. Until recently, at least, in the most peripheral dialects, the reflex present has still been that of COT + /u/, resulting in [ɔu~ɒu] (Rounded-LOUP). Over most of Scotland, however, the V1 was first centralised and then unrounded, with forms of the type of [ʌu] being the most common (Back-LOUP), with the intermediate [ɜu] found occasionally. Areas with OUT-Fronting also front this nucleus to [əʉ] (Central-LOUP) and even to [ɛ̈ʏ] (Front-LOUP).

Most words in this class existing in Standard dialects, such as *row* (a boat), *grow, glow, roll, gold, colt*, have the same [o(:)~ou~əu] as COAT words (reflecting Southumbrian Mid-Vowel Monophthongisation), and can only be spotted by the spelling, which usually contains ⟨ol, ow, ough⟩. However, forms that are of Scots origin, which sometimes appear in place-names such as *Coupland, Carrickknowe, Silverknowes*, are usually given the pronunciation of OUT in SSE, and following SSE norms, in other varieties also.

A few items, such as *loose*, belong to other vowel classes in SSE. Subsets of LOUP with following grave consonants, either labials (the ROUP subclass: *loup, coup, roup, golf*) or velars (the HOWK subclass: *folk, yolk, bowk*), might wind up with reflexes equalling COT, COAT or, in the first case, OUT as well in Scots; it is not known whether developments to /o/ followed an /ɔu/ > [ou] > [o(:)] (V1-Raising-first) or an /ɔu/ > [ɔ:] > [o:] (Monophthongisation-first) pathway, or results from a shortening process that is the back-series equivalent of what happens to *dike*.

11.6.8.1 LOUP in Insular Scots

The Insular Scots isolative realisation of LOUP is usually the CUT vowel + /u/, as in the rest of Scots. However, since the CUT vowel is often rounded, Rounded-LOUP forms predominate, ranging from [ɔu] to [ɒu]. The V1 has been fronted in outlying dialects in both archipelagoes, so that South Ronaldsay and North Ronaldsay, at the opposite ends of Orkney, roughly agree in having [au~ɑu], while Fair Isle has [æu]. Unrounded V1s are commoner in Orcadian than Shetlandic. *Howk* takes COT reflexes everywhere, but *roup* varies. The realisation /u/ = OUT is the most common form in Shetland (probably reflecting raising of the V1 before the /u/-like labial, then monophthongisation), and /ɒ~o/ = COT in Orkney, reflecting monophthongisation alone, in a pattern very similar to dialects like Ulster Scots, at the completely opposite end of this linguistic region (Mather and Speitel 1986: 13–17, 19–23, 26).

11.6.8.2 LOUP in Northern Scots

Northern Scots LOUP reflexes vary in backness according to whether (1) OUT-Fronting and (2) CUT-Centralisation are in evidence or not. In Caithness, where the Fronting process is pervasive, LOUP tends to have a very front [ɛʏ], with [əʉ] about the backest variant present (Mather and Speitel 1986: 27–36). In the Black Isle, where CUT is often central, [əu] forms are common. Much backer realisations, sometimes with rounded V1s, like [ɔu~ʌu~ɒu] are the rule from Nairn to north Angus, and even further south than that among older speakers. As Central Belt-style OUT-Fronting becomes usual in Angus, so does [əʉ], which is also prevalent among young Aberdonians. *Roup* and *howk* develop regularly for the most part, although *bowk* may be [b(j)ɔk~b(j)ok] and *yolk* is usually transferred to COT or COAT.

11.6.8.3 LOUP in Mid-Scots

Traditionally, all Mid-Scots except Ulster and Wigtownshire Scots and perhaps West Mid (where there was early Fronting) had a fully back [ʌu] LOUP realisation (Zai 1942: 110–11; Grant 1931: xxiv). While this still survives among older speakers in the eastern Borders, and has only recently disappeared around Crail and Pittenweem in Fife, Central-LOUP [əʉ] is now the most typical form all over the Mid-Scots region. The fronting of LOUP is continuing, so that Front-LOUP [ĕʉ~ĕʏ] may be the majority Central Belt form among those born since 1955 or so, and is not unknown even in Berwickshire or Tweeddale (Johnston 1980: 234). Most *howk* items are transferred to COAT, with the number of transfers greatest in South-west and South Mid B as well as in Argyll (Grant 1931: xxviii). The number of items tails off as one goes north and east, so that, for instance, Perthshire dialects only monophthongise *bowk* and *yolk*. Along the west coast from Greenock down, and in Campbeltown (Grant 1931: xxviii), *roup* may undergo the same monophthongisation, though generally this does not happen in Ulster.

11.6.8.4 LOUP in Southern Scots

Southern Scots once had Rounded [ɔu~ou] rather than [ʌu], roughly the usual traditional development in northern England, where [ɔu~ɒu] is the rule (Johnston 1980: 257; Orton et al. 1981: 192; Stursberg 1969: 105–7; Zai 1942: 110–11; Orton 1933: 86; Reaney 1927: 75;

Murray 1873: 116). Then, the realisation of OUT in final position did not fall together with LOUP, but was only an allophone of /u:/. However, LSS vol. 3 found this development only in Newcastleton, in Liddesdale (Mather and Speitel 1986: 159–60), with V1 unrounding even in east Dumfriesshire. The most frequent forms among younger Borderers, in fact, are Central-LOUP realisations like [əʉ], and Front ones are increasingly common (Johnston 1980: 230, 234). *Roup* and *howk* develop normally, except in *folk*, which is a COAT word here.

While border-area dialects in England do not front LOUP, and there is a much greater tendency towards erosion of the class and replacement of the vowels by COAT reflexes, those that do survive are undergoing the equivalent change to /ɔu/ > /əu/ and taking on the form found for OUT in final position, usually [ɤu] or [öu] (Johnston 1980: 257).

11.7 THE DIALECTOLOGY OF SCOTS CONSONANTS

11.7.1 Introduction

Germanic consonant systems are usually more historically stable than vowel systems (Lass 1976). English dialects of any kind, unless formed in second-language conditions (as many 'new Englishes' of the Third World were; see Wells 1982: 623–51), generally have nearly identical consonantal phonemic inventories. Most often, they share at least the stops /p b t d k g/, the affricates /ʧ ʤ/, the fricatives /f v θ ð s z ʃ/, the nasals /m n ŋ/, the lateral /l/ and the approximants /r j w/. Typical Scots and Scottish Standard English varieties add /ʒ/ and /h/, present also in RP, and two more to this array: (1) /ʍ/, as in *what, where, which*, in words that had Old English (and Older Scots) /xw/; and /x/, in words like *loch, dreich* and, in traditional Scots, *night, enough*, stemming from a native or borrowed /x/. There exist more profound differences between 'mainstream', southern-derived varieties and Scottish ones in phonetic realisations of specific phonemes (for instance, that /r/ is often a tap, and /l/ 'dark' or velarised [L] in all positions), and even more in phonotactics (such as the fact that SSE and Scots is fully rhotic), but there is still much in common among English dialectal consonantal phonological systems, despite distance in other aspects of the language.

One corollary of the similarity between systems is that the remaining differences can be enumerated in terms of a small 'checklist' of the results of historical processes which produce them. These may merely affect surface phonetic realisation, lexical incidence of phonemes in specific positions due to a phonemic split, phonotactic constraints on phonemic/phonetic sequences, or inventorial differences. Some of these, like /kn-, gn-/-Reduction, have English correlates and are extremely widespread; peripheral dialect groups are actually marked off by *non*-application of the rule. Others, like Glottalling, while distributed over a large area, are still diagnostic of membership of specific dialect groups or subgroups, while a few of the changes, like Scots /h/-Deletion, are highly localised to one and only one part of the country.

The analysis which follows is divided into parts dealing with the stop/affricate, fricative, nasal and liquid subsystems. The first part of each section consists of a list of phonemes belonging to the set, and their most common isolative phonetic realisations over the Scots area. A discussion of any relevant processes then follows, in which I discuss the geographical extent of each process inside and outside Scotland, the presence and amount of variability, if any, and the occurrence of recent spread or recession. Processes affecting the deeper phonology are treated before those merely changing the phonetic realisation, and rules affecting clusters are treated under the first-discussed consonant that appears in them.

11.7.2   The Stops and Affricates

The usual Scots isolative realisations of /p t k/, as found in syllable-onset positions in most dialects, are, traditionally, fully voiceless unaspirated or weakly aspirated bilabial, alveolar or dental, and velar stops respectively. The affricate /ʧ/, which exists in almost all dialects (though not always with a Standard-like lexical incidence), is a palato-alveolar affricate, or in a few dialects, notably Perthshire, an alveolo-palatal one (for the distinction, see Catford 1988: 96, who, however, disapproves of the terminology). The phonemes /b d g/ are voiced stops made in the same positions as /p t k/, while /ʤ/, if there is one, similarly corresponds to /ʧ/. Dialects with Palato-Alveolar Shift A lack this phoneme.

11.7.2.1   Processes Affecting Stop and Affricate Inventory: Palato-Alveolar Shift

Although mainstream English varieties have four palato-alveolar sounds, the voiced fricative /ʒ/ is fairly rare, and is not found initially at all, except in non-nativised foreign words and names like *Zhukov*. Some Scots varieties have pared this series down further. North Northern and Insular dialects, a few west Morayshire ones near the Highland Line, and some varieties of Hebridean English (Mather and Speitel 1986: 1–42, 44–8, 52, 54; Shuken 1985: 150; Johnston 1985b: 39, 44, 46) often devoice /ʒ/ to /ʃ/ and /ʤ/ to /ʧ/ (Palato-Alveolar Shift A and B), so that *job, jug, John* sound like they begin with *ch*. In most Caithnesian nowadays, some Shetlandic (including Lerwick and the north) and in Highland English, the /ʤ/ merges with the /ʧ/ already there. However, in the Shetland countryside, and more regularly in Orkney and the Black Isle and among older Caithnesians, a chain shift results, with the original /tʃ/ becoming /ʃ/, so that *chip = ship*. The latter change (Shift C) once happened unaccompanied by the devoicing of /ʤ/ in northern Northumberland in Glendale, around Chatton and Chillingham, and in mid-Berwickshire (Grant 1931: xxvi), but forms with /ʃ/ are at least recessive now, and may even be extinct. The dialects that devoice /ʒ/ do the same to initial /z/, which has a low functional load. It becomes /s/, so that *zoo = Sue*.

As a sporadic, lexically conditioned change, Palato-Alveolar Shift is more widespread, as General Scots forms like *cabbitch, parritch* for *cabbage, porridge* attest to (Zai 1942: 210; Dieth 1932: 136; Wilson 1915: 18; compare also Orton 1933: 165). The simplification of /lʧ nʧ/ to /lʃ nʃ/, though somewhat variable in Northern varieties (Dieth 1932: 136), is General Scots also, and quite common in Northumbrian and Cumbrian to the south. In the heart of the Northern/Insular shifting area, the inventory of palato-alveolars can be added to by /k, g/-Palatalisation, which follows the Shift. In Whalsay, Shetland, the [ʧ] in *ken* thus replaces the sound in *job*, which joins the sound in *chip* to equal *ship* as a fricative (Johnston 1985b: 46; Grant 1931: xxxvii, xl).

11.7.2.2   Processes Affecting Lexical Incidence and Phonotactics

(a)   Glottalling

A very common change in British dialects is the reinforcement or replacement of voiceless stops in coda positions by glottal stop, especially (and often exclusively) of word/syllable-final /t/, or syllable-final /t/ before a syllabic nasal. Glottalling can happen to /p k/ in these positions also, and affect all stops intervocalically and in intervocalic clusters. Glottalling as a Scottish phenomenon was first noticed in Glasgow in 1892 (Macafee 1994a: 27), though it is unclear whether it was an independent native development or an importation from England, or even whether the London development is of Scottish origin. SND (Grant 1931: xxvii) mentions it as a general West Mid feature, which had already spread into Stirlingshire. It seems to have occurred in the North Northern group independently. One or the other form of Glottalling has now spread throughout Scotland so that it may be encountered at least sporadically anywhere, though how common it is, what positions of a word are affected, and whether /k/ or /p/ undergo Glottalling differ widely from area to area.

The Central Scots version is similar to the well-known, widespread rule in most British dialects, especially urban ones (Wells 1982: 322–6).[29] This type of Glottalling affects /k/ less often than /t/, and /p/ even less often, and usually results in complete replacement of the stop. At present, it applies in all coda positions for many people throughout central Scotland, and younger north-easterners, Borderers and Highland English speakers are beginning to apply it intervocalically and in intervocalic clusters in addition to finally and pre-nasally, where it has been extant for a few generations (Shuken 1985: 152–6; Johnston 1985b: 27, 31; Johnston 1980: 90, 100). A few speakers in Fife, Stirling and Glasgow (and Perth or Edinburgh?) allow Glottalling in words like *hotel*, *pontoon*, where the /t/ is in a syllable onset, though this is rare (Lass 1976: 150) and often judged as impossible by working-class speakers. As majority forms, Edinburgh lower working-class speakers had [?] for final /t k/ and medial /t/, but most of the time had pre-glottalised syllable-final [?p] and regular [p k] medially, except before a syllabic nasal (Johnston 1983a: 29–37). Such a pattern is typical of Central Belt urban vernaculars, with a more restricted rule in outlying, more conservative dialects. A typical north-eastern rural dialect might have [?] only for final and pre-nasal /t/, for instance.

The North Northern form of Glottalling often has a different outcome and weighting of application, and serves to separate Caithnesian and Black Isle speech from the rest of Northern Scots. Except for /t k/ finally and pre-nasally to some extent, the Glottalling process does not seem to result in [?], but [?p ?t ?k] instead (Johnston 1985b: 40). Furthermore, /k/ is as likely to be Glottalled as /t/ is. However, this rule does apply in the same environments as the Central Belt one. There is a Northumbrian vernacular form of 'Partial Glottalling' giving the same result, spreading from Tyneside/Coalfields dialect, but the weighting of environments is different from either Scottish type of Glottalling (Milroy et al. 1994).

Since even Northern Isles dialects occasionally realise final/pre-nasal /t/ or /k/ as [?], it seems that Glottalling is on the way to becoming a general Scottish feature (Johnston 1985b: 46).

(b)   /kn/, /gn/-Reduction

At the time of SND and LSS vol. 3, a large region comprising the whole Insular and Northern areas as far south as Angus and north-east Fife variably retained /kn/ in *know*, *knee* and /gn/ in *gnaw*, *gnarled* (Mather and Speitel 1986: 1–3, 4–7, 14–17, 18–20, 22–9, 31–5, 37–9, 43–4, 46–7, 50–80, 82–5, 86–90, 109; Dieth 1932: 132; Grant 1931: xxii). The southern edge of this area had a possibility of [tn] instead of /kn/ (see the place-name *Gallet Knowe* for *Gallow Knowe* and Wilson 1915: 25). These forms still might be found, either as /kn gn/ or as [ŋn ~ hn] on the Orkney and Shetland archipelagoes or in some Moray and Banff vernaculars, but are recessive or jocular even there and are fast becoming extinct on the mainland (Melchers 1986). The realisation /nj/ instead of /gn/ in *gnaw* appeared sporadically in Caithness; this probably represents a simplified result of an earlier /gnj/, with the /j/ coming from /a:w/ > /jɑw/ > /jɑv/ (Robinson 1985: 239; Mather and Speitel 1986: 34–5).

On the Black Isle, /kn/ is not traditionally simplified to /n/, but becomes /kr/, a development also found in Gaelic (Borgstrom 1940: 136; Grant 1931: xxxvii). However, Mather and Speitel (1986: 43–4) found /kn/ there also. It is not recorded by Grant whether the /kr/ forms are followed by a nasalised vowel, which, in Gaelic, distinguishes underlying /kn/ from /kr/ clusters: *cnoc* is [kʰɪ̃ʰk] or the like. Murray (1873: 122) mentions /kn gn/ as obsolescent in Southern Scots, though it was not found by Grant (1931: xxxi) or Zai (1942: 212). The reduction rule apparently applied in the more urbanised regions of Scotland first, suggesting that it may have come in from SSE.

(c) /kl/, /gl/-Assimilation

Many peripheral dialects, including outlying Shetlandic and Orcadian, west Caithnesian and Nairn dialect, a few Berwickshire and Highland Line West Mid varieties, and those of the south-west of Scotland, such as western Border Scots from Annan westwards, Gallovidian, Ulster Scots and most Ayrshire varieties assimilate initial /kl gl/ to [tl dl], a change that is also widespread in the north of England (Mather and Speitel 1986; Reaney 1927: 126). Most of these dialects have clear /l/ either categorically or variably in this position, an easier realisation to assimilate to than the usual Scots dark one. Palatal clusters like [cʎ ɟʎ] may also result in some areas (Mather and Speitel 1986: 202–3, 206–8). The common factor among Scots dialects having this rule is close contact with either Norse or Gaelic, either one of which permits a clear /l/ in positions where English otherwise has 'weak', velarised allophones of /l/.[30]

(d) /nd/, /ld/-Simplification

The Simplification of the coda clusters /nd ld/ to /n l/ is a well-known feature of a number of Scots varieties (Mather and Speitel 1986; Grant 1931: xxii). The tendency is particularly strong in the whole Mid-Northern group, where /nd ld/ are simplified both finally and intervocalically, whether a morpheme boundary is present or not (Dieth 1932: 124). In North Northern, West and South-west Mid, western Border dialects and variably in the Lothians, a more restricted rule applies, where /nd/ simplifies to /n/ in all positions, but /ld/ becomes /l/ only finally, especially when a consonant begins the next word (Wilson 1923: 15–16). This form of Simplification is variable in Edinburgh and Angus, and is becoming increasingly common over the rest of the Mid-Scots region.

The Insular Scots group has developed an 'in-between' rule, by which syllable-final /ld nd/ are regularly simplified to /l n/, though medial /ld nd/ are retained more often than not. Originally, retention in almost all words characterised this group (Mather and Speitel 1986: 1–27; Johnston 1985b: 42, 47). Northern English dialects, on the other hand, have the mirror-image rule, simplifying medially but only rarely in final position (Orton 1933: 142, 147; Reaney 1927: 117).

Although this Simplification rule is of some antiquity, it did not arise due to the effects of a Gaelic substratum. The Middle Gaelic that first came into contact with English still possessed /ld nd/, though Brythonic had undergone simplification many centuries earlier

(Schrijver 1995: 351; Dieth 1932: 125). While the Pictish and Strathclyde Welsh heartlands do have the most extensive simplification, Scots replaced Gaelic in the north-east, not Pictish, and unless we know that the rule was there from the beginning, any connection with P-Celtic speech habits must remain speculative. The rule also happens in many other English dialects where Celtic influence is out of the question (Labov 1972: 216). It is more likely to be connected with the simplification of /mb ŋg/, which happens both finally and medially in Scots and northern English vernaculars (Zai 1942: 185–7; Dieth 1932: 125–6; Wilson 1923: 17–18; Wilson 1915: 22–3).

(e) /k g/-Palatalisation

Many peripheral dialects that undergo the previous consonantal changes also palatalise /k g/ to [kj gj] before front vowels. Palatalisation is most common in Galloway, the mainland far north and the Northern Isles, where a rich range of palatal reflexes are present, including true palatals [c ɟ], and palatal affricates [cç ~ tɕ ɟj ~ dʑ]. It can also happen variably in some forms of West Mid, notably Glaswegian, Clydemouth and Ayrshire varieties. It occurs sporadically in parts of the eastern Borders (Mather and Speitel 1986: 2–5, 12–15, 18–20, 21, 27–8, 37–8, 132, 149–50, 196–204). In some outlying parts of Shetland such as Whalsay, in North Ronaldsay in Orkney, or in parts of Ulster, the palatalisation may be so extreme as to go all the way to [tʃ dʒ], causing interactions with Palato-Alveolar Shift (Mather and Speitel 1986: 12–13; Johnston 1985b: 46).

Preceding front vowels may also palatalise velars, particularly /g/, in east Fife, Morayshire and North Northern varieties, and again in Ulster (Mather and Speitel 1986: 32–3, 54–5, 108, 198, 201–2). This may stem from an earlier diphthong in a word like egg, by which an earlier [ëɪg] > [ëɪ], with the /g/ assimilating to the palatal nature of the palatal offglide and ultimately absorbing it. In a few Highland Line dialects and in Ulster, /n/ after /i/, as in king and similar words, becomes [iɲ]. Occasionally, in Angus, Perthshire or North Fife varieties, /k/ around back vowels may become [q]; Mather and Speitel (1986: 82–3) describe this for Migvie, Angus, but I have heard it in Forfar also, and sporadically from Taysiders.

To assimilate velars in this way to surrounding vowels is a natural tendency; indeed, English /tʃ dʒ/, whether native or from Romance, mostly stem from palatalised velars before front vowels, including /a/ (Luick 1964: 835–41), and a form of restricted palatalisation was once prestigious in /ka ga/-combinations in words like card, garden in RP (Luick 1964: 1,116–17). It is therefore not necessary to invoke a Gaelic or Norse substratum, though the phonotactics of these languages both favour palatalisation (Haugen 1982: 65; Borgstrom 1940: 57–76), and no doubt the pronunciation habits of bilinguals aided the application and spread of these changes in the far north and south-west.

(f) /tj kj/-Interchange

It is quite normal for an initial /tj/ in a word like tube, tune to be realised as /tʃ/ in Mid-Scots and Southern Scots varieties. However, an alternative to this is to turn it into [cj] or even [kj] so that tube = cube (Mather and Speitel 1986: 33–5, 48, 52, 55, 59, 199, 208). This is quite common in both Caithnesian and Ulster Scots, but is also frequent in coastal Moray and Banff Mid-Northern varieties. All these dialects have a penchant for palatalising velars and assimilating parts of consonantal clusters to each other; it is likely that the merger is really under a fronted velar or palatal stop + /j/, and that this rule results from the same general tendency exhibited in other changes mentioned above.

(g) /kw/-Lenition

In dialects that are heavily Norse-influenced, such as those of the Northern Isles, initial /kw/ > [xw ~ ʍ], merging with the /xw/ that is already there, so that *wheen* = *queen*. In Orkney and southern Shetland, this process happens alone. In Lerwick, however, this rule interacts with its opposite, /xw/-Fortition (see below), resulting in a merger with either variant possible, and a crossover pattern is a stereotype of the Lerwick and south Shetland areas (Melchers 1985: 95). Traces of /kw/-Lenition are found in Cumbria (Reaney 1927: 100), suggesting that the change is due to Norse influence, as that area was heavily settled by Norwegians.

The cluster /skw/ as in *square* goes to /sw/ in all Shetlandic except that of the 'West Side'-Fortition area – and variably in northern and central varieties of Orcadian (Melchers 1986; Mather and Speitel 1986: 1–3, 8–11). This development is a corollary of Lenition, since /skw/ would become *[sxw ~ shw], which the phonotactics of no English dialect allow. The likely adjustment would be to [sʍw], which is how /sw/ is often realised anyway, given the tendencies of English sonorants in this position to begin voiceless.

The cluster /kw/ before front vowels in Mid-Scots or Angus dialects with OUT-Fronting is quite commonly realised as [kɥ], with the glide partially devoiced; this is becoming more widespread in conjunction with the Fronting rule. It is not related to the Insular lenitions mentioned above.

(h) Voicing of Stops in Unstressed Syllables

Caithnesian (and very sporadically, south-east Orcadian[31]) turns /t k/ in the coda of unstressed syllables to /d g/, so that the common verbal ending -*it* is -*id*, the diminutive suffix -*ock* is -*ag*, and words like *bucket* end in /d/. *It* is *hid*/*id*/*'d*, with a wider distribution, occurring in east and south-east Fife and coastal Berwickshire too (Grant 1931: xxv, xxxviii). Parallel voicing in a few words such as *loop* with final /p/ > /b/ occurs in a few Caithnesian and Black Isle varieties (Mather and Speitel 1986: 30, 47). The change is apparently shared by northern dialects of Gaelic, and may have come in from the Gaelic adstratum in Sutherland next door. It is not known if this change is related to the Aberdonian 'Lenisation' mentioned by Dieth (1932: 88–90), by which post-tonic medial /p t k/ become [b̥ d̥ g̊].

(i) /t/-Flapping

The flapping of /t/ in words like *butter* is generally associated with Irish, American and south-western English dialects (Wells 1982: 248–51, 344, 430), but may be encountered occasionally in West Mid (especially Glaswegian), Stirlingshire and West Lothian Scots dialects as a low-frequency competitor to Glottalling. The result is [ɾ], which has to be considered as /r/ here. Phonologically, this rule can be considered as a Scottish version of the Northern English T-to-R rule mentioned by Wells (1982: 370). It is not clear if the various Flapping rules are connected, but the distribution of the Scottish rule is similarly urban rather than rural.

(j) $/xt/ > /\theta/$

At the time of SND (Dieth 1932: 113; Grant 1931: xxxv), the cluster /xt/ in a few specific words such as *might, daughter* was realised as [θ] in north-eastern dialects. This feature is now highly recessive, and may survive, if at all, only in Angus. It must be an old change, recessive for years, if any of the ⟨th, tht⟩ spellings of Older Scots in the class of words really reflect [θ] and are not purely graphic. Lss vol. 3 failed to find any examples of this change. The type of change exhibited here seems odd, but there are parallels in the history of Brythonic (Schrijver 1995: 349–50). As with /ld nd/-Simplification, there may be a connection with Pictish or Strathclyde Welsh pronunciation habits, but we cannot prove this, since we do not know whether this change was present from the beginning. It may have covered a wider area in Older Scots.

11.7.2.3 Processes Affecting Phonetic Realisations

(a) Alveolar Dentalisation

Dental [t̪ d̪ n̪] are quite common variants of /t d n/ in many Scots dialects, most prevalent along the Highland Line, in Caithness and in the Northern Isles but also occurring idiolectally and variably in central Scotland, the Borders and Northumberland. A Gaelic or Norse substratum need not be invoked in all cases, though as for Palatalisation, the pronunciation habits of bilinguals might have fostered the change as the /t/ series tends to be dental in both languages. Alveolar sibilants /s z/ usually stay alveolar.

(b) Voiceless Stop Aspiration

While early authorities are united as to the unaspirated nature of Scots voiceless stops in syllable onsets (Zai 1942: 20; Dieth 1932: 100–1), aspirated ones equal to the equivalent /p t k/ allophones in other English dialects are now entering Scots (Johnston 1980: 78; 1983a: 16). The process, which results in weak rather than strong aspiration or affricated release, seems furthest advanced in Central Belt cities, especially Glasgow and Edinburgh, and in Ulster where the voice quality has a breathy-voiced component.

11.7.3 The Fricatives

Scots, like other English dialects, has the fricatives /f v/ (usually labiodental), the alveolars /s z/ and the palato-alveolar (or, on Tayside, alveolo-palatal) voiceless fricative /ʃ/. Most varieties have the other fricatives present in 'mainstream' English dialects, namely the palato-alveolar /ʒ/, the postdental or interdental pair /θð/, and the glottal /h/. In addition, traditional Scots possesses a voiceless velar fricative /x/, at least in words like *loch*, and, if no loss has taken place, in words like *bought, night, fight, laugh* and *enough* as well.

11.7.3.1 Changes Affecting the Phonemic Inventory

(a) /x/-Loss

The phoneme /x/ is somewhat recessive in Mid and, to a lesser extent, Southern Scots. Even in these areas, however, many speakers retain it variably in place-names like *Auchtermuchty*, personal names like *Lachlan*, and words without true English cognates like *pibroch*, while replacing /x/ in all 'ordinary' words like *right*, *bought* with /x/-less SSE forms. Some urban speakers in Edinburgh and Glasgow have even replaced /x/ in the 'special' words with /k/, so that *Sauchiehall* Street is regularly [sɔkehɔ:ɫ] and *Lochend* may be [lokɛ:n(d)] (Macafee 1994a: 28). The phoneme /ʌ/ seems to survive the best above the Forth/Clyde line, where even middle-aged people as far south as Kirkcaldy use forms like *night* = [nëçt ~ nëxt]. To the south of this line, it may be encountered from the oldest speakers, and in special registers involving fixed expressions such as *It's a braw bricht muinlicht nicht the nicht*, and in literary words. It is also quite recessive in Ulster Scots and in Shetlandic, where /h/ sometimes replaces it. Even in the north-east, there are a few items like *through* replaced by /x/-less cognates. As borrowing generally is, the process of /x/-Loss is lexically rather than phonologically conditioned.

(b)   /θ ð/-Stopping

The dental fricatives /θ ð/ are not very common sounds in the world, and are often unstable over time (Lass 1984: 151). The most frequent change within English is to turn them into the stops /t d/, merging them under any already existing phonemes. This can be observed, within native varieties of English, in Irish English, Caribbean dialects, and New York and other American urban vernaculars (Wells 1982: 428–31, 515–16, 565–6); it does not always happen in all positions, however, and sometimes results in a dental/alveolar contrast rather than a merger. In Scotland, Stopping has been traditionally usual in the Northern Isles, where /t d/ replaced /θ ð/ in all positions at the point of adoption (Grant 1931: xl), a rule that has been largely reversed in Orkney, and in final position everywhere. In the dialects of Pomona, Hoy and South Ronaldsay, Stopping is really only common in clusters, though Birsay dialect has it in single onsets. In *th*- pronouns, Shetland has mostly *d*- forms, while Orcadian often has the same vowel-initial forms that Northern Scots has, probably replacing earlier reflexes with /d/.

South Mid B and South-west Mid once also had regular Stopping of the same kind; this is now recessive in both places, with the older /t d/ forms persisting best in Wigtown and Antrim. Stopping is more common in Ireland, where it has support in other (non-Ulster) types of Hiberno-English (Wells 1982: 428–31). It can be sporadically found in Glasgow and elsewhere in West Mid urban Scots, mostly in clusters, and in pronouns and common adverbs such as *they*, *there*, *then*.

Traditionally in Aberdeenshire, /d/ appeared for /ð/ intervocalically in words like *mother*, *father*, *bother*, particularly in coastal localities, though this is sharply recessive now (Dieth 1932: 109). There seems to be a general interchange between stops and fricatives in all English to some extent where an /r/ follows immediately or in the next syllable; *father*, after all, goes back to an Old English *fæder*. The tendency towards generalising one type or the other one, usually the fricative at the expense of the stop, is furthest advanced in localities in North Britain, however (Zai 1942: 195; Wilson 1926: 29). Dialects which face the Solway Firth or Irish Sea have a tendency to have dental stops in this position from either original stop or fricative.

(c)   /θ ð/-Lenition/Deletion

Instead of Stopping, /ð/ may delete, particularly in pronouns and articles where it is in initial position. This is usual nearly everywhere after preceding alveolar consonants ending the preceding word, but is found in all positions in the Northern dialects above Angus, including Aberdonian, the Black Isle and Caithness, and occasionally elsewhere in the north and in Orkney (Grant 1931: xxxiii, xxxvii–xxxviii). For some reason, this development is not very well attested in the literature as a general feature except in North Northern, but it seems quite widespread in the rest of the north (Johnston 1985b: 31). Intervocalic /ð/ generally does not delete in these places, but may do quite frequently in Ulster Scots (L. Milroy 1980: 120), and may do in Galloway and Glasgow (Macafee 1983: 33). Final /ð/ is quite routinely dropped in *clothes, mouth, with* as a General Scots feature – much more widespread than that (non-Southern) in the case of the first and last.

The equivalent of /ð/-deletion for the voiceless sound is /θ/ > /h/. This can be found in initial and intervocalic position, including before /r/ (that is, in *thing, nothing, three*) in many Scots dialects, including all Southern and Central Belt varieties up to Perthshire (Zai 1942: 200; Wilson 1915: 30), and is becoming more common over time there, though still variable. However, the change is a little rarer in Northern Scots and Galloway. Final /θ/ is retained everywhere. In Angus and sporadically elsewhere, /θr/ generally becomes /fr/ rather than /hr/ (Mather and Speitel 1986: 84), though /θ/ routinely goes to /h/ between vowels as in Mid Scots. In other cases, /θ/ > /f/ is sporadic, though not unknown in Glasgow (Macafee 1994a: 29), but may occur in a few specific lexical items such as *Thursday* in North Northern and Insular Scots, and occasionally Gallovidian (Robinson 1991: 217; Dieth 1932: 115), attested as far back as the sixteenth century. The opposite change (/fr/ > /θr/) shows up in the word *thrae* < *frae* (Zai 1942: 187; Murray 1873: 228) in Southern Scots; other varieties generally have *fae* now, although in the last century this was strictly a Northern Scots feature (Grant 1931).

(d)   /h/-Deletion

In most dialects spoken in England, /h/, which is restricted to syllable-initial position anyway, has been deleted, and, parallel to this, /ʍ/ (which is phonologically /hw/) becomes /w/, so that *hat = at, hold = old*, and *which = witch*. This process has spread north in England as far as Cumberland and Durham (and well into Northumberland for /hw/ > /w/; Orton et al. 1978: 220–3; Orton 1933: 156), but Scots /h/-deletion is found only in Black Isle dialects (Grant 1931: xxxvii), while /hw/ > /w/ is more widespread and is in evidence in Glasgow and Edinburgh vernaculars, probably because of spread from England (Macafee 1994a: 28).

The realisation /hw/ stems from an earlier /xw/, retained around the periphery of Scotland (Mather and Speitel 1986: 37, 48, 52, 56–9, 62–6, 70–1, 75–6, 80, 82, 85, 87, 102–3, 154–5, 156–7). In Northern Scots except for the Black Isle, the two sounds must have coalesced with the labial element emphasised; the resulting [ɸ] then became the nearest regular English sound, [f], so that all the regular *wh-* pronouns (*who, where, when, why, how*) and, in North and Mid-Northern, other words as well (*whisky, while, wheen*) now begin with /f/[32] (Grant 1931: xxxiv–xxxv). The feature of /xw/-Labialisation is restricted to pronouns in Angus, and is very slowly becoming recessive in other words in North Northern and Moray varieties. However, in recent years, I have heard [ɸw] and even [ɸ] from Edinburgh speakers. This must be a recent development, independent from any Northern changes.

The realisation /xw/ must have gone to /hw/, and then /h/, in Black Isle dialects; the /h/ then dropped so that /xw/ words now have no consonant beginning the word (Grant 1931: xxxvii). Mather and Speitel (1986: 46) picked up a few cases of this in *wh-* pronouns, but found [xw ~ ɸw ~ kw] in other words. In the Northern Isles, /xw/ may become /kw/ by

/xw/-Fortition, particularly in northern, western and Lerwick Shetlandic, and on North Ronaldsay in Orkney (Mather and Speitel 1986: 1–8, 12–13; Melchers 1985: 95; Grant 1931: xl). This change is attested in Faroese and Norwegian dialects (Haugen 1982: 72, 75).

(e) /v w/-Interchange

Many English dialects, including Cockney, once merged /v/ and /w/ variably (Wakelin 1991: 218; Wells 1982: 333). Confusion between the two was once in evidence in Scots as well, particularly in coastal north-eastern varieties, according to SND (Grant 1931: xxv), taking the form of /w/ for /v/. The /v/ has been restored due to SSE influence, but the converse change happens to initial /wr/ in *wretch, wren, wrong, write*, which is generally /vr/ in all Mid- and North Northern dialects; and in originally (Old English) syllable-final /w/ in words like *blyaave* for *blow* or *chaave/tyaave/kyaave* (to toil) from Old English *teawian* in Mid Northern (Dieth 1932: 115–16). In the latter, the forms with /v/ are now recessive, except in the last item, which has no Standard English cognates.[33] The retention of /wr/ as such is found most commonly in Northern Isles dialects today, but /wr/ was also present a century ago in the Borders (Murray 1873: 130). There is usually an epenthetic schwa between the /w/ and /r/ in modern dialects (Mather and Speitel 1986: 1–4, 9–12).

(f) /ð/-Rhotacisation

A stereotype of Glaswegian that can be occasionally encountered in the rest of the West Mid area, and even Edinburgh vernacular as a very sporadic alternative to /ð/-Stopping or Deletion, is the change /ð/ > /r/, realised as either a tap or an approximant. Rhotacisation is particularly common in *th-* pronouns and for intervocalic /ð/ in words like *mother, brother, bother* (Macafee 1994a: 28).

(g) /s ʃ/-Interchange

There has been a tendency to interchange /s/ and /ʃ/ on a lexical basis ever since Older Scots times in most dialects, though the items affected may vary (Macafee 1983: 34; Zai 1942: 203–6; Dieth 1932: 103–5; Wilson 1923: 23; Wilson 1915: 29; Murray 1873: 126). Some of these cases, such as *creash* as compared to *grease*, may involve French loans with variation between Norman forms of Early Old French palatalised /s/ with the palato-alveolar and Francien ones with the straight alveolar (Pope 1934: 132, 429, 439). Other cases of /ʃ/ for /s/ involve /rs/ clusters, as *hoarse* in Midlothian and Roxburghshire Border Scots, where the /r/ may have pulled the /s/ back to palato-alveolar instead of retroflex position; retroflexion is quite usual in dialects with /r/ = [ɹ], and the resulting [ʂ] sounds [ʃ]-like. Still others may imply an earlier /sj/ cluster, as in *soon, suit* and the like.

The cluster /ʃr/ in *shrub, shrimp* is often /sr/ in a few different peripheral Scots dialects, such as those of Caithness, some Orcadian and Shetlandic, Moray Firth dialects and Ulster Scots (Mather and Speitel 1986: 33–40, 45–6, 48–9, 51–2, 56–7, 58–9, 65–6, 195–9, 202–4). More commonly, the cluster is broken up by an epenthetic schwa. This development is not restricted to Scots but occurs locally in many English dialects, and probably involves place assimilation.

11.7.3.2 Changes Affecting the Lexical Incidence or Phonotactics

(a)   The Ich/Ach *Rule*

Most Scots varieties have a German-like *Ich/Ach* rule governing the phonetic realisation of /x/ – that is, when the preceding vowel is front, the consonant is realised as a fronted velar [x̟], or more usually, a palatal fricative [ç]; if it is back, it is a plain velar [x], or more rarely, a uvular [χ]. Some dialects, such as East Mid B, Southern Scots and South Mid A, and further afield, varieties of Orcadian, have an *auch* allophone, an [xʷ], instead of [x] after back vowels (Mather and Speitel 1986: 14–15, 20–3, 150–9, 162, 164–5, 167–70, 172, 173–5, 177–81). Any of these may be weakened to [h] or, for the *auch-Laut*, [ʍ] (Mather and Speitel 1986: 164–5; Zai 1942: 216–17).

(b)   /hj/-Assibilation

The cluster /hj/, as in *Hugh, human* is generally assibilated to [ç] or even [ʃ] within Mid-Scots, excepting Gallovidian and Ulster Scots. The realisation [ʃ] is particularly common in Glaswegian, Lothian and Fife vernaculars (Mather and Speitel 1986: 99–100, 107–8, 110, 114–15, 140; Macafee 1983: 35). Assibilation is rarer in Northern Scots, though there are examples in Caithnesian and Angus (Mather and Speitel 1986: 34–5, 78–9, 82–3).

(c)   Obstruent + /t/-Simplification

The combination /st/ in codas may be simplified to /s/ as a sporadic change in Caithnesian, Angus and Perthshire dialects (Mather and Speitel 1986: 1–15, 17–22, 25–34, 35–6, 37–8, 86–9). It is most commonly simplified, however, in Shetlandic, where /xt ft/ in final positions may become /x f/ also. This change is probably an extension of the General Scots simplification of stop + /t/ (in *act, accept*), which is attested from Older Scots times onwards (Zai 1942: 193).

11.7.3.3 Changes Affecting Phonetic Realisations

(a)   Cacuminalisation

The phonemes /s z/ are quite commonly apico-alveolar [ŝ ẑ] (Catford 1977: 151) in Glasgow, Edinburgh, Dundee, south Fife and other Mid-Scots vernaculars, including the North Mid varieties along the Highland Line. The pronunciation is perceived to be due to badly fitting dentures by many native speakers, but, given that it correlates with class like other vernacular features and can be heard in children's speech, it must be counted as a Scots feature in the same way that /r/ > [ɰ] is in the south of England (Trudgill 1988: 43–6; Macafee 1983: 33–4). Some examples of /s ʃ/-Interchange, treated above, may have gone through a cacuminal stage (Macafee 1983: 34).

(b)   /f v/-Bilabialisation

The phonemes /f v/ may be realised as bilabial [ɸ β] in Ulster Scots, particularly around back sounds, where 'broad', plain Irish /f v/ would be realised this way in that language (Wells 1982: 434). Mather and Speitel (1986: 73–4) also uncovered a case of this in

Mid-Northern A, near the Highland Line, so that (South?) Gaelic influence can probably be invoked.

11.7.4 The Nasals

Scots has a typical set of nasals: a bilabial /m/, an alveolar or dental /n/ and a velar /ŋ/. The phonotactics are the same as in most other English dialects, except that intervocalic /ŋg/ > /ŋ/ throughout Scotland (as in northern England down to the Broad Northern line: Orton et al. 1978: 240–1), and often, intervocalic /mb/ > /m/ as well. Dialects that dentalise /t d/ do so also to /n/, and a few varieties near the Highland Line and in Ulster that palatalise /k g/ sometimes palatalise /ŋ/ to [ɲ] if it is preceded by /i/. Otherwise, there are few conditioned developments.

11.7.5 The Sonorants

Scots varieties possess the semi-vowels /j w ʍ (< /xw/)/ and the liquids /l r/. Changes affecting the former set such as /v w/-Interchange, /wr/-Simplification and /xw/-Voicing, Labialisation and Fortition have already been discussed, but otherwise, /j w/ are generally realised as in other English dialects, though there may be considerably more friction than in most varieties, especially if a high vowel follows.

11.7.5.1 The Phoneme /l/

Most Scots dialects realise /l/ as a 'dark' [ɫ], often strongly pharyngealised, with a marked [ɯ], [ɤ] or [ʌ] resonance. The darkness of /l/ is noteworthy even in early descriptions (Dieth 1932: 100), though Mutschmann (1908: 71) mentions a clear one in the north-east, now no longer extant, and Zai (1942: 30) seems to have clear /l/ when in an onset, as in RP. However, the dark /l/ variant has won out except around the periphery, and now distinguishes Scots from most traditional northern English vernaculars, especially Northumbrian and Cumbrian (Orton 1960). Dialects in the peripheral north and south, such as the Northern Isles and Caithness (and many types of Highland English; see Shuken 1985: 51) on one side, and the western Borders, Wigtownshire and Ulster on the other, however, retain clear /l/ in all positions, as northern English varieties do (Mather and Speitel 1986: 164–8, 172–85, 188; Johnston 1985b: 15). Berwickshire, Roxburghshire, west Dumfries and Kirkcudbrightshire agree with the Central Belt on this feature.

Besides the type of earlier Scots /l/-Vocalisation, a new, secondary vocalisation akin to the Cockney type described by Wells (1982: 313–16) has sprung up in Glasgow and, more rarely, other urban areas, resulting in [ɤ ~ o] (Macafee 1994: 2). Unlike the Older Scots change, this Vocalisation is not conditioned by the backness of the preceding vowel, nor is it retarded by the presence of a following /d/. The change has not reached Northern, Southern or Insular dialects, or even peripheral Mid varieties.

11.7.5.2 The Phoneme /r/

Traditionally, Scots had either a tap [ɾ] or a true trill [r] (still possible as an emphatic realisation) in all positions (Grant 1931: xxiv). The trill, counter to American stereotypes of what a Scottish accent is like, is now sporadic at best, but a tap in all positions is usual among older speakers everywhere, especially in rural Scots. The high-status SSE dialects of urban areas have [ɹ] instead, and this form is beginning to percolate into Scots, especially non-intervocalically. From my own observations, it seems more common in the west than the east, and more in codas than onsets (Johnston 1983a: 26–9).

In addition, the highly retroflex approximant [ɻ], which often backs following alveolars to the same place of articulation, has always been the norm where Celtic influence is strong, as in Ulster Scots, the North Northern dialects, and elsewhere along the Highland Line as in south Morayshire (Mather and Speitel 1986: 27–40, 41–9, 53–5). More variably, it may alternate with [ɾ] in codas in Insular Scots. Any /r/ + alveolar combination may be simplified to a retroflex consonant with the same manner of articulation of the alveolar if the /r/ realisation is [ɻ], as in Caithness or Ulster Scots (Mather and Speitel 1986: 27–50, 192– 208). The cluster /rs/ > [ʂ] in an even wider range of dialects, including Morayshire and parts of Banffshire (Grant 1931: xxxvi). Within Insular Scots, LSS vol. 3 material (Mather and Speitel 1986: 3–4, 14–15, 20–2) reveals this feature in Pomona, Hoy and Sanday in Orkney, and Hamnavoe in Shetland, areas where the retroflex /r/ is especially common.

Orcadian may also have a type of vocalisation to a plain or uvularised vowel, seemingly independently of the more widespread Mid-Scots vocalisation mentioned below. These developments do not occur farther south than Caithness, which provided several examples in Mather and Speitel (1986: 27–9, 30–4).

Postvocalic (and non-intervocalic) /r/-vocalisation is not traditionally associated with Scotland, but has become increasingly common in recent years. It is particularly characteristic of urban speech, and was first attested in Glasgow by Trotter (1901; cited by Macafee 1983: 33). It has become the rule now in all the Mid-Scots region except for South-west Mid, and is spreading both northwards and southwards into Angus (from Dundee, where it has been regular for some time) and even Aberdeen city on the one hand, and into Wigtownshire, Berwickshire and the Borders on the other (Johnston 1985b; Romaine 1978).

It is debatable whether /r/ should be counted as really deleted in most of these dialects, as it results in a 'coloured', distinctly pharyngealised vowel, similar to the well-attested uvularised vowels arising from /Vr/ combinations in Northumbrian (Wells 1982: 369; Johnston 1980: 80–4). Given the pharyngeal voice quality in most Mid-Scots, it is conceivable, however, that this is a 'default setting' (Macafee 1983: 34; Esling 1978), and that /r/ is as underlyingly deleted as in English non-rhotic dialects. Some recent examples of linking and intrusive /r/, as well as rhyme evidence, in Glasgow suggests that /Vr/ combinations have been reanalysed as non-rhotic (Macafee 1994a: 29).

When vocalised, /ar ʌr ɔr/ become pharyngealised as [ɑˤ: ʌˤ ɔˤ:] (see Northumbrian [ɑʁ: ɔʁ:]), but all other vowels are followed by an element [ʌˤ], so that here = [hi·ʌˤ], there = [ðɛ·ʌˤ] and the like (Northumbrian uses [ɑʁ ~ ɔʁ] the same way). Like /t/-Glottalling and OUT-Fronting, this change serves as a potent identifiable trait of Mid-Scots urban vernaculars, and is attractive to young rural speakers for its 'street-smart' associations. The three changes vary similarly, and seem to form a set, spreading in rough tandem.

The realisation [ʁ] is historical in Northumberland, although [ɹ], from other English dialects, is replacing it (Johnston 1980: 84). Within Scotland, it occurs as an idiolectal peculiarity in a few regions, especially Orkney, the Mid- and South Northern Scots region, and in Southern Scots (Johnston 1985b: 26, 31, 34).

NOTES

1. I realise that here (maybe because I am a native of a convergent dialect area, where what *traditional* lexis that existed died out before I was born), I am taking a controversial stand, the opposite one to Macafee (1994a), whose basic tack is that uniformation and convergence on the Standard is inevitable. I can see her point too; it depends on what one considers Scots to be, and what one's basic focus is. I am also aware that her viewpoint squares well with her older informants', and that of many of my own. I agree, too, that a typological break is inevitable. What one calls the result of modern changes, however, depends on one's emphasis, on dialect as lexis or non-accentual phonology.

2. I call it South-west Mid-Scots, since it has historical ties to both South and West Mid dialects (Gregg 1985: 6–9).

3. Some of these innovations, particularly those datable before the Industrial Revolution, did not necessarily *start* in cities. As I will show, some of the most distinctive 'Aberdonian' innovations really started in coastal fishing villages, and a few of the 'Glaswegian' ones seem to belong to the south-west of Scotland, to Ireland, or to the localities along the Highland Line. However, it seems that they are strictly local until carried by incomers to the cities and adopted there, and then the cities serve as 'transmitters' of the sound changes, spreading them widely throughout a wide area.

4. Note that peripherality does not necessarily mean that a region does not have a minor, local centre (such as Kirkwall and Lerwick) contained within it, but that these centres have little influence outside the region.

5. For this type of 'keyword' nomenclature in referring to descendants of Older Scots vowel classes, see Sections 11.4–11.6 and Wells (1982, vol. 1: 119–20) for the general methodology.

6. Nithsdale and North Dumfriesshire dialects are assigned to South Mid A in this classification, mostly on grounds of tradition (they have always been considered South Mid), linguistic perception (the speakers feel themselves to be Gallovidian) and lexical grounds. Phonologically, like Stirlingshire, it is a hard-to-place transition area, and could be called a putative South Mid C or a form of West Mid, with justification for this assignment in the shape and realisations of the vowel system.

7. A speculation on my part is that Pattern III communities, although common, did not exist until very recently, might have been Pattern II before 1940 or so, and are rapidly on the way to becoming Pattern IV.

8. All Argyllshire English is quite heavily West Mid-accented, however, as are varieties as far north as the Great Glen.

9. The dialects of Burnmouth and Eyemouth once had more North Northumbrian traits (Ellis 1889: 641–2), and Mather and Speitel (1986: 144–5) still show that BOOT takes [iː], and /Vr/ combinations are realised as uvularised vowels. When I visited that area in the 1970s, my impression was that the dialects were more Berwickshire in type than earlier descriptions would suggest. Berwick town is predominantly North Northumbrian-speaking (Mather and Speitel 1986: 190–2), with a few features shared with Scots.

10. C. I. Macafee at the University of Aberdeen has now started one.

11. The structure of the English Great Vowel Shift is somewhat disputed nowadays, and there are several viewpoints possible. Roger Lass (1988) has proposed that, while not monolithic, the changes affecting the top two heights of the system are more tightly linked than the other GVS changes. Robert Stockwell and Donka Minkova (1988) have denied the very existence of chains as such, seeking explanation in lexical transfers and dialect contact phenomena, where I have proposed (Johnston 1989, 1992) something of a compromise, postulating two chains operating on the top half and bottom half of the long vowel system (and allied diphthongs) separately. The arguments for such a structure are best summarised in the 1992 article, and the viewpoint on the GVS taken in both chapters rests on the two–chain hypothesis.

12. While Catford (1957b) does count this nucleus as part of the basic system, many north-eastern

varieties lack it, and one could argue that it is an 'extra' nucleus like the A and E vowels mentioned below. I am considering it as basic mostly for tradition's sake and to highlight the differences of the Northern dialects from the rest.

13. It is likely that Catford must have followed similar methodology, since his numbers of vowels square with the totals arrived at by this analysis.

14. In some dialects, including most Mid-Scots, these two words, and all Older Scots /ɛ·θ/, belong to MATE.

15. Fair Isle and Whalsay develop final MATE further, to [ɜi ~ ɤi], which implies transfer to BAIT.

16. See also *glebe* = [gləib] (Mather and Speitel 1986: 2, 26).

17. However, *weigh* and *swey* = [i:], indicating that they come from an early Older Scots */e:i/, not */ɛi/, as they have the same vowel as *fly*, *die* or *high* = MEET.

18. Lss vol. 3 denotes the Shetlandic vowel by [ɜ], and the Orcadian one by [ɛ].

19. The arguments for [ɔ:] rest on the fact that more peripheral and therefore conservative dialects have low-mid or lower forms for both COT and COAT, which derives from COT historically. The widespread occurrence of merger between the two in no way contradicts this hypothesis, and it brings the values into line with Middle English in the north and Midlands (Orton et al. 1978: 137), making for a more unified picture. Breaking up the Great Vowel Shift into two halves makes it easy to see how the raising of /ɔ:/, where it occurs, fits in. As in Standard English, it is a late part of the bottom-half raising process (Johnston 1992: 211). If we postulate that this raising applies to both front and back series, there is no contradiction with asserting that the top half is restricted in Scotland to front nuclei, as these are different processes.

20. The raising of /ɔ:/ is a relatively late rule in Standard English also (Dobson 1957: 672–3), although it may not have been in the Scandinavian Belt, the north-west Midlands, East Anglia or the far south-west of England (Johnston forthcoming).

21. Also BET.

22. Also CAUGHT.

23. Final /a/ often has CAUGHT reflexes.

24. *Hand*-Darkening should probably best be considered the Scots analogue of the English rule that affects START and *branch*, *dance*, *plant* in Southern vernaculars.

25. The /ɛi/ of Caithnesian and Black Isle Scots is better treated as an E1 vowel, since it is equivalent to /e/ in other dialects; one may also treat upgliding [ei ou] diphthongs as /e o/ in certain areas.

26. Mather and Speitel (1986: 63) list one south Banffshire variety with [ɛ̃i] for both BITE and TRY, but this could be an idiolectal peculiarity.

27. In Northern Scots only; Southern Scots has /ʌu/ too, but here it is likely that this is due to Pennine Diphthongisation from an earlier /u:/.

28. In peripheral dialects.

29. The Central Belt-based Glottalling is not identical to Southern English Glottalling, as Macaulay (1991: 35) points out. The Scottish rule (like Northern English versions) strongly disfavours two glottal stops in subsequent syllables unless the second one is before a syllabic /n/, so that *got it* is likely to be [gotʰɛ̃ʔ] rather than [goʔɛ̃ʔ]; Northern English would have a T-to-R Rule here (Wells 1982: 370). There seems to be no such constraint in broad Cockney, although there is in 'mesolectal' types (Wells 1982: 326).

30. Gaelic, however, has both 'clear' and 'dark' /l/ phonemes in contrast with each other (Borgstrom 1940: 68–70).

31. It is more common in Orcadian to devoice final voiced obstruents, and LSS vol. 3 records one South Ronaldsay informant doing so (Mather and Speitel 1986: 26–7).

32. See also a sixteenth-century Yorkshire case of Labialisation, which gave the place-name *Faulsgrave*, where the first syllable comes from an Old Norse *hvalr* (Orton 1933: 161).

33. A word *tew* or *taw* is attested in some south-western English vernaculars (Wright 1905).

12

Ongoing Change in Modern Scots

The Social Dimension

C. I. Macafee

12.1 THE SCOTS/ENGLISH CONTINUUM AND THE CURRENT STATUS OF SCOTS

Sociolinguistics in Lowland Scotland has so far been conducted within the broad framework of 'variation studies', or 'micro-sociolinguistics'. Work on the sociology of Scots (macro-sociolinguistics) is in its infancy, hampered by the absence of statistics on the language, and indeed by the difficulty of defining Scots as a language. The first variation studies (Romaine 1975; Reid 1976; Macaulay and Trevelyan 1977; Johnston 1983a; Pollner 1985a) took as their object of investigation the continuum between Scots and Scottish Standard English, assuming in effect that the Scottish situation could be handled with the same methodological tools as the linguistic situations of New York (Labov 1972) or Norwich (Trudgill 1974). The existence of a continuum has been treated as a working assumption (the parallel with post-creole continua was explicitly drawn by Romaine (1975)). Descriptions of its workings are confined to initial observations such as Aitken's (1979, 1984) discussion of style-switching (that is, code-switching) vs style-drifting.

The question of Scots as a separate language was not problematised in the variation studies mentioned above. Nevertheless, attention was paid by Macaulay and Pollner to Scots lexis; and Johnston, in a very important article (Johnston 1983b), raised theoretical questions about the applicability of the Labovian approach in what he called 'divergent dialect areas'. These studies showed that some, though not all, of the results of Labovian studies were replicable in urban Scotland. However, it was clear that the concentration on phonological variables, following the Labovian model, meant ignoring levels of variation that were much more salient in the Scottish context.

In his subsequent work, Macaulay (1991) investigated a wide range of grammatical and discourse features (with some attention also to vocabulary and phonology) in order to establish, without preconceptions, which variables were salient for stylistic variation in Scottish speech. He discovered distinctive narrative styles, as between middle-class and working-class speech, which in many ways belong to a folk vs literary dimension rather than to a Scots vs Standard English dimension. Macafee (1994a) concentrated on working-class speech, and therefore on the Scots end of the Scots–Scottish Standard English continuum. The usual sociolinguistic finding that men are more broad-spoken than women was not reproduced, presumably because the fieldworker was female, and also because the interviews were conducted in small groups. Phonological and morphological variables were extracted from tape-recordings, and a vocabulary questionnaire was also administered. No meaningful correlation was found between the interviewees' vocabulary scores and the breadth of their speech in the tape-recorded interviews. This again throws doubt on the relevance of the Labovian approach in the Scottish context.

Turning now to the sociology of language, the question of whether Scots is a language in its own right has been discussed in detail, notably by McClure (1980a, 1988, 1995). In recent years, the main pressure group for the language, the Scots Language Society, has achieved the notable success of obtaining recognition for Scots by the European Bureau for Lesser-Used Languages. This tends to underline how little is known about the present condition of the language. The *Mini-Guide to the Lesser-Used Languages of the EC*, for instance, contains a singularly uninformative entry (pp. 61–2):

> REGION: There is very little information on the use and spread of Scots language which is spoken south and east of the Highlands.
>
> DISTRIBUTION: There are no estimates or census data on the number of speakers.

Recently too, there has been a campaign to have a question on Scots in the 2001 census, along the same lines as the existing Gaelic question. At the time of writing, a case has been made to the relevant authorities, but no decision has yet been taken. Since Scots is an unfocused language variety, people do not necessarily identify themselves as speakers, and many have been taught at school that their language is simply incorrect English. Many, especially middle-class people, know and even use quite a large body of Scots vocabulary and idiom, but would not think of themselves as Scots-speakers. The draft question takes into account the problem that people may not identify themselves as speakers of 'Scots', and asks: *Can the person speak, read, write and understand Scots, or any of its dialects (for example Shetlandic, Glaswegian, Buchan)?*

An important recent study by Murdoch (1995) is the first serious attempt to estimate the proportion of the population of Scotland who consider themselves to be speakers of Scots. There have been other guesstimates: Görlach (1991) offers a figure of 20 per cent, Fladmark (1994) 80 per cent, the Aiberdeen Univairsitie Scots Leid Quorum (1995) 40 per cent. None of these sources gives any indication of how the figure was arrived at.[1] Murdoch asked the question: *What do you consider your native language? (Answers such as Doric, Shetlandic or Glaswegian will be taken to mean that dialect of Scots and not a dialect of English unless otherwise stated.)* Data were collected from 450 individuals in fifteen communities throughout Scotland, with Aberdeen and Glasgow specifically included to provide urban data, and Skye to provide data from Gaelic-speaking communities. Quota-sampling, largely via intermediaries, was used. As far as possible, interviews were conducted in the language most appropriate to the community. Being interviewed in Scots no doubt contributed to the high positive response rate: 57 per cent of the sample, or 67 per cent with the Gaelic communities omitted, declared themselves to be Scots-speakers. Murdoch's results were lower in the Central Belt and particularly in urban areas, so the estimate for Scotland has to be adjusted to take into account the concentration of population in these areas.

There are differences by social class (Figure 12.1), with professional/managerial and unskilled non-manual groups claiming English more often than Scots, while skilled non-manual and both skilled and unskilled manual groups claim Scots more often than English. Age differences (Figure 12.2) are not so marked, but are in the expected direction, with older age-groups more likely to claim Scots than younger ones. The most striking variability is by region. Murdoch (1995) presents figures both for region of residence and region of schooling (Figure 12.3). In both cases, the lowest figures in the Lowlands are for Strathclyde, Central and Glasgow, while the highest are for Shetland, Orkney and Grampian (excluding Aberdeen which is again somewhat lower). The low figure for Glasgow, for instance, probably means not that fewer Glaswegians speak Scots, but that the Scots they speak is less Scots. This lesser propensity of Glaswegians to identify themselves as Scots-speaking is apparently matched by the perception that other Scots have of Glaswegian speech.

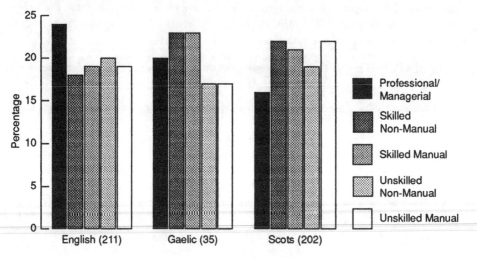

Figure 12.1:   Native language by occupational status (Murdoch 1995: figure 3).

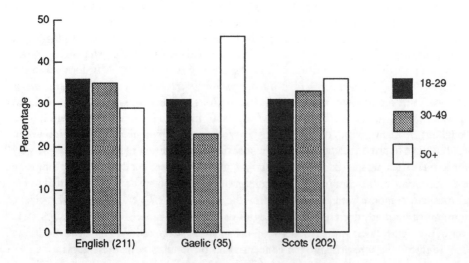

Figure 12.2:   Native language by age (Murdoch 1995: figure 2).

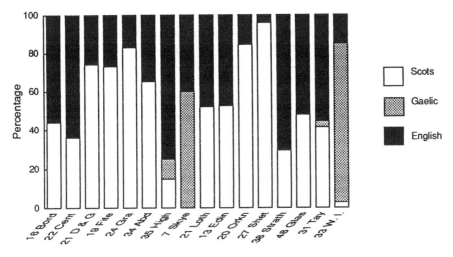

Figure 12.3:   Native language by region of schooling (Murdoch 1995: figure 9). The number of individuals is given at the base of each column.

In a small pilot study, Hardie (1995–6: 146) asked ten Scots living in Edinburgh to listen to a tape containing four speech varieties (Scottish English, Glasgow, Fife, and Aberdeenshire Doric). They were asked to place each variety on a scale ranging from Scottish English to Scots Language:

> The ranking of the four voices went more or less as predicted, i.e. the Fife Scots dialect and the Aberdeenshire dialect were both regarded as examples of Scots Language. The Scottish English example was seen exactly as that: Scottish English; the Glasgow one gave a spread result: people seemed uncertain about how to classify this speaker.

Murdoch also asked whether individuals had ever studied Scots. In Lothian and Grampian, over 50 per cent claimed to have studied the language. The lowest percentage was in Glasgow, with only 21 per cent. In Strathclyde, only three out of fifteen non–Scots-speakers expressed an interest in learning Scots, in contrast to nine out of eighteen in Central or ten out of twenty-one in Tayside.

   In the course of interviewing in Glasgow in 1984, Macafee (1994a) noticed a difference between older and younger interviewees in the terminology which they used to refer to their own language. The terms which she herself used in the interviews were 'Glasgow words' and 'Glaswegian (dialect)'. She observed that older people used the term 'Scotch' to refer to their own speech. This was in such contrast to the self-deprecating tendency, especially among younger people, to refer to their language as 'slang' that she decided to examine language labels in more detail, on the assumption that a systematic categorisation of language varieties was implicit in the terminology of each group. The terms 'Scots' and 'Scotch' (pronounced with either /o/ or /ɔ/) were absent from the terminology of females in the age-groups 26–45 and 10–25, and from the terminology of males in the age-group 10–25. The term 'slang' was applied to Scots or Scots vocabulary by females in the age-groups 46–65 and 10–25 and by males in all but the 46–65 age-groups. The difference, then, was more in the absence of the term 'Scots' than in the propensity to use 'slang' in this way as a derogatory (rather than as a descriptive) term. For those speakers who retained the term 'Scots', their language classification could be seen as an opposition between 'ordinary language' (containing both Scots and English) and 'colourful language' (containing slang and 'bad grammar').

Menzies (1991: 42) also found that in her sample of forty secondary-school children from Easterhouse in Glasgow, there was a tendency to describe Scots words as 'slang' alongside the use of the term 'Scots':

> Sadly, Scots is too often synonymous with 'slang' in the opinions of these school pupils. Words most unfavourably judged appear to be so because of unfamiliarity or pejorative meanings. There is a definite tendency throughout this section for females to rate Scots words as slang more frequently than males.

This elision of the distinction between Scots and slang reshapes the semantic field so that it resembles the middle-class three-way distinction (Standard English, 'Good Scots' and 'Bad Scots') as described by Aitken (1982): ordinary language (which is shifted a long way towards Standard English in comparison with an older generation) is contrasted with colourful language (consisting of 'old words' on the one hand and slang and bad language on the other). If there has indeed been such a change in perception, it brings with it the danger that many traditional Scots words – those that have passed from active everyday use into passive knowledge and occasional use – will come to be seen as simply the colourful and ephemeral slang of an older generation.

Attempts by language activists to increase the status of Scots include activities directed towards focusing the language, such as raising historical awareness and promoting access to literature in Scots.[2] The other main activity is language standardisation (McClure 1995). A number of spelling systems for a Standard Scots have been advanced. *The Scots Style Sheet* (1955) has been superseded by the Scots Language Society's *Spelling Recommendations* (1985). These are fairly radical, as are Stirling (1994) and Allan (1995). The Scots Language Resource Centre, when asked for advice on spelling, supplies the editorial guidelines of the Scottish National Dictionary Association, which are conservatively based on the literary tradition, flexible in allowing the main dialectal variants, and backed up by a range of one-volume dictionaries.[3] Many linguists have felt unable to take standardisation attempts seriously, sharing the view of Fishman (1980: 12) that 'corpus planning without status planning is a linguistic game, a technical exercise without social consequence'.

The reaction of linguists against what they see as subjective, extreme and even cranky views about Scots has led to a great deal of circumlocution to avoid the term 'Scots', and this operates, ideologically, as a force against the focusing of the language. The term 'Scottish Non-standard English' has enjoyed some currency. Although unwieldy in itself, it provides a neat parallel with 'Scottish Standard English' at the other end of the continuum. This means that the continuum as a whole can be referred to as 'Scottish English', and 'Scots' disappears from view altogether. This is unfortunate, and can only encourage the view that Scots is simply a part of 'everyday language' rather than a distinct code, which it certainly is in some parts of the country.

In Aitken's experience (1979, 1984), some speakers code-switch (he uses the term 'style-switching' and later 'dialect-switching'), selecting either Scots or English options fairly consistently. Others 'style-drift', mixing items from the Scots and English systems. In terms of Aitken's (1984: 522) five-column model (see Table 12.1),

> [they] display a tendency to 'drift' in the direction of the more prestigious, fully English, variety, by more frequently (though not necessarily invariably) preferring an 'English' (columns 4 or 5)

item when addressing 'English-speaking' interlocutors. As well as this common 'upwards convergence' phenomenon (towards the more socially prestigious variety, . . . Educated Scottish Standard English), the situation also offers opportunities for observing 'downwards convergence' . . . and, no doubt occasionally, of 'divergence' . . . (speakers reacting hostilely to what they take to be linguistic pretentiousness . . .). 'Style-drifters' may also be observed to drift away from preferring English (columns 4 and 5) options, as they become familiarized to a strange interlocutor or a formal setting.

He observed that the ability to switch cleanly 'seems to be most common with speakers from the most conservatively-spoken regions . . . but some working-class speakers from all regions possess it also' (1984: 523).

Table 12.1: A model of Modern Scottish speech (Aitken 1984: 520).

	Scots		English	
1	2	3	4	5
bairn	hame	name	home	child
brae	hale	hole	whole	slope
kirk	mare	before	more	church
ken	puir	soup	poor	know
darg	muin	room	moon	job of work
cuit	yuis (n.)	miss	use (n.)	ankle
kenspeckle	yaize (v.)	raise	use (v.)	conspicuous
birl	cauld		cold	spin
girn	auld	young	old	whine
mind	coo	row/rʌu/	cow	remember
sort	hoose	Loudon	house	mend
	loose	winter	louse	
	louse/lʌus/	feckless	loose	
ay/əi/	pay/pəi/	bite/bəit/	pay	always
gey/gəi/	way/wəi/	tide/təid/	way	very
kye/ka·e/		tie/ta·e/		cows
een	deed/did/	feed	dead	eyes
shuin	dee/di:/	see	die	shoes
deave/di:v/	scart	leave	scratch	deafen, vex
gaed	twaw, twae	agree	two	went
ben the hoose	no/no:/	he	not	in or into the inner part of the house
	-na, -nae	his	-n't	
		they		
		some		
	/ʌ/ (= I)	I		
	/o/ (= of)	of /ʌv/		
		'Obligatory covert Scotticisms'		
		Most of word order		
		Morphology		
		Syntax		
		Phonology (system and rules of realisation)		

Most sociolinguistic studies have been conducted in the Central Belt of Scotland and have observed style-drifting as the normal sociolinguistic behaviour along the Scots–Scottish Standard English continuum. Macaulay (1991: 48) considers it

> absurd to claim that Lang and Gemmill normally speak a 'vernacular' in which the realization of *out* is [ut] but that on occasions (for reasons of formality, recipient design, or speech convergence) they 'code-switch' to a 'Standard English' realization [aut]. Rather, both pronunciations are part of their language/dialect/competence/speech repertoire; and the choice of one or other will be governed by a number of factors, not all of which are dependent upon interactional features.

Romaine (1975: 225) likewise rejects the simultaneous existence of two linguistic systems:

> In the Scottish situation, dialect mixture is an adequate historical account of the situation which involves interference between Scots and English, but it is not a realistic picture of how speakers actually operate in this situation today. In this respect, I think that the application of Labov's method of correlating certain linguistic variables with social characteristics of speakers has made a tremendous step forward towards discovering 'system' in a speech community which was presumed by many investigators to vary randomly.

The view from Shetland, however, is rather different. Melchers (1985: 97) quotes a memorandum to teachers circulated by John J. Graham, former headmaster of the Anderson High School:

> The language situation in Shetland is clearly one of bilingualism, or rather bidialectalism, i.e. there is an either–or choice rather than slight changes along a continuum. In conversation, code-switching is realized on all linguistic levels, but to a varying degree. Most words connected with the traditional dialect are exchanged for English words (always with the exception of *peerie* for 'small', which is also the first Shetland word to be acquired by incoming children), some syntactic features are changed, such as *I am seen* for *I have seen*, and quite a few phonological ones, such as initial /t/ in *think* . . .

Code-switching has not yet come under sociolinguistic investigation in relation to Scots, except in fictional representations of Scots speech, notably in the works of John Galt and Sir Walter Scott (McClure 1995; Hewitt 1992). These fictional portrayals are very convincing, and probably do give us a real insight into the linguistic behaviour of educated Scots in the late eighteenth and nineteenth centuries. Some modern fictional examples are discussed briefly in Macafee (1983).

Any implicational hierarchy of linguistic forms remains to be discovered, apart from the sketchy observation (for example, Macafee 1994a) that the direction of linguistic change is towards intelligibility, with much of the distinctive lexis being allowed to fall into disuse, while grammatical and phonological (including word-form) peculiarities are maintained. It seems likely that for communities who characteristically keep the Scots and English codes fairly distinct, the language will also be more focused in other ways, and speakers readier to identify themselves as Scots-speaking. Murdoch's figures by region therefore offer the basis of a hypothesis about the regional distribution of both code-switching and style-drifting.

12.2 VARIATION STUDIES[4]

12.2.1 Glasgow: Macaulay

The first Scottish sociolinguistic study in the Labovian paradigm was, appropriately, conducted in the largest city, Glasgow. Macaulay and Trevelyan (1977) sampled a cross-section of the population of Glasgow in 1973. The sampling method centred on a quota sample of children. Sixteen primary and sixteen secondary-school children were selected, representative of four social classes. From among their parents, sixteen adults who had been resident from early childhood in Glasgow were selected. A quarter of each age-group were Catholics. Tape-recorded interviews were conducted around a questionnaire ostensibly concerned with changes taking place in Glasgow. The interviewees were also asked to reproduce sentences and a list of minimal pairs. The variables analysed were phonological (Macaulay and Trevelyan 1977: 27–8). They were:

(i)   the vowel in *hit, kill, risk* and so on
(u)   the vowel in *school, book, full, fool* and so on
(a)   the vowel in *hat, sad, back* and so on
(au)   the diphthong in *now, down, house* and so on
(gs)   the glottal stop as an alternative to /t/ in *butter, get* and so on.

The figures for the variable (gs) are expressed as percentages of glottal stops. Indices for the other variables are constructed in the usual way by arranging the phonetic variants along a continuum and assigning scores, with the lowest scores going to the variants closest to the 'standard' or RP pronunciation. In constructing some of his variables, Macaulay fell foul of the dialect differences between Scots and English; he was aware that differences of lexical incidence such as /e/ in *hame* versus /o/ in *home* give alternatives without intermediate variants, so that no phonetic continuum can be constructed as a sociolinguistic variable. However, he was not sufficiently familiar with the phonology of Scots to prevent this from becoming a confounding factor in one of the variables, namely (u) (1977: 30):

> In the case of (u) there is much more serious danger of confusion, which was not taken into account at the time of analysis. The tokens extracted for analysis were taken from those lexical items that belong to the RP /uː/ and /ʊ/ classes. Aitken points out that only some of these, e.g. *boot, school*, etc., will have unrounded front variants in the neighbourhood of [ɪ]; others, e.g. *pull, push*, etc., have unrounded back variants in the region of [ʌ]. Still other lexical items, e.g. *shoe, lose*, etc., will never have unrounded front variants. In the form of analysis adopted here no attempt was made to keep these word classes distinct, implying that an unrounded variant (coded u-4) was equally possible for all lexical items.

At first sight, it would appear that the same difficulty applies to his variable (au), which includes diphthongal realisations as in *house*, and also monophthongal realisations as in *hoose*. This is clearly another example of alternation between two different phonemes belonging to different dialect systems. Nevertheless, Macaulay argues convincingly that a phonetic continuum can be constructed, ranging from a wider through a narrower diphthong to monophthongal realisations, and the sociolinguistic patterning of the variable bears him out.[5] This is a troublesome anomaly, and one would like to see it explained in historical terms. The occurrence of compromise forms is not unprecedented, and Chambers and Trudgill (1980: 135) give us the case of [ɤ] as an intermediate form between [ʊ] and [ʌ] in the Midlands of England. In the Glasgow case, however, it is also possible, and perhaps more likely, that the very narrow diphthong represents a historically earlier stage. The historical development of this phoneme has been from a monophthong (Old English *ū*) through a narrower diphthong (which is still the typical realisation for many Scottish speakers, and occurs as an allophone in Canadian English) to the wider diphthong typical of RP.

A useful feature of Macaulay's presentation is the separation of the variants (for adults only), which shows that each social-class group has a clear preference for one or occasionally two of the variants. Originally, he analysed the data in terms of four social classes (1977: 18):

Class I   professional and managerial
Class IIa   white-collar, intermediate non-manual
Class IIb   skilled manual
Class III   semi-skilled and unskilled manual.

However, he found that the results for classes IIb and III tended to come close together. It was also these two classes who were likely to use dialect forms and constructions. Discussions with the adult interviewees about their perceptions of social class also indicated that there were three classes rather than four. Macaulay and Trevelyan (1977: 56) sum up the findings from this part of the study as follows:

> the linguistic variation displayed in the Glasgow survey . . . is systematically related to social class and sex, and the pattern is less clear at the age of ten though it is fairly well established by the age of fifteen. No clear indications of systematic variation according to differences of religion were found.

The variable (i) is typical (Figure 12.4). The average indices for this variable increase as we move down the social scale. Males have higher indices than females in each social-class group. On the whole, the average index also tends to increase with age, though this pattern is not so regular. At the top of the social scale, the distance between social-class groups clearly increases with age: 'The class I 10-year-olds . . . are closer to their peers in the other social class groups than are the adults or 15-year-olds' (Macaulay and Trevelyan 1977: 32, 33). There is also a sex-by-age difference, with the class I 15-year-old girls being much closer to adult women in their class than the boys are to the adult men. 'This may either reflect a greater awareness of the social significance of the variable among the girls, or indicate that for the class I boys, working-class speech holds the kind of favourable connotations Trudgill (1974) found among male speakers in Norwich.'

However, only a limited investigation of stylistic variation (in Labov's sense) was undertaken by Macaulay. Limitations of time prevented the arrangement of group sessions, which might have yielded more casual speech. In the interviews that were conducted, few clear examples of casual speech emerged, and he concludes (1977: 21) that 'it would be accurate to describe the speech of the informants in the interview as mono-stylistic, namely careful, rather formal speech'. For the variables (i) and (gs), the analysis was based on forty tokens from the second half of the tape-recorded interview and forty tokens from the first half. In the case of (i) there was a slight upward shift in the indices, taken as indicating a movement towards more informal speech towards the latter part of the interview, but this was slight; and no such clear tendency was discernible in the case of (gs). However, 'almost all informants showed a shift towards the "prestige" forms of (i) and (gs) in reading aloud' (1977: 52). But, surprisingly, men and 15-year-old boys in the lowest social class showed higher values in reading aloud than in speaking, for the variable (i). Even in this class, however, 10-year-olds showed much lower values in reading aloud. On the whole, therefore, the results for stylistic variation confirm the sociolinguistic prestige of the variants that were assigned the lowest values. The greatest stylistic differences were shown by the two social-class groups in the middle of the social-class spectrum.[6]

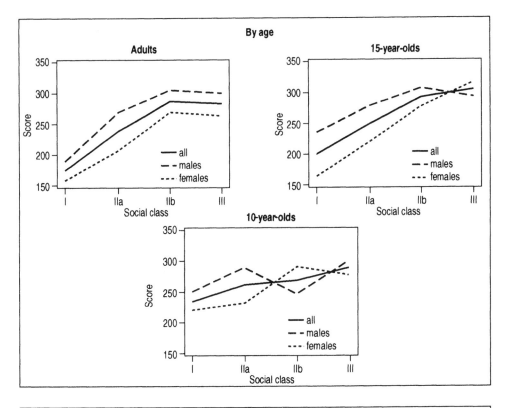

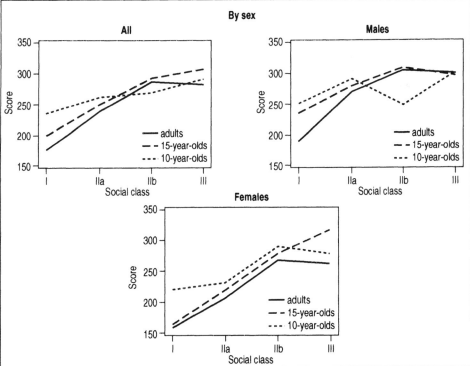

Figure 12.4: Indices for the variable (i) by age, sex and social class (based on Macaulay and Trevelyan 1977: table 3).

What Macaulay's study shows is that accent variables alone[7] are sufficient to differentiate the speech of Glaswegians by social class, sex and age. Given the right variables, it is possible to treat the continuum between Scots and Scottish Standard English as a unitary sociolect. However, it is possible to do this only by avoiding or circumventing all those linguistic features in which the two poles of the continuum are systemically different.

12.2.2   Edinburgh Children: Romaine and Reid

The replicability of the main findings of the Labovian paradigm was again confirmed in two separate studies of the speech of Edinburgh schoolchildren, Romaine (1975, 1978, 1979) and Reid (1976, 1978). Both studies demonstrate that sociolinguistic competence is established at an early age, contrary to the view of Macaulay and Trevelyan (1977: 53), who judged that the 'striking ability' of the 10-year-olds in the sample to switch to more prestigious forms in reading style was more likely to be a demonstration of 'a talent for mimicry' than evidence that the 10-year-olds are 'very sensitive to the social values that prevail in the adult world'. Reid (1978: 165) did indeed produce a remarkable example of mimicry: one boy who had 100 per cent glottal stops in interview style plummeted to 30 per cent in a playground recording where he was acting out the role of a boxing commentator. However, the bulk of Reid's evidence attests the now familiar pattern of stylistic variation matching social variation, with an increase in the more prestigious variants as we move either towards more formal styles or towards the top of the social scale.

Reid's study was based on the speech of sixteen male subjects, all 11-year-olds in Edinburgh primary schools. They were drawn from three schools according to the social profile of the catchment area served, with the addition of a fee-paying school (1978: 159):

> 'School 1' serves one of the bottom eight catchment areas . . . 'School 2' serves one of the top eight, and 'School 3' is the fee-paying day school, which was included so that the investigation would cover the children of those social groups in Edinburgh who did not use the publicly supported schools.

The boys were chosen to represent a range of fathers' occupations, and these were grouped into the same four classes initially used by Macaulay. Unlike Macaulay, Reid made the recording of a range of styles a research priority. Four different styles were recorded:

1. reading aloud a passage specially prepared to concentrate a number of linguistic variables: RP *style*
2. in a one-to-one interview with the investigator, intended to be fairly formal: IV *style*
3. talking with two classmates about topics of mutual interest with minimal participation by the investigator: GP *style*
4. in playground interaction, where the boy wore a radio-microphone and transmitter while playing with friends between school lessons, and was recorded via a receiver inside the school: PG *style*.

The results of the playground style were somewhat invalidated by the fact that the boys were encouraged to act as commentators on each other's games, and, as noted above, this produced several instances of (very good) mimicry.

Two variables were investigated: (gs) glottal as opposed to alveolar realisations of the phoneme /t/; (ng) alveolar as opposed to velar nasal in the *-ing* suffix. In each case, the score is effectively a percentage of the non-prestigious variant. As expected, the values in each case increase from the reading passage to the less formal styles, with some anomalies, as already noted, in the playground style (see Table 12.2). Reid also gives the scores for individuals (his tables 1 and 2), which show that for the glottal stop variable in particular, the shift in style from the interview to the group style is slight for those near the bottom of the social-class scale, who were already near 100 per cent in the interview style, but is larger for those at the top of the social scale; in the more casual style, the social classes are tending to converge.

Table 12.2   Indices for two variables by style (based on Reid 1978: tables 5 and 6).

Variable	Style			
	RP	IV	GP	PG
(gs)	25	71	84	79
(ng)	14	45	54	59

Social differences, both in terms of father's occupation and in terms of the three different schools, were also reported, and show the expected social stratification. Because of its high frequency, the glottal-stop variable did not spread the social classes as much as the (ng) variable. Reid also collected explicit comments on language variation from the boys interviewed, and is able to conclude (1978: 171) that 'already at the age of eleven, not only are patterns of social and stylistic variation well-established, but there is also a considerable degree of conscious awareness of variation'.

Romaine's (1975) study is based on tape-recorded interviews with twenty-four children at a single Edinburgh primary school, whose catchment area was in the bottom quartile on criteria of employment and housing. The social class was homogeneous in the sample in terms of father's occupation.[8] There were three age-groups: 6-, 8- and 10-year-olds. In each age group there were four males and four females. For the 10-year-olds only, the style provided by a one-to-one interview with Romaine was supplemented by a reading passage to give a more formal style. Linguistic variables were selected for their known social significance and the amount of phonetic differentiation exhibited. The variables were:

(gs)
(i)
(au)
(ng)
(th) as in *thing*, *think* and *something*, in which /θ/ alternates with /h/
-nae vs *-n't*
(r) postvocalic /r/

The (gs) and (ng) turned out not to be good measures of age and sex differences because of their very high overall values in the study. The best discriminator was (au). Romaine breaks down the glottal stops and (i) variables in particular by phonetic environment, and discusses the importance of being alert to the effects of phonetic environment as a confounding factor in this type of investigation.

In her 1979 study, Romaine once more takes up the theme of the early age at which Edinburgh schoolchildren demonstrate sociolinguistic competence. The variable (au) is used to illustrate differences between the age–groups, with the percentage of monophthongs declining with increasing age, particularly for the boys, who at the age of 8 and even more at the age of 10 are converging on the considerably lower figures produced by the girls in the context of a formal interview (see Table 12.3).

Table 12.3   The variable (au): percentage of monophthongs (Romaine 1979: table 1).

10-year-olds		8-year-olds		6-year-olds	
males	females	males	females	males	females
11	2	31	6	53	10

Romaine (1978) discusses a more complex variable, namely postvocalic /r/. Romaine had focused her attention on a particular area of Edinburgh, because she was aware of a sound change in progress there, namely the loss of postvocalic /r/. The three variants of /r/ which she examined are:

(r-1) [ɾ] [ɻ]
(r-2) [ɹ]
(r-3) zero.[9]

Romaine is reluctant to arrange the three variants into an index scale, since the selection among the different variants is not gradient in character, and she is unwilling to presuppose an ordering which would inevitably reflect a judgement about which was the 'standard' and which the 'non–standard' end of the scale. She therefore gives percentages separately for each variant. In this case, no clear pattern of age variation emerges (see Table 12.4).

Table 12.4   Percentage of (r) variants by age (Romaine 1978: table 3).

(r) type	10-year-olds	8-year-olds	6-year-olds
[ɹ]	50	44	46
[ɾ]	32	44	33
zero	18	12	21

However, there is a very strong pattern of sex differentiation, with the approximant (r) [ɹ] being the preferred variant among the girls (confirming the existing impression of linguists that this variant was associated with female speech), and the tap [ɾ] being more frequent among boys. The zero realisation of (r) was also more frequent among the boys.[10] The variant preferred by the females is expected to be the more prestigious variant, and this is partially confirmed by the pattern of style variation for 10-year-olds. Both males and females increase their use of the approximant in the reading passage as opposed to the one-to-one interview (see Table 12.5).

Table 12.5 Percentage of (r) variants by sex and style (Romaine 1978: table 4).

(r) Type	Single interview		Reading passage	
	Males	Females	Males	Females
[ɹ]	57	45	43	36
[ɾ]	15	54	24	48
zero	28	1	33	16

The variation of the zero realisation according to style is more difficult to explain. Females show a marked increase in this variant in the reading-passage style. It is highly unlikely that this innovative loss of postvocalic /r/ in Edinburgh is in any way connected with the prestigious RP pronunciation. If this were the case, it would be difficult to explain the fact that it is more a male variant in interview style. This is the sort of anomaly that Johnston was later to find in his Edinburgh sample. One thing that it *does* illustrate is the separateness of the Scottish sociolinguistic situation from the RP-dominated English situation.

12.2.3 The Borders: Johnston

Johnston's 1980 Ph.D. thesis provides a sociolinguistic study of four localities in the Borders, two in Scotland, two in England. The sample consisted of twenty-seven adults from Hawick, ten from Yetholm, fifteen from Wooler and fifteen from Bellingham, with roughly equal numbers of males and females in each sub-sample. Hawick is a town with a population over 16,000, while Wooler and Bellingham have populations of less than 2,000, and Yetholm less than 1,000. The sample was random, except that (as is usual) only people indigenous to the area were accepted, and it was intended to reflect the population structure of each locality. Unfortunately, differences among the localities meant that the study was conducted as, in effect, four separate sociolinguistic investigations, making the sample sizes rather too small. Comparability among the samples was lost at the outset by following Trudgill's (1974) method of using established sociolinguistic variables (in this case consonantal variables including (ng) and aspiration and glottalisation of voiceless plosives) to divide the samples into social-class groups. Each individual was given a social-class index on the basis of occupation, father's occupation and education. These scores run from 0 to 12 and are grouped separately for each locality by looking for natural breaks in the run of scores for the consonantal variables. In practice, the variability is such that there is a very wide scatter, and Johnston was probably not justified in basing a social-class breakdown on these data. It might as well have been made arbitrarily,[11] but having some kind of grouping of social-class index scores does mean that much of the inherent variability in the data is smoothed out, allowing a clearer picture to emerge. The number of classes identified is different in the different localities, with more in Hawick, as it has a larger population.

Johnston's study does provide further examples of regular sociolinguistic variation by class, sex and style, confirming that sociolinguistic variation at the level of accent is a feature of rural as well as urban Scotland. Where the findings are irregular, the weaknesses of the samples would suggest that too much weight should not be given to them. However, Johnston has an interesting explanation for one recurrent irregularity, namely anomalously low (in this case, low equates with non-standard) scores for some variables in reading the word-list. He concludes that some variants, given a low index because of their distance from RP, are actually conditioned by lento speech and have nothing to do with formality (word-list style usually being assumed in sociolinguistic studies to be near the most formal end of a style-continuum). This applies to ejective realisations of /t/, which had been scored as glottalised because they involve a simultaneous glottal and oral closure and vigorous release, and downgliding diphthongs such as [o(:)^] in words of the *home* class.[12] This is clearly a phenomenon of which sociolinguists should be aware.[13]

12.2.4   Livingston New Town: Pollner

Pollner, in his study of the speech of Livingston New Town (1985a, 1985b) aimed at comparability with Macaulay and Trevelyan (1977), in order to highlight the influence of Glasgow speakers in Livingston. It was expected that because of the high level of covert prestige of Glasgow speech, this influence would be out of proportion to the 29 per cent of the New Town population who actually came from Glasgow and the west of Scotland. Like Macaulay, Pollner constructed a sample based on schoolchildren and their parents (one secondary and one primary school; children aged 7–10 and 13). However, aware of criticisms that this method of selecting informants produces a bias against unmarried people, childless couples and the elderly, he supplemented the school sample with a random sample of households, providing an extra ten adult interviewees and giving a total of seventy interviewees. Like Macaulay, he recorded free speech in the interviews of a single, fairly careful, style, and also asked the interviewees to read a word-list. The variables selected were: phonological: (i), (au), (gs), (ng), (V+r) as in *fern, fir, burn*; morphological: *dinnae/ don't, go–went–went/go–went–gone*. The occurrence of Scots lexis was also examined.

Since Livingston as a New Town has, by definition, no native speakers, an individual's place of origin was not used as a basis for exclusion from the sample. The children were, however, chosen on the basis that they had been born in Livingston or had received their education in Livingston. Pollner again found regular patterns of sociolinguistic variation, despite the heterogeneity of the sample. He is probably correct, especially as his impression was confirmed by the comments of almost all the adult informants in the sample, that there was a disproportionate influence of Glasgow speech. However, this has not really been demonstrated by his study, as the variables on which his conclusion rests are by no means unique to Glasgow. Glasgow was probably the place of origin of the glottal stop in British urban speech, for instance, but it is by now so well established throughout Central Scotland that it would be extremely difficult to isolate the particular influence of present-day Glaswegian in spreading it.

12.2.5   The East Neuk of Fife: Hettinga

Like Johnston, Hettinga (1981) applied sociolinguistic methodology in rural Scotland. Again, the sample size was very small, twelve informants in four age-groups. Unfortunately, Hettinga does not state whether both males and females were interviewed. He found that variants historically associated with Central Scotland were infiltrating the area under investigation, as Johnston had also discovered in the Borders. For (u), he found that younger speakers had more centralised and fronted variants (see Table 12.6). His scoring system is: non-centralised 000; centralised 100; greatly centralised and fronted 200. As confirmation that this represents change in progress, he comments (1981: 43):

The older informants pronounce *fruit* in standard with a non-centralised /u/. Also their /u/ in a word like *house* is not centralised. The younger informants, however, pronounce both *fruit* and *house* with a very centralised /u/. It seems that the older informants model their standard pronunciation of a word like *fruit* in their dialect sound system, and that the younger informants model their dialect pronunciation of a word like *house* on their standard sound system. If this is true, then the standard may be taking over control.

Table 12.6 Indices for (u) by age-group (Hettinga 1981: 44).

(u) Index	Age group
85.3	Older folk
148.5	Middle-aged
179.0	Teenagers
190.0	Younger children

The other variable that he reports is (au). Three variants are identified, as in Macaulay and Trevelyan (1977). Here the age-trend is not so clear, with teenagers producing more vernacular forms than the middle-aged, and it seems likely that different responses to the interview situation are involved.

12.2.6 Edinburgh Adults: Johnston

A problem with all of the studies which we have so far considered – inherited of course with the Labovian methodology – is the small number of subjects investigated, and also the frequently non-random sampling methods. When the trends in the data are clear and consistent, and particularly when they replicate results from sociolinguistic studies elsewhere, we can accept that the findings are meaningful. However, when the quantitative differences among groups are small, statistical significance tests are not applicable to guide us in our interpretation. When the trends are not clear, we are deprived of statistical tools which would have pointed to the possibility of sampling error. Nevertheless, it is just as important for us to identify the ways in which the Scottish situation differs from that in New York or Norwich as it is for us to identify the ways in which it is the same. This is the challenge that is taken up by Johnston (1983a, 1983b).

Johnston's survey was conducted among adult speakers of both sexes and three age-groups (18–30, 31–55, and over 55) in four districts in Edinburgh chosen to reflect social-class differences. The subjects were mainly selected by random sampling from the electoral rolls, except in the Niddrie/Craigmillar area where the difficulty of obtaining interviews was met by resorting to contacts through a community organisation. There were ninety-one adults in the sample, of whom forty-five were males. The subjects were distributed across the four areas of the city, from the highest to the lowest proportion of owner-occupation, as follows:

Morningside	29 speakers
Portobello/Joppa	26 speakers
Gorgie/Dalry	25 speakers
Niddrie/Craigmillar	11 speakers

The subjects were interviewed[14] and a word-list was also recorded. The interviewees were encouraged to talk about their own interests and to reminisce, and Johnston felt able to distinguish two styles, formal style (FS) and casual style (CS), within the interviews. Word-list style (WLS) extends the range further in the formal direction. A limited sample of 'very casual style' was obtained by means of group recordings.

Johnston examined a very large number of variables, a number of which again take the form of alternations between forms from the Scots and from the English systems. The lack of correspondence between the systems in terms of lexical incidence again caused analytical problems: for instance, examples of the variable (u) include both English /u/ as in *boot* and Scots /u/ as in *out*.[15] However, a number of words that have /u/ in Scottish Standard English (/ʊ/ in RP) have /ʌ/ in Scots, for example *pull* and *wood*. These forms were left out of the analysis. Even with this sound knowledge of the philology, it is very difficult, as I also found in my Glasgow study (Macafee 1994a), to delimit variables of this kind because of what Johnston calls 'lexical transfer'. This is part of the ongoing process of anglicisation, whereby some of the historical Scots reflexes have disappeared and been replaced by their English equivalents; for example the north-eastern form *teel* of the word *tool* appears to have vanished from spoken language, although it occurs in William Alexander's nineteenth-century novel, *Johnny Gibb of Gushetneuk*. Unlike most sociolinguists, Johnston painstakingly transcribed his speech samples, so he was able to establish which individual lexical items were variable within his Edinburgh corpus before beginning the analysis.

Johnston's method of dividing the sample into social-class groupings was an improved version of that of Trudgill (1974). The social-class spectrum was first identified by giving the individuals scores on five factors – occupation, father's occupation, education, housing type, and housing area – combining to give an index value ranging from 2 to 20. The next stage, the division of the social scale into the number of groupings that best fits the linguistic data, was done by a kind of manual cluster analysis, which took into account individuals' scores across all variables. The largest split was taken to be the middle-class/working-class boundary, and five groupings were established: lower working class (LWC), middle working class (MWC), upper working class (UWC), lower middle class (LMC) and upper middle class (UMC).

Johnston classifies his variables according to Labov's (1972) terminology of markers and indicators. The only clear example of an indicator, that is, a variable that shows regular class and sex patterns (with females and the higher social classes using the more prestigious forms) but without style variation, is final /p/. Glottalised or glottal plosives are rare realisations for /p/ in this position. Most of the variables are markers, that is, they show regular patterns of class-, sex- and style-variation, though many have irregular style or sex patterns in at least some cells. One recurrent anomaly was the speech behaviour of young middle-class women, who in a number of cases went beyond men of their own class in their adoption of variants spreading up the social scale from working-class speech, notably glottalisation of final voiceless stops and of medial and final /t/, and the use of *-in* rather than *-ing*. Johnston interprets this young female middle-class behaviour in terms of a reaction against the stereotypical speech-style known as 'Morningside', and associated with upper middle class females and 'a certain put-on caricature of M[iddle]-C[lass] respectability' (Johnston 1984: 177). In the 1984 analysis, Johnston adds a number of additional phonetic variables, of which several are indicators. The Morningside accent is further discussed, along with its Glasgow equivalent, the 'Kelvinside' accent, and put in historical context in Johnston (1985a).

The other very striking finding from Johnston's survey concerned style variation; this is discussed in Johnston (1983b). He states (1983b: 1) the axiomatic finding of sociolinguistic studies with regard to style as follows: 'As formality of context increases, so will the frequency of more Standard-like forms, so long as the variable concerned is dependent on style. This is because these forms have overt prestige, derived from the social prestige of the groups using them habitually.' However, Johnston also found that his sample contained a minority of cases where stylistic variation did not follow this pattern but instead produced patterns that he terms 'humpbacks' (H), 'saddles' (S) and 'reversals' (R), from their appearance when graphed (see Figures 12.5, 12.6 and 12.7[16]). In humpback and saddle patterns, the graph does not move steadily in one direction as the style becomes more formal, but either rises or falls in the middle. In reversals, it moves in the opposite direction to that expected, showing the less prestigious variants becoming more common as the style becomes more formal. The occurrence of irregular style-patterns was itself treated as a variable and correlated with class, age and sex. No significant correlation with age was apparent, but irregular patterns (I) were found to be more common among men (see Table 12.7).

There is also a significant correlation with class, such that irregular patterns were more common among working-class than middle-class speakers, and it was the middle working-class in particular who produced the highest percentage of reversals (see Table 12.8). Johnston also constructed a crude measure of speakers' membership of local social networks, based on their known membership of organisations such as social clubs, works sports teams and so on, or indications that they had extensive social contacts with their

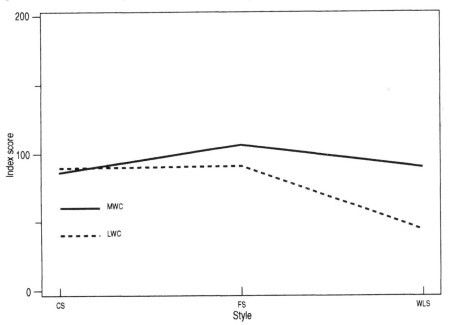

Figure 12.5 A humpback pattern: indices for the variable (u) for young men of the lower two social classes in three styles (unpublished Edinburgh data courtesy of Paul Johnston).

$$200 \ = \ [u(:)]$$
$$100 \ = \ [\textht{u}(:) \sim \textht{e}(:)]$$
$$000 \ = \ [\textht{y}(:) \sim \textht{e}(:)]$$

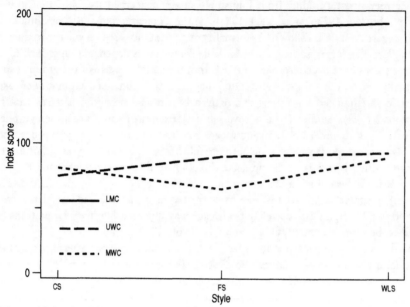

Figure 12.6   A saddle pattern: indices for the variable (a) for young men of the central three classes in three styles (unpublished Edinburgh data courtesy of Paul Johnston).

$$
\begin{aligned}
300 &= \quad [\varepsilon(:)] \\
200 &= \quad [e(:)] \\
100 &= \quad [a(:)] \\
000 &= \quad [\mathrm{D}(:) \sim \alpha(:)]
\end{aligned}
$$

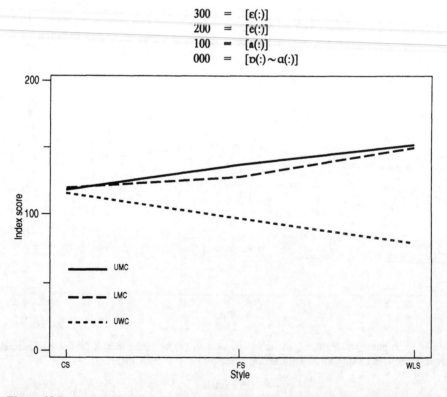

Figure 12.7   A reversal: indices for the variable (u) for young men of the upper three social classes (as Figure 12.5).

Table 12.7 Irregular style patterns by sex (Johnston 1983b: table 1.1.2).

Sex	N	I	%	H	%	S	%	R	%
Males	810	201	25	78	10	47	6	76	9
Females	702	144	21	62	9	45	6	36	5

workmates or neighbours. Again there was a strong correlation, and the occurrence of irregularities in general and reversals in particular was found to be highest among those who did participate in local working-class networks (see Table 12.9).

Johnston next looked at irregular style-patterns by variable, and found that the variables constructed of Scots vs English alternatives showed hardly any irregularities, nor did those that are the subject of overt stereotyping and stigmatisation, such as (gs) and (ng). 'Irregularities are almost totally confined to accent features, including some extremely subtle ones to the Edinburgh speaker . . . It seems that irregularities are associated with relatively low consciousness of the variable' (Johnston 1983b: 5). He divided the variables into three categories: 'high-consciousness', 'medium-consciousness' and 'low-consciousness' variables. He made this classification on the basis of the speech-samples produced by a small number of informants whom he asked to mimic other Edinburgh accents. He found that working-class speakers invited to imitate middle-class speech tended to aim at a 'Morningside' accent, successfully reproducing features that were rarely, if ever, explicitly commented upon: these are the 'medium-consciousness variables'. Other, 'low-consciousness variables', which remained unchanged from the speakers' own usage, included intervocalic /r/. He found that there was a connection with patterns of irregularity: the medium-consciousness variables typically showed reversals, that is the more formal the style, the more the vernacular variants were used; the low-consciousness variables typically showed humpback patterns, that is it was only in word-list style that unexpectedly high scores for the more vernacular variants were obtained.

Table 12.8 Irregular style patterns by class (Johnston 1983b: table 1.1.1).

Class	N	I	%	H	%	S	%	R	%
UMC	270	28	10	16	6	9	2	3	1
LMC	450	74	16	31	7	23	5	20	4
UWC	234	63	27	30	13	14	6	18	8
MWC	450	139	31	47	10	34	8	58	13
LWC	108	41	38	16	15	12	11	13	12

Table 12.9 Irregular style patterns by network participation (Johnston 1983b: table 1.1.4).

	N	I	%	H	%	S	%	R	%
Network	432	152	35	53	12	37	9	62	14
Non-network	360	91	25	40	11	23	7	28	8

Having discussed various possible sources of error, Johnston convincingly argues that the phenomenon which he has observed is a genuine one, and goes on to discuss various possible explanations. The data are partly explained by assuming that there is an ambivalence within the working-class Edinburgh groups about what the norms of the prestige Edinburgh accent are, or possibly indifference towards it: 'In Northern England and Scotland, the standard is defined more in terms of the editing out of dialect features than any conformity to an U[pper] M[iddle] C[lass] accent' (Johnston 1983b: 11). The increase in irregularities from high- to low-consciousness variables accords with this hypothesis; but if there really was no consensus about norms, 'one would expect random distribution of types of patterns among the speakers having the same sex and class characteristics' (ibid.), which is not the case. To some extent, it appears that the behaviour of speakers is expressing some consensual attitude towards linguistic variation in Edinburgh, and here the correlation with membership of networks (which also happened to be largely male) comes in. If humpback and saddle patterns can be seen as related to ambivalence about norms, reversals can be seen as expressing class solidarity. Conflicting speech goals are being met by moving towards the prestigious forms so far as dialect forms and other stereotypes are concerned, while moving towards the vernacular as far as low-consciousness variables are concerned. Since it is mainly 'the presence or absence of dialect features' (1983b: 13) that defines the difference between standard and vernacular, 'a compromise is easily reached'.

Johnston's explanation, then, is very much in terms of the peculiarity of a linguistic situation where two historically different dialects (in this case Scots and Standard English) are in contact. His findings are a major challenge to attempts to apply the Labovian approach in such areas. Indeed, it may be that there is something odd about the relatively homogeneous speech-situations that were the seedbed of Labovian sociolinguistics. Johnston (1983b: 16) concludes that minor accent variations can only become as salient as they have been shown to be in, for instance, New York and Norwich, when 'the two varieties are close in structure' so that 'every minor difference will stand out, and quickly pass into high-consciousness'.

12.2.7   Ayr: Macaulay

All of the studies discussed above are investigations of variation along a continuum between Scottish Standard English and Scots in which the Scots end of the continuum was only very rarely approached. We learn to what extent (and by which sex-, age- and class-groups) vestiges of Scots are retained in quite formal interview situations. But we learn little or nothing about Scots. It was with this goal in mind that Macaulay abandoned the classical Labovian approach and turned to the study of style in a more meaningful sense (Macaulay 1985, 1991). Macaulay also considered the question of which variables are the most salient in the Scottish context, and opened up a whole new area of investigation, namely discourse features.

His 1991 study looks at the speech of twelve informants from Ayr, of whom six are middle-class and six are working-class (Macaulay prefers the term 'lower-class'); three are women; the age-range is from 35 to 78.[17] Since Macaulay's aim was to investigate the range of variables and to establish which of these are most 'robust' in the sense that they discriminate between middle-class and working-class speech, the informants were selected not as a social sample but as a group of speakers who could provide a large volume of fairly natural, relaxed speech. The result is presented in Table 12.10.

Table 12.10 Summary of social-class differences (Macaulay 1991: table 13.1).

	Feature	Lower-class	Middle-class
I	Monophthongal (au)	very common	absent
	Variable (e)	common	absent
	Variable (a)	common	absent
	-ed devoicing	common	absent
	Homorganic stop deletion	common	absent
	Vocalisation of /1/	common	very rare
	Glottal stops	more	fewer
	Velar fricatives	more	fewer
II	Clitic -nae	very common	absent
	Negative operator no	very common	absent
	Subject/verb non-agreement	common	rare
	Multiple negative concord	rare	absent
III	wh-relative markers	very rare	very common
	Non-restrictive relative clauses	rare	common
	Subordinate clauses	fewer	more
	Noun clauses	fewer	more
	Subordinate clauses:		
	Reason, condition, concession, embedded questions	fewer	more
	Comparison, place, time	more	fewer
	Infinitives	fewer	more
	Gerunds	slightly fewer	slightly more
IV	Highlighting devices	more	fewer
	Adverbs	fewer	more
	Discourse markers	more	fewer

The breadth of variation covered here is extremely valuable. As Macaulay says, he has set out to discover what the differences are between two styles of speech (middle-class and working-class) rather than precluding any such discoveries by starting with a small number of predetermined variables. However, the lengthy discussion of phonological, grammatical and lexical variation that occupies chapters 4–6 of the book is a mere catalogue and is worryingly innocent of the knowledge of Scots philology that ought to inform any such discussion. For instance, he sometimes recognises Scots forms as the reflexes of a distinctive historical development, such as fifteenth-century vocalisation of /1/ (1991: 37), but in other cases he treats Scots forms as the output of synchronic rules within a unified Scots/English linguistic system: for example, the -it ending of verbs is treated as the outcome of a 'rule for devoicing' (1991: 36), and the loss of /d/ after /n/ is treated as 'homorganic voiced stop deletion' (1991: 37). Well-known differences between Scots and English are reinvented as differences between middle-class and 'lower-class' speech. It is unclear what the point is of describing so minutely the details of the variants as they occur in this corpus, which is acknowledged not to be any type of sample of the speech of Ayr. Nor are we being offered a description of the dialect of Ayr on the basis of a small number of typical speakers, as in traditional dialect monographs, since no attempt is made to reach beyond the *parole* that happens to be documented in the tapes towards the *langue* of the speakers. These data are of most value where they indicate change within the Scots of Ayr, for instance the addition of *them* alongside Scots *thae* (and English *those*) in the demonstrative system (1991: 72), or numerous indications that the Scots and English forms of particular words have specialised to different meanings, for example the exclusive use of *down* (as opposed to *doon*) in the idiom *down on* 'hostile to' (1991: 44).

Macaulay goes into considerable detail about the environmental conditioning of many variables, which would be useful to anyone trying to select and construct linguistic variables for a sociolinguistic investigation. His discussion of the glottal stop provides a useful summary of the findings of his own earlier Glasgow study and the Edinburgh studies of Romaine and Reid with regard to the ordering of environments according to how much or how little they favour the occurrence of glottal stops. All these studies agreed that the least favourable environment was within a word between vowels, and the figures for Ayr again confirm this. However, the other three environments (word-final before a following consonant, word-final before a following vowel, and word-final before a pause) were differently ranked in all three studies. The Ayr figures agree, as it happens, with Reid. The comparative dimension here is useful, because it reminds us of the statistical weaknesses of all sociolinguistic studies: the small numbers of informants and, indeed, the small numbers of linguistic tokens examined in these studies, make it inevitable that many chance results are arising and are being reported. The extremely time-consuming nature of this type of analysis means that data will always be limited in this way, but it is as well to be reminded from time to time of the problems, and of the need to replicate existing results.

Macaulay is enormously thorough in investigating the full range of linguistic variation in his corpus, with revealing results. Although measures such as syntactic complexity and lexical type–token ratios are not strictly speaking to do with Scots, they do give us an impression of the overall linguistic context in which Scots forms can be expected to occur. Macaulay's findings help to explain why it is so difficult, even for those very strongly motivated, to use Scots naturally and spontaneously in unfamiliar registers, for instance public speaking or academic lectures. On variation in the use of syntactic structures, Macaulay (1991: 106) concludes:

> [M]iddle–class speakers exhibit a greater use of subordination in general and a more frequent use of subordinate noun clauses in particular. Middle–class speakers also tend to use infinitives more frequently and, to a much less marked extent, gerunds. There are differences in the use of other subordinate clauses, with the middle–class speakers using more subordinate clauses of reason, concession, and condition and embedded questions and the lower–class speakers using more subordinate clauses of comparison, place, and time; but these differences are probably a reflection of differences in topic and gender between the two sets of interviews. No clear social class differences were found in the use of passives or present participles, in clause length, or in the frequency of *that*-deletion.

There were striking differences also in the ways that the middle–class and working–class speakers expressed intensity (1991: 136–7):

> The lower–class speakers make more use of differences in word order, universal quantifiers [*all*, *every*], and repetition. The middle–class speakers make much more use of a wide range of adverbs [including *really*, *quite*, *very* and 'evidentials' such as *basically*, *maybe*, and *seemingly*] . . .

spoken language tends to favor greater 'grammatical intricacy', while written language favors greater 'lexical density'. It is hardly surprising that lower-class speakers, with less education and probably less recourse to written materials in their daily lives, should employ discourse strategies that are characteristic of spoken language or that middle-class speakers should be more 'bookish' in their speech. (Though the greater frequency of *really* in the middle-class interviews cannot be attributed to the influence of the written language.)

Macaulay then goes on to discuss discourse features, which prove to discriminate very strongly between middle-class and working-class speech style in the corpus. Table 12.11[18] compares the distribution of discourse markers for the two classes. Discourse markers are short, propositionally empty items that have a pragmatic function modifying the utterance. It must be noted that the comparisons between the classes are to some extent distorted by strong idiosyncrasies in choice of discourse marker: for instance, a single speaker is responsible for 78 per cent of the examples of *(you) ken* (1991: 146). Nevertheless, it is a further striking confirmation of the coincidence between the social-class division and the linguistic division in Macaulay's corpus that none of the middle-class speakers used *(you) ken* at all.

Table 12.11   Frequency of discourse markers per 1,000 words (based on Macaulay 1991: tables 10.5, 2.1).

	WC	MC	Overall
oh	7.0	2.7	5.2
well	5.3	3.7	4.6
you see	3.7	1.6	2.8
I mean	3.9	0.8	2.6
(you) know	2.2	2.1	2.2
(you) ken	2.9	0.0	1.7
(of) course	0.7	1.2	0.9
anyway	0.8	0.3	0.6
in fact	0.7	0.4	0.5
now	0.4	0.7	0.5
here	0.4	0.04	0.3
mind you	0.1	0.06	0.1
Overall	28.2	13.6	22.0

Clause-final tags such as *and that, and one thing and another*, and *or that* are also overwhelmingly more frequent in the working-class interviews (95 per cent), but again a very high proportion (85 per cent) are contributed by a single interviewee (1991: 170). This same speaker provides another example of the phenomenon described by Johnston whereby Scots speakers move in contradictory stylistic directions:

Even without Sinclair's figures, . . . terminal tags are more frequent in the lower-class interviews than in the middle-class interviews, so that Sinclair is taking to an extreme a feature of lower-class speech. What is surprising about this is that in certain other respects (e.g., his use of relative clauses) Sinclair deviates from the other lower-class speakers in the direction of middle-class norms; in this case he moves in the other direction by exploiting so vigorously a feature that is not characteristic of middle-class speech.

In his Ayr study, Macaulay has expanded the boundaries of sociolinguistics in Scotland by going beyond the usual fairly tractable sociolinguistic variables into territory made difficult by earlier, class-biased, studies in England. Labov's criteria for linguistic variables – that they should be high in frequency, immune from conscious suppression, integral units of larger structures and easily quantified on a linear scale – are not met in the case of syntactic structures, lexis and discourse features. The latter are therefore measured in terms of the relative frequency of occurrence per 1,000 words (1991: 88). Unfortunately, Macaulay decided against dividing the corpus by genre, though he makes it clear that there are differences between narrative and non-narrative styles, and that quoted direct speech is also distinctive in relevant ways, in particular a very small range of discourse particles (1991: 143). At least one speaker produced no narrative at all, and narrative was more frequent overall in the working-class section of the corpus. To some extent, then, what is being measured, particularly in terms of syntactic structure, polysyllabic lexis and discourse features, is the propensity of the two classes to engage in a particular, narrative, style. Macaulay does indeed believe that the working-class speakers have superior narrative skills (Macaulay 1985, 1995–6), and these differences in conversational style are no doubt real. Nevertheless, many of the linguistic comparisons that he offers are not comparing like with like, and it would have been useful if the narrative and non-narrative sections had been separately tabulated and allowance made for the peculiarities of the embedded direct speech.

12.2.8   Glasgow: Macafee

In her Glasgow study, Macafee (1994a) did not attempt a Labovian approach, partly because this had already been done in Glasgow by Macaulay and partly because her main priority was to record broad Scots speech. She did succeed in recording very broad speech on the whole, as illustrated for instance by the fact that only six speakers in the sample failed to use -in 100 per cent of the time. Bearing in mind Johnston's use of group interviews (see above), Macafee recorded speakers in groups wherever possible. She did not record people in their own homes except by invitation. Paradoxically, the home can be a more public place than an all-male or all-female social setting, since mixed company and the presence of children demand higher standards of behaviour. She attempted to construct a situation in which she had a genuine interest in the *content* of what the interviewees were saying,[19] and in which the nature of the social transaction was clear, namely that significant information was being communicated by the interviewee to the fieldworker. Nevertheless, it is always the case in bidialectal or bilingual situations that the vernacular is not simply available to be recorded at will. The degree of rapport with the interviewees varied considerably, with older men in particular being more difficult to put at their ease, and teenagers of both sexes being more inclined to self-consciousness. The effect of this variation in the extent to which people actually moved into a truly vernacular style overwhelmed any other patterns of age or sex that might otherwise have existed. Class was not treated as a variable, since all of the people in the sample were working-class and no attempt was made to further differentiate the sample by class, as one of the conditions that secured vernacular speech in so many cases was to allow the speakers a degree of semi-anonymity. At some cost in goodwill, however, it was ascertained, for most individuals, whether they were Catholic or Protestant. Since Macaulay and Trevelyan (1977) had not been able to throw any light on the question of linguistic variation by religion in Glasgow, it seemed important to investigate this, and the most likely variable (the lowering of /e/ to /ɛ/ before /r/) was examined.

The sample of interviewees was obtained mainly through intermediaries such as members of local community councils and organisers of various types of social clubs, supplemented by other personal contacts in the fieldwork area. Many of the interviews were conducted over a series of meetings, and membership of the groups fluctuated somewhat. For this reason, the speech of only sixty-two individuals was examined quantitatively, although up to seventy-five people answered any given question on the lexical questionnaire (see below). The interviewees were drawn from four areas of the East End of Glasgow: one a sink housing estate, one a traditional Catholic working-class area, one a traditional Protestant working-class area, and the other a mixed middle-class and working-class area. The age of the interviewees ranged from 10 to 84. The age-group around the late 30s and early 40s was under-represented, because of the difficulty of finding people in this age-group with the time to spare. The core sample of sixty-two individuals consists of thirty-two females and thirty males.

The linguistic variables investigated were chosen for their salience, not for their frequency. Most of the Scots word-forms and morphological forms occurring in the sample were investigated. In most cases, the variables could be expressed as alternating Scots and English forms, like several of the variables mentioned above in other studies. The study is based, then, on a large number of low-frequency variables. In constructing variables that alternate between the Scots and Standard English forms, it is necessary, as we have seen, to be aware of the possibility of some historical Scots forms having been completely replaced within a particular speech community by Standard English equivalents. This situation is usefully conceptualised in terms of Aitken's (1984) five-column model (see Table 12.1). This makes it clear that forms that are not marked as Scots can belong either to column 3, the common core (items shared with English), or to column 5 (items used *qua* Standard English). The common core is enlarged by lexical transfer as English items are borrowed into Scots replacing historical Scots forms.

Following Johnston (1983a), the space of variation was defined in relation to the corpus analysed. For instance, the form *hae* occurs (albeit only once) in the corpus, and this allows the distinction between *hae* and *have* to be included, whereas *lea* happened not to occur, so speakers producing the form *leave* could not be 'penalised' for this. At first, it was intended that items should be quantified in broad philological categories such as 'l-vocalisation'. However, it became apparent that there was a great deal of lexical conditioning, that is, some words within a philological category were much more likely to occur in their vernacular form than others. The more frequent items in each philological category were therefore treated individually, and the residue treated together. This gives a total of eighty-eight separate categories of variation. An attempt was made to arrange the variables into an implicational scale. If successful, this would have indicated not only that some items were more likely to occur than others, but also that the fact of using some items would have predicted that a speaker would use others. However, in practice, the table showed very little tendency of this kind, leading to the conclusion that in each category the Scots form has its own likelihood of occurrence, and the occurrence of one is not dependent on the occurrence of the others. This may well not be true for more filtered styles of speech. For instance, the speaker who produced only a single type of Scots form, the *-in* form of the inflectional ending, was using the Scots form that occurred with highest overall frequency in the sample.

One variable was looked at in more detail, because of the belief in Glasgow that it varies between Catholics and Protestants. This is the lowering of /e/ to /ɛ/ before /r/ (Macafee 1994a: 226):

There is a quantitative difference in the data . . . with Catholics producing 70% local forms, Protestants 45%. But we have to notice that the Catholic speakers in the corpus were broader overall than the Protestants.[20] The percentages of Scots forms used . . . are 57% for Catholics (females 57%, males 58%) and 54% for Protestants (females 59%, males 48%). Bearing in mind this sex difference in the Protestant totals, the large contribution of /er/ forms from two male Protestants has perhaps exaggerated the gap . . . What we see here, then, is probably a small residual difference between Catholic and Protestant speakers. It may be that the ethnic difference is only manifest – as tends to be the case with many sociolinguistic variables – in conjunction with other social factors. Indeed it is sometimes suggested that middle–class Catholics, unlike middle–class Protestants, tend to use the /ɛr/ pronunciation. This is beyond the scope of the present study, which is concerned only with the working class.

Speakers were given a score for their range of Scots use. Given the low frequency of many of the variables, it was not meaningful to measure them quantitatively.[21] The occurrence of at least one instance of the Scots form of a given variable receives one mark.[22] The range of marks runs from 42 to 1 out of a possible 88. The percentage of Scots forms used was also calculated (with the eighty-eight variables simply aggregated), giving a percentage score. As shown in Figure 12.8, there is a good correlation between speakers' range and percentage use of Scots. This is in marked contrast to the lack of meaningful correlation (see Figure 12.9)[23] between percentage of Scots and the lexical score, leading to the conclusion that no prediction can be made about the survival of the lexical level of Scots from the type of speech that can be recorded and analysed in a sociolinguistic study. The fact that the range and quantity of Scots forms rise and fall together indicates that we are indeed dealing with a bipolar continuum, and not, as Macaulay (1991) often seems to suggest, with a single integrated linguistic system. I have been guilty of this assumption myself (Macafee 1983), and I am grateful to Miller (1985) for correcting me.

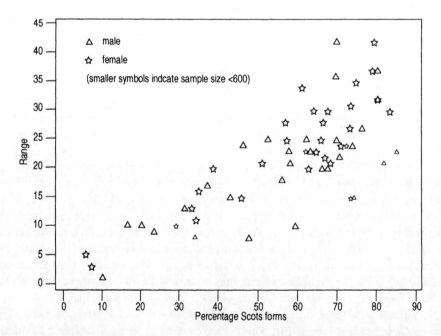

Figure 12.8   Range of Scots forms by percentage of Scots forms (based on Macafee 1994a: figure 5.3).

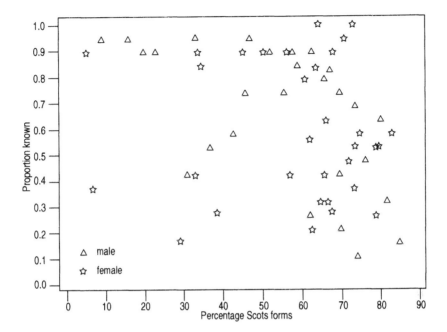

Figure 12.9 Claimed knowledge of selected 'old Scots' words by percentage of Scots forms in speech (based on Macafee 1994a: figure 5.5).

In the present state of knowledge, we simply do not know what the furthest reaches of Scots are like, nor how far they may now be from the historical models provided for instance by dialect monographs. Everyday experience suggests that the Scots extreme of the continuum is eroded, and that for some lexical items the English forms have replaced the Scots ones. Nevertheless, extremely broad forms of Scots can be produced in writing, and models still exist in song and popular literature, which we might suppose provide for the Scots extreme of the continuum a degree of focusing in the minds of at least the more educated speakers. The question of where the furthest Scots extent of the continuum lies in particular communities is an important one, particularly with regard to language maintenance, and we should not be deterred from asking it by the almost superstitious fear among sociolinguists of being caught in the act of seeking a 'pure' vernacular (*pace* L. Milroy 1987: 16).

12.3 LEXICAL EROSION

The twentieth century has seen enormous material and cultural changes, which have naturally been accompanied by a great deal of turnover of the vocabulary. Scots is not alone in having seen large amounts of vocabulary become old-fashioned and obsolescent within living memory: the same thing has happened to Standard English. The difference is that Scots does not regenerate itself to any large extent from internal resources, so that change (which in itself is inevitable) is by definition erosion. It has been argued that innovative 'slang' vocabulary compensates for the loss of traditional Scots vocabulary. This position is clearly stated by Agutter and Cowan (1981). My interviews in Glasgow, however, convinced me that it was not appropriate to equate the two. Whether or not the distinction between Scots and slang was being maintained by the younger speakers, middle-aged and older speakers in my study had very firm views about linguistic decorum and kept ordinary Scots and slang in separate registers. Lexical erosion is of concern because it reduces the intelligibility gap between Scots and English and thus diminishes the focus of the language, and because it increases the gap between Scots as it exists in spoken forms and the literary and traditional folk-culture in the language. A number of small studies have suggested that the rate of erosion may be very rapid, making this the single most important area of age difference.

The results of recent surveys are summarised in Table 12.12. In most of these studies, the subjects were presented with the words under investigation; in others (Agutter and Cowan 1981; Lawrie 1991), they were given a definition and asked to supply local words. Agutter and Cowan draw attention to new regionally marked items being introduced by the younger generation: *plug* joins *plunk* 'to play truant', and *beds* joins *peevers* 'hopscotch'. They also point out that the 12–13-year-olds may acquire some of the vocabulary known to the adults as they grow older (age-grading). Lawrie (1991) found some signs of age-grading. She notes that many of the terms used by the 10–12 age-group are superordinates: for example, *beastie* was given in response to 'beetle', 'caterpillar', 'earwig' and 'centipede', possibly an indication that the children's vocabulary is still limited by the stage of their mental development. Riach (1984) conducted a survey of thirty-eight primary schools in Galloway. In each school, he administered a questionnaire to a group of 9–11-year-olds. As in Wickens' (1980) study, both native and non-native children were present, and both contributed. He selected forty-four lexical items that had proved to be widely and well known in Galloway among adults aged 60 years or more in his earlier dialect survey (conducted in 1971–2) of Galloway (Riach 1979–82). It is not possible to construct a quantitative comparison between the two age-groups from the figures that Riach gives, but it is clear that there has been a considerable loss of vocabulary between the two age-groups. The highest number of words known in any one school was 36 out of a possible 101. While 97 of the 101 possible responses were given at least once, 35 per cent of these were elicited either by describing a context of use or by outright prompting.[24]

Despite the obvious weaknesses in many of these studies, and allowing for the possibility of a certain amount of age-grading, the general trend is so uniform and so large that we must conclude that significant lexical erosion is taking place, certainly far more than can be compensated for by the limited amount of non-slang neologism. In Agutter and Cowan's study, working-class speakers knew marginally more than middle-class ones (22.7 as opposed to 20.4 out of 33).[25] However, Macaulay found that his middle-class informants knew more of his ten 'old Scots words'. Pollner discovered that his middle-class informants scored better on the more arcane terms, for instance those gleaned from the *Linguistic Atlas of Scotland*. Aitken (1979: 108) explained Macaulay's results in terms of the middle classes being better read in Scottish literature.[26] Macaulay (1991: 261) compares his middle-class speakers to semi-speakers or near-passive bilinguals. Clearly, one can obtain very different results in this kind of investigation, depending on which words are chosen.

In her Glasgow questionnaire, Macafee (1994a) deliberately selected ninety-eight items so that both adults and children, males and females, would be likely to be able to respond positively to at least some of them. A variety of patterns emerged: some words are innovating (as Agutter and Cowan also found), others are declining, and there are large sex differences in slang terms and in some childish words. As Macafee (1994c) concludes, the approach to interpreting this has to be rather like that of linguistic geography, where we

Table 12.12   Mean percentages of lexical items known and used in several studies. In most case, the percentages have been calculated from the published figures. In some cases, the figures have been calculated from lists. In the case of Lawrie (1991), only Scots responses have been counted. In the case of Wickens (1980), two items where 'use' is higher than 'knowledge' have been dropped (these were presumably misprinted). 'No.' number of individuals.

Study	Place	Source of words	Number of words no.	Adults % known	Adults % used	Elderly no.	Elderly % known	Elderly % used	Middle-aged no.	Middle-aged % known	Teenagers no.	Teenagers % known	Teenagers % used	Children no.	Children % known	Children % used
Graham (1979)	Shetland	Jakobsen 1890s	360	29.1							1	18.1				
Wickens (1980)	Caithness	dialect glossary (Geddes)	461	44.8	27.2						34	26.1	13.5			
Macaulay and Trevelyan (1977)	Glasgow	'old Scots words'	10	78							16	33				
Pollner (1985c)	Livingston	"	23	45							9	26				
Nässén (1989)	Shetland	Jakobsen's dictionary (1921)	323	c.20												
Hettinga (1981)	Fife	'old Fife words'	21			3	81		3	57.1	3	23.8		3	7.1	
Aguter and Cowan (1981)	Stirlingshire	Linguistic Atlas of Scotland	33			10	77.3	52.1						10	52.1	33.6
Lawrie (1991)	Fife	"	20			16	23.3	12.2						16	9.8	6.9

can discern patterns of isogloss bundles, but there is also a great deal of 'noise'. Whether we can attach any significance to the observed patterns hinges very largely on whether we can relate them meaningfully to extralinguistic factors.

In Macafee's Glasgow study, adults frequently commented that a given word would not be known to children. On the whole, interviewees' comments about the status and usage of lexical items were confirmed by the results of the lexical questionnaire: for instance, words that were described as 'slang' were known and especially used more by men. Unusually, predictions about young people's ignorance of vocabulary items were often inaccurate. This appeared to be a stereotyped view within the community. The interviewees' comments imply that there has been an abrupt loss of vocabulary. In Figures 12.10 and 12.11, the results for nineteen lexical items that do show a pattern of decline by age have been combined in order to see whether there is an abrupt transition by age. On the contrary, the decline appears to be gradual. However, the graph for 'use' conceals as much as it reveals. In response to the question of whether they used a particular lexical item, interviewees frequently replied to the effect that they had formerly used a certain word but no longer did.[27] These comments came mostly from people aged over 40 (in 1984). Their insistent distinction between past and present usage was not anticipated in designing the questionnaire, and so the question about use was not subtle enough to detect the real difference between the older generation of adults and the younger, which lies in the distinction between using words as normal everyday terms, and using them, if at all, as stylistically marked alternatives to Standard English. The older generation, having participated in the changes, were particularly conscious of the demise of earlier speech habits.

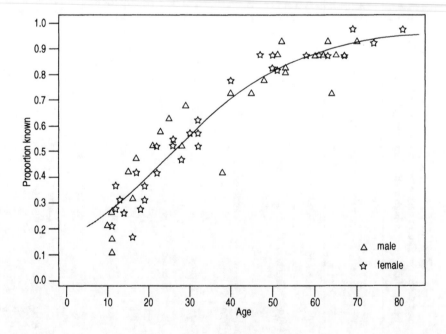

Figure 12.10   Claimed knowledge of selected 'old Scots' words by age (based on Macafee 1994a: figure 4.3).

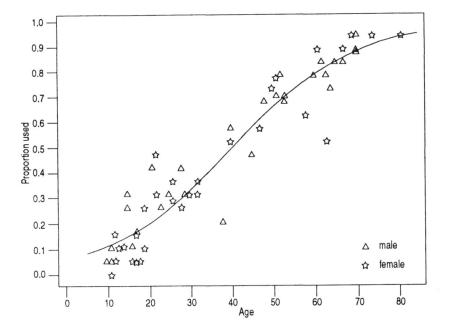

Figure 12.11   Claimed use of selected 'old Scots' words by age (based on Macafee 1994a: figure 4.6).

Also particularly striking were the recurrent accounts of adults (grandparents and even parents) altering their language in deference to their (grand-)children's education (Macafee 1994a: 189):[28]

> 46M7PS: But the whole point is, see, Caroline, Ah get – Ah cannae get sayin – see ma wee grankiddies? They [i.e. the parents]'re: 'Don't – [listen to] yer granda, that's no how ye say the things, that's – Ah'm gettin knoacked back. Ah'm gettin knoacked back wi sayin Scotch words. Ah'm – A'm feart tae – Ah'm feart tae say tae wee Graham, 'Dae –' – 'Get –' Ah try tae sometimes – an then Ah'll say, 'Oh, Christ, Ah better no say that, cos is faither disnae waant me.' He's – he's got tae get broat up wi – is Eng[lish] – is diction's goat tae be –

Word forms too show erosion, as we saw in the discussion of the difficulty of constructing sociolinguistic variables involving pairs of cognates such as *hoose* and *house*. In Macafee's Glasgow study, evidence was found of past erosion in the form of lexical conditioning. Some words are much more likely to occur in their Scots form, and some did not occur in this form at all in her data. In the word class exemplified by *hame* vs *home*, for instance, only /o/ forms occurred for the words *rope, toe, ghost* and *bone*. It was noticeable that items of general slang and colloquial idioms presumably imported into Glasgow speech from furth of Scotland were not scotticised in word form: for example, she recorded *deid* but *dead lucky*. Within her data, however, there was no evidence of age-differentiation in the use of word forms. In contrast, Hettinga (1981: 41) found that his three middle-aged subjects had shifted a small number of items (variably or absolutely) to Standard English phonemes, relative to the Scots system presented by the three older subjects. The six young subjects had shifted a large number of words (mostly invariably) to Standard English phonemes, for example giving *beat* the vowel of *beet*, whereas the traditional Fife dialect has a separate phoneme to which words of the *beat* class belong. These results were elicited by asking subjects to pronounce a word (spoken in English by the researcher) both as they would pronounce it in speaking to non-dialect speakers and as they would when speaking to local people. Another sign of erosion of word forms in Macafee's Glasgow data was the occurrence of etymologically incorrect forms, including interdialect forms such as *wroang* for Scots *wrang* and English *wrong*, or *broat* for Scots *brocht*, English *brought*.

The methodological obstacles to investigating lexical erosion in a systematic and reliable way are enormous. As we have seen, the results depend very much on which items are selected. However, some selection is unavoidable, given the sheer size of the lexicon. I estimate that for the north-east of Scotland and Angus, one would have to ask about 20,000 individual questions in order to cover all the senses and forms of items recorded in *The Concise Scots Dictionary* as current in this area in the twentieth century. In the North-East Language Project, presently under way at the University of Aberdeen, it is planned to develop proficiency tests in North-eastern Scots, based on lexis, word form and grammar. The intention is to stratify the lexis according to its present-day currency, so that this can be translated into levels of difficulty in a testing context. In order to do this, it is planned to recruit panels of local dialect speakers as experts. The indications of currency in the dictionary record are not, and probably could never be, adequate to this purpose. Only people who are immersed in the life of a Scots-speaking community can judge, without an enormous research effort, which words are in common use, which are passing out of use, and which are barely remembered, particularly as the situation is so fluid.[29]

As part of the North East Language Project, Briege McGarrity[30] is deriving measures of attitudes towards North-eastern Scots from an attitude questionnaire administered to a random sample of Aberdonians in three wards of the city. The development of these research instruments is the first phase of what is intended to be a large-scale sociolinguistic investigation. Proficiency and attitude scores, together with tape-recorded samples of speech, will be used as indicators of language maintenance and correlated with independent social variables. The aim is to arrive at a prognosis for the survival of North-eastern Scots, and to identify factors favouring its survival, in the hope that these can be strengthened by raising consciousness in the community and by educational intervention.

12.4   CONCLUSION

From the research surveyed above, we may conclude that Scots is already a long way along a trajectory which is taking it towards integration with English as the continuum between the two shrinks, apparently inexorably, towards the English pole. It seems likely that broad dialects of Scots will survive only in communities that have some degree of immunity to hegemonic external forces, which usually means rural communities with sufficient economic resources to prevent massive migration of the younger generation and sufficient self-assurance to absorb and nativise incomers. The north-east, Orkney and Shetland are the places that best fulfil these criteria. A particular characteristic of these areas is the vertical integration of the community. Middle-class people, including teachers, who have grown up in the area speaking the local dialect and participating in the local culture, are able to provide children with role models, demonstrating by example that local people can succeed, and that they can be bidialectal.[31]

Nevertheless, the corpus of the language is so large that a great deal could be lost and much would still remain, as we see in residual Scotticisms present even in the speech of the anglicised middle classes in the cities. There are reasons to hope that the process of decline may have reached a plateau. Much of the vocabulary loss within living memory is related to change in material culture. It may be that the surviving vocabulary has, to some extent, been stripped back to a semantic core that will not be so susceptible to external change.

NOTES

1. The discrepancy in the figures is not surprising since they are little more than guesses. Similarly oscillating figures have been offered for other minority languages: de Vries quotes estimates for Breton ranging from 600,000 to 3,200,000 and for Occitan from 950,000 to 14 million (1985: 214).
2. Menzies' small study (1991) indicated that short discussions with children about the historical differences between Scots and English, the status of Scots, Glasgow dialect and so on had the effect of changing their reaction to poetry readings in Scots in a more positive direction.
3. It will probably be clear which I favour.
4. The names of variables are standardised across studies below.
5. However, in Macaulay (1991) the variable (au) *is* treated as a simple alternation between a monophthongal and a diphthongal variant.
6. Macaulay's results at this point are presented in terms of the original four social classes.
7. This leaves aside the two variables which do in fact extend into the realm of dialect differences.
8. Unfortunately (in view of the unusual sound change affecting /r/), Romaine does not tell us exactly which area of Edinburgh this was, presumably in the interests of preserving the anonymity of her subjects.
9. Johnston (1983a: 28), however, interprets this variant phonetically as strongly pharyngealised colouring on the preceding vowel.
10. Romaine gives figures across a range of phonetic environments.
11. This *ad hoc* method of Trudgill's is extremely questionable.
12. The latter applies only to the Scottish localities. In this and other cases, Johnston sometimes uses different variant sets for the Scottish and English localities.
13. Johnston (personal communication) also points out that it has implications for the interpretation of data in the third volume of *The Linguistic Atlas of Scotland* (Mather and Speitel 1986), which is based on the elicitation of single words pronounced in isolation.
14. This used a questionnaire originally designed by Romaine, who preceded Johnston as researcher on the project.
15. The front–backness (and to a lesser extent the height) of the vowel is the variable dimension under examination.
16. I would like to thank Paul Johnston for providing the unpublished data on which Figures 12.5–12.7 are based.
17. Little reference is made to age differences, apart from the unjustified conclusion that because *for to* infinitives correlate with age in this corpus 'this construction may be about to disappear from Ayr speech' (1991: 106).
18. The figures here do not precisely correspond to those in Macaulay's text (1991: 144) or to his table 10.4 because of small discrepancies that crept into Macaulay's published figures (personal communication). For some reason, Macaulay subsumes the Scots forms *och* and *ach* under *oh* (1991: 151).
19. This is in contrast to the bland and desultory conversational ploys that are usually adopted in sociolinguistic interviews, merely to extract speech of some kind.
20. This is not a meaningful finding in itself, since the figures for Protestants and Catholics could not be cross-tabulated with any measure of social class.

21. Figures for the individual variables are given in Macafee (1988: table 5.2).
22. The broader /ɛr/ forms (see above) also receive a mark.
23. There is in fact a slight negative correlation, because of an effect of age and sex. As mentioned above, older men tended not to produce a very broad style. The children in the sample did tend to speak broadly.
24. The number of possible responses was 101 rather than 44 because the stimulus items often had a range of acceptable synonyms.
25. Figures are derived from Agutter and Cowan (1981: table 3).
26. In Lawrie's study also (1991: 22), a slight difference between males and females seemed to be attributable to females having read more in Scots than males.
27. Lawrie (1991: 22) also found that in a number of cases her Fife informants stated that they had used certain words when they were younger but no longer did so.
28. This speaker was unusually frank because he was under the influence of alcohol, and his speech is therefore rather disfluent. This was not characteristic of the interviews, which were notably articulate as well as insightful.
29. Ian Hendry has already developed proficiency tests for use with primary-school children, based on vocabulary known to middle-aged adults in the north-east (research in progress for a University of Aberdeen M.Litt.).
30. Research in progress for a University of Aberdeen M.Phil.
31. In the cultural realm, perhaps most important to the future survival of a lexically rich, elaborated register of Scots is its high status in the folk community. Because of the importance of performance and participation in folk song and storytelling, the language is able to propagate itself through this form of culture in a way that it does not through the written word.

Part III

Scots and Gaelic, and Scots furth of Scotland

13

The Scots–Gaelic Interface

Colm Ó Baoill

13.1 INTRODUCTION

Just as Scots is a sister of English, so also the Gaelic of Scotland is a sister of the Gaelic of Ireland and of the Gaelic of the Isle of Man (called Manx in English). The mother of all three, which we may call simply Gaelic, was still very much alive in the seventeenth century. Up until that time, those who wrote in Gaelic used a standard literary language, understood by the literati in all parts of the Gaelic world from Sutherland to Cork. An interesting account (from an Irish viewpoint) of how this standard language and the various vernacular dialects would have interacted in the sixteenth century may be found in Ó Cuív (1951: 48). The oldest form of the standard that we have is the language of the period c. AD 600–900, usually called 'Old Irish' – but this use of the word 'Irish' is a misapplication (popular among English-speakers in both Ireland and Scotland), for that period of the language would be more accurately called 'Old Gaelic'. Even in that early period, we find a few borrowings (such as *sebac* 'a hawk', *séol* 'a sail') into Gaelic from Anglo-Saxon, the parent of Scots, long before Scots emerges as distinct from English.

In spite of the conclusion in Jackson's (1951) famous paper that the spoken Gaelic of Scotland did not diverge noticeably from that of Ireland until about AD 1200, it is now accepted by scholars that the language probably started to diverge, to some degree, shortly after it reached Scotland, perhaps about the fourth century. MacAulay's review (1975: 86) of Jackson's (1972) edition of *The Gaelic Notes in the Book of Deer* seriously questions the suggestion there that the language of these *Notes*, written in Aberdeenshire in the 1130s, is indistinguishable from the Middle 'Irish' being spoken at the same time in Ireland. Some of the features which distinguish modern Scottish Gaelic from modern Irish Gaelic were already in place in the twelfth century. One example is the occurrence of 'hiatus', between two vowels, in certain words in the early language and in Scottish Gaelic, while Irish has dispensed with the hiatus since the twelfth century: thus in 'Old Irish' the word for a raven is *fïäch*, a disyllable maintained as such in Scottish Gaelic, where the spelling is *fitheach*; in Irish the hiatus between the two vowels has been lost, and *fiach* 'a raven' is monosyllabic.

13.2 BORROWINGS 1200–1300

Already probably in the process of developing distinctive Scottish features, Gaelic in the ninth century became the dominant language of the northern part of Scotland as the Scots expanded their power in Pictland. The further expansion of the Scots southwards in the eleventh century brings Gaelic place-names to the south and south-west, though the oldest element in Galloway place-names may date from a much earlier Gaelic settlement there, direct from Ireland (Nicolaisen 1976: 39–45). Just as Gaelic seems to have replaced Pictish remarkably quickly in the north-east, so the fortunes of Gaelic turned very quickly after 1100, with its replacement by Norman French as the court language. With the kingdom now centred on the eastern Lowlands, Gaelic goes speedily into retreat and English spreads quickly northwards. Thus begins the intimate relationship between Gaelic and English/ Scots which is still with us, and which has always involved some degree of societal and/or individual bilingualism. Loans in both directions are therefore to be expected from an early date.

We have the evidence of place-names, summarily set out by Murison (1974: 75, 1979b: 6), for early Gaelic loanwords in north-eastern Scots, showing, for instance, that the Early Gaelic word *carn* must have been borrowed into English/Scots (modern *cairn*) there before 1220. By that time, Gaelic 'had receded beyond Dunkeld and the foothills of Drumalban' (Murison 1979b: 8), but reasons for holding that the question is not a simple one, of Gaelic being pushed westwards by English, are given in Barrow (1989: 79). There, some Gaelic terms are noted from eastern Scotland in the period c. 1200–1400, together with instances of place-names which suggest coexistence, for a time, of the two languages. On the other hand, Dorian (1981: 13–14) gives us the example of the probably Flemish family of de Moravia, to whom the kings gave the earldom of Sutherland, and much besides, after 1200: for hundreds of years they and their successors conducted their business successively in Latin, French and English/Scots, but never in Gaelic, the language of their vassals/tenants (Dorian 1981: 48–54).

Bannerman (1990) has shown how some of the terminology of the kin-based Gaelic society reflected in the early Gaelic Laws (compiled in written form in the seventh and eighth centuries) was borrowed into Scots. Even though documents in Latin, after c. 1100, sometimes preferred to use Latin equivalents of the early terms, the Gaelic form frequently reasserts itself in the documents in Scots which are the norm by the fourteenth century. For example, the Old Gaelic term *cáin*, denoting a form of tribute, appears in these Latin documents as *canum* (but also as *can* in a twelfth-century Latin document from Kelso; DOST) and in Scots documents as *cane*. Doubtless many of the documents concerned belong to districts where the Gaelic way of life was coming into contact with the new way (D. S. Thomson 1968: 59), but we must recognise the pragmatic flexibility of the authorities in accepting important aspects of the Gaelic system (and the terminology that went with them).

Some of these legal or semi-legal terms borrowed into Scots are of special interest for Gaelic scholars, and not only because the terms reflect the medieval Scottish establishment's acceptance of Gaelic law (Kelly 1988: 125n.; Barrow 1989: 73–4). An early date of borrowing can be shown in words which contain dental fricatives taken from the Gaelic. O'Rahilly (1930) showed, by studying anglicisations of Irish Gaelic names, that the /θ/ and /ð/ of Early Gaelic, represented normally by <th> and <d> respectively in the early orthography, were still present in the thirteenth century, but were replaced in Ireland thereafter by /h/ and a voiced palatal or velar fricative respectively. O'Rahilly (1930: 194) believed that the same change happened in Scotland 'probably at much the same time', though no comparable study of Scottish names has been done to confirm that view. Words like *ranscauth* (for some kind of jurisdictional power), *conveth* (for an obligatory contribution to a superior) and *couthal* (or possibly *conthal*; for a kind of court), likely to be derived from Gaelic **rannsachad* ('searching'; itself a Norse borrowing in Gaelic), *coinnmed* ('billeting') and *comdál* ('assembly'; compare modern Manx *quaiyl* 'a court'), show the early Gaelic /ð/ being taken over into Scots with the digraph ⟨th⟩. *Conveth* is safely attested (1127, St Andrews/Coldingham; DOST) well before O'Rahilly's 'closing date' for the loss of the dental fricative (c. 1300), and *couthal* (c. 1317, Mearns, and 1329, Angus; Barrow (1981: 3, 1983: 68)) is not much later. And although *ranscauth* is apparently attested only in a Leuchars, Fife, document of 1431 (Barrow 1981: 2) – and the earliest Gaelic attestation of any part of the verb (*rannsaigh*) is much later – the implication of O'Rahilly's argument is that it had by then been in the Scots language for at least a century.

13.3 GAELIC LEARNING 1200–1600

Around 1200, it would seem, the Gaelic world reacted to changes being forced on it, especially by the loss of political control to Norman forces represented here by Queen Margaret's sons, and in Ireland by military adventurers after 1169; the loss of the distinctive 'Celtic' church in both countries (around 1150) was also a significant change. Whatever the cause (Murphy 1940), adjustments were made to the social structure at the end of the twelfth century, and the principal beneficiaries were the old Gaelic learned class. They organised themselves into a strong 'closed shop' for hereditary dynasties of learning, especially poetry, maintained on a professional basis by the local 'kings' or chiefs. To help exclude the ordinary aspirant to poetry, they tightened up and formalised the metrical requirements of professional verse to such an extent that this verse, which sold so readily as praise poetry to the kings, was both technically brilliant and in many cases devoid of originality of thought. As a further step towards that cultural revolution they updated the language, and the new standard then imposed is the earliest form of what we know as 'Modern Gaelic'. This standard form of Gaelic may even have been close to the spoken language (of some part of Gaeldom) around 1200, but for the next 400 years and more the poets saw to it that all the rules of 1200 were observed, literally to the letter, ignoring all developments in the spoken language. The details of what happened are once again mainly provided by evidence from Ireland (Knott 1966), and again we cannot be sure that Scotland followed in every step. But we do have solid evidence for some hereditary professional poets, and for their maintenance by the chiefs, in the Highlands during the period 1200–1650, in a structure very similar to that pertaining in the Gaelic parts of Ireland over the same period (Bannerman 1983: 223–30).

This period of Gaelic culture is sometimes viewed as one where Gaeldom turned in on itself, and away from Europe. It seems to have been a period of enormous Gaelic self-confidence, where Gaels developed their own life and culture with little regard for anyone else's. With their highly conservative view of the place of literary men in society, the Gaels played no significant part in the Renaissance when it came, nor did Renaissance ideas impinge very seriously on Gaeldom. The Gaels carried on blithely disregarding the fact that the rest of Europe, including the Lowlands, was linked together in a network of cultural, political and military ties: Scottish, Irish and Manx Gaels needed no-one but each other.

That simple picture would account for much that is distinctive about late medieval Gaelic literature, but it is far too simple (Mac Craith 1990: 58). All through the same period, when Gaelic links to the continent seem to be permanently cut by the presence of Anglophone cultures to the east, the literature shows signs of adaptation and change due to new ideas from England and the continent. Not that the Gaels simply followed or aped European literary and cultural trends; the evidence is for adaptation and absorption of new ideas into the already existing Gaelic pattern. And the weight of the input from outside is nowhere more obvious than in the matter of vocabulary. Large numbers of borrowings were made from French and English into Gaelic over the whole Early Modern period (c. 1200 to c. 1650), with the French element inevitably decreasing as the period goes on (Risk 1971: 593); on the evidence which we have, unfortunately, it is impossible to be sure whether the French impact on Gaelic in Scotland was stronger or weaker than that on Gaelic in Ireland.

It is rarely possible to say with certainty that a borrowing from 'English' at this period was in fact made from Scots, but one case seems to be the Scots word *frog(e)*, with the meaning of the English *frock*: what is clearly the Scottish form, with the ⟨g⟩, was borrowed into Gaelic early enough to appear in a somewhat vernacular pre-1514 poem in the *Book of the Dean of Lismore* (Gillies 1981: 274.10b). The word *prine* for 'a pin' in the same poem (Gillies 1981: 269.15a) is almost certainly borrowed from Scots *preen*. The distinctively Scots words *cunyie, spulyie* and *ulyie* were borrowed into Gaelic by the seventeenth century at the latest, to give the modern forms *cùinne* 'coin', *spùilleadh* (also *spùinneadh*) 'spoiling, plundering' and *ùille(adh)* 'oil'.

A contemporary borrowing in the other direction may be the word *pillion*, taken into standard English from Scots, where it occurs in 1503: the Classical Gaelic *pillín* from which it derives occurs in a poem of the period 1430–58 (Watson 1937: line 495; possible earlier instances at lines 63, 65). In the same way, it seems not at all unlikely that the Scots adjective *dour*, first attested in Barbour's *Brus* and later taken into Standard English, was borrowed from Gaelic *dúr*, 'hard, rigorous, hardy' (itself a borrowing from Latin *durus*), at almost any time before 1375. These evident Gaelic–Scots links, however, are only suggestions: the dates do seem to fit very conveniently, but (as Cathair Ó Dochartaigh has pointed out to me) the existence of such written evidence is largely fortuitous. Attestations in extant Gaelic (and other) writings of the time are so few that a datable written instance really tells us very little about the date of borrowing.

R. L. Thomson (1983b) offers a detailed discussion of medieval loans into Gaelic of words originating in French, again pointing out the difficulties involved in dating loans. He does, however, suggest that certain borrowed words ending in vowels in Classical Gaelic and modern Irish sources (like *cúpla, seomra*) are likely to be borrowed direct from French (*couple, chambre*), whereas their modern Scottish counterparts (*cupall, seòmar*) are more likely to have arrived through Scots (*cupple, chaumer*).

13.4   DOCUMENTS IN SCOTS AND GAELIC

The great cultural confidence of Gaeldom in the centuries following 1200 was probably reinforced in Scotland by the existence and power of the semi-independent Lordship of the Isles. Bannerman (Steer and Bannerman 1977: 201–9) would see the Lordship emerging in the twelfth century and remaining independent of the throne until forfeiture in 1493. He suggests (1977: 202) that the Lords of the Isles were probably 'more wholly committed to a purely Gaelic society and culture than the rest of Scotland'. But once the Norwegians ceded the Hebrides to Scotland in 1266, it is possible to detect influences from eastern Scotland. Bannerman even sees the influence of the Lowlands in the fact that, for a time after about 1200, Latin was the normal language used for stone inscriptions, dedicatory and funerary, in the West Highlands (Steer and Bannerman 1977: 90–1): 'as these inscriptions are of a formal or semi-official nature', it is likely that the use of Latin in them reflects 'closer contacts with a central government and church whose official written business was conducted principally in Latin'.

Scots emerges as a distinct language in full public use in the second half of the fourteenth century, replacing Latin as the language of legal documents: this new-found confidence in the language must surely owe much to the fact that the Scottish people had by 1350 finally brought the War of Independence against the English to a satisfactory end (though they did lose the Isle of Man to the English in 1346). So we must surely see Lowland influence in the existence of a small number of legal, semi-legal or political documents in Gaelic, the earliest one extant being dated 1408 (D. S. Thomson 1983: 9, 63–4, 148). It must be more than coincidence that these Gaelic documents all date from the period after Scots had become the normal language of government documents. The idea of a need for separately written charters and other documents was a new one in Gaelic tradition, but the Gaels were obviously adaptable enough to make use of written documents when necessary. They had done so when Gaelic documentation was inserted in the *Book of Deer* in the 1130s: this was to a considerable extent the result of the newly arrived Norman court's need for documents (Jackson 1972: 85–8).

By the second half of the fourteenth century, Murison (1979b: 8) tells us, 'French was fading out of the picture'. Written evidence of the Scots language appears in the mid-fourteenth century, and John Barbour's *Brus* follows quickly in 1375; by 1400, 'Inglis' is effectively the official language of the kingdom of Scotland (Murison 1974: 80, 1979b: 8). Legal documents in Scots appear in the Highlands as well, and even before 1500 some Gaelic leaders are found signing them in Scots; Bannerman (1983: 217) has shown how this practice spread more widely in the Highlands after 1550, following at an interval behind the spread of Scots documents in the Lowlands. It is worth pointing out that we have no evidence, as far as I know, of Scots-speakers showing any comparable acquaintance with Gaelic writing. Bannerman also provides evidence (1983: 223–34) for widespread literacy in Gaelic among the Highland aristocracy, major and minor, as well as among the various classes of learned men. 'The evidence from the sixteenth century indicates that in terms of the written word there were Gaelic-speaking Scots who operated at the interface of three languages, Gaelic, Latin and Scots, and, although the survival rate has been poor, there are contemporary documents extant and records of others that bear witness to this fact' (Bannerman 1983: 234).

13.5 'IRISH' AND 'SCOTTIS'

Scots, then, being accepted as the official language, was clearly in a mood of expansion and confidence after 1400, and Gaelic, despite the Lordship of the Isles, was in a weaker position. It is probably in the context of even greater growth of the confidence of Scots, later in the century, that we are to view the evidence for an attitude of contempt for and opposition to Gaelic, as shown in a number of pieces of literature examined in Murison (1974: 78–80).

The works which mimic Gaelic words and expressions include Richard Holland's *Buke of the Howlat* (?Elgin, c. 1450), Blind Harry's *Wallace* (1476) and the famous 'Flyting' of William Dunbar and Walter Kennedy (c. 1500) in the south-west (Kinsley 1979: 76–95). Kennedy was a Gaelic-speaker and defends himself and his language manfully (in Scots verse), but Dunbar has the added weapon of being able to abuse Gaelic by reference to its Irishness. Holland also emphasises this Irishness, ascribing the words which he mocks to 'ane bard owt of Irland' (Meek 1989a: 144.5), and preferring to list (for mockery) Irish-looking surnames: this clearly reflects a Lowland tendency at that time to refer to Gaelic as 'Irish' or 'Erse'. Walter Kennedy objected forcefully to the misapplication of the term 'Irish' in what Murison (1974: 80) sees as 'perhaps the first instance of linguistic nationalism to be found in Scottish literature'.

Since earlier documents (in Latin) had referred to Gaelic as *lingua Scotica*, it is reasonable to infer that this new tendency (to call it 'Irish') derives from a political will to mark Gaelic as a foreign language, and to upgrade the language of the Lowlands to be the national language (D. W. Riach 1986: 373). That language was becoming more distinct from the English of England, and by 1494 the name 'Scottis' had been appropriated for it.

MacKinnon (1991: 42–4; compare Dorian 1981: 17) suggests that Acts of the Scottish Parliament in 1496 and 1542 point to a practice of ignoring Gaelic at the official level, with a view to lowering its prestige. But even if so, Gaelic was far too strong at that time to suffer in any way from such a practice. A notable indication that the Gaelic culture retained considerable esteem in the eyes of at least some in the Lowlands is to be found in the career of William Elphinstone, Bishop of Aberdeen 1488–1514, Chancellor of Scotland during 1488 and founder (in 1495) of King's College, now part of the University of Aberdeen. Macfarlane's (1985: 381, 446) account of his life tells us that Elphinstone, himself a French-trained lawyer, had considerable interest in, and respect for, legal practices among the Gaels. His central role, as Bishop, in the publication in 1510 of the *Breviary of Aberdeen* is generally accepted, and the large corpus of traditional Highland hagiography that appears in the *Breviary* was collected, apparently from both written and oral sources, under his direction (Macfarlane 1985: 235, 237–8; Galbraith 1970: 225–8).

13.6 THE BOOK OF THE DEAN OF LISMORE

When James MacGregor (c. 1480–1551), Dean of Lismore, and his brother Duncan wrote their famous anthology of Gaelic verse (Adv. MS 72.1.37 in the National Library of Scotland) in the period 1512–42, the script which they used was the Middle Scots secretary hand, combined with a spelling system based on the Scots language. As D. S. Thomson (1983: 60) points out, this must have 'shocked' the Gaelic professional poets of the time. It may well be that the choice of script and spelling system is due, in some measure, to the continuing growth of the prestige of Scots, especially following the end of the Lordship of the Isles in 1493 (Meek 1989b: 390–4). Perhaps there was a corresponding decline in the prestige of their language as perceived by the Gaels, which led to the Dean's strange orthography. Meek (1989a) has identified instances of similar orthography in the writing of Gaelic before and after the Dean's time, but suggests that the fact that the Dean lived in Perthshire (at Fortingall), close to the Scots-speaking Lowlands, had a lot to do with the choice of Scots orthography. Perhaps, as he suggests (1989b: 394), some writers consciously thought that the spread of Scots was about to force major changes on Gaelic orthography, and decided to cooperate; the Dean and his brother might have been among these. The Dean, being also a notary public, was accustomed to using the same script and spelling for legal documents where he often had to include Gaelic names in the Scots text of the documents.

The most remarkable instance of Lowland regard for Gaelic is the rule, appearing among those of Aberdeen Grammar School in 1553 (Simpson 1906: 99, 107), that pupils might normally converse in Latin, Greek, Hebrew, French or Gaelic, but not in their own Scots vernacular:

> Loquantur omnes Latine, Graice, Hebraice,
> Gallice, Hybernice, nunquam vernacule,
> saltem cum his qui Latine noscunt.

In all the history of relations between the two languages, this is surely the most startlingly complimentary pronouncement ever made in relation to Gaelic by a Lowlander. It would be ungenerous, and almost certainly erroneous, to take it as an early pointer to a weakening of Scots confidence, though such a weakening did come about after the Reformation (decreed in 1560), when the only Bibles available in Scotland were English ones (D. F. Wright 1988: 160–1). In 1521, John Major had no compunction about simplifying the differences between Gaelic-speakers and Scots-speakers, very much as Lowland commentators had done before and have done on numerous occasions since (G. Donaldson 1970: 101):

> Just as among the Scots we find two distinct tongues, so we likewise find two different ways of life and conduct. For some are born in the forests and mountains of the north, and these we call men of the Highland, but the others men of the Lowland. By foreigners [including Major, apparently] the former are called Wild Scots, the latter householding Scots. The Irish tongue is in use among the former, the English tongue among the latter. One-half of Scotland speaks Irish, and all these as well as the Islanders we reckon to belong to the Wild Scots . . . One part of the Wild Scots have a wealth of cattle, sheep, and horses, and these, with a thought for the possible loss of their possessions, yield more willing obedience to the courts of law and the king. The other part of these people delight in the chase and a life of indolence . . .

It may be that the open-handed compliment in the rules of Aberdeen Grammar School represents an isolated legacy of the informed attitude of Bishop Elphinstone (d. 1514), rather than any more general Lowland appreciation of the dignity and value of Gaelic. Perhaps the rule was a conscious development of the rule, in force for centuries, that only Latin, Hebrew or Greek should be spoken at the university in that city (Innes 1854: 2,236); if so, the Grammar School, in giving places of honour to French and Gaelic, was well ahead of Elphinstone's more famous foundation in Old Aberdeen.

Lowland attitudes to the Gaels are very readably described in Nicholson (1968), and it is not surprising that people who thought them so 'wild' should seek to tame them. With the sustained attack on Gaelic to be found in the writings of educated Lowlanders, it must be asked if educated Gaels might not indeed have suffered some cumulative loss of confidence during the sixteenth century, or even before. Perhaps, as we have seen, such an uncertainty about his own literary tradition had a bearing on the Dean of Lismore's choice of a Lowland orthography for writing Gaelic (Meek 1989b: 394). While the old Gaelic script continues to be used in the majority of Gaelic manuscripts, there is, as Meek shows (1989a: 135–8), a succession of writings in Gaelic which use some kind of English-based orthography, right down to the crucially important *Fernaig Manuscript*, a verse collection made in Wester Ross in the period 1688–93. The spelling of this may be of great interest to dialectologists for what it tells us of the Wester Ross dialect of the seventeenth century, but it has obscured the text of some of the poems to such an extent that we are still frequently uncertain about what the poets are trying to say.

The seventeenth century emerges as the century for which we have the greatest number of surviving 'classical' manuscripts, those written in the old Gaelic hand (Black 1989: 160); but we must note that the old hand had virtually ceased to be used in Scotland by about 1750 (Black 1986: 12–13). A case could perhaps be made that the loss of confidence in the Gaelic script among the Gaelic literati of Scotland owes something to the fact that when, in 1567, Gaelic was printed for the first time, the type used (by the Edinburgh printer Robert Lekprevik) was the one normally used for English. Later texts printed in Scotland followed this practice, and the prestige of the printed page may have militated against that of manuscripts in the Gaelic orthography. Despite this use of the 'Lowland' script, however, we must remember that the correct Gaelic spelling was always adhered to in the printed books.

13.7 JOHN CARSWELL

John Carswell (c. 1520–72), Bishop of the Isles from 1567 until his death, brought printing to the Gaelic language for the first time when he published in 1567 *Foirm na n-Urrnuidheadh*, his translation of the *Book of Common Order* printed in Edinburgh in 1564. He is also given credit by Meek (1989b: 394) for having, in effect, single-handedly 'saved' the traditional Gaelic spelling system in Scotland. Manx had no Carswell, and in print has never used anything other than spelling systems based on English, and partly Welsh (R. L. Thomson 1969: 180–2). In Irish, the old orthography was never threatened in the way represented in Scotland by the attitudes reflected in the writing of the *Book of the Dean of Lismore*.

But it is seldom noted that Carswell deserves even greater credit for being the pioneer of a new Gaelic linguistic revolution. Before Carswell's time, Gaelic prose is perhaps best known as a vehicle for tales and sagas, often for flowery and frivolous romances, the sort of thing which he himself calls 'vain hurtful lying worldly tales' in his prefaced dedicatory epistle to the Earl of Argyll. Less 'vain' topics could, of course, be dealt with, and we have, for example, a long tradition of Gaelic saints' Lives and a body of medical treatises which are mainly, like Carswell's work, translations. But Carswell broke new ground by combining this kind of prose with the more formal language of the professional poets, to produce a prose form of 'Classical Gaelic'. As far as we know, Carswell was the first to use this formal Classical prose, though we are not yet in a position to say to what extent later prose writing of this formal kind, whether written in Scotland or in Ireland, is modelled on his work. The origin of his new style of Gaelic prose shines through in a goodly number of Scottish features, which are not to be found in the later Irish writings in classical Gaelic. Some borrowings by Carswell from English and Scots, as well as others appearing in religious works of c. 1630 and 1653, are discussed in detail in R. L. Thomson (1983b), many of them, of course, terms related to religion (R. L. Thomson 1970: xlix).

13.8 THE SEVENTEENTH CENTURY

If Scots suffered a serious blow when followers of the Reformation found that they had to rely on Bibles in English, Gaelic also came under attack about the same time as King James VI set out to extirpate Roman Catholicism, Gaelic and incivility from the western parts of his kingdom. When he moved his throne to England in 1603, his agents kept up the pressure on the Gaels: the Statutes of Iona, signed (with the aid of government trickery) by a number of Highland and Hebridean chiefs in 1609, obliged any gentleman in the Isles who was 'in goodis worth thriescore ky' to send his son to school in the Lowlands to learn 'to speik, reid, and wryte Inglische'. Doubtless this 'Inglische' would in many cases be Scots, but at least it was a step away from a Gaelic education! The Statutes also banned *bairdis* and ordered that they should be held in the stocks and then 'debarit furth of the cuntrey'. Much of the text of the Statutes can be seen in G. Donaldson (1970: 172–5).

We can probably take it that these *bairdis*, banned by the Statutes along with assorted troublemakers, were not the established professional poets who served the Gaelic aristocracy: more likely they were bands of wandering poets and minstrels who might really cause offence and trouble to the general public. Whatever the role of the old professional poetic caste in Scottish Gaelic society from 1200 until the sixteenth century, their importance wanes noticeably during the seventeenth century. Perhaps that has something to do with the fact that even after 1650 the last remaining professional poets still persisted in composing in the language of 1200, which meant that the number of people who could now understand them must have been small. Perhaps, too, the secure place which these poets had held was shaken by the defeat of the Irish Gaels at Kinsale in 1601: the loss of the Irish Gaelic aristocracy after that date meant a speedy decrease in patronage for Irish professional poetry, and possibly the Highlands were affected by the loss of the age-old Irish 'backdrop'.

In early comments on the Highland/Lowland divide, beginning with John of Fordun c. 1387 (Barrow 1989: 67), we find the writers (always Lowlanders) contrasting the civility and uprightness of the Lowlanders with the wildness and savagery of the Highlanders. The linguistic difference between the two peoples is duly noted, as we have seen in the case of John Major, quoted above, but no direct link is made between the barbarity and the Gaelic language. This link appears with the successors of Fordun and Major after the Reformation: the King, James VI (1567–1625), seems to deserve a good deal of the credit for linking Gaelic, barbarity and Roman Catholicism in public edicts, concerned as they were with his personal, and largely successful, mission to bring the Highlands under Edinburgh control.

The best-known link between Gaelic and barbarity is that made when the Statutes of Iona (1609), alluded to above, were ratified by the Privy Council in 1616 in order 'that the vulgar Inglishe toung be universallie plantit, and the Irishe language, whilk is one of the cheif and principall causis of the continewance of barbaritie and incivilitie amongis the inhabitantis of the Ilis and Heylandis, may be abolisheit and removit . . .' (G. Donaldson 1970: 178). The Statutes themselves do not, of course, contain this memorable stricture on Gaelic: the chiefs in 1609 might have had difficulty signing a document which contained it. But similar attitudes to the Gaelic language are displayed with depressing frequency over the next two centuries, especially among those concerned with education; good selections of such comments in the eighteenth century can be found in M. Macleod (1963: 308–10) and in Durkacz (1983: chapter 2).

After the Reformation, the prime purpose of education was, for many, to make it possible for all Scots to read the Bible, which was in English: so the Gaelic language must first be 'extirpated'. There are one or two notable exceptions, like the Reverend James Kirkwood (1650–1708), who worked hard, along with Sir Robert Boyle (1627–91), 'the son of the Earl of Cork and the Father of Chemistry', to bring the classical Gaelic Bible (publication completed in Ireland in 1685) to the Highlands; or like the Church of Scotland's occasional clear-sighted perception of the irrationality of not preaching to people in their own language (Durkacz 1983: 12–14).

But on the whole the process of spreading the Reformation in the Highlands at this early period involved what Durkacz (1983: 23) calls 'the alienation of language from literacy in the Scottish Highlands'. This same process, founded on the mindless notion that the education of a Gaelic speaker is incomplete if it is carried out in his own language, has been central to the whole history of Scottish education since that time. Even in 1994, Her Majesty's Inspectors of Schools could advise the Scottish Office that it was 'neither feasible nor desirable' to promote education through the medium of Gaelic in secondary schools in Gaelic-speaking areas. Such ideas would have been normal in the educational establishment of the eighteenth century; but one consolation is that the first secular Gaelic printed book, the *Galick and English Vocabulary* by Alexander M'Donald published in 1741, owes its existence, ironically, to the same anti-Gaelic mind-set: this work, in effect the first Gaelic dictionary, was commissioned by the Society in Scotland for the Propagation of Christian Knowledge for the purpose of teaching English to Gaelic-speakers – in order, of course, to 'extirpate the Irish language' (J. L. Campbell 1937: 53). However, it is important to note that, as Murison has pointed out (1979b: 10–11), the *Vocabulary* was intended to help replace Gaelic with English, not Scots, for by now Scots, like Gaelic, was statusless.

It is salutary to remember that, though the Reforming educators showed little interest in Gaelic, they were successful in establishing in the Highlands in the seventeenth century a considerable number of schools which taught through English. Withrington (1986: 68) has noted one exceptional instance of a teacher employed in 1703 because he could teach both English and Gaelic literacy: this happened in the Dunoon area, and there may have been other instances.

As well as seeing the spread of official Edinburgh prejudice against the Gaelic language, the beginning of the seventeenth century sees the rise to prominence of the Gaelic of the common people, in the form of song, which has come down to us in considerable volume from that time. We begin to have clear datable evidence for the history of the spoken language, even though our texts, those of a non-literate oral literature, very rarely survive in written form earlier than the eighteenth century: the rhyming systems, always more complex in Gaelic than in English/Scots, will often confirm for us genuine seventeenth-century forms in songs being sung even in the twentieth century.

Not surprisingly, this seventeenth-century verse contains a large array of borrowings, new and old, from English/Scots, and, as before, it is usually not possible to be sure whether the source language is Scots or English. It is necessary to think, from this time onwards, not of a simple Gaelic–Scots interface, but of one where Gaelic stands in opposition to both Scots and English. Linguistically, Scots is beginning to lose its distinctiveness from English; politically, speakers of both Scots and English see Gaelic as the barbarous and irreligious outsider.

Among the more notable borrowings which appear in the seventeenth century are those of terms connected with warfare, and it is easy (perhaps too easy) to assume that these are due to the close military relations between Highlands and Lowlands during all the wars and skirmishes, battles and massacres of that gory century. The list includes *adbhans* (in a song usually dated to 1649), *batailt* ('battle', c. 1660), *bragàda* (c. 1647), *cairbinn* (1649), *cnap saic* ('a knapsack', 1689), *còirneal* ('colonel', 1689), *combat* (1651), *cuilbheir* ('a gun, caliver', c. 1620), *cuinnseir* ('a whinger, a short stabbing sword', 1685), *fleisteir* ('a fletcher, arrowsmith', c. 1620), *frigeart* ('a frigate', 1647), *gòrsaid* ('a gorget, cuirass', 1645), *leibhidh* ('a levy', 1651), *lèigeard* ('a camp, siege', 1647), *màrsal* ('marching', 1647), *pàrlaidh* ('a parley', 1647), *randabù* ('a rendezvous, muster', 1685), *rèisimeid* ('a regiment', 1685) and *retreut* (1645).

A good few other such words, like *caiptean*, *piostal* and *sgonnsa* ('a sconce, fortification'), appear in the seventeenth century both in Scottish Gaelic verse and in the written Classical Gaelic common to both Scotland and Ireland, doubtless because in the borrowing of military terms the literary and vernacular forms of Gaelic were open to very similar influences. It will remain impossible to be at all confident about dates of borrowing until the long-awaited *Historical Dictionary of Scottish Gaelic* appears.

Some of the borrowed 'military' words seem to have come down to us in fairly unassimilated forms, like *cnap saic* in a vernacular song, and *màidseoir Sinirel* ('major general') and *reidsimeint* appearing in one version of the *Book of Clanranald* (?c. 1680). Some may well have been borrowed before the seventeenth century, for Carswell in 1567 used *Liuetenanda* in its non-military sense (R. L. Thomson 1970: 116). An instructive instance is *màidsear*, 'a major', which I have not seen attested from the seventeenth-century vernacular; but its derivative adjective *màidsearail*, '?manly, commanding', occurring in a version of a eulogy of perhaps the 1680s (Mackenzie 1964: 353: 1689), may constitute evidence that the basic noun had been fully accepted into Gaelic. These and later 'military' borrowings are studied in detail in Quick (1986).

13.9   THE DECLINE OF GAELIC SINCE 1700

The retreat of Gaelic north-westwards since the seventeenth century has been documented in detail in Withers (1984), where it is made very clear that we are not dealing, and probably never were, with a simple process of Gaelic being replaced, from the south-east and east, by Scots and/or English. The process (Withers 1984: 97–9) is much more insidious than that: English may first replace Gaelic among the upper levels of society or in a special context of discourse, such as trade, while Gaelic may remain normal in other contexts, as often for church purposes. The society may then still be seen by outsiders as a Gaelic-speaking one for a long time, but below the surface English spreads into more and more aspects of life. In this way, Withers sees a very significant degree of decline from within the Gaelic-speaking areas, under strong pressure, of course, from whatever educational facilities might be provided in the community. Dorian (1981: 39–40) goes further, speaking of eastern Sutherland in the early nineteenth century but with relevance to many other parts of Gaeldom: 'Gaelic quickly passed from the status of majority language to that of minority language once an English-speaking elite established itself in significant numbers – despite the fact that those numbers were tiny in comparison to the body of Gaelic speakers present in the area'.

MacKinnon (1977: 143–6, 172–4) describes the sociolinguistic pattern in present-day Harris, where Gaelic is widely spoken but where Gaelic literacy was until recently rare, and where Gaelic and English have clearly separate social roles. Different registers, within Gaelic and between Gaelic and English, are visible among the young, with the school always striving towards the prestigious register of standard English. The changing nature of these linguistic roles and registers is also important (MacKinnon 1977: 149–57), and even includes a 'backwash' of Gaelic into domains where it had not previously been widely used: for instance, MacKinnon (1977: 145–6, 168) attests a growing willingness among younger Gaelic-speakers in Harris to use the language in discussions with local councillors, a practice unknown among their elders and traditionally unknown even among the young. Similar complexities in the east Sutherland bilingual situation are described in detail in Dorian (1981: 84–102).

Education, as we have seen, has principally been aimed, since Reformation times, at making it possible for Gaels to read the Bible in English, and in the twentieth century at making Gaels English-speakers. This has been successful, as is well known (MacKinnon 1991: chapters 2–7). The result has been not only the drastic reduction of the Gaelic-speaking area in geographical terms, not only the inner corrosion of that area as English intrudes into more and more aspects of life, but also a notable impoverishment of the language itself (MacAulay 1978: 86–7, 1982a: 216; Dorian 1981: 114–15); the impoverishment can be seen in both the loss of considerable ranges of vocabulary and a strong tendency to remodel the syntax on English. Since there are now practically no Gaelic monoglots, increasing familiarity with English commonly leads to the 'code-switching' described in MacAulay (1982a: 223–32, 1982b: 30–42).

13.10 CODE-SWITCHING AND BORROWING

One tendency clearly is to switch to English in matters of commerce. Perhaps since as far back as the founding of the burghs in the twelfth century, trade between Gaels and non-Gaels has tended to be conducted principally in English/Scots, and we can no doubt attribute this to the import into the Gaelic world of ideas and commodities from the Lowlands – in other words, it is due to free-market forces. But education also bears some of the responsibility for the supremacy of English/Scots in the commercial domain: even where Gaelic has been taught in schools, it has rarely, until recently, been used as a means of teaching other subjects, such as arithmetic. And while Gaels have their own traditional system of counting in twenties (MacAulay 1982b: 30), the modern mathematical system, based on tens, has been taught to them in English and, as a result, as MacKinnon points out (1977: 146–7), most Gaels today find it easier to do their counting, and their commercial dealing, in English.

Incidentally, it is worth noting that the early Gaels (before AD 900) faced this same problem, where the same system of twenties ran up against the Latin decimal system, so they coined a set of terms to fit new concepts (such as 'thirty' and 'seventy') and to deal with the decimal system. This terminology fell out of practical use over the centuries, but there is no reason why the terms should not be restored for use in the modern business world: they would have been restored centuries ago if there had been a Gaelic education system.

One area where there is a good deal of English/Scots borrowing into Gaelic is sea-faring. Despite the fact that there is a long Gaelic tradition of sea-faring, and the terminology to go with it, there are numerous instances in Gaelic songs of the last two centuries or so of the use of sea-faring terms borrowed from English, even when Gaelic terms are available. In many cases, of course, there may be no genuine Gaelic term. Elaborate Gaelic terminologies for boats and sails are given in Dwelly's *Illustrated Gaelic–English Dictionary* of 1901–11 (1988), s.vv. *bàta, seòl*, and we need not necessarily take it that all the terms are equally authentic. English terms like *gangway, mate* and even *cuatar-deck* are quite acceptable in modern songs, and probably there never were precise Gaelic equivalents. One couplet that I have seen (National Library Acc. 9711/12/5, p. 18) goes:

> Dà *reef* againn 'na *foresail*
> S na *royals* a b'àirde

– with *foresail* and *royals*, incidentally, providing proper rhyme according to the Gaelic system. And despite evident reluctance on the part of dictionaries to accept the fact, the word *deck* seems to have been widely borrowed into Gaelic (*deic*), for want of a more accurate term. This evident facility for borrowing English sea-faring terminology is perhaps best explained by the long experience of Gaels, since the mid-eighteenth century at least, as sailors in the British navy or merchant navy, where all technical terminology would have reached them in English. And yet we must note that even in the early sixteenth century the word *top-chrann* occurs in a Gaelic poem where it has been translated 'top-mast' (W. J. Watson 1937: line 2,260).

Large-scale borrowing is, of course, significant, but MacAulay also notes (1982a: 219–21) the deeper spread of English influence, in contemporary spoken Gaelic, revealed by remodelling, which can drag Gaelic verb tenses towards English usage. For instance, Gaelic has what may be seen as two different present tenses of the verb to be, *tha* and *bithidh*. The former is sometimes called the 'stative' present, as in *tha e* 'he is', quite distinct from the 'iterative' present *bithidh e* 'he is in the habit of being'. But since English has only one present tense, 'he is', Gaelic has been affected to the extent of blurring the distinction, so that *tha* often comes to be used for both tenses.

It is likely that Irish Gaelic is under very similar pressure from English and that the syntactical effects are likely to be much the same, but at least one minor detail of likely English influence seems to distinguish the two languages. As W. J. Watson pointed out (1927: 326), the English preposition *for* has come to be equated with the Scottish Gaelic preposition *air son* in a great variety of contexts. The English preposition *for* has a large number of uses (the OED lists thirty-one), in meanings which include *in return for, on behalf of, in favour of*, whereas the Gaelic compound preposition *air son* originally had a narrower range (see RIA (1913–76) *Contributions* S:341.54). Irish has not moved very far from this narrower range, but Scottish Gaelic has spread the use of *air son* so that it almost equates in range of meaning with the English preposition *for*. This is probably to be attributed partly to the direct influence of spoken English; the extent to which translation of written English is involved will become clearer when the *Historical Dictionary* is published.

13.11 CALQUING

MacAulay also points (1978: 91, 1982a: 222) to the growth and expansion of calques, the borrowing from English/Scots of ways of expressing ideas other than single words. A simple example (MacAulay 1978: 91) is the calquing of the English *he has a cold*, where the Gaelic sometimes appearing in modern times is *tha fuachd aige*, which properly means that he has *cold* in the sense of 'coldness, low temperature'; for Gaelic has the specialised term *cnatan* for the affliction called in English 'a cold'. But *tha fuachd aige* is in fact a double calque, for *tha x aige*, meaning 'he has x', would not be used in traditional Gaelic with *cnatan*; instead, the usage is *tha cnatan air*, which means 'a cold is on him'. MacAulay (1982a: 217) shows how the excessive impact of the English verb 'have' has similarly led to a range of other calques founded on uses of its supposed equivalent in Gaelic, *tha x aige*. Other selections of calques may be seen in Watson (1927: 325) and MacAulay (1986: 122–3).

MacAulay suggests (1978: 91–2) that one widespread expression which looks like such a calque on English may well not be one. This is the use of *Tha agam ri* . . . for 'I have to . . .' or 'I must . . .'; though it looks like a simple calque, MacAulay argues that at least one internal Gaelic origin for the expression is possible. To support this possibility, it may be noted that, while many calques may well be of recent origin, this expression is on record in the Gaelic of Sutherland in the first half of the eighteenth century, and occurs also in the

Irish Gaelic of County Donegal, *tá agam le* . . . 'I have to' (Ó Baoill 1978: 173). Its presence there is possibly due, in some way, to that county's close historical links with Scotland.

Calquing very likely reflects a situation in which the influence of the dominant language has proceeded beyond mere borrowing of words by the weaker language, and it is valid to wonder if similar calquing did not occur in Scotland when Gaelic was the dominant language. It might be worthwhile to study the expression 'to let on' in Scots, English and Gaelic in order to seek evidence that this is originally a Scots calque on Gaelic. The expression can mean simply 'to pretend', but may also, in a negative construction, mean 'divulge' or 'admit' (as in *Never let on* . . .), in Scots and English. The expression (the normal one, for both meanings, in all three modern Gaelic languages) is firmly on record in the Gaelic of the twelfth century, and in a few later texts, meaning 'pretend', the form of the preposition used (for 'on') being the Gaelic personal form (*form* 'on me', *fair* 'on him', *forru* 'on them' and so on). Thus, in Middle Irish, *léicid fair* would mean 'he lets on him', that is, 'he pretends, feigns'.

There is then a gap in the evidence until shortly before 1589, when DOST (vol. 3, p. 574b.12c) gives, as the earliest Scots instance, a remarkably modern-sounding quotation: *He is not so daft as he lets on him*. The earliest instance of the negative use (which is not attested in early Gaelic) dates from 1629: *Christ letteth not on him, that hee either heareth or seeth me*; the next instance is in a text of 1637: *never let on him that He heareth*. The OED describes both usages as 'orig. *dial. and u.s.*', and the earliest non-Scottish instances there quoted date from 1828 for the positive meaning and 1848 for the negative one, both from east-coast American sources. It may be, therefore, that the expression *let on* reached English from Scots, though Irish Gaelic, operating via American English, is perhaps also a claimant. But if we are to hold that it reached Scots (by 1589) from Gaelic, then we have a large time-gap in the written record to account for (Aitken 1979: 106). The Royal Irish Academy's *Contributions* (L:79.21) note only three or four instances, two of which can be assigned to the twelfth century, the others perhaps up to two centuries later, for the dating is by no means certain.

A similar case may be the use of the Gaelic *agus*, 'and', in order 'to introduce a nominative absolute standing in adjectival relation to a foregoing noun' (RIA *Contributions* O: 97.7–29). Such a use of *and* is common in Scots (and not unknown in English) in sentences like *You ought not to do that and you pregnant* (Aitken 1979: 106). An instance is attested in the works of Robert Henryson, c. 1475, in DOST (vol. 1, p. 76a.c), which prefers to interpret it as a use of *and* in the meaning 'seeing that', occurring 'with ellipse of verb'. It is, of course, a commonplace in all three Gaelic languages, with a history dating back to the eighth century (*Contributions* O:161.21ff.), and is well attested in medieval Welsh also (Evans 1964: 231). It would therefore be worthwhile to investigate whether or not the Scots usage might be an early calque on Gaelic.

13.12 SOUND CHANGES

To return to the modern Gaelic–Scots interface, however, MacAulay (1978: 91–4) clearly shows how little we really know in detail about calquing and other remodellings, or about their geographical or historical spread. Even with word-borrowing there is still a lot to be done, for he shows that borrowing is not a simple matter. For example, the word *peann* for 'pen', borrowed 1,500 years ago from Latin, is rejected in some dialects for a more recent borrowing of the English to give *peana*; but we have evidence for this *peana* in a Lewis song from the 1690s. In MacAulay's view (1978: 92), 'the situation now, in general, is that any English word may be introduced into a Gaelic context unchanged. This marks an advanced state of bilingualism.' And MacAulay (1986: 121) suggests that instances of remodelling caused by pressure from English had by 1986 multiplied since the fieldwork was done for MacAulay (1978).

An earlier situation is discussed, for one group of dialects but probably with broad general application, in S. Watson (1983), where the words concerned are those whose initial consonants are foreign to Gaelic as radical initials. Gaelic has no native words beginning, in radical form, with the sounds represented by English ⟨ch-, h-, j-, wh-⟩ and ⟨y-⟩, and Watson shows how borrowing numerous words like *Charles*, *hall*, *jacket* and *wheel* seems to have involved the setting-up of patterns, doubtless varying from century to century and from place to place, of substitution of consonants to accommodate the borrowings. Thus ⟨ch-⟩ and ⟨j-⟩ have both most frequently been changed to /ʃ/, the sound of the Gaelic slender ⟨s-⟩, as in *seans* 'chance' and *Seumas*; but ⟨ch-⟩ can also appear as a slender ⟨t-⟩, as in *Teàrlach*, and the *j*-sound as a slender ⟨d-⟩, as in *Deòrsa* for 'George', and perhaps as a slender ⟨g-⟩, as in *giùisdis* 'justice' (in Carswell in 1564 (R. L. Thomson 1970), but possibly not a borrowing from English).

Such borrowings are fairly numerous, and the systems of consonant substitution may be fairly old. *Cuibhle* from 'wheel' is attested in Scottish Gaelic song at least as early as 1660 (Mackenzie 1964: line 910), *cuinnseir* from 'whinger, a short stabbing sword', occurs in a song of 1685 (ibid., line 2,183), and *togsaid* from 'hogshead' from about 1692 (ibid., line 2,665). Different systems of substitution of consonants presumably reflect, to some extent, the forms of English from which the borrowings were made (MacAulay 1978: 92), for probably few were made direct from standard English. This point is well illustrated by what can happen to the /θ/ of standard English in a word borrowed into Gaelic. It is well known that not nearly enough study has been done on the English of the Highlands and the Hebrides, but it is clear now that, in some places at least, /θ/ becomes /s/. This may well be due to the influence of Gaelic on Highland English for, as we have seen, Gaelic has not had the /θ/ sound since the Middle Ages. As a result, for instance, speakers of Highland English are sometimes mocked for replacing the standard English *think* with *sink* (*Éigse*, vol. 26, pp. 107–9). Frances Tolmie (1840–1926), the famous collector of songs, laughs at her fellow Skyewomen around 1902 for pronouncing the English word *south* as 'sous' (Bassin 1977: 154); in 1932, another Skye writer mocks the people of Barra for pronouncing *Yarmouth* as 'Yarmus' (*Éigse*, vol. 26, p. 109).

The old Gaelic 'difficulty' with /θ/, then, would seem to have affected the English of the Highlands to the extent of turning standard English /θ/ into /s/ in some places: this has certainly affected even the Gaelic-speaking area of Nova Scotia, but much more detailed study of the feature is clearly desirable. Some of the resultant Highland English words were then borrowed into Gaelic, or perhaps the same 'difficulty' with /θ/ affected a borrowing from some other dialect(s) of Scots: one good example is the word for a 'thousand', which appears as *sùsain* (plural) in a song of c. 1692 by Iain Lom (Mackenzie 1964: line 2,652). Obviously the ultimate source here is the Scots *thoosand*; even if we argue that the initial /s/ is not proven for this early date because the song was not written down until much later, at least the /u:/ is verified by rhyme in other songs. The word *sùsan* has in fact been accepted in east Sutherland dialects (Dorian 1978: 103, 168) as a normal word for 'a thousand', with status equivalent, apparently, to that of the old and respectable *mile* which is the usual word everywhere else. Why it was felt useful to borrow such a central word from Scots, when

Gaelic already has a word, is a question which may take a long time to answer: elsewhere Ó Dochartaigh (1996) offers some discussion of this difficulty in relation to other borrowed words.

MacAulay, in his survey of the English/Scots impact on modern Gaelic, comments (1982a: 208) on borrowings in the seventeenth century, when the Scottish Gaelic vernacular becomes clearly accessible to us. He traces the increase in borrowings in the eighteenth century and right down to modern times, noting conflicting pressures, especially in the literature, for and against the admission of numerous borrowings. He cites (1982a: 210–12) a South Uist text, published in 1972, containing the discourse of a crofter who was a renowned tradition-bearer, and therefore likely to resist excessive borrowing, as an illustration of the overwhelming extent to which English is 'now undeniably the dominant tongue' even in the most Gaelic parts of the Highlands. The next step in the loss of Gaelic has already been studied by Dorian (1981: chapter 4), who explored sociologically the dying stages of Embo and Golspie dialects in east Sutherland.

13.13 HIGHLAND ENGLISH

Murison tells us (1979b: 11) that 'the eighteenth century saw the disappearance of Scots as a full language . . .; not only its vocabulary and grammar, but also its pronunciation was displaced by English'. To Gaelic-speakers, the difference between Scots and English was generally minimal, and the same Gaelic term, *Beurla*, covers both English and Scots (Macinnes 1989: 92). As Gaelic recedes, the language which replaces it nowadays is generally taken to be a form of standard English rather than Scots. This language, or group of dialects, is usually referred to as 'Highland English', and includes 'Hebridean English'; it has been described as 'S[tandard] E[nglish] on a Gaelic substratum' (Mather and Speitel 1986: 8b). Some evidence examined by Shuken (1985: 151–6) suggests that this may be too simple, that there is also a Scots element in Highland English, at least among young Highlanders today. And as to the rule that where Gaelic dies out it is replaced by Highland English, one clear exception is Upper Deeside, where Gaelic has been receding for several centuries but has been replaced by Scots, not Highland English (A. Watson and Allan 1984: xiv).

It may be that in earlier centuries Highland English was closer to Scots than it is today. The case of the word *sùsan*, from Scots 'thoosand', noted above, is one where the borrowing (attested in different parts of the north-west) is obviously not from standard English. Much work remains to be done on this topic, but a start has been made by Ian Quick's interesting study of Gaelic domestic terminology, based on materials collected for the *Historical Dictionary of Scottish Gaelic*. While a few terms are likely to have been borrowed from standard English (Quick 1990: 39; *clabhda* from English 'clout', not Scots 'cloot'), most of those dealt with are consistent with being borrowed from Scots, and many can only be from Scots (like *babhstair* from Scots 'bowster', not English 'bolster'; and *noc* from Scots *knock* 'a clock'). Quick traces some of his borrowings back as far as c. 1700.

Although it might be held that the context of domestic furniture is one in which Highlanders are especially likely to borrow terms from their nearest, and longest-term, neighbours, it may not be excessive to suspect that Quick's findings may be paralleled in other contexts also. We may find, in due time, that other areas of Gaelic vocabulary in the last few centuries have likewise drawn not only on standard English but also to a considerable extent on Scots. Just as McClure found, on studying SND, that Scots owes a good deal more than is often assumed to Gaelic (McClure 1986: 85), so the evidence of the *Historical Dictionary* may yet show unexpectedly numerous Gaelic borrowings from Scots. As Mather and Speitel remark in their *Linguistic Atlas of Scotland* (1986: 9a), 'words travel more easily than sounds'.

Sabban (1985: 125) says of the Hebrides that English 'has been present in the area on a large-scale basis only since the Education Act of 1872, which made it compulsory in schools'. This will doubtless explain the direct changeover to English, rather than Scots, when Gaelic is lost in the present-day Hebrides, but we have seen that Gaelic was in close contact with Scots for many centuries before 1872: we have no good reason to assume that standard English was a more important influence than Scots before that year. The Gaelic of the eastern Highlands at least, and not just Deeside, must have been in close contact, until the twentieth century, with forms of English (Highland English) which were more Scottish than standard.

Studying the syntax of the verb in modern Hebridean English, Sabban points to the considerable impact made on it by the syntax of Gaelic, in which the morphologically marked perfect tense faded away 1,000 years ago. So it is not surprising that Sabban (1985: 128–35) finds frequent use of non-perfective forms where standard English would prefer a perfect: the Highlander says *I was smoking all my life* rather than *I have been smoking all my life*. Another likely sign of Gaelic input into Highland English is the 'difficulty' with /θ/ discussed above; but here we do not yet know nearly enough about the historical and geographical spread of the tendency to substitute /s/ for /θ/. The latter might also become /t/ in Gaelic, for Scots *graith* 'soapy water' was apparently borrowed into Gaelic in the nineteenth century as *great* (Quick 1990: 38–41).

And even if we accept that Highland English was once simply a form of spoken standard English strongly influenced by Gaelic, the situation has changed considerably: MacKinnon (1977: 174) notes 'increasing influence from Lowland Scots' in Highland English. This may imply that there was not always such influence, but the history of the Scots element in Highland English has still to be studied, and we have much to learn.

13.14 MODERN EDUCATION

Wherever there has been discussion above about historical developments affecting the relationship between Gaelic and Scots, public attitudes expressed, often in legal documents, by Scottish and British governments and their agents have been taken as expressing the views of speakers of Scots in general, and later of speakers of English in Scotland. Whether this assumption is valid or not is a question for historians, and may never be satisfactorily answered, but for the present we do seem to get the clearest picture of Lowland attitudes to Gaelic from what Lowland documents say about education. The deeds of Lowland educationalists have arguably been the most effective means used to weaken the Gaelic language: and this was always a one-way process, for Gaelic was never in a position to 'extirpate' Scots.

The assault on Gaelic, as we have seen, led at times to the complete banishment of the language from the schools, but Withrington (1986: 68) raises the possibility that national politics, especially Jacobitism, may have helped to dictate the degree of ferocity with which Gaelic was attacked at various times. Even when Gaelic did get into schools, though, it is important to remember that it was admitted only as a school subject, even for children who knew no English, to be studied as foreign languages are studied. It is probably the acceptance, even by some Gaelic-speakers, of this as right and natural that constitutes the greatest victory of Scotland's Lowland-based education system over the Gaelic world (Campbell 1945: 79–81). The situation has only as recently as 1975 begun to change, with the first genuine efforts to use Gaelic as a real medium of instruction in some primary schools in Gaelic-speaking areas (Murray and Morrison 1984: 16–25) – and even these efforts meet local resistance, from Gaelic-speakers as well as others.

One effect of all the centuries of efforts to 'educate' the speakers of Gaelic towards true religion and civility (for a summary, see Dorian 1981: 20–4) has been to deprive them of cultural self-confidence. Durkacz (1983: 226) offers one explanation for the present parlous state of Gaelic:

> Gaelic failed to adapt itself to the new protestant culture until the evangelical revival in the nineteenth century. By this time it had suffered some two centuries of neglect and distrust from Scottish cultural leaders who associated it with Catholicism and rebellion. Of course this damaged the self-confidence of the people, undermining their belief in the cultural worth of their mother tongue.

John Lorne Campbell prefers to put the blame not on the Gaelic language or people but on the Reformation: 'It is no accident, nor is it the result of any "inevitable historical process" that the decay of Scots and Gaelic in Scotland dates from 1560' (Campbell 1945: 41). The apportionment of blame, fortunately, is not the function of this chapter, and it must be left to others to find political explanations for language change.

Eventually the Established Church dropped its anti-Gaelic fury, and in general Gaelic suffers less positive persecution than it used to. Fifty years ago, Campbell (1945: 42) saw 'the now all-powerful Scottish Education Department' as the main enemy, but today Gaelic has found some friends even there. In the first half of the nineteenth century, Gaelic education had grown dramatically, following the weakening of the 'extirpate Gaelic' tendency of earlier days. But the Education Act of 1872, 'which laid the foundation of an educational system for the Highlands which was to be in close conformity with that for the rest of the country', does not even mention the Gaelic language (Macleod 1963: 319). MacKinnon (1991: 75–6) tells us that the 'writing out' of Gaelic in this Act was not due to mere carelessness or amnesia, but was a deliberate anglicising policy. On the other hand, Withers (1984: 157) emphasises the negative side of the causes of this 'writing out', noting a conviction, not only among the educational authorities currently in power but also among other educated people, even in the Highlands, that Gaelic really was a drawback and that to be of any value the main thrust of education must be towards English.

The omission of Gaelic from the 1872 Act was disastrous, but 'was not accepted with indifference' (Macleod 1963: 320). Spokespeople for the Gaels fought hard, and eventually new laws were passed. But the fighting has had to go on ever since, for the negative attitude, now internal as much as external, has unquestionably helped to eat away at the area over which Gaelic is spoken.

14

The Scots Language in Ulster

Michael B. Montgomery and Robert J. Gregg

14.1 INTRODUCTION AND DEFINITION OF TERMS

Just as the Celtic language Gaelic crossed the Moyle, the north channel of the Irish Sea, to Scotland beginning in the late fifth century of the modern era and developed a separate character through the experiences and contacts of its speakers there, so a millennium later the Germanic tongue Scots retraced this path in extending its own territory to the north of Ireland.[1] Thereby Scots became an international language, although in smaller dimensions than for many other European languages that migrated further west, and Ulster Scots[2] became the only recognisable variety of Scots outwith the mainland of Scotland. In these two extended migrations and countless other comings and goings, the narrowness of the channel (fourteen miles from Fair Head to the Mull of Kintyre, twenty-two from the Ards Peninsula to the Mull of Galloway) made this 'connection between West Scotland and North-East Ireland . . . a constant factor in history' (Trevelyan 1959: 60). It was pivotal in producing what we know today as 'Scottish Gaelic' and 'Ulster Scots'.

Ulster Scots developed primarily as a 'variant of West-Mid Scots' from Ayrshire and Renfrewshire, according to the *Scottish National Dictionary* (Grant 1931: xli), with influences also from the South Mid-Scots of Galloway and Kirkcudbrightshire (G. B. Adams 1964: 1). It has now been spoken in the historical province of Ulster[3] for more than 400 years and has had a stable community of speakers there since the early seventeenth century; through plantation schemes official and unofficial and a variety of less formal migrations, tens of thousands of Lowland Scots arrived in the first half of that century, establishing a rural heartland which further movement of people from Scotland and the internal migration of earlier settlers expanded as the century proceeded. In this territory, covering parts of four counties (Down, Antrim, (London)Derry and Donegal), Ulster Scots is still a medium of daily life. Soon after arriving, it developed complex relationships with Irish Gaelic and Ulster English, being almost from the beginning superposed by English, which became the language of urban life, education, government and social institutions. Because English and Scottish settlers from the time of the official Ulster Plantation (1610–25) have had continuing contact, there is today no absolute or altogether clear demarcation between Ulster Scots and Ulster English in terms of linguistic structure or geography. The 'core' Ulster Scots speech territory has been mapped, but in certain social contexts and in towns Ulster Scots tends to give way to English today, the logical result of a process of status differentiation that began in the early seventeenth century. This contrasting prestige may be the most prominent fact about their relationship in modern society, but it disguises much more complex relations between the two linguistically. Through much of Ulster, the two have penetrated one another in innumerable and subtle ways (as Irish Gaelic has penetrated them both), and they form a continuum, at one end of which is found a version of traditional Scots that is fully comprehensible only to native speakers, primarily because of its lexical density. A recent example of this is the following (Fenton 1996: 63):

> The McDonal boady frae Bristol (or neardher hame) wuz aksin wha should richtly be at the Ulster-Scots . . . It's nae guid ava jaist cloddin a gopin o the owl words inty a pome, lake pittin currans in fadge – whather it's Tam's fremd evenin or clabbery market, or Michel Langley's weefla lettin a guldher at his da. A boady micht think the lake of them could aiblins gie iz a hale pome or twa in the day's Ulster-Scots, but A wunther. It's a wile peety nether o them had it for their furst wie o takkin (an a peety, tae, Mossbawn wuznae a weethin neardher Buckna). For it haes enuch wee cleeks an thras tae sen even the brichtest ootsider heesmegairy; nae metther hoo able, he micht weel mak a sore han o it.

Like many other traditional European tongues, Ulster Scots has quite recently begun to experience a revival that has produced greater awareness, enhanced self-perception, and increased public use and attention (about which more below). It has yet to gain an official or institutional role, but its recent recognition as a Lesser-Used Language by the United Kingdom Committee of the European Commission and the efforts of the newly formed (1992) Ulster-Scots Language Society to document its history make predictions of its future livelihood rather different from those usually made for rural varieties of language in the modern era. This includes a statement of a few years ago by one author of this chapter, whose dissertation research mapped its boundaries more than thirty years ago:[4] 'the ultimate extinction of the dialect may be envisaged, probably within the next two or three generations' (Gregg 1972: 134).

The issue of whether to call Ulster Scots a language or a dialect, a concern in some quarters, is from a linguistic point of view not as meaningful or relevant as it used to be, as linguists sometimes use the terms interchangeably, recognising that both have speech communities, stylistic differentiation, functional domains in which they are used, and rule-based grammatical systems. There is little consensus on the linguistic and social criteria for distinguishing the two. The matter in any case cannot be addressed before two questions are answered: first, to which superordinate language is it related? and second, from what temporal point of view is the relationship viewed? Historically speaking, as the SND classification indicates, Ulster Scots is a dialect of Scots, the latter a close sibling language to English; many of its distinctive features, especially its phonological system, are traceable to Scotland. Synchronically, it has usually been classified by scholars in Ireland as a dialect of Irish English (standing along with Mid-Ulster English as the two main varieties in the north), by scholars in Scotland as a variety of Scots, and by the Ulster-Scots Language Society as a language. It has met the criteria of the European Commission's Bureau for Lesser-Used Languages as a minority or lesser-used language. Given the relative paucity of scholarly research on Ulster Scots and the fact that very few scholars have been speakers of it and have provided an insider's point of view, these labels are subject to revision. The designation 'language', whether applied by speakers of a language or by others in any particular case, may sometimes be symbolic, but no less real to many speakers themselves. All these issues of label aside, there is sufficient evidence of a shared linguistic system used by a speech community largely of Scottish ancestry for the term Ulster Scots to be justified, although much further description and analysis of this system is needed.

Perhaps the best term – the one employed hereinafter – for Ulster Scots is 'variety'. This designation (similar to the SND 'variant') avoids the connotations of 'dialect' as referring to a type of language that is peripheral and low in prestige and that usually has no literary tradition (Ulster Scots has the latter, though on a much smaller scale than mainland Scotland). 'Variety' also leaves open the issue of whether to stake a claim for linguistic autonomy. There can be no doubt that Ulster Scots is the traditional means of expression for part of the Ulster population, but disagreement over the status of Ulster Scots will likely continue for some time, for reasons of cultural politics as well as linguistic description and classification. Perhaps all parties can agree that speakers of Ulster Scots should have a principal say in the discussion. If the designation 'language' reflects the view of a speech community that it is a distinct entity and that the language of its nurture is part of this distinctiveness (as opposed to the language of education and other institutions of larger society), then the views of speakers are subject to change, as has happened elsewhere in Europe. Concerning this matter, one can make only tentative observations at the moment, as the work of the Ulster-Scots Language Society has hardly begun. It appears that the scholarly community has begun to give greater recognition to Ulster Scots: four Ph.D. dissertations, three in the 1980s; coverage in semi-popular books (Kay 1993, 1994) and in reference works (Todd 1992a; this chapter). For our purposes, it suffices to characterise it as a social and regional variety of Scots (as on the mainland, it was often called 'Scotch' or 'braid Scotch' in the eighteenth and nineteenth centuries) that is distinctive to Ireland.

About Ulster Scots, little systematic research has been undertaken outside the work of Robert J. Gregg, whose findings will form the core of this chapter's discussion on phonology. Much research that has been pursued is recent, published in journals not widely available, or not published at all. In the last category, for instance, is the Tape-Recorded Survey of Hiberno-English Speech, a cross-generational project undertaken in the 1970s, the data from which have occasionally been used for single-feature studies but never analysed in the comprehensive fashion intended (but perhaps this will be redressed by the phonetic atlas envisaged by John Kirk and outlined in Kirk forthcoming: 8).

This chapter reviews the existing, often disparate literature, assembling it here for the first time. In doing so, it inevitably highlights how much work needs to be done. The approach is to provide the following: first, additional historical and demographic background for Ulster Scots; second, a linguistic history using a chronological survey of documentary evidence; and third, a discussion of the affiliations and influences of Ulster Scots with and on other languages and other varieties of language. Then our attention shifts to the structure of Ulster Scots, focusing on its lexis, phonology and grammar, before considering recent developments and their implications.

14.2 HISTORICAL SKETCH

The migration of Lowland Scottish settlers brought the Scots language to Ulster four centuries ago, but it is proper to view this in the larger context of regular Scottish movements and contact dating back to the early fourteenth century. Following the defeat of Edward Bruce's army in Ulster in 1318, Gaelic lords, particularly in Antrim, began to recruit Scottish 'gallowglasses' to strengthen their defences; and, from that time through the Elizabethan wars of the late 1500s, Islanders and Highlanders served as professional soldiers in Ulster (sometimes known as 'Irish-Scots', according to Maxwell (1994: 10)) in return for money and land, and they sometimes settled there while maintaining connections with Scotland (Hayes–McCoy 1937). Also coming from Gaelic-speaking Scotland were landed families like the Macdonnells, Lords of the Isles, who in 1399 acquired Rathlin Island and the Glens of Antrim and became one of the most powerful families in Ulster for more than two centuries.[5] In bringing Scottish Gaelic to Ulster, where it was later influenced by its Irish counterpart and survived until the first half of the twentieth century, these Scots contributed to the complex linguistic landscape of the north of Ireland. With the supplanting of Irish Gaelic by Scottish Gaelic in parts of north-eastern Ulster and with the latter permeating the former throughout the province (O'Rahilly 1932: 161–91; Adams 1970–1: 164), the Scottish linguistic influence on Ireland can be seen as a vital, bilingual one.

Lowlanders speaking Scots began to trickle over the channel in the second half of the sixteenth century (indeed, it was their presence in Ulster which first alarmed and provoked the Tudors to attempt early but largely unsuccessful plantations), but their first significant infusion occurred around the turn of the seventeenth century, in the very earliest years of the reign of James VI/I.[6] Through private grants or other means, they arrived in east Ulster in numbers sizeable enough and were sufficiently successful in developing the land to exclude the counties of Antrim, Down and Monaghan from an official plantation.[7] It was James's official scheme, formulated in 1609 and begun in 1610, for the escheating of the remaining six counties of Ulster (all of them west of the River Bann) and the plantation of Protestants there that initiated the recruitment of Scots and English to take up land in the province; the coordination of the plan was doubtless assisted by the Union of the Crowns in 1603, as two different labour pools could now be solicited and government policy could be coordinated. 'Undertakers' and 'servitors' (mostly former soldiers of the crown) were granted parcels of land on conditions of improving, fortifying and populating them with tenants – farmers, artisans and the like (for details, see P. Robinson 1984: 63–5, Robinson 1989b). Because the identities of these grantees are often known, the allocation of land can be mapped according to their nationality or region of origin, but they represented only a small fraction of the settler population compared to their Scottish and English tenants. The latter were usually anonymous, meaning that patterns of comparative Scottish and English settlement can be discussed only somewhat later by using such indices as the occurrence of surnames on muster rolls and the establishment of church congregations. Unlike Antrim and Down, which were settled by private enterprise, (London)Derry was included in the official plantation plans. Its settlement was the prerogative of the London companies, which had little luck in the enterprise. The Lowland Scots, because of their closer bases, were able to take over a good portion of the north-east corner of the county and penetrate loosely the rest of (London)Derry and Tyrone. It was also as part of the official plantation plans that Scots were brought over to Donegal from 1610 onwards by the Ayrshire families of Cunningham and Stewart. They were settled in the northern parts of the low-lying east Donegal region known as the Laggan. The southern parts of the Laggan were English-settled, and most of the remainder of the county was left in the hands of the native Irish. Thus, Scottish settlers came to occupy solidly a wide band of coastal territory extending from the Ards in north-east Down northwards, taking in most of Antrim, the north-east corner of (London)Derry and the northern portion of the Laggan district in east Donegal.

The plantation was only one phase of a wider process of Scottish migration that can be sketched only in outline, because much of the later to-ing (and fro-ing) between Lowland Scotland and Ulster was anonymous and untraceable. Through the century, each was a safety valve for the other in periods of economic hardship or political and religious turmoil. Ulster, more often the place of refuge, was favoured by relative constants that included the pull of Irish land that was cheap (and free during the Plantation period, under certain conditions) and the push of population pressures, rent increases and ongoing tenurial reorganisation in Scotland. As a result, Scots were drawn in waves until the turn of the century – in the 1630s, the 1650s, the 1670s and especially the 1690s, the last a time of severe famine in Scotland and of dispossessions after the Williamite wars (one historian states that 'Ulster . . . was nearly colonised anew by the Scotch settlers and camp-followers of King William's foreign forces' (Prendergast 1887: 98). Indeed, one scholar cites contemporary estimates that '80,000 Scots had come to Ireland since the Battle of the Boyne', a figure probably reflecting Scotland's fear that it was losing valuable population (W. A. Macafee 1992: 107), but perhaps not too far off the mark.[8] Because of its proximity, Scots coming from the south-west were most numerous, but for the same economic and other reasons they also left from elsewhere in the Lowlands – the east (especially the Lothians), the north-east and the Borders.

Calculations of the size of British settler population, though usually based on inferences from incomplete records (e.g. muster rolls for c. 1630, a poll-tax survey of 1659) and using surnames for classification (which almost inevitably underestimates the Scottish proportion), consistently suggest the numerical superiority of Scots over the English, especially in Antrim and Down (Perceval-Maxwell 1973; Gillespie 1985; Macafee 1992). A broad survey such as that of Braidwood (1964: 5–45) and case studies such as Robinson's in County Tyrone indicate that the occupation of the landscape often shifted, with the competition of undertakers/landlords for tenants and other developments spurring internal migration that had significant effects on language diffusion. Nonetheless, a map such as that below from Robinson (1984: 94), based on the 1630 muster rolls, is suggestive for a comparative view of the two groups of British settlers.

The Scots predominated, naturally enough, in those parts of Ulster having the easiest access to Scotland: east Antrim, north-east Down (the passage from Portpatrick to Donaghadee was the most convenient one) and the broad river valleys along the north coast, particularly the Foyle Basin and the Laggan. Roughly speaking, this land area had a crescent shape with three discontinuous parts from Down in the south-east to Donegal in the west. According to Robinson (1984: 97), 'the population distribution of English and Scottish settlers had established into a coherent pattern circa 1622', and, even in areas of relatively mixed settlement, competition between Scots and English and segregation between their communities became a frequent pattern, though it could hardly have precluded contact between the two nationalities (or between either of them and the Irish) anywhere, and it must have varied from place to place. As settlement increased, those with English backgrounds more often favoured towns, but there too Scots were soon wont to go. In the second half of the century, Belfast (Agnew 1992: 152, 1994), as well as Londonderry and Coleraine (Robinson 1984: 158), became predominantly Scottish in population and were dominated by the Scottish merchant class. As Braidwood (1964: 31) states with regard to Scottish expansion,

[e]ven in what might well have been a purely English plantation the Scots intruded early and increasingly, till they eventually became predominant, encroaching at first across the Bann from Scots-settled Antrim, and in the later seventeenth century direct from Scotland through Derry city, a natural port for Scots immigrants.

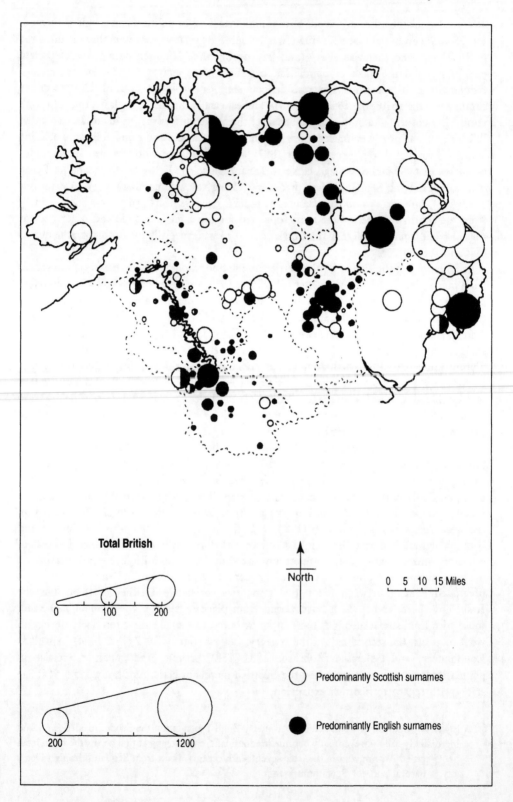

Total British

North

0 5 10 15 Miles

200   1200

○ Predominantly Scottish surnames

● Predominantly English surnames

The ratio of Scots to English during the century has often been put at five or six to one (Adams 1977: 57). This would have been much higher in Antrim and north Down and much more evenly balanced in the six escheated counties, but the native Irish were still in the majority in most Ulster parishes, according to the 1659 hearth money rolls. One calculation cited by Braidwood (1964: 6) 'reckons there were 100,000 Scots and 20,000 English in Ulster' at the time of the 1641 uprising by the native Irish. Regardless of the strict accuracy of any estimate, the patterns resulting from plantation settlements ensured that there were two, and sometimes three, cultural traditions in contact in much of the province.

Despite the 'coherent pattern' cited above, it would be wise to ask how stable the Scottish settlements in seventeenth-century Ulster were. Because of the fluidity of movement across the channel, a significant proportion of Ulster Scots were born in Scotland through the end of the century. There is substantial evidence that many considered mainland Scotland to be their homeland, in that they conducted such legal affairs as registering their deeds in Edinburgh rather than somewhere in Ireland (Agnew: personal communication). This suggests that Scots viewed their settlements in Ulster as a natural extension of Scotland rather than as a colony or outpost of settlers from the parent nation. In many ways, cultural relations between Ulster and Scotland were quite close and continued to be so for at least 200 years. For instance, the vast majority of Ulster Scots seeking tertiary education matriculated at Glasgow University, especially for theological training, until the nineteenth century (as dissenters, they were excluded from Trinity in Dublin). Close bonds between Ulster and Scotland were maintained through the eighteenth century in popular culture, intellectual currents, literary traditions and tastes (to be considered later in this chapter), and in other ways.

But there is other, more easily documentable evidence that in the early decades of the seventeenth century an Ulster Scots heartland had begun to form, and that it solidified and expanded as Scottish settlers continued to come until the turn of the century – long after the encouragement of official policy. Their spread can be tracked roughly by the growth of their most characteristic and important cultural institution, the Presbyterian church, the earliest congregation of which had a Scots Presbyterian minister from 1613, when Edward Brice became minister at Broadisland/Ballycarry in south-east Antrim. In a series of four maps, Gailey (1975: 4–8) tracks the founding of Presbyterian congregations and shows the gradual diffusion of Presbyterianism across Ireland from 1611–1720, including into areas that were originally settled by the English. In this and in a second essay (Gailey 1968–9), he cites a number of other Scottish cultural transfers to Ireland such as first-footing on New Year's Day. Thus, from modern-day linguistic, geographical and other research, and from our knowledge of settlement patterns of the Ulster plantations, we can infer the existence of a community of native speakers of Ulster Scots developing early in the seventeenth century.

14.3 THE DEMOGRAPHY OF ULSTER SCOTS

The historical dimensions of the Ulster Scots territory have been known for more than a century, being first sketched for Antrim and Down by the antiquarian/ethnologist Abraham Hume (1856: 162):

> The Scotch settlers . . . occupied the lowlands in Antrim, on the coast to near Glenarm, and in the interior of the county where there were fewest impediments of mountain, bog, or forest. In

Down, they passed over the bleak district near the north of Strangford lough, and passed on toward the centre of the county; having the hilly districts on the one side and the English on the other.

The work of Hill (1873, 1888–9) and Hume (1878) extended the account of Scottish settlement to west of the Bann and in the latter case related it to language: 'in numerous other districts – in Armagh, Tyrone and Fermanagh – the people of [Scotland and England] were mixed in varying proportions, so that the English language was introduced with unequal degrees of purity, and sometimes with a marked provincial accent' (Hume 1878: 8–9). Local historians in nineteenth-century Ulster frequently commented on the extent of Irish spoken and sometimes on Scots as well, as did Alexander Knox (1875: 48) for County Down:

> The Scottish idiom is most observable in the baronies of Ards and Castlereagh. and their confines, although extending as far as Hillsborough and Dromore. Until recently it was spoken as broadly as in Ayr or Wigtownshire, but it is gradually dying out, although innumerable words imported from Scotland are in daily use in the northern part of the county.

By the mid-1930s, W. F. Marshall (1936: 12) – antiquarian, clergyman, poet and consultant to Grant on SND – was speaking and writing on the three distinctive 'elements in Ulster speech, Elizabethan English, Lowland Scots, and Ulster Gaelic', while outlining the territory of Scots speech in Down, Antrim and (London)Derry (1936: 12, 25). However, it remained for G. B. Adams after the war to begin amassing evidence that confirmed the coextensiveness of Scottish settlement areas with modern-day linguistic districts. Early in his career, which later included more than twenty years as Dialect Archivist at the Ulster Folk Museum, he proposed the following outline (Adams 1964: 1): '[t]he northeastern dialect is spoken in most of Co. Antrim (except for the extreme south and the Glens in the north-east, together with the part of Co. Derry just across the River Bann, and from this centre it spreads westwards through Derry to parts of north Tyrone and north-east Donegal', but it was lexical data collected on behalf of *The Linguistic Survey of Scotland* that enabled him to be the first to draw maps of Scottish forms in Ulster. In the early 1950s, Angus McIntosh of Edinburgh University approached him to distribute the Scots section of the LSS lexical questionnaire in parts of Ulster, a task that Adams coordinated through the Belfast Naturalists' Field Club beginning in 1953. From the responses gathered, Adams mapped the distribution of four items, including terms for *earwig* and forms of *one*, and found (1956: 7) that *gellick* and *yann*, their Scottish variants, 'occupy the Northeastern or Coastal Crescent' of Ulster. In so doing, he carefully related both Scottish and non-Scottish responses to cultural geography and demographic history, proposing general principles for the diffusion of linguistic forms in the north of Ireland.

But fieldwork was necessary to determine the location and integrity of dialect boundaries. This challenge was met by Robert J. Gregg, a native of Larne, who learned Ulster Scots from his mother and other relatives native to Glenoe in south-east Antrim. Taking the generally known dimensions of the Ulster Scots zone as a given, Gregg conducted fieldwork from 1960–3 that aimed 'to collect the data that will polarise the systematic differences between the dialects' in phonology (1972: 110). (He had initially sought contrastive lexical items, but found this line of investigation unproductive; the multiplicity of responses was too great for mapping, and lexical isoglosses such as those identified by Adams failed to bundle.) From many years studying the speech of his home town, Gregg devised a questionnaire encompassing 683 items; then he interviewed 125 informants (thirty-four in Donegal, four in north-east (London)Derry, twenty-three in Antrim and sixty-four in Down) and analysed the patterning of fourteen features, twelve vocalic, one consonantal and one grammatical (these will be presented in detail in a later section).[9] Considering Antrim to be the 'heartland', he concentrated his efforts on locating the boundaries of Ulster Scots-speaking territory, and thus his interviews were most finely meshed in Donegal and in the areas of east Down where he expected to find contrasts. His goal thus was not to survey a geographically even spread of speakers in order to identify and compare varieties within the Ulster Scots area; however, the latter can be approached using the extensive data compilations and the ninety maps published in Gregg (1985): see Map 14.2.

The present distribution of dialects in Ulster reflects to a large extent the settlement patterns laid down in the seventeenth century. Antrim is the heartland of the Ulster Scots dialects. Apart from the English-settled parishes in the southern part, the formerly boggy corner between the River Bann and the north shores of Lough Neagh, and the mountainous glens in the north-east, the whole county is dominated by various forms of Ulster Scots among which it is possible to distinguish a northern subdialect with /e/ instead of /i/ as reflex of Early Scots or Middle Scots /ü/. Within the latter, it is possible to distinguish a distinctive coastal dialect in which /æ/ has largely replaced /ʌ/ in a wide range of words. North-east (London)Derry Ulster Scots is really an overspill of the northern subdialect of Antrim which straddles the Bann almost as far upstream as the Rasharkin–Kilrea crossing. The Magilligan area was settled as late as the nineteenth century by Lagganeers from east Donegal who brought with them their distinctive version of Ulster Scots with its typical forms such as [e'bin] 'above', [din] 'done', [gid] 'good' and so on. The Ulster Scots of Donegal is centred in the Laggan district extending northwards to the foothills of the mountain zone of the Inishowen Peninsula and to the Knockalla Range which cuts across the Fanad Peninsula. The mountains of central Donegal form the western limits of Ulster Scots, the watershed between the rivers Finn and Deele the southern limits, and the Foyle itself the eastern bounds of the dialect.

As far as the linguistic nature of the dialectal borders is concerned, Ulster Scots matches for the most part with various forms of Urban Hiberno-English, but in Fanad (along the southern boundary of Glenvar) and to the west of the Laggan the boundary is formed by Gaelic. The Ulster Scots dialect boundary stretching east–west across the south Ards is with a variety of standard English which in many ways resembles urban Ulster Scots, in other words the type of English used by educated bilingual speakers of rural Ulster Scots or used in the towns of the Ulster Scots areas. On the west side of Strangford Lough, Ulster Scots borders on the typical County Down version of Urban Hiberno-English, all the way west from Killyleagh to near Hillsborough and then northwards touching upon the outskirts of Belfast, which has, of course, its own particular urban version of Urban Hiberno-English, nowadays reaching out eastwards all the way along Belfast Lough's southern shore to Bangor and Groomsport. All these County Down Ulster Scots boundaries are quite sharply defined against Urban Hiberno-English, although the division at the eastern – Cloughey – end of the south Ards border is less clearly marked than at the Ardkeen end. The typical Scots forms have strayed much further south on the east coast than on the west, which may be explained partly by the poor communications on the west at an earlier date, before the drainage scheme had opened up the Ardkeen area.

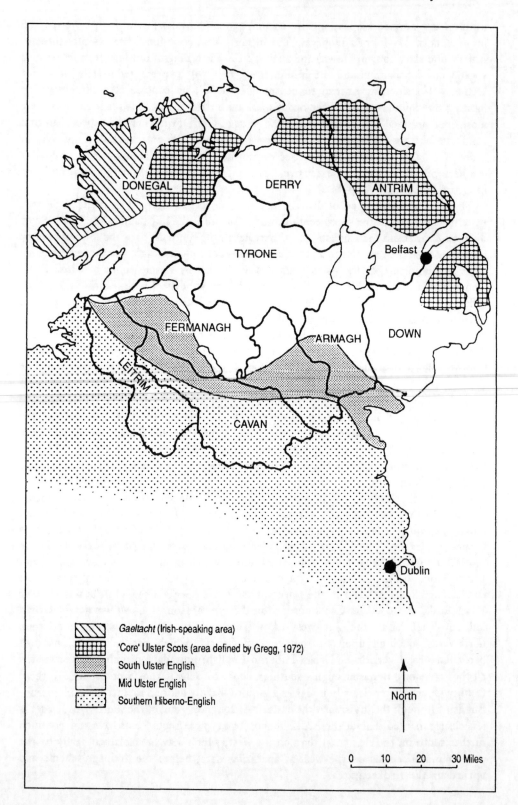

Gaeltacht (Irish-speaking area)

'Core' Ulster Scots (area defined by Gregg, 1972)

South Ulster English

Mid Ulster English

Southern Hiberno-English

Belfast Urban Hiberno–English also stretches along the northern shores of the Lough as far as Whitehead and forms a sharp boundary with east Antrim and, partly, with Mid-Antrim Ulster Scots. Further west, a more rural type of Urban Hiberno–English provides an equally clear-cut border running towards Lough Neagh and passing north of Antrim town. The rather mixed dialect of the area north of Lough Neagh and west to the Bann forms a vaguer boundary for the 100 per cent Ulster Scots of west Mid-Antrim, but the Urban Hiberno–English of the glens in the north-east corner of the county stands out in sharp contrast to the north Antrim and Braid versions of Ulster Scots. On the (London)Derry side of the Bann, the local Urban Hiberno–English, south and west of the Ulster Scots area, is again sharply contrastive, and the same holds true for the situation in Inishowen and the south Laggan in Donegal. The border with Gaelic to the west and north of the Laggan is, of course, the sharpest possible contrast, as it is part of one of the major European linguistic boundaries – that between Germanic and Celtic. Yet in spite of this apparently sudden transition, the Ulster Scots dialect of the Laggan has actually intruded across the line as the second language of most of the Gaelic speakers living near the border.

As we see from Map 14.2, Gregg finds that the Ulster Scots speech areas closely approximate those of Scottish settlement. These are discontinuous, indicating that they were settled directly from Scotland and spread inland and that, generally speaking, their population has remained static and rural over the past three centuries. Without a knowledge of settlement history, the Ulster Scots areas might appear to be remnants from a larger territory, but this is not the case. Indeed, a comparison of the earlier Map 14.1 with Map 14.3, which uses three indices (surnames, Presbyterian churches and speech), shows a consistent pattern, what P. Robinson (1989b: 28) calls 'distributional continuity'.

There has been no survey or census, of even the most informal nature, of people who identify themselves as Scots or of users of the Scots language in Ulster (however, at the time of writing there is a movement in Scotland to put a question regarding the Scots language on the 2001 census; if successful, this might have a follow-on effect for Northern Ireland). Estimates of the speakers of Ulster Scots can at present be only suggestive. The numbers would probably be in the tens of thousands, all of whom presumably would use both English and Scots and would have varying commands of the latter. Not long ago, James Milroy (1981: 23) offered the assessment, common in the literature, that 'in the Scots areas there are a great many rural speakers who speak a dialect of Scots rather than English; in its strongest forms it is also indistinguishable from the Scots dialects of West and Central Scotland', but neither he nor any other linguist reckons the numbers of Ulster Scots-speakers more precisely. G. B. Adams (1968: 2) stated that

> the rural population of [the three Ulster Scots areas] is about 170,000; not all of whom would be speakers of Ulster Scots, though some of the latter would be resident in towns within the area. Almost all speakers of Ulster Scots are now bidialectal using the regional form of standard English, or a close approximation to it, as an alternative to their native dialect under certain circumstances. Some are more conscious of the difference between dialect and standard usage than others and are better able to switch from one to the other depending on their audience.

The Ulster-Scots Language Society states that as many as 100,000 speakers can be found today, though it does not cite the criteria for arriving at this figure. There are likely no monoglot speakers, but this is a question at present unanswerable.

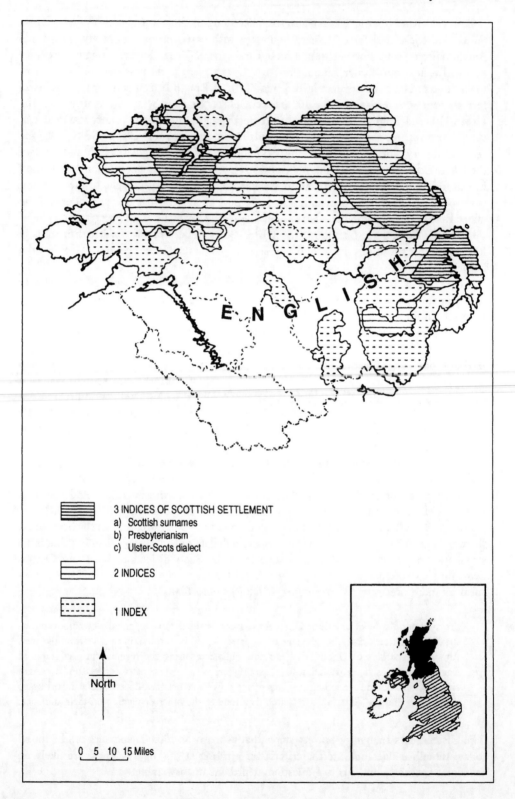

3 INDICES OF SCOTTISH SETTLEMENT
a) Scottish surnames
b) Presbyterianism
c) Ulster-Scots dialect

2 INDICES

1 INDEX

North

0   5   10 15 Miles

Given the present-day linguistic situation in the north of Ireland, the approximate number of Ulster Scots-speakers will undoubtedly remain a matter of conjecture, for several reasons that apply to many other minority 'languages' in Europe and elsewhere. First, Ulster English and Ulster Scots form a continuum ranging from a quasi-standard variety on the one hand to a vernacular one that is quite divergent to it on the other. From a linguistic point of view, it is difficult at best to formulate a method for consistently distinguishing the two, as the continuum between them includes different degrees of Scottish-influenced English. Gregg's approach is reasonable and thorough, but works only for phonology. Second, and perhaps more important, speakers of Ulster Scots often do not recognise it as distinct from Ulster English, either because they are acquainted with no written form of Ulster Scots that serves as a point of reference or because their native speech has been stigmatised as 'bad English' in the classroom. Third, there is an overwhelming tendency, because of prevailing contemporary political and social currents in Northern Ireland and the history of Irish–British relations, to see the island in terms of an English vs Irish dichotomy, with the former entirely subsuming Ulster Scots. These matters can hardly be resolved here, but it is instructive and important to point them out. As linguists who work on languages having mainly or exclusively oral forms well know, there is no necessary contradiction in a person's being a native speaker of a language which that person does not know to exist; the incongruity reflects how types of language are identified and labelled by a dominant society.

While the work of Gregg, Adams and others has confirmed the existence of Ulster Scots in the modern day, and, as we will see in the next section, we have documentary evidence of the use of Scots in Ulster in the early seventeenth century, the inference that the Ulster Scots territory has remained more or less stable may not be warranted unless a record of the continuous existence of Ulster Scots on the ground can be established. This evidence does exist and is of two kinds: contemporary commentary by travellers and observers who provide external evidence of when and where the variety was spoken; and actual documents exhibiting Scottish linguistic features, which constitutes the internal evidence for the variety.

If we take, for example, the first half of the nineteenth century, roughly the midpoint of the history of Ulster Scots, we find a number of striking remarks by outsiders that confirm the prevalence of Scottish speech in such places as north County Antrim and east County (London)Derry. The *Ordnance Survey Memoirs*, which were compiled in the 1830s by army officers and civil servants and which for some Ulster counties accompanied detailed maps, often briefly characterise the 'habits of the people' of a local parish as well as the landscape and the buildings. Three comments about local language from County Antrim, from which the memoirs are most detailed, will suffice to exemplify this commentary. Of the local people, the 1831 memoir for the Parish of Templecorran in south-east Antrim (Day et al. 1994: 106) states that

> their dialect, accent and idioms are strictly and disagreeably Scottish, partaking only of the broad and coarse accent and dialect of the southern counties of Scotland. Their manners are dry, blunt and uncommunicative, wanting in candour and courtesy, and to those unacquainted with them apparently uncivil.

In the 1838 memoir for the Parish of Templepatrick, towards the south-west of the county, we are told (Day et al. 1996: 141) that 'a great portion of [the inhabitants] are of Scotch origin and they all have a good deal of Scotch manner and accent. They are canny and inquisitive', while the 1832–3 memoir for the Parish of Donegore (Day and McWilliams 1995: 113) reports that the

> dialect, particularly in the more remote parts of the parish, is strongly Scottish, as are also their idioms and old saws, which are very quaint and pithy, and plainly indicate their extraction. In these respects they do not differ from the inhabitants of the adjoining parishes, from whom they can in few others be distinguished.

If the commentators are representative, we may infer that the use of Scots was becoming associated with rural areas and that it had by this time come under some censure in society at large, the object of some degree of social prejudice.

Some years earlier, in 1814, the Rev. John Graham of Maghera concluded the following about people in that east County (London)Derry town (Mason 1814: 592):

> In reporting the language and customs peculiar to this neighbourhood, attention must be made to the usual division of the inhabitants into English, Irish and Scotch. The dialect and customs of these distinct races are as different from each other as their respective creeds. The members of the established church are denominated Englishmen, they speak with an accent less provincial than the dissenters or Roman Catholics, the Scotch or Irish; and forming a kind of medium between these two discordant bodies of people in religious opinions, language and habits, are usually treated by respect and kindness by both. The Dissenters speak broad Scotch and are in the habit of using terms and expressions long since obsolete, even in Scotland, and which are only to be found in the glossary annexed to the bishop of Dunkeld's translation of Virgil.

Such statements can be multiplied, and are, in essays by Lunney (1994, 1996) and R. I. Connolly (1981) that assemble nineteenth-century comments on the Scottishness of local speech in Ulster. Collectively, the Ordnance Survey remarks, like the one cited above, suggest a negative assessment, at least on the part of government officials, that probably reflected the subordinate, 'coarse' status of people in the local community and resembled a similar disparagement of mainland Scottish speech at the time. Scottish observers on the other hand seem often to have expressed surprise and wonder at finding Scottish speech in Ulster, as did the traveller who in 1853 'met a woman on a farm near Londonderry [and] "was so struck with this that I asked her if she was herself really a Scotchwoman, but she assured me that her family had lived in the country for many generations"' (Lunney 1994: 60–1). This man and others hardly expected to find Scottish speech in the Irish countryside, but what surprises us somewhat is that they seemed quite unaware of the considerable published writing in Ulster Scots, which had been used for poetry since the previous century, as we will see below.

The general patterns, maps and anecdotes that have been presented so far contain many simplifications, however, and we must be careful not to understate the complexity of the linguistic landscape of Ulster over the past four centuries. Maps are two-dimensional, and anecdotes offer views that are largely subjective. Seeing the linguistic situation as one of bilingual contact between English and Irish Gaelic may be appropriate for much of Ireland, but for the north of the island it misses a great deal. Interestingly, the multilingual landscape in Ulster in recent centuries shows striking parallels with Scotland; the same languages were involved, with English gradually marginalising both Gaelic and Scots socially, geographically or in both ways. As in Scotland, the more widespread bilingualism/

bidialectalism in Ulster has involved English and Scots (at the time of writing, Gaelic is spoken by a historic speech community in the western part of Donegal and increasingly in urban enclaves such as Belfast as a learned language). Contact between the three has been more frequent in Ulster because of historical events, but the smaller land area of Ulster means that they have been more frequent and more intimate there. In some ways, the Ulster situation has been more complex than Scotland, in that there were varieties of English coming from both above (that is, administrative English from London) and below (spoken varieties from the English hinterland). In this crucible of language and dialect contact that is Ulster, much detail remains to be filled in, this chapter dealing primarily with the roles and contributions of Scots.

For instance, the recent language shift in Ireland away from Gaelic had its own dimensions in Ulster. Adams (1976: 86) suggests that this process was hardly uniform in Antrim:

> [By 1700] what had replaced Irish in many parts of this central area of east Ulster was not English in the strict sense, as happened in other parts of Ireland, but Scots. One must remember that in the seventeenth century Scots and English in the narrower sense were at their widest degree of divergence . . . They were as much two languages, say, as Danish and Swedish. Perhaps, therefore, bilingualism in Irish and English was replaced in many parts of the area not by English monoglottism, but by another if less blatant form of bilingualism, in Scots and English . . . One wonders to what extent the existence of what was in some ways a trilingual situation, embracing Irish, English and Scots, helped on the shift away from Irish, the one language in the situation which was least like the other two.

For Donegal, the situation was complicated in a different sense. There, contact between and bilingualism in Irish and Scots has been a continuing reality because of the proximity of the Gaeltacht to Scots-speaking areas of the Laggan Valley. Because of weaker and less frequent connections with mainland Scotland, the Scottish community in Donegal was smaller than in east Ulster, 'with the result that although individual features of Scots origin survive, one does not find an Ulster Scots dialect in the way that one does in the north-eastern crescent' (Adams 1977: 59). But what Irish-speakers sometimes learned from their neighbours was apparently more Scots than English, and a command of Scots had practical value at country fairs. A century and a half ago, Phelan (1838: 387) commented on this tendency in his *Letters from Ireland* after visiting Letterkenny: 'I had been told that the Irish language was very little spoken here; it is extremely prevalent, though few, if any, are entirely ignorant of English – or Scotch, as they call it'. At the turn of the twentieth century, Irish men hiring themselves out as farm workers spoke of ' "going up till the Lag[g]an, to lift the Scotch," i.e. to learn English' (Braidwood 1964: 35). Around the same time, a group of these workers are recorded as apologising to a traveller for their less-than-perfect English: 'It's the Irish we speak among wursels but we hae eunuch Scotch till speak till yer honer' (Gwynn 1899: 10). Complicating the picture further is the fact that Irish-speakers in recent times have also had contact with Scots on the mainland. Adams (1950: 300) refers to 'the Scottish tinge often heard in the more northerly part of the Donegal Gaeltacht, where many people, among the older generation at any rate, first learned [English] as a result of seasonal migrations to the Scottish lowlands'. It is worth noting that influences have flowed in the other direction too, as speakers of Irish English in the nineteenth century brought such forms as *youse* to Glasgow and elsewhere in North Britain.

Regional and social differentiation within Ulster Scots is also clear, though it is only

Gregg, and more recently Kingsmore (1995), who have investigated this. Both of these scholars examine urban vs rural variation, for south-east Antrim on the one hand and for Coleraine in County (London)Derry on the other. Gregg (1972: 110) summarises the situation as follows:

> within the Scotch-Irish (SI) districts the towns have developed their own version of Standard English which may be called Scotch-Irish Urban (SIU), important because it is also the second language of educated SI dialect speakers and because, when SI forms drop out, they tend to be replaced by SIU equivalents.

For individual speakers, more is involved, however, than adopting an urban variety when moving from the countryside. Using Labovian methodology that included having informants read lists of individual words, Kingsmore (1995) found that speakers systematically shifted away from Ulster Scots variants when more self-conscious. This suggests that they vary their speech according to context, using a deeper or denser version of Ulster Scots when talking among themselves but an approximation of the regional standard in talking to strangers. If this is true (and it is quite reasonable, though it needs more thorough investigation), the typical outsider or visitor may hear any number of linguistic features of Scottish ancestry in the local speech, but never hear Ulster Scots as a variety of language *per se*. Again, this situation parallels that for many other parts of Europe with minority languages, especially if they are of the same ultimate linguistic stock as their superordinate counterparts, so that the boundary between the two is indistinct.

We return to some of these issues later in discussing the affiliations with and influences of Ulster Scots on other varieties. At this point, we turn to exploring the documentary evidence for this largely rural variety of language found in the historical province of Ulster.

14.4 DOCUMENTARY HISTORY

We turn now to the internal history of Ulster Scots, insofar as this is revealed by Scottish features in written documents of Ulster provenance from the past 400 years. As has been suggested, the history of the Ulster Scots language variety – as opposed to the Ulster Scots people – was hardly documented until quite recently, and the sketchy account presented here will undoubtedly be revised as more material is recovered and assessed. Its existence is unnoted in standard accounts of the history of English (as mainland Scots routinely is as well), it rarely received the scantiest of consideration in the literature on Scots until very recent years (with the notable exceptions of the *Scottish National Dictionary* and the *Linguistic Atlas of Scotland*, as discussed below), and, other than for its synchronic phonology, it has drawn little interest from trained linguists (as opposed to amateur lexicographers). The existence of Ulster Scots is universally recognised in more recent literature, but, because of perspectives that differ from writer to writer, one finds variation in its nomenclature and its classification. Many linguists who have worked from an Irish perspective have, while using the term 'Ulster Scots', classified it as a variety of 'Anglo-Irish' (Henry 1958), 'Hiberno-English' (Barry 1982; Harris 1984), 'Ulster English' (Kirk forthcoming) or even 'Planter English' (Todd 1989a: 29). Among those who have stressed its derivation from Lowland Scots are Adams (1964: 1), who has referred to it as 'north-eastern dialect',[10] Braidwood (1964: 48) and Gregg (1958 etc.), both of whom have used

'Scotch-Irish' (Gregg, the only native speaker among all these scholars, now prefers 'Ulster Scots'). Superordinate labels with 'English' have some appropriateness in reference to the long-term, intensive contact between Scots and English in Ulster and in reflecting the obvious fact that Ulster Scots is found in Ireland, but they are only partially accurate from a historical point of view. To the extent that Ulster Scots is distinctive in Ireland, this is attributable to its inheritance of features from the Scottish mainland; the phonology and basic wordstock of traditional Ulster Scots are Scottish, as are most of the grammatical paradigms (to the extent that these have been described and are known). This is not to say that Ulster Scots does not exhibit lexical and grammatical features from contact with Irish and English, but it is doubtful that these distinguish it from varieties of English in Ireland. On a linguistic family tree, in other words, Ulster Scots would be a descendant of the Scottish parent.

From written documents, it is not always possible to achieve a very full, clear or direct view of speech, and this is especially true when one variety of language (in this case Scots) comes to be dominated by another (English) that becomes superordinate by developing a standard written form of great functional diversity and by acquiring social prestige. Many traditional spoken varieties in the British Isles have been evidenced only in the comments of external observers (of the type cited for Ulster Scots in the previous section) before the nineteenth century, when traditions of local-colour writing – usually by dilettantes – arose that employed these varieties in comic or stereotypical fashion, or when they may have received the attention of someone inspired by the English Dialect Society to compile a glossary of the local vocabulary. In Ulster, by contrast, Scots has been used in writing longer, more often, in more types of documents, for more diverse purposes and for wider audiences.

The use of Ulster Scots in writing over a course, albeit an irregular one, of four centuries is attributable to several things. As an extension of mainland Scots, which had already been used for written literature for two centuries (McClure 1988: 31–42) and which had achieved a near-standard written form by 1600, Ulster Scots maintained Scottish conventions of spelling and morphology for several decades (indeed, most of this writing was done by natives of Scotland who had migrated across the channel).

From plantation days, Ulster developments closely paralleled Scottish ones. In both places, literacy in Scots gave way to literacy in English, and by the second half of the seventeenth century Scottish forms had all but disappeared from writing. In Ulster, models of writing in Scots were lost, but Scottish vocabulary and morphology reappeared in certain types of early eighteenth-century writing, becoming more frequent in later decades as vernacular poetry flourished, and lasting well into the Victorian period (and to some degree into the twentieth century) for both poetry and prose. Not only is this popular literature, cumulatively speaking, persuasive evidence that Ulster Scots continued to be widely spoken, but it also reveals that writers sometimes preferred Ulster Scots for some purposes (such as expressing protest and dissent, asserting cultural identity – both Scottish and Irish). As in Scotland, the poetry that arose using Ulster Scots was based largely on the traditional spoken language, but new models of orthography and poetic conventions were introduced that, because of literacy in English, employed the spelling of the latter language to represent Scots. This tendency, which could disguise the broadness of Ulster Scots pronunciation, created a challenge to any writer using Scots who wanted to show how it differed from English, a challenge that was made more complex by the fact that vernacular poetry developed its own orthographic conventions that may not have been phonetic. From the volume of this poetry and its intended audience, we can infer the continuing vitality of spoken Ulster Scots.

Perhaps the earliest Ulster document in Scots to come to light is a letter to Elizabeth I written in March 1571 by Agnes Campbell, a member of the house of Argyll, on behalf of her husband Turlough O Neil and addressed from County Tyrone (Hayes-McCoy 1937: 116):

> It will ples your maiestie knaw yat I your maties suitore Agnes Campbell Lady of Cantire in Scotland hes happynit threw my chance and potoun to cum heir in Irland in yor maiesties realm and is marreid uponn Oneill quha is yor maiesties trew subject . . . I am maist desyrous of any erthlie thing that zour grace will accept and recive my said husband Oneill in zour hienes service and subiectioun quha is verrie earnestlie bent thr unto . . . And in takin up his obedience unto zour hienes he is content to randir and pay to yor maiesties assignayis in Irland ane certain tribute zeirlie as his missingeris will declair zour hienes counsile at mair linthe. Quhilk will extend grettielie to zour Maties grete proffitt and obedience nt only of Oneill but of all uthris in the north of Irland that rebellis agains yor hienes quha may be brocht to obedience and service throwch yor hienes power and be Oneillis means and force.

Herein we find numerous forms having distinctive Scottish orthography (*erthlie, zeirlie, grettielie, uthris, quha, quhilk, ane*), pronunciation (*maist, mair*) and morphology (*happynit*). Perhaps the most diagnostic feature in this and many other texts is the concord between subjects and verbs. This follows the traditional Scottish pattern of marking any present-tense verb with -*s* (or by analogy, using *is* or *has*) if its subject is not an adjacent personal pronoun (Murray 1873: 211–13; Montgomery 1994a).[11] Scots and English thus have concord paradigms based on two different systems, the one in Scots depending on the proximity between a subject and its verb and on the type of subject (noun vs pronoun), while the English one depends on the number and person of the subject. In the Campbell letter, four contexts for concord are found, all of which follow the Scottish rule: *I . . . hes happynit, I . . . is marreid, I am maist desyrous* and *all uthris . . . that rebellis*.

Ulster Scots during the plantation era is known from legal documents and correspondence (both domestic and semi-official letters) written in Ulster by individuals who, with one or two exceptions, were of Scottish nativity. This material was unknown to linguists (much of it in unpublished archival collections) until cited and excerpted in Robinson (1989a), an essay which surveys how the Scots language was used in 'letters, wills, indentures and leases written in Ulster between the late sixteenth century and the mid-seventeenth century' (1989a: 86) and which provides useful biographical information on the authors of these texts. At present, only a few dozen documents in Scots are known from the period, but they are sufficient to show that a fully-fledged variety of Scots was written by the first generation of migrants to Ulster. They also reveal that Scots as a written medium soon began to erode in favour of English.

Linguists have sometimes pointed out that, when Scots was brought to Ulster at the beginning of the seventeenth century, this was a time when 'it displayed the greatest difference from English' (Barry 1996: xi), a statement that pertains to speech but that can be surmised from surviving texts. For instance, the following excerpt comes from a legal document, an assignment of land from Robert McClelland to David Cunningham, dating from the second decade of the century (McClelland of Bombay Legal Documents 1614):

> I Sir Robert McClellane of Bomby knight be thir presentis does faithfullie promeiss to my gud freynd David Cunynghame of Heurt his airis and assignayis to set to thame ane sufficient Laice

of twell scoir aikeris of land that I haif of the Happerdaschers portion of Londary and that for the space of one and fiftie yeirs lyand within the Countie of Culraine in ony pairt of the said Happerdaschers proportioun now perteyning to me exceptand and reservand the stone hous and mannis . . .

In this short passage (only a part of the initial sentence, but consistent with the remainder), numerous Scottish forms occur, including the plural demonstrative adjective *thir*, noun plurals in *-is* (*presentis*, *airis*, *aikeris*), a non-adjacent verb marked with *-s* (*I Sir Robert McClellane . . . does*), the indefinite article *ane* before a consonant, present-participle forms in *-and* (*lyand*, *exceptand*, *reservand*) and variants such as *twell* 'twelve' and *haif* 'have'. The Scots used in the eighteen receipts, leases, promissory notes and land assignments in the McClelland papers (1612–24) is conservative, but the documents dating from the 1620s clearly begin to shift towards using English counterparts of the forms cited above.

Another collection in Scots, this time correspondence, is found among the papers of Archibald Edmonstone of Duntreath, a native of Stirlingshire who migrated to County Down c. 1604 and settled in Ballycarry, County Antrim, in 1609 with his brother and brother-in-law (Historical Manuscripts Commission 1909). Included are forty-five letters from twenty-eight different members of the aristocracy using some Scots, letters to family members, associates and members of other landed families (such as the Hamiltons, Montgomerys and MacDonnells), and written between 1609 and 1631. Though sometimes addressing intimate family subjects, these letters are generally formal in style, indicating that their writers were schooled in Scots. Two examples addressed from Ballymena follow.

W. Houstoun to [name missing], 25 April 1626, Ballemeanaghe: 'Worschipfull, my deuty unto your self rememberit and not forgetting my deuty and service to my Lord Clanneboyes. Theis ar to put yow in remembrance and also to intreate yow to do me the favour that ye wilbe in Craigfergus on Monday nixt, being May day, that I may haif your contenance thair at the tendur of Abrey Loo his money, as also for my meitting with Jhone McCulloch, becaus ye ar the man chosin for me as it fallis by our submissioun. Sunday nixt was the day of our meitting, bot I think we must put it off till Tuesday next. This hoiping ye will perform as I schalbe ever reddy to yow in the lyik of anything ellis that lyes in my power, and sua remaines, your faithfull freind, V. Houstoun.' (Historical Manuscripts Commission 1909: 123–4)

Sir Robert Adair of Kinhilt to his brother-in-law, Archibald Edmonston of Duntreath, 2 June 1627, Ballemenach. – 'Rycht worthie and loving brother, my love remembrit. We expectid to have sine yow longe sence. Ye shall wit that their hes bin servants of my Lord Cheichesters heir taking possesione in Gilform to the use of my Lord Cheichester. We have grait naid that ye and we war together to consult in this bussines and sindry other things. We ar mightilie trublit with the sogers monays daylie in this land, and your not agreement with Mr Houstoune drawis us still in farther inconvenients, as ye will heir at meiting. I have this day reseved letters from Scotland quich urgis me to go over with all the speid I can, quhich makes me the desyrus that we all sould be together befor my waygoing. So thinge els to meiting. With my love to your bedfellow and all our frends, I take leve and still remains, your loving brother to my uttermost, Ro. Adair.' (Historical Manuscripts Commission 1909: 126–7)

These two letters exhibit the same Scottish features as previously cited (for example, each places an *-s* on *remain* in the complementary clause where the verb is not adjacent to its subject), but these are markedly attenuated by comparison to the 1571 letter and 1614 land assignment.

In some cases, there seems to be competition between forms (*expectid/remembrit, trublit/reseved*), and in others the Scottish form has disappeared (for example, present participles only in *-ing*). Because the Duntreath letters span nearly a quarter of a century (though they are heavily skewed towards the end of this period), it is possible to observe the replacement of Scottish by English forms for a number of features. This same process of anglicisation, in which the written Scots language lost autonomy by the disappearance of a range of orthographic and grammatical features in favour of their English counterparts, had proceeded in Scotland since the mid-sixteenth century (Devitt 1989), for some genres of writing more quickly than for others. In family correspondence, distinctive Scots features prevailed longest in Scotland – well into the middle third of the 1600s – but in some types of national and public records the shift to English was not finally completed until the mid-eighteenth century (MacQueen 1957). In Ulster, the process apparently took place more rapidly, if the Duntreath letters are a reliable indicator. Table 14.1 shows the occurrence of five features over three equal subsets of these letters. That the preponderance of documents (thirty of the forty-five) dates from the last five years (1627–31) of the twenty-three-year period makes it more difficult to gauge the gradualness of shifts that appear to occur, and letters from so many different writers also vary in style. Even so, there is evidence of rapid erosion of written Scots in these few years.

Table 14.1   Attrition of Scottish forms in the Duntreath letters (based on Montgomery 1992).

	1609–26 (n = 15)		1627–9 (n = 14)		1630–1 (n = 16)	
verbal concord *-s**	12/23	52.2%	8/15	53.3%	6/27	22.2%
preterite/participle *-it*	45/76	59.2%	21/51	41.2%	23/79	29.1%
indefinite article *ane***	13/23	56.5%	10/20	50.0%	9/41	22.0%
relative pronoun *quha/quhilk*	40/56	71.4%	22/41	53.7%	28/62	45.2%
demonstrative *thir/thay*	5/9	55.6%	1/4	25.0%	0/5	0.0%

* All present-tense contexts except those that are third-person singular or that have personal pronoun subjects adjacent to their verbs.
** Only in contexts preceding a consonant.

Despite there being less data than we would like for some features, the cumulative evidence from Table 14.1 is that anglicisation was affecting written Ulster Scots. For four of the five features, a steady decline in the native Scots variant occurred across the three time periods, the only exception (and this is only a partial one) being verbal concord *-s*. It turns out that the decline is sharper than the table shows, because the 1630–1 subset of letters includes one from Isabel Haldane (mother of Archibald Edmonstone, and an older individual whose writing likely reflected the more conservative version of Scots learned in the late sixteenth century); she uses the preterite/past-participle suffix *-it* and relative pronouns spelled with *quh-* categorically (in all sixteen and all thirteen cases, respectively) and the indefinite article *ane* four times in seven contexts. If these figures are subtracted from the rightmost column, the percentages for the remaining letters drop sharply. For further citations and a more detailed analysis of these letters, see Montgomery (1992).

14.5 MID-SEVENTEENTH CENTURY

From the post-plantation period, few Ulster documents survive that are not written in a uniform, standard version of English, but session minute books from Presbyterian churches and a few letters can be cited as displaying Scottish forms. Presbyterianism came to Ulster as early as 1613, but formal organisation of a presbytery did not occur until 1642, under the auspices of the Scottish army arriving to assist compatriots after the 1641 Irish rebellion. Formal records apparently began shortly thereafter, as evidenced by early session books that have survived. Extracts from the minutes of two of these, transcribed and published a century ago by William T. Latimer, can be examined for their use of language. These include the complete minutes of the Templepatrick Presbyterian Church of south Antrim (a congregation dating back to at least 1626, when a grandson of John Knox became pastor) between 24 November 1646 and 14 September 1647 (Latimer 1895, 1901) and brief portions from the minute book of the Dundonald Presbyterian Church of north Down (1674–1713), published in Latimer (1897).

The language in these church records is overwhelmingly formal English, sometimes with Latinate terminology. Scottish forms show up from time to time (*leich* 'low', *robett* 'robbed', *buik* 'book', *coup* 'cup', *forgans* 'in front of'), but only three Scottish features occur with regularity: the spelling of *q-* for *wh-* in a variety of forms (*qlk* 'which', *qt* 'what', *qr* 'where', and *qm* 'whom'), *ane* before consonants, and the suffix *-s* on present-tense verbs other than those having adjacent personal pronouns. Except for this verbal suffix and a single instance of *-et* marking a preterite form, the morphology of the published portion of the Templepatrick minutes is English. The Scottish concord rule operates at the surprisingly high rate of nearly 60 per cent ($35/60 = 58.3$ per cent), which suggests that by the middle of the seventeenth century it had become characteristic of Ulster English through contact with Scots. The following sentences exemplify forms of Scottish origin.

(1) The qlk day it is inacted by the Session that no children be baptized till they first come to some of ye elders who presents them, and get their names inregistrated in the records; and yt the minister receave them not till he receive ane testimony from those elders of there so doing. (9 February 1647; Latimer 1901: 171)

(2) The qlk day Umphra browne being convened before ye Session and they not as yet satisfied with any signes of his repentance continues his standing the next lords day if so be the Lord may worke furder upon his heart. (16 February 1647; Latimer 1901: 172)

(3) To the wch agnes Dazell answered and called her ane Hell sow and said yt she cutted her keil and staw her peits. (27 July 1647; Latimer 1901: 268)

The Dundonald minutes attest no Scottish morphology and only a few forms which can only be called relic spellings: *qo* 'who' (1684), *ane* (1685, 1708), *qrof* 'whereof' (1702, 1707) and *qch* 'which' (1711).

Among surviving late seventeenth-century Ulster correspondence is the letterbook of Belfast merchant George McCartney (McCartney 1661–8), who was most likely a native of Kirkcudbright. In business correspondence with associates in Dublin, London, the Low Countries and France, McCartney used some Scottish spellings (for example, *zow* 'you', *zett* 'yet', *ze* 'you', *heawe/hawe* 'have', *serwis* 'service', *veshel* 'vessel', *persell* 'parcel', *money* 'many') and occasionally a morphological variant (for example, *yoursell* 'yourself'). The only grammatical feature which he employed with any frequency was the Scottish concord *-s*, as in the following:

I . . . saluts yow and desyres alyne from you (29 June 1661)
our nobles and great men remaines at London and dublin that makes things go the more in the
Contrie (30 June 1662)

McCartney's language would suggest his probable Scottish background if this were not known from other sources (Agnew 1994), but he uses far more English than Scottish conventions and thus his writing is English.

Much further documentation from the period may lie in archives awaiting linguistic analysis, but the evidence presently available requires us to conclude that Scots had more or less disappeared from the naive, unselfconscious writing of people in Ulster by the end of the seventeenth century, if not several decades earlier, other than occasional spellings such as with ⟨q-⟩ for ⟨wh-⟩. From the time of the Templepatrick session minutes forwards, writing was done in English that sometimes exhibited Scottish features. The same can be said about writing in the eighteenth and nineteenth centuries such as personal letters from Ulster emigrants to North America, whose written language is always English, but was in some respects influenced by Scots. If from a point in the seventeenth century there were no documents written in what we would call Scots and by those of Scottish ancestry except intentional, conscious renditions using Ulster Scots in prose and poetry, this could hardly have been otherwise. As English became the language of literacy, it took a deliberate decision for one to write in Scots, even if the latter was one's native speech.

Thus, as an unconscious written medium, the Scots language in Ulster represented an extension of mainland Scots and had a rather limited lifespan. If anything, features of Scots apparently gave way more quickly in Ulster than in Scotland. It is not difficult to understand why this could have been the case. English was not a language emanating from London or another governmental seat some distance away, but was the language of the local administration, the language of the bureaucracy of the plantation. Institutions using written language were more surely English than in Scotland, and any practice of using Scots could hardly have been established before being severed. Although English-speakers were outnumbered by Scots-speakers, the administrative requirement of writing in English must have added to the social and religious pressures already operating on written Scots (and well known on the mainland) to accelerate the process of anglicisation in Ulster.

On the other hand, that much of the population continued to speak Scots in parts of Ulster cannot be doubted, not only from the fact that Ulster Scots speech areas in the mid-twentieth century were almost exactly coextensive with the settlement patterns of Scots in the Ulster Plantation in the early 1600s, but also because of the geographical distribution, as we will see, of dozens of vernacular poets in the eighteenth and nineteenth centuries. Ulster Scots may have been replaced by English in the writing of clergymen, but did not necessarily disappear from their sermons; Patrick Adair (d. 1694) is said to have been accustomed to preaching in it (Killen 1866: xii–xiii). Most likely, spoken Ulster Scots declined in prestige only slowly until the strictures of schoolmasters began to make it an object of eradication beginning in the late eighteenth century and especially in the nineteenth century.

14.6   EIGHTEENTH CENTURY

A generation after the Williamite wars and the coming of stability to Ireland, evidence of interest in Scots-language literature and the use of Scots for literary expression began to appear in Ulster. As with other things, what happened in Ulster was inseparable from what happened in Scotland; in this case, there was certainly awareness of the work of Allan Ramsay and the vernacular revival. But developments were scarcely a mere imitation of Scottish ones. From a point in the eighteenth century, developments in Scottish areas of Ulster, whether literary, political, religious or otherwise, often began to take their own character – an Irish one. These were conditioned by and were responses to life in Ireland, as the Scottish community took deeper root and became integrated there. Accordingly, writers could have a dual identity, considering themselves as Irish (as citizens of a multicultural Ireland, not a monolithic one) and their language as Scots.

After a period of intermittent development, the use of Ulster Scots was to blossom, particularly for poetry, for several decades beginning around 1790, when popular verse was written by dozens of working-class poets (usually hand-loom weavers – hence the appellation 'Rhyming Weavers' given by Hewitt (1974)), printed in Belfast and other newspapers, and sometimes collected in small volumes and published by subscription. Most of these individuals were well read in both English and Scottish poets. Literate in English and having a native command of spoken Scots, many wrote poetry in each. Others produced English verse that was variably Scots, the choice of one over the other depending on a variety of factors, which will give us insight into the motivations for using Scots if we can sort these out. Nowhere in Ulster did publishing and writing in Scots ever take place to the exclusion of English, and for Scots these declined rapidly in the middle third of the nineteenth century under the pressures created by a national school system and other factors that marginalised the Ulster Scots language variety and gradually eroded the historic closeness between Ulster and Scotland. Scotland became no longer the only major point of cultural reference for the Scottish community in Ulster.

We will return to the use of Ulster Scots in poetry shortly, but will first consider its use in a strikingly different type of document. These are letters and sketches written in pseudo-dialect in the early eighteenth century and published as newspaper accounts or in pamphlet form. 'Pseudo-dialect' refers to the fact that these texts use a deliberate concentration of dialect for its rhetorical effect; their density of vernacular forms far exceeds what occurs in personal letters, the most colloquial type of documents from the hands of known semiliterate writers of the eighteenth or any other century. In fact, the putatively naive authors of these dialect pieces, whether anonymous or pseudonymous, appear to have been highly literate and skilful propagandists, perhaps even veterans of the fierce Irish pamphlet wars of the 1720s and 1730s. The unusual character and circumstances of production of these documents suggest the possibility of multiple audiences and purposes, but there is certainly much about them that we can never know, and we cannot absolutely rule out the possibility that they were produced in jest or as experiments. Though they are artificial in one sense, we may judge their validity, their authenticity as cultural statements, from how consistent their content is with the tempers of the day. Of course, linguistic analysis can proceed without reference to such considerations, relying on only our knowledge of eighteenth-century Scots and English, but this is hardly as easy as it might appear, since we know little about the spoken form of these languages from this period.

As greater equilibrium was achieved between the segments of Ulster society, Dublin and London became points of reference in addition to Glasgow and Edinburgh. Settled communities have their own politics. To say that from the early eighteenth century Ulster developments must be seen in their own light, as taking on a character different from Scotland, is in no sense more true than for emigration to North America, which by

1720 had become a matter of continuing awareness to the public and concern to the government. Scottish communities may have been firmly established in Ireland by this time, but the memory of the planting having been threatened in 1641 by the Irish uprising and in 1689 by the siege of Derry compounded with the passing of the Test Act in 1704 (which imposed civil disabilities on dissenters as well as Catholics) to instil the view among Ulster Presbyterians that they were on their own and could not necessarily depend on the Crown or the government for support. With the coming of rent and other economic crises in 1717, this memory produced the conviction that emigration was an appropriate response to their deprivation. This developing cultural psyche found direct expression in a noteworthy pseudo-dialect document whose earliest known form is a published version that appeared in North America. Ostensibly from a Mr James Murray in New York City to a Reverend Baptist Boyd in Aughnacloy, Country Tyrone, this lengthy letter was printed in October 1737 in two North American newspapers, the *Virginia Gazette* (Williamsburg) and the *Pennsylvania Gazette* (Philadelphia, which was edited by Benjamin Franklin).[12] It opens with an exhortation, as follows:

> Read this Letter, and look, and tell aw the poor Folk of your Place, that God has open'd a Door for their Deliverance; for here is ne Scant of Breed here, and if your Sons Samuel and James Boyd wad but come here, they wad get mere Money in ane Year for teechin a Letin Skulle, nor ye yer sell wad get for Three Years Preeching whar ye are. Reverend Baptist Boyd, there ged ane wee me in the Shep, that now gets ane Hundred Punds for ane Year for teechin a Letin Skulle, and God kens, little he is skill'd in Learning, and yet they think him a high learned Man: . . . for here aw that a Man warks for is his ane, there are ne ravenus Hunds to rive it fre uo here, ne sick Word as Herbingers is kend here, but every yen enjoys his ane, there is ne yen to tak awa yer Corn, yer Potatoes, yer Lint or Eggs . . .

Scottish forms abound here: *ken* (including its participial form, *kend*), *yer sell* 'yourself', *ged* 'went', *ane* 'own', *wee* 'with', *fre* 'from', *awa* 'away'. These are complemented by dozen of others, all of which appear to be authentic Scots, however extreme its use of vernacular is in a written document. The spellings are often semi-phonetic and close to representing the traditional Scots pronunciations of words, and the grammar is unmistakably Scots as well (such as verbal concord, though it is not found in this excerpt). The letter both protests and promotes. It calls for emigration from Ulster, especially by dissenters (such as Presbyterians), directly contravening the wishes of the British government, which of course had recruited Scottish Protestants a century earlier and, fearing destabilisation in Ireland, very much wanted to keep their descendants there to buffer the Irish, although on terms dictated from London. The letter articulates the theme of America as a Promised Land, known to have been prevalent in Presbyterian sermons of the day and a continuing expression of the Covenanting spirit that undergirded Scottish settlement in Ulster the previous century.

The documentary history of the Murray letter, though only partially known, is perhaps of even greater import than its content. The letter may have been first published in American newspapers in 1737, but in 1993 a manuscript version of it dated 1767 came to light that, though having the same content sentence by sentence, had innumerable variations in spelling, word choice, capitalisation and punctuation. One is a deliberate alteration of the other, or both are alterations of an unknown predecessor. The two known versions are apparently written in different varieties of Scots (see Montgomery (1994b) for a transcription of both texts), but these have yet to be identified. The remarkably different idioms of the versions (although both are internally consistent) suggest that the document may have had other manifestations and therefore may have enjoyed a life of its own as a rhetorical set piece that fulfilled one or more of the following functions: to express the continuing conviction of the Ulster Scots/Presbyterian community that it (or the Almighty) controlled its destiny, not the British government; to remind themselves of compatriots who had emigrated and of the endurance and sacrifice of these people; to supply the psychological assurance of having a place of refuge; to remind themselves of grievances against the established government; or even to serve as a kind of veiled warning to the authorities. The testimonial style and highly charged, passionate tone of the letter, along with its author's plea that the Rev. Boyd (whose existence and identity are known; he was in Aughnacloy in the early part of the century) read it to his parishioners, make it likely that the document was designed to be read in public and was circulated for public hearing at other churches and venues. It may have been read on public occasions for some time.

Another fictional letter of the same period using Ulster Scots is 'The North-Country Man's Description of Christ-Church in Dublin in a Letter to a Friend', purportedly written from Portaferry in County Down by an Ulster seaman who was laid over in Dublin on Sunday and sought a Presbyterian worship service, ending up instead in the Anglican cathedral (see Robinson (1995) for an analysis and transcript). The document was reprinted in the *Pennsylvania Gazette* in December 1733 after first being published in pamphlet form earlier that year with four other pieces (three in Ulster Scots), all of which caricatured dissenters. Irrespective of the identity of its author and the motivations for its composition (Robinson discusses these matters at some length and speculates on the possibility that it may actually have been penned by Jonathan Swift), the account is in Scots, though not as intense a version as the Murray letter. The sailor writes, in part (Robinson 1995: 41):

> WHAR I was I can ge ne Account of, but I can tell ye what I seed. When first I ged in, I ged doon a great place that a' the Floor was cover'd we bread Stens, and a Warld o' Foke going up and doon thro' yen another. We cam tell twa great Stairs, and ged under them, whar was a Door gaing in. This place was amest foo o' Foke; as well aboon as whar I was, this they cad the Kirk . . .

Though only four in number, these documents suggest the existence of a minor genre of letters designed to reflect speech, whose anonymous writers' adoption of a heavy dialect was intrinsic to their purpose, whether propaganda or satire. Interestingly, similar documents were written in the early eighteenth century in Highland English, one of them purportedly by an emigrant from Inverness-shire writing from Maryland (Miller forthcoming). Much work remains in seeking, among collections of ephemeral literature from the period, other documents like the two discussed here; at present, we can only begin to contextualise them and relate them to the political and publishing currents of the day.

14.7   EARLY VERNACULAR POETRY

Publishing came to Belfast early in the eighteenth century, reflecting a relatively high degree of literacy (attributable in large part to the emphasis placed by Presbyterianism on the individual's being able to read Scripture), and books in Scots were among those that were in demand. As previously stated, literacy would have been primarily in English, but this was often acquired at home, so it is difficult to know on what materials it was based or how often a taste for literature in Scots may have been involved. In any case, as early as

1714, James Blow of Belfast printed and sold an edition of the *Poems* of Sir David Lindsay, a Scots writer born in the late fifteenth century. Other early printings were of Alexander Montgomerie's *The Cherry and the Slae* (1731) and Allan Ramsay's *The Gentle Shepherd* (1748 and many subsequent editions; for a discussion of early printing in Ulster, see J. R. R. Adams 1987: 7). There is evidence that in the first quarter of the century vernacular verse in the form of poetic epistles was being written in Scots and exchanged with the mainland. An example is a sixty-four-line effort from a Mr William Starrat, a teacher of mathematics in Strabane, County Tyrone, that was written in 1722 to Ramsay (and answered in kind in fifty-two lines of his own). Starrat states: 'My Whistle frae my Blanket-nook I drew, and lifted owre thir twa three Lines to you', while Ramsay responds, 'Dear Friend of Mine, ye but o'er meikle roose/The lawly Mints of my poor moorland Muse' (Kinghorn and Law 1974: 69, 71). Starrat was likely also the 'Northern Bard' who penned 'An Elegy on the Much-Lamented Death of Quarter-Master Brice Blare; Who died at Strabane', a verse in Standard Habbie (a stanzaic form to be widely used by Ulster poets for more than a century) that was printed on a Dublin broadsheet in 1734 and that represents the first-known published poem in Ulster Scots (Marshall (1907); for further information on Starrat and other early poetry in Ulster Scots, see Robinson forthcoming b). At mid-century *The Ulster Miscellany*, an anthology of prose and poetry, was published in Belfast (1753) containing eighteen pages of 'Scotch Poems' that appear to have originated from the Laggan area of east Donegal; these are unattributed, but may also come from the pen of Starrat. Among these is 'TIT for TAT . . . A new Song, in Way of Dialogue, between a Laggan Farmer and his Wife', a satirical piece that still offers charms today:

> Ye're welcome hame, my Mar'gy,
> Frae the grim craving clergy;
> How deeply did they charge ye,
> Wi' fair oppressive tythe?
> While some are chous'd, and cheated;
> Some rattled are, and rated;
> Ye hae been better treated,
> I trow, ye luick sae blythe.
>   ('Scotch Poems': 380)

Because the work of early Ulster poets who used Scots has to date been identified only in private correspondence and ephemeral publications that chanced to survive, it is impossible at present to know how widespread this type of writing was.

It is surely significant, however, that any early poetry in Scots came from west Ulster at all. As would be expected, it was in more heavily Ulster Scots areas of Antrim and Down that vernacular poetry had its most vigorous existence; this involved the appearance, from the 1780s until past the mid-nineteenth century, of a remarkable number (for such a small area) of the aforementioned 'Rhyming Weaver' poets, a loose assemblage of popular versifiers so called because they were by trade either weavers of linen or otherwise involved in textile manufacture. We can never know how many there were – dozens at least – because often their work has now been lost. G. B. Adams' (1964: 4) characterisation that 'in Antrim and Down . . . throughout the eighteenth and nineteenth centuries many a hand-loom weaver or farmer could be found who would turn his hand to writing verse as easily as guiding the shuttle or the plough' may, however, be a slight exaggeration.

Although many of these poets had little formal education, they were well read in both poetry and current affairs, and some did have schooling in the rudiments of the classical languages. They were Presbyterians, mostly natives of small, rural communities where they remained weavers throughout their lives, and they assumed the stance of spokesman and advocate for the common folk who like themselves had little opportunity for schooling or social mobility. The definitive account of the movement and its principal members, from which much of the following is distilled, is *The Rhyming Weavers and Other Country Poets of Antrim and Down* (1974), a first critical account and selective anthology, by John Hewitt, a well-respected Ulster poet in his own right.

Though numbering in the dozens and writing over a period of several decades, some generalisations about the weaver poets can be offered that will help us to gauge the value of the work which they produced. Their poetry was often closely integrated with their communities, providing social commentary and dealing with local themes and interests, and the bards themselves strongly identified with these places (this hardly prevented them from taking an active interest in international events and democratic movements abroad or in the nationalist politics of the United Irishmen closer to home). Their identification with and status within local rural communities was signalled by their frequent appellations such as David Herbison, called 'the Bard of Dunclug', or James Orr, 'the Bard of Ballycarry'. They were most numerous and most familiar with one another's work in south Antrim (the small town of Cullybackey had eight published poets in the span of a century (R. I. Connolly 1981: 23), but were also concentrated in north Down and mid-Antrim and to be found occasionally west of the Bann (a map of their communities is provided in Connolly (1981: 64)). They often wrote and sometimes extemporised poetry for public rendering at village book clubs and country reading societies. Many of them were published, especially from the late 1790s through 1820 or so, primarily in such Belfast newspapers as *The Belfast Newsletter*, *The Northern Whig* and *The Northern Star*. Some had their work collected in small volumes, the first being Samuel Thomson (1793), but few were published in more than one collection, some never gathered their work into book form (being content to have an occasional piece appear in a newspaper), and others are known only from oral tradition. Almost none had steady patrons, which meant that they had to finance publication by enlisting subscriptions from individuals and booksellers beforehand (usually several hundred were needed), a time-consuming if not ego-testing process which they usually undertook themselves after many years of composition. Most maintained their work as weaver/farmers and their status as peasant or 'folk poets' until the end of their lives; none made more than a modest, part-time income from writing.

A poetic movement of such size and span had its share of diversity, reflecting the religious and political cross-currents of the day. Social protest was among its expressions, but this was sometimes tempered because support from middle-class subscribers was needed for publication. Over the decades, the movement underwent some cultivation, but it remained largely rooted in the speech of the day; the weaver poets were using their own language, not that of an artificial literary tradition.

The movement paralleled and sometimes drew inspiration from Robert Burns, but, in view of the dating of the poetry cited earlier, it seems more likely to have been an indigenous, parallel Ulster development rather an imitation and derivation from Scotland. (There were minor Ulster poets, like Francis Boyle of Gransha and Robert Dinsmoor of New Hampshire, an emigrant from north Antrim, who were writing vernacular poetry in the 1770s, drawing inspiration from Ramsay and perhaps others.) The weavers doubtless saw themselves as writing in a vernacular tradition having the same sources as those of

Burns, these going back to Ramsay. They read Burns, whose collected works were first published in Belfast in the same year as the first Edinburgh edition (1787) and then reprinted three times before the end of the century. They enthusiastically admired his poetry, sometimes used it as a model for their own, and celebrated his work in theirs (his popularity is maintained today in Ulster, reflected in an association of Burns Clubs). But they did the same for other Scottish poets, and for some English ones too; more than anything else, they 'were acutely conscious of their Scottish literary heritage. In particular, they valued an independent literary tradition which could trace its ancestry back to the Middle Scots writers Barbour, Lindsay, Dunbar and Henryson' (Herbison 1993: 14). They thus saw themselves as belonging within the same inclusive tradition as Burns. The avid demand for poetry in Scots from both Scotland and Ulster suggests a readership in Ulster of some size. Ivan Herbison's (1989: 5) assessment is a thoughtful one:

> The true importance of Burns for the Ulster poets lay in what he had achieved: the establishment of a regional literature and a distinctive Scottish poetic. They shared with Burns a similar rural environmental and social background, a common cultural heritage, a common vernacular language, and a rich inheritance of verse-forms and poetic genres. It was this achievement which they sought to recreate in Ulster.

These vernacular poets identified with and used Scots to different degrees. Many appeared to be more comfortable in Scots than in English, but others were equally at home in English, in which all of them wrote at least some verse; the latter is no surprise, since many were members of local book clubs and country reading societies that met to discuss contemporary poetry, much of which was from Britain. Even when the use of Scots was heavy, poets and their publishers almost never attached a glossary to their collection.[13] Having two mediums at hand gave advantages beyond the ability to address different audiences; it afforded two sets of rhyming possibilities, at least as many options as their mainland versifying counterparts. Their degree of Scots depended on their subject matter; according to Herbison (1993: 14),

> [i]n the use of Ulster Scots, one can detect the operation of some principles of literary decorum. The vernacular is used for satirical and humorous pieces, for poetic addresses, epistles, songs, and ballads, for domestic subjects and (occasionally) social commentary. English is preferred for pastorals, elegies and topographical pieces.

It also depended on their intended readership's tastes and facility with vernacular language; these things could be surmised because their subscribers were often known. If poets relied on middle-class patronage or sought to reach a dispersed audience, they would dilute their use of dialect. Sarah Leech of east County Donegal is apparently the only female who made poetry in Scots in the period. A sample stanza of hers follows: 'Ilk lass maun ha'e a snaw-white goun/Wi' span-lang flounces wavin' roun',/Some weel-plait straw upon her croun,/ And ribbons gay,/While hose weel starched an' right-left shoon her feet display' (Hewitt 1974: 37).

Perhaps the best-known and most skilful user of Scots among these poets was James Orr. In the introduction to a recent collection of his poems, *The Country Rhymes of James Orr, the Bard of Ballycarry, 1770–1816*, his editor states (P. Robinson 1992: ix) that he provides us with the stereotype of the Ulster weaver-poet of the 1790s and early 1800s – a radical thinker, a patriot, a United Irishman, a 'New Light' Presbyterian, a humanist with a penetrating social concern for the poor, a contented weaver and small farmer who never sought social elevation, and a man who until his death in 1817 continued to speak 'braid Scotch'.

Orr's 'The Irish Cottier's Death and Burial', a work inspired and influenced by Burns, exemplifies the social sentiments of the poetic movement well; it is also a work judged by more than one critic to be superior to Orr's Ayrshire counterpart (Hewitt 1974: 5). An excerpt from another of Orr's poems, 'The Dying Mason', shows his mastery of Scots (Robinson 1992: 96):

> Nae mair shall I gang, while in this side o' time . . .
> Nae mair, while ilk mouth's clos'd, an' fast the door bar'd,
> Initiate the novice, baith curious and scaur'd;
> Nae mair join wi' scores in the grand chorus saft,
> Nor fandly toast 'Airlan' – and peace to the craft';
> I aye cud been wi' ye, but now I maun stay
> Confin'd in my lang hame – the cauld house o' clay.

Other common sentiments of the poets, light-hearted ones, can be seen in a short verse that Hugh Porter of Moneyslane, County Down, wrote to address readers of his collection of poems published in 1813 (A. Adams and J. R. R. Adams 1992: xxix):

> READER,
> SINCE ye hae gie'n your five an' fi'ppence.
> For this bit Beuk, that's no worth tippence,
> Anither page or twa o' paper,
> Wad mak it aye leuk something cheaper.

Because many identified intensely with a local native community and contributed occasional verse to its life, these bards often did achieve a degree of celebrity there. But their publication in newspapers and other mass outlets meant that their reputations could extend widely enough to interest subscribers when a collection was prospected. Those enlisting had their names, titles and locales compiled in the book, so that a profile of them can be made and we can gauge the extent of literacy in Scots. Andrew McKenzie, a County Down poet, managed to recruit an impressive count of 144 subscribers from western Scotland, an unusually high number but ample evidence that vernacular poetry did not flow in only one direction across the channel. Samuel Thomson had a dozen subscribers from Boston, Massachusetts, for his *Poems in Different Subjects Partly in the Scottish Dialects* (1793).

In choosing to write in Scots, these writers were well aware of making a cultural statement. Their self-consciousness about language is revealed on occasion in their verse, in that they sometimes made a point of refusing to apologise for using the vernacular:

> Thomson: 'In costume Scotch, o'er bog and park/My hame bred Muse delighted plays' [orig. 1806];
> Porter: 'And thirdly, in the style appears/The accent o' my earlier years/Which is not Scotch, nor English either,/But part o' baith mixed up thegither./Yet it's the sort my neighbors use,/ Wha think "shoon" prettier far than "shoes".' [orig. 1813]

> Orr: 'My rude Scotch rhymes the tasteful justly slight, The Scotch-tongued rustics scorn each
> nobler flights' [n.d., cited in Robinson 1992: xxiii]

Hewitt shows how the poetic tradition waned in response to changing conditions of the
day, primarily the decline of cottage-based home weaving due to the advent of mechanised
production, and the disappearance of the tightly knit, organic rural communities from
which many poets drew their inspiration. As a result, Ulster Scots increasingly lost its
status as a vehicle of literary expression. Barriers to publication arose, as newspapers
became less and less willing to carry vernacular poetry after mid-century, which forced
writers like David Herbison, who is considered the last of the weavers and who wrote
poetry until his death in 1880, 'to adopt Standard English as his principal medium'
(Herbison 1993: 14).

Poets were also aware of this declining estimation of their native tongue, feeling that their
voice was being taken away. One in particular, Robert Huddleston (1814–87), the 'Bard of
Moneyrea' (County Down), was apparently so embittered by the poor reception of his
vernacular work that he refused to have his poetry published in the last forty years of his life
and left the following acerbic statement among his unpublished papers (1993: 10–11):

> To strangers who may say that I am the follower of Burns and the Scottish Bards both in idiom
> and rhythm. To such men I say how could it be otherwise, unless I walked out of my country
> and idiom – a thing that the poetic bosom won't do – nay, unless I outstepped my nature, a thing
> no man can do. You may as well say a man will write out of his senses as out of his dialect . . .
> People who imagine the Irish idiom, in every part of the isle, to be smattering of English coupled
> with a brogue, are quite mistaken. Almost the half of Ulster, my native province, speak the very
> dialect in which my poems is written. Born and brought up in the County of Down and the
> parish of Comber on the northern shores of the island, within forty miles of Scotland, what
> wonder if my language and that of the Scot almost agree. What a mockery it is then, for
> intelligent men, to be calling the writings of some authors those of others, because they resemble
> them in language. This it is, that so many rustic authors of Ulster are said to be sprung from
> Burns. Alas, what a mistake! And what a mischance that people who even talk the very dialect
> cannot even read it – nay – even when they see it in print.

After their heyday, the reputation of these poets slowly ebbed until their modern-day
rediscovery by Hewitt in the 1970s. Contemporary critics had begun to deprecate their work
in their own lifetime (Herbison 1996), but Abraham Hume could write a balanced, even
admiring view of their achievements at mid-century (1858: 58):

> [t]he rustic poets in Ulster, especially in Antrim, Down, and Londonderry, seemed to let their
> ideas flow insensibly in Scottish verse. There were two reasons, however, for the practice. One
> was, that their taste had been formed almost exclusively on Scottish models; the other, that by
> using more or fewer Scotticisms at will, they had nearly a double power in the matter of rhymes.

The weaver poets maintained a token representation in anthologies of Irish verse until the
early twentieth century, but in more recent years it has become increasingly difficult to find
any trace of them in collections, guides or survey discussions of Anglo-Irish literature. Of a
dozen such volumes examined, only three had any mention or inclusion of them: John
Montague's *The Faber Book of Irish Verse* (1974) has Samuel Thomson's 'To a Hedgehog';
A. Norman Jeffares' *Anglo-Irish Literature* (1982: 109) has one rather puzzling comment on
James Orr, stating that 'Northern dialect was aimed at by' him; and Loreto Todd's *The*

Language of Irish Literature (1989a) has commentary and brief excerpts from Orr and Thomson. None of these works refers to the weavers as a group.

One contemporary critic, Ivan Herbison, views the declining awareness of vernacular poetry in Ulster Scots since the nineteenth century, as well as its subsequent downgrading and disappearance from anthologies and consideration in schools, in unambiguous political terms:

> [s]tate control of education through the National School system enabled the Anglo-Irish establishment to frame a curriculum that privileged English language, literature and cultural values and marginalised Ulster's Scottish cultural heritage . . . The exclusion of Ulster Scots from the *Field Day Anthology of Irish Writing* (1991) is merely the most recent and the most blatant example of a more widespread reluctance to acknowledge the presence of a Scottish cultural heritage in Ulster. In the compass of three ample volumes, containing translations from Latin, Norman French and Irish, as well as works in English, there is, apparently, no room for a single poem in the vernacular Scots. (Herbison 1993: 14–15)

Herbison may be justified in taking Seamus Deane, the editor of the *Field Day* anthology, sharply to task for a version of the 'canon' of Irish writing that is too narrow, or worse; but one may hope that in our day of redefining 'canons' in more sociologically valid and inclusive ways, one or more weaver poets may shortly be admitted on the basis of their reflecting the popular temper and tastes of their time. If this happens, it may give a fuller view of the many cultures that have contributed to and that constitute Ireland, and the use of tradition in Ulster writing may be seen as in a different light, as the weavers drew more on Scottish models than English ones, but in their own way, giving them the status of genuine literary figures of a time and place.

At the least, it seems that vernacular poetry in Ulster Scots has fallen between the cracks of Anglo-Irish and Scottish literatures, as it has *de facto* been considered under neither broad rubric. We have noted how rarely it has merited attention in works on Irish writing, but it is even more conspicuously absent in works on Scottish writing. There is no mention of the weaver poets (or in fact any literature in Ulster Scots) in the four-volume *History of Scottish Literature* (Craig 1987), which has at least passing reference to literature in Irish Gaelic. Literature in Ulster Scots obviously presents a problem of classification for established taxonomies.

Until Hewitt's rediscovery of these writers in *The Rhyming Weavers* (1974), a volume that established their place in the literary history of the province and vindicated them from rejection as slavish imitators of Burns, they had become almost completely unknown. Following Hewitt's lead, scholars have begun to consider the work of the weavers from the context of social history and linguistics, and it is now clear that this poetry provides the major source of documentation for the period for these and other disciplines. Using James Orr as an example, Akenson and Crawford (1977) show, among other things, how much we may learn about rural society, material culture and local life of the day from one poet's work (indeed, Gailey (1996) argues that the weaver poetry is sometimes the only source). Akenson followed this volume with a study (Akenson 1980) that is less rigorous but does provide useful lists of pronunciations and vocabulary items extracted from Orr's poetry. By using rhymes, unconventional spellings and metrical patterns from forty-nine poets, R. I. Connolly (1981) undertakes a much more sophisticated and ambitious analysis that attempts to reconstruct pronunciation in Ulster from the late eighteenth to the mid-nineteenth centuries. Because these poets' verse is a window on the social life of the day, it is a valuable source not only of information – sometimes the only source, according to Gailey (1996) – on aspects of material culture and rural life in the north of Ireland in an earlier day, but also of early nineteenth-century attestations of terms like *ingle* 'hearth' and *spence* 'pantry, inner apartment', of Scottish and English derivation, respectively.

The vernacular poetry itself was out of print until collections of the work of Orr, Porter and Thomson were recently published in the Folk Poets of Ulster series (P. Robinson 1992; Adams and Adams 1992; J. R. R. Adams 1992).

Linguistically speaking, it is not always easy to tell whether the vernacular poetry drew upon an earlier tradition (documentation of this is scarce) or how to interpret variation between poets (does this reflect local, historical or other differences?). Some conventions, including spellings, may have been indigenous to Ulster or adopted from Scotland (it is probably impossible to determine which), but in other cases poets seemed keenly aware that English spelling did not approximate to spoken Scots very closely, and they experimented with different forms in order to approach a more phonetic rendering of the language. Even the common word *with* 'will be spelt *wi*', *we* or *wae*, with the added confusion that *wae* also represents the word *woe*. So that the reader has to judge . . . what makes sense in a particular context' (Hewitt 1974: 15). R. I. Connolly's research throws light on many of the relevant issues here, especially by comparing the tentatively-reconstructed historical evidence with more modern spoken data, but much work remains to be done with the weaver-poet material. Connolly has also sought to 'explain why so much poetry was produced in the Ulster-Scots areas in the period studied' (1981: 1). A perhaps striking answer is that the use of Ulster Scots expressed resistance to the dominant English culture (Connolly 1981: 16):

> expressions of this resistance are to be found in certain nineteenth-century poets, notably Huddleston . . . [Ulster Scots] did suffer from 'the encroachment of standard English' and the change in attitudes. The result was that Ulster-Scots increasingly lost status in the community. The evidence suggests that it was not regarded even in the eighteenth century as a standard, but it had certainly more prestige then than it has in the present day.

The volume and the quality of this vernacular poetry make it the primary resource for the lexis of the day. It is from this poetry that innumerable citations would be drawn in the composition of a historical dictionary of Ulster Scots (indeed, Ulster Scots forms could hardly be neglected in a comprehensive lexicographical work on the entire island, as Michael Traynor (1953) discovered in editing his work on Donegal). The subject matter ranges widely over many domains of daily life. As intensely rooted to their localities as these poets were, it may also be possible to identify local variations of terms. As in any poetry, however, the weavers' verse did employ some conventional forms, some more than others, and it is difficult to surmise the actual currency of the language being used.

This poetry is also the principal source from which we may draw clues about pronunciation 200 years ago. As suggested above, a number of difficulties confront the analyst, but the sheer volume of material and the absence of other contemporary data make this poetry invaluable. As Connolly (1981: 3) points out, 'orthopoeistic, which would have been most useful, is largely lacking'. The verse itself is largely free from the phonetic spellings and other orthographical contortions that are found in much dialect verse and prose elsewhere. This was perhaps because the weavers were native speakers of Ulster Scots and because their standing as amateur poets in rural, working-class society permitted fewer pretensions; they had first and foremost to be comprehensible to their neighbours, to the local folk.

However well their lexis and idiom may reflect that of their localities, or the manipulated spelling may approximate their pronunciation, it is doubtful whether the grammar used by the weaver poets regularly reflects the vernacular. For instance, there is only occasional appearance of the Scottish verbal concord rule cited for earlier documents, and many poets employ (like Burns) the form *wha* as a relative pronoun when *that* (or its clipped form '*at*) is traditional Scots; in both of these respects, the poetry is less colloquial than emigrant letters of the time, although the latter are written in English that exhibits only occasional influence from Scots. Still, the linguist may usefully mine the poetry for citations of select grammatical features and find some that are rarely attested elsewhere, such as the ellipsis of *have* in the verb phrase *cud been* in the excerpt from Orr above.

14.8 NINETEENTH CENTURY

It is easy to track the declining use of Ulster Scots in vernacular poetry, what may be considered the second stage of Ulster Scots writing, and to identify the social and educational forces that caused it to wane in the course of the nineteenth century, forces that are all too familiar on the mainland as well. So far did it sink in status that one of Ireland's best-known literary artists of the period, a native of western County Tyrone who must have had first-hand acquaintance with it, told his readers that he was scrupulously avoiding the medium of Ulster Scots. This was William Carleton, whose *Traits and Stories of the Irish Peasantry* (first serialised and then published in the 1830s) presented the frankness and foibles of the common people. In the preface to an early version, Carleton stated: 'In the language and expressions of the northern peasantry [the author] has studiously avoided that intolerable Scoto-Hibernic jargon that pierces the ear so unmercifully, but he has preserved everything Irish . . . so that the book, wherever it may go, will exhibit a truly Hibernian spirit' (Herbison 1989: 3).

But after the demise of Scots in Ulster correspondence and legal documents in the seventeenth century, only for Scots to reappear in other types of writing a century later, one might not be surprised if it found voice anew in still other guises. This is precisely what happened in the middle of the nineteenth century in the form of a third stage of writing in Ulster Scots, material from which has slowly come to light. This was a tradition of ephemeral prose – fiction and non-fiction – that overlapped with the poetry just surveyed. Extending steadily well past the turn of the present century and as an occasional phenomenon more recently, this involved popular sketches, commentaries and stories (sometimes serialised and published later as novels, as W. G. Lyttle's *Robin's Readings* was in 1879) in newspapers in such towns as Ballymena, Belfast, Downpatrick and Newtownards. Like some earlier Ulster Scots literature, these items were pseudonymous or anonymous (though their authorship must inevitably have been known to local citizens) and were typically written in a folksy, intimate, first-person style, with both the narrative/ commentary and any dialogue being in dialect. Many social, political and other topics and issues were addressed in these highly anecdotal items, but they were most often local-colour sketches or ruminations about local life. The authors, in viewing themselves as a 'voice of the people', formed a striking parallel to what appeared simultaneously in Scottish newspapers, as demonstrated by William Donaldson (1986, 1989) on the vernacular revival in Victorian Scotland, when 'a radical new speech-based prose came into being reflecting the regional diversity of the spoken language and dealing with every aspect of contemporary life' (1986: 206), and also in English newspapers especially in the industrial north – Lancashire and Yorkshire, according to Joyce (1991). Whether or not its rise was patterned on Scotland is presently unknown, but the Ulster phenomenon does appear not to have drawn consciously from earlier writing in Ulster Scots (it employs different spelling conventions, for instance, including considerable eye dialect). While the vernacular persona was intrinsic to their point of view (which often performed the function, if it did not follow the form, of newspaper editorials), spoken models probably played a role in their composition also.

An early example of this literature is two letters written by Thomas McIlwham to the editor of the *Belfast Newsletter* in 1836 and published in pamphlet form as the McIlwham Papers (McIlwham 1838: 7):

> Roseybank, by Lanerick, 20th o' November, 1836
> Dear Frien' and Schulefellow,
>   Mony a time, sin' we parted, hae I thoct o' ye, an' o' writin' till ye, just for the sake of auld lang syne. Bonny Rafrilan' crownin' the hill-tap like a diadem, and the blue big mountains o' Mourne frownin' i' the distance, like the ruined wa's o' a giant's castle, and the wee bit craft whaur we pu'd the gowans, an' the wumplin burn whaur we fished an' paiddled; oh! how they come ower me i' the lonely evenings, till I begin amaist till greet, wi' a mixture o' joy an' vexation, that nae man can comprehend, but ane that has been estranged from the hame o' his fathers, an' dreed an acquaintance in a foreign lan'.

Like Scottish counterparts adduced by Donaldson, this passage contains salient Scottish phonological forms (*mony, whaur, amaist, nae* and so on) and liberal use of the apostrophe to suggest sandhi and consonantal differences from English. Lexically, it displays not only typical (*wee, burn, wumple*) and symbolic (*auld lang syne*) Scotticisms but also a few terms from classical languages (*comprehend, estrange, acquaintance, diadem*). The paratactic syntax is quite reminiscent of speech.

McIlwham called himself a weaver, meaning that he probably saw his writing as within the compass of the rhyming weavers' vernacular work; at the very least, his effort was a precursor to what followed later in the century. In Ulster, such prose was neither unique to Ulster Scots nor restricted to newspapers. It was also written in mid-Ulster English and sometimes in a mixture of the two varieties (a generalised, diffuse variety coming to represent the everyday speech of Belfast, a prosperous city that was drawing people from the Ulster hinterland). Such a mixed version was used in *Poor Rabin's Almanac* (1861–3), written by Abraham Hume (alias Billy McCart), one of numerous short-lived almanacs, which was 'prentit jest the way people spaiks' and published in 'Bilfawst'. It was newspapers, however, that featured such writing most often. It was the *Newtownards Chronicle* that serialised W. G. Lyttle's tales of Robin Gordon, a country man from County Down (later compiled as *Robin's Readings*), and it was Lyttle, the paper's editor, who contributed such pseudonymous pieces to its pages (Lyttle 1879):

> Newtownards Chronicle, 18th November 1882
> AN ECHT-DAYS RETROSPECK O CUMMER DOINS.
> To the editur o the 'Newtoun Chronickel.'
> SUR – You wull nae doot wunner at my lang silonse, but the awfu things that hae hapened ye ken gies me a terble time o truble, gest to think that ony thief can gang intil yer back yeard and steel

pig troughs, and make three-legged pots rin awa wi hachets is enuff to mack yen's hair stan on thar heed; and day a this, mind ye, an get off scot frae. It ocurs to my mind that the star wi the lang tale has sumthin to day wi these miricals, but mebbe the aturney wha sayed sich quare things ti the fella that the pot and ither things rin awa frae hes som nollege o astronmy, and caused the lang tailed comit to dezzel the eyes o folk a could name, wha think it no crime to day the like . . .

In mid-Antrim, Mr John Weir wrote verse and prose in the same vein under the nom de plume of Bab McKeen for his own newspaper, the *Ballymena Observer*, in the early decades of the twentieth century. In general terms, this writing formed a rather loose tradition of individual, speech-based styles, in which the degree of Scottishness very gradually declined as the decades passed. The genre itself with its folksy commentary on local matters has continued to thrive in recent years, with, among others, columnists like Tom McDevitt (alias Barney McCool) writing for the *Tyrone Constitution*.

These excerpts suggest that it is not unthinkable that Donaldson's work in Scotland could be replicated on a smaller scale for Ulster and that a previously inaccessible popular literature using several varieties and styles of vernacular language might be documented. As one reviewer notes (P. Scott 1994: 323), Donaldson 'single-handedly turned upside down the long-conventional account of nineteenth-century Scottish literature. By examining the dusty files of old Scottish newspapers, he has brought to critical attention, for the first time, the sheer wealth of late Victorian writing in Scots.' Ulster Scots culture has so often paralleled that on the mainland that perhaps it did so here as well.

The extent of Ulster Scots literature is easily underestimated if we consider only the weaver poets, its best-known and best-documented writers. A few years ago, J. R. R. Adams (1989) identified more than 100 published items (poetry, fiction and some early glossaries, but ignoring ephemeral writing and twentieth-century works) in a checklist of works with Ulster dialect from 1700–1900, the vast majority of these using Scots; Adams emphasises that his list is only preliminary.

Scots has continued to be a resource for literature written in Ulster or by Ulster natives in the twentieth century. Poets include George F. Savage-Armstrong, Adam Lynn and W. F. Marshall earlier in the century, and Michael Longley today. Among novelists is Sam Hanna Bell, whose *Across the Narrow Sea: A Romance* (1987), set in County Down during plantation times, features dozens of Scotticisms such as *stoor* 'conflict', *swither* and *thrawn*, Scottish variants of English forms (*mair, maist, puir* and so on), and the stereotypical *auld, aye* 'always', *bonny, brae, ken* and *wheen*. Bell uses Scottish forms in his narrative and descriptive passages as well as in dialogue, but his grammar, like other Ulster Scots writers since the eighteenth century, is English, reflecting his literacy. Some years ago G. B. Adams (1958: 63) stated that 'the tradition of a separate Scottish language for some types of literature still persists'. If in the writing of Longley, Bell and others this is the case, it suggests that Scots in Ulster remains a resilient spoken language variety that creative writers can draw on.

A general estimation of four centuries of Ulster writing that uses Scots is difficult because of its uneven nature, involving stages that are discontinuous and unrelated (to one another, that is, but most of these parallel, if they are not related to, developments in Scotland), but it is also difficult because it is still only partially known. Much of that discussed here was buried in libraries ten years ago, and writing in Ulster Scots is only gradually becoming known to its speakers, through the work of the Ulster-Scots Language Society and otherwise. The journal of the society, *Ullans*, has published new and traditional items

604 MICHAEL B. MONTGOMERY AND ROBERT J. GREGG

(poetry, prose and translations) in an effort to increase awareness of literature and literacy in Ulster Scots and to promote it for more diverse uses. Because, for most of its history, literature using Ulster Scots has been self-conscious, as writers literate in English have for one social reason or another deliberately represented voices from the Ulster Scots community, this will probably continue to be the case for some time.

Ulster Scots literature cannot and should not be compared with the canons established for national languages that have long enjoyed a great variety of formal uses, widespread literacy, and popular education in them. Even the few documents cited in this chapter may come as something of a surprise, because Ulster Scots, like many other European 'minority languages' that once had the reputation of 'rural dialects' used only in the home and the countryside and for intimate discourse, has often not been known to have a literature at all. It is not our purpose to suggest which writings should be admitted to a revised canon of writings of Anglo-Irish literature from Ireland. Indeed, those who have had much to say about such matters recently (for example, Greenblatt 1992) contend that the foremost issue is how the 'canon' is to be redefined, not which items have suffered neglect and need to be re-evaluated. If this implies that it is literature which articulates the diversity of voices within a culture that should be included, then literature written in Ulster Scots, as well as literature produced in and for the Ulster Scots community, might be considered; for Ulster Scots, the latter might well include religious prose before anything else.

14.9 AFFILIATIONS AND INFLUENCES

How Scottish is Ulster Scots? How distinct is it from mainland Scots after three centuries of separation and how different from other language varieties in Ireland after four centuries of contact? What differences exist within Ulster Scots? Except for phonology, in which Gregg, Milroy, Harris, Barry and others have elucidated the relations, such questions can be dealt with at present only in outline form and with reference to individual features. It is to be hoped that linguists will work towards a comprehensive understanding of these matters in the future. Addressing such questions presupposes a corpus of material and basic descriptive works from which to extract data on Ulster Scots, items which either do not exist or have only begun to appear.[14] Two dictionaries of Ulster speech, the *Concise Ulster Dictionary* (Macafee 1996) and *The Hamely Tongue: A Personal Record of Ulster Scots in County Antrim* (Fenton 1995), are now available, and the publication of a grammatical conspectus, *Ulster Scots: A Grammar of the Traditional Written and Spoken Language* (P. Robinson forthcoming a), is on the horizon.

As suggested earlier, the outline of the Ulster Scots speech area was known informally long before its mapping by Robert Gregg. His fieldwork was based on his refinement, through years of observation, of an intuitive idea of its limits. However real it may be on the ground, the boundary of Ulster Scots (and to some extent the variety itself) is from a linguistic viewpoint an abstraction both geographically and socially, in the same manner as for minority European languages in close proximity to a related national standard language. The Gregg line, established a third of a century ago, was unquestioned in the literature until Fenton's 1995 work.[15] Even if we considered only what may be called the folk speech used in rural areas of its heartland, and even if voluminous data and comprehensive reference works were at hand, characterising Ulster Scots and accurately identifying its relations with other language varieties in the north of Ireland (namely English and Irish) would present complex challenges today.

One reason is that in the course of 400 years Ulster Scots has been penetrated by both Irish and English, producing effects which one may discern especially in lexis and grammar. On the other hand, because Scots has been spoken in parts of the province since the seventeenth century, it has strongly influenced Ulster English, giving rise to mixed varieties, as in Belfast, and leading linguists to state that Mid–Ulster English 'is essentially an English-based dialect with varying degrees of discernible Scots influence' (Barry 1996: xi). Moreover, Scottish forms and features have diffused beyond Ulster, into Ireland more generally, where their influence has been less marked.

In working through the relevant literature on Ulster speech, one is often reminded that three formative stocks contributed to the province's distinctive and varying speech patterns – English, Irish and Scots. This understanding for some reason seems rather more prevalent in the popular than in the scholarly literature, especially with reference to Ulster Scots vocabulary, and it may be growing in the public mind. For example, W. F. Marshall gave a series of BBC talks on Ulster speech in 1935 (subsequently published in 1936), three of which were 'The Brand of the Rose', 'The Brand of the Thistle' and 'The Brand of the Shamrock'. A more recent, representative statement comes from a book-length glossary of Ulster speech (O'Kane 1991):

> [Our English] bears the imprint of infusions from other blood-lines; from Irish, Scots-Gaelic, and Lowland Scots, as well as variants of dialects from northern and central England. The tortuous course of our history has ensured this intermingling. From earliest times there was commerce between Ireland and Scotland, then with the successive waves of soldiers, adventurers, traders and planters that swirled over the country in later ages were implanted the chief ingredients of Ulster's rich linguistic brew.

Taken in conjunction with what historians and cultural geographers have established, the threefold presence of English, Irish and Scots in Ulster suggests a range of contact situations over the past four centuries, a proper sorting-out of which would involve knowledge of three historic languages and something of the functional domains and types of interaction between speakers in earlier times, when there were probably invisible barriers of cultural identification as there are today. Degrees and types of contact between the three have produced the linguistic differentiation between Ulster Scots, Mid-Ulster English and South Ulster English, the three-way division generally accepted by dialectologists today on the basis of vocalic phonology (Harris 1984; Barry 1982; and others), and that accords well with the settlement history detailed by Braidwood (1964). (By extension, the broader distinction between Northern and Southern Irish English is also based in part on the differential manifestation of such Scottish features as the lack of systematic vowel length.)

However, if Ulster speech has three formative elements, these were hardly discrete in the late sixteenth/early seventeenth century, when they came into what was to be continuous contact. As a close sibling to English, mainland Scots shared innumerable features with its southern neighbour – especially with varieties of English spoken north of the Humber. Irish Gaelic was not discrete from Scots, in the sense that the latter had been considerably influenced by centuries of contact with the former's close relative Scottish Gaelic and already shared features of lexis and grammar traceable to a common Gaelic source. Moreover, it is likely that, among the Scots who settled in Ulster during plantation times, there were some from Galloway or Carrick who were bilingual in Scots and Gaelic.[16]

Thus, any attempt to separate and assess the different linguistic streams that have flowed together to make modern Ulster English and Ulster Scots faces difficulties. Generalisations are hazardous and impressions can easily be mistaken. The effort itself involves dangers if it highlights only differences between these varieties rather than what they share. As we consider the questions posed above, we will draw principally on lexical data, leaving summary discussion of phonology and grammar of Ulster Scots until later.

14.10 RELATIONSHIP TO SCOTS

As demonstrated throughout this chapter, Ulster Scots shares innumerable features with mainland Scots; it is this core of features which justifies its very classification as a variety of Scots. But beyond this, little is known about the relative debt owed by Ulster Scots to different varieties in Scotland. The *Scottish National Dictionary* classifies Ulster Scots as a 'variant of West-Mid Scots', but does not indicate whether this is based on reflexes of historic vowels, on vocabulary or on something else.[17] Presumably this designation is provisional and based on external settlement history, and this is of course most plausible. Although Grant in his introduction to the dictionary identifies Ulster as one of the three main areas of Scottish speech, the other two being the Lowlands and the Northern Isles, he makes only the aforementioned brief statement about Ulster Scots in an otherwise greatly detailed thirty-three-page essay on the history and geography of the language.

In surveying the modern-day reflexes of English vowels in Ulster, Braidwood (1964: 46–80) occasionally relates his material to one variety of Scots or another (most often that of his native Renfrewshire) or to Scots in general, but this appears to be the only published effort at comparative analysis. The Scottish character of Ulster Scots has been very widely acknowledged over the past thirty years for phonology by Gregg, Harris, Barry, J. Milroy and others (especially with regard to vowel length), and over the past century for vocabulary (from Patterson (1880)[18] to Fenton (1995)), but it seems never to have been suggested for grammar or morphology outside scattered comments by Braidwood (1964: 85–102), even for such a common and presumably salient feature as verbal concord.

For a view of what may be distinctive to Ulster Scots today, one can isolate items labelled '*now Uls*' by SND/CSD and identify vocabulary items from the published volumes of the *Linguistic Atlas of Scotland* that were collected in Ulster but not in Scotland. This is as close as we can at present come to distinguishing Ulster Scots from other varieties of Scots. The *Linguistic Atlas of Scotland* routinely maps items for Ulster, as a result of fieldwork in the 1950s. At the beginning of that decade, Angus McIntosh approached G. B. Adams to distribute the Scots section of the project's lexical questionnaire to investigate the traditional lexis in the province. Under the auspices of the Belfast Naturalists' Field Club, questionnaires were collected from 131 individuals in seven counties, more than half (71) of whom were in Antrim and Down; areas well outside the Ulster Scots territory, such as Counties Armagh and Fermanagh, were also surveyed, because the BNFC had already conceived the idea of compiling a dictionary. Members of the LSS staff worked closely with Adams through the 1950s, with J. S. Woolley visiting in 1953 and J. Y. Mather in 1957 and 1959 to record speakers, using the project's phonological questionnaire.

A synoptic statement based on LAS materials is not attempted here, but maps in the published volumes (Mather and Speitel 1975, 1977, 1986) suggest that a number of lexical items are now apparently restricted to Ulster Scots, including *clootie* 'left-handed', *lap* 'small heap of hay', *(hay)pike* 'haystack', *mitch* 'play truant', *clib* 'colt', *crew* 'pigsty' and *goosebag* 'gooseberry' (the first three of these are confirmed by regional labels in CSD). Items identified by CSD as '*now Uls*' include *baigle* 'a disagreeable, dirty person', *boon* 'a band of reapers, shearers', *bottle* 'a bundle of hay or straw, a sheaf', *champ* 'mashed potatoes', *claggy* 'muddy, glutinous', *in course* 'of course', *crisp* 'to fold cloth lengthwise', *elbow grass* 'foxtail grass', and *fadge* 'type of prattie-scone'. Given that it came to Ulster in the migration of speakers who established what was in many respects a colony there, Ulster Scots has in some respects been more conservative than varieties on the mainland, exhibiting what has been called 'colonial lag' (Marckwardt 1958: 60–80), probably an appropriate label for some terms designated '*now Uls*'. That Ulster Scots maintains archaic phonological features has been suggested by G. B. Adams (1964: 2):

> In some particulars it shows interesting variations which appear to represent older Scots sounds now lost or driven back to the outer edges of the Scots dialect area in their native land. A good example is provided by words of the type *old, cold, hold* which appear in parts of Antrim with a diphthong like that in Standard English *owl, cowl, howl*, where one might expect *auld, cauld, hauld*, as in Scots.

Other scholars have cited the voiceless velar fricative /x/ in the same regard.

We cannot assume, however, that features of conservative Ulster Scots that have exact counterparts in mainland Scots are necessarily attributable simply to Scottish migrations. An item that is distinctively Modern Scots may not have been distinctively Scottish centuries ago. Braidwood (1964: 48) discusses this fallacy:

> Because Scotch-Irish is the dominant form of the Ulster dialect, and because we are very familiar with modern Scots dialectal forms like, for example, *han', win', spinnel*, 'spindle', *fowk*, 'folk', *jine*, 'join', *warm* rhyming with *arm*, etc., we must not jump to the conclusion that these forms in Ulster are necessarily of Scots origin; they are only a few of the early modern English traits shared by Scots and English . . . The same difficulty arises with vocabulary . . . we are apt in Ulster to regard words like *bonny, Lammas Fair, ken*, 'know' etc. as of Scots origin, but they were standard vocabulary in Shakespeare's day, and could have been brought by both Scots and English settlers; again we have recourse to non-linguistic evidence.

14.11 RELATIONSHIP TO ULSTER ENGLISH

There is of course much overlap between English and Scots, both in Britain and Ireland, because of common Germanic ancestry. The more immediate issues at hand are the relation between Mid-Ulster English (the dominant form of spoken English in the province) and Ulster Scots today and between Scots and varieties of British English, especially in the seventeenth century. Gregg's work, which is largely responsible for the modern-day Ulster Scots/Mid-Ulster demarcation, bases the division on thirteen phonological variables (twelve vocalic and one consonantal – the voiceless velar fricative) and a closely related group of grammatical forms (mostly enclitic negation, but also cases of 'morphological fusion' or reduction such as *gin* as the past participle of *give*).

Although Gregg found support for some lexical isoglosses, his principal goal was to use the data gathered with his extensive questionnaire to establish the phonological boundaries of Ulster Scots. Thus, much mapping of vocabulary and comparative reconstruction of English vs Scots in Ulster remains to be done. Since Gregg has published so much of the data which he collected, more recent quantitatively based mapping methods may yet demarcate some forms, although this would pertain only to the Ulster Scots territory and its periphery.

If in viewing Ulster as an English/Scottish language complex we sought to describe the relations between the two using published material, the Scots element would be easier to identify and characterise, for two reasons. It is better documented in glossaries, dictionaries and other resources (Patterson 1880; SND; Fenton 1995; and others) than is Ulster English (Marshall 1904–6 and Lutton 1923 being the main glossaries, the former particularly having many Scots forms). When collecting material for the EDD, Joseph Wright had several consultants from Ulster, but he did not usually localise them, so we cannot tell if they provided material from an Ulster Scots area (an exception to this is William Patterson (1880)). We can hold SND or CSD on one side to check on Scots, but there is no comparable source on English for the other side. A more difficult problem is that varieties of regional British English brought to Ulster have subsequently mixed and are not easy to separate from one another or to cross-reference to their progenitors in England. Except for the work of Braidwood (1964), there has been almost no tracing of Ulster forms to one region of England or another. This does not mean that the literature on Ulster speech does not have much to say about English antecedents, but rather that these are customarily grouped under the broad rubric of 'Elizabethan' or 'Jacobin' (Braidwood 1964; Marshall 1936; Byers 1916). Ulster Scots had not only more homogeneity of origin than did Ulster English, but also reinforcement from the mainland throughout the seventeenth century. Ulster English and its local varieties are not yet classifiable with relation to its mainland ancestors. Apparently, speakers from no English region maintained an identity in Ireland, and there is no vernacular poetry in Ulster varieties of English.

14.12 INFLUENCE OF IRISH GAELIC

There can be no doubt about a large Gaelic component in Scots, in Scotland and especially in Ulster, the most obvious being the lexical influence of Irish Gaelic on Ulster Scots. As speakers are transplanted to a new environment, they naturally tend to adopt (and then to modify in form) terms for new flora, fauna, landscape features, cultural items and the like. If so, we would expect most lexical borrowings to be nouns, and indeed a quick look at a few terms given an Irish etymology in Fenton and the CUD (Macafee 1996) confirms this.

A selection of terms that Fenton attributes to Irish include *ban-daisy* 'ox-eye daisy', *banshee*, *blockan* 'coalfish', *bockan* 'coward', *caleery* 'silly person', *camman*, *clabber* 'soft mud', *clib* 'year-old horse', *cullion* 'small potato', *doran* 'doleful person', *dullachan* 'brown trout', *glaiks* 'lever to aid churning' and *gullion* 'quagmire'. The larger and more etymologically based CUD enters many hundreds of items attributed to Irish, including the following beginning with *ba*: *bacan* 'wooden peg for tethering an animal', *baghran* 'a type of wild flower', *ballan* 'a shellfish', *ballyboe* 'division of land', *banafan* 'chubby youngster', *bardock* 'a creel with a collapsible bottom', *barneagh* 'a type of crustacean', *barradugh* 'a cluster of plant roots for scouring pans', *bart* 'an oblong haystack' and *baukey* 'lame'. These lists are only suggestive, including only terms with an obvious Irish source. As the editor of the CUD appropriately advises in the introduction (Macafee 1996: xxxiii),

> a significant proportion of the [Ulster] population descends from Irish speakers, and traces of their older language remain with them, while those whose line of descent is from Scots or English dialect speakers have been interacting with their neighbours over four centuries . . . The influences of Irish on Ulster English/Scots are therefore extensive, and can, moreover, be very subtle . . . The reinforcement of Irish may have subtly affected which senses, phrases, etc. survived in Ulster use.

Grammatical influence from Gaelic is also manifest in Ulster Scots, although considerably less so than on Ulster English both in the number and currency of features. Two representative constructions are progressive verbs formed with *be* (such as 'A'*m waiting* this twa hours', 'A'*m waiting* fae last nicht') and habitual expressions using the verb *be* or *bes* ('A aye *bes* bad wi a sair heid in tha sun'); the first may be due in part to Scottish Gaelic.

Undoubtedly the vast majority of the forms in Ulster Scots of Celtic derivation come from Irish Gaelic, but some are traceable to the latter's sibling language, Scottish Gaelic; they are products of the centuries-long contact between Scots and Gaelic in Lowland Scotland or were borrowed into Scots in the speech of bilinguals. Given the historical closeness of Ulster Irish and Scottish Gaelic, there are often plausible etyma from both languages, so that we cannot know whether a term has a single source or dual ones. This is especially true when a word is attested in several forms, such as *moiley* (the CUD lists eight distinct forms) or *greeshoch* (which has more than a dozen, according to Braidwood (1964: 9)). The CUD cites two possible sources for many items, including *beddy, beltane, bin*[1], *blockan, bothy, bourach*[1], *brallion* and *brochan*. In other cases, a difference between the two Celtic languages, especially involving sound changes, is decisive; according to G. B. Adams (1958: 69), 'many Gaelic borrowings at present used in Ulster . . . were already embedded in [Scots] before its establishment here, for they show sound changes which either belong to Scottish rather than Irish Gaelic or they belong to an earlier stage of Lowland Scots than that at which it was brought to Ulster'.

However, a word like *sheugh* is often, but mistakenly, attributed to Irish because it looks and sounds like a borrowing from that language. To judge whether an Ulster Scots grammatical construction or idiom may be a calque on Gaelic, one must identify not only Irish and Scottish Gaelic analogues but also possible English ones from early modern times. English usages from that period have been maintained in Ireland because of relative isolation or because they have been reinforced by parallel constructions in Irish. Constructions of apparent English origin include the 'split-perfect' construction 'I'*ve* it *eaten*' (Harris 1983), the idiom *think long*, subordinating *and* ('I was washing the dishes and him just standing there' (Klemola and Filppula 1992; Hacker 1994) and *sheugh*.

14.13 EXTENSION OF SCOTS

If Irish Gaelic has penetrated Ulster Scots, a reciprocal process has occurred as features of Scots have spread beyond Ulster Scots territory into Ulster and Ireland more generally. Though their language lacked the prestige of English, speakers of Ulster Scots, because of their number and dominance of the rural economy, probably exercised influence beyond the north-east of Ireland where they were concentrated. At present we cannot estimate how much Scots has entered varieties of English in Ireland, but the CUD, even though it does not indicate the modern-day currency (its principal sources dating from the early twentieth century) or the regionalisation of its items (since its material was not derived from a systematic survey), will provide useful points of departure for future scholars, such as to investigate the currency or the phonetic and semantic variation of items identified as having a Scots source.

There is much evidence that Scottish vocabulary diffused into varieties of Ulster English; for instance, Todd (1989b: 341) states that 'throughout Northern Ireland we can find vocabulary items *ark* "meal chest", *dab-han* "expert", *drouth* "thirst", *gawk* "stare, stupid person", *hogo* "bad smell" and idioms *a fiddler's biddin'* "a late invitation" . . . which indicate that Scottish influence did not stop with the isoglosses'. There is also some indication that lexical influence from Scots extended over much of the island, as from J. M. Clark (1917: 43): 'The Hibernicisms to be considered here, have never at any time been literary English, but have always been provincialisms. By far the greater part of them are Scotch or Northern English'; a similar point is made by Bliss (1972) with regard to the vocabulary of J. M. Synge. But the absence of any dictionary or other island-wide reference work makes this difficult to assess, and the literature on Irish English focuses over-whelmingly on borrowings from Irish Gaelic into Irish English.

The influence of Scots outside north-east Ireland is clearest in grammar, especially for verbal concord, evidence for which has been published for Irish emigrant letters from the eighteenth and nineteenth centuries (Montgomery 1995), literary dialect employed by nineteenth-century works of fiction from southern Ireland (Kallen 1991), the English of Donegal emigrants to America whose first language was Irish (O'Duill 1994), and modern-day Belfast (Policansky 1981). Another feature of Scottish origin is 'punctual *whenever*', the use of the subordinator in referring to a single event or state in the past (the first two sentences below come from an Ulster English area, the third from southern Ireland):

1. It was a lovely job whenever it was finished.
2. Whenever I was in my teens, we had a hall up here.
3. I was kind of really surprised whenever I had the first one.

These two features are widely known in Ulster today (*whenever* has become something of a shibboleth for Ulster), but are nowhere cited in the literature as being of Scottish origin. The problem has been a lack of knowledge of Scots, whether in Ulster or on the mainland, an amnesia about the prominence of Scots in the history of the province over the past four centuries, or an assumption that the influence of Scots occurs only for more superficial aspects of language like vocabulary. Whatever the cause, a lack of knowledge of Scots in many recent studies of Ulster speech has led to the misleading characterisation of verbal concord with plural nouns as 'singular concord' (Policansky 1981) or 'complete lack of agreement' (Henry 1995: 170). A historical perspective would reveal the synchronic regularity of this pattern and provide a diachronic generalisation. Along the same line, Todd (1971: 37–8) states that with regard to 'this feature of plural subject + singular verb, . . . a factor which probably contributed to its widespread use is the fact that, in Gaelic there is no agreement between NP and the VP', here as elsewhere attempting to associate grammatical features in Ulster English with a Gaelic source but never a Scottish one.

It is true that in Belfast and elsewhere in Ulster, English and Scots have blended so completely that they have formed new varieties of Ulster speech. Almost inevitably, the tendency that has arisen in the study of Irish English in recent years to compare structures has, in addition to the view of Ireland as a bilingual island, led to the presumption of only two possible sources – English or Irish.

Parallel research with Scots is needed like that of Harris and others who have shown how Early Modern English contributed grammatical patterns to Irish English. To sort the antecedents out, we need historical and descriptive work by researchers who know both English and Scots. Another imperative is recovery of documentary evidence from earlier periods, because one recent study (Montgomery forthcoming b) suggests not only that, grammatically speaking (in terms of the Scots verbal concord system), the influence of Scots is also discernible in southern Ireland, but also that this may have been more pronounced in the eighteenth century, before large-scale transfer from Irish to English brought substratal influence more strongly into varieties of southern Irish English.

The extension of Scots within Ireland demonstrates the obvious fact that linguistic features take on a life of their own in a new environment, and it accentuates the shortcomings of identifying only their ultimate sources. Some Scottish features (such as punctual *whenever*) have greatly increased in currency in Ireland, while others (such combinations of modals as *might could*) have receded. As a result, some features that were Ulster Scots have lost their distinctiveness because they have spread, while others have done so by becoming more rare. The demarcation of Ulster Scots is difficult not only because of its attrition, but also because of its diffusion into other areas.

14.14 VARIATION IN ULSTER SCOTS

Within Ulster, the degree of Scots in an individual's speech appears to depend on macro-social factors such as region, social position, urban vs rural residence/orientation, age and education, the degree used on a particular occasion depending on micro-factors such as topic of conversation, formality of occasion, accommodation to audience and so on. Speakers vary widely in their command of Ulster Scots, those with the greatest competence being able to shift, according to the occasion and the interlocutor, from a 'deeper' to 'shallower' type or from Scots to English (Douglas-Cowie 1978, 1984), and they can magnify the use of some features for rhetorical purposes, as has been shown by Gunn (1990) for the Unionist politician Peter Robinson.

What we know of variation within Ulster Scots is drawn from four sources (all quantitatively based), two on phonology (Gregg 1972, 1985; Kingsmore 1995) and two on vocabulary (Skea 1982; Fenton 1995). Beyond determining the geographical boundary of Ulster Scots, a principal focus of Gregg's work (1964, 1972, 1976) has been to contrast varieties of Ulster Scots with one another, especially urban and rural Ulster Scots, and to identify the phonological shifts that rural speakers make as they adopt more educated, urban speech (the latter based in part on Mid-Ulster English) when they move into towns like Larne, and the dialect mixture that results. Gregg finds that attrition in some distinctive elements of Ulster Scots is the result of this process, but that it is appropriate to conclude that the shift is primarily a stylistic one, from one variety of Ulster Scots to another. Elsewhere, Gregg (1972: 135) presents the contrasting phonemic systems of vowels for three rural types of Ulster Scots (Antrim/north Down, north Antrim/north-east (London)Derry, Donegal/east Down). Kingsmore's study, based on extensive interviews with twenty-three speakers in Coleraine, north-east (London)Derry, finds striking social stratification within the Protestant community, between Presbyterians, Congregationalists and those with no church affiliation for three phonological variables – (ng), (l) and (t).

Popular literature on Ulster language varieties sometimes presents the nostalgic view of thorough insularity and asserts that little or no change in language has occurred since the seventeenth century (compare the notion of 'Elizabethan' speech cited earlier). For instance, Akenson (1980) calls Ballycarry, scarcely a dozen miles from Belfast, a 'linguistic museum' and touts the archaicness of the vocabulary used by James Orr of that town as preserved since days of the Ulster plantation. Such an assertion is doubtful for a host of reasons, just as people in Ballycarry today would have great difficulty understanding much of Orr's vocabulary of 200 years ago, but perhaps no more than modern-day speakers would have with two-centuries-old rural vocabulary anywhere. Attrition of many facets of Ulster

Scots vocabulary has been unmistakable, reflecting sociodemographic changes experienced by the Ulster Scots community in the twentieth century. Skea (1982) is the only systematic, cross-generational investigation of this subject. She investigates the extent to which items in Patterson (1880) are retained or have undergone semantic shift in five north-east Down localities, three on the Ards Peninsula and two west of Strangford Lough, by surveying 120 speakers equally distributed across four age-groups. In sum, she 'demonstrates the resilience of traditional vocabulary within a standardised grammatical system, and offers a clear rebuke to earlier predictions that Ulster Scots would, by now, be virtually extinct' (Kirk forthcoming: 15).

Fenton's work is a compilation by a native speaker based on lifelong observation and collection of material from rural parts of the northern two-thirds of County Antrim, where 'Ulster Scots was and is the everyday spoken medium of the great majority of the people' (1995: v). The growing obsolescence of 'much of the expressive and often colourful language' of rural society of half a century ago was a prime motivation behind his work, but to confirm the modern currency of many items he systematically surveyed thirteen speakers (each entry identifies those speakers who attested that item).

Lexical–domain studies such as G. B. Adams (1966) and Braidwood (1972, 1974) on *left-handed* and *the runt of the litter* have also revealed complex variation in many parts of Ulster, showing not only the threefold nature of Ulster speech but also, just as important, the diversity within each of these, which produces quite complex distributions for many lexical items in a rather small territory.

14.15 PHONOLOGY

14.15.1 Vowels

In his study of Ulster Scots, Gregg investigated contrastive vowel and diphthongal nuclei using a questionnaire of 683 items, administered in 125 localities. On the basis of this, the following summary is provided of heartland rural Ulster Scots as exemplified in Glenoe, east Antrim. Glenoe has a range of fourteen vocalic phonemes, itemised in the following paragraphs.

(1) /i/ (close, front) is best regarded as basically short with a long allophone in final syllables, in hiatus, and before voiced fricatives including [r]: [gin] 'gave, given' but [giː] 'give'; [dif] 'deaf' but [diːv] 'deafen'; [briːər] 'briar'; [miːr] 'mare'.

(2) /e/ (half-close, front) is realised as a long vowel in syllables with primary or secondary stress, but as a short variant in weakly-stressed positions: [əˈbɛːʈədeː] 'a better day'; [əˈsɛːʈde] 'a Saturday'; [ˈsʌmˌdeː] 'some day'; [ˈsʌndeː] 'Sunday'; [ˈsʌne] 'sunny'. Some speakers use a diphthongal variant with a schwa-glide in preconsonantal positions: [weən] 'child'; [heəm] 'home'; [seəl] 'sail'; [geət] 'gate'. A diphthong with an even closer starting point, [iə], may occur in such words.

(3) /ɛ/ (half-open, front) is generally realised as a long vowel: [ˈɛːfʈərˌgrɛːs] 'aftermath'; [hɛːsp] 'hasp'; [ˈhɛːrvəst] 'harvest'; [ˈdɛːʀər] 'dinner'.

(4) /ü/ has four positional variants. The main one (close, front-central, rounded) occurs in open syllables, in hiatus, and before voiced fricatives [v] and [z]. It always occurs long: [küː] 'cow'; [ˈʃüːər] 'shower'; [ˈθüːzn] 'thousand'. A short, more open allophone /ü/ occurs in closed syllables generally and in disyllables having at least one medial consonant other than [v], [z] or [r] and a strongly stressed first syllable: [hüs] 'house'; [ˈhüsəz] 'houses'; [küʈər]

'coulter, nose'; ['püðər] 'powder'. The third allophone is long and rounded, but is lowered to the half-close position and occurs only before [r]: [ø:r] 'our'; [pø:r] 'pour'; [kø:rs] 'coarse'; [kø:rt] 'court'. The fourth allophone [ÿ], occurring after a yod, a palatalised consonant or an affricate, is often the result of an earlier palatalisation: [bljÿ:] 'blue' (earlier [bl'ÿ:]); [pjÿ:] 'plough' (earlier [pl'ÿ:]); ['l'ÿ:k'warm] 'lukewarm'. It must be noted that morphology affects the distribution of these allophones: for example, monosyllables such as [smüð] 'smooth', [smü:ðər] 'smoother'. In these forms, [ü:] points to a morphological juncture following [ð], whereas in non-derivative forms such as ['püðər] 'powder' and ['ʃüðər] 'shoulder', [ü] points to a solid morpheme. The occurrence of [ÿ:] in ['bjÿ:te] 'beauty' and ['ʤÿ:te] over against [ü] in ['büte] 'booty', [füte] 'small, trifling' (and so on) seems to be due to the preceding palatal elements (the yod in ['bjÿ:te] and [ʤ] ⟨earlier [d'] in [ʤÿ:te], coupled with another, following yod element, for [e] is undoubtedly from earlier [i].

(5) /ï/ (between close and half-close, between front and central) has one slightly lowered variant [ë], which occurs before [r]: [flë:r] 'floor'; [pë:r] 'poor'. The main allophone occurs in ['əbïn] 'above'; [dïn] 'done'; [gïs] 'goose'; [gïd] 'good'; [pït] 'put'; [skïl] 'school'.

(6) /æ/ (open, between front and central) occurs with primary stress in most cases: [blæn] 'blind'; [ræm] 'ram'; [bræg] 'bridge'; [ræd] 'red'; but it occurs with secondary stress in ['bɛ:d,tæk] 'bed tick'; [ə'ræðmə,tæk] 'arithmetic'.

(7) /o/ (between close and half-close, back, heavily rounded) is realised mostly as a long vowel: [bo:k] 'retch'; [go:pən] 'double handful'; ['lo:nən] 'lane'; ['mo:rnən] 'morning'. A short variant of this vowel occurs in a few words, including [spok] 'spoke' (noun); [pok] 'small bag'; these are thus in phonological contrast with [spo:k] 'spoke' (verb); [po:k] 'poke' (verb).

(8) /ʌ/ (half-open, fully back, that is, further back than standard Southern British [ʌ]) is always short and occurs in ['wʌnTər] 'winter'; ['mʌne] 'many'; [dʌg] 'dog'; [grʌn] 'ground'; ['brʌkl̩] 'brittle'; ['stʌde] 'steady'.

(9) /ɔ/ (half-open, back, rounded) is always long and occurs in [stRɔ:ŋ] 'strong'; [fɔ:] 'fall'; [twɔ:] 'two'; [blɔ:] 'blow'; ['bɔ:rə] 'wheel-barrow'.

(10) /ɑ/ (open, back) is always long and occurs in ['ɑ:Tər,kɑ:p] 'peevish person'; ['ɑ:pən] 'open'; [stɑ:p] 'stop'; [bɑ:b] 'bob'; [sɑ:ft] 'soft'; ['bɑ:tl] (bottle of straw and so on)'; [lɑ:ŋ] 'long'; [wɑ:t] 'wet'.

For comparative and historical purposes, it is convenient to treat the four diphthongal vocalic nuclei as distinct phonological units:

1. /əi/ as in [fəif] 'fife'; [məin] 'mine' (noun); [pəi] 'pay'; [wəiər] 'wire'.
2. /ae/ as in [faev] 'five'; [maen] 'mine' (adjective); [pae] 'pie'; [taeər] 'tire; tyre'.
3. /ɔe/ as in [bɔe] 'boy'; ['mɔele] 'hornless cow'; [stɔex] 'stench'.
4. /əü/ as in [nəü] 'knoll'; [rəü] 'roll'; ['fəüər] 'four'.

These diphthongs are all of the descending type, with a relatively strong stress on the first element and various glides making up the second. Thus the glide in /əi/ reaches the close front position, in /ae/ and /ɔe/ the half-close front position only, and in /əü/ the close position, between front and central, rounded. The schwa as first element is quite short, especially in closed syllables ending with an unvoiced consonant: [rəis] 'rice; [bəit] 'bite'; [ləüs] 'loose'. Both elements of this diphthong may be slightly longer before voiced consonants or in open syllables and may be closely transcribed as follows: [rə·i·z] 'rise'; [bə·i·d] 'bide'; [jə·ü·] 'ewe'; [hə·i·] 'hay'; [lə·ü·z] 'loosen'. The [ɑ] and [ɔ] as first elements are, however, long and may even be overlong, which gives the impression of two syllables instead of one: [kɑ:e] or ['kɑ::e] 'cows'; [tɔ:e] or [tɔ::e] 'toys'.

The distribution of /ɔi/ and /ae/ in Glenoe is typical of Ulster Scots. In this respect, the latter contrasts with Ulster English varieties, which have only one diphthong of this type. Traces of an allophonic distribution are clearly marked in Glenoe, in that /ae/ occurs before voiced fricatives (including [r]), in hiatus, and in most final open syllables, whereas /əi/ occurs in other situations, thus [praez] 'prize' vs [prəis] 'price'; [faeəl] 'phial' vs [fəil] 'file'; [tae] 'tie' vs [təid] 'tide'.

This simple picture has been disturbed, however, by factors such as the historical development of certain Middle English diphthongs, for example [əi] (< Middle English *ei/ai*), which in final open syllables is in contrast with the regular [ae] (< Middle English /ī/) and gives rise to many meaningful contrasts, as shown in Table 14.2. Verb forms occasionally have 'irregular' diphthongs which can be ascribed to the conservative effect of analogy operating within the subset of strong verbs: [drəiv] 'drive' vs [dro:v]; [strəiv] 'strive' vs [stro:v] 'strove'; [θrəiv] 'thrive' vs [θro:v] 'throve'; [rəiz] 'rise' vs [ro:z] 'rose'. These verbs perhaps owe their [əi] (for which [ae] would be expected) to the analogy with [rəid] 'ride' vs [ro:d] 'rode'; [rəit] 'write' vs [ro:t] 'wrote'. A weak verb like *dive* (*dived*), on the other hand, is always pronounced [daev].

Table 14.2

Middle English *ei/ai*	Middle English *ī*
[əi] 'always'	[ae] 'I'
[bəi] 'bay'	[bae] 'buy', 'by'
[ɣəl] 'very'	[gae] 'guy'
[məi] 'May'	[mae] 'my'
[pəi] 'pay'	[pae] 'pie'
[stəi] 'stay'	[stae] '(pig)sty'

A more obvious case involving analogy is heard in the plural forms [ləif] / [ləivz] 'life/lives' (not [laevz]; [nəif] / [nəivz] 'knife/knives' (not naevz]); [wəif] / [wəivz] 'wife/wives' (not [waevz]). With these plurals, compare [haevz] < [haev] 'hive'.

Following /w/ or /ʍ/, the diphthong /əi/ is used to the exclusion of /ae/, regardless of what follows: [ʍəi] 'why' (in an open syllable); [wəiz] 'wise' (before a voiced fricative); [wəiər] 'wire'; ['kwəiər] 'choir, quire' (in hiatus). Dialect borrowing may explain the incidence of /əi/ in ['əirlən] 'Ireland'; ['əirtʃ] 'Irish'; [ʃəi] 'shy' (the normal dialect word is [ble:t]). It is worth noting, in respect to this, that in a number of words which have /i/, Ulster Scots urban and regional standard speech has /əi/, presumably borrowed from local Ulster English, as shown in Table 14.3. The Ulster Scots urban forms are thus phonemically opposed to [dae] 'dye'; [ae] 'I'; [lae] 'lie' (assume a recumbent position).

Table 14.3

Ulster Scots	Ulster English	Ulster Scots Urban	Meaning
[di:]	[dəi]	[dəi]	'die'
[i:]	[əi]	[əi]	'eye'
[li:]	[ləi]	[ləi]	'lie' (untruth)

Apart from the fourteen vocalic phonemes discussed above (all occur with primary or secondary stress), there is a vowel quality, [ɪ] (between close and half-close, front), which in syllables with relatively strong stress is found only at morphological junctures, and which arises from a contextual shortening of [eː]. Examples are to be found in the fused form of verb plus negative particle, preposition or pronoun; preposition plus pronoun, and so on: [deː] 'do' vs ['dɪne] 'don't'; [heː] 'have' vs ['hɪte] 'have to'; [feː] 'from' vs ['fɪine] 'from me'; [neː] 'no' (adjective) vs ['nɪθən] 'nothing'. The same vowel quality also occurs in weakly stressed syllables: ['gɛːlɪk] 'earwig'; ['pɑːrɪtʃ] 'porridge'; ['tiθɪk] 'toothache'.

A half-close, central vowel, [ə] (the schwa), is of course heard also in weakly stressed syllables: ['wʌndə] 'window'; ['hüsəz] 'houses'; ['wɑntəd] 'wanted'; [ə'bin] 'above'.

14.15.2   Consonants

Most Glenoe consonants correspond to those of standard Southern British, but at the phonetic level there is (in addition to the various phones of the standard language) a series of voiceless ejective or glottalised plosives, a full range of interdental and of alveolar palatalised consonants, and a voiceless velar fricative. This range of consonants is not confined to Ulster Scots varieties but is found in Ulster English as well. Hence, in seeking among the consonants differential criteria that would separate the two groups of varieties, we are thrown back on distributional contrasts. It is, for example, not the velar fricative /x/ in itself that distinguishes Ulster Scots from Ulster English, but its incidence. This sound may even be common to all or most varieties of whatever origin in certain words of clearly Scottish provenance such as [pɛːx] 'pant', ['sprɑːx]] 'sprawl' and so on, where the Scottish phonology was not in obvious conflict with that of a corresponding standard word. In many words without orthographic ⟨gh⟩, however, Ulster Scots (like Scots) has preserved /x/, which in Ulster English (as in standard Southern British) has become [f] or zero. This feature was found to be by far the most valuable consonantal criterion for separating Ulster Scots from other varieties and provided the basis for the first part of the phonological questionnaire.

14.16   INFLUENCE OF THE ULSTER SCOTS URBAN SPEECH OF LARNE ON GLENOE

Although the phonetic repertoire of Larne is almost identical with that of Glenoe, the two are, in effect, different languages phonologically by virtue of the wide range of discrepancies in the incidence of the sounds in question, particularly as regards vowels.

The importance of Larne is that it is the 'other' language of bilingual Ulster Scots speakers and that, as the local version of the standard language, it enjoys special prestige and exercises considerable influence over Glenoe; when a markedly Scots element in Glenoe has fallen into disuse, it has usually been replaced by the corresponding Larne form. A comparison of Glenoe with other forms of Ulster Scots reveals that all these varieties are closely parallel. They form a unity that remains very close to the speech of south-west Scotland, although generally more archaic in character. The similarities are naturally most marked between Glenoe and the varieties of Mid-Antrim, although those of north Antrim, which extend into north-east (London)Derry, are still very close. The speech of Magilligan, County (London)Derry, represents a nineteenth-century expansion of the Ulster Scots of the Laggan Valley in east Donegal, which diverges most widely from Glenoe in preserving archaisms and in certain peculiarities related undoubtedly to the local Gaelic substratum which must have differed in a few details from that of north-east Ulster. The Laggan Valley variety links up in some typical features with the Mid-Ards and a large part of west Strangford Ulster Scots, not, obviously, because of geographical contiguity but because County Down Ulster Scots has also in many areas preserved the same archaisms as Donegal.

It must be emphasised that all Ulster Scots varieties agree on an overwhelming number of points with regard to their reflexes of Middle English sounds. The main criteria by which they may be separated are the various developments of Middle English, which give the subdivision set out in Table 14.4. Elsewhere, partial summaries of Ulster Scots phonological features are provided in Barry (1982: 111–15), Adams (1964: 1–2) and Harris (1984: 119–25), all of which are founded on the work of Gregg. J. Milroy (1981), the most detailed examination of Belfast English within a sociohistorical framework, finds that although it 'is usually said to be "Mid-Ulster" in type, [it] also exhibits more Scots features than are generally recognised (in particular a progressive tendency to back /a/ to [ɒ] in words like *hand*, *man*, *bad* pronounced like *haund*, *maun*, *baud*)'. Adams (1964: 3–4) has a brief summary of Belfast pronunciation. Using data from the Tape-Recorded Survey of Hiberno-English, Harris (1984, 1985) shows that the three geographical divisions of Ulster speech are distinguished by the relative prevalence of Scottish vowel length, a feature which is largely followed in Mid-Ulster as well as Ulster Scots areas.

Table 14.4 Reflexes of Middle English or Old/Middle Scots

Laggan/ Mid-Ards/ West Strangford/ Magilligan	Mid-Antrim/ North Ards/ North-west Strangford	North Antrim/ North-east (London)Derry	Meaning
[ə'bin]	[ə'bɪn]	[ə'ben]	'above'
[šin]	[šin]	[šen]	'soon'
[stil]	[stɨl]	[stel]	'stool'

14.17 GRAMMAR

Until recently, as with most regional varieties in the British Isles (except for mainland Scots), one had to glean extra bits and pieces of grammatical information (primarily inflectional morphology) on Ulster Scots from historical documents and from sentences in linguistic studies that were cited for some other purpose (one could undertake a useful culling of grammatical data from Fenton (1995), for example). Virtually nothing has been published on the grammar of Ulster Scots; Milroy (1981: 10–15) deals with punctual *whenever*, verbal concord, perfectives and so on in Belfast English, but does not consider them with relation to Ulster Scots. In his study, Gregg (1985) investigated a group of morphological forms, finding that the most salient characteristics proved to be the negatives in [-ne], contrasting with Ulster English [not] or [nt], in addition to the archaic Ulster Scots plurals [in] 'eyes'; [ʃin] 'shoes'; [kae] 'cows'. Verb forms such as [de] 'do'; [din] 'did, done'; [giː] 'give'; [gin] 'gave, given'; [heː] 'have'; [maːn] 'must' proved to be reliable markers of Ulster Scots vs [dü], [dön], [giv], [gïv] or [geːv], [hav], [möst] for Ulster English, as was the syntactic use of *can* as infinitive in phrases like [‚ɑːl 'no: kən 'stəi] vs [əil 'nɒt be 're:bl tə 'ste:] *I'll not be able to stay.*

Ulster Scots: A Grammar of the Traditional Written and Spoken Language (Robinson forthcoming a) will be the first substantial presentation of both morphology and syntax by a native of south-east Antrim who is a near-native speaker and a lifetime observer of Ulster Scots. A late draft of this work shows chapters or sections on such topics as negation, demonstratives, habitual verbs, sentence tags, modal verbs, verbal concord and subordination. For most of these, Ulster Scots patterns very closely to mainland Scots, an interesting exception being the expression of habituality; Ulster Scots has four forms that do this (exemplified by 'I *be* going', 'I *bes* going', 'I *does be* going' and 'I *goes*'). It is unknown whether these are exact semantic/pragmatic equivalents, and even though there has undoubtedly been change and attrition between mainland and Ulster Scots for grammar,[19] it is premature, even with the Robinson grammatical sketch in hand, to say which other features do not occur in Ulster Scots. Long-term fieldwork is needed, preferably by members of the Ulster Scots community, to establish the currency and details of features presented in Robinson's work. At the same time, that volume will identify innumerable points for scholars to explore, such as the evolution of Ulster Scots features that came to North America (Montgomery 1989, 1995).

14.18 RECENT DEVELOPMENTS

In late 1995, the UK Committee of the European Bureau for Lesser-Used Languages approved 'the Scots language in Ulster' as a second lesser-used language within Northern Ireland, giving it status alongside Irish Gaelic in the province, four other languages in the UK (Welsh, Cornish/Kernewek, Scottish Gaelic and Lowland Scots/Lallans) and more than thirty in Western Europe (James 1986). Like Ulster Scots, most of these have been spoken for centuries in the home and associated with traditional rural life. Having rarely if ever been used for public functions, recognised by the institutions of society or acknowledged by educational establishments, most have enjoyed neither prestige nor status in modern times. Many of their speakers are ambivalent about using and promoting them, making it difficult in the extreme to estimate their numbers of speakers. This was hardly surprising, since Ulster Scots lacked any public role, there was no account of its history or literature, and most speakers had never seen a written version of it. These speakers, all bilingual/bidialectal in English and Ulster Scots, had been taught in school to consider their native speech a rural or uneducated variety of English.

As we have seen, writing in Ulster Scots was normally grounded closely on speech, which gave it immediacy and a first-person perspective. Because many texts have come to light only in the 1990s, we cannot yet gauge adequately the dimensions of this literature or the roles which it played in Ulster society. As these are steadily pieced together, they provide cumulative support for recognising Ulster Scots as having an identity of its own. Far more is known about Ulster Scots today than only ten years ago, and the confidence inspired by this growing knowledge gave rise in 1992 to the founding of the Ulster-Scots Language Society, which now has more than 200 members. Its goals are fivefold:

1. To promote the use of Ulster Scots in writing, education and speech.
2. To encourage interest in Ulster Scots literature, prose, poetry and speech. In 1993, the society began publishing *Ullans: The Magazine for Ulster Scots*, an annual featuring new and reprinted creative writing in Ulster Scots, word-lists on aspects of traditional life, translations into Ulster Scots of historical passages and of Scripture, and other items on language, names and culture.

3. To encourage confidence in the use of Ulster Scots.
4. To encourage contemporary writing in Ulster Scots. Writing in Ulster Scots today finds itself in a state of experimentation, having no established orthography and few models to guide spelling, style and the other facets of writing in a language in which very few people are literate (the aforementioned literature has had very little circulation in the present day) and no-one is schooled. The written version of Ulster Scots is far from being standardised, and at best this will come slowly, although the publication of Fenton's dictionary and Robinson's grammar, as well as any public use of the language, may hasten the process considerably. For the foreseeable future, Ulster Scots writing will be based on speech, which of course varies according to social and regional factors. One goal of the envisaged Ulster Scots Academy is to consider the advisability of recommending certain spellings.
5. To encourage interest in the Ulster Scots traditions of music, dance and song.

In June 1995, the Ulster-Scots Language Society joined forces at Belfast City Hall with several other groups, including the Belfast Burns Association and Burns Clubs, the Presbyterian Historical Society, the Royal Scottish Pipe Band Association and the Royal Scottish Country Dance Society, to launch the Ulster-Scots Heritage Council, an umbrella body covering Ulster Scots culture and artistic expression. A further plan of the language society is to establish the Ulster Scots Academy as a permanent, independent institution to undertake the more formal aspects of language revival, including the teaching of courses, the publication of reference works and research on Ulster Scots.

The future of Ulster Scots would seem to depend on several things, including diversification of its domains and development of public uses and continued reconstruction of its history. Because Ulster Scots has become more and more steadily identified with rural life over the past three centuries, it needs to increase associations with the modern world; Ulster Scots needs contemporary written texts and public spoken uses. Developing these will require the society to navigate a challenging, if not to say uncharted path, to permit differences of view on orthography and similar questions for some time in the face of sceptics who may view the lack of a standard written form as evidence against its legitimacy. Of crucial importance is appreciation of Ulster Scots by younger generations; this may follow from attention being given in the new national curriculum announced in 1989, which led to the Department of Education for Northern Ireland commissioning the *Concise Ulster Dictionary*, designed to be primarily a schools dictionary that would meet the objectives of the curriculum for children to 'know about some regional differences in accent and dialect and understand that these have been influenced by other parts of Ireland, the UK, and the world' and 'explore a wide range of colloquial words and expressions which occur in everyday speech in Northern Ireland' (Macafee 1994b: 177).

14.19 IMPLICATIONS AND CONCLUSIONS

Named and recognised by linguists for two-thirds of a century, Ulster Scots is a regional and social variety of language spoken in parts of the historical province of Ulster for the past 400 years. Variation in its use occurs mainly along the dimensions of individual style, urban vs rural orientation, and age. Ulster Scots should not be considered the medium of one social group or orientation. Within its territory, Ulster Scots is used by both Protestants and Catholics; Todd states that Catholic speakers whose ancestral language was Irish Gaelic 'approximate to the Anglo-Irish or Ulster Scots norms of the area in which they live' (1992b: 469). The primacy of the geographical division of Ulster speech implies that all varieties are cross-sectarian.

The Scottish component of the Ulster Scots lexicon was documented for east Ulster (Antrim and Down) over a century ago by Patterson (1880), but, other than the lifetime work of Robert Gregg on its phonology and geographical boundaries, there was until recently scant scholarly attention to it. This chapter has attempted to assemble what is known about Ulster Scots and also to make a modest contribution to its description and reconstruction.

Today, Ulster Scots is inseparable from rural life, the result of a process of association that began with the weaver poets, but there are good reasons to regard statements about its impending extinction as being the social evaluation of it by the dominant culture, which is often schizophrenic about traditional language – assigning it low prestige and general condemnation in the classroom but at the same time reminiscing nostalgically about its heritage and character. The death of Ulster Scots was predicted over a century ago by Patterson, who stated that many words in his glossary were obsolete, yet they very often show up in Fenton's (1995) work. As a rural variety tied closely to and identified with a traditional way of life, Ulster Scots will thrive in that domain as long as that lifestyle does; as it continues to be rediscovered and revived, its uses and associations will diversify.

Ulster Scots is a language variety that has probably not been autonomous from English since the early seventeenth century, just as English has not been autonomous from Scots in Britain. Its continuous interchange with English has blurred the lines between the two in many respects today, but one cannot consider Ulster Scots merely a variety of English, for two reasons. First, it has its own separate external history: though some of its distinctiveness derives from interaction with other languages and varieties in Ireland, the core of its vocabulary, grammar and phonology is easily traceable to Scotland. Second, the elements of Scots preserved in the everyday speech of Northern Ireland today are by no means restricted to individual forms, but include phonological processes and grammatical paradigms.

Historically speaking, Ulster Scots cannot be classified as one among many surviving language varieties brought from Britain during plantation times. English settlers came from disparate areas (especially the north-west Midlands, but also the south-west and elsewhere), but none of the varieties of British English which they brought established a speech community in Ireland. The links between Ulster speech and earlier English that are cited in the literature (W. F. Marshall 1936; Braidwood 1964) are usually assigned the collective label of 'Elizabethan' or 'Shakespearean' English by academics and lay people alike.[20] Though in Ulster it was rapidly supplanted in the seventeenth century by English for administrative purposes, Scots was a language with a variety of registers and a literary tradition behind it, unlike varieties of English brought during plantation times.

Though connections between Ulster and Scotland can be traced back for centuries and are older, more profound and more varied than those between Ulster and any part of England, it is paradoxical today that there is generally speaking only a vague awareness of what Scotland has contributed to Ulster beyond the institution of the Presbyterian church; the cultural and linguistic connections are there (see Wood 1994), but there is little specific knowledge of them. The general obscurity of Scottish influences has unfortunately led to the default presumption that anything different from English in Ulster has an Irish Gaelic source. The evolution of modern Ireland as a bilingual island in popular and scholarly consciousness has produced a general tendency, including among linguists, to view language issues, whether synchronic or diachronic, as dichotomous. The uncertain relationship of Scots to English, especially synchronically, has reinforced this. Recognition of Ulster Scots as a lesser-used language alongside Irish Gaelic and of Scottish contributions to Ulster present the opportunity for understanding the cultural and linguistic diversity of the province, an appreciation that must be careful to point out the shared as well as the distinct elements.

Linguists in the British Isles and beyond will need to pay increased attention to Ulster Scots. The effect of its rediscovery on writing the complete linguistic history of Ireland will be profound, as information on Ulster Scots throws into sharp relief the need for a full accounting of the language situation in Ulster over the past four centuries as involving continuing contact between English, Scots and Irish Gaelic, the first two of which were superstrate languages brought from Britain. With increasing documentation of Ulster Scots will come a fuller appreciation of the complexity of language variation in the British Isles during the early modern period and a more accurate description of American English as it developed from contact between varieties of English and Scots that came from both Britain and Ireland to the Western Hemisphere and there had contact with African, Amerindian and a host of other European languages. Although work on North American English has begun, the latter lies somewhat in the future because much work recovering and documenting Ulster Scots, the third European language historically spoken in Ireland, remains to be done.

In terms of both Scots and Gaelic, Ulster and Scotland have enjoyed a long-term linguistic partnership, with similar relationships to English and with frequent interchange of peoples and languages. We cannot understand one without the other at any time in recent centuries.

NOTES

1. The first author is grateful to many people for support in writing this chapter. Without the assistance of many others in providing bibliography and answering queries, and in myriad other ways, it could not have been written. Particular gratitude is extended to Jack Aitken, Bruce Boling, Roger Dixon, John Erskine, Jeff Kallen, John Kirk, Catherine Macafee, Iseabail Macleod and Philip Robinson, but none of these special people is responsible for the presentation or interpretation of material here.

2. Although some scholars until recently used other terms (for example, Scotch-Irish by Gregg and Braidwood, and Scots-Irish by Barry (1982: 110–11)), today the preferred nomenclature for the Scots language in Ulster is Ulster Scots, a term that Gregg also now prefers. As far as can be determined, 'Ulster Scots' was first used by William Grant (1931) in his introduction to SND.

3. The historic province of Ulster comprises nine counties, six of which now constitute Northern Ireland (Antrim, Armagh, Down, Fermanagh, (London)Derry and Tyrone) and three of which are in the Republic of Ireland (Eire): Monaghan, Cavan and Donegal. As will become clear, the Ulster Scots speech territory cuts across the modern political boundary.

4. As the honorary president of the Ulster-Scots Language Society, Gregg would agree with changes in predictions.

5. Although these were Gaelic-speakers, there is some evidence that their descendants learned English and even occasionally became trilingual in Gaelic, English and Scots; see the letters from Randal Macdonnell, Earl of Antrim, dated 1626, 1630, 1631 in Historical Manuscripts Commission (1909: 124, 132, 135, 139–40, 142–4).

6. The most prominent of these were grants to Hugh Montgomery and James Hamilton in north Down; according to Robinson (1984: 53), 'through these grants to Montgomery and Hamilton

foundations were laid for the most concentrated and substantial colony of British to arrive in Ulster in the first half of the seventeenth century'. According to Perceval-Maxwell (1973: 1), Hamilton, probably a native of Ayrshire, was already well acquainted with Ireland, having arrived in 1587. In the early years of the seventeenth century, Macdonnell, Earl of Antrim, brought many Lowland Scots to settle his estates.

7. A number of English settlement schemes in Ulster were pursued under the Tudors, but none with notable success. For a survey of these, see Robinson (1984: 46–52).

8. Interestingly enough, it was the conjunction of similar factors – including economic difficulties and religious pressures in Ulster and the attraction of land elsewhere – that led to a similar exodus of Ulster Scots to North America in the eighteenth century.

9. Of these speakers, the majority were in the 60–80 age-group. Only three were under 50, and only three were over 90. The oldest (97) and the youngest (25) had perfect control of Ulster Scots.

10. G. B. Adams did use the term 'Ulster Scots' in unpublished papers (for example, Adams c. 1968).

11. This concord rule has also characterised the speech of northern England since late Middle English times (McIntosh (1983), who refers to it as the 'northern paradigm') and until the present (Ihalainen (1994: 221), who calls it the 'northern subject rule').

12. It is probably insignificant that the first known appearance of this letter was in American newspapers. Such publications frequently cribbed materials from one another or from British counterparts without attribution. An earlier copy or version could easily have disappeared.

13. The only two exceptions to this are Hugh Porter's collection (1813) and Henry Fletcher's *Poems, Songs and Ballads* (1866).

14. The interviews conducted by the Tape-Recorded Survey of Hiberno-English (Barry 1981) in the 1970s might presumably be employed in this respect, but those from Antrim and Down are generally acknowledged to have been too formal for the purpose. Respondents there used the variety of public English reserved for outsiders to the community.

15. Using a checklist of key pairs and groups of words, Fenton (1995: viii) revises Gregg's southern boundary running from Antrim town to Whitehead, concluding that it 'has in places clearly shifted northwards' (ibid.).

16. Despite the evidence being indirect at best, writers like Padraig O'Snodaigh, on the basis of the Gaelic surnames of plantation settlers, and Roger Blaney, on the basis of the use of Irish and the existence of Irish-speaking Presbyterian churches in the seventeenth century, have found it irresistible to estimate the proportion of Gaelic speakers who crossed the channel from south-western Scotland. If the figures are as high as they believe ('possibly the majority', according to O'Snodaigh (1995: 30); 'at least half of early Presbyterians in Ulster', according to Blaney (1996: 17)), this would offer strong circumstantial evidence for significant Scottish Gaelic influence on Ulster Scots and Ulster English. In the absence of historical comments about the speech of plantation settlers, we can do little more than hazard inferences about such matters. Very few forms of Celtic origin appear in the Ulster Scots vernacular documents of the eighteenth and nineteenth centuries, nor is there any documentary evidence in Gaelic among the plantation settlers; they left no documents written in the language.

The degree of Scottish Gaelic monolingualism or Scottish Gaelic/Scots bilingualism among plantation settlers has been, and will probably continue to be, a highly debatable matter, primarily because most of the fragmentary evidence that exists is anecdotal and subject to distinctly different inferences. Lorimer (1949, 1951), easily the fullest and most objective consideration of the matter, concludes not only that in Carrick and Galloway Gaelic was moribund by the early seventeenth century and probably extinct by mid-century, but that Scots was universally known by the end of the previous century, meaning that any Gaelic-speakers who came to Ulster during the plantation period were most likely bilingual:

> [T]he evidence relating to Carrick shows that Scots was already in 1562 widely understood over that region. Gaelic monoglottism was evidently not a problem in the South-West as it was in the North . . . Gaelic wilted fast before Scots and English in the next hundred years,

and perhaps by the middle, and probably by the end of the 17th century, it was extinct.
(Lorimer 1951: 27, 42)

17. Grant (1931: xli) relies on W. F. Marshall's *Ballads and Verses from Tyrone* (1929) for information
on the Ulster plantation and perhaps did so as well for examples from Ulster Scots.

18. Patterson's work is in many ways the foundation for the study of Ulster Scots, featuring the first
significant coverage of Scottish areas in the province, but it did not attempt to isolate the Ulster
Scots element, the Scotticisms being interleaved among English (and Irish) forms. He did
recognise the Scottish character of many of his entries (1880: vii–viii):

> The words and phrases in the accompanying Glossary will be found in the main to be of
> Scottish origin, and many of them have already found a place in Jamieson's dictionary and
> in the various glossaries already printed by the English Dialect Society . . . In some districts
> in the east of the two counties people still talk a Scotch dialect, but with a modified Scotch
> accent; the old people talk more 'broadly' than the young.

19. Punctual *whenever* apparently extended in Ulster, expanding its meaning and currency after
coming from Scotland.

20. Of the numerous, closely similar comments on this that could be cited, especially from local and
popular glossaries, we cite the following as representative: 'Many words in common use here have
died out in England or changed their meanings, in fact it has been said that more Shakespearean
words are used in Armagh today than in Warwickshire' (Blaney 1985: 6).

15

The Scots Language in Australia

Graham Tulloch

Arriving in Port Phillip (in present-day Victoria) in 1839, Neil Black found that it was 'a Scotch colony' in which 'two thirds of the inhabitants are Scotch' (Richards 1988: 9). While there is no doubt some rhetorical exaggeration here, Hugh Watson, who arrived in South Australia in the same year, also reported that there were plenty of Scots to talk to in that colony (Richards 1985: 487). These comments offer a personal light on a wider phenomenon, the nineteenth-century emigration of Scots to Australia. Although, as Eric Richards has reported, this emigration has not been as thoroughly studied as that to North America, it was certainly significant. Scots came to Australia from the very beginning of European settlement: there were seventy Scots among the just over 1,000 people who came in the First Fleet of convict settlement in 1788. Later, three early governors were Scots and there were two sets of Scottish political prisoners, but it was with the growth in the numbers of free settlers in the nineteenth century that Scottish emigration to Australia really got under way. In the later twentieth century, Scots migration has continued but has provided a much smaller percentage of the total number of immigrants. The exact number of Scots people coming to Australia is impossible to determine, but some idea is given by the fact that, between 1853 and 1880, 138,036 Scots arrived in Australasia under government-assisted migration schemes, representing 13 per cent of the total of assisted migrants. Scots migrants were not equally distributed across Australia, and the 1891 censuses of the Australian colonies show the proportion of the population born in Scotland ranging from 11 per cent in South Australia to 15.7 per cent in Victoria (Richards 1988: 12). These percentages are not high (though they are also not insignificant), and generally Scots dispersed among the wider population. As Richards notes, even though there were a few places where Scots collected in greater concentrations, like Mount Gambier in South Australia or the Western Districts of Victoria, 'none of these became permanent enclaves, nor exclusively Scottish settlements' (Richards 1988: 13).

Of course, not all people coming from Scotland spoke Scots; many Highlanders would have spoken Gaelic and some educated Lowlanders would have spoken Scottish Standard English. As it happens, however, at almost all stages, the bulk of the Scottish migrants came from the Lowlands (Richards 1985: 476). Moreover, although the Scots immigrants came from diverse social backgrounds, they certainly included a large number of members of the urban and rural working classes who might be expected, at this stage in Scottish history, to be speakers of Scots. Given this, we can be sure that Scots was spoken in Australia, at least within some families of Scottish immigrants and when some Scottish people met together.

624 GRAHAM TULLOCH

As far as I know, there has been no scholarly study of the use of Scots speech in Australia, so that we need to turn to other evidence, both anecdotal and literary. One still hears strongly marked Scottish accents in Australia even with people who have lived in the country a long time. Although some such speakers consciously avoid using Scots vocabulary (except such terms as *wee* which are readily intelligible to non-Scots), they are likely to use some features of Scottish idiom, often probably without being conscious of their Scottishness, as I suspect was the case with a Scotsman who said to me *there are lots of houses around here that has big windows*. This use of *has* in a relative clause referring back to a plural subject is a long-established feature of Scots but not of Australian English. Among my students, I have also encountered young people of Scottish birth who can easily switch between Scots speech which they say they use at home and fully Australian speech which they use with their friends at university.

Written texts also provide us with evidence of the presence of Scots speech in Australia. They need, however, to be treated with caution even if their testimony broadly conforms with what one would expect. My own family provides a pertinent example. My grandmother's great-grandfather Hepburn Reid came to Adelaide from Scotland in 1859 with his family, including a son, also called Hepburn, then aged 16. Since the elder Hepburn is described in 1855 in the parish records as a miner, it is quite probable that he and his family were speakers of Scots. In her unpublished, semi-fictional recollections of her early life – *The Top Note* – my grandmother presents the younger Hepburn Reid as still speaking Scots at the end of his life early in the twentieth century. His dialogue includes such items as, *Come Lassie, . . . I'll gie ye saxpence if you can sing 'Bonny Charlie' right through, Well done lassie, I kent you'd reach it* and *Lassie the aufu pains are coming on again, maybe if I lie down they'll gang awa*. While it is not at all unlikely that he did continue to speak Scots, it is worth noting that the representation of Scots is entirely conventional and such as could have been created by anyone acquainted with Scott, Burns or many other Scottish writers. Is this then an accurate recollection of the degree to which Hepburn Reid's Scots speech survived, or is it simply a conventional literary creation?

Turning to better-known literary texts, it is easy to find evidence of Scots speech in realistic texts such as novels. Catherine Helen Spence, who arrived in Adelaide in 1839 at the age of 13 and who is of particular interest because of her deep concern with both Australia and Scotland, includes a number of Scots-speakers in the Australian settings of her novels. The kind of Scots which her characters speak varies in ways that both Scottish literary texts and modern sociolinguistic studies have led us to expect. In *Clara Morison* (1854), Mrs Duncanson, who has come straight from Orkney to South Australia, speaks in broad Scots (Spence 1854, vol. 2: 156):

> We have appointed to bide wi' you a towmont, sir, an' we are nae gangrel bodies, Sandy or me; we hae nae will to leave a gude place when we find ane. There's just twa things I dinna like – nae kirk, an' nae schule for the bairns, puir things! – but Sandy micht gie them a lesson at an orra time, at nicht, when there is na muckle thrang?

It is true that she does not speak a specifically Orkney Scots, probably because Spence was unable to reproduce a dialect she did not know from personal experience or from reading, but this need not prevent us from accepting Spence's introduction of working-class Scots into the realistic setting of her novel as evidence of the presence of Scots-speakers in Australia. Spence herself, with a Melrose lawyer as a father and a daughter of well-off tenant farmers as a mother, is likely to have spoken Scottish Standard English rather than Scots as a child, although she never lost her Scottish accent (Magarey 1985: 17). She would have heard Scots in Scotland before leaving at the age of 13, but it was perhaps equally, or even more, important that she could draw on literary texts to provide a conventional representation of Scots in her picture of South Australian life in the 1850s. Her heroine is of a higher social class, as are her cousins; they speak and write English but with a leavening of Scots words and proverbs, as when her cousin Grace advises Clara to speak to her employer: *Tell her that you have found relations in us, and keep your spirits up, for as the old Scotch proverb says, 'Tine heart, tine a'.* (vol. 1: 230), or when her cousin George writes to his sister: *I fear it is but 'water-brose and muslin-kail' hospitality that you can give your cousin, Miss Morison* (vol. 2: 47). In *Gathered In* (serialised 1881–2), Spence's hero, though a Scots-speaker as a child in Scotland, is educated and becomes an English-speaker. Coming to Australia, he meets his relatively uneducated but very successful uncle whose speech has been influenced by his many years in Australia but retains many Scots features, as the following passage illustrates (Spence 1977: 131):

> Say ye so, Kenneth, say ye so? But I hear you're just like the rest, carried away by a bonny face, and I'll no deny she's real bonny, though no to hold the candle to the lassie Gray – for I went to Castlehurst yesterday to see that Ellerton woman with my own eyes in her own house, and there was Edith, as she called her, with a face and look and a voice and a way with her that makes her worth twenty milk-and-water boarding school misses, that are only fit to sit at a piano, and skirl out songs in foreign tongues. I'm no denying that I like the Scotch songs the other one sings, but that's neither here nor there. William Gray's daughter has been at the head of his table and managed his house since she was sixteen . . . Ay, if it had been only Edith Gray.

Thus Spence presents us with a sociolinguistic range of different kinds of Scots such as we might expect in the speech of people who have migrated from Scotland. If the fine detail of the representation of Scots perhaps owes more to what Spence has read than to what she has heard, the broad picture is clear enough.

Catherine Martin, another South Australian, likewise includes conventional broad Scots in her novel *An Australian Girl* (1894) in the speech of the servant Kirsty. Little is known about Martin, but she was born in Skye and her novels show her to be highly educated. In the circumstances of the time, this makes it unlikely that she was a Scots-speaker. Indeed, other writers without any Scottish background at all have been willing to introduce Scots-speaking characters into their novels. This is in part testimony to the enormous influence of Scott, who had made the Scots literary dialect entirely familiar to Scots and non-Scots alike – so much so that knowledge of the literary tradition is sometimes more helpful than having lived in Scotland. The Australian children's writer David McRobbie, who was born and educated in Scotland and emigrated at the age of 20, has written a novel, *Mandragora* (1991), dealing with early Scots emigrants to Australia. *Mandragora* has been justly acclaimed, and McRobbie expresses his pride in his Scottish background in an after-word, but he apparently lacks the knowledge of works like the Waverley Novels which were so familiar to earlier writers, and he makes several mistakes in his representation of Scots speech. On the other hand, 'Steele Rudd' (Arthur Hoey Davis), born of a Welsh father and an Irish mother on the Darling Downs in Queensland in 1868, handles Scots quite well. It is true that his wife's parents were Scottish, but he would also have known writers who used Scots including, perhaps, such contemporaries as the Kailyarder 'Ian Maclaren' (John Watson), whose *Beside the Bonnie Brier Bush* (1894) and *The Days of Auld Lang Syne* (1895) seem, to judge by the ease with which one can find them in Australian second-hand bookshops, to have been just as popular in Australia as they were in Britain and America. Rudd became the writer of immensely popular stories of outback life in which he created a gallery of portraits of bush characters including the Scots-speaking Duncan McClure, who figures prominently in *The Poor Parson* (1907). When the play *On Our Selection* (1912) was fashioned from his work, it became even more popular than his novels and helped establish his characters as the national stereotypes of Australian bush battlers. The characters of the play include a Scots-speaking minister, his right to be seen as part of a typically Australian scene apparently accepted unchallenged. Rudd's representation of Scots shows very clearly his two sources of knowledge, reading Scottish books and hearing Scottish speakers: most of the spelling is of the conventional kind used in Scottish texts of the nineteenth century, but the use of *rr* in words like *pairrson*, *larrk* and *yairrd* (Rudd 1968: 11) to indicate the rhotic nature of Scots derives from observation of Scots-speakers, since this is not a feature of Scots to which Scots-speakers normally draw attention by their spelling. It represents, in fact, the outsider's view of Scots, but outsiders can use Scots effectively. Another classic Australian text containing Scots-speaking characters is Joseph Furphy's *Such is Life* (1903). Here, Tom Collins, the narrator and ostensible author, wins over the Scots-speaking 'Tam Airmstrang' by pretending to be himself a Scots-speaker. Collins' linguistic virtuosity (he speaks in very credible Scots) mirrors that of the real author Furphy and reminds us of how easy it was for writers steeped in Burns, Scott and their followers to imitate their language.

Thus in realistic novels, whether written by Scots or not, Scots-speakers are often present; this presumably reflects a perception that they were a recognised part of the Australian scene. Their recurring appearance provides evidence, if evidence is needed, that Scots was widely used by some members of Australian society.

Naturally, non-fiction adds to this picture, although the examples of Scots speech which it records are often quite short, as in Jane Isabella Watts' story of 'An old Scotchwoman, who . . . generally went about miserably clad and barefoot, and only *pit on her shoon when she cam' to wait upon the leddies*, as she informed them' (Watts 1890: 103) and in the story of John Dunmore Lang's mother who, when the Governor refused her a favour, retorted with: *Weel . . . ye needna gie yoursel airs an' be sae high aboot it. I mind your mither when she used to drive her ain mulk cairt into Largs, and she sitting on the barrel* (Gilchrist 1951, vol. 1: 75).

Scots words borrowed into Australian English provide another indicator of the presence of users of Scots language in Australia. The term *billy*, used to denote a kind of container with a lid for boiling water and making tea over a open fire, is first recorded in New Zealand in 1839 and in Australia in 1849 and is a development from Scots *billy-pot* 'pot used for boiling', recorded by the *Scottish National Dictionary* as occurring in 1828 in Scotland (Ramson 1988: s.v. *billy* n.[1]). *Darg* 'a day's work', a word found in Britain mainly in Scots and northern English dialects, occurs in Australia in the twentieth century with the slightly different meaning of 'a fixed or allotted amount of work', often used for the agreed amount of work that workers will perform when working to rule as a form of industrial action. The normal Australian term for a woodlouse is *slater*, which likewise derives from British usage found chiefly in Scotland and the north of England. The Scots use of *change* or *change-house* to mean 'an alehouse' may have helped in the development of the sense 'a changing-place for coach-horses' for the word *change* in Australian English: inevitably where horses were changed there would be an alehouse. In Scotland, an *upset price* is one publicly announced before an auction as the lowest price acceptable to the seller. The practice of announcing such a price in advance (rather than having a secret *reserve price*) was continued in Australia with the sale of land, and the term was taken over from Scots. Another phrase, *back of beyond*, occurs in Scott and other Scottish writers meaning 'somewhere very remote' or even 'somewhere non-existent', but in Australia refers to the far outback. It occurs in De Quincey but seems to be overwhelmingly a Scots usage until its appearance in Australia, the *Australian National Dictionary*'s first attestation being in Rolf Boldrewood's *Robbery under Arms* (1888). The child's word *googie* 'egg' is perhaps a more doubtful case; it is attested in Australian English from the early twentieth century, but whether it is from Scots *goggie* (first recorded in 1954) or the now obsolete use of the same word in northern English, or even conceivably from the Gaelic *gogaidh* (recorded by Dwelly in the early twentieth century), is hard to say. Thus Scots can be seen to have made its contribution, along with other British dialects, to the vocabulary of Australian English.

Many Australian place-names are of Scottish origin, although they are not always named directly after the Scottish place. Two British Secretaries of State for the Colonies are commemorated in Glenelg in South Australia and Perth in Western Australia – Lord Glenelg, and Sir George Murray who was born in Perthshire – while the Wemyss River in New South Wales was probably named after a certain William Wemyss, Deputy Commissary-General, and Buccleuch in South Australia after the Duke of Buccleuch. These should not perhaps be considered as elements of Scots in Australia, except insofar as they contain Scots words such as *glen* 'valley', *weem* 'cave' and *cleuch* 'narrow gorge' and, even then, the meaning of the Scots word cannot be said to have been consciously applied where, as often happens, it has no relevance to the newly named place. However, the term 'Scots' can legitimately be applied to manufactured names composed of Scots elements and recognised as such. An alternative name, now dropped, for Delamere in South Australia was Glenburn. The Rev. Dr Burgess explained the origin of the name (Cockburn 1984: s.v. *Glenburn*):

> A Methodist Church and Sunday School were opened down in the hollow under a precipitous hill at a place then known as Stockyards Creek, which was considered a very inappropriate name. I found that the native designation of the locality (Etchecowinga) was long and clumsy. The physical geography of the place suggested glen and burn, and at a public meeting in the Church I proposed the adoption of Glenburn, and the motion was carried.

The cultural attitudes embodied in this are fascinating, not least the assumption that a manufactured Scots place-name is entirely appropriate for an Australian locality. *Glen* seems to be a favoured element in the creation of names, whether in descriptive compounds like *Glenside* (SA) or in combination with personal names like *Glen Annie* (SA), *Glen Emily* (SA), *Glenora* (Tasmania, elided from *Glen Norah*), *Glen Innes* (NSW) and *Glen Osmond* (SA). *Glenunga*, the name of a suburb near Glen Osmond, unusually combines *glen* with the aboriginal termination *unga* meaning 'close to', while *Glenalta* (SA) joins it to Latin *alta* 'high'. *Strath* is similarly used in *Strathewin* (Victoria) named after Ewin Cameron and *Strathalbyn*, the name of a town established by Scots in South Australia, in which *Albyn* is a variant of *Albion*. *Burn* is less common in compounds but is found in *Burnside* (SA) and, due to a conflation of *Glynde* and *Burnside*, in *Glynburn Road* in Adelaide. Individuals also expressed their Scottishness by naming their houses or property with Scots names. For instance, the McColls named their station near Quorn *Braeside* (Quorn 1978: 123). However, the use of Scots terms does not always mean that they were correctly understood: both of the explanations of the house-name *Urrbrae* in Adelaide suggest that *brae* was misunderstood. It has been explained as 'Scottish for "our valley"' or as 'named after Urr,

the town in Scotland where [the owner] was born, and the "brae" added to it because there
was a burn running through the town' (Cockburn 1984: s.v. *Urrbrae*). It would seem that a
desire to identify oneself as Scots is more important in this case than an actual knowledge of
Scots. This was very likely the case with others, but it would be wrong to end on that note.
There can be no doubt that over time there have been people living in Australia who have
had a thorough knowledge of spoken Scots and who would not have made these mistakes.

It is not surprising that we can find plenty of evidence for the use of spoken Scots in
Australia given the number of Scots people who settled in the country; but, at first sight, the
amount of written Scots is rather more surprising, especially as the authors who use it are
not always Scots by birth. However, the language of Scott and Burns was, as I have already
noted, well known to Australian readers. Indeed, all readers in the English-speaking world
were familiar with an alternative literary dialect which they were free to use if they chose.
However, for the most part, since the choice of using Scots as a literary medium has long
been associated with a strong sense of Scottish national identity, few writers have chosen to
use Scots (except as an aspect of realism of dialogue in novels) without themselves having a
sense of identity with Scotland in some way or other.

I have already considered the use of Scots in novel dialogue as part of the evidence for the
use of Scots in speech in Australia, but it is worth looking again at a passage of such dialogue
to emphasise how much it can be a literary construct drawing on literary sources. Take, for
instance, the following passage in W. H. Lang's *The Thunder of the Hoofs* (1909: 85):

> She was awfu' bonny, and Maister Elliot fair wurshipit the vera grund she steppit on. But folk
> aye thocht her a glaikit, ne'r-do-weel, flichty kind of a body. Aweel, afore yer faither had
> foregathered wi' her – Eellen Mather was her name – there was an unco clash throu' the coonty
> that her and Lord Torsonce were ower chief, and that it was his lordship that should hae mairit
> her, and no yer papaw. But Maister Elliot was clean wud ower her . . .

This is old Nancy, a servant, speaking. It reads smoothly as a piece of spoken Scots and is
likely to strike the reader as realistic. But it should be noted that old Scottish servant women
(and their language) are a long-standing literary tradition. I do not know if Lang had any
particular source for this incident (although in general terms it resembles the story of Sybil
Knockwinnock in *The Antiquary*),[1] but it has very much the feeling of phrases picked up
from here and there, and it is probably significant that the phrase *glaiket ne'er-do-weel*
occurs in *Redgauntlet* and *clean wud* in *Old Mortality* and in *Rob Roy*.[2] Anyone writing Scots
of this kind in 1909 has plenty of literary models to draw on.

Nevertheless, it would be unfair to Scots novelists in Australia to suggest that they are
merely imitators. In particular, in the narrative of novels there is at least one case of striking
innovation. *The Life and Recollections of Dr Duguid of Kilwinning* (1887), *The Memorables of
Robin Cummell* (1899) and *Thir Notandums Being the Literary Recreations of Laird Canticarl
of Mongrynen* (1890) all by John Service, a Scotsman who had lived in Sydney since the
mid-1880s, are less novels than loosely structured anecdotal narratives but are remarkable
for being written entirely in Scots. While Scott's *Wandering Willie's Tale* and Stevenson's
Thrawn Janet and *The Tale of Tod Lapraik* are all written in Scots, none of them is of novel
length. Service employs the same device as Scott and Stevenson in having a Scots-speaking
character as the narrator, but Service's characters, Cummell, Canticarl and Duguid are
presented as writing their stories down and not relating them verbally. For a full-length
work, this breaks a barrier which had remained unbroken since Scott first brought Scots in a

major way into novels but confined it to dialogue.[3] The opening of *The Memorables of Robin Cummell* provides a specimen of the sort of narrative language that Service was able to use with the narrators which he created (Service 1913: 1–2):

> The wind was roarin' at the lum-heid and soughin' like a spate among the auld trees o' the gairden – I mean the gairden of the monks that is kent noo as the Bean-yaird, and whaur I mysel' can mind, langsyne, of seeing the yellow plooms and the peaches and pears beeking bonniely in the sun, and hinging, drap-ripe, frae the ruined wa'.
>
> But it was the winter time noo, and, as I sat by the cosie ingle neuck and hearkened to the rairin' storm, my thochts gaed awa back to the far-off years when the auld abbey was in a' its glory and its spoliawtors were yet unborn. It maun hae been a grand and glorious biggin' in its day. Mony a time, in my waukin' oors, have I tried to rear it again as it stood there in a' its stately beauty in the green deeps o' the forest, but it aye seemed to me like ettlin' wi' a thrawcruk to make rapes oot o' the saun'. There was a confusion o' gavels and oriels and lang lance windows and carven doors, but naething o' a wysse-like kirk that would rise before my een. Now, however, there cam to me a dream, in which it stood revealed.

Service copies a familiar, late nineteenth-century novelistic style of writing but introduces a substantial amount of Scots vocabulary and spelling and some Scots grammar. All the same, the spelling is not as fully Scots as it could have been – for instance, the last sentence could have contained spellings like *noo, hooiver* and *stude*. Various explanations of this could be offered – that Service does not want to make his text look too unlike English, that he reverts unconsciously to the English novelistic style which underlies his Scots, that he is simply following the inconsistencies of Scott and Burns, even that the mention of a significant dream calls forth memories of the Bible or, more particularly, the Authorised Version – but it is impossible to be certain quite why Service stops short of a fully realised Scots. Galt, writing of the same Ayrshire district as Service but at the beginning of the nineteenth century, provides an instructive comparison here. In a narrative like *The Howdie* which is supposedly written by a poorly educated woman, the midwife of the title, Galt makes good use of Scots vocabulary and idiom but rarely uses Scots spelling. The language remains in this way more or less within the bounds of realism as a written narrative given that, since at least the eighteenth century, Scots have been taught to write English and not Scots. A language such as Service uses with its many Scottish spellings is hardly realistic for a written narrative, but by the end of the nineteenth century it had come to seem a fairly natural choice for a literary text, especially a text dealing, as do all three of Service's novels, with a Scottish setting. (I know of nothing so radical in Australian writing as the work of the New Zealand writer John Summers, whose novel *Fernie Brae* (1984) is not only written throughout in a form of Scots but also set in New Zealand.)

The Memorables of Robin Cummell was printed with a glossary for all three novels prepared by Henry Paterson Cameron, another Scot living in Sydney. Cameron was also an innovator in his own way, and, in the same year, 1913, he published his own fully Scots text, but it was a different kind of text and a different kind of Scots. Cameron's *Of the Imitation of Christ by Thomas à Kempis frae Latin intil Scots* aims at a more elevated Scots appropriate to a much-admired religious text. At the same time, the strongly colloquial bias of modern Scots shows through in some of the diction. This is evident, for example, in the opening section of Book I, chapter 10 (Cameron 1913: 14):

> Evite as faur as ye can the rippet o' men; for the han'lin o' warldlie things, alpuist saiklesslie unertaen is a trachle, sae radly are we kilhab'd an' fyled be ydilheid. Aften I wuss that I hed

been whush, an' hedna mell'd wi' men. Bot whatfor dae we sae fainly tauk an' claver ane wi' anither, sin' we retour tae quateness sae seenil withoot a kennin skaith dune tae oor conscience? Mairower, we are fu' fain tae tauk, sith throwe oor corrieneuchins we houp tae obteen some easedom ane wi' anither, an' tae cule oor forfochen hert wi' a hantle o' thochts. An' we are geyan gled tae tauk an' think o' what we loe or grien for, or o' thae things whilk are contrair tae us.

This is clearly not an imitation of early twentieth-century Scots speech with its archaisms like *alpuist* 'although' (an eighteenth-century term, no doubt taken from Jamieson who spells it *allpuist*) and *kilhab* 'lure, seduce' (otherwise recorded in SND only in Hogg (1865, vol. 1: 322)), but it includes some modern colloquialisms like *corrieneuchin* 'intimate conversation'. Writing before MacDiarmid, Cameron had already learned the value of drawing on works like Jamieson's *Etymological Dictionary of the Scottish Language* as a way of enriching current Scots, as he was to continue to demonstrate in his translation of Genesis (1921) – see Tulloch (1989: 64–8). There are similarities between Cameron's language and that of P. Hately Waddell's translations of the Psalms (1871) and Isaiah (1879), but Cameron's style of Scots has its own unique characteristics, and he was an innovator in translating a religious text other than the Bible into Scots. It would seem that being away from the Scottish literary scene sometimes freed writers of the Scots diaspora to try out new ways of using Scots. Such is the case with Service and Cameron in Australia, the poet Charles Murray in South Africa and William Wye Smith, translator of the New Testament into Scots, in Canada. (Smith was not the first modern writer to translate from the Bible into Scots, but earlier translations had either been of poetic books of the Old Testament or publications of limited circulation intended for linguists. Smith's translation was intended for ordinary readers.) It is perhaps symbolic of this that Cameron, while in Scotland, wrote a book on the history of the English Bible but in Australia translated Genesis into Scots.

Needless to say, poetry, though not of Waddell's kind, has been a recognised vehicle for the use of Scots. In the nineteenth and earlier twentieth centuries, the Burns tradition was alive and well in Australia, and comic and sentimental verse in Scots was quite common. A typical example is the poetry of Joan Torrance, a collection of whose poems was published in 1904 in Scots and English called *Twixt Heather and Wattle*, a title which neatly positions her both culturally and linguistically. For sentimentality, one might choose her *Nannie* which begins (Torrance 1904: 24–5):

'Tae puir-house, Nannie, come awa',
'There's hame an 'claes [sic] baith there,
'The winter's cauld, yer getting auld,
'Come, dinna greet sae sair.'

Thae doctor paused, his heart was full,
A tear crept down his cheek –
I kent her when a bonnie lass,
'O Gavin, ye maun speak!'

'Have faith, dear Nannie,' Gavin said,
'Now kneel wi' me in prayer:
'Creator, smile upon the ane
'Whae's bowed in great despair.'

This kind of Scots, using only the most familiar Scots terms such as *greet, ken, bairn, jouk* and *dykes* along with a leavening of Scots spelling, is very much in the *Whistle-Binkie* mould which had dominated Scottish poetry for much of the nineteenth century. The use of *thae* to mean 'the' suggests that Torrance was familiar with the literary dialect (from which she has misunderstood the use of *thae* as being a simple alternative to *the*) but was not so familiar with the spoken language where *thae* still strongly survives in its correct and historic usage even today (though often apprehended as a use of *they*). When we turn to 'The First Parade of the Scottish Regiment. 28th June, 1899', where Torrance addresses soldiers about to set off for the Boer War, the incongruities of the situation are very obvious – an *Australian* poet addressing soldiers in *Australia* and urging them in *Scots* to invade *Africa* for *Scotland's* sake. These incongruities manifest themselves linguistically (Torrance 1904: 36–7):

> The nicht's the nicht for clannish folk,
> The Scots braw regiment's noo nae jouk,
> Wi' colours o' the forty twa,
> The bonniest sicht ye ever saw!
> Wi' jewell'd dirk, an' skene that's true,
> They march like shades o' Roderick Dhu . . .
>
> Shame! Sons of Scotia standing aff
> In fear of idlers' windy chaff!
> Roll up! Roll up!! wi' richt gude will,
> And show ye lo'e Auld Reekie still!
> Fill up the ranks! mak nae delay –
> To Afric's veldts ye're sune to gae!

Torrance's grip of the language is uncertain (*jouk* seems to have been misunderstood as meaning 'joke'), and the reference to *Afric's veldts* sits a little uneasily here.

Torrance is an easy target for criticism, and, to be fair to her, some of her other poems handle Scots with rather more assurance. Other poets, too, can handle Scots with reasonable confidence: an example is a neat little poem called *Bereaved* by Mary Ann Robertson:

> A lane fireside, ah me!
> Gang doon, O fire, and dee!
> O laughin, lispin, livin thing, waes me!
>
> O wheesht noo, clock, ah me!
> Ye deave like ony three!
> O feet that patted ye tae sleep, waes me!
>
> I lift my een, Ah me!
> Is that my Man I see?
> O Faither of my bairnie gaen, waes me!

Like some of the best of MacDiarmid's lyrics, this strikes me as having had its origin in an evocative phrase, in this case *Waes me*. It first appeared in *The Bulletin* (4 January 1902), where Scots poems were not uncommon at the time, and it is surely significant that a journal that saw itself as quintessentially Australian was quite willing to publish poems in Scots.

George Mure Black's *Yin Wee Drappie* provides an example of that other staple of nineteenth-century Scots verse, the comic poem about drink (Mure Black 1923: 91):

> Gin a chappie's dour, unhappy,
>   Tired o' fechtin care;
> Yin wee drappie o' the nappy
>   Gars him loup and rair.
> Ilka chappie taks his drappie,
>   Warkin' maks folks dry:
> Gin a drappie maks ye happy,
>   'Swig it doun,' say I.
>
> Gin a body meet a body
>   Stottin', drucken hame,
> Need a body spier if toddy
>   Wambles in his wame?
> Ilka fogie taks his cogie,
>   Ilka body's dry;
> Tak your liquor, toom the bicker,
>   Nane the waur am I!

A poem like this shows the possibility of fairly dense and accurate Scots written in Australia within the Burns tradition. If the use of *yin* as an attributive adjective is ultimately from Standard English (*yae* or *ae* would have been the traditional Scots form), Mure Black was not the first to adopt this usage, which SND records in Scotland from the later nineteenth century onwards.

As with novels, the use of Scots by poets of non-Scottish origin reminds us of how well established Scots was as an alternative literary language. For instance, Henry Lawson, that most Australian of writers, published a short poem called *The Scots: A Dirge* in *The Bulletin* of 3 February 1910. Lawson in fact uses Scots to abuse the Scots, perhaps somewhat tongue in cheek. Such feelings were not likely to be shared by Australians of Scottish descent who, while not Scots-speakers themselves, could use Scots as a tribute to their Scottish ancestry, as seems to be the case with Mary Gilmore's *The Owing* and Hugh Macrae's *The Gaberlunzie, The Bairnie and the Birdie* and *To Mary Gilmore* or because they were dealing with Scottish subject matter, as in Douglas Stewart's *Glencoe*.

These poets are attempting, with various degrees of success, to write Scots. But this need not be the only way in which Scots is used. A sprinkling of Scots terms can perform a useful literary function even when the base of the language seems to be English. In these cases, Scots figures primarily as an element of poetic diction or an assertion of national affiliation. Particularly from their associations with Burns and with various Scottish songs, Scots terms can evoke an image of Scotland and the Scots with overtones of nostalgia, melancholy and tenderness or pithiness, hardheadedness and even ribaldry. For instance, in John Macleod's *Lament of the '45* there are a number of Scots terms and spellings which contribute to the poem's air of melancholy and nostalgia. To quote the first four stanzas:

> The wild woods bloom as though there was nae care;
>   As though bleak winter never had been there.
> The bluebells and the snowdrops come and go,
>   And life goes on as though it didn'a know.

The Stuart, tae Scotland's sorrow, passed this glen,
   An' took wi' him oor ain hame-lovin' men.
Noo nane among them ever will come back.
   What hae we got for a' the love we lack?

There is nae song, nae music in the breeze,
   Nae whispered message in the soochin' trees;
Nae hope, nae comfort in the glow o' spring,
   Noo feckless fate has taken everything.

Wild Nature in its beauty noo is still;
   And that way it'll stay for me, until
The last bird sings its song, the last bloom's gone,
   And I can join my ain man, further on.[4]

The rhymes here are English (*care*, *go* and *gone* rather than *caur*, *gae* and *gane*) and the rhythms are also those of English verse, so that the presence of Scottish terms cannot turn this into fully Scots verse; but this does not invalidate the function of the Scots terms that are included.

As is so often the case in the presentation of dialect texts, typography can be all-important in defining what is seen as the language of the poem. When *A Scotch Night* by Will Ogilvie first appeared in *The Bulletin* (28 August 1897: p. 18), the Scots words were surrounded by quotation marks, as we can see in the first verse:

If you chance to strike a gathering of half-a-dozen friends
Where the drink is Highland whisky or some chosen 'Border Blends,'
And the room is full of 'spierin,' and the 'gruppin'' of brown 'han's,'
And the talk is all of 'tartans' and of 'plaidies' and of 'clans,'
You can take things 'douce' and easy, you can judge you're going right,
For you've had the luck to stumble on a 'wee Scotch night.'

The quotation marks define the Scots as 'other' and establish the basic medium of discourse as English. When this same poem was published in *The Bulletin Reciter*, the quotation marks were removed, very likely simply because they are distracting for anyone reciting the poem.[5] However, the effect, probably not intended, is to redefine the basic medium as what might be called 'Australian Scottish English'.

Insofar as many Australian poems using Scots are following in the tired tradition exemplified in Scotland in the *Whistle-Binkie* anthology, their language is likely to lack inventiveness and vigour. Stevenson, it is true, had reinvigorated and reinvented this tradition to some degree, as had Charles Murray whose work may also have been known in Australia, but neither poet's Scots is so strongly different from that of the Burns tradition that it would be likely to provoke a radical change in the kind of Scots used by Australian poets. We might expect the influence of Hugh MacDiarmid to have a stronger effect on Australian Scots poetry; but, firstly, there are fewer Australian poets writing in Scots in the twentieth century, and, secondly, MacDiarmid's model is one that only some poets are temperamentally inclined to follow. It is not all poets who are willing to write with Jamieson open at their side.

One of the most interesting of the twentieth-century poets who have used Scots is J. M. Couper. Couper was certainly aware of MacDiarmid's work – his *Sydney Cricket Ground on*

Judgment Day, a public holiday is subtitled 'from Hugh MacDiarmid's *Crowdieknowe*' and
provides an Australian version of it (Couper 1979: 67). But Couper does not imitate
MacDiarmid's synthetic Scots; there is very little revival of unusual words or long-obsolete
terms, although there is plenty of variety in his diction. For the most part, he writes in
English but often with a good sprinkling of Scots vocabulary, as in the seventh sonnet of his
sequence 'A series of letters to Mark Alexander Boyd' (Couper 1967: 23–33):

> Well, when yon lassie kept you in torment
> and played you mince, or pert, or douce, or dour,
> as though she never leapt clean out of her sark
> but wore through life in all yon heap of clothes,
> then maybe you clapped down and cursed your days,
> or threw off your bit of a sonnet out to stark
> peelie-wallie despair . . .

One thing he has learnt from Scottish poetry is its strong tradition of using colloquial
language. This reveals itself, as one of his translations of Horace shows, in some of his
poems in Australian English, as in *For You Angela* (Couper 1967: 63):

> What cheerful bastard
> reeking of sun-tan
> goes for you, Angela,
> flat on the sands? . . .

> My, but he's in for a
> tough old time there,
> tossing the seas of your
> greedy libido.

At other times, this colloquial tone takes him into the colloquial base of modern spoken
Scots, as happens in the tenth sonnet of the Boyd sequence:

> Well, for the like of your days it was braly, was't no?
> Wishart there birling like a football match, a splore
> to warm the tail end of the winter, the starving poor,
> as good's the Cup Final – Beaton in the grandstand, too . . .

> John canted the queyns, forby. I ken that fine.
> As randy a yoking of buckies as ever you'd see, man,
> I'm doubting there never a one of them thick with God.

Here, the basic medium comes close to being Scots rather than English. This happens,
however, in only a small proportion of Couper's work. When writers choose to write in
Scots, they generally build on existing styles of Scots writing. Even MacDiarmid did this to
some degree. Here, I think Couper is drawing on traditions of the representation of Scots
speech in the dialogue of novels. Mostly, however, he draws on the traditions of poets
writing in English, particularly those of the twentieth century. While the style which he has
learnt from these writers can accommodate quite large numbers of Scots words, it is not in
most cases a suitable basis for the development of a fully Scots poetic style.

The use of Scots remains an option open to Australian writers, but the cultural pressures which, for instance, led Lorimer to forge a new Scots style for his New Testament in Scotland operate with far less force in Australia. As the tradition of writing Burns-type Scots dies away, no new tradition has taken hold, and, as a consequence, Scots is more likely to be introduced as an element in writing in English than as part of a fully developed Scots style. At the same time, the fact that Scots has any currency at all in later twentieth-century Australian writing is a tribute to the extraordinary position which Scots developed in the English-speaking world as an alternative literary language to English. No other strongly regional form of English has ever achieved anything like that status in the English-speaking world, and the special position which Burns, Scott and others won for Scots has even now not been entirely lost in a country to which so many Scots emigrated.

NOTES

1. Walter Scott, *The Antiquary*, Border Edition, pp. 328–9 (chapter 24). References to Scott are, where available, to The Edinburgh Edition of the Waverley Novels (Edinburgh: Edinburgh University Press, 1993–), referred to as 'EEWN'; otherwise to Lang (1898–9), referred to as 'Border Edition'.
2. *Redgauntlet*, Border Edition, p. 238 (chapter 2); *Old Mortality*, EEWN, p. 291 (chapter 37); *Rob Roy*, Border Edition, p. 194 (chapter 14).
3. Such at least is the case with printed books. As William Donaldson notes in his Introduction to William Alexander's *The Laird of Drammochdyle and his Contemporaries* (1986), 'Scottish papers carried original fiction in serial form throughout the second half of the nineteenth century and some thousands of Scottish novels are preserved in this as yet largely unexplored source' (p. xii), and it may be that there are novels entirely in Scots among them.
4. *Where Old Friends Meet* (Sydney: Currawong, 1964), p. 23. It is worth noting that all the poems in this collection had been read aloud on a radio programme before being printed here; broad Scots would probably not have been seen as appropriate for radio.
5. *The Bulletin Reciter: A Collection of Verses for Recitation from 'The Bulletin' 1880–1901* (Sydney: The Bulletin, 1901), pp. 200–3.

Bibliography

Abercrombie, D. (1979), 'The accents of Standard English in Scotland', in A. J. Aitken and T. McArthur (eds), *Languages of Scotland*, Edinburgh: Chambers, pp. 68–81.

Ackerman, A. (1898), *Die Sprache der ältesten schottischen Urkunden (A.D. 1385–1440)*, Berlin: Buchdruckerei Gustav Schade.

Adam Smith, J. (1970), 'Some eighteenth-century ideas of Scotland', in N. T. Phillipson and R. Mitchison (eds), *Scotland in the Age of Improvement*, Edinburgh: Edinburgh University Press, pp. 107–24.

Adams, A. and J. R. R. Adams (eds) (1992), *The Country Rhymes of Hugh Porter, the Bard of Moneyslane*, Folk Poets of Ulster series, vol. 1, Bangor: Pretani.

Adams, G. B. (1948), 'Introduction to the study of Ulster dialect', *Royal Irish Academy Proceedings*, Section C 52, pp. 1–26.

Adams, G. B. (1950), 'Phonological notes on the English of south Donegal', *Royal Irish Academy Proceedings*, Section C 53, pp. 299–310.

Adams G. B. (1956), 'Patterns of word distribution', *Ulster Folklife*, 2, pp. 6–13.

Adams, G. B. (1958), 'The emergence of Ulster as a distinct dialect area', *Ulster Folklife*, 4, pp. 61–73.

Adams, G. B. (1964), 'Introduction', in idem (ed.), *Ulster Dialects: An Introductory Symposium*, Holywood: Ulster Folk Museum, pp. 1–4.

Adams, G. B. (1966), 'The work and words of hay-making', *Ulster Folklife*, 12, pp. 66–91.

Adams, G. B. (1967), 'Northern England as a source of Ulster dialects (review and discussion of E. Kolb (ed.), *Linguistic Atlas of England – Phonological Atlas of the Northern Region*)', *Ulster Folklife*, 13, pp. 69–74.

Adams, G. B. (c. 1968), 'A brief guide to Ulster Scots', typescript.

Adams, G. B. (1970–1), 'Language and man in Ireland', *Ulster Folklife*, 15–16, pp. 140–71.

Adams, G. B. (1971), 'Ulster dialect origins', *Ulster Folklife*, 17, pp. 99–102.

Adams, G. B. (1976), 'Aspects of monoglottism in Ulster', *Ulster Folklife*, 22, pp. 76–87.

Adams, G. B. (1977), 'The dialects of Ulster', in D. O'Muirithe (ed.), *The English Language in Ireland*, Cork: Mercier, pp. 56–69.

Adams, G. B. (1982), 'Report on dialect work in Ulster', *Scottish Language*, 1, pp. 6–12.

Adams, G. B. (1986), 'Language and man in Ireland', in M. Barry and P. M. Tilling (eds), *The English Dialects of Ulster*, Holywood: The Ulster Folk and Transport Museum, pp. 1–32.

Adams, J. (1794), *Euphonologia Linguae Anglicanae: English Linguistics 1500–1800*, 112, ed. R. C. Alston (1968), Menston: Scolar Press.

Adams, J. (1799), *The Pronunciation of the English Language Vindicated from Imputed Anomaly and Caprice*, Edinburgh: *English Linguistics 1500–1800*, 72, ed. R. C. Alston (1968), Menston: Scolar Press.

Adams, J. R. R. (1987), *The Printed Word and the Common Man: Popular Culture in Ulster 1700–1900*, Belfast: Institute of Irish Studies.

Adams, J. R. R. (1989), 'A preliminary checklist of works containing Ulster dialect 1700–1900', *Linen Hall Review*, 6:3, pp. 10–12.

Adams, J. R. R. (1992), *The Country Rhymes of Samuel Thomson, the Bard of Carngranny*, Folk Poets of Ulster series, vol. 3, Bangor: Pretani.

Adie, W. (1769), *A New Spelling-Book: In which the Rules of Spelling and Pronouncing the English Language are Exemplified and Explained*, Paisley.

Agnew, J. (1992), 'Sources for the history of Belfast in the seventeenth and early eighteenth centuries', *Familia*, 2, pp. 150–8.

Agnew, J. H. (1994), 'The merchant community of Belfast, 1660–1707', Dissertation, Queen's University of Belfast.

Agutter, A. (1987), 'A taxonomy of Older Scots orthography', in C. I. Macafee and I. Macleod (eds), *The Nuttis Schell. Essays on the Scots Language presented to A. J. Aitken*, Aberdeen: Aberdeen University Press, pp. 75–82.

Agutter, A. (1989a), 'Standardisation in Middle Scots', *Scottish Language*, 8, pp. 17–24.

Agutter, A. (1989b), 'Restandardisation in Middle Scots', in S. Adamson, V. Law, N. Vincent and S. Wright (eds), *Papers from the 5th International Conference on English Historical Linguistics*, Amsterdam: John Benjamins, pp. 1–11.

Agutter, A. J. and L. N. Cowan (1981), 'Changes in the vocabulary of Lowland Scots dialects', *Scottish Literary Journal*, Supplement 14, pp. 49–62.

Aitken, A. J. (1954), 'Sources of the vocabulary of Older Scots', unpublished paper.

Aitken, A. J. (1964), 'Completing the record of Scots', *Scottish Studies*, 8, pp. 129–40.

Aitken, A. J. (1971a), 'Variation and variety in written Middle Scots', in A. J. Aitken, A. McIntosh and H. Pálsson (eds), *Edinburgh Studies in English and Scots*, London: Longman, pp. 177–209.

Aitken, A. J. (1971b), 'Historical dictionaries and the computer', in R. A. Wisbey (ed.), *The Computer in Literary and Linguistic Research*, London: Cambridge University Press, pp. 3–17.

Aitken, A. J. (1973a), 'Definitions and citations in a period dictionary', in R. I. McDavid and A. R. Duckert (eds), *Lexicography in English*, New York: New York Academy of Sciences, pp. 259–65.

Aitken, A. J. (1973b), 'Sense-analysis for a historical dictionary', *Zeitschrift für Dialektologie und Linguistik*, Neue Folge, 9, pp. 5–16.

Aitken, A. J. (ed.) (1973c), *Lowland Scots: Occasional Papers no. 2*, Edinburgh: Association for Scottish Literary Studies.

Aitken, A. J. (1977a), 'Textual problems and the *Dictionary of the Older Scottish Tongue*', in P. G. J. van Sterkenburg (ed.), *Lexicologie, een bundel opstellen voor F. de Tollenaere*, Groningen: Walters-Noundhoff, pp. 13–15.

Aitken, A. J. (1977b), 'How to pronounce Older Scots', in A. J. Aitken, M. P. McDiarmid and D. S. Thomson (eds), *Bards and Makars: Scots Language and Literature, Mediaeval and Renaissance*, Glasgow: Glasgow University Press, pp. 1–21.

Aitken, A. J. (1978a), 'Historical dictionaries, word frequency distributions and the computer', *Cahiers de lexicologie*, 33, pp. 28–47.

Aitken, A. J. (1978b), 'Oral narrative style in Middle Scots', in J.-J. Blanchot and C. Graf (eds), *Actes du 2ᵉ colloque de langue et de littérature écossaises*, Strasbourg [n.pub.], pp. 98–112.

Aitken, A. J. (1979), 'Scottish speech: a historical view with special reference to the standard English of Scotland', in A. J. Aitken and T. McArthur (eds), *Languages of Scotland*, Edinburgh: Chambers, pp. 85–118.

Aitken, A. J. (1981a), 'The Scottish vowel-length rule', in M. Benskin and M. L. Samuels (eds), *So Meny People, Longages and Tonges: Philological Essays in Scots and Medieval English Presented to Angus McIntosh*, Edinburgh: Edinburgh University Press, pp. 131–57.

Aitken, A. J. (1981b), 'DOST: How we made it and what's in it', in R. J. Lyall and F. Riddy (eds), *Proceedings of the Third International Conference on Scottish Language and Literature, Medieval and Renaissance*, Stirling and Glasgow, University of Stirling, pp. 33–51.

Aitken, A. J. (1981c), 'The good old Scots tongue: does Scots have an identity?', in E. Haugen, J. D. McClure and D. Thomson (eds), *Minority Languages Today*, Edinburgh: Edinburgh University Press, pp. 72–90.

Aitken, A. J. (1982), 'Bad Scots: some superstitions about Scots speech', *Scottish Language*, 1, pp. 30–44.

Aitken, A. J. (1983), 'The languages of Older Scots poetry', in J. D. McClure, A. J. Aitken and D. Murison (eds), *Scotland and the Lowland Tongue*, Aberdeen: Aberdeen University Press, pp. 18–49.

Aitken, A. J. (1984), 'Scots and English in Scotland', in P. Trudgill (ed.), *Language in the British Isles*, Cambridge: Cambridge University Press, pp. 517–32.

Aitken, A. J. (1988), 'The lexicography of Scots: the current position', in K. Hyldgaard-Jensen (ed.), *Proceedings of the Third International Symposium on Lexicography*, Tübingen: Niemeyer, pp. 323–33.

Aitken, A. J. (1991), 'Progress in Older Scots philology', in G. Ross Roy (ed.), *Studies in Scottish Literature*, vol. 26, *The Language and Literature of Early Scotland*, Columbia: South Carolina University Press, pp. 19–37.

Aitken, A. J. and T. McArthur (eds) (1979), *Languages of Scotland*, Edinburgh: Chambers.

Aitken, A. J., M. P. McDiarmid and D. S. Thomson (eds) (1977), *Bards and Makars: Scots Language and Literature, Mediaeval and Renaissance*, Glasgow: Glasgow University Press.

Aitken, A. J., A. McIntosh and H. Pálsson (eds) (1971), *Edinburgh Studies in English and Scots*, London: Longman.

Akenson, D. H. (1980), 'Listening to rural language: Ballycarry Co. Antrim 1798–1817', in idem (ed.), *Canadian Papers in Rural History*, Langdale: Ganacoque, pp. 155–72.

Akenson, D. H. and W. H. Crawford (1977), *Local Poets and Social History: James Orr Bard of Ballycarry*, Belfast: Public Record Office of Northern Ireland.

Alexander, W. (1884), *Johnny Gibb of Gushetneuk*, 8th edn, Edinburgh: Douglas.

Alexander, W. (1986), *The Laird of Drammochdyle and his Contemporaries, or Random Sketches Done in Outline with a Burnt Stick*, ed. with an intro. by W. Donaldson, Aberdeen: Aberdeen University Press.

Allan, A. (1995), 'Scots spellin – ettlin efter the quantum loup', *English World-Wide*, 16:1, pp. 61–103.

Allardyce, A. (1888), *Scotland and Scotsmen in the 18th Century from the MSS of John Ramsay. Esqu. of Ochtertyre*, 2 vols, Edinburgh and London: Blackwood.

Amours, F. J. (ed.) (1896), *Scottish Alliterative Poems*, Scottish Text Society, 1st series, Edinburgh and London: Blackwood.

Anderson, J. M. and C. J. Ewen (1987), *Principles of Dependency Phonology*, Cambridge: Cambridge University Press.

Anderson, J. M. and C. Jones (eds) (1974a), *Historical Linguistics*, 2 vols, Amsterdam: North-Holland.

Anderson, J. M. and C. Jones (1974b), *Phonological Structure and the History of English*, Amsterdam: North-Holland.

Anderson, P. M. (1987), *A Structural Atlas of the English Dialects*, London: Croom Helm.

Angus, W. (1800a), *A Pronouncing Vocabulary of the English Language: Exhibiting the Most Appropriate Mode of Pronunciation: English Linguistics 1500–1800*, 164, ed. R. C. Alston (1969), Menston: Scolar Press.

Angus, W. (1800b), *An Epitome of English Grammar*, Glasgow.

Angus, W. (1814a), *An English Spelling and Pronouncing Vocabulary*, Glasgow.

Angus, W. (1814b), *An Introduction to Angus' Vocabulary and Fulton's Dictionary*, Glasgow.

Angus, W. (1814c), *English Spelling and Pronouncing Dictionary*, Glasgow.

Anon. (1711), *The Needful Attempt to Make Language and Divinity Plain and Easy*, London: English Linguistics 1500–1800, 154, ed. R. C. Alston (1969), Menston: Scolar Press.

Anon. (1784), *A General View of English Pronunciation: to which are added EASY LESSONS for the use of the English Class*, London: English Linguistics 1500–1800, 96, ed. R. C. Alston (1968), Menston: Scolar Press.

Anon. (1795), *The Child's Guide*, Aberdeen.

Anon. (1796), *A Spelling-Book upon a New Plan*, Glasgow.

Anon. (1798), *The Instructor: or An Introduction to Reading and Spelling*, London.

Anon. (1820), 'Sketches of Village Character. No. II', *Blackwood's Edinburgh Magazine*, 8, pp. 7–11.

Anon. (1826), *The Vulgarities of Speech Corrected, with Elegant Expressions for Provincial and Vulgar English, Scots and Irish*, London: Bulcock.

Anon. (1855), *Scotticisms Corrected*, London: Shaw.

Aylmer, J. (1559), *An Harborowe for Faithful and Trew Servants*, London.

Baildon, H. B. (1899), *On the Rimes in the Authentic Poems of William Dunbar*, Edinburgh: Neill.

Bald, M. (1926), 'The anglicisation of Scottish printing', *Scottish Historical Review*, 23, pp. 107–15.

Bald, M. (1927), 'The pioneers of anglicised speech in Scotland', *Scottish Historical Review*, 24, pp. 179–93.

Bald, M. (1928), 'Contemporary references to the Scottish speech of the sixteenth century', *Scottish Historical Review*, 25, pp. 163–79.

Bannerman, J. (1983), 'Literacy in the Highlands', in I. B. Cowan and D. Shaw (eds), *The Renaissance and Reformation in Scotland*, Edinburgh: Scottish Academic Press, pp. 214–35.

Bannerman, J. (1990), 'The Scots language and the kin-based society', in D. S. Thomson (ed.), *Gaelic and Scots in Harmony: Proceedings of the Second International Conference on the Languages of Scotland*, Glasgow: Department of Celtic, University of Glasgow, pp. 1–19.

Barber, C. (1976), *Early Modern English*, London: Deutsch.

Barbour, J. (1968), *The Bruce*, ed. Walter Skeat, vols 1–2, Early English Text Society E.S. 11, 21, 29, 55, Oxford: Oxford University Press.

Barke, J. and S. Goodsir Smith (eds) (1965), *Robert Burns, The Merry Muses of Caledonia*, London: W. H. Allen.

Barnes, M. P. (1984), 'Orkney and Shetland Norn', in P. Trudgill (ed.), *Language in the British Isles*, Cambridge: Cambridge University Press, pp. 352–66.

Barnes, M. P. (1991), 'Reflections on the structure and the demise of Shetland and Orkney Norn', in P. S. Ureland and G. Broderick (eds), *Language Contact in the British Isles*, Tübingen: Niemeyer, pp. 429–60.

Barrie, A. (1794), *A Spelling and Pronouncing Dictionary of the English Language for the Use of Schools*, Edinburgh.

Barrie, A. (1796), *A Spelling and Pronouncing Catechism*, Edinburgh.

Barrie, A. (1799), *A Spelling and Pronouncing Dictionary of the English Language*, Edinburgh.

Barrie, A. (1800a), *An Epitome of English Grammar*, Edinburgh.

Barrie, A. (1800b), *The Tyro's Guide to Wisdom and Wealth with Exercises in Spelling*, Edinburgh: George Caw.

Barrow, G. W. S. (1981), 'Popular courts in early medieval Scotland: some suggested place-name evidence', *Scottish Studies*, 25, pp. 1–24.

Barrow, G. W. S. (1983), 'Popular courts in early medieval Scotland: some suggested place-name evidence – Additional note', *Scottish Studies*, 27, pp. 67–8.

Barrow, G. W. S. (1989), 'The lost Gàidhealtachd of medieval Scotland', in W. Gillies (ed.), *Gaelic and Scotland: Alba agus a' Ghàidhlig*, Edinburgh: Edinburgh University Press, pp. 67–88.

Barry, M. V. (ed.) (1981), *Aspects of English Dialects in Ireland*, Belfast: Institute of Irish Studies.

Barry, M. V. (1982), 'English language in Ireland', in R. W. Bailey and M. Görlach (eds), *English as a World Language*, Ann Arbor: University of Michigan Press, pp. 84–133.

Barry, M. V. (1996), 'Historical introduction to the dialects of Ulster', in C. I. Macafee (ed.), *Concise Ulster Dictionary*, Oxford: Oxford University Press, pp. ix–xii.

Barry, M. and P. M. Tilling (eds) (1986), *The English Dialects of Ulster*, Holywood: The Ulster Folk and Transport Museum.

Bartsch, R. (1987), *Norms of Language: Theoretical and Practical Aspects*, London and New York: Longman.

Basker, J. G. (1993), 'Scotticisms and the problem of cultural identity in eighteenth-century Britain', in J. Dwyer and R. B. Sher (eds), *Sociability and Society in Eighteenth-Century Scotland*, Edinburgh: Mercat Press, pp. 81–95.

Bassin, E. (1977), *The Old Songs of Skye: Frances Tolmie and her Circle*, London: Routledge and Kegan Paul.

Baugh, A. C. and T. Cable (1982), *A History of the English Language*, 3rd edn, London: Routledge and Kegan Paul.

Bawcutt, P. (1976), *Gavin Douglas: A Critical Study*, Edinburgh: Edinburgh University Press.

Beal, J. C. (1993), 'The grammar of Tyneside and Northumbrian English', in J. Milroy and L. Milroy (eds), *Real English: The Grammar of English Dialects in the British Isles*, Harlow: Longman, pp. 187–213.

Beattie, J. (1787), *Scoticisms Arranged in Alphabetical Order*, Edinburgh.

Beattie, J. (1788), *The Theory of Language: English Linguistics 1500–1800*, 88, ed. R. C. Alston (1968), Menston: Scolar Press.

Bell, S. H. (1987), *Across the Narrow Sea: A Romance*, Belfast: Blackstaff.

Bennett, J. A. W. and G. V. Smithers (eds) (1968), *Early Middle English Verse and Prose*, 2nd edn, Oxford: Oxford University Press.

Benskin, M. and M. L. Samuels (eds) (1981), *So Meny People, Longages and Tonges: Philological Essays in Scots and Medieval English Presented to Angus McIntosh*, Edinburgh: Edinburgh University Press.

Biber, D. (1988), *Variation across Speech and Writing*, Cambridge: Cambridge University Press.

Bickley, F. (1928), *The Diaries of Sylvester Douglas*, 2 vols, London: Constable.

Bitterling, K. (1970), *Der Wortschatz von Barbours 'Bruce'*, Dissertation, Berlin: Dissertationsdruckstelle.

Bitterling, K. (1975), '*Till* "While" in Barbour's *Bruce*', *Neuphilologische Mitteilungen*, 76, pp. 428–30.

Björkman, E. (1900), *Scandinavian Loan Words in Middle English*, Halle: Ehrhardt Karras.

Black, R. (1986), *Mac Mhaighstir Alasdair: The Ardnamurchan Years*, Coll: Society of West Highland and Island Historical Research.

Black, R. (1989), 'The Gaelic manuscripts of Scotland', in W. Gillies (ed.), *Gaelic and Scotland: Alba agus a' Ghàidhlig*, Edinburgh: Edinburgh University Press, pp. 146–74.

Blaney, J. (1985), 'Upper Ards folk and glossary of words', *Journal of the Upper Ards Historical Society*, 9, pp. 6–7.

Blaney, R. (1996), *Presbyterians and the Irish Language*, Belfast: Ulster Historical Foundation.

Bliss, A. J. (1948–9), 'Three Middle English studies', *English and Germanic Studies*, 2, pp. 40–54.

Bliss, A. J. (1952), 'Vowel quantity in Middle English borrowings from Anglo-Norman', *Archivum Linguisticum*, 4, pp. 71–86.

Bliss, A. J. (1955–6), 'Quantity in Old French and Middle English', *Archivum Linguisticum*, 5, pp. 22–47, 121–47.

Bliss, A. J. (1972), 'The language of J. M. Synge', in M. Harmon (ed.), *J. M. Synge Centenary Papers*, Dublin: Dolmen, pp. 35–62.

Boldrewood, R. (1888), *Robbery under Arms*, London: Oxford University Press.

Book of British Towns (1982), London: Drive Publications.

Borger, J. (1980), *The Dialect of Holy Island*, Bern: Peter Lang.

Borgstrom, C. H. (1940), *A Linguistic Survey of the Gaelic Dialects of Scotland*, 3 vols, Oslo: Norwegian Universities.

Bosworth, J. (ed.) (1882–98), *An Anglo-Saxon Dictionary*, enlarged by T. Northcote Toller, Oxford: Clarendon Press.

Bourcier, G. (1978), *L'orthographe de l'anglais*, Paris: Presses Universitaires de France.

Braidwood, J. (1964), 'Ulster and Elizabethan English', in G. B. Adams (ed.), *Ulster Dialects: An Introductory Symposium*, Holywood: Ulster Folk Museum, pp. 5–109.

Braidwood, J. (1965), 'Towards an Ulster dialect dictionary', *Ulster Dialect Archives Bulletin*, 4, pp. 3–14.

Braidwood, J. (1972), 'Terms for "left-handed" in the Ulster dialects', *Ulster Folklife*, 18, pp. 98–110.

Braidwood, J. (1974), 'Crowls and runts: Ulster dialect terms for "the runt of the litter"', *Ulster Folklife*, 20, pp. 71–84.

Brand, J. (1701), *A Brief Description of Orkney, Zetland, Pightland-Firth and Caithness*, Edinburgh.

Breivik, L.-E., A. Hille and S. Johannson (eds) (1981), *Essays on English Language in Honour of Bertil Sundby*, Oslo: Novus.

Brilioth, B. (1913), *A Grammar of the Dialect of Lorton (Cumberland)*, Oxford: Oxford University Press.

Britton, D. (1991), 'On ME *she/sho*: a Scots solution to an English problem', *North-Western European Language Evolution*, 17, pp. 3–51.

Brown, E. K. and J. Miller (1982), 'Aspects of Scottish English syntax', *English World-Wide*, 3, pp. 3–17.

Brown, G. (1979), *Intonation of Scottish English*, SSRC Final Report, London.

Buchanan, J. (1757), *Linguae Britannicae Vera Pronunciatio: English Linguistics 1500–1800*, 39, ed. R. C. Alston (1968), Menston: Scolar Press.

Buchanan, J. (1762), *The British Grammar: English Linguistics 1500–1800*, 97, ed. R. C. Alston (1968), Menston: Scolar Press.

Buchanan, J. (1766), *An Essay Towards Establishing a Standard for an Elegant and Uniform Pronunciation of the English Language throughout the British Dominions*, London.

Buchanan, J. (1770), *A Plan for an English Grammar-School Education*, London.

Burn, J. (1766–99), *A Practical Grammar of the English Language for the Use of Schools*, Glasgow.

Burn, J. (1796), *A Pronouncing Dictionary of the English Language: English Linguistics 1500–1800*, 173, ed. R. C. Alston (1969), Menston: Scolar Press.

Burns, R. (1965), *The Merry Muses of Caledonia*, ed. J. Barke and S. Goodsir Smith, London: Allen.

Burton-Roberts, N. (1986), *Analysing Sentences: An Introduction to English Syntax*, London: Longman.

Buss, P. (1886), 'Sind die von Horstmann herausgegebenen Schottischen Legenden ein Werk Barbere's?', Dissertation, Göttingen.

Buthlay, K. (ed.) (1987), *A Drunk Man Looks at the Thistle*, Edinburgh: Scottish Academic Press.

Buuren-Veenenbos, C. C. van (ed.) (1982), *The Buk of the Sevyne Sagis*, Leiden: Leiden University Press.

Buuren-Veenenbos, C. C. van (forthcoming), *The Buke of the Chess*, in preparation for the Scottish Text Society.

Byers, J. W. (1916), 'Shakespeare and the Ulster dialect', *Northern Whig*, 22 April. Reprinted in pamphlet form.

Caldwell, S. J. G. (1974), *The Relative Pronoun in Early Scots*, Helsinki: Société Néophilologique.

Callander, J., of Craigforth (1782), *Two Ancient Scottish Poems; the Gaberlunzie-man, and Christ's Kirk on the Green*, Edinburgh.

Cameron, H. P. (trans.) (1913), *Thomas à Kempis, Of the Imitation of Christ by Thomas à Kempis frae Latin intil Scots*, Paisley: Gardner.

Cameron, H. P. (1921), *Genesis in Scots*, Paisley: Gardner.

Campbell, A. (1959), *An Old English Grammar*, Oxford: Clarendon Press.

Campbell, G. (1776), *The Philosophy of Rhetoric*, Edinburgh.

Campbell, J. L. (1937), 'The first printed Gaelic vocabulary', *The Scots Magazine*, pp. 51–7.

Campbell, J. L. (1945), *Gaelic in Scottish Education and Life, Past, Present and Future*, Edinburgh: W. and A. K. Johnston, Saltire Society.

Carruthers, M. (1990), *The Book of Memory*, Cambridge: Cambridge University Press.

Carter, R. (1975), 'Some theoretical implications of the Great Vowel Shift', in D. L. Goyvaerts and G. K. Pullum (eds), *Essays on the Sound Pattern of English*, Ghent: Story Scientia, pp. 369–76.

Carver, C. (1989), *American Regional Dialects*, Ann Arbor: University of Michigan Press.

Cassidy, F. (ed.) (1985–), *Dictionary of American Regional English*, Cambridge, MA: Belknap.

Catford, J. C. (1957a), 'Shetland dialect', in *Shetland Folk-Book*, 3, Lerwick: Shetland Times, pp. 71–5.

Catford, J. C. (1957b), 'Vowel systems of Scots dialects', *Transactions of the Philological Society*, pp. 107–17.

Catford, J. C. (1957c), 'The Linguistic Survey of Scotland', *Orbis*, 6, pp. 105–21.

Catford, J. C. (1977), *Fundamental Problems in Phonetics*, Edinburgh: Edinburgh University Press.

Catford, J. C. (1988), *A Practical Introduction to Phonetics*, Oxford: Clarendon Press.

Chambers, J. K. (1995), *Sociolinguistic Theory. Linguistic Variation and its Social Significance*, Oxford: Blackwell.

Chambers, J. K. and P. Trudgill (1980), *Dialectology*, Cambridge: Cambridge University Press.

Chambers, R. (1870), *Popular Rhymes of Scotland*, London: Chambers.

Cheshire, J. (ed.) (1991), *English Around the World: Sociolinguistic Perspectives*, Cambridge: Cambridge University Press.

Cheshire, J., V. K. Edwards and P. Whittle (1993), 'Non-standard English and dialect levelling', in J. Milroy and L. Milroy (eds), *Real English: The Grammar of English Dialects in the British Isles*, London: Longman, pp. 53–96.

Chomsky, N. and M. Halle (1968), *The Sound Pattern of English*, New York: Harper and Row.

Clark, C. (1970), *The Peterborough Chronicle 1070–1154*, Oxford: Oxford University Press.

Clark, J. M. (1917), *The Vocabulary of Anglo-Irish*, St Gallen.

Cleishbotham the Younger (1858), *Handbook of the Scottish Language*, Edinburgh.

Clyne, M. G. (1984), *Language and Society in the German-Speaking Countries*, Cambridge: Cambridge University Press.

Cockburn, R. (1984), *What's in a Name?: Nomenclature of South Australia*, Adelaide: Ferguson Publications.

Coldwell, D. F. C. (ed.) (1950–6), *Virgil's Aeneid*, trans. G. Douglas, Scottish Text Society, 2nd series, 4 vols, Edinburgh and London: Blackwell.

Collin, Z. (1862), *An Essay on the Scoto-English Dialect*, Lund: Berlings.

Collins, S. L. (1989), *From Divine Cosmos to Sovereign State*, Oxford: Oxford University Press.

Connolly, L. (1982), 'Spoken English in Ulster in the eighteenth and nineteenth centuries', *Ulster Folklife*, 28, pp. 33–9.

Connolly, R. I. (1981), 'An analysis of some linguistic information observed from eighteenth and nineteenth-century Ulster poetry', Dissertation, Queen's University of Belfast.

Couper, J. M. (1967), *East of Living*, Sydney: Edwards and Shaw.

Couper, J. M. (1979), *The Lee Shore*, Sydney: Edwards and Shaw.

Cowling, G. H. (1915), *The Dialect of Hackness (North-East Yorkshire)*, Cambridge: Cambridge University Press.

Craig, C. (ed.) (1987), *The History of Scottish Literature*, 4 vols, Aberdeen: Aberdeen University Press.

Craig, D. (1961), *Scottish Literature and the Scottish People 1680–1830*, London: Chatto and Windus.

Craig, Sir W. G. (ed.) (1935), *Facsimiles of National Manuscripts of Scotland*, 1867–71, 3 vols, Southampton: Ordnance Survey Office.

Craigie, J. (ed.) (1939), 'Fowler's language', in *The Works of William Fowler*, vol. 3, Scottish Text Society, 3rd series, vol. 13, pp. li–lxxix.

Craigie, J. (1941a), 'The language', in idem (ed.), *Thomas Hudson. The Historie of Judith*, Scottish Text Society, 3rd series, vol. 14, Edinburgh and London: Blackwell, pp. xlviii–lxxxxv.

Craigie, J. (ed.) (1941b), *Thomas Hudson. The Historie of Judith*, Scottish Text Society, 3rd series, vol. 14, Edinburgh and London: Blackwell.

Craigie, J. (ed.) (1948–58), *The Poems of King James VI*, Scottish Text Society, 2nd series, Edinburgh and London: Blackwell.

Craigie, J. (1950), 'The language of MS ROYAL 18 B XV', in *Basilikon Doron*, Scottish Text Society, 3rd series, vol. 18, pp. 117–35.

Craigie, W. A. (1925), 'The earliest records of the Scottish tongue', *Scottish Historical Review*, 22, pp. 61–7.

Craigie, W. A. (1935), 'Older Scottish and English: a study in contrasts', *Transactions of the Philological Society*, pp. 1–15.

Craigie, Sir William, A. J. Aitken, J. M. Templeton, H. Watson and J. A. C. Stevenson (eds) (1937–), *A Dictionary of the Older Scottish Tongue* [DOST], Chicago: University of Chicago Press; London: Oxford University Press. 8 vols to *s(c)hake*.

Cranstoun, J. (ed.) (1887), *The Poems of Alexander Montgomerie*, Scottish Text Society, 1st series, vol. 36, Edinburgh and London: Blackwell.

Crockett, S. R. (1904), *Strong Mac*, London: Ward Lock.

Crowley, T. (1991), *Proper English? Readings in Language, History and Cultural Identity*, London: Routledge.

Cruttenden, A. (1994), revision of A. C. Gimson (1980 edn), *An Introduction to the Pronunciation of English*, London: Edward Arnold.

Currie, K. (1979), 'Intonation systems of Scottish English', Ph.D. dissertation, University of Edinburgh.

Curtis, F. J. (1893, 1894), 'An investigation of the rimes and phonology of the Middle-Scotch romance *Clariodus*', *Anglia*, 16, pp. 387–450; 17, pp. 1–68, 125–60.

Dante Alighieri (1890), *De Vulgaria Eloquentia*, trans. A. G. Ferrers Howell, London: Kegan Paul, Trench, Trübner, Book 1, Chapters 6 and 7.

Dareau, M., E. Finlayson, M. McNeill, L. Pike, H. Watson and J. A. C. Stevenson (1987), 'A re-editing of *Gif*', in C. I. Macafee and I. Macleod (eds), *The Nuttis Schell. Essays on the Scots Language presented to A. J. Aitken*, Aberdeen: Aberdeen University Press, pp. 25–7.

Davidson, C. (ed.) (1993), *A Tretise of Miraclis Pleyinge*, Mediaeval Institute, Western Michigan University, Kalamazoo, Michigan.

Day, A. and P. McWilliams (eds) (1995), *Ordnance Survey Memoirs of Ireland*, vol. 29, *Parishes of County Antrim XI: Antrim Town and Ballyclare*, Belfast: Institute of Irish Studies.

Day, A., P. McWilliams and N. Dobson (eds) (1994), *Ordnance Survey Memoirs of Ireland*, vol. 26, *Parishes of County Antrim X: Glynn, Inver, Kilroot, and Templecorran*, Belfast: Institute of Irish Studies.

Day, A., P. McWilliams and L. English (eds) (1996), *Ordnance Survey Memoirs of Ireland*, vol. 35, *Parishes of County Antrim XIII: Templepatrick and District*, Belfast: Institute of Irish Studies.

Dearing, B. (1951), 'Gavin Douglas' *Eneados*, a reinterpretation', *Publications of the Modern Language Association*, 67, pp. 845–62.

Denison, D. (1993), *English Historical Syntax*, London: Longman.

Devitt, A. J. (1989), *Standardizing Written English: Diffusion in the Case of Scotland 1520–1659*, Cambridge: Cambridge University Press.

Dickinson, W. C. (1961), *Scotland from the Earliest Times to 1603*, Edinburgh: Thomas Nelson.

Dickinson, W. C. (1977), revised by A. Duncan, *Scotland from the Earliest Times to 1603*, 3rd edn, Oxford: Clarendon.

Dieth, E. (1932), *A Grammar of the Buchan Dialect*, Cambridge: Heffer.

Dieth, E. (1955), 'Hips. A geographical contribution to the *she* puzzle', *English Studies*, 36, pp. 209–17.

Dietz, K. (1981), 'ME *oi* heimischer Provenienz', in P. Kunsmann and O. Kuhn (eds), *Weltsprache Englisch in Forschung und Lehre*, Festschrift für Kurt Wächtler, Berlin: Schmidt, pp. 17–30.

Dobson, E. J. (1957), *English Pronunciation, 1500–1700*, vol. 2, *Phonology*, Oxford: Clarendon.

Donaldson, D. (1887), *Supplement to Jamieson's Scottish Dictionary*, Paisley: Gardner.

Donaldson, G. (1970), *Scottish Historical Documents*, New York: Barnes and Noble.

Donaldson, W. (1986), *Popular Literature in Victorian Scotland: Language, Fiction and the Press*, Aberdeen: Aberdeen University Press.

Donaldson, W. (1989), *The Language of the People: Scots Prose from the Victorian Revival*, Aberdeen: Aberdeen University Press.

Dorian, N. C. (1978), *East Sutherland Gaelic*, Dublin Institute for Advanced Studies.

Dorian, N. C. (1981), *Language Death: The Life Cycle of a Scottish Gaelic Dialect*, Philadelphia: University of Pennsylvania Press.

Dorsch, T. S. (trans.) (1965), *Horace, On the Art of Poetry*, in *Aristotle, Horace, Longinus*, Harmondsworth: Penguin.

Douglas-Cowie, E. (1978), 'Linguistic code-switching in a northern Irish village: social interaction and social ambition', in P. Trudgill (ed.), *Sociolinguistic Patterns in British English*, London: Edward Arnold, pp. 37–51.

Douglas-Cowie, E. (1984), 'The sociolinguistic situation in northern Ireland', in P. Trudgill (ed.), *Language in the British Isles*, Cambridge: Cambridge University Press, pp. 533–45.

Drummond, J. (1767), *A Grammatical Introduction to the Modern Pronunciation and Spelling of the English Tongue*, Edinburgh.

Dubourdieu, J. (1812), *Statistical Study of the County of Antrim*, 2 vols, Dublin: Gill and McMillan. Reprinted in 1993 by Ulster Historical Foundation, Belfast.

Dun, J. (1766), *The Best Method of Teaching to Read and Spell English, Demonstrated in Eight Parts*, Edinburgh.

Duncan, A. M. (1975), *Scotland: The Making of the Kingdom*, Edinburgh: Oliver and Boyd.

Dunlap, A. R. (1940), 'Vicious pronunciation in eighteenth-century England', *American Speech*, 15, pp. 364–7.

Durkacz, V. E. (1983), *The Decline of the Celtic Languages*, Edinburgh: John Donald.

Dwelly, E. (ed.) (1988), *The Illustrated Gaelic–English Dictionary, Containing every Gaelic word and meaning given in all previously published Dictionaries and a great number never in print before. To which is prefixed a Concise Gaelic Grammar*, 10th edn, Glasgow: Gairm.

Dwyer, J. (1987), *Virtuous Discourse: Sensibility and Community in Late Eighteenth-Century Scotland*, Edinburgh: Edinburgh University Press.

Eckhardt, E. (1910), *Die Dialekt- und Ausländertypen des älteren englischen Dramas*, 2 vols, Louvain.

Edel, A. (1973), *Hochsprache und Mundart in Nordengland*, Zürich: Juris.

Edgeworth, M. (1814), *Letters for Literary Ladies*, London.

Éigse. A Journal of Irish Studies (1939–), Dublin: Colm O Lochlainn, for the National University of Ireland.

Ekwall, E. (1975), *A History of Modern English Sounds and Morphology*, Oxford: Blackwell.

Ellis, A. J. (1889), *On Early English Pronunciation*, vol. 5, London: Trübner.

Elphinston, J. (1766), *The Principles of the English Language Digested for the Use of Schools*, London.

Elphinston, J. (1786, 1787), *Propriety Ascertained in her Picture, or Inglish Speech and Spelling Rendered Mutual Guides, Secure Alike from Distant, and from Domestic, Error*, 2 vols, London.

Elphinston, J. (1790), *English Orthoggraphy Epittomized*: *English Linguistics 1500–1800*, 288, ed. R. C. Alston (1971), Menston: Scolar Press.

Elphinston, J. (1795), *Miniature of English Orthography*: *English Linguistics 1500–1800*, 28, ed. R. C. Alston (1967), Menston: Scolar Press.

Emerson, O. F. (1921), 'John Dryden and a British Academy', *Proceedings of the British Academy*, London.

Emsley, B. (1933), 'James Buchanan and the 18th-century regulation of English usage', *Publications of the Modern Language Association*, 48:3, pp. 54–66.

Erasmus, D. (1526), in J. K. Sowards (ed.) (1985), *Collected Works*, vol. 26, Toronto: University of Toronto Press.

Esling, J. H. (1978), 'Voice quality in Edinburgh – a sociolinguistic and phonetic study', Dissertation, University of Edinburgh.

Evans, D. S. (1964), *A Grammar of Middle Welsh*, Dublin Institute for Advanced Studies.

Ewen, C. J. (1977), 'Aitken's law and the phonatory gesture in dependency phonology', *Lingua*, 41, pp. 307–29.

Feilitzen, O. von (1937), *The Pre-Conquest Personal Names of the Domesday Book*, Nomina Germanica 3, Uppsala: Almqvist and Wiksell.

Fenton, A. (1978), *The Northern Isles: Orkney and Shetland*, Edinburgh: John Donald.

Fenton, A. and D. A. MacDonald (eds) (1994), *Studies in Scots and Gaelic: Proceedings of the Third International Conference on the Languages of Scotland, 1991*, Edinburgh: Canongate Academic.

Fenton, J. (1995), *The Hamely Tongue: A Personal Record of Ulster Scots in County Antrim*, Newtownards: Ulster Scots Academic Press.

Fenton, J. (1996), 'Postscript', *Ullans: The Magazine for Ulster Scots*, 4, p. 63.

Finkenstaedt, T. and D. Wolff (1973), *Ordered Profusion: Studies in Dictionaries and the English Lexicon*, Heidelberg: Carl Winter.

Fisher, G. (1789), *The Instructor or Young Man's Best Companion*, London: Rivington.

Fisher, J. H. (1996), *The Emergence of Standard English*, Lexington: University Press of Kentucky.

Fisher, J. H., M. Richardson and J. L. Fisher (eds) (1984), *An Anthology of Chancery English*, Knoxville: University of Tennessee Press.

Fishman, J. (1980), 'Bilingual education, language planning and English', *English World-Wide*, 1, pp. 11–24.

Fisiak, J. (1968), *A Short Grammar of Middle English 1*, Warsaw: Panstwowe Wydawnictwo Naukowe.

Fladmark, J. M. (1994), *The Wealth of a Nation: Heritage as a Cultural and Competitive Asset*, Aberdeen: The Robert Gordon University Professorial Lectures.

Fowler, A. (ed.) (1991), *The New Oxford Book of Seventeenth-Century Verse*, Oxford and New York: Oxford University Press.

Fox, D. (ed.) (1981), *Robert Henryson: The Poems*, Oxford: Clarendon Press.

Francis, W. N. (1983), *Dialectology: An Introduction*, London: Longman.

Freeborn, D. (1992), *From Old English to Standard English*, Basingstoke: Macmillan.

Freeman, E. (1924), 'A proposal for an English Academy in 1660', *Modern Language Review*, 19, pp. 291–300.

Füchsel, H. (1901), 'Die Sprache der northumbrischen Interlinearversion zum Johannes-Evangelium', *Anglia*, 24, pp. 1–99.

Fulton, G. and G. Knight (1813), *Principles of English Pronunciation: A General Pronouncing and Explanatory Dictionary of the English Language*, Edinburgh.

Furphy, J. (1903), *Such is Life*, Sydney: The Bulletin Newspaper Company.

Gailey, A. (1968–9), 'Cultural connections in north-west Britain and Ireland', *Ethnologia Europaea*, 2–3, pp. 138–43.

Gailey, A. (1975), 'The Scots element in north Irish popular culture', *Ethnologia Europaea*, 8, pp. 2–22.

Gailey, A. (1996), 'The Ulster poets and local life: 1790–1870', in J. Gray and W. McCann (eds), *An Uncommon Bookman: Essays in Memory of J. R. R. Adams*, Belfast: Linen Hall Library, pp. 159–74.

Galbraith, J. D. (1970), 'The sources of the Aberdeen Breviary', Dissertation, Aberdeen University.

Galt, J. (1823), *The Spaewife*, 3 vols, Edinburgh: Oliver and Boyd.

Galt, J. (1984), *Ringan Gilhaize; or The Covenanters*, ed. P. J. Wilson, Edinburgh: Scottish Academic Press.

Gburek, H. (1984), 'Changes in the structure of the English verb system: evidence from Scots', *Scottish Studies*, 4, pp. 115–23.

Geddes, A. (1792), 'Three Scottish poems. With a previous dissertation on the Scoto-Saxon dialect', *Transactions of the Society of Antiquaries of Scotland*, vol. 1, Edinburgh, pp. 402–68.

Geeson, C. (1969), *A Northumberland and Durham Word Book*, Newcastle-upon-Tyne: Harold Hill.

Gibb, A. D. (1946), *Student's Glossary of Scottish Legal Terms*, Edinburgh: Green.

Giegerich, H. J. (1992), *English Phonology*, Cambridge: Cambridge University Press.

Gilchrist, A. (ed.) (1951), *John Dunmore Lang, Chiefly Autobiographical 1799 to 1878*, 2 vols, Melbourne: Jedgarm Publications.

Gillespie, R. (1985), *Colonial Ulster: The Settlement of East Ulster 1600–1741*, Cork: Cork University Press.

Gillies, W. (1981), 'The Gaelic poems of Sir Duncan Campbell of Glenorchy (II)', *Scottish Gaelic Studies*, 13:2, pp. 263–88.

Gillies, W. (ed.) (1989), *Gaelic and Scotland: Alba agus a' Ghàidhlig*, Edinburgh: Edinburgh University Press.

Gimson, A. C. (1962), *An Introduction to the Pronunciation of English*, London: Edward Arnold.

Girvan, R. (1939), 'Introduction', in *Ratis Raving and Other Early Scots Poems on Morals*, Scottish Text Society, 3rd series, vol. 11, pp. vii–lxxvii.

Glauser, B. (1974), *The Scottish–English Linguistic Border*, Bern: Francke.

Glawe, E. (1908), *Der Sprachgebrauch in den altschottischen Gesetzen der Handschrift, Adv. Libr. 25.4.16*, Berlin.

Glenn, J. A. (1987), 'Linguistic analysis in *Sir Gilbert Haye's Buke of the Ordre of Knychthede*', Dissertation, Bloomington, Indiana.

Good, J. (1896 [1973]), *A Glossary of Collection of Words, Phrases, Place Names and Superstitions Current in East Lincolnshire*, Skegness: Major.

Goodsir Smith, S. (1959), *Figs and Thistles*, Edinburgh and London: Oliver and Boyd.

Gordon, E. V. (1957), *An Introduction to Old Norse*, Oxford: Oxford University Press.

Görlach, M. (1985a), 'Scots and Low German: the social history of two minority languages', in idem (ed.), *Focus on Scotland. Varieties of English Around the World*, General series, 5, Amsterdam: Benjamins, pp. 19–36.

Görlach, M. (ed.) (1985b), *Focus on Scotland. Varieties of English Around the World*, General series, 5, Amsterdam: Benjamins.

Görlach, M. (1987), 'Lexical loss and lexical survival: the case of Scots and English', *Scottish Language*, 6, pp. 1–20.

Görlach, M. (1991), 'Jamaica and Scotland – bilingual or bidialectal?', in idem (ed.), *Englishes: Studies in Varieties of English 1984–1988*, Amsterdam: Benjamins, pp. 69–89.

Graham, J. J. (1979), *The Shetland Dictionary*, Stornoway: Thule Press.

Grant, W. (1913), *The Pronunciation of English in Scotland*, Cambridge: Cambridge University Press.

Grant, W. (1931), 'Introduction', *The Scottish National Dictionary*, vol. 1, Edinburgh: Scottish National Dictionary Association.

Grant, W. and J. Main Dixon (1921), *Manual of Modern Scots*, Cambridge: Cambridge University Press.

Grant, W. and D. D. Murison (eds) (1931–76), *The Scottish National Dictionary* [SND], Aberdeen: Aberdeen University Press.

Gray, J. (1794), *A Concise Spelling Book for the Use of Children*, Edinburgh: George Caw.

Greenbaum, S. and R. Quirk (1990), *A Student's Grammar of the English Language*, London: Longman.

Greenblatt, S. J. (1992), *Redrawing the Boundaries: The Transformation of English and American Literary Studies*, New York: Modern Language Association.

Gregg, R. J. (1958), 'Notes on the phonology of a County Antrim Scotch-Irish dialect', *Orbis*, 7, pp. 392–406.

Gregg, R. J. (1964), 'Scotch-Irish urban speech in Ulster', in G. B. Adams (ed.), *Ulster Dialects: An Introductory Symposium*, Holywood: Ulster Folk Museum, pp. 163–92.

Gregg, R. J. (1972), 'The Scotch-Irish dialect boundaries in Ulster', in M. Wakelin (ed.), *Patterns in the Folk Speech of the British Isles*, London: Athlone, pp. 109–39.

Gregg, R. (1975), 'The distribution of raised and lowered diphthongs as reflexes in two Scotch-Irish dialects', in W. U. Dressler and F. V. Mares (eds), *Phonologica 1972: Akten der 2. internationalen Phonologie-Tagung. Wien. 1972*, Munich: Fink, pp. 101–5.

Gregg, R. J. (1976), 'Dialect mixture in Scotch-Irish urban speech', *Northern Ireland Speech and Language Forum Journal*, 2, pp. 35–7.

Gregg, R. J. (1985), *The Scotch-Irish Dialect Boundaries in the Province of Ulster*, Ottawa: Canadian Federation for the Humanities.

Gregg, R. J. (1989), 'The feature "dentality" in Ulster Scots dialects and its role as a sociolinguistic marker', paper read at the Linguistics Association of Great Britain Spring Meeting, Belfast.

Gregory Smith, G. (ed.) (1904 [1937]), *Elizabethan Critical Essays*, 2 vols, Oxford: Clarendon Press.

Greig, J. Y. T. (1932), *The Letters of David Hume*, Oxford: Oxford University Press.

Gullans, C. B. (ed.) (1955), *The English and Latin Poems of Sir Robert Ayton*, Scottish Text Society, 4th series, Edinburgh and London: Blackwell.

Gunn, B. (1990), 'The politic word', Dissertation, University of Ulster, Jordanstown.

Gwynn, S. (1899), *Highways and Byways in Donegal and Antrim*, London.

Hacker, M. (1994), 'Subordinate *and*-clauses in Scots and Hiberno-English: origins and development', *Scottish Language*, 13, pp. 34–50.

Halliday, M. A. K. (1985 [1989]), *Spoken and Written Language*, Oxford: Oxford University Press.

Hamilton, E. (1808), *The Cottagers of Glenburnie*, Edinburgh: Manners and Miller.

Hamp, E. (1975–6), 'Miscellanea Celtica I, II, III, IV', *Studia Celtica*, 10–11, pp. 54–73.

Hanley, C. (1958), *Dancing in the Streets*, London: White Lion.

Hardie, K. (1995–6), 'Scots: matters of identity and nationalism', *Scottish Language*, 14–15, pp. 141–7.

Harris, J. (1983), 'The Hiberno-English *I've it eaten* construction: what is it and where does it come from?', *Teanga*, 3, pp. 30–43.

Harris, J. (1984), 'English in the north of Ireland', in P. Trudgill (ed.), *Language in the British Isles*, Cambridge: Cambridge University Press, pp. 115–34.

Harris, J. (1985), *Phonological Variation and Change: Studies in Hiberno-English*, Cambridge: Cambridge University Press.

Harris, J. (1991), 'Ireland', in J. Cheshire (ed), *English around the World: Sociolinguistic Perspectives*, Cambridge: Cambridge University Press, pp. 37–50.

Harris, J. (1993), 'The grammar of Irish English', in J. Milroy and L. Milroy (eds), *Real English: The Grammar of English Dialects in the British Isles*, Harlow: Longman, pp. 139–86.

Haugen, E. (1982), *Scandinavian Language Structures*, Minneapolis: University of Minnesota.

Haugen, E., J. D. McClure and D. Thomson (eds) (1981), *Minority Languages Today*, Edinburgh: Edinburgh University Press.

Hay Fleming, D. (ed.) (1901), *Patrick Walker, Six Saints of the Covenant*, 2 vols, London: Hodder and Stoughton.

Hayes-McCoy, G. (1937), *Scots Mercenary Forces in Ireland*, Dublin: Burns, Oates and Washbourn.

Hedevind, B. (1967), *The Dialect of Dentdale*, Uppsala: Appelberg.

Henderson, T. F. (1900), *Scottish Vernacular Literature*, 2nd edn, London: David Nutt.

Henry, A. (1995), *Belfast English and Standard English: Dialect Variation and Parameter Setting*, Oxford: Oxford University Press.

Henry, P. L. (1958), 'A linguistic survey of Ireland: preliminary report', *Lochlann*, 1, pp. 49–208.

Herbison, I. (1989), *Language, Literature, and Cultural Identity: An Ulster-Scots Perspective*, Ballymena: Dunclug Press.

Herbison, I. (1993), 'Oor ain native tung: talking Scots', *Special Supplement. Fortnightly*, 318, pp. 13–15.

Herbison, I. (1996), '"The rest is silence": some remarks on the disappearance of Ulster-Scots poetry', paper read at Varieties of Scottishness Conference, Belfast. Forthcoming in J. Erskine (ed.), *Varieties of Scottishness*.

Hettinga, J. (1981), 'Standard and dialect in Anstruther and Cellardyke', *Scottish Literary Journal*, Supplement 14, pp. 37–48.

Heuser, W. (1896), 'Offenes und geschlossenes *ee* im Schottischen und Nordenglischen', *Anglia*, 18, pp. 114–28, 319–47.

Heuser, W. (1897a), 'Die Dehnung vor *-nd* im Mittelschottischen', *Anglia*, 19, pp. 401–5.

Heuser, W. (1897b), 'Die Lautveränderung von *A, E, I* im Mittelschottischen', *Anglia*, 19, pp. 405–8.

Heuser, W. (1897c), 'Die Ursprung des Unorganischen *I* in der Mittelschottischen Schreibung', *Anglia*, 19, pp. 409–12.

Hewitt, D. (1987), 'James Beattie and the languages of Scotland', in J. J. Carter and J. H. Pittock (eds), *Aberdeen in the Enlightenment*, Aberdeen: Aberdeen University Press, pp. 251–60.

Hewitt, J. (1974), *The Rhyming Weavers and Other Country Poets of Antrim and Down*, Belfast: Blackstaff.

Hewitt, L. (1992), 'A sociolinguistic approach to the study of literary dialect in the work of John Galt and Christian Johnstone', Dissertation, University of Glasgow.

Hill, G. (1873), *Historical Account of the Plantation in Ulster 1608–1620*, Belfast.

Hill, G. (1888–9), *Plantation Papers*, parts I and II, Belfast.

Hirst, T. O. (1913), *A Grammar of the Dialect of Kendal*, Heidelberg: Winter.

Historical Manuscripts Commission (1909), *The Manuscripts of Sir Archibald Edmonstone of Duntreath, Bart*. Report on manuscripts in various collections, vol. 5, London, pp. 72–195.

Hogg, J. (1865), *The Shepherd's Calendar*, in *The Works of the Ettrick Shepherd*, 2 vols, London: Blackie and Son.

Holmberg, B. (1956), *James Douglas on English Pronunciation c. 1740*, Lund: Gleerup.

Holmes, F. (1989), 'The Scots-Irish', in P. Loughery (ed.), *The People of Ireland*, Belfast: Appletree, pp. 98–111.

Houston, R. A. (1985), *Scottish Literacy and Scottish Identity. Illiteracy and Society in Scotland and Northern England*, Cambridge, New York and Melbourne: Cambridge University Press.

Houston, R. A. and I. D. Whyte (eds) (1989), *Scottish Society 1500–1800*, Cambridge, New York and Melbourne: Cambridge University Press.

Huddleston, R. (1993), unattributed piece, *Ullans: The Magazine for Ulster Scots*, 1, pp. 10–11.

Hughes, G. A. and P. Trudgill (1987), *English Accents and Dialects*, London: Edward Arnold.

Hume, A. (1616), *Of the Orthographie and Congruitie of the Britan Tongue*, MS ed. H. B. Wheatley, Early English Text Society, original series, vol. 5, 1865.

Hume, A. (1856), 'Ethnology of the counties of Down and Antrim', *Ulster Journal of Archaeology*, 1st series, vol. 4, pp. 154–63.

Hume, A. (1858), 'The Irish dialect of the English language', *Ulster Journal of Archaeology*, 1st series, vol. 6., pp. 47–56.

Hume, A. (1859), 'The elements of population in Down and Antrim illustrated by the statistics of religious belief', *Ulster Journal of Archaeology*, 1st series, vol. 7, pp. 116–30.

Hume, A. (1878), *Remarks on the Irish Dialect of the English Language*, Liverpool.

Hume, D. (1760), 'Scoticisms', *Scots Magazine*, Appendix, pp. 686–7.

Huygens, R. B. C. (ed.) (1970), *Accessus ad Auctores: Bernard d'Utrecht; Conrad of Hirsau*, Leiden: Leiden University Press.

Ihalainen, O. (1994), 'The dialects of England since 1776', in R. Burchfield (ed.), *The Cambridge History of the English Language*, vol. 5, *English in Britain and Overseas: Origins and Development*, Cambridge: Cambridge University Press, pp. 197–274.

Innes, C. (1854), *Fasti Aberdonenses: Selections from the Records of the University and King's College of Aberdeen 1494–1854*, Aberdeen: Spalding Club.

Jack, R. D. S. (ed.) (1978), *A Choice of Scottish Verse 1550–1660*, London: Hodder.

Jack, R. D. S. (1981), 'The prose of John Knox: a re-assessment', *Prose Studies*, 4, pp. 239–51.

Jack, R. D. S. (ed.) (1988), *The History of Scottish Literature*, vol. 1, *Origins to 1660*, Aberdeen: Aberdeen University Press.

Jack, R. D. S. (1994), 'Burns as Sassenach poet', in K. Simpson (ed.), *Burns Now*, Edinburgh: Canongate, pp. 150–66.

Jack, R. D. S. and R. J. Lyall (eds) (1983), *Sir Thomas Urquhart, The Jewel*, Edinburgh: Scottish Academic Press.

Jackson, K. (1951), '*Common Gaelic*: the evolution of the Goidelic languages', *Proceedings of the British Academy*, 37, pp. 71–97.

Jackson, K. (1972), *The Gaelic Notes in the Book of Deer*, London: Cambridge University Press.

James, C. (1986), 'Indigenous non-English language communities in the United Kingdom', *Contact Bulletin* 3, pp. 1–4.

Jamieson, J. (1808), *An Etymological Dictionary of the Scottish Language*, Edinburgh: Creech.

Jeffares, A. N. (1982), *Anglo-Irish Literature*, London: Gill and McMillan.

Jespersen, O. (1946), *Mankind, Nation and Individual from a Linguistic Point of View*, Bloomington: Indiana University Press.

Jespersen, O. (1949), *A Modern English Grammar on Historical Principles*, Heidelberg: Carl Winters.

Johnson, S. (1747), *A Plan of a Dictionary for the English Language. Idler*, London.

Johnston, P. A. (1980), 'A synchronic and historical view of border area bimoric vowel systems', Dissertation, University of Edinburgh.

Johnston, P. A. (1983a), *A Sociolinguistic Investigation of Edinburgh Speech*, Social Science Research Council End of Grant Report, C/00/23/0023/1.

Johnston, P. A. (1983b), 'Irregular style variation patterns in Edinburgh speech', *Scottish Language*, 2, pp. 1–19.

Johnston, P. A. (1984), 'Variation in the Standard Scottish English of Morningside', *English World-Wide*, 5, pp. 133–85.

Johnston, P. A. (1985a), 'The rise and fall of the Morningside/Kelvinside accent', in M. Görlach (ed.), *Focus on Scotland. Varieties of English Around the World*, General series, 5, Amsterdam: Benjamins, pp. 37–56.

Johnston, P. A. (1985b), 'Work sheets on Scots dialects', unpublished handouts, University of Glasgow. Based on material collected under funding of the Nuffield Foundation, 1984.

Johnston, P. A. (1989), 'Lass's Law and West Germanic vowel shifts', *Folia Linguistica Historica*, 10:2, pp. 299–361.

Johnston, P. A. (1992), 'English vowel shifting: one great vowel shift or two small vowel shifts?', *Diachronica*, 9:2, pp. 189–213.

Johnston, P. A. (1993), 'The dialect of *A Tretise of Miraclis Pleyinge*', in C. Davidson (ed.), *A Tretise of Miraclis Pleyinge*, Mediaeval Institute, Western Michigan University, Kalamazoo, Michigan, pp. 53–93.

Johnston, P. A. (forthcoming), 'The mid vowel merger reappraised: or, what really happened to ME /ai au/ and /ɔu/', unpublished manuscript.

Johnston, W. (1764), *A Spelling and Pronouncing Dictionary: English Linguistics 1500–1800*, 95, ed. R. C. Alston (1968), Menston: Scolar Press.

Jones, C. (1972), *An Introduction to Middle English*, New York: Holt, Rinehart and Winston.

Jones, C. (1988), *Grammatical Gender in English 950 to 1250*, London: Croom Helm.

Jones, C. (1989), *A History of English Phonology*, London: Longman.

Jones, C. (ed.) (1991), *A Treatise on the Provincial Dialect of Scotland, by Sylvester Douglas*, Edinburgh: Edinburgh University Press.

Jones, C. (1993), 'Scottish Standard English in the late eighteenth century', *Transactions of the Philological Society*, 9, pp. 95–131.

Jones, C. (1994), 'Alexander Geddes: an eighteenth-century Scottish orthoepist and dialectologist', *Folia Linguistica Historica*, sv/1, pp. 71–103.

Jones, C. (1996), *A Language Suppressed: The Pronunciation of the Scots Language in the Eighteenth Century*, Edinburgh: John Donald.

Jones, C. (forthcoming), 'An eighteenth-century Scottish ladies' spelling book', *English Studies*.

Jones, J. W. and E. F. Jones (eds) (1977), *Bernardus Sylvestris, Commentary on the First Six Books of the Aeneid of Vergil*, Lincoln, NB and London: University of Nebraska Press.

Jordan, R. (1934), *Handbuch der Mittelenglischen Grammatik*, part 1, *Lautlehre*, Heidelberg: Matthes.

Jordan, R. (1974), *Handbook of Middle English Grammar: Phonology*, trans. and revised E. J. Crook, The Hague: Mouton.

Joyce, P. (1991), 'The people's English: language and class in England c.1840–1920', in P. Burke and R. Porter (eds), *Language, Self, and Society*, Cambridge: Polity, pp. 27–34.

Kallen, J. (1991), 'Intra-language transfer and plural subject concord in Irish and Appalachian English', *Teanga*, 11, pp. 11–21.

Kastner, L. E. (ed.) (1912), *The Poetical Works of William Drummond of Hawthornden*, Scottish Text Society, 2 vols, Edinburgh and London: Blackwell.

Kastner, L. E. and H. B. Charlton (eds) (1921, 1929), *The Poetical Works of Sir William Alexander of Stirling*, Scottish Text Society, 2 vols, Edinburgh and London: Blackwell.

Kastovsky, D. and G. Bauer (eds) (1988), *Luick Revisited: Papers read at the Luick-Symposium at Schloss Liechtenstein, 15–18.9.1985*, Tübingen: Gunter Narr.

Kay, B. (1993), *The Mither Tongue*, Ayrshire: Alloway.

Kay, B. (1994), 'The Scots ower the Sheugh', in I. S. Wood (ed.), *Scotland and Ulster*, Edinburgh: Mercat Press, pp. 88–96.

Kelly, F. (1988), *A Guide to Early Irish Law*, Dublin Institute for Advanced Studies.

Kelly, F. M. (1957), 'The origin of the use of i as a sign of length in Middle Scots', Dissertation, Columbia University.

Kennedy, A. G. (1926), 'Authorship of *The British Grammar*', *Modern Language Notes*, 41, pp. 388–91.

Kenrick, W. (1784), *A Rhetorical Grammar of the English Language: English Linguistics 1500–1800*, 332, ed. R. C. Alston (1972), Menston: Scolar Press.

Kenworthy, J. (1978), 'The intonation of questions in one variety of Scottish English', *Lingua*, 44, pp. 267–82.

Kerswill, P. (1987), 'Levels of linguistic variation in Durham', *Journal of Linguistics*, 23, pp. 25–49.

Killen, W. D. (1866), 'Introduction' to *A True Narrative of the Rise and Progress of the Presbyterian Church in Ireland (1623–1670)*, Belfast: C. Aitchison.

Kindrick, R. L. (1993), *Henryson and the Medieval Arts of Rhetoric*, New York and London: Garland.

King, A. (1986), 'The Ruthwell Cross – a linguistic monument (runes as evidence for Old English)', *Folia Linguistica Historica*, 7:1, pp. 43–79.

King, A. (forthcoming), *An Introduction to Scots and Scottish English*, London: Longman.

Kinghorn, A. M. and A. Law (eds) (1974), *The Works of Allan Ramsay*, Edinburgh: Blackwood and Sons.

Kingsmore, R. (1995), *Ulster Scots Speech: A Sociolinguistic Study*, Tuscaloosa: University of Alabama Press.

Kinsley, J. (ed.) (1979), *The Poems of William Dunbar*, Oxford: Clarendon Press.

Kirk, J. M. (forthcoming), 'Ulster English: the state of the art', in H. Tristram (ed.), *Proceedings of a Colloquium on 'Celtic Englishes', Potsdam, 1995*, Heidelberg: Carl Winter.

Klein, L. (1994), '*Politeness* as linguistic ideology in late seventeenth- and eighteenth-century England', in D. Stein and I. Tieken-Boon van Ostade (eds), *Towards a Standard English 1600–1800*, Berlin and New York: Mouton de Gruyter, pp. 31–50.

Klemola, J. and M. Filppula (1992), 'Subordinating uses of *and* in the history of English', in M. Rissanen, O. Ihalainen, T. Nevalainen and I. Taavitsainen (eds), *History of Englishes: New Methods and Interpretations in Historical Linguistics*, Berlin: Mouton de Gruyter, pp. 310–18.

Kniezsa, V. (1981a), 'On the origin of ⟨ei, ey⟩ spellings in Middle English', in S. Rot (ed.), *On the Development of English*, Budapest: MTA Hzinyomda, pp. 88–100.

Kniezsa, V. (1981b), 'Some problems of early Scots', *Annales Universitatis Scientorum Budapestinensis. Sectio Linguistica*, 12, Budapest, pp. 207–13.

Kniezsa, V. (1983a), '⟨ai⟩–⟨a⟩ in Mediaeval Northern English manuscripts', *Folia Linguistica Historica*, 4:1, pp. 45–53.

Kniezsa, V. (1983b), 'EI, EY in fourteenth and fifteenth-century North Midland and Northern English manuscripts', in S. Rot (ed.), *The Functions of Language*, Budapest: MTA Sokszoroslt. Fzem, pp. 173–88.

Kniezsa, V. (1983c), 'The problem of the merger of Middle English /a:/–/ai/ in Northern English', in M. Davenport, E. Hansen and H. F. Nielsen (eds), *Current Topics in Historical Linguistics*, Odense: Odense University Press, pp. 95–102.

Kniezsa, V. (1986), 'What happened to Old French *ai* in Britain?', in D. Strauss and H. W. Drescher (eds), *Scottish Language and Literature, Medieval and Renaissance: Fourth International Conference. Scottish Studies*, Frankfurt am Main: Lang, pp. 95–102.

Kniezsa, V. (1989), 'The origin of the ⟨i⟩ digraphs: the place-name evidence', in J. D. McClure and M. R. G. Spiller (eds), *Bryght Lanternis: Essays on the Language and Literature of Medieval and Renaissance Scotland*, Aberdeen: Aberdeen University Press, pp. 442–50.

Kniezsa, V. (1991), '*Scotica Pronunciatione*: sixteenth and seventeenth-century English authors on Scots', *Scottish Language*, 10, pp. 1–8.

Kniezsa, V. (1994), 'Early Scots: its origin and development', in W. Viereck (ed.), *The Computer-Developed Linguistic Atlas of England*, vol. 1, Tübingen: Niemeyer, pp. 132–9.

Knott, E. (1966), 'The court poet and his work', in E. Knott and G. Murphy (eds), *Early Irish Literature*, London: Routledge and Kegan Paul, pp. 60–93.

Knox, A. (1875), *A History of the County of Down*, Dublin: Hodges.

Kohler, K. J. (1966a), 'A late eighteenth-century comparison of the "Provincial Dialect of Scotland" and the "Pure Dialect"', *Linguistics*, 23, pp. 30–69.

Kohler, K. J. (1966b), 'Aspects of the history of English pronunciation in Scotland', Ph.D. dissertation, University of Edinburgh.

Kohler, K. J. (1967), 'Aspects of Middle Scots phonemics and graphemics', *Transactions of the Philological Society*, pp. 32–61.

Kolb, E. (1964), *Phonological Atlas of the Northern Region*, Bern: Franke.

Kristensson, G. (1967), *A Survey of Middle English Dialects 1290–1350: The Six Northern Counties and the Isle of Man*, Lund: Gleerup.

Kristensson, G. (1987), *A Survey of Middle English Dialects 1290–1350: The West Midland Counties*, Lund and Bromley: Lund University Press.

Kubuzono, H. (1982), 'The genesis of the English *Great Vowel Shift*', *Studies in Linguistic Change*, Tokyo: Kenkyusha, pp. 39–52.

Kuipers, C. H. (ed.) (1964a), '*Quintin Kennedy (1520–1564): Two Eucharistic Tracts*. A critical edition', Dissertation, University of Nijmegen.

Kuipers, C. H. (1964b), 'Kennedy's language', in idem (ed.), '*Quintin Kennedy (1520–1564): Two Eucharistic Tracts*. A critical edition', Dissertation, University of Nijmegen, pp. 7–24.

Kurath, H. and S. Kuhn (eds) (1954–), *Middle English Dictionary* [MED], Ann Arbor: University of Michigan Press. 11 vols to *thufe*.

Kytö, M. (1993), *Manual to the Diachronic Part of the Helsinki Corpus of English Texts: Coding Conventions and Lists of Source Texts*, 2nd edn, Helsinki: Helsinki University Press.

Kytö, M., M. Rissanen and S. Wright (eds) (1994), *Corpora Across the Centuries. Proceedings of the First International Colloquium on English Diachronic Corpora*, Amsterdam and Atlanta: Rodopi.

Labov, W. (1966), *The Social Stratification of English in New York City*, Washington, DC: Center for Applied Linguistics.

Labov, W. (1972), *Sociolinguistic Patterns*, Oxford: Blackwell.

Labov, W. (1987), 'Are Black and White vernaculars diverging? Papers from the NWAVE XIV panel discussion', *American Speech*, 87, pp. 5–12, 62–74.

Labov, W. (1994), *Principles of Linguistic Change: Internal Factors*, Oxford: Blackwell.

Laing, M. (1994), 'The linguistic analysis of medieval vernacular texts: two projects at Edinburgh', in M. Kytö, M. Rissanen and S. Wright (eds), *Corpora Across the Centuries. Proceedings of the First International Colloquium on English Diachronic Corpora*, Amsterdam and Atlanta: Rodopi, pp. 121–41.

Landau, S. (1984), *Dictionaries. The Art and Craft of Lexicography*, New York: Scribner Press.

Lang, A. (ed.) (1898–9), *Sir Walter Scott. Waverley Novels*, Large Type Border Edition, London: Nimmo.

Lang, W. H. (1909), *The Thunder of the Hoofs*, London: Long.

Lass, R. (ed.) (1969), *Approaches to English Historical Linguistics*, New York: Holt Rinehart.

Lass, R. (1976), *English Phonology and Phonological Theory*, Cambridge: Cambridge University Press.

Lass, R. (1980), *On Explaining Language Change*, London: Cambridge University Press.

Lass, R. (1984), *Phonology: An Introduction to Basic Concepts*, Cambridge: Cambridge University Press.

Lass, R. (1988), 'Vowel shifts, great and otherwise: remarks on Stockwell and Minkova', in D. Kastovsky and G. Bauer (eds), *Luick Revisited: Papers read at the Luick-Symposium at Schloss Liechtenstein, 15–18.9.1985*, Tübingen: Gunter Narr, pp. 395–410.

Lass, R. (1990), 'What, if anything, was the Great Vowel Shift?', paper read at the Sixth International Conference on English Historical Linguistics, Helsinki.

Lass, R. (1992), 'Phonology and morphology', in N. Blake (ed.), *The Cambridge History of the English Language*, vol. 2, *1066–1476*, Cambridge: Cambridge University Press, pp. 23–155.

Lass, R. and J. M. Anderson (1975), *Old English Phonology*, Cambridge: Cambridge University Press.

Latimer, Rev. W. T. (1895, 1901), 'The old session-book of Templepatrick Presbyterian church', *Journal of the Royal Society of Antiquaries of Ireland*, Part I, 25, pp. 130–4; Part II, 31, pp. 162–75; Part III, 31, pp. 259–72.

Latimer, Rev. W. T. (1897), 'The old session-book of the Presbyterian congregation at Dundonald, Co. Down', *Ulster Journal of Archaeology*, 2nd series, vol. 3, pp. 227–32; vol. 4, pp. 33–6.

Laver, J. (1994), *Principles of Phonetics*, Cambridge: Cambridge University Press.

Law, A. (1965), *Education in Edinburgh in the Eighteenth Century*, Publications of the Scottish Council for Research in Education, 52, London: University of London Press.

Lawrie, S. (1991), 'A linguistic survey of the use of Scottish dialect terms in North-East Fife', *Scottish Language*, 10, pp. 18–29.

Lawson-Tancred, H. C. (trans.) (1965), *Aristotle, The Art of Rhetoric*, Harmondsworth: Penguin.

Lea, E. M. (1893), 'The language of the Northumbrian gloss to the Gospel of St. Mark', *Anglia*, 16, pp. 62–206.

Leith, D. (1983), *A Social History of English*, London: Routledge and Kegan Paul.

Lennie, W. (1823), *The Principles of English Grammar*, 2nd edn with Large Additions, Edinburgh.

Leonard, A. S. (1929), *The Doctrine of Correctness in English Usage 1700–1800*, Madison: University of Wisconsin Press.

Lodge, K. R. (1984), *Studies in the Phonology of Colloquial English*, London: Croom Helm.

Loey, A. von (1951), *Introduction à l'étude du Moyen-Neêrlandais*, Paris: Aubier.

Logan, J. (1924), *Ulster in the X-rays*, London: Arthur Stockwell.

Longmuir, J. and D. Donaldson (eds) (1879–82), *J. Jamieson, An Etymological Dictionary of the Scottish Language*, Paisley: Gardner.

Lorimer, W. T. (1949, 1951), 'The persistence of Gaelic in Galloway and Carrick', *Scottish Gaelic Studies*, 6, pp. 114–36; 7, pp. 26–46.

Lovie, R. (1995), *Innin ti the Scots Leid/An Introduction to the Scots Language*, Aiberdeen Univairsitie Scots Leid Quorum.

Luick, K. (1896), *Untersuchungen zur englischen Lautgeschichte*, Strassburg.

Luick, K. (1898 [1964]), *Studien zur englischen Lautgeschichte*, 2 vols, Oxford: Blackwell; New York: Johnson.

Luick, K. (1964), *Historische Grammatik der englischen Sprache*, vols 1–2, Cambridge, MA: Harvard University Press.

Lunney, L. [Connolly] (1994), 'Ulster attitudes to Scottishness: the eighteenth century and after', in I. S. Wood (ed.), *Scotland and Ulster*, Edinburgh: Mercat Press, pp. 56–70.

Lunney, L. [Connolly] (1996), 'The nature of the Ulster-Scots language community', paper read at Varieties of Scottishness Conference, Belfast. Forthcoming in J. Erskine (ed.), *Varieties of Scottishness*.

Lutton, W. (1923), *Montiaghisms – Ulster Words and Phrases*, ed. F. J. Bigger, Armagh [n.pub.]. Reprinted in 1976 by Linen Hall Library, Belfast.

Lyall, R. J. (1988), 'Vernacular prose before the Reformation', in C. Craig (ed.), *The History of Scottish Literature*, 4 vols, vol. 1, *Origins to 1660*, ed. R. D. S. Jack, Aberdeen: Aberdeen University Press, pp. 163–82.

Lyall, R. (ed.) (1989), *Sir David Lindsay, The Thrie Estaitis*, Edinburgh: Canongate.

Lynch, M. (1992), *Scotland: A New History*, London: Pimlico.

Lyttle, W. G. (1879), *Robin's Readings. Part I. The Adventures of Paddy McQuillan*, Belfast: Carswell and Sons.

Macafee, C. I. (n.d.), 'Characteristics of non-standard grammar in Scotland', unpublished MS.

Macafee, C. I. (1978–9), *An Outline of Scots Phonology*, table 1: Sources. MS, Department of English Language, University of Glasgow.

Macafee, C. I. (1981), 'Nationalism and the Scots Renaissance now', *English World-Wide*, 2:1, pp. 29–38.

Macafee, C. I. (1982), 'Glasgow dialect in literature', *Scottish Language*, 1, pp. 45–53.

Macafee, C. I. (1983), *Varieties of English Around the World: Glasgow*, Amsterdam: Benjamins.

Macafee, C. I. (1985), 'Nationalism and the Scots Renaissance now', in M. Görlach (ed.), *Focus on Scotland. Varieties of English Around the World*, General series, 5, Amsterdam: Benjamins, pp. 7–17.

Macafee, C. I. (1987), 'Language and modern life: notes from Glasgow', in C. I. Macafee and I. Macleod (eds), *The Nuttis Schell. Essays on the Scots Language presented to A. J. Aitken*, Aberdeen: Aberdeen University Press, pp. 182–94.

Macafee, C. I. (1988), 'Some studies in the Glasgow vernacular', Dissertation, University of Glasgow.

Macafee, C. I. (1989), 'Middle Scots dialects – extrapolating backwards', in J. D. McClure and M. R. G. Spiller (eds), *Bryght Lanternis: Essays on the Language and Literature of Medieval and Renaissance Scotland*, Aberdeen: Aberdeen University Press, pp. 429–41.

Macafee, C. I. (1992–3), 'A short grammar of Older Scots', *Scottish Language*, 11–12, pp. 10–36.

Macafee, C. I. (1994a), *Traditional Dialect in the Modern World: A Glasgow Case Study*, Bamberger Beiträge zur Englischen Sprachwissenschaft 35, Frankfurt am Main: Lang.

Macafee, C. I. (1994b), 'The Ulster dictionary project', *Belfast Working Papers in Language and Linguistics*, 12, pp. 177–93.

Macafee, C. I. (1994c), 'Dialect erosion with special reference to urban Scots', in A. Fenton and D. A. MacDonald (eds), *Studies in Scots and Gaelic: Proceedings of the Third International Conference on the Languages of Scotland, 1991*, Edinburgh: Canongate Academic, pp. 69–80.

Macafee, C. I. (1994d), 'How it feels to be thick as a brick', in A. Fenton and D. A. MacDonald (eds), *Studies in Scots and Gaelic: Proceedings of the Third International Conference on the Languages of Scotland, 1991*, Edinburgh: Canongate Academic, pp. 111–17.

Macafee, C. I. (ed.) (1996), *Concise Ulster Dictionary*, Oxford: Oxford University Press.

Macafee, C. I. and A. Anderson (forthcoming), 'A sample of Older Scots lexis'.

Macafee, C. I. and I. Macleod (eds) (1987), *The Nuttis Schell. Essays on the Scots Language presented to A. J. Aitken*, Aberdeen: Aberdeen University Press.

Macafee, C. I. and C. Ó Baoill (forthcoming), 'Why Scots is not a Celtic English', in H. Tristram (ed.), *Proceedings of a Colloquium on 'Celtic Englishes', Potsdam, 1995*, Heidelberg: Carl Winter.

Macafee, W. A. (1992), 'The movement of British settlers into Ulster in the seventeenth century', *Familia*, 2, pp. 94–111.

MacAulay, D. (1975), 'The Gaelic notes in the Book of Deer', *Scottish Historical Review*, 54, pp. 84–7.

MacAulay, D. (1978), 'Intra-dialectal variation as an area of Gaelic linguistic research', *Scottish Gaelic Studies*, 13:1, pp. 81–97.

MacAulay, D. (1982a), 'Borrow, calque and switch: the law of the English frontier', in J. M. Anderson (ed.), *Language Form and Linguistic Variation: Papers Dedicated to Angus McIntosh*, Amsterdam: John Benjamins, pp. 203–37.

MacAulay, D. (1982b), 'Register range and choice in Scottish Gaelic', *International Journal of the Sociology of Language*, 35, pp. 25–48.

MacAulay, D. (1986), 'New Gaelic?', *Scottish Language*, 5, pp. 120–5.

Macaulay, R. K. S. (1978), 'Variation and consistency in Glaswegian English', in P. Trudgill (ed.), *Sociolinguistic Patterns in British English*, London: Edward Arnold, pp. 132–43.

Macaulay, R. K. S. (1985), 'The narrative skills of a Scottish coal miner', in M. Görlach (ed.), *Focus on Scotland. Varieties of English Around the World*, General series, 5, Amsterdam: Benjamins, pp. 101–24.

Macaulay, R. K. S. (1991), *Locating Dialect in Discourse: The Language of Honest Men and Bonny Lasses in Ayr*, Oxford: Oxford University Press.

Macaulay, R. K. S. (1995–6), 'Remarkably common eloquence: the aesthetics of urban dialect', *Scottish Language*, 14–15, pp. 66–80.

Macaulay, R. K. S. and G. D. Trevelyan (1977), *Language, Social Class and Education. A Glasgow Study*, Edinburgh: Edinburgh University Press.

Mac Craith, M. (1990), 'Gaelic Ireland and the Renaissance', in G. Williams and R. Owen Jones (eds), *The Celts and the Renaissance*, Cardiff: University of Wales Press, pp. 57–89.

Macfarlane, L. J. (1985), *William Elphinstone and the Kingdom of Scotland 1431–1514: The Struggle for Order*, Aberdeen: Aberdeen University Press.

Macinnes, J. (1989), 'The Gaelic perception of the Lowlands', in W. Gillies (ed.), *Gaelic and Scotland: Alba agus a' Ghàidhlig*, Edinburgh: Edinburgh University Press, pp. 89–100.

Mack, D. (ed.) (1976), *James Hogg. The Brownie of Bodsbeck*, Edinburgh: Scottish Academic Press.

Mackay, C. (1888), *Dictionary of Lowland Scotch*, London: Whittaker & Co.

Mackay, M. A. (1973), 'The Scots of the Makars', in A. J. Aitken (ed.), *Lowland Scots: Occasional Papers no. 2*, Edinburgh: Association for Scottish Literary Studies, pp. 20–31.

MacKenna, G. E. (1989), 'Vowel duration in the Standard English of Scotland', Dissertation, University of Edinburgh.

Mackenzie, A. M. (1964), *Orain Iain Luim*, Edinburgh: Scottish Gaelic Texts Society.

Mackie, A. (1881), *Scotticisms Arranged and Corrected, Solecisms Corrected*, London: Hamilton Adams.

MacKinnon, K. (1977), *Language, Education and Social Processes in a Gaelic Community*, London: Routledge and Kegan Paul.

MacKinnon, K. (1991), *Gaelic: A Past and Future Prospect*, Edinburgh: Saltire Society.

Maclaren, I. (1894), *Beside the Bonnie Brier Bush*, London: Hodder and Stoughton.

Maclaren, I. (1895), *The Days of Auld Lang Syne*, London: Hodder and Stoughton.

Macleod, I., P. Cairns, C. I. Macafee and R. Martin (eds) (1990), *The Scots Thesaurus*, Aberdeen: Aberdeen University Press.

Macleod, M. (1963), 'Gaelic in Highland education', *Transactions of the Gaelic Society of Inverness*, 43, pp. 305–34.

MacMahon, A. M. S. (1990), 'Constraining lexical phonology: evidence from English vowels', Dissertation, University of Edinburgh.

MacMahon, A. M. S. (1991), 'Lexical phonology and sound change: the case of the *Scottish Vowel Length Rule*', *Journal of Linguistics*, 27, pp. 29–53.

MacMahon, A. M. S. (1992), 'Lexical phonology and diachrony', in M. Rissanen, O. Ihalainen, T. Nevalainen and I. Taavitsainen (eds), *History of Englishes: New Methods and Interpretations in Historical Linguistics*, Berlin: Mouton de Gruyter, pp. 167–90.

MacMahon, A. M. S. (1994), *Understanding Language Change*, Cambridge: Cambridge University Press.

MacQueen, J. (1967), *Robert Henryson: A Study of the Major Narrative Poems*, Oxford: Clarendon Press.

MacQueen, J. (ed.) (1970), *Ballattis of Luve 1470–1570*, Edinburgh: Edinburgh University Press.

MacQueen, J. (1988), 'Scottish Latin poetry', in R. D. S. Jack (ed.), *The History of Scottish Literature*, vol. 1, Aberdeen: Aberdeen University Press, pp. 213–26.

MacQueen, J. and T. Scott (1966), *The Oxford Book of Scottish Verse*, Oxford: Clarendon Press.

MacQueen, L. E. C. (1957), 'The last stages of the older literary language of Scotland: a study of the surviving Scottish elements in Scottish prose, 1700–1750, especially of the records, national and local', Dissertation, University of Edinburgh.

MacRae, G. D. (1975), 'An edition of nine Early Scots texts from 1379 to 1402', Dissertation, University of Edinburgh.

Mactaggart, J. (1824), *The Scottish Gallovidian Encyclopedia*, London, printed for the author.

Magarey, S. (1985), *Unbridling the Tongues of Women: A Biography of Catherine Helen Spence*, Sydney: Hale and Iremonger.

Marckwardt, A. (1958), *American English*, New York: Oxford University Press.

Markus, R. A. (1972), 'St Augustine on signs', in idem (ed.), *Augustine: A Collection of Critical Essays*, Garden City, New York: Doubleday, pp. 61–91.

Marshall, J. J. (1904–6), 'The dialect of Ulster: a glossary of words in the Ulster dialect, chiefly used in the midland and north-western counties', *Ulster Journal of Archaeology*, 2nd series, vol. 10, pp. 121–30; vol. 11, pp. 64–70, 122–5, 175–9; vol. 12, pp. 18–21.

Marshall, J. J. (1907), 'An elegy/The epitaph', *Ulster Journal of Archaeology*, 2nd series, vol. 13, pp. 160–1.

Marshall, W. F. (1936), *Ulster Speaks*, London: British Broadcasting Corporation.

Martin, M. A. R. (1979), '*The Concise Scots Dictionary*: an interim report', *Scottish Literary Journal*, Supplement 9, pp. 28–40.

Mason, W. S. (1814), *A Statistical Account or Parochial Survey of Ireland, Drawn up by W. S. Mason from the Communications of the Clergy*, vol. 1, Dublin.

Mather, J. Y. (1973), 'The Scots we speak today', in A. J. Aitken (ed.), *Lowland Scots: Occasional Papers no. 2*, Edinburgh: Association for Scottish Literary Studies, pp. 56–71.

Mather, J. Y. (1978), 'The dialect of Caithness', *Scottish Literary Journal*, Supplement 6, pp. 1–16.

Mather, J. Y. (1980), 'The dialect of the Eastern Borders', *Scottish Literary Journal*, Supplement 12, pp. 30–42.

Mather, J. Y. and H. H. Speitel (1975, 1977, 1986), *The Linguistic Atlas of Scotland*, 3 vols, London: Croom Helm.

Matsumoto, N. (1982), 'On the uses of *Do* in William Dunbar's English', *Hiroshima Studies in English Language and Literature*, 27, pp. 32–41.

Matthiesen, F. O. (1931), *Translation: An Elizabethan Art*, Cambridge, MA: Harvard University Press.

Maxwell, S. (1994), 'Arms and armour', in D. S. Thomson (ed.), *The Companion to Gaelic Scotland*, Glasgow: Gairm, pp. 9–11.

McArthur, T. (ed.) (1992), *The Oxford Companion to the English Language*, Oxford: Oxford University Press.

McCartney, G. (1661–8), [Letter book], Manuscript on deposit in Linen Hall Library, Belfast.

McClelland of Bombay Legal Documents (1612–24), Collection T640, Belfast: Public Record Office of Northern Ireland.

McClure, J. D. (1977), 'Vowel duration in a Scottish accent', *Journal of the International Phonetic Association*, 7, pp. 10–16.

McClure, J. D. (1979), 'Scots, its range of uses', in A. J. Aitken and T. McArthur (eds), *Languages of Scotland*, Edinburgh: Chambers, pp. 26–48.

McClure, J. D. (1980a), 'Developing Scots as a national language', in J. D. McClure, A. J. Aitken and J. T. Low (eds), *The Scots Language: Planning for Modern Usage*, Edinburgh: Ramsay Head Press, pp. 11–41.

McClure. J. D. (1980b), 'Western Scottish intonation: a preliminary study', in L. R. Waugh and C. H. van Schooneveld (eds), *The Melody of Language*, Baltimore: University Park Press, pp. 201–17.

McClure, J. D. (1981a), 'The synthesisers of Scots', in E. Haugen, J. D. McClure and D. Thomson (eds), *Minority Languages Today*, Edinburgh: Edinburgh University Press, pp. 91–9.

McClure, J. D. (1981b), 'Scottis, Inglis, Suddron: language labels and language attitudes', in R. J. Lyall and F. Riddy (eds), *Proceedings of the Third International Conference on Scottish Language and Literature, Medieval and Renaissance*, Stirling and Glasgow: University of Stirling, pp. 52–69.

McClure, J. D. (ed.) (1983), *Scotland and the Lowland Tongue*, Aberdeen: Aberdeen University Press.

McClure, J. D. (1986), 'What Scots owes to Gaelic', *Scottish Language*, 5, pp. 85–98.

McClure, J. D. (1988), *Why Scots Matters*, Edinburgh: Saltire Society.

McClure, J. D. (1990), 'Douglas Young and Sorley Maclean', in D. S. Thomson (ed.), *Gaelic and*

Scots in Harmony: Proceedings of the Second International Conference on the Languages of Scotland, Glasgow: Department of Celtic, University of Glasgow, pp. 136–48.

McClure, J. D. (1994), 'English in Scotland', in R. Burchfield (ed.), *The Cambridge History of the English Language*, vol. 5, *English in Britain and Overseas: Origins and Development*, Cambridge: Cambridge University Press, pp. 23–93.

McClure, J. D. (1995), *Scots and its Literature*, Amsterdam: Benjamins.

McClure, J. D., T. Low, J. K. Annand, A. D. Mackie and J. J. Graham (1981), 'Our ain leid? The predicament of a Scots writer', *English World-Wide*, 2:1, pp. 3–28.

McClure, J. D. and M. R. G. Spiller (eds) (1989), *Bryght Lanternis: Essays on the Language and Literature of Medieval and Renaissance Scotland*, Aberdeen: Aberdeen University Press.

McCrum, R., W. Cran and R. MacNeil (eds) (1986), *The Story of English*, New York: Viking.

McDiarmid, M. P. (ed.) (1959–60), *Hary's Wallace*, Scottish Text Society, 4th series, 2 vols, Edinburgh and London: Blackwood.

McDiarmid, M. P. (ed.) (1973), *The Kingis Quair of James Stewart*, London: Heinemann.

McDiarmid, M. P. and J. Stevenson (eds) (1981–5), *Barbour's Bruce*, Scottish Text Society, 4th series, 3 vols, Edinburgh and London: Blackwood.

McElroy, D. D. (1969), *Scotland's Age of Improvement: A Survey of Eighteenth-Century Literary Clubs and Societies*, Washington: Washington State University Press.

McElroy, L. and D. McElroy (1969), 'The literary clubs and societies of the eighteenth century in Scotland', Dissertation, University of Edinburgh.

McGavin, J. J. (1993), 'The dramatic prosody of Sir David Lindsay', in R. D. S. Jack and K. McGinley (eds), *Of Lion and of Unicorn*, Edinburgh: Quadriga, pp. 17–27.

McIllquam, W. (1781), *A Comprehensive Grammar*, Glasgow.

McIlwham, T. (1838), *The McIlwham Papers: Two Letters from Thomas McIlwham Weaver to his Friend Mr. James McNeight*, ed. and illustrated with notes and a glossary by John Morrison, Belfast: W. McComb.

McIntosh, A. (1966), 'A new approach to Middle English dialectology', *English Studies*, 44, pp. 1–11.

McIntosh, A. (1978 [1989]), 'The dialectology of mediaeval Scots: some possible approaches to its study', in M. Laing (ed.), *Middle English Dialectology. Essays on Some Principles and Problems*, Aberdeen: Aberdeen University Press, pp. 81–5.

McIntosh, A. (1983), 'Present indicative plural forms in the later Middle English of the North Midlands', in D. Gray and E. G. Stanley (eds), *Middle English Studies Presented to Norman Davis*, Oxford: Clarendon Press, pp. 235–44.

McIntosh, A., M. L. Samuels and M. Benskin (eds) (1986), *Linguistic Atlas of Late Medieval English* [LALME], 4 vols, Aberdeen: Aberdeen University Press.

McMordie, Rev. W. ('One Who Listens') (1897), *Our Ulster Accent and Ulster Provincialisms*, Belfast.

McNaught, D. (1901), 'The raucle tongue of Burns', *Burns Chronicle and Club Directory*, 10, pp. 26–37.

McNeill, P. and R. Nicholson (eds) (1975), *An Historical Atlas of Scotland*, St Andrews: Atlas Committee.

Meek, D. E. (1989a), 'Gàidhlig is Gaylick anns na meadhon aoisean', in W. Gillies (ed.), *Gaelic and Scotland: Alba agus a' Ghàidhlig*, Edinburgh: Edinburgh University Press, pp. 131–45, 233–5.

Meek, D. E. (1989b), 'The Scots-Gaelic scribes of late medieval Perthshire: an overview of the orthography and contents of the Book of the Dean of Lismore', in J. D. McClure and M. R. G. Spiller (eds), *Bryght Lanternis: Essays on the Language and Literature of Medieval and Renaissance Scotland*, Aberdeen: Aberdeen University Press, pp. 387–404.

Meier, H. H. (1977), 'Scots is not alone: the Swiss and Low German analogues', in A. J. Aitken, M. P. McDiarmid and D. S. Thomson (eds), *Bards and Makars: Scots Language and Literature, Mediaeval and Renaissance*, Glasgow: Glasgow University Press, pp. 201–13.

Melchers, G. (1980), 'The Norn element in Shetland dialect today – a case of "never-accepted" language death', in E. Ejerhed and I. Henrysson (eds), *Tvåspråkighet, Föredag från tredje Nordiska Tvåspråkighetsymposiet 4–5 juni 1980, Umeå Universitet*, Umeå University, pp. 254–61.

Melchers, G. (1981), 'Hween, Kenee, Tlock: on the realisation of initial /k/-clusters in some varieties of English', in L. E. Breivik, A. Hille and S. Johannson (eds), *Essays on English Language in Honour of Bertil Sundby*, Oslo: Novus, pp. 237–44.

Melchers, G. (1985), '*Knappin, Proper English, Modified Scottish*. Some language attitudes in the Shetland Isles', in M. Görlach (ed.), *Focus on Scotland. Varieties of English Around the World*, General series, 5, Amsterdam: Benjamins, pp. 87–100.

Melchers, G. (1986), 'Narrowing and extension of meaning in the Scandinavian-based vocabulary of Shetland dialect', *Scottish Language*, 5, pp. 110–19.

Melchers, G. (1991), 'Norn–Scots: a complicated language contact situation in Shetland', in P. S. Ureland and G. Broderick (eds), *Language Contact in the British Isles*, Tübingen: Niemeyer, pp. 461–77.

Melchers, G. and N.-L. Johanneson (eds) (1994), *Non-Standard Varieties of Language*, Stockholm: Almqvist and Wiksell.

Mennie Shire, H. (1969), *Song, Dance and Poetry of the Court of Scotland under King James VI*, Cambridge: Cambridge University Press.

Menzies, J. (1991), 'An investigation of attitudes to Scots and Glasgow dialect among secondary school pupils', *Scottish Language*, 10, pp. 30–46.

Meurman-Solin, A. (1992), 'On the morphology of verbs in Middle Scots: present and present perfect indicative', in M. Rissanen, O. Ihalainen, T. Nevalainen and I. Taavitsainen (eds), *History of Englishes: New Methods and Interpretations in Historical Linguistics*, Berlin: Mouton de Gruyter, pp. 611–23.

Meurman-Solin, A. (1993a) *Variation and Change in Early Scottish Prose: Studies Based on the Helsinki Corpus of Older Scots*, Helsinki: Suomalainen Tiedeakatemia.

Meurman-Solin, A. (1993b), 'The author–addressee relationship and the marking of stance in the characterisation of sixteenth- and seventeenth-century genre styles', in *New Horizons in Stylistics?* Belgisch Tijdschrift voor Filologie en Geschiedenis, 71:3, pp. 733–45.

Meurman-Solin, A. (1993c), 'Introduction to the Helsinki Scots corpus', in M. Rissanen, M. Kytö and M. Palander-Collin (eds), *Early English in the Computer Age: Explorations through the Helsinki Corpus*, Topics in English Linguistics 11, Berlin and New York: Mouton de Gruyter, pp. 75–82.

Meurman-Solin, A. (1993d), 'Periphrastic and auxiliary *do* in early Scottish prose genres', in M. Rissanen, M. Kytö and M. Palander-Collin (eds), *Early English in the Computer Age: Explorations through the Helsinki Corpus*, Topics in English Linguistics 11, Berlin and New York: Mouton de Gruyter, pp. 235–51.

Meurman-Solin, A. (1994a), 'The Helsinki Corpus of Older Scots', in M. Kytö, M. Rissanen and S. Wright (eds), *Corpora Across the Centuries. Proceedings of the First International Colloquium on English Diachronic Corpora*, Amsterdam and Atlanta: Rodopi, pp. 53–63.

Meurman-Solin, A. (1994b), 'On the evolution of prose genres in Older Scots', *Nowele*, 23, pp. 91–138.

Meurman-Solin, A. (1995a), 'A new tool: the Helsinki Corpus of Older Scots (1450–1700)', ICAME *Journal*, 19, pp. 49–62.

Meurman-Solin, A. (1995b), 'Marking of stance in Early Modern English imaginative narration', in W. Görtschacher and H. Klein (eds), *Narrative Strategies in Early English Fiction*, Salzburg: Mellen, pp. 25–52.

Meurman-Solin, A. (forthcoming a), 'Text profiles in the study of language variation and change', in R. Hickey, K. Kytö, I. Lancashire and M. Rissanen (eds), *Tracing the Trail of Time. Proceedings from the Diachronic Corpora Workshop*, Toronto, May 1995.

Meurman-Solin, A. (forthcoming b), 'Towards reconstructing a grammar of point of view. Textual roles of adverbials and adjectives in early non-literary prose', Berlin and New York: Mouton de Gruyter.

Meurman-Solin, A. (forthcoming c), 'Women's Scots: gender-based variation in Renaissance letters'; paper read at the International Conference on Mediaeval and Renaissance Scottish Literature and Language, Oxford, 1996.

Michael, I. (1970), *English Grammatical Categories and the Tradition to 1800*, London: Cambridge University Press.

Michel, F. (1882), *A Critical Inquiry into the Scottish Language with the View of Illustrating the Rise and Progress of Civilisation in Scotland*, Edinburgh and London: Blackwood.

Millar, R. M. (1996), 'English a creoloid? Possible examples of, and explanation for, only partial creolization', paper delivered at the 32nd Annual International Mediaeval Congress, Western Michigan University, Kalamazoo, Michigan.

Millar, R. M. (forthcoming), 'Gaelic-influenced Scots in pre-revolutionary Maryland', in S. P. Ureland (ed.), *Language Contact across the North Atlantic*, Tübingen: Max Niemeyer.

Miller, J. (1985), 'Review of C. I. Macafee, *Varieties of English Around the World: Glasgow*, *Scottish Language*, 4, pp. 32–6.

Miller, J. (1993), 'The grammar of Scottish English', in J. Milroy and L. Milroy (eds), *Real English: The Grammar of English Dialects in the British Isles*, Harlow: Longman, pp. 99–138.

Milroy, J. (1981), *Regional Accents of English: Belfast*, Belfast: Blackstaff.

Milroy, J. (1982), 'Some connections between Galloway and Ulster speech', *Scottish Language*, 1, pp. 23–9.

Milroy, J. (1992), *Linguistic Variation and Change*, Language in Society 19, Oxford and Cambridge, MA: Blackwell.

Milroy, J. (1994), 'The notion of "standard language" and its applicability to the study of Early Modern English pronunciation', in D. Stein and I. Tieken-Boon van Ostade (eds), *Towards a Standard English 1600–1800*, Berlin and New York: Mouton de Gruyter, pp. 19–29.

Milroy, J. and L. Milroy (1985), *Authority in Language. Investigating Language Prescription and Standardisation*, London, Boston and Henley: Routledge and Kegan Paul.

Milroy, J. and L. Milroy (eds) (1993), *Real English: The Grammar of English Dialects in the British Isles*, Harlow: Longman.

Milroy, J., L. Milroy, S. Hartley and D. Walstow (1994), 'Glottal stops and Tyneside Glottalisation: competing patterns of variation and change in British English', *Language Variation and Change*, 13:3, pp. 327–58.

Milroy, L. (1980), *Language and Social Networks*, Oxford: Blackwell.

Milroy, L. (1987), *Observing and Analysing Natural Language*, Oxford: Blackwell.

Milroy, L. (1994), 'Interpreting the role of extralinguistic variables in linguistic variation and change', in G. Melchers and N.-L. Johanneson (eds), *Non-Standard Varieties of Language*, Stockholm: Almqvist and Wiksell, pp. 131–45.

Mini-Guide to the Lesser-Used Languages of the EC (1993), Dublin: European Bureau for Lesser Used Languages.

Minkova, D. (1982), 'The environment for Open Syllable Lengthening', *Folia Linguistica Historica*, 3:1, pp. 29–58.

Minkova, D. (1991), *The History of Final Vowels in English*, Berlin: Mouton de Gruyter.

Minkova, D. and R. Stockwell (1992), 'Homorganic clusters as moric busters in the history of English: the case of *-ld*, *-nd*, *-mb*', in M. Rissanen, O. Ihalainen, T. Nevalainen and I. Taavitsainen (eds), *History of Englishes: New Methods and Interpretations in Historical Linguistics*, Berlin: Mouton de Gruyter, pp. 191–206.

Minnis, A. J. (1991), 'Dante, *Epistle to Can Grande*', in idem (ed.), *Medieval Literary Theory and Criticism c.1100–c.1375*, 2nd rev. edn, Oxford: Oxford University Press.

Mitchell, H. (1799), *Scotticisms, Vulgar Anglicisms, and Grammatical Improprieties Corrected*, Glasgow.

Mohr, V. (1990), 'ESc /a:/ and ESc /ai/ reconsidered', Dissertation, Anglistisches Seminar der Universität Heidelberg.

Monboddo, J. B. (Lord) (1774), *Of the Origin and Progress of Language*, London.

Monroe, B. S. (1910), 'An English Academy', *Modern Philology*, 8, pp. 107–16.

Montague, J. (ed.) (1974), *The Faber Book of Irish Verse*, London: Faber and Faber.

Montgomery, M. (1989), 'Exploring the roots of Appalachian English', *English World-Wide*, 10, pp. 227–78.

Montgomery, M. (1992), 'The anglicization of Ulster Scots', *Studies in Scottish Literature*, 26, pp. 50–64.

Montgomery, M. (1994a), 'The evolution of verbal concord in Scots', in A. Fenton and D. A. MacDonald (eds), *Studies in Scots and Gaelic: Proceedings of the Third International Conference on the Languages of Scotland, 1991*, Edinburgh: Canongate Academic, pp. 81–95.

Montgomery, M. (1994b), 'An early letter in Ulster Scots', *Ullans: The Magazine for Ulster Scots*, 2, pp. 45–51.

Montgomery, M. (1995), 'The linguistic value of Ulster emigrant letters', *Ulster Folklife*, 41, pp. 26–41.

Montgomery, M. (1996), 'Speaking like Shakespearean: another Ulster-Appalachian connection?', paper read at the eleventh Ulster American Heritage Symposium, Ulster American Folk Park, Omagh, Northern Ireland.

Montgomery, M. (forthcoming a), 'A tale of two Georges: the language of Irish Indian traders in colonial America', in J. Kallen (ed.), *Focus on Ireland*, Amsterdam: Benjamins.

Montgomery, M. (forthcoming b), 'Making the Trans-Atlantic connection', *Journal of English Linguistics*.

Montgomery, M. and S. J. Nagle (1994), 'Double modals in Scotland and the southern United States: trans-Atlantic inheritance or independent development?', *Folia Linguistica Historica*, 14, pp. 91–107.

Moore, S., S. B. Meech and H. Whitehall (1935), *Middle English Dialectal Characteristics and Dialect Boundaries*, Ann Arbor: University of Michigan Press.

Morsbach, L. (1896), *Mittelenglische Grammatik*, Halle.

Mugglestone, L. (1995), *Talking Proper*, Oxford: Clarendon Press.

Müller, P. (1908), *Die Sprache der aberdeener Urkunden des sechzehnten Jahrhunderts*, Berlin: Gustav Schade.

Mulrine, S. (1985), 'Poetry in Glasgow dialect', in M. Görlach (ed.), *Focus on Scotland. Varieties of English Around the World*, General series, 5, Amsterdam: Benjamins, pp. 227–35.

Munro, M. (1985), *The Patter: A Guide to Current Glasgow Usage*, Glasgow: Glasgow District Libraries.

Munro, M. (1988), *The Patter: Another Blast*, Edinburgh: Canongate.

Munro, N. (1935), *John Splendid*, Inveraray Edition, Edinburgh: Blackwood.

Murdoch, S. (1995), *Language Politics in Scotland*, Aiberdeen Univairsitie Scots Leid Quorum.

Mure Black, G. (1923), *Anzac Areopagus*, Sydney: Tyrrells.

Murison, D. (1970), 'The two languages of Scott', in A. N. Jeffares (ed.), *Scott's Mind and Art*, London: Oliver and Boyd, pp. 206–29.

Murison, D. (1971), 'The Dutch element in the vocabulary of Scots', in A. J. Aitken, A. McIntosh and H. Pálsson (eds), *Edinburgh Studies in English and Scots*, London: Longman, pp. 159–76.

Murison, D. (1972), 'The Scottish National Dictionary', *University of Edinburgh Journal*, 25, pp. 305–89.

Murison, D. (1974), 'Linguistic relationships in medieval Scotland', in G. W. S. Barrow (ed.), *The Scottish Tradition: Essays in Honour of Ronald Gordon Cant*, Edinburgh: Scottish Academic Press, pp. 71–83.

Murison, D. (1977), *The Guid Scots Tongue*, Edinburgh: Blackwood.

Murison, D. (1979a), 'Norse influence on Scots', *Lallans*, 13, pp. 58–62.

Murison, D. (1979b), 'The historical background', in A. J. Aitken and T. McArthur (eds), *Languages of Scotland*, Edinburgh: Chambers, pp. 2–13.

Murison, D. (1980), 'The language problem in Hugh MacDiarmid's work', in P. H. Scott and A. C. Davis (eds), *The Age of MacDiarmid: Essays on Hugh MacDiarmid and his Influence on Contemporary Scotland*, Edinburgh: Mainstream, pp. 93–9.

Murphy, G. (1940), 'Bards and Filidh', *Éigse*, 2, pp. 200–7.

Murray, J. and C. Morrison (1984), *Bilingual Primary Education in the Western Isles, Scotland: Report of the Bilingual Education Project 1975–81*, Stornoway: Acair.

Murray, J. A. H. (1873), *The Dialect of the Southern Counties of Scotland*, London: The Philological Society.

Murray, J. A. H. et al. (eds.) (1989), *The Oxford English Dictionary* [OED], 2nd edn, London: Oxford University Press.

Mustanoja, T. F. (1960), *A Middle English Syntax, Part I: Parts of Speech*, Helsinki: Société Néophilologique.

Mutschmann, H. (1908), *A Phonology of the Northeastern Scotch Dialect on an Historical Basis*, Bonn: Hanstein.

Nares, R. (1784), *Elements of Orthoepy: English Linguistics 1500–1800*, 56, ed. R. C. Alston (1968), Menston: Scolar Press.

Nässén, G. (1989), 'Norn weather words. 323 meteorological terms in Jakobsen's dictionary and their extent in present-day Shetland dialect', Report no. 3, *Norn: The Scandinavian Element in Shetland Dialect*, Department of English, Stockholm University; Department of Linguistics, Trondheim University.

Neill, P. (1808–10), 'A list of fishes found in the Firth of Forth, and rivers and lakes near Edinburgh, with remarks', *Memoirs of the Wernerian National History Society*, 1, pp. 526–55.

Nevalainen, T. and H. Raumolin-Brunberg (1989), 'A corpus of Early Modern Standard English in a socio-historical perspective', *Neuphilologische Mitteilungen*, 90, pp. 67–110.

Newbrook, M. (1981), *Sociolinguistic Reflexes of Dialect Interference in West Wirral*, Frankfurt: Peter Lang.

Nicholson, R. (1968), 'Domesticated Scots and wild Scots: the relationship between Lowlanders and Highlanders in mediaeval Scotland', *Scottish Colloquium Proceedings*, University of Guelph, Ontario.

Nicholson, R. (1974), *Scotland: The Later Middle Ages*, Edinburgh: Edinburgh University Press.

Nicolaisen, W. F. H. (1976), *Scottish Place-names: Their Study and Significance*, London: Batsford.

Nicolaisen, W. F. H. (1977), *The Place-names of Scotland*, London: Batsford.

Nims, M. F. (trans.) (1967), *Poetria Nova of Geoffrey of Vinsauf*, Toronto: Universal Press.

Ó Baoill, C. (1978), *Contributions to a Comparative Study of Ulster Irish and Scottish Gaelic*, Belfast: Institute of Irish Studies.

Ó Cuív, B. (1951), *Irish Dialects and Irish-Speaking Districts*, Dublin Institute for Advanced Studies.

Ó Dochartaigh, C. (1996), 'Two loans in Scottish Gaelic', *Scottish Gaelic Studies*, 17, pp. 305–13.

O'Duill, G. (1994), 'Emigrant letters from the Donegal Gaeltacht', in T. W. Ihde (ed.), *The Irish Language in the United States: A Historical, Sociolinguistic, and Applied Linguistic Survey*, Westport, CT: Bergin and Garvey, pp. 57–66.

O'Kane, W. (1991), *You Don't Say?: The Tyrone Crystal Book of Ulster Dialect*, Dungannon: Irish World.

Onions, C. T. (ed.) (1966 [1979]), *The Oxford Dictionary of English Etymology*, London: Oxford University Press.

O'Rahilly, T. F. (1930), 'Notes on Middle-Irish pronunciation', *Hermathena*, 20, pp. 152–95.

O'Rahilly, T. F. (1932), *Irish Dialects Past and Present*, Dublin.

Orton, H. (1929), 'Medial development of ME $\bar{o}_1$ (tense), F $\bar{u}$ (= [ȳ]) and ME *eu* (OE *ēow*) in the dialects of the North of England', *Englische Studien*, 63, pp. 229–51.

Orton, H. (1933), *The Phonology of a South Durham Dialect*, London: Kegan Paul, Trench, Trübner.

Orton, H. (1960), 'An English dialect survey: Linguistic Atlas of England', *Orbis*, 8, pp. 331–48.

Orton, H. and M. V. Barry (1969), *The Survey of English Dialects: Basic Material*, vol. 2, *The West Midland Counties*, 3 parts, Leeds: Arnold.

Orton, H. and W. H. Halliday (1962), *The Survey of English Dialects: Basic Material*, vol. 1, *The Six Northern Counties and the Isle of Man*, 3 parts, Leeds: Arnold.

Orton, H., S. Sanderson and J. Widdowson (1978), *The Linguistic Atlas of England*, London: Croom Helm.

Orton, H. and P. M. Tilling (1967), *The Survey of English Dialects: Basic Material*, vol. 3, *The East Midland Counties and East Anglia*, 3 parts, Leeds: Arnold.

Orton, H. and M. F. Wakelin (eds) (1968), *The Survey of English Dialects: The Southern Counties*, Leeds: Arnold.

Orton, H. and N. Wright (1974), *A Word Geography of England*, London: Seminar Press.

O'Snodaigh, P. (1995), *Hidden Ulster: Protestants and the Irish Language*, Belfast: Lagan.

Parker, W. M. (ed.) (1971), *Sir Walter Scott. The Heart of Midlothian*, London: Dent.

Partridge, E. (1966), *Origins: An Etymological Dictionary of Modern English*, 4th edn, London: Routledge.

Partridge, E. (1984), *A Dictionary of Slang and Unconventional English*, 8th edn, ed. P. Beale, London: Routledge and Kegan Paul.

Patterson, D. (1868), *The Provincialisms of Belfast and the Surrounding Districts Pointed out and Corrected, to Which is Added an Essay on Mutual Improvement Societies*, Belfast.

Patterson, W. H. (1880), *A Glossary of Words in Use in the Counties of Antrim and Down*, London: English Dialect Society.

Paulin, T. (1995), *Braid Scots*, Belfast: D. Hammond.

Perceval-Maxwell, M. (1973), *The Scottish Migration to Ulster in the Reign of James I*, London: Routledge and Kegan Paul. Repr. (1990) Belfast: Ulster Historical Foundation.

Perry, W. (1775), *The Royal Standard English Dictionary*, Edinburgh.

Perry, W. (1802 [1776]), *The Only Sure Guide to the English Tongue or a New Pronouncing Spelling Book*, Edinburgh.

Petyt, K. M. (1980), *The Study of Dialect*, London: Deutsch.

Phelan, T. (1838), *Letters from Ireland*.

Plummer, C. (1892), *Two of the Saxon Chronicles Parallel*, Oxford: Clarendon Press.

Pódör, D. (1995–6), 'The phonology of Scottish Gaelic loanwords in Lowland Scots', *Scottish Language*, 14–15, pp. 174–89.

Policansky, L. (1981), 'Grammatical variation in Belfast English', *Belfast Working Papers in Language and Linguistics*, 6, pp. 37–66.

Pollner, C. (1985a), *Englisch in Livingston. Ausgewählte sprachliche Erscheinungen in einer schottischen new town*, Frankfurt: Peter Lang.

Pollner, C. (1985b), 'Linguistic fieldwork in a Scottish new town', in M. Görlach (ed.), *Focus on Scotland. Varieties of English Around the World*, General series, 5, Amsterdam: Benjamins, pp. 57–68.

Pollner, C. (1985c), 'Old words in a young town', *Scottish Language*, 4, pp. 5–15.

Pope, M. K. (1934), *From Latin to Modern French with Especial Consideration of Anglo-Norman*, Manchester: Manchester University Press.

Porter, T. and C. Cunningham (1987), 'Mourne dialect', *12 Miles of Mourne*, 1, pp. 26–9.

Porterfield, J. (1695), *Edinburghs English School-Master*, Glasgow.

Pottle, F. A. (ed.) (1952), *Boswell in Holland 1763–1764, including his Correspondence with Belle de Zuyten (Zelide)*, London: Heinemann.

Prendergast, J. P. (1887), *Ireland from the Restoration to the Revolution, 1660 to 1690*, London: Longmans.

Prins, A. A. (1972), *A History of English Phonemes*, Leiden: Leiden University Press.

Pyles, T. and J. Algeo (1982), *The Origins and Development of the English Language*, 3rd edn, San Diego: Harcourt Brace Jovanovich.

Quick, I. (1986), 'English and Scots military loanwords in Scottish Gaelic', *Scottish Language*, 5, pp. 99–105.

Quick, I. (1990), 'The Scots element in the Gaelic vocabulary of domestic furnishings and utensils', in D. S. Thomson (ed.), *Gaelic and Scots in Harmony: Proceedings of the Second International Conference on the Languages of Scotland*, Glasgow: Department of Celtic, University of Glasgow, pp. 36–42.

Quirk, R., S. Greenbaum, G. Leech and J. Svartvik (eds) (1985), *A Comprehensive Grammar of the English Language*, London: Longman.

Quirk, R. and C. L. Wrenn (1957), *An Old English Grammar*, London: Methuen.

Quorn Centenary Book Committee (1978), *Quorn and District Centenary 1878–1978*, Adelaide: Lutheran Publishing House.

Ramsay, A. (1944–74), *The Works of Allan Ramsay*, ed. B. Martin and J. W. Oliver, Scottish Text Society, 3rd series, Edinburgh: Blackwood.

Ramson, W. S. (1988), *The Australian National Dictionary*, Melbourne: Oxford University Press.

Read, A. W. (1938), 'Suggestions for an Academy in England in the latter half of the 18th century', *Modern Philology*, 36, pp. 145–56.

Reaney, P. H. (1927), *A Grammar of the Dialect of Penrith*, Manchester: Manchester University Press.

Reid, E. (1976), 'Social and stylistic variation in the speech of some Edinburgh schoolchildren', Dissertation, University of Edinburgh.

Reid, E. (1978), 'Social and stylistic variation in the speech of children', in P. Trudgill (ed.), *Sociolinguistic Patterns in British English*, London: Edward Arnold, pp. 158–72.

Reid, J. B. (1889), *A Complete Word and Phrase Concordance to the Poems and Songs of Robert Burns*, Glasgow: Kerr and Richardson.

RIA (1913–76), *Contributions*, The Royal Irish Academy, *(Contributions to a) Dictionary of the Irish Language*, Dublin.

Riach, D. W. (1986), 'Walter Kennedy's part in *The Flyting of Dunbar and Kennedie*', in D. Strauss and H. W. Drescher (eds), *Scottish Language and Literature, Medieval and Renaissance: Fourth International Conference. Scottish Studies*, Frankfurt am Main: Lang, pp. 369–79.

Riach, W. A. D. (1979–82), 'A dialect study of comparative areas in Galloway', *Scottish Literary Journal*, Supplement 9 (1979), pp. 1–16, Supplement 12 (1980), pp. 43–51; *Scottish Language*, 1 (1982), pp. 13–22.

Riach, W. A. D. (1984), 'Galloway schools dialect survey', *Scottish Language*, 3, pp. 49–59.

Riach, W. A. D. (1988), *A Galloway Glossary*, Association for Scottish Literary Studies, Occasional Papers, 7, Aberdeen.

Richards, E. (1985), 'Varieties of Scottish emigration in the nineteenth century', *Historical Studies*, 21, pp. 473–92.

Richards, E. (1988), 'Scottish Australia 1788–1914', in *That Land of Exiles: Scots in Australia*, Edinburgh: HMSO, pp. 9–39.

Riddell, H. S. (1857), *The Book of Psalms in Lowland Scotch from the Authorised Version*, London: printed by Robson, Levey and Franklin for Prince Louis Lucien Bonaparte.

Risk, H. (1971), 'French loan-words in Irish', *Études Celtiques*, 12, pp. 585–655.

Rissanen, M. (1991), 'Spoken language and the history of the *Do*-periphrasis', in D. Kastovsky (ed.), *Historical English Syntax*, Topics in English Linguistics 2, Berlin: Mouton de Gruyter, pp. 321–42.

Rissanen, M., O. Ihalainen, T. Nevalainen and I. Taavitsainen (eds) (1992), *History of Englishes: New Methods and Interpretations in Historical Linguistics*, Berlin: Mouton de Gruyter.

Rissanen, M., M. Kytö and M. Palander-Collin (eds) (1993), *Early English in the Computer Age: Explorations through the Helsinki Corpus*, Topics in English Linguistics 11, Berlin and New York: Mouton de Gruyter.

Robertson, J. (1722), *The Ladies Help to Spelling*, Glasgow.

Robinson, M. (1973), 'Modern literary Scots: Fergusson and after', in A. J. Aitken (ed.), *Lowland Scots: Occasional Papers no. 2*, Edinburgh: Association for Scottish Literary Studies, pp. 38–55.

Robinson, M. (1983), 'Language choice in the Reformation: the Scots Confession of 1560', in J. D. McClure (ed.), *Scotland and the Lowland Tongue*, Aberdeen: Aberdeen University Press, pp. 59–78.

Robinson, M. (1985), *The Concise Scots Dictionary*, Aberdeen: Aberdeen University Press.

Robinson, M. (1987), '*The Concise Scots Dictionary* as a tool for linguistic review', in C. I. Macafee and I. Macleod (eds), *The Nuttis Schell. Essays on the Scots Language presented to A. J. Aitken*, Aberdeen: Aberdeen University Press, pp. 59–72.

Robinson, P. (1984), *The Plantation of Ulster: British Settlement in an Irish Landscape, 1600–1670*, Dublin: Gill and McMillan. Repr. (1993) Belfast: Ulster Historical Foundation.

Robinson, P. (1989a), 'The Scots language in seventeenth-century Ulster', *Ulster Folklife*, 35, pp. 86–99.

Robinson, P. (1989b), 'The Ulster plantation', *Ulster Local Studies*, 11:2, pp. 20–30.

Robinson, P. (ed.) (1992), *The Country Rhymes of James Orr, the Bard of Ballycarry, 1770–1816*, Folk Poets of Ulster series, vol. 2, Bangor: Pretani.

Robinson, P. (1995), 'Jonathan Swift: his early writings in Ulster Scots?', *Ullans: The Magazine for Ulster Scots*, 3, pp. 37–48.

Robinson, P. (forthcoming a), *Ulster Scots: A Grammar of the Traditional Written and Spoken Language*, Newtownards: Ulster Scots Academic Press.

Robinson, P. (forthcoming b), 'Burns and the Ulster-Scots poets', in R. W. Dixon (ed.), *Belfast, Burns and the Ulster Scots*, Newtownards: Ulster Scots Academic Press.

Rogers, P. (1991), 'Boswell and the Scotticism', in G. Cligham (ed.), *New Light on Boswell*, London: Cambridge University Press, pp. 56–71.

Rohlfing, H. (1984), *Die Werke James Elphinstons (1721–1809) als Quellen der englischen Lautgeschichte*, Heidelberg.

Romaine, S. (1975), 'Linguistic variability in the speech of some Edinburgh schoolchildren', Dissertation, University of Edinburgh.

Romaine, S. (1978), 'Postvocalic /r/ in Scottish English: sound change in progress?', in P. Trudgill (ed.), *Sociolinguistic Patterns in British English*, London: Edward Arnold, pp. 144–57.

Romaine, S. (1979), 'The language of Edinburgh schoolchildren: the acquisition of sociolinguistic competence', *Scottish Literary Journal*, Supplement 9, pp. 54–60.

Romaine, S. (1980), 'The relative clause marker in Scots English: diffusion, complexity, and style as dimensions of syntactic change', *Language in Society*, 9, pp. 221–47.

Romaine, S. (1981), 'Syntactic complexity, relativization and stylistic levels in Middle Scots', *Folia Linguistica Historica*, 2:1, pp. 71–97.

Romaine, S. (1982a), *Socio-Historical Linguistics: Its Status and Methodology*, Cambridge: Cambridge University Press.

Romaine, S. (1982b), 'The English language in Scotland', in R. W. Bailey and M. Görlach (eds), *English as a World Language*, Ann Arbor: University of Michigan Press, pp. 56–83.

Romaine, S. (1984a), 'Some historical and social dimensions of syntactic change in Middle Scots relative clauses', in N. F. Blake and C. Jones (eds), *English Historical Linguistics: Studies in Development*, Centre for English Cultural Tradition and Language, University of Sheffield, pp. 101–22.

Romaine, S. (1984b), 'The sociolinguistic history of [t/d] deletion', *Folia Linguistica Historica*, 5, pp. 221–55.

Rudd, S. (1968), *The Poor Parson*, St Lucia: University of Queensland Press.

Russell, C. C. (1910), *The Language and People of Ulster*, Belfast: Linenhall Press.

Sabban, A. (1982), *Gälisch–englischer Sprachkontakt: Zur Variabilität des Englischen im gälischsprachigen Gebiet Schottlands: Eine empirische Studie*, Heidelberg: Groos.

Sabban, A. (1985), 'On the variability of Hebridean English syntax: the verbal group', in M. Görlach (ed.), *Focus on Scotland. Varieties of English Around the World*, General series, 5, Amsterdam: Benjamins, pp. 125–43.

Samuels, M. L. (1985), 'The Great Scandinavian Belt', in R. Eaton (ed.), *Current Issues in Linguistic Theory 41. Papers from the 4th International Conference on English Historical Linguistics*, Amsterdam: Benjamins, pp. 269–81.

Samuels, M. L. (1989), 'The Great Scandinavian Belt', in A. McIntosh, M. L. Samuels and M. Laing (eds), *Middle English Dialectology*, Aberdeen: Aberdeen University Press, pp. 17–26.

Sandred, K. I. (1983), *Good or Bad Scots?*, Stockholm: Almqvist and Wiksell.

Sandred, K. I. (1987), 'Measurement by the hand in Lowland Scots: a study of four Scandinavian loanwords', in C. I. Macafee and I. Macleod (eds), *The Nuttis Schell. Essays on the Scots Language presented to A. J. Aitken*, Aberdeen: Aberdeen University Press, pp. 227–35.

Schendl, H. (1996), 'The present plural indicative in Early Modern English – variation and linguistic contact', in D. Britton (ed.), *English Historical Linguistics 1994*, Amsterdam: Benjamins, pp. 143–60.

Schlemilch, W. (1914), *Beiträge zur Sprache und Orthographie spätaltenglischer Sprachdenkmäler der Übergangszeit (1000–1150)*, Halle/Saale: Max Niemeyer.

Schrijver, P. (1995), *Studies in British Celtic Historical Phonology*, Amsterdam: Rodopi.

Scot, A. (1779), *The Contrast: A Specimen of the Scotch Dialect. In Prose and Verse. According to the Latest Improvements; With an English Version.*

Scotch Poems (1753), *The Ulster Miscellany*, Belfast, pp. 369–86.

Scots Language Society, *Spelling Recommendations* (1985), *Lallans*, 24, pp. 18–19.

Scots Style Sheet, (1955), *The Lines Review*, 9, pp. 30–1.

Scott, A. (1805), *Poems*, Edinburgh.

Scott, J. (1774), *The School-Boy's Sure Guide; or, Spelling and Reading Made Agreeable and Easy*, Edinburgh.

Scott, P. (1994), 'Review of W. Donaldson (1989), *The Language of the People: Scots Prose from the Victorian Revival*, Aberdeen University Press', *Studies in Scottish Literature*, 27, pp. 323–6.

Scott, W. (1793), *A Short System of English Grammar*, Edinburgh.

Scott, W. (1796), *An Introduction to Reading and Spelling*, Edinburgh.

Scott, W. (1807), *A New Spelling, Pronouncing, and Explanatory Dictionary of the English Language*, Edinburgh.

Scragg, D. G. (1974), *A History of English Spelling*, Manchester: Manchester University Press.

Service, J. (1913), *The Memorables of Robin Cummell*, Paisley: Gardner.

Sheldon, E. K. (1971), 'Pronouncing systems in eighteenth-century dictionaries', *Language*, 22, pp. 27–41.

Sheppard, E. A. (1936), 'Studies in the language of Bellenden's *Boece*', Dissertation, University of London.

Sheridan, T. (1762), *Course of Lectures on Elocution*, London: *English Linguistics 1500–1800*, 129, ed. R. C. Alston (1968), Menston: Scolar Press.

Sheridan, T. (1780), *A General Dictionary of the English Language*, London.

Sheridan, T. (1781), *A Rhetorical Grammar of the English Language*, Dublin: *English Linguistics 1500–1800*, 146, ed. R. C. Alston (1969), Menston: Scolar Press.

Shire, H. (1969), *Song, Dance and Poetry of the Court of Scotland under King James VI*, London: Cambridge University Press.

Shuken, C. R. (1985), 'Variation in Hebridean English', in M. Görlach (ed.), *Focus on Scotland. Varieties of English Around the World*, General series, 5, Amsterdam: Benjamins, pp. 145–58.

Sibbald, Sir R. (1845), *Description of the Islands of Orkney and Shetland*, Edinburgh: Stevenson.

Simpson, G. (1975), *Scottish Handwriting 1150–1650*, Edinburgh: Bratton.

Simpson, H. F. Morland (1906), *Bon Record: Records and Reminiscences of Aberdeen Grammar School from the Earliest Times by Many Writers*, Edinburgh: Ballantyne.

Sinclair, J. (1782), *Observations on the Scottish Dialect*, Edinburgh.

Skea, M. (1982), 'Change and variation in the lexicon of a non-standard dialect: a sociolinguistic study of dialect semantics in north Down', Dissertation, Ulster Polytechnic, Jordanstown.

Skeat, W. W. (ed.) (1884), *The Kingis Quair*, Scottish Text Society, 1st series, Edinburgh and London: Blackwood.

Skeat, W. W. (1887), *Principles of English Etymology: First Series. The Native Element*, Oxford: Clarendon Press.

Skeat, W. W. (ed.) (1896), *Barbour's Bruce*, Early English Text Society, London.

Slater, J. (1952), 'An edition of Early Scots texts from the beginnings to 1410', Dissertation, 2 vols, University of Edinburgh.

Smith, G. G. (1902), *Specimens of Middle Scots*, Edinburgh: W. Blackwell.

Smith, J. J. (1994), 'Norse in Scotland', *Scottish Language*, 13, pp. 18–33.

Smith, Sir T. (1568), *De Recta et emendata Linguae Anglicae Scriptione Dialogus*, in B. Danielsson (ed.) (1963), *Sir Thomas Smith: Literary and Linguistic Works*, 3, Stockholm Studies in English, 56, Stockholm: Almqvist and Wiksell.

SOED (1991), *The Curriculum and Assessment in Scotland: National Guidelines: English Language 5–14*, Scottish Office Education Department, Circular 19/21.

Soutar, W. (1935), *Poems in Scots*, Edinburgh and London: Moray Press.

Speirs, J. (1940), *The Scots Literary Tradition*, London: Chatto and Windus.

Speitel, H. H. (1969a), 'Some studies in the dialect of Midlothian', Dissertation, University of Edinburgh.

Speitel, H. H. (1969b), 'An early specimen of Edinburgh speech', *Work in Progress*, 3, Department of Phonetics and Linguistics, University of Edinburgh, pp. 26–36.

Speitel, H. H. (1978), 'The word geography of the Borders', *Scottish Literary Journal*, Supplement 6, pp. 17–37.

Speitel, H. H. and J. Y. Mather (1968), 'Schottische Dialektologie', in L. E. Schmitt (ed.), *Germanische Dialektologie: Festschrift für Walter Mitzka*, Wiesbaden: Franz Steiner, pp. 520–41.

Spence, C. H. (1854), *Clara Morison*, 2 vols, London: Parker.

Spence, C. H. (1977), *Gathered In*, ed. B. L. Waters and G. A. Wilkes, Sydney: Sydney University Press.

Spence, T. (1775), *The Grand Repository of the English Language*, Newcastle: *English Linguistics 1500–1800*, 155, ed. R. C. Alston (1969), Menston: Scolar Press.

Spence, T. (1782), *Crusonia: or Robinson Crusoe's Island. A Supplement to the History of Robinson Crusoe*, Newcastle.

Sprague, T. B. (1881), 'On som differences between the speech ov Edinboro and London', *Transactions of the Philological Society*, 1880–1881, pp. 106–16.

Steele, J. (1775), *An Essay towards Establishing the Melody and Measure of Speech: English Linguistics 1500–1800*, 172, ed. R. C. Alston (1969), Menston: Scolar Press.

Steer, K. A. and J. W. M. Bannerman (1977), *Late Medieval Monumental Sculpture in the West Highlands*, Edinburgh: Royal Commission on the Ancient and Historical Monuments of Scotland.

Stein, D. and I. Tieken-Boon van Ostade (eds) (1994), *Towards a Standard English 1600–1800*, Berlin and New York: Mouton de Gruyter.

Stevenson, J. A. C. and I. Macleod (1989), *Scoor-Oot: A Dictionary of Scots Words and Phrases in Current Use*, London: Athlone Press.

Stirling, A. (1994), 'On a standardised spelling for Scots', *Scottish Language*, 13, pp. 88–93.

Stockwell, R. (1961 [1969]), 'The Middle English "long close" and "long open" mid vowels', *Texas Studies in Literature and Language*, 2, pp. 259–68. Reprinted in R. Lass (ed.) (1969), *Approaches to English Historical Linguistics*, New York: Holt Rinehart, pp. 154–63.

Stockwell, R. and D. Minkova (1988), 'The English Vowel Shift: problems of coherence and explanation', in D. Kastovsky and G. Bauer (eds), *Luick Revisited: Papers read at the Luick-Symposium at Schloss Liechtenstein, 15–18.9.1985*, Tübingen: Gunter Narr, pp. 355–93.

Stockwell, R. and D. Minkova (1990), 'The Early English modern vowels: more O' Lass', *Diachronica*, 7:2, pp. 199–214.

Strang, B. M. H. (1968), *Modern English Structure*, 2nd edn, London: Edward Arnold.

Strang, B. M. H. (1970), *A History of English*, London: Methuen.

Strang, B. M. H. (1982), 'Some aspects of the *be + ing* construction', in J. M. Anderson (ed.), *Language Form and Linguistic Variation: Papers Dedicated to Angus McIntosh*, Amsterdam: John Benjamins, pp. 427–74.

Strout, A. L. (1959), *A Bibliography of Articles in Blackwood's Magazine 1817–1825*, Lubbock, TX: Texas Technological College Library.

Stuart, J. (1992), *The Glasgow Gospel*, Edinburgh: St Andrew Press.

Stursberg, M. (1969), 'The stressed vowels in the dialects of Longtown, Abbey Town, and Hunsonby (Cumberland): a structural approach', Dissertation, University of Basel.

Sweet, H. (ed.) (1966), *The Oldest English Texts*, Early English Text Society, repr. Oxford: Oxford University Press.

Swift, J. (1712), *A Proposal for Correcting, Improving, and Ascertaining the English Tongue*, London.

Tannahill, R. (1911), *Poetical Works*, Paisley: Parlane.

Tasker, R. V. G. (ed.) (1967), *St Augustine, The City of God*, London: Dent.

Taylor, M. V. (1974), 'The great southern Scots conspiracy: patterns in the development of Northern English', in J. M. Anderson and C. Jones (eds), *Historical Linguistics*, 2 vols, Amsterdam: North-Holland, pp. 403–6.

Telfair, C. (1775), *The Town and Country Spelling Book*, Edinburgh: Elliot.

Templeton, J. M. (1973), 'Scots: an outline history', in A. J. Aitken (ed.), *Lowland Scots: Occasional Papers no. 2*, Edinburgh: Association for Scottish Literary Studies, pp. 4–11.

Thelander, M. (1979), *Språkliga variationsmodeller tillampade pa nutida Burtrasktal*, Stockholm: Almqvist and Wiksell.

Thomas, A. R. (1980), *Areal Analysis of Dialect Data by Computer: A Welsh Example*, Cardiff: University of Wales Press.

Thomason, S. G. and T. Kaufman (1988), *Language Contact, Creolization, and Genetic Linguistics*, Berkeley: University of California Press.

Thompson, E. P. (1983), *The Making of the English Working Class*, Harmondsworth: Penguin.

Thomson, D. S. (1968), 'Gaelic learned orders and literati in medieval Scotland', *Scottish Studies*, 12, pp. 57–78.

Thomson, D. S. (ed.) (1983), *The Companion to Gaelic Scotland*, Oxford: Blackwell.

Thomson, H. W. (1927), *The Anecdotes and Egotisms of Henry Mackenzie, 1745–1831*, London: Oxford University Press.

Thomson, R. L. (1969), 'The study of Manx Gaelic', *Proceedings of the British Academy*, 55, pp. 177–210.

Thomson, R. L. (1970), *Foirm na n-Urrnuidheadh: John Carswell's Translation of the Book of Common Order, in part from materials collected by the late Angus Matheson*, Scottish Gaelic Texts Society, vol. 11, Edinburgh: Oliver and Boyd.

Thomson, R. L. (1983a), 'Loanwords, English and Scots', in D. S. Thomson (ed.), *The Companion to Gaelic Scotland*, Oxford: Blackwell, pp. 152–3.

Thomson, R. L. (1983b), 'Loanwords, Gaelic, in English', in D. S. Thomson (ed.), *The Companion to Gaelic Scotland*, Oxford: Blackwell, pp. 153–4.

Thomson, T. and C. Innes (eds) (1814–75), *Acts of Parliament of Scotland*, 12 vols, Records Commission, Edinburgh.

Thun, N. (1963), 'Reduplicative words in English. A study of formations of the types Tick-tick, Hurly-burly and Shilly-shally', Dissertation, University of Uppsala.

Todd, L. (1971), 'Tyrone English', *Yorkshire Dialect Society Transactions*, 13, pp. 29–40.

Todd, L. (1989a), *The Language of Irish Literature*, New York: St Martins.

Todd, L. (1989b), 'Cultures in conflict: varieties of English in northern Ireland', in O. Garcia and R. Otheguy (eds), *English across Cultures/Cultures across English*, Berlin: Mouton de Gruyter, pp. 335–55.

Todd, L. (1992a), 'Ulster Scots', in T. McArthur (ed.), *The Oxford Companion to the English Language*, Oxford: Oxford University Press, pp. 1,087–8.

Todd, L. (1992b), 'Hiberno English', in T. McArthur (ed.), *The Oxford Companion to the English Language*, Oxford: Oxford University Press, pp. 469–70.

Toon, T. E. (1983), *The Politics of Early Old English Sound Change*, New York: Academic Press.

Torrance, J. (1904), *Twixt Heather and Wattle*, Melbourne: Robertson.

Trask, W. (trans.) (1994), *E. R. Curtius, European Literature and the Latin Middle Ages*, London: Routledge.

Traugott, E. C. (1992), 'Syntax', in R. Hogg (ed.), *The Cambridge History of the English Language*, vol. 1, *The Beginnings to 1066*, Cambridge: Cambridge University Press, pp. 168–289.

Traynor, M. (1953), *The English Dialect of Donegal: A Glossary, Incorporating the Collections of H. C. Hart, etc.*, Dublin: Royal Irish Academy.

Trevelyan, G. M. (1959), *A Shortened History of England*, Baltimore: Penguin.

Trotter, R. de B. (1901), 'The Scottish language', *The Gallovidian*, vol. 3, pp. 22–9.

Trudgill, P. (1974), *The Social Differentiation of English in Norwich*, Cambridge: Cambridge University Press.

Trudgill, P. (ed.) (1978), *Sociolinguistic Patterns in British English*, London: Edward Arnold.

Trudgill, P. (1983), *On Dialect*, Oxford: Blackwell.

Trudgill, P. (ed.) (1984), *Language in the British Isles*, Cambridge: Cambridge University Press.

Trudgill, P. (1986), *Dialects in Contact*, Oxford: Blackwell.

Trudgill, P. (1988), 'Norwich revisited: changes in an English urban dialect', in *English World-Wide*, 9:1, pp. 33–49.

Trudgill, P. (1990), *Dialects of England*, Oxford: Blackwell.

Trudgill, P. and J. K. Chambers (eds) (1992), *Dialects of English: Studies in Grammatical Variation*, London: Longman.

Trudgill, P., V. K. Edwards and B. Weltens (1983), *Grammatical Characteristics of Non-Standard Dialects of English in the British Isles: A Survey of Research*, Report to the Social Science Research Council, London.

Tuchman, B. W. (1978), *A Distant Mirror: The Calamitous Fourteenth Century*, New York: Ballantine.

Tuite, T. (1726), *The Oxford Spelling-Book (Being a Complete Introduction to English Orthography)*: *English Linguistics 1500–1800*, 41, ed. R. C. Alston (1967), Menston: Scolar Press.

Tulloch, G. (1980), *The Language of Walter Scott: A Study of his Scottish and Period Language*, London: André Deutsch.

Tulloch, G. (1989), *A History of the Scots Bible with Selected Texts*, Aberdeen: Aberdeen University Press.

Ureland, P. S. and G. Broderick (eds) (1991), *Language Contact in the British Isles*, Tübingen: Niemeyer.

Viana, M. (1972), 'A study of the dialect of the southern counties of Scotland', Dissertation, University of Indiana.

Viereck, W. (1991), *The Computer-Developed Linguistic Atlas of England*, vol. 1, Tübingen: Niemeyer.

Vikar, A. (1922), *Contributions to the History of the Durham Dialect*, Malmö: Rohr's Boktrykevi.

Visser, F. Th. (1973), *An Historical Syntax of the English Language*, Leiden: E. J. Brill.

Vries, J. de (1985), 'Secondary data analysis on ethno-linguistic minorities: problems and pitfalls', *Plurilingua*, 5, pp. 209–16.

Waddell, P. H. (1859), *Genius and Morality of Burns*, Ayr: Ayrshire Express.

Waddell, P. H. (1871), *The Psalms frae Hebrew intil Scottis*, Edinburgh: Menzies.

Waddell, P. H. (1879), *Isaiah frae Hebrew intil Scottis*, Edinburgh: Menzies.

Wakelin, M. (1972), *English Dialects: An Introduction*, London: Athlone.

Wakelin, M. (1991), 'The Cornishness of Cornwall's English', in P. S. Ureland and G. Broderick (eds), *Language Contact in the British Isles*, Tübingen: Niemeyer, pp. 199–225.

Walker, I. C. (1968), 'Dr. Johnson and *The Weekly Magazine*', *Review of English Studies*, 19, pp. 14–24.

Walker, J. (1791), *A Critical Pronouncing Dictionary*: *English Linguistics 1500–1800*, 117, ed. R. C. Alston (1968), Menston: Scolar Press.

Wall, A. A. (1898), 'A contribution towards the study of the Scandinavian elements in the English dialects', *Anglia*, 20, pp. 45–135.

Warden, J. (1753), *A Spelling Book*, Edinburgh.

Warrack, A. (ed.) (1911), *Chambers' Scots Dialect Dictionary*, London: Chambers.

Watson, A. and E. Allan (1984), *The Place Names of Upper Deeside*, Aberdeen: Aberdeen University Press.

Watson, G. (1923), *The Roxburghshire Word-Book*, Cambridge: Cambridge University Press.

Watson, R. (1959), *The Poetry of Scotland: Gaelic, Scots and English*, Edinburgh: Edinburgh University Press.

Watson, R. (1984), *The Literature of Scotland*, Basingstoke: Macmillan.

Watson, S. (1983), 'Loan-words and initial mutations in a Gaelic dialect', *Scottish Gaelic Studies*, 14:1, pp. 100–13.

Watson, W. J. (1927), 'Some interactions between Gaelic and English', *Transactions of the Gaelic Society of Inverness*, 33, pp. 310–26.

Watson, W. J. (1937), *Scottish Verse from the Book of the Dean of Lismore*, Edinburgh: Scottish Gaelic Texts Society.

Watt, L. M. (1920), *Douglas' Æneid*, Cambridge: Cambridge University Press.

Watts, J. I. (1890), *Family Life in South Australia Fifty Three Years Ago, Dating from October, 1837*, Adelaide: Thomas.

Wells, J. C. (1982), *Accents of English*, 3 vols, Cambridge: Cambridge University Press.

Weston, J. C. (ed.) (1967), *The Collected Poems of Hugh MacDiarmid*, New York: Macmillan.

Wettstein, P. (1942), *The Phonology of a Berwickshire Dialect*, Bienne: Schüler.

Weyl, H. (trans.) (1948), *Ortega Y Gasset, The Dehumanization of Art*, Princeton: Princeton University Press.

Wickens, B. (1980, 1981), 'Caithness speech', *Scottish Literary Journal*, Supplement 12, pp. 61–76; Supplement 14, pp. 25–36.

Williams, O. T. (1907–10), 'The development of *ai* and *ei* in Middle Scotch', *Transactions of the Philological Society*, pp. 285–7.

Williams, O. T. (1911–14), 'On OE *a*, *ā* and *æ* in the rimes of Barbour's *Brus* and in modern Scotch dialects', *Transactions of the Philological Society*, pp. 7–16.

Wilson, D. (1974), *Staffordshire Dialect Words: A Historical Survey*, Stafford: Moorland.

Wilson, J. (1855–6), *Noctes Ambrosianae*, 4 vols, Edinburgh: Blackwood.

Wilson, J. (1915), *Lowland Scotch, as Spoken in the Lower Strathearn District of Perthshire*, London: Oxford University Press.

Wilson, J. (1923), *The Dialect of Robert Burns as Spoken in Central Ayrshire*, Oxford: Oxford University Press.

Wilson, J. (1926), *The Dialects of Central Scotland*, Oxford: Oxford University Press.

Wilson, J. M. (n.d.), *Historical, Traditionary and Imaginative Tales of the Borders, and of Scotland*, Manchester: Ainsworth.

Withers, C. W. J. (1979), 'The language geography of Scottish Gaelic', *Scottish Literary Journal*, Supplement 9, pp. 41–53.

Withers, C. W. J. (1984), *Gaelic in Scotland 1698–1981: The Geographical History of a Language*, Edinburgh: John Donald.

Withrington, D. (1986), 'Education in the seventeenth century Highlands', in L. Maclean of Dochgarroch (ed.), *The Seventeenth Century in the Highlands*, Inverness Field Club, pp. 60–9.

Wittig, K. (1958), *The Scottish Tradition in Literature*, Edinburgh and London: Oliver and Boyd.

Wollstonecraft, M. (1792), *A Vindication of the Rights of Women*, London.

Wood, I. S. (ed.) (1994), *Scotland and Ulster*, Edinburgh: Mercat Press.

Wright, D. F. (1988), '*The Commoun Buke of the Kirke*: the Bible in the Scottish Reformation', in idem (ed.), *The Bible in Scottish Life and Literature*, Edinburgh: St Andrew Press, pp. 155–78.

Wright, J. (1892), *A Grammar of the Dialect of Windhill in the West Riding of Yorkshire*, London: Kegan Paul, Trench, Trübner.

Wright, J. (1905), *The English Dialect Dictionary*, London: Frowde.

Wright, J. and E. M. Wright (1928), *An Elementary Middle English Grammar*, Oxford: Oxford University Press.

Wyld, H. C. (1937), *A Short History of English*, London: John Murray.

Yorke, B. (1990), *Kings and Kingdoms in Early Anglo-Saxon England*, London: Seaby.

Young, D. (1950), *Selected Poems*, Edinburgh and London: Oliver and Boyd.

Zai, R. (1942), *The Phonology of the Morebattle Dialect*, Lucerne: Raeber.

Index

Numbers in italics refer to tables or figures.